T0210913

Lecture Notes in Computer Science   13438

More information about this series at https://link.springer.com/bookseries/558

Linwei Wang · Qi Dou · P. Thomas Fletcher ·
Stefanie Speidel · Shuo Li (Eds.)

Medical Image Computing and Computer Assisted Intervention – MICCAI 2022

25th International Conference
Singapore, September 18–22, 2022
Proceedings, Part VIII

 Springer

Editors
Linwei Wang
Rochester Institute of Technology
Rochester, NY, USA

Qi Dou
Chinese University of Hong Kong
Hong Kong, Hong Kong

P. Thomas Fletcher
University of Virginia
Charlottesville, VA, USA

Stefanie Speidel
National Center for Tumor Diseases
(NCT/UCC)
Dresden, Germany

Shuo Li
Case Western Reserve University
Cleveland, OH, USA

ISSN 0302-9743   ISSN 1611-3349 (electronic)
Lecture Notes in Computer Science
ISBN 978-3-031-16451-4   ISBN 978-3-031-16452-1 (eBook)
https://doi.org/10.1007/978-3-031-16452-1

This Springer imprint is published by the registered company Springer Nature Switzerland AG
The registered company address is: Gewerbestrasse 11, 6330 Cham, Switzerland

Preface

We are pleased to present the proceedings of the 25th International Conference on Medical Image Computing and Computer-Assisted Intervention (MICCAI) which – after two difficult years of virtual conferences – was held in a hybrid fashion at the Resort World Convention Centre in Singapore, September 18–22, 2022. The conference also featured 36 workshops, 11 tutorials, and 38 challenges held on September 18 and September 22. The conference was also co-located with the 2nd Conference on Clinical Translation on Medical Image Computing and Computer-Assisted Intervention (CLINICCAI) on September 20.

MICCAI 2022 had an approximately 14% increase in submissions and accepted papers compared with MICCAI 2021. These papers, which comprise eight volumes of Lecture Notes in Computer Science (LNCS) proceedings, were selected after a thorough double-blind peer-review process. Following the example set by the previous program chairs of past MICCAI conferences, we employed Microsoft's Conference Managing Toolkit (CMT) for paper submissions and double-blind peer-reviews, and the Toronto Paper Matching System (TPMS) to assist with automatic paper assignment to area chairs and reviewers.

From 2811 original intentions to submit, 1865 full submissions were received and 1831 submissions reviewed. Of these, 67% were considered as pure Medical Image Computing (MIC), 7% as pure Computer-Assisted Interventions (CAI), and 26% as both MIC and CAI. The MICCAI 2022 Program Committee (PC) comprised 107 area chairs, with 52 from the Americas, 33 from Europe, and 22 from the Asia-Pacific or Middle East regions. We maintained gender balance with 37% women scientists on the PC.

Each area chair was assigned 16–18 manuscripts, for each of which they were asked to suggest up to 15 suggested potential reviewers. Subsequently, over 1320 invited reviewers were asked to bid for the papers for which they had been suggested. Final reviewer allocations via CMT took account of PC suggestions, reviewer bidding, and TPMS scores, finally allocating 4–6 papers per reviewer. Based on the double-blinded reviews, area chairs' recommendations, and program chairs' global adjustments, 249 papers (14%) were provisionally accepted, 901 papers (49%) were provisionally rejected, and 675 papers (37%) proceeded into the rebuttal stage.

During the rebuttal phase, two additional area chairs were assigned to each rebuttal paper using CMT and TPMS scores. After the authors' rebuttals were submitted, all reviewers of the rebuttal papers were invited to assess the rebuttal, participate in a double-blinded discussion with fellow reviewers and area chairs, and finalize their rating (with the opportunity to revise their rating as appropriate). The three area chairs then independently provided their recommendations to accept or reject the paper, considering the manuscript, the reviews, and the rebuttal. The final decision of acceptance was based on majority voting of the area chair recommendations. The program chairs reviewed all decisions and provided their inputs in extreme cases where a large divergence existed between the area chairs and reviewers in their recommendations. This process resulted in the acceptance of a total of 574 papers, reaching an overall acceptance rate of 31% for MICCAI 2022.

In our additional effort to ensure review quality, two Reviewer Tutorials and two Area Chair Orientations were held in early March, virtually in different time zones, to introduce the reviewers and area chairs to the MICCAI 2022 review process and the best practice for high-quality reviews. Two additional Area Chair meetings were held virtually in July to inform the area chairs of the outcome of the review process and to collect feedback for future conferences.

For the MICCAI 2022 proceedings, 574 accepted papers were organized in eight volumes as follows:

- Part I, LNCS Volume 13431: Brain Development and Atlases, DWI and Tractography, Functional Brain Networks, Neuroimaging, Heart and Lung Imaging, and Dermatology
- Part II, LNCS Volume 13432: Computational (Integrative) Pathology, Computational Anatomy and Physiology, Ophthalmology, and Fetal Imaging
- Part III, LNCS Volume 13433: Breast Imaging, Colonoscopy, and Computer Aided Diagnosis
- Part IV, LNCS Volume 13434: Microscopic Image Analysis, Positron Emission Tomography, Ultrasound Imaging, Video Data Analysis, and Image Segmentation I
- Part V, LNCS Volume 13435: Image Segmentation II and Integration of Imaging with Non-imaging Biomarkers
- Part VI, LNCS Volume 13436: Image Registration and Image Reconstruction
- Part VII, LNCS Volume 13437: Image-Guided Interventions and Surgery, Outcome and Disease Prediction, Surgical Data Science, Surgical Planning and Simulation, and Machine Learning – Domain Adaptation and Generalization
- Part VIII, LNCS Volume 13438: Machine Learning – Weakly-supervised Learning, Machine Learning – Model Interpretation, Machine Learning – Uncertainty, and Machine Learning Theory and Methodologies

We would like to thank everyone who contributed to the success of MICCAI 2022 and the quality of its proceedings. These include the MICCAI Society for support and feedback, and our sponsors for their financial support and presence onsite. We especially express our gratitude to the MICCAI Submission System Manager Kitty Wong for her thorough support throughout the paper submission, review, program planning, and proceeding preparation process – the Program Committee simply would not have be able to function without her. We are also grateful for the dedication and support of all of the organizers of the workshops, tutorials, and challenges, Jianming Liang, Wufeng Xue, Jun Cheng, Qian Tao, Xi Chen, Islem Rekik, Sophia Bano, Andrea Lara, Yunliang Cai, Pingkun Yan, Pallavi Tiwari, Ingerid Reinertsen, Gongning Luo, without whom the exciting peripheral events would have not been feasible. Behind the scenes, the MICCAI secretariat personnel, Janette Wallace and Johanne Langford, kept a close eye on logistics and budgets, while Mehmet Eldegez and his team from Dekon Congress & Tourism, MICCAI 2022's Professional Conference Organization, managed the website and local organization. We are especially grateful to all members of the Program Committee for their diligent work in the reviewer assignments and final paper selection, as well as the reviewers for their support during the entire process. Finally, and most importantly, we thank all authors, co-authors, students/postdocs, and supervisors, for submitting and presenting their high-quality work which made MICCAI 2022 a successful event.

We look forward to seeing you in Vancouver, Canada at MICCAI 2023!

September 2022

Linwei Wang
Qi Dou
P. Thomas Fletcher
Stefanie Speidel
Shuo Li

Organization

General Chair

Shuo Li — Case Western Reserve University, USA

Program Committee Chairs

Linwei Wang — Rochester Institute of Technology, USA
Qi Dou — The Chinese University of Hong Kong, China
P. Thomas Fletcher — University of Virginia, USA
Stefanie Speidel — National Center for Tumor Diseases Dresden, Germany

Workshop Team

Wufeng Xue — Shenzhen University, China
Jun Cheng — Agency for Science, Technology and Research, Singapore
Qian Tao — Delft University of Technology, the Netherlands
Xi Chen — Stern School of Business, NYU, USA

Challenges Team

Pingkun Yan — Rensselaer Polytechnic Institute, USA
Pallavi Tiwari — Case Western Reserve University, USA
Ingerid Reinertsen — SINTEF Digital and NTNU, Trondheim, Norway
Gongning Luo — Harbin Institute of Technology, China

Tutorial Team

Islem Rekik — Istanbul Technical University, Turkey
Sophia Bano — University College London, UK
Andrea Lara — Universidad Industrial de Santander, Colombia
Yunliang Cai — Humana, USA

Clinical Day Chairs

Jason Chan	The Chinese University of Hong Kong, China
Heike I. Grabsch	University of Leeds, UK and Maastricht University, the Netherlands
Nicolas Padoy	University of Strasbourg & Institute of Image-Guided Surgery, IHU Strasbourg, France

Young Investigators and Early Career Development Program Chairs

Marius Linguraru	Children's National Institute, USA
Antonio Porras	University of Colorado Anschutz Medical Campus, USA
Nicole Rieke	NVIDIA, Deutschland
Daniel Racoceanu	Sorbonne University, France

Social Media Chairs

Chenchu Xu	Anhui University, China
Dong Zhang	University of British Columbia, Canada

Student Board Liaison

Camila Bustillo	Technische Universität Darmstadt, Germany
Vanessa Gonzalez Duque	Ecole centrale de Nantes, France

Submission Platform Manager

Kitty Wong	The MICCAI Society, Canada

Virtual Platform Manager

John Baxter	INSERM, Université de Rennes 1, France

Program Committee

Ehsan Adeli	Stanford University, USA
Pablo Arbelaez	Universidad de los Andes, Colombia
John Ashburner	University College London, UK
Ulas Bagci	Northwestern University, USA
Sophia Bano	University College London, UK
Adrien Bartoli	Université Clermont Auvergne, France
Kayhan Batmanghelich	University of Pittsburgh, USA

Hrvoje Bogunovic   Medical University of Vienna, Austria
Ester Bonmati   University College London, UK
Esther Bron   Erasmus MC, the Netherlands
Gustavo Carneiro   University of Adelaide, Australia
Hao Chen   Hong Kong University of Science and
                            Technology, China
Jun Cheng   Agency for Science, Technology and Research,
                            Singapore
Li Cheng   University of Alberta, Canada
Adrian Dalca   Massachusetts Institute of Technology, USA
Jose Dolz   ETS Montreal, Canada
Shireen Elhabian   University of Utah, USA
Sandy Engelhardt   University Hospital Heidelberg, Germany
Ruogu Fang   University of Florida, USA
Aasa Feragen   Technical University of Denmark, Denmark
Moti Freiman   Technion - Israel Institute of Technology, Israel
Huazhu Fu   Agency for Science, Technology and Research,
                            Singapore
Mingchen Gao   University at Buffalo, SUNY, USA
Zhifan Gao   Sun Yat-sen University, China
Stamatia Giannarou   Imperial College London, UK
Alberto Gomez   King's College London, UK
Ilker Hacihaliloglu   University of British Columbia, Canada
Adam Harrison   PAII Inc., USA
Mattias Heinrich   University of Lübeck, Germany
Yipeng Hu   University College London, UK
Junzhou Huang   University of Texas at Arlington, USA
Sharon Xiaolei Huang   Pennsylvania State University, USA
Yuankai Huo   Vanderbilt University, USA
Jayender Jagadeesan   Brigham and Women's Hospital, USA
Won-Ki Jeong   Korea University, Korea
Xi Jiang   University of Electronic Science and Technology
                            of China, China
Anand Joshi   University of Southern California, USA
Shantanu Joshi   University of California, Los Angeles, USA
Bernhard Kainz   Imperial College London, UK
Marta Kersten-Oertel   Concordia University, Canada
Fahmi Khalifa   Mansoura University, Egypt
Seong Tae Kim   Kyung Hee University, Korea
Minjeong Kim   University of North Carolina at Greensboro, USA
Baiying Lei   Shenzhen University, China
Gang Li   University of North Carolina at Chapel Hill, USA

Fuyong Xing	University of Colorado Denver, USA
Ziyue Xu	NVIDIA, USA
Yanwu Xu	Baidu Inc., China
Pingkun Yan	Rensselaer Polytechnic Institute, USA
Guang Yang	Imperial College London, UK
Jianhua Yao	Tencent, China
Zhaozheng Yin	Stony Brook University, USA
Lequan Yu	University of Hong Kong, China
Yixuan Yuan	City University of Hong Kong, China
Ling Zhang	Alibaba Group, USA
Miaomiao Zhang	University of Virginia, USA
Ya Zhang	Shanghai Jiao Tong University, China
Rongchang Zhao	Central South University, China
Yitian Zhao	Chinese Academy of Sciences, China
Yefeng Zheng	Tencent Jarvis Lab, China
Guoyan Zheng	Shanghai Jiao Tong University, China
Luping Zhou	University of Sydney, Australia
Yuyin Zhou	Stanford University, USA
Dajiang Zhu	University of Texas at Arlington, USA
Lilla Zöllei	Massachusetts General Hospital, USA
Maria A. Zuluaga	EURECOM, France

Reviewers

Alireza Akhondi-asl	Manas Nag
Fernando Arambula	Tianye Niu
Nicolas Boutry	Seokhwan Oh
Qilei Chen	Theodoros Pissas
Zhihao Chen	Harish RaviPrakash
Javid Dadashkarimi	Maria Sainz de Cea
Marleen De Bruijne	Hai Su
Mohammad Eslami	Wenjun Tan
Sayan Ghosal	Fatmatulzehra Uslu
Estibaliz Gómez-de-Mariscal	Fons van der Sommen
Charles Hatt	Gijs van Tulder
Yongxiang Huang	Dong Wei
Samra Irshad	Pengcheng Xi
Anithapriya Krishnan	Chen Yang
Rodney LaLonde	Kun Yuan
Jie Liu	Hang Zhang
Jinyang Liu	Wei Zhang
Qing Lyu	Yuyao Zhang
Hassan Mohy-ud-Din	Tengda Zhao

Yingying Zhu
Yuemin Zhu
Alaa Eldin Abdelaal
Amir Abdi
Mazdak Abulnaga
Burak Acar
Iman Aganj
Priya Aggarwal
Ola Ahmad
Seyed-Ahmad Ahmadi
Euijoon Ahn
Faranak Akbarifar
Cem Akbaş
Saad Ullah Akram
Tajwar Aleef
Daniel Alexander
Hazrat Ali
Sharib Ali
Max Allan
Pablo Alvarez
Vincent Andrearczyk
Elsa Angelini
Sameer Antani
Michela Antonelli
Ignacio Arganda-Carreras
Mohammad Ali Armin
Josep Arnal
Md Ashikuzzaman
Mehdi Astaraki
Marc Aubreville
Chloé Audigier
Angelica Aviles-Rivero
Ruqayya Awan
Suyash Awate
Qinle Ba
Morteza Babaie
Meritxell Bach Cuadra
Hyeon-Min Bae
Junjie Bai
Wenjia Bai
Ujjwal Baid
Pradeep Bajracharya
Yaël Balbastre
Abhirup Banerjee
Sreya Banerjee

Shunxing Bao
Adrian Barbu
Sumana Basu
Deepti Bathula
Christian Baumgartner
John Baxter
Sharareh Bayat
Bahareh Behboodi
Hamid Behnam
Sutanu Bera
Christos Bergeles
Jose Bernal
Gabriel Bernardino
Alaa Bessadok
Riddhish Bhalodia
Indrani Bhattacharya
Chitresh Bhushan
Lei Bi
Qi Bi
Gui-Bin Bian
Alexander Bigalke
Ricardo Bigolin Lanfredi
Benjamin Billot
Ryoma Bise
Sangeeta Biswas
Stefano B. Blumberg
Sebastian Bodenstedt
Bhushan Borotikar
Ilaria Boscolo Galazzo
Behzad Bozorgtabar
Nadia Brancati
Katharina Breininger
Rupert Brooks
Tom Brosch
Mikael Brudfors
Qirong Bu
Ninon Burgos
Nikolay Burlutskiy
Michał Byra
Ryan Cabeen
Mariano Cabezas
Hongmin Cai
Jinzheng Cai
Weidong Cai
Sema Candemir

Qing Cao
Weiguo Cao
Yankun Cao
Aaron Carass
Ruben Cardenes
M. Jorge Cardoso
Owen Carmichael
Alessandro Casella
Matthieu Chabanas
Ahmad Chaddad
Jayasree Chakraborty
Sylvie Chambon
Yi Hao Chan
Ming-Ching Chang
Peng Chang
Violeta Chang
Sudhanya Chatterjee
Christos Chatzichristos
Antong Chen
Chao Chen
Chen Chen
Cheng Chen
Dongdong Chen
Fang Chen
Geng Chen
Hanbo Chen
Jianan Chen
Jianxu Chen
Jie Chen
Junxiang Chen
Junying Chen
Junyu Chen
Lei Chen
Li Chen
Liangjun Chen
Liyun Chen
Min Chen
Pingjun Chen
Qiang Chen
Runnan Chen
Shuai Chen
Xi Chen
Xiaoran Chen
Xin Chen
Xinjian Chen

Xuejin Chen
Yuanyuan Chen
Zhaolin Chen
Zhen Chen
Zhineng Chen
Zhixiang Chen
Erkang Cheng
Jianhong Cheng
Jun Cheng
Philip Chikontwe
Min-Kook Choi
Gary Christensen
Argyrios Christodoulidis
Stergios Christodoulidis
Albert Chung
Özgün Çiçek
Matthew Clarkson
Dana Cobzas
Jaume Coll-Font
Toby Collins
Olivier Commowick
Runmin Cong
Yulai Cong
Pierre-Henri Conze
Timothy Cootes
Teresa Correia
Pierrick Coupé
Hadrien Courtecuisse
Jeffrey Craley
Alessandro Crimi
Can Cui
Hejie Cui
Hui Cui
Zhiming Cui
Kathleen Curran
Claire Cury
Tobias Czempiel
Vedrana Dahl
Tareen Dawood
Laura Daza
Charles Delahunt
Herve Delingette
Ugur Demir
Liang-Jian Deng
Ruining Deng

Yang Deng
Cem Deniz
Felix Denzinger
Adrien Depeursinge
Hrishikesh Deshpande
Christian Desrosiers
Neel Dey
Anuja Dharmaratne
Li Ding
Xinghao Ding
Zhipeng Ding
Ines Domingues
Juan Pedro Dominguez-Morales
Mengjin Dong
Nanqing Dong
Sven Dorkenwald
Haoran Dou
Simon Drouin
Karen Drukker
Niharika D'Souza
Guodong Du
Lei Du
Dingna Duan
Hongyi Duanmu
Nicolas Duchateau
James Duncan
Nicha Dvornek
Dmitry V. Dylov
Oleh Dzyubachyk
Jan Egger
Alma Eguizabal
Gudmundur Einarsson
Ahmet Ekin
Ahmed Elazab
Ahmed Elnakib
Amr Elsawy
Mohamed Elsharkawy
Ertunc Erdil
Marius Erdt
Floris Ernst
Boris Escalante-Ramírez
Hooman Esfandiari
Nazila Esmaeili
Marco Esposito
Théo Estienne

Christian Ewert
Deng-Ping Fan
Xin Fan
Yonghui Fan
Yubo Fan
Chaowei Fang
Huihui Fang
Xi Fang
Yingying Fang
Zhenghan Fang
Mohsen Farzi
Hamid Fehri
Lina Felsner
Jianjiang Feng
Jun Feng
Ruibin Feng
Yuan Feng
Zishun Feng
Aaron Fenster
Henrique Fernandes
Ricardo Ferrari
Lukas Fischer
Antonio Foncubierta-Rodríguez
Nils Daniel Forkert
Wolfgang Freysinger
Bianca Freytag
Xueyang Fu
Yunguan Fu
Gareth Funka-Lea
Pedro Furtado
Ryo Furukawa
Laurent Gajny
Francesca Galassi
Adrian Galdran
Jiangzhang Gan
Yu Gan
Melanie Ganz
Dongxu Gao
Linlin Gao
Riqiang Gao
Siyuan Gao
Yunhe Gao
Zeyu Gao
Gautam Gare
Bao Ge

Rongjun Ge
Sairam Geethanath
Shiv Gehlot
Yasmeen George
Nils Gessert
Olivier Gevaert
Ramtin Gharleghi
Sandesh Ghimire
Andrea Giovannini
Gabriel Girard
Rémi Giraud
Ben Glocker
Ehsan Golkar
Arnold Gomez
Ricardo Gonzales
Camila Gonzalez
Cristina González
German Gonzalez
Sharath Gopal
Karthik Gopinath
Pietro Gori
Michael Götz
Shuiping Gou
Maged Goubran
Sobhan Goudarzi
Alejandro Granados
Mara Graziani
Yun Gu
Zaiwang Gu
Hao Guan
Dazhou Guo
Hengtao Guo
Jixiang Guo
Jun Guo
Pengfei Guo
Xiaoqing Guo
Yi Guo
Yuyu Guo
Vikash Gupta
Prashnna Gyawali
Stathis Hadjidemetriou
Fatemeh Haghighi
Justin Haldar
Mohammad Hamghalam
Kamal Hammouda

Bing Han
Liang Han
Seungjae Han
Xiaoguang Han
Zhongyi Han
Jonny Hancox
Lasse Hansen
Huaying Hao
Jinkui Hao
Xiaoke Hao
Mohammad Minhazul Haq
Nandinee Haq
Rabia Haq
Michael Hardisty
Nobuhiko Hata
Ali Hatamizadeh
Andreas Hauptmann
Huiguang He
Nanjun He
Shenghua He
Yuting He
Tobias Heimann
Stefan Heldmann
Sobhan Hemati
Alessa Hering
Monica Hernandez
Estefania Hernandez-Martin
Carlos Hernandez-Matas
Javier Herrera-Vega
Kilian Hett
David Ho
Yi Hong
Yoonmi Hong
Mohammad Reza Hosseinzadeh Taher
Benjamin Hou
Wentai Hou
William Hsu
Dan Hu
Rongyao Hu
Xiaoling Hu
Xintao Hu
Yan Hu
Ling Huang
Sharon Xiaolei Huang
Xiaoyang Huang

Yangsibo Huang
Yi-Jie Huang
Yijin Huang
Yixing Huang
Yue Huang
Zhi Huang
Ziyi Huang
Arnaud Huaulmé
Jiayu Huo
Raabid Hussain
Sarfaraz Hussein
Khoi Huynh
Seong Jae Hwang
Ilknur Icke
Kay Igwe
Abdullah Al Zubaer Imran
Ismail Irmakci
Benjamin Irving
Mohammad Shafkat Islam
Koichi Ito
Hayato Itoh
Yuji Iwahori
Mohammad Jafari
Andras Jakab
Amir Jamaludin
Mirek Janatka
Vincent Jaouen
Uditha Jarayathne
Ronnachai Jaroensri
Golara Javadi
Rohit Jena
Rachid Jennane
Todd Jensen
Debesh Jha
Ge-Peng Ji
Yuanfeng Ji
Zhanghexuan Ji
Haozhe Jia
Meirui Jiang
Tingting Jiang
Xiajun Jiang
Xiang Jiang
Zekun Jiang
Jianbo Jiao
Jieqing Jiao

Zhicheng Jiao
Chen Jin
Dakai Jin
Qiangguo Jin
Taisong Jin
Yueming Jin
Baoyu Jing
Bin Jing
Yaqub Jonmohamadi
Lie Ju
Yohan Jun
Alain Jungo
Manjunath K N
Abdolrahim Kadkhodamohammadi
Ali Kafaei Zad Tehrani
Dagmar Kainmueller
Siva Teja Kakileti
John Kalafut
Konstantinos Kamnitsas
Michael C. Kampffmeyer
Qingbo Kang
Neerav Karani
Turkay Kart
Satyananda Kashyap
Alexander Katzmann
Anees Kazi
Hengjin Ke
Hamza Kebiri
Erwan Kerrien
Hoel Kervadec
Farzad Khalvati
Bishesh Khanal
Pulkit Khandelwal
Maksim Kholiavchenko
Ron Kikinis
Daeseung Kim
Jae-Hun Kim
Jaeil Kim
Jinman Kim
Won Hwa Kim
Andrew King
Atilla Kiraly
Yoshiro Kitamura
Stefan Klein
Tobias Klinder

Lisa Koch
Satoshi Kondo
Bin Kong
Fanwei Kong
Ender Konukoglu
Aishik Konwer
Bongjin Koo
Ivica Kopriva
Kivanc Kose
Anna Kreshuk
Frithjof Kruggel
Thomas Kuestner
David Kügler
Hugo Kuijf
Arjan Kuijper
Kuldeep Kumar
Manuela Kunz
Holger Kunze
Tahsin Kurc
Anvar Kurmukov
Yoshihiro Kuroda
Jin Tae Kwak
Francesco La Rosa
Aymen Laadhari
Dmitrii Lachinov
Alain Lalande
Bennett Landman
Axel Largent
Carole Lartizien
Max-Heinrich Laves
Ho Hin Lee
Hyekyoung Lee
Jong Taek Lee
Jong-Hwan Lee
Soochahn Lee
Wen Hui Lei
Yiming Lei
Rogers Jeffrey Leo John
Juan Leon
Bo Li
Bowen Li
Chen Li
Hongming Li
Hongwei Li
Jian Li

Jianning Li
Jiayun Li
Jieyu Li
Junhua Li
Kang Li
Lei Li
Mengzhang Li
Qing Li
Quanzheng Li
Shaohua Li
Shulong Li
Weijian Li
Weikai Li
Wenyuan Li
Xiang Li
Xingyu Li
Xiu Li
Yang Li
Yuexiang Li
Yunxiang Li
Zeju Li
Zhang Li
Zhiyuan Li
Zhjin Li
Zi Li
Chunfeng Lian
Sheng Lian
Libin Liang
Peixian Liang
Yuan Liang
Haofu Liao
Hongen Liao
Ruizhi Liao
Wei Liao
Xiangyun Liao
Gilbert Lim
Hongxiang Lin
Jianyu Lin
Li Lin
Tiancheng Lin
Yiqun Lin
Zudi Lin
Claudia Lindner
Bin Liu
Bo Liu

Chuanbin Liu
Daochang Liu
Dong Liu
Dongnan Liu
Fenglin Liu
Han Liu
Hao Liu
Haozhe Liu
Hong Liu
Huafeng Liu
Huiye Liu
Jianfei Liu
Jiang Liu
Jingya Liu
Kefei Liu
Lihao Liu
Mengting Liu
Peirong Liu
Peng Liu
Qin Liu
Qun Liu
Shenghua Liu
Shuangjun Liu
Sidong Liu
Tianrui Liu
Xiao Liu
Xingtong Liu
Xinwen Liu
Xinyang Liu
Xinyu Liu
Yan Liu
Yanbei Liu
Yi Liu
Yikang Liu
Yong Liu
Yue Liu
Yuhang Liu
Zewen Liu
Zhe Liu
Andrea Loddo
Nicolas Loménie
Yonghao Long
Zhongjie Long
Daniel Lopes
Bin Lou

Nicolas Loy Rodas
Charles Lu
Huanxiang Lu
Xing Lu
Yao Lu
Yuhang Lu
Gongning Luo
Jie Luo
Jiebo Luo
Luyang Luo
Ma Luo
Xiangde Luo
Cuong Ly
Ilwoo Lyu
Yanjun Lyu
Yuanyuan Lyu
Sharath M S
Chunwei Ma
Hehuan Ma
Junbo Ma
Wenao Ma
Yuhui Ma
Anderson Maciel
S. Sara Mahdavi
Mohammed Mahmoud
Andreas Maier
Michail Mamalakis
Ilja Manakov
Brett Marinelli
Yassine Marrakchi
Fabio Martinez
Martin Maška
Tejas Sudharshan Mathai
Dimitrios Mavroeidis
Pau Medrano-Gracia
Raghav Mehta
Felix Meissen
Qingjie Meng
Yanda Meng
Martin Menten
Alexandre Merasli
Stijn Michielse
Leo Milecki
Fausto Milletari
Zhe Min

Jorg Peters
Terry Peters
Eike Petersen
Jens Petersen
Micha Pfeiffer
Dzung Pham
Hieu Pham
Ashish Phophalia
Tomasz Pieciak
Antonio Pinheiro
Kilian Pohl
Sebastian Pölsterl
Iulia A. Popescu
Alison Pouch
Prateek Prasanna
Raphael Prevost
Juan Prieto
Federica Proietto Salanitri
Sergi Pujades
Kumaradevan Punithakumar
Haikun Qi
Huan Qi
Buyue Qian
Yan Qiang
Yuchuan Qiao
Zhi Qiao
Fangbo Qin
Wenjian Qin
Yanguo Qin
Yulei Qin
Hui Qu
Kha Gia Quach
Tran Minh Quan
Sandro Queirós
Prashanth R.
Mehdi Rahim
Jagath Rajapakse
Kashif Rajpoot
Dhanesh Ramachandram
Xuming Ran
Hatem Rashwan
Daniele Ravì
Keerthi Sravan Ravi
Surreerat Reaungamornrat
Samuel Remedios

Yudan Ren
Mauricio Reyes
Constantino Reyes-Aldasoro
Hadrien Reynaud
David Richmond
Anne-Marie Rickmann
Laurent Risser
Leticia Rittner
Dominik Rivoir
Emma Robinson
Jessica Rodgers
Rafael Rodrigues
Robert Rohling
Lukasz Roszkowiak
Holger Roth
Karsten Roth
José Rouco
Daniel Rueckert
Danny Ruijters
Mirabela Rusu
Ario Sadafi
Shaheer Ullah Saeed
Monjoy Saha
Pranjal Sahu
Olivier Salvado
Ricardo Sanchez-Matilla
Robin Sandkuehler
Gianmarco Santini
Anil Kumar Sao
Duygu Sarikaya
Olivier Saut
Fabio Scarpa
Nico Scherf
Markus Schirmer
Alexander Schlaefer
Jerome Schmid
Julia Schnabel
Andreas Schuh
Christina Schwarz-Gsaxner
Martin Schweiger
Michaël Sdika
Suman Sedai
Matthias Seibold
Raghavendra Selvan
Sourya Sengupta

Carmen Serrano
Ahmed Shaffie
Keyur Shah
Rutwik Shah
Ahmed Shahin
Mohammad Abuzar Shaikh
S. Shailja
Shayan Shams
Hongming Shan
Xinxin Shan
Mostafa Sharifzadeh
Anuja Sharma
Harshita Sharma
Gregory Sharp
Li Shen
Liyue Shen
Mali Shen
Mingren Shen
Yiqing Shen
Ziyi Shen
Luyao Shi
Xiaoshuang Shi
Yiyu Shi
Hoo-Chang Shin
Boris Shirokikh
Suprosanna Shit
Suzanne Shontz
Yucheng Shu
Alberto Signoroni
Carlos Silva
Wilson Silva
Margarida Silveira
Vivek Singh
Sumedha Singla
Ayushi Sinha
Elena Sizikova
Rajath Soans
Hessam Sokooti
Hong Song
Weinan Song
Youyi Song
Aristeidis Sotiras
Bella Specktor
William Speier
Ziga Spiclin

Jon Sporring
Anuroop Sriram
Vinkle Srivastav
Lawrence Staib
Johannes Stegmaier
Joshua Stough
Danail Stoyanov
Justin Strait
Iain Styles
Ruisheng Su
Vaishnavi Subramanian
Gérard Subsol
Yao Sui
Heung-Il Suk
Shipra Suman
Jian Sun
Li Sun
Liyan Sun
Wenqing Sun
Yue Sun
Vaanathi Sundaresan
Kyung Sung
Yannick Suter
Raphael Sznitman
Eleonora Tagliabue
Roger Tam
Chaowei Tan
Hao Tang
Sheng Tang
Thomas Tang
Youbao Tang
Yucheng Tang
Zihao Tang
Rong Tao
Elias Tappeiner
Mickael Tardy
Giacomo Tarroni
Paul Thienphrapa
Stephen Thompson
Yu Tian
Aleksei Tiulpin
Tal Tlusty
Maryam Toloubidokhti
Jocelyne Troccaz
Roger Trullo

Chialing Tsai
Sudhakar Tummala
Régis Vaillant
Jeya Maria Jose Valanarasu
Juan Miguel Valverde
Thomas Varsavsky
Francisco Vasconcelos
Serge Vasylechko
S. Swaroop Vedula
Roberto Vega
Gonzalo Vegas Sanchez-Ferrero
Gopalkrishna Veni
Archana Venkataraman
Athanasios Vlontzos
Ingmar Voigt
Eugene Vorontsov
Xiaohua Wan
Bo Wang
Changmiao Wang
Chunliang Wang
Clinton Wang
Dadong Wang
Fan Wang
Guotai Wang
Haifeng Wang
Hong Wang
Hongkai Wang
Hongyu Wang
Hu Wang
Juan Wang
Junyan Wang
Ke Wang
Li Wang
Liansheng Wang
Manning Wang
Nizhuan Wang
Qiuli Wang
Renzhen Wang
Rongguang Wang
Ruixuan Wang
Runze Wang
Shujun Wang
Shuo Wang
Shuqiang Wang
Tianchen Wang

Tongxin Wang
Wenzhe Wang
Xi Wang
Xiangdong Wang
Xiaosong Wang
Yalin Wang
Yan Wang
Yi Wang
Yixin Wang
Zeyi Wang
Zuhui Wang
Jonathan Weber
Donglai Wei
Dongming Wei
Lifang Wei
Wolfgang Wein
Michael Wels
Cédric Wemmert
Matthias Wilms
Adam Wittek
Marek Wodzinski
Julia Wolleb
Jonghye Woo
Chongruo Wu
Chunpeng Wu
Ji Wu
Jianfeng Wu
Jie Ying Wu
Jiong Wu
Junde Wu
Pengxiang Wu
Xia Wu
Xiyin Wu
Yawen Wu
Ye Wu
Yicheng Wu
Zhengwang Wu
Tobias Wuerfl
James Xia
Siyu Xia
Yingda Xia
Lei Xiang
Tiange Xiang
Deqiang Xiao
Yiming Xiao

Hongtao Xie
Jianyang Xie
Lingxi Xie
Long Xie
Weidi Xie
Yiting Xie
Yutong Xie
Fangxu Xing
Jiarui Xing
Xiaohan Xing
Chenchu Xu
Hai Xu
Hongming Xu
Jiaqi Xu
Junshen Xu
Kele Xu
Min Xu
Minfeng Xu
Moucheng Xu
Qinwei Xu
Rui Xu
Xiaowei Xu
Xinxing Xu
Xuanang Xu
Yanwu Xu
Yanyu Xu
Yongchao Xu
Zhe Xu
Zhenghua Xu
Zhoubing Xu
Kai Xuan
Cheng Xue
Jie Xue
Wufeng Xue
Yuan Xue
Faridah Yahya
Chaochao Yan
Jiangpeng Yan
Ke Yan
Ming Yan
Qingsen Yan
Yuguang Yan
Zengqiang Yan
Baoyao Yang
Changchun Yang

Chao-Han Huck Yang
Dong Yang
Fan Yang
Feng Yang
Fengting Yang
Ge Yang
Guanyu Yang
Hao-Hsiang Yang
Heran Yang
Hongxu Yang
Huijuan Yang
Jiawei Yang
Jinyu Yang
Lin Yang
Peng Yang
Pengshuai Yang
Xiaohui Yang
Xin Yang
Yan Yang
Yifan Yang
Yujiu Yang
Zhicheng Yang
Jiangchao Yao
Jiawen Yao
Li Yao
Linlin Yao
Qingsong Yao
Chuyang Ye
Dong Hye Ye
Huihui Ye
Menglong Ye
Youngjin Yoo
Chenyu You
Haichao Yu
Hanchao Yu
Jinhua Yu
Ke Yu
Qi Yu
Renping Yu
Thomas Yu
Xiaowei Yu
Zhen Yu
Pengyu Yuan
Paul Yushkevich
Ghada Zamzmi

Ramy Zeineldin
Dong Zeng
Rui Zeng
Zhiwei Zhai
Kun Zhan
Bokai Zhang
Chaoyi Zhang
Daoqiang Zhang
Fa Zhang
Fan Zhang
Hao Zhang
Jianpeng Zhang
Jiawei Zhang
Jingqing Zhang
Jingyang Zhang
Jiong Zhang
Jun Zhang
Ke Zhang
Lefei Zhang
Lei Zhang
Lichi Zhang
Lu Zhang
Ning Zhang
Pengfei Zhang
Qiang Zhang
Rongzhao Zhang
Ruipeng Zhang
Ruisi Zhang
Shengping Zhang
Shihao Zhang
Tianyang Zhang
Tong Zhang
Tuo Zhang
Wen Zhang
Xiaoran Zhang
Xin Zhang
Yanfu Zhang
Yao Zhang
Yi Zhang
Yongqin Zhang
You Zhang
Youshan Zhang
Yu Zhang
Yubo Zhang
Yue Zhang

Yulun Zhang
Yundong Zhang
Yunyan Zhang
Yuxin Zhang
Zheng Zhang
Zhicheng Zhang
Can Zhao
Changchen Zhao
Fenqiang Zhao
He Zhao
Jianfeng Zhao
Jun Zhao
Li Zhao
Liang Zhao
Lin Zhao
Qingyu Zhao
Shen Zhao
Shijie Zhao
Tianyi Zhao
Wei Zhao
Xiaole Zhao
Xuandong Zhao
Yang Zhao
Yue Zhao
Zixu Zhao
Ziyuan Zhao
Xingjian Zhen
Haiyong Zheng
Hao Zheng
Kang Zheng
Qinghe Zheng
Shenhai Zheng
Yalin Zheng
Yinqiang Zheng
Yushan Zheng
Tao Zhong
Zichun Zhong
Bo Zhou
Haoyin Zhou
Hong-Yu Zhou
Huiyu Zhou
Kang Zhou
Qin Zhou
S. Kevin Zhou
Sihang Zhou

Outstanding Area Chairs

Outstanding Reviewers

Honorable Mentions (Reviewers)

Ruisheng Su	Erasmus MC, the Netherlands
Liyan Sun	Xiamen University, China
Raphael Sznitman	University of Bern, Switzerland
Elias Tappeiner	UMIT - Private University for Health Sciences, Medical Informatics and Technology, Austria
Mickael Tardy	Hera-MI, France
Juan Miguel Valverde	University of Eastern Finland, Finland
Eugene Vorontsov	Polytechnique Montreal, Canada
Bo Wang	CtrsVision, USA
Tongxin Wang	Meta Platforms, Inc., USA
Yan Wang	Sichuan University, China
Yixin Wang	University of Chinese Academy of Sciences, China
Jie Ying Wu	Johns Hopkins University, USA
Lei Xiang	Subtle Medical Inc, USA
Jiaqi Xu	The Chinese University of Hong Kong, China
Zhoubing Xu	Siemens Healthineers, USA
Ke Yan	Alibaba DAMO Academy, China
Baoyao Yang	School of Computers, Guangdong University of Technology, China
Changchun Yang	Delft University of Technology, the Netherlands
Yujiu Yang	Tsinghua University, China
Youngjin Yoo	Siemens Healthineers, USA
Ning Zhang	Bloomberg, USA
Jianfeng Zhao	Western University, Canada
Tao Zhou	Nanjing University of Science and Technology, China
Veronika Zimmer	Technical University Munich, Germany

Mentorship Program (Mentors)

Ulas Bagci	Northwestern University, USA
Kayhan Batmanghelich	University of Pittsburgh, USA
Hrvoje Bogunovic	Medical University of Vienna, Austria
Ninon Burgos	CNRS - Paris Brain Institute, France
Hao Chen	Hong Kong University of Science and Technology, China
Jun Cheng	Institute for Infocomm Research, Singapore
Li Cheng	University of Alberta, Canada
Aasa Feragen	Technical University of Denmark, Denmark
Zhifan Gao	Sun Yat-sen University, China
Stamatia Giannarou	Imperial College London, UK
Sharon Huang	Pennsylvania State University, USA

Contents – Part VIII

Machine Learning – Model Interpretation

Machine Learning – Uncertainty

Machine Learning Theory and Methodologies

Machine Learning – Weakly-Supervised Learning

CS²: A Controllable and Simultaneous Synthesizer of Images and Annotations with Minimal Human Intervention

Xiaodan Xing[1], Jiahao Huang[1,5], Yang Nan[1], Yinzhe Wu[1,2], Chengjia Wang[3], Zhifan Gao[4], Simon Walsh[1], and Guang Yang[1,5(✉)]

[1] National Heart and Lung Institute, Imperial College London, London, UK
g.yang@imperial.ac.uk
[2] Department of Biomedical and Engineering, Imperial College London, London, UK
[3] Edinburgh Centre for Robotics, Heriot-Watt University, Edinburgh, UK
[4] School of Biomedical Engineering, Sun Yat-sen University, Guangdong, China
[5] Cardiovascular Research Centre, Royal Brompton Hospital, London, UK

Abstract. The destitution of image data and corresponding expert annotations limit the training capacities of AI diagnostic models and potentially inhibit their performance. To address such a problem of data and label scarcity, generative models have been developed to augment the training datasets. Previously proposed generative models usually require manually adjusted annotations (e.g., segmentation masks) or need pre-labeling. However, studies have found that these pre-labeling based methods can induce hallucinating artifacts, which might mislead the downstream clinical tasks, while manual adjustment could be onerous and subjective. To avoid manual adjustment and pre-labeling, we propose a novel controllable and simultaneous synthesizer (dubbed CS²) in this study to generate both realistic images and corresponding annotations at the same time. Our CS² model is trained and validated using high resolution CT (HRCT) data collected from COVID-19 patients to realize an efficient infections segmentation with minimal human intervention. Our contributions include 1) a conditional image synthesis network that receives both style information from reference CT images and structural information from unsupervised segmentation masks, and 2) a corresponding segmentation mask synthesis network to automatically segment these synthesized images simultaneously. Our experimental studies on HRCT scans collected from COVID-19 patients demonstrate that our CS² model can lead to realistic synthesized datasets and promising segmentation results of COVID infections compared to the state-of-the-art nnUNet trained and fine-tuned in a fully supervised manner.

Keywords: Generative model · Semi-supervised segmentation · Data augmentation

---

S. Walsh and G. Yang—Co-last senior authors.

Supplementary Information The online version contains supplementary material available at https://doi.org/10.1007/978-3-031-16452-1_1.

1 Introduction

Medical images with ample annotations are difficult to obtain. This paucity of medical images and labels compromises the performance of AI-based computer-aided diagnosis, including medical image segmentation and classification. Medical image synthesis [3,4] provides an effective and practical strategy for data augmentation that can mitigate the problem of data and labeling scarcity. Generative Adversarial Networks (GAN) [6] is a potent paradigm for realistic medical image synthesis, which can be potentially used for effective data augmentation. In medical image synthesis, three types of GANs are widely used:

The first type of model is called vector-to-image (V2I) GANs, which synthesize augmented images from a vector of noises (Fig. 1 (a)). A recent study [21] used a V2I styleGAN model to produce annotated augmented images from a vector of noises without a pre-labeled dataset. By labeling a handful of those synthesized images and re-inferencing their styleGAN, augmented images with annotations could be obtained. However, the generation of anatomy and the location of the lesions could not be controlled in these V2I models, and the explainability of these generative models was limited, which might sabotage following clinical interpretation and decision making.

The second type is called mask-to-image (M2I) GANs (Fig. 1 (b)). The annotations of these algorithms could be manually adjusted, i.e., combining existing segmentation masks [19,20], or transferred from a labeled dataset in another domain [9]. Unfortunately, fully paired mask-to-image synthesis reduces the variance of synthetic data. Moreover, these models require large human input to feed them with manual pre-labeling, conflicting with our primary aim to alleviate manual labeling workload. Besides, cross-modality models require the labeled dataset in another domain, which might not always be available due to exorbitant costs of additional scanning and patients' physiological limitations.

The third type is vector-to-mask-to-image (V2M2I) GANs. To obtain the segmentation mask, a particular synthesis network in addition to the networks in M2I was designed and trained [1,16]. However, the added segmentation mask synthesis network demanded a large number of labeled samples to make it well trained, which could be up to hundreds for example in [1] thus labor-intensive.

To constrain the synthesis of images and annotations at the same time without using a large scale of pre-labeling, we propose a novel controllable and simultaneous synthesizer (so-called CS^2) in this study. The novelty of our work is three-fold: 1) we develop a novel unsupervised mask-to-image synthesis pipeline that generates images controllably without human labeling; 2) instead of directly using the numeric and disarranged unsupervised segmentation masks, which are cluttered with over-segmented super-pixels, we assign the mean Hounsfield unit (HU) value for each cluster in the unsupervised segmentation masks to obtain an ordered and well-organized labeling; and 3) we propose a new synthesis network structure featured by multiple adaptive instance normalization (AdaIN) blocks that handles unaligned structural and tissue information. The code is publicly available at https://github.com/ayanglab/CS2.

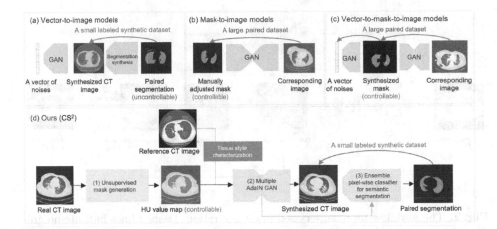

Fig. 1. The rationale of our developed CS² compared to previously proposed data augmentation methods, including vector-to-image (a), mask-to-image (b), and vector-to-mask-to-image (c). Our CS² model can produce a large labeled synthetic dataset controllably without using large-scale pre-labeling or human-labeled datasets.

2 Methods

Our model consists of three major components, including 1) an **unsupervised mask generation** module, which generates unsupervised segmentation masks from input images; 2) a **multiple AdaIN GAN** that receives an unsupervised mask and a reference CT image as inputs, and outputs a synthetic CT image; then we use a small labeled subset of synthetic images and leverage the feature maps from the mask-to-image model to train 3) an **ensemble pixel-wise classifier for semantic segmentation**. Once trained, our model can produce synthetic images and corresponding annotations simultaneously. We present the overall network structure in Fig. 1 (d) and introduce the details of each component as follows.

2.1 Unsupervised Mask Generation

To achieve a controllable synthesis, an adjustable input that contains the structure of synthetic images must be provided. As we mentioned in the Introduction section, the supervised generation of structural masks requires a large scale of pre-labeling. Thus, in our algorithm, we adopt an unsupervised structural mask generation [13] as shown in Fig. 2. Unsupervised segmentation masks are obtained by a super-pixel guided CNN.

Instead of using the disarrayed unsupervised masks directly, we compute the average HU value inside each class and assign this value to each cluster to create the structural guidance maps. In so doing, we can achieve an ordered and well-organized labeling for our unsupervised segmentation mask generation. We refer to this step as the mean HU assignment. According to the mean HU assignment,

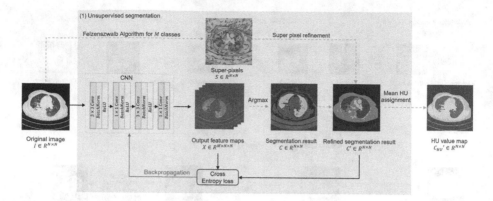

Fig. 2. The workflow for unsupervised mask generation. Dashed lines indicate no gradient back-propagation during the training procedure.

we can easily edit the unsupervised segmentation mask. For example, by adding a patch with an approximate HU value of the COVID infections, we can artificially add a lesion in the synthesized healthy lungs. It is of note that this mean HU assignment step is also crucial for the content matching loss defined in Sect. 2.2.

The unsupervised segmentation algorithm is optimized by the cross-entropy loss between CNN output X and the super-pixel refined mask C'. M is the number of classes initialized for our algorithm and is a pre-defined super parameter. For each cluster m in the super-pixel mask S, we extract the corresponding region $C^{(m)}$ in segmentation result C. Then we count the mostly appeared class in $C^{(m)}$, and assign this value C_{max} as the new label to all elements in $C^{(m)}$ The elements in $C^{(m)}$ is mathematically defined as

$$C_{i,j}^{(m)} = \begin{cases} 0 & S_{i,j} \neq m \\ 1 & S_{i,j} = m \end{cases}.$$

Here, $C_{max}, m, C_{i,j}, S_{i,j}$ are class numbers in the range of $(0, M]$. The refined mask $C' = \sum_{m=1}^{M} C^{(m)}$. This refinement can decrease the number of classes in the segmentation results. Once the number of clusters in the refined segmentation result reaches four or the number of iterations reaches 60, we stop the training of the CNN and use the refined segmentation result C' as our unsupervised masks.

2.2   Multiple AdaIN GAN

For the image synthesis branch, we use a multiple AdaIN GAN shown in Fig. 3. The input of our generator is one HU value map and one non-corresponding reference CT image. An additional reference CT image helps the synthesis network to adopt the style of the whole dataset better, and the unpaired inputs increase the variability of the synthetic images. The encoder extracts feature from both

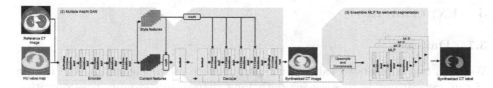

Fig. 3. The network structure of our UM2I model and the ensemble MLP pixel-wise classifier for the segmentation synthesis. Dashed lines indicate no gradient back-propagation during training in this operation.

HU value maps and CT images simultaneously, and an Adaptive Instance Normalization (AdaIN) [8] block normalize the content feature (from the HU value map) with the style feature (e.g., from the CT image). In our multiple AdaIN GAN, AdaIN blocks are added in all convolutional blocks except for the residual blocks (ResBlocks) [7]. This is because AdaIN changes the distribution of feature maps; thus, it corrupts the identity mapping between input feature maps and output feature maps in residual blocks.

The final loss function is composed of three parts: 1) a discriminator loss, which is computed by a patch-based discriminator [5]; 2) a style matching loss, which is the VGG loss [12] between the reference CT and our synthesized CT images; and 3) a content matching loss that is the Mean Squared Error (MSE) loss between the content and our synthesized CT.

In the previously published style transfer network using AdaIN [8], the content matching loss was computed by the VGG loss between content features and the feature maps extracted from the synthesized images. However, this loss function required extra GPU memory and limited the training batch size. We observed in our experiments that a large batch size led to a stable optimization procedure, which was also in accordance with a previous study [2]. Therefore, we replace the content matching loss using the MSE between the HU value map and our synthesized CT images. Due to our mean HU assignment step, this MSE loss function performs better compared to using the original content matching loss.

2.3 Ensemble MLP Classifier for Semantic Segmentation

Once the generative model is trained, we can generate synthetic images. The multiple AdaIN GAN provides effective image representations for synthetic images. We label several synthetic images (30 in our experiments) and then up-sample their features from the decoder into the same size as the original CT image. The features in the decoder are so powerful that even labeling a handful of synthetic images can lead to an accurate segmentation synthesis. We then train an ensemble multi-layer perceptron (MLP) classifier for the pixel-wise classification, as shown in Fig. 3. The ensemble MLP classifier and multiple AdaIN GAN are trained separately. During inference, synthesized CT images and corresponding annotations are produced. In our experiments, we trained 10 MLP classifiers and obtained the final segmentation mask by majority voting. The number of pixel-wise classifiers was selected based on empirical studies according to [21].

3   Experiments

3.1   Dataset

We used two datasets to validate the performance of our algorithm. The target of our experiment is to segment both lung tissues and ground glass opacities (GGOs) from CT images in those datasets. The first dataset is our in-house multi-center chest CT dataset, which contains 7,140 3D CT volumes from 2,071 COVID patients. An experienced radiologist manually labeled 1,192 volumes for this dataset. We randomly selected 192 volumes for independent testing. Detailed descriptions of our private dataset can be found in our supplementary file. The second is an open-access chest CT dataset, COVID-19-CT-Seg, containing 20 3D CT volumes of COVID patients [15]. All CT images from this open-access dataset have left lung, right lung, and infections labeled by two radiologists and verified by an experienced radiologist. It should be noted that we only used the open-access dataset for independent testing.

Our experiments were performed on 4-channel 2.5D CT images, i.e., we selected 4 2D slices from the 3D CT volume and stacked them channel-wise. The 2.5D concept [18] is widely used to represent 3D medical imaging volumes and to reduce computational costs. In this study, we used 2.5D CT representation to handle the varied slice thickness among multi-centered CT data. The selection strategy was a uniform selection from the middle (25%–75%) slices.

3.2   Experimental Settings

We compared our CS^2 with three state-of-the-art models, as shown in Fig. 1. For vector-to-image (V2I) synthesis, we used StyleGAN [14]. For mask-to-image synthesis (M2I), we used the pix2pix [11] model, and the masks are generated by randomly adding circular GGO patches to lung segmentation masks. For the vector-to-mask-to-image synthesis (V2M2I), we used styleGAN to generate synthesis masks and then used the pix2pix model to generate patches. For each generative model, we created synthetic datasets with 4,000 2.5D CT images. We will refer to 2.5D CT images as images or samples in the following section.

We further trained a UNet on these synthetic images together for lung and GGO segmentation. To prove that our synthetic data are representative, we also compared the segmentation result with the transfer-learning based method, i.e., we used a pretrained nnUNet model [10] (task numbered 115 [17]) and fine-tuned the last layer according to 10 volumes from our labeled in-house training dataset.

3.3   Results

Our Model Can Successfully Synthesize Both the Overall Shape of Lungs and Textures of the GGOs. Examples of synthetic images and annotations are shown in Fig. 4. The V2I model, although generates a realistic overall shape of the lung and human body, falsely captures the texture of lung tissues, as shown in Fig. 4 (a1). Since the segmentation mask of the M2I model is manually

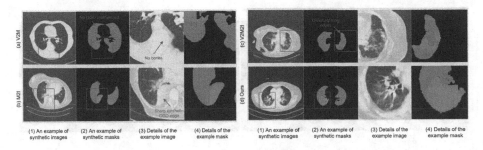

Fig. 4. Example synthetic images from four generative models. The masks are synthetic segmentation masks that corresponded with these images. Red pixels indicate lung tissues and green pixels are GGOs. **We also include synthetic samples of different modalities in our supplementary file.** (Color figure online)

generated, the M2I model failed to capture the gradual change between normal tissues and GGOs, as shown in Fig. 4 (b3). As for the V2M2I synthesized masks shown in Fig. 4 (c2), the lung edges are unnatural. Our model successfully generates realistic synthetic images and annotations. Both M2I and V2M2I models are trained with 500 2.5D CT images.

The Downstream Segmentation Model Trained on CS^2 Synthesized Images Can Reach an Accuracy as High as Fully Supervised Pretrained nnUNet. We trained our ensemble MLP classifier with a different number of labeled synthetic 2.5D CT images and generated 4,000 synthetic masks for each group. Then we trained our segmentation network with these synthetic data. The result is shown in Fig. 5 (a). In our in-house dataset, the UNets trained on CS^2 synthetic datasets with 20, 25, and 30 manual labels even outperform nnUNet which was trained on 199 manually labeled 3D CT volumes and fine-tuned by 10 volumes in a fully supervised manner. It is of note that in the public dataset, the UNet trained on our synthetic datasets did not perform

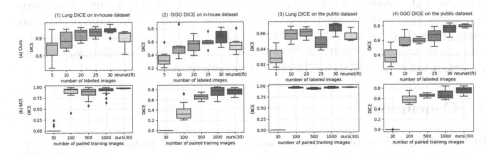

Fig. 5. Dice scores of the lung and GGO on both in-house and public datasets from models trained on CS^2 synthesized (a) and M2I model synthesized (b) datasets.

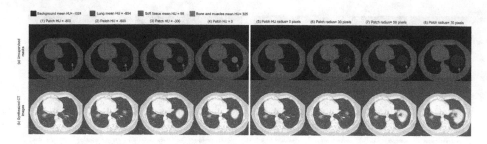

Fig. 6. An example of our synthetic images (b) structurally edited with the Unsupervised masks (a) by adding circular patches of different HU values (1–4) and radii (5–8). The patches in (a1) to (a4) have a radius of 30 pixels, and the patches in (a1) to (a4) have a mean HU value of −600.

as well as the fine-tuned nnUNet. However, our segmentation results are still comparable in such a low-labeled data scenario.

Our CS² Demonstrate Promising Results for Large-Scale Annotated Data Synthesis When Only a Limited Number of Annotations is Required. However, when the number of annotations increased, the performance of the M2I model and V2M2I model improved, as shown in Fig. 5 (b). We only plotted the M2I model performance here because the performance of the V2M2I model was limited by its M2I component. To achieve similar synthesis performance, the M2I model required at least 500 paired training images.

The Synthetic Images of Our Model are Structurally Editable. As shown in Fig. 6, we added circular patches in the lung masks with different mean HU values and different shapes. The mean HU values of the added patches are more decisive than their radius. For example in (b2) to (b4), even though we did not increase the radius of the added patches, our model detected a change from GGOs patches toward background tissue patches, thus automatically adjusting the size of the generated infectious areas. In contrast, as (b4) to (b8) show, once the mean HU value is fixed, the corresponding object is synthesized (e.g., no extraneous tissue or lesion is generated). The example HU values were given by an experienced radiologist, and we present the statistical distributions of HU values in unsupervised masks in our supplementary file.

4   Conclusion

In this study, a generative model called CS² has been proposed for data augmentation. By labeling only a handful of synthetic images (e.g., 30 2.5D CT images in our experimental studies), our CS² model has been able to generate realistic images and annotations at the same time. In addition, our algorithm has no requirement of any large pre-labeling or manually adjusted segmentation masks. Our experiments have proven our hypothesis that the proposed CS^2 has produced realistic synthetic images with annotations, which have enhanced the accuracy of lung tissues and infections segmentation of COVID-19 CT images. One limitation of our work is that we obtained our segmentation masks from a pixel-wise classifier, so the segmentation masks are fuzzy and have a few (8%) scattered wrongly labeled pixels. Post-processing algorithms on segmentation masks such as connected component analysis can remove these artifacts easily.

Acknowledgement. This study was supported in part by the ERC IMI (101005122), the H2020 (952172), the MRC (MC/PC/21013), the Royal Society (IEC\NSFC\211235), the NVIDIA Academic Hardware Grant Program, the SABER project supported by Boehringer Ingelheim Ltd, and the UKRI Future Leaders Fellowship (MR/V023799/1).

References

1. Bailo, O., Ham, D., Min Shin, Y.: Red blood cell image generation for data augmentation using conditional generative adversarial networks. In: Proceedings of the IEEE/CVF Conference on Computer Vision and Pattern Recognition Workshops (2019)
2. Brock, A., Donahue, J., Simonyan, K.: Large scale GAN training for high fidelity natural image synthesis. arXiv preprint arXiv:1809.11096 (2018)
3. Tsaftaris, S.A., Gooya, A., Frangi, A.F., Prince, J.L. (eds.): SASHIMI 2017. LNCS, vol. 10557. Springer, Cham (2017). https://doi.org/10.1007/978-3-319-68127-6
4. Dalmaz, O., Yurt, M., Çukur, T.: ResViT: residual vision transformers for multimodal medical image synthesis. arXiv preprint arXiv:2106.16031 (2021)
5. Demir, U., Unal, G.: Patch-based image inpainting with generative adversarial networks. arXiv preprint arXiv:1803.07422 (2018)
6. Goodfellow, I., et al.: Generative adversarial nets. In: Advances in Neural Information Processing Systems, vol. 27 (2014)
7. He, K., Zhang, X., Ren, S., Sun, J.: Deep residual learning for image recognition. In: Proceedings of the IEEE Conference on Computer Vision and Pattern Recognition, pp. 770–778 (2016)
8. Huang, X., Belongie, S.: Arbitrary style transfer in real-time with adaptive instance normalization. In: Proceedings of the IEEE International Conference on Computer Vision, pp. 1501–1510 (2017)
9. Huo, Y., Xu, Z., Bao, S., Assad, A., Abramson, R.G., Landman, B.A.: Adversarial synthesis learning enables segmentation without target modality ground truth. In: 2018 IEEE 15th International Symposium on Biomedical Imaging (ISBI 2018), pp. 1217–1220. IEEE (2018)
10. Isensee, F., Kickingereder, P., Wick, W., Bendszus, M., Maier-Hein, K.H.: No New-Net. In: Crimi, A., Bakas, S., Kuijf, H., Keyvan, F., Reyes, M., van Walsum, T. (eds.) BrainLes 2018. LNCS, vol. 11384, pp. 234–244. Springer, Cham (2019). https://doi.org/10.1007/978-3-030-11726-9_21
11. Isola, P., Zhu, J.Y., Zhou, T., Efros, A.A.: Image-to-image translation with conditional adversarial networks. In: Proceedings of the IEEE Conference on Computer Vision and Pattern Recognition, pp. 1125–1134 (2017)

12. Johnson, J., Alahi, A., Fei-Fei, L.: Perceptual losses for real-time style transfer and super-resolution. In: Leibe, B., Matas, J., Sebe, N., Welling, M. (eds.) ECCV 2016. LNCS, vol. 9906, pp. 694–711. Springer, Cham (2016). https://doi.org/10.1007/978-3-319-46475-6_43

13. Kanezaki, A.: Unsupervised image segmentation by backpropagation. In: 2018 IEEE International Conference on Acoustics, Speech and Signal Processing (ICASSP), pp. 1543–1547. IEEE (2018)

14. Karras, T., Laine, S., Aila, T.: A style-based generator architecture for generative adversarial networks. In: Proceedings of the IEEE/CVF Conference on Computer Vision and Pattern Recognition, pp. 4401–4410 (2019)

15. Ma, J., et al.: Towards efficient Covid-19 CT annotation: a benchmark for lung and infection segmentation. arxiv 2020, arXiv preprint arXiv:2004.12537 (2020)

16. Pandey, S., Singh, P.R., Tian, J.: An image augmentation approach using two-stage generative adversarial network for nuclei image segmentation. Biomed. Signal Process. Control **57**, 101782 (2020)

17. Roth, H., et al.: Rapid artificial intelligence solutions in a pandemic-the Covid-19-20 lung CT lesion segmentation challenge (2021). researchsquare.com

18. Roth, H.R., et al.: A new 2.5D representation for lymph node detection using random sets of deep convolutional neural network observations. In: Golland, P., Hata, N., Barillot, C., Hornegger, J., Howe, R. (eds.) MICCAI 2014. LNCS, vol. 8673, pp. 520–527. Springer, Cham (2014). https://doi.org/10.1007/978-3-319-10404-1_65

19. Shin, H.-C., et al.: Medical image synthesis for data augmentation and anonymization using generative adversarial networks. In: Gooya, A., Goksel, O., Oguz, I., Burgos, N. (eds.) SASHIMI 2018. LNCS, vol. 11037, pp. 1–11. Springer, Cham (2018). https://doi.org/10.1007/978-3-030-00536-8_1

20. Sun, Y., Yuan, P., Sun, Y.: MM-GAN: 3D MRI data augmentation for medical image segmentation via generative adversarial networks. In: 2020 IEEE International Conference on Knowledge Graph (ICKG), pp. 227–234. IEEE (2020)

21. Zhang, Y., et al.: DatasetGAN: efficient labeled data factory with minimal human effort. In: Proceedings of the IEEE/CVF Conference on Computer Vision and Pattern Recognition, pp. 10145–10155 (2021)

Stabilize, Decompose, and Denoise: Self-supervised Fluoroscopy Denoising

Ruizhou Liu[1], Qiang Ma[1], Zhiwei Cheng[1], Yuanyuan Lyu[1], Jianji Wang[2], and S. Kevin Zhou[3,4]

[1] Z2Sky Technologies Inc., Suzhou, China
[2] Affiliated Hospital of Guizhou Medical University, Guiyang, China
[3] Center for Medical Imaging, Robotics, Analytic Computing and Learning (MIRACLE), School of Biomedical Engineering & Suzhou Institute for Advanced Research, University of Science and Technology of China, Suzhou, China
skevinzhou@ustc.edu.cn
[4] Key Laboratory of Intelligent Information Processing of Chinese Academy of Sciences (CAS) Institute of Computing Technology, CAS, Beijing, China

Abstract. Fluoroscopy is an imaging technique that uses X-ray to obtain a real-time 2D video of the interior of a 3D object, helping surgeons to observe pathological structures and tissue functions especially during intervention. However, it suffers from heavy noise that mainly arises from the clinical use of a low dose X-ray, thereby necessitating the technology of fluoroscopy denoising. Such denoising is challenged by the relative motion between the object being imaged and the X-ray imaging system. We tackle this challenge by proposing a self-supervised, three-stage framework that exploits the domain knowledge of fluoroscopy imaging. (i) Stabilize: we first construct a dynamic panorama based on optical flow calculation to stabilize the non-stationary background induced by the motion of the X-ray detector. (ii) Decompose: we then propose a novel mask-based Robust Principle Component Analysis (RPCA) decomposition method to separate a video with detector motion into a low-rank background and a sparse foreground. Such a decomposition accommodates the reading habit of experts. (iii) Denoise: we finally denoise the background and foreground separately by a self-supervised learning strategy and fuse the denoised parts into the final output via a bilateral, spatiotemporal filter. To assess the effectiveness of our work, we curate a dedicated fluoroscopy dataset of 27 videos (1,568 frames) and corresponding ground truth. Our experiments demonstrate that it achieves significant improvements in terms of denoising and enhancement effects when compared with standard approaches. Finally, expert rating confirms this efficacy.

Keywords: Fluoroscopy Denoising · Image decomposition · Self-supervised learning

Supplementary Information The online version contains supplementary material available at https://doi.org/10.1007/978-3-031-16452-1_2.

1 Introduction

Fluoroscopy is a medical imaging technique that uses X-ray to monitor the interior structure of human body in real-time. It helps surgeons to observe pathological structures and tissue functions especially during intervention, without destroying the external epidermis. While it is desirable to reduce a radiation dose for less harm in clinical practice, the use of low dose results in heavy noise in raw fluoroscopy, thereby necessitating the technology of fluoroscopy denoising. But, fluoroscopy denoising is challenging due to the relative motion of the object being imaging with respect to the imaging system as well as a lack of ground truth clean data.

Video denoising, one of the most fundamental tasks in computer vision, is a procedure that eliminates measurement noise from corrupted video data and recovers the original clean information. In mathematical terms, a corrupted video y can be represented as $y = x + n$, where x is clean video data and n is measurement noise. Conventionally, not only edge-preserving adaptive filters [5], non-local means [2,7,8,18] denoising methods, but Robust Principle Components Analysis (RPCA) [3,11,14,15,19,21], a prominent method on foreground-background problem, is often used on video denoising task, which uses a low-rank subspace model to estimate the background and a spatially sparse model to estimate the foreground. Some models [12,13] employing Total Variation (TV) on RPCA to separate foreground and background, like TVRPCA [4]. While Inc-PCP [21] can iteratively align the estimated background component. However, for non-static background video, a RPCA-based [9] model was proposed, but the approach considers only the common view of the video. In addition, when processing such video data with the Inc-PCP method, the decomposed background information is lost due to the moving background.

Recently, deep learning based denoising approaches become prominent. Fully supervised methods usually train a neural network with *corrupted/clean data pairs* [6,24,25]. However, they require collecting paired data and also have the likelihood of learning an identity mapping instead of statistic feature of noise. Self-supervised models aim to avoid this issue by either inferring real data by the local perceived corrupted data, or predicting clean images based on characteristics of noise [1,10,16,17,20]. Meanwhile, most approaches are designed for natural images, while denoising algorithms for medical imaging data are less common.

In this paper, we propose a novel self-supervised, three-stage fluoroscopy denoising framework for processing a fluoroscopy video with a non-static background. In the first stage, **Stabilize.** In order to preserve temporal consistency and stabilize the given fluoroscopy imaging data, which might still undergo a global motion, a dynamic panorama is constructed for frame registration. In the second stage, **Decompose.** We proposed a simple but novel mask-based RPCA decomposition method to separate the given imaging video with detector motion into a low-rank background and a sparse foreground. In the third stage, **Denoise.** The background and foreground will be denoised, respectively, with a self-supervised denoising strategy, and the foreground is denoised again with spatiotemporal bilateral filtering. Finally, these parts are fused together to obtain final result. We improve the denoising performance of our framework by

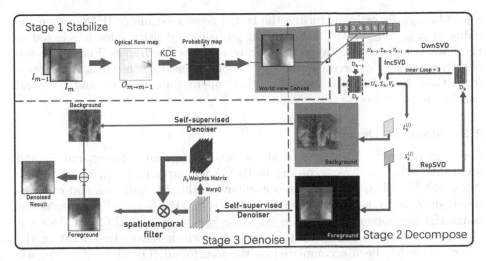

Fig. 1. Overview of the Stabilize, Decompose, and Denoise framework for fluoroscopy denoising.

5–6 dB on a dedicated fluoroscopy imaging video dataset comparing with other approaches. Expert evaluations confirm the efficacy of our framework on clinical images too.

2 Method

We design a self-supervised framework for reducing the noise in fluoroscopy, tackling problem of background shift in RPCA decomposition, and supporting fast data processing. As in Fig. 1, our framework consists of three stages—Stabilize, Decompose and Denoise, whose details are elaborated below.

2.1 Stage 1 - Stabilize

In a fluoroscopy video, the motion of X-ray detector results in a shift in the background, which makes temporal denoising challenging. Inspired by [19], we construct a panorama on a world view canvas for each input video frame to preserve the temporal consistency of input video by compensating the translation between frames.

For a given video stream $Y := \{Y_0, Y_1, ..., Y_{T-1}\} \in \mathbb{R}^{M \times N \times T}$, we first construct a world view canvas. We use the first frame Y_0 as the reference frame of the entire video and place it at the center of the world view canvas. When any given frame Y_m is fed into this stage, we calculate an optical flow field $\mathcal{O}_{m \to m-1} \in \mathbb{R}^{M \times N \times 2}$ between Y_{m-1} and Y_m with optical flow estimator $\mathcal{G}_{flow}$, which is implemented by PWC-Net [23].

Though it is likely that the video foreground possesses more pixels than background, the motion patterns of foreground pixels are random, while those of background pixels are consistent. Thus, the distribution of the optical flow field $\mathcal{O}_{m\to m-1}$ is estimated using the kernel density estimator (KDE), then the value of $[u_{max}, v_{max}]$ with a maximum probability density value is selected as the background offset between the current and previous frames. Finally, we can obtain a panoramic current frame Y_m^{pano} by compensating the translation transformation. Each frame is placed on their appropriate position and temporal consistency of video is preserved.

2.2   Stage 2 - Decompose

For a given frame Y_i, it can be decomposed into sparse foreground S_i and low-rank background L_i according to RPCA assumption. Then, given a mask $\mathcal{M}_i \in \mathbb{R}^{MN\times 1}$ of S_i, in which ones elements in the $\mathcal{M}_i$ indicates non-zero elements of S_i, so we have $\|\mathcal{M}_i\|_F \ll \|1 - \mathcal{M}_i\|_F$, and the $\|\cdot\|_F$ is Frobenius norm. Since the component L_i complies with the assumption of RPCA, it does not change significantly along the temporal axis, which means that most of the noise energy has been accumulated on the foreground. Therefore, if we denoise the background L_i to obtain $\hat{L}_i$ and denoise the foreground S_i to obtain $\hat{S}_i$, then noise energy of $\hat{Y}_i = \hat{L}_i + \hat{S}_i$ must be no more than that of $\hat{X}_i$, which is the result obtained by directly denoising the corrupted image Y_i. Assuming that X_i is a clean version of Y_i, we can prove (in supplementary materials) that

$$\|(1 - \mathcal{M}_i) \odot (X_i - \hat{L}_i)\|_F^2 \leq \|(1 - \mathcal{M}_i) \odot (X_i - \hat{X}_i)\|_F^2, \qquad (1)$$

where the $\odot$ is element-wise multiplication. Denoting the errors in the denoised results $\hat{Y}_i$ and $\hat{X}_i$ by $\epsilon(X_i, \hat{Y}_i)$ and $\epsilon(X_i, \hat{X}_i)$, respectively, using (1), we can further prove that $\epsilon(X_i, \hat{Y}_i) \leq \epsilon(X_i, \hat{X}_i)$ (refer to supplementary materials for more details), which means that **video decomposition results in better denoising performance**.

However, since two consecutive frames after translation compensation do not perfectly overlap with each other in the canvas, we need to deal with this issue. We use $\mathcal{P}_M$ and $\mathcal{P}_{\bar{M}}$ to indicate non-overlapped area and overlapped area between Y_{i-1} and Y_i, respectively. Generally speaking, the non-overlapped area introduces new information, which makes $\mathcal{P}_M(S_i) = 0$ and $\mathcal{P}_M(L_i) = \mathcal{P}_M(Y_i)$. Therefore, we have

$$\begin{cases} \mathcal{P}_{\bar{M}}(\|(1 - \mathcal{M}_i) \odot (X_i - \hat{L}_i)\|_F^2) \leq \mathcal{P}_{\bar{M}}(\|(1 - \mathcal{M}_i) \odot (X_i - \hat{X}_i)\|_F^2), \\ \mathcal{P}_M(\|X_i - \hat{L}_i\|_F^2) = \mathcal{P}_M(\|X_i - \hat{X}_i\|_F^2). \end{cases} \qquad (2)$$

With the help of (2), the same statement $\epsilon(X_i, \hat{Y}_i) \leq \epsilon(X_i, \hat{X}_i)$ still holds (again refer to supplementary materials).

Because the conventional RPCA decomposition methods cannot tackle aforementioned problem, such as Inc-PCP [21], we proposed mask-based RPCA decomposition method as decomposition module in the framework. It inherits four operations from Inc-PCP, PartialSVD, IncSVD, RepSVD and DwnSVD. Through these operations, the U matrix reserving previous background information and two weight matrices Σ and V in the algorithm are maintained and updated. However, because the positions of two consecutive panoramic frames on world view are not the same, we need to fill the non-overlapped areas on Y_i and U before decomposition using the below equations:.

$$\begin{cases} \mathcal{P}_{M_Y}(Y_i) = \mathcal{P}_{M_Y}(U)\text{diag}(\Sigma)(\mathcal{P}_{\bar{M}}(U)\text{diag}(\Sigma))^+\mathcal{P}_{\bar{M}}(Y_i); \\ \mathcal{P}_{M_U}(U) = \mathcal{P}_{M_U}(Y_i)\mathcal{P}_{\bar{M}}(Y_i)^+ (\mathcal{P}_{\bar{M}}(U)\text{diag}(\Sigma))\text{diag}(\Sigma)^+, \end{cases} \tag{3}$$

where $\mathcal{P}_{M_U}$ indicates unknown area on U relatively to known area on Y_i, and $\mathcal{P}_{M_Y}$ refers as unknown area on Y_i corresponding to known area on U. The $(\cdot)^+$ is pseudo inverse matrix. The first equation of (3) is used to complete non-overlapped area on Y_i, and the second equation of (3) is used to fill non-overlapped blank area on U. The aforementioned Inc-PCP operations are then used to decompose Y_i into the foreground S_i and background L_i and update the U matrix, Σ matrix and V matrix.

2.3   Stage 3 - Denoise

At this stage, a single-frame self-supervised denoising network $\mathcal{F}_\theta(\cdot)$ is deployed to denoise the background L_i and foreground S_i decomposed from a corrupted frame Y_i, and the denoised results are denoted by $\hat{L}_i$ and $\hat{S}_i$, respectively. In this work, the Self2Self [20] denoising network is used, and it is worth noting that the Denoise stage is a general stage for self-supervised denoising, which means the denoising model can be substituted with other self-supervised denoising approaches. In the training phase of the Self2Self network, we first generate a lot of training samples through Bernoulli sampling $x^i \sim \mathcal{X}$, donated as $\{\hat{x}_m^i\}_{m=1}^M$, where $\hat{x}_m^i := b_m \odot x^i$. Next, let $\bar{x}_m^i := (1 - b_m) \odot x^i$ and b_m is a down sampling mask. The network is then trained by minimizing the following loss function

$$\mathcal{L}(\theta) = \mathbb{E}_{x \sim \mathcal{X}} \left[\sum_{m=1}^M \|\mathcal{F}_\theta(\hat{x}_m) - \bar{x}_m\|_{b_m}^2 \right]. \tag{4}$$

But in the testing stage, for reducing prediction time, a U-Net [22] as a student module $\mathcal{D}_\omega(\cdot)$ is added into the framework, learning the features of Self2Self network in a fully-supervised manner. The loss function $\mathcal{L}_{student}(\omega)$ is given as

$$\mathcal{L}_{student}(\omega) = \mathbb{E}_{x \sim \mathcal{X}} \left[\sum_{m=1}^M \|\mathcal{D}_\omega(x) - \mathcal{F}_\theta(x)\|_F^2 \right]. \tag{5}$$

Finally, an optical flow based spatiotemporal bilateral filter on foregrounds is adopted for multi-frame denoising. Given $2K + 1$ consecutive foregrounds $\hat{S}_{t-K}, ..., \hat{S}_t, ..., \hat{S}_{t+K}$, for each $k \in \{-K, ..., K\}$, the optical flow $\mathcal{O}_{t+k \to t} \in \mathbb{R}^{M \times N \times 2}$ is calculated. Then we use a bilateral filter to average the warped $2K + 1$ frames for denoising $\overline{S}_t$,

$$\overline{S}_t = \sum_{k=-K}^K \beta_k \cdot \mathcal{W}(\hat{S}_{t+k}, \mathcal{O}_{t+k \to t}), \tag{6}$$

$$\beta_k \propto exp\{-(\mathcal{W}(\hat{S}_{t+k}, \mathcal{O}_{t+k \to t}) - \hat{S}_t)/\rho\}, \sum_k \beta_k = 1, \tag{7}$$

where $\mathcal{W}(\cdot)$ is a warping function and ρ is a parameter controlling the smoothness, with a larger ρ value producing a smoother denoising result.

Table 1. Denoising performances of various self-supervised denoising methods. In each cell, the PSNR and SSIM values are presented. The italics shows our framework adopted other denoiser in Denoise stage. The **bold** shows the best scores.

Gaussian	Method					
	Noise2Void	*Ours w/ N2V*	Noise2Self	*Ours w/ N2S*	Self2Self	*Ours w/ S2S*
0.001	19.27/.919	25.13/**.960**	30.69/.935	34.78/.948	34.39/.941	**36.47**/.941
0.003	15.74/.856	21.98/**.920**	23.99/.854	29.80/.895	29.96/.870	**34.18/.864**
0.005	14.25/.820	19.29/.890	21.01/.801	26.86/.854	27.72/.819	**32.78/.938**

3 Experiment

3.1 Setup Details

Fluoroscopy Dataset. We collect 27 clean fluoroscopy videos (1,568 frames in total) with a high X-ray dose as ground truth, including 20 static-background videos and 7 non-static background videos. For evaluation, we add Gaussian noise with different variances of 0.001, 0.003, and 0.005 into clean images to simulate corrupted data with different noise levels.

Clinical Dataset. We collect 60 groups of real corrupted samples by sampling low dose X-ray videos. Each group consists of 5 images, one of which is the original noisy image, and the remaining four are denoised results obtained by feeding the original noisy image into our method, Noise2Self, Noise2Void and Self2Self, respectively. In addition, for each group, the five images are permuted randomly.

Implementation and Training Stage. We adopt the Self2Self as denoiser, which is trained on X-ray Coronary Angiograms dataset (XCA) of 22 videos and set the probability of Bernoulli sampling as 0.3. When we train student network, the Adam optimizer is used and the learning rate is set as 10^{-4}, and it is trained with 100 epochs with a batch size of 8. In the Stabilize stage, the size of world view canvas is 2048×2048 and frame size $M \times N$ is 1024×1024. The Inc-PCP algorithm is implemented on GPU except the part of filling blank area, with the rank $r = 1$, and the windows size is 30. In spatiotemporal bilateral filter, we set $\rho = 0.02$. All experiments are implemented on an NVIDIA GeForce RTX 2080Ti GPU and using PyTorch.

Metrics. We use peak signal-to-noise ratio (PSNR) and structural similarity index (SSIM) to evaluate denoising performance by comparing the denoised images and its corresponding clean images. To evaluate the extend of blurriness for a given image, image entropy (IE) is used for quantification.

Expert Rating. A proficient radiologist with about 20 years of reading experience is invited to rate the denoised image quality for our Clinical dataset. The criteria include perceived noisiness and completeness of micro-structures like small vessels. The radiologist is asked to rate all the images from each group presented in a random order, from 1 (bad) to 5 (good).

3.2 Results and Discussion

Restoration. We select some state-of-the-art self-supervised deep models, including Noise2Void [16], Noise2Self [1], Self2Self [20] for comparison. The comparison performances are demonstrated in Table 1. It is evident that the PSNR and SSIM scores of our framework (Ours+S2S, the last column) among these self-supervised denoising methods are the best, contributing an improvement of about 5–6 dB compared with other self-supervised methods. Especially the comparison between our results and the results of Self2Self (the second to last column) clearly demonstrates the effectiveness of the Stabilize and Decompose stages. Similarly, in terms of SSIM, ours framework records the best performance. It is noted that even when the noise level increases, our framework is robust too. Figure 2 visualizes the processed results of these methods.

Table 2. Denoising performances of our framework with and without the Stabilize stage. In each cell, the PSNR and SSIM values are presented.

Method	Gaussian			FPS
	0.001	0.003	0.005	
Full three-stage	**36.466/.941**	**34.183/.864**	**32.783/.938**	0.72
w/o Stabilize	36.223/.939	33.229/.852	30.239/.933	4.20

Input	GT	N2V	N2S	S2S	Ours

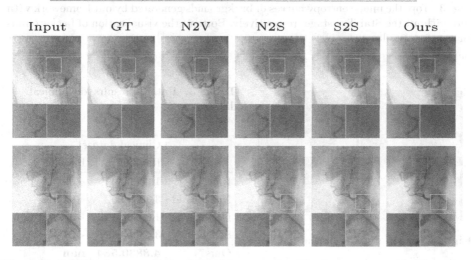

Fig. 2. Left: Visual comparison of denoising results. The images are with Gaussian noise ($\sigma = 0.003$).

Ablation Study. First of all, the detector motion in fluoroscope yields background shifting, which leads to serious blurriness in the background obtained in video decomposition stage. To quantify this artifact, we calculate the image entropy (IE) for the background to verify the effectiveness of the Stabilize stage for preserving temporal consistency of video. The higher IE is, the better. We plot the IE curves of one fluroscopy video with and without the Stabilize stage as shown in Fig. 3. It is clear that the existence of the Stabilize stage preserves more information on the background. Table 2 indicates that preserving more background information can improve the denoising performance. In addition, in order to verify the generalization of our framework, we replace the denoiser in the Denoise stage with other self-supervised models, like Noise2Void, Noise2Self, the result is shown in Table 1. It is clear that our framework boosts a significant performance for all denoising network.

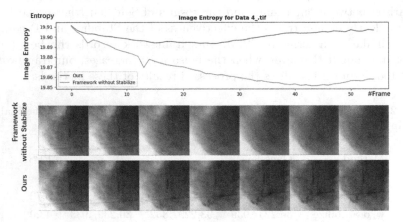

Fig. 3. Top: the image entropy curves of backgrounds generated by our framework with and without the Stabilize stage, respectively. Bottom: the visualization of backgrounds for the two results.

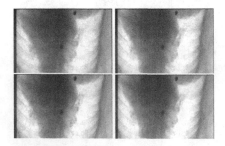

Fig. 4. Visualization of clinical dataset.

Table 3. Ratings results on clinical dataset

	Clinical dataset	
	Ranking	P-value
Raw	1.6000.693	<0.001
Noise2Void	3.3000.962	<0.001
Noise2Self	1.8670.769	<0.001
Self2Self	3.3500.840	<0.001
Ours	**4.8830.584**	**nan**

Clinical Study. Table 3 summarizes the average ratings and P-values for comparison between our model and other competing methods. The performance of our framework is significantly better than Noise2Self [1], Noise2Void [16], Self-2Self [20] on our clinical dataset. Figure 4 shows one group of denoising results of real corrupted data. The top-left, top-right, bottom-left, and bottom-right are denoised by Noise2Void [16], Noise2Self [1], Self2Self [20] and our framework, respectively. It is obvious that the denoised image generated by our framework possesses less noise and better preserves the micro-structures in the image.

4   Conclusion

We propose a three-stages self-supervised denoising framework, consisting of the Stabilize, Decompose, and Denoise stages. In the Stabilize stage, we firstly estimate the optical flow map and then the background offset for each frame to build a panorama. Then in the second Decompose stage, a mask-based RPCA decomposition method is proposed for separating foreground and background. Finally, we invoke a self-supervised denoising method to denoise foreground and background, respectively, and fuse them together with a bilateral temporal-spatial filter as final denoised result. In experiments, visual comparisons and qualitative evaluations demonstrate that our framework yields better image quality than competing methods and exhibits a great potential of boosting self-supervised learning denoising method on Fluoroscopy dataset and Clinical dataset. In the future, we plan to employ deep learning model to estimate affine parameters so that our framework can work on more complex circumstance.

References

1. Batson, J., Royer, L.: Noise2Self: blind denoising by self-supervision. In: International Conference on Machine Learning, pp. 524–533. PMLR (2019)
2. Buades, A., Coll, B., Morel, J.M.: Non-local means denoising. Image Processing On Line **1**, 208–212 (2011)
3. Candès, E.J., Li, X., Ma, Y., Wright, J.: Robust principal component analysis? J. ACM (JACM) **58**(3), 1–37 (2011)
4. Cao, X., Yang, L., Guo, X.: Total variation regularized RPCA for irregularly moving object detection under dynamic background. IEEE Trans. Cybern. **46**(4), 1014–1027 (2016). https://doi.org/10.1109/TCYB.2015.2419737
5. Cerciello, T., Romano, M., Bifulco, P., Cesarelli, M., Allen, R.: Advanced template matching method for estimation of intervertebral kinematics of lumbar spine. Med. Eng. Phys. **33**, 1293–302 (07 2011). https://doi.org/10.1016/j.medengphy.2011.06.009
6. Claus, M., van Gemert, J.: ViDeNN: deep blind video denoising. In: Proceedings of the IEEE/CVF Conference on Computer Vision and Pattern Recognition Workshops (2019)

7. Dabov, K., Foi, A., Egiazarian, K.: Video denoising by sparse 3D transform-domain collaborative filtering. In: 2007 15th European Signal Processing Conference, pp. 145–149 (2007)
8. Dabov, K., Foi, A., Katkovnik, V., Egiazarian, K.: Image denoising by sparse 3-D transform-domain collaborative filtering. IEEE Trans. Image Process. **16**(8), 2080–2095 (2007). https://doi.org/10.1109/TIP.2007.901238
9. Ebadi, S.E., Guerra-Ones, V., Izquierdo, E.: Approximated robust principal component analysis for improved general scene background subtraction. arXiv abs/1603.05875 (2016)
10. Ehret, T., Davy, A., Morel, J.M., Facciolo, G., Arias, P.: Model-blind video denoising via frame-to-frame training. In: Proceedings of the IEEE/CVF Conference on Computer Vision and Pattern Recognition, pp. 11369–11378 (2019)
11. Feng, J., Xu, H., Yan, S.: Online robust PCA via stochastic optimization. In: Advances in Neural Information Processing Systems, pp. 404–412. Citeseer (2013)
12. Guyon, C., Bouwmans, T., Hadi Zahzah, E.: Foreground detection via robust low rank matrix decomposition including spatio-temporal constraint. In: ACCV Workshops (2012)
13. Guyon, C., Bouwmans, T., Zahzah, E.H.: Foreground detection via robust low rank matrix factorization including spatial constraint with iterative reweighted regression, November 2012
14. Han, S., Cho, E.-S., Park, I., Shin, K., Yoon, Y.-G.: Efficient neural network approximation of robust PCA for automated analysis of calcium imaging data. In: de Bruijne, M., et al. (eds.) MICCAI 2021. LNCS, vol. 12907, pp. 595–604. Springer, Cham (2021). https://doi.org/10.1007/978-3-030-87234-2_56
15. He, J., Balzano, L., Szlam, A.: Incremental gradient on the Grassmannian for online foreground and background separation in subsampled video. In: 2012 IEEE Conference on Computer Vision and Pattern Recognition, pp. 1568–1575. IEEE (2012)
16. Krull, A., Buchholz, T.O., Jug, F.: Noise2Void-learning denoising from single noisy images. In: Proceedings of the IEEE/CVF Conference on Computer Vision and Pattern Recognition, pp. 2129–2137 (2019)
17. Lehtinen, J., et al.: Noise2Noise: learning image restoration without clean data. arXiv preprint arXiv:1803.04189 (2018)
18. Maggioni, M., Boracchi, G., Foi, A., Egiazarian, K.: Video denoising using separable 4D nonlocal spatiotemporal transforms. In: Proceedings of SPIE - The International Society for Optical Engineering, vol. 7870, February 2011. https://doi.org/10.1117/12.872569
19. Moore, B.E., Gao, C., Nadakuditi, R.R.: Panoramic robust PCA for foreground-background separation on noisy, free-motion camera video. IEEE Trans. Comput. Imaging **5**(2), 195–211 (2019)
20. Quan, Y., Chen, M., Pang, T., Ji, H.: Self2Self with dropout: learning self-supervised denoising from single image. In: Proceedings of the IEEE/CVF Conference on Computer Vision and Pattern Recognition, pp. 1890–1898 (2020)
21. Rodriguez, P., Wohlberg, B.: Incremental principal component pursuit for video background modeling. J. Math. Imaging Vision **55**(1), 1–18 (2016)
22. Ronneberger, O., Fischer, P., Brox, T.: U-Net: convolutional networks for biomedical image segmentation. In: Navab, N., Hornegger, J., Wells, W.M., Frangi, A.F. (eds.) MICCAI 2015. LNCS, vol. 9351, pp. 234–241. Springer, Cham (2015). https://doi.org/10.1007/978-3-319-24574-4_28

23. Sun, D., Yang, X., Liu, M.Y., Kautz, J.: PWC-Net: CNNs for optical flow using pyramid, warping, and cost volume. In: Proceedings of the IEEE Conference on Computer Vision and Pattern Recognition, pp. 8934–8943 (2018)
24. Wang, C., Zhou, S.K., Cheng, Z.: First image then video: a two-stage network for spatiotemporal video denoising. arXiv preprint arXiv:2001.00346 (2020)
25. Zhang, K., Zuo, W., Zhang, L.: FFDNet: toward a fast and flexible solution for CNN-based image denoising. IEEE Trans. Image Process. 27(9), 4608–4622 (2018)

Discrepancy-Based Active Learning for Weakly Supervised Bleeding Segmentation in Wireless Capsule Endoscopy Images

Fan Bai[1], Xiaohan Xing[2], Yutian Shen[1], Han Ma[1], and Max Q.-H. Meng[1,3(✉)]

[1] Department of Electronic Engineering, The Chinese University of Hong Kong,
Shatin, Hong Kong
{fanbai,yt.shen,hanma}@link.cuhk.edu.hk
[2] Department of Electrical Engineering, City University of Hong Kong,
Kowloon, Hong Kong
xiaoxing@cityu.edu.hk
[3] Department of Electronic and Electrical Engineering,
Southern University of Science and Technology, Shenzhen, China
max.meng@sustech.edu.cn

Abstract. Weakly supervised methods, such as class activation maps (CAM) based, have been applied to achieve bleeding segmentation with low annotation efforts in Wireless Capsule Endoscopy (WCE) images. However, the CAM labels tend to be extremely noisy, and there is an irreparable gap between CAM labels and ground truths for medical images. This paper proposes a new Discrepancy-basEd Active Learning (DEAL) approach to bridge the gap between CAMs and ground truths with a few annotations. Specifically, to liberate labor, we design a novel discrepancy decoder model and a CAMPUS (CAM, Pseudo-label and groUnd-truth Selection) criterion to replace the noisy CAMs with accurate model predictions and a few human labels. The discrepancy decoder model is trained with a unique scheme to generate standard, coarse and fine predictions. And the CAMPUS criterion is proposed to predict the gaps between CAMs and ground truths based on model divergence and CAM divergence. We evaluate our method on the WCE dataset and results show that our method outperforms the state-of-the-art active learning methods and reaches comparable performance to those trained with full annotated datasets with only 10% of the training data labeled. The source code is available at https://github.com/baifanxxx/DEAL.

Keywords: Active learning · Segmentation · WCE images

1 Introduction

Wireless Capsule Endoscopy (WCE) [10] is a first-line diagnostic tool for GI tract cancers due to its non-invasiveness to patients. It can capture images of the entire gastrointestinal tract, allowing visualization and diagnosis of the abnormalities and diseases in the GI tract. In recent years, researchers have paid more

L. Wang et al. (Eds.): MICCAI 2022, LNCS 13438, pp. 24–34, 2022.
https://doi.org/10.1007/978-3-031-16452-1_3

attention to the problem of abnormality classification [11, 22] and detection [6], such as bleeding, polyps, inflammatory and other abnormalities in WCE images. Compared to these, abnormality segmentation [9] is more challenging due to the complexity of the task and the mass annotation cost caused by pixel-level labels.

Weakly supervised methods, especially CAM-based [16, 23], have attracted increasing attention due to high data efficiency [20, 21]. Without any pixel-level labels, these methods are capable of achieving segmentation relying on the CAMs. However, there is an irreparable gap between the generated CAMs and the ground truths, even though weakly supervised learning is constantly evolving. We experimentally find that existing weakly supervised methods [16] perform poorly on the WCE bleeding segmentation task due to the gaps between CAMs and ground truths. Since medical diagnosis requires exceptionally high accuracy, bridging the gap is critical to the practical application of weakly supervised methods. Intuitively, replacing the nasty CAMs with more accurate pseudo labels and ground truths will revitalize these methods from a data perspective and makes the performance of weakly supervised learning infinitely close to that of full supervision. But how to pick out the nasty CAMs is a critical problem.

Active learning is an efficient data selection strategy that selects the most informative samples for annotation based on uncertainty [2], data distribution [17, 19], model gradient [4], and other criteria. These methods work well utilizing only unlabeled data. However, in weakly supervised training, all data are annotated by rough CAMs rather than nothing. Therefore, estimating the CAM uncertainty is far more important than traditional criteria under weak supervision. Moreover, previous active learning mainly focused on selecting the human labels, ignoring the accurate pseudo labels from model predictions. However, these accurate pseudo labels can also be selected to replace the nasty CAMs under weak supervision. Since pseudo labels do not increase the labeling burden, it is cost-effective to design a criterion that skillfully combines pseudo labels and ground truths in active learning.

In this paper, we propose the first label selection method to advance weakly supervised to approach fully supervised performance. Our contribution consists of three parts: (1) We design a novel Discrepancy-basEd Active Learning (DEAL) pipeline to select the nasty CAMs and replace them with pseudo labels and a few human annotations, which achieves superior performance; (2) We build a new discrepancy decoder model and design a novel scheme to train it with different propensities to produces standard, coarse and fine predictions, while avoiding unstable single predictions and noisy CAMs; (3) We propose the CAMPUS criterion based on model divergence and CAM divergence, selecting pseudo labels and ground truths to trade off labeling burden and performance. The results show our DEAL outperforms other active learning methods, achieving a comparable performance of full annotated training and saving 90% human labels.

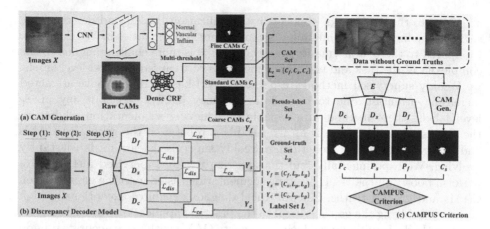

Fig. 1. The overview of our proposed DEAL method. (a) The CAM generation with three different propensities. (b) The training of discrepancy decoder model with three steps. (c) The CAMPUS criterion based on model divergence and CAM divergence.

2   Methodology

The overview of our work with three components is demonstrated in Fig. 1: (a) CAM generation, (b) discrepancy decoder model, (c) CAMPUS criterion. First, we train a classification model based on image-level labels to generate standard CAMs C_s, coarse CAMs C_c and fine CAMs C_f. For segmentation, there are CAMs in the initial label set L_c, and the discrepancy decoder model M_d is trained by L_c under a novel training scheme. In each active learning cycle, guided by DEAL, we select K_g samples for human labeling to form ground-truth set L_g and K_p samples for pseudo labels to form pseudo-label set L_p. Since the pseudo labels have no label burden, K_p is an adaptive parameter rather than a hyperparameter. In the end, our label set L consists of CAM set L_c, pseudo-label set L_p, and ground-truth set L_g, which guarantees the performance of the segmentation model M_d with as little labor cost as possible.

2.1   CAM Generation

Image segmentation requires a huge amount of pixel-level labels, resulting in labeling burden, especially in medical images which need expert experience. Fortunately, supervised by image-level labels only, the CAMs can roughly locate the foreground regions and provide good seeds for segmentation. In this paper, we follow the main-stream approach to train a fully supervised classification model with image-level labels. We replace the stride with dilation in the last layer to increase the map size on ResNet-50. Meanwhile, we also use regularization terms, drop blocks, and data augmentation to guarantee a good performance. After training, we calculate the CAMs via the Grad-CAM method [16]:

$$\alpha_i^c = \frac{1}{Z} \sum_{h=1}^{m} \sum_{w=1}^{n} \frac{\partial S_c}{\partial A_{hw}^i} \tag{1}$$

$$L_{Grad-CAM}^c = ReLU(\sum_i \alpha_i^c A^i) \tag{2}$$

where α_i^c is the weight connecting the ith feature map with the cth class, S_c is the classification score of class c, A_{hw}^i is the value of ith feature map h^{th} row wth column, Z is the number of pixels in the feature map ($Z = \sum_h \sum_w 1$).

To deal with the high false positives problem [12] in medical images, we post process the CAMs with dense CRF [3] to refine the boundaries and reduce noise. Nevertheless, we can not eliminate the noise completely. To evaluate the uncertainty of the CAM generation, we leverage multi-threshold to generate standard, coarse and fine CAMs, and prepare to train the discrepancy decoder model. In Fig. 1(a), we set the best, low and high thresholds to generate the standard, coarse and fine CAMs, respectively. Compared with the standard CAMs, the coarse CAMs have coarser boundaries with higher false positives and the fine CAMs have more detailed textures with higher false negatives. These different CAMs train the discrepancy decoders to form corresponding propensities, described in detail below.

2.2   Discrepancy Decoder Model

Intuitively, the straightforward way to assess the CAM uncertainty is to measure the difference between model predictions and CAMs. However, due to the noisy CAMs and the unstable model with noisy training, we can not accurately judge whether this gap is caused by CAM uncertainty or model uncertainty. With the help of multiple discrepancy models, we can estimate model uncertainty and CAM uncertainty, respectively. Different from the model ensemble approach [1], these discrepancy models should not be arbitrary. They should have two properties: (1) The decision boundary between discrepancy models and the standard model should be adjacent to prevent departure from the standard model; (2) The prediction discrepancy should be positively related to the CAM uncertainty instead of being arbitrary. Next, we will detail the discrepancy decoder model and training scheme.

Network Architecture: Our novel discrepancy decoder model is shown in Fig. 1(b). Without loss of generality, we directly leverage U-Net [13] used in medical image segmentation. For the encoder E, we adopt ResNet-18 [8] and replace the stride with dilation to increase the receptive field. We use the same structure of three U-Net decoders D_s, D_c and D_f. For fairness, the model's performance is evaluated by D_s, and other decoders only work in label selection.

Training Procedure: Let E denotes the encoder parameterized by θ_E. The decrepancy decoders D_s, D_c and D_f are parameterized by θ_{D_s}, θ_{D_c} and θ_{D_f}, respectively. For input images X, there are label sets Y_s, Y_c and Y_f from the standard CAMs C_s, coarse CAMs C_c and fine CAMs C_f, respectively. After active label selection, we replace some CAMs with pseudo labels or ground truths. In Fig. 1(b), our novel training scheme consists of three steps:

(1) We train the encoder E and decoder D_s using Y_s. The objective is

$$\min_{\theta_E, \theta_{D_s}} \mathcal{L}_{ce}(D_s(E(X)), Y_s), \tag{3}$$

where $\mathcal{L}_{ce}$ denotes the loss function with Cross-Entropy and Dice loss.

(2) We duplicate θ_{D_s} to θ_{D_c} and θ_{D_f}, fix the encoder E, and train the two decoders D_c and D_f with Y_c and Y_f to maximize the prediction discrepancy, which forms different prediction propensities and makes the discrepancy larger. To get a coarse decoder and a fine decoder, the objective is:

$$\min_{\theta_{D_c}, \theta_{D_f}} \mathcal{L}_{ce}(D_c(E(X)), Y_c) + \mathcal{L}_{ce}(D_f(E(X)), Y_f) - \mathcal{L}_{dis}(D_c(E(X)), D_f(E(X))), \tag{4}$$

where $\mathcal{L}_{dis}$ denotes the L1 distance between the two discrepancy predictions, which is proved effective in [14].

(3) We fine-tune the decoders D_c and D_f to minimize the prediction discrepancy with D_s, making the boundary of the discrepancy decoders always surround the boundary of the standard decoder. The objective function is defined as:

$$\min_{\theta_{D_c}, \theta_{D_f}} \mathcal{L}_{dis}(D_c(E(X)), D_s(E(X))) + \mathcal{L}_{dis}(D_f(E(X)), D_s(E(X))). \tag{5}$$

In the training process, we first train the model according to step (1). Then we iterate steps (2) and (3) for several epochs. After that, we obtain a model with a shared encoder, a standard decoder and two discrepancy decoders.

2.3 CAMPUS Criterion

Evaluating the CAM uncertainty and the model uncertainty is crucial for selection. In this regard, we define the model divergence and the CAM divergence for selecting pseudo labels and ground truths in the CAMPUS criterion. To avoid weights that are difficult to balance between different criteria, we do not use additive combinations but better multiplicative combinations.

Model Divergence: The model divergence represents the model uncertainty, including prediction entropy and divergence among three discrepancy decoders. The prediction divergence is related to the standard prediction P_s, coarse prediction P_c and fine prediction P_f. If one sample has three very different predictions, the prediction is likely to be unreliable. In detail, we measure the score of model divergence S_{md} based on the formula below.

$$S_{md} = S_e \cdot (\mathcal{D}(P_s, P_c) + \mathcal{D}(P_s, P_f) + \mathcal{D}(P_c, P_f)), \tag{6}$$

Table 1. The segmentation performance of the competing approaches. The 95% of the performance with 100% ground truths is 0.7840, which is a line for achieving comparable performance to fully supervised learning in active learning [18]

Method	Dice with ground truths				
	0%	10%	20%	30%	100%
Random	0.7364	0.7598(0.0250)	0.7836(0.0214)	0.7837(0.0223)	0.8253
Dice	(0.0254)	0.7645(0.0274)	0.7871(0.0253)	0.7933(0.0187)	(0.0163)
VAAL [19]		0.7644(0.0252)	0.7810(0.0248)	0.7973(0.0171)	
CoreSet [17]		0.7598(0.0245)	0.7762(0.0279)	0.7937(0.0202)	
CoreGCN [2]		0.7697(0.0215)	0.7845(0.0167)	0.7899(0.0251)	
UncertaintyGCN [2]		0.7598(0.0233)	0.7796(0.0266)	0.7953(0.0225)	
GGS [4]		0.7618(0.0163)	0.7836(0.0204)	0.7988(0.0227)	
DEAL (w/o pseudo labels)		0.7735(0.0242)	0.7967(0.0134)	0.8066(0.0172)	
DEAL	**0.7626**	**0.7947**	**0.7973**	**0.8083**	
	(0.0270)	**(0.0211)**	**(0.0149)**	**(0.0215)**	

where $\mathcal{D} = 1 - \frac{2TP}{FP+2TP+FN}$ defines the Dice distance between predictions. Here TP, FP, TN, and FN are true positive, false positive, true negative and false negative. The prediction entropy $S_e = -\frac{1}{N}\sum_{i=1}^{N} p_{si} \log p_{si}$ denotes the prediction uncertainty of the standard decoder, where p_{si} is the probability of the ith pixel in P_s.

CAM Divergence: The CAM divergence defines the divergence between predictions and CAMs, positively related to the CAM uncertainty. To eliminate the outliers of the prediction, we design the score S_{cd} by the distance between CAMs and two predictions that are closest to the CAMs.

$$S_{cd} = sum\{D_3\} - max\{D_3\}, \mathcal{D}_3 = \{\mathcal{D}(P_s,Y_s), \mathcal{D}(P_c,Y_s), \mathcal{D}(P_f,Y_s)\} \qquad (7)$$

In pseudo-label selection, we should pick out the samples with small model divergence and large CAM divergence for pseudo labels, implying noisy CAMs and accurate predictions. The criterion S_p is

$$S_p = (3 - S_{md}) \cdot S_{cd}. \qquad (8)$$

We sort the images in increasing order, locate the knee point K_p of the score curve by KneeLocator [15], and select the higher point.

In ground-truth selection, we select uncertainty samples with large model divergence and CAM divergence for human labeling. The criterion S_g is

$$S_g = S_{md} \cdot S_{cd}. \qquad (9)$$

We sort S_g in increasing order and select top K_g values to annotate manually.

Table 2. The ablation studies for our proposed method. We show the changes compared to the initial under different settings in pseudo-label and 20% ground-truth selection.

Discrepancy model	Model divergence	CAM divergence	Pseudo-label selection	Ground-truth selection
×	×	✓	−8.70%	+3.77%
✓	✓	×	+2.01%	+3.51%
✓	×	✓	+2.07%	+4.42%
✓	✓	✓	+2.62%	+6.09%

3   Experiments and Results

3.1   Experimental Settings

Datasets: We conducted experiments on the CAD-CAP WCE dataset [5]. It contains 1812 images with both image-level and pixel-level labels available (600 normal images, 605 vascular images and 607 inflammatory images). In data preprocessing, we adopted the deformation field [7] to preprocess all images to 320×320. We split labeled data by 5-fold cross-validation and calculated the $Dice = \frac{2TP}{FP+2TP+FN}$ as the metric to evaluate the performance.

Competing Approaches: For label selection, we compared our DEAL with various types of active learning methods: (1) Random; (2) Dice, which computes the CAM uncertainty naively using the Dice between predictions and CAMs; (3) VAAL [19] (diversity-based); (4) CoreSet [17] (representativeness-based); (5) CoreGCN [2] (representativeness-based); (6) UncertaintyGCN [2] (uncertainty-based); (7) GGS [4] (gradient-based). (8) Our DEAL without pseudo labels; (9) Our DEAL. Since methods (3)–(7) require an initial label set as a reference, we randomly initialized half of the budget and actively selected the other half in the first cycle. From the second cycle, all methods selected labels normally to reach the budget.

Training Setup: We conducted our experiment on a single GTX 3090 GPU with Pytorch. In CAM generation, we trained a ResNet-50 model to classify images into normal, vascular and inflammatory to generate high-quality CAMs. The standard, coarse and fine CAMs about vascular were generated by thresholds 0.8, 0.75, and 0.85 as multi-threshold masks for segmentation. In segmentation, we trained our discrepancy decoder model to segment the bleeding and background with the Adam optimizer of learning rate 0.003 for 50 epochs. To eliminate the effects of the model ensemble and training process, we only used the output of the standard decoder as the model's predictions in the test. We conducted all segmentation experiments under fixed random seeds and 5-fold cross-validation and calculated the mean and variance.

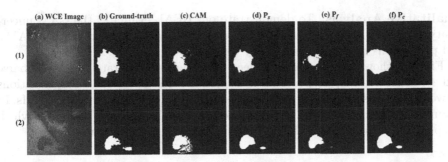

Fig. 2. (1) In ground-truth selection, we pick out samples with large divergence in three predictions and the CAM. (2) In pseudo-label selection, we select samples with small model divergence and large CAM divergence.

3.2 Results

Evaluation of Label Selection: After training with CAMs as the initial, all methods selected 10% CAMs actively replaced by ground truths via human labeling in each cycle. Three rounds of active selection were performed. Our DEAL selected pseudo labels before the first cycle because of the CAMPUS criterion. Table 1 shows the selection performance of the competing approaches. We can see that our DEAL (w/o pseudo labels) and DEAL outperform other methods on 10%, 20%, and 30% ground truths, respectively. By comparing DEAL and DEAL (w/o pseudo labels), we concluded labeling gain of pseudo-label selection is significant. After pseudo-label selection, our DEAL is 2.6% higher than the initial model without any ground truth. We surprisingly find that our DEAL outperforms 95% performance of full supervised training with only 10% ground truths, which is much better than other methods. Our DEAL can reach performance saturation quickly under a few ground truths and achieve 0.8083 on Dice finally. Obviously, other methods are far inferior to ours. Our DEAL saves 90% ground truths and achieves the comparable performance of full supervised training, which is of great significance to medical image segmentation.

Ablation Studies: We conducted ablation studies on the discrepancy decoder model, model divergence, and CAM divergence, respectively. Specifically, we compared the pseudo-label and 20% ground-truth selection performance under different settings and showed the performance changes compared with the initial model. Note that the none-discrepancy decoder model can not obtain model divergence. Table 2 shows the effect of each part of DEAL on model performance. We find the single network without model divergence evaluation can not accurately select the pseudo labels, resulting in −8.80% performance degradation. In the CAMPUS criterion, both the model divergence and the CAM divergence play a crucial role, and lacking any of them is massive destruction of performance.

Qualitative Analysis: To demonstrate our DEAL evaluates the CAM uncertainty more intuitively, we visualized the WCE images, ground truths, CAMs, and predictions from the discrepancy decoder model on Fig. 2, respectively.

Figure 2 shows our discrepancy decoder model can generate standard, coarse and fine predictions, respectively. In pseudo-label selection, the predictions between three discrepancy decoders are similar but very different from CAMs. In ground-truth selection, both three predictions and CAMs have large gaps which are positively correlated with the gaps between CAMs and ground truths.

4   Conclusions

In this paper, we propose a novel Discrepancy-basEd Active Learning (DEAL) approach to bridge the gaps between the CAMs and the ground truths with pseudo labels and a few annotations. With the designed discrepancy decoder model and CAMPUS criterion, our approach can detect the samples with noisy CAMs and replace them with high-quality pseudo labels and ground truths to minimize human labeling costs. As the first label selection method to advance weakly supervised to approach fully supervised performance, our DEAL saves labeling burden significantly. In the future, our method can be transferred to a wide variety of medical image applications and save the labeling burden.

Acknowledgements.. The work described in this paper was supported by National Key R&D program of China with Grant No. 2019YFB1312400, Hong Kong RGC CRF grant C4063-18G, and Hong Kong RGC GRF grant # 14211420.

References

1. Beluch, W.H., Genewein, T., Nürnberger, A., Köhler, J.M.: The power of ensembles for active learning in image classification. In: Proceedings of the IEEE Conference on Computer Vision and Pattern Recognition, pp. 9368–9377 (2018)
2. Caramalau, R., Bhattarai, B., Kim, T.K.: Sequential graph convolutional network for active learning. In: Proceedings of the IEEE/CVF Conference on Computer Vision and Pattern Recognition, pp. 9583–9592 (2021)
3. Chen, L.C., Papandreou, G., Kokkinos, I., Murphy, K., Yuille, A.L.: DeepLab: semantic image segmentation with deep convolutional nets, atrous convolution, and fully connected CRFs. IEEE Trans. Pattern Anal. Mach. Intell. **40**(4), 834–848 (2017)
4. Dai, C., et al.: Suggestive annotation of brain tumour images with gradient-guided sampling. In: Martel, A.L., et al. (eds.) MICCAI 2020. LNCS, vol. 12264, pp. 156–165. Springer, Cham (2020). https://doi.org/10.1007/978-3-030-59719-1_16
5. Dray, X., et al.: Cad-cap: une base de données française à vocation internationale, pour le développement et la validation d'outils de diagnostic assisté par ordinateur en vidéocapsule endoscopique du grêle. Endoscopy **50**(03), 000441 (2018)
6. Goel, N., Kaur, S., Gunjan, D., Mahapatra, S.: Dilated CNN for abnormality detection in wireless capsule endoscopy images. Soft Comput. **26**, 1231–1247 (2022)

7. Guo, X., Yuan, Y.: Semi-supervised WCE image classification with adaptive aggregated attention. Med. Image Anal. **64**, 101733 (2020)

8. He, K., Zhang, X., Ren, S., Sun, J.: Deep residual learning for image recognition. In: Proceedings of the IEEE Conference on Computer Vision and Pattern Recognition, pp. 770–778 (2016)

9. Jia, X., Mai, X., Xing, X., Shen, Y., Wang, J., Meng, M.Q.H.: Multibranch learning for angiodysplasia segmentation with attention-guided networks and domain adaptation. In: 2021 IEEE International Conference on Robotics and Automation (ICRA), pp. 12373–12379. IEEE (2021)

10. Jia, X., Xing, X., Yuan, Y., Xing, L., Meng, M.Q.H.: Wireless capsule endoscopy: a new tool for cancer screening in the colon with deep-learning-based polyp recognition. Proc. IEEE **108**(1), 178–197 (2019)

11. Muruganantham, P., Balakrishnan, S.M.: Attention aware deep learning model for wireless capsule endoscopy lesion classification and localization. J. Med. Biol. Eng. **42**, 157–168 (2022)

12. Qu, H., et al.: Weakly supervised deep nuclei segmentation using partial points annotation in histopathology images. IEEE Trans. Med. Imaging **39**(11), 3655–3666 (2020)

13. Ronneberger, O., Fischer, P., Brox, T.: U-Net: convolutional networks for biomedical image segmentation. In: Navab, N., Hornegger, J., Wells, W.M., Frangi, A.F. (eds.) MICCAI 2015. LNCS, vol. 9351, pp. 234–241. Springer, Cham (2015). https://doi.org/10.1007/978-3-319-24574-4_28

14. Saito, K., Watanabe, K., Ushiku, Y., Harada, T.: Maximum classifier discrepancy for unsupervised domain adaptation. In: Proceedings of the IEEE Conference on Computer Vision and Pattern Recognition, pp. 3723–3732 (2018)

15. Satopaa, V., Albrecht, J., Irwin, D., Raghavan, B.: Finding a "Kneedle" in a haystack: detecting knee points in system behavior. In: 2011 31st International Conference on Distributed Computing Systems Workshops, pp. 166–171. IEEE (2011)

16. Selvaraju, R.R., Cogswell, M., Das, A., Vedantam, R., Parikh, D., Batra, D.: Grad-CAM: visual explanations from deep networks via gradient-based localization. In: Proceedings of the IEEE International Conference on Computer Vision, pp. 618–626 (2017)

17. Sener, O., Savarese, S.: Active learning for convolutional neural networks: a core-set approach. arXiv preprint arXiv:1708.00489 (2017)

18. Siddiqui, Y., Valentin, J., Niebner, M.: ViewAL: active learning with viewpoint entropy for semantic segmentation. In: 2020 IEEE/CVF Conference on Computer Vision and Pattern Recognition (CVPR) (2020)

19. Sinha, S., Ebrahimi, S., Darrell, T.: Variational adversarial active learning. In: Proceedings of the IEEE/CVF International Conference on Computer Vision, pp. 5972–5981 (2019)

20. Tang, W., et al.: M-SEAM-NAM: multi-instance self-supervised equivalent attention mechanism with neighborhood affinity module for double weakly supervised segmentation of COVID-19. In: de Bruijne, M., et al. (eds.) MICCAI 2021. LNCS, vol. 12907, pp. 262–272. Springer, Cham (2021). https://doi.org/10.1007/978-3-030-87234-2_25

21. Wu, K., Du, B., Luo, M., Wen, H., Shen, Y., Feng, J.: Weakly supervised brain lesion segmentation via attentional representation learning. In: Shen, D., et al. (eds.) MICCAI 2019. LNCS, vol. 11766, pp. 211–219. Springer, Cham (2019). https://doi.org/10.1007/978-3-030-32248-9_24

22. Xing, X., Hou, Y., Li, H., Yuan, Y., Li, H., Meng, M.Q.-H.: Categorical relation-preserving contrastive knowledge distillation for medical image classification. In: de Bruijne, M., et al. (eds.) MICCAI 2021. LNCS, vol. 12905, pp. 163–173. Springer, Cham (2021). https://doi.org/10.1007/978-3-030-87240-3_16
23. Zhou, B., Khosla, A., Lapedriza, A., Oliva, A., Torralba, A.: Learning deep features for discriminative localization. In: Proceedings of the IEEE Conference on Computer Vision and Pattern Recognition, pp. 2921–2929 (2016)

Diffusion Models for Medical Anomaly Detection

Julia Wolleb$^{(\boxtimes)}$, Florentin Bieder, Robin Sandkühler, and Philippe C. Cattin

Department of Biomedical Engineering, University of Basel, Allschwil, Switzerland
julia.wolleb@unibas.ch

Abstract. In medical applications, weakly supervised anomaly detection methods are of great interest, as only image-level annotations are required for training. Current anomaly detection methods mainly rely on generative adversarial networks or autoencoder models. Those models are often complicated to train or have difficulties to preserve fine details in the image. We present a novel weakly supervised anomaly detection method based on denoising diffusion implicit models. We combine the deterministic iterative noising and denoising scheme with classifier guidance for image-to-image translation between diseased and healthy subjects. Our method generates very detailed anomaly maps without the need for a complex training procedure. We evaluate our method on the BRATS2020 dataset for brain tumor detection and the CheXpert dataset for detecting pleural effusions.

Keywords: Anomaly detection · Diffusion models · Weak supervision

1 Introduction

In medical image analysis, pixel-wise annotated ground truth is hard to obtain, often unavailable and contains a bias to the human annotators. Weakly supervised anomaly detection has gained a lot of interest in research as an essential tool to overcome the aforementioned issues. Compared to fully supervised methods, weakly supervised models rely only on image-level labels for training. In this paper, we present a novel pixel-wise anomaly detection approach based on Denoising Diffusion Implicit Models (DDIMs) [25]. Figure 1 shows an overview of the proposed method. We assume two unpaired sets of images for the training, the first containing images of healthy subjects and the second images of subjects affected by a disease. Only the image and the corresponding image-level label (healthy, diseased) are provided during training.

Our method consists of two main parts. In the first part, we train a Denoising Diffusion Probabilistic Models (DDPM) [10] and a binary classifier on a dataset of healthy and diseased subjects. In the second part, we create the actual anomaly map of an unseen image. For this, we first encode the anatomical information of an

---

Supplementary Information The online version contains supplementary material available at https://doi.org/10.1007/978-3-031-16452-1_4.

L. Wang et al. (Eds.): MICCAI 2022, LNCS 13438, pp. 35–45, 2022.
https://doi.org/10.1007/978-3-031-16452-1_4

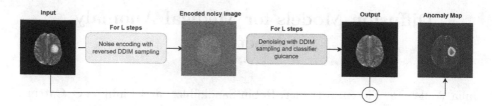

Fig. 1. Proposed sampling scheme for image-to-image translation between a diseased input image and a healthy output image. The anomaly map is defined as the difference between the two.

image with the reversed sampling scheme of DDIMs. This is an iterative noising process. Then, in the denoising process, we use the deterministic sampling scheme proposed in DDIM with classifier guidance to generate an image of a healthy subject. The final pixel-wise anomaly map is the difference between the original and the synthetic image. With this encoding and denoising procedure, our method can preserve many details of the input image that are not affected by the disease while re-painting the diseased part with realistic looking tissue. We apply our algorithm on two different medical datasets, i.e., the BRATS2020 brain tumor challenge [2,3,16], and the CheXpert dataset [11], and compare our method against standard anomaly detection methods. The source code and implementation details are available at https://gitlab.com/cian.unibas.ch/diffusion-anomaly.

Related Work. In classical anomaly detection, autoencoders [13,29] are trained on data of healthy subjects. Any deviations from the learned distribution then lead to a high anomaly score. This idea has been applied for unsupervised anomaly detection in medical images [6,14,30], where the difference between the healthy reconstruction and the anomalous input image highlight pixels that are perceived as anomalous. Other approaches focus on Generative Adversarial Networks (GANs) [9] for image-to-image translation [5,24,27].

However, training of GANs is challenging and requires a lot of hyperparameter tuning. Furthermore, additional loss terms and changes to the architecture are required to ensure cycle-consistent results. In [1,19], the gradient of a classifier is used to obtain anomaly maps. O Recently, transformer networks [21] were also successfully applied on brain anomaly detection [20]. Non-synthesis based methods such as density estimation, feature modeling or self-supervised classification also provide state-of-the-art techniques for anomaly detection [28]. In [15], a new thresholding method is proposed for anomaly segmentation on the BRATS dataset.

Lately, DDPMs were in focus for there ability to beat GANs on image synthesis [8]. In the flow of this success, they were also applied on image-to-image translation [7,23], segmentation [4], reconstruction [22] and registration [12]. As shown in [25], DDIMs are closely related to score-based generative models [26], which can be used for interpolation between images. However, there is no diffusion model for anomaly detection so far to the best of our knowledge.

2   Method

A typical example for image-to-image translation in medicine is the transformation of an image of a patient to an image without any pathologies. For anomaly detection it is crucial that only pathological regions are changed, and the rest of the image is preserved. Then, the difference between the original and the translated image defines the anomaly map. Our detail-preserving image-to-image translation is based on diffusion models. We follow the formulation of DDPMs given in [10,17]. In Algorithm 1, we present the workflow of our approach.

The general idea of diffusion models is that for an input image x, we generate a series of noisy images $\{x_0, x_1, ..., x_T\}$ by adding small amounts of noise for many timesteps T. The noise level t of an image x_t is steadily increased from 0 to T. A U-Net ϵ_θ is trained to predict x_{t-1} from x_t according to (5), for any step $t \in \{1, ..., T\}$. During training, we know the ground truth for x_{t-1}, and the model is trained with an MSE loss. During evaluation, we start from $x_T \sim \mathcal{N}(0, \mathbf{I})$ and predict x_{t-1} for $t \in \{T, ..., 1\}$. With this iterative denoising process, we can generate a a fake image x_0. The forward noising process q with variances $\beta_1, ..., \beta_T$ is defined by

$$q(x_t|x_{t-1}) := \mathcal{N}(x_t; \sqrt{1 - \beta_t}x_{t-1}, \beta_t\mathbf{I}). \tag{1}$$

This recursion can be written explicitly as

$$x_t = \sqrt{\bar{\alpha}_t}x_0 + \sqrt{1 - \bar{\alpha}_t}\epsilon, \quad \text{with } \epsilon \sim \mathcal{N}(0, \mathbf{I}). \tag{2}$$

with $\alpha_t := 1 - \beta_t$ and $\bar{\alpha}_t := \prod_{s=1}^{t} \alpha_s$. The denoising process p_θ is learned by optimizing the model parameters θ and is given by

$$p_\theta(x_{t-1}|x_t) := \mathcal{N}(x_{t-1}; \mu_\theta(x_t, t), \Sigma_\theta(x_t, t)). \tag{3}$$

The output of the U-Net is denoted as ϵ_θ, and the MSE loss used for training is

$$\mathcal{L} := ||\epsilon - \epsilon_\theta(\sqrt{\bar{\alpha}_t}x_0 + \sqrt{1 - \bar{\alpha}_t}\epsilon, t)||_2^2, \quad \text{with } \epsilon \sim \mathcal{N}(0, \mathbf{I}). \tag{4}$$

As shown in [25], we use the DDPM formulation to predict x_{t-1} from x_t with

$$x_{t-1} = \sqrt{\bar{\alpha}_{t-1}} \left(\frac{x_t - \sqrt{1 - \bar{\alpha}_t}\epsilon_\theta(x_t, t)}{\sqrt{\bar{\alpha}_t}} \right) + \sqrt{1 - \bar{\alpha}_{t-1} - \sigma_t^2}\epsilon_\theta(x_t, t) + \sigma_t\epsilon, \tag{5}$$

with $\sigma_t = \sqrt{(1 - \bar{\alpha}_{t-1})/(1 - \bar{\alpha}_t)}\sqrt{1 - \bar{\alpha}_t/\bar{\alpha}_{t-1}}$. DDPMs have a stochastic element ϵ in each sampling step (5). In DDIMs however, we set $\sigma_t = 0$, which results in a deterministic sampling process. As derived in [25], (5) can be viewed as the Euler method to solve an ordinary differential equation (ODE). Consequently, we can reverse the generation process by using the reversed ODE. Using enough discretization steps, we can encode x_{t+1} given x_t with

$$x_{t+1} = x_t + \sqrt{\bar{\alpha}_{t+1}} \left[\left(\sqrt{\frac{1}{\bar{\alpha}_t}} - \sqrt{\frac{1}{\bar{\alpha}_{t+1}}} \right) x_t + \left(\sqrt{\frac{1}{\bar{\alpha}_{t+1}} - 1} - \sqrt{\frac{1}{\bar{\alpha}_t} - 1} \right) \epsilon_\theta(x_t, t) \right]. \tag{6}$$

By applying (6) for $t \in \{0, ..., T - 1\}$, we can encode an image x_0 in a noisy image x_T. Then, we recover the identical x_0 from x_T by using (5) with $\sigma_t = 0$ for $t \in \{T, ..., 1\}$.

For anomaly detection, we train a DDPM on a dataset containing images of healthy and diseased subjects. For evaluation, we define a noise level $L \in \{1, ..., T\}$ and a gradient scale s. Given an input image x, we encode it to a noisy image x_L using (6) for $t \in \{0, ..., L - 1\}$. With this iterative noising process, we can induce anatomical information of the input image. During the denoising process, we follow (5) with $\sigma_t = 0$ for $t \in \{L, ..., 1\}$. We apply classifier guidance as introduced in [8] to lead the image generation to the desired healthy class h. For this, we pretrain a classifier network C on the noisy images x_t for $t \in \{1, ..., T\}$, to predict the class label of x. During the denoising process, the scaled gradient $s\nabla_{x_t} \log C(h|x_t, t)$ of the classifier is used to update $\epsilon_\theta(x_t, t)$. This iterative noising and denoising scheme is presented in Algorithm 1. We generate an image x_0 of the desired class h that preserves the basic structure of x. The anomaly map is then defined by the difference between x and x_0. The choice of the noise level L and the gradient scale s is crucial for the trade-off between detail-preserving image reconstruction and freedom for translation to a healthy subject.

Algorithm 1. Anomaly detection using noise encoding and classifier guidance

Input: input image x, healthy class label h, gradient scale s, noise level L
Output: synthetic image x_0, anomaly map a
for all t from 0 to $L - 1$ **do**
$$x_{t+1} \leftarrow x_t + \sqrt{\bar{\alpha}_{t+1}} \left[\left(\sqrt{\tfrac{1}{\bar{\alpha}_t}} - \sqrt{\tfrac{1}{\bar{\alpha}_{t+1}}} \right) x_t + \left(\sqrt{\tfrac{1}{\bar{\alpha}_{t+1}} - 1} - \sqrt{\tfrac{1}{\bar{\alpha}_t} - 1} \right) \epsilon_\theta(x_t, t) \right]$$
end for
for all t from L to 1 **do**
$$\hat{\epsilon} \leftarrow \epsilon_\theta(x_t, t) - s\sqrt{1 - \bar{\alpha}_t}\nabla_{x_t} \log C(h|x_t, t)$$
$$x_{t-1} \leftarrow \sqrt{\bar{\alpha}_{t-1}} \left(\tfrac{x_t - \sqrt{1 - \bar{\alpha}_t}\hat{\epsilon}}{\sqrt{\bar{\alpha}_t}} \right) + \sqrt{1 - \bar{\alpha}_{t-1}}\hat{\epsilon}$$
end for
$$a \leftarrow \sum_{channels} |x - x_0|$$
return x_0, a

---

3   Experiments

The DDPM is trained as proposed in [17] without data augmentation. We choose the hyperparameters for the DDPM model as described in the appendix of [8], for $T = 1000$ sampling steps. The model is trained with the Adam optimizer and the hybrid loss objective described in [17], with a learning rate of 10^{-4}, and a batch size of 10. By choosing the number of channels in the first layer as 128, and using one attention head at resolution 16, the total number of parameters is 113,681,160 for the diffusion model and 5,452,962 for the classifier. We train the class-conditional DDPM model for 50,000 iterations and the classifier network for 20,000 iterations, which takes about one day on an NVIDIA Quadro RTX

6000 GPU. We used Pytorch 1.7.1 as software framework. The CheXpert and the BRATS2020 dataset are used for the evaluation of our method.

CheXpert. This dataset contains lung X-ray images. For training, we choose 14,179 subjects of the healthy control group, as well as 16,776 subjects suffering from pleural effusions. The images are of size 256×256 and normalized to values between 0 and 1. The test set comprises 200 images of each class.

BRATS2020. This dataset contains 3D brain Magnetic Resonance (MR) images of subjects with a brain tumor, as well as pixel-wise ground truth labels. Every subject is scanned with four different MR sequences, namely, T1-weighted, T2-weighted, FLAIR, and T1-weighted with contrast enhancement. Since we focus on a 2D approach, we only consider axial slices. Each slice contains the aforementioned four channels, is padded to a size of 256×256, and normalized to values between 0 and 1. Since tumors mostly occur in the middle of the brain, we exclude the lowest 80 slices and the uppermost 26 slices. A slice is considered healthy if no tumor is found on the ground truth label mask. All other slices get the image-level label *diseased*. Our training set includes 5,598 healthy slices, and 10,607 diseased slices. The test set consists of 1,082 slices containing a tumor, and 705 slices without.

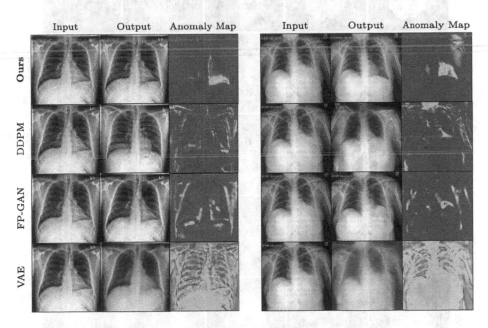

Fig. 2. Results for two X-ray images of the CheXpert dataset for $L = 500$ and $s = 100$.

4   Results and Discussion

For the evaluation of our method, we compare our method to the Fixed-Point GAN (FP-GAN) [24], and the variational autoencoder (VAE) proposed in [6]. As an ablation study, we add random noise for L steps to the input image using and perform the sampling using the DDPM sampling scheme with classifier guidance. In all experiments, we set $s = 100$ and $L = 500$. In Fig. 2, we show two exemplary patient images of the CheXpert dataset, and apply all comparing methods to generate the corresponding healthy image. We observe that compared to the other methods, our approach generates realistic looking images and preserves all the details of the input image, which leads to a very detailed anomaly map. The other methods either change other parts image, or are not able to find an anomaly. Figure 3 shows the results for all four MR sequences for an exemplary image of the BRATS2020 dataset. More examples can be found in the supplementary material. Of all methods, only the VAE tries to reconstruct the right ventricle. Comparing our results to the results of DDPM, we see that encoding

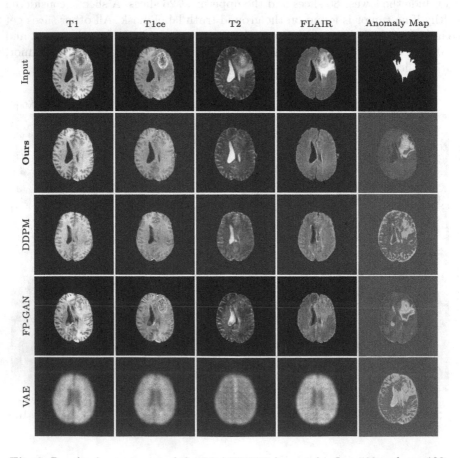

Fig. 3. Results for an image of the BRATS2020 dataset for $L = 500$ and $s = 100$.

information in noise using the deterministic noising process of DDIM brings the advantage that all details of the input image can be reconstructed. In contrast, we see that sampling with the DDPM approach changes the basic anatomy of the input image. The computation of a complete image translation takes about 158 s. This longish running time is mainly due to the iterative image generation process. We could speed up this process by choosing a smaller L, or by skipping timesteps in the DDIM sampling scheme. However, we observed that this degrades the image quality.

In [15], using the reconstruction error as anomaly score has received some criticism. It was shown that a simple method based on histogram equalization could outperform neural networks and state that reconstruction quality does not correlate well with the Dice score. As an alternative, anomaly scores of other types of methods, i.e., the log-likelihood of density estimation models, will be explored in future work.

Hyperparameter Sensitivity. Our method has two major hyperparameters, the classifier gradient scale s and the noise level L. We performed experiments to evaluate the sensitivity of our method to changes of s and L. On the BRATS2020 dataset, we have pixel-wise ground truth labels, which enable us to calculate the Dice score and the Area under the receiver operating statistics (AUROC) for diseased slices. For the Dice score, we use the average Otsu thresholding [18] on the anomaly maps. In Fig. 4, we show the average Dice and AUROC scores on the test set with respect to the gradient scale s for different noise levels L. The scores for the comparing methods FP-GAN and VAE are shown in horizontal bars in Fig. 4.

Figure 5 shows an exemplary FLAIR image. We fix $L = 500$ and show the sampled results for various values of s. If we choose s too small, the tumor cannot be removed. However, if we choose s too large, additional artefacts are

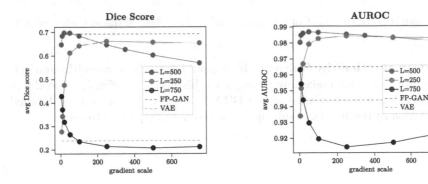

Fig. 4. Average Dice and AUROC scores on the test set for different s and L.

introduced to the image. Those artefacts are mainly at the border of the brain, and lead to a decrease in the Dice score. In Fig. 6, we fix $s = 100$, and show the sampled results for the same image for varying noise levels L. If L is chosen too large, this results in a destruction of the images. If L is chosen too small, the model does not have enough freedom to remove the tumor from the image.

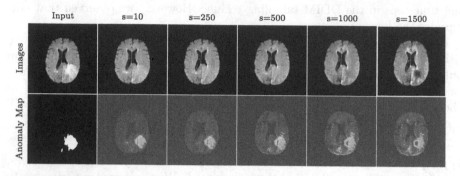

Fig. 5. Illustration of the effect of the gradient scale s for a fixed noise level $L = 500$.

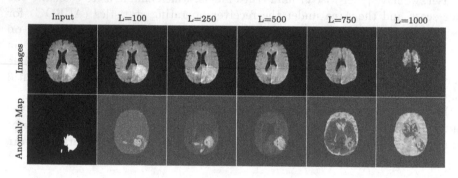

Fig. 6. Illustration of the effect of the noise level L, for a fixed gradient scale $s = 100$.

Translation of a Healthy Subject. If an input image shows a healthy subject, our method should not make any changes to this image. In Fig. 7, we evaluate our approach on a healthy slice of the BRATS dataset. We get a very detailed reconstruction of the image, resulting in an anomaly map close to zero.

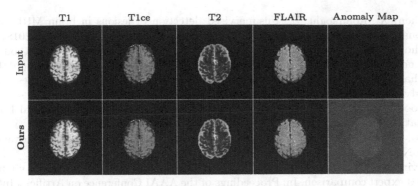

Fig. 7. Results of the presented method for an image without a tumor. The difference between the input image and the synthetic image is close to zero.

5   Conclusion

In this paper, we presented a novel weakly supervised anomaly detection method by combining the iterative DDIM noising and denoising schemes, and classifier guidance. No changes were made to the loss function or the training scheme of the original implementations, making the training on other datasets straightforward. We applied our method for anomaly detection on two different medical datasets and successfully translated images of patients to images without pathologies. Our method only performs changes in the anomalous regions of the image to achieve the translation to a healthy subject. This improves the quality of the anomaly maps. We point out that we achieve a detail-consistent image-to-image translation without the need of changing the architecture or training procedure. We achieve excellent results on the BRATS2020 and the CheXpert dataset.

Acknowledgements. This research was supported by the Novartis FreeNovation initiative and the Uniscientia Foundation (project #147-2018).

References

1. Arun, N.T., et al.: Assessing the validity of saliency maps for abnormality localization in medical imaging. arXiv preprint arXiv:2006.00063 (2020)
2. Bakas, S., et al.: Advancing the cancer genome atlas glioma MRI collections with expert segmentation labels and radiomic features. Sci. Data **4**(1), 1–13 (2017)
3. Bakas, S., et al.: Identifying the best machine learning algorithms for brain tumor segmentation, progression assessment, and overall survival prediction in the BRATS challenge. arXiv preprint arXiv:1811.02629 (2018)
4. Baranchuk, D., Voynov, A., Rubachev, I., Khrulkov, V., Babenko, A.: Label-efficient semantic segmentation with diffusion models. In: International Conference on Learning Representations (2022)
5. Baumgartner, C.F., Koch, L.M., Tezcan, K.C., Ang, J.X., Konukoglu, E.: Visual feature attribution using Wasserstein GANs. In: Proceedings of the IEEE Conference on Computer Vision and Pattern Recognition, pp. 8309–8319 (2018)

6. Chen, X., Konukoglu, E.: Unsupervised detection of lesions in brain MRI using constrained adversarial auto-encoders. arXiv preprint arXiv:1806.04972 (2018)
7. Choi, J., Kim, S., Jeong, Y., Gwon, Y., Yoon, S.: ILVR: conditioning method for denoising diffusion probabilistic models. arXiv preprint arXiv:2108.02938 (2021)
8. Dhariwal, P., Nichol, A.: Diffusion models beat GANs on image synthesis. In: Advances in Neural Information Processing Systems, vol. 34 (2021)
9. Goodfellow, I., et al.: Generative adversarial nets. In: Advances in Neural Information Processing Systems, vol. 27 (2014)
10. Ho, J., Jain, A., Abbeel, P.: Denoising diffusion probabilistic models. In: Advances in Neural Information Processing Systems, vol. 33, no. 6840–6851 (2020)
11. Irvin, J., et al.: CheXpert: a large chest radiograph dataset with uncertainty labels and expert comparison. In: Proceedings of the AAAI Conference on Artificial Intelligence, vol. 33, pp. 590–597 (2019)
12. Kim, B., Han, I., Ye, J.C.: DiffuseMorph: unsupervised deformable image registration along continuous trajectory using diffusion models. arXiv preprint arXiv:2112.05149 (2021)
13. Kingma, D.P., Welling, M.: An introduction to variational autoencoders. arXiv preprint arXiv:1906.02691 (2019)
14. Marimont, S.N., Tarroni, G.: Anomaly detection through latent space restoration using vector quantized variational autoencoders. In: 2021 IEEE 18th International Symposium on Biomedical Imaging (ISBI), pp. 1764–1767. IEEE (2021)
15. Meissen, F., Kaissis, G., Rueckert, D.: Challenging current semi-supervised anomaly segmentation methods for brain MRI. arXiv preprint arXiv:2109.06023 (2021)
16. Menze, B.H., et al.: The multimodal brain tumor image segmentation benchmark (BRATS). IEEE Trans. Med. Imaging **34**(10), 1993–2024 (2014)
17. Nichol, A.Q., Dhariwal, P.: Improved denoising diffusion probabilistic models. In: Proceedings of the 38th International Conference on Machine Learning, vol. 139, pp. 8162–8171. PMLR (2021)
18. Otsu, N.: A threshold selection method from gray-level histograms. IEEE Trans. Syst. Man Cybern. **9**(1), 62–66 (1979)
19. Panwar, H., Gupta, P., Siddiqui, M.K., Morales-Menendez, R., Bhardwaj, P., Singh, V.: A deep learning and grad-CAM based color visualization approach for fast detection of COVID-19 cases using chest X-ray and CT-scan images. Chaos Solitons Fractals **140**, 110190 (2020)
20. Pinaya, W.H.L., et al.: Unsupervised brain anomaly detection and segmentation with transformers. arXiv preprint arXiv:2102.11650 (2021)
21. Pirnay, J., Chai, K.: Inpainting transformer for anomaly detection. arXiv preprint arXiv:2104.13897 (2021)
22. Saharia, C., et al.: Palette: image-to-image diffusion models. arXiv preprint arXiv:2111.05826 (2021)
23. Sasaki, H., Willcocks, C.G., Breckon, T.P.: UNIT-DDPM: UNpaired Image Translation with Denoising Diffusion Probabilistic Models. arXiv preprint arXiv:2104.05358 (2021)
24. Siddiquee, M.M.R., et al.: Learning fixed points in generative adversarial networks: from image-to-image translation to disease detection and localization. In: Proceedings of the IEEE/CVF International Conference on Computer Vision, pp. 191–200 (2019)
25. Song, J., Meng, C., Ermon, S.: Denoising diffusion implicit models. arXiv preprint arXiv:2010.02502 (2020)

26. Song, Y., Sohl-Dickstein, J., Kingma, D.P., Kumar, A., Ermon, S., Poole, B.: Score-based generative modeling through stochastic differential equations. arXiv preprint arXiv:2011.13456 (2020)
27. Wolleb, J., Sandkühler, R., Cattin, P.C.: DeScarGAN: disease-specific anomaly detection with weak supervision. In: Martel, A.L., et al. (eds.) MICCAI 2020. LNCS, vol. 12264, pp. 14–24. Springer, Cham (2020). https://doi.org/10.1007/978-3-030-59719-1_2
28. Yang, J., Xu, R., Qi, Z., Shi, Y.: Visual anomaly detection for images: a survey. arXiv preprint arXiv:2109.13157 (2021)
29. Zhou, C., Paffenroth, R.C.: Anomaly detection with robust deep autoencoders. In: Proceedings of the 23rd ACM SIGKDD International Conference on Knowledge Discovery and Data Mining, pp. 665–674 (2017)
30. Zimmerer, D., Kohl, S.A., Petersen, J., Isensee, F., Maier-Hein, K.H.: Context-encoding variational autoencoder for unsupervised anomaly detection. arXiv preprint arXiv:1812.05941 (2018)

Few-Shot Generation of Personalized Neural Surrogates for Cardiac Simulation via Bayesian Meta-learning

Xiajun Jiang[1(✉)], Zhiyuan Li[1], Ryan Missel[1], Md Shakil Zaman[1],
Brian Zenger[2], Wilson W. Good[2], Rob S. MacLeod[2], John L. Sapp[3],
and Linwei Wang[1]

[1] Rochester Institute of Technology, Rochester, NY 14623, USA
{xj7056,zl7904,rxm7244,mz1482,linwei.wang}@rit.edu
[2] The University of Utah, Salt Lake City, UT 84112, USA
brian.zenger@hsc.utah.edu,macleod@sci.utah.edu
[3] Dalhousie University, Halifax, NS, Canada
john.sapp@nshealth.ca

Abstract. Clinical adoption of personalized virtual heart simulations faces challenges in model personalization and expensive computation. While an ideal solution is an efficient neural surrogate that at the same time is personalized to an individual subject, the state-of-the-art is either concerned with personalizing an expensive simulation model, or learning an efficient yet generic surrogate. This paper presents a completely new concept to achieve *personalized neural surrogates* in a single coherent framework of meta-learning (metaPNS). Instead of learning a single neural surrogate, we pursue the process of learning a personalized neural surrogate using a small amount of context data from a subject, in a novel formulation of few-shot generative modeling underpinned by: 1) a set-conditioned neural surrogate for cardiac simulation that, conditioned on subject-specific context data, learns to generate query simulations not included in the context set, and 2) a meta-model of amortized variational inference that learns to condition the neural surrogate via simple feed-forward embedding of context data. As test time, metaPNS delivers a personalized neural surrogate by fast feed-forward embedding of a small and flexible number of data available from an individual, achieving – for the first time – personalization and surrogate construction for expensive simulations in one end-to-end learning framework. Synthetic and real-data experiments demonstrated that metaPNS was able to improve personalization and predictive accuracy in comparison to conventionally-optimized cardiac simulation models, at a fraction of computation.

Keywords: Cardiac electrophysiology · Personalization · Meta-learning

1 Introduction

Personalized virtual hearts, customized to the observational data of individual subjects, have shown promise in clinical tasks such as treatment planning [25]

L. Wang et al. (Eds.): MICCAI 2022, LNCS 13438, pp. 46–56, 2022.
https://doi.org/10.1007/978-3-031-16452-1_5

and risk stratification [2]. Their wider clinical adoption, however, is hindered by two major bottlenecks. First, it remains challenging and time-consuming to calibrate these simulation models to an individual's physiology (*i.e.*, personalization), especially for model parameters that are not directly observable (*e.g.*, material properties) [23]. Second, it is not yet possible to run these simulations at scale due to their high computational cost: this prevents comprehensive testing in clinical pipelines, or rigorous assessment of simulation uncertainties [23].

Significant progress has been made in personalizing the parameters of a cardiac model [8,21,27–29]. Earlier methods typically rely on iterative optimization processes involving repeated calls to the expensive simulation model [27,28]. Increasing recent works start to leverage modern machine learning (ML) methods such as active learning [9], reinforcement learning [22], and ML of the input-output relationship between the parameter of interest and available measurements [7,14]. While the optimization process is being accelerated with these recent advances, model personalization remains a non-trivial and time-consuming process. Furthermore, the outcome of personalization is still concerned with a simulation model too expensive for clinical adoption at scale.

In parallel, advances in deep learning (DL) have led to a surge of interests in developing efficient neural approximations of expensive scientific simulations [18]. Progress in building neural surrogates for cardiac electrophysiology simulations, however, has been relatively limited: initial successes have been mainly demonstrated in 2D settings [5,17] with a recent work reporting 3D results on the left atrium [13]. A significant challenge arises from the dependence of these simulations on various model parameters such as material properties, denoted here as θ. Most existing works attempt to learn a single neural function $f(\theta)$ as the surrogate of a simulation model $\mathcal{M}(\theta)$. This raises two challenges. First, to learn an accurate $f(\theta)$ requires a significant amount of training data pairs of $\{\theta_i, \mathcal{M}(\theta_i)\}$ simulated across the input space of θ: this is computationally challenging, and has not been demonstrated possible in existing works. Second, the resulting neural surrogate is generic and requires the knowledge of a proper patient-specific θ – which is often unknown – in order to become personalized.

In summary, ideally we would like in the clinical workflow an efficient simulation surrogate that at the same is personalized to an individual subject. The state-of-the-art, however, is either concerned with optimizing a personalized but expensive simulation model, or learning an efficient yet generic surrogate. One may consider naively combining existing works by first building an accurate neural surrogate $f(\theta)$, and then having it optimized to a subject. This however has not been demonstrated feasible, especially considering the challenge of learning a $f(\theta)$ accurate across the space of θ. Even if feasible, it is a solution that combines two disconnected processes to achieve an otherwise intertwined objective.

In this paper, we present a completely new concept to achieve *personalized neural surrogates* in a single coherent framework of meta-learning (metaPNS). Our guiding principle is that we are interested in a set of, rather then one single, neural functions as the simulation surrogate: therefore, instead of *learning a single neural surrogate*, we would *learn the process of learning* a personalized neural surrogate from a small number of available data of a subject (*context* data).

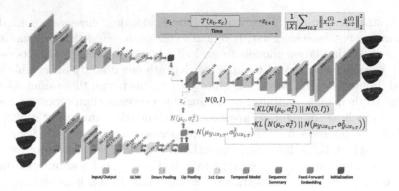

Fig. 1. Overview of framework. Green arrows show the flow of meta-inference using context set, and red arrows show how target set participates in meta-training. (Color figure online)

We cast this in a novel formulation of few-shot generative modeling via Bayesian meta-learning. It has two main elements: 1) a set-conditioned generative model as the neural surrogate for cardiac simulation that, conditioned on the *context* data of an individual, learns to generate *target* simulations not included in the context set, and 2) a meta-model of amortized variational inference (VI) that learns to condition (*i.e.,* personalize) the generative model via feed-forward embedding of context data of *variable* sizes. Compared to optimization-based meta-learning methods [12, 26], this type of feed-forward meta-models remove the need of further training and obtain a model at meta-test time via simple feed-forward embedding of context data. With this, at test time, a personalized neural surrogate can be quickly obtained by simple feed-forward embedding of a small and flexible number of data available from a subject. This 1) replaces expensive personalizatoin with fast feed-forward meta-embedding, and 2) delivers a personalized neural surrogate for efficient predictive simulations. To our knowledge, this is the first time personalization and surrogate constructions are achieved in an end-to-end framework of few-shot generative modeling.

We evaluated metaPNS in synthetic and real-data experiments, in comparison to 1) personalized cardiac simulation models obtained via published optimization methods [10] and 2) a conditional generative model similar to what is presented but without set conditioning or meta-inference. We demonstrated that metaPNS was able to deliver improved personalization and predictive performance at a fraction of computation cost of conventionally-optimized simulation models. Furthermore, we showed that the presented meta-learning elements are critical to the predictive capacity of the resulting neural surrogates.

2   Methodology

Figure 1 gives an overview of metaPNS. Consider a cardiac electrophysiology simulation model $x_{1:T} = \mathcal{M}(s; \theta)$ with both known input s and unknown parameter

θ: in predictive tasks, a typical example of s is the electrical stimulation applied to the virtual heart, whereas a typical example of θ is the material property to be tailored to an individual. Consider observations $y_{1:T}$ of $x_{1:T}$ that, for instance, can be sparse heart surface voltage mapping, or body-surface potential recordings. The goal of model personalization is to obtain an estimated $\hat{\theta}$ to minimize the actual and simulated observations. The goal of personalized neural surrogate is then to obtain a neural function $f(s, \hat{\theta})$ that 1) can approximate and accelerate the computation of $\mathcal{M}(s; \hat{\theta})$ and 2) is calibrated to an individual's observations.

It is natural to approach this by learning a neural function $f(s, \theta)$ that approximates $\mathcal{M}(s; \theta)$ across the space of θ [13,17]—a generic surrogate that, once learned, requires an input of θ or a separate optimization process to become personalized. Departing from the common practice, we will aim to obtain a set of personalized neural surrogates that change with a small set of context observations, $\mathcal{Y} = \{y_{1:T}^{(i)}\}_{i=1}^{\nu}$ with variable size ν, from an individual subject:

$$p(\hat{x}_{1:T}|s, \mathcal{Y}) = \int p(\hat{x}_{1:T}|s, \mathbf{c})q_\zeta(\mathbf{c}|\mathcal{Y})dc, \tag{1}$$

where the neural surrogate $p(\hat{x}_{1:T}|s, \mathcal{Y})$ is a stochastic process learned in the context of Bayesian meta-learning: $p(\hat{x}_{1:T}|s, \mathbf{c})$ is a generative model conditioned on known s and personalized by latent embedding $\mathbf{c}$ derived from subject-specific context data; $q_\zeta(\mathbf{c}|\mathcal{Y})$ is the meta-model that, parameterized by ζ, learns to personalize the generative model via feed-forward embedding of $\mathcal{Y}$.

2.1 Set-Conditioned Generative Model

The generative neural surrogate is conditioned on context-set embedding $p(\mathbf{c})$ and known stimulation s. It has a temporal transition model $\mathcal{T}$ of the latent state z_t, and a spatial model $\mathcal{G}$ for emission to x_t at the high-dimensional cardiac mesh:

$$\begin{aligned}\text{Transition} &: z_{t+1} = \mathcal{T}(z_t), \\ \text{Emission} &: \hat{x}_{t+1} = \mathcal{G}(z_{t+1}).\end{aligned} \tag{2}$$

where the initial state z_0 is obtained by applying a neural function consisting a linear layer to the embedding of the known stimulation input s: $z_0 = f_\rho(s)$.

Spatial Modeling via Graph CNNs (GCNNs): As x lives on 3D geometry of the heart, we describe $\mathcal{G}$ with GCNNs. We represent triangular meshes of the heart as undirected graphs, with edge attributes between vertices as normalized differences in their 3D coordinates if an edge exists. Encoding and decoding are performed over hierarchical graph representations of the heart geometry, obtained by a specialized mesh coarsening method [4]. A continuous spline kernel for spatial convolution is used such that it can be applied across graphs [11]. To make the network deeper and more expressive, we introduce residual blocks here through a skip connection with 1D convolution [15].

Temporal Modeling via Set-Conditioned Transition Function: The temporal transition function $\mathcal{T}$ is inspired by Gated Recurrent Units (GRUs) [6]. Note that, with regular GRUs, $\mathcal{T}$ would be global to the training data rather than subject-specific. Instead, we condition $\mathcal{T}$ on the context-set embedding by creating conditional gated transition functions:

$$g_t = \sigma(W_1 z_t^{(1)} + b_1), \quad z_t^{(1)} = \text{ELU}(\alpha_1 z_t + \beta_1 \mathbf{c} + \gamma_1),$$

$$h_t = \text{ELU}(W_2 z_t^{(2)} + b_2), \quad z_t^{(2)} = \text{ELU}(\alpha_2 z_t + \beta_2 \mathbf{c} + \gamma_2) \tag{3}$$

$$z_{t+1} = (1 - g_t) \odot (W_3 z_t^{(3)} + b_3) + g_t \odot h_t, \quad z_t^{(3)} = \alpha_3 z_t + \beta_3 \mathbf{c} + \gamma_3$$

where $\mathbf{c}$ is sampled from the context-set embedding, and $\{W_i, b_i, \alpha_i, \beta_i, \gamma_i\}_{i=1}^3$ are learnable parameters. The model has flexibility to choose a linear transition for some dimensions and non-linear transition for the others.

2.2   Meta-model for Amortized Variational Inference

Amortized Variational Inference: Consider a multi-subject dataset $\mathcal{X} = \{\mathcal{X}^k\}_{k=1}^K, k \in \{1, 2, ..., K\}$, where $\mathcal{X}^k = \{x_{1:T}^{(1)}, x_{1:T}^{(2)}, ..., x_{1:T}^{(N_k)}\}$ are heart signals from subject k with N_k samples. For each subject k, a subset of $\mathcal{X}^k$ is associated with observations $\mathcal{Y}^k = \{y_{1:T}^{(1)}, y_{1:T}^{(2)}, ..., y_{1:T}^{(M_k)}\}, M_k \ll N_k$, such that $\mathcal{Y}^k$ is the context set. The rest of $\mathcal{X}^k$ is unobserved target set. Stimulation inputs s^k are known on all samples in $\mathcal{X}^k$. The evidence lower bound (ELBO) we optimize is:

$$\sum_k \sum_{x_{1:T} \in \mathcal{X}^k} \log p(\hat{x}_{1:T} | s^k, \mathcal{Y}^k) \geq \sum_k \sum_{x_{1:T} \in \mathcal{X}^k} \mathbb{E}_{q_\zeta(\mathbf{c}^k | \mathcal{Y}^k)} \left[\log p(\hat{x}_{1:T} | \mathbf{c}^k, s^k)\right]$$
$$- \text{KL}\left(q_\zeta(\mathbf{c}^k | \mathcal{Y}^k \cup x_{1:T}) || p(\mathbf{c}^k | \mathcal{Y}^k)\right), \tag{4}$$

where we let $p(\mathbf{c}^k | \mathcal{Y}^k)$ and $q_\zeta(\mathbf{c}^k | \mathcal{Y}^k \cup x_{1:T})$ share the same meta set-embedding networks to parameterize their means and variances. We further regularize $p(\mathbf{c}^k | \mathcal{Y}^k)$ to be close to a standard Gaussian distribution $\mathcal{N}(0, I)$. Therefore, the overall loss function is:

$$\arg \min_\theta \sum_k \sum_{x_{1:T} \in \mathcal{X}^k} \mathbb{E}_{q_\zeta(\mathbf{c}^k | \mathcal{Y}^k)} \left[\log p(\hat{x}_{1:T} | \mathbf{c}^k, s^k)\right]$$
$$- \lambda_1 \text{KL}\left(q_\zeta(\mathbf{c}^k | \mathcal{Y}^k \cup x_{1:T}) || p(\mathbf{c}^k | \mathcal{Y}^k)\right) - \lambda_2 \text{KL}\left(p(\mathbf{c}^k | \mathcal{Y}^k) || \mathcal{N}(0, I)\right), \tag{5}$$

where λ_1 and λ_2 are regularization multipliers.

Context-Set Feed-Forward Embedding: We use the meta-model $q_\zeta(c|\mathcal{D}_c)$ to get the feed-forward embedding for each context set. First, each sample $y_{1:T} \in \mathcal{D}_c$ is embedded through a neural function $h_\phi(y_{1:T})$ that uses a GCN-GRU cell [16] to obtain the sequential information from the graph, and aggregate it across time with a linear layer. We then average all latent embedding in $\mathcal{D}_c$:

$$\frac{1}{|\mathcal{D}_c|} \sum_{y_{1:T} \in \mathcal{D}_c} h_\phi(y_{1:T}), \tag{6}$$

Table 1. Performance metrics of 1) the presented metaPNS, 2) PNS without meta-model, 3) FS-BO, and 4) VAE-BO on context and target sets.

Model	Context set			Target set		
	MSE	CC	DC	MSE	CC	DC
metaPNS	4.5 ± 1.2e−4	0.74 ± 0.089	**0.88 ± 0.10**	4.4 ± 1.1e−4	**0.72 ± 0.092**	**0.88 ± 0.089**
PNS	**2.7 ± 0.54e−4**	**0.83 ± 0.068**	0.77 ± 0.13	1.2 ± 0.29e−3	0.44 ± 0.13	0.75 ± 0.13
FS-BO	5.3 ± 6.5e−4	0.69 ± 0.25	0.48 ± 0.34	5.3 ± 5.9e−4	0.69 ± 0.24	0.48 ± 0.34
VAE-BO	4.8 ± 2.5e−4	0.46 ± 0.15	0.48 ± 0.09	5.0 ± 3.3e−4	0.48 ± 0.11	0.48 ± 0.12

which then parameterizes $q_\zeta = \mathcal{N}(\boldsymbol{\mu}_c, \boldsymbol{\sigma}_c^2)$ via two separate linear layers. The conditional factor $\mathbf{c}$ is then sampled by $\mathbf{c} = \boldsymbol{\mu}_c + \boldsymbol{\epsilon} \odot \boldsymbol{\sigma}_c$, where $\boldsymbol{\epsilon} \sim \mathcal{N}(0, \mathbf{I})$ [20].

The loss in Eq. 5 is optimized in episodic training. In each training episode across all subjects, the input data is divided into two separate sets: a context set $\mathcal{D}_c^k$ consists of small sets of samples from each subject and the target set formed by the remaining data. The model is asked to take $\mathcal{D}_c^k$ for each subject k, and generate samples in $\mathcal{D}_x^k$ including both context and target sets.

3 Experiments

In all experiments, metaPNS consists of 4 GCNN blocks and 2 regular convolution layers in the encoders, 1 context-set aggregator with a GCN-GRU block followed by a linear layer to compress time and another linear layer for feature extraction, 1 conditional gated transition unit for the generation of latent dynamics, and 4 GCNN blocks and 2 regular convolution layers in the decoder. We used Adam optimizer [19]. The learning rate is set at 1×10^{-3} with a learning rate decreasing rate 0.5 every 50 episodes. The two KL multipliers are: $\lambda_1 = 10^{-4}$ and $\lambda_2 = 0.1$. All experiments were run on NVIDIA Tesla T4s with 16 GB memory. Our implementation is available here: https://github.com/john-x-jiang/epnn.

3.1 Synthetic Experiments

Data and Training. We generated propagation of action potential by the Aliev-Panfilov model [1] and the corresponding sparse heart-surface potential as measurements. We considered 3 heart meshes with a combination of 16 different tissue parameter settings (15 scar and one healthy) and approximately 200 different locations of stimulations. This is treated as 16 unique subjects. In each episode of meta-training, for each subject, we randomly sample 25 origins with a variable number (1–5) of origins as the context and the rest 20 as the target. Each training episode took on average 8.5 min.

Testing and Comparisons. In meta-testing, we considered the same 16 subjects with 2,731 unique simulations. For each subject, 3 different context sets with a varying number of samples (1–5) were used to obtain the personalized surrogate, to each then simulation 1,638 target samples with distinct stimulations.

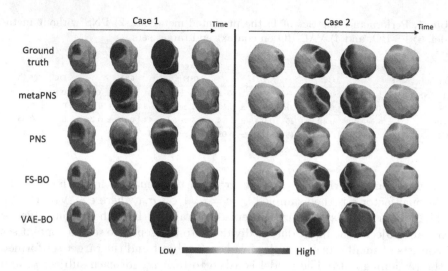

Fig. 2. Examples of generated simulations on target sets.

The closest related works are those utilizing expensive optimizations to personalize the parameters of a cardiac simulation model, and using the expensive personalized model in predictions. Therefore, for a subset of 11 subjects and 165 unique simulations, we compared metaPNS with published personalized cardiac simulation workflows where *tissue excitability* within the Alieve-Panfilov model was estimated by derivative-free Bayesian optimization [10] using the same context sets used for metaPNS. We considered two optimization formulations where the tissue excitability was represented either using a seven-segment division of the cardiac mesh (FS-BO) or a modern VAE-based generative model as described in [10] (VAE-BO). Predictive simulations were then performed with the personalized cardiac model and compared to metaPNS on the same target samples.

Alternative neural surrogates of cardiac simulations [5,13,17] are also related, although existing works are either 2D on image grids or on atria [13]. Once learned, they all have to be separately optimized to a subject's data for personalized predictions - the latter we have not seen in published works. Thus, for a neural baseline, we considered a version of metaPNS without the set-conditioning or meta-model, *i.e.*, a regular generative model $p(x_{1:T}|s, \mathbf{c})$ where the embedding c is directly inferred from $y_{1:T}$ as $q(\mathbf{c}|y_{1:T})$. We term this PNS.

Results. The performance of all methods was quantitatively measured by mean square error (MSE) and spatial correlation coefficient (CC) between the predicted and actual target simulations, and the dice coefficient (DC) of the abnormal tissue region obtained by thresholding signals with Otsu's method [24]. Performance on the context set shows how well each method fits the data, whereas that on the target set shows how well each personalized model predicts new simulations. As shown in Table 1 and Fig. 2, metaPNS has the strongest predictive performance on target sets. Due to the difficulty in convergence, for FS-BO we

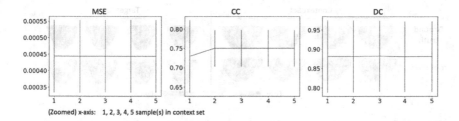

Fig. 3. Performance of metaPNS as the number of context data decreases.

set the optimization bound to consider the ground-truth tissue-property setting. Despite this, metaPNS was able to deliver comparable performance in some cases (*e.g.*, Case 1 in Fig. 2), and the highest average accuracy across all samples in target sets. Notably, this performance gain was achieved at a fraction of computation cost: one Alieve-Panfilov simulation took on average 5 min versus 0.24 s by the neural surrogate; furthermore, an average BO personalization required 100 calls to the simulation model, whereas metaPNS took on average 0.032 s for the feed-forward embedding of the context set.

Compared to metaPNS, PNS was able to well reconstruct the context set (and thus capture the abnormal tissue). It however was not able to generate any new simulations in target sets. This provided evidence for the importance of the presented meta-model of context-set embedding. We further compared metaPNS using different number of samples in the context set. As shown in Fig. 3, the predictive performance of metaPNS seldomly changed as the context data decreased, demonstrating its strong ability as a few-shot generative model.

3.2 Clinical Data

We then evaluated the trained metaPNS on *in-vivo* recordings from an animal model experiment [3]. Several cardiac activation sequences were generated using bipolar stimulation from intramural plunge needles at four sites: left ventricular (LV) base, LV Apex, LV freewall, and LV septum. The cardiac potentials were recorded at the epicardial surface with an epicardial sock with 247 electrodes (inter-electrode spacing 6.5 ± 1.3 mm). Geometric surfaces were constructed based on electrode locations acquired during each experiment.

We carried out cross validation by leaving out one stimulated site as the target sample each time, and the rest as the context set (15 sequences). Accuracy of metaPNS prediction on the target sample was evaluated by MSE and CC with the epicardial sock measurements. Across all samples, metaPNS obtained MSE 1.0 ± 0.015e-3 and CC 0.36 ± 0.038 on context sets, MSE 1.0 ± 0.073e-3 and CC 0.33 ± 0.087 on target sets. Figure 4 show the performance of the presented model on both context and target sets. Despite the performance gap with synthetic experiments, this experiment demonstrated the ability of metaPNS to generalize outside the geometry and simulations seen at the meta-training time.

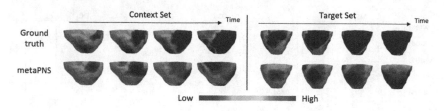

Fig. 4. Examples of generated target simulations in real-data experiments.

4   Conclusion

In this work, we demonstrated the promising potential of metaPNS – a novel framework for obtaining a personalized neural surrogate by simple feed-forward embedding of a small and flexible number of data available from a subject. Future work will evaluate use of metaPNS for higher-fidelity cardiac simulations, extend its ability to personalize using different types of observational data, and improve its generalization ability to more complex real-data applications.

Acknowledgement. This work is supported by the National Institutes of Health (NIH) under Award Numbers R01HL145590 and F30HL149327; the NIH NIGMS Center for Integrative Biomedical Computing (www.sci.utah.edu/cibc), NIH NIGMS grants P41GM103545 and R24 GM136986; the NSF GRFP; the Utah Graduate Research Fellowship; and the Nora Eccles Harrison Foundation for Cardiovascular Research.

References

1. Aliev, R.R., Panfilov, A.V.: A simple two-variable model of cardiac excitation. Chaos Solitons Fractals **7**(3), 293–301 (1996)
2. Arevalo, H.J., et al.: Arrhythmia risk stratification of patients after myocardial infarction using personalized heart models. Nat. Commun. **7**(1), 1–8 (2016)
3. Bergquist, J.A., Good, W.W., Zenger, B., Tate, J.D., Rupp, L.C., MacLeod, R.S.: The electrocardiographic forward problem: A benchmark study. Comput. Biol. Med. **134**, 104476 (2021)
4. Cacciola, F.: Triangulated surface mesh simplification. In: Board, C.E. (ed.) CGAL User and Reference Manual, 3.3 edn. (2007). http://www.cgal.org/Manual/3.3/doc_html/cgal_manual/packages.html#Pkg:SurfaceMeshSimplification
5. Cantwell, C.D., et al.: Rethinking multiscale cardiac electrophysiology with machine learning and predictive modelling. Comput. Biol. Med. **104**, 339–351 (2019)
6. Chung, J., Gulcehre, C., Cho, K., Bengio, Y.: Empirical evaluation of gated recurrent neural networks on sequence modeling. arXiv preprint arXiv:1412.3555 (2014)
7. Coveney, S., Corrado, C., Oakley, J.E., Wilkinson, R.D., Niederer, S.A., Clayton, R.H.: Bayesian calibration of electrophysiology models using restitution curve emulators. Front. Physiol. **12**, 1120 (2021)
8. Dhamala, J., et al.: Quantifying the uncertainty in model parameters using gaussian process-based Markov chain Monte Carlo in cardiac electrophysiology. Med. Image Anal. **48**, 43–57 (2018)

9. Dhamala, J., et al.: Embedding high-dimensional Bayesian optimization via generative modeling: parameter personalization of cardiac electrophysiological models. Med. Image Anal. **62**, 101670 (2020)
10. Dhamala, J., Ghimire, S., Sapp, J.L., Horáček, B.M., Wang, L.: High-dimensional Bayesian optimization of personalized cardiac model parameters via an embedded generative model. In: Frangi, A.F., Schnabel, J.A., Davatzikos, C., Alberola-López, C., Fichtinger, G. (eds.) MICCAI 2018. LNCS, vol. 11071, pp. 499–507. Springer, Cham (2018). https://doi.org/10.1007/978-3-030-00934-2_56
11. Fey, M., Eric Lenssen, J., Weichert, F., Müller, H.: SplineCNN: fast geometric deep learning with continuous B-spline kernels. In: The IEEE Conference on Computer Vision and Pattern Recognition (CVPR), pp. 869–877 (2018)
12. Finn, C., Abbeel, P., Levine, S.: Model-agnostic meta-learning for fast adaptation of deep networks. In: International Conference on Machine Learning, pp. 1126–1135. PMLR (2017)
13. Fresca, S., Manzoni, A., Dedè, L., Quarteroni, A.: POD-enhanced deep learning-based reduced order models for the real-time simulation of cardiac electrophysiology in the left atrium. Front. Physiol. **12**, 1431 (2021)
14. Giffard-Roisin, S., et al.: Noninvasive personalization of a cardiac electrophysiology model from body surface potential mapping. IEEE Trans. Biomed. Eng. **64**(9), 2206–2218 (2016)
15. Jiang, X., Ghimire, S., Dhamala, J., Li, Z., Gyawali, P.K., Wang, L.: Learning geometry-dependent and physics-based inverse image reconstruction. In: Martel, A.L., et al. (eds.) MICCAI 2020. LNCS, vol. 12266, pp. 487–496. Springer, Cham (2020). https://doi.org/10.1007/978-3-030-59725-2_47
16. Jiang, X., et al.: Label-free physics-informed image sequence reconstruction with disentangled spatial-temporal modeling. In: de Bruijne, M., et al. (eds.) MICCAI 2021. LNCS, vol. 12906, pp. 361–371. Springer, Cham (2021). https://doi.org/10.1007/978-3-030-87231-1_35
17. Kashtanova, V., Ayed, I., Cedilnik, N., Gallinari, P., Sermesant, M.: EP-Net 2.0: out-of-domain generalisation for deep learning models of cardiac electrophysiology. In: Ennis, D.B., Perotti, L.E., Wang, V.Y. (eds.) FIMH 2021. LNCS, vol. 12738, pp. 482–492. Springer, Cham (2021). https://doi.org/10.1007/978-3-030-78710-3_46
18. Kasim, M.F., et al.: Building high accuracy emulators for scientific simulations with deep neural architecture search. Mach. Learn. Sci. Technol. **3**(1), 015013 (2021)
19. Kingma, D.P., Ba, J.: Adam: a method for stochastic optimization. arXiv preprint arXiv:1412.6980 (2014)
20. Kingma, D.P., Welling, M.: Auto-encoding variational Bayes. arXiv preprint arXiv:1312.6114 (2013)
21. Miller, R., Kerfoot, E., Mauger, C., Ismail, T.F., Young, A.A., Nordsletten, D.A.: An implementation of patient-specific biventricular mechanics simulations with a deep learning and computational pipeline. Front. Physiol. **12**, 1398 (2021)
22. Neumann, D., Mansi, T.: Machine learning methods for robust parameter estimation. In: Artificial Intelligence for Computational Modeling of the Heart, pp. 161–181. Elsevier (2020)
23. Niederer, S., et al.: Creation and application of virtual patient cohorts of heart models. Phil. Trans. R. Soc. A **378**(2173), 20190558 (2020)
24. Otsu, N.: A threshold selection method from gray-level histograms. IEEE Trans. Syst. Man Cybern. **9**(1), 62–66 (1979)
25. Prakosa, A., et al.: Personalized virtual-heart technology for guiding the ablation of infarct-related ventricular tachycardia. Nat. Biomed. Eng. **2**(10), 732–740 (2018)

26. Ravi, S., Larochelle, H.: Optimization as a model for few-shot learning (2016)
27. Sermesant, M., et al.: Patient-specific electromechanical models of the heart for the prediction of pacing acute effects in CRT: a preliminary clinical validation. Med. Image Anal. **16**(1), 201–215 (2012)
28. Wong, K.C., et al.: Velocity-based cardiac contractility personalization from images using derivative-free optimization. J. Mech. Behav. Biomed. Mater. **43**, 35–52 (2015)
29. Zettinig, O., et al.: Fast data-driven calibration of a cardiac electrophysiology model from images and ECG. In: Mori, K., Sakuma, I., Sato, Y., Barillot, C., Navab, N. (eds.) MICCAI 2013. LNCS, vol. 8149, pp. 1–8. Springer, Heidelberg (2013). https://doi.org/10.1007/978-3-642-40811-3_1

Aggregative Self-supervised Feature Learning from Limited Medical Images

Jiuwen Zhu[1], Yuexiang Li[2], Lian Ding[3], and S. Kevin Zhou[1,4(✉)]

[1] Key Laboratory of Intelligent Information Processing of Chinese Academy of Sciences (CAS) Institute of Computing Technology, CAS, Beijing, China
jiuwen.zhu@miracle.ict.ac.cn
[2] Jarvis Lab, Tencent, Shenzhen, China
vicyxli@tencent.com
[3] Huawei Cloud Computing Technologies Company Limited, Shenzhen, China
dinglian@huawei.com
[4] Center for Medical Imaging, Robotics, Analytic Computing and Learning (MIRACLE), School of Biomedical Engineering & Suzhou Institute for Advanced Research, University of Science and Technology of China, Suzhou, China
skevinzhou@ustc.edu.cn

Abstract. Limited training data and annotation shortage are challenges for developing automated medical image analysis systems. As a potential solution, self-supervised learning (SSL) causes an increasing attention from the community. The key part in SSL is its proxy task that defines the supervisory signals and drives the learning toward effective feature representations. However, most SSL approaches usually focus on a single proxy task, which greatly limits the expressive power of the learned features and therefore deteriorates the network generalization capacity. In this regard, we hereby propose two strategies of **aggregation** in terms of complementarity of various forms to boost the robustness of self-supervised learned features. We firstly propose a **principled framework** of multi-task aggregative self-supervised learning from limited medical samples to form a unified representation, with an intent of exploiting feature complementarity among different tasks. Then, in self-aggregative SSL, we propose to **self-complement** an existing proxy task with an auxiliary loss function based on a linear centered kernel alignment metric, which explicitly promotes the exploring of where are uncovered by the features learned from a proxy task at hand to further boost the modeling capability. Our extensive experiments on 2D and 3D medical image classification tasks under limited data and annotation scenarios confirm that the proposed aggregation strategies successfully boost the classification accuracy.

Keywords: Self-supervised learning · Feature complementarity

Supplementary Information The online version contains supplementary material available at https://doi.org/10.1007/978-3-031-16452-1_6.

L. Wang et al. (Eds.): MICCAI 2022, LNCS 13438, pp. 57–66, 2022.
https://doi.org/10.1007/978-3-031-16452-1_6

1   Introduction

Recently, self-supervised learning (SSL) [9,12] gains an increasing attention in the community as it attempts to loose the requirement of large annotated data for neural networks by exploiting the rich information contained in unlabeled data, especially in the scenario of small number of data such as medical image data [19,21]. A conventional SSL approach starts with a formulated proxy task to encourage the learning of informative features from raw data. A multitude of proxy tasks, dealing with 2D natural images or 3D medical volumes, have been proposed, including grayscale image colorization [14,17], images rotation [5], Jigsaw puzzles [16], instance discrimination based on contrastive prediction [3,6], Rubik's cube [24,25], Model Genesis [23], and D2D-CNNs [2].

Most SSL approaches usually focus on a single proxy task, which limits their representation capacity of the learned features, and therefore decreases their generalization. Nevertheless, there are few studies trying to exploit the potential of assembling multiple SSL tasks. Concretely, Doersch and Zisserman [4] made the first attempt in the area exploring the way to combine multiple self-supervised tasks. Those approaches [22,23] demonstrate that the integration of proxy tasks improves the generalization of pre-trained networks and thus boosts the performance of subsequent target tasks.

The above task integration approaches are usually derived from ad-hoc assumptions and *there is a lack of a principled way of aggregation*. In this paper, we attempt to bridge the gap by exploiting two different forms of complementarity. (i) We first systematically explore the *feature complementarity* between multiple SSL approaches and propose a greedy algorithm to aggregate multiple proxy tasks. Based on the hypothesis: *a weaker correlation means a higher complementarity between two features*, we first calculate the correlation measure (*i.e.,* linear centered kernel alignment (LCKA) [13]) between the features yielded by different proxy tasks, and then employ the proposed greedy algorithm to iteratively add a proxy task with the lowest LCKA to the proxy tasks in the current task pool, and finally form a multi-task SSL framework. (ii) We implement a self-aggregation method to enlarge the feature space explored by a proxy task in a mode of *self-complementarity*. To achieve this, an auxiliary loss function based on LCKA is proposed as an add-on to the existing loss function to promote the exploring of where a single proxy task fails to cover.

In summary, our paper contributes two SSL aggregation strategies to exploit the complementarity. Specifically, 1) our *multi-task aggregative SSL (MT-ASSL)* provides new insights into multiple proxy task integration and systematically designs a greedy algorithm to combine complementary tasks; and 2) our *self-aggregative SSL (Self-ASSL)* provides a powerful add-on for improving the performance of an existing SSL approach. Such aggregative SSL methods boost the robustness of the learned feature representation with limited samples as demonstrated by our extensive evaluations on 2D and 3D medical datasets.

2   Formulation of SSL on Limited Samples

Here, we first mathematically illustrate the procedure of SSL training with the limited data. Assume $x = \{x^i\}$ and $y_p = \{y_p^i\}$ are a small group of data and pseudo label of proxy task p, respectively, and $x_t = \{x_t^j\}$ and $y_t = \{y_t^j\}$ are the data and labels of target task, respectively. The optimization problem for proxy task p can be written as:

$$\min_{\phi, h_p} F_p(\phi, h_p | x, y_p) = \sum_i L_p[h_p(\phi(x^i)), y_p^i], \tag{1}$$

where ϕ, h_p, and L_p denote the backbone model, projection layer and loss function for proxy task, respectively. Following that, ϕ is fine-tuned on the target task:

$$\min_{\phi, h_t} F_t(\phi, h_t | x_t, y_t) = \sum_j L_t[h_t(\phi(x_t^j)), y_t^j], \tag{2}$$

where y_t, h_t, and L_t denote the label, projection layer, and loss function for target task. After the training on target task, the model performance, such as classification accuracy, can be evaluated:

$$ACC(\phi | x_t, y_t) = \sum_j Eval[h_t(\phi(x_t^j)), y_t^j], \tag{3}$$

where $Eval[.]$ is the specific function for model performance evaluation. The goal of SSL is to obtain a robust ϕ, which achieves the better performance ACC than the train-from-scratch model.

3   Multi-task Aggregative SSL

Existing studies have demonstrated the effectiveness of multi-task learning for the extraction of a robust feature representation. In this regard, to further boost the robustness of self-supervised feature representations, we propose a principled framework for the integration of multiple SSL approaches to exploit more useful information from the limited raw data. Assume there is a pool of candidate proxy tasks $\mathcal{P} = \{p_1, p_2, ..., p_{|\mathcal{P}|}\}$, where $|\mathcal{P}|$ denotes the number of candidate proxy tasks, the conventional multi-task integrates all $\mathcal{P}$ can be formulated as:

$$\min_{\phi} F_{\mathcal{P}}(\phi | x) = \sum_{p \in \mathcal{P}} F_p(\phi, h_p | x, y_p) = \sum_{p \in \mathcal{P}} \sum_i L_p[h_p(\phi(x^i)), y_p^i]. \tag{4}$$

However, since the feature subspaces explored by different proxy tasks are heterogeneous; they might highly overlap or isolated. A blind integration of such feature subspaces brings limited (if not damaged) performance improvement. To address the problem, we systematically explore the feature complementarity between multiple SSL approaches, and propose a novel multi-task aggregative

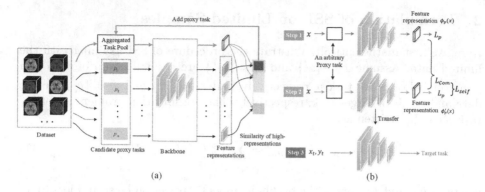

(a)   (b)

Fig. 1. (a) **The proposed MT-ASSL strategy**. In each iteration, we evaluate the similarity between feature representations learned by aggegated task pool and candidate proxy tasks using LCKA, and accordingly integrate the proxy task with the low similarity into the proposed MT-ASSL framework. The green and black arrows indicate aggregation SSL and single proxy task training. (b) **The proposed Self-ASSL pipeline**. It includes three different training steps. The feature representation $\phi_p'(x)$ gains a better generalization by aggregating a latent space complement to $\phi_p(x)$. (Color figure online)

self-supervised learning (MT-ASSL) strategy to **iteratively integrate** the features extracted by different-yet-complementary proxy tasks. The objective of our MT-ASSL can be defined as:

$$\min_{\phi,\mathcal{A}} F_{MT}(\phi|x) = \sum_{p\in\mathcal{A}} F_p(\phi, h_p|x, y_p) \tag{5}$$

where $\mathcal{A}$ denotes the selected subset of proxy tasks for aggregation, *which is optimized* too.

Initially, for each $p \in \mathcal{P}$ we train the network from scratch according to (1) to obtain its representation ϕ_p, which is then fined-tuned based on (2). Suppose that task $\hat{p}$ has with the highest evaluating performance of target task,

$$\hat{p} = \arg\max_{p\in\mathcal{P}} ACC(\phi_p|x_t, y_t), \tag{6}$$

then it is added to $\mathcal{A} = \{\hat{p}\}$, and removed from $\mathcal{P}$. The initial aggregation feature representation is set as $\phi_\mathcal{A} = \phi_{\hat{p}}$. We then attempt to add into $\mathcal{A}$ with more proxy tasks from $\mathcal{P}$ in order to learn a stronger aggregation feature representation. We follow a greedy algorithm by adding one proxy task at one iteration. To achieve so, we leverage the hypothesis underlying our MT-ASSL, that is, *a weaker correlation means a higher complementarity among features*.

To measure the complementarity between features learned by two different proxy task, we choose to use **linear centered kernel alignment (LCKA)** proposed by Kornblith et al. [13], who conducted a careful study on measuring similarity between the representations learned by neural networks, among other choices [15,20]. Mathematically, the LCKA between two feature representations, say ϕ_A and ϕ_p, are defined as

$$S[\phi_A, \phi_p] = \frac{\|G[\phi_A] \odot G[\phi_p]\|_1}{\sqrt{\|G[\phi_A]\|_1 \|G[\phi_p]\|_1}}, \quad G[\phi] = C(\phi(x)^T \phi(x)), \tag{7}$$

where $\phi(x)$ is a matrix that contains the features for all samples in x, $(.)^T$ and $\odot$ denote matrix multiplication and element-wise multiplication, respectively; $C(.)$ denotes the centered alignment operation, which is defined as $C(M) = M(I_d - \mathbf{1}\mathbf{1}^T/d)$, where d denotes the dimension of a square matrix $M_{d \times d}$, I_d is an identity matrix of size $d \times d$, and $\mathbf{1}$ is a $d \times 1$ vector of ones.

LCKA offers a simple yet concrete measurement of task correlation, which can be used as the guideline for aggregation of multiple proxy tasks. We update the task pool A by adding one more task that has the lowest correlation with the existing tasks in the pool and remove the selected task from $\mathcal{P}$:

$$p_x = \arg\min_{p \in \mathcal{P}} S[\phi_A, \phi_p], \quad A = A \cup \{p_x\}. \tag{8}$$

Following this selection criterion, a greedy training strategy is proposed to aggregate different proxy tasks for feature learning in an iterative fashion (from Eqs. (5) to (8)) The algorithm stops as long as there is no performance gain by adding a new proxy task or $\mathcal{P}$ is blank. Therefore, as the training iteration increases, the features exploited by different proxy tasks are gradually integrated, which yields a feature representation of better generalization. The process of the proposed aggregative training is described in Algorithm 1 (in supplementary materials).

4   Self-aggregative SSL

While MT-ASSL integrates different SSL proxy tasks, we further propose a novel aggregation strategy based on **self-complementarity**, namely self-aggregative SSL (Self-ASSL), to boost the generalization of features learnt from a limited sample, going beyond the limitation of a single SSL.

The pipeline of our Self-ASSL is shown in Fig. 1(b), which includes three steps. First, we train the backbone network by Eq. (1) to obtain a feature representation $\phi_p(x)$. Then in Step 2 of Fig. 1(b), we attempt to learn a new, self-complementary representation $\phi'_p(x)$, which ideally should have a low similarity with $\phi_p(x)$, using the following objective:

$$\min_{\phi'_p, h'_p} F_{Self}(\phi'_p, h'_p | \phi_p, x, y_p) = L_{self} + L_{com}; \tag{9}$$

$$L_{self} = \sum_{i=1} L_p(h'_p(\phi'_p(x^i)), y_p^i), L_{com} = -S[\phi'_p, \phi_p]. \tag{10}$$

where the trained backbone ϕ_p is frozen. After several iterations, the model ϕ'_p, achieving the better generalization, can further boost the improvement of the subsequent target task, by optimizing $F_t(\phi'_p, h_t | x_t, y_t)$ in Eq. (2). The process of Self-ASSL is summarized in Algorithm 2 (in supplementary materials).

5   Experiments

In this section, we conduct extensive experiments on medical image datasets with a limited number of samples to validate the effectiveness of the proposed self-supervised learning paradigms (i.e. MT-ASSL and Self-ASSL).

2D Medical Image Dataset: APTOS. APTOS kaggle benchmark dataset which consists of 3,662 fundus images, is a diabetic retinopathy (DR) classification contest available at [10]. The images are graded manually on a scale of 0 to 4 to indicate the severity levels.

3D Medical Volume Dataset: Brain Hemorrhage. The brain hemorrhage dataset, containing 1,486 brain CT volumes, is collected from our collaborative hospital with IRB approval. The CT volumes can be separated to four classes: aneurysm, arteriovenous malformation, moyamoya disease and hypertension. The size of CT volumes is standardized to $30 \times 270 \times 230$ voxels.

Implementation Details. Two datasets are separated into training and testing sets according to the ratio of 80:20. For 2D medical image classification, several state-of-the-art SSL approaches, including SRC [1], MCPC [1], 2D jigsaw puzzles (2D Jigsaw) [16], image rotation (2D Rot) [5], image inpainting (Inpaint) [17] and SimCLR [3], are involved to form a pool of proxy tasks for our MT-ASSL and Self-ASSL. The 2D ResNet-18 [7] is adopted as backbone network. For 3D SSL method, several 3D-based SSL approaches are included, *i.e.*, 3D SCA [1], 3D rotation (3D Rot) [5], Model genesis (MG) [23], 3D CPC (3D version of [8]) and Rubik's cube (Cube) [25]. The 3D ResNet-18 is utilized as backbone for MT-ASSL and Self-ASSL.

All the SSL methods are implemented using PyTorch and Adam solver optimizer [11]. We only use random horizontal flip for data augmentation. The network is trained with a mini-batch size of 64 and 16 for APTOS and brain hemorrhage datasets, respectively. The initial learning rate for the proxy task and target task are set to $3e^{-4}$ and $1e^{-4}$ for APTOS, $2e^{-5}$ and $15e^{-6}$ for brain hemorrhage dataset. For APTOS, network training stop at the 50th and 250th iterations for pre-training and supervised fine-tuning. And 50th and 200th iterations are set for brain hemorrhage dataset. The classification accuracy (ACC) is employed as the metric for evaluation.

5.1   Evaluation of MT-ASSL

APTOS. We first evaluate the proposed MT-ASSL on APTOS dataset. The results are shown in Table 1, following the greedy algorithm as presented in Algorithm 1. We first pre-train and fine-tune the ResNet-18 using each proxy task and record accuracy in the first iteration. It can be found that SRC achieves the best transferring performance of 79.64%, then it is added to the aggregation

Table 1. Results of our multi-task aggregative SSL (MT-ASSL) on APTOS dataset. The '$\mathcal{A}$' and '$\mathcal{P}$' indicate aggregated task pool and candidate proxy tasks, respectively. '$\mathcal{P}$' are sorted by the LCKA similarity in an increasing order.

Iter.	$\mathcal{A}$	$\mathcal{P}$	Similarity	ACC of $\mathcal{A}$	MT-ASSL ACC	δACC
1	–	SRC	–	–	**79.64**	–
	–	Inpaint	–	–	79.63	–
	–	MCPC	–	–	79.50	–
	–	2D Jigsaw	–	–	79.09	–
	–	2D Rot	–	–	78.82	–
	–	SimCLR	–	–	78.55	–
2	{SRC}	SimCLR	0.3448	79.64	**85.03**	**+5.39**
		2D Rot	0.4037		85.00	+5.36
		2D Jigsaw	0.4964		84.78	+5.14
		Inpaint	0.4968		80.19	+0.55
		MCPC	0.9756		79.23	−0.41
3	{SRC,SimCLR}	2D Rot	0.4069	85.03	**85.82**	**+0.79**
		2D Jigsaw	0.4989		85.11	+0.08
		Inpaint	0.4996		84.43	−0.60
		MCPC	0.5003		84.46	−0.57
4	{SRC,SimCLR,2D Rot}	2D Jigsaw	0.4989	85.82	83.74	−2.08
		Inpaint	0.4995		**84.84**	**−0.98**
		MCPC	0.5004		84.69	−1.13

task pool. The SimCLR and 2D Rot proxy tasks with the lowest similarity to the aggregation task pool are involved during iteration two and three, respectively. The MT-ASSL is completed after four iterations since no further performance improvement is observed, as the similarities of the remaining three proxy tasks are nearly the same (around 0.5). Therefore, our MT-ASSL obtains the best combination of proxy tasks (*i.e.*, SRC + SimCLR + 2D Rot) for the fundus image classification on APTOS dataset, which achieves a test accuracy of 85.82%.

Brain Hemorrhage. The results of MT-ASSL with five 3D-based SSL methods on brain hemorrhage dataset refer to Table 3 (in *supplementary material*). The best model is the combination of SCA and Cube.

Performances on Extremely Limited Data. We also conduct an experiment in Fig. 2(b) to evaluate the variation of accuracy achieved by different SSL approaches while training with different numbers of images from APTOS.

5.2 Evaluation of Self-ASSL

For the evaluation of Self-ASSL, apart from the ResNet-18 model, we also use the VGG [18] model as a backbone. From Table 2, it is observed that the Self-ASSL strategy consistently boosts the accuracy of proxy tasks, *e.g.*, +2.46% for SRC with VGG and +2.33% for 2D Jigsaw with ResNet-18. The SRC with Self-ASSL outperforms the benchmarking algorithms on APTOS dataset, *i.e.*, an ACC of

Table 2. Accuracy (ACC %) of different proxy tasks tested on APTOS and Brain hemorrhage datasets. δACC lists the improvements of ACC obtained by Self-ASSL against the original SSL. "T.f.s." stands for "Train from scratch".

Backbone	Method	2D APTOS ACC	w/Self-ASSL	δACC	3D Brain hemorrhage Backbone	ACC	w/Self-ASSL	δACC
VGG	T. f. s	79.09	–	–	T. f. s	72.30	–	–
	2D Jigsaw	79.91	80.87	+0.96	3D CPC	77.02	83.44	**+6.42**
	Inpaint	79.37	80.23	+0.86	3D Rot	76.68	79.05	+2.37
	2D Rot	79.92	80.32	+0.40	Cube	77.36	81.08	+3.72
	SimCLR	79.64	80.05	+0.41	MG	85.81	86.15	+0.34
	SRC	79.23	**81.69**	**+2.46**	SRC	85.81	87.50	+1.69
	MCPC	**80.05**	80.46	+0.41	MCPC	87.50	**89.52**	+2.02
ResNet18	T. f. s	78.82	–	–	T. f. s	81.08	–	–
	2D Jigsaw	79.09	**81.42**	**+2.33**	3D CPC	83.79	88.17	**+4.38**
	Inpaint	**79.64**	79.91	+0.27	3D Rot	85.81	85.47	−0.34
	2D Rot	78.82	78.96	+0.14	Cube	87.50	88.85	+1.35
	SimCLR	78.55	79.09	+0.54	MG	87.50	88.17	+0.67
	SRC	**79.64**	79.78	+0.14	SRC	87.16	88.51	+1.35
	MCPC	79.50	79.78	+0.28	MCPC	88.51	88.85	+0.34

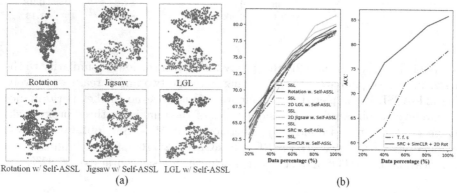

Fig. 2. (a) T-SNE visualizations of SSL and Self-ASSL on 2D medical dataset, where each color represents one specific class. (b) The performances of networks trained with different amounts of labeled data on APTOS dataset. The left figure shows the results of various SSLs with/without Self-ASSL and the right shows improvement of MT-ASSL, respectively. (Color figure online)

81.69% is achieved using VGG as backbone. A similar trend of improvement is observed on the brain hemorrhage dataset. Our Self-ASSL training strategy boosts the 3D CPC and Cube with VGG by large margins of +6.42% and +3.72%, respectively. And a margin of +4.38% for 3D CPC with 3D ResNet18. Also, the exception happens to 3D Rot with ResNet-18. The exact reason of such an exception is unclear and worthy of further investigation.

Visualization of Self-ASSL. We visualize the features using t-SNE (Fig. 2(a)), which shows that Self-ASSL leads to less intra-class distance and more clustered, compared to the original single SSL task. This expansive behavior is exactly what we want and where the strength arises.

6 Conclusion

We propose two approaches for SSL aggregation training from a limited medical sample by exploiting the complementarity of multiple proxy tasks and self-complementarity to a single proxy task itself, respectively. Our extensive experiments on two datasets with limited annotations show that the proposed aggregation strategies expose new insights for self-supervised learning and significantly improve the accuracy of learned features on the target tasks. These improvements are **essentially free performance boosts** as our models introduce no extra computation. Future works include mining the feature complementarity among off-the-shelf networks for various vision tasks, and constructing a unified framework that features both MT-ASSL and Self-ASSL.

References

1. Zhu, J., Li, Y., Hu, Y., Zhou, S.K.: Embedding task knowledge into 3D neural networks via self-supervised learning. arXiv preprint arXiv:2006.05798 (2020)
2. Blendowski, M., Nickisch, H., Heinrich, M.P.: How to learn from unlabeled volume data: self-supervised 3D context feature learning. In: Shen, D., et al. (eds.) MICCAI 2019. LNCS, vol. 11769, pp. 649–657. Springer, Cham (2019). https://doi.org/10. 1007/978-3-030-32226-7_72
3. Chen, T., Kornblith, S., Norouzi, M., Hinton, G.E.: A simple framework for contrastive learning of visual representations. arXiv: Learning (2020)
4. Doersch, C., Zisserman, A.: Multi-task self-supervised visual learning. In: IEEE International Conference on Computer Vision, pp. 2070–2079 (2017)
5. Gidaris, S., Singh, P., Komodakis, N.: Unsupervised representation learning by predicting image rotations. arXiv:1803.07728 (2018)
6. Grill, J.B., et al.: Bootstrap your own latent: A new approach to self-supervised learning. ArXiv abs/2006.07733 (2020)
7. He, K., Zhang, X., Ren, S., Sun, J.: Deep residual learning for image recognition. In: IEEE Conference on Computer Vision and Pattern Recognition, pp. 770–778 (2016)
8. Henaff, O.J., Razavi, A., Doersch, C., Eslami, S.M.A., Den Oord, A.V.: Data-efficient image recognition with contrastive predictive coding. In: IEEE Conference on Computer Vision and Pattern Recognition (2019)
9. Jakab, T., Gupta, A., Bilen, H., Vedaldi, A.: Self-supervised learning of interpretable keypoints from unlabelled videos. In: IEEE Conference on Computer Vision and Pattern Recognition, pp. 8784–8794 (2020)
10. Kaggle: Aptos 2019 blindness detection (2019). https://www.kaggle.com/c/aptos2019-blindness-detection
11. Kingma, D.P., Ba, J.: Adam: a method for stochastic optimization. arXiv preprint arXiv:1412.6980 (2014)

12. Kolesnikov, A., Zhai, X., Beyer, L.: Revisiting self-supervised visual representation learning. In: IEEE Conference on Computer Vision and Pattern Recognition, pp. 1920–1929 (2019)
13. Kornblith, S., Norouzi, M., Lee, H., Hinton, G.E.: Similarity of neural network representations revisited. In: International Conference on Machine Learning (2019)
14. Larsson, G., Maire, M., Shakhnarovich, G.: Colorization as a proxy task for visual understanding. In: IEEE Conference on Computer Vision and Pattern Recognition, pp. 840–849 (2017)
15. Morcos, A.S., Raghu, M., Bengio, S.: Insights on representational similarity in neural networks with canonical correlation. In: Conference on Neural Information Processing Systems (2018)
16. Noroozi, M., Favaro, P.: Unsupervised learning of visual representations by solving Jigsaw puzzles. In: Leibe, B., Matas, J., Sebe, N., Welling, M. (eds.) ECCV 2016. LNCS, vol. 9910, pp. 69–84. Springer, Cham (2016). https://doi.org/10.1007/978-3-319-46466-4_5
17. Pathak, D., Krähenbühl, P., Donahue, J., Darrell, T., Efros, A.A.: Context encoders: feature learning by inpainting. In: IEEE Conference on Computer Vision and Pattern Recognition, pp. 2536–2544 (2016)
18. Simonyan, K., Zisserman, A.: Very deep convolutional networks for large-scale image recognition. In: International Conference on Learning Representations (2015)
19. Tajbakhsh, N., Jeyaseelan, L., Li, Q., Chiang, J., Wu, Z., Ding, X.: Embracing imperfect datasets: a review of deep learning solutions for medical image segmentation. Med. Image Anal. **63**, 101693 (2020)
20. Wilks, D.: Canonical correlation analysis (CCA). Int. Geophys. **100**, 563–582 (2011)
21. Zhou, S., et al.: A review of deep learning in medical imaging: image traits, technology trends, case studies with progress highlights, and future promises. In: Proceedings of the IEEE, August 2020
22. Zhou, Z., Sodha, V., Pang, J., Gotway, M.B., Liang, J.: Models genesis. Med. Image Anal. **67**, 101840 (2020)
23. Zhou, Z., et al.: Models genesis: generic autodidactic models for 3D medical image analysis. In: Medical Image Computing and Computer Assisted Intervention, pp. 384–393 (2019)
24. Zhu, J., Li, Y., Hu, Y., Ma, K., Zhou, S.K., Zheng, Y.: Rubik's Cube+: a self-supervised feature learning framework for 3D medical image analysis. In: Medical Image Analysis, vol. 64, p. 101746 (2020)
25. Zhuang, X., Li, Y., Hu, Y., Ma, K., Yang, Y., Zheng, Y.: Self-supervised feature learning for 3D medical images by playing a Rubik's cube. In: Shen, D., et al. (eds.) MICCAI 2019. LNCS, vol. 11767, pp. 420–428. Springer, Cham (2019). https://doi.org/10.1007/978-3-030-32251-9_46

Learning Underrepresented Classes from Decentralized Partially Labeled Medical Images

Nanqing Dong[1]([✉]) [iD], Michael Kampffmeyer[2] [iD], and Irina Voiculescu[1] [iD]

[1] Department of Computer Science, University of Oxford, Oxford, UK
nanqing.dong@cs.ox.ac.uk
[2] UiT The Arctic University of Norway, Tromsø, Norway

Abstract. Using decentralized data for federated training is one promising emerging research direction for alleviating data scarcity in the medical domain. However, in contrast to large-scale fully labeled data commonly seen in general object recognition tasks, the local medical datasets are more likely to only have images annotated for a subset of classes of interest due to high annotation costs. In this paper, we consider a practical yet under-explored problem, where underrepresented classes only have few labeled instances available and only exist in a few clients of the federated system. We show that standard federated learning approaches fail to learn robust multi-label classifiers with extreme class imbalance and address it by proposing a novel federated learning framework, Fed-Few. FedFew consists of three stages, where the first stage leverages federated self-supervised learning to learn *class-agnostic* representations. In the second stage, the decentralized partially labeled data are exploited to learn an energy-based multi-label classifier for the common classes. Finally, the underrepresented classes are detected based on the energy and a *prototype*-based nearest-neighbor model is proposed for few-shot matching. We evaluate FedFew on multi-label thoracic disease classification tasks and demonstrate that it outperforms the federated baselines by a large margin.

Keywords: Federated learning · Partially supervised learning · Multi-label classification

1 Introduction

Learning from partially labeled data, or partially supervised learning (PSL), has become an emerging research direction in label-efficient learning on medical images [4,6,8,20,27]. Due to high data collection and annotation costs, PSL utilizes multiple available partially labeled datasets when fully labeled data are difficult to acquire. Here, a partially labeled dataset refers to a dataset with only a specific *true subset* of classes of interest annotated. For example, considering a multi-label thoracic disease task on chest X-ray (CXR) images (*i.e.* a CXR

© The Author(s), under exclusive license to Springer Nature Switzerland AG 2022
L. Wang et al. (Eds.): MICCAI 2022, LNCS 13438, pp. 67–76, 2022.
https://doi.org/10.1007/978-3-031-16452-1_7

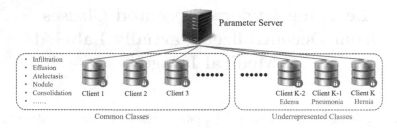

Fig. 1. An example problem setup with multi-label thoracic disease classification. In this example, each client in the red dashed box has only one underrepresented class, while the clients in the green dashed box share a set of common classes. (Color figure online)

could contain several diseases at the same time), a pneumonia dataset may only have labels for pneumonia and not the labels for the other diseases of interest.

In this work, we extend the discussion of PSL to an unexplored federated setup, where the partially labeled datasets are stored separately in different clients (*e.g.* hospitals and research institutes). In this work, we denote the common classes (CCs) as the classes with enough labels to learn a multi-label classifier. Meanwhile, in a *open-world* scenario, there are also newly-found or under-examined classes, which tend to have much fewer labeled instances than the CCs. This extreme class imbalance makes learning these underrepresented classes (UCs) a difficult task. Furthermore, the main assumption of this work is that the CCs and UCs are annotated at disjoint clients, which makes this practical problem even more challenging. While a formal problem setup will be described in Sect. 2, an intuitive illustration of the problem is presented in Fig. 1. Due to decentralization and extreme class imbalance, improving the performance of UCs can inevitably decrease the performance of CCs, while maintaining the performance of CCs might lead to UCs being completely ignored. To the best of our knowledge, this is the first study on decentralized partially labeled rare classes.

Contributions. We formalize this under-explored problem and present FedFew, the first solution to it. FedFew is a three-stage federated learning (FL) framework. Firstly, we utilize federated self-supervised learning (FSSL) to learn *class-agnostic* transferable representations in a pre-training stage. Secondly, in the fine-tuning stage, we propose an energy-based multi-label classifier that aims to utilize the knowledge from the CCs to learn representations for the UCs. Finally, we utilize a *prototype*-based nearest-neighbor classifier for few-shot matching given only few partially labeled examples for the UCs. We evaluate FedFew on a set of multi-label thoracic disease classification tasks on the Chest-Xray14 dataset [25] in a simulated federated environment. The empirical results show that the proposed framework outperforms existing methods by a large margin.

2   Problem Setup

Task and Data Setup. The task of interest is multi-label classification (MLC) with C non-mutually exclusive classes of interest, where the decentralized data are stored in a federated system with $K > 1$ clients. Let $\mathcal{D}_k$ denote the data stored in client $k \leq K$, we have $\mathcal{D}_k \cap \mathcal{D}_l = \emptyset$ for $k \neq l$ and $\{\mathcal{D}_k\}_{k=1}^K$ are non-IID data. For convenience, we define $\mathcal{D}_k = \mathcal{P}_k \cup \mathcal{U}_k$, where $\mathcal{P}_k$ is a *partially labeled* dataset and $\mathcal{U}_k$ is an *unlabeled* dataset. We define $n_k^p = |\mathcal{P}_k|$ and $n_k^u = |\mathcal{U}_k|$.[1] We assume that the classes of interest, denoted as $\mathcal{C}$, can be split into two mutually exclusive subsets, namely a set of UCs (denoted as $\mathcal{C}_u \subset \mathcal{C}$), which is also the primary target of this work, and a set of CCs (denoted as $\mathcal{C}_c = \mathcal{C} \setminus \mathcal{C}_u$). For simplicity, we consider a representative case that there are $|\mathcal{C}_u| < K$ clients and each of these clients is annotated for only one UC[2]. For the remaining $K - |\mathcal{C}_u|$ clients, we assume that each client has *partially labeled*[3] data for all CCs ($\mathcal{C}_c$). We additionally require $n_i^p \ll n_j^p \ \forall \ i \in \mathcal{C}_u, j \in \mathcal{C}_c$ to enforce the assumption of UCs. The learning outcome is to leverage the decentralized training data to train an MLC model for $\mathcal{C}$.

Federated Environment Setup. In addition to K clients, there is a parameter server (PS) [16] for model aggregation. Let f_θ be the model of interest. In the PS, the parameter set θ_0 is randomly initialized and sent out to K clients as K copies $\{\theta_k\}_{k=1}^K$ for full synchronization. During the federated optimization phase, the client k updates θ_k by training on $\mathcal{D}_k$ independently for a number of local epochs. Then, the PS aggregates $\{\theta_k\}_{k=1}^K$ collected from K clients to update θ_0. Under the data regulations in the medical domain [7,22], we assume that the patients' data (either raw data or encoded data) in a client can not be uploaded to the PS or other clients, *i.e.* only parameters $\{\theta_k\}_{k=0}^K$ and *metadata* (*e.g.* the statistics of data) can be exchanged between the PS and the clients.

3   Method

In this section, we first provide the preliminaries that FedFew builds on in Sect. 3.1. The first training stage of FSSL is briefly described in Sect. 3.2, while the second training stage of energy-based FL with partial labels is described in Sect. 3.3. Finally, in Sect. 3.4, we present the prototype-based nearest-neighbor classifier for few-shot matching.

---

[1] $|\cdot|$ is the cardinality of a set.

[2] This is the most fundamental case. As a trivial extension, each client could have labels for more than one class and multiple clients could have labels for the same set of classes. The proposed method could be easily adapted to these extensions.

[3] Here, the images with CCs are partially labeled with respect to the missing labels of the UCs, *i.e.* they are fully labeled if we only consider CCs. The assumption here is that the CCs are diseases with high prevalence, which can be easily collected and diagnosed; but the UCs are rare and only spotted in certain clients.

3.1   Preliminaries

FedAvg. As a seminal FL model, FedAvg [18] aggregates the model weights $\{\theta_k\}_{k=1}^{K}$ as a weighted average. Mathematically, we have

$$\theta_0 = \sum_{k=1}^{K} a_k \theta_k, \tag{1}$$

where $a_k = \frac{n_k}{n_{tot}}$. The metadata n_k is the number of labeled training examples stored in client k and $n_{tot} = \sum_{k=1}^{K} n_k$ is the total number of training examples.
Energy Function. Given a discriminative neural network classifier f, the energy function $E(x; f) : \mathbb{R}^{H \times W} \to \mathbb{R}$ maps an image with shape $H \times W$ to a scalar, which is also known as *Helmholtz free energy* [15]. The energy is defined as

$$E(x; f) = -\tau \log \int_y \exp^{\frac{f^y(x)}{\tau}}, \tag{2}$$

where $f^y(x)$ is the logit of the yth class label and τ is the temperature parameter.

3.2   Federated Self-supervised Learning

The first training stage consists of FSSL, where a feature extractor f_θ is pretrained to learn class-agnostic representations. Theoretically, multiple existing self-supervised learning frameworks (*e.g.* [1,9,10]) could serve as the local backbone. In this work, however, due to its lightweight nature, we leverage SimSiam [2]. Let θ_0^t denote the aggregated model weights in the PS at the end of the tth training round. Thus, at the beginning of the $t+1^{\text{th}}$ round, the model weights at client k should be synchronized to θ_0^t. After the local updates of the $t + 1^{\text{th}}$ round, the local model weights of client k are now θ_k^{t+1} and, θ_0^{t+1} is computed by applying Eq. 1 on $\{\theta_k^{t+1}\}_{k=1}^{K}$.

3.3   Energy-Based Federated Learning with Partial Labels

For standard MLC, it is common to use a C-dimensional binary vector to encode the label information for a given input. When all binary entries are 0s, the input does not contain any class of interest. However, with limited partial labels of UCs, it is difficult to train an MLC model for $\mathcal{C}$ or $\mathcal{C}_u$ directly. Instead, we first train an MLC model for CCs $\mathcal{C}_c$. In contrast to previous studies [19,25], we encode the label into a $(C_c + 1)$-dimensional vector, where $C_c = |\mathcal{C}_c|$. That is to say, we use an additional dimension (denoted as 0th class[4]) to specifically determine whether the patient contains any CCs. Note, this 0th class only reflects the information on CCs, as we have no label information for the UCs.

---

[4] When the additional dimension is 0, the rest of C_c dimensions should have at least one 1; when the additional dimension is 1, C_c dimensions should all be 0s.

Without loss of generality, let us consider a client $k \in \mathcal{K}_c$ with only $\mathcal{C}_c$ labeled, where $\mathcal{K}_c$ denotes the clients with the CCs. Given an example x in client k with corresponding partial label y, the binary cross-entropy loss is

$$\mathcal{L}_{BCE}(x, y) = - \sum_{j \in \{0\} \cup \mathcal{C}_c} y_j \log(f_\theta^j(x)) + (1 - y_j) \log(1 - f_\theta^j(x)), \qquad (3)$$

where $f_\theta^j(x)$ is the probability score for the jth class. As MLC can be decomposed into multiple binary classification tasks, the energy of x for class j degenerates to $E(x; f_\theta^j) = -\tau \log(1 + \exp^{\frac{f_\theta^j(x)}{\tau}})$ (c.f. Eq. (2)) and the *joint energy* [24] of x is then the sum of energies over all CCs $\mathcal{C}_c$:

$$E(x, f_\theta) = \sum_{j \in \{0\} \cup \mathcal{C}_c} E(x; f_\theta^j) = - \sum_{j \in \{0\} \cup \mathcal{C}_c} \tau \log(1 + \exp^{\frac{f_\theta^j(x)}{\tau}}). \qquad (4)$$

We include a regularization term [17] to penalize the energy of x with a squared hinge loss:

$$\mathcal{L}_{E_c}(x) = \lambda \| \max(0, E(x; f_\theta) - m_c) \|_2^2, \qquad (5)$$

where the margin m_c is a hyperparameter chosen empirically to decrease the energy of x and λ is a weight hyperparameter. The final optimization goal for client $k \subset \mathcal{C}_c$ is to minimize the sum of the two losses:

$$\mathcal{L}_c = \mathcal{L}_{BCE}(x, y) + \mathcal{L}_{E_c}(x). \qquad (6)$$

For clients with only UC (*i.e.* no CCs), we only minimize a regularization term:

$$\mathcal{L}_u = \lambda \| \max(0, m_u - E(x; f_\theta)) \|_2^2, \qquad (7)$$

where the margin m_u is chosen empirically to increase the energy of x. Note, Eq. (5) and Eq. (7) are both designed to enlarge the *energy gap* between $\mathcal{C}_c$ and $\mathcal{C}_u$. We aggregate the models weights $\{\theta_k\}_{k=1}^K$ via Eq. (1), where $a_k = \frac{n_k^P}{\sum_{j=1}^K n_j^P}$. The complete pseudo-code is given in Algorithm 1.

3.4 Prototype-Based Inference

After the federated training in Sect. 3.3, f_θ can be directly used as an MLC model to predict CCs.[5] Now, we use the energy (Eq. (4)) to detect UCs, *i.e.* if the energy of an example is lower than a threshold[6], then the example is deemed to contain no UCs; if the energy is higher than the threshold, we further match the test example to the nearest neighbor, given few partially labeled examples. However, due to the constraint of data regulations, the training data and the test data are

---

[5] Given the $(C_c + 1)$-dimensional output vector, we drop the 0th dimension and only use the C_c-dimensional vector as the final prediction.

[6] The threshold is chosen to maximize the number of correctly classified training examples.

Algorithm 1. Energy-Based Federated Partially Supervised Training. T is the total number of rounds. θ_k^t denotes the weights stored in client k at the tth round.

    Input: θ_0^0, $\{\mathcal{P}_k\}_{k=1}^K$, T_w, T
    Output: θ_0^T
1: **for** $t = 1, 2, \cdots, T_w$ **do**   ▷ Warm up
2:     **for** $k \in \mathcal{K}_c$ **do**
3:         $\theta_k^t \leftarrow \theta_0^{t-1}$ ▷ Synchronize with PS
4:         $\theta_k^t \leftarrow local\_update(\theta_k^t)$ ▷ Eq. (6)
5:     $\theta_0^t \leftarrow \sum_{k \in \mathcal{K}_c} a_k^t \theta_k^t$ ▷ Aggregate with Eq. (1)
6: **for** $t = T_w + 1, T_w + 2, \cdots, T$ **do**
7:     **for** $k = 1, 2, \cdots, K$ **do**
8:         $\theta_k^t \leftarrow \theta_0^{t-1}$ ▷ Synchronize with PS
9:         $\theta_k^t \leftarrow local\_update(\theta_k^t)$ ▷ Eq. (6) or Eq. (7)
10:    $\theta_0^t \leftarrow \sum_{k=1}^K a_k^t \theta_k^t$ ▷ Aggregate with Eq. (1)

---

stored in separated clients. Thus, similar to [5], we transfer the metadata of UCs to the PS. Here, the metadata is the mean of the extracted features. For class $c \in \mathcal{C}_u$, we have $\boldsymbol{\mu}_c^{pos} = \frac{\sum_{i=1}^{n_c^{pos}} g_\theta(x_i^{pos})}{n_c^{pos}}$, $\boldsymbol{\mu}_c^{neg} = \frac{\sum_{i=1}^{n_c^{neg}} g_\theta(x_i^{neg})}{n_c^{neg}}$, where we use pos and neg to denote the positive and negative examples of class c, respectively, and use g_θ to denote the feature extractor. Note, $\boldsymbol{\mu}_c^{pos}$ and $\boldsymbol{\mu}_c^{neg}$ factually define the *prototypes* in the few-shot learning literature [21]. With the *dual*-prototypes for class c, we match the test example to the closer one by computing the distance between the features of test example and the two prototypes[7].

4 Experiments

4.1 Experimental Setup

To provide empirical insights into the problem and ensure fair comparisons with the baselines, we share the same experimental setup among all experiments.
Implementation. We explore two network backbones (f_θ), ResNet34 (RN) [11] and DenseNet121 (DN) [12], which are lightweight models commonly used for FL. We use SimSiam [9], a state-of-the-art SSL framework, to pre-train f_θ locally, and use a standard Adam [14] optimizer with fixed learning rate 10^{-3} and batch-size 64 for both pre-training and fine-tuning. We set $\tau = 1$ when computing the energy, following [17]. The values of m_c and m_u can be chosen around the mean of energy scores from a model trained without energy-based loss (*e.g.* warm-up stage in this work) for images from the clients of CCs and the clients of UCs, respectively. In this work, we simply set $m_c = -5$ and $m_u = -25$ to intentionally enlarge the energy gap and we use $\lambda = 0.01$. We follow the same data pre-processing and augmentation procedure as [5]. The synchronization and

---

[7] Again, this is a simple case. When there are multiple prototypes collected from different clients for class c, majority voting is adopted.

aggregation for federated methods are performed every 10 epochs. For the second stage, $T_w = 20$ and $T = 100$. All models are implemented in PyTorch (1.10.1) on an NVIDIA Tesla V100.

Data. We use the multi-label dataset ChestX-ray14[8] [25] and adopt its default batch splits to ensure reproducibility. Based on the label statistics of the dataset, we choose *edema, pneumonia,* and *hernia* as the three UCs and use the remaining 11 classes as CCs. Note, most CXR images do not contain any diseases. We use 6 batches[9] to simulate the $K = 6$ clients, where we use the first three batches to simulate the partially labeled datasets for CCs, where we randomly sample $n_k^p = 5 \times 10^3$ images to keep partial labels for CCs. Each of the remaining three batches contains one of the three UCs. We sample 10 positive examples and 90 negative examples to simulate the class imbalance for UCs, *i.e.* $n_k^p = 100$. See Fig. 1 for an illustration of the class assignment. From the remaining batches, we hold out 100 positive and 100 negative examples for each class as the test set.

4.2 Results

Empirical Analysis of FSSL. Following previous SSL studies, we examine the FSSL performance via the *linear classification protocol* [1,9,10]. Similar to [5], we fix all the weights of f_θ except the last layer and only fine-tune the last layer on a public pneumonia dataset[10] [13]. In this dataset, there are three mutually exclusive classes, *normal, bacteria pneumonia,* and *virus pneumonia.* We randomly split the images of each class into two halves as the training and test sets. We use the test accuracy as the *proxy* measure to assess the representation learning performance. Firstly, we provide a counter-intuitive observation that more disease images might not improve the performance. We create two clients with Chest-Xray14 data, where one client contains 10^4 images without any diseases and the other client contains $r \times 10^4$ images with various diseases. The results in Table 1 show that FedAvg does not always benefit from large r and it might be unnecessary to collect a large number of images with related diseases for pre-training. Secondly, we examine the impact of the training epochs for federated SSL in Fig. 2, where we pre-train f_θ on the 6 clients described in Sect. 4.1. In contrast to the empirical findings collected from general images [1,2,9,10], more epochs will not lead to diminishing performance gain but decreasing results. We will use DenseNet121 as the default network and use the pre-trained weights with 100 epochs in the following experiments.

Evaluation of FedFew. Following the experimental setup in Sect. 4.1, we evaluate FedFew against a few seminal baselines from two aspects, *i.e.* we aim to achieve high accuracy on UCs while maintaining robust performance on CCs. The first baseline is a standard MLC model [19], which is trained with FedAvg on decentralized partially labeled data of all 14 classes and weighted binary cross-entropy [19]. We use *MLC w/o FSSL* and *MLC w/FSSL* to differentiate

---

[8] https://nihcc.app.box.com/v/ChestXray-NIHCC.

[9] We use batch 2 to 7. Each batch has 10^4 CXR images and similar label distributions.

[10] https://data.mendeley.com/datasets/rscbjbr9sj/2.

Table 1. Impact of class imbalance on FSSL. We report the mean accuracy over three random seeds.

Epoch	$r = 1$		$r = 0.5$		$r = 0.1$	
	RN	DN	RN	DN	RN	DN
100	61.69	70.47	69.34	71.94	65.92	73.81
200	62.96	71.22	68.32	71.36	65.24	74.43

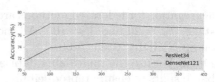

Fig. 2. Impact of the number of training epochs on FSSL.

whether f_θ is pre-trained with FSSL. The second baseline is a hypothetical local nearest-neighbor classifier (*NN*) that does not use prototypes, where g_θ is either pre-trained with FSSL alone or further fine-tuned with *MLC w/FSSL*. Note, *NN* can not be used in a federated system due to data regulations. For FedFew, we use *EBM* to denote the energy-based loss in the training. The results on UCs are presented in Table 2 and include the mean accuracy (A), precision (P), recall (R), and F-1 (F) score over three random seeds. Note, standard MLC models fail to detect any images of the UCs due to extreme class imbalance. With only proto-types (as only metadata can be transferred to the PS), NNs struggle to improve over random guessing. FedFew (*w/o EBM*) outperforms the two baselines by a large margin while *EBM* further improves the performance of FedFew with higher precision. Similar to Table 2, we report the mean *area under the receiver operating characteristic* (AUROC) for the 11 CCs over three runs in Table 3. We find that FSSL can boost the performance for standard MLC. While FedFew (*w/o EBM*) and FedFew (*w/EBM*) both outperform *MLC w/FSSL*, including *EBM* slightly improves the performance on CCs. We conjecture that *EBM* can play a role as regularization in the federated training. By combining the results from both Table 2 and Table 3, we conclude that FedFew (*w/EBM*) provides a robust solution to the problem of interest.

Analysis on Energy. As an ablation study, we visualize the energy density plots between images with and without UCs in Fig. 3, which demonstrates that including *EBM* in the training does increase the energy gap, thus leading to improved performance.

Distance Metric. We consider three distance metrics for the nearest-neighbor matching is Sect. 3.4, which are cosine distance [23], Euclidean distance [21], and earth mover's distance [26] (computed with Sinkhorn-Knopp algorithm [3]). We choose the cosine distance based on its empirical robustness. It achieves an average F-1 score over the UCs of 0.67, while the Euclidean distance obtains 0.6 and the earth mover's distance obtains 0.43.

Table 2. Performance comparison on the UCs. The standard MLC and NN models fail to predict the UCs. A, P, R, and F denote the mean accuracy, precision, recall, and F1-score over three random seeds, respectively.

Method	Edema				Pneumonia				Hernia			
	A	P	R	F	A	P	R	F	A	P	R	F
MLC w/o FSSL	0.50	0.00	0.00	0.00	0.50	0.00	0.00	0.00	0.50	0.00	0.00	0.00
MLC w/FSSL	0.50	0.00	0.00	0.00	0.50	0.00	0.00	0.00	0.50	0.00	0.00	0.00
NN (FSSL)	0.53	0.53	0.50	0.52	0.51	0.51	0.46	0.48	0.50	0.50	0.54	0.52
NN (MLC w/FSSL)	0.53	0.53	0.50	0.52	0.51	0.51	0.46	0.48	0.50	0.50	0.54	0.52
FedFew w/o EBM	0.71	0.85	0.50	0.63	0.69	0.84	0.46	0.59	0.72	0.83	0.54	0.65
FedFew w/EBM	**0.75**	**1.00**	**0.50**	**0.67**	**0.73**	**1.00**	**0.46**	**0.63**	**0.77**	**1.00**	**0.54**	**0.70**

Table 3. Performance comparison on the CCs. AUROC denotes the mean AUROC over three random seeds.

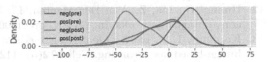

Fig. 3. Energy gaps between positive and negative cases before (pre) and after (post) *EBM* training in Client 1.

Method	AUROC
MLC w/o FSSL	0.6905
MLC w/FSSL	0.7227
FedFew w/o EBM	0.7423
FedFew w/EBM	**0.7479**

5 Conclusion

In this work, we raise awareness of an under-explored problem, namely the learning of underrepresented classes from decentralized partially labeled medical images. We not only provide a solution to this novel problem but also provide the first empirical understanding of federated partially supervised learning with extreme class imbalance, a new research direction on label-efficient learning.

References

1. Chen, T., Kornblith, S., Norouzi, M., Hinton, G.: A simple framework for contrastive learning of visual representations. In: ICML, pp. 1597–1607. PMLR (2020)
2. Chen, X., He, K.: Exploring simple Siamese representation learning. In: CVPR, pp. 15750–15758 (2021)
3. Cuturi, M.: Sinkhorn distances: lightspeed computation of optimal transport. In: NIPS, vol. 26, pp. 2292–2300 (2013)
4. Dong, N., Kampffmeyer, M., Liang, X., Xu, M., Voiculescu, I., Xing, E.: Towards robust partially supervised multi-structure medical image segmentation on small-scale data. Appl. Soft Comput. 108074 (2022)
5. Dong, N., Voiculescu, I.: Federated contrastive learning for decentralized unlabeled medical images. In: de Bruijne, M., et al. (eds.) MICCAI 2021. LNCS, vol. 12903, pp. 378–387. Springer, Cham (2021). https://doi.org/10.1007/978-3-030-87199-4_36

6. Dong, N., Wang, J., Voiculescu, I.: Revisiting vicinal risk minimization for partially supervised multi-label classification under data scarcity. In: CVPR Workshops, pp. 4212–4220 (2022)

7. European Commission. General data protection regulation (2016). https://ec.europa.eu/info/law/law-topic/data-protection/data-protection-eu_en

8. Fang, X., Yan, P.: Multi-organ segmentation over partially labeled datasets with multi-scale feature abstraction. IEEE TMI (2020)

9. Grill, J.B., et al.: Bootstrap your own latent: a new approach to self-supervised learning. In: NIPS, vol. 33, pp. 21271–21284 (2020)

10. He, K., Fan, H., Wu, Y., Xie, S., Girshick, R.: Momentum contrast for unsupervised visual representation learning. In: CVPR, pp. 9729–9738 (2020)

11. He, K., Zhang, X., Ren, S., Sun, J.: Deep residual learning for image recognition. In: CVPR, pp. 770–778 (2016)

12. Huang, G., Liu, Z., Van Der Maaten, L., Weinberger, K.Q.: Densely connected convolutional networks. In: CVPR, pp. 4700–4708 (2017)

13. Kermany, D.S., et al.: Identifying medical diagnoses and treatable diseases by image-based deep learning. Cell **172**(5), 1122–1131 (2018)

14. Kingma, D.P., Ba, J.: Adam: a method for stochastic optimization. In: ICLR (2015)

15. LeCun, Y., Chopra, S., Hadsell, R., Ranzato, M., Huang, F.: A tutorial on energy-based learning. Predict. Struct. Data **1** (2006)

16. Li, M., Andersen, D.G., Smola, A.J., Yu, K.: Communication efficient distributed machine learning with the parameter server. In: NIPS, pp. 19–27 (2014)

17. Liu, W., Wang, X., Owens, J., Li, Y.: Energy-based out-of-distribution detection. In: NIPS. **33**, 21464–21475 (2020)

18. McMahan, B., Moore, E., Ramage, D., Hampson, S., Agueray Arcas, B.: Communication-efficient learning of deep networks from decentralized data. In: AISTATS, pp. 1273–1282. PMLR (2017)

19. Rajpurkar, P., et al.: Chexnet: radiologist-level pneumonia detection on chest x-rays with deep learning. arXiv preprint arXiv:1711.05225 (2017)

20. Shi, G., Xiao, L., Chen, Y., Zhou, S.K.: Marginal loss and exclusion loss for partially supervised multi-organ segmentation. Med. Image Anal. 101979 (2021)

21. Snell, J., Swersky, K., Zemel, R.: Prototypical networks for few-shot learning. In: NIPS, pp. 4077–4087 (2017)

22. US Department of Health and Human Services. Health insurance portability and accountability act (2017). https://www.cdc.gov/phlp/publications/topic/hipaa.html

23. Vinyals, O., Blundell, C., Lillicrap, T., Wierstra, D., et al.: Matching networks for one shot learning. In: NIPS, pp. 3630–3638 (2016)

24. Wang, H., Liu, W., Bocchieri, A., Li, Y.: Can multi-label classification networks know what they don't know? In: NIPS, vol. 34 (2021)

25. Wang, X., Peng, Y., Lu, L., Lu, Z., Bagheri, M., Summers, R.M.: Chestx-ray8: hospital-scale chest x-ray database and benchmarks on weakly-supervised classification and localization of common thorax diseases. In: CVPR, pp. 2097–2106 (2017)

26. Zhang, C., Cai, Y., Lin, G., Shen, C.: Deepemd: few-shot image classification with differentiable earth mover's distance and structured classifiers. In: CVPR, pp. 12203–12213 (2020)

27. Zhou, Y., et al.: Prior-aware neural network for partially-supervised multi-organ segmentation. In: ICCV, pp. 10672–10681 (2019)

Adversarially Robust Prototypical Few-Shot Segmentation with Neural-ODEs

Prashant Pandey[1]([⊠])[iD], Aleti Vardhan[2], Mustafa Chasmai[1], Tanuj Sur[3], and Brejesh Lall[1]

[1] Indian Institute of Technology Delhi, New Delhi, India
getprashant57@gmail.com
[2] Manipal Institute of Technology, Manipal, India
[3] Chennai Mathematical Institute, Chennai, India

Abstract. Few-shot Learning (FSL) methods are being adopted in settings where data is not abundantly available. This is especially seen in medical domains where the annotations are expensive to obtain. Deep Neural Networks have been shown to be vulnerable to adversarial attacks. This is even more severe in the case of FSL due to the lack of a large number of training examples. In this paper, we provide a framework to make few-shot segmentation models adversarially robust in the medical domain where such attacks can severely impact the decisions made by clinicians who use them. We propose a novel robust few-shot segmentation framework, Prototypical Neural Ordinary Differential Equation (PNODE), that provides defense against gradient-based adversarial attacks. We show that our framework is more robust compared to traditional adversarial defense mechanisms such as adversarial training. Adversarial training involves increased training time and shows robustness to limited types of attacks depending on the type of adversarial examples seen during training. Our proposed framework generalises well to common adversarial attacks like FGSM, PGD and SMIA while having the model parameters comparable to the existing few-shot segmentation models. We show the effectiveness of our proposed approach on three publicly available multi-organ segmentation datasets in both in-domain and cross-domain settings by attacking the support and query sets without the need for ad-hoc adversarial training.

Keywords: Few-shot segmentation · Neural-ODE · Adversarial robustness

---

P. Pandey and A. Vardhan—Equal contribution.

Supplementary Information The online version contains supplementary material available at https://doi.org/10.1007/978-3-031-16452-1_8.

1   Introduction

Modern day safety-critical medical systems are vulnerable to different kinds of attacks that can cause danger to life. With the penetration of AI, Machine Learning and Deep Neural models to healthcare and medical systems, it is imperative to make such models robust against different kinds of attacks. By design, these models are data-hungry and need a significant amount of labelled data to improve their performance and generalizability. Past studies have shown that it is not always feasible to annotate medical data, especially for segmentation problems due to the huge time and specific skills it needs to do so. Lack of well-annotated data, make these models vulnerable to different kind of attacks like adversarial white and black box attacks [2,5,13] on Deep Neural models. ML practitioners employ FSL [1,7] to learn patterns using well-annotated base classes, finally to transfer the knowledge to scarcely annotated novel classes. This knowledge transfer is severely impacted in the presence of adversarial attacks when *support* and *query* samples from novel classes are injected with adversarial noise [29].

Commonly used Adversarial Training mechanisms [2,13,17] require adversarially perturbed examples shown to the model during training. [34] introduced standard adversarial training (SAT) procedure for semantic segmentation. These methods do not guarantee defense when the type of attack is different from the adversarially perturbed examples [18,30] and it is impractical to expose the model with different kind of adversarial examples during training itself. Also, a common method that handles attacks both on support and query examples of novel classes, is non-existent. To the best of our knowledge, the adversarial attacks on few-shot segmentation (FSS) with Deep Neural models and their defense mechanisms have not yet been explored and the need for such robust models is inevitable. To this end, we propose **P**rototypical **N**eural **O**rdinary **D**ifferential **E**quation (PNODE), a novel prototypical few-shot segmentation framework based on Neural-ODEs [14] that provides defense against different kinds of adversarial attacks in different settings. Owing to the fact that the integral curves of Neural-ODEs are non-intersecting, adversarial perturbations in the input lead to small changes in the output as opposed to existing FSS models where the output is unpredictable. In this paper, we make the following contributions:

- We extend SAT for FSS task to handle attacks on both support and query.
- We propose a novel adversarially robust FSS framework, PNODE, that can handle different kinds of adversarial attacks like FGSM [2], PGD [13] and SMIA [33] differing in intensity and design, even without an expensive adversarial training procedure.
- We show the effectiveness of our proposed approach with publicly available multi-organ segmentation datasets like BCV [3], CT-ORG [25] and DECATHLON [23] for both in-domain and cross-domain settings on novel classes.

2 Related Works

Neural ODEs: Deep learning models such as ResNets [4] learn a sequence of transformation by mapping input $\mathbf{x}$ to output $\mathbf{y}$ by composing a sequence of transformations to a hidden state. In a ResNet block, computation of a hidden layer representation can be expressed using the following transformation: $\mathbf{h}(t + 1) = \mathbf{h}(t) + f_\theta(\mathbf{h}(t), t)$ where $t \in \{0, \ldots, T\}$ and $\mathbf{h} : [0, \infty] \to \mathbb{R}^n$. As the number of layers are increased and smaller steps are taken, in the limit, the continuous dynamics of the hidden layers are parameterized using an ordinary differential equation (ODE) [14] specified by a neural network $\frac{d\mathbf{h}(t)}{dt} = f_\theta(\mathbf{h}(t), t)$ where $f : \mathbb{R}^n \times [0, \infty] \to \mathbb{R}^n$ denotes the non-linear trainable layers parameterized by weights θ and $\mathbf{h}$ represents the n-dimensional state of the Neural-ODE. These layers define the relation between the input h(0) and output h(T), at time $T > 0$, by providing solution to the ODE initial value problem at terminal time T. Neural-ODEs are the continuous equivalent of ResNets where the hidden layers can be regarded as discrete-time difference equations.

Recent studies [27, 28, 31] have applied Neural-ODEs to defend against adversarial attacks. [27] proposes time-invariant steady Neural-ODE that is more stable than conventional convolutional neural networks (CNNs) in the classification setting.

Few-Shot Learning: FSL methods seek good generalization and learn transferable knowledge across different tasks with limited data [1, 20, 21]. Few-shot segmentation (FSS) [19, 24, 26] aims to perform pixel-level classification for novel classes in a query image when trained on only a few labelled support images. The commonly adopted approach for FSS is based on prototypical networks [6, 19, 32] that employ prototypes to represent typical information for foreground objects present in the support images. In addition to prototype-based setting, [24] incorporates 'squeeze & excite' blocks that avoids the need of pre-trained models for medical image segmentation. [26] uses a relation network [12] and introduced FSS-1000 dataset that is significantly smaller as compared to contemporary large-scale datasets for FSS.

Adversarial Robustness: Adversarial attacks for natural image classification has been extensively explored. FGSM [2] and PGD [13] generate adversarial examples based on the CNN gradients. Besides image classification, several attack methods have also been proposed for semantic segmentation [9, 10, 22, 33]. [10] introduced Dense Adversary Generation (DAG) that optimizes a loss function over a set of pixels for generating adversarial perturbations. [15] studied the effects of adversarial attacks on brain segmentation and skin lesion classification. Recently, [33] proposes an adversarial attack (SMIA) for images in medical domain that employs a loss stabilization term to exhaustively search the perturbation space. While adversarial attacks expose the vulnerability of deep neural networks, adversarial training [2, 8, 13] is effective in enhancing the target model by training it with adversarial samples. However, none of existing methods have explored SAT procedure for few-shot semantic segmentation.

3   Proposed Method

The objective is to build a FSS model robust to various gradient-based attacks on support and query images. Our methodology focuses on two aspects. First, we extend SAT as a defense mechanism. Second, we propose our framework, PNODE, which alleviates existing limitations faced by SAT.

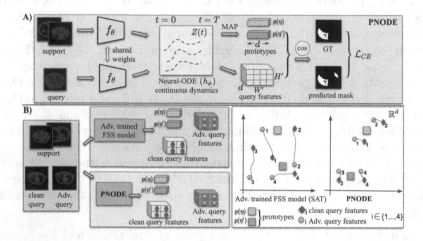

Fig. 1. A) Robust features for query and support images are obtained by the feature extractor followed by the continuous dynamics and integral solutions of a Neural-ODE. Class-wise prototypes are obtained by applying Masked Average Pool (MAP) on support features. Pixel-level cosine similarities of query features with the prototypes provide query mask predictions. **B)** d-dimensional representation of clean and adversarial query features. Adversarial query features lie closer to the clean ones unlike Adversarially trained FSS model (or SAT). In SAT, perturbations from one class may be closer to prototypes of another class (model is confused), while for PNODE, they tend to remain closer.

3.1   Problem Setting

FSS setting includes train $\mathcal{D}_{\text{train}}$ and test $\mathcal{D}_{\text{test}}$ datasets having non-overlapping class sets. Each dataset consists of a set of episodes with each episode containing a N-way K-shot task $\mathcal{T}_i = (\mathcal{S}_i, \mathcal{Q}_i)$ where $\mathcal{S}_i$ and $\mathcal{Q}_i$ are support and query sets for the ith episode having class set C_i. Formally, $\mathcal{D}_{\text{train}} = \{(\mathcal{S}_i, \mathcal{Q}_i)\}_{i=1}^{E_{\text{train}}}$ and $\mathcal{D}_{\text{test}} = \{(\mathcal{S}_i, \mathcal{Q}_i)\}_{i=1}^{E_{\text{test}}}$ where E_{train} and E_{test} denote the number of episodes during training and testing. The support set $\mathcal{S}_i$ has K image ($\mathcal{I}_\mathcal{S}$), mask ($L_\mathcal{S}$) pairs per class with a total of N semantic classes i.e. $\mathcal{S}_i = \{(\mathcal{I}_\mathcal{S}^k, L_\mathcal{S}^k(\eta))\}$ where $L_\mathcal{S}^k(\eta)$ is the ground-truth mask for k-th shot corresponding to class $\eta \in C_i$, $|C_i| = N$ and $k = 1, 2, \ldots, K$. The query set $\mathcal{Q}_i$ has $N_\mathcal{Q}$ image ($\mathcal{I}_\mathcal{Q}$), mask ($L_\mathcal{Q}$) pairs. The FSS model $\mathcal{F}(.)$ is trained on $\mathcal{D}_{\text{train}}$ across the episodes with support sets and query images as inputs, and predicts the segmentation mask $M_\mathcal{Q} = \mathcal{F}(\mathcal{S}_i, \mathcal{I}_\mathcal{Q})$ in the i-th episode for query image $\mathcal{I}_\mathcal{Q}$. During testing, the trained model $\mathcal{F}(.)$ is used to predict masks for unseen novel classes with the corresponding support set samples and query images as inputs from $\mathcal{D}_{\text{test}}$.

Further, the trained FSS model is adversarially attacked to record the drop in performance. An adversarial version of a clean sample can be generated by exploiting gradient information from the model $\mathcal{F}(.)$ employing [2]. Specific to the case of FSS, the prediction of query mask not only depends on the query image but also on the information from support set. This enables the attacks to be designed in such a way that either attacked query or support can deteriorate the query prediction. These perturbations are specifically chosen so that the loss between ground-truth and the predicted masks of the query increases.

3.2 Adversarial Training

To ensure that the segmentation model $\mathcal{F}(.)$ is robust to adversarial perturbations for both support and query images, we extend $\mathcal{D}_{\text{train}}$ in each batch during training with two additional batches generated for the ith episode using update rule from [2] as follows: (a) generate adversarial example for support image $\mathcal{I}_{\mathcal{S}}$:

$$\mathcal{I}_{\mathcal{S}}^{\text{adv}} = \mathcal{I}_{\mathcal{S}} + \epsilon.\text{sign}(\nabla_{\mathcal{I}_{\mathcal{S}}} \mathcal{L}(\mathcal{F}(\mathcal{S}_i, \mathcal{I}_{\mathcal{Q}}), L_{\mathcal{Q}}(\eta))) \tag{1}$$

(b) generate adversarial example for query image $\mathcal{I}_{\mathcal{Q}}$:

$$\mathcal{I}_{\mathcal{Q}}^{\text{adv}} = \mathcal{I}_{\mathcal{Q}} + \epsilon.\text{sign}(\nabla_{\mathcal{I}_{\mathcal{Q}}} \mathcal{L}(\mathcal{F}(\mathcal{S}_i, \mathcal{I}_{\mathcal{Q}}), L_{\mathcal{Q}}(\eta))) \tag{2}$$

This is a single-step attack, which minimises the l_∞ norm of the perturbation bounded by parameter ϵ. The detailed procedure of SAT is listed in Algorithm 1.

Algorithm 1. Standard Adversarial Training (SAT) for FSS

Require: Clean training data $\mathcal{D}_{\text{train}} = \{(\mathcal{S}_i, \mathcal{Q}_i)\}_{i=1}^{E_{train}}$, segmentation network $\mathcal{F}(.)$.
1. for $i \in \{1, \ldots, E_{train}\}$ do
2:     Sample episode $\mathcal{E}^{\text{orig}} = \{(\mathcal{S}_i, \mathcal{Q}_i)\}$ from $\mathcal{D}_{\text{train}}$.
3:     Calculate gradients w.r.t support and query images using $\mathcal{F}(.)$.
4:     Get $\mathcal{E}^{\mathcal{S}} = \{(\mathcal{S}_i^{\text{adv}}, \mathcal{Q}_i)\}$ by perturbing support images using Eq. 1.
5:     Get $\mathcal{E}^{\mathcal{Q}} = \{(\mathcal{S}_i, \mathcal{Q}_i^{\text{adv}})\}$ by perturbing query images using Eq. 2.
6:     for $\mathcal{E} \in \{\mathcal{E}^{\text{orig}}, \mathcal{E}^{\mathcal{S}}, \mathcal{E}^{\mathcal{Q}}\}$ do
7:         Train $\mathcal{F}$ on episode $\mathcal{E}$.
8:     end for
9: end for

SAT requires prior knowledge on the type of adversarial attacks to include the corresponding samples during training which is practically infeasible, compute intensive and also doesn't guarantee robustness to unseen attacks. Our PNODE framework addresses these shortcomings.

3.3 Prototypical Neural ODE (PNODE)

The proposed framework is based on existing prototypical few-shot segmentation models [11,19]. Given an episode i with task $\mathcal{T}_i = (\mathcal{S}_i, \mathcal{Q}_i)$, the feature extractor f_θ generates intermediate feature representations $Z_\mathcal{S}^k$ and $Z_\mathcal{Q}$ for the support and query images $\mathcal{I}_\mathcal{S}^k$, $\mathcal{I}_\mathcal{Q}$. The outputs from the feature extractor f_θ are considered as initial states for the Neural-ODE block at time t=0, denoted as $Z_\mathcal{S}^k(0)$, $Z_\mathcal{Q}(0)$.

The Neural-ODE block consists of hidden layers h_ϕ parameterized by ϕ and its dynamics are governed by h_ϕ which control how the intermediate state changes at any given time t. The output representation at fixed terminal time $T(T > 0)$ for query features $Z_\mathcal{Q}$ is given by $Z_\mathcal{Q}(T) = Z_\mathcal{Q}(0) + \int_0^T h_\phi(Z_\mathcal{Q}(t), t)dt$. Similarly, the output representation at fixed terminal time $T(T > 0)$ for support features $Z_\mathcal{S}^k$ are generated. The support feature maps $Z_\mathcal{S}^k(T)$ from the Neural-ODE block of spatial dimensions $(H' \times W')$ are upsampled to the same spatial dimensions of their corresponding masks $L_\mathcal{S}$ of dimension $(H \times W)$. Inspired by late fusion [19] where the ground-truth labels are masked over feature maps, we employ Masked Average Pooling (MAP) between $Z_\mathcal{S}^k(T)$ and $L_\mathcal{S}^k(\eta)$ to form a d-dimensional prototype $p(\eta)$ for each foreground class $\eta \in C_i$ as shown:

$$p(\eta) = \frac{1}{K} \sum_k \frac{\sum_{x,y} \{Z_\mathcal{S}^k(T)\}^{(x,y)} \cdot \mathbb{1}[\{L_\mathcal{S}^k(\eta)\}^{(x,y)} = \eta]}{\sum_{x,y} \mathbb{1}[\{L_\mathcal{S}^k(\eta)\}^{(x,y)} = \eta]} \tag{3}$$

where (x, y) are the spatial locations in the feature map and $\mathbb{1}(.)$ is an indicator function. The background is also treated as a separate class and the prototype for it is calculated by computing the feature mean of all the spatial locations excluding the ones that belong to the foreground classes.

The probability map over semantic classes η is computed by measuring the cosine similarity (cos) between each of the spatial locations in $Z_\mathcal{Q}(T)$ with each prototype $p(\eta)$ as given by:

$$M_\mathcal{Q}^{(x,y)}(\eta) = \frac{\exp(\cos(\{Z_\mathcal{Q}(T)\}^{(x,y)}, p(\eta)))}{\sum_{\eta' \in \mathcal{C}_i} \exp(\cos(\{Z_\mathcal{Q}(T)\}^{(x,y)}, p(\eta')))} \tag{4}$$

The predicted mask $M_\mathcal{Q}$ is generated by taking the argmax of $M_\mathcal{Q}(\eta)$ across semantic classes. We use Binary Cross Entropy loss $\mathcal{L}_{CE}$ between $M_\mathcal{Q}$ and the ground-truth mask for training. For detailed overview of PNODE, refer to Fig. 1. During evaluation, PNODE's robustness against adversarial attacks is attributed to the fact that the integral curves corresponding to the features are non-intersecting. Thus, if a clean sample (support or query) is adversarially perturbed, the integral curves associated with other similar samples constrain the adversrial features to remain bounded in the representation space. Consequently, the perturbed sample's feature representations are closer to the clean or original feature representations as shown in Fig. 1 which leads to accurate predictions of the query masks.

4   Implementation Details

PNODE framework consists of a CNN-based feature extractor followed by a Neural-ODE block consisting of 3 convolutional layers. The architecture of PNODE consists of a total of 14.7M trainable parameters, while PANet and FSS1000 have 14.7M and 18.6M parameters, respectively. The solution for Neural-ODE is obtained by using Runge-Kutta ODE solver [14]. To understand the effect of adversarial training on prototype-based networks, we employ SAT with PANet [19] and name it AT-PANET. It is trained with FGSM with $\epsilon = 0.025$. To test the trained models, we perturb the support and query images by setting $\epsilon = 0.02, 0.01$ and 0.04 for FGSM, PGD and SMIA, respectively. For the iterative adversarial attacks SMIA and PGD, we take 10 iterations each. These hyperparameters for the attacks were chosen so as to keep the perturbed images human perceptible. We use one A100 GPU to conduct our experiments. For statistical significance, we run each experiment twice and report the mean and standard deviation. All our implementations can be found here[1].

5   Experiments and Results

We experiment on three publicly available multi-organ segmentation datasets, BCV [3], CT-ORG [25], and Decathlon [23] to evaluate the generalisability of our method. We train on the smaller BCV dataset and use CT-ORG and Decathlon for cross-domain FSS. To have a more uniform size of the test set, we sample 500 random slices per organ from the much larger CT-ORG and Decathlon datasets. For the 3D volumes in all three datasets, we extract slices with valid masks and divide them into fixed train, test, and validation splits. We do not crop the slices class-wise and handle multiple organs in the same slice since cropping in the test set would require labels, leading to an unfair test set evaluation. For baseline models we use PANet [19], FSS1000 [26], SENet [24] and AT-PANET. Of the organs available in these datasets, we report results on Liver and Spleen (as novel classes) due to their medical significance and availability in multiple datasets.

Table 1. 1-shot query attack results for BCV $\rightarrow$ BCV in-domain Liver and Spleen organs (novel classes). The dice scores are rounded off to two decimals.

Method	BCV $\rightarrow$ BCV (Liver)				BCV $\rightarrow$ BCV (Spleen)			
	Clean	FGSM	PGD	SMIA	Clean	FGSM	PGD	SMIA
PANet [19]	.61 ± 01	.29 ± .01	.21 ± .01	.20 ± .01	.38 ± .03	.16 ± .01	.11 ± .01	.07 ± .01
FSS1000 [26]	.37 ± .04	.10 ± .03	.04 ± .02	.18 ± .01	.41 ± .02	.19 ± .01	.08 ± .01	.17 ± .01
SENet [24]	.61 ± .01	.30 ± .06	.22 ± .02	.12 ± .02	.57 ± .01	.04 ± .01	.21 ± .04	.01 ± .01
AT-PANet	.65 ± .01	.35 ± .03	.27 ± .02	.36 ± .01	.46 ± .01	.32 ± .08	.19 ± .03	.11 ± .01
PNODE	**.83 ± .01**	**.52 ± .02**	**.46 ± .01**	**.38 ± .03**	**.60 ± .01**	**.36 ± .01**	**.27 ± .03**	**.20 ± .02**

---

[1] https://github.com/prinshul/Prototype_NeuralODE_Adv_Attack.

Table 2. 3-shot query attack results for Liver BCV in-domain and BCV → CT-ORG cross-domain settings. The dice scores are rounded off to two decimals.

Method	BCV → BCV (Liver)				BCV → CT-ORG (Liver)			
	Clean	FGSM	PGD	SMIA	Clean	FGSM	PGD	SMIA
PANet [19]	.67 ± .01	.38 ± .01	.31 ± .01	.16 ± .01	.60 ± .01	.23 ± .01	.21 ± .01	.17 ± .01
FSS1000 [26]	.49 ± .04	.15 ± .01	.05 ± .01	.19 ± .03	.14 ± .02	.03 ± .01	.01 ± .01	.08 ± .01
AT-PANet	.69 ± .01	.36 ± .09	.39 ± .01	.23 ± .01	.64 ± .03	.09 ± .05	.21 ± .02	.18 ± .01
PNODE	**.76 ± .02**	**.53 ± .01**	**.52 ± .01**	**.39 ± .02**	**.68 ± .01**	**.43 ± .02**	**.42 ± .01**	**.31 ± .02**

As shown in Table 1, PNODE outperforms all of our baselines by atleast 27%, 48%, 70% and 5% on clean, FGSM, PGD and SMIA attacks respectively for BCV in-domain Liver setting. While PNODE provides a better defense against the adversarial attacks, it also outperforms the baselines for clean samples. This indicates that PNODE also learns a better representation space of unperturbed support and query samples which is attributed to the continuous dynamics of the Neural-ODE. With small perturbations, the integral curves with respect to the perturbed samples are sandwiched between the curves that correspond to the neighbouring samples ensuring that outputs of the perturbed samples do not change drastically. This is not the case with traditional CNNs, as there are no such intrinsic constraints [27]. To further show the Neural-ODE's role in robustness, we conduct a set of ablation studies. Upon removing the Neural-ODE block from PNODE, maintaining the remaining architecture and training procedure, we observed 0.41, 0.36, 0.36 and 0.31 units of drop in performance for clean, FGSM, PGD and SMIA, respectively. Further, using SAT made this model more robust, but PNODE outperformed it by 0.28, 0.19, 0.20 and 0.31 units, respectively. An interesting observation is that the baseline results tend to perform well for some attacks, while fail for others. For example, SENet [24] does very well on PGD [13] attack with a dice of 0.21, but performs very poorly on SMIA [33]. PNODE, on the other hand performs consistently across the different attacks. As can be seen in Fig. 2, PNODE also performs well on a wider range of attack intensities. Some other experimental analyses in the cross-domain setting can be seen in Fig. 2, which follow similar patterns with consistently better performance of PNODE. We also perform experiments on the 3-shot setting in Table 2. While there is a consistent drop between in-domain and cross-domain performance of all models, the drops corresponding to PNODE are relatively smaller. Thus, similar to distribution shifts between clean and perturbed samples, PNODE is also robust to cross-domain distribution shifts. We visualise the predictions by each of these models for the different attacks in Fig. 3. For the clean samples, PANet, AT-PANet and PNODE are visually very similar, while FSS1000 and SENet have relatively poorer performance. For FGSM, AT-PANet performs much better than PANet, most likely because of encountering similar data during training. For PGD, all of PANet, FSS1000, SENet and AT-PANet predict shapes that resemble the true organ, but are at wrong locations. PNODE is able to localise the organ better. For SMIA, all the predictions are poor and

PNODE is the only one even closely resembling the actual labels. For additional results, please refer to the supplementary material.

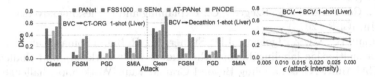

Fig. 2. Performance of models for attacks on BCV $\rightarrow$ CT-ORG (left), BCV $\rightarrow$ Decathlon (middle) and for different intensities of FGSM (right), on Liver 1-shot.

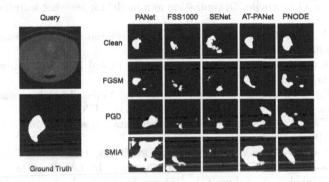

Fig. 3. Predicted masks by different models for different attacks. On the left are the query sample being tested and its ground-truth.

6   Conclusion

Defense against adversarial attacks on few-shot segmentation models is of utmost importance as these models are data-scarce. With their applications in the medical domain, it is critical to provide robust mechanisms against attacks of varying intensity and design. Although adversarial training can alleviate the risk associated with these attacks, the training procedure's computational overhead and poor generalizability render it less favourable as a robust defense strategy. We overcome its limitations by employing Neural-ODEs to propose adversarially robust prototypical few-shot segmentation framework PNODE that stabilizes the model against adversarial support and query attacks. PNODE is shown to have better generalization abilities against attacks while maintaining performance on clean examples. To the best of our knowledge, we are the first to study effects of different adversarial attacks on few-shot segmentation models and provide a robust defense strategy that we hope will help the medical community.

References

1. Li, F.-F., Rob, F., Pietro, P.: One-shot learning of object categories. IEEE TPAMI, vol. 28 (2006)
2. Ian, J., Goodfellow, J.S., Szegedy, C.: Explaining and harnessing adversarial examples. In: ICLR (2015)
3. Landman, B., Xu, Z., Igelsias, J.E., Styner, M., Robin, Thomas, Langerak, A.K.: Miccai multi-atlas labeling beyond the cranial vault-workshop and challenge. In: MICCAI Multi-Atlas Labeling Beyond Cranial Vault-Workshop Challenge (2015)
4. He, K., Zhang, X., Ren, S., Sun, J.: Deep residual learning for image recognition. In: CVPR (2016)
5. Kurakin, A., Goodfellow, I.J., Bengio, S.: Adversarial examples in the physical world. In: ICLR (Workshop) (2017)
6. Snell, J., Swersky, K., Zemel, R.S.: Prototypical networks for few-shot learning. In: NeurIPS (2017)
7. Ravi, S.: Hugo Larochelle. Optimization as a model for few-shot learning. In: ICLR (2017)
8. Kurakin, A., Goodfellow, I.J., Bengio, S.: Adversarial machine learning at scale. In: ICLR (2017)
9. Moosavi-Dezfooli, S.-M., Fawzi, A., Fawzi, O.: Pascal Frossard. Universal adversarial perturbations. In: CVPR (2017)
10. Xie, C., Wang, J., Zhang, Z., Zhou, Y., Xie, L., Yuille, A.: Adversarial examples for semantic segmentation and object detection. In: ICCV (2017)
11. Dong, N., Xing, E.P.: Few-shot semantic segmentation with prototype learning. In: BMVC (2018)
12. Sung, F., Yang, Y., Zhang, L., Xiang, T., Torr, P.H.S., Hospedales, T.M.: Learning to compare: relation network for few-shot learning. In: CVPR (2018)
13. Madry, A., Makelov, A., Schmidt, L., Tsipras, D., Vladu, A.: Towards deep learning models resistant to adversarial attacks. In: ICLR (2018)
14. Ricky, T.Q., Chen, Y.R., Bettencourt, J., Duvenaud, D.: Neural ordinary differential equations. In: NeurIPS (2018)
15. Paschali, M., Conjeti, S., Navarro, F., Navab, N.: Generalizability vs. Investigating medical imaging networks using adversarial examples. In: MICCAI, Robustness (2018)
16. Arnab, A., Miksik, O., Torr, P.H.S.: On the robustness of semantic segmentation models to adversarial attacks. In: CVPR (2018)
17. Zhang, H., Yu, Y., Jiao, J., Xing, E., El Ghaoui, L., Jordan, M.: Theoretically principled trade-off between robustness and accuracy. In: ICML (2019)
18. Zhang, H., Chen, H., Song, Z., Boning, D., Dhillon, I., Hsieh, C.-J.: The limitations of adversarial training and the blind-spot attack. In: ICLR (2019)
19. Wang, K., Liew, J.H., Zou, Y., Zhou, D., Feng, J.: Panet: few-shot image semantic segmentation with prototype alignment. In: ICCV (2019)
20. Zhao, A., Balakrishnan, G., Durand, F., Guttag, J.V., Dalca, A.V.: Data augmentation using learned transformations for one-shot medical image segmentation. In: CVPR (2019)
21. Ouyang, C., Kamnitsas, K., Biffi, C., Duan, J., Rueckert, D.: Data efficient unsupervised domain adaptation for cross-modality image segmentation. In: MICCAI (2019)
22. Ozbulak, U., Van Messem, A., De Neve, W.: Impact of adversarial examples on deep learning models for biomedical image segmentation. In: MICCAI (2019)

23. Simpson, A.L., et al.: A large annotated medical image dataset for the development and evaluation of segmentation algorithms. arXiv preprint arXiv:1902.09063 (2019)
24. Roy, A.G., Siddiqui, S., Pölsterl, S., Navab, N., Wachinger, C.: 'Squeeze & Excite' Guided few-shot segmentation of volumetric images. In: MedIA, vol. 59 (2020)
25. Rister, B., Yi, D., Shivakumar, K., Nobashi, T., Rubin, D.L.: CT-ORG, a new dataset for multiple organ segmentation in computed tomography. Sci. Data (2020). https://doi.org/10.1038/s41597-020-00715-8
26. Li, X., Wei, T., Chen, Y.P., Tai, Y.-W., Tang, C.-K.: FSS-1000: a 1000-class dataset for few-shot segmentation. In: CVPR (2020)
27. Yan, H., Du, J., Vincent, Y.F.T., Feng, J.: On robustness of neural ordinary differential equations. In: ICLR (2020)
28. Liu, X., Xiao, T., Si, S., Cao, Q., Kumar, S., Hsieh, C.-J.: How does noise help robustness? Explanation and exploration under the neural SDE framework. In: CVPR (2020)
29. Goldblum, M., Fowl, L., Goldstein, T.: A meta-learning approach. In: NeurIPS, Adversarially Robust Few-Shot Learning (2020)
30. Park, S., So, J.: On the effectiveness of adversarial training in defending against adversarial example attacks for image classification. Appl. Sci. **10**(22), 8079 (2020). https://doi.org/10.3390/app10228079
31. Kang, Q., Song, Y., Ding, Q., Tay, W.P.: Stable neural ode with Lyapunov-stable equilibrium points for defending against adversarial attacks. In: NeurIPS (2021)
32. Tang, H., Liu, X., Sun, S., Yan, X., Xie, X.: Recurrent mask refinement for few-shot medical image segmentation. In: ICCV (2021)
33. Qi, G., Gong, L., Song, Y., Ma, K., Zheng, Y.: Stabilized medical image attacks. In: ICLR (2021)
34. Xiaogang, X., Zhao, H., Jia, J.: Dynamic divide and conquer adversarial training for robust semantic segmentation. In: ICCV (2021)

Uni4Eye: Unified 2D and 3D Self-supervised Pre-training via Masked Image Modeling Transformer for Ophthalmic Image Classification

Zhiyuan Cai[1], Li Lin[1,2], Huaqing He[1], and Xiaoying Tang[1(✉)]

[1] Department of Electronic and Electrical Engineering,
Southern University of Science and Technology, Shenzhen, China
tangxy@sustech.edu.cn

[2] Department of Electrical and Electronic Engineering, The University of Hong Kong, Pok Fu Lam, Hong Kong SAR, China

Abstract. A large-scale labeled dataset is a key factor for the success of supervised deep learning in computer vision. However, a limited number of annotated data is very common, especially in ophthalmic image analysis, since manual annotation is time-consuming and labor-intensive. Self-supervised learning (SSL) methods bring huge opportunities for better utilizing unlabeled data, as they do not need massive annotations. With an attempt to use as many as possible unlabeled ophthalmic images, it is necessary to break the dimension barrier, simultaneously making use of both 2D and 3D images. In this paper, we propose a universal self-supervised Transformer framework, named Uni4Eye, to discover the inherent image property and capture domain-specific feature embedding in ophthalmic images. Uni4Eye can serve as a global feature extractor, which builds its basis on a Masked Image Modeling task with a Vision Transformer (ViT) architecture. We employ a Unified Patch Embedding module to replace the origin patch embedding module in ViT for jointly processing both 2D and 3D input images. Besides, we design a dual-branch multitask decoder module to simultaneously perform two reconstruction tasks on the input image and its gradient map, delivering discriminative representations for better convergence. We evaluate the performance of our pre-trained Uni4Eye encoder by fine-tuning it on six downstream ophthalmic image classification tasks. The superiority of Uni4Eye is successfully established through comparisons to other state-of-the-art SSL pre-training methods.

Keywords: Self-supervised pre-training · Unified 2D and 3D · Vision transformer · Ophthalmic disease classification · Multitask

Z. Cai and L. Lin—Contributed equally to this work.

Supplementary Information The online version contains supplementary material available at https://doi.org/10.1007/978-3-031-16452-1_9.

L. Wang et al. (Eds.): MICCAI 2022, LNCS 13438, pp. 88–98, 2022.
https://doi.org/10.1007/978-3-031-16452-1_9

1   Introduction

Recently, supervised deep learning methods have been found to perform comparably to human experts in various medical image analysis tasks such as disease classification [19] and structure segmentation [14,22], benefiting from supervision of large-scale labeled datasets [27]. However, manual delineation is time-consuming and labor-intensive, especially for large-scale datasets. Besides, fully supervised learning may somehow limit the model performance in some scenarios, such as in the Noisy Label [8] scenario.

   To address these issues, self-supervised learning (SSL) methods have been gaining increasing research interest in the medical image analysis realm. SSL methods can be mainly categorized into generative and discriminative approaches [1]. For generative approaches, [10] models the distribution of the data based on a GAN [13] framework, which is very computationally expensive. On the other hand, discriminative approaches focus on obtaining better generalized representations with relatively low computational burdens. Typically, discriminative approaches are implemented with contrastive learning frameworks [3,7,16,17] or through novel pre-text tasks [12,29]. The main shortcoming of contrastive learning methods is that they often focus on the main part of a medical image of interest but disregard contextual representations. Since the main parts are highly similar across different medical images, contrastive learning methods might fail, in which situation pre-text tasks accommodate better [1]. Recently, novel pre-text tasks have been explored, such as the Rubik's Cube Recovery task [31] and the Masked Image Modeling (MIM) task [15,28]. MIM originates from the idea of masked signal modeling which refers to masking a portion of the input signals and trying to predict the masked signals. Lately, based on Vision Transformer (ViT) backbones, MIM attains huge success in SSL on natural image. For example, [2] and [15] employ MIM and get pre-trained on ImageNet-1k [9], which respectively achieve 86.3% and 87% Top-1 accuracy.

   Nevertheless, the success of SSL has a prerequisite of massive datasets [24]. For instance, the recent success of Transformers on image classification [11] is mainly due to the large-scale ImageNet [9] dataset. However, for intelligent analyses of ophthalmic images, the sample sizes are usually very small. Ophthalmic image modalities can be categorized into 2D (e.g., fundus image [21] and Fundus Fluorescein Angiography (FFA)) and 3D (e.g., Optical Coherence Tomography (OCT) and Optical Coherence Tomography Angiography (OCTA)). Because of the dimension barrier, current SSL approaches are typically designed for dimension-specific images [4,5,26,30]; that is, an SSL model can only accommodate either 2D or 3D images, which contradicts the intuitive motivation of employing as many as possible data for better performance.

   In such context, we propose a simple yet effective framework that can learn universal representations from both 2D and 3D ophthalmic images, named Uni4Eye. Uni4Eye is designed to perform dual MIM tasks with a ViT architecture. We design a two-branch switchable patch embedding layer in Uni4Eye to replace the origin patch embedding layer, which allows it to switch to different branches for patch embedding of 2D and 3D images. Furthermore, we employ a dual-branch decoder in our network and train it with different modeling/reconstruction tasks, so as to achieve more robust convergence and better representation. Additionally, we create so far the largest ophthalmic image dataset of multiple modalities as well as multiple dimensions, consisting a total of 95,978 samples. We name it as *mmOphth*-v1, on which our proposed Uni4Eye gets pre-trained.

Collectively, our main contributions are three-fold: (1) To the best of our knowledge, this is the first time that a self-supervised pre-training framework is proposed to learn general visual representations of both 2D and 3D ophthalmic images. (2) We collect and create the largest ophthalmic image dataset of multiple modalities and of both 2D and 3D dimensions, named as *mmOphth*-v1. This dataset will be made publicly available. (3) We conduct extensive experiments on six downstream classification tasks with four datasets involving common eye diseases. The superiority of our proposed Uni4Eye over other state-of-the-art (SOTA) self-supervised pre-training methods is successfully established on these tasks. The source code is available at https://github.com/Davidczy/Uni4Eye.

2   Methodology

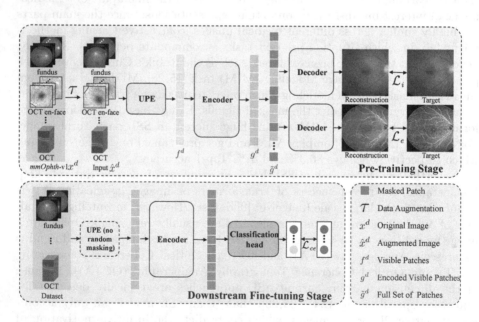

Fig. 1. The overall framework of Uni4Eye.

The overview of our Uni4Eye is provided in Fig. 1. There are three main components, including a Unified Patch Embedding (UPE) module, a ViT encoder and a dual-branch decoder. We first pre-train our encoder on two MIM self-supervised tasks in the pre-training stage and then fine-tune our model on different downstream tasks. As shown in Fig. 1, the pre-training stage and downstream fine-tuning stage are respectively denoted as P and D. Stage P aims at training the encoder to generate more generalized and discriminative representations from different input ophthalmic images. Then, the UPE module and the ViT encoder in D are utilized to load pre-trained parameters and continue to fine-tune on different downstream tasks to achieve better performance. For a downstream classification task, we adopt a fully-connected layer as the classification head to process features generated by the encoder and output prediction. We now delve into the details of UPE and the dual-branch decoder.

2.1 Unified Patch Embedding Module

To make our self-supervised framework compatible with both 2D and 3D data and accommodate different downstream scenarios, we employ UPE as the patch embedding module. As shown in Fig. 1, different images in the $mmOphth$-v1 dataset can be directly fed into the UPE module, regardless of their dimensions.

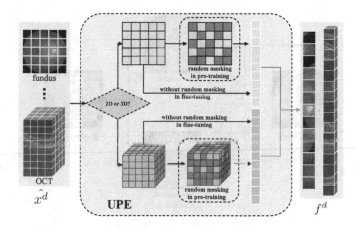

Fig. 2. The structure of the Unified Patch Embedding module.

Figure 2 illustrates the structure of UPE. Let an unlabeled training image sampled from $mmOphth$-v1 be denoted by x^d, where $d \in \{2, 3\}$ represents the dimension of the image. Then, data augmentation τ is applied to x^d to generate an input $\hat{x}^d$ of the UPE module. UPE switches $\hat{x}^d$ to specific patch embedding depending on the dimension of $\hat{x}^d$. Afterwards, a random masking strategy is employed to generate the masked patch embedding f^d in stage P, while the strategy is skipped in stage D. To be more specific, since we divide an image into regular non-overlapping patches (2D square patches for 2D input and 3D cubic patches for 3D input), we follow a uniform distribution to sample random patches without replacement. Then, the remaining ones are masked out, which means these patches will not be fed into the encoder. Thus, the ViT encoder operates only on the visible patches but not the masked ones, which differs our proposed method from inpainting methods.

2.2   Dual-Decoder for Intensity and Edge Reconstruction

Compared with natural images, ophthalmic images are more similar across different samples, which makes diagnoses of eye diseases challenging. Some detailed information, such as that on the retinal vessels, is important for disease dignosis but is easily to be ignored due to the redundancy in image information. For example, the reconstructed images in [2] are blurry with little edge information, which is not suitable for medical images. Therefore, we employ two decoders, namely an intensity decoder and an edge decoder, to encourage the network to learn representations containing both local and global information. The intensity decoder and edge decoder share the same network structure and the same input $\tilde{g}^d$. As shown in Fig. 1, $\tilde{g}^d$ denotes the full set of patches consisting both the encoded visible patches g^d and the masked patches. $\tilde{g}^d$ is simultaneously fed into the intensity decoder and the edge decoder. The difference between the two decoders lies in the reconstruction objectives.

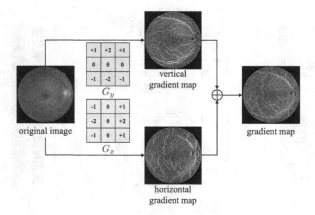

Fig. 3. Generation of the gradient map. Please note the original image is the reconstruction objective of the intensity decoder and the gradient map is the reconstruction target of the edge decoder. Keys: G_x - Sobel operator in the horizontal direction; G_y - Sobel operator in the vertical direction.

As shown in Fig. 3, taking the fundus image as an example, the left side is the original input, which is the reconstruction objective of the intensity decoder. We apply Sobel operators [18] at both horizontal G_x and vertical G_y directions to the original image, to get the horizontal gradient map and the vertical gradient map. Afterwards, we integrate these two gradient maps and obtain the gradient map of the fundus image, which is the reconstruction target of the edge decoder. We apply this operation to all 2D images and the 2D slices of each 3D volume. Compared with the original image, the gradient map uniformly characterizes the edge of the retinal structure and more clearly depicts tiny retinal vessels. In summary, in stage P, with trade-off parameters λ_1 and λ_2, the total objective function of our self-supervised learning framework is

$$\mathcal{L}_{ssl} = \lambda_1 \mathcal{L}_i + \lambda_2 \mathcal{L}_e, \tag{1}$$

where $\mathcal{L}_i$ and $\mathcal{L}_e$ are mean squared error (MSE) losses of the masked patches between the predictions from the intensity/edge decoders and the corresponding targets. λ_1 and λ_2 are set as 0.5 and 0.5 to make the network concentrate equally on global intensity information and local edge information of the ophthalmic images of interest.

3 Experiments and Results

3.1 Experimental Setup

In the pre-training phase, the input images of $mmOphth$-v1 are downsampled as 224×224 for 2D images and $112 \times 224 \times 112$ for 3D images. The batch size is 64 for 2D and 4 for 3D. The data augmentation strategy is a combination of random color jitter, random grayscaling, random cropping and random horizontal flipping. The model is optimized by an AdamW optimizer [23] with an initial learning rate of 0.0005. Our model is implemented in PyTorch [25] with 2 NVIDIA GeForce RTX 3090 GPUs, which takes 50 epochs and 20 h to converge. In the fine-tuning phase, the input keeps consistent with the aforementioned settings. AdamW is also used as the optimizer with an initial learning rate of 0.0001 and the batch sizes are respectively set to be 8 and 1 for 2D and 3D images. Since all downstream tasks are classification tasks, we employ the area under curve (AUC), accuracy, precision, recall, F1-score and Kappa as our evaluation metrics. Details of the $mmOphth$-v1 ophthalmic dataset and the evaluation datasets are presented in Fig. A1 and Table A1 of the appendix.

Table 1. Results obtained by fine-tuning on four 2D datasets. Rand denotes randomly-initialized model parameters. ViT-base and ViT-large respectively denote ViT-base-patch16-224 and ViT-large-patch16-224. - denotes the result is not available from the original article. (Unit: %)

Method	Ichallenge-AMD						Ichallenge-PM					
	AUC	Accuracy	Precision	Recall	F1-score	Kappa	AUC	Accuracy	Precision	Recall	F1-score	Kappa
	Convolutional neural network											
Rand [20]	77.19	87.09	82.98	77.82	79.27	–	98.04	97.66	97.30	98.04	97.53	–
Invariant [29]	81.62	87.51	81.92	81.62	81.35	–	98.02	97.84	97.56	98.02	97.75	–
Li et al. [20]	83.17	89.37	85.71	83.17	83.67	–	98.41	98.38	98.31	98.41	98.33	–
Method	Vision transformer											
Rand	64.92	82.25	77.47	64.92	67.59	36.78	96.65	96.48	96.13	96.65	96.36	92.73
ImageNet	73.75	86.00	82.68	73.75	76.79	54.00	97.70	97.74	97.60	97.70	97.65	95.30
SiT [1]	78.81	88.25	85.32	78.81	81.38	62.92	97.80	97.49	97.10	97.80	97.41	94.82
Ours (ViT-base)	83.13	89.95	86.86	83.13	84.78	69.60	98.22	98.24	**98.12**	98.22	98.17	96.35
Ours (ViT-large)	**85.85**	**90.45**	**86.44**	**85.85**	**86.14**	**72.28**	**98.53**	**98.24**	97.90	**98.53**	**98.18**	**96.37**
Method	OCTA-500 (2D)						GAMMA (2D)					
	AUC	Accurancy	Precision	Recall	F1-score	Kappa	AUC	Accurancy	Precision	Recall	F1-score	Kappa
	Vision transformer											
Rand	73.63	73.60	74.35	73.63	73.41	47.24	90.04	90.00	90.04	90.04	90.00	78.01
ImageNet	74.65	74.60	76.50	74.65	74.16	49.25	91.00	91.00	91.02	91.00	91.00	82.00
SiT [1]	81.72	81.73	81.73	81.72	81.73	63.45	93.83	93.88	93.98	93.83	93.87	87.74
Ours (ViT-base)	82.10	82.13	82.32	82.10	82.09	64.32	94.92	94.90	94.90	94.92	94.90	89.80
Ours (ViT-large)	**83.40**	**83.34**	**83.33**	**83.40**	**83.33**	**66.67**	**97.00**	**97.00**	**97.02**	**97.00**	**97.00**	**94.00**

3.2   Comparison with State-of-the-Art

We compare Uni4Eye with other SOTA SSL methods employing convolutional neural network (CNN) or ViT as the backbone. The binary classification results of different pre-training methods on four 2D datasets are shown in Table 1. Li et al. [20] feeds paired fundus and FFA data into a CNN for self-supervised contrastive learning, and achieves SOTA performance on Ichallenge-AMD and Ichallenge-PM datasets. Self-supervised Vision Transformer (SiT) [1] conducts image reconstruction, rotation prediction and contrastive learning tasks for pre-training, which outperforms randomly-weighted initialization and ImageNet pre-training. Although these SSL methods are beneficial in improving the classification performance, it is worth emphasizing that our Uni4Eye outperforms all compared methods regardless of the backbone. On the Ichallenge-AMD dataset, our method outperforms the second best method in terms of the F1-score by 2.2%.

Table 2. Results obtained by fine-tuning on 3D OCT volumes from the GAMMA and OCTA-500 datasets. (Unit: %)

Method	GAMMA (3D)						OCTA-500 (3D)					
	AUC	Accurancy	Precision	Recall	F1-score	Kappa	AUC	Accurancy	Precision	Recall	F1-score	Kappa
	Convolutional neural network											
Med3D [6]	86.23	86.73	87.24	86.23	86.50	73.07	66.07	67.87	78.29	66.07	63.17	33.27
Method	Vision transformer											
Rand	85.79	85.71	85.91	85.79	85.71	71.46	60.33	60.64	77.15	60.33	53.25	20.78
ImageNet	85.28	85.71	86.01	85.28	85.50	71.04	65.12	66.87	75.45	65.12	62.32	31.27
Ours	**86.39**	**86.73**	**86.90**	**86.39**	**86.57**	**73.16**	**66.18**	**67.87**	76.13	**66.18**	**63.75**	**33.43**

For 3D downstream tasks, we fine-tune Uni4Eye on the OCT volumes from the GAMMA dataset and the OCTA-500 dataset. As shown in Table 2, our proposed Uni4Eye performs better than random initialization and ImageNet pre-training. Please note that ImageNet pre-training means we only replace the patch embedding module of ViT with a 3D version, and maintain all other pre-trained parameters of ViT. Since there is relatively few amount of 3D ophthalmic data, the classification performance of the 3D model is worse than that of the 2D model.

Table 3. Results obtained by first training a self-supervised model on $mmOphth$-v1 with different mask ratios α and then fine-tuning on the Ichallenge-AMD dataset. (Unit: %)

Metrics	AUC	Accurancy	Precision	Recall	F1-score	Kappa
$\alpha = 0.25$	80.80	89.45	87.32	80.8	83.42	66.97
$\alpha = 0.5$	**85.85**	90.45	86.44	**85.85**	**86.14**	**72.28**
$\alpha = 0.75$	83.38	**91.00**	**89.56**	83.38	85.94	71.96

3.3   Reconstruction Results

We visualize the reconstruction results of different ophthalmic modalities from the same network pre-trained on *mmOphth*-v1 to highlight the universality of our learned features. As shown in Fig. 4, we feed the input of different modalities to the network and obtain the reconstruction results. We set the mask ratio in UPE as 25%, 50%, 75%. It is clear that a smaller mask ratio enables the model to generate better reconstruction results. However, better reconstruction is not equivalent to better performance on downstream tasks. We fine-tune these three models on Ichallenge-AMD with the same settings. As shown in Table 3, the network pre-trained with a 50% mask ratio achieves the best performance on the specific downstream task of interest. For ophthalmic image analysis, this result may suggest the encoder cannot generate discriminative representations through a too-easy (mask ratio = 25%) or a too-difficult (mask ratio = 75%) reconstruction task. Ablation analysis results are presented in Tables A2–A3 of the appendix, demonstrating the importance of resolving the dimension barrier and that of employing the dual-branch decoder.

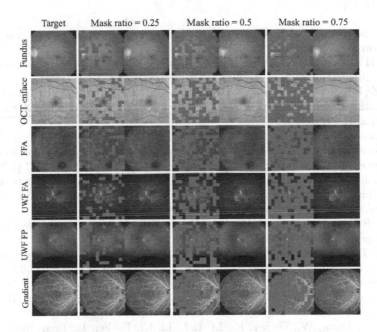

Fig. 4. The reconstruction results for six common modalities (from top to bottom), with different mask ratios in stage P.

4   Conclusion

This paper proposes a simple, unified and powerful self-supervised framework, namely Uni4Eye, for ophthalmic image analysis. Specifically, by modifying the patch embedding module to generate UPE in ViT, Uni4Eye can easily break the dimension barrier and process both 2D and 3D images. We also design a dual-decoder structure based on the MIM task, to make Uni4Eye take advantage of not only intensity information but also edge information in ophthalmic images. Extensive experiments on four 2D datasets and two 3D datasets show that our Uni4Eye achieves better classification performance than representative SOTA methods for eye disease diagnoses. Our results also demonstrate the potential of MIM for self-supervised pre-training in various medical image analyses. Our future work will involve investigating the feasibility of our framework for other types of medical images and exploring methods to further improve the efficiency of our framework.

Acknowledgement. This study was supported by the Shenzhen Basic Research Program (JCYJ20190 809120205578); the National Natural Science Foundation of China (62071210); the Shenzhen Science and Technology Program (RCYX2021060910305 6042); the Shenzhen Basic Research Program (JCYJ20200925153847004).

References

1. Atito, S., Awais, M., Kittler, J.: Sit: self-supervised vision transformer. arXiv preprint arXiv: 2104.03602 (2021)
2. Bao, H., Dong, L., et al.: BEIT: BERT pre-training of image transformers. In: International Conference on Learning Representations, ICLR (2022)
3. Cai, Z., Lin, L., He, H., Tang, X.: Corolla: an efficient multi-modality fusion framework with supervised contrastive learning for glaucoma grading. arXiv preprint arXiv: 2201.03795 (2022)
4. Chaitanya, K., Erdil, E., Karani, N., Konukoglu, E.: Contrastive learning of global and local features for medical image segmentation with limited annotations. In: Advances in Neural Information Processing Systems, NeurIPS, vol. 33 (2020)
5. Chen, L., Bentley, P., et al.: Self-supervised learning for medical image analysis using image context restoration. IEEE Trans. Med. Imaging **58**, 101539 (2019). https://doi.org/10.1016/j.media.2019.101539
6. Chen, S., Ma, K., et al.: Med3D: transfer learning for 3D medical image analysis. arXiv preprint arXiv: 1904.00625 (2019)
7. Chen, T., Kornblith, S., Norouzi, M., Hinton, G.: A simple framework for contrastive learning of visual representations. arXiv preprint arXiv: 2002.05709 (2020)
8. Cordeiro, F.R., Sachdeva, R., et al.: LongReMix: robust learning with high confidence samples in a noisy label environment. arXiv preprint arXiv: 2103.04173 (2021)
9. Deng, J., Dong, W., Socher, R., Li, L.J., Li, K., Fei-Fei, L.: ImageNet: a large-scale hierarchical image database. In: Proceedings of the IEEE/CVF Conference on Computer Vision and Pattern Recognition, CVPR, pp. 248–255 (2009)
10. Donahue, J., Simonyan, K.: Large scale adversarial representation learning. In: Advances in Neural Information Processing Systems, NeurIPS, vol. 32 (2019)
11. Dosovitskiy, A., Beyer, L., et al.: An image is worth 16x16 words: transformers for image recognition at scale. arXiv preprint arXiv: 2010.11929 (2021)

12. Gidaris, S., Singh, P., Komodakis, N.: Unsupervised representation learning by predicting image rotations. arXiv preprint arXiv:1803.07728 (2018)
13. Goodfellow, I.J., Pouget-Abadie, J., et al.: Generative adversarial nets. In: Advances in Neural Information Processing Systems, NeurIPS, vol. 27 (2014)
14. He, H., Lin, L., Cai, Z., Tang, X.: JOINED: prior guided multi-task learning for joint optic disc/cup segmentation and fovea detection. In: International Conference on Medical Imaging with Deep Learning, MIDL (2022)
15. He, K., Chen, X., Xie, S., Li, Y., Dollár, P., Girshick, R.: Masked autoencoders are scalable vision learners. arXiv preprint arXiv: 2111.06377 (2021)
16. He, K., Fan, H., Wu, Y., Xie, S., Girshick, R.: Momentum contrast for unsupervised visual representation learning. In: Proceedings of the IEEE/CVF Conference on Computer Vision and Pattern Recognition, CVPR, pp. 9729–9738 (2020)
17. Huang, Y., Lin, L., Cheng, P., Lyu, J., Tang, X.: Lesion-based contrastive learning for diabetic retinopathy grading from fundus images. In: de Bruijne, M., et al. (eds.) MICCAI 2021. LNCS, vol. 12902, pp. 113–123. Springer, Cham (2021). https://doi.org/10.1007/978-3-030-87196-3_11
18. Kanopoulos, N., Vasanthavada, N., Baker, R.L.: Design of an image edge detection filter using the Sobel operator. IEEE J. Solid State Circuits **23**(2), 358–367 (1988)
19. Li, X., Hu, X., et al.: Rotation-oriented collaborative self-supervised learning for retinal disease diagnosis. IEEE Trans. Med. Imaging **40**(9), 2284–2294 (2021)
20. Li, X., Jia, M., Islam, M.T., Yu, L., Xing, L.: Self-supervised feature learning via exploiting multi-modal data for retinal disease diagnosis. IEEE Trans. Med. Imaging **39**(12), 4023–4033 (2020)
21. Lin, L., et al.: The SUSTech-SYSU dataset for automated exudate detection and diabetic retinopathy grading. Sci. Data **7**(1), 1–10 (2020)
22. Lin, L., et al.: BSDA-Net: a boundary shape and distance aware joint learning framework for segmenting and classifying OCTA images. In: de Bruijne, M., et al. (eds.) MICCAI 2021. LNCS, vol. 12908, pp. 65–75. Springer, Cham (2021). https://doi.org/10.1007/978-3-030-87237-3_7
23. Loshchilov, I., Hutter, F.: Fixing weight decay regularization in adam. arXiv preprint arXiv: 1711.05101 (2017)
24. Oliver, A., Odena, A., Raffel, C., Cubuk, E.D., Goodfellow, I.J.: Realistic evaluation of deep semi-supervised learning algorithms. In: Advances in Neural Information Processing Systems, NeurIPS, vol. 31 (2019)
25. Paszke, A., Gross, S., et al.: PyTorch: an imperative style, high-performance deep learning library. In: Advances in Neural Information Processing Systems, NeurIPS, vol. 32 (2019)
26. Taleb, A., Loetzsch, W., et al.: 3D self-supervised methods for medical imaging. In: Advances in Neural Information Processing Systems, NeurIPS, vol. 33 (2020)
27. Tan, M., Le, Q.V.: EfficientNet: rethinking model scaling for convolutional neural networks. In: International Conference on Machine Learning, ICML, pp. 6105–6114 (2019)
28. Wei, C., Fan, H., Xie, S., Wu, C.Y., Yuille, A., Feichtenhofer, C.: Masked feature prediction for self-supervised visual pre-training. arXiv preprint arXiv: 2112.09133 (2021)
29. Ye, M., Zhang, X., Yuen, P.C., Chang, S.F.: Unsupervised embedding learning via invariant and spreading instance feature. In: Proceedings of the IEEE/CVF Conference on Computer Vision and Pattern Recognition, CVPR, pp. 6210–6219 (2019)

30. Zhou, H.Y., Lu, C., et al.: Preservational learning improves self-supervised medical image models by reconstructing diverse contexts. In: The IEEE International Conference on Computer Vision, ICCV, pp. 3499–3509 (2021)
31. Zhuang, X., Li, Y., Hu, Y., Ma, K., Yang, Y., Zheng, Y.: Self-supervised feature learning for 3D medical images by playing a Rubik's cube. In: Shen, D., et al. (eds.) MICCAI 2019. LNCS, vol. 11767, pp. 420–428. Springer, Cham (2019). https://doi.org/10.1007/978-3-030-32251-9_46

Self-supervised Learning of Morphological Representation for 3D EM Segments with Cluster-Instance Correlations

Chi Zhang[1,2], Qihua Chen[1,2], and Xuejin Chen[1,2]($\boxtimes$)

[1] National Engineering Laboratory for Brain-Inspired Intelligence Technology and Application, University of Science and Technology of China, Hefei 230027, China
{chih,cqh}@email.ustc.edu.cn, xjchen99@ustc.edu.cn
[2] Institute of Artificial Intelligence, Hefei Comprehensive National Science Center, Hefei 230088, China

Abstract. Morphological analysis of various cells is essential for understanding brain functions. However, the massive data volume of electronic microscopy (EM) images brings significant challenges for cell segmentation and analysis. While obtaining sufficient data annotation for supervised deep learning methods is laborious and tedious, we propose the first self-supervised approach for learning 3D morphology representations from ultra-scale EM segments without any data annotations. Our approach, MorphConNet, leverages contrastive learning in both instance level and cluster level to enforce similarity between two augmented versions of the same segment and the compactness of representation distributions within clusters. Through experiments on the dense segmentation of the full-brain EM volume of an adult fly FAFB-FFN1, our MorphConNet shows effectiveness in learning morphological representation for accurate classification of cellular subcompartments such as somas, neurites, and glia. The self-supervised morphological representation will also facilitate other morphological analysis tasks in neuroscience.

Keywords: Morphological representation · Self-supervised learning · Neuron classification · EM segmentation · FAFB

1 Introduction

The advanced electronic microscopy (EM) imaging technology supports fine biomedical observation on the nanometer scale and significantly facilitates the development of neuroscience. Recently, many EM data have been published for the community, including the 12-terabyte EM images of a full adult fly brain (FAFB) [23], the EM volume MICrONS [22] of a 1.4 mm × .87 mm × .84 mm volume of cortex in a P87 mouse, and the 1.4 petabyte EM images H01 [21] of a 1 mm^3 volume of a human cerebral cortex. The super-high-resolution EM

Supplementary Information The online version contains supplementary material available at https://doi.org/10.1007/978-3-031-16452-1_10.

brings massive data volumes, which are unfeasible for neuroscientists to analyze manually. Many approaches have been proposed for automatic data processing and efficient analysis by introducing algorithms from computer vision.

A deep-learning-based segmentation approach FFN [14] is first applied to the FAFB EM volume and results in millions of over-segmented 3D fragments of neurons, glia, and other non-neuron tissues. Although well-trained experts can classify a segment to its corresponding cellular subcompartment type, the huge amount of over-segmented pieces in high-resolution EM images poses significant challenges for biological analysis. Particularly for neuron tracing that involves super long range across a brain, it is non-trivial to select the right segments from such a massive volume, even for human experts. Therefore, it is imperative to filter out desired cellular subcompartments, such as dendrites, axons, somas, and glia, from massive segments for the subsequent reconstruction and analysis.

The length of the 3D segments in FAFB-FFN1 ranges from $1 \sim 10^3 \, \mu m$. In this scale, morphology is a feasible feature for cellular subcompartment selection. How to effectively represent the segment morphology for accurate classification is a key problem. Several approaches have been proposed for neuron classification based on 3D neuron morphology [1,3,8,11]. Given relatively complete neuron skeletons, these methods typically rely on hand-crafted morphological features, such as the neuron length, the number of branches, etc. Some deep learning methods [15,20] have been proposed for correcting merge errors of 3D EM segments by classifying neuron skeleton nodes. However, these methods do not provide a general representation of the entire 3D morphology of cellular subcompartments. In computer vision, some deep learning methods have been proposed for 3D shape classification [17,19]. These supervised approaches require large-scale training data with annotations. However, data labeling of various brain tissues in EM images is extremely laborious and tedious. Moreover, specialized biology knowledge is also required.

Self-supervised learning provides a new direction to solve this problem. Recently, many contrastive self-supervised methods have been proposed to learn image representations in computer vision [4–7,12,13]. The underlying concept is to pull similar instances close in the embedding space. Typically, those self-supervised learning methods use different image augmentations for the same sample to create positive pairs while considering different samples as negative pairs to train the latent representation network without any manual annotations. We adopt self-supervised learning to learn the morphological representation for cellular segments, avoiding time-consuming manual labeling and bias to easy-to-label categories.

In this paper, we propose the first self-supervised approach named MorphConNet to learn representations of 3D morphology from massive EM cellular segments. Instead of requiring data annotations and human pre-defined priors, we leverage contrastive learning at both instance level and cluster level. In the instance-level contrast module, we follow the typical contrastive learning framework that adopts an online network and a target network to enforce similarity between two augmented versions of the same segment. In our cluster-instance

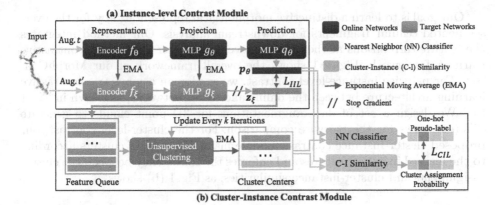

Fig. 1. Overview of our MorphConNet. It consists of two parts to leverage instance-level and cluster-level feature correlations. (a) An asymmetric architecture consists of an online network and a target network for instance-level pairwise comparison of two augmented views of an input 3D segment. (b) A cluster-instance correlation module exploits the cluster-level correlations between an instance and its cluster. By contrastive learning, the bootstrapped encoder f_θ can generate discriminative morphological representations for downstream analysis tasks.

contrast module, we cluster the latent representations and enforce the compactness of representation distributions in the same cluster. Instead of comparing the cluster assignments of two augmentations, our cluster-instance contrast module enforces the in-cluster concentration and between-cluster dispersion in the entire representation vector space. The target network and the cluster centers are progressively updated using moving averages to bootstrap the online network to learn the morphological representation. To evaluate the learned morphological representation, we annotated a dataset that consists of 1165 segments of three cellular subcompartment classes, including somas, neurites, and glia. Experiments show that our self-supervised morphological representation greatly improves the performance of the downstream classification task on the proposed dataset than the supervised method with limited annotated data. Our MorphConNet also outperforms existing self-supervised learning methods by exploiting the cluster-level feature correlation.

2   Our Method

For each fragment in the FAFB-FFN1 segmentation results [16], we first transfer it into the form of point clouds. We extract the contours of the fragment on each image slice along the z direction and collect all the contour points to compose a point cloud. While the number of points of all the fragments varies greatly, we uniformly downsample the dense surface point cloud to a fixed number of points and normalize it inside a unit cube.

Our goal is to learn a distinctive morphological representation **y** for the over-segmented cellular fragments for downstream analysis. Our method integrates the feature correlations at the instance level and cluster level in the contrastive learning framework. Figure 1 shows the overall framework of our MorphCon-Net. For pairwise instance-level contrast, we employ an asymmetric contrastive learning architecture between the online and target networks, as shown in Fig. 1 (a). We design a set of data augmentations for 3D point clouds to generate different views for the pairwise comparison. For the cluster-level contrast, our proposed cluster-instance contrast module maintains a set of clusters according to the learned instance features and enforces the consistency between the cluster assignments and cluster-instance similarities, as Fig. 1 (b) shows.

2.1 Instance-Level Contrastive Learning

In the instance-level contrast module, we follow a common contrastive learning framework that employs an asymmetric architecture to perform pairwise comparisons. It includes an online network and a target network to embed a point cloud **x** under two augmented views. The online network consists of three parts: an encoder f_θ, a projector g_θ, and a predictor q_θ, where θ is a set of weights. The target network consists of an encoder f_ξ and a projector g_ξ, which have the same architecture as the online network but different weights ξ, which is an exponential moving average of the online parameters θ during training.

From a large set of point clouds $\mathcal{P}$ of various cellular segments, we randomly sample a point cloud $\mathbf{x} = \{\mathbf{p}_i\}_{i=1,\ldots,N}$ which consists of N 3D points. From a predefined data augmentation distribution $\mathcal{T}$ for 3D point clouds, two data augmentation functions $t(\cdot)$ and $t'(\cdot)$ can be randomly selected and used to produce two augmented views $\mathbf{v} = t(\mathbf{x})$ and $\mathbf{v}' = t'(\mathbf{x})$ respectively. The online network outputs a representation $\mathbf{y}_\theta = f_\theta(\mathbf{v})$, a projection $\mathbf{z}_\theta = g_\theta(\mathbf{y}_\theta)$, and a prediction $\mathbf{p}_\theta = q_\theta(\mathbf{z}_\theta)$ for the first view. The target network outputs a representation $\mathbf{y}'_\xi = f_\xi(\mathbf{v}')$ and a projection $\mathbf{z}'_\xi = g_\xi(\mathbf{y}'_\xi)$ for the second view. To enforce the consistence between the morphological representations of the two augmented point clouds, we compute the mean squared error between the normalized predictions

$$L_{ins}(\mathbf{v}, \mathbf{v}'; \theta, \xi) = \left| \frac{q_\theta(\mathbf{z}_\theta)}{|q_\theta(\mathbf{z}_\theta)|} - \frac{\mathbf{z}'_\xi}{|\mathbf{z}'_\xi|} \right|^2 = 2 - 2\frac{q_\theta(\mathbf{z}_\theta) \cdot \mathbf{z}'_\xi}{|q_\theta(\mathbf{z}_\theta)||\mathbf{z}'_\xi|}. \tag{1}$$

At each training iteration, we swap the input $\mathbf{v}$ and $\mathbf{v}'$ to the online and target networks and compute another loss $L_{ins}(\mathbf{v}', \mathbf{v}; \theta, \xi)$. We only update parameters θ by minimizing the instance-level contrast loss $L_{IIL} = L_{ins}(\mathbf{v}, \mathbf{v}'; \theta, \xi) + L_{ins}(\mathbf{v}', \mathbf{v}; \theta, \xi)$ through stochastic optimization algorithm. Note the stop-gradient for parameters ξ which are estimated by the exponential moving average of θ.

2.2 Cluster-Instance Contrast Module

While the instance-level contrast module only performs a pairwise comparison of instances, we design a novel cluster-instance contrast module to combine the cluster-level correlations among all instances. It consists of a cluster center updating step and a cluster assignment step, as shown in Fig. 1 (b). In comparison with the pairwise comparison of features of two views in the instance-level contrast module, we compare the coherence of an instance with the cluster to which it belongs.

Cluster-Instance Contrast. Assuming there is a set of clusters in the embedding space for all samples in $\mathcal{P}$, the cluster centers are denoted as $C = \{c_1, c_2, \ldots, c_K\}$, where K is the cluster number. For an instance point cloud x, the online network generates its prediction vector $p_\theta = q_\theta(g_\theta(f_\theta(x)))$. We compute its corresponding cosine similarity s_j with each cluster center c_j and then transfer the similarities to a cluster assignment probability $\hat{s}_j$ using softmax:

$$\hat{s}_j = \frac{e^{s_j/\tau}}{\sum_{j=1}^{K} e^{s_j/\tau}}, \tag{2}$$

where τ is the temperature parameter, empirically set to 0.05 in our experiments.

We assign the instance x to the m-th cluster with the maximum probability, i.e., $y = m$, and compute the cluster-instance contrast loss L_{CIL} as

$$L_{CIL} = -\sum_{j=1}^{K} \mathbb{I}(y = j) log(\hat{s}_j) = -log(\hat{s}_m), \tag{3}$$

where $\mathbb{I}(\cdot)$ is the indicator function. Different from the swapped prediction [4] which compares the cluster predictions of two augmented views, our cluster-instance contrastive loss compares the hard cluster assignment and the soft cluster assignment of the same augmentation.

Memory Feature Queue. The cluster centers are expected to convey the feature distribution in the embedded space for all the training samples. However, it is impossible to store all the sample features for the large-scale training dataset at each training iteration. On the other hand, the samples in a mini-batch are very limited. Considering memory limits and data diversity, we sample a subset of instances from the training set to estimate the feature clusters. Meanwhile, the features learned by the networks are progressively updated during the training process. Therefore, we adopt a first-in-first-out feature memory queue Q in size of N_Q to store the features generated by target networks in the training process. At each training iteration, we can get the feature projection z_ξ by the target network for an instance. We push all the projection vectors for all the sampled instances in a mini-batch to the memory feature queue Q. When the queue is large enough, the features in the memory queue well approximate the feature distribution of the training data.

Cluster Center Initialization. Since there is no data category annotation, the number of clusters is unknown. For unsupervised clustering of the features, we can use the k-means algorithm by manually defining the cluster number K or DBSCAN [10] by specifying a minimum radius to determine the number of clusters K. Thus, we can get the initial cluster centers $C^0 = \{c_1^0, c_2^0, \ldots, c_K^0\}$.

Cluster Center Updating. During training, the feature vectors in the queue are dynamically updated, so that the cluster centers need to be updated accordingly. Different from estimating the initial cluster centers, the updated cluster centers evolve from previous ones. Given the previous cluster centers $C^{t-1} = \{c_1^{t-1}, c_2^{t-1}, \ldots, c_K^{t-1}\}$, we take them as the initial cluster centers and perform K-means clustering for all the feature vectors in the memory feature queue Q. Thus, a new set of cluster centers $\tilde{C}^t = \{\tilde{c}_1^t, \tilde{c}_2^t, \ldots, \tilde{c}_K^t\}$ can be obtained. To ensure the stability of cluster centers, we use the moving average of the cluster centers $c_i^t = \beta c_i^{t-1} + (1-\beta)\tilde{c}_i^t$. During the training, we update the cluster centers every k iterations. $k = 100$ in our experiments.

Based on the constantly updated cluster centers and feature projections of randomly selected instances, we combine the cluster-instance contrast loss L_{CIL} with the instance-level contrast loss L_{IIL} for all instances in a mini-batch as the overall training loss:

$$L = \alpha L_{CIL} + (1 - \alpha)L_{IIL}, \tag{4}$$

where the weight α balances the instance-level correlations and cluster-level correlations for learning morphological representations.

2.3 Data Augmentation

In contrastive learning, data augmentation indicates the invariance desired to be encoded in the learned representations. There are many data augmentation for images, such as rotation, cropping, and adding noises. However, those operations are not suitable for point clouds. We propose four data augmentations for point clouds, especially for cellular structures.

Part Dropping. For a point cloud $\mathbf{x}$, we divide it into eight parts $P_i, i = 1, \ldots, 8$ according to the eight quadrants in the 3D space whose origin is located at the center of $\mathbf{x}$. In part dropping, a part P_k is randomly selected and all of the points in this part are discarded. It implies that the morphological representation should be robust to structural incompleteness.

Varying Sparsity. A good morphological representation should be robust to various densities of 3D point clouds, that is, the network should output similar representations in the embedding space for the instances with similar morphology but different point densities. To formulate this property, we design this varying-sparsity augmentation. Given a point cloud, we randomly choose a part P_i and down-sample the M points in P_i to kM points by farthest point sampling (FPS) [18], where $k \in (0, 1]$ is a parameter to control the point sparsity.

Adding Noise. We add noise to a point cloud for data augmentation to promote the tolerance of the morphological representation to segmentation noises. The adding-noise augmentation samples λN points from an i.i.d. uniform distribution on a unit sphere and merges these λN points to the original point cloud that is also normalized, where $\lambda \in (0, 1]$ is used to control the portion of noisy points.

Rotation. The rotation augmentation rotates a point cloud by a randomly sampled rotation angle and an axis in a random direction, in order to ensure that our morphological representation is invariant to the orientations of cellular segments.

During the training process, for each instance, we randomly select the four augmentation operations with probabilities of $0.1, 0.6, 0.5, 0.5$ respectively and apply the combination of the selected augmentations to the point cloud. Then we down-sample the augmented point cloud to a fixed point number $N = 1024$ by FPS as the input of the encoder f.

3 Experiments and Results

Dataset. We conduct experiments on the over-segmented results FAFB-FFN1 [16] on the FAFB EM volume. We sample the points on the surface of each segment at resolution of $256\,\text{nm} \times 256\,\text{nm} \times 320\,\text{nm}$. There are $84,560$ 3D volumetric segments after remove segments that contain a small number of points. To evaluate the effectiveness of the learned 3D morphological representation, we contribute a new dataset, named **FAFB-CellSeg**, that consists of labeled $1,165$ cellular subcompartments from FAFB-FFN1. We asked three experts to select three types of cellular subcompartments, including 591 somas, 464 neurite segments, and 110 glia segments. These labeled segments are split into a training set with 50% samples and a test set with 50% samples for subcompartment classification.

Table 1. Comparison of 3D cellular subcompartment classification accuracy on our FAFB-CellSeg Dataset.

Method	Soma	Neurite	Glia	OA	AA
PointNet++	0.852	0.938	0.232	0.846	0.674
SwAV (Linear)	0.919	0.968	0.465	0.891	0.784
SwAV (Fine-tuned)	0.927	0.963	0.386	0.906	0.759
BYOL (Linear)	0.950	0.963	0.582	0.921	0.832
BYOL (Fine-tuned)	0.955	0.971	0.587	0.927	0.838
Ours (Linear)	0.953	0.974	0.673	0.935	0.867
Ours (Fine-tuned)	**0.960**	**0.980**	**0.740**	**0.944**	**0.893**

Cellular Subcompartment Classification. The learned 3D representations of our MorphConNet are expected to facilitate the selection of specific cellular subcompartments for further neuron reconstruction and analysis. To evaluate the effectiveness of the self-supervised representations in cellular subcompartment classification, we follow a common protocol for contrastive learning [5] to conduct both linear classification and semi-supervised evaluation. For the linear classification evaluation, we first train our MorphConNet with all unlabelled 3D segments. Then we freeze the encoder f and train a linear classifier in a supervised manner with the training samples of labeled subcompartments in FAFB-CellSeg. For semi-supervised evaluation, we fine-tune the encoder f as well as the linear classifier with the training samples in FAFB-CellSeg.

Comparison with Other Methods. While our MorphConNet is the first contrastive learning method for 3D morphological representation, we modify two state-of-the-art methods that are applied to images, *i.e.* SwAV [4] and BYOL [12], to point clouds for comparison. Specifically, we replace their original encoder networks with PointNet++ [19]. The training and data augmentation settings are the same as our method. To quantitatively evaluate the classification performance, we use the top-1 accuracy of each class, overall accuracy (OA), and average accuracy (AA). The OA is the ratio of the number of correctly classified segments to the number of all test segments. The AA is the average of top-1 accuracy of the three classes. The results are reported in Table 1. Our method outperforms all the competing approaches for the segment classification task. The poor performance of the supervised method PointNet++ is mainly due to the limited annotated data. Our method significantly outperforms SwAV by combining pairwise instance comparison and cluster-level correlation. Our MorphConNet is equivalent to BYOL when trained with the instance-level pairwise loss L_{IIL} only. By exploiting cluster-level correlation to bootstrap the morphological representation, our MorphConNet outperforms BYOL, especially for the neurite and glia classes which exhibit more diverse morphology than somas.

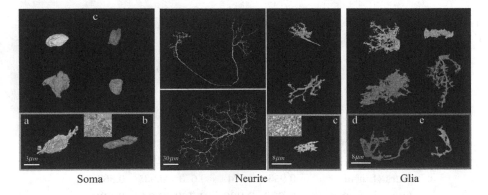

Soma   Neurite   Glia

Fig. 2. Visualization of some cellular segments on the test set with ground-truth labels. Most segments are correctly classified. We highlight some samples of the wrong classification in color boxes. (a)(b) Two somas and a neurite segment (c) are misclassified as glia. (d)(e) two glia segments are classified as neurites.

Quantitative Performance. We show a group of samples of our FAFB-CellSeg test set in Fig. 2. Most samples are correctly classified by our method with the classification accuracies of 0.960 for somas, 0.980 for neurites, and 0.740 for glia. While somas and neurites show more within-class morphology consistency, the glia segments exhibit significantly diverse morphology. We also show some samples that are misclassified in the color boxes. For example, morphological confusion of glia and neurite is demonstrated by Fig. 2 (c, d, e). Particularly, it is hard to label the neurite segment (c) only from its morphology even for experts without checking the corresponding EM images. We also observe that several long flat somas at the periphery of the brain were predicted as glia by our method. More experimental settings, ablation studies, and results are reported in the supplementary materials.

4   Conclusion

In this paper, we propose the first self-supervised learning approach, MorphCon-Net, to automatically learn representation for 3D EM segments. Our MorphCon-Net bootstraps 3D representation learning by integrating instance-level correlations and cluster-level correlations among a large-scale unlabeled dataset. While the instance-level contrast module enforces similarity between two augmented versions of the same instance, the proposed cluster-level contrast module enforces representation compactness within clusters. The experiments conducted on the massive segmentation of the FAFB volume show that our MorphConNet outperforms existing approaches in learning 3D representations for distinguishing cell subcompartments such as somas, neurites, and glia. Note that our method for learning 3D representations can be applied to classify any 3D segments. We believe that our approach could greatly facilitate the neuron reconstruction and analysis for massive EM data. One limitation of our approach is that it currently only considers morphological features of 3D EM segments. Incorporating the point-cloud morphology with additional biology information such as synapses [2], neurotransmitters [9], and relative positions could help more precise classification of cellular subcompartments in the future.

Acknowledgments. This work was supported by the National Natural Science Foundation of China under Grant 62076230 and the University Synergy Innovation Program of Anhui Province GXXT-2019-025.

References

1. Basu, S., Condron, B., Acton, S.T.: Path2path: hierarchical path-based analysis for neuron matching. In: International Symposium on Biomedical Imaging, pp. 996–999 (2011)
2. Buhmann, J., et al.: Automatic detection of synaptic partners in a whole-brain Drosophila electron microscopy data set. Nat. Methods **18**(7), 771–774 (2021)
3. Cardona, A., Saalfeld, S., Arganda, I., Pereanu, W., Schindelin, J., Hartenstein, V.: Identifying neuronal lineages of Drosophila by sequence analysis of axon tracts. J. Neurosci. **30**(22), 7538–7553 (2010)
4. Caron, M., Misra, I., Mairal, J., Goyal, P., Bojanowski, P., Joulin, A.: Unsupervised learning of visual features by contrasting cluster assignments. Neural Inf. Process. Syst. **33**, 9912–9924 (2020)

5. Chen, T., Kornblith, S., Norouzi, M., Hinton, G.E.: A simple framework for contrastive learning of visual representations. In: International Conference on Machine Learning, vol. 119, pp. 1597–1607 (2020)
6. Chen, X., Fan, H., Girshick, R., He, K.: Improved baselines with momentum contrastive learning. arXiv preprint arXiv:2003.04297 (2020)
7. Chen, X., He, K.: Exploring simple Siamese representation learning. In: Computer Vision and Pattern Recognition, pp. 15750–15758 (2021)
8. Costa, M., Manton, J.D., Ostrovsky, A.D., Prohaska, S., Jefferis, G.S.: NBLAST: rapid, sensitive comparison of neuronal structure and construction of neuron family databases. Neuron **91**(2), 293–311 (2016)
9. Eckstein, N., Bates, A.S., Du, M., Hartenstein, V., Jefferis, G.S., Funke, J.: Neurotransmitter classification from electron microscopy images at synaptic sites in Drosophila. BioRxiv (2020)
10. Ester, M., Kriegel, H.P., Sander, J., Xu, X., et al.: A density-based algorithm for discovering clusters in large spatial databases with noise. In: Conference on Knowledge Discovery and Data Mining, vol. 96, pp. 226–231 (1996)
11. Ganglberger, F., et al.: Structure-based neuron retrieval across Drosophila brains. Neuroinformatics **12**(3), 423–434 (2014)
12. Grill, J.B., et al.: Bootstrap your own latent - a new approach to self-supervised learning. Neural Inf. Process. Syst. **33**, 21271–21284 (2020)
13. He, K., Fan, H., Wu, Y., Xie, S., Girshick, R.: Momentum contrast for unsupervised visual representation learning. In: Computer Vision and Pattern Recognition, pp. 9729–9738 (2020)
14. Januszewski, M., et al.: High-precision automated reconstruction of neurons with flood-filling networks. Nat. Methods **15**(8), 605–610 (2018)
15. Li, H., Januszewski, M., Jain, V., Li, P.H.: Neuronal subcompartment classification and merge error correction. In: Medical Image Computing and Computer-Assisted Intervention, pp. 88–98 (2020)
16. Li, P.H., et al.: Automated reconstruction of a serial-section EM Drosophila brain with flood-filling networks and local realignment. Microsc. Microanal. **25**(S2), 1364–1365 (2019)
17. Li, Y., Bu, R., Sun, M., Wu, W., Di, X., Chen, B.: PointCNN: convolution on x-transformed points. Neural Inf. Process. Syst. **31** (2018)
18. Qi, C.R., Su, H., Mo, K., Guibas, L.J.: PointNet: deep learning on point sets for 3D classification and segmentation. In: Computer Vision and Pattern Recognition, pp. 652–660 (2017)
19. Qi, C.R., Yi, L., Su, H., Guibas, L.J.: PointNet++: deep hierarchical feature learning on point sets in a metric space. Neural Inf. Process. Syst. **30** (2017)
20. Schubert, P.J., Dorkenwald, S., Januszewski, M., Jain, V., Kornfeld, J.: Learning cellular morphology with neural networks. Nature Commun. **10**(1), 1–12 (2019)
21. Shapson-Coe, A., et al.: A connectomic study of a petascale fragment of human cerebral cortex. bioRxiv (2021)
22. Turner, N.L., et al.: Reconstruction of neocortex: organelles, compartments, cells, circuits, and activity. Cell (2022)
23. Zheng, Z., et al.: A complete electron microscopy volume of the brain of adult Drosophila melanogaster. Cell **174**(3), 730–743 (2018)

Calibrating Label Distribution
for Class-Imbalanced Barely-Supervised
Knee Segmentation

Yiqun Lin[1], Huifeng Yao[1], Zezhong Li[3], Guoyan Zheng[3(✉)],
and Xiaomeng Li[1,2(✉)]

[1] The Hong Kong University of Science and Technology, Hong Kong, China
eexmli@ust.hk
[2] Shenzhen Research Institute, The Hong Kong University of Science
and Technology, Hong Kong, China
[3] Shanghai Jiao Tong University, Shanghai, China
guoyan.zheng@sjtu.edu.cn

Abstract. Segmentation of 3D knee MR images is important for the assessment of osteoarthritis. Like other medical data, the volume-wise labeling of knee MR images is expertise-demanded and time-consuming; hence semi-supervised learning (SSL), particularly barely-supervised learning, is highly desirable for training with insufficient labeled data. We observed that the class imbalance problem is severe in the knee MR images as the cartilages only occupy 6% of foreground volumes, and the situation becomes worse without sufficient labeled data. To address the above problem, we present a novel framework for barely-supervised knee segmentation with noisy and imbalanced labels. Our framework leverages label distribution to encourage the network to put more effort into learning cartilage parts. Specifically, we utilize 1) label quantity distribution for modifying the objective loss function to a class-aware weighted form and 2) label position distribution for constructing a cropping probability mask to crop more sub-volumes in cartilage areas from both labeled and unlabeled inputs. In addition, we design dual uncertainty-aware sampling supervision to enhance the supervision of low-confident categories for efficient unsupervised learning. Experiments show that our proposed framework brings significant improvements by incorporating the unlabeled data and alleviating the problem of class imbalance. More importantly, our method outperforms the state-of-the-art SSL methods, demonstrating the potential of our framework for the more challenging SSL setting. Our code is available at https://github.com/xmed-lab/CLD-Semi.

Keywords: Semi-supervised learning · Class imbalance · Knee segmentation · MRI image

1 Introduction

The most common form of arthritis in the knee is osteoarthritis, a degenerative, "wear-and-tear" type of arthritis that occurs most often in people 50 years of age

© The Author(s), under exclusive license to Springer Nature Switzerland AG 2022
L. Wang et al. (Eds.): MICCAI 2022, LNCS 13438, pp. 109–118, 2022.
https://doi.org/10.1007/978-3-031-16452-1_11

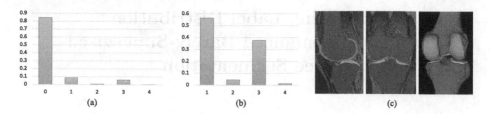

Fig. 1. (a) Quantity distribution of all background (labeled as 0) and foreground categories (labeled as 1, 2, 3, 4). (b) Quantity distribution of foreground categories including distal femur, femoral cartilage, tibia, and tibial cartilage, which are labeled as 1, 2, 3, 4, respectively. (c) Visualization of segmentation ground truth (left and middle) and reconstructed mesh (right). Red, green, blue, yellow color refer to the above 4 categories, respectively. (Color figure online)

and older. Magnetic resonance imaging (MRI) is a widely used medical imaging technology [9]. It is ideally suited for the assessment of osteoarthritis because it can clearly show soft-tissue contrast without ionizing radiation. For an objective and quantitative analysis, high-precision segmentation of cartilages from MR images is significant. With the development of deep learning technology, automatic knee segmentation has drawn more and more attention [1,13,17]. However, different from natural images, the segmentation of knee MR images suffers from a class imbalance problem. As shown in Fig. 1a–b, the foreground volumes (cartilages and hard tissues) occupy 16% of the entire image, and the cartilages only occupy 6% of foreground volumes, which implies a severe class imbalance between foreground and background and between cartilage and hard tissue.

Though deep learning methods can achieve better performance than morphological analysis, they require massive pixel-wise annotation to be trained in full supervision. In the medical field, sufficient labeled data is more difficult to obtain than natural images as manual annotation is expertise-demanded and time-consuming. Therefore, semi-supervised learning was introduced to solve this problem by utilizing only a small amount of labeled data and an arbitrary amount of unlabeled data for training. Recently, many semi-supervised learning (SSL) methods were proposed to solve insufficient labeled data problems on the natural images [3,4,12,18,19] and medical images [7,10,11,15,20,22]. In particular, [2,23] are proposed to generate pseudo labels for unlabeled data with model parameter fixed for the next round training. [18,22] proposed to guide the model to be invariant to random noises in the input domain. [3,5,14,15] proposed to design several models or decoders and use consistency regularization for unsupervised learning. [15,22] leveraged the uncertainty information to enable the framework to gradually learn from meaningful and reliable targets. Although appealing results have been achieved by these SSL methods, they cannot handle the class imbalance problem with barely labeled data. Recent work AEL (Adaptive Equalization Learning [6]) proposed adaptive augmentation, re-weighting, and sampling strategies to solve the class imbalance for natural images in SSL.

However, Table 1 shows the improvement of AEL is limited since the proposed strategies are not suitable for medical data.

In this work, we aim to address the problem of class imbalance in semi-supervised knee segmentation with barely labeled data. We regard CPS (Cross Pseudo Supervision [3]) as the baseline framework as it achieves the state-of-the-art performance on the SSL segmentation task for natural images. We further present a novel SSL framework named CLD (Calibrating Label Distribution) by leveraging the label distribution and uncertainty information to guide the model to put more effort into the learning of cartilage parts and enhance the learning of low-confident categories. Specifically, we firstly modify the objective loss function to a class-aware weighted form by utilizing the quantity distribution of labels. As shown in Fig. 1c, the soft cartilages are much thinner than hard tissues and occupy fewer volumes along the z-axis (from up to down), resulting in the cartilages being less cropped in random cropping augmentation, which further exacerbates the class imbalance problem. Therefore, we propose probability-aware random cropping to crop more in cartilage areas of both labeled and unlabeled input images by incorporating the position distribution of labels. Furthermore, we observe that the output confidence of cartilage volumes is lower than hard tissues due to the class imbalance. Hence we design dual uncertainty-aware sampling supervision to enhance the supervision of low-confident categories (i.e., cartilages). Concretely, instead of using a constant sampling rate, We maintain an uncertainty bank for each of the two models to estimate the sampling rate for each category.

To summarize, the main contributions of this work include 1) we are the first to address the class imbalance problem in barely-supervised knee segmentation; 2) we propose a novel SSL framework CLD for knee segmentation, consisting of class-aware weighted loss, probability-aware random cropping, and dual uncertainty-aware sampling supervision; 3) we conduct extensive experiments and ablation studies to validate the effectiveness of the proposed methods on a clinical knee segmentation dataset.

2   Method

As illustrated in Fig. 2, our framework consists of two models with the same architecture but different initial parameters. We modify the objective loss function to a class-aware weighted form and replace the random cropping with probability-aware random cropping to address the problem of class imbalance. In addition, we design dual uncertainty-aware sampling supervision to enhance the supervision on low-confident categories by maintaining two uncertainty banks for two models.

2.1   Cross Supervision for Semi-supervised Segmentation

In this work, we study the task of semi-supervised segmentation for knee MR imaging scans. We follow CPS [3] to firstly initialize two models with the same

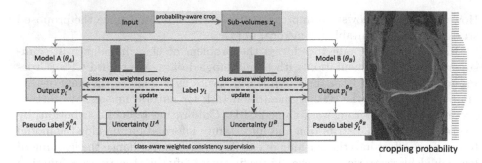

Fig. 2. Overview of the proposed semi-supervised segmentation framework. We modify the original supervised/unsupervised loss to a weighted form by leveraging the quantity distribution of segmentation labels. We replace the random cropping with a probability-aware cropping strategy by incorporating the position distribution (right) of cartilages. In addition, we design dual uncertainty-aware sampling to enhance the supervision on low-confident categories for efficient unsupervised learning.

architecture but different parameters θ_A and θ_B, respectively. To formulate, let the labeled set be $\mathcal{D}_L = \{(x_i, y_i)\}_{i=1}^{N_L}$ with N_L data and the unlabeled set be $\mathcal{D}_U = \{x_i\}_{i=1}^{N_U}$ with N_U data, where $x_i \in \mathbb{R}^{H \times W \times D}$ is the input volume and $y_i \in \{0, 1, 2, 3, 4\}^{H \times W \times D}$ is the ground-truth annotation (4 foreground categories). Denote the output probability of the segmentation model as $p_i^{\theta} = f(x_i; \theta)$ and the prediction (pseudo label) as $\hat{y}_i^{\theta} = \mathrm{argmax}(p_i^{\theta})$, where θ indicates the model parameters. The goal of our semi-supervised segmentation framework is to minimize the following objective function:

$$\mathcal{L} = \sum_{i=1}^{N_L} \left[L_s(p_i^{\theta_A}, y_i) + L_s(p_i^{\theta_B}, y_i) \right] + \lambda \sum_{i=1}^{N_L+N_U} \left[\mathcal{L}_u(p_i^{\theta_A}, \hat{y}_i^{\theta_B}) + \mathcal{L}_u(p_i^{\theta_B}, \hat{y}_i^{\theta_A}) \right], \quad (1)$$

where $\mathcal{L}_s$ is the supervised loss function to supervise the output of labeled data, and $\mathcal{L}_u$ is the unsupervised loss function to measure the prediction consistency of two models by taking the same input volume x_i. Note that both labeled and unlabeled data are used to compute the unsupervised loss. In addition, λ is the weighting coefficient, ramping up from 0 to $\lambda_{\max}$ for controlling the trade-off between the supervised loss and the unsupervised loss.

In practice, we employ V-Net [16] as the backbone network and regard CPS [3] as the SSL baseline framework. We follow [22] to remove the short residual connection in each convolution block. In the baseline, we use cross-entropy (CE) loss as the unsupervised loss, and a joint cross-entropy loss and soft dice loss as the supervised loss function, which are given as follows:

$$\mathcal{L}_u(x, y) = \mathcal{L}_{\mathrm{CE}}(x, y), \quad \mathcal{L}_s(x, y) = \frac{1}{2} \left[\mathcal{L}_{\mathrm{CE}}(x, y) + \mathcal{L}_{\mathrm{Dice}}(x, y) \right]. \quad (2)$$

In addition, we empirically choose $\lambda_{\max}$ as 0.1 and use the epoch-dependent Gaussian ramp-up function $\lambda(t) = \lambda_{\max} * e^{-5\left(1 - \frac{t}{t_{\max}}\right)^2}$, where t is the current training epoch and $t_{\max}$ is the total number of training epochs.

2.2   Calibrating Label Distribution (CLD)

To solve the class imbalance problem in barely-supervised knee segmentation, we propose a novel framework CLD, by leveraging the label distribution of soft cartilages and hard tissues for addressing the class imbalance problem.

Class-Aware Weighted Loss. We firstly modify the supervised and unsupervised loss function to a weighted form by introducing class-aware weights. We utilize the category distribution of labeled data by counting the number of voxels for each category, denoted as $N_i, i = 0, \ldots, C$, where C is the number of foreground categories, and N_0 indicates the number of background voxels. We construct the weighting coefficient w_i for i^{th} category as follows

$$w_i = \left(\frac{\max\{n_j\}_{j=0}^{C}}{n_i} \right)^{\alpha}, \quad n_i = \frac{N_i}{\sum_{j=0}^{C} N_j}, \quad i = 0, \ldots, C. \tag{3}$$

The exponential term α is empirically set to $\frac{1}{3}$ in the experiments. For cross-entropy loss calculation, the loss of each voxel will be multiplied by a weighting coefficient depending on using true label ($\mathcal{L}_s$) or pseudo label ($\mathcal{L}_u$). The soft dice loss will be calculated on the input image for each category separately and then multiplied by the weighting coefficient.

Probability-Aware Random Cropping. As mentioned in Sect. 1, the soft cartilages are thinner, and we propose probability-aware random cropping replacing random cropping to crop more sub-volumes in cartilage areas from both labeled and unlabeled inputs. Since the distributions of foreground categories along x-axis and y-axis are quite similar, we only consider the cropping probabilities along z-axis (from up to down). Suppose that the total length is D and the cropping size is D' along z-axis. To formulate, for each labeled image x_i, we calculate a vector v_i with the length of D, where the jth value of v_i is 1 only when there are more than k_1 voxels labeled as soft cartilages in the cropping window centered at j^{th} voxel along z-axis. Then we sum all v_i to obtain $v = \sum_{i=1}^{N_l} v_i$ and increase the cropping probability by a factor of β at j^{th} position if j^{th} value of v is greater than k_2. In the experiments, we empirically choose both k_1 and k_2 as 1, and β as 2.0.

Dual Uncertainty-Aware Sampling Supervision. To alleviate the uncertainty imbalance brought by class imbalance and limited labeled data, we adopt the sampling strategy to sample fewer voxels of low-uncertainty categories and more voxels of high-uncertainty categories for supervision. Instead of using a constant sampling rate, maintain an uncertainty bank for each category as $U \in \mathbb{R}^C$ for estimating the sampling rate on-the-fly. Assume that the output is $p \in \mathbb{R}^{C \times WHD}$ and the one-hot label is $y \in \mathbb{R}^{C \times WHD}$, then the uncertainty of ith category is given by

$$u_i = 1 - \frac{\sum y_i \cdot p_i}{\sum y_i}, \tag{4}$$

where $p_i, y_i \in \mathbb{R}^{WHD}$ are i^{th} values in the first dimension, indicating the prediction and label value for i^{th} category. Due to the class-imbalance problem, the cropped sub-volumes sometimes cannot contain all categories. In practice, we accumulate the values of $\sum y_i \cdot p_i$ and $\sum y_i$ for k_3 times to obtain a more stable uncertainty estimation:

$$u_i = 1 - \frac{\sum_{j=1}^{k_3} \sum y_i^j \cdot p_i^j}{\sum_{j=1}^{k_3} \sum y_i^j}, \tag{5}$$

where p^j, y^j is the output and label of jth input sub-volume. In addition, the uncertainty values are initialized randomly and updated as an exponential moving average (EMA) with a momentum γ, i.e., $u_i^t = \gamma u_i^{t-1} + (1 - \gamma)u_i^{t'}$. Note that the uncertainty values are only measured from the output of labeled data, and we maintain two uncertainty banks for two models respectively. Then we define the sampling rate for each category as $s_i = \left(\frac{u_i}{\max_j u_j}\right)^{1/2}$. Taking the supervision on model A as an example. Let pseudo labels from model B be $\hat{y}^{\theta_B}$, and the uncertainty bank and sampling rates of model A be $U^A = \{u_1^A, \ldots, u_C^A\}$ and $S^A = \{s_1^A, \ldots, s_C^A\}$, respectively. For those voxels predicted as i^{th} category in $\hat{y}^{\theta_B}$, we randomly sample a subset of voxels with the sampling rate s_i^A and construct the binary sampling mask as $m_i^A \in \{0, 1\}^{WHD}$. Compute all m_i^A and denote the union sampling mask as $m^A = \bigcup m_i^A$. Therefore, only the voxels with the value of 1 in m^A (i.e., sampled voxels) will contribute to the unsupervised loss. k_3 and γ are empirically set to 8 and 0.999 in the experiments.

3 Experiments

We conducted comprehensive experiments to validate the effectiveness of our proposed methods on a collected knee segmentation dataset. In addition, we conduct extensive ablation experiments to analyze the working mechanism of different proposed modules in the framework.

Dataset and Pre-processing. We collected a knee segmentation dataset with 512 MR imaging scans, containing 412 for training, 50 for validation, and 50 for testing. The size of each imaging scan is $384 \times 384 \times 160$. All the image data are publicly available from Osteoarthritis Initiative (OAI[1]). Ground-truth segmentation of the data were done by orthopaedic surgeons from local institution. There are 4 foreground categories, including distal femur (DF), femoral cartilage (FC), tibia (Ti), and tibial cartilage (TC), which have extremely imbalanced distribution. Some example slices and the category quantity distribution are shown in Fig. 1. We follow the previous work [22] to normalized the input scans as zero mean and unit variance before being fed into the network.

Implementation. We implement the proposed framework with PyTorch, using a single NVIDIA RTX 3090 GPU. The network parameters are optimized with SGD with a momentum of 0.9 and an initial learning rate of 0.01. The learning rate is divided by $0.001^{1/300} \approx 0.9772$ per epoch. Totally 300 epochs are trained

---

[1] https://oai.nih.gov.

Table 1. Comparison between our method with previous methods. DF: distal femur, FC: femoral cartilage, Ti: tibia, and TC: tibial cartilage.

Method	# scans used		Dice [%]↑/ASD [voxel]↓				
	Labeled	Unlabeled	Avg.	DF	FC	Ti	TC
V-Net [16]	412	0	90.5/3.4	97.2/7.4	86.4/1.2	97.3/3.7	81.1/1.3
	4	0	25.9/–	68.3/35.1	69.9/13.4	0.0/–	0.0/–
UA-MT [22]	4	408	32.0/–	67.7/51.5	60.1/24.2	0.0/–	0.0/–
URPC [15]	4	408	76.6/26.2	88.7/26.9	74.4/5.2	82.6/46.7	60.5/25.9
CPS [3]	4	408	83.4/16.3	93.1/17.2	81.1/2.4	91.5/24.5	67.7/20.9
CPS+AEL [3,6]	4	408	83.6/15.1	93.2/16.8	81.3/2.7	90.8/27.3	69.2/13.5
CLD (ours)	4	408	**87.2/8.8**	**93.8/14.9**	**83.7/1.1**	**92.8/17.9**	**78.6/1.2**

as the network has well converged. The batch size is 4, consisting of 2 labeled data and 2 unlabeled data. We choose $160 \times 160 \times 48$ as the cropping size of sub-volumes in the training and testing. In the inference (testing) stage, final segmentation results are obtained using a sliding window strategy [22] with a stride size of $64 \times 64 \times 16$, where the outputs of overlapped volumes are averaged over all windows' outputs. Standard data augmentation techniques [21,22] are used one-the-fly to avoid overfitting, including randomly flipping, and rotating with 90, 180 and 270 °C along the axial plane.

Evaluation Metrics and Results. We evaluate the prediction of the network with two metrics, including Dice and the average surface distance (ASD). We use 4 scans (1%) as labeled data and the remaining 408 scans as unlabeled data. In Table 1, we present the segmentation performance of different methods on the testing set. The first two rows show the results of V-Net [16] trained with the full training set and with only 1% labeled data, revealing that the lack of efficient labels makes the class imbalance problem worse, and brings a dramatic performance drop. By utilizing the unlabeled data, our proposed SSL framework significantly improves the performance in all categories. To validate our network backbone design (V-Net [16]), we also conduct the experiments with nnUNet [8], and the final testing Dice score is 90.8% (Avg.) with the full labeled set (412 data) for training, which shows that we can regard the revised V-Net [16] as a standard backbone model.

Furthermore, we implemented several state-of-the-art SSL segmentation methods for comparison, including UA-MT [22], URPC [15], and CPS [3] in Table 1. Although utilizing the unlabeled data, the Dice scores of two cartilages are still much worse than hard tissues. In addition, we adopted the learning strategies in AEL [6] to CPS, but the improvement is still limited. Compared with the baseline model (CPS), our proposed learning strategies further improve the performance by 3.8% Dice on average. The results also show that the proposed framework alleviates the class imbalance problem and improves the performance by 2.6% and 10.9% Dice for two cartilages, respectively. Visual results

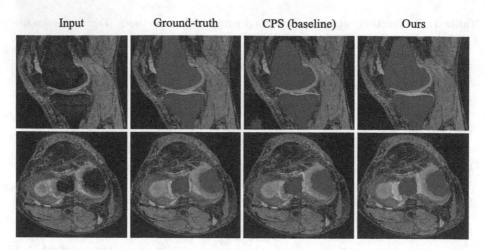

Fig. 3. Comparison of segmentation results with CPS [3]. As the cartilages (colored in green and yellow) are much thinner and tightly connected to hard tissues, CPS does not perform well in the junction areas of cartilages and hard tissues, while ours can. (Color figure online)

Table 2. Ablative study on different proposed modules. WL: class-aware weighted loss function, DUS: dual uncertainty-aware sampling supervision, and PRC: probability-aware random cropping.

WL	DUS	PRC	Dice [%]↑/ASD [voxel]↓				
			Avg.	DF	FC	Ti	TC
			83.4/16.3	93.1/17.2	81.1/2.4	91.5/24.5	67.7/20.9
√			84.8/14.4	90.8/23.9	82.2/1.5	89.2/31.0	77.0/1.1
√	√		86.1/9.7	92.5/**11.4**	82.5/1.3	91.0/24.9	77.1/**1.0**
√	√	√	**87.2/8.8**	**93.8**/14.9	**83.7/1.1**	**92.8**/17.9	**78.6**/1.2

in Fig. 3 show our method can perform better in the junction areas of cartilages and hard tissues.

Analysis of Our Methods. To validate the effectiveness of the proposed learning strategies, including class-aware weighted loss (WL), dual uncertainty-aware sampling supervision (DUS), and probability-aware random cropping (PRC), we conduct ablative experiments, as shown in Table 2. We can see that WL improves the Dice scores of two cartilages 1.1% and 9.3% but brings a 2.3% performance drop for hard tissues, which means WL can improve the learning of cartilages, but in turn negatively affect the learning of hard tissues. DUS maintains the improvements on cartilages and alleviates the performance drop of hard tissues. PRC can further boost the performance of both soft cartilages and hard tissues.

4   Conclusion

In this work, we propose a novel semi-supervised segmentation framework CLD by introducing class-aware weighted loss (WL), probability-aware random cropping (PRC), and dual uncertainty-aware sampling supervision (DUS) to enhance the learning and supervision in the areas of cartilages in knee MR images. Among them, WL and DUS are general solutions for solving the class imbalance problem in semi-supervised segmentation tasks. PRC is the specific design for the knee dataset, where the cartilages are extremely thin and have a smaller cropping probability along the z-axis than hard tissues. Extensive experiments show that the proposed framework brings significant improvements over the baseline and outperforms previous SSL methods by a considerable margin.

Acknowledgement. This work was supported by a grant from HKUST-Shanghai Jiao Tong University (SJTU) Joint Research Collaboration Fund (SJTU21EG05), a grant from HKUST-BICI Exploratory Fund (HCIC-004), and a grant from Shenzhen Municipal Central Government Guides Local Science and Technology Development Special Funded Projects (2021Szvup139).

References

1. Ambellan, F., Tack, A., Ehlke, M., Zachow, S.: Automated segmentation of knee bone and cartilage combining statistical shape knowledge and convolutional neural networks: data from the osteoarthritis initiative. Med. Image Anal. **52**, 109–118 (2019)
2. Bai, W., et al.: Semi-supervised learning for network-based cardiac MR image segmentation. In: Descoteaux, M., Maier-Hein, L., Franz, A., Jannin, P., Collins, D.L., Duchesne, S. (eds.) MICCAI 2017. LNCS, vol. 10434, pp. 253–260. Springer, Cham (2017). https://doi.org/10.1007/978-3-319-66185-8_29
3. Chen, X., Yuan, Y., Zeng, G., Wang, J.: Semi-supervised semantic segmentation with cross pseudo supervision. In: CVPR (2021)
4. Ding, X., Wang, N., Gao, X., Li, J., Wang, X., Liu, T.: KFC: an efficient framework for semi-supervised temporal action localization. IEEE Trans. Image Process. **30**, 6869–6878 (2021)
5. Fang, K., Li, W.-J.: DMNet: difference minimization network for semi-supervised segmentation in medical images. In: Martel, A.L., et al. (eds.) MICCAI 2020. LNCS, vol. 12261, pp. 532–541. Springer, Cham (2020). https://doi.org/10.1007/978-3-030-59710-8_52
6. Hu, H., Wei, F., Hu, H., Ye, Q., Cui, J., Wang, L.: Semi-supervised semantic segmentation via adaptive equalization learning. Advances in Neural Information Processing Systems 34 (2021)
7. Huang, H., et al.: 3D graph-S^2Net: shape-aware self-ensembling network for semi-supervised segmentation with bilateral graph convolution. In: de Bruijne, M., et al. (eds.) MICCAI 2021. LNCS, vol. 12902, pp. 416–427. Springer, Cham (2021). https://doi.org/10.1007/978-3-030-87196-3_39
8. Isensee, F., Jaeger, P.F., Kohl, S.A., Petersen, J., Maier-Hein, K.H.: nnU-Net: a self-configuring method for deep learning-based biomedical image segmentation. Nat. Meth. **18**(2), 203–211 (2021)

9. Li, X., et al.: 3D multi-scale FCN with random modality voxel dropout learning for intervertebral disc localization and segmentation from multi-modality MR images. Med. Image Anal. **45**, 41–54 (2018)

10. Li, X., Yu, L., Chen, H., Fu, C.W., Heng, P.A.: Semi-supervised skin lesion segmentation via transformation consistent self-ensembling model. In: BMVC (2018)

11. Li, X., Yu, L., Chen, H., Fu, C.W., Xing, L., Heng, P.A.: Transformation-consistent self-ensembling model for semisupervised medical image segmentation. IEEE Trans. Neural Netw. Learn. Syst. **32**(2), 523–534 (2020)

12. Liang, X., Lin, Y., Fu, H., Zhu, L., Li, X.: RSCFed: random sampling consensus federated semi-supervised learning. In: CVPR (2022)

13. Liu, F., Zhou, Z., Jang, H., Samsonov, A., Zhao, G., Kijowski, R.: Deep convolutional neural network and 3d deformable approach for tissue segmentation in musculoskeletal magnetic resonance imaging. Magn. Reson. Med. **79**(4), 2379–2391 (2018)

14. Luo, X., Chen, J., Song, T., Wang, G.: Semi-supervised medical image segmentation through dual-task consistency. arXiv preprint arXiv:2009.04448 (2020)

15. Luo, X., et al.: Efficient semi-supervised gross target volume of nasopharyngeal carcinoma segmentation via uncertainty rectified pyramid consistency. In: de Bruijne, M., et al. (eds.) MICCAI 2021. LNCS, vol. 12902, pp. 318–329. Springer, Cham (2021). https://doi.org/10.1007/978-3-030-87196-3_30

16. Milletari, F., Navab, N., Ahmadi, S.A.: V-Net: fully convolutional neural networks for volumetric medical image segmentation. In: 2016 4th International Conference on 3D Vision (3DV), pp. 565–571. IEEE (2016)

17. Prasoon, A., Petersen, K., Igel, C., Lauze, F., Dam, E., Nielsen, M.: Deep feature learning for knee cartilage segmentation using a triplanar convolutional neural network. In: Mori, K., Sakuma, I., Sato, Y., Barillot, C., Navab, N. (eds.) MICCAI 2013. LNCS, vol. 8150, pp. 246–253. Springer, Heidelberg (2013). https://doi.org/10.1007/978-3-642-40763-5_31

18. Tarvainen, A., Valpola, H.: Mean teachers are better role models: weight-averaged consistency targets improve semi-supervised deep learning results. In: Advances in Neural Information Processing Systems 30 (2017)

19. Xie, Q., Luong, M.T., Hovy, E., Le, Q.V.: Self-training with noisy student improves imagenet classification. In: CVPR, pp. 10687–10698 (2020)

20. Yao, H., Hu, X., Li, X.: Enhancing pseudo label quality for semi-superviseddomain-generalized medical image segmentation. In: AAAI (2022)

21. Yu, L., et al.: Automatic 3D cardiovascular MR segmentation with densely-connected volumetric convnets. In: Descoteaux, M., Maier-Hein, L., Franz, A., Jannin, P., Collins, D.L., Duchesne, S. (eds.) MICCAI 2017. LNCS, vol. 10434, pp. 287–295. Springer, Cham (2017). https://doi.org/10.1007/978-3-319-66185-8_33

22. Yu, L., Wang, S., Li, X., Fu, C.-W., Heng, P.-A.: Uncertainty-aware self-ensembling model for semi-supervised 3D left atrium segmentation. In: Shen, D., et al. (eds.) MICCAI 2019. LNCS, vol. 11765, pp. 605–613. Springer, Cham (2019). https://doi.org/10.1007/978-3-030-32245-8_67

23. Zhou, Y., et al.: Semi-supervised 3d abdominal multi-organ segmentation via deep multi-planar co-training. In: 2019 IEEE Winter Conference on Applications of Computer Vision (WACV), pp. 121–140. IEEE (2019)

Semi-supervised Medical Image Classification with Temporal Knowledge-Aware Regularization

Qiushi Yang[1], Xinyu Liu[1], Zhen Chen[1], Bulat Ibragimov[2], and Yixuan Yuan[1(✉)]

[1] Department of Electrical Engineering, City University of Hong Kong, Hong Kong SAR, China
yxyuan.ee@cityu.edu.hk

[2] Department of Computer Science, University of Copenhagen, 2100 Copenhagen, Denmark

Abstract. Semi-supervised learning (SSL) for medical image classification has achieved exceptional success on efficiently exploiting knowledge from unlabeled data with limited labeled data. Nevertheless, recent SSL methods suffer from misleading hard-form pseudo labeling, exacerbating the confirmation bias issue due to rough training process. Moreover, the training schemes excessively depend on the quality of generated pseudo labels, which is vulnerable against the inferior ones. In this paper, we propose TEmporal knowledge-Aware Regularization (TEAR) for semi-supervised medical image classification. Instead of using hard pseudo labels to train models roughly, we design Adaptive Pseudo Labeling (AdaPL), a mild learning strategy that relaxes hard pseudo labels to soft-form ones and provides a cautious training. AdaPL is built on a novel theoretically derived loss estimator, which approximates the loss of unlabeled samples according to the temporal information across training iterations, to adaptively relax pseudo labels. To release the excessive dependency of biased pseudo labels, we take advantage of the temporal knowledge and propose Iterative Prototype Harmonizing (IPH) to encourage the model to learn discriminative representations in an unsupervised manner. The core principle of IPH is to maintain the harmonization of clustered prototypes across different iterations. Both AdaPL and IPH can be easily incorporated into prior pseudo labeling-based models to extract features from unlabeled medical data for accurate classification. Extensive experiments on three semi-supervised medical image datasets demonstrate that our method outperforms state-of-the-art approaches. The code is available at https://github.com/CityU-AIM-Group/TEAR.

Keywords: Semi-supervised learning · Medical image classification · Temporal knowledge · Pseudo labeling · Prototype harmonizing

---

Supplementary Information The online version contains supplementary material available at https://doi.org/10.1007/978-3-031-16452-1_12.

1 Introduction

Deep learning methods have achieved remarkable success on medical image classification with a large number of human-craft annotated data. Nevertheless, medical data annotations are usually costly expensive and not available in many clinical scenarios [32,37]. Semi-supervised learning (SSL), as an efficient machine learning paradigm, is widely used to tackle this issue and achieves exceptional advances with limited labeled data, due to its superiority in exploiting knowledge from a large amount of unlabeled data.

Recent SSL approaches [4,7,11,14–16,23,29,34] in medical image analysis target to obtain relatively reliable predictions for unlabeled samples and reduce the risk of *confirmation bias* [3,33], i.e., mistakes accumulation caused by incorrect pseudo labels, by employing two types of techniques: (1) Pseudo labeling paradigm [4,17,21,28], generating pseudo labels by current model and training the model in an ad-hoc manner. For example, FixMatch [28] produces pseudo labels from weak-augmented samples with high-confidence and regards them as the supervision for strong-augmented samples. FedPerl [4] utilizes peer learning to ensemble the results of multiple models and encourages them to learn from each other. Other methods [17,21,23] extend FixMatch through designing addition constraints and exploiting latent relation among unlabeled data to generate more accurate pseudo labels. (2) Consistency regularization [11,15,29,33,34], enforcing the predictions drawn from different views of data to be consistent. GLM [15] adopts both data and latent feature mixup to obtain augmented samples and corresponding labels, and NM [34] aims to refine pseudo labels by matching neighbor samples from a dynamic memory queue with a feature similarity-based attention mechanism to re-weight pseudo labels. Mean-teacher based methods [11,29,33] encourage consistent predictions between a learnable model and its exponential moving average model.

However, most previous methods with pseudo labeling paradigm [4,21,23,28] adhere to the entropy minimization principle [13] and utilize *hard pseudo labels* as supervision, which represent a kind of extreme distribution and may produce strong biased supervision with over-confident predictions. Thus, hard pseudo labels would lead a *rough training* process and exacerbate the overfitting problem. To remedy this issue, although cautious training schemes [15,16,29,34] that employ mixup and intuitively design soft labeling strategies are proposed, their mild supervision with *soft pseudo labels* may weaken the discrimination ability of the model [28]. Moreover, recent consistency regularization-based methods [5,6,12,20,28,33,36] aim to achieve the consistency between the predictions of weak and strong augmented samples, yet their excessive reliance on pseudo labels makes them vulnerable to the label quality and the risk of overfitting to misleading pseudo labels.

To deal with these problems, as shown in Fig. 1, we propose TEmporal knowledge-Aware Regularization (TEAR) to adaptively soften pseudo labels and relieve the corresponding dependency simultaneously. To balance the trade-off between cautious training and rough training, we first theoretically derive an upper bound of the potential loss of unlabeled samples according to the

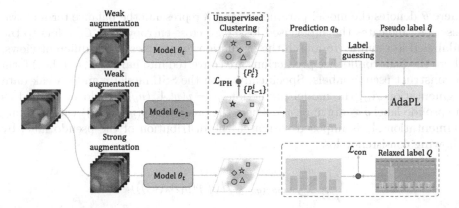

Fig. 1. Framework of the proposed method. The hard pseudo labels are relaxed by Adaptive Pseudo Labeling (AdaPL) according to both current and historical model predictions. The modulated pseudo labels and the predictions of strong augmented samples are encouraged to be consistent by $\mathcal{L}_{\text{con}}$. Moreover, in the feature space, the clustered prototypes obtained by unsupervised clustering from different training iterations are matched by Iterative Prototype Harmonizing (IPH) constraint $\mathcal{L}_{\text{IPH}}$.

models from different training iterations, and leverage it to estimate the discrepancy between pseudo labels and unavailable ground-truth labels. On basis of this, *Adaptive Pseudo Labeling* (AdaPL) is designed to calibrate unreliable hard pseudo labels by adaptive relaxation. Moreover, to release the excessive dependency of biased pseudo labels in the consistency constraints, we propose a temporal self-supervised constraint, *Iterative Prototype Harmonizing* (IPH), by taking advantage of the knowledge from different training iterations and relieving the reliance on the pseudo label guidance. It encourages the prototypes of the unsupervised clustering processes to be harmonious across different iterations. In practice, we maintain the feature prototypes obtained by the unsupervised clustering approach from current and historical models to be matched from the perspective of feature distribution. As such, IPH can provide a regularization to reduce the risk of confirmation bias in a pseudo label independent way.

2   Methodology

The SSL framework with the proposed TEAR aims to learn labeled and unlabeled data simultaneously. Precisely, given a batch of labeled data $\mathcal{X} = \{(x_b, y_b); b \in (1, \ldots, B)\}$ and unlabeled data $\mathcal{U} = \{u_b; b \in (1, \ldots, \mu B)\}$, where B denotes the batch size, and μ is the ratio of unlabeled and labeled data within a mini-batch. SSL models are optimized by minimizing the following loss function:

$$\sum_{(x_b, y_b) \in \mathcal{X}} \mathcal{L}_s(x_b, y_b, \theta) + \lambda \sum_{u_b \in \mathcal{U}} \mathcal{L}_u(u_b, \theta), \tag{1}$$

where θ denotes the model parameters and λ represents the balance term of two losses. $\mathcal{L}_s$ indicates the supervised loss, e.g., cross-entropy loss. $\mathcal{L}_u$ refers to the unlabeled loss aiming to match the predictions of samples under different views, where the high-confidence predictions are converted into hard (i.e., one-hot) form to construct pseudo labels. Specifically, with the SSL model p and a weak data augmentation $\mathcal{A}_w$, the model prediction $q_b = p(y|\mathcal{A}_w(u_b))$ would be formed as the pseudo label $\hat{q} = \arg\max(q_b)$. Then, the prediction $p(y|\mathcal{A}_s(u_b))$ with a strong augmentation $\mathcal{A}_s$ is imposed to match the distribution of the pseudo label by following consistency loss:

$$\frac{1}{\mu B} \sum_{b=1}^{\mu B} \mathbb{1}_{\max(q_b) \geq \tau} H(\hat{q}, p(y|\mathcal{A}_s(u_b))), \tag{2}$$

where $H(\cdot)$ refers to cross-entropy loss, and τ is the threshold used to select eligible samples.

2.1 Adaptive Pseudo Labeling (AdaPL)

To adaptively calibrate pseudo labels and alleviate the confirmation bias, we take advantage of the predictions produced by different training iterations to model the loss related information in the process of pseudo labeling. Rather than intuitively measuring the uncertainty of pseudo labels [26, 34], we theoretically design a novel strategy to estimate the unlabeled sample loss according to predictions of current and previous models. The estimated loss can represent the reliability of unlabeled sample and provide a specific level of label relaxation for better pseudo labeling.

Definition 1 (Loss Estimating (LE) Function). *Given an unlabeled sample u, and its model predictions $p(y|u; \theta_t)$ and $p(y|u; \theta_{t-1})$ of the models at the t-th and $(t-1)$-th training iterations, the cross-entropy loss estimator for unlabeled sample is defined as:*

$$LE(u; t) \stackrel{\text{def}}{=} \|p(y|u; \theta_t) \odot log(p(y|u; \theta_t))\|_1 \cdot \|p(y|u; \theta_t) - p(y|u; \theta_{t-1})\|_2, \tag{3}$$

where $\odot$ represents the Hadamard product. LE function calculates the product of the entropy of current prediction, and the discrepancy of two predictions produced by models from current and previous iterations, respectively.

Given a sample u and model parameters θ_t, for model prediction $p(y|u; \theta_t)$, we assume $\|\nabla p(y|u; \theta_t)\|_2$ is upper bounded by a constant in the context of neural network, which has been theoretically proved and empirically observed in [2, 18, 31]. According to this, we justify that the LE function can approximate the upper bound of sample loss without the availability of ground-truth label:

Theorem 1. *With the cross-entropy as loss function $\mathcal{L}_{gt}(\cdot)$, LE can approximate the upper bound of unlabeled sample loss:*

$$LE(u; t) \geq \eta \mathcal{L}_{gt}(u; \theta_t) \|\nabla p(y|u; \theta_t)\|_2^2, \tag{4}$$

where η is the learning rate. Detailed proof is provided in supplementary materials. Considering that the LE function as the estimation towards the loss upper bound can represent the relative discrepancy between the pseudo label and ground-truth label, we apply it to modulate hard pseudo labels to generate more reliable soft ones. Specifically, given the prediction q_b of sample u, we first sharpen it to be one-hot form $\hat{q} = \arg\max(q_b)$. Then, to rectify the rough hard pseudo label, we normalize LE function to be the modulation function $R(u;t)$, where $\max R(u;t) = 1.0$, thereby guaranteeing the probability of soft label relaxed by modulation function is: $\bar{q} \leq 1.0$. The formulation of $R(u;t)$ is:

$$R(u;t) = b - \sigma(LE(u;t)), \tag{5}$$

where $\sigma(\cdot)$ and b represent the normalization function and constant bias, respectively. Afterward, we employ the modulation function to relax hard pseudo label $\hat{q}$ to obtain a soft one: $\bar{q} = R(u;t) \cdot (\hat{q})$.

Then the relaxed pseudo labels are reconstructed by setting the probabilities of non-target classes equally to convert the $\bar{q}$ into the form of the probability vector. Therefore, we can obtain the modulated pseudo label Q as:

$$Q_i = \begin{cases} \max(\bar{q}) & \text{if } i = \arg\max(\bar{q}) \\ \frac{1-\max(\bar{q})}{C-1} & \text{otherwise}, \end{cases} \tag{6}$$

where C is the number of classes across the dataset. The final pseudo label Q calibrated by the information of both current and historical models can provide cautious supervision and mitigate confirmation bias.

With the calibrated pseudo labels Q, the consistency loss Eq. 2 can be rewritten as:

$$\mathcal{L}_{con} = \frac{1}{\mu B} \sum_{b=1}^{\mu B} \mathbb{1}_{\max(q_b) \geq \tau} H(Q, p(y|\mathcal{A}_s(u_b))). \tag{7}$$

By enforcing eligible pseudo labels to match the predictions of the strong-augmented samples, we can reduce the risk of confirmation bias and train our model more efficiently. Moreover, the modulated pseudo label contains the information of both current and historical models, which provides more sufficient supervision and facilitates the model performance.

2.2 Iterative Prototype Harmonizing (IPH)

Most prior consistency regularization-based works [4,7,21,28,29] mainly enforce the model predictions of samples with different augmentations to be consistent, yet depends on the quality of pseudo labels and suffers from confirmation bias. To address this issue, we propose Iterative Prototype Harmonizing (IPH) to match the feature prototypes P, i.e., cluster-wise feature centroids, across different training iterations in a self-supervised manner. Specifically, IPH takes advantage of the knowledge from different training iterations and provides the coherent optimization. Moreover, it considers the harmonization from the perspective of feature distribution, thus can avoid the affects of misleading pseudo labels and tolerate biased clustered samples. Therefore, IPH can regularize the training process to reduce the risk of overfitting to misleading supervision with the pseudo label independent constraint in the feature level.

To be specific, given unlabeled samples u, we leverage the feature extractor $f_t(\cdot)$ to extract the latent representation $z_t = f_t(u)$ at t training iteration. Then, the prototype P_t^c for each cluster is calculated by: $P_t^c = \frac{1}{N_c} \sum_{i=1}^{N_c} z_t^i$, where c is the cluster index, and N_c is the number of samples within the mini-batch belonging to the c-th cluster. Note that the cluster-aware information is obtained by the unsupervised clustering method within a mini-batch, and we adopt K-Means in this work. Finally, we enforce the clustered prototypes to be harmonious across different training iterations via IPH loss as:

$$\mathcal{L}_{\text{IPH}} = \frac{1}{C} \sum_{i=1}^{C} h(P_t^i, P_{t-1}^i), \tag{8}$$

where C is the number of clusters that is equal to the number of classes. $h(\cdot)$ denotes the metric function and we use cosine similarity as $h(v, w) = \frac{v \cdot w}{\|v\|_2 \cdot \|w\|_2}$. IPH loss regularizes the model to capture pseudo label independent information in a self-supervised manner. Compared with the training paradigm [17,21,28] guided by pseudo labels, IPH can avoid the model learning from biased supervision, thereby alleviating confirmation bias in the process of pseudo labeling.

2.3   Optimization

In general, our framework is optimized by AdaPL and IPH with labeled and unlabeled medical images simultaneously. The overall loss function is written as:

$$\mathcal{L} = \mathcal{L}_s + \lambda_1 \mathcal{L}_{\text{con}} + \lambda_2 \mathcal{L}_{\text{IPH}}, \tag{9}$$

where the $\mathcal{L}_s$ is the supervision for labeled samples with standard cross-entropy loss. λ_1 and λ_2 are factors for balancing two proposed components. The consistency loss encourages the model to achieve alignment between the prediction of the strong-augmented sample and pseudo label calibrated by AdaPL, while the IPH loss enforces clustered prototypes obtained by unsupervised clustering to be harmonious across different training iterations. Both AdaPL and IPH provide adaptive regularizations for SSL models with temporal knowledge and alleviate confirmation bias for consistently performance improvement.

3   Experiments and Results

3.1   Dataset and Implementation Details

Dataset 1 - Kvasir-Capsule (KC). KC dataset [27] contains 47,238 endoscopic images including 14 classes. Considering that most of images belong to the normal category and some categories only consist of few images, we randomly select 3,560 images from ten categories to create a class-balanced dataset.

Table 1. Quantitative comparison with state-of-the-art algorithms on Kvasir-Capsule (KC), RSNA and ISIC 2018 datasets.

Dataset	Method	5%		10%		20%		30%	
		AUC	MCA	AUC	MCA	AUC	MCA	AUC	MCA
KC	GLM [36]	77.09	43.83	80.27	45.54	85.27	52.39	87.35	54.48
	NM [22]	76.53	45.01	79.85	47.36	83.22	53.52	86.70	55.57
	SimPLE [17]	78.05	44.61	80.96	48.23	85.81	54.27	87.87	56.09
	CoMatch [21]	78.24	45.13	81.67	49.17	85.68	54.62	88.13	56.83
	FixMatch [28]	77.17	44.44	80.81	47.78	85.86	53.89	87.42	55.33
	TEAR	**80.24**	**46.70**	**83.17**	**50.62**	**87.33**	**55.96**	**88.74**	**58.26**
RSNA	GLM [36]	73.31	37.53	77.99	46.79	83.47	52.51	84.88	55.69
	NM [22]	72.47	38.08	77.54	47.23	82.68	52.88	84.40	56.28
	SimPLE [17]	72.92	38.66	78.29	46.38	82.47	52.75	85.47	56.15
	CoMatch [21]	74.37	39.20	80.41	47.44	83.87	53.06	85.92	57.31
	FixMatch [28]	72.71	38.15	78.96	46.52	83.17	52.70	85.15	55.77
	TEAR	**76.25**	**40.78**	**82.17**	**48.78**	**85.20**	**54.36**	**87.49**	**58.80**

Dataset	Method	350		800		1200		2000	
		AUC	MCA	AUC	MCA	AUC	MCA	AUC	MCA
ISIC	GLM [36]	78.70	38.56	84.79	45.15	87.54	50.34	88.56	53.47
	NM [22]	77.43	41.45	83.03	49.33	85.47	55.39	86.18	56.21
	SimPLE [17]	77.87	40.58	84.07	49.22	87.32	54.16	88.25	56.68
	CoMatch [21]	79.24	40.83	84.71	49.65	87.64	54.90	88.93	57.31
	FixMatch [28]	78.36	40.29	84.30	48.77	86.61	53.29	87.77	55.79
	TEAR	**80.63**	**42.36**	**85.50**	**51.24**	**88.52**	**56.56**	**89.87**	**58.24**

Dataset 2 - RSNA Intracranial Hemorrhage (ICH) Detection. RSNA ICH Detection dataset [1] consists of brain CT slices across 5 categories of ICH disease. We randomly sample 10,000 slices containing 5 disease categories from RSNA as our dataset.

Dataset 3 - ISIC 2018 Skin Lesion. ISIC 2018 Skin Lesion dataset [9] includes 10,015 dermoscopy images across 7 types of skin lesions. It is a more challenging dataset due to the class-imbalanced issue.

Implementation Details. In the evaluation, we conduct experiments in 5%, 10%, 20% and 30% label regimes (LRs) on KC and RSNA datasets, and 350, 800, 1200 and 2000 LRs on ISIC 2018. All models are optimized by SGD [30] with the initial learning rate of 1×10^{-3}, a momentum of 0.9 and a weight decay [24] of 5×10^{-4}. We follow prior methods [15,34] and use AlexNet [19] as the backbone to train models with a mini-batch size of 128 for 256 epochs (except for 100 epochs on RSNA dataset for efficiency). Each dataset is divided into 70%, 10% and 20% for training, validation and testing. All images are resized to 128×128, randomly rotated in the range of $(-10°, 10°)$ and translated (horizontal and vertical) in the range of $(0, 0.1)$ as the weak augmentation, and the RandAugmentation [10] is used as the strong augmentation. The loss balance terms λ_1 and λ_2 in Eq. 9 are set as 1.0 and 0.1, respectively. All experiments are conducted on NVIDIA RTX 2080Ti GPUs with PyTorch [25] framework.

3.2 Comparison with State-of-the-Arts

We compare TEAR with various state-of-the-art methods [15,17,21,28,34] to verify the effectiveness of the proposed strategies on three datasets in multiple LRs. Table 1 shows the results on three datasets. Our model achieves consistent improvements over state-of-the-art methods [15,17,21,28,34] on mean AUC (area under the ROC curve) and mean MCA (mean class accuracy) in all LRs. On *KC* dataset, TEAR exhibits 80.24%, 83.17%, 87.33% and 88.74% AUC scores with 5%, 10%, 20%, 30% labeled samples per class, surpassing CoMatch [21] with 2.0%, 1.5%, 1.65% and 0.61%, respectively, indicating that TEAR is powerful even when labeled samples are extremely scarce. It is because TEAR can fit to more reliable calibrated pseudo labels with AdaPL and IPH. Moreover, the proposed method delivers the best results on *RSNA*, better than the second best ones CoMatch [21] with 1.88%, 1.76%, 1.33% and 1.49% AUC scores in four LRs. In addition, on *ISIC 2018*, TEAR outperforms other comparisons in all LRs. Particularly, we obtain 80.63% AUC and 42.36% MCA in 350-label split, superior than CoMatch [21] with 1.39% and 1.53%, respectively. Those results demonstrate the proposed TEAR can improve the SSL performance consistently.

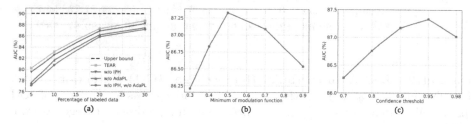

Fig. 2. Ablation study of our models. (a) Ablations on TEAR model, without IPH, without AdaPL, without IPH and AdaPL, and the upper bound, i.e., the fully supervised model. (b) Minimum of modulation function. (c) The confidence threshold.

3.3 Ablation Study

Effects of AdaPL and IPH. To investigate the effects of AdaPL and IPH, we conduct ablation studies on KC dataset in four LRs. From Fig. 2(a), both of them increase the classification performance in all LRs. The dash line represents the upper bound results obtained from the model trained with all labels. We notice that even with 30% labeled data, TEAR achieves 88.74% AUC score with only

1.3% lower than fully-supervised trained one. These experiments demonstrate both AdaPL and IPH can constantly improve the performance in all LRs.

Impact of Modulation Function $R(u; t)$**.** In AdaPL, according to the normalization process in Eq. 5, the range of modulation function is: $R(u) \in (\xi, 1.0)$, where ξ is the maximum level of label relaxation. It means if the unlabeled sample loss estimated by Eq. 3 is very large, indicating with the unreliable pseudo label, the AdaPL will impose a strong relaxation on the pseudo label with the maximum level of ξ. To evaluate the effects of ξ, we train models using various ξ with different levels of pseudo label relaxation on KC dataset with 20% labels. From Fig. 2(b), the optimal choice of ξ is 0.5, and either increasing or decreasing ξ leads to the drop of results, which suggests too strong and too weak label relaxation would be harmful to pseudo labeling.

Effect of Threshold τ**.** Our method focuses on adaptively adjusting pseudo labels and uses a fixed threshold τ in Eq. 7 to train models, which is different from previous methods [8,35] utilizing dynamic thresholding strategies to pick up samples. To study the effects of the threshold in our model, we conduct experiments with various thresholds on KC dataset in 20% LR and record the corresponding results in Fig. 2(c). Our model performs stably with the threshold τ in the value range of $(0.90, 0.98)$, while the results show a remarkable drop when the threshold is smaller than 0.90, since it is hard to optimize models without a strong threshold to select reliable samples for pseudo labeling, especially in the early training stage. It implies instead of designing intricate thresholding strategies, our model can achieve superior performance only with the threshold in a suitable range to roughly filter the most unreliable samples.

4 Conclusion

In this paper, we take advantage of temporal knowledge and propose TEAR to improve the performance of semi-supervised medical image classification. We design AdaPL to mitigate confirmation bias by modulating pseudo labels based on a theoretically derived loss estimator. To further regularize the training process, we propose IPH to encourage the harmonious clustered prototypes across different training iterations in a pseudo label independent manner. Extensive experiments on three semi-supervised medical image datasets verify the effectiveness of the proposed method.

Acknowledgement. This work was supported by Hong Kong Research Grants Council (RGC) Early Career Scheme grant 21207420 (CityU 9048179) and the Novo Nordisk Foundation under the grant NNF20OC0062056.

References

1. RSNA: Intracranial hemorrhage detection challenge (2019). https://www.kaggle.com/c/rsna-intracranial-hemorrhage-detection/
2. Allen-Zhu, Z., Li, Y., Song, Z.: A convergence theory for deep learning via over-parameterization. In: Proceedings of the ICML (2019)
3. Arazo, E., Ortego, D., Albert, P., O'Connor, N.E., McGuinness, K.: Pseudo-labeling and confirmation bias in deep semi-supervised learning. In: IEEE IJCNN (2020)
4. Bdair, T., Navab, N., Albarqouni, S.: FedPerl: semi-supervised peer learning for skin lesion classification. In: de Bruijne, M., et al. (eds.) MICCAI 2021. LNCS, vol. 12903, pp. 336–346. Springer, Cham (2021). https://doi.org/10.1007/978-3-030-87199-4_32
5. Berthelot, D., et al.: ReMixMatch: semi-supervised learning with distribution alignment and augmentation anchoring. In: Proceedings of the ICLR (2019)
6. Berthelot, D., Carlini, N., Goodfellow, I., Papernot, N., Oliver, A., Raffel, C.A.: MixMatch: a holistic approach to semi-supervised learning. In: Proceedings of the NeurIPS (2019)
7. Bortsova, G., Dubost, F., Hogeweg, L., Katramados, I., de Bruijne, M.: Semi-supervised medical image segmentation via learning consistency under transformations. In: Shen, D., et al. (eds.) MICCAI 2019. LNCS, vol. 11769, pp. 810–818. Springer, Cham (2019). https://doi.org/10.1007/978-3-030-32226-7_90
8. Cascante-Bonilla, P., Tan, F., Qi, Y., Ordonez, V.: Curriculum labeling: revisiting pseudo-labeling for semi-supervised learning. In: AAAI (2020)
9. Codella, N., et al.: Skin lesion analysis toward melanoma detection 2018: a challenge hosted by the international skin imaging collaboration (ISIC). arXiv preprint arXiv:1902.03368 (2019)
10. Cubuk, E.D., Zoph, B., Shlens, J., Le, Q.V.: RandAugment: practical automated data augmentation with a reduced search space. In: Proceedings of the CVPR Workshops (2020)
11. Cui, W., et al.: Semi-supervised brain lesion segmentation with an adapted mean teacher model. In: Chung, A.C.S., Gee, J.C., Yushkevich, P.A., Bao, S. (eds.) IPMI 2019. LNCS, vol. 11492, pp. 554–565. Springer, Cham (2019). https://doi.org/10.1007/978-3-030-20351-1_43
12. Gong, C., Wang, D., Liu, Q.: AlphaMatch: improving consistency for semi-supervised learning with alpha-divergence. In: Proceedings of the CVPR (2021)
13. Grandvalet, Y., Bengio, Y., et al.: Semi-supervised learning by entropy minimization. In: CAP (2005)
14. Guo, X., Yuan, Y.: Semi-supervised WCE image classification with adaptive aggregated attention. Med. Image Anal. **64**, 101733 (2020)
15. Gyawali, P.K., Ghimire, S., Bajracharya, P., Li, Z., Wang, L.: Semi-supervised medical image classification with global latent mixing. In: Martel, A.L., et al. (eds.) MICCAI 2020. LNCS, vol. 12261, pp. 604–613. Springer, Cham (2020). https://doi.org/10.1007/978-3-030-59710-8_59
16. Gyawali, P.K., Li, Z., Ghimire, S., Wang, L.: Semi-supervised learning by disentangling and self-ensembling over stochastic latent space. In: Shen, D., et al. (eds.) MICCAI 2019. LNCS, vol. 11769, pp. 766–774. Springer, Cham (2019). https://doi.org/10.1007/978-3-030-32226-7_85
17. Hu, Z., Yang, Z., Hu, X., Nevatia, R.: Simple: Similar pseudo label exploitation for semi-supervised classification. In: Proceedings of the CVPR (2021)

18. Huang, S., Wang, T., Xiong, H., Huan, J., Dou, D.: Semi-supervised active learning with temporal output discrepancy. In: Proceedings of the ICCV (2021)
19. Krizhevsky, A., Sutskever, I., Hinton, G.E.: ImageNet classification with deep convolutional neural networks. In: Proceedings of the NeurIPS, vol. 25 (2012)
20. Laine, S., Aila, T.: Temporal ensembling for semi-supervised learning. In: Proceedings of the ICLR (2017)
21. Li, J., Xiong, C., Hoi, S.C.: CoMatch: semi-supervised learning with contrastive graph regularization. In: Proceedings of the ICCV (2021)
22. Lienen, J., Hüllermeier, E.: Credal self-supervised learning. In: Proceedings of the NeurIPS (2021)
23. Liu, Q., Yang, H., Dou, Q., Heng, P.-A.: Federated semi-supervised medical image classification via inter-client relation matching. In: de Bruijne, M., et al. (eds.) MICCAI 2021. LNCS, vol. 12903, pp. 325–335. Springer, Cham (2021). https://doi.org/10.1007/978-3-030-87199-4_31
24. Loshchilov, I., Hutter, F.: SGDR: stochastic gradient descent with warm restarts. In: Proceedings of the ICLR (2016)
25. Paszke, A., et al.: PyTorch: an imperative style, high-performance deep learning library. In: Proceedings of the NeurIPS (2019)
26. Ren, Z., Yeh, R., Schwing, A.: Not all unlabeled data are equal: learning to weight data in semi-supervised learning. In: Proceedings of the NeurIPS (2020)
27. Smedsrud, P.H., et al.: Kvasir-capsule, a video capsule endoscopy dataset (2020)
28. Sohn, K., et al.: FixMatch: simplifying semi-supervised learning with consistency and confidence. In: Proceedings of the NeurIPS (2020)
29. Su, H., Shi, X., Cai, J., Yang, L.: Local and global consistency regularized mean teacher for semi-supervised nuclei classification. In: Shen, D., et al. (eds.) MICCAI 2019. LNCS, vol. 11764, pp. 559–567. Springer, Cham (2019). https://doi.org/10.1007/978-3-030-32226-7_62
30. Sutskever, I., Martens, J., Dahl, G., Hinton, G.: On the importance of initialization and momentum in deep learning. In: Proceedings of the ICML (2013)
31. Szegedy, C., et al.: Intriguing properties of neural networks. In: Proceedings of the ICLR (2014)
32. Tao, X., Li, Y., Zhou, W., Ma, K., Zheng, Y.: Revisiting Rubik's cube: self-supervised learning with volume-wise transformation for 3D medical image segmentation. In: Martel, L., et al. (eds.) MICCAI 2020. LNCS, vol. 12264, pp. 238–248. Springer, Cham (2020). https://doi.org/10.1007/978-3-030-59719-1_24
33. Tarvainen, A., Valpola, H.: Mean teachers are better role models: weight-averaged consistency targets improve semi-supervised deep learning results. In: Proceedings of the NeurIPS (2017)
34. Wang, R., Wu, Y., Chen, H., Wang, L., Meng, D.: Neighbor matching for semi-supervised learning. In: de Bruijne, M., et al. (eds.) MICCAI 2021. LNCS, vol. 12902, pp. 439–449. Springer, Cham (2021). https://doi.org/10.1007/978-3-030-87196-3_41
35. Xu, Y., et al.: Dash: semi-supervised learning with dynamic thresholding. In: Proceedings of the ICML (2021)
36. Zhang, B., et al.: FlexMatch: boosting semi-supervised learning with curriculum pseudo labeling. In: Proceedings of the NeurIPS (2021)
37. Zhou, Z., Sodha, V., Pang, J., Gotway, M.B., Liang, J.: Models genesis. Med. Image Anal. 67, 101840 (2021)

GaitForeMer: Self-supervised Pre-training of Transformers via Human Motion Forecasting for Few-Shot Gait Impairment Severity Estimation

Mark Endo[1], Kathleen L. Poston[1], Edith V. Sullivan[1], Li Fei-Fei[1], Kilian M. Pohl[1,2], and Ehsan Adeli[1(✉)]

[1] Stanford University, Stanford, CA 94305, USA
eadeli@stanford.edu
[2] SRI International, Menlo Park, CA 94025, USA

Abstract. Parkinson's disease (PD) is a neurological disorder that has a variety of observable motor-related symptoms such as slow movement, tremor, muscular rigidity, and impaired posture. PD is typically diagnosed by evaluating the severity of motor impairments according to scoring systems such as the Movement Disorder Society Unified Parkinson's Disease Rating Scale (MDS-UPDRS). Automated severity prediction using video recordings of individuals provides a promising route for non-intrusive monitoring of motor impairments. However, the limited size of PD gait data hinders model ability and clinical potential. Because of this clinical data scarcity and inspired by the recent advances in self-supervised large-scale language models like GPT-3, we use human motion forecasting as an effective self-supervised pre-training task for the estimation of motor impairment severity. We introduce **GaitForeMer**, Gait Forecasting and impairment estimation transforMer, which is first pre-trained on public datasets to forecast gait movements and then applied to clinical data to predict MDS-UPDRS gait impairment severity. Our method outperforms previous approaches that rely solely on clinical data by a large margin, achieving an F_1 score of 0.76, precision of 0.79, and recall of 0.75. Using GaitForeMer, we show how public human movement data repositories can assist clinical use cases through learning universal motion representations. The code is available at https://github.com/markendo/GaitForeMer.

Keywords: Few-shot learning · Gait analysis · Transformer

1 Introduction

Large-scale language models [1], such as the third generation Generative Pre-trained Transformer (GPT-3) [2] and Contrastive Language-Image Pre-Training (CLIP) [20], have gained great success in solving challenging problems under few or zero-shot settings. They owe their success to self-supervised pre-training on an

© The Author(s), under exclusive license to Springer Nature Switzerland AG 2022
L. Wang et al. (Eds.): MICCAI 2022, LNCS 13438, pp. 130–139, 2022.
https://doi.org/10.1007/978-3-031-16452-1_13

abundant amount of raw and unlabeled data while completing a downstream task fine-tuned on small datasets. These methods can be of great interest in clinical applications, where data are regularly scarce and limited. For instance, one such application could be automatically estimating motor and gait impairments. This is a crucial step in the early diagnosis of Parkinson's disease (PD).

PD is a chronic, progressive brain disorder with degenerative effects on mobility and muscle control [5]. It is one of the most common neurodegenerative disorders, affecting around 0.57% of people age 45 and over [16]. Motor symptoms are typically used to diagnose PD, as non-motor symptoms such as cognitive symptoms lack specificity and are complicated to assess [27]. Most of the prior methods for automated prediction of motor-related PD signs and symptoms use wearable sensors [4,11,12], but these systems can be expensive and intrusive [14].

Recent methods have shown that video technology can be a scalable, contactless, and non-intrusive solution for quantifying gait impairment severity [15]. They use recordings of clinical gait tests from the Movement Disorder Society Unified Parkinson's Disease Rating Scale (MDS-UPDRS) [8], a widely used clinical rating scale for the severity and progression of PD. One of its components is a motor examination where participants walk 10 m away from and toward an examiner. Specialists assess the severity of motor impairment on a score from 0 to 4. Score 0 indicates no motor impairment, 1 means slight impairment, 2 indicates mild impairment, 3 specifies moderate impairment, and 4 means severe impairment. The goal is automated prediction of this universally-accepted scale.

At the same time, most clinical studies are limited by the difficulty of large-scale data collection, since recruiting patients requires costly multi-site national or international efforts. Recent self-supervised pre-training frameworks have been used to learn useful representations that can be applied to downstream tasks [3,6,9,10,21]. Yet, their translation to clinical applications is under-explored. There is a growing number of 3D human motion capture repositories that can be used for self-supervised pre-training of motion representation learning, the same way GPT-3 [2] and CLIP [20] are trained for language-related tasks. Such pre-trained models can then be adapted for motor impairment estimation.

In this paper, we develop a novel method, **GaitForeMer**, that forecasts motion and gait (pretext task) while estimating impairment severity (downstream task). Our model is based on the recent advances in convolution-free, attention-based Transformer models. GaitForeMer can take advantage of large-scale public datasets on human motion and activity recognition for learning reliable motion representations. To this end, we pre-train the motion representation learning on 3D motion data from the NTU-RGB+D dataset [22]. The learned motion representations are then fine-tuned to estimate the MDS-UPDRS gait scores. Our approach outperforms previous methods on MDS-UPDRS score prediction by a large margin. The benefits of GaitForeMer are twofold: (1) we use motion forecasting as a self-supervised pre-training task to learn useful motion features for the task of motor impairment severity prediction; (2) the joint training of motion and MDS-UPDRS score prediction helps improve the model's

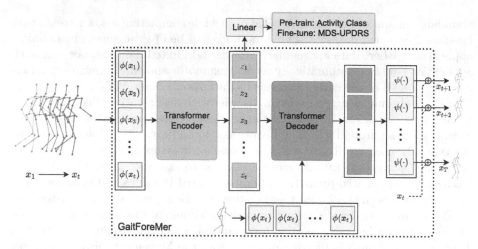

Fig. 1. The proposed GaitForeMer framework for motor impairment severity estimation. A Transformer model based on body skeletons is first pre-trained on a large dataset jointly for human motion prediction and activity prediction. The model is subsequently fine-tuned on the task of MDS-UPDRS gait score prediction using extracted 3D skeleton sequences from clinical study participants using VIBE (Video Inference for Body pose and shape Estimation) [13].

understanding of motion, therefore leading to enhanced differentiation of motor cues. To the best of our knowledge, we are the first to use motion prediction from natural human activity data as an effective pre-training task for the downstream task of motor impairment severity estimation. We expect this method to be useful in decreasing the reliance on large-scale clinical datasets for the detection of factors defining gait disturbance.

2   GaitForeMer: <u>Gait</u> <u>Fore</u>casting and Impairment Estimation Transfor<u>Mer</u>

We first introduce a Transformer model that operates on sequences of 3D human body skeletons for the pre-training task of human motion forecasting, and we subsequently adapt it to the downstream task of MDS-UPDRS gait score estimation. Given a sequence of t 3D skeletons $\mathbf{x}_{1:t}$, we predict the next M skeletons $\mathbf{x}_{t+1:T}$ and the motion class y (either activity or MDS-UPDRS score). We follow the original setup of the pose Transformer model defined in [17]. Specifically, our model comprises a skeleton encoding neural network ϕ, a Transformer encoder and decoder, a pose decoding neural network ψ that reconstructs the 3D poses, and a linear classifier for MDS-UPDRS score/activity prediction. The model takes $\mathbf{x}_{1:t}$ as input, and the skeleton encoding network ϕ embeds this joint data into dimension D for each skeleton vector. Then, the Transformer encoder takes in this sequence of skeleton embeddings aggregated with positional embeddings and computes a latent representation $\mathbf{z}_{1:t}$ using L multi-head self-attention layers. The outputs of the encoder embeddings, $z_{1:t}$, are fed into a single linear layer to predict class probabilities. The classification loss L_c (a multi-class cross-entropy) is used to train activity or score prediction. Note that the class prediction uses the motion representation (i.e., the latent space of the Transformer) as input and outputs the activity classes in the pre-training stage and MDS-UPDRS scores in the downstream task.

In addition, the encoder outputs $z_{1:t}$ and a query sequence $q_{1:M}$ are fed into the Transformer decoder. The query sequence is filled with the last element of the input sequence x_t. The decoder uses L multi-head self- and encoder-decoder attention layers. The output of the decoder is fed into a skeleton decoding network ψ to generate the future skeleton predictions $x_{t+1:T}$. The motion forecasting branch is trained using a layerwise loss calculated as:

$$ L_l = \frac{1}{M \cdot N} \sum_{m=t+1}^{T} \|\hat{x}_m^l - x_m^*\|_1, $$

where $\hat{x}_m^l$ is the predicted sequence of N-dimensional skeleton vectors at layer l of the Transformer decoder, and x_m^* is the ground-truth future skeleton. The motion forecasting loss L_f is then computed by averaging the layerwise loss over all decoder layers L_l. See Fig. 1 for an overview of the model architecture.

2.1 Pre-training Procedure

For pre-training, we jointly train the activity and motion branches of the Gait-ForeMer. For the classification loss L_c, we use a standard categorical cross-entropy loss. The final loss is calculated as $L_{pre} = L_c + L_f$, where there is an equal weighting of the two different losses. We train the model for 100 epochs using an initial learning rate of 0.0001.

2.2 Fine-Tuning Procedure

For our downstream task of MDS-UPDRS score prediction, we initialize the model using the learned weights from pre-training. We set the classification loss L_c as a weighted categorical cross-entropy loss since there is a significant class imbalance in the clinical data. We experiment with a variety of training procedures for fine-tuning the model. In one setup, we solely fine-tune the class prediction branch by setting $L_{fine} = L_c$. In another setup, we fine-tune both the class prediction branch and the motion prediction branch by setting $L_{fine} = L_c + L_f$. We also experiment with first fine-tuning both branches for 50 epochs then additionally solely fine-tuning the class prediction branch for 50 epochs. All fine-tuning setups are trained for 100 epochs using an initial learning rate of 0.0001.

2.3 Baselines

We compare our GaitForeMer method to a similar setup without pre-training on the NTU RGB+D dataset as well as various other motion impairment severity estimation models for MDS-UPDRS score prediction. The GaitForeMer model trained from scratch (GaitForeMer-Scratch) uses the loss function $L = L_c + L_f$ and follows the same configuration as the fine-tuning setups except it is trained for an additional 100 epochs. Hybrid Ordinal Focal DDNet (OF-DDNet) [15] uses a Double-Features Double-Motion Network with a hybrid ordinal-focal objective. This previous method has shown promising results on this MDS-UPDRS dataset. Spatial-Temporal Graph Convolutional Network (ST-GCN) is a graphical approach for learning spatial and temporal characteristics that can be used for action recognition [26]. For this method, we add slow and fast motion features and pass the input through a Graph Attention Network (GAT) [23] layer first to allow for additional spatial message passing. DeepRank [18] is a ranking CNN, and the Support Vector Machine (SVM) [24] is using the raw 3D joints.

3   Datasets

In this work, we use a clinical dataset for estimation of gait impairment severity from MDS-UPDRS videos and a public 3D human gait dataset for pre-training the motion forecasting component. Both datasets are described below.

3.1   NTU RGB+D Dataset

We use NTU RGB+D [22] to pre-train our GaitForeMer model. This dataset includes 56,880 video samples with 60 action classes. We use the skeletal data containing 3D coordinates of 25 joints and class labels. We pre-train our model using the joints as input and the activity labels for supervision of the activity branch. The activity branch is the same as our MDS-UPDRS branch (see Fig. 1), except that during pre-training we train the linear layers to predict the activity class in the NTU RGB+D dataset.

3.2   MDS-UPDRS Dataset

For the downstream task of gait impairment severity estimation, we use the MDS-UPDRS dataset defined in [15]. This dataset contains video recordings of MDS-UPDRS exams from 54 participants. Following previously published protocols [19], all participants are recorded during the off-medication state. During the examinations, participants are recorded walking towards and away from the camera twice at 30 frames per second. Each sample is scored by three board-certified movement disorders neurologists and we use the majority vote among the raters as the ground-truth score, randomly breaking ties. Note that, in this work, we do not aim to model the uncertainty among raters. The raters score the videos on a scale from 0 to 4 based on MDS-UPDRS Section 3.10 [7]. In our work, we combine scores 3 and 4 due to the difficulty of obtaining video recordings for participants with extreme motor impairment. The data setup and protocols are the same as in [15], except in their previous work two sets of scores were counted from one of the neurologists. Using the gait recordings as input, we use Video Inference for Body Pose and Shape Estimation (VIBE) to extract

Table 1. Comparison with baseline methods. Performance is evaluated using macro F_1 score, precision, and recall. We find that pre-training results in significantly improved performance over training from scratch and the other methods. ♮ refers to results directly cited from [15]. * indicates statistical difference at ($p < 0.05$) compared with our method, measured by the Wilcoxon signed rank test [25]. Note that this is a 4-class classification problem and hence 0.25 recall implies a random classifier. Best results are in bold. See text for details about compared methods.

Method	F_1	Pre	Rec
GaitForeMer (Ours)	**0.76**	**0.79**	**0.75**
GaitForeMer-Scratch (Ours)	0.60	0.64	0.58
OF-DDNet♮* [15]	0.58	0.59	0.58
ST-GCN [26]*	0.52	0.55	0.52
DeepRank♮* [18]	0.56	0.53	0.58
SVM♮* [24]	0.44	0.49	0.40

3D skeletons [13]. This joint data is then preprocessed by normalization and splitting of samples into clips of 100 frames each. We then use these clips for estimating motor impairment severity.

4 Experiments

In this section, we first evaluate how motion forecasting helps improve a system estimating the MDS-UPDRS scores. We compare our results with several baselines (Sect. 4.1). We then evaluate how the fine-tuning strategy contributes to better results (Sect. 4.2). We further experiment on how our few-shot learning paradigm can be adopted for clinical approaches using pre-training (Sect. 4.3). Qualitative results on motion forecasting of PD patients validate that GaitForeMer is able to learn good motion representations (Sect. 4.4).

4.1 Using Motion Forecasting as an Effective Pre-training Task

We investigate the efficacy of using human motion forecasting as a self-supervised pre-training task for the downstream task of motor impairment severity estimation. We evaluate each model using macro F_1 score, precision, and recall. These metrics are calculated on a per subject level with leave-one-out-cross-validation settings. We compare our GaitForeMer method to baseline methods in Table 1.

We find that our GaitForeMer method pre-trained on the NTU RGB+D dataset results in improved performance over training the model from scratch and all baselines trained on the MDS-UPDRS dataset. Our best setup achieves an F_1 score of 0.76, precision of 0.79, and recall of 0.75. In comparison, training the model from scratch results in an F_1 score of 0.60, precision of 0.64, and recall of 0.58, which is still superior to other baselines. The OF-DDNet baseline (previous state-of-the-art approach in MDS-UPDRS score prediction) has an F_1 score of 0.58, precision of 0.59, and recall of 0.58.

Table 2. Comparison of different training/fine-tuning strategies of our method (ablation study on fine-tuning strategy). Performance is evaluated using macro F_1 score, precision, and recall. We find that first fine-tuning both branches (forecasting and score prediction) then additionally fine-tuning the score prediction branch yields best results.

Pre-trained	Fine-tune strategy	F_1	Pre	Rec
Yes	Both branches then class branch	**0.76**	**0.79**	**0.75**
Yes	Both branches	0.72	0.75	0.71
Yes	Class branch	0.66	0.72	0.63
No		0.60	0.64	0.58

4.2 Evaluating Fine-Tuning Strategies

We experiment with various fine-tuning strategies in order to evaluate different approaches for training our GaitForeMer method. Our best approach of first fine-tuning both the class prediction and motion prediction branches then solely fine-tuning the class prediction branch achieves an F_1 score of 0.76, precision of 0.79, and recall of 0.75. Another approach of fine-tuning both branches achieves an F_1 score of 0.72, precision of 0.75, and recall of 0.71. We observe that solely fine-tuning the class branch results in worse performance than also training the motion branch with an F_1 score of 0.66, precision of 0.72, and recall of 0.63. The relatively poor performance could be due to the data shift between the NTU RGB+D and MDS-UPDRS datasets that requires training of the motion forecasting branch. Results are shown in Table 2.

4.3 Few-Shot Estimation of Gait Scores

To better understand the few-shot capabilities of GaitForeMer, we experiment with limiting the training dataset size and evaluating performance compared to

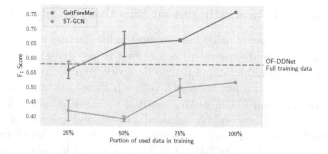

Fig. 2. Few-shot performance of GaitForeMer compared to ST-GCN with different portions of data used in training. Error bars represent standard deviation across 3 runs. Our GaitForeMer method using only 25% of training data maintains comparable performance to the second-best performing method with full training data (OF-DDNet).

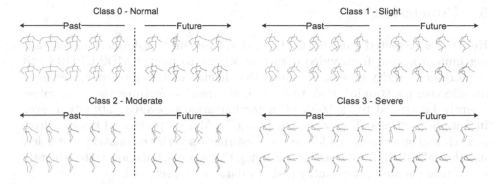

Fig. 3. Visualization of human motion forecasting for different levels of motor impairment severity. The purple skeletons are ground-truth data, and the blue ones are predictions from GaitForeMer with fine-tuning both branches. (Color figure online)

ST-GCN. We sample either 25%, 50%, or 75% of the data (analogous to 13, 26, or 39 videos) for training in each fold, preserving the same samples across the two methods. We maintain class balance by sampling one-fourth of the required subsamples from each class when permitted. We resample and run each method three times. The results are illustrated in Fig. 2.

We find that our GaitForeMer method maintains relatively strong performance with only a fraction of the data. GaitForeMer with access to 25% of training data achieves an average F_1 score of 0.56, which is higher than ST-GCN using 100% of training data with an F_1 score of 0.52 and comparable to OF-DDNet (second-best performing method) using 100% training data with an F_1 score of 0.58. This shows the power of using motion forecasting as a self-supervised pre-training task for few-shot gait impairment severity estimation.

4.4 Motion Forecasting Visualization

In Fig. 3, we visualize the predicted outputs of the GaitForeMer model jointly trained on MDS-UPDRS score prediction and motion forecasting. Although accurate pose forecasting is not necessary for the prediction of MDS-UPDRS scores, it can help demonstrate the utility of learned motion features. Qualitatively, we see that the predicted poses most closely match the ground-truth at the beginning of the output. This might be because using the last input entry x_t as the query sequence $q_{1:M}$ helps the prediction in the short term [17]. A larger error exists for longer horizons where the outputted poses become less similar to the query sequence. In addition, the non-autoregressive approach of GaitForeMer can lead to an increased accumulation of error.

Clinically, the results illustrated in Fig. 3 show normal movement behavior in class 0 (normal), while classes 1 and 2 show increased stiffness, decreased mobility, and reduced arm swing and pedal motion. Participants in class 3 are imbalanced and require assistive devices for safe walking. These results verify that the forecasting module is able to properly predict future motion that encodes motor impairments.

5 Conclusion

Herein, we presented a model, GaitForeMer, based on transformers for forecasting human motion from video data that we use to predict MDS-UPDRS gait impairment severity scores. We found that human motion forecasting serves as an effective pre-training task to learn useful motion features that can subsequently be applied to the task of motor impairment severity estimation, even in few-shot settings. The pre-trained GaitForeMer outperformed training from scratch and other methods for motor impairment severity estimation that solely use the MDS-UPDRS dataset for training. Our approach demonstrates the utility of using motion pre-training tasks in data-limited settings.

Acknowledgements. This work was supported in part by NIH grants (AA010723, NS115114, P30AG066515), the Michael J Fox Foundation for Parkinson's Research, UST (a Stanford AI Lab alliance member), and the Stanford Institute for Human-Centered Artificial Intelligence (HAI) Google Cloud credits.

References

1. Bommasani, R., et al.: On the opportunities and risks of foundation models. arXiv preprint arXiv:2108.07258 (2021)
2. Brown, T., et al.: Language models are few-shot learners. In: Advances in Neural Information Processing Systems 33, pp. 1877–1901 (2020)
3. Chen, T., Kornblith, S., Norouzi, M., Hinton, G.: A simple framework for contrastive learning of visual representations (2020)
4. Daneault, J., et al.: Accelerometer data collected with a minimum set of wearable sensors from subjects with Parkinson's disease. Sci. Data **8**, 48 (2021)
5. DeMaagd, G., Philip, A.: Parkinson's disease and its management: part 1: disease entity, risk factors, pathophysiology, clinical presentation, and diagnosis. P& T: Peer-rev. J. Formulary Manage. **40**, 504–32 (2015)
6. Devlin, J., Chang, M.W., Lee, K., Toutanova, K.: BERT: pre-training of deep bidirectional transformers for language understanding (2019)
7. Goetz, C., Fahn, S., Martinez-Martin, P., Poewe, W., Sampaio, C.: The MDS-sponsored revision of the unified Parkinson's disease rating scale. J. Mov. Disord. **1**, 1–33 (2008)
8. Goetz, C.G., et al.: Movement disorder society-sponsored revision of the unified Parkinson's disease rating scale (MDS-UPDRS): scale presentation and clinimetric testing results: MDS-UPDRS: clinimetric assessment. Mov. Disord. **23**(15), 2129–2170 (2008). https://doi.org/10.1002/mds.22340
9. He, K., Chen, X., Xie, S., Li, Y., Dollár, P., Girshick, R.: Masked autoencoders are scalable vision learners (2021)
10. He, K., Fan, H., Wu, Y., Xie, S., Girshick, R.: Momentum contrast for unsupervised visual representation learning (2020)
11. Hobert, M.A., Nussbaum, S., Heger, T., Berg, D., Maetzler, W., Heinzel, S.: Progressive gait deficits in Parkinson's disease: a wearable-based biannual 5-year prospective study. Front. Aging Neurosci. **11** (2019). https://doi.org/10.3389/fnagi.2019.00022, https://www.frontiersin.org/article/10.3389/fnagi.2019.00022

12. Hssayeni, M.D., Jimenez-Shahed, J., Burack, M.A., Ghoraani, B.: Wearable sensors for estimation of parkinsonian tremor severity during free body movements. Sensors (Basel, Switz.) **19**, 4215 (2019)

13. Kocabas, M., Athanasiou, N., Black, M.J.: VIBE: video inference for human body pose and shape estimation. In: Proceedings of the IEEE/CVF Conference on Computer Vision and Pattern Recognition (CVPR), June 2020

14. Lu, M., et al.: Vision-based estimation of MDS-UPDRS gait scores for assessing Parkinson's disease motor severity. In: Martel, A.L., et al. (eds.) MICCAI 2020. LNCS, vol. 12263, pp. 637–647. Springer, Cham (2020). https://doi.org/10.1007/978-3-030-59716-0_61

15. Lu, M., et al.: Quantifying Parkinson's disease motor severity under uncertainty using MDS-UPDRS videos. Med. Image Anal. **73**, 102179 (2021)

16. Marras, C., et al.: Prevalence of Parkinson's disease across North America. npj Parkinson's Dis. **4** (2018). https://doi.org/10.1038/s41531-018-0058-0

17. Martínez-González, A., Villamizar, M., Odobez, J.M.: Pose transformers (POTR): human motion prediction with non-autoregressive transformers. In: Proceedings of the IEEE/CVF International Conference on Computer Vision (ICCV) Workshops, pp. 2276–2284, October 2021

18. Pang, L., Lan, Y., Guo, J., Xu, J., Xu, J., Cheng, X.: DeepRank. In: Proceedings of the 2017 ACM on Conference on Information and Knowledge Management, November 2017. https://doi.org/10.1145/3132847.3132914

19. Poston, K.L., et al.: Compensatory neural mechanisms in cognitively unimpaired Parkinson disease. Ann. Neurol. **79**(3), 448–463 (2016) https://doi.org/10.1002/ana.24585, https://onlinelibrary.wiley.com/doi/abs/10.1002/ana.24585

20. Radford, A., et al.: Learning transferable visual models from natural language supervision. In: International Conference on Machine Learning, pp. 8748–8763. PMLR (2021)

21. Ramesh, A., et al.: Zero-shot text-to-image generation. In: International Conference on Machine Learning, pp. 8821–8831. PMLR (2021)

22. Shahroudy, A., Liu, J., Ng, T.T., Wang, G.: NTU RGB+D: a large scale dataset for 3d human activity analysis. In: 2016 IEEE Conference on Computer Vision and Pattern Recognition (CVPR), pp. 1010–1019 (2016). https://doi.org/10.1109/CVPR.2016.115

23. Veličković, P., Cucurull, G., Casanova, A., Romero, A., Liò, P., Bengio, Y.: Graph attention networks (2018)

24. Weston, J., Watkins, C.: Support vector machines for multi-class pattern recognition (1999)

25. Wilcoxon, F.: Individual comparisons by ranking methods. In: Kotz, S., Johnson, N.L. (eds.) Breakthroughs in Statistics, pp. 196–202. Springer, New York (1992). https://doi.org/10.1007/978-1-4612-4380-9_16

26. Yan, S., Xiong, Y., Lin, D.: Spatial temporal graph convolutional networks for skeleton-based action recognition (2018)

27. Zesiewicz, T.A., Sullivan, K.L., Hauser, R.A.: Nonmotor symptoms of Parkinson's disease. Exp. Rev. Neurother. **6**(12), 1811–1822 (2006)

Semi-supervised Medical Image Segmentation Using Cross-Model Pseudo-Supervision with Shape Awareness and Local Context Constraints

Jinhua Liu[1], Christian Desrosiers[2], and Yuanfeng Zhou[1(✉)]

[1] School of Software, Shandong University, Jinan, China
yfzhou@sdu.edu.cn
[2] Software and IT Engineering Department, École de technologie supérieure, Montreal, Canada

Abstract. In semi-supervised medical image segmentation, the limited amount of labeled data available for training is often insufficient to learn the variability and complexity of target regions. To overcome these challenges, we propose a novel framework based on cross-model pseudo-supervision that generates anatomically plausible predictions using shape awareness and local context constraints. Our framework consists of two parallel networks, a shape-aware network and a shape-agnostic network, which provide pseudo-labels to each other for using unlabeled data effectively. The shape-aware network implicitly captures information on the shape of target regions by adding the prediction of the other network as input. On the other hand, the shape-agnostic network leverages Monte-Carlo dropout uncertainty estimation to generate reliable pseudo-labels to the other network. The proposed framework also comprises a new loss function that enables the network to learn the local context of the segmentation, thus improving the overall segmentation accuracy. Experiments on two publicly-available datasets show that our method outperforms state-of-the-art approaches for semi-supervised segmentation and better preserves anatomical morphology compared to these approaches. Code is available at https://github.com/igip-liu/SLC-Net.

Keywords: Semi-supervised segmentation · Shape awareness · Cross-model pseudo-supervision · Local context loss

1 Introduction

Medical image segmentation is an essential step for various clinical applications. Recently, segmentation methods based on deep learning have achieved remarkable success in fully supervised scenarios [8,18]. However, the success of these

Supplementary Information The online version contains supplementary material available at https://doi.org/10.1007/978-3-031-16452-1_14.

methods largely depends on the availability of large datasets of labeled images for training. Since acquiring annotations is a time- and labor-intensive process that often requires trained experts, the use of fully-supervised methods in clinical practice remains limited. Semi-supervised segmentation methods alleviate the high cost of delineating ground truth data by exploiting a set of unlabeled images, which are readily-available, in addition to a few labeled images. A broad range of semi-supervised methods based on deep learning have been proposed for medical image segmentation, including pseudo-labeling [4,14,22], entropy minimization [21], data augmentation [2], deep co-training [25,26], deep adversarial learning [28], multi-task learning [10,13,23], self-ensembling [5,19,20,27], and contrastive learning [6,17].

Despite the important achievements of these methods, semi-supervised segmentation remains a challenging problem in many application settings. In such settings, the limited amount of annotated data is insufficient for the segmentation network to learn to full variability of input images and corresponding segmentation, even though using unlabeled data can alleviate this to some extent. In light of this, there have been considerable efforts in recent years to improve the performance of semi-supervised segmentation methods and bring it closer to full supervision. A notable approach to achieve this exploits uncertainty [15,23,26,27] to guide the semi-supervised segmentation process. Other approaches use multi-task learning [10,13,23] to boost segmentation accuracy in semi-supervised scenarios, or leverage contrastive learning to effectively utilize unsupervised data [6,17]. Another line of work exploits shape information to produce more anatomically-plausible results [3,7,10,23,24], which is a critical factor in various clinical applications. For example, the approaches in [10,23] employ a multi-task learning framework that generates both the segmentation class probabilities and a signed distance map (SDM) measuring the nearest distance of each pixel to the segmentation boundary. Furthermore, [7] combines bilateral graph convolutions and a self-ensembling technique to learn relationships between semantics and geometry in semi-supervised segmentation. The method in [24] uses a strategy based on reinforcement learning to incorporate non-differentiable segmentation constraints like connectivity and convexity. Last, [3] adopts a variational autoencoder (VAE) trained on segmentation masks to learn a shape prior from data.

In this paper, inspired by [4,9], we propose a novel segmentation framework to improve accuracy and generate anatomically-plausible results in semi-supervised scenarios. Unlike the methods mentioned above, the proposed framework does not impose explicit shape constraints, and instead exploits shape-related information at the input level to capture shape constraints implicitly. We employ two parallel networks in a cross-teaching strategy, each network generating pseudo-labels for the other on unlabeled data. The first network receives the raw images as input to perform standard segmentation operations. On the other hand, the second receives the same input as well as the corresponding probability maps produced by the first network to capture shape information implicitly. This *shape-aware* network corrects prediction boundaries to generate more accurate pseudo-labels for the other one. To mitigate the impact of noisy pseudo-labels,

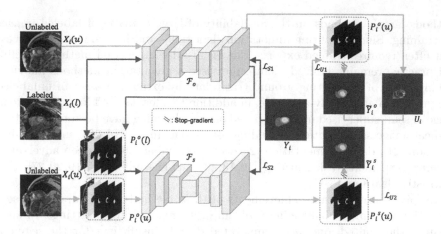

Fig. 1. The pipeline of our cross-model pseudo-supervision framework with shape awareness and local context constraints. $P_i^o(l)$ and $P_i^o(u)$ represent supervised and unsupervised probability maps from network $\mathcal{F}_o$, respectively.

we enhance the shape-agnostic network with an uncertainty estimation strategy that filters out unreliable regions. Moreover, we also design a new loss function called *local context loss* that enforces an accurate prediction in local regions across the image. This contrasts with the standard Dice loss [16] which focuses on *global* overlap and thus can lead to a poor representation of shape in certain regions of the image, and with the popular cross-entropy loss that corrects individual pixel predictions without considering their local context. Compared to [4], our method adds two innovative strategies to make the segmentation pipeline more robust and boost performance: a shape awareness for enhanced guidance and a local context loss for enforcing accuracy in local regions. While the instance segmentation method of [9] also exploits shape priors, we do not use such priors in an iterative process but instead through the cross-teaching of shape-agnostic and shape-aware networks.

To sum up, our work makes three important contributions to semi-supervised segmentation of medical images: (1) We design a novel cross-model pseudo-supervision framework for this task, which combines shape-aware and local context constraints to produce accurate results with limited labeled data. (2) To our knowledge, our semi-supervised segmentation framework is the first to incorporate shape information at the input level of the semi-supervised network, without the need for complex shape constraints. (3) We propose a new loss function that helps the network learn the local context of the segmentation, which enhances the representation of shape across the entire image.

2   Methods

For our semi-supervised learning task, we have N labeled examples in a set $\mathcal{S} = \{(X_i, Y_i)\}_{i=1}^N$ and M unlabeled examples in a set $\mathcal{U} = \{X_i\}_{i=N+1}^{N+M}$, where

$X_i \in \mathbb{R}^{H \times W}$ is a raw image and $Y_i \in \{0,1\}^{H \times W \times C}$ is the corresponding ground-truth annotation. Here, $H \times W$ is the image size and C is the number of ground truth classes. As in standard semi-supervised problems, the number of labeled images is much less than unlabeled images, i.e. $N \ll M$. Given the full training set $\mathcal{D} = \mathcal{S} \cup \mathcal{U}$, we aim to learn a segmentation model $\mathcal{F}$ mapping an image X to its corresponding ground-truth segmentation Y. In the following sections, we describe the details of the proposed semi-supervised segmentation framework.

2.1 Cross-Model Pseudo-Supervision with Shape Awareness and Local Context Constraints

Our framework is illustrated in Fig. 1. It comprises two networks: the shape-agnostic network $\mathcal{F}_o$ and shape-aware network $\mathcal{F}_s$. The networks, respectively parameterized by weights Θ^o and Θ^s, teach each other to yield correct predictions during training. For a labeled example $(X_i, Y_i) \in \mathcal{S}$, both networks are supervised with a standard segmentation loss using the ground truth Y_i. On the other hand, for unlabeled data $X_i \in \mathcal{U}$, the networks mutually provide pseudo-labels to guide each other's parameter update.

To build our framework, we use different configurations for the two networks. The shape-agnostic network $\mathcal{F}_o$ receives the raw image as input to perform segmentation and generate pseudo-labels for network $\mathcal{F}_s$. This process is defined as follows:

$$P_i^o = \mathcal{F}_o(X_i; \Theta^o); \quad \widetilde{Y}_i^o = \arg\max(P_i^o). \tag{1}$$

For the shape-aware network $\mathcal{F}_s$, we adopt a simple yet effective method to incorporate shape information: in addition to the raw image, we also feed $\mathcal{F}_s$ the output probability maps of $\mathcal{F}_o$. This enables the network to implicitly capture shape information from the input and ultimately produce more reliable predictions and pseudo-labels. The process for this second network is defined as

$$P_i^s = \mathcal{F}_s([X_i, P_i^o]; \Theta^s); \quad \widetilde{Y}_i^s = \arg\max(P_i^s) \tag{2}$$

where $[\cdot]$ is the concatenation operator.

Finally, the objective loss to optimize the entire semi-supervised framework is the following:

$$\mathcal{L} = \sum_{i=1}^{N} \left(\mathcal{L}_{S1}(P_i^o, Y_i) + \mathcal{L}_{S2}(P_i^s, Y_i) \right) + \lambda \sum_{i=N+1}^{N+M} \left(\mathcal{L}_{U1}(P_i^o, \widetilde{Y}_i^s) + \mathcal{L}_{U2}(P_i^s, \widetilde{Y}_i^o) \right). \tag{3}$$

In this loss, $\mathcal{L}_{S1/2}$ are supervised losses and $\mathcal{L}_{U1/2}$ are unsupervised losses, which will be introduced in the next section. λ is a weight factor balancing the two types of losses. To limit resource consumption and have a fair comparison with other semi-supervised approaches, at inference time, we only use the output of the shape-agnostic network $\mathcal{F}_o$ to obtain the final segmentation prediction.

2.2 Loss Functions

Supervised Loss. The overall supervised loss $\mathcal{L}_S$ combines two separate terms based on the widely used cross-entropy loss $\mathcal{L}_{CE}$ and the proposed local context loss $\mathcal{L}_{LC}$:

$$\mathcal{L}_S = \mathcal{L}_{CE}(P_i, Y_i) + \mathcal{L}_{LC}(P_i, Y_i). \tag{4}$$

The local context loss extends the popular Dice segmentation loss by constraining it to multiple local regions in the image:

$$\mathcal{L}_{LC} = \sum_{k=1}^{K} \sum_{l=1}^{L} \mathcal{L}_{Dice}(P_i^{(k,l)}, Y_i^{(k,l)}). \tag{5}$$

Here, $K \times L$ is the number of local regions obtained by dividing the image. The size of local prediction $P_i^{(k,l)}$ and ground-truth mask $Y_i^{(k,l)}$ is ($h = H/K$, $w = W/L$), and a coordinate (r, s) in these local maps corresponds to position $[h \times (k-1) + r, w \times (l-1) + s]$ in P_i and Y_i.

Compared to the standard Dice loss which maximizes the *global* overlap between the prediction and ground-truth mask, our local context loss gives an equal importance to each local region, which helps the network learn fine-grained shape information. It also has an advantage over the cross-entropy loss which focuses on single-pixel predictions without considering the information of neighboring pixels.

Unsupervised Loss. For unlabeled data, the two parallel networks provide pseudo-labels to each other. For the shape-agnostic network $\mathcal{F}_o$, the pseudo-labels $\tilde{Y}_i^s$ provided by $\mathcal{F}_s$ are relatively more accurate due to the integration of shape information. Therefore, these pseudo-labels are directly used to construct a loss for guiding $\mathcal{F}_o$:

$$\mathcal{L}_{U1} = \mathcal{L}_{CE}(P_i^o, \tilde{Y}_i^s). \tag{6}$$

In comparison, the pseudo-labels provided by $\mathcal{F}_o$ have a lower accuracy. To alleviate this problem, we use an uncertainty estimation strategy based on Monte Carlo Dropout so that $\mathcal{F}_s$ can focus its learning on more reliable pseudo-labels. Specifically, we calculate an uncertainty map to filter out unreliable (high uncertainty) regions, preventing $\mathcal{F}_s$ to learn from noisy information. Then, the unsupervised loss for network $\mathcal{F}_s$ is defined as

$$\mathcal{L}_{U2} = -\frac{1}{H \times W} \sum_{z=1}^{H \times W} \sum_{c=1}^{C} \mathcal{W}_{iz} \tilde{Y}_{iz,c}^o \log P_{iz,c}^s, \tag{7}$$

where $\mathcal{W}_i = \mathbb{I}(U_i < thres)$ is the weight map after thresholding. Here, $\mathbb{I}(\cdot)$ is the indicator function and $thres$ is a given uncertainty threshold.

To get the uncertainty map U_i, we perform K forward passes on $\mathcal{F}_o$ for each input image to obtain a set of temporary predictions $\{P_{ik}^o\}_{k=1}^{K}$. These predictions can then be used to compute U_i based on entropy,

$$P_{im} = \frac{1}{K} \sum_{k=1}^{K} P_{ik}^o; \quad U_i = -\sum_{c=1}^{C} P_{im}^c \log P_{im}^c, \tag{8}$$

where P_{im}^c is the c-th channel of P_{im} and C is the number of classes.

Table 1. DSC (%) and ASSD (mm) with 7 labeled samples on the ACDC test set. Values are the mean (stdev) obtained over three random seeds. $*$ indicates that our method significantly outperforms others with $p < 0.05$.

Method	RV		Myo		LV	
	DSC ↑	ASSD ↓	DSC ↑	ASSD ↓	DSC ↑	ASSD ↓
LS	60.98 (1.93)*	5.52 (1.75)	71.23 (1.68)*	2.74 (0.67)*	77.21 (1.20)*	3.45 (0.88)*
EM	69.46 (1.32)*	3.68 (0.67)	75.32 (1.36)*	2.12 (0.40)*	81.14 (0.61)*	3.00 (0.41)*
MT	66.18 (2.40)*	4.90 (1.11)	74.87 (0.28)*	2.07 (0.20)*	80.38 (1.30)*	2.94 (0.45)*
DAN	69.20 (1.13)*	4.41 (0.59)*	74.97 (0.70)*	2.28 (0.80)	80.03 (1.78)*	2.90 (1.06)
UAMT	68.47 (1.45)*	3.95 (0.81)*	75.14 (0.71)*	2.03 (0.36)*	81.04 (1.16)*	2.67 (0.65)*
ICT	67.10 (2.13)*	3.48 (0.36)*	75.43 (0.62)*	2.07 (0.14)*	81.01 (1.45)*	2.96 (0.31)*
URPC	68.52 (1.88)*	2.73 (0.22)*	74.37 (0.89)*	1.94 (0.25)*	82.41 (2.41)	3.53 (0.67)*
CPS	68.42 (1.02)*	2.81 (0.40)	75.93 (0.90)*	1.80 (0.69)	81.11 (1.94)	2.83 (0.71)
Ours	**78.87** (1.63)	**1.64** (0.53)	**81.06** (0.39)	**0.64** (0.09)	**87.56** (0.82)	**0.89** (0.16)
Baseline	69.33 (1.07)	3.05 (0.41)	76.05 (0.45)	1.49 (0.18)	82.64 (0.40)	2.12 (0.31)
S (w/o. UE)	71.70 (1.30)	3.22 (0.40)	78.51 (1.30)	1.88 (0.22)	83.74 (1.23)	2.26 (0.10)
S + $\mathcal{L}_{Dice}$	72.61 (1.76)	3.82 (1.37)	79.51 (0.80)	1.49 (0.37)	85.20 (0.29)	2.09 (0.55)
S + $\mathcal{L}_{LC}$ (2, 2)	75.01 (1.12)	2.68 (0.42)	80.78 (0.56)	1.23 (0.24)	85.34 (1.38)	2.23 (0.55)
S + $\mathcal{L}_{LC}$ (4, 4)	**78.87** (1.63)	1.64 (0.53)	**81.06** (0.39)	0.64 (0.09)	87.56 (0.82)	0.89 (0.16)
S + $\mathcal{L}_{LC}$ (6, 6)	77.35 (1.50)	**1.43** (0.36)	80.35 (1.68)	**0.62** (0.03)	**87.91** (1.22)	**0.81** (0.13)
S + $\mathcal{L}_{LC}$ (8, 8)	77.17 (1.38)	1.53 (0.20)	80.01 (1.04)	0.77 (0.05)	85.79 (0.48)	1.17 (0.09)
FS	88.24 (0.21)	1.07 (0.17)	87.19 (0.37)	0.48 (0.13)	93.44 (0.27)	0.46 (0.15)

3   Experiments and Results

Datasets and Evaluation Metrics. We evaluate our method on two public benchmarks, the Automated Cardiac Diagnosis Challenge (ACDC) dataset [1] and Prostate MR Image Segmentation (PROMISE12) Challenge dataset [11]. The ACDC dataset contains 200 annotated short-axis cardiac cine-MRI scans from 100 subjects. We randomly selected 140 scans from 70 subjects, 20 scans from 10 subjects, and 40 scans from 20 subjects as training, validation, and test sets, ensuring that each set contains data from *different* subjects. The PROMISE12 dataset contains 50 transverse T2-weighted MRI scans. We randomly divided the data into 35, 5, and 10 cases as training, validation, and test sets. Due to the low cross-slice resolution, and following previous work on the datasets [17], both datasets are segmented in 2D (slice by slice). Each slice is resized to 256×256, and the intensities of pixels are normalized to the [0, 1] range. We use two standard evaluation metrics to measure the accuracy of the predicted 3D segmentation, obtained by stacking the predictions for each 2D slice: Dice Similarity Coefficient (DSC) and Average Symmetric Surface Distance (ASSD).

Implementation Details. All comparisons and ablation experiments are performed using the same experimental setting for a fair comparison. They are conducted on PyTorch using an Intel(R) Xeon(R) CPU and NVIDIA GeForce RTX 2080 Ti GPU. Our training process uses an SGD optimizer with an initial learning rate set to 0.01 and a poly learning rate strategy to update the learning rate. During training, our batch size is set to 24, each batch containing 12 labeled examples and 12 unlabeled examples. Moreover, a data augmentation strategy

Table 2. DSC (%) and ASSD (mm) on the PROMISE12 test set for 7 labeled samples.

N. Labeled	Method	DSC ↑	ASSD ↓
$L = 7$	LS	57.93 (0.89)*	14.08 (0.90)*
	EM	62.16 (2.32)*	10.11 (2.68)
	MT	62.52 (2.18)*	12.24 (2.64)*
	DAN	61.55 (4.57)	11.80 (2.73)*
	UAMT	61.43 (0.30)*	13.94 (1.58)*
	ICT	62.13 (1.40)*	13.81 (3.34)
	URPC	61.55 (1.37)*	9.63 (1.00)*
	CPS	60.32 (2.40)*	19.45 (10.09)
	Ours	**70.30** (1.91)	**4.69** (2.06)
All	FS	84.76 (0.77)	1.58 (0.13)

including random flipping and random rotation is exploited to alleviate overfitting. We adopt U-net [12,18] as our base network, and only add dropout layers with a dropout rate of 0.5 between the encoder and decoder of the network. For estimating uncertainty in the unsupervised loss, we perform $K = 8$ Monte Carlo dropouts. Following [27], hyperparameter λ is set using a time-dependent Gaussian warming up function, $\lambda(t_i) = 0.1 \cdot e^{-5(1-t_i/t_{max})^2}$, where t_i represents the current training iteration, and t_{max} is the maximum number of iterations. The same function is used to increase the uncertainty threshold $thres$ from $0.75 \cdot U_{max}$ to U_{max}, where U_{max} is $\ln(2)$.

Comparison with Other Methods. To verify the effectiveness of our method, we compare it with full/limited supervision (FS/LS) baselines and several state-of-the-art approaches for semi-supervised segmentation, including: (1) Entropy Minimization (EM) [21]; (2) Deep Adversarial Network (DAN) [28]; (3) Mean Teacher (MT) [19]; (4) Uncertainty Aware Mean Teacher (UAMT) [27]; (5) Interpolation Consistency Training (ICT) [20]; (6) Uncertainty Rectified Pyramid Consistency (URPC) [15]; (7) Cross Pseudo Supervision (CPS) [4]. All tested methods use the same experimental configuration and do not employ any post-processing operations at the inference stage. Table 1 and 2 report quantitative results on the ACDC dataset and PROMISE12 dataset, respectively, using only 7 labeled examples for training. Additional results comparing the methods trained with more labeled examples can be found in the supplementary material. As can be seen, our method achieves statistically better performance than other approaches, with paired t-test p < 0.05, for all datasets and performance metrics. Compared with the limited supervision (LS) baseline, our method improves DSC by 17.89%, 9.83% and 10.35% for the RV, Myo and LV classes of the ACDC dataset, respectively, and by 12.37% for prostate segmentation in the PROMISE12 dataset. It also yields considerable improvements compared to state-of-the-art approaches like Cross Pseudo Supervision (CPS), proving its ability to effectively use unsupervised data. Figure 2 provides a visual

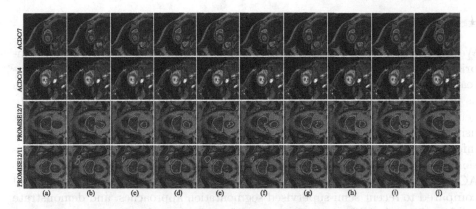

Fig. 2. Visual comparison of different methods for test samples. (a) GT; (b) LS; (c) EM; (d) DAN; (e) MT; (f) UAMT; (g) URPC; (h) ICT; (i) CPS; (j) Ours.

comparison of tested methods on the ACDC and PROMISE12 datasets. We see that our method produces more reliable predictions than other approaches, and better preserves anatomical morphology. As reported in the supplementary material, similar improvements are also obtained by our method when using a different number of labeled examples.

Ablation Study. Table 1 gives the results of ablation experiments performed on the ACDC dataset, showing the effectiveness of adding shape information (S) to the input layer and the benefit of our local context loss with different parameter configurations ($\mathcal{L}_{LC}(K, L)$). When adding shape information to the input layer and using a standard Dice loss (S+$\mathcal{L}_{Dice}$), DSC improves by 3.28%, 3.46% and 2.56% for RV, Myo and LV, respectively, compared to the Baseline (the plain cross-model pseudo-supervision). On the other hand, removing the uncertainty estimation (UE) from the shape-enhanced model decreases this DSC improvement by 0.91%, 1.00% and 1.46% for the same classes. These results show that incorporating shape priors as additional input to a network helps improve accuracy, and that using uncertainty estimation to filter out low-confidence regions can further boost performance. The ablation visualization in the supplementary material also illustrates the benefit of shape priors.

Table 1 also demonstrates the usefulness of our local context loss, $\mathcal{L}_{LC}$. In particular, replacing the standard Dice loss by $\mathcal{L}_{LC}$ with ($K = 4$, $L = 4$) subregions, increases the DSC by 6.26%, 1.55%, and 2.36% for the RV, Myo and LV classes, respectively. This shows the benefit of constraining the loss to local regions on overall performance. And compared to Myo and LV, which are mostly circular, the RV has a more complex and irregular shape (see Fig. 2), thus benefits more from our $\mathcal{L}_{LC}$. The supplementary material provides results for different numbers of labeled examples and visualizations of ablation experiments.

4   Conclusion

We presented a novel framework for semi-supervised image segmentation comprised of two networks that provide pseudo-labels to each other in a cross-teaching strategy: 1) a shape-agnostic network which only receives raw images as input and employs uncertainty estimation based on Monte-Carlo dropout to generate reliable pseudo-labels for the other network; 2) a shape-aware network using prediction of the first network as additional input to incorporate shape information. We also propose a loss term that helps the network learn a precision segmentation in local regions across the image. Experimental results on the ACDC and PROMISE12 datasets show the better performance of our method compared to recent semi-supervised segmentation approaches, and demonstrate the benefit of the different components of our framework.

In some cases, giving an equal importance to each region in the local context loss may not be optimal for learning to segment complex structures. In future work, to further boost accuracy, we will investigate adaptive strategies that assign an importance weight to individual regions. We will also explore other uncertainty estimation approaches to improve the reliability of pseudo-labels.

Acknowledgement. This work is supported by the National Key R&D Plan on Strategic International Scientific and Technological Innovation Cooperation Special Project (No. 2021YFE0203800), the NSFC-Zhejiang Joint Fund of the Integration of Informatization and Industrialization (No. U1909210), the National Natural Science Foundation of China under Grant (No. 62172257, 61902217), the Natural Science Foundation of Shandong Province (ZR2019BF043).

References

1. Bernard, O., et al.: Deep learning techniques for automatic MRI cardiac multi-structures segmentation and diagnosis: is the problem solved? IEEE Trans. Med. Imaging **37**(11), 2514–2525 (2018)
2. Chaitanya, K., Karani, N., Baumgartner, C.F., Becker, A., Donati, O., Konukoglu, E.: Semi-supervised and task-driven data augmentation. In: Chung, A.C.S., Gee, J.C., Yushkevich, P.A., Bao, S. (eds.) IPMI 2019. LNCS, vol. 11492, pp. 29–41. Springer, Cham (2019). https://doi.org/10.1007/978-3-030-20351-1_3
3. Chen, L., Zhang, W., Wu, Y., Strauch, M., Merhof, D.: Semi-supervised instance segmentation with a learned shape prior. In: Cardoso, J., et al. (eds.) IMIMIC/MIL3ID/LABELS -2020. LNCS, vol. 12446, pp. 94–102. Springer, Cham (2020). https://doi.org/10.1007/978-3-030-61166-8_10
4. Chen, X., Yuan, Y., Zeng, G., Wang, J.: Semi-supervised semantic segmentation with cross pseudo supervision. In: Computer Vision Foundation, CVPR 2021, pp. 2613–2622. IEEE (2021)
5. Cui, W., et al.: Semi-supervised brain lesion segmentation with an adapted mean teacher model. In: Chung, A.C.S., Gee, J.C., Yushkevich, P.A., Bao, S. (eds.) IPMI 2019. LNCS, vol. 11492, pp. 554–565. Springer, Cham (2019). https://doi.org/10.1007/978-3-030-20351-1_43

6. Hu, X., Zeng, D., Xu, X., Shi, Y.: Semi-supervised contrastive learning for label-efficient medical image segmentation. In: de Bruijne, M., et al. (eds.) Medical Image Computing and Computer Assisted Intervention – MICCAI 2021: 24th International Conference, Strasbourg, France, September 27–October 1, 2021, Proceedings, Part II, pp. 481–490. Springer, Cham (2021). https://doi.org/10.1007/978-3-030-87196-3_45

7. Huang, H., et al.: 3D graph-S^2Net: shape-aware self-ensembling network for semi-supervised segmentation with bilateral graph convolution. In: de Bruijne, M., et al. (eds.) MICCAI 2021. LNCS, vol. 12902, pp. 416–427. Springer, Cham (2021). https://doi.org/10.1007/978-3-030-87196-3_39

8. Isensee, F., Jaeger, P.F., Kohl, S.A., Petersen, J., Maier-Hein, K.H.: nnU-Net: a self-configuring method for deep learning-based biomedical image segmentation. Nat. Meth. **18**(2), 203–211 (2021)

9. Li, K., Hariharan, B., Malik, J.: Iterative instance segmentation. In: CVPR 2016, pp. 3659–3667. IEEE Computer Society (2016)

10. Li, S., Zhang, C., He, X.: Shape-aware semi-supervised 3D semantic segmentation for medical images. In: Martel, A.L., et al. (eds.) MICCAI 2020. LNCS, vol. 12261, pp. 552–561. Springer, Cham (2020). https://doi.org/10.1007/978-3-030-59710-8_54

11. Litjens, G., et al.: Evaluation of prostate segmentation algorithms for MRI: the PROMISE12 challenge. Med. Image Anal. **18**(2), 359–373 (2014)

12. Luo, X.: SSL4MIS (2020). https://github.com/HiLab-git/SSL4MIS

13. Luo, X., Chen, J., Song, T., Wang, G.: Semi-supervised medical image segmentation through dual-task consistency. In: AAAI 2021, pp. 8801–8809. AAAI Press (2021)

14. Luo, X., Hu, M., Song, T., Wang, G., Zhang, S.: Semi-supervised medical image segmentation via cross teaching between CNN and transformer. CoRR abs/2112.04894 (2021)

15. Luo, X., et al.: Efficient semi-supervised gross target volume of nasopharyngeal carcinoma segmentation via uncertainty rectified pyramid consistency. In: de Bruijne, M., et al. (eds.) MICCAI 2021. LNCS, vol. 12902, pp. 318–329. Springer, Cham (2021). https://doi.org/10.1007/978-3-030-87196-3_30

16. Milletari, F., Navab, N., Ahmadi, S.A.: V-Net: fully convolutional neural networks for volumetric medical image segmentation. In: 2016 4th International Conference on 3D Vision (3DV), pp. 565–571. IEEE (2016)

17. Peng, J., Wang, P., Desrosiers, C., Pedersoli, M.: Self-paced contrastive learning for semi-supervised medical image segmentation with meta-labels. In: Advances in Neural Information Processing Systems 34 (2021)

18. Ronneberger, O., Fischer, P., Brox, T.: U-Net: convolutional networks for biomedical image segmentation. In: Navab, N., Hornegger, J., Wells, W.M., Frangi, A.F. (eds.) MICCAI 2015. LNCS, vol. 9351, pp. 234–241. Springer, Cham (2015). https://doi.org/10.1007/978-3-319-24574-4_28

19. Tarvainen, A., Valpola, H.: Mean teachers are better role models: weight-averaged consistency targets improve semi-supervised deep learning results. In: Guyon, I., et al. (eds.) NIPS 2017, pp. 1195–1204 (2017)

20. Verma, V., et al.: Interpolation consistency training for semi-supervised learning. Neural Netw. **145**, 90–106 (2022)

21. Vu, T., Jain, H., Bucher, M., Cord, M., Pérez, P.: ADVENT: adversarial entropy minimization for domain adaptation in semantic segmentation. In: CVPR 2019, pp. 2517–2526. Computer Vision Foundation/IEEE (2019)

22. Wang, G., et al.: Semi-supervised segmentation of radiation-induced pulmonary fibrosis from lung CT scans with multi-scale guided dense attention. IEEE Trans. Med. Imaging **41**, 531–542 (2021)
23. Wang, K., et al.: Tripled-uncertainty guided mean teacher model for semi-supervised medical image segmentation. In: de Bruijne, M., et al. (eds.) MICCAI 2021. LNCS, vol. 12902, pp. 450–460. Springer, Cham (2021). https://doi.org/10.1007/978-3-030-87196-3_42
24. Wang, P., Peng, J., Pedersoli, M., Zhou, Y., Zhang, C., Desrosiers, C.: Context-aware virtual adversarial training for anatomically-plausible segmentation. In: de Bruijne, M., et al. (eds.) MICCAI 2021. LNCS, vol. 12901, pp. 304–314. Springer, Cham (2021). https://doi.org/10.1007/978-3-030-87193-2_29
25. Wang, P., Peng, J., Pedersoli, M., Zhou, Y., Zhang, C., Desrosiers, C.: Self-paced and self-consistent co-training for semi-supervised image segmentation. Med. Image Anal. **73**, 102146 (2021)
26. Xia, Y., et al.: Uncertainty-aware multi-view co-training for semi-supervised medical image segmentation and domain adaptation. Med. Image Anal. **65**, 101766 (2020)
27. Yu, L., Wang, S., Li, X., Fu, C.-W., Heng, P.-A.: Uncertainty-aware self-ensembling model for semi-supervised 3D left atrium segmentation. In: Shen, D., et al. (eds.) MICCAI 2019. LNCS, vol. 11765, pp. 605–613. Springer, Cham (2019). https://doi.org/10.1007/978-3-030-32245-8_67
28. Zhang, Y., Yang, L., Chen, J., Fredericksen, M., Hughes, D.P., Chen, D.Z.: Deep adversarial networks for biomedical image segmentation utilizing unannotated images. In: Descoteaux, M., Maier-Hein, L., Franz, A., Jannin, P., Collins, D.L., Duchesne, S. (eds.) MICCAI 2017. LNCS, vol. 10435, pp. 408–416. Springer, Cham (2017). https://doi.org/10.1007/978-3-319-66179-7_47

MUSCLE: Multi-task Self-supervised Continual Learning to Pre-train Deep Models for X-Ray Images of Multiple Body Parts

Weibin Liao[1], Haoyi Xiong[1(✉)] [iD], Qingzhong Wang[1], Yan Mo[1], Xuhong Li[1], Yi Liu[1], Zeyu Chen[1], Siyu Huang[2], and Dejing Dou[1]

[1] Baidu, Inc., Beijing, China
xionghaoyi@baidu.com
[2] Harvard University, Cambridge, MA, USA

Abstract. While self-supervised learning (SSL) algorithms have been widely used to pre-train deep models, few efforts [11] have been done to improve representation learning of X-ray image analysis with SSL pre-trained models. In this work, we study a novel self-supervised pre-training pipeline, namely *Multi-task Self-super-vised Continual Learning* (MUSCLE), for multiple medical imaging tasks, such as classification and segmentation, using X-ray images collected from multiple body parts, including heads, lungs, and bones. Specifically, MUSCLE aggregates X-rays collected from multiple body parts for MoCo-based representation learning, and adopts a well-designed continual learning (CL) procedure to further pre-train the backbone subject various X-ray analysis tasks jointly. Certain strategies for image pre-processing, learning schedules, and regularization have been used to solve *data heterogeneity, over-fitting,* and *catastrophic forgetting* problems for multi-task/dataset learning in MUSCLE. We evaluate MUSCLE using 9 real-world X-ray datasets with various tasks, including pneumonia classification, skeletal abnormality classification, lung segmentation, and tuberculosis (TB) detection. Comparisons against other pre-trained models [7] confirm the *proof-of-concept* that self-supervised multi-task/dataset continual pre-training could boost the performance of X-ray image analysis.

Keywords: X-ray images (X-ray) · Self-supervised learning

1 Introduction

While deep learning-based solutions [1] have achieved great success in medical image analysis, such as X-ray image classification and segmentation tasks for

_____

Supplementary Information The online version contains supplementary material available at https://doi.org/10.1007/978-3-031-16452-1_15.

L. Wang et al. (Eds.): MICCAI 2022, LNCS 13438, pp. 151–161, 2022.
https://doi.org/10.1007/978-3-031-16452-1_15

diseases in bones, lungs and heads, it might require an extremely large number of images with fine annotations to train the deep neural network (DNN) models and deliver decent performance [2] in a supervised learning manner. To lower the sample size required, the self-supervised learning (SSL) paradigm has been recently proposed to boost the performance of DNN models through learning visual features from images [3] without using labels.

Among a wide range of SSL methods, contrastive learning [4] algorithms use a similarity-based metric to measure the distance between two embeddings derived from two different views of a single image, where the views of image are generated through data augmentation, e.g., rotation, clip, and shift, and embeddings are extracted from the DNN with learnable parameters. In particular, for computer vision tasks, the contrastive loss is computed using the feature representations of the images extracted from the encoder network, resulting in the clustering of similar samples together and the dispersal of different samples. Recent methods such as SwAV [5], SimCLR [6], MoCo [7], and PILR [8] have been proposed to outperform supervised learning methods on natural images. While contrastive learning methods have demonstrated promising results on natural image classification tasks, the attempts to leverage them in medical image analysis are often limited [9,10]. While Sowrirajan et al. [11] proposed MoCo-CXR that can produce models with better representations for the detection of pathologies in chest X-rays using MoCo [7], the superiority of SSL for *other X-ray analysis tasks, such as detection and segmentation, on various body parts, such as lung and bones, is not yet known.*

Our Contributions. In this work, we proposed MUSCLE–*MUlti-task Self-supervised Continual LEarning* (shown in Fig. 1) that pre-trains deep models using X-ray images collected from multiple body parts subject to various tasks, and made contributions as follow.

1. We study the problem of multi-dataset/multi-task SSL for X-ray images. To best of our knowledge, only few works have been done in related area [11,12], especially by addressing *data heterogeneity* (e.g., image sizes, resolutions, and gray-scale distributions), *over-fitting* (e.g., to any one of the tasks), and *catastrophic forgetting* (e.g., ejection of knowledge learned previously) in multi-dataset/multi-task learning settings.
2. We present MUSCLE that pre-trains the backbone in multi-dataset/multi-task learning settings with task-specific heads, including Fully-Connected (FC) Layer, DeepLab-V3 [13], and FasterRCNN [14] for classification, segmentation, and abnormal detection tasks respectively. As shown in Fig. 1, MUSCLE (1) adopts MoCo to learn representations with a backbone network from multiple datasets, with pre-processing to tackle *data heterogeneity*, and further (2) pre-trains the backbone to learn discriminative features with continual learning (CL) subject to multiple tasks, while avoiding over-fitting and "catastrophic forgetting" [15,16]. MUSCLE finally (3) fine-tunes the pre-trained backbone to adapt every task independently and separately.

3. In this work, we collect 9 X-ray datasets to evaluate MUSCLE, where we pretrain and fine-tune the network to adapt all tasks using training subsets, and validate the performance using testing subsets. The experimental results show MUSCLE outperforms ImageNet/MoCo pre-trained backbones [11] using both ResNet-18 and ResNet-50 as backbones. The comparisons confirm the *proof-of-concept* of MUSCLE–self-supervised multi-task/dataset continual pre-training can boost performance of X-ray image analysis.

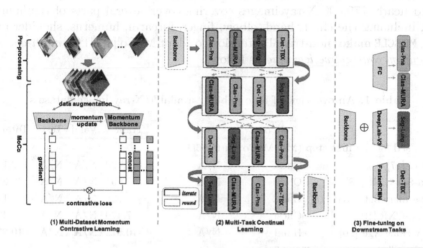

Fig. 1. The pipeline of MUSCLE, consists of three parts (1) Multi-Dataset Momentum Contrastive (Multi-Dataset MoCo) Learning, (2) Multi-Task Continual Learning and (3) Fine-tuning on Downstream Tasks.

2   Methodologies

In this section, we present the framework and algorithms design for MUSCLE. As was shown in Fig. 1, MUSCLE consists of three steps as follows.

1. *Multi-dataset momentum contrastive learning.* (MD-MoCo)   Give multiple datasets of X-ray images collected from different body parts and based on different image resolution and gray-scale distributions, MUSCLE aggregates these datasets with pre-processing (e.g., resize, re-scale, and normalization), then adopts a MoCo-based SSL algorithm [11] to pre-train the backbone networks and learn the representation of X-ray images within the aggregated dataset.
2. *Multi-task continual learning.* Given the MD-MoCo pre-trained backbone and the datasets for different X-ray analysis tasks, e.g., pneumonia classification, skeletal abnormality classification, and lung segmentation, MUSCLE leverages continual learning algorithms and further pre-trains a unified backbone network with alternating heads to learn the various sets of discriminative features subject to the different tasks.

3. *Fine-tuning with downstream tasks.* Given the pre-trained backbone and every downstream X-ray image analysis task, MUSCLE fine-tunes and outputs a neural network using pre-trained weights as the initialization and its own task-specific head to fit the task independently.

2.1   Multi-Dataset Momentum Contrastive Learning (MD-MoCo)

To pre-train the backbone with multiple datasets, MUSCLE collects and aggregates nine X-ray image datasets listed in Table 1. While these datasets have offered nearly 179,000 X-ray images covering cover several parts of the human body, including the chest, hand, elbow, finger, forearm, humerus, shoulder and wrist, MUSCLE makes non-trivial extension to adopt MoCo [4, 11] for *multi-dataset momentum contrastive learning* as follows.

Table 1. An overview of nine publicly available X-ray image datasets

Datasets	Body part	Task	Train	Valid	Test	Total
Only Used for the first step (MD-MoCo) of MUSCLE						
NIHCC [17]	Chest	N/A	112,120	N/A	N/A	112,120
China-Set-CXR [18]	Chest	N/A	661	N/A	N/A	661
Montgomery-Set-CXR [18]	Chest	N/A	138	N/A	N/A	138
Indiana-CXR [19]	Chest	N/A	7,470	N/A	N/A	7,470
RSNA Bone Age [20]	Hand	N/A	10,811	N/A	N/A	10,811
Used for all three steps of MUSCLE						
Pneumonia [21]	Chest	Classification	4,686	585	585	5,856
MURA [22]	Various Bones	Classification	32,013	3,997	3,995	40,005
Chest Xray Masks [18]	Chest	Segmentation	718	89	89	896
TBX [23]	Chest	Detection	640	80	80	800
Total	N/A	N/A	169,257	4,751	4,749	178,757

Re-sizing, Re-scaling, Normalization, and Aggregation. The major challenge to work with multiple X-ray image datasets collected from different body part is the heterogeneity of images, including X-ray image resolutions and the distribution of gray-scales. To aggregate these datasets, several image pre-processing schemes have been used, where MUSCLE transforms and normalizes the gray-scale distribution of these datasets using the Z-score method with the mean of 122.786 and a standard deviation of 18.390. Further to fully utilize GPU for the resource-consuming MoCo algorithms, MUSCLE re-sizes all images into a 800 × 500 resolution which balances the effectiveness and efficiency of deep learning.

MoCo-Based Pre-training with Aggregated Datasets. To utilize MoCo algorithm [4] for X-ray images pre-training, MUSCLE further extends MoCo-CXR [11] with advanced settings on data augmentation strategies and initialization tricks. Specifically, while MoCo uses random data augmentation to generate contrastive views, MUSCLE disables random cropping, gaussian blurring, color/gray-scale jittering to preserve the semantic information for medical images. Furthermore, MUSCLE initializes the MoCo-based pre-training procedure with Kaiming's initialization [24] to setup the convolution layers, so as to ensure the stability of back-propagation in contrastive learning.

Note that, in this work, the training sets of all nine datasets have been used for *multi-dataset momentum contrastive learning*, while four of them with specific X-ray image analysis tasks are further used for *multi-task continual learning*.

2.2   Multi-task Continual Learning

To further pre-train the backbone subject to task-specific representations, MUSCLE adopts the continual learning (CL) [25] with four X-ray image analysis tasks, including pneumonia classification from Pneumonia [21], skeletal abnormality classification from MURA [22], lung segmentation from Chest Xray Masks and Labels [18], and Tuberculosis(TB) detection from TBX [23]. Specifically, MUSCLE extends the vanilla CL for neural network, which iterates the training procedures of the backbone network with alternating task-specific heads subject to tasks, with two major advancements as follows.

Cyclic and Reshuffled Learning Schedule.   MUSCLE splits the continual learning procedure into 10 **rounds** of learning process, where each round of learning process **iterates** the 4 learning tasks one-by-one and each iterate of learning task trains the backbone network with 1 epoch using a task-specific head, i.e., Fully-Connected (FC) Layer for classification tasks, DeepLab-V3 [13] for segmentation tasks, and FasterRCNN [14] for detection tasks. Furthermore, to avoid overfitting to any task, MUSCLE reshuffle the order of tasks in every round of learning process, and adopts Cosine annealing learning rate schedule as follow.

$$\eta_t = \eta_{\min}^i + \frac{1}{2}\left(\eta_{\max} - \eta_{\min}\right)\left(1 + \cos\left(\frac{t}{T}\cdot 2\pi\right)\right) \tag{1}$$

where η_t refers to the learning rate of the tth iteration, $\eta_{\max}$ and $\eta_{\min}$ and T_i refer to the maximal and minimal learning rates, and T refers to the total number of iterations within a period of cyclic learning rate schedule.

Cross-Task Memorization with Explicit Bias.   Yet another challenge of multi-task CL is "catastrophic forgetting", where the backbone would "forget" the knowledge learned from the previous iterates. To solve the problem, MUSCLE leverages a knowledge transfer regularization derived from L^2-SP [15]. In each iterate of learning task, given the pre-trained model obtained from previous iterates, MUSCLE sets the pre-trained weights as w_S^0 and trains the backbone using the following loss, where w_S is the learning outcome and α is the hyper-parameter.

$$\Omega(\boldsymbol{w}_S) = \underbrace{\alpha \left\| \boldsymbol{w}_S - \boldsymbol{w}_S^0 \right\|_2^2}_{\text{outcome of CL}} + \underbrace{(1-\alpha) \left\| \boldsymbol{w}_S \right\|_2^2}_{\text{pre-trained by previous iterates}} \qquad (2)$$

distance to the model pre-trained by previous iterates.

Ridge-based regularization.

Thus, above regularization constrains the distance between the learning outcome and the backbone trained by the previous iterates.

2.3 Fine-Tuning on Downstream Tasks

Finally, given the backbone pre-trained using above two steps, MUSCLE fine-tunes the backbone on each of the four tasks independent and separately. Again, MUSCLE connects the pre-trained backbone with Fully-Connected (FC) Layer for classification tasks, DeepLab-V3 [13] for segmentation tasks, and Faster-RCNN [14] for detection tasks. Finally, MUSCLE employs the standard settings, such as vanilla weight decay as stability regularization and step-based decay of learning rate schedule, for such fine-tuning.

Table 2. Performance comparisons for pneumonia classification (pneumonia) and skeletal abnormality classification (MURA) using various pre-training algorithms.

Datasets	Backbones	Pre-train	Acc.	Sen.	Spe.	AUC (95%CI)
Pneumonia	ResNet-18	Scratch	91.11	93.91	83.54	96.58 (95.09–97.81)
		ImageNet	90.09	93.68	80.38	96.05 (94.24–97.33)
		MD-MoCo	96.58	97.19	94.94	98.48 (97.14–99.30)
		MUSCLE⁻⁻	96.75	**97.66**	94.30	99.51 (99.16–99.77)
		MUSCLE	**97.26**	97.42	**96.84**	**99.61 (99.32–99.83)**
	ResNet-50	Scratch	91.45	92.51	88.61	96.55 (95.08–97.82)
		ImageNet	95.38	95.78	94.30	98.72 (98.03–99.33)
		MD-MoCo	97.09	**98.83**	92.41	99.53 (99.23–99.75)
		MUSCLE⁻⁻	96.75	98.36	92.41	99.58 (99.30–99.84)
		MUSCLE	**98.12**	98.36	**97.47**	**99.72 (99.46–99.92)**
MURA	ResNet-18	Scratch	81.00	68.17	**89.91**	86.62 (85.73–87.55)
		ImageNet	81.88	73.49	87.70	88.11 (87.18–89.03)
		MD-MoCo	82.48	72.27	89.57	88.28 (87.28–89.26)
		MUSCLE⁻⁻	82.45	74.16	88.21	88.41 (87.54–89.26)
		MUSCLE	**82.62**	**74.28**	88.42	**88.50 (87.46–89.57)**
	ResNet-50	Scratch	80.50	65.42	90.97	86.22 (85.22–87.35)
		ImageNet	81.73	68.36	**91.01**	87.87 (86.85–88.85)
		MD-MoCo	82.35	73.12	88.76	87.89 (87.06–88.88)
		MUSCLE⁻⁻	81.10	69.03	89.48	87.14 (86.10–88.22)
		MUSCLE	**82.60**	**74.53**	88.21	**88.37 (87.38–89.32)**

3   Experiment

In this section, we present our experimental results to confirm the effectiveness of MUSCLE on various tasks.

Experiment Setups. In this experiments, we include performance comparisons on pneumonia classification (Pneumonia) [21], skeletal abnormality classification (MURA) [22], lung segmentation (Lung) [18], and tuberculosis detection (TBX) [23] tasks. We use the training sets of these datasets/tasks to pre-train and fine-tune the network with MUSCLE or other baseline algorithms, tune the hyper-parameters using validation sets, and report results on testing datasets.

As the goal of MUSCLE is to pre-train backbones under multi-task/dataset settings, we propose several baselines for comparisons as follows. **Scratch**: the models are all initialized using Kaiming's random initialization [24] and fine-tuned on the target datasets (introduced in Sect. 2.3). **ImageNet**: the models are initialized using the officially-released weights pre-trained by the ImageNet dataset and fine-tuned on the target datasets. **MD-MoCo**: the models are pre-trained using *multi-dataset MoCo* (introduced in Sect. 2.2) and fine-tuned accordingly; we believe MD-MoCo is one of our proposed methods and can prove the concepts,

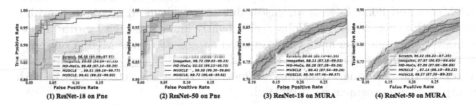

(1) ResNet-18 on Pne   (2) ResNet-50 on Pne   (3) ResNet-18 on MURA   (4) ResNet-50 on MURA

Fig. 2. Receiver Operating Characteristic (ROC) Curves with AUC value (95%CI) on pneumonia classification (Pne) and skeletal abnormality classification (MURA)

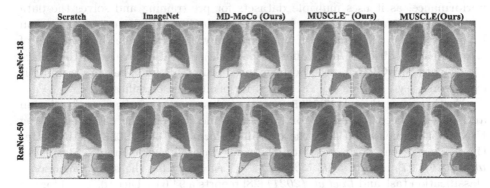

Fig. 3. Results using various pre-training algorithms on lung segmentation, where green lines indicate ground truth and red areas indicate model prediction results, and the blue and orange boxes cover regions of the main differences in these results. (Color figure online)

as MD-MoCo extends both vanilla MoCo [7] and MoCo-CXR [11] with additional data pre-processing methods to tackle the multi-dataset issues. MUSCLE^{--}: all models are pre-trained and fine-tuned with MUSCLE but with *Cross-Task Memorization* and *Cyclic and Reshuffled Learning Schedule* turned off. All models here are built with ResNet-18 and ResNet-50.

To compare these algorithms, we evaluate and compare *Accuracy* (Acc.), *Area under the Curve* (AUC), *Sensitivity* (Sen.), *Specificity* (Sep.) and *Receiver Operating Characteristic (ROC) Curve* for Pneumonia and MURA classification tasks, *Dice Similarity Coefficient* (Dice), *mean Intersection over Union* (mIoU) for lung segmentation (Lung) task, and *mean Average Precision* (mAP), *Average Precision of Active TB* (AP_{active}) and *Average Precision of Latent TB* (AP_{latent}) for tuberculosis detection (TBX), all of them at the IoU threshold of 0.5. AUC values are reported with 95% confidence intervals estimated through bootstrapping with 100 independent trials on testing sets.

Overall Comparisons. We present the results on Pneumonia and MURA classification tasks in Table 2 and Fig. 2, where we compare the performance of MUSCLE with all baseline algorithms and plot the ROC curve. Results show that our proposed methods, including MUSCLE, MUSCLE^{--} and MD-MoCo can significantly outperform the one based on ImageNet pre-trained models and Scratch. Furthermore, in terms of overall accuracy (Acc. and AUC), MUSCLE outperforms MD-MoCo and MUSCLE^{--} in all cases, due to its advanced continual learning settings. However, we can still observe a slightly lower sensitivity on the Pneumonia classification task and a slightly lower specificity on the MURA delivered by MUSCLE. Similar observations could be found in Table 3 and Fig. 3, where we report the performance on lung segmentation and TB detection tasks with examples of lung segmentation plotted.

More Comparisons. Please note that MD-MoCo indeed surpasses **MoCo** [7] and **MoCo-CXR** [11] (state of the art in X-rays pre-training), in terms of performance, as it uses multiple datasets for pre-training and solves the data heterogeneity problem (the performance of MoCo might be even worse than ImageNet-based pre-training, if we don't unify the gray-scale distributions of X-ray images collected from different datasets). We also have tried to replace MoCo with **SimCLR** [6], the performance of SimCLR for X-ray pre-training is even worse, e.g., 87.52% (9.57%↓) Acc. for pneumonia classification.

Furthermore, though MUSCLE is proposed as a *"proof-of-concept"* solution and has not been optimized for any single medical imaging task, e.g., using U-Net for segmentation [26], the overall performance of MUSCLE is still better than many recent works based on the same datasets. For example, *Stephen et al. (2019)* [27] reports a 93.73% (4.42%↓) accuracy for the same pneumonia classification task and *Li et al. (2021)* [28] reports a 94.64% Dice (0.73%↓) for the lung segmentation. For MURA, *Bozorgtabar et al. (2020)* [29] reports an AUC of 82.45% (6.05%↓), while *Liu et al. (2020)* [23] reports a 58.70% (4.76%↓) AP_{active} and a 9.60% (2.61%↓) AP_{latent} for TBX based on FasterRNN. The advantages of MUSCLE demonstrate the feasibility of using multiple tasks/datasets to pre-train the backbone with SSL and CL. For more results, please refer to the appendix.

Ablation Studies. The comparisons between Scratch versus MD-MoCo, between MD-MoCo versus MUSCLE⁻⁻, and between MUSCLE⁻⁻ versus MUSCLE confirm the contributions made by each step of our algorithms. Frankly speaking, in many cases, MD-MoCo achieved the most performance improvement (compared to ImageNet or Scratch), while continual learning without *Cyclic & Reshuffled Learning Schedule* and *Cross-Task Memorization* may even make MUSCLE⁻⁻ performs worse, due to over-fitting or catastrophic forgetting. However, MUSCLE, pipelining MD-MoCo and advanced continual learning strategies, successfully defends her dominant position and outperforms other algorithms in most cases.

Table 3. Performance comparisons for lung segmentation (lung) and TB Detection (TBX) using various pre-training algorithms.

Backbones	Pre-train	Lung		TBX		
		Dice	mIoU	mAP	AP_{Active}	AP_{Latent}
ResNet-18	Scratch	95.24	94.00	30.71	56.71	4.72
	ImageNet	95.26	94.10	29.46	56.27	2.66
	MD-MoCo	95.31	94.14	36.00	**67.17**	4.84
	MUSCLE⁻⁻	95.14	93.90	34.70	63.43	5.97
	MUSCLE	**95.37**	**94.22**	**36.71**	64.84	**8.59**
ResNet-50	Scratch	93.52	92.03	23.93	44.85	3.01
	ImageNet	93.77	92.43	35.61	58.81	12.42
	MD-MoCo	04.33	93.04	36.78	**04.37**	9.18
	MUSCLE⁻⁻	95.04	93.82	35.14	57.32	**12.97**
	MUSCLE	**95.27**	**94.10**	**37.83**	63.46	12.21

4   Discussion and Conclusion

In this work, we present MUSCLE a self-supervised continual learning pipeline that pre-trains deep neural networks using multiple X-ray image datasets collected from different body parts, e.g., hands, chests, bones and etc., for multiple X-ray analysis tasks, e.g., TB detection, lung segmentation, and skeletal abnormality classification. MUSCLE proposes *multi-dataset momentum contrastive learning* (MD-MoCo) and *multi-task continual learning* to tackle the data heterogeneity, over-fitting, and catastrophic forgetting problems in pre-training, and finally fine-tunes the network to adapt every task independently and separately. Experiment results on 9 X-ray image datasets show MUSCLE outperforms other pre-training methods, including ImageNet-based and MoCo-based [11] solutions. We do acknowledge that MUSCLE might NOT be an optimized solution for any specific task in this study, we however claim MUSCLE as a *"proof-of-concept"* that demonstrates the feasibility of using multiple datasets/tasks to pre-train X-ray models with advanced strategies of self-supervised continual learning.

References

1. LeCun, Y., Bengio, Y., Hinton, G.: Deep learning. Nature **521**(7553), 436–444 (2015)
2. Balki, I., et al.: Sample-size determination methodologies for machine learning in medical imaging research: a systematic review. Can. Assoc. Radiol. J. **70**(4), 344–353 (2019)
3. Jing, L., Tian, Y.: Self-supervised visual feature learning with deep neural networks: a survey. IEEE Trans. Pattern Anal. Mach. Intell. **43**(11), 4037–4058 (2020)
4. Chen, T., Kornblith, S., Norouzi, M., Hinton, G.: A simple framework for contrastive learning of visual representations. In: International Conference on Machine Learning, pp. 1597–1607. PMLR (2020)
5. Caron, M., Misra, I., Mairal, J., Goyal, P., Bojanowski, P., Joulin, A.: Unsupervised learning of visual features by contrasting cluster assignments. In: Advances in Neural Information Processing Systems, vol. 33, pp. 9912–9924 (2020)
6. Chen, T., Kornblith, S., Norouzi, M., Hinton, G.: A simple framework for contrastive learning of visual representations. arXiv:2002.05709 (2020)
7. He, K., Fan, H., Wu, Y., Xie, S., Girshick, R.: Momentum contrast for unsupervised visual representation learning. In: Proceedings of the IEEE/CVF Conference on Computer Vision and Pattern Recognition, pp. 9729–9738. IEEE (2020)
8. Misra, I., Maaten, L.V.D.: Self-supervised learning of pretext-invariant representations. In: Proceedings of the IEEE/CVF Conference on Computer Vision and Pattern Recognition, pp. 6707–6717. IEEE (2020)
9. Maithra, R., Chiyuan, Z., Jon, K., Samy B.: Transfusion: understanding transfer learning for medical imaging. arXiv:1902.07208 (2019)
10. Cheplygina, V., de Bruijne, M., Pluim, J.P.: Not-so-supervised: a survey of semi-supervised, multi-instance, and transfer learning in medical image analysis. Med. Image Anal. **54**, 280–296 (2019)
11. Sowrirajan, H., Yang, J., Ng, A.Y., Rajpurkar, P.: MoCo pretraining improves representation and transferability of chest X-ray models. In: Medical Imaging with Deep Learning, pp. 728–744. PMLR (2021)
12. Memmel, M., Gonzalez, C., Mukhopadhyay, A.: Adversarial continual learning for multi-domain hippocampal segmentation. In: Albarqouni, S., et al. (eds.) DART/FAIR -2021. LNCS, vol. 12968, pp. 35–45. Springer, Cham (2021). https://doi.org/10.1007/978-3-030-87722-4_4
13. Chen, L.C., Papandreou, G., Schroff, F., Adam, H.: Rethinking atrous convolution for semantic image segmentation. arXiv:1706.05587 (2017)
14. Girshick, R.: Fast R-CNN. In: Proceedings of the IEEE International Conference on Computer Vision, pp. 1440–1448 (2015)
15. Xuhong, L.I., Grandvalet, Y., Davoine, F.: Explicit inductive bias for transfer learning with convolutional networks. In: International Conference on Machine Learning, pp. 2825–2834. PMLR (2018)
16. Gotmare, A., Keskar, N.S., Xiong, C., Socher, R.: A closer look at deep learning heuristics: learning rate restarts, warmup and distillation. arXiv:1810.13243 (2018)
17. Wang, X., Peng, Y., Lu, L., Lu, Z., Bagheri, M., Summers, R.M.: ChestX-ray8: hospital-scale chest X-ray database and benchmarks on weakly-supervised classification and localization of common thorax diseases. In: Proceedings of the IEEE Conference on Computer Vision and Pattern Recognition, pp. 2097–2106. IEEE (2017)

18. Jaeger, S., Candemir, S., Antani, S., Wáng, Y.X.J., Lu, P.X., Thoma, G.: Two public chest X-ray datasets for computer-aided screening of pulmonary diseases. Quant. Imaging Med. Surg. **4**(6), 475 (2014)

19. Demner-Fushman, D., et al.: Preparing a collection of radiology examinations for distribution and retrieval. J. Am. Med. Inform. Assoc. **23**(2), 304–310 (2016)

20. Halabi, S.S., et al.: The RSNA pediatric bone age machine learning challenge. Radiology **290**(2), 498–503 (2019)

21. Kermany, D.S., et al.: Identifying medical diagnoses and treatable diseases by image-based deep learning. Cell **172**(5), 1122–1131 (2018)

22. Rajpurkar, P., et al.: MURA: large dataset for abnormality detection in musculoskeletal radiographs. arXiv:1712.06957 (2017)

23. Liu, Y., Wu, Y.H., Ban, Y., Wang, H., Cheng, M.M.: Rethinking computer-aided tuberculosis diagnosis. In: Proceedings of the IEEE/CVF Conference on Computer Vision and Pattern Recognition, pp. 2646–2655. IEEE (2020)

24. He, K., Zhang, X., Ren, S., Sun, J.: Delving deep into rectifiers: surpassing human-level performance on ImageNet classification. In: Proceedings of the IEEE International Conference on Computer Vision, pp. 1026–1034. IEEE (2015)

25. Parisi, G.I., Kemker, R., Part, J.L., Kanan, C., Wermter, S.: Continual lifelong learning with neural networks: a review. Neural Netw. **113**, 54–71 (2019)

26. Ronneberger, O., Fischer, P., Brox, T.: U-Net: convolutional networks for biomedical image segmentation. In: Navab, N., Hornegger, J., Wells, W.M., Frangi, A.F. (eds.) MICCAI 2015. LNCS, vol. 9351, pp. 234–241. Springer, Cham (2015). https://doi.org/10.1007/978-3-319-24574-4_28

27. Stephen, O., Sain, M., Maduh, U.J., Jeong, D.U.: An efficient deep learning approach to pneumonia classification in healthcare. J. Healthc. Eng. **2019** (2019)

28. Li, D., Yang, J., Kreis, K., Torralba, A., Fidler, S.: Semantic segmentation with generative models: semi supervised learning and strong out-of-domain generalization. In: Proceedings of the IEEE/CVF Conference on Computer Vision and Pattern Recognition, pp. 8300–8311. IEEE (2021)

29. Bozorgtabar, B., Mahapatra, D., Vray, G., Thiran, J.-P.: SALAD: self-supervised aggregation learning for anomaly detection on X-rays. In: Martel, A.L., et al. (eds.) MICCAI 2020. LNCS, vol. 12261, pp. 468–478. Springer, Cham (2020). https://doi.org/10.1007/978-3-030-59710-8_46

ShapePU: A New PU Learning Framework Regularized by Global Consistency for Scribble Supervised Cardiac Segmentation

Ke Zhang and Xiahai Zhuang[✉]

School of Data Science, Fudan University, Shanghai, China
zxh@fudan.edu.cn
https://www.sdspeople.fudan.edu.cn/zhuangxiahai

Abstract. Cardiac segmentation is an essential step for the diagnosis of cardiovascular diseases. However, pixel-wise dense labeling is both costly and time-consuming. Scribble, as a form of sparse annotation, is more accessible than full annotations. However, it's particularly challenging to train a segmentation network with weak supervision from scribbles. To tackle this problem, we propose a new scribble-guided method for cardiac segmentation, based on the Positive-Unlabeled (PU) learning framework and global consistency regularization, and termed as *ShapePU*. To leverage unlabeled pixels via PU learning, we first present an Expectation-Maximization (EM) algorithm to estimate the proportion of each class in the unlabeled pixels. Given the estimated ratios, we then introduce the marginal probability maximization to identify the classes of unlabeled pixels. To exploit shape knowledge, we apply cutout operations to training images, and penalize the inconsistent segmentation results. Evaluated on two open datasets, *i.e.*, ACDC and MSCMRseg, our scribble-supervised ShapePU surpassed the fully supervised approach respectively by 1.4% and 9.8% in average Dice, and outperformed the state-of-the-art weakly supervised and PU learning methods by large margins. Our code is available at https://github.com/BWGZK/ShapePU.

Keywords: Weakly supervised learning · PU learning · Segmentation

1 Introduction

Curating a large scale of fully annotated dataset is burdensome, particularly in the field of medical image analysis. However, most of advanced segmentation

This work was funded by the National Natural Science Foundation of China (grant no. 61971142, 62111530195 and 62011540404) and the development fund for Shanghai talents (no. 2020015).

Supplementary Information The online version contains supplementary material available at https://doi.org/10.1007/978-3-031-16452-1_16.

models are fully supervised and rely on pixel-wise dense labeling [19,27,28]. To alleviate it, existing literature [5,11,20,22,25] have explored weaker form of annotations (e.g. image-level label, sparse label, noisy label), among which scribbles in Fig. 1 are particularly attractive in medical image segmentation [5]. Therefore, we propose to utilize only scribble-annotated data for model training, which is a specific form of weakly supervised segmentation.

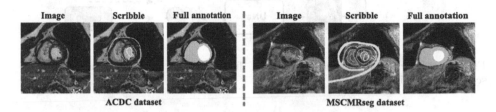

Fig. 1. Examples from ACDC and MSCMRseg datasets.

Two challenges are presented for scribble-guided segmentation, *i.e.*, insufficient supervision and incomplete shape of the annotated object. Existing methods exploited labeled pixels [1,10,16], but the supervision from unlabeled pixels is rarely explored. To capture complete shape features, several methods proposed to learn from unpaired fully annotated segmentation masks, meaning additional resources are required [13,22,23].

To exploit supervision from unlabeled data, a line of researches have been proposed to learn from positive and unlabeled data, well known as *PU learning* [6,9,12,15]. This framework is designed for binary classification task and aims to extract negative samples from unlabeled data. In medical imaging, PU learning has been applied to classification [17] and object detection tasks [29]. Many methods have been proposed for binary mixture proportion estimate [3,9,18] and PU learning [7,8,12]. However, these methods generate independent estimate of mixture ratio for each class, which is unreasonable in multi-class image segmentation. Correspondingly, *existing PU learning methods for classification task cannot be directly adapted for image segmentation.*

To tackle the above challenges, we propose a novel shape-constrained PU learning method, *i.e.*, *ShapePU*, for scribble-guided cardiac segmentation. As Fig. 2 shows, ShapePU consists of a PU learning framework for seeking supervision from unlabeled pixels and consistency constraint for shape regularization. Firstly, We adopt EM algorithm to estimate the multi-class mixture ratios in unlabeled pixels. Then, we conduct PU learning to identify classes of unlabeled pixels by maximizing marginal probability. Finally, we regularize the segmentation by global consistency, which captures shape features by leveraging cutout-equivalence of image. As illustrated in Fig. 2, cutout-equivalence requires the prediction of an image should obtain the same cutout of the input. Therefore, ShapePU enables the model to exploit supervision from unlabeled pixels and capture the global shape features.

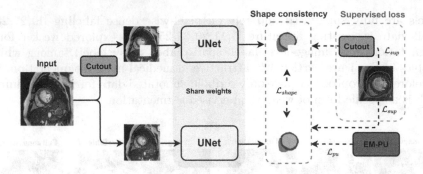

Fig. 2. Overview of the proposed ShapePU framework for cardiac segmentation from scribble supervision.

Our contributions are summarized as follows: (1) To the best of our knowledge, this is the first PU learning framework formulated for weakly supervised segmentation, incorporated with shape knowledge. (2) We propose the novel PU learning framework for multi-class segmentation, which implements EM estimation of mixture ratios and PU learning to identify classes of unlabeled pixels. (3) We introduce the global consistency regularization by leveraging the cutout equivalence, which can enhance the ability of model to capture global shape features. (4) The proposed *ShapePU* consistently outperformed the fully supervised methods, the state-of-the-art weakly supervised approaches, and the competitive PU learning methods on two cardiac segmentation tasks.

2   Method

As shown in Fig. 2, our method takes UNet [2] as backbone. Besides the supervised loss of annotated pixels, we leverage the unlabeled pixels via a new PU framework regularized by global consistency. The proposed ShapePU consists of three components: (1) multi-class mixture proportion estimation based on EM algorithm; (2) PU learning step to distinguish unlabeled pixels by maximizing the marginal probability; and (3) the global consistency leveraging cutout equivalence.

2.1   EM Estimation of Multi-class Mixture Proportion

For multi-class segmentation with $m+1$ label classes including background c_0, we denote $P_j, j = 0, \cdots, m$ as the class-conditional distributions of label class $c_j, j = 0, \cdots, m$, and p_j as its density. Let P_u be the distribution of unlabeled pixels with density p_u. We formulate P_u as the mixture of $\{P_j\}_{j=0}^m$, i.e., $P_u = \sum_{j=0}^m \alpha_j P_j$. $\alpha_j \in [0, 1]$ is the mixture proportion of class c_j, which satisfying $\sum_{j=0}^m \alpha_j = 1$. In weakly supervised segmentation with scribble annotations, we treat each pixel of label c_j as an i.i.d sample from the class-conditional distribution P_j. Similarly, the unlabeled pixels are taken as i.i.d samples from mixed distribution P_u. The goal of mixture proportion estimation is to estimate $\{\alpha_j\}_{j=0}^m$.

We employ the EM algorithm [14] to estimate the multi-class mixture proportions. For class c_j and labeled pixel x, one has $\hat{p}_l(x|c_j) = \frac{\hat{p}_l(c_j|x)p(x)}{\hat{p}_l(c_j)}$ based on Bayes' theorem, where $\hat{p}_l(x|c_j)$ denotes the within-class probability of labeled pixels. Similarly, we obtain the within-class probability of unlabeled pixels by $\hat{p}_u(x|c_j) = \frac{\hat{p}_u(c_j|x)\hat{p}_u(x)}{\hat{p}_u(c_j)}$. We assume the within-class probability $\hat{p}(x|c_j)$ of labeled and unlabeled pixels be the same, i.e., $\hat{p}_l(x|c_j) = \hat{p}_u(x|c_j)$. Given the condition that $\sum_{j=0}^{m} \hat{p}_u(c_j|x) = 1$, we can solve that:

$$\alpha_j = \frac{1}{n_u} \sum_{i=1}^{n_u} \hat{p}_u(c_j|x_i) = \frac{1}{n_u} \sum_{i=1}^{n_u} \frac{\hat{p}_u(c_j)\hat{p}_l(c_j|x_i)/\hat{p}_l(c_j)}{\sum_{j=0}^{m}[\hat{p}_u(c_j)\hat{p}_l(c_j|x_i)/\hat{p}_l(c_j)]}, \tag{1}$$

where the mixture ratio α_j equals $\hat{p}_u(c_j)$; $\hat{p}_u(c_j|x_i)$ is the probability of pixel x_i belonging to c_j, which is predicted by segmentation network; $\hat{p}_l(c_j)$ is the proportion of class c_j in labeled pixels; n_u is the number of unlabeled pixels. The mixture ratios $\hat{p}_u(c_j)$ of unlabeled pixels are initialized with the class frequencies of labeled pixels, i.e., $\hat{p}_l(c_j)$. Then, we substitute the estimated α_j into $\hat{p}_u(c_j)$ on the right side of the formula, and repeat it until the value of α_j converges. The detailed derivation of Eq. (1) is provided in the supplementary material.

2.2 PU Learning with Marginal Probability

Given the estimated mixture proportions, we aim to identify the classes of unlabeled pixels. Firstly, positive samples of each class are distinguished from unlabeled pixels. Secondly, we design the negative loss ($\mathcal{L}^-$) to maximize the marginal probability of negative samples.

For class c_j, we rank the unlabeled pixels according to their probability belongs to class c_j, which is predicted by the segmentation network. After that, the pixels within the α_j proportion are considered as positive samples, denoted as Ω_j. The remain $1 - \alpha_j$ proportion is taken as a set of negative samples, which is represented as $\bar{\Omega}_j$.

We apply loss only to foreground classes. Given the observation that the ratios of foreground classes tend to be over-estimated [9], we do not directly compute the loss on the predicted positive samples. Instead, we apply a loss function to the set of predicted negative samples ($\bar{\Omega}_j$). Firstly, we fuse other classes together except c_j, and denote the fused class as $\bar{c}_j$. Then the marginal probability of $\bar{c}_j$ is equal to the sum of the probabilities belonging to related classes, i.e., $\hat{p}(\bar{c}_j|x) = \sum_{k=1}^{m}[\mathbb{1}_{[k \neq j]}\hat{p}(c_k|x)]$. Finally, we formulate the negative loss $\mathcal{L}^-$ to maximize the marginal probabilities, i.e.,

$$\mathcal{L}^- = -\sum_{j=1}^{m} \sum_{i \in \bar{\Omega}_j} \log(\hat{p}(\bar{c}_j|x_i)). \tag{2}$$

2.3 Global Consistency

In segmentation tasks, We need to consider not only individual pixels, but also global shape features. Taking an input image, denoted as X, we first randomly *cutout* a square area of X. Let z be the binary cutout mask in $[0, 1]$ and $T(\cdot)$ be the transformation of rotation and flipping. The perturbed image is represented as $X' = T(z \odot X)$. Then, we require the segmentation result of the image X and masked image X' to be consistent except the cutout area. Therefore, we have $T(z \odot f(X)) = f(T(z \odot X))$, where f denotes the segmentation network. Defining $f'(X) = T(z \odot f(X))$, we formulate global consistency loss $\mathcal{L}_{global}$ as:

$$\mathcal{L}_{global} = \frac{1}{2}\mathcal{L}_{cos}(f'(X), f(X') + \frac{1}{2}\mathcal{L}_{cos}(f(X'), f'(X)), \tag{3}$$

where $\mathcal{L}_{cos}$ indicates cosine similarity distance, *i.e.*, $\mathcal{L}_{cos}(a, b) = -\frac{a \cdot b}{(||a||_2 \cdot ||b||_2)}$.

Given scribble annotations, we calculate the supervised cross entropy loss $\mathcal{L}^+$ for annotated pixels of both X and X'. Let the set of labeled pixels be Ω_l and the label of pixel x_i be a vector of dimension m, *i.e.*, $\boldsymbol{y}_i = \{y_{i1}, \cdots, y_{im}\}$. We denote the predicted label of pixel x_i as $\hat{\boldsymbol{y}}_i = \{\hat{y}_{i1}, \cdots, \hat{y}_{im}\}$. Then, the supervised cross entropy loss $\mathcal{L}^+$ is written as:

$$\mathcal{L}^+ = -\sum_{i \in \Omega_l} \sum_{j=1}^{m} [y_{ij} \log(\hat{y}_{ij})]. \tag{4}$$

Finally, the optimization objective is represented as:

$$\mathcal{L} = \mathcal{L}^+ + \lambda_1 \mathcal{L}^- + \lambda_2 \mathcal{L}_{global}, \tag{5}$$

where λ_1 and λ_2 are balancing parameters.

3   Experiment

In the experiments, we first performed the ablation study on the ACDC dataset [4]. Then, we compared our ShapePU to weakly supervised methods and PU learning approaches using ACDC and MSCMRseg dataset [26,27], respectively. We further analyzed the stability of model training and presented estimated mixture ratios in the supplementary material.

3.1   Experiment Setup

Datasets. ACDC[1] consists of fully annotated cardiac MR images from 100 patients. The goal is to automatically segment right ventricle (RV), left ventricle (LV) and myocardium (MYO). We randomly divided the 100 subjects into 3 sets of 70 (training), 15 (validation), and 15 (test) subjects for experiments. The expert-made scribble annotations in [22] were leveraged for weak-supervision studies. **MSCMRseg**[2] includes late gadolinium enhancement (LGE) cardiac MR images from 45 patients with cardiomyopathy. MSCMRseg is more challenging compared to ACDC, as LGE CMR segmentation per se is more complex

---

[1] https://www.creatis.insa-lyon.fr/Challenge/acdc/databasesTraining.html.
[2] http://www.sdspeople.fudan.edu.cn/zhuangxiahai/0/mscmrseg19/data.html.

Table 1. Results in Dice scores of the ablation study. **Bold** denotes the best result, underline indicates the best but one. Significant improvement compared to previous model given by Wilcoxon test (p<0.05) is denoted with [†].

Methods	$\mathcal{L}^+$	Cutout	$\mathcal{L}^-$	$\mathcal{L}_{global}$	LV	MYO	RV	Avg
#1	✓	✗	✗	✗	.808±.161	.749±.099	.779±.133	.779
#2	✓	✓	✗	✗	.815±.172	.758±.134	.817±.123[†]	.797[†]
#3	✓	✗	✓	✗	.870 ± .141[†]	.798 ± .104[†]	.832±.133	.833[†]
#4	✓	✓	✓	✗	.859±.150	.794±.113	.850 ± .104	.834
ShapePU	✓	✓	✓	✓	**.888±.103**[†]	**.813±.095**[†]	**.854±.089**	**.851**[†]

and the training set is smaller. We generated scribble annotations for RV, LV and MYO following the similar protocol of [22]. We randomly divided the 45 images into 25 training images, 5 validation images, and 15 test images.

Implementation. We warmly started training the networks with supervised loss and global consistency loss for 100 epochs, and then invoked the negative loss. Since the images are of different resolutions, we first re-sampled all images to a fixed resolution of 1.37×1.37 mm and then extracted the central patch of size 212×212 as input. Then, we normalized the intensity to zero mean and unit variance. A square area of 32×32 was randomly cut out for each image. Hyper-parameters λ_1 and λ_2 were empirically set to be 1 and 0.05. All models were trained with batch size 16 and learning rate 1e^{-4}. For testing, we kept the largest connected area of foreground to eliminate false positives. Dice scores and Haussdorff Distance (HD) are reported to measure the accuracy of segmentation models. We implemented our framework with Pytorch and conducted experiments on one NVIDIA 3090Ti 24GB GPU for 1000 epochs.

3.2   Ablation Study

We performed an ablation study to verify effects of the two key components of the proposed ShapePU, *i.e.*, the negative loss ($\mathcal{L}^-$) and the global consistency loss ($\mathcal{L}_{global}$). Table 1 reports the results. One can see that cutout augmentation showed marginal improvement over model #1. Having supervision for unlabeled pixels, model #3 included the negative loss ($\mathcal{L}^-$) and obtained remarkable performance gain over model #1 by 5.5% (83.3% vs 77.8%) on the average Dice. When combined with Cutout, PU (without shape) improved the average Dice marginally from 83.3% to 83.4%. Cutout enhances the localization ability, but may change the shape of target structure. Therefore, it could be difficult for the segmentation model to learn the shape priors, leading to the performance drop in some structures. When combined with global consistency ($\mathcal{L}_{global}$), which overcomes the disadvantage by requiring the cutout equivalence, the performance is evidently better with a significant improvement of 1.7% on average Dice (85.1% vs 83.4%). This indicated that the combination of PU learning and global consistency endows the algorithm with supervision of unlabeled pixels and with knowledge of global shapes.

Table 2. Comparisons of ShapePU trained on 35 scribbles with other scribble-guided models, GAN-based models, and fully supervised method. The results cited from [22], which did not report standard deviation, are denoted with *.

Methods	Dice				HD (mm)			
	LV	MYO	RV	Avg	LV	MYO	RV	Avg
35 scribbles								
PCE	.795±.193	.745±.143	.755 ± .204	.765	16.9±24.1	23.4 ± 25.7	40.6±28.4	26.9
WPCE*	.784	.675	.563	.674	97.4	99.6	120.5	105.8
CRF*	.766	.661	.590	.672	99.6	103.2	117.8	106.9
ShapePU (ours)	.860±.122	.791±.091	**.852±.102**	**.834**	**12.0±10.5**	**13.8±10.5**	**11.9±7.60**	**12.6**
35 scribbles + 35 unpaired full annotations								
PostDAE*	.806	.667	.556	.676	80.6	88.7	103.4	90.9
ACCL*	.878	.797	.735	.803	16.6	28.8	26.1	23.8
MAAG*	**.879**	**.817**	.752	.816	25.2	26.8	22.7	24.9
35 full annotations								
UNet_F	.849±.152	.792±.140	.817±.151	.820	15.7±13.9	13.8±12.2	13.2±13.4	14.2

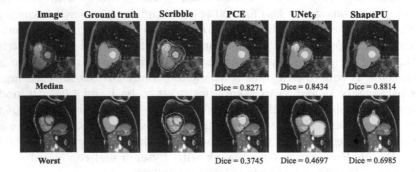

Fig. 3. Visualization on two typical ACDC cases for illustration and comparison.

3.3 Comparisons with Weakly Supervised Methods

We performed two groups of experiments. One included three scribble-guided models, *i.e.*, partial cross entropy (PCE) [21], weighted partial cross entropy (WPCE) [22], conditional random fields post-processing (CRF) [24]. The other consisted of three GAN-based models trained with *additional unpaired full annotations* to provide shape priors, *i.e.*, post-processing with denoising auto-encoders (PostDAE) [13], adversarial constrained CNN (ACCL) [23], multi-scale attention gates (MAAG) [22]. Finally, the results from *fully supervised* UNet [2] (UNet_F), were provided for reference.

Table 3. The performance on MSCMRseg and comparisons with other PU methods based on scribble supervision. GTα indicates the ground truth mixture proportions of α are provided for model training; UNet$_F$ is a fully supervised approach solely for reference, and n/a means not applicable.

Methods	GTα	Dice				HD (mm)			
		LV	MYO	RV	Avg	LV	MYO	RV	Avg
PCE	×	.514±.078	.582±.067	.058±.023	.385	259.4±14.2	228.1±21.4	257.4±12.4	248.3
(TED)^n	×	.524±.098	.443±.122	.363±.125	.443	107.8±63.6	82.0±70.2	30.0±21.3	73.2
CVIR	✓	519±.042	.519±.081	.443±.089	.493	73.2±7.22	65.3±68.9	69.3±86.3	69.3
nnPU	✓	.516±.075	.536±.085	.442±.121	.498	76.7±11.0	41.7±13.3	**23.9±20.6**	47.4
PU w/o Shape(ours)	×	.911 ± .042	.808 ± .063	.793 ± .101	.837	45.4 ± 73.8	36.5 ± 61.1	43.1±52.5	41.7
ShapePU(ours)	×	**.919±.029**	832±.042	**.804±.123**	**.852**	**10.3±13.0**	**10.6±10.1**	24.3 ± 19.6	**15.0**
UNet$_F$	n/a	.856±.040	.722±.061	.684±.122	.754	17.2±20.6	16.6±15.4	81.5±7.06	38.4

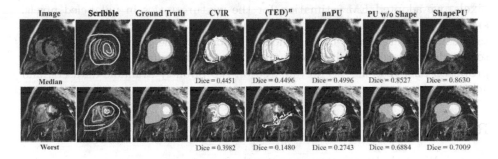

Fig. 4. Visualization on two typical MSCMRseg cases for illustration and comparisons with PU learning methods.

Table 2 provides the quantitative results. ShapePU outperformed all other methods by a large margin. Notably, the weakly supervised ShapePU matched the performance of fully supervised UNet (UNet$_F$) with a significant better HD on LV (p=0.041), demonstrating its outstanding learning ability from scribble supervision. Figure 3 visualizes results from the median and worst cases selected using the mean Dice of compared methods. ShapePU was more robust to diverse shapes and densities of heart than the fully supervised UNet (UNet$_F$), thanks to the effective learning of unlabeled pixels and shape features.

3.4   Comparisons with PU Learning Methods

We performed the scribble-guided segmentation on MSCMR LGE CMR images and compared ShapePU with other state-of-the-art PU learning approaches, including Transform-Estimate-Discard ((TED)^n) [9], PU learning with conditional value ignoring risk (CVIR) [9], and positive-unlabeled learning with non-negative risk estimator (nnPU) [12].

Table 3 reports the quantitative results. Without additional information of ground truth mixture ratio α (GT α), our basic PU learning framework (PU w/o Shape) still significantly outperformed the peers with at least 33.9% average

Dice, demonstrating the challenge of directly applying PU learning for image segmentation, and the effectiveness of our PU formulation for this task. By leveraging shape features, the proposed ShapePU further boosted the performance to 85.2% (85.2% vs 83.7%), with an improvement of 26.7 mm (15.0 mm vs 41.7 mm) on average HD. Figure 4 visualizes the worst and median cases selected using the average Dice scores of all compared PU methods. One can observe that ShapePU achieved the best performance on both the two cases.

4   Conclusion

This paper presents a shape-constrained PU learning (ShapePU) method for weakly supervised cardiac segmentation. To provide supervision for unlabeled pixels, we adopted EM estimation for the mixture ratios in unlabeled pixels, and employed PU framework to distinguish the classes of unlabeled pixels. To tackle incomplete shape of scribbles, we proposed the shape-consistency loss to regularize cutout equivalence and capture global shape of the heart. The proposed ShapePU has been evaluated on two publicly available datasets, and achieved the new state-of-the-art performance.

References

1. Bai, W., et al.: Recurrent neural networks for aortic image sequence segmentation with sarse annotations. In: Frangi, A.F., Schnabel, J.A., Davatzikos, C., Alberola-López, C., Fichtinger, G. (eds.) MICCAI 2018. LNCS, vol. 11073, pp. 586–594. Springer, Cham (2018). https://doi.org/10.1007/978-3-030-00937-3_67
2. Baumgartner, C.F., Koch, L.M., Pollefeys, M., Konukoglu, E.: An exploration of 2D and 3D deep learning techniques for cardiac MR image segmentation. In: Pop, M., et al. (eds.) STACOM 2017. LNCS, vol. 10663, pp. 111–119. Springer, Cham (2018). https://doi.org/10.1007/978-3-319-75541-0_12
3. Bekker, J., Davis, J.: Estimating the class prior in positive and unlabeled data through decision tree induction. In: Proceedings of the AAAI Conference on Artificial Intelligence, vol. 32 (2018)
4. Bernard, O., et al.: Deep learning techniques for automatic MRI cardiac multi-structures segmentation and diagnosis: is the problem solved? IEEE Trans. Med. Imaging 37(11), 2514–2525 (2018)
5. Can, Y.B., et al.: Learning to segment medical images with scribble-supervision alone. In: Stoyanov, D., et al. (eds.) DLMIA/ML-CDS -2018. LNCS, vol. 11045, pp. 236–244. Springer, Cham (2018). https://doi.org/10.1007/978-3-030-00889-5_27
6. De Comité, F., Denis, F., Gilleron, R., Letouzey, F.: Positive and unlabeled examples help learning. In: Watanabe, O., Yokomori, T. (eds.) ALT 1999. LNCS (LNAI), vol. 1720, pp. 219–230. Springer, Heidelberg (1999). https://doi.org/10.1007/3-540-46769-6_18
7. Du Plessis, M., Niu, G., Sugiyama, M.: Convex formulation for learning from positive and unlabeled data. In: International Conference on Machine Learning, pp. 1386–1394. PMLR (2015)
8. Du Plessis, M.C., Niu, G., Sugiyama, M.: Analysis of learning from positive and unlabeled data. Adv. Neural Inf. Process. Syst. 27, 703–711 (2014)

9. Garg, S., Wu, Y., Smola, A.J., Balakrishnan, S., Lipton, Z.: Mixture proportion estimation and PU learning: a modern approach. Adv. Neural Inf. Process. Syst. **34** (2021)

10. Ji, Z., Shen, Y., Ma, C., Gao, M.: Scribble-based hierarchical weakly supervised learning for brain tumor segmentation. In: Shen, D., et al. (eds.) MICCAI 2019. LNCS, vol. 11766, pp. 175–183. Springer, Cham (2019). https://doi.org/10.1007/978-3-030-32248-9_20

11. Khoreva, A., Benenson, R., Hosang, J., Hein, M., Schiele, B.: Simple does it: weakly supervised instance and semantic segmentation. In: Proceedings of the IEEE Conference on Computer Vision and Pattern Recognition, pp. 876–885 (2017)

12. Kiryo, R., Niu, G., du Plessis, M.C., Sugiyama, M.: Positive-Unlabeled Learning with Non-negative Risk Estimator, vol. 30 (2017)

13. Larrazabal, A.J., Mart'inez, C., Glocker, B., Ferrante, E.: Post-DAE: anatomically plausible segmentation via post-processing with denoising autoencoders. IEEE Trans. Med. Imaging **39**, 3813–3820 (2020)

14. Latinne, P., Saerens, M., Decaestecker, C.: Adjusting the outputs of a classifier to new a priori probabilities may significantly improve classification accuracy: evidence from a multi-class problem in remote sensing. In: ICML, vol. 1, pp. 298–305. Citeseer (2001)

15. Letouzey, F., Denis, F., Gilleron, R.: Learning from positive and unlabeled examples. In: International Conference on Algorithmic Learning Theory, pp. 71–85. Springer (2000). https://doi.org/10.1016/j.tcs.2005.09.007

16. Lin, D., Dai, J., Jia, J., He, K., Sun, J.: Scribblesup: scribble-supervised convolutional networks for semantic segmentation. In: Proceedings of the IEEE Conference on Computer Vision and Pattern Recognition, pp. 3159–3167 (2016)

17. Nagaya, M., Ukita, N.: Embryo grading with unreliable labels due to chromosome abnormalities by regularized pu learning with ranking. IEEE Trans. Med. Imaging **41**(2), 320–331 (2021)

18. Ramaswamy, H., Scott, C., Tewari, A.: Mixture proportion estimation via kernel embeddings of distributions. In: International Conference on Machine Learning, pp. 2052–2060. PMLR (2016)

19. Ronneberger, O., Fischer, P., Brox, T.: U-Net: convolutional networks for biomedical image segmentation. In: Navab, N., Hornegger, J., Wells, W.M., Frangi, A.F. (eds.) MICCAI 2015. LNCS, vol. 9351, pp. 234–241. Springer, Cham (2015). https://doi.org/10.1007/978-3-319-24574-4_28

20. Shi, G., Xiao, L., Chen, Y., Zhou, S.K.: Marginal loss and exclusion loss for partially supervised multi-organ segmentation. Med. Image Anal. **70**, 101979 (2021)

21. Tang, M., Djelouah, A., Perazzi, F., Boykov, Y., Schroers, C.: Normalized cut loss for weakly-supervised CNN segmentation. In: Proceedings of the IEEE Conference on Computer Vision and Pattern Recognition, pp. 1818–1827 (2018)

22. Valvano, G., Leo, A., Tsaftaris, S.A.: Learning to segment from scribbles using multi-scale adversarial attention gates. IEEE Trans. Med. Imaging **40**(8), 1990–2001 (2021)

23. Zhang, P., Zhong, Y., Li, X.: ACCL: adversarial constrained-CNN loss for weakly supervised medical image segmentation (2020)

24. Zheng, S., et al.: Conditional random fields as recurrent neural networks. In: Proceedings of the IEEE International Conference on Computer Vision, pp. 1529–1537 (2015)

25. Zhou, Y., et al.: Prior-aware neural network for partially-supervised multi-organ segmentation. In: Proceedings of the IEEE/CVF International Conference on Computer Vision, pp. 10672–10681 (2019)

26. Zhuang, X.: Multivariate mixture model for cardiac segmentation from multi-sequence MRI. In: Ourselin, S., Joskowicz, L., Sabuncu, M.R., Unal, G., Wells, W. (eds.) MICCAI 2016. LNCS, vol. 9901, pp. 581–588. Springer, Cham (2016). https://doi.org/10.1007/978-3-319-46723-8_67
27. Zhuang, X.: Multivariate mixture model for myocardial segmentation combining multi-source images. IEEE Trans. Pattern Anal. Mach. Intell. **41**(12), 2933–2946 (2019)
28. Zhuang, X., Shen, J.: Multi-scale patch and multi-modality atlases for whole heart segmentation of MRI. Med. Image Anal. **31**, 77–87 (2016)
29. Zuluaga, M.A., et al.: Learning from only positive and unlabeled data to detect lesions in vascular CT images. In: Fichtinger, G., Martel, A., Peters, T. (eds.) MICCAI 2011. LNCS, vol. 6893, pp. 9–16. Springer, Heidelberg (2011). https://doi.org/10.1007/978-3-642-23626-6_2

ProCo: Prototype-Aware Contrastive Learning for Long-Tailed Medical Image Classification

Zhixiong Yang[1], Junwen Pan[1], Yanzhan Yang[1], Xiaozhou Shi[1],
Hong-Yu Zhou[2], Zhicheng Zhang[1(✉)], and Cheng Bian[1(✉)]

[1] Xiaohe Healthcare, ByteDance, Guangzhou, China
{biancheng,zc.zhang}@bytedance.com
[2] Department of Computer Science, The University of Hong Kong,
Pokfulam, Hong Kong, China

Abstract. Medical image classification has been widely adopted in medical image analysis. However, due to the difficulty of collecting and labeling data in the medical area, medical image datasets are usually highly-imbalanced. To address this problem, previous works utilized class samples as prior for re-weighting or re-sampling but the feature representation is usually still not discriminative enough. In this paper, we adopt the contrastive learning to tackle the long-tailed medical imbalance problem. Specifically, we first propose the category prototype and adversarial proto-instance to generate representative contrastive pairs. Then, the prototype recalibration strategy is proposed to address the highly imbalanced data distribution. Finally, a unified proto-loss is designed to train our framework. The overall framework, namely as **Prototype-aware Contrastive learning (ProCo)**, is unified as a single-stage pipeline in an end-to-end manner to alleviate the imbalanced problem in medical image classification, which is also a distinct progress than existing works as they follow the traditional two-stage pipeline. Extensive experiments on two highly-imbalanced medical image classification datasets demonstrate that our method outperforms the existing state-of-the-art methods by a large margin. Our source codes are available at https://github.com/skyz215/ProCo.

Keywords: Contrastive learning · Prototype · Imbalanced dataset

1 Introduction

Convolution neural network has been proved to be successful in many visual tasks [11–13,20,23,25]. Although impressive breakthrough has been achieved, recent advances are still driven by the balanced dataset in the corresponding tasks. However, in real-world medical practice, the acquired dataset often exhibits long-tail distribution [19], where the head categories dominate most of the data, whereas tailed categories only have a handful of samples. Such skewed

---

Z. Yang and J. Pan—Contributed equally.

© The Author(s), under exclusive license to Springer Nature Switzerland AG 2022
L. Wang et al. (Eds.): MICCAI 2022, LNCS 13438, pp. 173–182, 2022.
https://doi.org/10.1007/978-3-031-16452-1_17

dataset is commonly originated from the difficulty of collecting rare diseases, or insufficient annotation from the proficient expertise. For this reason, the well-trained model is prone to make decision bias towards head classes due to the numerical superiority, weakening the model performance on tailed classes.

To address the long-tailed imbalance, follow-up studies have been conducted in recent years. Common solutions include class-rebalancing [8,27], information supplement [29,32], and module modification [14,15,34]. Unfortunately, these works are heavily depended on manual designs or prior knowledge, causing low efficacy and poor generalization of their proposed models. To this end, we propose **Pro**totype-aware **Co**ntrastive learning (**ProCo**) to address the long-tailed problem with decent performance and high efficiency.

Different from previous works, with the assistance of well-designed loss function Proto-loss, the main innovation of ProCo is that the proposed framework is a combination of the contrastive learning, category prototype, and proto-instance and can commendably tackle the long-tailed medical image classification. Formally, our technical contributions can be summarized in four-fold:

- We propose a category prototype and adversarial proto-instance for feature modeling. Specifically, the category prototype can model the arbitrary category distribution adaptively. Especially, adversarial proto-instance is generated from category prototype and representative instance to enhance the robustness of contrastive learning over all classes in the long-tailed setting.
- We present a prototype recalibration strategy to ensure the updated frequency on category prototypes of tailed classes and eliminate the prototype bias, which is an imbalance updating process resulting in an incorrect distribution prediction.
- To unify the contrastive learning together with prototype-based supervised learning, we propose a proto-loss, which can significantly boost the efficiency of our end-to-end framework ProCo.
- Extensive experiments on two long-tailed medical classification datasets show that ProCo yields the best over state-of-the-arts by a large margin, demonstrating the effectiveness of the proposed method.

2   Related Work

Existing practices on the class-rebalancing aim to adjust the distribution of training samples to achieve balanced data over all categories, e.g., over-sampling [17] on tailed classes or under-sampling [16] on head classes. While these techniques have successfully improved the performance on tailed classes, the performance on head classes will be sacrificed [33]. In this regards, information supplement methods are investigated by introducing prior expertise into the entire framework to overcome the performance degradation, e.g., transfer learning [30], model pre-training [31], knowledge distillation [28], and self-supervised learning [29]. Other studies explore module modification paradigms. For instance, Kang et al. [15] proposed a two-stage decoupling training method, in which the backbone and classifier were trained separately for the tailed class accommodation. Dong et al. [7] proposed a metric learning approach for batch incremental

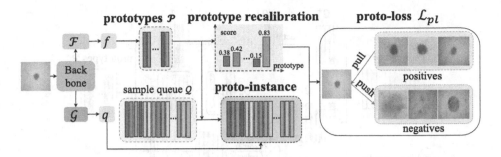

Fig. 1. Our proposed Prototype-aware Contrastive Learning (ProCo) framework. $\mathcal{F}$ and $\mathcal{G}$ are two projectors, f is the image feature, q is the query feature. Prototypes $\mathcal{P}$ and sample queue $\mathcal{Q}$ are used to generate adversarial proto-instances. All negatives and positives enter into the proposed proto-loss $\mathcal{L}_{pl}$ for optimization. Besides, a prototype recalibration strategy is used for adjusting the weight of each prototype in proto-loss.

hard sample mining of minority attribute classes from imbalanced large-scale training data. However, one limitation of these methods is that the prior expertise relies on cumbersome manipulation, which is an obstacle to real-world application. In this paper, we attempt to address the long-tail problem in a contrastive way, which can not only tackle above challenges but also achieve promising performance with competence of high efficiency.

3 Methodology

Figure 1 demonstrates the diagram of our proposed ProCo framework. It originates from MoCo [10], which consists of an online encoder and a momentum updated encoder. Here we omit the momentum encoder for simplicity. As these two encoders share the same architecture, in the following text we only describe the structure of the online encoder.

Notation. The long-tailed classification training set with N training samples and C categories is denoted as $\mathcal{X} = \{(x_j, y_j) | 1 \leq j \leq N\}$. The network consists of a shared backbone and two projection heads notated as $\mathcal{G}$ and $\mathcal{F}$, respectively. The feature produced by projection head $\mathcal{F}$ is used for classification, while $\mathcal{G}$ for the contrastive learning. The sample queue $\mathcal{Q} = \{q_j \in \mathbb{R}^k | 1 \leq j \leq M\}$ with M instances is maintained via the momentum fashion [10].

3.1 Category Prototype and Adversarial Proto-instance

Classic contrastive training pairs (*i.e.*, positive and negative pairs) are used to learn the representation of instances. However, in the long-tailed dataset, the head classes dominate most of negative pairs via the conventional contrastive methods, causing the under-learning of tailed classes. Previous works [2,24]

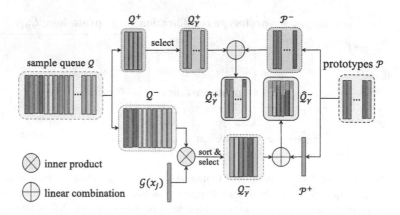

Fig. 2. Illustration of the proposed adversarial proto-instance.

reveal that not all negative pairs facilitate the contrastive learning. Therefore, the key to improve the performance of the long-tailed problem is to reduce the redundancy of contrastive negative pairs and mine recognizable positive pairs. To this end, we propose a new concept named category prototype. The prototype is a set of learnable parameters $\mathcal{P} = \{p_c \in \mathbb{R}^k | 1 \leq c \leq C\}$ for predefined C categories and is optimized by our proto-loss as described in Sect. 3.3. Then, we generate the adversarial proto-instance from the category prototype and representative sample, $i.e.$, confusing samples from the alternative sample queue, via a linear interpolation in the feature space, which will be utilized to form a training pair in ProCo. Theoretically, the adversarial proto-instance is designed as a special outlier, which can encourage ProCo to rectify the decision boundaries of the tailed categories during the contrastive learning.

Figure 2 illustrates the diagram of the adversarial proto-instance. First, for each instance (x_j, y_j), the queue $\mathcal{Q}$ is divided into two disjoint subsets $\mathcal{Q}^+ = \{s_i | y_i = y_j\}$ and $\mathcal{Q}^- = \{s_i | y_i \neq y_j\}$ that comprise positive and negative instances, respectively. Similarly, $\mathcal{P}$ is also grouped into a singleton set $\mathcal{P}^+ = \{p_c^+ | c = y_j\}$ with exactly one prototype p_c^+ and a negative set $\mathcal{P}^- = \mathcal{P} \setminus \mathcal{P}^+$, where p_c^+ is the positive prototype feature corresponding to the current instance. Then, the adversarial positive proto-instances are derived from $\mathcal{P}^-$ and $\mathcal{Q}^+$ while the negative ones are from $\mathcal{P}^+$ and $\mathcal{Q}^-$.

To synthesize the adversarial negative proto-instances, we prioritize those negative instances that are likely to be confused with the current instance. The distance between the current feature $\mathcal{G}(x_j)$ and negative feature $s_i^- \in \mathcal{Q}^-$ can be utilized as an indicator, and is represented as:

$$d(x_j, s_i^-) = 1 - \frac{\mathcal{G}(x_j)^\top \cdot s_i^-}{\|\mathcal{G}(x_j)\|_2 \|s_i^-\|_2}, \tag{1}$$

where the superscript $\top$ represents the transpose operation. Then, we rank the negative instances in $\mathcal{Q}^-$ in ascending order according to their distance to $\mathcal{G}(x_j)$

and select the top γ instances to compose the adversarial proto-instance set $\mathcal{Q}_\gamma^-$:

$$\mathcal{Q}_\gamma^- = \left\{ s_i^- | s_i^- \in \mathcal{Q}^-, d(x_j, s_i^-) \leq d(x_j, s_\gamma^-) \right\}, \tag{2}$$

where s_γ is the γ-th element in the sorted $\mathcal{Q}^-$. Finally, for more challenging negative instances, we randomly perturb each element in $\mathcal{Q}^-$ with the positive prototype p_c^+:

$$\hat{\mathcal{Q}}_\gamma^- = \left\{ \frac{(1-\epsilon_i)s_i + \epsilon_i p_c^+}{\|(1-\epsilon_i)s_i + \epsilon_i p_c^+\|_2} \;\middle|\; s_i \in \mathcal{Q}_\gamma^- \right\}, \tag{3}$$

where $\epsilon_i \in (0, E)$ is a random interpolation coefficient for each sample and the upper bound E is a hyperparameter with a small value. We assume that prototype p_c^+ always contributes less than s_i to the generated proto-instance, which guarantees that the negative semantic within s_i can be held.

As for the adversarial positive proto-instances, the strategy is to select samples in $\mathcal{Q}^+$ that are misclassified and combine them with the incorrectly assigned prototype, where the interpolation manner is identical to that of Eq. 3.

3.2 Prototype Recalibration

Although the problem of constructing contrastive pairs has been addressed by the proposed category prototype and adversarial proto-instance, the learning of category prototype is still potentially affected by the class imbalance problem. We argue that the underlying reason is the prototype bias, where the generated proto-instance will incline to head classes, jeopardizing the performance on tailed classes. For this reason, this work proposes a prototype recalibration strategy, which estimates the representative level of each category prototype showing the importance of tailed class prototype features.

Specifically, inspired by the similarity between the projected features and prototype, we introduce a rectified sigmoid function to achieve recalibration. In formal, the calibration factor for each category prototype $p_c \in \mathcal{P}$ is defined as:

$$\omega_c (p_c, \{x_j \mid y_j = c\}) = \frac{1}{N_c} \sum_{1 \leq j \leq N_c} \frac{1}{1 + e^{-\mathcal{F}(x_j)^\top \cdot p_c}}, \tag{4}$$

where $\{x_j | y_j = c\}$ is a subset of samples in the associated category c, and N_c is the total number of them. To allow end-to-end calibration for batch-based training, we keep a running mean via the exponential moving average for the global calibration factor:

$$\bar{\omega}_c = \beta \cdot \bar{\omega}_c + (1 - \beta) \cdot \omega_c (p_c, \{x_j \mid y_j = c\}), \tag{5}$$

where $\{x_j | y_j = c\}$ are samples in a batch with label c, and β is a smoothing coefficient.

The calibration factor reflects the *difficulty* of each category and the *representativeness* of the corresponding prototype in the model learning. Eventually, we impose all prototypes in $\mathcal{P}$ by the calibration factors as:

$$\hat{\mathcal{P}} = \{\log(\bar{\omega}_c) + p_c \mid p_c \in \mathcal{P}\}. \tag{6}$$

3.3 Proto-loss for Training

To integrate the contrastive learning into our work in an end-to-end manner, we refer to the concept of InfoNCE [22]. Unfortunately, it only supports single positive pair, which is incompatible to our work. Therefore, inspired by the unified contrastive loss [6], we extend it to include prototypes and involve both positive and negative adversarial proto-instance for training, which ensures the optimization consistency of supervised and contrastive training so as to achieve decent performance compared with the former studies.

Formally, considering $\mathcal{H}^- = \mathcal{Q}^- \cup \hat{\mathcal{Q}}_\gamma^-$ as negative set, and $\mathcal{H}^+ = \mathcal{Q}^+ \cup \hat{\mathcal{Q}}_\gamma^+$ as positive set. For an instance x_j, the proto-loss is formulated as:

$$
\mathcal{L}_j = \log \left[1 + \left(\sum_{s_i^- \in \mathcal{H}^-} e^{\mathcal{G}(x_j)^\top s_i^-} + \sum_{p_i^- \in \hat{\mathcal{P}}^-} e^{\mathcal{F}(x_j)^\top p_i^-} \right) \cdot \left(\sum_{s_i^+ \in \mathcal{H}^+} e^{-\mathcal{G}(x_j)^\top s_i^+} + \sum_{p_i^+ \in \hat{\mathcal{P}}^+} e^{-\mathcal{F}(x_j)^\top p_i^+} \right) \right].
\tag{7}
$$

Note that the proposed proto-loss can also be applied to general contrastive settings.

4 Experiments

4.1 Datasets and Evaluation

We conduct the experiment on two publicly available datasets. The ISIC2018 is accessed by the Skin Lesion Analysis Toward Melanoma Detection 2018 challenge [5]. The other dataset is APTOS2019, which is provided by [1]. For a better illustration, the details of datasets are listed in Table 1. Notably, the imbalance ratio denotes as N_{max}/N_{min}, where N is the number of samples in each class. We follow the same protocol in [21] and randomly split the original dataset into train and test sets with the ratio of 7:3. All experimental results will be reported with the criterion of accuracy and F1-score.

Table 1. The details of long-tailed medical datasets.

Dataset	# of classes	# of samples	Imbalance ratio
ISIC2018	7	10015	58
APTOS2019	5	3662	10

In this work, we selected 9 existing methods as the comparison methods. To be specific, we use cross-entropy (CE) as the baseline. Further, based on CE, the balanced resampling strategy is used to address the imbalanced classification

Table 2. Comparison with the state-of-the-art methods

Methods	ISIC2018		APTOS2019	
	Accuracy	F1-score	Accuracy	F1-score
CE	0.850	0.716	0.812	0.608
CE+resample	0.861	0.735	0.802	0.583
Focal loss	0.849	0.728	0.815	0.629
LDAM	0.857	0.734	0.813	0.620
OHEM	0.818	0.660	0.813	0.631
MTL	0.811	0.667	0.813	0.632
DANIL	0.825	0.674	0.825	0.660
CL	0.865	0.739	0.825	0.652
CL+resample	0.868	0.751	0.816	0.608
ProCo (ours)	**0.887**	**0.763**	**0.837**	**0.674**

problem. The contrastive learning method can be treated as another comparison method. By integrating the balanced resampling strategy, "CL+resample" is proposed in [21], which is a two-stage approach by training the backbone firstly, then freezing the backbone and training the classifier with balanced sampling. To down-weight easy negatives in one-stage detector, focal loss [18] is also useful in classification problem. LDAM [3] focuses on label distribution margin, and is regarded as a simple but effective training strategy. OHEM [26] is a hard negative mining method based on the model. DANIL [9] explores distractors to learn better CNN features (Table 2).

4.2 Implementation Details

The data augmentation policy and update ratio we utilized of the contrastive learning is identical to MoCoV2 [4]. ResNet50 [11] is used as our backbone. We implement projector $\mathcal{G}$ with 2 fully-connected layers, of which the hidden layer size is set to 2048, followed by ReLU activation function. The projector $\mathcal{F}$ is realized by a single fully-connected layer with ReLU activation function. For simplicity, category prototype $\mathcal{P}$ can be regarded as a classifier in our framework. The batch size is 128 and the default optimizer is SGD with a momentum of 0.9 and a weight decay of 0.0001. The initial learning rate is set to 0.05. The initial similarity value ω_c is set to 0.01 and β is set to 0.95. Hyperparameters γ and E are set at 20 and 0.4 via a grid search. Referring to [21], the training epochs of ISIC2018 and APTOS2019 are set at 1,000 and 2,000, respectively. Particularly in the test phase, we only utilize $\mathcal{F}(x)$ and $\mathcal{P}$ to acquire the prediction.

4.3 Comparison with the State-of-the-Art

In this part, we compare the proposed ProCo with the state-of-the-art methods on two open-release datasets: ISIC2018 and APTOS2019. Table 1 presents the

Table 3. Effectiveness of each module in our ProCo framework

Proto-loss	Proto-instance	Prototype recalibration	Accuracy	F1-score
✓			0.857	0.742
✓	✓		0.875	0.751
✓		✓	0.862	0.754
✓	✓	✓	**0.887**	**0.763**

entire experimental results. We can see that the proposed method achieves optimal performance regardless of the data set, demonstrating its excellent generalization. Apart from this observation, the performance of Focal loss and LDAM is comparable to the baseline on both datasets. In addition, OHEM, MTL, and DANIL obtain comparable accuracy and F1-score on the APTOS2019 while inferior performance on the ISIC2018, illustrating their weak generalization. The results from the two CL-based methods are uniform and outperform the baseline. Note that the role of the balanced resampling strategy is inconsistent across different data sets.

4.4   Ablation Study

In this work, the proposed framework has three fundamental modules. To validate the effectiveness of each module, we carried out ablation studies as shown in Table 3. For this ablation study, four extra experiments have been designed by arranging and combining these three modules: 1) We discarded the proto-instance and prototype recalibration strategy and only used Proto-loss to train the proposed method. 2) Based on the above experiment setting, we introduced the proto-instance module to re-train the proposed method. 3) Integrating the prototype recalibration strategy into the first experiment setting. 4) Employing all the three modules which is our entire proposed framework. From Table 3, we can clearly observe that with all the three modules, the proposed method can obtain the best performance in terms of accuracy and F1-score as shown in the last row. To be specific, the modified framework with only the Proto-loss as the loss function obtained an inferior performance to other three experiments. To this end, we can benefit from proto-instance module and prototype recalibration strategy, which is consistent with the results from experiment 1 and 2. In addition, to evaluate the superiority of the Proto-loss over other commonly-used loss functions: cross-entropy (CE) and InfoNCE, we re-trained the proposed network using different loss functions, respectively. The final results of F1-score were: 0.716 (CE), 0.739 (InfoNCE), and 0.742 (Proto-loss). We can see that using Proto-loss as the loss function will improve the final F1-score by 3.63% compared to that from CE.

5   Conclusion

This paper proposes a novel paradigm called ProCo, addressing the long-tailed classification problem in a contrastive way. Our ProCo mainly consists of three components: i) category prototype and the adversarial proto-instance; ii) prototype recalibration strategy and iii) a unified proto-loss. Extensive experiments on two publicly available datasets show that the efficacy of our proposed components, and our proposed framework outperforms the existing state-of-the-art long-tailed methods by a large margin.

References

1. APTOS 2019 blindness detection (2019). https://www.kaggle.com/c/aptos2019-blindness-detection/data
2. Cai, T.T., Frankle, J., Schwab, D.J., Morcos, A.S.: Are all negatives created equal in contrastive instance discrimination? arXiv preprint arXiv:2010.06682 (2020)
3. Cao, K., Wei, C., Gaidon, A., Arechiga, N., Ma, T.: Learning imbalanced datasets with label-distribution-aware margin loss. In: NeurIPS, vol. 32 (2019)
4. Chen, X., Fan, H., Girshick, R., He, K.: Improved baselines with momentum contrastive learning. arXiv preprint arXiv:2003.04297 (2020)
5. Codella, N.C., et al.: Skin lesion analysis toward melanoma detection: a challenge at the 2017 international symposium on biomedical imaging (ISBI), hosted by the international skin imaging collaboration (ISIC). In: ISBI, pp. 168–172 (2018)
6. Dai, Z., Cai, B., Lin, Y., Chen, J.: UniMoCo: unsupervised, semi-supervised and full-supervised visual representation learning. arXiv preprint arXiv:2103.10773 (2021)
7. Dong, Q., Gong, S., Zhu, X.: Class rectification hard mining for imbalanced deep learning. In: ICCV, pp. 1851–1860 (2017)
8. Estabrooks, A., Jo, T., Japkowicz, N.: A multiple resampling method for learning from imbalanced data sets. Comput. Intell. **20**(1), 18 36 (2004)
9. Gong, L., Ma, K., Zheng, Y.: Distractor-aware neuron intrinsic learning for generic 2D medical image classifications. In: Martel, A.L., et al. (eds.) MICCAI 2020. LNCS, vol. 12262, pp. 591–601. Springer, Cham (2020). https://doi.org/10.1007/978-3-030-59713-9_57
10. He, K., Fan, H., Wu, Y., Xie, S., Girshick, R.: Momentum contrast for unsupervised visual representation learning. In: CVPR, pp. 9729–9738 (2020)
11. He, K., Zhang, X., Ren, S., Sun, J.: Deep residual learning for image recognition. In: CVPR, pp. 770–778 (2016)
12. Isensee, F., et al.: nnU-Net: self-adapting framework for u-net-based medical image segmentation. arXiv preprint arXiv:1809.10486 (2018)
13. Ji, W., et al.: Learning calibrated medical image segmentation via multi-rater agreement modeling. In: Proceedings of the IEEE/CVF Conference on Computer Vision and Pattern Recognition (CVPR), pp. 12341–12351, June 2021
14. Kang, B., Li, Y., Xie, S., Yuan, Z., Feng, J.: Exploring balanced feature spaces for representation learning. In: ICLR (2020)
15. Kang, B., et al.: Decoupling representation and classifier for long-tailed recognition. In: ICLR (2020)
16. Koziarski, M.: Radial-based undersampling for imbalanced data classification. Pattern Recogn. **102**, 107262 (2020)

17. Last, F., Douzas, G., Bacao, F.: Oversampling for imbalanced learning based on K-Means SMOTE. arXiv preprint arXiv:1711.00837 (2017)
18. Lin, T.Y., Goyal, P., Girshick, R., He, K., Dollár, P.: Focal loss for dense object detection. In: ICCV, pp. 2980–2988 (2017)
19. Liu, Z., Miao, Z., Zhan, X., Wang, J., Gong, B., Yu, S.X.: Large-scale long-tailed recognition in an open world. In: CVPR, pp. 2537–2546 (2019)
20. Long, J., Shelhamer, E., Darrell, T.: Fully convolutional networks for semantic segmentation. In: CVPR, pp. 3431–3440 (2015)
21. Marrakchi, Y., Makansi, O., Brox, T.: Fighting class imbalance with contrastive learning. In: de Bruijne, M., et al. (eds.) MICCAI 2021. LNCS, vol. 12903, pp. 466–476. Springer, Cham (2021). https://doi.org/10.1007/978-3-030-87199-4_44
22. van den Oord, A., Li, Y., Vinyals, O.: Representation learning with contrastive predictive coding. arXiv preprint arXiv:1807.03748 (2018)
23. Ren, S., He, K., Girshick, R.B., Sun, J.: Faster R-CNN: towards real-time object detection with region proposal networks. IEEE TPAMI **39**(6), 1137–1149 (2017)
24. Robinson, J.D., Chuang, C., Sra, S., Jegelka, S.: Contrastive learning with hard negative samples. In: ICLR (2021)
25. Ronneberger, O., Fischer, P., Brox, T.: U-Net: convolutional networks for biomedical image segmentation. In: Navab, N., Hornegger, J., Wells, W.M., Frangi, A.F. (eds.) MICCAI 2015. LNCS, vol. 9351, pp. 234–241. Springer, Cham (2015). https://doi.org/10.1007/978-3-319-24574-4_28
26. Shrivastava, A., Gupta, A., Girshick, R.: Training region-based object detectors with online hard example mining. In: CVPR, pp. 761–769 (2016)
27. Wang, T., et al.: The devil is in classification: a simple framework for long-tail instance segmentation. In: Vedaldi, A., Bischof, H., Brox, T., Frahm, J.-M. (eds.) ECCV 2020. LNCS, vol. 12359, pp. 728–744. Springer, Cham (2020). https://doi.org/10.1007/978-3-030-58568-6_43
28. Wang, X., Lian, L., Miao, Z., Liu, Z., Yu, S.X.: Long-tailed recognition by routing diverse distribution-aware experts. arXiv preprint arXiv:2010.01809 (2020)
29. Wei, C., Sohn, K., Mellina, C., Yuille, A., Yang, F.: CReST: a class-rebalancing self-training framework for imbalanced semi-supervised learning. In: CVPR, pp. 10857–10866 (2021)
30. Weng, Z., Ogut, M.G., Limonchik, S., Yeung, S.: Unsupervised discovery of the long-tail in instance segmentation using hierarchical self-supervision. In: CVPR, pp. 2603–2612 (2021)
31. Yang, Y., Xu, Z.: Rethinking the value of labels for improving class-imbalanced learning. In: NeurIPS, vol. 33, pp. 19290–19301 (2020)
32. Zang, Y., Huang, C., Loy, C.C.: FASA: feature augmentation and sampling adaptation for long-tailed instance segmentation. In: ICCV, pp. 3457–3466 (2021)
33. Zhang, Y., Kang, B., Hooi, B., Yan, S., Feng, J.: Deep long-tailed learning: a survey. arXiv preprint arXiv:2110.04596 (2021)
34. Zhou, B., Cui, Q., Wei, X.S., Chen, Z.M.: BBN: Bilateral-branch network with cumulative learning for long-tailed visual recognition. In: CVPR, pp. 9719–9728 (2020)

Combining Mixed-Format Labels for AI-Based Pathology Detection Pipeline in a Large-Scale Knee MRI Study

Micha Kornreich[✉], JinHyeong Park, Joschka Braun, Jayashri Pawar, James Browning, Richard Herzog, Benjamin Odry, and Li Zhang

Covera Health, New York, NY 10013, USA
micha.kornreich@coverahealth.com
https://www.coverahealth.com/

Abstract. Labeling for pathology detection is a laborious task, performed by highly trained and expensive experts. Datasets often have mixed formats, including a mix of pathology positional labels and categorical labels. Successfully combining mixed-format data from multiple institutions for model training and evaluation is critical for model generalization. Herein, we describe a novel machine-learning method to augment a categorical dataset with positional information. This is inspired by the emerging data-centric AI paradigm, which focuses on systematically changing data to improve performance, rather than changing the model. In order to improve on a baseline of reducing the positional labels to categorical data, we propose a generalizable two-stage method that directs model attention to regions where pathologies are highly likely to occur, exploiting all the mixed-format data. The proposed approach was evaluated using four different knee MRI pathology detection tasks, including anterior cruciate ligament (ACL) integrity and injury age (5082 cases), and medial compartment cartilage (MCC) high-grade defects and subchondral edema detection (4251 cases). For these tasks, we achieved specificities and sensitivities between 90–94% and 78–93%, respectively, which were comparable to the inter-reader agreement results. On all tasks, we report an increase in AUC score, and an average of 8% specificity and 4% sensitivity improvement, as compared to the baseline approach. Combining a UNet network with a morphological peak-finding algorithm, our method also provides defect localization, with average accuracies between 4.3–5.1 mm. In addition, we demonstrate that our model generalizes well on a publicly available ACL tear dataset of 717 cases, without re-training, achieving 90% specificity and 100% sensitivity. The proposed method can be used to optimize image classification tasks in other medical or non-medical domains, which often have a mixture of categorical and positional labels.

Keywords: MRI · Pathology detection · ACL · Cartilage · Data-centric

Supplementary Information The online version contains supplementary material available at https://doi.org/10.1007/978-3-031-16452-1_18.

L. Wang et al. (Eds.): MICCAI 2022, LNCS 13438, pp. 183–192, 2022.
https://doi.org/10.1007/978-3-031-16452-1_18

1 Introduction

One of the key challenges to the clinical deployment of artificial intelligence models in medical imaging is the failure of models to generalize across institutions, demographics, and imaging protocols [7]. Accordingly, it is important to train and evaluate models over a broad variety of data sources, and to be able to combine these sources efficiently in training.

However, different data sources which focus on the same pathology detection task could include different label data types, as well as different image types. This is especially true in knee MRI studies, where MRI orientations, protocols, and scanners can significantly differ between unassociated institutions. In addition, some data sources include positional labels such as point-landmarks or bounding boxes, while others only include labels in the form of text or categories.

Combining defect bounding box labels with categorical labels was recently explored in a large scale chest x-ray study, using multiple instance learning [8]. The results suggested that combining positional and categorical *defect* labels can improve network attention and performance over purely categorical training. Such attention focusing was previously accomplished in MRI studies by using *anatomical* landmarks (*i.e.*, that do not label a defect), including in recent knee ACL and cartilage studies [1,9–11]. However, models combining different defect label types were not addressed.

We present a two stage model to combine positional point-like defect landmark labels with categorical defect labels. The first stage was trained on positional labels to predict possible defect locations. A compact volume-of-interest (VOI) was cropped around each predicted defect location, to improve network attention. The second stage classified the pathologies in the VOIs using a convolutional network, and was trained on a combination of positional and categorical labels. This two-stage technique overcomes the difficulties object and point detection models face while training on class imbalanced sets [12] - a common scenario in the medical field.

Our method was evaluated on four knee MRI defect detection and localization tasks, including anterior cruciate ligament (ACL) integrity and injury age, as well as medial compartment cartilage (MCC) high-grade defect and subchondral osteoarthritis related edema underlying the cartilage defect. The classification performance was comparable to the inter-reader agreement levels in the radiologists' reviews, and superior to a purely categorical baseline.

For a recent general review of pathology detection in MRI for ACL and cartilage, we refer readers to [6].

The main contributions of this paper are:

- A method to efficiently combine categorical-label datasets with positional-label datasets during training.
- The proposed method can train and infer on studies that include one or multiple series.
- First models, to our knowledge, trained at this scale for ACL injury-age and Osteoarthritis associated subchondral edema underlying the high grade cartilage defect pathology detection.

– Leveraging the above-mentioned series and label type flexibility during training, we were able to use over 5,000 studies from over 25 institutions, as well as validate on a publicly available dataset.

2 Data

The dataset included 5676 ACL reviews collected from 5082 imaging studies, and 4759 MCC reviews, collected from 4251 studies. Studies were split between training (66%), validation (21%) and test sets (13%). The split was performed in two stages. First, we randomly sampled at a 70-30-10% ratio. Then, we randomly sampled positive cases from the training set, until each positive category in the test set had at least 100 cases. The data did not include multiple studies for any single patient.

Studies were collected at over 25 different institutions, and differed in scanner manufacturers, magnetic field strengths, and imaging protocols (Supplementary Fig. 1). The most common series types included fat-suppressed (FS) sagittal (Sag), coronal (Cor) and axial (Ax) orientations, using either T2-weighted (T2) or proton-density (PD) protocols (Supplementary Table 1). For pathology detection, we used either SagFS, SagPD, or both.

Ground Truth Labeling Process. Each study was reviewed by at least one of eight board-certified radiologists with an MSK fellowship. The review was performed using either a structured form (for categorical labels) or a custom viewer. Radiologists using the viewer also annotated the position of the defect. In both formats, the same ACL and MCC defect categories were used (see Supplementary Tables 2 and 3). ACL categories included *ACL defect* (normal, degeneration, partial tear, or complete tear) and *ACL injury age* (non-acute, or acute). For the MCC, structured report categories included *Cartilage defects* (normal or slight thinning, small high-grade defect, moderate high-Grade defect, or large high-grade defect) and *Edema underlying cartilage defects* (none or trace edema, or more than trace edema). The edema labeled in our dataset differs from the one labeled in previous studies [1], since it is limited to non-traumatic, osteoarthritis associated edema that is underlying a high-grade defect. This distinction is

Table 1. Available categorical and position-labeled data for different pathologies.

Labels	Class	ACL C. Tear	ACL acute	MCC edema	MCC grade
Categorical	0	2323	2161	1327	1122
	1	147	80	198	403
Positional	0	1794	1907	2260	1808
	1	818	705	466	918
Total		5082	4853	4251	4251

clinically important, since Osteoarthritis associated edema is a good predictor of structural deterioration in knee osteoarthritis [5].

Notably, an annotated review could include the same location label type (*e.g.*, a small high-grade defect) multiple times in the same series, one for each such observed defect on the cartilage surface.

Labels Used by Models. For model training and evaluation, we grouped label categories to create 4 tasks that can assist in surgical decision making. For ACL, we trained a model to differentiate *Complete tear* from *Not-complete tear*, and another to predict *Acute* vs. *Non-acute* states. In the MCC, one task was *High-grade defect* vs. *Not-high-grade defect*, and another was *Underlying edema* vs. *None or trace edema* (Table 1 and Supplementary Table 4).

Inter-reader agreement analysis was conducted on 1398 studies with multiple reviews. For training and testing, if two conflicting reviews for the same study existed, the position-annotated review was preferred over the categorical-only one.

3   Methods

Preprocessing Using Deep Reinforcement Learning. Images were automatically cropped around the ACL or MCC prior to pathology detection. Two anatomical landmarks, the Intercondylar Eminence and the Fibular Styloid, were detected using a deep reinforcement learning model [2], and a VOI was positioned with respect to the location of the landmarks. VOI dimensions were determined by clinical experts to include the anatomy of interest (ACL or MCC).

The ACL VOI was a $75 \times 75 \times 75$ mm^3 cube, centered 2.5 mm anteriorly and 2.5 mm medially from the Intercondylar Eminence. The MCC VOI dimensions were 80 mm (superior-inferior), 95 mm (Anterior-posterior) and 75 mm (left-right). The VOI was located 27.5 mm superior, 12.5 mm anterior, and 12.5 mm medial to the Intercondylar Eminence.

Cropped images were linearly interpolated in-plane to a 0.325 mm resolution. Images with out-of plane resolution below 2 mm were sub-sampled (but never interpolated out of plane) to approximately a 4 mm resolution. Images were then intensity-standardized by clipping the 1st and 99th percentile intensities, followed by volume normalization to 0 mean intensity and 1 standard deviation.

Baseline Convolutional Network. As a baseline to our proposed method, we trained a 3D ResNet50 for each of the four tasks using the same preprocessing steps described above. In order to include the position-annotated labels in baseline training, we used their categorical labels only. Following preprocessing, the VOI was in-plane padded to a square, and resized to 256×256 pixels. The number of slices was fixed to 24, by either padding or slicing. We also experimented with 128×128 and 320×320 pixel images, which both achieved slightly worse baseline results and were discarded.

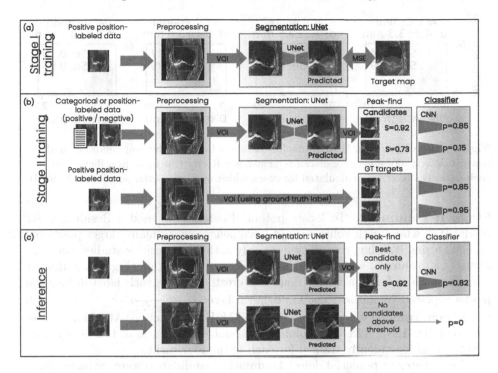

Fig. 1. Architecture. (a) The segmentation UNet is trained during Stage I, using MSE loss to the Target map. (b) The classifier is trained during Stage II, using cropped VOI that were centered either around a positional label created by the expert annotator, or around a candidate label predicted by the UNet and peak-finding algorithm. (c) During inference, positional labels are not used. If the peak-finding failed for the case, the model predicts Class 0 (negative).

A dropout modification to the convolutional network allowed us to train a single model on studies with either Sag FS, Cor FS, or both. The network had two parallel encoders, one for Sag and another for Cor images. The features from the encoders were concatenated and forwarded to a fully connected network. Whenever one of the series was missing, its corresponding feature vector was dropped-out, while the other feature vector was multiplied by two. This was performed both in training and inference.

3.1 Proposed Model Using Mixed-Format Labels

The proposed method utilizes both categorical and positionally-labeled data formats during training, which is performed in two stages, as explained below. Models were trained using PyTorch 1.7.1 and Albumentations 1.1.0 software on an AWS *p3.x2large* instance (16 GB v100 Tesla GPU), where 200 Stage I followed by 50 Stage II epochs took 24 h. GPU memory allowed batch sizes up to 10 and 36 in Stage I and II, respectively.

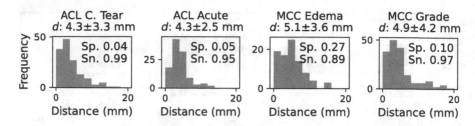

Fig. 2. Stage I results. Histograms for distances between the best candidate and the nearest defect, along average distance $d\pm$std, sensitivity (Sn.) and Specificity (Sp.) for each task. Distances are calculated for cases which were predicted positive by Stage II.

Stage I: Landmark. To locate potential defects, we used a Residual UNet model [13], where each volume could have none, one, or many target positional labels. During training, this stage used only pathology-positive studies, and only series (*i.e.*, volumes) with at least one positional annotation (Fig. 1a). Following [15], for each volume, a target map was created, where each label in location μ was replaced by an isotropic Gaussian sphere: $I_G = \frac{1}{\sigma\sqrt{2\pi}}e^{-\|x-\mu\|^2/2\sigma^2}$, with $\sigma = 10$ mm. Training was performed with an MSE loss function, ADAM optimizer (lr $= 0.0001$), $128 \times 128 \times 24$ volume size, and a batch size of ten. A separate UNet was independently trained for each of the four tasks.

Coordinates of potential defect landmarks (candidates) were extracted from the UNet output, using a fast peak-finding algorithm, originally developed for particle-tracking [3]. During training, all candidates were forwarded to Stage II. During test and validation, only the "best" candidate was selected from each series for stage II (see Supplementary Fig. 2). Whenever Stage I found no defect candidates, the full model prediction was negative (class 0).

Stage II: Pathology Detection. Classification was performed using a 3D ResNet50 with an ADAM optimizer (lr $= 0.0001$). For each task, the model was trained and evaluated on $40 \times 40 \times 40$ mm^3 defect-VOI cubes, which were resized to $128 \times 128 \times 12$ pixels. Each cube was centered around a single candidate defect location that was predicted in stage I, or a location provided by our ground-truth annotations (Fig. 1b). Limiting the classifier to these compact VOIs was meant to improve network attention, and subsequent performance. Series for which stage I found no candidates were not included in stage II training. Training was performed by cross-entropy loss on each series, where the categorical ground truth for the study (rather than series) was used. To assess the performance of our complete model on unlabeled data, we only used locations predicted by the trained stage I model during inference (Fig. 1c).

Perturbations and Augmentation Strategy. In both stages, augmentations included blurring, uniform noise, gamma shift, horizontal flips (for Cor only) and reverse ordering of slices (for Sag only). In addition, during stage II training, the defect location was shifted uniformly in the $[-3.5, 3.5]$ mm range in all axes.

4   Results and Discussion

Baseline Convolutional Network Performance. The baseline convolutional model was evaluated on two datasets: 1) including only categorical labels (Labels = *Categ.* and Method = *ResNet* in Table 2) and, 2) a unified dataset which included categorical labels originating from both the categorical and the positional-annotated datasets (Labels = *Both* and Method = *ResNet* in Table 2). When training the baseline model using the unified dataset, all positional-annotated data was reduced to categorical format by taking the most severe label for each study, and removing the positional information.

4.1   Performance of Proposed Model Using Mixed-Format Labels

Stage I: Landmark. Stage I training was designed to achieve high sensitivity, since false positive studies would be filtered by stage II. Indeed, in three tasks we observed sensitivity exceeding 95% (Fig. 2). By training on positive samples only at stage I and using stage II for filtering, we circumvent difficulties encountered when training object detection models on mostly negative samples.

The localization accuracy of stage I confirms that the defects are captured by the $40 \times 40 \times 40\,mm^3$ VOI cubes used by the following stage (see Fig. 2).

Table 2. Ablation study of different training methods and datasets, where each model was run 5 times using randomly initialized weights to produce average ± std. Inter-reader sensitivity and specificity appear in the last row.

Labels method perturb		Categ ResNet	Positional two-stage	Positional two-stage +	Both ResNet	Both two-stage	Both two-stage +	Inter-reader
ACL C. Tear	Sp.	82.8±1.3	**92.4±0.8**	90.2±0.7	89.4±0.8	92.2±0.4	**92.2±0.7**	97
	Sn.	47.8±5.8	65.4±1.9	89.4±1.0	**91.0±0.6**	76.4±1.2	**92.6±0.5**	84
	AUC	72.0±0.6	90.8±0.4	94.8±0.4	**95.8±0.3**	91.8±0.4	**97.0±0.2**	
ACL acute	Sp.	65.8±1.7	89.8±0.7	**93.4±1.0**	**94.0±1.4**	89.8±1.0	92.2±0.7	97
	Sn.	**74.8±3.0**	69.8±1.5	73.0±1.4	64.0±0.9	72.4±1.0	**78.4±1.0**	74
	AUC	75.6±1.6	84.4±0.5	87.6±0.5	**88.0±0.6**	85.8±0.4	**89.2±0.4**	
MCC edema	Sp.	73.6±2.4	89.2±0.7	**94.0±0.9**	82.8±1.2	90.8±0.7	**92.8±0.7**	92
	Sn.	64.4±2.7	68.3±0.8	74.2±0.7	**80.8±0.4**	70.2±0.7	**78.4±0.5**	69
	AUC	74.2±1.2	86.4±0.5	**88.4±0.5**	87.4±0.5	87.0±0.9	**90.2±0.4**	
MCC grade	Sp.	66.2±1.5	**92.4±0.8**	**89.8±0.7**	87.6±1.0	83.2±1.2	89.0±0.6	87
	Sn.	77.8±1.6	75.2±0.7	80.4±1.0	77.4±0.5	**85.4±0.5**	**88.2±0.4**	84
	AUC	79.6±1.4	90.4±0.5	**91.6±0.5**	90.4±0.5	91.0±0.6	**93.8±0.4**	

Stage II: Pathology Detection. Final classification results were obtained at stage II inference, using the cropped volumes. Each volume was centered around a best defect candidate predicted by stage I. The sensitivity, specificity, and AUC are detailed under *Two-stage* method in Table 2. For ablation research, four different models were trained. Two models only used positional-labels in training (Labels = *Positional* in Table 2). This was achieved by removing the positional information from the annotations, and using only the categorical information. The other two used both categorical and positional datasets, facilitated by our two-stage combined approach (Labels = *Both* in Table 2). In addition, in two of the four models we added a random perturbation shift to the best candidate location, sampled uniformly in the range [−3.5, 3.5] mm in each direction. Evaluation was performed on the same data set for all four models.

Our combined method achieved specificities and sensitivities between 89–94% and 78–93%, respectively, which were comparable to the inter-reader agreement results. These results were, on average, 8% specificity and 4% sensitivity over the baseline model. A McNemar's test [4] comparing our method with the baseline model (columns 7 and 5 in Table 2, respectively) yielded a 10^{-6} p-value. Since the dataset is not class balanced, we also computed the p-values for positive cases (sensitivity, p-value = 0.0001) and negative cases (specificity, p-value = 0.0008), indicating that the performance improvement was statistically significant.

Our best results are comparable to the inter-reader agreement between the board-certified MSK fellowship trained radiologists that labeled our ground-truth data. Notably, it is unusual for a model to outperform noisy ground-truth agreement rates in evaluation, unless the evaluation set is obtained from a higher-quality source. However, our test set had disproportionately more positional-annotated studies, which the radiologists established as more reliable (Supplementary Table S5). Therefore, we maintain that higher performance evaluation is possible, given the assumption that the test had higher quality labels.

Public Dataset Validation. The trained model utilized data from multiple institutions, using various protocols, with either Cor, Sag or both orientations. To further validate its generalizability, we evaluated performance, without any re-training, on a publicly available ACL dataset [14]. The dataset included 917 Sag PDFS 12-bit grayscale images. 717 studies (≈76%) were classified as non-injured, 182 (≈19%) partially injured, 45 (≈5%) completely ruptured. Since our model differentiates complete tear from not complete tears, we mapped their class labels from 1 to 0 and 2 to 1. Even though our network was trained on data that typically had both Sag and Cor series, it achieved 90% specificity and 100% sensitivity, which were comparable to results on our test set.

5 Conclusions

We proposed a novel method to flexibly combine categorical labels with positional labels during training, and demonstrated its applicability in four knee MRI pathology detection tasks. Our method leverages available positional-annotated data to attach location to categorical labels, which improves the overall model performance. In addition, it reliably localizes the defects, which is useful in several potential applications, such as computer aided diagnosis and AI-based quality assurance. We show that without any re-training, our model, which was trained to use either one or two MRI orientations, can generalize well to a publicly available, which included one orientation (Sag) only. Notably, our method can be employed in other computer vision domains, such as captioning, where similar mixed-format label types are often available during training.

References

1. Astuto, B., et al.: Automatic deep learning-assisted detection and grading of abnormalities in knee MRI studies. Radiol. Artif. Intell. **3**(3), e200165 (2021)
2. Browning, J., et al.: Uncertainty aware deep reinforcement learning for anatomical landmark detection in medical images. In: de Bruijne, M., et al. (eds.) MICCAI 2021. LNCS, vol. 12903, pp. 636–644. Springer, Cham (2021). https://doi.org/10.1007/978-3-030-87199-4_60
3. Crocker, J.C., Grier, D.G.: Methods of digital video microscopy for colloidal studies. J. Colloid Interface Sci. **179**(1), 298–310 (1996)
4. Everitt, B.S.: The Analysis of Contingency Tables. CRC Press, New York (1992)
5. Felson, D.T., et al.: Bone marrow edema and its relation to progression of knee osteoarthritis. Ann. Internal Med. **139**(5(1)), 330–336 (2003)
6. Fritz, B., Fritz, J.: Artificial intelligence for MRI diagnosis of joints: a scoping review of the current state-of-the-art of deep learning-based approaches. Skeletal Radiol. **51**(2), 315–329 (2021)
7. Futoma, J., Simons, M., Panch, T., Doshi-Velez, F., Celi, L.A.: The myth of generalisability in clinical research and machine learning in health care. Lancet Digital Health **2**(9), e489–e492 (2020)
8. Li, Z., et al.: Thoracic disease identification and localization with limited supervision. In: Proceedings of the IEEE Conference on Computer Vision and Pattern Recognition, pp. 8290–8299 (2018)
9. Liu, F., et al.: Fully automated diagnosis of anterior cruciate ligament tears on knee MR images by using deep learning. Radiol. Artif. Intell. **1**(3), 180091 (2019)
10. Liu, F., et al.: Deep learning approach for evaluating knee MR images: achieving high diagnostic performance for cartilage lesion detection. Radiology **289**(1), 160–169 (2018)
11. Namiri, N.K., et al.: Deep learning for hierarchical severity staging of anterior cruciate ligament injuries from MRI. Radiol. Artif. Intell. **2**(4), e190207 (2020)
12. Oksuz, K., Cam, B.C., Kalkan, S., Akbas, E.: Imbalance problems in object detection: a review. IEEE Trans. Pattern Anal. Mach. Intell. **43**(10), 3388–3415 (2020)
13. Ronneberger, O., Fischer, P., Brox, T.: U-Net: convolutional networks for biomedical image segmentation. In: Navab, N., Hornegger, J., Wells, W.M., Frangi, A.F. (eds.) MICCAI 2015. LNCS, vol. 9351, pp. 234–241. Springer, Cham (2015). https://doi.org/10.1007/978-3-319-24574-4_28

14. Štajduhar, I., Mamula, M., Miletić, D., Uenal, G.: Semi-automated detection of anterior cruciate ligament injury from MRI. Comput. Methods Programs Biomed. **140**, 151–164 (2017)
15. Yang, D., et al.: Automatic vertebra labeling in large-scale 3D CT using deep image-to-image network with message passing and sparsity regularization. In: Niethammer, M., et al. (eds.) IPMI 2017. LNCS, vol. 10265, pp. 633–644. Springer, Cham (2017). https://doi.org/10.1007/978-3-319-59050-9_50

Task-Oriented Self-supervised Learning for Anomaly Detection in Electroencephalography

Yaojia Zheng[1,2], Zhouwu Liu[1,2], Rong Mo[3], Ziyi Chen[3], Wei-shi Zheng[1,2], and Ruixuan Wang[1,2(✉)]

[1] School of Computer Science and Engineering,
Sun Yat-sen University, Guangzhou, China
wangruix5@mail.sysu.edu.cn
[2] Key Laboratory of Machine Intelligence and Advanced Computing,
MOE, Guangzhou, China
[3] The First Affiliated Hospital, Sun Yat-sen University, Guangzhou, China

Abstract. Accurate automated analysis of electroencephalography (EEG) would largely help clinicians effectively monitor and diagnose patients with various brain diseases. Compared to supervised learning with labelled disease EEG data which can train a model to analyze specific diseases but would fail to monitor previously unseen statuses, anomaly detection based on only normal EEGs can detect any potential anomaly in new EEGs. Different from existing anomaly detection strategies which do not consider any property of unavailable abnormal data during model development, a task-oriented self-supervised learning approach is proposed here which makes use of available normal EEGs and expert knowledge about abnormal EEGs to train a more effective feature extractor for the subsequent development of anomaly detector. In addition, a specific two-branch convolutional neural network with larger kernels is designed as the feature extractor such that it can more easily extract both larger-scale and small-scale features which often appear in unavailable abnormal EEGs. The effectively designed and trained feature extractor has shown to be able to extract better feature representations from EEGs for development of anomaly detector based on normal data and future anomaly detection for new EEGs, as demonstrated on three EEG datasets. The code is available at https://github.com/ironing/EEG-AD.

Keywords: Anomaly detection · Self-supervised learning · EEG

1 Introduction

Electroencephalography (EEG) is one type of brain imaging technique and has been widely used to monitor and diagnose brain status of patients with various brain diseases (e.g., epilepsy) [2,10–12,16]. EEG data typically consists of multiple sequences (or channels) of waveform signals, with each sequence obtained by densely sampling electrical signals of brain activities from a unique electrode

© The Author(s), under exclusive license to Springer Nature Switzerland AG 2022
L. Wang et al. (Eds.): MICCAI 2022, LNCS 13438, pp. 193–203, 2022.
https://doi.org/10.1007/978-3-031-16452-1_19

attached to a specific position on patient's head surface. While brain activities can be recorded by EEG equipment over hours or even days, clinicians often analyze EEG data at the level of seconds, considering that cycles of most brain activities varies between 0.5 Hz and 30 Hz. Therefore, it is very tedious to manually analyze long-term EEG data and automated analysis of EEG would largely alleviate clinician efforts in timely monitoring patient statuses.

Currently, most automated analyses of EEGs focus on specific diseases [1, 8,17], where labelled EEGs at the onset of disease and normal (healthy) status are collected to train a classifier for prediction of patient status at the level of seconds. However, such automated systems can only help analyze specific diseases and would fail to recognize novel unhealthy statuses which do not appear during classifier training. In contrast, developing an anomaly detector based on only normal EEGs has the potential to detect any possible unhealthy status (i.e., anomaly) in new EEG data. While multiple anomaly detection strategies have been developed for both natural and medical image analyses [22,24], including statistical approaches [13,18], discriminative approaches [4,25]reconstruction approaches [19,27]and self-supervised learning approaches [5,15], very limited studies have been investigated on anomaly detection based on normal EEGs only [26]. Furthermore, all these strategies build anomaly detectors without considering any property of anomaly due to absence of abnormal data during model development. One exception is the recently proposed CutPaste method for anomaly detection in natural images [14], where simulated abnormal images were generated by cutting and pasting small image patches in normal images and then used to help train a more effective feature extractor and anomaly detector.

Inspired by the CutPaste method, we propose a novel task-oriented self-supervised learning approach to train an effective feature extractor based on normal EEG data and expert knowledge (key properties including increased amplitude and unusual frequencies) about unavailable abnormal EEGs. In addition, a specific two-branch convolutional neural network (CNN) with larger kernels is designed for effective extraction of both small-scale and large-scale features, such that the CNN feature extractor can be trained to extract features of both normal and abnormal EEGs. The feature extractor with more powerful representation ability can help establish a better anomaly detector. State-of-the-art anomaly detection performance was obtained on one internal and two public EEG datasets, confirming the effectiveness of the proposed approach.

2   Methodology

In this study, we try to solve the problem of anomaly detection in EEGs when only normal EEG data is available for training. A two-stage framework is proposed here, where the first stage aims to a train a feature extractor using a novel self-supervised learning method, and the second stage can adopt any existing generative or discriminative method to establish an anomaly detector based on the feature representations from the well-trained feature extractor.

2.1   Task-Oriented Self-supervised Learning

Various self-supervised learning (SSL) strategies have been proposed to train feature extractors for downstream tasks in both natural and medical image analysis.
To make a feature extractor more generalizable for downstream tasks, existing
SSL strategies are often designed purposely without regard to any specific downstream task. That means, SSL strategies often do not consider characteristics
in specific downstream tasks. However, when applying any such SSL technique
to an anomaly detection task, the feature extractor based on only normal data
would less likely learn to extract features of abnormal data, and therefore may
negatively affect model performance in the subsequent anomaly detection task.

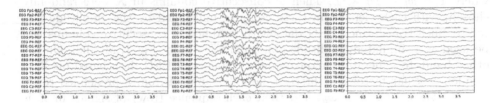

Fig. 1. Transformation of normal EEG (Left) to generate simulated amplitude-
abnormal (Middle) and frequency-abnormal (Right) EEGs. One EEG data consists
of multiple sequences (channels, y-axis) of wave signals. x-axis: time (seconds).

Different from most SSL strategies, a novel SSL strategy is proposed here to
train a feature extractor which can extract features of both normal and abnormal EEG data. Specifically, considering that abnormal EEGs are characterized
by increased wave amplitude or temporally slowed or abrupt wave signals, two
special transformations are designed to generate simulated abnormal EEG data.
One transformation is to temporally locally increase amplitude of normal EEG
signals (Fig. 1, Middle), and the other transformation is to temporally increase or
decrease the frequency of normal EEG signals (Fig. 1, Right). These amplitude-
abnormal and frequency-abnormal data, together with original normal EEGs,
form a 3-class dataset for the training of a 3-class CNN classifier. The feature
extractor part of the well-trained classifier would be expected to learn to extract
features of both normal and (simulated) abnormal EEGs. While the simulated
abnormal data are different from real abnormal EEGs, empirical evaluations
show the feature extractor trained with simulated abnormal EEGs helps improve
the performance of anomaly detection significantly.

Generation of Self-labeled Abnormal EEG Data: Denote a normal EEG
data by a matrix $\mathbf{X} \in \mathbb{R}^{K \times L}$, where K represents the number of channels
(sequences) and L represents the length of each sequence. To generate an
amplitude-abnormal EEG data based on $\mathbf{X}$, a scalar amplitude factor α is firstly
sampled from a predefined range $[\alpha_l, \alpha_h]$ where $1 < \alpha_l < \alpha_h$, followed by sampling a segment length w from a predefined sequence segment range $[w_l, w_h]$

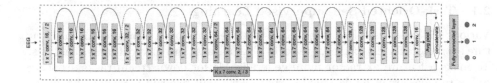

Fig. 2. The two-branch architecture for feature extractor training. The second branch (lower part) consists of only one convolutional layer for extraction of small-scale features. The part in the blue dotted box is the feature extractor. (Color figure online)

where $1 < w_l < w_h < L$. Then w consecutive columns in $\mathbf{X}$ were randomly chosen, with each element in these columns multiplied by the amplitude factor α. Such transformed EEG data with modified w consecutive columns can be used as a simulated amplitude-abnormal EEG data (Fig. 1, Middle). On the other hand, to generate a lower-frequency abnormal EEG data based on $\mathbf{X}$, a frequency scalar factor ω is firstly randomly sampled from a predefined range $[\omega_l, \omega_h]$ where $1 < \omega_l < \omega_h$, and then each sequence (row) of signals in $\mathbf{X}$ is linearly interpolated (i.e., upsampled) by the factor ω to generate an elongated EEG data $\mathbf{X}' \in \mathbb{R}^{K \times L'}$, where $L' = \lfloor \omega L \rfloor$ is the largest number which is equal to or smaller than ωL. One frequency-abnormal EEG data can be generated by randomly choosing L consecutive columns from $\mathbf{X}'$. Similarly, to alternatively generate a higher-frequency abnormal EEG data from $\mathbf{X}$, the frequency scalar factor ω' is firstly randomly sampled from another predefined range $[\omega'_l, \omega'_h]$ where $0 < \omega'_l < \omega'_h < 1$, and then each row of signals in $\mathbf{X}$ is down-sampled by the factor ω' to generate a shortened EEG data. The shortened EEG data is then concatenated by itself multiple times along the temporal (i.e., row) direction to obtain a temporary EEG data $\mathbf{X}'' \in \mathbb{R}^{K \times L''}$ where $L'' = \lfloor \omega' L \rfloor \cdot \lceil \frac{1}{\omega'} \rceil \geq L$. One higher-frequency abnormal EEG data can be obtained by randomly choosing L consecutive columns from $\mathbf{X}''$ (when $L'' > L$) or just be $\mathbf{X}''$ (when $L'' = L$).

Using these simple transformations and based on multiple normal EEG data, two classes of self-labeled abnormal data will be generated, with one class representing anomaly in amplitude, and the other representing anomaly in frequency. Although more complex transformations can be designed to generate more realistic amplitude- and frequency-abnormal EEGs, empirical evaluations show the simple transformations are sufficient to help train an anomaly detector for EEGs.

Architecture Design for Feature Extractor: To train a feature extractor with more powerful representation ability, we designed a specific CNN classifier based on the ResNet34 backbone (Fig. 2). Considering that two adjacent channels (rows) in the EEG data do not indicate spatial proximity between two brain regions, one-dimensional (1D) convolutional kernels are adopted to learn to extract features from each channel over convolutional layers as in previous studies [9]. However, different from the previously proposed 1D kernels of size 1×3, kernels of longer size in time (i.e., 1×7 here) is adopted in this study. Such longer kernels are used considering that lower-frequency features may last for a longer period (i.e., longer sequence segment) in EEGs and therefore would not be well captured by shorter kernels even over multiple convolutional layers. On the other hand, considering that some other anomalies in EEGs may last for very short time and therefore such abnormal features may be omitted after multiple times of pooling or down-sampling over layers, we propose adding a shortcut branch from the output of the first convolutional layer to the penultimate layer. Specifically, the shortcut branch consists of only one convolutional layer in which each kernel is two-dimensional (i.e., number of EEG channels × 7) in order to capture potential correlation across all the channels in short time interval. By combining outputs from the two branches, both small-scale and large-scale features in time would be captured. The concatenated features are fed to the last fully connected layer for prediction of EEG category. The output of the classifier consists of three values, representing the prediction probability of 'normal EEG', 'amplitude-abnormal EEG', and 'frequency-abnormal EEG' class, respectively.

The feature extractor plus the 3-class classifier head can be trained by minimizing the cross-entropy loss on the 3-class training set. After training, the classifier head is removed and the feature extractor is used to extract features from normal EEGs for the development of anomaly detector. Since the feature extractor is trained without using real abnormal EEGs and the simulated abnormal EEGs are transformed from normal EEGs and self-labelled, the training is an SSL process. The SSL is task-oriented because it considers the characteristics (i.e., crucial anomaly properties in both amplitude and frequency of abnormal EEGs) in the subsequent specific anomaly detection task. The feature extractor based on such task-oriented SSL is expected to be able to extract features of both normal and abnormal EEGs for more accurate anomaly detection.

2.2   Anomaly Detection

While in principle any existing anomaly detection strategy can be applied based on feature representations of normal EEGs from the well-trained feature extractor, here the generative approach is adopted to demonstrate the effectiveness of the proposed two-stage framework considering that a large amount of normal EEG data are available to estimate the distribution of normal EEGs in the feature space. Note discriminative approaches like one-class SVM may be a better choice if normal data is limited. As one simple generative approach, multivariate Gaussian distribution $\mathcal{G}(\boldsymbol{\mu}, \boldsymbol{\Sigma})$ is used here to represent the distribution of normal EEGs, where the mean $\boldsymbol{\mu}$ and the covariance matrix $\boldsymbol{\Sigma}$ are directly estimated from the feature vectors of all normal EEGs in the training set, with each vector being the output of the feature extractor given a normal EEG input.

With the Gaussian model $\mathcal{G}(\boldsymbol{\mu}, \boldsymbol{\Sigma})$, the degree of abnormality for any new EEG data $\mathbf{z}$ can be estimated based on the Mahalanobis distance between the mean $\boldsymbol{\mu}$ and the feature representation $f(\mathbf{z})$ of the new data $\mathbf{z}$, i.e.,

$$A(\mathbf{z}) = \sqrt{(f(\mathbf{z}) - \boldsymbol{\mu})^\top \Sigma^{-1} (f(\mathbf{z}) - \boldsymbol{\mu})}. \tag{1}$$

Larger $A(\mathbf{z})$ score indicates that $\mathbf{z}$ is more likely abnormal, and vice versa.

3   Experiments and Results

Experimental Settings: Three EEG datasets were used to evaluate the proposed approach, including the public Children's Hospital Boston-Massachusetts Institute of Technology Database ('CHB-MIT') [21] and the UPenn and Mayo Clinic's Seizure Detection Challenge dataset ('UPMC') [23], and an internal dataset from a national hospital ('Internal'). See Table 1 for details. While only the ictal stage of seizure is included as anomaly in UPMC, both ictal and various interictal epileptiform discharges (IEDs) were included in Internal and CHB-MIT. Particularly, the abnormal waveforms in Internal include triphasic waves, spike-and-slow-wave complexes, sharp-and-slow-wave complex, multiple spike-and-slow-wave complexes, multiple sharp-and-slow-wave complex and ictal discharges. 2 out of 23 patients were removed from CHB-MIT due to irregular channel naming and electrode positioning. For normal EEG recordings lasting for more than one hour in CHB-MIT, only the first hour of normal EEG recordings were included to partly balance data size across patients. In UPMC, only dog data were used because of inconsistent recording locations across human patients. For CHB-MIT and Internal, each original EEG recording was cut into short segments of fixed length (3 s in experiments). For UPMC, one-second short segments have been provided by the organizer. Each short segment was considered as one EEG data during model development and evaluation. Therefore the size of each EEG data is [number of channels, sampling rate × segment duration]. For each dataset, signal amplitude in EEG data was normalized to the range [0, 1] based on the minimum and maximum signal values in the dataset.

Table 1. The statistics of three EEG datasets.

Dataset	Sampling rate	Channels	Patients	Normal EEGs (seconds)	Abnormal EEGs (seconds)
Internal	1024	19	50	30008	14402
CHB-MIT	256	18	21	70307	11506
UPMC	400	16	4	9116	1087

On each dataset, while all abnormal EEG data were used for testing, normal EEG data were split into training and test parts in two ways. One way (Setting I, default choice) is to randomly choose the same number of normal EEGs as that of abnormal EEGs for testing and the remaining is for training, without considering patient identification of EEGs. The other (Setting II, subject level) is to split patients with the cross-validation strategy, such that all normal EEGs of one patient were used either for training or test at each round of cross validation.

In training the 3-class classifier, for each batch of 64 normal EEGs, correspondingly 64 amplitude-abnormal EEGs and 64 frequency-abnormal (32 higher-frequency and 32 lower-frequency) EEGs were generated (see Sect. 2.1). Adam optimizer with learning rate 0.0001 and weight decay coefficient 0.00003 were

Table 2. Performance comparison on three datasets with Setting I. Bold face indicates the best, and italic face for the second best. Standard deviations are in brackets.

Method	Internal			CHB-MIT			UPMC		
	EER↓	F1↑	AUC↑	EER↓	F1↑	AUC↑	EER↓	F1↑	AUC↑
OC-SVM	0.30(0.008)	0.71(0.008)	0.75(0.02)	0.33(0.001)	0.69(0.001)	0.73(0.003)	0.33(0.01)	0.51(0.02)	0.74(0.01)
KDE	0.24(0.001)	0.76(0.001)	0.87(0.001)	0.32(0.002)	0.69(0.002)	0.75(0.003)	0.24(0.003)	0.70(0.004)	0.83(0.003)
AE	0.35(0.01)	0.65(0.01)	0.69(0.02)	0.46(0.007)	0.54(0.007)	0.56(0.01)	0.32(0.02)	0.61(0.02)	0.75(0.02)
MSCRED	0.37(0.02)	0.64(0.03)	0.67(0.03)	0.34(0.03)	0.67(0.03)	0.72(0.03)	0.28(0.02)	0.70(0.02)	0.76(0.02)
USAD	0.25(0.02)	0.76(0.02)	0.83(0.03)	0.30(0.02)	0.69(0.03)	0.79(0.02)	0.24(0.02)	0.75(0.02)	0.82(0.02)
ScaleNet	*0.18(0.01)*	*0.82(0.01)*	*0.90(0.01)*	0.26(0.03)	0.73(0.03)	0.81(0.03)	*0.20(0.03)*	*0.75(0.03)*	*0.89(0.03)*
CutPaste	0.26(0.02)	0.74(0.02)	0.83(0.03)	*0.26(0.01)*	*0.74(0.01)*	*0.83(0.01)*	0.21(0.01)	0.74(0.01)	0.87(0.006)
Ours	**0.11(0.01)**	**0.89(0.01)**	**0.95(0.004)**	**0.16(0.01)**	**0.84(0.02)**	**0.92(0.02)**	**0.13(0.007)**	**0.83(0.01)**	**0.95(0.006)**

adopted, and training was consistently observed convergent within 300 epochs. $[\alpha_l, \alpha_h] = [2.0, 4.0]$, $[w_l, w_h] = [4, L]$, $[\omega_l, \omega_h] = [2, 4]$, and $[\omega'_l, \omega'_h] = [0.1, 0.5]$. The ranges of amplitude and frequency scalar factors were determined based on expert knowledge about potential changes of abnormal brain wave compared to normal signals. The area under ROC curve (AUC) and its average and standard deviation over five runs (Setting I) or multiple rounds of validation (Setting II), the equal error rate (EER), and F1-score (at EER) were reported.

Effectiveness Evaluation: Our method was compared with well-known anomaly detection methods including the one-class SVM (OC-SVM) [20], the statistical kernel density estimation (KDE), and the autoencoder (AE) [7], the recently proposed methods Multi-Scale Convolutional Recurrent Encoder-Decoder (MSCRED) [28] and Unsupervised Anomaly Detection (USAD) [3] for multivariate time series, and the recently proposed SSL methods for anomaly detection, including ScaleNet [26] and CutPaste [14]. Note that ScaleNet [26] uses frequencies of normal EEGs at multiple scales to help detect abnormal EEGs, without considering any characteristics in abnormal EEGs. Similar efforts were taken to tune relevant hyper-parameters for each method. In particular, to obtain feature vector input for OC-SVM and KDE, every row in each EEG data was reduced to a 64-dimensional vector by principal component analysis (PCA) based on all the row vectors of all normal EEGs in each dataset, and then all the dimension-reduced rows were concatenated as the feature representation of the EEG data. For AE, the encoder consists of three convolutional layers and one fully connected (FC) layer, and symmetrically the decoder consists of one FC and three deconvolutional layers. For CutPaste, each normal EEG in each training set is considered as a gray image of size $K \times L$ pixels, and the suggested hyper-parameters from the original study [14] were adopted for model training. For ScaleNet, the method was re-implemented with suggested hyper-parameters [26]. As Table 2 shows, on all three datasets, our method (last row) outperforms all the baselines by a large margin. Consistently, as Fig. 3 (Left) demonstrates, our method performed best as well at the subject level (i.e., Setting II), although the performance decreases a bit due to the more challenging setting. All these results clearly confirm the effectiveness of our method for anomaly detection in EEGs.

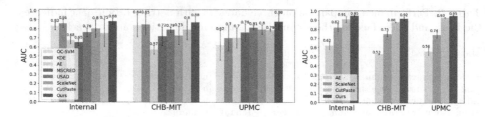

Fig. 3. Performance comparison at the subject level (i.e., Setting II) on each dataset (Left), and the ablation study of the feature extractor training (Right). AUC values were included in figure for each method. Vertical line: standard deviation.

Table 3. The effect of simulated anomaly classes and the two-branch architecture on anomaly detection with 'Internal' dataset.

Amplitude-abnormal		✓		✓	✓	✓	✓
Frequency-abnormal			✓	✓	✓	✓	✓
Two-branch					✓		✓
Larger kernel						✓	✓
AUC	0.71(0.04)	0.91(0.001)	0.89(0.01)	0.93(0.01)	0.94(0.006)	0.94(0.005)	0.95(0.004)

Ablation Studies: To specifically confirm the effectiveness of the proposed task-oriented SSL strategy in training a feature extractor for EEG anomaly detection, an ablation study is performed by replacing this SSL strategy with several other SSL strategies, including (1) training an autoencoder and then keeping the encoder part as the feature extractor, (2) training a ScaleNet and then keeping its feature extractor part whose structure is the same as the proposed one, and (3) contrastive learning of the proposed two-branch feature extractor using the well-known SimCLR method [6]. As Fig. 3 (Right) shows, compared to these SSL strategies which do not consider any property of anomalies in EEGs, our SSL strategy performs clearly better on all three datasets.

Another ablation study was performed to specifically confirm the role of the proposed two-branch backbone and self-labeled abnormal EEGs during feature extractor training. From Table 3, it is clear that the inclusion of the two types of simulated anomalies boosted the performance from AUC = 0.71 to 0.93, and additional inclusion of the second branch ('Two-branch') and change of kernel size from 1×3 to 1×7 ('Larger kernel') further improved the performance.

In addition, one more evaluation showed the proposed simple transformations (based on simulated anomalies in frequency and amplitude individually) performed better than the more complex transformations (based on combinations of simulated abnormal frequency and amplitude), with AUC 0.954 vs. 0.901 on dataset Internal, 0.924 vs. 0.792 on CHB-MIT, and 0.952 vs. 0.918 on UPMC. Although simulated combinations of anomalies could be more realistic, they may not cover all possible anomalies in real EEGs and so the feature extractor could be trained to extract features of only the limited simulated complex anomalies. In contrast, with simple transformations, the feature extractor is trained to extract features which are discriminative enough between normal EEGs and simulated abnormal EEGs based on only abnormal frequency or amplitude features, therefore more powerful and effective in extracting discriminative features.

Sensitivity Studies: The proposed task-oriented SSL strategy is largely insensitive to the hyper-parameters for generating simulated abnormal EEGs. For example, as shown in Fig. 4, when respectively varying the range $[\alpha_l, \alpha_h]$ from $[2.0, 3.0]$ to $[2.0, 7.0]$, the range $[w_l, w_h]$ from $[4, L/5]$ to $[4, L]$, the range $[\omega_l, \omega_h]$ from $[2, 3]$ to $[2, 7]$, and the range $[\omega_l', \omega_h']$ from $[0.1, 0.4]$ to $[0.1, 0.8]$, the final anomaly performance changes in a relatively small range and all of them are clearly better than the baselilne methods. These results support that the proposed task-oriented SSL strategy is quite stable in improving anomaly detection.

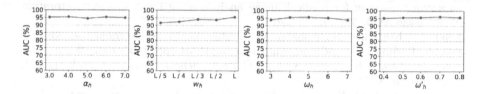

Fig. 4. Sensitivity study of hyper-parameters.

In addition, it is expected the proposed SSL strategy works stably even when injecting incompatible transformations. For example, during training the feature extractor, when a proportion (5%, 10%, 15%, 20%) of simulated abnormal EEGs were replaced by fake abnormal EEGs (each fake EEG randomly selected from real normal EEGs but used as abnormal), the AUC is respectively 0.927, 0.916, 0.898, and 0.883 on Internal, lower than original 0.954 but still kept at high level.

4   Conclusion

In this study, we propose a two-stage framework for anomaly detection in EEGs based on normal EEGs only. The proposed task-oriented self-supervised learning together with the two-branch feature extractor from the first stage was shown to be effective in helping improve the performance of the anomaly detector learned at the second stage. This suggests that although only normal data are available for anomaly detection in some scenarios, transformation of normal data with embedded key properties of anomalies may generate simulated abnormal data which can be used to greatly help develop a more effective anomaly detector.

Acknowledgments. This work is supported by NSFCs (No. 62071502, U1811461), the Guangdong Key Research and Development Program (No. 2020B1111190001), and the Meizhou Science and Technology Program (No. 2019A0102005).

References

1. Achilles, F., Tombari, F., Belagiannis, V., Loesch, A.M., Noachtar, S., Navab, N.: Convolutional neural networks for real-time epileptic seizure detection. Comput. Meth. Biomech. Biomed. Eng. Imaging Vis. **6**, 264–269 (2018)
2. Alturki, F.A., AlSharabi, K., Abdurraqeeb, A.M., Aljalal, M.: EEG signal analysis for diagnosing neurological disorders using discrete wavelet transform and intelligent techniques. Sensors **20**(9), 2505 (2020)
3. Audibert, J., Michiardi, P., Guyard, F., Marti, S., Zuluaga, M.A.: USAD: unsupervised anomaly detection on multivariate time series. In: KDD, pp. 3395–3404 (2020)
4. Chalapathy, R., Menon, A.K., Chawla, S.: Anomaly detection using one-class neural networks. arXiv preprint arXiv:1802.06360 (2018)
5. Chen, L., Bentley, P., Mori, K., Misawa, K., Fujiwara, M., Rueckert, D.: Self-supervised learning for medical image analysis using image context restoration. Med. Image Anal. **58**, 101539 (2019)
6. Chen, T., Kornblith, S., Norouzi, M., Hinton, G.: A simple framework for contrastive learning of visual representations. In: ICML, pp. 1597–1607 (2020)
7. Chen, Z., Yeo, C.K., Lee, B.S., Lau, C.T.: Autoencoder-based network anomaly detection. In: WTS (2018)
8. Craley, J., Johnson, E., Venkataraman, A.: A novel method for epileptic seizure detection using coupled hidden Markov models. In: Frangi, A.F., Schnabel, J.A., Davatzikos, C., Alberola-López, C., Fichtinger, G. (eds.) MICCAI 2018. LNCS, vol. 11072, pp. 482–489. Springer, Cham (2018). https://doi.org/10.1007/978-3-030-00931-1_55
9. Dai, G., Zhou, J., Huang, J., Wang, N.: HS-CNN: a CNN with hybrid convolution scale for motor imagery classification. J. Neural Eng. **17**, 016025 (2020)
10. Dhar, P., Garg, V.K.: Brain-related diseases and role of electroencephalography (EEG) in diagnosing brain disorders. In: ICT Analysis and Applications, pp. 317–326 (2021)
11. Fiest, K.M., et al.: Prevalence and incidence of epilepsy: a systematic review and meta-analysis of international studies. Neurology **88**(3), 296–303 (2017)
12. Gemein, L.A., et al.: Machine-learning-based diagnostics of EEG pathology. Neuroimage **220**, 117021 (2020)
13. Jia, W., Shukla, R.M., Sengupta, S.: Anomaly detection using supervised learning and multiple statistical methods. In: ICML (2019)
14. Li, C.L., Sohn, K., Yoon, J., Pfister, T.: CutPaste: self-supervised learning for anomaly detection and localization. In: CVPR, pp. 9664–9674 (2021)
15. Li, Z., et al.: Superpixel masking and inpainting for self-supervised anomaly detection. In: BMVC (2020)
16. Megiddo, I., Colson, A., Chisholm, D., Dua, T., Nandi, A., Laxminarayan, R.: Health and economic benefits of public financing of epilepsy treatment in India: an agent-based simulation model. Epilepsia **57**, 464–474 (2016)
17. Pérez-García, F., Scott, C., Sparks, R., Diehl, B., Ourselin, S.: Transfer learning of deep spatiotemporal networks to model arbitrarily long videos of seizures. In: de Bruijne, M., et al. (eds.) MICCAI 2021. LNCS, vol. 12905, pp. 334–344. Springer, Cham (2021). https://doi.org/10.1007/978-3-030-87240-3_32
18. Rippel, O., Mertens, P., Merhof, D.: Modeling the distribution of normal data in pre-trained deep features for anomaly detection. In: ICPR (2021)

19. Schlegl, T., Seeböck, P., Waldstein, S.M., Langs, G., Schmidt-Erfurth, U.: f-AnoGAN: fast unsupervised anomaly detection with generative adversarial networks. Med. Image Anal. **54**, 30–44 (2019)
20. Schölkopf, B., Williamson, R.C., Smola, A.J., Shawe-Taylor, J., Platt, J.: Support vector method for novelty detection. In: NeurIPS (1999)
21. Shoeb, A.H.: Application of machine learning to epileptic seizure onset detection and treatment. Ph.D. thesis, Massachusetts Institute of Technology (2009)
22. Shvetsova, N., Bakker, B., Fedulova, I., Schulz, H., Dylov, D.V.: Anomaly detection in medical imaging with deep perceptual autoencoders. IEEE Access **9**, 118571–118583 (2021)
23. Temko, A., Sarkar, A., Lightbody, G.: Detection of seizures in intracranial EEG: UPenn and Mayo clinic's seizure detection challenge. In: EMBC, pp. 6582–6585 (2015)
24. Tian, Y., et al.: Constrained contrastive distribution learning for unsupervised anomaly detection and localisation in medical images. In: de Bruijne, M., et al. (eds.) MICCAI 2021. LNCS, vol. 12905, pp. 128–140. Springer, Cham (2021). https://doi.org/10.1007/978-3-030-87240-3_13
25. Wang, J., Cherian, A.: GODS: generalized one-class discriminative subspaces for anomaly detection. In: CVPR, pp. 8201–8211 (2019)
26. Xu, J., Zheng, Y., Mao, Y., Wang, R., Zheng, W.S.: Anomaly detection on electroencephalography with self-supervised learning. In: BIBM (2020)
27. Zavrtanik, V., Kristan, M., Skočaj, D.: Reconstruction by inpainting for visual anomaly detection. Pattern Recogn. **112**, 107706 (2021)
28. Zhang, C., Song, D., Chen, Y., Feng, X., Lumezanu, C., Cheng, W., Ni, J., Zong, B., Chen, H., Chawla, N.V.: A deep neural network for unsupervised anomaly detection and diagnosis in multivariate time series data. In: AAAI, pp. 1409–1416 (2019)

Multiple Instance Learning with Mixed Supervision in Gleason Grading

Hao Bian[1], Zhuchen Shao[1], Yang Chen[1], Yifeng Wang[2],
Haoqian Wang[1], Jian Zhang[3], and Yongbing Zhang[2(✉)]

[1] Tsinghua Shenzhen International Graduate School, Tsinghua University,
Beijing, China
bianh21@mails.tsinghua.edu.cn
[2] Harbin Institute of Technology (Shenzhen), Shenzhen, China
ybzhang08@hit.edu.cn
[3] School of Electronic and Computer Engineering, Peking University, Beijing, China

Abstract. With the development of computational pathology, deep learning methods for Gleason grading through whole slide images (WSIs) have excellent prospects. Since the size of WSIs is extremely large, the image label usually contains only slide-level label or limited pixel-level labels. The current mainstream approach adopts multi-instance learning to predict Gleason grades. However, some methods only considering the slide-level label ignore the limited pixel-level labels containing rich local information. Furthermore, the method of additionally considering the pixel-level labels ignores the inaccuracy of pixel-level labels. To address these problems, we propose a mixed supervision Transformer based on the multiple instance learning framework. The model utilizes both slide-level label and instance-level labels to achieve more accurate Gleason grading at the slide level. The impact of inaccurate instance-level labels is further reduced by introducing an efficient random masking strategy in the mixed supervision training process. We achieve the state-of-the-art performance on the SICAPv2 dataset, and the visual analysis shows the accurate prediction results of instance level. The source code is available at https://github.com/bianhao123/Mixed_supervision.

Keywords: Gleason grading · Mixed supervision · Multiple instance learning

1 Introduction

Prostate cancer is the second most common cancer in men, with a large number of new cases every year. For the diagnosis of prostate cancer, whole slide images (WSIs) are currently the gold standard for clinical diagnosis. Pathologists analyze WSIs by visual inspection, classify tissue regions, detect the presence of one or more Gleason patterns, and ultimately make a diagnosis based on a composite

---

H. Bian, Z. Shao, and Y. Chen—-Co-first authors.

© The Author(s), under exclusive license to Springer Nature Switzerland AG 2022
L. Wang et al. (Eds.): MICCAI 2022, LNCS 13438, pp. 204–213, 2022.
https://doi.org/10.1007/978-3-031-16452-1_20

Gleason score. For example, a composite grade of $5 + 4 = 9$ would be assigned to a sample where the primary Gleason grade is 5 and the secondary is 4. However, pathologists still face many challenges in Gleason grading: (1) Since WSIs are of enormous data volume, observation and analysis are time-consuming; (2) WSIs are of poor quality, with artifacts and tissue folding. Therefore, some machine learning and deep learning algorithms provide automatic solutions for Gleason grading. However, due to the long labeling time and the need for professional medical knowledge in Gleason grading, WSIs usually only contain slide-level labels or some limited pixel-level labels. In addition, the refined pixel-level labels may be overlapping and inaccurate sometimes.

When only slide-level labels are available, some weakly supervised multiple instance learning (MIL) algorithms are proposed to predict the slide-level labels of WSIs automatically. At present, commonly embedding-based MIL methods can be divided into two categories: attention-based MIL methods [7,10,13], and correlated MIL methods [9,11,12]. The attention-based MIL method is mainly based on the bypass attention mechanism, which provides additional contribution information for each instance through learnable attention weight. Correlated MIL method mainly includes non-local attention mechanism and self-attention mechanism. These methods can capture the dependencies between instances by calculating the attention scores.

When both slide-level label and limited pixel-level labels are available, methods such as [2,15] are proposed to deal with mixed supervision scenarios, which can promote the classification performance. However, these mixed supervision methods do not consider the impact of limited inaccurate pixel-level labels on model performance.

In this work, we propose a mixed supervision Transformer based on the MIL framework. First, pixel-level labels are converted into instance-level labels through the superpixel-based instance feature and label generation. The slide-level multi-label classification task and the instance-level multi-classification task are jointly trained in the training process. Second, we adopt an effective random masking strategy to avoid the performance loss caused by the inaccurate instance-level labels. At the same time, we perform 2D sinusoidal position encoding on the spatial information of the instance, which is beneficial for the correlation learning between instances. Our method achieves the best slide-level classification performance, and the visual analysis shows the instance-level accuracy of the model in Gleason pattern prediction.

2   Method

2.1   Problem Fomulation

Gleason grading is a multi-label MIL classification task. A WSI is regarded as a bag X, which contains N instances $\{x_1, x_2, \ldots, x_N\}$ and each instance represents a pixel set with a proper size. The instance-level labels $\{y_1, y_2, \ldots, y_N\}$ are unknown, and the bag-level label Y is a ground truth set of ℓ binary labels $\{p_1, p_2, \ldots, p_\ell\}, p_i \in \{0, 1\}$.

In practice, besides slide-level labels, Gleason grading task also has limited pixel-level labels sometimes. Therefore, based on mixed supervision, it would be beneficial to improve the accuracy of Gleason grading by effectively utilizing the two types of labels. However, pixel-level labels may be inaccurate. Therefore, the mixed supervision of the Gleason grading can be divided into two steps, as shown in Fig. 1. First, the inaccurate pixel-level labels are employed to get more reliable instance-level labels. Next, both some instance-level labels and the slide-level label are utilized for mixed supervision model training. In the following, we will provide the description of two steps in detail.

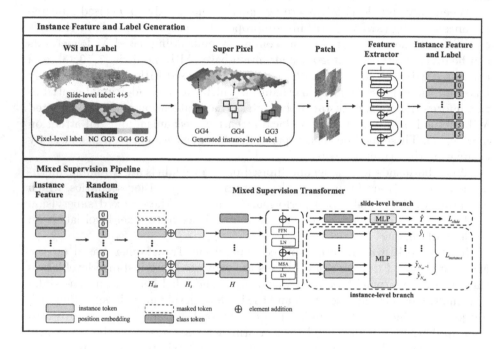

Fig. 1. Overview of our proposed method. In the first step, we obtain instance-level features and labels according to the generated superpixel regions. In the second step, we adopt a random masking strategy to train a mixed supervision Transformer, which utilizes both slide-level label and instance-level labels.

2.2   Instance Feature and Label Generation

Although pixel-level labels in Gleason grading are not always accurate, we can convert the inaccurate pixel-level labels into more reliable instance-level labels. However, patch-based methods cannot obtain a reliable instance-level label containing same tissue structures within one rectangular patch. Inspired by the method in [2], we first filter the blank area and use stain normalization on different WSIs. Then we employ the simple linear iterative clustering (SLIC) algorithm [1] to extract superpixel tissue regions. The area of each superpixel can be considered as an instance. Since the superpixel region is generated according to the similarity of tissue texture structure, each superpixel region contains most of the same tissues and has a smoother boundary than the rectangular block. Therefore, we assign the pixel-level labels with the largest proportion as the labels of instance-level.

Considering the irregularities and different sizes of the generated superpixel regions, we extract the instance feature as follows. First, based on the centroid of each superpixel region, we cut it into one or more patches sized of 224×224. Then, we employ ImageNet pre-trained mobilenetv2 to extract d dimensional features (d is 1280). It is worth noting that in the case of cutting out multiple patches, we average the feature of each patch as the instance-level feature corresponding to each superpixel region.

2.3   Mixed Supervision Pipeline

This section introduces the training pipeline of mixed supervision. Firstly, a random masking strategy is employed to generate the unmasking instance tokens. Then, a mixed supervision Transformer is designed by utilizing both slide-level label and instance-level labels to achieve more accurate Gleason grading at slide level.

Random Masking Strategy. For Gleason grading, pixel-level labels may be inaccurate, which will cause the error in generated instance-level labels and poor performance of mixed supervision. To assist the training of mixed-supervised network, we adopted an effective sampling strategy (random masking) to optimize the training process, inspired by MAE [6]. In each training epoch, we sampled the instance token and corresponding label without replacement according to the uniform distribution. Therefore, unmasked instance tokens $H_{un} = \{z_1, \ldots, z_{N_{un}}\}$ are obtained, where $N_{un} = (1 - m) \times N$, $z_i \in R^d$ and m is masking ratio. The uniform distribution sampling ensures that the unmasked instance tokens are distributed in the entire WSI area, enabling the mixed supervision Transformer to encode the information of the entire WSI as much as possible. The advantages of random masking strategy are two folds: (1) Reducing the impact of label inaccuracy. (2) Reducing computation and memory occupation.

Mixed Supervision Transformer. The Gleason grading task has slide-level and instance-level supervision information. The Transformer structure contains two types of token: class token and instance token, which correspond exactly to the two types of supervision information in the Gleason grading. Based on this property, we design the mixed supervision Transformer. The whole structure can be divided into two branches: slide-level branch and instance-level branch, corresponding to class token output and instance token output, respectively.

Algorithm 1: Class Token and Instance Token Calculation

Input: unmasking tokens $H_{un} = \{z_1, \ldots, z_{N_{un}}\}, z_i \in R^d, H_{un} \in R^{N_{un} \times d}$
Output: class token outputs $\tilde{Y}$, instance token output $\tilde{y}_1, \ldots, \tilde{y}_{N_{un}}$
// 1. add 2D spatial position encoding to unmasking token H_{un}

1 $(p_{i,h}, p_{i,w}) \leftarrow$ centroid coordinate of each instance z_i ;

2 $PE_{(i,pos,2j)} = \sin\left(\frac{pos}{10000^{2j/d_{half}}}\right), PE_{(i,pos,2j+1)} = \cos\left(\frac{pos}{10000^{2j/d_{half}}}\right)$
   $\triangleright pos \in \{\frac{p_{i,h}}{100}, \frac{p_{i,w}}{100}\}, d_{half} = \frac{d}{2}, j \in [0, d_{half} - 1]$;

3 $s_i \in R^d \leftarrow$ CONCAT$[PE_{i,h}, PE_{i,w}]$ $\triangleright$ encoding $p_{i,h}$ and $p_{i,w}$, and concatenate
   two-dimensional embeddings;

4 $h_i \leftarrow z_i + ws_i$ $\triangleright$ add instance token and spatial position token, w is 0.1;
   // 2. correlation learning between instances by Transformer

5 $h_{class} \in R^d \leftarrow$ set a learnable class token ;

6 $H^{(0)} = \{h_{class}, h_1, \ldots, h_{N_{un}}\} \in R^{(N_{un}+1) \times d}$ $\triangleright$ concatenate class token and
   instance token ;

7 **for** $l \in [0 : 1 : L - 1]$ **do**

8 | $H^{(l+1)} =$ Transformer$(H^{(l)})$

9 **end**
   // 3. class token output and instance token output

10 $\tilde{Y} \leftarrow H^{(L)}[0]$ $\triangleright$ input to slide-level branch;

11 $\tilde{y}_1, \ldots, \tilde{y}_{N_{un}} \leftarrow H^{(L)}[1], \ldots, H^{(L)}[N_{un}]$ $\triangleright$ input to instance-level branch;

To obtain class token output and instance token output, firstly, we encode the spatial information of unmasking instance tokens. We obtain the centroid coordinates (p_x, p_y) of the superpixel area corresponding to each instance and encode coordinate information by 2D sinusoidal position encoding [16]. Then, similar to [3–5], we add a learnable class token. The class token and all the instance tokens are combined and fed into Transformer, which can capture slide-level and instance-level information, respectively. The detailed calculation of class token and instance token is shown in Algorithm 1.

The slide-level branch is actually a multi-label classification task. We use multi-layer perception to predict $\hat{Y}$ for the class token output $\tilde{Y}$. Through the sigmoid layer, the slide-level loss L_{bag} is calculated via a multi-label weighted cross entropy loss function L_1 with slide-level label Y:

$$L_{slide} = L_1(Y, sigmoid(\hat{Y})). \tag{1}$$

For the instance-level branch, since we generate an instance-level label for each superpixel instance, it is regarded as a multi-category task. So we use multi-layer perception to predict $\hat{y}_i$ for the instance token output $\tilde{y}_i$. Through the softmax layer, the instance-level loss $L_{instance}$ is calculated by a multi-category weighted cross entropy loss function L_2 with the instance-level label y_i:

$$L_{instance} = L_2(y_i, softmax(\hat{y}_i)). \tag{2}$$

To optimize the model parameters, we minimize the following loss function:

$$L_{total} = \lambda L_{slide} + (1 - \lambda) \sum_k L_{instance}, \tag{3}$$

where $\lambda \in [0, 1]$, and λ is set to 0.5 in our experiment.

3 Experiments

Dataset. We evaluate our method on the SICAPv2 dataset [14] for the Gleason grading task. SICAPv2 is a public collection of prostate H&E biopsies containing slide-level labels (i.e., Gleason scores for each slide) and pixel-level annotations (18783 patches of size 512×512). SICAPv2 database includes 155 slides from 95 different patients. The tissue samples are sliced, stained, and digitized by the Ventana iScan Coreo scanner at $40\times$ magnification. Then the WSIs are obtained by downsampling to $10\times$ resolution, and Gleason's total score is assigned for each slide tissue. The main Gleason grade (GG) distribution in each slide is as follows: 36 noncancerous areas, 40 samples are Gleason grade 3, 64 samples are Gleason grade 4, and 15 samples are Gleason grade 5 (NC, GG3, GG4, and GG5). We randomly split the patient data in the ratio of training: validation: test = 60: 15: 25 and use 4-fold cross-validation for all experiments. Due to unbalanced data distribution, we use the StratifiedKFold method to ensure similar label ratios on the training, validation, and test sets.

Implementations. We implement our method in PyTorch-Lightning and train it on a single NVIDIA GeForce RTX 3090 24 GB GPU. In the mixed supervision Transformer, we employ 2 stacked Transformer blocks with 6 heads, and other configurations are similar to [8]. For 2D sinusoidal position encoding, we set the maximum *pos* as 200. And the embedded dimension is set to 1280 as the instance feature dimension. For the training process, the batch size is 1, and the grad accumulation step is 8. The Ranger optimizer [17] is employed with a learning rate of 2e−4 and weight decay of 1e-5. The validation loss is used as the monitor metric, and the early stopping strategy is adopted, with the patience of 20. We use macro AUC as the evaluation metric.

Baselines. We compared our method with attention based methods such as ABMIL [7], CLAM [10], Loss-Attention [13], correlated based methods such as DSMIL [9], AttnTrans [11], TransMIL [12], and GNN based method SegGini [2]. In our experiment, we reproduce the baselines' code in the Pytorch-Lightning framework based on the existing code. The data processing flow of SegGini is consistent with our method. Other methods follow the CLAM standard processing step to extract patch features with the patch size of 224. And their parameters refer to the default parameter template used for segmenting biopsy slides.

Table 1. Evaluations results on SICAPv2 dataset as $Mean \pm std$. The bold font is the best score and the underline is the second score.

Supervision	Method	AUC
Slide-level supervision	ABMIL [7]	0.6574 ± 0.0825
	CLAM [10]	0.6096 ± 0.0783
	DSMIL [9]	0.5920 ± 0.0656
	LossAttn [13]	0.5778 ± 0.0484
	ATMIL [11]	$\underline{0.9373 \pm 0.0294}$
	TransMIL [12]	0.9152 ± 0.0314
Mixed supervision	SegGini [2]	0.7941 ± 0.1011
	Ours	$\mathbf{0.9429 \pm 0.0094}$

Result and Discussion. According to Table 1, the AUCs of some current SOTA methods, such as ABMIL, CLAM, DSMIL, LossAttn, are ranged from 0.5778 to 0.6574, which is far from satisfaction. The main reason is that Gleason grading is a multi-label task, each instance has different categories, and the correlation between instances should be considered when classifying. The above methods are based on bypass attention, and the model scale is too small to efficiently fit the data, so the performance is relatively poor. ATMIL and TransMIL models are Transformer-based models, which mainly adopt the multi-head self-attention mechanism. These models both consider the correlation between different instances and achieve better performance. However, the network structure of above methods does not utilize the instance-level labels, causing the AUC to be lower than our method from 0.0056 to 0.0277. GNN based method SegGini is also a mixed supervision method, but it adopts all the instance-level label, which will be seriously affected by inaccurate labels. The model we propose employs the random masking strategy and integrates the spatial position information of the instances in WSIs into the Transformer learning process to achieve the performance of SOTA (0.9429).

Table 2. Effects of masking instance token ration and spatial position encoding.

	w/o spatial position encoding	w/ spatial position encoding
Masking 0%	0.9273 ± 0.0103	0.9267 ± 0.0148
Masking 10%	0.9337 ± 0.0118	0.9405 ± 0.021
Masking 25%	0.9247 ± 0.0153	0.9415 ± 0.0163
Masking 50%	$\mathbf{0.9339 \pm 0.0210}$	$\mathbf{0.9429 \pm 0.0094}$
Only slide label	0.9172 ± 0.0145	0.9190 ± 0.0201

According to Table 2, we have the following observations: (1) The performance of the model using slide-level label alone is not better than other models

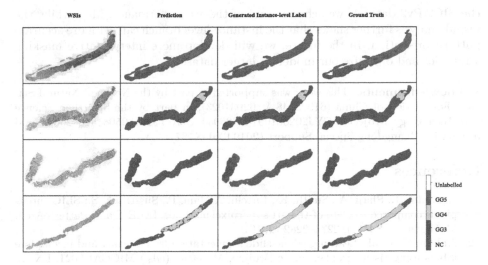

Fig. 2. Gleason pattern prediction visualization.

with mixed supervision. It indicates that adding the instance-level label to each instance token in the Transformer model can improve the slide-level classification. (2) When random masking ratios are 10%, 25% and 50%, the model's performance is about 0.0160 better than using full instance token labels (masking 0%), which shows that the strategy of random masking is effective. (3) The spatial position encoding can improve the performance in most experiment settings.

Visual Analysis. The motivation of our mixed supervision Transformer is that the class token corresponds to the slide information, and the instance token corresponds to the local superpixel information. The combination of these two types of label can improve the utilization of supervision information. In Fig. 2, we show the Gleason pattern prediction of the instance-level branch. It can be seen that the label of each superpixel area can be predicted more accurately.

4 Conclusion

Gleason grading is a multi-label MIL classification task, which has slide-level labels and limited pixel-level labels sometimes. For this task, we propose a method composed of two steps: (1) instance feature and label generation; (2) mixed supervision Transformer. In the first step, we adopt the SILC algorithm to obtain more reliable instance-level labels from inaccurate pixel-level labels. In the second step, both instance-level labels and slide-level labels are utilized for training the mixed supervision Transformer model. Besides, we employ the random masking strategy to further reduce the impact of inaccurate labels. In the SICAPv2 dataset, we achieve state-of-the-art performance. Meanwhile, the visual analysis further shows that the instance-level branch can get more accurate pattern prediction. In the future, we will develop more interpretative masking strategies and optimize our model on larger datasets.

Acknowledgements. This work was supported in part by the National Natural Science Foundation of China (61922048 & 62031023), in part by the Shenzhen Science and Technology Project (JCYJ20200109142808034 & JCYJ20180508152042002), and in part by Guangdong Special Support (2019TX05X187).

References

1. Achanta, R., Shaji, A., Smith, K., Lucchi, A., Fua, P., Süsstrunk, S.: SLIC superpixels compared to state-of-the-art superpixel methods. IEEE Trans. Pattern Anal. Mach. Intell. **34**(11), 2274–2282 (2012)
2. Anklin, V., et al.: Learning whole-slide segmentation from inexact and incomplete labels using tissue graphs. In: de Bruijne, M., et al. (eds.) MICCAI 2021. LNCS, vol. 12902, pp. 636–646. Springer, Cham (2021). https://doi.org/10.1007/978-3-030-87196-3_59
3. Cai, Y., et al.: Mask-guided spectral-wise transformer for efficient hyperspectral image reconstruction. In: Proceedings of the IEEE/CVF Conference on Computer Vision and Pattern Recognition, pp. 17502–17511 (2022)
4. Cai, Y., et al.: MST++: multi-stage spectral-wise transformer for efficient spectral reconstruction. In: Proceedings of the IEEE/CVF Conference on Computer Vision and Pattern Recognition, pp. 745–755 (2022)
5. Dosovitskiy, A., et al.: An image is worth 16×16 words: transformers for image recognition at scale. In: International Conference on Learning Representations (2021). https://openreview.net/forum?id=YicbFdNTTy
6. He, K., Chen, X., Xie, S., Li, Y., Dollár, P., Girshick, R.: Masked autoencoders are scalable vision learners. In: Proceedings of the IEEE/CVF Conference on Computer Vision and Pattern Recognition, pp. 16000–16009 (2022)
7. Ilse, M., Tomczak, J., Welling, M.: Attention-based deep multiple instance learning. In: International Conference on Machine Learning, pp. 2127–2136. PMLR (2018)
8. Jiang, Z.H., et al.: All tokens matter: token labeling for training better vision transformers. In: Advances in Neural Information Processing Systems, vol. 34 (2021)
9. Li, B., Li, Y., Eliceiri, K.W.: Dual-stream multiple instance learning network for whole slide image classification with self-supervised contrastive learning. In: Proceedings of the IEEE/CVF Conference on Computer Vision and Pattern Recognition, pp. 14318–14328 (2021)
10. Lu, M.Y., Williamson, D.F., Chen, T.Y., Chen, R.J., Barbieri, M., Mahmood, F.: Data-efficient and weakly supervised computational pathology on whole-slide images. Nat. Biomed. Eng. **5**(6), 555–570 (2021)
11. Myronenko, A., Xu, Z., Yang, D., Roth, H.R., Xu, D.: Accounting for dependencies in deep learning based multiple instance learning for whole slide imaging. In: de Bruijne, M., Cattin, P.C., Cotin, S., Padoy, N., Speidel, S., Zheng, Y., Essert, C. (eds.) MICCAI 2021. LNCS, vol. 12908, pp. 329–338. Springer, Cham (2021). https://doi.org/10.1007/978-3-030-87237-3_32
12. Shao, Z., Bian, H., Chen, Y., Wang, Y., Zhang, J., Ji, X., et al.: TransMIL: transformer based correlated multiple instance learning for whole slide image classification. In: Advances in Neural Information Processing Systems, vol. 34 (2021)

13. Shi, X., Xing, F., Xie, Y., Zhang, Z., Cui, L., Yang, L.: Loss-based attention for deep multiple instance learning. In: Proceedings of the AAAI Conference on Artificial Intelligence, vol. 34, pp. 5742–5749 (2020)
14. Silva-Rodríguez, J., Colomer, A., Sales, M.A., Molina, R., Naranjo, V.: Going deeper through the Gleason scoring scale: an automatic end-to-end system for histology prostate grading and cribriform pattern detection. Comput. Methods Programs Biomed. **195**, 105637 (2020)
15. Tourniaire, P., Ilie, M., Hofman, P., Ayache, N., Delingette, H.: Attention-based multiple instance learning with mixed supervision on the camelyon16 dataset. In: MICCAI Workshop on Computational Pathology, pp. 216–226. PMLR (2021)
16. Vaswani, A., et al.: Attention is all you need. In: Advances in Neural Information Processing Systems, vol. 30 (2017)
17. Wright, L.: Ranger - a synergistic optimizer (2019). https://github.com/lessw2020/Ranger-Deep-Learning-Optimizer

An Accurate Unsupervised Liver Lesion Detection Method Using Pseudo-lesions

He Li[1], Yutaro Iwamoto[1], Xianhua Han[2], Lanfen Lin[3(✉)], Hongjie Hu[4], and Yen-Wei Chen[1(✉)]

[1] Graduate School of Information Science and Engineering, Ritsumeikan University, Shiga 5250058, Japan
chen@is.ritsumei.ac.jp
[2] Faculty of Science, Yamaguchi University, Yamaguchi 7538511, Japan
[3] College of Computer Science and Technology, Zhejiang University, Hangzhou 310000, China
llf@zju.edu.cn
[4] Department of Radiology, Sir Run Run Shaw Hospital, Zhejiang University, Hangzhou 310000, China

Abstract. Anomaly detection using an unsupervised learning scheme has become a challenging research topic. Unsupervised learning requires only unlabeled normal data for training and can detect anomalies in unseen testing data. In this paper, we propose an unsupervised liver lesion detection framework based on generative adversarial networks. We present a new perspective that learning anomalies positively affect learning normal objects (e.g., liver), even if the anomalies are fake. Our framework uses only normal and pseudo-lesions data for training, and the pseudo-lesions data comes from normal data augmentation. We train our framework to predict normal features by transferring normal and augmented data into each other. In addition, we introduce a discriminator network containing a U-Net-like architecture that extracts local and global features effectively for providing more informative feedback to the generator. Further, we also propose a novel reconstruction-error score index based on the image gradient perception pyramid. A higher error-index score indicates a lower similarity between input and output images, which means lesions detected. We conduct extensive experiments on different datasets for liver lesion detection. Our proposed method outperforms other state-of-the-art unsupervised anomaly detection methods.

Keywords: Unsupervised learning · Liver lesion detection · Generative adversarial network

1 Introduction

Liver cancer is the sixth most diagnosed cancer and the third leading cause of death worldwide [1]. Anomalies in the shape and texture of the liver and visible lesions in

Supplementary Information The online version contains supplementary material available at https://doi.org/10.1007/978-3-031-16452-1_21.

computed tomography (CT) are important biomarkers for disease progression in primary and secondary hepatic tumor disease [2]. In clinical routine, manual techniques are applied, doctors need plenty of hours to annotate the shape and location of liver lesions. However, this process is very subjective and time-consuming. To improve doctors' productivity, automated live lesion detection methods in CT images play an essential role in computer-aided diagnosis systems [3,4].

Following recent trends in the anomaly detection field, there has been a significant increase in deep learning algorithms. In general, these methods can be classified into supervised learning and unsupervised learning methods. The supervised learning methods [5,6], with the help of ground truths guidance, learn anomaly images' feature distribution from global to local. Several supervised methods have been proposed for liver lesion detection in CT images [7,8]. However, supervised learning methods learn features only from annotated anomaly images, which faces the problem of limited training data.

Unsupervised learning-based methods [9–11] are currently increasingly becoming popular for various tasks. These methods do not require manual annotations because they only use normal data training. These methods can rebuild normal areas better than the anomaly areas, and the high reconstruction error (RE) shows the anomalies. In [9] author propose a GAN-based [12] unsupervised anomaly detection approach. The anomaly in the output image is classified using latent space vectors. The network is improved in [10,11] by introducing latent loss and an extra encoder network. However, these techniques still has a high false-positive rate during testing and fails to detect anomalies effectively. In our previous work [13], we proposed a weakly-supervised detection method. We used both normal and image-level annotated abnormal data for training and demonstrated that the detection accuracy could be significantly improved. Compared to unsupervised methods, the limitation of the weakly-supervised method is that we need to use image-level annotated abnormal data for training.

In this paper, to address these issues, we propose a liver lesion detection framework using an unsupervised learning approach. We bring the CycleGAN [14] structure with pseudo-lesions and normal data training into our framework. Our proposed data augmentation technique can create pseudo liver lesions with various shapes, sizes, intensities, and locations. This technique addresses the issue of a lack of training data while also improving the network's capacity to reconstruct normal images. We introduce a U-Net [15] discriminator network to pursue the framework to generate detailed images. Further, we propose a novel reconstruction-error (RE) index based on the image gradient perception pyramid. The RE is also a part of our loss function for image gradient awareness. Extensive experiments conducted on different datasets for liver lesion detection demonstrate that our proposed method outperforms the state-of-the-art methods.

2   Method

The overview of our proposed unsupervised learning framework is shown in Fig. 1(b). Unlike the conventional method in Fig. 1(a), which only training for

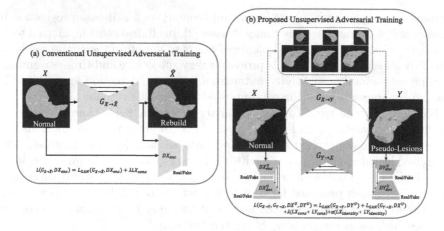

Fig. 1. The illustration of the conventional GAN-based method (a) and the proposed method (b) for unsupervised learning.

rebuilding normal images into their owns ($X \rightarrow \hat{X}$). The CycleGAN [14] structure inspires us, and we bring it into our liver lesion detection framework. Using the proposed data augmentation approach, we first create the pseudo-lesion images (Y) from normal images (X). Then, we learn how to translate normal (X) and pseudo-lesion (Y) images into each other using our networks. The generator and discriminator networks have a U-Net-like [15] structure. Our framework employs two generators and two discriminators. The generator $G_{X \rightarrow Y}$ transforms normal images (X) into pseudo-lesions images (Y). The output of $G_{X \rightarrow Y}$ is classified as real or fake by one discriminator, DY^U. The second generator, $G_{Y \rightarrow X}$, transforms Y to X, while the second discriminator, DX^U, determines if the result of $G_{Y \rightarrow X}$ is real or fake. During the testing stage, we use one generator, $G_{Y \rightarrow X}$, to rebuild input images. Liver lesions can be detected by a high reconstruction error (RE) score between input and output images.

2.1 Unsupervised Learning with Pseudo-lesions

Unsupervised Learning. We believe that learning anomalies positively affect learning normal objects (e.g., liver), and we bring the CycleGAN [14] structure into our framework for learning normal (X) and anomaly features (Y) at the same time. We set pseudo-lesions as Y, and they come from normal data augmentation. Our proposed unsupervised learning in Fig. 1(b) mainly serves for solveing:

$$G_{X \rightarrow Y}, G_{Y \rightarrow X} = argmin_{(G_{X \rightarrow Y}, G_{Y \rightarrow X})} max_{(DX^U, DY^U)}$$
$$L(G_{X \rightarrow Y}, G_{Y \rightarrow X}, DX^U, DY^U). \tag{1}$$

We set pseudo-lesions as Y, and they come from normal data augmentation. Our proposed unsupervised learning in Fig. 1(b) mainly serves for transforming

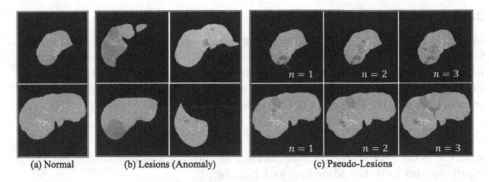

(a) Normal   (b) Lesions (Anomaly)   (c) Pseudo-Lesions

Fig. 2. The examples show normal (a), real lesions (b), and pseudo-lesions (c) images. Augmented samples in (c) come from our proposed strategy producing $n = 1, 2, 3$ pseudo lesion parts.

$X \to Y$ and $Y \to X$. With the help of our cycle learning steps, we can learn normal features more accurately than the conventional method.

Pseudo-lesions. Our data augmentation strategy for producing pseudo-lesions (Y) is inspired by the Cutout [16] method. The Cutout approach wipes out a randomly small rectangular area of a normal image for providing model anomaly data training. Unlike the Cutout approach, we use several normal liver images (without liver lesions) to create anomalies (pseudo-lesions). First, we set a normal image as background. Next, we randomly down-sample and rotate other normal images. Then we place the down-sampled images on the top of the background image and jitter its internal pixel values. We show the pseudo-lesions argumentation process in Fig. 1(b), Fig. 2(a) shows some normal liver images, Fig. 2(b) shows some authentic lesion images, and Fig. 2(c) shows pseudo-lesions examples.

2.2 U-Net Based Discriminator

The U-Net [15] architecture has shown excellent performance for a variety of tasks, particularly for medical images. To construct our discriminator, we employ the U-Net design. The conventional discriminator (in Fig. 1(a)) performs an image-based two-class classification. It extracts features from the whole image and classifies it as either fake or true. The conventional discriminator uses only global information, while our U-Net-based discriminator performs pixel-wise classification for local discrimination and uses both global and local information for discrimination. For stable training, we use spectral-normalization [17] instead of instance-normalization [18]. We set identical design for our two discriminator networks (DX^U, DY^U), and we refer the discriminator encoder as D_{enc}^U and the decoder as D_{dec}^U. The new discriminator loss is now can be defined as two components, i.e., $L_{DX^U} = L_{DX_{enc}^U} + L_{DX_{dec}^U}$.

2.3   Loss Function

We added the GMSD [19] based reconstruction error loss (RE_{GMSD}) into our training process, which will be discussed in Sect. 2.4. For better consistency between normal images (X) and pseudo-lesion images (Y) and their rebuilds during training, we also add structure similarity index (SSIM) [20] and mean squared error (MSE) losses. Our consistency loss is shown below:

$$LX_{cons}(x, \hat{x}) = MSE(x, \hat{x}) + SSIM(x, \hat{x}) + RE_{GMSD}(x, \hat{x}), \quad (2)$$

where $\hat{x}$ is the rebuild image that image x go through two generators. For the y input we also have the same loss as $LY_{cons}(y, \hat{y})$.

Our full loss function is:

$$L(G_{X \to Y}, G_{Y \to X}, DX^U, DY^U) = L_{GAN}(G_{X \to Y}, DY^U) + L_{GAN}(G_{Y \to X}, DX^U)$$
$$+ \lambda(LX_{cons} + LY_{cons}) + \alpha(LX_{identity} + LY_{identity}), \quad (3)$$

where L_{GAN} represents the GAN loss [14], λ and α controls the relative importance of consistency and identity loss. The identity loss is:

$$LX_{identity}(x, G_{Y \to X}(x)) = MSE(x, G_{Y \to X}(x))$$
$$+ SSIM(x, G_{Y \to X}(x)) + RE_{GMSD}(x, G_{Y \to X}(x)). \quad (4)$$

2.4   Liver Lesion Detection by Image Gradient Perception

To detect liver lesions during the testing stage, we use the reconstruction error (RE), liver lesion images having a higher RE index than the normal liver images. RE is used to compute structural differences between the input and the output of our trained model. Unlike conventional MSE-based methods [9], we employ the gradient magnitude similarity deviation (GMSD) [19] as a criterion for liver lesion detection. The GMSD provides image gradient perception, and the GMSD-based RE is more accurate than the MSE-based. The x is the input test sample, and the $\hat{x}$ is the output, the GMSD is defined as:

$$Gri(x) = \sqrt{(x * p_h)^2 + (x * p_v)^2}, \quad (5)$$

$$Gri(\hat{x}) = \sqrt{(\hat{x} * p_h)^2 + (\hat{x} * p_v)^2}, \quad (6)$$

$$GMSD(x, \hat{x}) = \frac{2Gri(x)Gri(\hat{x}) + \sigma}{Gri(x)^2 + Gri(\hat{x})^2 + \sigma}, \quad (7)$$

where $*p_h$ and $*p_v$ denotes the convolution computation by the Prewitt filters along horizontal and vertical directions, σ is a constant for numerical stability. Moreover, to focus on multi-scale feature representation, we build an image pyramid for GMSD. Finally, our GMSD-based RE index is defined as:

$$RE_{GMSD}(x, \hat{x}) = 1 - \frac{1}{4} \sum_{s=1}^{4} GMSD(x_s, \hat{x}_s), \quad (8)$$

the x_s and $\hat{x}_s$ mean the image at scale s, and each scale's image is formed by average pooling.

3   Experiments and Results

3.1   Datasets and Implementation

We train and test our proposed framework on public and private datasets. The LiTS dataset [21] from the MICCAI 2017 Challenge is the public dataset. It has 131 patients' abdominal CT scans. The private dataset contains 90 patients' abdominal CT scans. The liver and lesion areas are labeled by experienced doctors. For all CT scans, pixel intensity values between $[-200, +250]$ HU are employed. We down-sample all images into 256×256 pixels. From these two datasets, we train a segmentation network [22] to extract the liver regions from the CT images. We select normal and anomaly slices (with lesions) based on the lesion masks. Table 1 shows the details of the training and testing datasets. For more details of network backbone architectures and hyperparameters, see supplementary material. We used the entire network for training, but we only use one generator $(G_{Y \rightarrow X})$ for testing. Both datasets are passed five-fold cross-validation in the deep-learning box with the i9-9820X CPU and RTX 8000 GPU.

Table 1. Datasets distribution.

	LiTS	Private
Train	104 Patients	62 Patients
Normal	3443 Slices	1338 Slices
Pseudo-lesions	10329 Slices	4014 Slices
Test	27 Patients	18 Patients
Normal	947 Slices	341 Slices
Lesions (Anomaly)	1436 Slices	383 Slices

3.2   Comparison with State-of-the-Art Methods

We demonstrate that the proposed method is effective by comparing it to several state-of-the-art unsupervised learning methods. The area under the curve (AUC) of the receiver operational characteristic (ROC) is used to evaluate the methods' ability to detect liver lesions. This function plots the true-positive and false-positive rates using different threshold values. The results of single-model training and testing are utilized to compare with other approaches on both datasets. The quantitative results for the methods are shown in Table 2, and Fig. 3 illustrates the curves. The curve is determined by the RE index values. The AUC of our proposed method is 0.861 for the LiTS dataset and 0.844 for the private dataset. Our method surpasses existing methods by a wide margin. Figure 4 shows some examples of prediction outcomes along with the anomaly map generated by our RE index. According to the results, our model effectively localizes the lesion areas from the anomaly map.

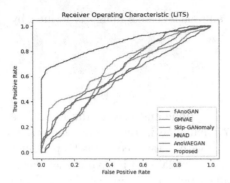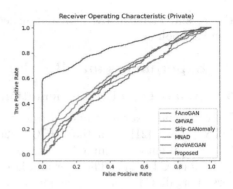

Fig. 3. Area under the curve (AUC) results for the LiTS and private datasets. The better results tend to curve toward the upper left corner.

Table 2. Quantitative results of different methods. The best results are highlighted in bold.

Methods	AUC (LiTS)	AUC (Private)
f-AnoGAN [23]	0.610	0.591
GMVAE [24]	0.666	0.642
Skip-GANomaly [11]	0.642	0.618
MNAD [25]	0.629	0.623
AnoVAEGAN [26]	0.624	0.611
Proposed	**0.861**	**0.844**

3.3   Ablation Study

As a baseline, we use a conventional GAN network with a U-Net generator [11], a discriminator that only contains encoder parts, and MSE and SSIM [20] losses. Using the LiTS dataset, we analyze each component. The results of the ablation experiments are shown in Table 3. Our pseudo-lesions (PL) data augmentation approach provides a considerable AUC in ablation studies. For learning normal features, PL is an effective and efficient method. The discriminator network (U-Net D), which consists of both encoder and decoder parts, encourages the generator to learn the features significantly. When recognizing small changes in the gradient, consistency loss with multi-scale gradient perception (RE_{GMSD}) is more effective in identifying the lesions. Comparison of the different AUC results obtained using the regular RE_{MSE} [9] and proposed RE_{GMSD}, it is noticeable that the image gradient-based RE index outperforms the standard measure index. We also analyze the performance of detecting different types of lesions, see supplementary material.

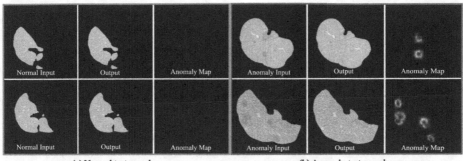

(a) Normal test samples   (b) Anomaly test samples

Fig. 4. Examples show the normal test samples (a, green), their output and anomaly maps, anomaly test samples (b, red), their output, and anomaly maps. We use the RE_{GMSD} to compute the anomaly maps. According to the results, our model localizes the regions of lesion areas from the anomaly maps, and the lesion areas have a brighter color than the surrounding places. (Color figure online)

Table 3. Ablation Study on LiTS dataset. The best result is highlighted in **bold**.

Methods	+PL	+U-Net D	+RE_{GMSD}	AUC(RE_{MSE})	AUC(RE_{GMSD})
Baseline				0.576	0.589
Baseline	✓			0.787	0.829
Baseline	✓	✓		0.817	0.847
Baseline	✓		✓	0.809	0.853
Baseline	✓	✓	✓	0.827	**0.861**

4 Conclusion

In this paper, we present a novel framework for unsupervised liver lesion detection. The unsupervised learning approach is successfully implemented using the pseudo-lesions data augmentation strategy. The U-Net discriminator provides accurate identifications for training results. The combination of multi-scale gradient perception consistency loss and the reconstruction-error (RE) score results in a more accurate and effective detection of liver lesions. In compared to other state-of-the-art methods, our proposed method achieves the major superior performance. In the future, we will explore into more approaches for optimizing training in a more consistent manner.

Acknowledgements. We would like to thank Profs. Ikuko Nishikawa and Gang Xu of Ritsumeikan University, Japan for their advice on this research. This work was supported in part by the Grant in Aid for Scientific Research from the Japanese Ministry for Education, Science, Culture and Sports (MEXT) under the Grant Nos. 20KK0234, 21H03470, and 20K21821, and in part by the Natural Science Foundation of Zhejiang Province (LZ22F020012), in part by Major Scientific Research Project of Zhejiang Lab

(2020ND8AD01), and in part by the National Natural Science Foundation of China (82071988), the Key Research and Development Program of Zhejiang Province.

References

1. Global cancer statistics 2020: GLOBOCAN estimates of incidence and mortality worldwide for 36 cancers in 185 countries. CA Cancer J. Clin. **71**(3), 209–249 (2021). https://doi.org/10.3322/caac.21660
2. Heimann, T., et al.: Comparison and evaluation of methods for liver segmentation from CT datasets. IEEE Trans. Med. Imaging **28**(8), 1251–1265 (2009)
3. Xu, Y., et al.: PA-ResSeg: a phase attention residual network for liver tumor segmentation from multiphase CT images. Med. Phys. **48**(7), 3752–3766 (2021)
4. Zhang, Y., et al.: DeepRecS: from RECIST diameters to precise liver tumor segmentation. IEEE J. Biomed. Health Inform. **26**(2), 614–625 (2021)
5. Girshick, R.: Fast R-CNN. In: Proceedings of the IEEE International Conference on Computer Vision, pp. 1440–1448 (2015)
6. He, K., Gkioxari, G., Dollár, P., Girshick, R.: Mask R-CNN. In: Proceedings of the IEEE International Conference on Computer Vision, pp. 2961–2969 (2017)
7. Ben-Cohen, A., Klang, E., Kerpel, A., Konen, E., Amitai, M.M., Greenspan, H.: Fully convolutional network and sparsity-based dictionary learning for liver lesion detection in CT examinations. Neurocomputing **275**, 1585–1594 (2018)
8. Yan, K., et al.: MULAN: multitask universal lesion analysis network for joint lesion detection, tagging, and segmentation. In: Shen, D., et al. (eds.) MICCAI 2019. LNCS, vol. 11769, pp. 194–202. Springer, Cham (2019). https://doi.org/10.1007/978-3-030-32226-7_22
9. Schlegl, T., Seeböck, P., Waldstein, S.M., Schmidt-Erfurth, U., Langs, G.: Unsupervised anomaly detection with generative adversarial networks to guide marker discovery. In: Niethammer, M., et al. (eds.) IPMI 2017. LNCS, vol. 10265, pp. 146–157. Springer, Cham (2017). https://doi.org/10.1007/978-3-319-59050-9_12
10. Akcay, S., Atapour-Abarghouei, A., Breckon, T.P.: GANomaly: semi-supervised anomaly detection via adversarial training. In: Jawahar, C.V., Li, H., Mori, G., Schindler, K. (eds.) ACCV 2018. LNCS, vol. 11363, pp. 622–637. Springer, Cham (2019). https://doi.org/10.1007/978-3-030-20893-6_39
11. Akçay, S., Atapour-Abarghouei, A., Breckon, T.P.: Skip-GANomaly: skip connected and adversarially trained encoder-decoder anomaly detection. In: 2019 International Joint Conference on Neural Networks (IJCNN), pp. 1–8. IEEE (2019)
12. Goodfellow, I., et al.: Generative adversarial nets. In: Advances in Neural Information Processing Systems 27 (2014)
13. Li, H., et al.: A weakly-supervised anomaly detection method via adversarial training for medical images. In: 2022 IEEE International Conference on Consumer Electronics (ICCE), pp. 1–4. IEEE (2022)
14. Zhu, J.Y., Park, T., Isola, P., Efros, A.A.: Unpaired image-to-image translation using cycle-consistent adversarial networks. In: Proceedings of the IEEE International Conference on Computer Vision, pp. 2223–2232 (2017)
15. Ronneberger, O., Fischer, P., Brox, T.: U-Net: convolutional networks for biomedical image segmentation. In: Navab, N., Hornegger, J., Wells, W.M., Frangi, A.F. (eds.) MICCAI 2015. LNCS, vol. 9351, pp. 234–241. Springer, Cham (2015). https://doi.org/10.1007/978-3-319-24574-4_28
16. DeVries, T., Taylor, G.W.: Improved regularization of convolutional neural networks with cutout. arXiv preprint arXiv:1708.04552 (2017)

17. Miyato, T., Kataoka, T., Koyama, M., Yoshida, Y.: Spectral normalization for generative adversarial networks. arXiv preprint arXiv:1802.05957 (2018)
18. Ulyanov, D., Vedaldi, A., Lempitsky, V.: Instance normalization: the missing ingredient for fast stylization. arXiv preprint arXiv:1607.08022 (2016)
19. Xue, W., Zhang, L., Mou, X., Bovik, A.C.: Gradient magnitude similarity deviation: a highly efficient perceptual image quality index. IEEE Trans. Image Process. **23**(2), 684–695 (2013)
20. Wang, Z., Bovik, A.C., Sheikh, H.R., Simoncelli, E.P.: Image quality assessment: from error visibility to structural similarity. IEEE Trans. Image Process. **13**(4), 600–612 (2004)
21. Bilic, P., et al.: The liver tumor segmentation benchmark (LiTS). arXiv preprint arXiv:1901.04056 (2019)
22. Huang, H., et al.: UNet 3+: a full-scale connected UNet for medical image segmentation. In: 2020 IEEE International Conference on Acoustics, Speech and Signal Processing (ICASSP), ICASSP 2020, pp. 1055–1059. IEEE (2020)
23. Schlegl, T., Seeböck, P., Waldstein, S.M., Langs, G., Schmidt-Erfurth, U.: f-AnoGAN: fast unsupervised anomaly detection with generative adversarial networks. Med. Image Anal. **54**, 30–44 (2019)
24. You, S., Tezcan, K.C., Chen, X., Konukoglu, E.: Unsupervised lesion detection via image restoration with a normative prior. In: International Conference on Medical Imaging with Deep Learning, pp. 540–556. PMLR (2019)
25. Park, H., Noh, J., Ham, B.: Learning memory-guided normality for anomaly detection. In: Proceedings of the IEEE/CVF Conference on Computer Vision and Pattern Recognition, pp. 14372–14381 (2020)
26. Baur, C., Wiestler, B., Albarqouni, S., Navab, N.: Deep autoencoding models for unsupervised anomaly segmentation in brain MR images. In: Crimi, A., Bakas, S., Kuijf, H., Keyvan, F., Reyes, M., van Walsum, T. (eds.) BrainLes 2018. LNCS, vol. 11383, pp. 161–169. Springer, Cham (2019). https://doi.org/10.1007/978-3-030-11723-8_16

Addressing Class Imbalance
in Semi-supervised Image Segmentation:
A Study on Cardiac MRI

Hritam Basak[1]([⊠]), Sagnik Ghosal[1], and Ram Sarkar[2]

[1] Department of Electrical Engineering, Jadavpur University, Kolkata, India
hritambasak48@gmail.com
[2] Department of Computer Science and Engineering, Jadavpur University,
Kolkata, India

Abstract. Due to the imbalanced and limited data, semi-supervised medical image segmentation methods often fail to produce superior performance for some specific tailed classes. Inadequate training for those particular classes could introduce more noise to the generated pseudo labels, affecting overall learning. To alleviate this shortcoming and identify the under-performing classes, we propose maintaining a confidence array that records class-wise performance during training. A fuzzy fusion of these confidence scores is proposed to adaptively prioritize individual confidence metrics in every sample rather than traditional ensemble approaches, where a set of predefined fixed weights are assigned for all the test cases. Further, we introduce a robust class-wise sampling method and dynamic stabilization for a better training strategy. Our proposed method considers all the under-performing classes with dynamic weighting and tries to remove most of the noises during training. Upon evaluation on two cardiac MRI datasets, ACDC and MMWHS, our proposed method shows effectiveness and generalizability and outperforms several state-of-the-art methods found in the literature.

Keywords: Class imbalance · Fuzzy fusion · Semi-supervised learning · Cardiac MRI · Image segmentation

1 Introduction

In the context of medical imaging, access to large volumes of labelled data is difficult owing to the high cost, required domain-specific expertise, and protracted process involved in generating accurate annotations. Using a lesser amount of training data, on the other hand, significantly affects the model's performance. To solve this bottleneck, researchers shifted towards the domain of Semi-Supervised Learning

Supplementary Information The online version contains supplementary material available at https://doi.org/10.1007/978-3-031-16452-1_22.

L. Wang et al. (Eds.): MICCAI 2022, LNCS 13438, pp. 224–233, 2022.
https://doi.org/10.1007/978-3-031-16452-1_22

(SSL) which exploits unlabeled data information to compensate for the substantial requirement of data annotation [6]. Recently SSL-based medical image segmentation strategies have been widely adopted due to their competing performance and ability to learn from very few annotations. To this end, adversarial learning is a very promising direction where Peng et al. [17] proposed an adversarial co-training strategy to enforce diversity across multiple models. Li et al. [13] took a generative adversarial-based approach for cardiac magnetic resonance imaging (MRI) segmentation, where they proposed utilizing the predictive result as a latent variable to estimate the distribution of the latent. Nie et al. [16] proposed ASDNet, an adversarial attention-based SSL method utilizing a fully convolutional confidence map. Besides, Luo et al. [15] proposed a dual-task consistent network to utilize geometry-aware level-set as well as pixel-level predictions. Contrastive Learning (CL) based strategies [4,24] have also been instrumental in this purpose by enforcing representations in latent space to be similar for similar representations. Chaitanya et al. [4] showed the effectiveness of global and local contexts to be of utmost importance in contrastive pretraining to mine important latent representations. Lately, Peng et al. [18] tried to address the limitations of these CL-based strategies by proposing a dynamic strategy in CL by adaptively prioritizing individual samples in an unsupervised loss. Other directions involve consistency regularization [23], domain adaptation [22], uncertainty estimation [21], etc.

However, a significant problem to train the existing SSL-based techniques is that they are based on the assumption that every class has an almost equal number of instances [19]. On the contrary, most real-life medical datasets have some classes with notably higher instances in training samples than others, which is technically termed as *class imbalance*. For example, the class *myocardium* in ACDC [3] is often missing or too small to be detected in apical slices, leading to substandard segmentation performance for this class [3]. This class-wise bias affects the performance of traditional deep learning networks in terms of convergence during the training phase, and generalization on the test set [10].

This paper addresses a relatively new research topic, called the class imbalance problem in SSL-based medical image segmentation. Though explicitly not focusing on class imbalance, our proposed method aims to improvise the segmentation performance of tail classes by keeping track of category-wise confidence scores during training. Furthermore, we incorporate fuzzy adaptive fusion using the Gompertz function where priority is given to individual confidence scores in every sample in this method rather than traditional ensemble approaches (average, weighted average, etc.), where a set of predefined fixed weights is assigned for all the test cases.

2   Proposed Method

Let us assume that the dataset consists of N_1 number of labelled images $\mathbb{I}_{\mathcal{L}}$ and N_2 number of unlabelled images $\mathbb{I}_{\mathcal{U}}$ (where $\{\mathbb{I}_{\mathcal{L}}, \mathbb{I}_{\mathcal{U}}\} \in \mathbb{I}$ and $N_1 << N_2$). First, we define the standard student-teacher architecture, and then formulate our dynamic training strategy by redefining the loss terms.

2.1 Basic Student-Teacher Framework

Similar to [20], our network consists of a student-teacher framework, where the network learns through the student branch only, and the weights of the teacher model are updated by using an Exponential Moving Average (EMA). The student model is used to generate pseudo labels $\bar{\mathcal{Y}}$ on both labelled data $\mathbb{I}_{\mathcal{L}}$ with weak augmentations and unlabelled data $\mathbb{I}_{\mathcal{U}}$ with strong augmentations. In contrast, the teacher model only generates pseudo labels on weakly augmented unlabelled data $\mathbb{I}_{\mathcal{U}}$. The base student-teacher model is shown in Fig. 1(A). The standard supervised and unsupervised loss functions ($\mathcal{L}^S$ and $\mathcal{L}^U$) can, therefore, be defined as:

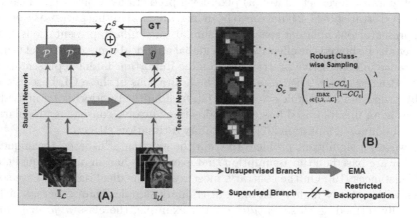

Fig. 1. Overall training strategy of the proposed method: (A) the basic student-teacher network, used as a backbone in our work, and (B) the Robust Class-wise Sampling that adaptively samples more pixels from the under-performing classes

$$\mathcal{L}^S = \frac{1}{\mathbb{N}_1} \sum_{n=1}^{\mathbb{N}_1} \frac{1}{h \times w} \sum_{i=1}^{h \times w} \mathcal{L}_{CE}(\mathcal{P}_{n,i}, GT_{n,i}) \qquad (1)$$

$$\mathcal{L}^U = \frac{1}{\mathbb{N}_2} \sum_{n=1}^{\mathbb{N}_2} \frac{1}{h \times w} \sum_{i=1}^{h \times w} \mathcal{L}_{CE}(\mathcal{P}_{n,i}, \bar{y}_{n,i}) \qquad (2)$$

where, $h \times w$ is the image dimension, $\mathcal{L}_{CE}$ represents the standard pixelwise cross-entropy loss, $\mathcal{P}_{n,i}$ represents the prediction of ith pixel of nth image, GT is the ground truth label, and $\bar{y}_{n,i} \in \bar{\mathcal{Y}}$ is the generated pseudo label for the corresponding pixel of the corresponding image.

2.2 Dynamic Class-Aware Learning

Formulation of Confidence Array. Some of the methods in literature [8,14] address the imbalanced training in natural scene images by relying on class-wise sample counts followed by ad-hoc weighting and sampling strategies. To this end, we propose maintaining three different performance indicators, namely *Entropy*, *Variance*, and *Confidence*, in a class-wise confidence array to assess the performance of every class. We define *Entropy* indicator $\mathbb{E}_c$ for class c as:

$$\mathbb{E}_c = \frac{1}{\mathbb{N}_1} \sum_{n=1}^{\mathbb{N}_1} \frac{1}{\mathbb{N}_c^n} \sum_{i=1}^{\mathbb{N}_c^n} \sum_{j=1}^{\mathbb{C}} \mathcal{P}_{n,i}^c \log \mathcal{P}_{n,i}^j \; ; \; \forall c \in \{1,2,3,...,\mathbb{C}\} \tag{3}$$

where $\mathcal{P}_{n,i}^j$ is the jth channel prediction for the ith pixel of nth image. Similarly, we define *Variance* and *Confidence* indicators $\mathbb{V}_c$ and $\mathbb{C}on_c$ respectively as:

$$\mathbb{V}_c = \frac{1}{\mathbb{N}_1} \sum_{n=1}^{\mathbb{N}_1} \frac{1}{\mathbb{N}_c^n} \sum_{i=1}^{\mathbb{N}_c^n} \left(\max_{j \in \{1,2,..,\mathbb{C}\}} [\mathcal{P}_{n,i}^j] - \mathcal{P}_{n,i}^c \right) \; ; \; \forall c \in \{1,2,3,...,\mathbb{C}\} \tag{4}$$

$$\mathbb{C}on_c = \frac{1}{\mathbb{N}_1} \sum_{n=1}^{\mathbb{N}_1} \frac{1}{\mathbb{N}_c^n} \sum_{i=1}^{\mathbb{N}_c^n} \mathcal{P}_{n,i}^c \; ; \; \forall c \in \{1,2,3,...,\mathbb{C}\} \tag{5}$$

Fuzzy Confidence Fusion. We combine the three class-wise performance indicators $\mathbb{E}_c$, $\mathbb{V}_c$, and $\mathbb{C}on_c$ to generate the final CC score using a fuzzy fusion scheme. Gompertz function was experimentally adopted for fuzzy fusion as explained in the supplementary material. First, we generate a class-wise fuzzy rank of different performance indicators using a re-parameterized Gompertz function [12] as:

$$\mathbb{R}_c^k = 1 - e^{-e^{-2 \cdot norm(x_c^k)}}, \text{ where } x_c^k \in \{\mathbb{E}_c, \mathbb{V}_c, \mathbb{C}on_c\}, \tag{6}$$

where, $norm()$ signifies normalization function, $\mathbb{R}_c^k$ is in range $[0.127, 0.632]$, where a higher confidence score gives better (lower) rank. The selection of the objective fuzzy function is based on model performance. For detailed analysis, please refer to the supplementary file. Now, if M^k represents top m ranks for class c, then we compute a complement of confidence factor sum (CCF_c) and fuzzy rank sum (FR_c) as follows:

$$CCF_c = \sum_k \begin{cases} norm(x_c^k), & \text{if } \mathbb{R}_c^k \in M^k \\ P_c^{CCF}, & \text{otherwise} \end{cases} \text{ and } FR_c = \sum_k \begin{cases} \mathbb{R}_c^k, & \text{if } \mathbb{R}_c^k \in M^k \\ P_c^{FR}, & \text{otherwise} \end{cases}$$
$$\tag{7}$$

where, P_c^{CCF} and P_c^{FR} are the penalty values (set to 0 and 0.632 respectively) for class c to suppress the unlikely winner. The final cumulative confidence (CC) score is thereafter computed as:

$$CC_c = CCF_c \times FR_c \; \forall c \in \{1,2,...\mathbb{C}\} \tag{8}$$

The obtained CC score is updated after t^{th} training iteration as:

$$CC_c^t \longleftarrow \alpha CC_c^{t-1} + (1-\alpha)CC_c^t \; ; \forall c \in \{1,2,3,...,\mathbb{C}\} \tag{9}$$

where, α is the momentum parameter, set to 0.999 experimentally.

Robust Class-Wise Sampling. We obtain the category-wise confidence score and identify the under-performing classes as described in Sect. 2.2. To alleviate the problem of class-wise training bias, i.e., preventing well-performing classes from overwhelming model training and anchoring the training on a sparse set of under-performing classes, we propose a class-wise sampling rate $\mathcal{S}_c$ as:

$$\mathcal{S}_c = \left(\frac{[1 - CC_c]}{\max\limits_{c \in \{1,2,...,\mathbb{C}\}} [1 - CC_c]} \right)^{\lambda} \tag{10}$$

where λ is a tunable parameter. Instead of sampling all the available pixels for the unsupervised loss formulation, we sample random pixels from class c with sampling rate of $\mathcal{S}_c$. So $\mathcal{L}^U$ in Eq. 2 can be reformulated as:

$$\mathcal{L}^U = \frac{1}{\mathbb{N}_2} \sum_{n=1}^{\mathbb{N}_2} \frac{1}{\left(\sum\limits_{i=1}^{h \times w} \mathbb{1}_{n,i} \right)} \sum_{i=1}^{h \times w} \mathbb{1}_{n,i} \mathcal{L}_{CE}(\mathcal{P}_{n,i}, \bar{y}_{n,i}) \tag{11}$$

where $\mathbb{1}$ is the binary value operator. The value $\mathbb{1}_{n,i} = 0$ if the ith pixel from the nth image is not sampled according to sampling rate $\mathcal{S}_c$, otherwise set to 1. Figure 1(B) represents the proposed class-wise sampling strategy.

Dynamic Training Stabilization. As the model performance strictly relies upon the quality of pseudo labels, the under-performing categories insert a significant amount of noise in the pseudo label, hindering the training process. Methods in literature [11] set a higher threshold value to remove the under-performing classes, although this firm criterion leads to lower recall value for those categories, affecting the overall training. We utilize a dynamic modulation of weights to alleviate this problem for better training stabilization. This aims to redistribute the loss contribution from convincing and under-performing samples, i.e., more weights to the convincing classes. The unsupervised loss in Eq. 11 can be reformulated as:

$$\mathcal{L}^U = \frac{1}{\mathbb{N}_2} \sum_{n=1}^{\mathbb{N}_2} \frac{1}{\left(\sum\limits_{i=1}^{h \times w} \mathcal{W}_{n,i} \right)} \sum_{i=1}^{h \times w} \mathcal{W}_{n,i} \mathcal{L}_{CE}(\mathcal{P}_{n,i}, \bar{y}_{n,i}) \tag{12}$$

where $\mathcal{W}_{n,i}$ is the weight provided for the ith pixel in n^{th} image in the final unsupervised loss formulation, and can be defined as:

$$\mathcal{W}_{n,i} = \mathbb{1}_{n,i} \max_{c \in \{1,2,...,\mathbb{C}\}} [\mathcal{P}_{n,i}]^{\beta} \tag{13}$$

where β is a tunable parameter. The final loss function is computed as:

$$\mathcal{L}_{total} = \mathcal{L}^U + \zeta \mathcal{L}^S, \tag{14}$$

where ζ is a tunable parameter. The value of ζ decreases with an increase in the number of iterations, limiting the contribution of supervised loss term $\mathcal{L}^S$ in the overall loss in the later stage of training.

3   Experiments and Results

3.1   Dataset and Implementation Details

The model is evaluated on two publicly available cardiac MRI datasets. (1) the **ACDC dataset** [3], hosted in MICCAI17, contains 100 patients' cardiac MR volumes, where for every patient it has around 15 volumes covering the entire cardiac cycle, and expert annotations for left and right ventricles and myocardium. (2) The **MMWHS dataset** [25] consists of 20 cardiac MRI samples with expert annotations for seven structures: left and right ventricles, left and right atrium, pulmonary artery, myocardium, and aorta. The datasets are distributed into a 4 : 1 ratio of training and validation sets for both cases. To validate the model performance on different label percentages, we use 1.25%, 2.5%, and 10% labelled data from ACDC and 10%, 20%, and 40% labelled data from MMWHS for training purposes (label percentage is taken in accordance to other methods in literature). The values of β in Eq. 13 and λ in Eq. 10 are taken as 1.5 and 2.5, respectively (experimental analysis in supplementary file). The experimentation is implemented using Tesla K80 GPU with 16 GB RAM. An SGD optimizer with an initial learning rate $1e-4$, momentum of 0.9, and weight decay of 0.0001 was employed. Three widely used metrics are used for the evaluation purpose: Dice Similarity Score (DSC), Average Symmetric Distance (ASD), and Hausdorff Distance (HD) [2].

3.2   Quantitative Performance Evaluation

To empirically illustrate the effective segmentation ability of the proposed model in a semi-supervised environment, we evaluate our proposed method on the ACDC and MMWHS datasets by training the model using different percentages of labelled data (see Fig. 2). For the ACDC dataset, the reported DSC, ASD and HD values are 0.746, 0.677, 2.409, respectively while using 1.25% training samples, 0.842, 0.614, 2.009 corresponding to 2.5% training labels, 0.889, 0.511, 1.804 for 10% and 0.902, 0.489, 1.799 while using 100% samples for training. We consider the 100% training labels utilization as a fully supervised functioning for comparative analysis. As can be inferred from Fig. 2A, the segmentation performance of the proposed model utilizing only a handful of labels is comparable to the fully supervised counterpart. A similar trend is also observed in Fig. 2B, where the DSC score while using 10%, 20%, 40% and 100% training samples are 0.626, 0.791, 0.815 and 0.826 respectively. The reported ASD scores for the respective cases are 2.397, 1.798, 1.355 and 1.317, respectively. The HD score for the 10% case is 5.001, which is slightly higher, but while using 40% of the labels for training, the HD score drops down to 2.221, comparable to the fully supervised case with an HD of 2.183.

3.3   Comparison with State-of-the-Art

To prove the effectiveness of the proposed model, we have performed its comparative analysis with some state-of-the-art models [5–7,9] which is shown in

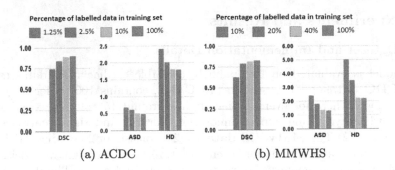

(a) ACDC   (b) MMWHS

Fig. 2. Quantitative segmentation performance of our proposed method using different percentage of labelled data of ACDC and MMWHS.

Table 1. As can be inferred, for the ACDC dataset, the average DSC score as reported by our model while using 1.25% and 2.5% training samples is the second best with the state-of-the-art performance given by Global + Local CL [4], and PCL [24] respectively. For 10% training samples, on the other hand, the state-of-the-art performance is reported by the proposed model (DSC = 0.889). For the MMWHS dataset, the proposed model surpasses all the existing models in terms of the average DSC score while using 10%, 20% or 40% of the training samples, with an average 5% margin over the second-best performing model. Another important observation is that methods like [1,9,24] fail to produce satisfactory results using very few annotations (1.25% and 10% labelled data for ACDC and MMWHS, respectively). In contrast, our proposed method performs quite consistently as compared to those. We record class-wise DSC and sensitivity to observe the improvements for under-performing classes. Observed DSC and sensitivity are (0.934, 0.883, 0.877) and (0.964, 0.925, 0.911) for classes LV, RV, and MYO respectively using 10% labelled data of ACDC. Our method achieves an improvement of ≈2–5% for under-performing classes (RV, MYO) than the baseline and literature. Similar improvements are observed across the classes in other experimental settings, both for ACDC and MMWHS.

3.4   Ablation Studies

To find out the potency of different components used in the formulation of our proposed scheme, we perform a detailed ablation study, as shown in Table 2. We use a student-teacher framework as the baseline for all the ablation experiments, which produces an average DSC of 0.819 and 0.734 upon evaluation on ACDC and MMWHS datasets, respectively, as a standalone model. Then, we perform two sets of experiments to identify the importance of Robust Class-wise Sampling (RCS) and fuzzy fusion. Instead of fuzzy fusion, as described in Eq. 8, first we form the CC score by just simple averaging the three performance indicators: $CC_c = (\mathbb{E}_c + \mathbb{V}_c + \mathbb{C}on_c)/3$. This, along with the RCS, improves the baseline performance by 4.65% and 6.40% in terms of DSC on ACDc and

Table 1. Comparison of the proposed method with state-of-the-art frameworks on ACDC and MMWHS datasets.

Method	Average DSC (ACDC)			Average DSC (MMWHS)		
	L = 1.25%	L = 2.5%	L = 10%	L = 10%	L = 20%	L = 40%
Global CL [7]	0.729	–	0.847	0.5	0.659	0.785
PCL [24]	0.671	**0.85**	0.885	–	–	–
Context Restoration [6]	0.625	0.714	0.851	0.482	0.654	0.783
Label Efficient [9]	–	–	–	0.382	0.553	0.764
Data Aug [5]	0.731	0.786	0.865	0.529	0.661	0.785
Self Train [1]	0.69	0.749	0.86	0.563	0.691	0.801
Global + Local CL [4]	**0.757**	0.826	0.886	0.617	0.710	0.794
Ours	0.746	0.842	**0.889**	**0.626**	**0.791**	**0.815**

Table 2. Ablation study to identify the effectiveness of Robust Class-wise Sampling (RCS), Dynamic Training Stabilization (DTS), Fuzzy Fusion on ACDC and MMWHS datasets using 10% and 40% labelled data respectively.

Student-teacher (base model)	RCS		DTS	ACDC			MMWHS		
	Simple avg. rule	Fuzzy fusion		DSC	ASD	HD	DSC	ASD	HD
✓				0.817	2.697	0.653	0.734	2.808	2.119
✓	✓			0.855	2.118	0.580	0.781	2.419	1.662
✓		✓		0.861	1.978	0.541	0.792	2.328	1.461
✓	✓		✓	0.872	1.803	0.522	0.809	2.291	1.377
✓		✓	✓	**0.889**	**1.804**	**0.511**	**0.815**	**2.221**	**1.355**

MMWHS, respectively. To fully utilize the potential of RCS, when we evaluate it along with fuzzy fusion, the model outperforms the baseline DSC by a margin of 6.73% and 7.91% respectively on the two datasets. The fuzzy fusion scheme adaptively prioritizes the confidence scores for individual samples rather than using any preset fixed weights to combine the confidence scores. On the other hand, Dynamic Training Stabilization (DTS) and RCS alleviate the problem of class-wise biased training by adaptively prioritizing the under-performing sample classes. This is also justified by the improvements of $\approx$2% and $\approx$3% on ACDC and MMWHS brought by DTS when used on top of RCS with a simple average rule. Furthermore, we present our proposed scheme using DTS and a fuzzy fusion scheme in RCS to achieve the best DSC of 0.889 and 0.815 on ACDC and MMWHS, respectively. Additionally, we also observe the variation of model performance by using three confidence indicators individually (refer to supplementary file).

4   Conclusion

The scarcity of pixel-level annotations has always been a significant hurdle for medical image segmentation. Besides, a limitation of the deep-learning-based strategies is that they get biased toward the majority class, thereby affecting the overall model performance. To this end, our work addresses both issues by forming a class-wise performance-aware dynamic learning strategy. Experimentation on two publicly available cardiac MRI datasets exhibits the superiority of the proposed method over the state-of-the-art methods. In future, we plan to extend the work by designing it as a fine-tuning strategy on top of a contrastive pre-training for more effective utilization of the global context.

References

1. Bai, W., et al.: Semi-supervised learning for network-based cardiac MR image segmentation. In: Descoteaux, M., Maier-Hein, L., Franz, A., Jannin, P., Collins, D.L., Duchesne, S. (eds.) MICCAI 2017. LNCS, vol. 10434, pp. 253–260. Springer, Cham (2017). https://doi.org/10.1007/978-3-319-66185-8_29
2. Basak, H., Bhattacharya, R., Hussain, R., Chatterjee, A.: An embarrassingly simple consistency regularization method for semi-supervised medical image segmentation. arXiv preprint arXiv:2202.00677 (2022)
3. Bernard, O., et al.: Deep learning techniques for automatic MRI cardiac multi-structures segmentation and diagnosis: is the problem solved? IEEE Trans. Med. Imaging 37(11), 2514–2525 (2018)
4. Chaitanya, K., Erdil, E., Karani, N., Konukoglu, E.: Contrastive learning of global and local features for medical image segmentation with limited annotations. arXiv preprint arXiv:2006.10511 (2020)
5. Chaitanya, K., Karani, N., Baumgartner, C.F., Becker, A., Donati, O., Konukoglu, E.: Semi-supervised and task-driven data augmentation. In: Chung, A.C.S., Gee, J.C., Yushkevich, P.A., Bao, S. (eds.) IPMI 2019. LNCS, vol. 11492, pp. 29–41. Springer, Cham (2019). https://doi.org/10.1007/978-3-030-20351-1_3
6. Chen, L., Bentley, P., Mori, K., Misawa, K., Fujiwara, M., Rueckert, D.: Self-supervised learning for medical image analysis using image context restoration. Med. Image Anal. 58, 101539 (2019)
7. Chen, T., Kornblith, S., Norouzi, M., Hinton, G.: A simple framework for contrastive learning of visual representations. In: International Conference on Machine Learning, pp. 1597–1607. PMLR (2020)
8. Hu, H., Wei, F., Hu, H., Ye, Q., Cui, J., Wang, L.: Semi-supervised semantic segmentation via adaptive equalization learning. In: Advances in Neural Information Processing Systems 34 (2021)
9. Hu, X., Zeng, D., Xu, X., Shi, Y.: Semi-supervised contrastive learning for label-efficient medical image segmentation. In: de Bruijne, M., et al. (eds.) MICCAI 2021. LNCS, vol. 12902, pp. 481–490. Springer, Cham (2021). https://doi.org/10.1007/978-3-030-87196-3_45
10. Japkowicz, N., Stephen, S.: The class imbalance problem: a systematic study. Intell. Data Anal. 6(5), 429–449 (2002)
11. Ke, Z., Qiu, D., Li, K., Yan, Q., Lau, R.W.H.: Guided collaborative training for pixel-wise semi-supervised learning. In: Vedaldi, A., Bischof, H., Brox, T., Frahm, J.-M. (eds.) ECCV 2020. LNCS, vol. 12358, pp. 429–445. Springer, Cham (2020). https://doi.org/10.1007/978-3-030-58601-0_26

12. Kundu, R., Basak, H., Singh, P.K., Ahmadian, A., Ferrara, M., Sarkar, R.: Fuzzy rank-based fusion of CNN models using Gompertz function for screening COVID-19 CT-scans. Sci. Rep. **11**(1), 1–12 (2021)

13. Li, S., Zhang, Y., Yang, X.: Semi-supervised cardiac MRI segmentation based on generative adversarial network and variational auto-encoder. In: 2021 IEEE International Conference on Bioinformatics and Biomedicine (BIBM), pp. 1402–1405. IEEE (2021)

14. Li, Y., et al.: Overcoming classifier imbalance for long-tail object detection with balanced group softmax. In: Proceedings of the IEEE/CVF conference on computer vision and pattern recognition, pp. 10991–11000 (2020)

15. Luo, X., Chen, J., Song, T., Wang, G.: Semi-supervised medical image segmentation through dual-task consistency. In: Proceedings of the AAAI Conference on Artificial Intelligence, vol. 35, pp. 8801–8809 (2021)

16. Nie, D., Gao, Y., Wang, L., Shen, D.: ASDNet: attention based semi-supervised deep networks for medical image segmentation. In: Frangi, A.F., Schnabel, J.A., Davatzikos, C., Alberola-López, C., Fichtinger, G. (eds.) MICCAI 2018. LNCS, vol. 11073, pp. 370–378. Springer, Cham (2018). https://doi.org/10.1007/978-3-030-00937-3_43

17. Peng, J., Estrada, G., Pedersoli, M., Desrosiers, C.: Deep co-training for semi-supervised image segmentation. Pattern Recogn. **107**, 107269 (2020)

18. Peng, J., Wang, P., Desrosiers, C., Pedersoli, M.: Self-paced contrastive learning for semi-supervised medical image segmentation with meta-labels. In: Advances in Neural Information Processing Systems 34 (2021)

19. Stanescu, A., Caragea, D.: Semi-supervised self-training approaches for imbalanced splice site datasets. In: Proceedings of the 6th International Conference on Bioinformatics and Computational Biology, BICoB 2014, pp. 131–136 (2014)

20. Tarvainen, A., Valpola, H.: Mean teachers are better role models: weight-averaged consistency targets improve semi-supervised deep learning results. arXiv preprint arXiv:1703.01780 (2017)

21. Wang, K., et al.: Tripled-uncertainty guided mean teacher model for semi-supervised medical image segmentation. In: de Bruijne, M., et al. (eds.) MICCAI 2021. LNCS, vol. 12902, pp. 450–460. Springer, Cham (2021). https://doi.org/10.1007/978-3-030-87196-3_42

22. Xia, Y., et al.: Uncertainty-aware multi-view co-training for semi-supervised medical image segmentation and domain adaptation. Med. Image Anal. **65**, 101766 (2020)

23. Xie, Y., Zhang, J., Liao, Z., Verjans, J., Shen, C., Xia, Y.: Intra-and inter-pair consistency for semi-supervised gland segmentation. IEEE Trans. Image Process. **31**, 894–905 (2021)

24. Zeng, D., et al.: Positional contrastive learning for volumetric medical image segmentation. In: de Bruijne, M., et al. (eds.) MICCAI 2021. LNCS, vol. 12902, pp. 221–230. Springer, Cham (2021). https://doi.org/10.1007/978-3-030-87196-3_21

25. Zhuang, X., Shen, J.: Multi-scale patch and multi-modality atlases for whole heart segmentation of MRI. Med. Image Anal. **31**, 77–87 (2016)

Scribble2D5: Weakly-Supervised Volumetric Image Segmentation via Scribble Annotations

Qiuhui Chen and Yi Hong[(✉)]

Department of Computer Science and Engineering, Shanghai Jiao Tong University,
Shanghai, China
yi.hong@sjtu.edu.cn

Abstract. Image segmentation using weak annotations like scribbles has gained great attention, since such annotations are easier to obtain compared to time-consuming and labor-intensive labeling at the pixel/voxel level. However, scribbles lack structure information of the region of interest (ROI), thus existing scribble-based methods suffer from poor boundary localization. Moreover, current methods are mostly designed for 2D image segmentation, which do not fully leverage volumetric information. In this paper, we propose a scribble-based volumetric image segmentation, Scribble2D5, which tackles 3D anisotropic image segmentation and improves boundary predictions. To achieve this, we augment a 2.5D attention UNet with a proposed label propagation module to extend semantic information from scribbles and a combination of static and active boundary prediction to learn ROI's boundaries and regularize its shape. Extensive experiments on three public datasets demonstrate Scribble2D5 significantly outperforms existing scribble-based methods and approaches the performance of fully-supervised ones. Our code is available at https://github.com/Qybc/Scribble2D5.

Keywords: Weakly-supervised learning · Scribble annotation · Volumetric image segmentation

1 Introduction

Deep learning based methods have achieved impressive accuracy in many medical segmentation tasks, especially in a fully-supervised manner [19,30]. However, such segmentation methods typically require a large amount of dense annotations for pixels or voxels to train a deep model. While dense annotations sometimes are not easy to obtain in practice because annotating at the image pixel-/voxel-level is time-consuming and needs medical expertise to provide high-quality labels. On the other hand, fully-unsupervised segmentation methods [6,24] have shown promising results; however, their performance gap with respect to fully-supervised approaches is too large to make them practical. Therefore, weakly-supervised approaches by using weak annotations have gained great attention to

© The Author(s), under exclusive license to Springer Nature Switzerland AG 2022
L. Wang et al. (Eds.): MICCAI 2022, LNCS 13438, pp. 234–243, 2022.
https://doi.org/10.1007/978-3-031-16452-1_23

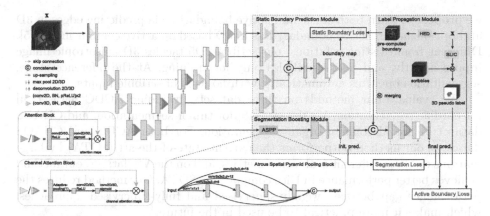

Fig. 1. Our Scribble2D5 architecture for volumetric image segmentation: 1) pseudo label propagation (gray box): generating pseudo 3D segmentation masks and pre-computed boundaries; 2) static boundary prediction (green box): incorporating object boundary information from the input image; 3) segmentation boosting (pink box): further considering active boundaries via an active boundary loss (Best view in color). (Color figure online)

greatly reduce the workload of manual annotations while having promising and comparable results compared to fully-supervised approaches.

Commonly-used weak annotations include image-level annotations [2,26], bounding boxes [15,19], scribbles [7,11,20,21], and extreme points [13,17], etc. Compared to image-level and bounding box annotations, scribbles provide rough positions of Region of Interests (ROIs) to allow a better location of ROI. Also, scribbles are more flexible than bounding boxes and extreme points when annotating, especially for ROIs with irregular shapes. In addition, extreme point annotations are more suitable for convex shapes and may not work well for non-convex ones. Therefore, we choose scribbles as our weak annotations. However, scribbles are often sparse with no structure information of ROIs; as a result, scribble-based methods have difficulty in accurately locating ROI boundaries [20]. Moreover, existing methods [11,12,21,23,28,29] are typically designed for segmenting 2D image slices, which do not fully leverage the whole image volume, with missing continuity between slices. Researchers attempt to alleviate such issue by regularizing the volume size of segmentation outputs [10]. Another solution [7] performs 3D segmentation with transfer learning, which learns with dense annotations in the source domain and with scribbles in the target domain.

Inspired by two recent works [23,28], we propose a volumetric segmentation network based on scribble annotations, called scribble2D5. As shown in Fig. 1, we adopt a 2.5D attention UNet [19] to handle anisotropic medical volumes with different voxel spacings, which is very common in practice like our datasets. To amplify the influence of sparse scribbles and suit for volumetric segmentation, we use a label propagation module based on supervoxels to generate 3D pseudo masks from scribbles for supervision. To address the boundary localization issue, we propose to learn both static and active boundaries via predicting edges in 3D and optimizing an active boundary loss in 3D based on active contour model [5]. Different from existing solutions, our scribble2D5 tackles 3D anisotropic image inputs directly, and needs scribbles only for training. At the inference stage, segmentation operates automatically, with no need of scribble inputs.

We evaluate our methods on three datasets, including ACDC dataset [4] for cardiac segmentation, VS dataset [18] for tumor segmentation, and CHAOS dataset [9] for abdominal organ segmentation. For both ACDC and CHAOS datasets, our method outperforms the current state-of-the-art (SOTA) by large margins on three different evaluation metrics; and on the VS dataset, our method achieves better performance in Dice compared to SOTA. Our method reduces the performance gap between weakly-supervised and fully-supervised approaches, which makes it more practical to be used in the future.

Overall, our contributions in the paper are summarized as follows:

- We propose a scribble2D5 network for segmenting medical image volumes with scribbles for training only. Our method is compared to five baselines and significantly outperforms scribble-based methods on three datasets.
- We propose a label propagation module for 3D pseudo mask generation and an active boundary loss to regularize 3D segmentation results. These modules are general and could be used in other segmentation networks.

2   Scribble2D5: Scribbles-Based Volumetric Segmentation

Figure 1 presents the framework of our Scribble2D5, a weakly-supervised image segmentation network based on scribble annotations. Scribble2D5 has a 2.5D attention UNet [19] as the backbone network, which is augmented by three modules, i.e., a label propagation module for generating 3D pseudo masks and boundaries, a static boundary prediction module for incorporating object boundary information from images, and a segmentation boosting module for further considering active boundaries via an active boundary loss.

2.1   3D Pseudo Label Generation via Label Propagation

Scribble annotations are often sparse, which cover a small amount of pixels on each slice of an image volume. As a result, the supervision information from scribbles is not strong enough to produce good guidance, like UNet$_{PCE}$ [20]. To address this issue, we propose to magnify the effects of scribble annotations in 3D by leveraging supervoxels. That is, we adopt SLIC [1], which generates supervoxels from images using an adaptive k-means clustering by considering both image intensity and distance similarities. We collect the supervoxels that scribbles pass through, resulting in 3D pseudo segmentation masks for ROIs.

Except for the pseudo mask we generate from the scribble annotations, we generate the pseudo static boundary of ROI from an image volume by stacking 2D edges detected on each slice. This boundary is static since it is precomputed from the image and keeps unchanged during training, which is different from the active boundary we will discuss later. To obtain 2D edges, we directly use an existing method, HED [25], which is pretrained on the generic edges of BSDS500 [3]. In this way, we have a Label Propagation Module (LPM) to generate 3D pseudo labels from scribbles and images for ROI segmentation and pre-computed boundary for static boundary prediction, respectively.

2.2   Scribble2D5 Network

Backbone. The image volumes studied in the experiments have different voxel spacings. Roughly, the in-plane resolution within a slice is about four times the thickness of a slice. Since 2D CNNs ignore the important correlations among slices and 3D CNNs typically handle isotropic image volumes, we choose a 2.5D neural network that considers the anisotropic properties of an image volume. In particular, we adopt an attention UNet2D5 [19] as our backbone network, which augments UNet2D5 by adding a simple attention block at each deconvolutional layer, as shown in Fig. 1. Specifically, at the top two layers of both encoder and decoder branches, we have 2D convolutional operations; while at other layers, the feature maps are isotropic, which are suitable for 3D convolutions. The attention blocks are colored in purple in Fig. 1. Their attention maps are estimated via two layers of convolutions, i.e., one with ReLU and the other with a Sigmoid activation function. This 2.5D network suits for all images in our experiments.

Static Boundary Prediction Module (SBPM). This module encourages the backbone network to extract image features with rich boundary structures at different scales. Following [28], we collect feature maps from different layers of the network decoder, and concatenate them at different resolutions right after one convolutional layer with a filter of size $1 \times 1 \times 1$. To fuse these features, we feed them to a residual channel attention block (as shown by a green triangle in Fig. 1) and a $1 \times 1 \times 1$ convolutional layer to produce a boundary map b in 3D. Under the supervision of the previously generated 3D pseudo boundary B, the network is trained with a cross-entropy loss: $\mathcal{L}_{bry}(b, B) = -\sum_{c=1}^{N} B_c log(b_c)$. Here, N is the total number of classes for segmenting in a dataset.

Segmentation Boosting Module (SBM). This module performs segmentation under the supervision of the pseudo mask generated with supervoxels and a regularization on segmentation output. The module includes an initial segmentation and a final one with further considering static and active boundaries. To predict a preliminary mask, we employ a dense atrous spatial pyramid pooling (DenseASPP) block [27] right after the bottom layer of the backbone network in Fig. 1, which enlarges its receptive fields by utilizing different dilation rates. In this block, the convolutional layers are connected in a dense way to cover a larger scale range without significantly increase the model size.

To generate the initial segmentation mask M^{init}, we adopt two additional 3D convolutional layers followed by a $1 \times 1 \times 1$ convolution, resulting in the initial prediction supervised by the generated pseudo mask M^{pseudo}. Considering the oversegment nature of supervoxels, one supervoxel may be selected by multiple

Table 1. Quantitative comparison among baselines and our method for volumetric segmentation on three datasets. Mean and standard deviation (subscript) are reported. The upper bounds are colored in blue, and the best results by using scribbles are marked in **bold**. †P is short for Point, indicating extreme points such annotations are available only in the VS dataset. *These numbers are taken from [8]. (Best viewed in color)

Approach			ACDC			VS			CHAOS		
			Dice (%,↑)	HD95 (mm,↓)	Precision (%,↑)	Dice (%,↑)	HD95 (mm,↓)	Precision (%,↑)	Dice (%,↑)	HD95 (mm,↓)	Precision (%,↑)
Supervision type	Scribble	UNet$_{PCE}$ [20]	79.0_{06}	6.9_{04}	77.3_{06}	44.6_{08}	6.5_{03}	43.8_{05}	34.4_{06}	9.4_{03}	36.6_{05}
		MAAG [21]	83.4_{04}	8.6_{04}	78.5_{05}	69.4_{06}	5.9_{05}	56.8_{05}	66.4_{05}	3.8_{05}	57.2_{06}
		Ours w/o LPM	83.2_{05}	7.7_{03}	84.1_{05}	78.8_{05}	4.6_{01}	77.6_{05}	81.2_{07}	5.8_{08}	82.0_{06}
		Ours w/o SBPM	85.6_{05}	4.6_{04}	85.5_{04}	80.6_{05}	7.1_{03}	$\mathbf{81.6_{04}}$	84.6_{05}	5.5_{05}	83.1_{05}
		Ours w/o ABL	88.7_{04}	5.1_{08}	$\mathbf{86.0_{05}}$	81.0_{03}	4.8_{01}	80.1_{05}	85.6_{04}	4.8_{05}	81.3_{02}
		Scribble2D5$_{(ours)}$	$\mathbf{90.6_{03}}$	$\mathbf{2.3_{05}}$	84.7_{05}	$\mathbf{82.6_{07}}$	4.7_{04}	81.5_{06}	$\mathbf{86.0_{04}}$	$\mathbf{2.9_{02}}$	$\mathbf{88.2_{03}}$
	P†	InExtremeIS [8]	–	–	–	81.9_{03}	3.7_{03}^{*}	92.9_{02}^{*}	–	–	–
	Mask	2D UNet [16]	93.0_{05}	3.5_{15}	90.2_{07}	80.4_{03}	7.3_{04}	81.2_{03}	82.3_{04}	3.3_{01}	81.7_{05}
		2.5D UNet [19]	96.1_{03}	0.3_{00}	95.3_{04}	87.3_{02}	6.8_{04}	84.7_{03}	90.8_{03}	1.1_{00}	91.4_{05}

different classes. To avoid this confusion, we only consider those supervoxels with a unique label, which are set as 1 in the mask M^{voxel} with others being zeros. We use the partial cross entropy to supervise the initial segmentation: $\mathcal{L}_{seg}(M^{init}, M^{pseudo}, M^{voxel}) = -\sum_{c=1}^{N} M_{c}^{voxel} \cdot M_{c}^{pseudo} log(M_{c}^{init})$. This loss function allows early feedback to fasten the network convergence.

To refine the initial estimation and obtain a boundary-preserving mask for a final prediction, we merge SBPM outputs with those from the initial mask prediction for a refinement. These feature maps are fed to a residual channel attention block, followed by a $1 \times 1 \times 1$ convolutional layer to predict the final mask M^{final}. Similarly, we use the partial cross-entropy loss to predict the final mask under the supervision of the generated pseudo mask M^{pseudo}.

<u>Active Boundary (AB) Loss.</u> The pseudo masks are imperfect because supervoxels are coarse segmentation masks of ROIs and have oversegment issues, resulting in a potential of having many false positives. To mitigate this issue, we propose regularizing the surface and volume of the 3D segmentation region by upgrading the active contour loss [5] to a 3D version. We apply an AB loss as following: $\mathcal{L}_{AB} = Surface + \lambda_{1} \cdot Volume_{In} + \lambda_{2} \cdot Volume_{Out}$, where $Surface = \int_{S} |\nabla u| ds$ and u is the prediction; $Volume_{In} = \int_{V} (c_{1} - v)^{2} u dx$, c_{1} is the mean image intensity inside of interested regions V, and v is the input image; $Volume_{Out} = \int_{\bar{V}} (c_{2} - v)^{2} u dx$ and c_{2} is the mean image intensity outside of the region. These items are balanced by two hyper-parameters λ_{1} and λ_{2}. In the experiments, we set $\lambda_{1} = 1$ and $\lambda_{2} = 0.1$, to emphasis more on the inside region of the volume. This new loss function considers the shape and intensity of an image in 3D, which regularizes ROI's shapes and reduces false positives.

The final loss function is $\mathcal{L}_{total} = \beta_{1}\mathcal{L}_{bry}(b, B) + \mathcal{L}_{seg}(M^{init}, M^{pseudo}, M^{voxel}) + \mathcal{L}_{seg}(M^{final}, M^{pseudo}, M^{voxel}) + \beta_{2}\mathcal{L}_{AB}$. Here, β_{1} and β_{2} are weights for balancing loss terms, which are both set as 0.3.

3   Experiments

3.1   Datasets and Experimental Settings

ACDC Dataset [4]. This dataset consists of Cine MR images collected from 100 patients. Manual segmentation masks of the left and right ventricles and myocardium are provided at the end-diastolic and end-systolic cardiac phases. The slice size is 256×208 with the pixel spacing varying from 1.37 to 1.68 mm. The number of slices is between 28 and 40, and the slice thickness is 5 mm or 8 mm. We subject-wisely divide the ACDC dataset into sets of 70%, 15% and 15% for training, validation, and test, respectively.

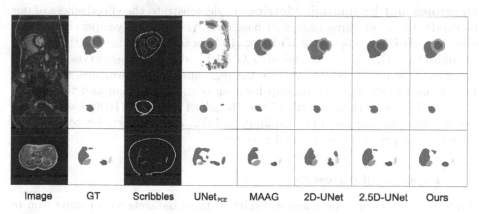

| Image | GT | Scribbles | UNet$_{PCE}$ | MAAG | 2D-UNet | 2.5D-UNet | Ours |

Fig. 2. Qualitative comparison among scribble-based (UNet$_{PCE}$ and MAAG), mask-based (2D and 2.5D UNets), and our methods (Best viewed in color). (Color figure online)

VS Dataset [18]. This dataset collects T2-weighted MRIs from 242 patients with a single sporadic vestibular schwannoma (VS) tumor. The size of an image slice is 384×384 or 448×448, with a pixel spacing of 0.5×0.5 mm^2. The number of slices varies from 19 to 118, with a thickness of 1.5 mm. The VS tumor masks are manually annotated by neurosurgeons and physicists. The dataset is subject-wisely split into 172 for training, 20 for validation, and 46 for test.

CHAOS Dataset [9]. This dataset has abdominal T1-weighted MR images collected from 20 subjects and the corresponding segmentation masks for liver, kidneys, and spleen. The image slice size is 256×256 with a resolution of 1.36–1.89 mm (average 1.61 mm). The number of slices is between 26 and 50 (average 36) with the slice thickness varying from 5.5 to 9 mm (average 7.84 mm). We also subject-wisely divide this dataset into sets of 70%, 15% and 15% for training, validation, and test, respectively.

Scribble Generation and Other Settings. For the ACDC dataset, we use the scribbles provided in [21], which are manually drawn by experts at both end-diastolic and end-systolic phases. For both VS and CHAOS datasets, following [14], we simulate scribbles by an iterative morphological erosion and closing of segmentation masks, which results in a one-pixel skeleton for each object.

Since the resulting background scribble is winding, we use ITK-Snap to annotate background with 1-pixel width curves.

For all datasets, we randomly crop an image volume and obtain patches of size $224 \times 224 \times 32$ as the network inputs. An image volume is padded with zeros if its size is smaller than the input size.

We train all models for 200 epochs with early stopping. The weights of the network are initialized by following a normal distribution with a mean of 0 and variance of 0.01. We use Adam optimizer with a weight decay 10^{-7} and an initial learning rate $1e-4$. The whole training takes about 6 h with a batch size of 4 on one NVIDIA GeForce RTX 3090 GPU.

Baselines and Evaluation Metrics. To demonstrate the effectiveness of our methods, we select three groups of baselines, including fully-supervised methods (i.e., 2D UNet [16] and 2.5D UNet [19]), weakly-supervised methods using scribbles (i.e., UNet$_{PCE}$ [20] and MAAG [21]) and a weakly-supervised method using extreme points [8]. To evaluate the segmentation performance, we use the Dice score to calculate the overlap between our segmentation and the ground truth (GT), the 95th percentile of the Hausdorff Distance (HD95) to measure the distance between our ROI boundary and GT, and the precision to check the purity of the positively-segmented voxels.

3.2   Experimental Results

Table 1 presents our experimental results on three datasets with comparison to five baselines. For all datasets, the upper bounds of the segmentation performance are mainly provided by the 2.5D UNet, which are colored in blue in Table 1. Compared to the scribble-based SOTA method on ACDC and CHAOS datasets, i.e., MAAG [21], scribble2D5 improves the Dice score by 7% and 19.5%, reduces the HD95 by 6.3 mm and 1.8 mm, and improves the precision by 6.2% and 29.5%, respectively. In addition, our method outperforms the most recent two methods, i.e., ScribbleSeg [12] and CycleMix [29], on ACDC Dataset, with our 0.903 mean dice vs 0.872 in [12] (using the same 5-fold cross validation), our 0.896 mean dice vs 0.848 in [29] (similarly, using 35 subjects for training). Compared to the extreme-point-based SOTA method on the VS dataset, i.e., InExtremeIS [8], although our method has a lower precision and HD95 value, it improves the Dice score by 0.7%. We do not report InExtremeIS' results on ACDC and CHAOS datasets because extreme points for these two datasets are not available or easy to be generated.

Figure 2 demonstrates the sampled qualitative results of our method compared to the baselines. Overall, we have fewer false positives compared to scribble-based methods, i.e., UNet$_{PCE}$ and MAAG, and better boundary localization with more accurate boundary prediction for each ROI. Regarding the comparison with mask-based methods, our method sometimes generates even better masks than 2D UNet, while needs improvements at details compared to 2.5D UNet.

Ablation Study. To check the effectiveness of each module in our method, we perform an ablation study with three variants: a) **Ours w/o LPM**: Scribble2D5 without the label propagation module (LPM); b) **Ours w/o SBPM**: Scribble2D5 without the static boundary prediction model (SBPM), including SBPM and active boundary loss; and c) **Ours w/o ABL**: Scribble2D5 without the active boundary loss (ABL). Take the ACDC dataset as an example, as shown in Table 1, without LPM but all others, the Dice score reduces from 90.4% to 80.6%. With LPM but without SBPM, the Dice score is 85.6%; then the static boundary prediction module contributes an improvement of 3.1%, and the active boundary loss contributes an additional improvement of 1.7% in Dice score. Figure 3 visualizes two samples from the ACDC dataset with our intermediate and final prediction results. Without LPM, our method suffers from false positives far away from the ROI; without SBPM, our method has oversegment issues of the ROI; by adding the boundary map and active boundary regularization, our method adjusts the prediction based on the image edge and texture information, resulting the closest results compared to GT.

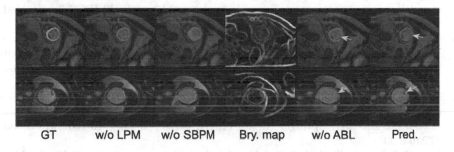

GT   w/o LPM   w/o SBPM   Bry. map   w/o ABL   Pred.

Fig. 3. Visualization of our intermediate and final results on image samples from ACDC dataset. The ground truth (GT) is colored in blue, like the blue region in the first column and the blue contours in other images, while our predictions are colored in red. Yellow arrows show the effect of the active boundary loss (ABL) (Best viewed in color). (Color figure online)

4   Conclusion and Discussion

In this paper, we proposed a weakly-supervised volumetric image segmentation network, Scribble2D5, which significantly outperforms existing scribble-based methods and reduces the performance gap between weakly-supervised and full-supervised segmentation methods. One limitation of our method is that our pseudo boundary labels are not purely 3D, which will be explored in the future. Currently, we do not consider the case of missing scribble annotations on some slices or further reducing the manual work via an adaptive annotation. One potential solution for this is using the watershed technique [22] in 3D. Also, We observe that the shape and location of scribbles would affect the segmentation accuracy, summarizing a way to make scribble annotations for different shapes of ROIs will be useful in practice by providing some rules for users to make annotations, which will benefit the segmentation and be left as the future work.

Acknowledgment. This work was supported by Shanghai Municipal Science and Technology Major Project 2021SHZDZX0102.

References

1. Achanta, R., Shaji, A., Smith, K., Lucchi, A., Fua, P., Süsstrunk, S.: SLIC superpixels compared to state-of-the-art superpixel methods. IEEE Trans. Pattern Anal. Mach. Intell. **34**(11), 2274–2282 (2012)
2. Ahn, J., Kwak, S.: Learning pixel-level semantic affinity with image-level supervision for weakly supervised semantic segmentation. In: Proceedings of the IEEE Conference on Computer Vision and Pattern Recognition, pp. 4981–4990 (2018)
3. Arbelaez, P., Maire, M., Fowlkes, C., Malik, J.: Contour detection and hierarchical image segmentation. IEEE Trans. Pattern Anal. Mach. Intell. **33**(5), 898–916 (2010)
4. Bernard, O., et al.: Deep learning techniques for automatic MRI cardiac multi-structures segmentation and diagnosis: is the problem solved? IEEE Trans. Med. Imaging **37**(11), 2514–2525 (2018)
5. Chen, X., Williams, B.M., Vallabhaneni, S.R., Czanner, G., Williams, R., Zheng, Y.: Learning active contour models for medical image segmentation. In: Proceedings of the IEEE/CVF Conference on Computer Vision and Pattern Recognition, pp. 11632–11640 (2019)
6. Dey, R., Hong, Y.: ASC-Net: adversarial-based selective network for unsupervised anomaly segmentation. In: de Bruijne, M., et al. (eds.) MICCAI 2021. LNCS, vol. 12905, pp. 236–247. Springer, Cham (2021). https://doi.org/10.1007/978-3-030-87240-3_23
7. Dorent, R., et al.: Scribble-based domain adaptation via co-segmentation. In: Martel, A.L., et al. (eds.) MICCAI 2020. LNCS, vol. 12261, pp. 479–489. Springer, Cham (2020). https://doi.org/10.1007/978-3-030-59710-8_47
8. Dorent, R., et al.: Inter extreme points geodesics for end-to-end weakly supervised image segmentation. In: de Bruijne, M., et al. (eds.) MICCAI 2021. LNCS, vol. 12902, pp. 615–624. Springer, Cham (2021). https://doi.org/10.1007/978-3-030-87196-3_57
9. Kavur, A.E., et al.: Chaos challenge-combined (CT-MR) healthy abdominal organ segmentation. Med. Image Anal. **69**, 101950 (2021)
10. Kervadec, H., Dolz, J., Tang, M., Granger, E., Boykov, Y., Ayed, I.B.: Constrained-CNN losses for weakly supervised segmentation. Med. Image Anal. **54**, 88–99 (2019)
11. Lin, D., Dai, J., Jia, J., He, K., Sun, J.: ScribbleSup: scribble-supervised convolutional networks for semantic segmentation. In: Proceedings of the IEEE Conference on Computer Vision and Pattern Recognition, pp. 3159–3167 (2016)
12. Luo, X., et al.: Scribble-supervised medical image segmentation via dual-branch network and dynamically mixed pseudo labels supervision. arXiv preprint arXiv:2203.02106 (2022)
13. Maninis, K.K., Caelles, S., Pont-Tuset, J., Van Gool, L.: Deep extreme cut: from extreme points to object segmentation. In: Proceedings of the IEEE Conference on Computer Vision and Pattern Recognition, pp. 616–625 (2018)

14. Rajchl, M., et al.: Employing weak annotations for medical image analysis problems. arXiv preprint arXiv:1708.06297 (2017)
15. Rajchl, M., et al.: DeepCut: object segmentation from bounding box annotations using convolutional neural networks. IEEE Trans. Med. Imaging **36**(2), 674–683 (2016)
16. Ronneberger, O., Fischer, P., Brox, T.: U-Net: convolutional networks for biomedical image segmentation. In: Navab, N., Hornegger, J., Wells, W.M., Frangi, A.F. (eds.) MICCAI 2015. LNCS, vol. 9351, pp. 234–241. Springer, Cham (2015). https://doi.org/10.1007/978-3-319-24574-4_28
17. Roth, H.R., Yang, D., Xu, Z., Wang, X., Xu, D.: Going to extremes: weakly supervised medical image segmentation. Mach. Learn. Knowl. Extr. **3**(2), 507–524 (2021)
18. Shapey, J., et al.: Segmentation of vestibular schwannoma from magnetic resonance imaging: an open annotated dataset and baseline algorithm. The Cancer Imaging Archive (2021)
19. Shapey, J., et al.: An artificial intelligence framework for automatic segmentation and volumetry of vestibular schwannomas from contrast-enhanced T1-weighted and high-resolution T2-weighted MRI. J. Neurosurg. **134**(1), 171–179 (2019)
20. Tang, M., Djelouah, A., Perazzi, F., Boykov, Y., Schroers, C.: Normalized cut loss for weakly-supervised CNN segmentation. In: Proceedings of the IEEE Conference on Computer Vision and Pattern Recognition, pp. 1818–1827 (2018)
21. Valvano, G., Leo, A., Tsaftaris, S.A.: Learning to segment from scribbles using multi-scale adversarial attention gates. IEEE Trans. Med. Imaging **40**(8), 1990–2001 (2021)
22. Vincent, L., Soille, P.: Watersheds in digital spaces: an efficient algorithm based on immersion simulations. IEEE Trans. Pattern Anal. Mach. Intell. **13**(06), 583–598 (1991)
23. Wang, B., et al.: Boundary perception guidance: a scribble-supervised semantic segmentation approach. In: IJCAI International Joint Conference on Artificial Intelligence (2019)
24. Xia, X., Kulis, B.: W-Net: a deep model for fully unsupervised image segmentation. arXiv preprint arXiv:1711.08506 (2017)
25. Xie, S., Tu, Z.: Holistically-nested edge detection. In: Proceedings of the IEEE International Conference on Computer Vision, pp. 1395–1403 (2015)
26. Xu, J., Schwing, A.G., Urtasun, R.: Learning to segment under various forms of weak supervision. In: Proceedings of the IEEE Conference on Computer Vision and Pattern Recognition, pp. 3781–3790 (2015)
27. Yang, M., Yu, K., Zhang, C., Li, Z., Yang, K.: DenseASPP for semantic segmentation in street scenes. In: Proceedings of the IEEE Conference on Computer Vision and Pattern Recognition, pp. 3684–3692 (2018)
28. Zhang, J., Yu, X., Li, A., Song, P., Liu, B., Dai, Y.: Weakly-supervised salient object detection via scribble annotations. In: Proceedings of the IEEE/CVF Conference on Computer Vision and Pattern Recognition, pp. 12546–12555 (2020)
29. Zhang, K., Zhuang, X.: CycleMix: a holistic strategy for medical image segmentation from scribble supervision. In: Proceedings of the IEEE/CVF Conference on Computer Vision and Pattern Recognition, pp. 11656–11665 (2022)
30. Zhou, Z., Rahman Siddiquee, M.M., Tajbakhsh, N., Liang, J.: UNet++: a nested U-Net architecture for medical image segmentation. In: Stoyanov, D., et al. (eds.) DLMIA/ML-CDS -2018. LNCS, vol. 11045, pp. 3–11. Springer, Cham (2018). https://doi.org/10.1007/978-3-030-00889-5_1

Self-learning and One-Shot Learning Based Single-Slice Annotation for 3D Medical Image Segmentation

Yixuan Wu[1], Bo Zheng[2], Jintai Chen[3], Danny Z. Chen[4], and Jian Wu[5(✉)]

[1] School of Medicine, Zhejiang University, Hangzhou, China
[2] Polytechnic Institute, Zhejiang University, Hangzhou, China
[3] College of Computer Science and Technology,
Zhejiang University, Hangzhou, China
[4] Department of Computer Science and Engineering, University of Notre Dame,
Notre Dame, USA
[5] Second Affiliated Hospital School of Medicine, School of Public Health,
and Institute of Wenzhou, Zhejiang University, Hangzhou, China
wujian2000@zju.edu.cn

Abstract. As deep learning methods continue to improve medical image segmentation performance, data annotation is still a big bottleneck due to the labor-intensive and time-consuming burden on medical experts, especially for 3D images. To significantly reduce annotation efforts while attaining competitive segmentation accuracy, we propose a self-learning and one-shot learning based framework for 3D medical image segmentation by annotating only one slice of each 3D image. Our approach takes two steps: (1) self-learning of a reconstruction network to learn semantic correspondence among 2D slices within 3D images, and (2) representative selection of single slices for one-shot manual annotation and propagating the annotated data with the well-trained reconstruction network. Extensive experiments verify that our new framework achieves comparable performance with less than 1% annotated data compared with fully supervised methods and generalizes well on several out-of-distribution testing sets.

Keywords: 3D medical image segmentation · Sparse annotation · Self-learning · One-shot learning

1 Introduction

Recent development of deep learning (DL) methods has revolutionized the medical image segmentation landscape and achieved remarkable successes [5–8,14,21,22,25]. However, such DL-based segmentation models commonly use large amounts of fine-annotated data in training and the manual annotation process is very time-consuming. Since medical experts, the main annotation providers, are normally busy in daily clinical work, it is highly desirable to develop effective DL segmentation methods with limited annotation, especially for 3D images.

L. Wang et al. (Eds.): MICCAI 2022, LNCS 13438, pp. 244–254, 2022.
https://doi.org/10.1007/978-3-031-16452-1_24

There are two main types of known approaches for alleviating the annotation burden. One type is to explore the potential of non-annotated data [29–31] and use weak-annotation strategies (e.g., using rough annotation as supervision, such as sparse slice labelling [3,41], bounding box-level labelling [17,23,28], and image-level labelling [4,13,19], for medical image segmentation). However, empirical evidences [40] suggested that such approaches typically resulted in suboptimal performance. The second type seeks to annotate only "worthy" samples that help improve the final segmentation accuracy, often using active learning methods [9,26,36,38], which iteratively conduct two steps: (i) a model selects valuable samples from the unlabeled set; (ii) experts annotate the selected samples. However, such a process implies that experts should be readily available for queries in each round, and that the active learning process needs to be suspended until queried samples are annotated. To address this, some studies [40,41] managed to avoid human-machine iterations by only selecting representative samples for annotation, but still needed to annotate a considerable amount of samples. Motivated by previous work [11,24,33] which suggested that a high proportion of pixels in an image (e.g., 80%) is redundant and most pixels can be reconstructed from other pixels with self-learning, our work investigates to annotate only a single slice of each 3D image and reconstruct full annotation of 3D images using self-learning.

To this end, in this paper, we propose a new self-learning and one-shot learning based framework to predict annotation of any 3D image X if labeled annotation of a selected slice in X is provided. Note that the word "one-shot" in this paper means conducting specific processes only once (i.e., manual annotation and representative slices selection). In general, we train a reconstruction network to learn semantic correspondence among 2D slices of 3D images by self-learning, which is then used to reconstruct and propagate the annotated data. Specifically, a *screening module* (Sect. 2.4) is proposed to build a *representative set* in one-shot for training and select a most representative single slice of each 3D image for one-shot manual annotation in testing. Meanwhile, we design an *information bottleneck* (Sect. 2.3) to force the model to focus more on high-level semantic features of the images, further contributing to segmentation accuracy. To reduce error accumulation when propagating annotation in testing, two training strategies called *scheduled sampling* and *cycle consistency* (Sect. 2.6) are adopted to enhance robustness of the reconstruction network.

Contributions. (1) We employ self-learning to capture semantic correspondence among slices, which facilitates propagation of annotation data provided by experts. (2) By sharing semantics, a most representative single slice per 3D image is selected for one-shot manual annotation to address inter-slice redundancy, thus reducing manual annotation efforts. (3) Experiments show that our method performs well with less than 1% slices manually annotated and generalizes promisingly on several out-of-distribution testing sets.

2   Method

2.1   Problem Formulation

In clinical scenarios, a certain amount of unannotated volumes (3D images) of patients is often available, regarded as a training set, $X_{tra} = \{X_1, \ldots, X_N\}$, containing enormous semantics to be utilized (though unannotated). Meanwhile, raw volumes of new patients are constantly produced, regarded as an testing set, $X_{inf} = \{X'_1, \ldots, X'_M\}$, needed to be segmented for clinical diagnosis and analysis. Each volume has D slices (D could be different for volumes), $X_i = \{S_{i1}, \ldots, S_{iD}\}$, with $S_{id} \in \mathbb{R}^{H \times W}$. In this setting, we propose a novel framework to attain full annotation, i.e., $\{\hat{A}'_{i1}, \ldots, \hat{A}'_{iD}\}$ of any volume X'_i in the testing set with only one slice's ground truth annotation A'_{id} provided.

2.2   Pipeline

The main idea of our method is to learn feature representations that enable semantic correspondence matching among slices, which is used to reconstruct and propagate expert-provided single 2D slices' annotation in testing. To this end, during training, a proxy task is proposed as reconstructing a target slice S_{tar} based on a reference slice S_{ref} by self-learning within a *representative slice-pair* $\{S_{ref}, S_{tar}\}$.

Training Stage. As illustrated in Fig. 1(a), with our *feature extraction module* (Sect. 2.3) and *screening module* (Sect. 2.4), a series of *representative slice-pairs* is selected from the unannotated training volumes in one-shot (for simplicity, Fig. 1(a) shows only one input volume and one *representative slice-pair*). Then, a reference slice S_{ref} and corresponding high-level features $\{S_{ref}^f, S_{tar}^f\}$ obtained by the *feature extraction module* are fed to the *reconstruction module* (Sect. 2.5) to reconstruct $\hat{S}_{tar}$.

Testing Stage. As shown in Fig. 1(b), for any volume X', its most representative single slice $S_{rep}^{\prime*}$ is screened out by the well-trained *feature extraction* and *screening modules* in one-shot, and manual annotation is needed only for this single slice. Then, the obtained ground truth annotation $A_{rep}^{\prime*}$ and its corresponding high-level features $\{S_{rep}^{\prime f}, S_{rep+1}^{\prime f}\}$ are computed by the *reconstruction module* in which an adjacent slice's annotation $\hat{A}'_{rep+1}$ is reconstructed. In this manner, annotation will be propagated slice-by-slice, until all slices in this volume are (computationally) annotated, i.e., $\hat{A}'_1, \ldots, A_{rep}^{\prime*}, \ldots, \hat{A}'_D$.

2.3   Feature Extraction Module

To obtain feature representations of slices for the *screening* and *reconstructing* processes, we design the *feature extraction module* to extract high-level features, as:

$$S_i^f = \Phi(g(S_i), \theta), \tag{1}$$

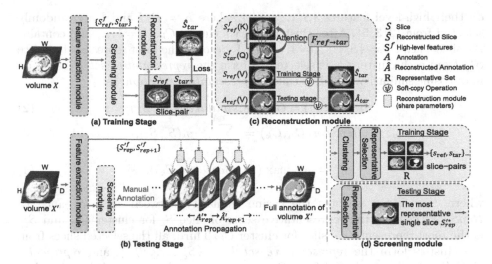

Fig. 1. The pipeline of our framework. (a) Illustrating the self-learning process of one *representative slice-pair* from one input training volume. (b) Illustrating the testing process. (c)–(d) Specification of *Reconstructing* and *Screening modules*, respectively.

where S_i^f denotes the extracted high-level features of a slice S_i, $\Phi(\cdot, \theta)$ refers to the ResNet-18 [12] feature encoder, and $g(\cdot)$ denotes our *information bottleneck*. The *information bottleneck* aims to force the model to focus more on high-level semantic features instead of simple pixel intensities when learning correspondences between slices. We adopt the Gabor filter [10] as the *information bottleneck* to emphasize the edge and texture features. For each slice $S_i \in \mathbb{R}^{H \times W}$, after the Gabor feature extraction, we obtain S different scales and O different orientations of filtered features, which are pixel-wise concatenated along the channel dimension to obtain $g(S_i) \in \mathbb{R}^{H \times W \times S \times O}$. Then, after processed by ResNet-18, high-level features $S_i^f \in \mathbb{R}^{H \times W \times C}$ are obtained. In our implementation, S, O, and C are set to $4, 8$, and 256, respectively.

2.4 Screening Module

One challenge to our method is how to select suitable slice-pairs for self-learning and how to screen out the most "worthy" single slice to annotate in testing. To this end, we propose the *screening module* to select suitable samples in one-shot, as shown in Fig. 1(d).

Training Stage. For a medical volume, its adjacent slices are often similar but all the slices may be divided into several consecutive subsequences based on anatomical structures. To deal with redundancy between adjacent slices and learn correspondences between slices with diverse anatomical structures, the *screening module* selects a *representative set R* from all the slices of each training volume X. First, K-Means clustering [20] is performed on all the slices based on their high-level features $\{S_1^f, \ldots, S_D^f\}$, where $K = D/I$ and I are randomly selected from $\{2,3,5\}$. After clustering, each cluster C_k $(k = 1, \ldots, K)$ contains N_k slices, i.e., $C_k = \{S_{kj} \mid j = 1, \ldots, N_k\}$. Second, the most representative slice $S_{c_k}^*$ from each cluster C_k is selected to form the *representative set* R based on max cosine similarity, which is called *representative selection*, as:

$$Sim(S_i, S_j) = Cosine\_similarity(S_i^f, S_j^f), \tag{2}$$

$$RepScore(S_i, C_k) = \sum_{S_j \in C_k} Sim(S_i, S_j), \tag{3}$$

$$S_{c_k}^* = \arg \max_{S_i \in C_k} \left(RepScore(S_i, C_k) \right), \tag{4}$$

where $Sim(S_i, S_j)$ denotes the cosine similarity between slices S_i and S_j, *RepScore* denotes the representative score of slice S_i for cluster C_k, and $S_{c_k}^*$ is the most representative slice for cluster C_k. Third, all the selected slices from the clusters form the *representative set* $R = \{S_{c_1}^*, \ldots, S_{c_K}^*\}$, and *representative slice-pairs* are selected from R one-by-one for subsequent self-learning, i.e., $\{S_{c_1}^*, S_{c_2}^*\}, \{S_{c_2}^*, S_{c_3}^*\}, \ldots$. Note that the above process is conducted on one volume, and all the volumes in the training set are processed in this way.

Testing Stage. *Representative selection* is conducted to screen out the most representative slice $S_{rep}'^*$ for each testing volume $X' = \{S_1', \ldots, S_D'\}$, as:

$$RepScore(S_i', X') = \sum_{S_j' \in X'} Sim(S_i', S_j'), \tag{5}$$

$$S_{rep}'^* = \arg \max_{S_i' \in X'} \left(RepScore(S_i', X') \right). \tag{6}$$

2.5   Reconstruction Module

The *reconstruction module* aims to reconstruct a target slice S_{tar} by linearly combining pixels from a reference slice S_{ref}, with weights measuring the strengths of correspondences between pixels. In detail, in order to reconstruct pixel i in the target slice, an attention mechanism [34] is applied to measure the similarity between pixel i in the target slice and a related pixel j in the reference slice, denoted as *reconstruction factor* $F_{ref \rightarrow tar}^{ji}$, which is used to weight and copy pixel j to reconstruct pixel i. All the pixels in the target slice are reconstructed in this manner to obtain the reconstructed target slice $\hat{S}_{tar}$:

$$F_{ref \rightarrow tar}^{ji} = \frac{\exp\langle Q_{tar}^i, K_{ref}^j \rangle}{\sum_p \exp\langle Q_{tar}^i, K_{ref}^p \rangle}, \tag{7}$$

$$\hat{S}_{tar} = \Psi(F_{ref \rightarrow tar}, V_{ref}) = \sum_i \sum_j F_{ref \rightarrow tar}^{ij} V_{ref}^j, \tag{8}$$

where $\langle \cdot, \cdot \rangle$ denotes the *dot product* between two vectors, query (Q) and key (K) are high-level features computed by the *feature extraction module* (i.e., $Q_{tar} =$

$\Phi(g(S_{tar}), \theta), K_{ref} = \Phi(g(S_{ref}), \theta))$, V is a reference slice in training (i.e., $V_{ref} = S_{ref}$) and refers to the reference slice's annotation in testing (i.e., $V_{ref} = A_{ref}$), i, j denote corresponding pixels in the target and reference slices respectively, p denotes a pixel in a square patch of size $P \times P$ surrounding pixel j ($P = 13$ in our implementation), and $\Psi(\cdot, \cdot)$ denotes the soft-copy operation for pixel-wise reconstruction.

2.6   Training Strategies

Scheduled Sampling. In our original setting above, a **ground truth** reference slice is used to reconstruct a target slice in training, while in testing, it is a **reconstructed** annotation that is used to reconstruct its adjacent annotation iteratively, which may lead to possible error accumulation. To bridge this gap between training and testing, we adopt *scheduled sampling* [1] to replace some ground truth reference slices by reconstructed slices in training. We define the loss as $\mathcal{L}_{sche}$:

$$\mathcal{L}_{sche} = \alpha_1 \cdot \sum_{i=1}^{n} \|S_{i+1} - \Psi(F_{i \to i+1}, S_i)\|_1 + \alpha_2 \cdot \sum_{i=1}^{n} \|S_{i+1} - \Psi(F_{i \to i+1}, \hat{S}_i)\|_1,$$

(9)

where $\{S_i, S_{i+1}\}$ denotes *representative slice-pairs* from *representative set R*, and n denotes the number of *representative slice-pairs* for training. $\Psi(\cdot, \cdot)$ is the soft-copy operation for pixel-wise reconstruction, and $F_{i \to i+1}$ denotes *reconstruction factor*. The weight α_1 starts from a high value of 0.9 in early training stage and is uniformly annealed to 0.5, keeping $\alpha_1 + \alpha_2 = 1$.

Cycle Consistency. Normally, in testing, the expert-provided single slice's annotation A_i is around the middle of the slices along the depth dimension of a volume, and the annotation is propagated in two directions, i.e., $A_i \to \hat{A}_{i+1}$ and $A_i \to \hat{A}_{i-1}$. *Cycle consistency* [35] is adopted to enhance the model's robustness for reconstruction in both directions. Specifically, for one *representative slice-pairs*, $\{S_i, S_{i+1}\}$, S_i is used to reconstruct $\hat{S}_{i+1}$ in one direction, i.e., $i \to i + 1$, and, in turn, the reconstructed slice $\hat{S}_{i+1}$ is also utilized to reconstruct the initial one $\hat{S}_i$ in the other direction, i.e., $i + 1 \to i$. The loss $\mathcal{L}_{cyc}$ is defined as:

$$\mathcal{L}_{cyc} = \sum_{i=1}^{n} \|S_i - \Psi(F_{i+1 \to i}, \Psi(F_{i \to i+1}, S_i))\|_1.$$

(10)

Thus, the overall learning objective loss $\mathcal{L}$ is defined as:

$$\mathcal{L} = \lambda_1 \mathcal{L}_{sche} + \lambda_2 \mathcal{L}_{cyc},$$

(11)

where the weights λ_1 and λ_2 are set to 0.9 and 0.1, respectively.

3   Experiments

3.1   Datesets and Metrics

We conduct experiments on four public benchmark datasets with different imaging modalities: LiTS [2], CHAOS [15], Sliver07 [32], and Decathlon-Liver [27]. For CT, our model is trained on LiTS that includes 130 contrast-enhanced abdominal CT scans, and is tested on CHAOS (a CT subset), Sliver07, and Decathlon-Liver which contain 20, 20, and 131 abdominal CT scans, respectively. For MRI, our model is both trained and tested on CHAOS (an MRI subset) that includes 60 training samples and 60 testing samples (20 T1-DUAL in-phase, 20 opposephase, and 20 T2-SPIR, respectively). Following the assessment criteria of the CHAOS challenge [15], we use Dice coefficient (DICE), relative absolute volume difference (RAVD), and average symmetric surface distance (ASSD) as metrics to evaluate results based on overlapping, volumetric, and spatial differences.

3.2   Implementation

Our model is implemented with PyTorch 1.8.0, and all the experiments are conducted on an NVIDIA GeForce RTX 2080 GPU with 11 GB memory. The batch size during training is 2 and during testing is 1. The Adam optimizer [18] is used with an initial learning rate of 0.0001, which is halved every epoch. In pre-processing, all slices are resized to 256×256.

Table 1. Segmentation performances of different methods on CHAOS.

Modality (organ)	MRI (spleen)			CT (liver)		
Method	DICE ↑	RAVD ↓	ASSD ↓	DICE ↑	RAVD ↓	ASSD ↓
(1) 2D U-Net (one slice annotated) [25]	0.64	39.36	31.57	0.80	17.75	14.94
(2) 3D U-Net (one slice annotated) [8]	0.47	37.52	34.25	0.57	19.78	17.54
(3) Pseudo annotation [39]	0.69	22.41	14.36	0.63	22.24	25.34
(4) Scribble-level annotation [16]	0.72	21.67	13.54	0.81	11.37	12.22
(5) Box-level annotation [37]	0.73	21.25	9.98	0.79	15.79	9.97
Ours	**0.85**	**11.58**	**4.35**	**0.93**	**7.48**	**3.34**
(6) 3D U-Net (fully annotated) [8]	0.89	9.74	4.21	0.94	13.74	3.47

3.3   Compared Methods and Results

Compared Methods. To investigate the segmentation accuracy of our method, we compare it with common known methods that use different annotation strategies, including: (1) 2D U-Net [25] trained on one annotated slice in each 3D training volume, (2) 3D U-Net [8] trained on 3D training volumes with one 2D slice annotated and other slices unannotated, (3) 3D CNN [39] trained on one fully annotated volume and augmented pseudo annotation, (4) 3D CNN [16] trained on scribble annotation where the location of a target organ in all slices

Table 2. Results of two methods when the testing set shifted from the training set.

Training set (organ)	LiTS (liver)		
Testing set (organ)	Sliver07 (liver)	CHAOS (liver)	Decathlon (liver)
Method	DICE ↑	DICE ↑	DICE ↑
3D U-Net (fully annotated) [8]	0.71	0.75	0.63
Ours	**0.92**	**0.93**	**0.89**

Table 3. Ablation study on the effect of each module on CHAOS (a CT subset).

Method	DICE ↑	RAVD ↓	ASSD ↓
w/o Screening module	0.74	27.54	18.24
w/o Information bottleneck	0.84	14.12	10.23
w/o Scheduled sampling	0.80	21.02	12.24
w/o Cycle consistency	0.89	8.24	7.94
Full model, $\lambda_1 = 0.1, \lambda_2 = 0.9$	0.83	15.44	11.78
Full model, $\lambda_1 = 0.5, \lambda_2 = 0.5$	0.87	10.23	9.13
Full model, $\lambda_1 = 0.9, \lambda_2 = 0.1$	**0.93**	**7.48**	**3.34**

in each training volume is specified by a small number of voxels, (5) 3D CNN [37] trained on bounding box annotation of all slices in each training volume, (6) 3D U-Net [8] trained on all fully annotated training volumes (representing the performance of a fully-supervised model). For fair comparison, the annotated slices in (1) and (2) are randomly selected and kept the same. All the compared methods work in the original settings of their papers, which are trained/tested on the CT and MRI subsets of CHAOS, respectively, based on official division [15].

Performance. From the results in Table 1, (1) and (2) are trained with the same amount of annotation data as our method, but show inferior performance, which suggests that single slice annotation is too sparse for conventional fully supervised models. Besides, compared with other weakly-supervised methods ((3), (4), and (5)), our method achieves superior accuracy by a large margin. Moreover, our method shows close results to (6) while utilizing only less than 1% annotation (i.e., one 2D slice vs. a 3D volume). Notably, our method even outperforms (6) in the ASSD metric that is for evaluating model performance with boundary and spatial variations.

Generalizability. To explore the generalizability of our method, we compare it with fully supervised 3D U-Net [8] by testing on several out-of-distribution testing sets. Specifically, both the methods are trained on LiTS and tested on CHAOS, Sliver07, and Decathlon-Liver, respectively. In Table 2, the performances of fully-supervised 3D U-Net drop considerably when shifting to other datasets for testing, even when the target organ and modality remain the same.

In contrast, our method shows promising generalizability. Medical images are commonly collected from different machines, often leading to domain shift. In such scenarios, the generalizability allows our model to attain good performances on out-of-distribution testing sets, thus achieving robustness in predicting annotation for new images.

3.4   Ablation Study

To evaluate the effectiveness of our method, we assess our full model against the absence of each its module on CHAOS (a CT subset). Table 3 shows that the *screening module* contributes to the results by 0.19 in DICE, compared to randomly taking a single slice for manual annotation. Besides, without *information bottleneck*, only ResNet-18 is used to extract features, which leads to an accuracy drop of 0.09 in DICE. Moreover, the two training strategies, *scheduled sampling* and *cycle consistency*, also improve the performance by 0.13 and 0.04 in DICE, respectively. Meanwhile, we try different weights of these two strategies and $\lambda_1 = 0.9, \lambda_2 = 0.1$ work well. Thus, it is evident that each our module contributes to the segmentation performance.

4   Conclusions

In this paper, we proposed a new self-learning and one-shot learning based framework for 3D medical image segmentation with only single slice annotation. A most representative single slice of each 3D image is selected for one-shot manual annotation, thus reducing annotation efforts. Self-learning of a reconstruction network facilitates to match semantic correspondences among slices and propagate annotation. Extensive experiments showed that with less than 1% annotated data, our method achieves competitive results and promising generalizability.

Acknowledgments. This research was partially supported by National Key R&D Program of China under grant No. 2019YFC0118802, National Natural Science Foundation of China under grants No. 62176231, Zhejiang public welfare technology research project under grant No. LGF20F020013, D. Z. Chen's research was supported in part by NSF Grant CCF-1617735.

References

1. Bengio, S., Vinyals, O., et al.: Scheduled sampling for sequence prediction with recurrent neural networks. In: NIPS, vol. 28 (2015)
2. Bilic, P., Christ, P.F., et al.: The liver tumor segmentation benchmark (LiTS). ArXiv preprint arXiv:1901.04056 (2019)
3. Bitarafan, A., Nikdan, M., et al.: 3D image segmentation with sparse annotation by self-training and internal registration. JBHI **25**(7), 2665–2672 (2020)
4. Chang, Y.T., Wang, Q., et al.: Weakly-supervised semantic segmentation via subcategory exploration. In: CVPR, pp. 8991–9000 (2020)
5. Chen, L.C., Papandreou, G., et al.: Semantic image segmentation with deep convolutional nets and fully connected CRFs. ArXiv preprint arXiv:1412.7062 (2014)

6. Chen, L.C., Papandreou, G., et al.: DeepLab: semantic image segmentation with deep convolutional nets, atrous convolution, and fully connected CRFs. TPAMI **40**, 834–848 (2017)
7. Chen, L.C., Zhu, Y., et al.: Encoder-decoder with atrous separable convolution for semantic image segmentation. In: ECCV (2018)
8. Çiçek, Ö., Abdulkadir, A., Lienkamp, S.S., Brox, T., Ronneberger, O.: 3D U-Net: learning dense volumetric segmentation from sparse annotation. In: Ourselin, S., Joskowicz, L., Sabuncu, M.R., Unal, G., Wells, W. (eds.) MICCAI 2016. LNCS, vol. 9901, pp. 424–432. Springer, Cham (2016). https://doi.org/10.1007/978-3-319-46723-8_49
9. Dai, C., et al.: Suggestive annotation of brain tumour images with gradient-guided sampling. In: Martel, A.L., et al. (eds.) MICCAI 2020. LNCS, vol. 12264, pp. 156–165. Springer, Cham (2020). https://doi.org/10.1007/978-3-030-59719-1_16
10. Gabor, D.: Theory of communication. Part 1: the analysis of information. J. Inst. Electr. Eng. Part III: Radio Commun. Eng. **93**(26), 429–441 (1946)
11. He, K., Chen, X., et al.: Masked autoencoders are scalable vision learners. ArXiv preprint arXiv:2111.06377 (2021)
12. He, K., Zhang, X., et al.: Deep residual learning for image recognition. In: CVPR, pp. 770–778 (2016)
13. Huang, Z., Wang, X., et al.: Weakly-supervised semantic segmentation network with deep seeded region growing. In: CVPR, pp. 7014–7023 (2018)
14. Isensee, F., Jaeger, P.F., et al.: nnU-Net: a self-configuring method for deep learning-based biomedical image segmentation. Nat. Methods **18**, 203–211 (2021)
15. Kavur, A.E., Gezer, N.S., et al.: CHAOS challenge-combined (CT-MR) healthy abdominal organ segmentation. MIA **69**, 101950 (2021)
16. Kervadec, H., Dolz, J., et al.: Constrained-CNN losses for weakly supervised segmentation. MIA **54**, 88–99 (2019)
17. Khoreva, A., Benenson, R., et al.: Simple does it: weakly supervised instance and semantic segmentation. In: CVPR, pp. 876–885 (2017)
18. Kingma, D.P., Ba, J.: Adam: a method for stochastic optimization. arXiv preprint arXiv:1412.6980 (2014)
19. Kolesnikov, A., Lampert, C.H.: Seed, expand and constrain: three principles for weakly-supervised image segmentation. In: Leibe, B., Matas, J., Sebe, N., Welling, M. (eds.) ECCV 2016. LNCS, vol. 9908, pp. 695–711. Springer, Cham (2016). https://doi.org/10.1007/978-3-319-46493-0_42
20. Krishna, K., Murty, M.N.: Genetic K-means algorithm. IEEE Trans. Syst. Man Cybern. Part B (Cybern.) **29**(3), 433–439 (1999)
21. Long, J., Shelhamer, E., et al.: Fully convolutional networks for semantic segmentation. In: CVPR (2015)
22. Milletari, F., Navab, N., et al.: V-Net: fully convolutional neural networks for volumetric medical image segmentation. In: 3DV (2016)
23. Papandreou, G., Chen, L.C., et al.: Weakly-and semi-supervised learning of a deep convolutional network for semantic image segmentation. In: ICCV, pp. 1742–1750 (2015)
24. Pathak, D., Krahenbuhl, P., et al.: Context encoders: feature learning by inpainting. In: CVPR, pp. 2536–2544 (2016)
25. Ronneberger, O., Fischer, P., Brox, T.: U-Net: convolutional networks for biomedical image segmentation. In: Navab, N., Hornegger, J., Wells, W.M., Frangi, A.F. (eds.) MICCAI 2015. LNCS, vol. 9351, pp. 234–241. Springer, Cham (2015). https://doi.org/10.1007/978-3-319-24574-4_28

26. Shi, X., Dou, Q., Xue, C., Qin, J., Chen, H., Heng, P.-A.: An active learning approach for reducing annotation cost in skin lesion analysis. In: Suk, H.-I., Liu, M., Yan, P., Lian, C. (eds.) MLMI 2019. LNCS, vol. 11861, pp. 628–636. Springer, Cham (2019). https://doi.org/10.1007/978-3-030-32692-0_72

27. Simpson, A.L., Antonelli, M., et al.: A large annotated medical image dataset for the development and evaluation of segmentation algorithms. ArXiv preprint arXiv:1902.09063 (2019)

28. Song, C., Huang, Y., et al.: Box-driven class-wise region masking and filling rate guided loss for weakly supervised semantic segmentation. In: CVPR, pp. 3136–3145 (2019)

29. Tajbakhsh, N., Hu, Y., et al.: Surrogate supervision for medical image analysis: effective deep learning from limited quantities of labeled data. In: ISBI, pp. 1251–1255. IEEE (2019)

30. Taleb, A., Lippert, C., Klein, T., Nabi, M.: Multimodal self-supervised learning for medical image analysis. In: Feragen, A., Sommer, S., Schnabel, J., Nielsen, M. (eds.) IPMI 2021. LNCS, vol. 12729, pp. 661–673. Springer, Cham (2021). https://doi.org/10.1007/978-3-030-78191-0_51

31. Taleb, A., Loetzsch, W., et al.: 3D self-supervised methods for medical imaging. In: NIPS, vol. 33, pp. 18158–18172 (2020)

32. Van Ginneken, B., Heimann, T., et al.: 3D segmentation in the clinic: a grand challenge. In: MICCAI Workshop on 3D Segmentation in the Clinic: A Grand Challenge, vol. 1, pp. 7–15 (2007)

33. Vincent, P., Larochelle, H., et al.: Stacked denoising autoencoders: learning useful representations in a deep network with a local denoising criterion. JMLR 11(12), 3371–3408 (2010)

34. Vondrick, C., Shrivastava, A., et al.: Tracking emerges by colorizing videos. In: ECCV, pp. 391–408 (2018)

35. Wang, X., Jabri, A., et al.: Learning correspondence from the cycle-consistency of time. In: CVPR, pp. 2566–2576 (2019)

36. Wang, Z., Yin, Z.: Annotation-efficient cell counting. In: de Bruijne, M., et al. (eds.) MICCAI 2021. LNCS, vol. 12908, pp. 405–414. Springer, Cham (2021). https://doi.org/10.1007/978-3-030-87237-3_39

37. Yang, G., Wang, C., et al.: Weakly-supervised convolutional neural networks of renal tumor segmentation in abdominal CTA images. BMC Med. Imaging 20(1), 1–12 (2020)

38. Yang, L., Zhang, Y., Chen, J., Zhang, S., Chen, D.Z.: Suggestive annotation: a deep active learning framework for biomedical image segmentation. In: Descoteaux, M., Maier-Hein, L., Franz, A., Jannin, P., Collins, D.L., Duchesne, S. (eds.) MICCAI 2017. LNCS, vol. 10435, pp. 399–407. Springer, Cham (2017). https://doi.org/10.1007/978-3-319-66179-7_46

39. Zhao, A., Balakrishnan, G., et al.: Data augmentation using learned transformations for one-shot medical image segmentation. In: CVPR, pp. 8543–8553 (2019)

40. Zheng, H., Yang, L., et al.: Biomedical image segmentation via representative annotation. In: AAAI, vol. 33, pp. 5901–5908 (2019)

41. Zheng, H., Zhang, Y., et al.: An annotation sparsification strategy for 3D medical image segmentation via representative selection and self-training. In: AAAI, vol. 34, pp. 6925–6932 (2020)

Longitudinal Infant Functional Connectivity Prediction via Conditional Intensive Triplet Network

Xiaowei Yu[1,3], Dan Hu[2], Lu Zhang[1], Ying Huang[3], Zhengwang Wu[3], Tianming Liu[4], Li Wang[3], Weili Lin[3], Dajiang Zhu[1], and Gang Li[3(✉)]

[1] Department of Computer Science and Engineering, University of Texas at Arlington, Arlington, TX 76013, USA
dajiang.zhu@uta.edu

[2] Department of Neuroscience, College of Medicine, Medical University of South Carolina, Charleston, SC 29425, USA

[3] Department of Radiology and Biomedical Research Imaging Center, University of North Carolina at Chapel Hill, Chapel Hill, NC 27599, USA
gang_li@med.unc.edu

[4] Department of Computer Science, University of Georgia, Athens, GA 30602, USA

Abstract. Longitudinal infant brain functional connectivity (FC) constructed from resting-state functional MRI (rs-fMRI) has increasingly become a pivotal tool in studying the dynamics of early brain development. However, due to various reasons including high acquisition cost, strong motion artifact, and subject dropout, there has been an extreme shortage of usable longitudinal infant rs-fMRI scans to construct longitudinal FCs, which hinders comprehensive understanding and modeling of brain functional development at early ages. To address this issue, in this paper, we propose a novel conditional intensive triplet network (CITN) for longitudinal prediction of the dynamic development of infant FC, which can traverse FCs within a long duration and predict the target FC at any specific age during infancy. Targeting at accurately modeling of the progression pattern of FC, while maintaining the individual functional uniqueness, our model effectively disentangles the intrinsically mixed age-related and identity-related information from the source FC and predicts the target FC by fusing well-disentangled identity-related information with the specific age-related information. Specifically, we introduce an intensive triplet auto-encoder for effective disentanglement of age-related and identity-related information and an identity conditional module to mix identity-related information with designated age-related information. We train the proposed model in a self-supervised way and design downstream tasks to help robustly disentangle age-related and identity-related features. Experiments on 464 longitudinal infant fMRI scans show the superior performance of the proposed method in longitudinal FC prediction in comparison with state-of-the-art approaches.

Keywords: Functional connectivity · Longitudinal prediction · Autoencoder

L. Wang et al. (Eds.): MICCAI 2022, LNCS 13438, pp. 255–264, 2022.
https://doi.org/10.1007/978-3-031-16452-1_25

1 Introduction

Functional connectivity (FC) constructed from resting-state fMRI is one of the most prevalent data for revealing brain functional organization [1, 2]. Typically, brain functional connectivity is represented as an undirected graph encoded in a symmetric connectivity matrix, where each element is the Pearson's correlation coefficient (PCC) of the average blood-oxygen-level-dependent (BOLD) signal between a pair of regions of interest (ROIs) [3]. Being demonstrated as an effective way to represent a comprehensive mapping of neural activities, FC has been widely used in many applications, such as mutual prediction between FC and structural connectivity (SC) [4, 5], brain development and aging studies [6–8], and early detection of brain diseases [9–12]. To answer questions raised in brain research for early ages with extremely dynamic neurodevelopment, it is critical to obtain sufficient longitudinal FC data. However, the usable longitudinal infant FC data are still scarce due to many reasons, e.g., strong motion effect, subject dropout, high acquisition costs, few volunteers, and long-time acquisition time [13]. As a result, predicting infant FC development at specific ages from limited samples becomes extremely challenging in neuroscience study, though it is of great importance in understanding normal brain development and early diagnosing neurodevelopmental abnormalities [14–16]. Some learning-based methods have been proposed for the longitudinal prediction of missing structural images and features [17–22], but these methods generally fail in predicting functional connectivity due to the large heterogeneity of FCs between individuals and developmental stages. Besides, the multi-view brain graph synthesis methods designed for cortical morphological connectomes usually cannot perform well in FC prediction [23, 24]. To the best of our knowledge, computational techniques for predicting the longitudinal development of FCs in infants remain unexplored.

To address this issue, in this paper, we propose a novel conditional intensive triplet network (CITN) for longitudinal prediction of the dynamic development of infant FC, which can traverse FCs within a long duration and predict the target FC at any specific age during infancy. Specifically, 1) we introduce an intensive triplet auto-encoder for effective disentanglement of age-related and identity-related information, which accurately disentangles brain development-related and identity-related features; 2) we design an identity conditional module to fuse identity-related information with designated age-related information, which effectively models the progression process of FC, while maintaining the individualized intrinsic brain functional patterns; 3) our method enables FC prediction at any time period during infancy by concatenating the trained identity extractor and identity conditional module. We validate our proposed CITN on the Baby Connectome Project (BCP) [25] dataset, including 464 longitudinal scans from 119 subjects, and achieve better FC prediction than state-of-the-art methods.

2 Methods

2.1 Model Overview

The framework of our proposed conditional intensive triplet network is shown in Fig. 1 and detailed below. Specifically, the whole framework is divided into two parts: the training stage and the testing stage.

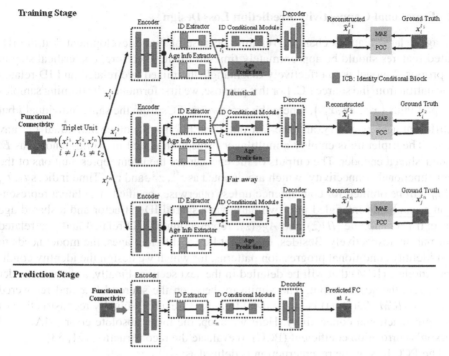

Fig. 1. The framework of the proposed conditional intensive triplet network (CITN). In the training stage, the model has a structure in the form of a triplet network. Each branch consists of six components: 1) Encoder, mapping the source FC to a mixed latent representation; 2) ID Extractor, extracting ID-related features from mixed latent features; 3) Age Info Extractor, extracting age-related features from mixed latent features; 4) Age prediction, utilizing age-related features for age prediction to enforce the age-specific information in age-related features; 5) ID Conditional Module, learning ID conditional age progression patterns; 6) Decoder, reconstructing the source functional connectivity.

The goal is to predict infantile functional connectivity at any age by capturing the FC progression pattern during early brain development. In the training stage, a triplet network is the backbone with three parallel branches and identical modules, such as encoder, ID (identify) extractor, decoder, etc. Specifically, the proposed model is composed of six parts in each branch: 1) learning the latent representations of individual FC by an encoder; 2) disentangling ID-related and age-related features by corresponding ID extractor and age Info (information) extractors; 3) strengthening the similarity/difference between the FCs acquired from the same/different individuals by delicately designed triplet loss of ID-related features; 4) using age-related information for a downstream task, i.e., age prediction; 5) learning ID conditional age features by ID conditional module; 6) reconstructing the input functional connectivity by the decoder. In the prediction stage, the trained model takes an available FC as input to extract ID-related features for predicting the target FC at any age during infancy.

2.2 Functional Connectivity Prediction Loss Design

The age-related features change over time because of brain development, but the ID-related features should be approximately time-invariant. Therefore, one critical step in the proposed model is to effectively disentangle the mixed age-related and ID-related information from the source FC. For this purpose, we first formulate the training samples in triplet units $\left(x_i^{t_1}, x_i^{t_2}, x_j^{t_n}\right)$, where the first two are FCs from the same individual i but at different ages t_1 and t_2, and the last one is an FC from another individual j at any age t_n. The triplet units employ a multilayer perceptron neural network, denoted as E, as their shared encoder. The outputs of the encoder are the latent representations of the input functional connectivity, which are denoted as $z_i^{t_1}, z_i^{t_2}$, and $z_j^{t_n}$. Time indices t_1, t_2, and t_n will be omitted for convenience unless otherwise specified. The latent representation z can be disentangled into two parts via a shared ID extractor and a shared age Info extractor module: $ID(z)$ and $Age(z)$, representing the ID-related and age-related information, respectively. Besides, to predict FCs at different ages, the model needs to learn identity conditional progression patterns, for which we design the identity conditional module (ICM) that will be detailed in the next section. Finally, a shared decoder G recovers the source input. The similarity between the source FC x and recovered FC $\hat{x} = G(ICM(ID(z), t))$ is maximized to make sure a high-quality reconstruction of the input functional connectivity. Here we adopt the mean absolute error (MAE) and Pearson's correlation coefficient (PCC) to evaluate the reconstruction [21, 33].

The PCC loss of the reconstruction is defined as:

$$\mathcal{L}_{recon}^{PCC} = \sum_{x=x_i^{t_1}, x_i^{t_2}, x_j^{t_n}} \mathbb{E}_x corr(x, G(ICM(ID(E(x)), t))) \tag{1}$$

where $t \in \{t_1, t_2, t_n\}$, $corr$ represents the Pearson's correlation and $\mathbb{E}$ represents the expectation. The MAE loss of the reconstruction is defined as:

$$\mathcal{L}_{recon}^{MAE} = \sum_{x=x_i^{t_1}, x_i^{t_2}, x_j^{t_n}} \mathbb{E}_x |x - G(ICM(ID(E(x)), t))| \tag{2}$$

The whole reconstruction loss is defined as a weighted sum of the reconstruction PCC and MAE loss:

$$\mathcal{L}_{recon} = \lambda \mathcal{L}_{recon}^{MAE} - \beta \mathcal{L}_{recon}^{PCC} \tag{3}$$

where λ and β control the balance of different loss terms.

The disentanglement of the ID-related features is an essential step to the success of our proposed model. The disentangled ID-related features from the same subject should be as close as possible while being distinct from other subjects. Therefore, we introduced the intensive triplet loss to distinguish ID-related features from different subjects. We borrow the concept from the triplet loss models, where we consider the anchor and positive as the ID-related features of $ID(E(x_i^{t_1}))$ and $ID(E(x_i^{t_2}))$, while the negative is the ID-related features of $ID(E(x_j^{t_n}))$. The distance between anchor and positive is minimized, while the distances between the anchor/positive and negative are maximized in the latent space. However, the original triplet loss only considers the relative distance between (Anchor, Positive) and (Anchor, Negative) pairs. Since (Positive, Negative) is also a pair of distinct labels, the relative distance between (Anchor, Positive) and (Positive, Negative) is measured as an additional constraint to increase the inter-subject dissimilarity [33]. Therefore, we define a new intensive triplet loss as follows:

$$\mathcal{L}_{I-tri} = \mathcal{L}_{tri} + \mathcal{L}_I \tag{4}$$

$$\mathcal{L}_{tri} = corr\left(ID\left(E\left(x_i^{t_1}\right)\right), ID\left(E\left(x_j^{t_n}\right)\right)\right) - corr\left(ID\left(E\left(x_i^{t_1}\right)\right), ID\left(E\left(x_i^{t_2}\right)\right)\right) \tag{5}$$

$$\mathcal{L}_I = corr\left(ID\left(E\left(x_i^{t_2}\right)\right), ID\left(E\left(x_j^{t_n}\right)\right)\right) - corr\left(ID\left(E\left(x_i^{t_1}\right)\right), ID\left(E\left(x_i^{t_2}\right)\right)\right) \tag{6}$$

To encourage the proposed model to disentangle the latent representation robustly, we use a downstream task, i.e., age estimation, to supervise the feature disentanglement. The output of age Info extractor module $Age(z)$ is further fed into the age predictor module P for age estimation. Its loss function is defined as:

$$\mathcal{L}_{age} = \sum_{x=x_i^{t_1}, x_i^{t_2}, x_j^{t_n}} \mathbb{E}_x |y_x - P(Age(E(x)))| \tag{7}$$

where y_x is the real age corresponding to FC x.

On the whole, the FC prediction loss is formulated as

$$\mathcal{L}_{overall} = \mathcal{L}_{recon} + \alpha \mathcal{L}_{age} + \delta \mathcal{L}_{I-tri} \tag{8}$$

where α and δ controls the influence of age estimation loss and intensive triplet loss, respectively.

2.3 Identity Conditional Module

The identity conditional module (ICM) is built by cascading several identity conditional blocks (ICBs) to improve the age smoothness of synthesized FCs. The detailed structure of ICBs is shown in Fig. 2.

In our work, the number of ICBs is set as six after multiple empirical tries. Specifically, the designed ICB takes the identity-related feature from the ID extractor as input to learn the general FC progression pattern with the condition of identity. The ICBs shown in Fig. 2 contains a fully connected feed-forward network (FFN), which consists of two linear projections with a ReLU activation in between.

$$FFN(v) = mask(mask(max(0, vW_1 + b_1), t_n)W_2 + b_2, t_n) \tag{9}$$

where v represents the input vector. While the linear projections are the same across the ICBs, they use different parameters from layer to layer. The $mask()$ function is to filter out the features of the target age group, which is the ID-Age features as shown in Fig. 2. Then, with a dedicated designed weights-sharing strategy, the age smoothness of synthesized FCs is enforced by sharing part of ID-Age features across adjacent age groups. A hyper-parameter p is further introduced to adjust the percentage of the ID-Age features shared between two adjacent age groups, which is empirically set to 0.1. In the training process, the ICM synthesizes the corresponding ID-Age features under the guidance of the age label of source functional connectivity. In the prediction process, the ICM fuses the target age label and ID-related features together to synthesize the corresponding target ID-Age features.

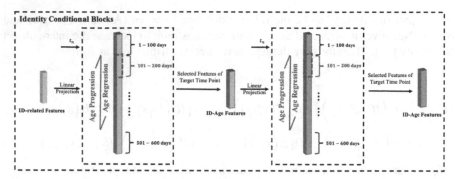

Fig. 2. The architecture of the identity conditional blocks (ICBs). The proposed ICBs aim to learn the general FC progression pattern with the conditionality of identity. It takes the ID-related feature from the ID extractor as input to learn an identity-level progression pattern. Here the target age is set to be the period of 101–200 days for illustration.

3 Experiments

3.1 Dataset

In this work, we use 464 longitudinal resting-state fMRI scans of 119 typically developing infants before 600 days of age from the Baby Connectome Project (BCP) dataset [25]. Since the individuals have two different types of scan orders, anterior to posterior (AP) and posterior to anterior (PA), we divide the dataset into two separate groups, AP and PA, for independent validation, where each group has 232 scans. After a detailed investigation of the dataset, we uniformly divide the dataset into six partitions forming a relatively balanced data distribution. The six temporal partitions are [1, 100], [101, 200], ..., [501, 600], corresponding to six ages. Note that none of the individuals has complete scans of six ages. For structural and functional MRI processing, we follow the strategies in [28, 29], resulting in average fMRI time series in each of 35 cortical regions for each hemisphere. We construct the functional connectivity by calculating the Pearson's correlation coefficient between time series of each pair of regions and performing Fishers r-to-z transformation. The flattened vector of the upper triangle of FC is taken as the input of our model. Of note, we use the absolute value of FCs, which means we narrow the range of FCs from $[-1, 1]$ to $[0, 1]$, since we focus more on predicting the strength of the connection [30] in this study.

3.2 Results and Visualization

The encoder E and decoder G were designed as a two-layer perceptron neural network. The ID extractor and age Info extractor both consist of densely connected layers of dimension (1500, 1000) and (1500, 500), respectively, with ReLU as the activation function. The age predictor comprises 3 densely connected layers of dimension (256, 32, 1) with a nonlinear activation function of ReLU. There are six identical ICBs in ICM, where each ICB project ID-related features to a high dimension (1000, $((\varphi - (\varphi - 1) \times p) \times 1500)$), in which φ is the number of age groups and corresponding to the number of partitions 6 in our experiments. The ID-Age features that match the target age were then correspondingly selected out as shown in Fig. 2.

We show the predicted results of two representative individuals that have three FCs at different ages. Each individual takes one of the three FCs as the source input and the other two as target FC to predict. To evaluate the stability and effectiveness of the proposed method, we display the FCs of ground truth and predictions in Fig. 3. For each subject, there are two target predictions at two ages. The prediction results demonstrate that our method can maintain the stability of the FC prediction at any specific age regardless of different source FCs, where the average correlation between the predicted FCs obtained from different source FC achieves above 0.90.

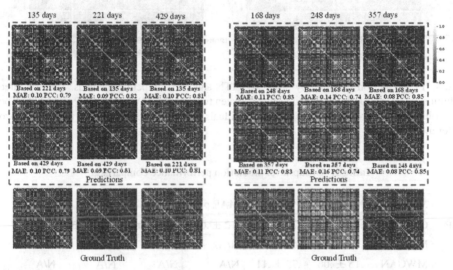

Fig. 3. Visual comparison between the ground truth and the predicted FCs of two representative individuals. Each column represents a specific age, and each row includes the FCs in three different ages. The first two rows are the predicted FCs, and the last row is the ground truth FCs. For each predicted FC, the text below it describes the MAE and PCC between the predicted and ground truth FCs.

3.3 Evaluation and Comparison

To quantitatively evaluate the performance, we compare our conditional intensive triplet network with two well-recognized approaches. The first one is the MLP-type network [31], which incorporates source FC with the target age information by one-hot encoding. The other one is multi-marginal Wasserstein GAN (MWGAN) [32], which defines a generator for target FC prediction at each age. We display the comparison results of the prediction of two representative individuals at two time periods in Fig. 4, where the first three columns represent the predicted results and the last column is the ground truth, while the rows represent the ages. MLP deteriorates the performance rapidly when the FC pattern changes a lot along the time, while the target results of WMGAN are not stable when input source FCs from different ages. We also tried different filter-sharing strategies by setting the hyper-parameter p with a range of values. Table 1 shows the group-level performance comparison between the proposed method and two baselines, where p0, p1, and p2 mean the hyper-parameter p set to be 0.0, 0.1, 0.2. From the comparisons in Fig. 4 and Table 1, we can see our proposed model achieves better performance in both AP and PA groups and under different settings.

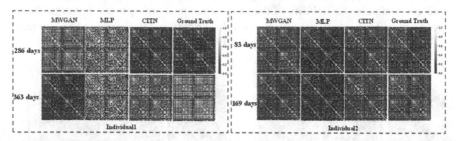

Fig. 4. FC prediction obtained by proposed CITN and two competing methods. The first three columns are the mutually predicted results between two ages by MWGAN, MLP and CITN. The last column is the ground truth. The two individuals shown in this figure have two FCs at two different ages.

Table 1. Group-level prediction performance comparison.

	Method	MAE p0	PCC p0	MAE p1	PCC p1	MAE p2	PCC p2
AP	CITN	**.12 ± .03**	**.77 ± .07**	.12 ± .03	.77 ± .07	.12 ± .03	.76 ± .07
	MLP	.18 ± .04	.62 ± .06	N/A	N/A	N/A	N/A
	MWGAN	.15 ± .06	.75 ± .11	N/A	N/A	N/A	N/A
PA	CITN	**.12 ± .04**	**.76 ± .07**	.13 ± .04	.75 ± .08	.12 ± .04	.76 ± .08
	MLP	.18 ± .09	.60 ± .04	N/A	N/A	N/A	N/A
	MWGAN	.17 ± .06	.73 ± .08	N/A	N/A	N/A	N/A

4   Conclusion

In this work, we proposed a conditional intensive triplet deep learning network, which is a novel approach for predicting longitudinal infant functional connectivity from severely irregularly-distributed data. To this end, we formulate triplet units to augment training samples, design identity and age information extractors to disentangle the identity-related and age-related features from the latent representations, and devise identity conditional module to fuse the identity-related features with the target age information, thus enabling generate functional connectivity at any specific age. The promising results on the BCP dataset demonstrate the practicality and feasibility of our model in the application for infant functional connectivity prediction.

Acknowledgments. This work was supported in part by NIH grants (MH116225, MH117943, MH123202, MH127544, and AG075582). This work also utilizes approaches developed by an NIH grant (1U01MH110274) and the efforts of the UNC/UMN Baby Connectome Project Consortium.

References

1. Heuvel, M., Pol, H.: Exploring the brain network: a review on resting-state fMRI functional connectivity. Eur. Neuropsychopharmacol. **20**(8), 519–534 (2010)
2. Bastos, A.M., Schoffelen, J.M.: A tutorial review of functional connectivity analysis methods and their interpretational pitfalls. Front. Syst. Neurosci. **9**, 175 (2016)
3. Power, J.D., Barnes, K.A., Snyder, A.Z., Schlaggar, B.L., Petersen, S.E.: Steps toward optimizing motion artifact removal in functional connectivity MRI; a reply to Carp. Neuroimage **76** (2013)
4. Zhang, L., Wang, L., Zhu, D.: Recovering brain structural connectivity from functional connectivity via multi-GCN based generative adversarial network. In: Martel, A.L., et al. (eds.) MICCAI 2020. LNCS, vol. 12267, pp. 53–61. Springer, Cham (2020). https://doi.org/10.1007/978-3-030-59728-3_6
5. Zhang, L., Wang, L., Zhu, D.: Predicting brain structural network using functional connectivity. Med. Image Anal. **79** (2022)
6. Yamada, H., et al.: A rapid brain metabolic change in infants detected by fMRI. NeuroReport **8**(17), 3775–3778 (1997)
7. Zhang, H., Shen, D., Lin, W.: Resting-state functional MRI studies on infant brains: a decade of gap-filling efforts. Neuroimage **185**, 664–684 (2019)
8. Wen, X., et al.: First-year development of modules and hubs in infant brain functional networks. Neuroimage **185**, 664–684 (2019)
9. Zhang, L., et al.: Deep fusion of brain structure-function in mild cognitive impairment. Med. Image Anal. **72**, 102082 (2021)
10. Zhang, L., Wang, L., Zhu, D.: Jointly analyzing alzheimer's disease related structure-function using deep cross-model attention network. In: IEEE 17th International Symposium on Biomedical Imaging (ISBI), pp. 563–567 (2020)
11. Zhang, L., Zaman, A., Wang, L., Yan, J., Zhu, D.: A cascaded multi-modality analysis in mild cognitive impairment. In: Suk, H.-I., Liu, M., Yan, P., Lian, C. (eds.) MLMI 2019. LNCS, vol. 11861, pp. 557–565. Springer, Cham (2019). https://doi.org/10.1007/978-3-030-32692-0_64
12. Wang, L., Zhang, L., Zhu, D.: learning latent structure over deep fusion model of mild cognitive impairment. In: IEEE 17th International Symposium on Biomedical Imaging (ISBI), pp. 1039–1043 (2020)
13. Logothetis, N.K.: What we can do and what we cannot do with fMRI. Nature **453**(7197), 869–878 (2008)
14. Yu, X., Zhang, L., Zhao, L., Lyu, Y., Liu, T., Zhu, D.: Disentangling spatial-temporal functional brain networks via twin-transformers. arXiv preprint arXiv:2204.09225 (2022)
15. Lin, W., et al.: Functional connectivity MR imaging reveals cortical functional connectivity in the developing brain. Am. J. Neuroradiol. **29**(10), 1883–1889 (2008)
16. Yu, X., Scheel, N., Zhang, L., Zhu, D.C., Zhang, R., Zhu, D.: Free water in T2 FLAIR white matter hyperintensity lesions. Alzheimer's Dementia **17** (2021)
17. Zhao, F., et al.: Spherical deformable U-Net: application to cortical surface parcellation and development prediction. IEEE Trans. Med. Imaging **40**(4), 1217–1228 (2021)
18. Meng, Y., et al.: Can we predict subject-specific dynamic cortical thickness maps during infancy from birth? Hum. Brain Mapp. **38**(6), 2865–2874 (2017)

19. Rekik, I., Li, G., Pew-Thian, Y., Chen, G., Lin, W., Shen D.: Joint prediction of longitudinal development of cortical surfaces and white matter fibers from neonatal MRI. NeuroImage **152**, 411–424 (2017)

20. Zhang, Z., Song, Y., Qi, H.: Age progression/regression by conditional adversarial autoencoder. In: Proceedings of the IEEE Conference on Computer Vision and Pattern Recognition, pp. 5810–5818 (2017)

21. Nie, J., Li, G., Wang, L., Gilmore, J., Lin, W., Shen, D.: A computational growth model for measuring dynamic cortical development in the first year of life. Cereb. Cortex **22**(10), 2272–2284 (2012)

22. Zhao, F., et al.: Spherical U-Net on cortical surfaces: methods and applications. In: Chung, A.C.S., Gee, J.C., Yushkevich, P.A., Bao, S. (eds.) IPMI 2019. LNCS, vol. 11492, pp. 855–866. Springer, Cham (2019). https://doi.org/10.1007/978-3-030-20351-1_67

23. Bessadok, A., Mahjoub, M.A., Rekik, I.: Brain multigraph prediction using topology-aware adversarial graph neural network. Med. Image Anal. **72**(3), 102090 (2021)

24. Gurbuz, M.B., Rekik, I.: Deep graph normalizer: a geometric deep learning approach for estimating connectional brain templates. In: Martel, A.L., et al. (eds.) MICCAI 2020. LNCS, vol. 12267, pp. 155–165. Springer, Cham (2020). https://doi.org/10.1007/978-3-030-59728-3_16

25. Howell, B.R., et al.: The UNC/UMN Baby Connectome Project (BCP): an overview of the study design and protocol development. Neuroimage **185**, 891–905 (2019)

26. Amico, E., Goñi, J.: The quest for identifiability in human functional connectomes. Sci. Rep. **8**(1), 1–14 (2018)

27. Finn, E.S., et al.: Functional connectome fingerprinting: identifying individuals using patterns of brain connectivity. Nat. Neurosci. **18**(11), 1664–1671 (2015)

28. Hu, D., et al.: Disentangled-multimodal adversarial autoencoder: application to infant age prediction with incomplete multimodal neuroimages. IEEE Trans. Med. Imaging **39**(12), 4137–4149 (2020)

29. Hu, D., et al.: Existence of functional connectome fingerprint during infancy and its stability over months. J. Neurosci. **42**, 377–389 (2021)

30. Ran, Q., Jamoulle, T., Schaeverbeke, J., Meersmans, K., Vandenberghe, R., Dupont, P.: Reproducibility of graph measures at the subject level using resting-state fMRI. Brain Behav. **10**(8), 2336–2351 (2020)

31. Tolstikhin, I.O., et al.: MLP-mixer: an all-MLP architecture for vision. Adv. Neural Inf. Process. Syst. **34**, 24261–24272 (2021)

32. Cao, J., Mo, L., Zhang, Y., Jia, K., Shen, C., Tan, M.: Multi-marginal wasserstein GAN. Adv. Neural Inf. Process. Syst. **32** (2019)

33. Hu, D., et al.: Disentangled intensive triplet autoencoder for infant functional connectome fingerprinting. In: Martel, A.L., et al. (eds.) MICCAI 2020. LNCS, vol. 12267, pp. 72–82. Springer, Cham (2020). https://doi.org/10.1007/978-3-030-59728-3_8

Leveraging Labeling Representations in Uncertainty-Based Semi-supervised Segmentation

Sukesh Adiga Vasudeva$^{(\boxtimes)}$ ⓘ, Jose Dolz ⓘ, and Herve Lombaert ⓘ

ETS Montreal, Montreal, Canada
sukesh.adiga-vasudeva.1@ens.etsmtl.ca

Abstract. Semi-supervised segmentation tackles the scarcity of annotations by leveraging unlabeled data with a small amount of labeled data. A prominent way to utilize the unlabeled data is by consistency training which commonly uses a teacher-student network, where a teacher guides a student segmentation. The predictions of unlabeled data are not reliable, therefore, uncertainty-aware methods have been proposed to gradually learn from meaningful and reliable predictions. Uncertainty estimation, however, relies on multiple inferences from model predictions that need to be computed for each training step, which is computationally expensive. This work proposes a novel method to estimate the pixel-level uncertainty by leveraging the labeling representation of segmentation masks. On the one hand, a labeling representation is learnt to represent the available segmentation masks. The learnt labeling representation is used to map the prediction of the segmentation into a set of plausible masks. Such a reconstructed segmentation mask aids in estimating the pixel-level uncertainty guiding the segmentation network. The proposed method estimates the uncertainty with a single inference from the labeling representation, thereby reducing the total computation. We evaluate our method on the 3D segmentation of left atrium in MRI, and we show that our uncertainty estimates from our labeling representation improve the segmentation accuracy over state-of-the-art methods. Code is released at GitHub.

Keywords: Semi-supervised learning · Segmentation · Labeling representation · Uncertainty

1 Introduction

Segmentation of organs or abnormal regions is a fundamental task in clinical applications, such as diagnosis, intervention and treatment planning. Deep learning techniques are driving progress in automating the segmentation task under the full-supervision paradigm [5,16]. Training these models, however, relies on a large amount of pixel-level annotations, which require expensive clinical expertise [4].

Semi-supervised learning techniques alleviate the annotation scarcity by leveraging unlabeled data with a small amount of labeled data. Current semi-supervised

© The Author(s), under exclusive license to Springer Nature Switzerland AG 2022
L. Wang et al. (Eds.): MICCAI 2022, LNCS 13438, pp. 265–275, 2022.
https://doi.org/10.1007/978-3-031-16452-1_26

segmentation methods typically utilize the unlabeled data either in the form of pseudo labels [1,32], regularization [6,17,19] or knowledge priors [8,31]. For instance, self-training methods [1] generate pseudo labels from unlabeled data, which are used to retrain the network iteratively. A wide range of regularization-based methods has been explored for semi-supervised segmentation using adversarial learning [3,17], consistency learning [2,12,14,30], or co-training [19,25,27]. Adversarial methods encourage the segmentation of unlabeled images to be closer to those of the labeled images. In contrast, consistency and co-training methods encourage two or more segmentation predictions, either from the same or different networks, to be consistent under different perturbations of the input data. Such consistency-based methods are popular in semi-supervision due to their simplicity. Consequently, self-ensembling [9] and mean teacher-based [22] methods are often used in semi-supervised segmentation of medical images [2,6,12]. However, their generated predictions from the unlabeled images may not always be reliable. To alleviate this issue, uncertainty-aware regularization methods [15,21,24,26,30] are proposed to gradually add reliable target regions in predictions. This uncertainty scheme is also employed in co-training [27] and self-training [32] approaches to obtain reliable predictions. Although these methods perform well in low-labeled data regimes, their high computation and complex training techniques might limit their applicability to broader applications in practice. For instance, the uncertainty estimation is approximated via Monte-Carlo Dropout [7] or an ensembling, which requires multiple predictions per image. Co-training methods require two or more networks to be trained simultaneously, whereas self-training-based methods rely on costly iterations. Lastly, adversarial training is challenging in terms of convergence [20].

Prior-based methods in semi-supervised segmentation typically incorporate anatomical knowledge of the target object during training the model. For instance, He et al. [8] encode the unlabeled images in an autoencoder and combine the learnt features as prior knowledge in the segmentation networks. Recent attempts use signed distance maps (SDM) as shape constraints during training [11,24,29]. For instance, Le et al. [11] propose an additional task of predicting SDM and enforcing consistency with an adversarial loss. Zheng et al. [31] exploit a probabilistic atlas in their loss function. These knowledge-based methods require an additional task to constraints shape prior, or it requires aligned images.

These limitations motivate our approach, which leverages a learnt labeling representation to approximate the uncertainty. Our main idea is to mimic a shape prior by learning a representation using segmentation masks such that each prediction is mapped into a set of plausible segmentations. In contrast to [31], our approach does not require aligned images. The mapped segmentation is subsequently used to estimate the uncertainty maps to guide the segmentation network. We hypothesize that the proposed uncertainty estimates are more robust than those derived from the entropy variance, requiring multiple inferences strategy.

Our Contributions. We propose a novel way to estimate the pixel-wise uncertainty to guide the training of a segmentation model. In particular, we integrate

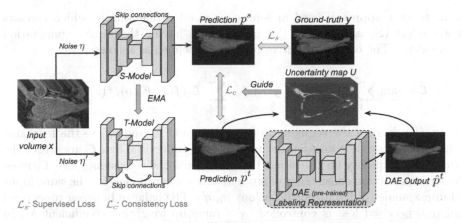

Fig. 1. Overview of our uncertainty estimation from labeling representation for semi-supervised segmentation. A pre-trained labeling representation (DAE) is integrated into the training of the mean teacher method, which maps the teacher predictions p^t into plausible segmentation $\hat{p}^t$. The uncertainty map (U) is subsequently estimated with the teacher and DAE predictions, guiding the student model.

a pre-trained denoising autoencoder (DAE) into the training, whose goal is to leverage a learnt labeling representation on unlabeled data. The DAE maps the segmentation predictions into a set of plausible segmentation masks. Then, we approximate the uncertainty by computing the pixel-wise difference between predicted segmentation and its DAE reconstruction. In contrast to commonly used uncertainty-based approaches, our uncertainty map needs a single inference from the DAE model, reducing computation complexity. Our method is extensively evaluated on the 2018 Atrial Segmentation Challenge dataset [28]. The results demonstrate the superiority of our approach over the state-of-the-art.

2   Method

The schematic of the proposed label representation-based uncertainty estimation is shown in Fig. 1. The main idea is to exploit a labeling representation that maps the predictions of the segmentation into set of plausible masks. The reconstructed segmentations will be later employed to estimate an uncertainty map. Following current literature [30], we adopt a mean teacher approach to train a segmentation network. These steps are detailed next.

2.1   Mean Teacher Formulation

The standard semi-supervised learning consists of N labeled and M unlabeled data in the training set, where $N \ll M$. Let $D_L = \{(x_i, y_i)\}_{i=1}^{N}$ and $D_U = \{(x_i)\}_{N+1}^{(N+M)}$ denote the labeled and unlabeled sets, where an input volume is represented as $x_i \in R^{H \times W \times D}$ and its corresponding segmentation mask is $y_i \in \{0, 1, ..., C\}^{H \times W \times D}$, with C being the number of classes. We use the common mean teacher approach used in semi-supervised segmentation, which consists of a student (S) and teacher (T) model, both having the same segmentation architecture. The overall objective function is defined as follows:

$$\mathcal{L} = \min_{\theta_s} \sum_{i=1}^{N} \mathcal{L}_s(f(x_i; \theta_s), y_i) + \lambda_c \sum_{i=1}^{N+M} \mathcal{L}_c(f(x_i; \theta_s, \eta), f(x_i; \theta_t; \eta')),$$

where $f(\cdot)$ denotes the segmentation network, and θ_s and θ_t are the learnable weights of the student and teacher models. The supervised loss $\mathcal{L}_s$ measures the segmentation quality on the labeled data, whereas the consistency loss $\mathcal{L}_c$ measures the prediction consistency of student and teacher models for the same input volume x_i under different perturbations (η, η'). The balance between supervised and unsupervised loss is controlled by a ramp-up weighting co-efficient λ_c. In the mean teacher training, the student model parameters are optimized with stochastic gradient descent (SGD), whereas exponential moving average (EMA) is employed at each training step t, i.e., $\theta_t = \alpha\theta_{t-1} + (1 - \alpha)\theta_s$ to update the teacher model parameters. Note that α is the smoothing coefficient of EMA that controls the update rate.

2.2   Labeling Representation Prior

Incorporating object shape prior in deep segmentation models is not obvious. One of the reasons is that, in order to integrate such prior knowledge during training, one needs to augment the learning objective with a differentiable term, which in the case of complex shapes is not trivial. To circumvent these difficulties, a simpler solution is to resort to an autoencoder trained with pixel-wise labels, which can represent anatomical priors and be used as a global regularizer during training. This strategy has been adopted for fully supervised training in [18] and as a post-processing step in [10] to correct the segmentation predictions. Motivated by this, we represent the available labels in a non-linear latent space using a denoising autoencoder (DAE) [23], which somehow mimics a shape prior. The DAE model consists of an encoder $f_e(\cdot)$ and a decoder module $f_d(\cdot)$ with a d-dimensional latent space as shown in the Fig. 1. The DAE is trained to reconstruct the clean labels y_i from its corrupted version $\tilde{y}_i$, which can be achieved with a mean squared error loss: $\frac{1}{H \times W \times D} \sum_v ||f_d(f_e(\tilde{y}_{i,v})) - y_{i,v}||^2$.

2.3   Uncertainty from a Labeling Representation

The role of the uncertainty is to gradually update the student model with reliable target regions from the teacher predictions. Our proposed method estimates the uncertainty directly from the labeling representation network $f_d(f_e(\cdot))$, requiring only one inference step. First, we map the prediction from the teacher model p_i^t with a DAE model to produce a plausible segmentation $\hat{p}_i^t$. We subsequently estimate the uncertainty as the pixel-wise difference between the DAE output and the prediction, i.e., $U_i = ||\hat{p}_i^t - p_i^t||^2$. Then, the reliable target for the consistency loss is obtained as $e^{-\gamma U_i}$, similarly to [15], where γ is an uncertainty weighting factor empirically set to 1. Finally, our consistency loss is defined as:

$$\mathcal{L}_c(p_i^s, p_i^t) = \frac{\sum_v e^{-\gamma U_{i,v}} \|p_{i,v}^s - p_{i,v}^t\|^2}{\sum_v e^{-\gamma U_{i,v}}}$$

where v is a voxel. We jointly optimize the consistency loss $\mathcal{L}_c$ and supervised loss $\mathcal{L}_s$ as learning objectives, where $\mathcal{L}_s$ uses the cross-entropy and dice losses.

3   Results

Our proposed method is compared with the state-of-the-art semi-supervised segmentation methods [11,14,15,30]. We group the uncertainty-based methods to assess the effectiveness of our uncertainty estimation for segmentation. For a fair comparison, all experiments are run three times with a fixed set of seeds on the same machines, and their average results are reported.

Dataset and Evaluation Metrics. Our method is evaluated on the Left Atrium (LA) dataset from the 2018 Atrial Segmentation Challenge [28]. The dataset consists of 100 3D MR volumes of LA with an isotropic resolution of 0.625 mm^3 and corresponding segmentation masks. In our experiments, we use a 80/20 training/testing split and apply the same preprocessing as in [11,14,30]. The training set is partitioned into N/M labeled/unlabeled splits, fixed across all methods for each setting. We employ Dice Score Coefficient (DSC) and 95% Hausdorff Distance (HD) metrics to assess quantitative segmentation performance.

Implementation and Training details. Following [11,14,30], we use V-net [16] as backbone architecture for teacher, student and DAE models. The skip connections are removed, and a dense layer is added at the bottleneck layer for the DAE model. The student model is trained by a SGD optimizer with an initial learning rate (lr) of 0.1 and momentum 0.9 for 6000 iterations with a cosine annealing [13] decaying. The teacher weights are updated by an EMA with an update rate of $\alpha = 0.99$ as in [22]. The consistency weight is updated with Gaussian warming up function $\lambda_c = \beta * e^{-5(1-t/t_{max})^2}$, where t and t_{max} denotes current and maximum training iterations, and β is set to 0.1, as in [30]. The DAE model is also trained with SGD with $lr = 0.1$, momentum of 0.9 and decaying the lr by 2 for every 5000 iterations. Input to both segmentation and DAE networks are random cropped to 112 × 112 × 80 size and employ online standard data augmentation techniques such as random flipping and rotation. In addition, input labels to the DAE model are corrupted with a random swapping of pixels around class boundaries, morphological operations (erosion and dilation), resizing and adding/removing shapes. The batch size is set to 4 in both networks. Input batch for segmentation network uses two labeled and unlabeled data. For testing, generating segmentation predictions uses the sliding window strategy, and the method is evaluated at the last iteration as in [30]. Our experiments were run on an NVIDIA RTX A6000 GPU with PyTorch 1.8.0.

Table 1. Segmentation results on the LA test set for 10% labeled data experiments averaged over three runs. Uncertainty methods with K inferences are grouped at the bottom, while $K = -$, indicates non-uncertainty methods.

Methods	#K	N/M	DSC (%)	HD (mm)
Upper bound	–	80/0	91.23 ± 0.44	6.08 ± 1.84
Lower bound	–	8/0	76.07 ± 5.02	28.75 ± 0.72
MT [22]	–	8/72	78.22 ± 6.89	16.74 ± 4.80
SASSnet [11]	–	8/72	83.70 ± 1.48	16.90 ± 1.35
DCT [14]	–	8/72	83.10 ± 0.26	12.62 ± 1.44
UAMT [30]	8	8/72	85.09 ± 1.42	18.34 ± 2.80
URPC [15]	1	8/72	84.47 ± 0.31	17.11 ± 0.60
Ours	1	8/72	**86.58 ± 1.03**	**11.82 ± 1.42**

Comparison with the State-of-the-Art. We now compare our method with relevant semi-supervised segmentation approaches under the 10% and 20% labeled data settings and report their results in Tables 1 and 2. Non-uncertainty-based method such as MT [22], DCT [14], and SASSnet [11] are grouped in the middle of the table, while uncertainty-based methods UAMT [30], URPC [15][1] and our methods are grouped at the bottom of each table. The upper and lower bound from the backbone architecture V-net [16] are reported in the top.

In the first setting, 10% of labeled data is used, and the remaining images are used as unlabeled data. From Table 1, we can observe that leveraging unlabeled data improves the lower bound in all baselines. The uncertainty-based baselines seem to improve the segmentation performance by 1% in Dice score compared to non-uncertainty-based baselines. However, their performance drops in terms of HD up to 5 mm. Among baseline methods, UAMT and DCT achieve the best Dice and HD scores, respectively. Compared to these best performing baselines, our method brings 1.5% and 0.8 mm improvements in Dice and HD scores. Moreover, uncertainty estimation in our method requires a single inference from a labeling representation, whereas UAMT uses $K = 8$ inferences per training step to obtain an uncertainty map.

Furthermore, we also validate our method on the 20% of labeled data scenario, whose results are reported in Tables 2. Results demonstrate a similar trend as compared to the 10% experiments. The uncertainty-based baselines improve 1% in terms of Dice and drop up to 1 mm in HD, compared to non-uncertainty-based methods. Our method improves the best performing baseline in both Dice and HD scores. Particularly, our method improves the HD score by 2.5 mm compared to the best performing baseline (SASSnet).

Visual results of different segmentation results are depicted in Fig. 2. In the top row of the figure, the segmentation of SASSnet produces holes in segmentation, and their method employs a post-processing tool to improve the segmenta-

---

[1] Note that URPC [15] use multi-scale 3D U-Net [5] architecture.

Table 2. Segmentation results on the LA test set for 20% labeled data experiments averaged over three runs. Uncertainty methods with K inferences are grouped at the bottom, while $K = -$, indicates non-uncertainty methods.

Methods	#K	N/M	DSC (%)	HD (mm)
Upper bound	–	80/0	91.23 ± 0.44	6.08 ± 1.84
Lower bound	–	16/0	81.46 ± 2.96	23.61 ± 4.94
MT [22]	–	16/64	86.06 ± 0.81	11.63 ± 3.4
SASSnet [11]	–	16/64	87.81 ± 1.45	10.18 ± 0.55
DCT [14]	–	16/64	87.35 ± 1.26	10.25 ± 2.49
UAMT [30]	8	16/64	87.78 ± 1.03	11.1 ± 1.91
URPC [15]	1	16/64	88.58 ± 0.10	13.1 ± 0.60
Ours	1	16/64	**88.60 ± 0.82**	**7.61 ± 0.78**

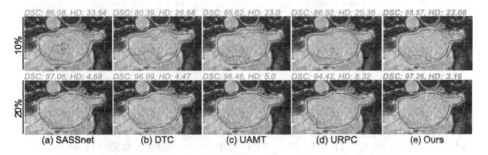

DSC: 86.08, HD: 33.54   DSC: 80.39, HD: 26.68   DSC: 85.62, HD: 23.0   DSC: 86.52, HD: 25.35   DSC: 88.57, HD: 22.08

DSC: 97.06, HD: 4.68   DSC: 96.99, HD: 4.47   DSC: 96.46, HD: 5.0   DSC: 94.42, HD: 8.32   DSC: 97.26, HD: 3.16

(a) SASSnet   (b) DTC   (c) UAMT   (d) URPC   (e) Ours

Fig. 2. Qualitative comparison under 10% and 20% annotation setting. DSC (%) and HD (mm) scores are mentioned at the top of each image. Coloring is the prediction (Red) and ground truth (Blue). (Color figure online)

tion, which is avoided for a fair comparison. DTC captures the challenging top right side region in segmentation; however, the prediction is under-segmented and noisy. The uncertainty-based methods improve the segmentation in UAMT and produce smooth segmentation boundaries in URPC. Our method improves the segmentation region further compared to URPC. In the case of 20% labeled data experiments, all methods improve the segmentation due to having access to more labels during training, while the boundary regions are either under or over-segmented. Our method produces better and smoother segmentation, which can be due to the knowledge derived from the labeling representation.

Ablation Study. To validate the effectiveness of our uncertainty estimation on segmentation performance, two experiments are conducted by adopting threshold strategy and entropy scheme from UAMT. Particularly, a threshold strategy is used in consistency, whereas entropy is used to estimate the uncertainty, and their results are reported in Table 3. Compared to UAMT, our threshold and entropy experiments significantly improve the segmentation performance in HD and Dice scores, while our proposed method (L2-based exponential uncertainty) achieves the best performance. These results show the merit of our labeling representation for uncertainty estimation. Furthermore, we report the ablation on uncertainty weight γ and consistency weight β, in Table 4. Results demonstrate that $\gamma = 1$ is best for our method, while for $\beta = 1$ our method further improves Dice and HD scores; however, we report on $\beta = 0.1$ in all experiments for a fair comparison. Overall, for most of the γ and β values, our method is consistently better than UAMT baselines, demonstrating the robustness of our approach.

Table 3. Effectiveness of our proposed uncertainty estimation on segmentation results using different strategies.

Methods	N/M	DSC (%)	HD (mm)
UAMT [30]	8/72	85.09 ± 1.42	18.34 ± 2.80
Ours (threshold)	8/72	85.39 ± 0.91	12.96 ± 3.05
Ours (entropy)	8/72	85.92 ± 1.52	**11.16 ± 0.82**
Ours	8/72	**86.58 ± 1.03**	11.82 ± 1.42

Table 4. Evaluating the γ and β values under 10% annotation setting.

γ, $\beta = 0.1$	DSC (%)	HD (mm)	β, $\gamma = 1$	DSC (%)	HD (mm)
0.1	85.30 ± 1.17	13.51 ± 2.66	0.01	84.89 ± 0.92	11.84 ± 2.79
0.5	85.28 ± 0.60	14.01 ± 4.44	0.05	85.88 ± 1.44	10.98 ± 1.85
1	**86.58 ± 1.03**	**11.82 ± 1.42**	0.1	86.58 ± 1.03	11.82 ± 1.42
2	85.84 ± 1.39	12.13 ± 3.43	0.5	86.54 ± 0.74	12.42 ± 1.31
5	84.87 ± 0.85	15.28 ± 1.76	1	**86.89 ± 0.6**	**9.85 ± 0.82**

4   Conclusion

We presented a novel labeling representation-based uncertainty estimation for the semi-supervised segmentation. Our method produces an uncertainty map from a labeling representation network, which guides the reliable regions of prediction for the segmentation network, thereby achieving better segmentation results. Results demonstrate that the proposed method achieves the best performance compared to state-of-the-art baselines on left atrium segmentation from 3D MR volumes in two different settings. The ablation studies demonstrate the effectiveness and robustness of our uncertainty estimation compared to the entropy-based method. Our proposed uncertainty estimation from the labeling representation approach can be adapted to a broader range of applications where it is crucial to obtain a reliable prediction.

Acknowledgments. This research work was partly funded by the Canada Research Chair on Shape Analysis in Medical Imaging, the Natural Sciences and Engineering Research Council of Canada (NSERC), and the Fonds de Recherche du Quebec (FQRNT).

References

1. Bai, W., et al.: Semi-supervised learning for network-based cardiac MR image segmentation. In: Descoteaux, M., Maier-Hein, L., Franz, A., Jannin, P., Collins, D.L., Duchesne, S. (eds.) MICCAI 2017. LNCS, vol. 10434, pp. 253–260. Springer, Cham (2017). https://doi.org/10.1007/978-3-319-66185-8_29

2. Bortsova, G., Dubost, F., Hogeweg, L., Katramados, I., de Bruijne, M.: Semi-supervised medical image segmentation via learning consistency under transformations. In: Shen, D., et al. (eds.) MICCAI 2019. LNCS, vol. 11769, pp. 810–818. Springer, Cham (2019). https://doi.org/10.1007/978-3-030-32226-7_90

3. Chaitanya, K., Karani, N., Baumgartner, C.F., Becker, A., Donati, O., Konukoglu, E.: Semi-supervised and task-driven data augmentation. In: Chung, A.C.S., Gee, J.C., Yushkevich, P.A., Bao, S. (eds.) IPMI 2019. LNCS, vol. 11492, pp. 29–41. Springer, Cham (2019). https://doi.org/10.1007/978-3-030-20351-1_3

4. Cheplygina, V., de Bruijne, M., Pluim, J.P.: Not-so-supervised: a survey of semi-supervised, multi-instance, and transfer learning in medical image analysis. Media **54**, 280–296 (2019)

5. Çiçek, Ö., Abdulkadir, A., Lienkamp, S.S., Brox, T., Ronneberger, O.: 3D U-Net: learning dense volumetric segmentation from sparse annotation. In: Ourselin, S., Joskowicz, L., Sabuncu, M.R., Unal, G., Wells, W. (eds.) MICCAI 2016. LNCS, vol. 9901, pp. 424–432. Springer, Cham (2016). https://doi.org/10.1007/978-3-319-46723-8_49

6. Cui, W., et al.: Semi-supervised brain lesion segmentation with an adapted mean teacher model. In: Chung, A.C.S., Gee, J.C., Yushkevich, P.A., Bao, S. (eds.) IPMI 2019. LNCS, vol. 11492, pp. 554–565. Springer, Cham (2019). https://doi.org/10.1007/978-3-030-20351-1_43

7. Gal, Y., Ghahramani, Z.: Dropout as a Bayesian approximation: representing model uncertainty in deep learning. In: ICML, pp. 1050–1059. PMLR (2016)

8. He, Y., et al.: Dense biased networks with deep priori anatomy and hard region adaptation: semi-supervised learning for fine renal artery segmentation. Media **63**, 101722 (2020)

9. Laine, S., Aila, T.: Temporal ensembling for semi-supervised learning. arXiv preprint arXiv:1610.02242 (2016)

10. Larrazabal, A.J., Martínez, C., Glocker, B., Ferrante, E.: Post-DAE: anatomically plausible segmentation via post-processing with denoising autoencoders. IEEE TMI **39**(12), 3813–3820 (2020)

11. Li, S., Zhang, C., He, X.: Shape-aware semi-supervised 3D semantic segmentation for medical images. In: Martel, A.L., et al. (eds.) MICCAI 2020. LNCS, vol. 12261, pp. 552–561. Springer, Cham (2020). https://doi.org/10.1007/978-3-030-59710-8_54

12. Li, X., Yu, L., Chen, H., Fu, C.W., Xing, L., Heng, P.A.: Transformation-consistent self-ensembling model for semisupervised medical image segmentation. IEEE Trans. Neural Netw. Learn. Syst. **32**(2), 523–534 (2020)

13. Loshchilov, I., Hutter, F.: SGDR: stochastic gradient descent with warm restarts. arXiv preprint arXiv:1608.03983 (2016)

14. Luo, X., Chen, J., Song, T., Wang, G.: Semi-supervised medical image segmentation through dual-task consistency. In: AAAI, vol. 35, pp. 8801–8809 (2021)
15. Luo, X., et al.: Efficient semi-supervised gross target volume of nasopharyngeal carcinoma segmentation via uncertainty rectified pyramid consistency. In: de Bruijne, M., et al. (eds.) MICCAI 2021. LNCS, vol. 12902, pp. 318–329. Springer, Cham (2021). https://doi.org/10.1007/978-3-030-87196-3_30
16. Milletari, F., Navab, N., Ahmadi, S.A.: V-Net: fully convolutional neural networks for volumetric medical image segmentation. In: 3DV, pp. 565–571. IEEE (2016)
17. Nie, D., Gao, Y., Wang, L., Shen, D.: ASDNet: attention based semi-supervised deep networks for medical image segmentation. In: Frangi, A.F., Schnabel, J.A., Davatzikos, C., Alberola-López, C., Fichtinger, G. (eds.) MICCAI 2018. LNCS, vol. 11073, pp. 370–378. Springer, Cham (2018). https://doi.org/10.1007/978-3-030-00937-3_43
18. Oktay, O., et al.: Anatomically constrained neural networks (ACNNs): application to cardiac image enhancement and segmentation. IEEE TMI 37(2), 384–395 (2017)
19. Peng, J., Estrada, G., Pedersoli, M., Desrosiers, C.: Deep co-training for semi-supervised image segmentation. Pattern Recogn. 107, 107269 (2020)
20. Salimans, T., Goodfellow, I., Zaremba, W., Cheung, V., Radford, A., Chen, X.: Improved techniques for training GANs. In: NeurIPS, vol. 29 (2016)
21. Sedai, S., et al.: Uncertainty guided semi-supervised segmentation of retinal layers in OCT images. In: Shen, D., et al. (eds.) MICCAI 2019. LNCS, vol. 11764, pp. 282–290. Springer, Cham (2019). https://doi.org/10.1007/978-3-030-32239-7_32
22. Tarvainen, A., Valpola, H.: Mean teachers are better role models: weight-averaged consistency targets improve semi-supervised deep learning results. In: NeurIPS, vol. 30 (2017)
23. Vincent, P., Larochelle, H., Lajoie, I., Bengio, Y., Manzagol, P.A., Bottou, L.: Stacked denoising autoencoders: learning useful representations in a deep network with a local denoising criterion. JMLR 11(12), 3371–3408 (2010)
24. Wang, K., et al.: Tripled-uncertainty guided mean teacher model for semi-supervised medical image segmentation. In: de Bruijne, M., et al. (eds.) MICCAI 2021. LNCS, vol. 12902, pp. 450–460. Springer, Cham (2021). https://doi.org/10.1007/978-3-030-87196-3_42
25. Wang, P., Peng, J., Pedersoli, M., Zhou, Y., Zhang, C., Desrosiers, C.: Self-paced and self-consistent co-training for semi-supervised image segmentation. Media 73, 102146 (2021)
26. Wang, Y., et al.: Double-uncertainty weighted method for semi-supervised learning. In: Martel, A.L., et al. (eds.) MICCAI 2020. LNCS, vol. 12261, pp. 542–551. Springer, Cham (2020). https://doi.org/10.1007/978-3-030-59710-8_53
27. Xia, Y., et al.: 3D semi-supervised learning with uncertainty-aware multi-view co-training. In: IEEE/CVF WCCV, pp. 3646–3655 (2020)
28. Xiong, Z., et al.: A global benchmark of algorithms for segmenting the left atrium from late gadolinium-enhanced cardiac magnetic resonance imaging. Media 67, 101832 (2021)
29. Xue, Y., et al.: Shape-aware organ segmentation by predicting signed distance maps. In: AAAI, vol. 34, pp. 12565–12572 (2020)
30. Yu, L., Wang, S., Li, X., Fu, C.-W., Heng, P.-A.: Uncertainty-aware self-ensembling model for semi-supervised 3D left atrium segmentation. In: Shen, D., et al. (eds.) MICCAI 2019. LNCS, vol. 11765, pp. 605–613. Springer, Cham (2019). https://doi.org/10.1007/978-3-030-32245-8_67

31. Zheng, H., et al.: Semi-supervised segmentation of liver using adversarial learning with deep atlas prior. In: Shen, D., et al. (eds.) MICCAI 2019. LNCS, vol. 11769, pp. 148–156. Springer, Cham (2019). https://doi.org/10.1007/978-3-030-32226-7_17

32. Zheng, H., et al.: Cartilage segmentation in high-resolution 3D micro-CT images via uncertainty-guided self-training with very sparse annotation. In: Martel, A.L., et al. (eds.) MICCAI 2020. LNCS, vol. 12261, pp. 802–812. Springer, Cham (2020). https://doi.org/10.1007/978-3-030-59710-8_78

Analyzing Brain Structural Connectivity as Continuous Random Functions

William Consagra[1(✉)], Martin Cole[1], and Zhengwu Zhang[2]

[1] Department of Biostatistics and Computational Biology, University of Rochester, Rochester, NY 14642, USA
william_consagra@urmc.rochester.edu
[2] Department of Statistics and Operations Research, UNC Chapel Hill, Chapel Hill, NC 27599, USA

Abstract. This work considers a continuous framework to characterize the population-level variability of structural connectivity. Our framework assumes the observed white matter fiber tract endpoints are driven by a latent random function defined over a product manifold domain. To overcome the computational challenges of analyzing such complex latent functions, we develop an efficient algorithm to construct a data-driven reduced-rank function space to represent the latent continuous connectivity. Using real data from the Human Connectome Project, we show that our method outperforms state-of-the-art approaches applied to the traditional atlas-based structural connectivity matrices on connectivity analysis tasks of interest. We also demonstrate how our method can be used to identify localized regions and connectivity patterns on the cortical surface associated with significant group differences.

Keywords: Point process · Functional data · Continuous connectomics

1 Introduction

The structural connectivity (SC) describes connectivity patterns between regions of the brain generated by the white matter (WM) fiber tracking results from diffusion-weighted MRI (dMRI). Understanding the heterogeneity of SC across individuals and its relationship to various traits of interest is of fundamental importance for understanding the brain. The most common approach for analyzing SC data is to represent it as a symmetric adjacency matrix, i.e., a network, denoted A, referred to as the (structural) connectome matrix. To obtain A, the brain surface is discretized into V disjoint regions of interest (ROIs) using some predefined parcellation [5,6]. The element A_{ab} quantifies the extent of structural

---

Supplementary Information The online version contains supplementary material available at https://doi.org/10.1007/978-3-031-16452-1_27.

L. Wang et al. (Eds.): MICCAI 2022, LNCS 13438, pp. 276–285, 2022.
https://doi.org/10.1007/978-3-031-16452-1_27

connectivity between ROIs a and b. Joint analysis of a sample of SC from multiple subjects can be performed utilizing network analysis models. For example, in [1,7,25], the proposed techniques learn a shared latent space characterizing the variability of a sample of networks. Subsequent statistical analysis and inference to relate this variability to cognitive and psychiatric traits of interest can then be performed in the latent space.

The dependence on the pre-specification of an atlas in the discrete ROI-based framework of analyzing SC is problematic for at least two major reasons. First, analyses are known to be sensitive to the choice of atlas [24] and therefore studies can draw different conclusions for different parcellation schemes of the same data. Second, the ROIs can be large and thus introduce information loss, since fine-grained connectivity information on the sub-ROI level is aggregated in the construction of the adjacency matrix. Studies indicate that connectivity information at higher resolutions can capture more valuable information for many traits of interest [14].

A series of recent works [4,13,15] have addressed these problems by transitioning from the discrete, ROI-based representation of brain connectivity to a fully continuous model. These works assume the observed pattern of WM fiber tract endpoints is driven by an unobserved continuous function, referred to as the *continuous connectivity*. This function is defined on the product space of the cortical surface with itself and governs the strength of connectivity between any pair of points on the surface. Critically, the continuous model of connectivity does not depend on the pre-specification of an atlas and therefore avoids the previously outlined issues which plague traditional discrete network based approaches. Despite these advantages, the current approaches suffer from significant computational hurdles for multi-subject analysis. This is because the continuous connectivity is represented as an extremely high-dimensional matrix, obtained through discretization over a high-resolution grid on the cortical surface. For instance, the popular surface mesh from [22] results in matrices of dimension $\approx 64,000 \times 64,000$. Applying the existing joint network analysis approaches to a sample of matrices of this size is prohibitive.

In this work, we extend the continuous connectivity framework to explicitly model the population variability of the SC by considering a random intensity function which governs the distribution of the observed WM fiber tract endpoints. Utilizing techniques from functional data analysis (FDA), we develop a novel methodology and accompanying estimation algorithm which learns a data-adaptive reduced-rank function space for parsimonious and efficient data representation, allowing us to overcome the enormous computational challenges involved in analyzing a sample of super high-dimensional connectivity matrices. We apply the proposed method to a sample of Human Connectome Project (HCP) subjects and show that our method outperforms traditional atlas-based approaches on tasks related to identifying group differences in SC associated with cognitive and psychiatric traits.

2 Methodology

A Model for Continuous Connectivity: For a sample of $i = 1, ..., N$ subjects, let O_i be endpoints of the WM fiber tracts connecting cortical surfaces for subject i. Let $\mathbb{S}_1^2$ and $\mathbb{S}_2^2$ be two independent copies of the 2-sphere and let $\Omega = \mathbb{S}_1^2 \cup \mathbb{S}_1^2$. Since the the left and right cortical surfaces are diffeomorphic to a 2-sphere, O_i can be modeled as a point process on $\Omega \times \Omega$ [15]. Define the intensity function $U_i : \Omega \times \Omega \mapsto [0, \infty)$, such that U_i is symmetric and L^2, i.e. $U_i(\omega_1, \omega_2) = U_i(\omega_2, \omega_1)$ and $\int_\Omega \int_\Omega U_i^2 < \infty$. For any two distinct/non-overlapping and Borel measurable regions $E_1 \subset \Omega$ and $E_2 \subset \Omega$, denote $N(E_1, E_2)$ as the counting process of the number of WM fiber tracts ending in (E_1, E_2). Then U_i satisfies $\mathbb{E}[N(E_1, E_2)] = \int_{E_1} \int_{E_2} U_i(\omega_1, \omega_2) d\omega_1 d\omega_2 < \infty$. Said another way, U_i determines, up to first-order moment, the pattern of fiber tract endpoints on the cortical surface. For any pair of points $(\omega_1, \omega_2) \in \Omega \times \Omega$, subject-level estimates of $U_i(\omega_1, \omega_2)$ can be formed from O_i using the point-wise product heat kernel density estimator (KDE) proposed in [15].

In order to properly account for the population variability of the SC, we model the sample of N point patterns using the theory of doubly stochastic point-processes. In this framework, we assume that intensity function U_i governing O_i is itself a realization of an underlying *random function*, which we denote as U. We analyze the variability in the SC using the sample of continuous connectivity $\{U_1, ..., U_N\}$.

Reduced-Rank Embedding of a Sample of Continuous Connectivity: Due to the infinite dimensionality of the continuous connectivity, we must construct an efficient representation before conducting meaningful statistical analysis. In this section, we propose a data-adaptive reduced-rank space for the joint embedding of a sample of continuous connectivity.

Since we are interested in characterizing the variability of the SC, without loss of generality, assume that U has been centered, i.e. $\mathbb{E}[U] = 0$. Define the symmetric separable orthogonal function set of rank K:

$$\mathcal{V}_K = \{\xi_k \otimes \xi_k : \xi_k \in L^2(\Omega), \langle \xi_k, \xi_j \rangle_{L^2(\Omega)} = \delta_{kj}, \text{ for } k = 1, 2, ..., K\},$$

where $\xi \otimes \xi(\omega_1, \omega_2) := \xi(\omega_1)\xi(\omega_2)$ and δ_{ik} is the Kronecker delta. The i'th continuous connectivity can be written as a linear combination of basis functions in $\mathcal{V}_K$ plus a residual: $U_i = \sum_{k=1}^{K} S_{ik} \xi_k \otimes \xi_k + R_{K,i}$, with $S_{ik} = \langle U_i, \xi_k \otimes \xi_k \rangle_{L^2(\Omega \times \Omega)}$ and symmetric residual $R_{K,i}$, which is orthogonal to $\text{span}(\mathcal{V}_K)$. As such, any U_i can be identified with a K-dimensional Euclidean vector $\boldsymbol{s}_i := [S_{i1}, ..., S_{iK}]^T$. The mapping $U_i \mapsto \boldsymbol{s}_i$ is an isometry between $(\text{span}(\mathcal{V}_K), \langle \cdot, \cdot \rangle_{L^2(\Omega \times \Omega)})$ and $(\mathbb{R}^K, \langle \cdot, \cdot \rangle_2)$, where $\langle \cdot, \cdot \rangle_2$ is the standard Euclidean metric. Therefore, we can properly embed the continuous connectivity into a K-dimensional Euclidean vector space and utilize a multitude of existing tools from multivariate statistics for analysis and inference.

To facilitate powerful embeddings, we construct a $\mathcal{V}_K$ that is adapted to the distribution of U. This is accomplished utilizing a greedy learning procedure. In particular, given a sample of N realizations of $U_i \sim U$, we iteratively construct $\mathcal{V}_K$ by repeating the following steps

$$\xi_k = \sup_{\xi \in \mathbb{S}^\infty(\Omega)} N^{-1} \sum_{i=1}^N | \langle R_{k-1,i}, \xi \otimes \xi \rangle_{L^2(\Omega \times \Omega)} |^2 \tag{1}$$

$$R_{k,i} = U_i - P_{\mathcal{V}_k}(U_i), \quad \mathcal{V}_k = \mathcal{V}_{k-1} \cup \{\xi \otimes \xi\}$$

for $k = 1, ..., K$, where $P_{\mathcal{V}_k}$ is the L^2 orthogonal projection operator onto span $(\mathcal{V}_k)$, $\mathbb{S}^\infty(\Omega) := \{\xi \in L^2(\Omega) : \|\xi\|_{L^2(\Omega)} = 1\}$ and the process is initialized with $R_{0,i} = U_i$ and $\mathcal{V}_0 = \emptyset$. In order to understand the theoretical performance of our representation space constructed using the updates in (1), Theorem 1 establishes an asymptotic universal approximation property as a function of the rank.

Theorem 1. *Let $U_1, ..., U_N$ be i.i.d. with $U_i \sim U$. Under some minor assumptions on the distribution of U, the asymptotic mean residual L^2 error resulting from the greedy algorithm defined in (1) is bounded as*

$$\lim_{N \to \infty} N^{-1} \sum_{i=1}^N \|R_{K,i}\|^2_{L^2(\Omega \times \Omega)} \leq \frac{B \left(\sum_{k=1}^\infty \sqrt{\rho_k} \right)^2}{K+1}$$

where B is a finite positive constant related to the smoothness of U and ρ_k is the k'th eigenvalue of the covariance operator of U.

Our functional greedy learning procedure (1) facilitates efficient computation in multiple ways. It requires solving an optimization problem over $L^2(\Omega)$, opposed to the full space $L^2(\Omega \times \Omega)$. Optimization for functions directly in $L^2(\Omega \times \Omega)$ square the number of unknown parameters compared to $L^2(\Omega)$, a manifestation of the curse of dimensionality. Additionally, in practice, we are able to utilize the smoothness of elements in $L^2(\Omega)$ to further reduce the dimensionality using basis expansion over $\mathbb{S}^2$.

Deriving the Optimization Problem: The optimization problem in (1) is intractable since the search space $\mathbb{S}^\infty(\Omega)$ is infinite-dimensional. In practice, we address this by approximating the infinite dimensional parameter ξ_k using basis expansion. Let $\boldsymbol{\phi}_{M_d} = (\phi_1, ..., \phi_{M_d})^\intercal$ be the spherical splines basis of degree 1 defined over spherical Delaunay triangulation $\mathcal{T}_d$ [12] for $d = 1, 2$. We form the approximation: $\xi_k(\omega) = \boldsymbol{c}_{1,k}^\intercal \boldsymbol{\phi}_{M_1}(\omega) \mathbb{I}\{\omega \in \mathbb{S}_1^2\} + \boldsymbol{c}_{2,k}^\intercal \boldsymbol{\phi}_{M_2}(\omega) \mathbb{I}\{\omega \in \mathbb{S}_2^2\}$, where the $\boldsymbol{c}_{d,k} \in \mathbb{R}^{M_d}$ are the vectors of coefficients with respect to the basis $\boldsymbol{\phi}_{M_d}$. Denote the collected vector of coefficients $\boldsymbol{c}_k = (\boldsymbol{c}_{1,k}^\intercal, \boldsymbol{c}_{2,k}^\intercal)^\intercal$ and basis functions $\boldsymbol{\phi}_M = (\boldsymbol{\phi}_{M_1}^\intercal, \boldsymbol{\phi}_{M_2}^\intercal)^\intercal$, where $M = M_1 + M_2$.

For tractable computation of the $L^2(\Omega \times \Omega)$ inner product, we form a discrete approximation using a dense grid of n points in Ω, denoted as $\boldsymbol{X}$. Define $\boldsymbol{\Phi} \in \mathbb{R}^{n \times M}$ to be the matrix of evaluations of $\boldsymbol{\phi}_M$ over $\boldsymbol{X}$ and denote the matrix of $L^2(\Omega)$ inner products of $\boldsymbol{\phi}_M$ as $\boldsymbol{J}_\phi \in \mathbb{R}^{M \times M}$, with $\langle \phi_i, \phi_j \rangle_{L^2(\Omega)} = 0$

if splines ϕ_i and ϕ_j are not on the same copy of $\mathbb{S}^2$. The k'th discretized residual for the i'th subject is approximately $\mathbf{R}_{k,i} = \mathbf{Y}_i - \sum_{j=1}^{k-1} s_{ij}(\mathbf{\Phi}c_j)(\mathbf{\Phi}c_j)^\mathsf{T}$, where $\mathbf{Y}_i$ is the mean-centered KDE estimate of the continuous connectivity over $\mathbf{X}$ for the i'th subject, the c_j's are from the previous $k-1$ selections and $s_{ij} = n^{-2} \langle \mathbf{R}_{j-1,i}, (\mathbf{\Phi}c_j)(\mathbf{\Phi}c_j)^\mathsf{T} \rangle_F$. Introducing the auxiliary variable $\mathbf{s} = (s_1, ..., s_N)^\mathsf{T} \in \mathbb{R}^N$, we propose the following discretized formulation of the optimization problem in (1):

$$\hat{c}_k = \underset{c \in \mathbb{R}^M}{\mathrm{argmax}} \sum_{i=1}^N s_i \langle \mathbf{R}_{k-1,i}, \mathbf{\Phi}c \otimes \mathbf{\Phi}c \rangle_F - \alpha_1 c^\mathsf{T} \mathbf{Q}_\phi c$$

$$\mathrm{s.t.} \quad c^\mathsf{T} \mathbf{J}_\phi c = 1, c^\mathsf{T} \mathbf{J}_\phi c_j = 0 \text{ for } j = 1, 2, ..., k-1$$

$$\|c\|_0 \leq \alpha_2, \quad s_i = \langle \mathbf{R}_{k-1,i}, (\mathbf{\Phi}c) \otimes (\mathbf{\Phi}c) \rangle_F, \text{ for } i = 1, ..., N.$$

(2)

where $\mathbf{Q}_\phi$ is a matrix encoding the quadratic variation of the candidate solution c and is used to control the "roughness" of the basis functions via tuning parameter $\alpha_1 > 0$. For certain applications it may be of interest to promote the estimation of locally supported ξ_k, e.g., in order to localize the effect of the k'th basis function on the cortical surface. Owing to the local support of the spherical spline basis functions, this can be done by employing an l_0 constraint to encourage sparsity in the c_k's, with α_2 controlling the degree of localization. Efficient algorithms exist for evaluating spherical splines, computing their directional derivatives as well as performing integration [12]. As a result, the matrices $\mathbf{J}_\phi$ and $\mathbf{Q}_\phi$ can be constructed cheaply.

Algorithm: We apply an alternating optimization (AO) scheme to form an approximate solution to the problem (2), iteratively maximizing c given s and vice versa. Denote the singular value decomposition $\mathbf{\Phi} = \mathbf{U}\mathbf{D}\mathbf{V}^\mathsf{T}$, and let $\mathbf{G}_{k,i} := \mathbf{U}^\mathsf{T} \mathbf{R}_{k,i} \mathbf{U}$ and define the tensor $\mathcal{G}_k$ to be the mode-3 stacking of the $\mathbf{G}_{k,i}$. Under the AO scheme, the update for the block variable c_k at iteration $t+1$ is given by

$$c^{(t+1)} = \max \quad c^\mathsf{T} \left[\mathbf{V}\mathbf{D} (\mathbf{I} - \mathbf{P}_{k-1}) \left[\mathcal{G}_{k-1} \times_3 s^{(t)} - \alpha_1 \mathbf{D}^{-1} \mathbf{V}^\mathsf{T} \mathbf{Q}_\phi \mathbf{V}\mathbf{D}^{-1} \right] (\mathbf{I} - \mathbf{P}_{k-1}^\mathsf{T}) \mathbf{D}\mathbf{V}^\mathsf{T} \right] c$$

$$\mathrm{s.t.} \quad c^\mathsf{T} \mathbf{J}_\phi c = 1, \quad \|c\|_0 \leq \alpha_2,$$

(3)

where $\times_d$ denotes the d-mode tensor-matrix multiplication and

$$\mathbf{P}_{k-1} = \mathbf{D}\mathbf{V}^\mathsf{T} \mathbf{C}_{k-1} \left[\mathbf{C}_{k-1}^\mathsf{T} \mathbf{J}_\phi \mathbf{C}_{k-1} \right]^{-1} \mathbf{C}_{k-1}^\mathsf{T} \mathbf{J}_\phi \mathbf{V}\mathbf{D}^{-1} \quad \mathbf{C}_{k-1} := [c_1, ..., c_{k-1}],$$

(4)

For s, the update at iteration $t+1$ is given in closed form by

$$s^{(t+1)} = \mathcal{G}_{k-1} \times_1 (\mathbf{D}\mathbf{V}^\mathsf{T} c_k^{(t+1)}) \times_2 (\mathbf{D}\mathbf{V}^\mathsf{T} c_k^{(t+1)}).$$

(5)

We apply the fast truncated power iterations method from [23] to approximate the solution to the sparse eigenvector problem in (3). Notice that the tensor $\mathcal{G}_k$ is $M \times M \times N$ and thus the complexity of the AO-updates are independent of the number of grid points used in the discretization. Since the computational grid X can be made arbitrarily dense, typically $M \ll n$ which can amount to an enormous savings in computation when compared to an alternative approach of performing tensor decomposition directly on the super high-dimensional discretized continuous connectivity matrices Y_i. For example, the tensor decomposition method from [25] failed when applied directly to the high-resolution connectivity data described in Sect. 3 on a HPC cluster with 120GB of RAM.

3   Experiments and Conclusions

Dataset Description, Preprocessing, Modeling and Implementation:
In this work, we use brain imaging data and associated measurements related to various cognitive and psychiatric factors from a sample of 437 female subjects in the HCP young adult cohort, publicly available at https://db.humanconnectome. org. For each subject, we use both the dMRI and the structural T1-weighted images collected using a 3T Siemens Connectome scanner (Erlangen, Germany). The full imaging acquisition protocol as well as the minimal preprocessing pipeline applied to the dMRI data are given in [10]. fODFs were estimated from the preprocessed diffusion data using CSD [21] and then SET [20] was used to estimate the underlying WM fiber tracts and endpoints on the surface. The T1 images were registered to the dMRI using ANTs [2] and the cortical white surfaces were extracted using Freesurfer. To alleviate the misalignment issue resulting from the joint analysis of N cortical surfaces, we parameterized each using a spherical coordinate via the surface inflation techniques from [9] and then applied the warping function from freesurfer to bring the endpoints to a template space.

To estimate $\mathcal{V}_K$, we use a spherical spline basis with $M_1 = M_2 = 410$ over a spherical Delaunay triangulation. In accordance with [4], the KDE bandwidth was set to be 0.005 and a grid of $4,121$ points on Ω was used for discretization. We set $\alpha_1 = 10^{-8}$ and $\alpha_2 = 40$ to encourage locally supported basis functions. The rank was selected to be $K = 100$ using a threshold criteria on the proportion of variance explained, estimated efficiently by $\|\mathcal{G}_K\|_F^2 / \|\mathcal{G}\|_F^2$.

For comparison, we apply several state-of-the-art network embedding methods, namely Tensor-Network PCA (TN-PCA) [25], Multiple Random Dot-Product Graph model (MRDPG) [16] and Multiple Adjacency Spectral Embedding method (MASE) [1] to the sample of SC matrices obtained using the Destriex atlas [6]. TN-PCA can be applied directly to the streamline endpoint count data, while MRDPG and MASE require a binarization of the connectome matrices. Embedding spaces of $K = 100$ were constructed using the publicly available implementations for each method. Analysis was performed using R/4.0.2 and MATLAB/2020b on a Linux machine equipped with a 2.4 GHz Intel Xeon CPU E5-2695 and 120 GB of RAM.

Hypothesis Testing: We compare the power of the embeddings produced by our continuous connectivity framework, denoted as CC, to the network-embeddings produced by TN-PCA, MDRPG and MASE on a set of two group hypothesis tests. We use a set of 80 measurements of traits spanning the categories of cognition, emotion, and sensory. For each trait, two groups are created by selecting the top 100 and bottom 100 of the 437 HCP females, in terms of their measured trait score. Between-subject pairwise distance matrices were computed in the embedding space for each of the methods and p-values for the two group comparison were formed using the Maximum Mean Discrepancy (MMD) test [11]. The p-values were corrected for false discovery rate (FDR) control using [3].

The four panels in Fig. 1 show the results for each of the embedding methods. The y-axis gives the negative log transformed p-values and the colors indicate significant discoveries under a couple FDR control levels. With a threshold of FDR ≤ 0.05, the embeddings produced by our method are able to identify 22 significant discoveries, compared to 7 or less for the competitors. These results suggests potentially large gains in statistical power for detecting group differences when modeling the SC data at much higher resolutions than are commonly being used currently.

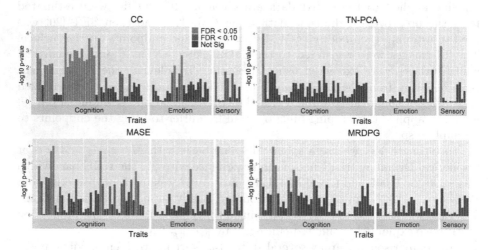

Fig. 1. Results from the two-group hypothesis tests for the collection of cognition, emotion and sensory traits. The y-axis gives the $-$log-transformed p-values.

Continuous Subnetwork Discovery: We now demonstrate how our method can be utilized for atlas-independent identification of brain regions and connectivity patterns that are related to traits of interest. We consider the cognitive trait *delay discounting*, which refers to the subjective decline in the value of a reward when its arrival is delayed in time and is measured for HCP subjects by the subjective value of \$200 at 6 months [8]. We define the steep and low discounting groups using thresholds on this subjective value of $\leq\$40$ and $\geq\$160$, respectively. Sub-selecting individuals from our sample who met these criteria resulted in a total sample size of 142: 64 in the steep discounting group and 78 in the low discounting group. We test for group differences in each embedding dimension using univariate permutation tests on the associated embedding coefficients. 10,000 permutations were used to compute the empirical p-values for each test. A Bonferroni-Holm correction was applied to the p-values to ensure family-wise error rate control ≤ 0.10.

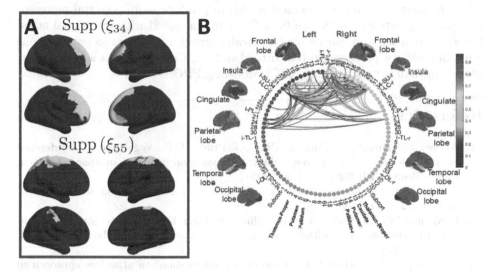

Fig. 2. A: Support sets (yellow) of the two basis functions found to be significantly associated with connectivity differences in the delay discounting groups. B: Top 50% of the edges in $\boldsymbol{A}^{CC}$. (Color figure online)

The k = 34 and k = 55 embedding dimensions were found to be significantly different between steep and low discounting groups. Figure 2 A shows the non-zero support sets: $\text{Supp}(\xi_k) := \{\omega \in \Omega : \xi_k(\omega) \neq 0\}$, of the selected basis functions (yellow) plotted on the cortical surface. To visualize the associated connectivity patterns, we coarsened the continuous support sets using integration over the Desikan atlas [5]. Specially, we define the (a, b)-th element in the coarsened adjacency matrix as

$$\boldsymbol{A}_{ab}^{CC} := |E_a|^{-1}|E_b|^{-1} \int_{E_a} \int_{E_b} \sum_{k \in \{34,55\}} \mathbb{I}\{\xi_k(\omega_1)\xi_k(\omega_2) \neq 0\} d\omega_1 d\omega_2$$

where $E_a, E_b \in \Omega$ are any two parcels from the Desikan atlas, $\mathbb{I}$ is the indicator function and $|E_a|$ denotes the surface measure. Figure 2 B provides a circular network plot showing the top 50% of the edges in $\boldsymbol{A}_{ab}^{CC}$. Together, these views indicate the affected brain regions and connectivity patterns are predominantly within and between areas in the left and right frontal lobes and the left parietal lobe. Previous studies have shown these areas to be strongly related to delay discounting [17–19].

Conclusion: This work introduces a novel modeling framework for structural connectivity using latent random functions defined on the product space of the cortical surface. To facilitate tractable representation and analysis, we formulate a data-adaptive reduced-rank function space that avoids the curse of dimensionality while also retaining a reasonable convergence rate. To form a basis for this space, we derive a penalized optimization problem and propose a novel computationally efficient algorithm for estimation. Experiments on real data from the HCP demonstrate that our method is able to produce more powerful representations for group-wise inference from SC data compared with traditional atlas-based approaches and can be used to localize group differences to brain regions and connectivity patterns on the cortical surface. Code and data is available at https://github.com/sbci-brain/SBCI_Modeling_FPCA.

References

1. Arroyo, J., Athreya, A., Cape, J., Chen, G., Priebe, C.E., Vogelstein, J.T.: Inference for multiple heterogeneous networks with a common invariant subspace. J. Mach. Learn. Res. JMLR **22**(141), 1–49 (2021)
2. Avants, B.B., Tustison, N., Song, G.: Advanced normalization tools (ANTs). Insight J **2**(365), 1–35 (2009)
3. Benjamini, Y., Hochberg, Y.: Controlling the false discovery rate: a practical and powerful approach to multiple testing. J. R. Stat. Soc. Ser. B (Methodol.) **57**(1), 289–300 (1995)
4. Cole, M., et al.: Surface-based connectivity integration: an atlas-free approach to jointly study functional and structural connectivity. Hum. Brain Mapp. **42**(11), 3481–3499 (2021)
5. Desikan, R.S., et al.: An automated labeling system for subdividing the human cerebral cortex on MRI scans into gyral based regions of interest. Neuroimage **31**(3), 968–980 (2006)
6. Destrieux, C., Fischl, B., Dale, A., Halgren, E.: Automatic parcellation of human cortical gyri and sulci using standard anatomical nomenclature. Neuroimage **53**(1), 1–15 (2010)
7. Durante, D., Dunson, D.B., Vogelstein, J.T.: Nonparametric Bayes modeling of populations of networks. J. Am. Stat. Assoc. **112**(520), 1516–1530 (2017)
8. Estle, S.J., Green, L., Myerson, J., Holt, D.D.: Differential effects of amount on temporal and probability discounting of gains and losses. Mem. Cognit. **34**(4), 914–928 (2006). https://doi.org/10.3758/BF03193437
9. Fischl, B., Sereno, M.I., Dale, A.M.: Cortical surface-based analysis: II: inflation, flattening, and a surface-based coordinate system. Neuroimage **9**(2), 195–207 (1999)
10. Glasser, M.F., et al.: The minimal preprocessing pipelines for the Human Connectome Project. Neuroimage **80**, 105–124 (2013)
11. Gretton, A., Borgwardt, K.M., Rasch, M.J., Schölkopf, B., Smola, A.: A kernel two-sample test. J. Mach. Learn. Res. **13**(25), 723–773 (2012)
12. Lai, M.J., Schumaker, L.L.: Spline Functions on Triangulations. Encyclopedia of Mathematics and its Applications. Cambridge University Press (2007)
13. Mansour, S., Seguin, C., Smith, R.E., Zalesky, A.: Connectome spatial smoothing (CSS): concepts, methods, and evaluation. Neuroimage **250**, 118930 (2022)

14. Mansour, S., Tian, Y., Yeo, B.T., Cropley, V., Zalesky, A.: High-resolution connectomic fingerprints: mapping neural identity and behavior. Neuroimage **229**, 117695 (2021)
15. Moyer, D., Gutman, B.A., Faskowitz, J., Jahanshad, N., Thompson, P.M.: Continuous representations of brain connectivity using spatial point processes. Med. Image Anal. **41**, 32–39 (2017). Special Issue on the 2016 Conference on Medical Image Computing and Computer Assisted Intervention (Analog to MICCAI 2015)
16. Nielsen, A.M., Witten, D.: The multiple random dot product graph model. arXiv preprint arXiv:1811.12172 (2018)
17. Olson, E.A., Collins, P.F., Hooper, C.J., Muetzel, R., Lim, K.O., Luciana, M.: White matter integrity predicts delay discounting behavior in 9- to 23-year-olds: a diffusion tensor imaging study. J. Cogn. Neurosci. **21**(7), 1406–1421 (2009)
18. Owens, M.M., Gray, J.C., Amlung, M.T., Oshri, A., Sweet, L.H., MacKillop, J.: Neuroanatomical foundations of delayed reward discounting decision making. Neuroimage **161**, 261–270 (2017)
19. Sebastian, A., Jung, P., Krause-Utz, A., Lieb, K., Schmahl, C., Tüscher, O.: Frontal dysfunctions of impulse control - a systematic review in borderline personality disorder and attention-deficit/hyperactivity disorder. Front. Hum. Neurosci. **8**, 698 (2014)
20. St-Onge, E., Daducci, A., Girard, G., Descoteaux, M.: Surface-enhanced tractography (SET). Neuroimage **169**, 524–539 (2018)
21. Tournier, J.D., Calamante, F., Connelly, A.: Robust determination of the fibre orientation distribution in diffusion MRI: non-negativity constrained super-resolved spherical deconvolution. Neuroimage **35**(4), 1459–1472 (2007)
22. Van Essen, D.C., Glasser, M.F., Dierker, D.L., Harwell, J., Coalson, T.: Parcellations and hemispheric asymmetries of human cerebral cortex analyzed on surface-based atlases. Cereb. Cortex **22**(10), 2241–2262 (2012)
23. Yuan, X.T., Zhang, T.: Truncated power method for sparse eigenvalue problems. J. Mach. Learn. Res. **14**, 899–925 (2011)
24. Zalesky, A., et al.: Whole-brain anatomical networks: does the choice of nodes matter? Neuroimage **50**(3), 970–983 (2010)
25. Zhang, Z., Allen, G.I., Zhu, H., Dunson, D.: Tensor network factorizations: relationships between brain structural connectomes and traits. Neuroimage **197**, 330–343 (2019)

Learning with Context Encoding
for Single-Stage Cranial Bone Labeling
and Landmark Localization

Jiawei Liu[1]([✉]), Fuyong Xing[1], Abbas Shaikh[1], Marius George Linguraru[2,3],
and Antonio R. Porras[1,4,5]

[1] Department of Biostatistics and Informatics, Colorado School of Public Health,
University of Colorado Anschutz Medical Campus, Aurora, CO 80045, USA
`jiawei.liu@cuanschutz.edu`
[2] Sheikh Zayed Institute for Pediatric Surgical Innovation, Children's National Hospital,
Washington DC 20010, USA
[3] Departments of Radiology and Pediatrics, George Washington University School of Medicine
and Health Sciences, Washington DC 20052, USA
[4] Department of Pediatrics, School of Medicine, University of Colorado Anschutz Medical
Campus, Aurora, CO 80045, USA
[5] Departments of Pediatric Plastic and Reconstructive Surgery and Neurosurgery,
Children's Hospital Colorado, Aurora, CO 80045, USA

Abstract. Automatic anatomical segmentation and landmark localization in medical images are important tasks during craniofacial analysis. While deep neural networks have been recently applied to segment cranial bones and identify cranial landmarks from computed tomography (CT) or magnetic resonance (MR) images, existing methods often provide suboptimal and sometimes unrealistic results because they do not incorporate contextual image information. Additionally, most state-of-the-art deep learning methods for cranial bone segmentation and landmark detection rely on multi-stage data processing pipelines, which are inefficient and prone to errors. In this paper, we propose a novel context encoding-constrained neural network for single-stage cranial bone labeling and landmark localization. Specifically, we design and incorporate a novel context encoding module into a U-Net-like architecture. We explicitly enforce the network to capture context-related features for representation learning so pixel-wise predictions are not isolated from the image context. In addition, we introduce a new auxiliary task to model the relative spatial configuration of different anatomical landmarks, which serves as an additional regularization that further refines network predictions. The proposed method is end-to-end trainable for single-stage cranial bone labeling and landmark localization. The method was evaluated on a highly diverse pediatric 3D CT image dataset with 274 subjects. Our experiments demonstrate superior performance of our method compared to state-of-the-art approaches.

Keywords: Cranial segmentation · Landmark localization · Context encoding

Supplementary Information The online version contains supplementary material available at
https://doi.org/10.1007/978-3-031-16452-1_28.

1 Introduction

The assessment of cranial pathology in pediatric patients usually involves the acquisition of computed tomography (CT) images, since other imaging modalities do not provide an accurate visualization of the cranial bones. In these patients, image evaluation is often centered around the calvaria, which is the part of the skull that encloses the brain. The reason is that any abnormality in the development of the calvaria, which is induced by brain growth, can provide insight into an underlying brain anomaly or can cause a secondary brain pathology.

Most methods that quantitatively analyze cranial anomalies rely on the accurate segmentation of the calvaria from the rest of the skull and the identification of the different cranial bones forming it [1–5]. Because manual annotations are tedious, the large cranial suture variability among children and the limited image resolution, bone labeling is a challenging task and different automatic segmentation methods have been presented in the literature. Traditional methods were based on the automatic identification of a series of landmarks at the cranial base using image registration to a manually annotated template [1, 2, 5, 6]. Similarly, early methods for calvarial bone labeling were also driven or initialized by manually segmented templates given the challenges to identify the narrow cranial sutures that separate the bone plates [2, 7]. However, template-driven methods are dependent on variable image registration accuracy and highly affected by the anatomical variability between subjects, so manual adjustments are often needed.

Recently, convolutional neural networks (CNN) such as fully convolutional networks (FCN) [8–11] and U-net [12, 13] have been used to automatically segment cranial bones and/or identify anatomical landmarks. Taking advantage of the anatomical relationships between bone structures and landmark locations, Liu et al. [14] proposed a two-stage coarse-to-fine method for bone segmentation and landmark identification. However, their approach did not account for any contextual information, which has been proven to improve results [15–17]. Attempting to incorporate image context, Zhang et al. [18] proposed two cascaded U-Nets to perform joint bone segmentation and landmark digitization in CT images. Torosdagli et al. [19] employed a DenseNet-backbone FCN for mandible segmentation, and then a modified U-Net and a long short-term memory (LSTM) network for landmark detection. However, these methods [18, 19] required multi-stage training, which is inefficient and exhibits high variability. Although Lian et al. [20] proposed an end-to-end dynamic transformer network addressing the potential heterogeneity caused by different training steps, their model lacked specific contextual information to guide the training of attention networks.

In this paper, we propose a novel context encoding-constrained neural network for single-stage cranial bone segmentation and landmark detection. We designed a new context encoding module into a U-Net-like architecture for feature learning that considers the global image context. We used landmark-based displacement vector maps to regularize training and learn features that consider contextual information. Furthermore, we introduced an auxiliary regression task that models the relative spatial configuration of the anatomical landmarks to promote realistic and refined landmark configurations. The entire network can be trained end-to-end in one single stage.

2   Methods

Figure 1 presents the overall pipeline of the proposed method. We aim to automatically localize four anatomical landmarks at the cranial base [2] and segment the five major bone plates in the calvaria from CT images. The four landmarks are located at the glabella (G), the clinoid processes of the dorsum sellae (D1 and D2) and the opisthion (Op) (see Fig. 2(b)). The five bone plates correspond to the left and right frontal (LF and RF), left and right parietal (LP and RP) and occipital bones (O) (see Fig. 2(c)).

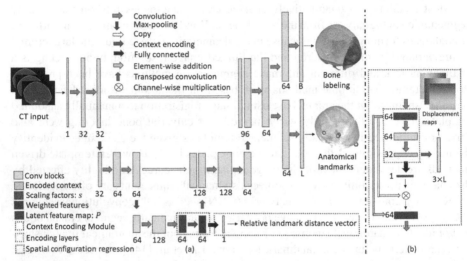

Fig. 1. (a) Proposed network architecture. The red dashed area represents the context encoding module. Regularization with relative landmark distance vector regression (green dashed area) is only used during training. (b) Architecture of the context encoding module. Context features are guided by landmark displacement vector maps, which are only used during training. (Color figure online)

2.1   Joint Cranial Bone Segmentation and Landmark Detection

Cranial bone segmentation and landmark detection are highly related, since the landmarks are located at specific locations of the cranial bones. Benefitting from these relationships, we propose to perform these two tasks into a single deep network. Since heatmap regression has achieved great performance in landmark detection tasks [21], we propose representing each landmark using heatmaps generated from Gaussian kernels centered at the landmark locations, with normalized probabilistic output range between 0 and 100.

All CT images were masked to exclude the background similar to the method proposed in [22], and the intensities were normalized to the range between 0 and 1. Let X, Y and Z represent 3D training CT images, ground-truth landmark heatmaps and segmentation labels, respectively. Our goal is to learn a non-linear mapping $M : X \rightarrow Y, Z$ that can automatically segment cranial bones and identify landmarks given a CT image. We propose to learn the mapping M using a novel deep network based on a U-Net-like architecture [18] that jointly conducts multi-bone labeling and landmark localization, as presented in Fig. 1.

We denote X_i, $i \in [1, N]$ the 3D CT image of subject i, $Y_{i,v}^l$, $v \in [1, V]$, $l \in [1, L]$ the vth voxel value of the heatmaps associated with the lth landmark, and $Z_{i,v}^b$, $b \in [1, B]$ the vth voxel value of the binary segmentation of the bth bone label. Then, we formulate bone segmentation as a multi-class pixel-wise classification problem whose training error can be optimized based on a weighted cross entropy loss expressed as

$$\mathcal{L}_{seg} = -\frac{1}{N_s BV} \sum_i^{N_s} \sum_b^B \sum_v^V \lambda_b 1(Z_{i,v}^b = 1) \log(P(Z_{i,v}^b = 1 | X_i, M)) \qquad (1)$$

where N_s is the number of images, $1(\cdot)$ represents the indicator function, and λ_b is a weight of the relative contribution from different labeled regions to the loss function compensating for different bone volumes.

We approached the landmark detection problem using a mean squared error (MSE) loss formulation based on the regressed heatmaps as

$$\mathcal{L}_{heat} = \frac{1}{N_s LV} \sum_i^{N_s} \sum_l^L \sum_v^V ||Y_{i,v}^l - \widehat{Y}_{i,v}^l||_2^2 \qquad (2)$$

where $\widehat{Y}_{i,v}^l$ is the predicted value from image X_i using the learned mapping M.

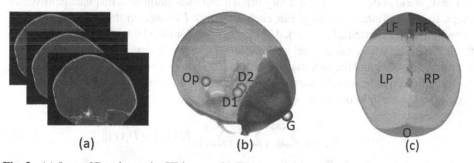

Fig. 2. (a) Input 3D volumetric CT image. (b) Four cranial base landmarks annotated as gray spheres on an example cranial surface mesh: glabella (G), left and right clinoid processes of the dorsum sellae (D1 and D2), and opisthion (Op). (c) Superior view of an example cranial surface mesh, color-coded with cranial bone labels.

2.2 Context Encoding

Because contextual information in the input images can significantly improve segmentation and landmark detection accuracies [15, 18], we introduce a novel context encoding module into our network (see Fig. 1(b)) to incorporate global context during feature representation learning. Our context encoding module is based on [15] but it presents several substantial differences introduced for our specific application: (1) we extended it from 2D to 3D to model the spatial relationships between cranial landmarks and bones; (2) we used displacement vector maps to introduce landmark context learning to improve representation learning; and (3) we propose an attention mechanism that uses previous context features to upweight relevant information in the latent space to improve learning, instead of using a simple classification-based attention framework [15]. Our context encoding module upweights global features that are indicative of the anatomical location and orientation of the cranial base encoded as landmark displacement maps. This module is differentiable and can be optimized in one single stage with our bone labeling and landmark detection network, unlike previous works [14, 18, 19] using multi-stage model training.

The context encoding layers operate on the latent feature maps P with shape $C \times H \times W \times E$ where C is the number of channels, H, W, E are the height, width and depth of the feature maps, producing the encoded context (see Fig. 1(b)). This encoded context learned a set of C scaling factors s that upweight the channel-specific features that are most relevant to our task (see Fig. 1(b)). These scaling factors were activated using a sigmoid function and used as a channel-wise attention mechanism. To avoid suppressing features via zero-weighting and to facilitate backpropagation, the residuals from the original latent space were aggregated together with the scaled features [15], as shown in Fig. 1(b). Hence, the output features from this attention module can be expressed as $P + s \otimes P$, where $\otimes$ is channel-wise multiplication.

To promote learning channel-wise scaling factors s that upweight relevant features to our task, we also designed an auxiliary branch that uses landmarks displacement vector maps to guide context learning. For each landmark l located in the training image of subject i, we calculated a landmark displacement vector map D_i^l with the same size than the input image where each voxel v containing a vector that represents the displacement between the voxel and the landmark coordinates. Then, we propose to promote learning features that encode specific landmark location information by incorporating an MSE regularization term to our training loss with the form

$$\mathcal{L}_{coe} = \frac{1}{3N_s LV} \sum_{i=1}^{N_s} \sum_{l=1}^{L} \sum_{v=1}^{V} \|D_i^l(v) - \widehat{D}_i^l(v)\|_2^2 \tag{3}$$

where $\widehat{D}_i^l$ is the predicted value of D_i^l. Note that the landmarks displacement vector maps are only used during training.

2.3 Regression of Spatial Landmark Configuration

Since the landmark displacement vector maps D_i^l were generated based on the independent coordinates of individual landmarks, they did not consider their spatial relationships. Hence, we propose to further regularize our training to account for these relationships. For every landmark l in the image X_i of subject i, we calculated its displacement vector $a_i^{l,k} \in \mathbb{R}^3$ to every other landmark k in the same subject, where $k \neq l$. These displacement vectors provide an explicit encoding of their spatial configuration in each training subject. We propose to incorporate this spatial configuration information as a regularization term in our training loss with the form:

$$\mathcal{L}_{scr} = \frac{1}{N_s L(L-1)} \sum_i^N \sum_l^L \sum_k^L 1(l \neq k) ||a_i^{l,k} - \hat{a}_i^{l,k}||_2^2 \qquad (4)$$

where $\hat{a}_i^{l,k}$ represents the predicted values for $a_i^{l,k}$. The complete objective for the proposed model was constructed as

$$\mathcal{L}_{tot} = \lambda_{seg}\mathcal{L}_{seg} + \lambda_{heat}\mathcal{L}_{heat} + \lambda_{coe}\mathcal{L}_{coe} + \lambda_{scr}\mathcal{L}_{scr} \qquad (5)$$

where λ_{seg}, λ_{heat}, λ_{coe} and λ_{scr} are the constant weights for different tasks.

3 Experiments and Results

3.1 Data Description

Retrospective incidental CT images of 274 pediatric subjects (147 male, 127 female, age 0.85 ± 0.57 years, range 0–2 years) were collected with IRB approval at University of Colorado Anschutz Medical Campus (protocol #20-1563) and Children's National Hospital (protocol #3792). The images have an average in-plane resolution of 0.38 ± 0.05 mm, and slice thickness of 1.14 ± 0.62 mm. The anatomical landmarks and bone labels shown in Fig. 2 were manually annotated at each CT image by an expert.

3.2 Implementation Details

Cranial segmentation and landmarks identification is especially challenging during the first two years of age (the age of the patients in our dataset), since most cranial anatomical changes occur during that time and there is a large variability in shape and volume among subjects [23]. Image sampling to a uniform spatial resolution in millimeters would create a large image variability that would translate into additional challenges during training. Therefore, we resampled all images to a uniform size of $96 \times 96 \times 96$ voxels. Heatmaps were generated using a Gaussian filter with a standard deviation of 5 voxels. The dataset was randomly split into training, validation, and test sets with a ratio of 80:10:10. The contracting and expanding path of U-Net was built based on [18] but with $5 \times 5 \times 5$ convolutions similar to [19] for improved accuracies. In the training phase, the training data was split into batches of size two and the stochastic gradient descent

(SGD) algorithm was used to optimize the model coefficients with a learning rate of 0.001 and a momentum of 0.9. The weighting parameters λ_{seg}, λ_{heat}, λ_{coe} and λ_{scr} were empirically selected at 3, 1, 3, and 3, respectively, and λ_b was set to 30 (the ratio between background and bone volumes). The method was implemented using PyTorch 1.10.0 in Python 3.8.5, and the expriments were run on a Intel Xeon CPU with 12 cores, 32 GB RAM and a NVIDIA Titan V GPU with 12 GB. The model was trained for a maximum of 200 epochs and stopped if the validation loss did not improve for successive 20 epochs. It occupied 1.85 GB in memory during evaluation and the average evaluation time was 3.65 s/image. The model is available at https://github.com/cuMIP/ctImage.

3.3 Performance Evaluation

Landmark detection was evaluated using the Euclidean distance between the ground truth and the predicted coordinates measured in voxel units. We obtained an average landmark detection error of 1.15 ± 0.61 voxels (1.43 ± 0.69, 1.02 ± 0.56, 1.05 ± 0.53, and 1.09 ± 0.65 voxels for the G, D1, D2 and Op, respectively). We evaluated bone segmentation using three different metrics: Dice coefficient (DSC), sensitivity (SEN), and specificity (SPE). Our model provided an average DSC of $81.96 \pm 2.71\%$ for the five bone plates and background, with average SEN of $97.02 \pm 1.07\%$ and SPE of $99.67 \pm 0.10\%$.

Table 1. Landmark detection using different methods (prediction errors in voxels).

Methods	Glabella	D1	D2	Opisthion	Average
CG-FCN [18]	1.53 ± 0.89	1.24 ± 0.66	1.24 ± 0.51	1.54 ± 0.94	1.38 ± 0.77
Baseline	1.49 ± 0.73	1.06 ± 0.55	1.04 ± 0.54	1.29 ± 0.70	1.22 ± 0.64
COE-UNet	1.43 ± 0.73	1.09 ± 0.61	$\mathbf{1.00 \pm 0.64}$	1.18 ± 0.72	1.18 ± 0.68
SCR-UNet	$\mathbf{1.41 \pm 0.70}$	1.11 ± 0.60	1.02 ± 0.57	1.21 ± 0.70	1.19 ± 0.65
Proposed	1.43 ± 0.69	$\mathbf{1.02 \pm 0.56}$	1.05 ± 0.53	$\mathbf{1.09 \pm 0.65}$	$\mathbf{1.15 \pm 0.61}$

We compared the proposed method with the state-of-the-art approach context-guided FCN (CG-FCN) [18], and we conducted ablation studies to evaluate the improvements from each novel component in our method. Specifically, we evaluated the performance of (1) our base U-net architecture without context encoding and spatial configuration regression (Baseline in Tables 1 and 2); (2) our base U-net architecture with only the context encoding module (COE-UNet); and (3) our base U-net architecture with only spatial configuration regression module (SCR-UNet). Table 1 presents the landmark identification error with the different architectures evaluated, and Table 2 presents the bone segmentation results. Please, see supplementary figures for qualitative comparisons.

Table 2. Bone segmentation using different methods. DSC, SEN and SPE represent Dice coefficient, sensitivity and specificity, respectively. BS represents binary segmentation of the skull. ** Both bone and background segmentation were considered to calculate the average values.

		LF	RF	LP	RP	O	BS	Average**
CG-FCN [18]	DSC	74.12 ± 4.52	72.17 ± 4.66	77.34 ± 4.82	75.57 ± 4.38	75.40 ± 4.42	82.03 ± 3.37	77.35 ± 3.40
	SEN	81.13 ± 6.32	88.74 ± 5.27	95.46 ± 2.50	94.82 ± 3.09	92.84 ± 3.09	92.04 ± 2.74	91.67 ± 2.17
	SPE	**99.85 ± 0.03**	**99.77 ± 0.04**	99.68 ± 0.05	99.71 ± 0.05	**99.76 ± 0.05**	**99.73 ± 0.05**	**99.70 ± 0.04**
Baseline	DSC	71.27 ± 4.10	73.52 ± 4.66	75.61 ± 4.56	79.64 ± 4.28	73.56 ± 4.72	82.96 ± 3.26	78.09 ± 2.99
	SEN	95.91 ± 2.29	96.96 ± 1.78	**98.42 ± 0.95**	97.33 ± 2.25	**97.09 ± 1.94**	**98.21 ± 0.79**	**97.38 ± 0.90**
	SPE	99.69 ± 0.07	99.73 ± 0.05	99.70 ± 0.07	99.73 ± 0.06	99.70 ± 0.05	99.72 ± 0.08	99.69 ± 0.09
COE-UNet	DSC	73.18 ± 4.04	71.52 ± 4.41	78.08 ± 4.53	**82.38 ± 3.68**	75.98 ± 4.28	84.77 ± 3.03	79.58 ± 3.06
	SEN	**96.62 ± 2.00**	**97.28 ± 1.86**	98.32 ± 1.18	96.18 ± 3.28	96.90 ± 2.09	97.96 ± 0.94	97.31 ± 1.11
	SPE	99.64 ± 0.07	99.69 ± 0.07	99.66 ± 0.07	**99.76 ± 0.05**	99.73 ± 0.05	99.77 ± 0.08	99.66 ± 0.10
SCR-UNet	DSC	70.83 ± 4.08	72.33 ± 4.21	79.44 ± 4.01	81.70 ± 3.77	72.85 ± 4.11	84.32 ± 3.47	79.06 ± 2.94
	SEN	95.76 ± 2.26	95.70 ± 1.99	98.34 ± 1.09	97.68 ± 2.08	96.32 ± 2.40	97.53 ± 0.80	97.06 ± 0.91
	SPE	99.69 ± 0.06	99.71 ± 0.05	99.69 ± 0.06	99.74 ± 0.06	99.66 ± 0.07	99.68 ± 0.09	99.66 ± 0.10
Proposed	DSC	**77.04 ± 3.48**	**75.01 ± 3.77**	**81.72 ± 3.66**	82.28 ± 3.28	**76.21 ± 4.19**	**87.02 ± 2.97**	**81.96 ± 2.71**
	SEN	95.26 ± 2.57	95.86 ± 2.04	98.27 ± 1.19	**97.94 ± 2.05**	95.96 ± 2.89	96.77 ± 1.03	97.02 ± 1.07
	SPE	99.78 ± 0.05	99.76 ± 0.05	**99.73 ± 0.06**	99.75 ± 0.05	99.75 ± 0.05	**99.77 ± 0.05**	99.67 ± 0.10

4 Discussion

We proposed a novel neural network for single-stage joint cranial bone segmentation and landmark detection that benefits from the close relationships between these two tasks. Our results presented in Tables 1 and 2 show that the proposed architecture outperforms current state-of-the-art approaches. Specifically, our architecture provided a significant improvement of 17.21% over the state-of-the-art alternative CG-FCN [18] for landmark detection, with $p < 0.001$ (estimated using a paired Wilcoxon test). Our network also significantly outperformed the CG-FCN by a 2.95% ($p < 0.001$) DSC score for bone segmentaions.

We also show in Tables 1 and 2 the improvements of our two novel modules over our baseline U-net-like architecture: spatial landmark configuration regression and context-encoding modules. As it can be observed, the independent incorporation of each of these two modules improves the results from the baseline architecture and their joint integration provides the best results. Hence, our results indicate quantitatively the importance of considering both context information and spatial relationships during anatomical segmentation tasks.

Our results and all comparative frameworks provided a higher accuracy detecting the two landmarks at the clinoid processes of the dorsum sellae (D1 and D2) compared to the glabella (G) and the opisthion (OP). These results are consistent with the higher variability observed in the manual annotations since the exact placement of the glabella and opisthion is affected by the subjective identification of the cranial midline. This subjective placement is one of the main motivators to construct fully automated methods that can reduce inter- and intra-observer variability such as the one presented in this work. In our case, all models tend to produce higher DSC scores for the parietal bones, since they have larger volumes than the other bone plates. Additionally, since the background volume is substantially higher than any bone plates, all models tend to produce slightly thinner bone segmentations than the ground truth. This has led to all models providing high SPE and relative low DSC score for all bones. We will further explore countering the effects of this region imbalance in future work. Another limitation of the presented study is the empirical estimation of our weights λ based on the observed loss ranges. In future work, we will also explore a more automated mechanism to increase model robustness for different datasets.

5 Conclusion

We proposed a novel end-to-end context encoding-constrained neural network for concurrent cranial bone segmentation and landmark detection using CT images. We proposed a new context encoding module that was incorporated into a U-Net-like network, and we used an attention mechanism based on landmark displacement vector maps to improve context learning. In addition, we used an additional regression task to promote learning features that account for the spatial anatomical configuration of the predicted landmarks. Our experiments demonstrated superior performance of the proposed model compared to recent state-of-the-art approaches.

Acknowledgments. The research reported in this publication was supported by the National Institute Of Dental & Craniofacial Research of the National Institutes of Health under Award Number R00DE027993. The content is solely the responsibility of the authors and does not necessarily represent the official views of the National Institutes of Health.

References

1. Wood, B.C., et al.: What's in a name? Accurately diagnosing metopic craniosynostosis using a computational approach. Plast. Reconstr. Surg. **137**, 205–213 (2016)
2. Mendoza, C.S., Safdar, N., Okada, K., Myers, E., Rogers, G.F., Linguraru, M.G.: Personalized assessment of craniosynostosis via statistical shape modeling. Med. Image Anal. **18**, 635–646 (2014)
3. Porras, A.R., et al.: Quantification of head shape from three-dimensional photography for presurgical and postsurgical evaluation of craniosynostosis. Plast. Reconstr. Surg. **144**, 1051e–1060e (2019)
4. Rodriguez-Florez, N., et al.: Statistical shape modelling to aid surgical planning: associations between surgical parameters and head shapes following spring-assisted cranioplasty. Int. J. Comput. Assis. Radiol. Surg. **12**, 1739–1749 (2017)
5. Lamecker, H., et al.: Surgical treatment of craniosynostosis based on a statistical 3D-shape model: first clinical application. Int. J. Comput. Assis. Radiol. Surg. **1**, 253 (2006)
6. Porras, A.R., et al.: Locally affine diffeomorphic surface registration and its application to surgical planning of fronto-orbital advancement. IEEE Trans. Med. Imaging **37**, 1690–1700 (2018)
7. Liu, L., et al.: Interactive separation of segmented bones in CT volumes using graph cut. In: Metaxas, D., Axel, L., Fichtinger, G., Székely, G. (eds.) MICCAI 2008. LNCS, vol. 5241, pp. 296–304. Springer, Heidelberg (2008). https://doi.org/10.1007/978-3-540-85988-8_36
8. Long, J., Shelhamer, E., Darrell, T.: Fully convolutional networks for semantic segmentation. In: IEEE Conference on Computer Vision and Pattern Recognition, pp. 3431–3440 (2014)
9. Lian, C., Liu, M., Zhang, J., Shen, D.: Hierarchical fully convolutional network for joint atrophy localization and alzheimer's disease diagnosis using structural MRI. IEEE Trans. Pattern Anal. Mach. Intell. **42**, 880–893 (2020)
10. Lian, C., et al.: Multi-channel multi-scale fully convolutional network for 3D perivascular spaces segmentation in 7T MR images. Med. Image Anal. **46**, 106–117 (2018)
11. Egger, J., Pfarrkirchner, B., Gsaxner, C., Lindner, L., Schmalstieg, D., Wallner, J.: Fully convolutional mandible segmentation on a valid ground-truth dataset. In: The 40th Annual International Conference of the IEEE Engineering in Medicine and Biology Society, pp. 656–660 (2018)
12. Ronneberger, O., Fischer, P., Brox, T.: U-Net: convolutional networks for biomedical image segmentation. In: Navab, N., Hornegger, J., Wells, W.M., Frangi, A.F. (eds.) MICCAI 2015. LNCS, vol. 9351, pp. 234–241. Springer, Cham (2015). https://doi.org/10.1007/978-3-319-24574-4_28
13. González Sánchez, J.C., Magnusson, M., Sandborg, M., Carlsson Tedgren, Å., Malusek, A.: Segmentation of bones in medical dual-energy computed tomography volumes using the 3D U-Net. Physica Medica **69**, 241–247 (2020)
14. Liu, Q., et al.: SkullEngine: a multi-stage CNN framework for collaborative CBCT image segmentation and landmark detection. In: Lian, C., Cao, X., Rekik, I., Xu, X., Yan, P. (eds.) MLMI 2021. LNCS, vol. 12966, pp. 606–614. Springer, Cham (2021). https://doi.org/10.1007/978-3-030-87589-3_62

15. Zhang, H., et al.: Context encoding for semantic segmentation. In: IEEE/CVF Conference on Computer Vision and Pattern Recognition, pp. 7751–7160 (2018)

16. Oliva, A., Torralba, A.: The role of context in object recognition. Trends Cogn. Sci. **11**, 520–527 (2007)

17. Tu, Z., Bai, X.: Auto-context and its application to high-level vision tasks and 3D brain image segmentation. IEEE Trans. Pattern Anal. Mach. Intell. **32**, 1744–1757 (2009)

18. Zhang, J., et al.: Joint Craniomaxillofacial Bone Segmentation ans Landmark Digitization by Context-Guided Fully Convolutional Networks. Springer, Cham (2017)

19. Torosdagli, N., Liberton, D.K., Verma, P., Sincan, M., Lee, J.S., Bagci, U.: Deep geodesic learning for segmentation and anatomical landmarking. IEEE Trans. Med. Imaging **38**, 919–931 (2018)

20. Lian, C., et al.: Multi-task dynamic transformer network for concurrent bone segmentation and large-scale landmark localization with dental CBCT. In: Martel, A.L., et al. (eds.) MICCAI 2020. LNCS, vol. 12264, pp. 807–816. Springer, Cham (2020). https://doi.org/10.1007/978-3-030-59719-1_78

21. Payer, C., Štern, D., Bischof, H., Urschler, M.: Regressing heatmaps for multiple landmark localization using CNNs. In: Ourselin, S., Joskowicz, L., Sabuncu, M.R., Unal, G., Wells, W. (eds.) MICCAI 2016. LNCS, vol. 9901, pp. 230–238. Springer, Cham (2016). https://doi.org/10.1007/978-3-319-46723-8_27

22. Dangi, S., et al.: Robust head CT image registration pipeline for craniosynostosis skull correction surgery. In: Healthcare Technology Letters, pp. 174–178. Institution of Engineering and Technology (2017)

23. Sgouros, S., Goldin, J.H., Hockley, A.D., Wake, M., Natarajan, K.: Intracranial volume change in childhood. J. Neurosurg. **94**, 610–616 (1999)

Warm Start Active Learning with Proxy Labels and Selection via Semi-supervised Fine-Tuning

Vishwesh Nath[1(✉)], Dong Yang[2], Holger R. Roth[2], and Daguang Xu[2]

[1] NVIDIA, Nashville, TN, USA
vnath@nvidia.com
[2] Bethesda, MD, USA

Abstract. Which volume to annotate next is a challenging problem in building medical imaging datasets for deep learning. One of the promising methods to approach this question is active learning (AL). However, AL has been a hard nut to crack in terms of which AL algorithm and acquisition functions are most useful for which datasets. Also, the problem is exacerbated with which volumes to label first when there is zero labeled data to start with. This is known as the cold start problem in AL. We propose two novel strategies for AL specifically for 3D image segmentation. First, we tackle the cold start problem by proposing a proxy task and then utilizing uncertainty generated from the proxy task to rank the unlabeled data to be annotated. Second, we craft a two-stage learning framework for each active iteration where the unlabeled data is also used in the second stage as a semi-supervised fine-tuning strategy. We show the promise of our approach on two well-known large public datasets from medical segmentation decathlon. The results indicate that the initial selection of data and semi-supervised framework both showed significant improvement for several AL strategies.

Keywords: Active learning · Deep learning · Semi-supervised learning · Self-supervised learning · Segmentation · CT

1 Introduction

Active learning (AL) [21] for medical image segmentation can help reduce the burden of annotation effort as it focuses on selection of the *more* relevant data that may lead to a better performing model. However, there is disagreement among which acquisition function for ranking the unlabeled data is the best [3–5,20,22] and also which framework is the best for uncertainty generation [2,6,7,15–17,26]. Apart from these challenges for AL, there are two other critical

Supplementary Information The online version contains supplementary material available at https://doi.org/10.1007/978-3-031-16452-1_29.

problems to be addressed as well: (1) When faced with an entirely unlabeled pool of data, how does one select the initial set of data to start annotation? This falls under the problem of the "cold start" in AL [9,32]. (2) Current acquisition functions utilize supervised models which learn using labeled data. There is a lack of 3D-based AL algorithm that leverages the knowledge of unlabeled data in uncertainty generation and data ranking. The models based on semi-supervised learning (SSL) can become better data selectors [22,28]. So far SSL has only been shown to be effective for helping AL algorithms in generic computer vision tasks [3,4,22] or 2D medical segmentation [28]. Unfortunately, SSL models for 3D segmentation are not straightforward, as the entire 3D volume cannot be used as input, unlike the 2D variants due to memory constraints. They face the challenge of appropriate patch selection, which needs to focus on the desired region of interest (ROI). In this work, we propose novel strategies to tackle these challenges. The experiments have been performed on two well-known large public computed tomography (CT) datasets [23].

2   Related Work

Cold Start AL: The knowledge of which data to annotate first, given a completely unlabeled pool of data, can serve as an excellent starting point for the active learning process. Prior work has been done for natural language processing [1,32]. In [32] an embedding is generated for sentences using a pre-trained transformer model. Clustering is performed on the embeddings; the sentences closest to cluster centers are selected first for annotation. Compared to random selection, such a strategy improves the data annotation process when there is zero labeled data. This is highly relevant in the medical imaging domain where there is an abundance of unlabeled data, but annotations are costly and often unavailable.

Semi-supervised AL: There is prior work that has shown that semi-supervised learning is beneficial for AL where it makes the models a better selector of annotation data while improving the performance [4,22]. However, these have only been shown for either classification [22] or for 2D segmentation [13,27]. There is no AL work combined with 3D semi-supervised learning to the best of our knowledge.

Meanwhile, multiple methods have been proposed that fall under semi-supervised learning techniques for 3D segmentation, such as [29] which utilizes an ensemble of models for SSL, [31] which uses a student-teacher method, [14] which proposes to use a shape constraint for SSL, as well as prediction consistency-based approaches or contrastive approaches [25]. Ensembles are computationally expensive, while student-teacher and shape constraints are not ideal for AL either. Hence, we explore towards consistency-based approaches for AL SSL.

3   Proposed Method

The proposed method starts with ranking of a zero-labeled data pool via a proxy task that utilizes pseudo labels, which can also be considered as a self-supervised

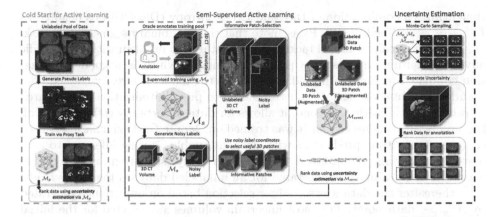

Fig. 1. The proposed pipeline of the entire AL framework. Left to right: First, we generate the pseudo-labels for a proxy task to perform data ranking via uncertainty. The pre-trained model and the ranking both are used in the semi-supervised AL framework, which is a two-stage learning process. After semi-supervised learning is done, the final model is used to select data for annotation to repeat the cyclic process.

learning task (Ref Fig. 1). After the annotation of selected unlabeled data, a fully supervised training is performed. The trained model is consecutively fine-tuned via a semi-supervised approach. Finally, the fine-tuned semi-supervised model is used for data selection of which 3D volumes should be labeled next by the annotator. The cycle continues till the desired performance is achieved. Please refer to Algorithm 1 for more details.

We utilize a U-Net [19] like 5-level encoder-decoder network architecture with residual blocks at every level. In the experiments, only the number of output channels are modified based upon the number of classes of the segmentation task. We consistently utilize a softmax function for activation to probability maps $p(x_i)$, for proxy, supervised and semi-supervised learning.

3.1   Pre-ranking of Data via Pseudo Labels as a Proxy Task

Consider an unlabeled pool of data $\mathcal{U}$ which consists of n samples, forming a set as $\mathcal{U} = \{x_1, x_2, ...x_n\}$. To generate a pseudo label denoted as y_i^p for a given sample data point x_i, we threshold x_i within a typical abdominal soft-tissue windows for CT data (W:50 L:125) Hounsfield Units (HU)[1], then utilize largest connected component analysis to select ROIs that are well connected. Intuitively, the expectation is to select all major organs of the abdomen as foreground. All prior approaches regarding pseudo-labels have been 2D or on a slice-by-slice basis [18, 28]. Here, we provide an efficient and effective 3D extension.

After the generation of pseudo labels, we form a pseudo-labeled dataset $\mathcal{U}^p = \{(x_1, y_1^p), (x_2, y_2^p), ...(x_n, y_n^p)\}$. A proxy model is trained using the pseudo-labels

---

[1] https://radiopaedia.org/articles/windowing-ct.

that utilizes a combination of Dice and Cross-entropy (DiceCE) loss denoted as L_{DiceCE} as outlined in [10]. Please note that this is a binary segmentation task.

The proxy-trained model tackles the cold start AL problem with two specific advantages. First, it acts as a pre-trained model, which is a good initialization compared to random initialization. Since the model is already trained on a pseudo segmentation task, it is better suited to prior initialization as compared to random initialization. Second, it allows for data uncertainty estimation of all the unlabeled volumes $\mathcal{U}$ that it was trained on. Monte Carlo simulation is used to generate multiple predictions with dropout enabled during inference to estimate the uncertainty [6]. More details on uncertainty estimation can be found in Sect. 3.4. Uncertainty was generated for all unlabeled data via the proxy model $\mathcal{M}_p$, thereafter the data was sorted for selection based on uncertainty generated by $\mathcal{M}_p$ per data point. The most uncertain volumes are selected for the initial pool denoted as T^l with the pre-trained checkpoint of the model. The initially selected training pool data points are annotated by the annotator for supervised learning. Once a volume is labeled it is removed from $\mathcal{U}$. k volumes are selected for T^l. At every active learning iteration, k volumes are added to T^l.

3.2 Fully Supervised Training

The fully supervised model denoted as $\mathcal{M}_s$ is trained on all the available labeled data from the training pool T^l. L_{DiceCE} as defined in Sect. 3.1 is used for training. The network uses all the layers of the pre-trained checkpoint from the proxy task. If the number of classes for segmentation are more than 2, then the number of output channels are increased and the last layer of the proxy model $\mathcal{M}_p$ is ignored when loading the pre-trained model.

3.3 Semi-supervised Training

Due to the computational expense of 3D training and maintaining a balance between labeled and unlabeled data, we cannot use all the unlabeled volumes for training. Hence, $\mathcal{M}_s$ is used to select the most *certain* 3D volumes from the remaining unlabeled pool of data $\mathcal{U}$. The number of selected unlabeled volumes for semi-supervised training is equivalent to the number of labeled data in T^l. The biggest challenge with 3D training of unlabeled data is the selection of the more informative cubic patches that contain the specific ROI, which is crucial for the segmentation task. To overcome this challenge, we generate noisy labels denoted as $\hat{y}^n$ of the selected most certain unlabeled 3D volumes using $\mathcal{M}_s$. The generated labels are so called "noisy" because the $\mathcal{M}_s$ is trained on a small sample size and hence is a low-performance model which is unlikely to lead to good and clean predictions. Thus, we use a threshold τ on the probability maps $p(x_i)$ to remove false positive predictions.

The semi-supervised learning is performed as a fine-tuning step to the existing trained model $\mathcal{M}_s$. The model trained from the semi-supervised learning framework is denoted as $\mathcal{M}_{semi}$. The training process utilizes both labeled T^l and unlabeled data T^n. Please note that all samples from T^l are also used in

---

Algorithm 1: Semi-Supervised AL Algorithm

---

1 **Input:** Unlabeled Pool $\mathcal{U}$
2 Generate Pseudo Labels for $\mathcal{U}$ forming $\mathcal{U}^p = \{(x_1, y_1^p), ...(x_n, y_n^p)\}$
3 Train $\mathcal{M}_p$ using $\mathcal{U}^p$, generate uncertainty for $\mathcal{U}$
4 Sort $\mathcal{U}$ based on uncertainty via $\mathcal{M}_p$
5 Select most uncertain k data from $\mathcal{U}$ for annotation, add k to $\mathcal{T}_j^l$
6 **for** $j \in \{0, 1...\}$ **do**
7 $\quad$ $\mathcal{M}_s =$ Supervised Training on $\mathcal{M}_p$ using $\mathcal{T}_j^l$
8 $\quad$ **if** *Semi-Supervised is True* **then**
9 $\quad\quad$ Extract most certain $len(\mathcal{T}_j^l)$data from $\mathcal{U}$ & add to $\mathcal{U}_n$
10 $\quad\quad$ Generate Noisy Labels for $\mathcal{U}_n$ & form $\mathcal{T}_j^n$
11 $\quad\quad$ $\mathcal{M}_{semi} =$ Semi-Supervised Fine-Tuning on $\mathcal{M}_s$ using $\{\mathcal{T}_j^l, \mathcal{T}_j^n\}$
12 $\quad\quad$ Generate uncertainty via $\mathcal{M}_{semi}$ for $\mathcal{U}$
13 $\quad\quad$ Select the most uncertain k data from $\mathcal{U}$ & add to $\mathcal{T}_j^l$
14 $\quad$ **else**
15 $\quad\quad$ Generate uncertainty via $\mathcal{M}_s$ for $\mathcal{U}$
16 $\quad\quad$ Select the most uncertain k data from $\mathcal{U}$ for annotation & add to $\mathcal{T}_j^l$
17 $\quad$ **end if**
18 **end for**

---

semi-supervised training (Fig. 1). The training process for a single step is defined by the following loss function:

$$L_{total} = \alpha L_{DiceCE}^{Supervised}(\hat{y}_j, y_j) \mid \beta L_{DiceCE}^{Semi-Supervised}(\hat{y}_i^{v1}, \hat{y}_i^{v2}) \tag{1}$$

where supervised and semi-supervised, L_{DiceCE} loss is the same as in Sect. 3.1. The semi-supervised loss is based on a randomly chosen unlabeled volume x_i^U from which a cubic patch is selected that focuses on the required ROI. This ROI patch is extracted based on the noisy label $\hat{y}_i^n$. Consecutively, two views x_i^{v1}, x_i^{v2} of the cubic patch are generated, x_i^{v1} is kept unaugmented for best prediction from $\mathcal{M}_{semi}$ while the other view x_i^{v2} is augmented. $\hat{y}_i^{v1}$, $\hat{y}_i^{v2}$ are predictions from $\mathcal{M}_{semi}$. α and β allow for weighing the loss function terms for supervised and semi-supervised, respectively.

3.4 Uncertainty Estimation and AL

We use epistemic or model uncertainty as defined in [5,30] for variance and entropy. The uncertainty measure is estimated based on the number of MC simulations m. To obtain a score, we use the mean across all the 3D voxels in the 3D uncertainty map $\mathcal{H}$.

4 Datasets and Experiments

4.1 Datasets

Liver and Tumor: This dataset comes from task 3 of Medical Segmentation Decathlon (MSD) [23]. It consists of 131 3D CT volumes. The data was split into 105 volumes for training and 26 for validation. The 105 volumes represent the unlabeled pool $\mathcal{U}$ for experimentation. The validation set was kept consistent for all experiments ranging from pseudo-label pre-training to AL results. For pre-processing, all data were re-sampled to $1.5 \times 1.5 \times 2$ mm^3 spacing for rapid experimentation. Augmentation of shifting, scaling intensity and gaussian noise were used. The CT window was used as per [8].

Hepatic Vessels and Tumor: This dataset comes from task 8 of MSD and consists of 303 3D CT volumes. The data was split into 242 volumes for training and 61 for validation. The 242 volumes represent $\mathcal{U}$ for experimentation. The validation set was kept consistent for all experiments ranging from pseudo-label pre-training to AL results. Pre-processing is similar as for liver & tumor except for CT window for normalization which was adapted as per [8].

4.2   Experiments

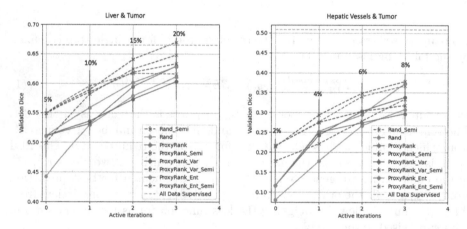

Fig. 2. The percentage represents the amount of data used at the current active iteration with respect to all available data. Solid lines represent fully supervised approaches and dashed lines represent semi-supervised approaches. Solid lines are baselines, while dashed lines include our proposed methods. "Proxyrank" indicates that the initial training pool was estimated using proxy task. "Var" → "Variance" [30], "Ent" → "Entropy" [16], "Rand" → "Random", "Semi" → "Semi-supervised learning". Refer Supplementary Table 1. for more details.

Proxy Training Hyper-parameters: All proxy models trained with pseudo-labels were trained for 100 epochs on all data; the validation set for selecting the best model is consistent with the other experiments. The validation frequency was once every 5 epochs. L_{DiceCE} loss was used for training. Cubic patch size of $96 \times 96 \times 96$ was used with random selection of patches from the 3D CT volumes. Learning rate was set to $1e^{-4}$ and Adam optimizer [11] was used.

Uncertainty Hyper-parameters: To estimate uncertainty, m was set to 10 and the dropout ratio was set to 0.2. A dropout layer was kept at the end of every level of the U-Net for both the encoder and decoder.

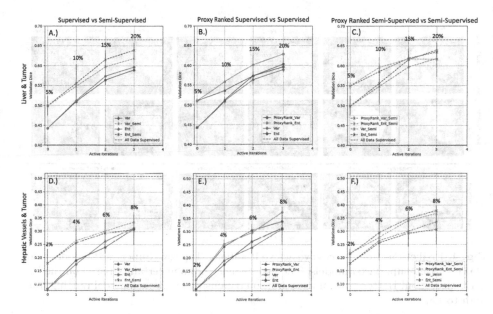

Fig. 3. Top row: results for hepatic vessels & tumor. Bottom row: results for liver & tumor. The percentage represents the amount of data used at current active iteration with respect to all available data. Solid lines are baselines, while dashed lines include our proposed methods. "Proxyrank" indicates that the initial training pool was estimated using proxy task. "Var" → "Variance" [30], "Ent" → "Entropy" [16], "Rand" → "Random", "Semi" → "Semi-supervised learning". Refer Supplementary Table 1. for more details.

AL Acquisition Functions: To gauge the benefit of the combined strategies of semi-supervised learning with proxy ranking, we compare them with random based acquisition and also with two well-known AL acquisition functions of entropy and variance [5,6,30]. We also utilize proxy ranking by itself as a strategy for acquisition of data, as that eliminates the need to compute uncertainty at the end of every active iteration. Advanced acquisition functions such as coreset [20], maximum-cover [30], knapsack [12], Fisher information [24] were not tested as the purpose of this study was to evaluate if the proposed strategies are beneficial for basic components of AL. Though more advanced acquisition functions could be added.

SSL AL with Proxy Ranking: One active iteration consists of supervised learning with the existing labeled data and a secondary semi-supervised fine-tuning if needed. All AL experiments were executed for $j = 4$ active iterations.

For both datasets, liver & tumor and hepatic vessels & tumor, k was set to 5 volumes which were being acquired at every active iteration to be annotated by the annotator. The validation set was kept the same for all active iterations as also defined in Sect. 4.1 for all datasets.

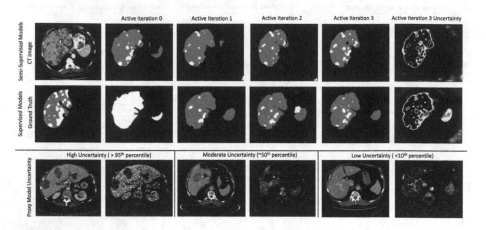

Fig. 4. Predictions from successive active iterations. Top row: Supervised models, middle row: Semi-supervised models. The last column shows uncertainty based on the last active iteration. Bottom row: uncertainty on data using proxy task model ranging from high to low

Table 1. The validation Dice at the end of last active iteration are reported to show the benefits of proxy ranking and semi-supervised learning

Proxy rank & Semi-Supervised Learning Adv.				
Supervised				
Dataset	Variance	Entropy	Proxy variance	Proxy entropy
Liver & Tumor	0.5891 ± 0.0039	0.5962 ± 0.0048	0.6032 ± 0.0207	0.6287 ± 0.0092
Hepatic & Tumor	0.3083 ± 0.0568	0.3116 ± 0.0494	0.3378 ± 0.0257	0.3723 ± 0.0217
Semi-supervised				
Dataset	Variance	Entropy	Proxy variance	Proxy entropy
Liver & Tumor	0.6178 ± 0.0218	0.6335 ± 0.0183	$\mathbf{0.6383 \pm 0.0091}$	0.6162 ± 0.0439
Hepatic & Tumor	0.3351 ± 0.0379	0.3060 ± 0.0567	$\mathbf{0.3779 \pm 0.0188}$	0.3670 ± 0.0162

We utilize a fixed number of steps strategy for an equivalent amount of training per active iteration instead of a fixed number of epochs. 2,000 steps were used for both datasets. These steps were estimated from all data training. Learning rate, optimizer and patch size were kept consistent with proxy task hyper-parameters. The selected patches had a foreground and background ratio of 1:1. For semi-supervised learning with noisy labels, this ratio was kept at 9:1.

The semi-supervised loss function hyper-parameters α and β were set to 1 and 0.001, respectively. The threshold τ for probability maps $p(x_i)$ was set to 0.9 for noisy label generation.

All AL strategies were repeated three times with different random initializations. The mean and standard deviation of Dice scores are reported in plots and tables.

Adv. of Proxy Ranking and SSL: To gauge the advantage of proxy ranking for the unlabeled data, we conduct experiments with and without proxy rank to assess both supervised and semi-supervised training. We also gauge the advantage of using semi-supervised over supervised learning. All AL settings are kept the same as described above.

Implementation: All deep learning networks were implemented using PyTorch v1.10. MONAI v0.8[2] was used for data transformations and pre-processing. The experiments were conducted on Tesla V100 16GB & 32GB GPUs.

5   Results

SSL AL with Proxy Ranking: Quantitatively, semi-supervised & proxy-ranked approaches provide a benefit over just using supervised methods for AL (Ref Fig. 2). It should also be noted that the proxy ranking of data is helpful at the first active iteration for both datasets and gives a better starting point for the AL models for both supervised and also semi-supervised methods. Surprisingly, the best performing method for liver & tumor is given just proxy ranking coupled with semi-supervised learning. While for hepatic vessel & tumor the best performance is given by the variance acquisition function coupled with semi-supervised learning.

Adv. of Proxy Ranking and SSL: Quantitatively, the semi-supervised approaches offer a significant benefit for both datasets (Fig. 3A & 3D). A similar observation can be made when the proxy ranking is added to either supervised (Fig. 3B and 3E) or semi-supervised (Fig. 3C and 3F). This is also summarized in Table 1. All methods when inter-compared by validation Dice score per volume are statistically significant ($p \ll 0.05$) using Wilcoxon signed rank test.

Qualitatively, the quality of labels generated by semi-supervised models per active iterations are better as compared to supervised models (Ref Fig. 4). The uncertainty maps indicate more relevant ROIs which assists in selecting more relevant data. The bottom row shows an intuition of how proxy rank selects data, we can observe that unlabeled volumes with abnormalities (tumor) tend to have a higher uncertainty as compared to volumes without abnormalities.

6   Conclusion

Proxy-based ranking and semi-supervised learning both add much needed tools to AL. Where we see typical supervised learning based AL fail or lack in performance, the proposed strategies can add significant leverage. It should be noted

---

[2] https://github.com/Project-MONAI/MONAI.

that the HU-based proxy ranking is limited to CT datasets; future work could focus on how a proxy rank could be estimated for other imaging modalities such as magnetic resonance imaging, ultra-sound, etc.

References

1. Ash, J.T., Zhang, C., Krishnamurthy, A., Langford, J., Agarwal, A.: Deep batch active learning by diverse, uncertain gradient lower bounds. arXiv preprint arXiv:1906.03671 (2019)
2. Beluch, W.H., Genewein, T., Nürnberger, A., Köhler, J.M.: The power of ensembles for active learning in image classification. In: Proceedings of the IEEE Conference on Computer Vision and Pattern Recognition, pp. 9368–9377 (2018)
3. Bengar, J.Z., Raducanu, B., Weijer, J.v.d.: When deep learners change their mind: learning dynamics for active learning. In: International Conference on Computer Analysis of Images and Patterns, pp. 403–413. Springer (2021). https://doi.org/10.48550/arXiv.2107.14707
4. Bengar, J.Z., van de Weijer, J., Twardowski, B., Raducanu, B.: Reducing label effort: Self-supervised meets active learning. In: Proceedings of the IEEE/CVF International Conference on Computer Vision, pp. 1631–1639 (2021)
5. Chitta, K., Alvarez, J.M., Lesnikowski, A.: Large-scale visual active learning with deep probabilistic ensembles. arXiv preprint arXiv:1811.03575 (2018)
6. Gal, Y., Ghahramani, Z.: Dropout as a bayesian approximation: Representing model uncertainty in deep learning. In: International Conference on Machine Learning, pp. 1050–1059 (2016)
7. Gal, Y., Islam, R., Ghahramani, Z.: Deep bayesian active learning with image data. In: Proceedings of the 34th International Conference on Machine Learning, vol. 70, pp. 1183–1192. JMLR. org (2017)
8. He, Y., Yang, D., Roth, H., Zhao, C., Xu, D.: Dints: differentiable neural network topology search for 3d medical image segmentation. In: Proceedings of the IEEE/CVF Conference on Computer Vision and Pattern Recognition, pp. 5841–5850 (2021)
9. Houlsby, N., Hernández-Lobato, J.M., Ghahramani, Z.: Cold-start active learning with robust ordinal matrix factorization. In: International Conference on Machine Learning, pp. 766–774. PMLR (2014)
10. Isensee, F., Jaeger, P.F., Kohl, S.A., Petersen, J., Maier-Hein, K.H.: nnu-net: a self-configuring method for deep learning-based biomedical image segmentation. Nat. Methods **18**(2), 203–211 (2021)
11. Kingma, D.P., Ba, J.: Adam: a method for stochastic optimization. arXiv preprint arXiv:1412.6980 (2014)
12. Kuo, W., Häne, C., Yuh, E., Mukherjee, P., Malik, J.: Cost-sensitive active learning for intracranial hemorrhage detection. In: International Conference on Medical Image Computing and Computer-Assisted Intervention, pp. 715–723. Springer (2018)
13. Lai, Z., Wang, C., Oliveira, L.C., Dugger, B.N., Cheung, S.C., Chuah, C.N.: Joint semi-supervised and active learning for segmentation of gigapixel pathology images with cost-effective labeling. In: Proceedings of the IEEE/CVF International Conference on Computer Vision, pp. 591–600 (2021)

14. Li, S., Zhang, C., He, X.: Shape-aware semi-supervised 3D semantic segmentation for medical images. In: Martel, A.L., et al. (eds.) MICCAI 2020. LNCS, vol. 12261, pp. 552–561. Springer, Cham (2020). https://doi.org/10.1007/978-3-030-59710-8_54

15. Nath, V., et al.: The power of proxy data and proxy networks for hyper-parameter optimization in medical image segmentation. In: de Bruijne, M., et al. (eds.) MICCAI 2021. LNCS, vol. 12903, pp. 456–465. Springer, Cham (2021). https://doi.org/10.1007/978-3-030-87199-4_43

16. Nath, V., Yang, D., Landman, B.A., Xu, D., Roth, H.R.: Diminishing uncertainty within the training pool: Active learning for medical image segmentation. IEEE Trans. Med. Imaging 40(10), 2534–2547 (2020)

17. Nguyen, V.L., Shaker, M.H., Hüllermeier, E.: How to measure uncertainty in uncertainty sampling for active learning. Mach. Learn. 111, 1–34 (2021)

18. Ouyang, C., Biffi, C., Chen, C., Kart, T., Qiu, H., Rueckert, D.: Self-supervision with superpixels: training few-shot medical image segmentation without annotation. In: Vedaldi, A., Bischof, H., Brox, T., Frahm, J.-M. (eds.) ECCV 2020. LNCS, vol. 12374, pp. 762–780. Springer, Cham (2020). https://doi.org/10.1007/978-3-030-58526-6_45

19. Ronneberger, O., Fischer, P., Brox, T.: U-Net: Convolutional networks for biomedical image segmentation. In: Navab, N., Hornegger, J., Wells, W.M., Frangi, A.F. (eds.) MICCAI 2015. LNCS, vol. 9351, pp. 234–241. Springer, Cham (2015). https://doi.org/10.1007/978-3-319-24574-4_28

20. Sener, O., Savarese, S.: Active learning for convolutional neural networks: A coreset approach. arXiv preprint arXiv:1708.00489 (2017)

21. Settles, B.: Active learning. Synth. Lect. Artif. Intell. Mach. Learn. 6(1), 1–114 (2012)

22. Siméoni, O., Budnik, M., Avrithis, Y., Gravier, G.: Rethinking deep active learning: Using unlabeled data at model training. In: 2020 25th International Conference on Pattern Recognition (ICPR), pp. 1220–1227. IEEE (2021)

23. Simpson, A.L., et al.: A large annotated medical image dataset for the development and evaluation of segmentation algorithms. arXiv preprint arXiv:1902.09063 (2019)

24. Sourati, J., Gholipour, A., Dy, J.G., Kurugol, S., Warfield, S.K.: Active deep learning with fisher information for patch-wise semantic segmentation. In: DLMIA/ML-CDS -2018. LNCS, vol. 11045, pp. 83–91. Springer, Cham (2018). https://doi.org/10.1007/978-3-030-00889-5_10

25. Tang, Y., et al.: Self-supervised pre-training of swin transformers for 3d medical image analysis. arXiv preprint arXiv:2111.14791 (2021)

26. Wang, G., Li, W., Aertsen, M., Deprest, J., Ourselin, S., Vercauteren, T.: Test-time augmentation with uncertainty estimation for deep learning-based medical image segmentation (2018)

27. Wang, J., et al.: Semi-supervised active learning for instance segmentation via scoring predictions. arXiv preprint arXiv:2012.04829 (2020)

28. Wang, S., et al.: Annotation-efficient deep learning for automatic medical image segmentation. Nat. Commun. 12(1), 1–13 (2021)

29. Xia, Y., et al.: 3d semi-supervised learning with uncertainty-aware multi-view co-training. In: Proceedings of the IEEE/CVF Winter Conference on Applications of Computer Vision, pp. 3646–3655 (2020)

30. Yang, L., Zhang, Y., Chen, J., Zhang, S., Chen, D.Z.: Suggestive annotation: A deep active learning framework for biomedical image segmentation. In: Descoteaux, M., Maier-Hein, L., Franz, A., Jannin, P., Collins, D.L., Duchesne, S. (eds.) MICCAI

2017. LNCS, vol. 10435, pp. 399–407. Springer, Cham (2017). https://doi.org/10.1007/978-3-319-66179-7_46

31. Yu, L., Wang, S., Li, X., Fu, C.-W., Heng, P.-A.: Uncertainty-aware self-ensembling model for semi-supervised 3d left atrium segmentation. In: Shen, D., et al. (eds.) MICCAI 2019. LNCS, vol. 11765, pp. 605–613. Springer, Cham (2019). https://doi.org/10.1007/978-3-030-32245-8_67

32. Yuan, M., Lin, H.T., Boyd-Graber, J.: Cold-start active learning through self-supervised language modeling. arXiv preprint arXiv:2010.09535 (2020)

Intervention & Interaction Federated Abnormality Detection with Noisy Clients

Xinyu Liu, Wuyang Li, and Yixuan Yuan[✉]

Department of Electrical Engineering, City University of Hong Kong,
Kowloon, Hong Kong, China
yxyuan.ee@cityu.edu.hk

Abstract. Federated learning (FL), which trains a shared global model by collaboration between distributed clients (e.g. medical institutions) and preserves the privacy of local data, has been widely deployed in the medical field to benefit abnormality diagnosis. However, it is inevitable that local data contains noise across clients, resulting in notably performance deterioration in the global model. To this end, a practical yet challenging FL problem is studied in this paper, namely Federated abnormality detection with noisy clients (FADN). We represent the first effort to reason the FADN task as a structural causal model, and identify the main issue that leads to the performance deterioration, namely *recognition bias*. To tackle the problem, an Intervention & Interaction FL framework (FedInI) is proposed, comprising two key strategies: (1) Intervention: considering the data distribution heterogeneity caused by different noisy levels within each client, we use the global model to intervene the training of local models, by shuffling and mixing features extracted from different models and suppress the noise gradually; (2) Interaction: we devise an adaptive sample-wise weighting strategy that jointly considers the local training statuses and global noisy levels with a shared interactive layer. Extensive experiments on class-conditional noise and instance-dependant noise settings are conducted, FedInI outperforms state-of-the-arts by a remarkable margin. Code is available at github.com/CityU-AIM-Group/FedInI.

Keywords: Federated learning · Learning with noisy labels · Abnormality detection · Causal intervention

1 Introduction

Deep neural networks have found pervasive suite of applications in computer-aided diagnosis and gradually become a standard to detect abnormalities [2,8,12,19,20,24,29,34], attributing to the increasing availability of computational resources as well as datasets. However, it is still infeasible to train a

Supplementary Information The online version contains supplementary material available at https://doi.org/10.1007/978-3-031-16452-1_30.

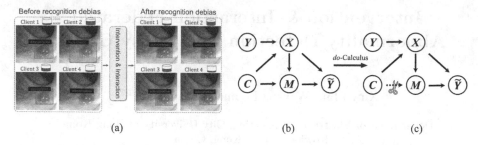

Fig. 1. (a) The proposed FedInI uses intervention & interaction to perform recognition debias among clients. (b) The biased structural causal model (SCM) assumption of the FADN task. (c) The intervened SCM where the confounding impact from C is cut out.

powerful abnormality detection model as collecting large datasets from multiple hospitals is hampered by data privacy concerns and security limitations. Recently, federated learning (FL) has emerged as a promising solution [1,28] to train a shared global model in a decentralized manner. The paradigm optimizes each local model with separated private data, and aggregates the model parameters at a certain frequency without exchanging the data. Most existing FL approaches are based on the training paradigm of FedAvg [13], i.e., using supervised learning to train distributed local models and averaging their parameters to build a generalized global model. These approaches excessively rely on well-annotated data to train local models, yet the label quality may vary significantly across clients, due to different labeling standards and ambiguous samples [22,38]. Therefore, the noisy data will degrade the generalization ability of local models, and consequently magnify the negative impact on the averaged global model, which may lead to false abnormalities diagnosis and even dreadful results.

Some recent studies have been focusing on learning with noisy labels (LNL), such as regularization methods [11,17,18,26,33,35], sample selection [6,9], and robust losses [5,25,36,37]. However, simply adopting these LNL methods to FL abnormality detection only leads to sub-optimal solutions. Firstly, these LNL methods only work with a local dataset and model, while ignoring the potential benefits for noise suppression with mutual information among multiple local models in the FL scenario. Secondly, compared with the traditional LNL methods, the global model has no access to local data in FL, thus the aggregated performance may fluctuate severely due to inconsistent noisy reduction degree of client models. Thirdly, the noisy levels are often unknown and variable among clients, thus the methods require client-by-client tuning.

To this end, we aim to solve the practical problem of Federated abnormality detection with noisy clients (FADN). As shown in Fig. 1(a), although different clients are trained with their correspondent labeled data, they generate diversified false predictions for the same abnormality image (termed as *recognition bias*). This phenomenon is caused by the noise heterogeneity among clients, since each local model attempts to extract features utilizing the relative cues within their training data. Intuitively, when making predictions for the same testing data, each local model attempts to correlate it with their memorized local data, but could be prone to fallacious predictions if the local data contains heterogeneous noise. Therefore, the correlation between unseen testing data and the knowledge inherited from the noisy local data is spurious, and the authentic causality of recognizing abnormalities should be unbiased of the client-side data partition.

To tackle the *recognition bias* issue, we refer to the causal mechanism and propose to formulate FADN into a structural causal model (SCM) [16], which has been recently developed to provide a rational way to mitigate biases [3,7,30,32], as shown in Fig. 1(b). With the SCM, it is identified that client serves as a confounder that leads to the recognition bias. Therefore, based on backdoor adjustment [16], we propose a debiasing solution namely Intervention & Interaction FL framework (FedInI) to alleviate the client confounder effect with two key strategies. The first is **Intervention**. Considering the heterogeneity is caused by different noisy levels within each client, we use the global model as an approximation of the stratified confounder C to intervene the training of local models. Specifically, we shuffle and mix features extracted from both global and local models, generating synthetic interpolated samples for training. With these intervened samples as regularization, the original useless and harmful noisy samples are transferred to be contributive, and the noise is suppressed consequently. The second is **Interaction**. As the global model is ignorant of the training statuses and noise heterogeneities of local models, we propose a synchronization measurement and a shared interactive layer to adaptively generate mixup weights. The interactive layer is designed to learn the global knowledge of noise heterogeneity among all clients and aims to perform optimal mixing strategies for noise suppression. Extensive experiments on class-conditional noise and instance-dependant noise demonstrate the effectiveness of FedInI.

2   Intervention & Interaction Framework

2.1   Structural Causal Model for FADN

Recall in Fig. 1(a), the recognition bias is the bottleneck of FADN. To fundamentally conduct debiasing, in this section, we depict the SCM of FADN task in Fig. 1(b) and reveal the confounding impact of the client. We first describe the causal relationships as follows:

$Y \to X$. X is the input image content and Y is the true label. The causality stands that changes in true labels will definitely result in changes in images.

$C \to X$. C refers to the client that corresponds to the hospital that conducts medical diagnosis (e.g. abnormality detection). The direct link implies that C induces the abnormality images X.

$C \to M \leftarrow X$. Here M pictures the feature representations of X, and C serves as the confounder that causes biased recognition and generalization abilities of the local models, due to the data distribution heterogeneity caused by noise.

$X \to \tilde{Y} \leftarrow M$. $\tilde{Y}$ refers to the detection result that also corresponds to the noisy labels, which is determined by $X \to M \to \tilde{Y}$, as the prediction is explicitly based on the image X and implicitly based on the feature representation M.

Then according to the graph, we observe that the causality of FPDN aims to directly learn $P(\tilde{Y}|M)$ without considering the client confounder set C. The non-interventional prediction can be expressed using Bayes rule as:

$$P(\tilde{Y}|M) = \sum_c P(\tilde{Y}|M,c)P(c|M). \tag{1}$$

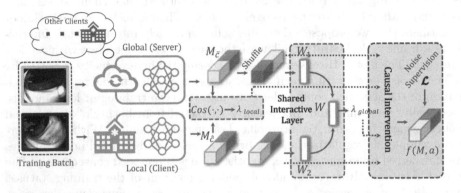

Fig. 2. The overall framework of FedInI. Each local client performs causal intervention with the global model, and the weights are adaptively determined by feature similarity and shared interactive layer.

The above objective learns not only the main direct correlation $X \to \tilde{Y} \leftarrow M$ but also the one from the unblocked backdoor path $X \leftarrow C \to M \to \tilde{Y}$. However, the correlation between feature M and the client C is spurious, as recognizing abnormalities should be unbiased and invariant of the client-side data partition. Hence, an intervention that uses $P(\tilde{Y}|do(M))$ instead of $P(\tilde{Y}|M)$ as the new objective is proposed, as shown in Fig. 1(c), we use do-Calculus [16] to cut the pathway from C to M:

$$P(\tilde{Y}|do(M)) = \sum_c P(\tilde{Y}|do(M),c)P(c|do(M)) = \sum_c P(\tilde{Y}|M,c)P(c), \tag{2}$$

where $P(c)$ is the prior of client data distribution, and the aim is to force the feature to fairly interact with all clients for making unbiased predictions. To implement the recognition debiasing, we propose an Intervention & Interaction FL framework (FedInI) in this paper, which is divided into two steps: Intervention and Interaction. The overall framework is shown in Fig. 2.

2.2 Intervention

To perform the recognition debiasing with the *do*-Calculus in Eq. (2), a stratification of the confounder set C is required [16]. However, in the FL paradigm, it is infeasible to stratify other confounders $C = \{c_1, c_2, ..., c_n\}$, due to the unavailability of the local models of other clients. Hence, we propose to utilize an approximation that the global model $\bar{c}$ serves as an aggregation of the confounder set as it is an average of all local models. Based on the approximation, we have:

$$P(\tilde{Y}|do(M)) = \sum_c P(\tilde{Y}|M, c)P(c) \approx \sum_{a \in A} P(\tilde{Y}|M, a)P(a), \quad A = \{\bar{c}, \hat{c}\}, \quad (3)$$

where $\hat{c}$ is the current local model. Specifically, $P(\tilde{Y}|do(M))$ is implemented as $\mathbb{E}_a[\sigma(f(M, a))]$, where σ is the normalization function and f is the intervention. With Normalized Weighted Geometric Mean (NWGM) [27], the outer expectation $\mathbb{E}_a$ can be moved into the normalization function as $\sigma(\mathbb{E}_a[f(M, a)])$ thus the feed-forward process is simplified to one round.

To intervene the confounder with $\mathbb{E}_a[f(M, a)]$, both the global and local model features are leveraged for prediction. For arbitrary two images within a training batch, the extracted global features and local features are denoted as $M_{\bar{c}1}, M_{\bar{c}2}$ and $M_{\hat{c}1}, M_{\hat{c}2}$, respectively. Then, the features are shuffled and mixed regarding the following equation:

$$f(M, a) = \phi[(\lambda M_{\hat{c}1} + (1 - \lambda)M_{\bar{c}2}) \oplus (\lambda M_{\hat{c}2} + (1 - \lambda)M_{\bar{c}1})], \quad A = \{\hat{c}, \bar{c}\}, \quad (4)$$

where ϕ is the predictor of the detector, λ is the manifold mixup weight [23], and $\oplus$ is the concatenation operation. The intuitive behind this design is that mixing different sample features could prevent the detrimental memorizing effect of local models [26,31], meanwhile alleviate the overfitting problem when the dataset is noisy. Moreover, the decision boundary of each class is forced smoother and provides a more precise estimation of uncertainty [17,23,33]. By increasing the communication rounds between local and global models, the variety of mixed samples is increased and the robustness and the generalization ability of local model is further enhanced.

2.3 Interaction

In FedInI, we devise a feature intervention strategy in Eq. (4), and λ is the weight that controls the sample-wise manifold mixup. Instead of randomly sampling from a prior beta distribution, an interaction strategy is presented to adaptively determine the value of λ for the training of each local model. Choosing the manifold mixup weight λ is non-trival as larger weights on noisy samples may damage the training process and smaller weights will only provide negligible interventional effect. An optimal intervention with mixing should consider both local training status and global noise heterogeneity. To evaluate the synchronism of local training statuses, we utilize the cosine similarity between the features extracted from current local and global model as measurement, which is computed via:

$$\lambda_{local} = \frac{1}{\sum_{(u,v)}} \frac{(M_{\bar{c}1} \oplus M_{\bar{c}2}) \cdot (M_{\hat{c}1} \oplus M_{\hat{c}2})}{\| M_{\bar{c}1} \oplus M_{\bar{c}2} \|_2 \cdot \| M_{\hat{c}1} \oplus M_{\hat{c}2} \|_2}, \tag{5}$$

where (u, v) are the locations within the feature maps. According to the equation, stronger synchronization will assign larger weight to the local features $M_{\hat{c}1}, M_{\hat{c}2}$ in the manifold space to improve of the abnormality detection performance of the network, while weaker synchronization requires to assign larger weight to global features $M_{\bar{c}1}, M_{\bar{c}2}$, and interpolated features are generated for regularizing the training process. Hence, this local measurement could balance the promoting of the recognition ability and preventing overfitting to recognition bias.

To adaptively generate weights for different samples by simultaneously considering the synchronism of training statuses and the noise heterogeneities among clients, we construct an interactive layer with three linear mapping units $\mathbf{W}_1$, $\mathbf{W}_2$, $\mathbf{W}$ that are shared among server and clients, and the global measurement λ_{global} is written as:

$$\lambda_{global} = \sigma(\mathbf{W}^T(\mathbf{W}_1(M_{\bar{c}1} \oplus M_{\bar{c}2}) \odot \mathbf{W}_2(M_{\hat{c}1} \oplus M_{\hat{c}2}))), \tag{6}$$

where $\mathbf{W}_1, \mathbf{W}_2 \in \mathbb{R}^{\frac{d}{4} \times d}$ and $\mathbf{W} \in \mathbb{R}^{\frac{d}{4}}$, d is the channel dimension of the concatenated features, and $\odot$ is the Hadamard product, which serves as the *interaction operation*. The aim of the interactive layer is to adapt to different noisy levels within each client automatically. Having obtained λ_{local} and λ_{global}, the final λ is computed via $\lambda = \lambda_{local} + \lambda_{global}$, which jointly considers the training status synchronization and the noise heterogeneity to generate sample-wise manifold mixup weight adaptively.

2.4   Learning Objective and Inference

In the training stage of FedInI, the images are simultaneously fed into the global and local models to obtain corresponding features, and Interaction is conducted to compute the mixup weights. Then, the global feature is utilized as the Intervention of the local feature. With both features before and after intervention, the overall learning objective is expressed as:

$$\mathcal{L} = \mathbb{E}_{M \sim P_{\hat{c}}}[\ell(\phi(M), \tilde{Y})] + \mathbb{E}_{M \sim P_A}[\ell(f(M, a), \tilde{Y})], \tag{7}$$

where $P_{\hat{c}}$ and P_A refers to the feature prior distribution of the current client and the intervened client, and ℓ is the loss function of the detector [21]. During inference, both Intervention and Interaction are deactivated thus no extra computation is required.

3   Experiments

3.1   Dataset and Experimental Setup

Dataset and Noise Settings. We validate our method on the large-scale abnormality detection benchmark GLRC [10,14], which has 76 colonoscopy video sequences with box labels. It contains hyperplastic and adenomatous polyps and is uniformly split into 4 clients, each client comprises 70% training and 30% testing data. To simulate the annotation mistakes, two types of noise are considered: *Class-conditional noise*, where the noisy level in each client is randomly sampled from a truncated gaussian distribution with mean 0.3 and standard deviation 0.05. *Instance-dependant noise*, we utilize a centralized model trained with clean data to measure the confidence score of each sample, then treat the low-confident ones (<80%) as easily mislabeled samples and flip their labels.

Implementation Details. We implement FedInI and state-of-the-arts using FCOS [21] in PyTorch [15]. Experiments are conducted on NVIDIA V100 GPUs. For data preprocessing, the long edge and short edge are restricted to 1333 and 800 respectively, and random horizontal flipping is adopted. The learning rate is fixed to $1e-4$ and SGD is utilized as the optimizer. We train 15 communication rounds when the global model has converged stably, with 1500 iterations per round. For evaluation, VOC average precision (mAP) [4] is computed for each client and class, and we also report the macro average for all clients.

Baselines. To validate our approach FedInI in the FADN task, we compare it with multiple baselines, which are the combinations of state-of-the-art LNL methods and FL framework. *Fed-CP* [18] performs confidence penalty for low entropy outputs within each client; *Fed-AFM* [17], which groups instances in each client and use self-attention and mixup to suppress noise; *Fed-CDR* [26] uses different update rules for critical and non-critical parameters; *Fed-SR* [37] restricts the network output to the set of permutations over a fixed vector and makes the loss robust. We also add *FedAvg* [13] and *Oracle* (training without noisy labels) for clearer comparison.

3.2   Comparison with State-of-the-Arts

As illustrated in Table 1, our method achieves the best performance on both FADN settings, with an average mAP of 89.91% in class-conditional noise and 90.15% in instance-dependant noise, meanwhile shows consistent performance advantages over other state-of-the-arts on all clients and classes. Although utilizing LNL methods such as Fed-AFM [17] and Fed-CDR [26] could improve the performance over the baseline FedAvg, their improvements are limited and restricted to certain noise scenarios. Compared with them, FedInI shows 3.13% and 6.48% gain on class-conditional noise, 1.64% and 1.58% gain on instance-dependant noise, demonstrating the significance of addressing recognition bias

Table 1. Comparisons with state-of-the-arts on different noise settings (%).

Method	Class-conditional noise						
	Client 1	Client 2	Client 3	Client 4	hyper	ade	Avg
FedAvg [13]	85.90	84.33	82.61	84.29	84.10	84.46	84.28
Fed-CP [18]	87.40	86.56	86.42	88.90	85.86	88.77	87.31
Fed-AFM [17]	87.28	87.67	84.89	87.31	87.02	86.55	86.78
Fed-CDR [26]	83.35	83.36	82.25	84.77	85.16	81.70	83.43
Fed-SR [37]	84.05	82.98	83.36	84.69	87.23	80.30	83.77
FedInI w/o Interv.	86.47	88.86	87.49	88.65	88.27	87.46	87.87
FedInI w/o Intera.	88.37	88.81	86.36	88.87	87.61	88.59	88.10
FedInI (ours)	**88.87**	**89.02**	**90.22**	**91.52**	**90.28**	**89.53**	**89.91**
Method	Instance-dependant noise						
	Client 1	Client 2	Client 3	Client 4	hyper	ade	Avg
FedAvg [13]	85.74	87.77	87.27	88.73	88.80	85.95	87.37
Fed-CP [18]	86.44	85.89	87.13	89.62	88.58	85.96	87.27
Fed-AFM [17]	88.24	88.63	88.11	89.07	89.43	87.58	88.51
Fed-CDR [26]	86.77	88.08	88.99	90.49	90.68	86.47	88.57
Fed-SR [37]	86.72	87.88	87.03	90.15	89.23	86.66	87.94
FedInI w/o Interv.	86.28	87.71	88.10	89.26	87.20	88.47	87.83
FedInI w/o Intera.	87.61	88.40	88.65	89.65	89.78	87.34	88.58
FedInI (ours)	**88.58**	**89.59**	**89.67**	**92.77**	**90.99**	**89.32**	**90.15**
Oracle	94.82	94.36	92.30	99.75	94.14	96.47	95.30

in FADN. Moreover, compared with oracle when there is no noise, FedInI only has ∼5% mAP drop on both settings with approximately 30% samples being mislabeled, which verifies the efficacy of FedInI in enhancing the robustness of the network by eliminating the bias issue caused by noise.

3.3   Further Analysis

Ablation Studies of the Components. To further validate the effectiveness of the two key operations, Intervention and Interaction, we perform detailed ablation study in Table 1. Specially, we record the performance of FedInI without Intervention (denoted as w/o Interv.) and Interaction (denoted as w/o Intera.) for both noise settings. From the Table, the model with only Interaction (using only non-shuffled local samples) and with only Intervention (using random λ and no interactive layer) bring average mAP improvements of 3.59% and 3.82% in class-conditional noise, 0.46% and 1.21% improvements in instance-dependant noise, respectively. With both strategies, the full FedInI model displays 5.63% and 2.78% improvements, demonstrating that both Intervention and Interaction play critical roles in addressing recognition bias.

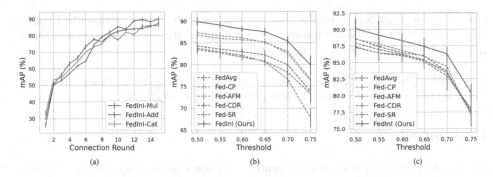

Fig. 3. (a) Performance (%) of different interaction operations with increasing the connection round. (b) Performance (%) with the variation of IOU thresholds on the class-conditional noise setting. (c) Performance (%) with the variation of IOU thresholds on the instance-dependant noise setting.

Analysis of the Interaction Operation. To study the impact of different interaction operations in Eq. (6), we conduct experiments with varying the operations and record the results in Fig. 3(a). Add and concat operations only show accuracy improvements at the beginning and saturate gradually, which may due to the diversities of their generated features are limited and the recognition bias could not be fully alleviated. When using Hadamard product (multiplication), the performance improves steadily and achieves the highest mAP of 89.91% when FI. terminates, demonstrating the effectiveness of the design in FedInI.

Analysis of the Performance with the Variation of IOU Thresholds. To evaluate the detection performance of different methods with more strict metrics, we present performance comparison of different methods with the variation of IOU thresholds from 0.5 to 0.75 in Fig. 3(b)–(c). With the threshold increases, the mAP of all methods drops continuously. However, it is noteworthy that FedInI shows superiority over other methods on all thresholds in both noise settings, demonstrating the robustness of the proposed method and its efficacy in generating unbiased and precise box predictions.

4   Conclusion

This paper presents a causality-inspired method for federated abnormality detection with noisy clients, namely FedInI. It comprises two key strategies: To decounfound the client variable that causes recognition bias, we propose Intervention to utilize server model as an approximation of the confounder set to intervene the local training; To address the issue that the global model is unconscious of the local training, an Interaction strategy is presented, which jointly considers the training status synchronization and the noise heterogeneity between clients and adaptively generate manifold mixup weights. Extensive experiments demonstrate the advantages of our framework over state-of-the-arts on class-conditional noise and instance-dependant noise settings.

Acknowledgements. This work was supported by Hong Kong Research Grants Council (RGC) General Research Fund 11211221(CityU 9043152).

References

1. Ali, S., et al.: PolypGen: a multi-center polyp detection and segmentation dataset for generalisability assessment. arXiv preprint arXiv:2106.04463 (2021)
2. Bernal, J., Histace, A.: Computer-Aided Analysis of Gastrointestinal Videos. Springer, Cham (2021). https://doi.org/10.1007/978-3-030-64340-9
3. Deng, X., Zhang, Z.: Comprehensive knowledge distillation with causal intervention. In: NeurIPS, vol. 34 (2021)
4. Everingham, M., Van Gool, L., Williams, C.K., Winn, J., Zisserman, A.: The pascal visual object classes (VOC) challenge. Int. J. Comput. Vis. **88**(2), 303–338 (2010)
5. Ghosh, A., Kumar, H., Sastry, P.: Robust loss functions under label noise for deep neural networks. In: AAAI, vol. 31 (2017)
6. Han, B., et al.: Co-teaching: robust training of deep neural networks with extremely noisy labels. In: NeurIPS, vol. 31 (2018)
7. Hu, X., Tang, K., Miao, C., Hua, X.S., Zhang, H.: Distilling causal effect of data in class-incremental learning. In: CVPR, pp. 3957–3966 (2021)
8. Jia, X., et al.: Automatic polyp recognition in colonoscopy images using deep learning and two-stage pyramidal feature prediction. IEEE Trans. Autom. Sci. Eng. **17**(3), 1570–1584 (2020)
9. Jiang, L., Zhou, Z., Leung, T., Li, L.J., Fei-Fei, L.: MentorNet: learning data-driven curriculum for very deep neural networks on corrupted labels. In: ICML, pp. 2304–2313. PMLR (2018)
10. Li, K., et al.: Colonoscopy polyp detection and classification: dataset creation and comparative evaluations. PLoS ONE **16**(8), e0255809 (2021)
11. Liu, S., Niles-Weed, J., Razavian, N., Fernandez-Granda, C.: Early-learning regularization prevents memorization of noisy labels. In: NeurIPS, vol. 33, pp. 20331–20342 (2020)
12. Liu, X., Guo, X., Liu, Y., Yuan, Y.: Consolidated domain adaptive detection and localization framework for cross-device colonoscopic images. Med. Image Anal. **71**, 102052 (2021)
13. McMahan, B., Moore, E., Ramage, D., Hampson, S., y Arcas, B.A.: Communication-efficient learning of deep networks from decentralized data. In: AISTATS, pp. 1273–1282. PMLR (2017)
14. Mesejo, P., et al.: Computer-aided classification of gastrointestinal lesions in regular colonoscopy. IEEE Trans. Med. Imag. **35**(9), 2051–2063 (2016)
15. Paszke, A., et al.: PyTorch: an imperative style, high-performance deep learning library. arXiv preprint arXiv:1912.01703 (2019)
16. Pearl, J.: Causal inference in statistics: an overview. Stat. Surv. **3**, 96–146 (2009)
17. Peng, X., Wang, K., Zeng, Z., Li, Q., Yang, J., Qiao, Yu.: Suppressing mislabeled data via grouping and self-attention. In: Vedaldi, A., Bischof, H., Brox, T., Frahm, J.-M. (eds.) ECCV 2020. LNCS, vol. 12361, pp. 786–802. Springer, Cham (2020). https://doi.org/10.1007/978-3-030-58517-4_46

18. Pereyra, G., Tucker, G., Chorowski, J., Kaiser, Ł., Hinton, G.: Regularizing neural networks by penalizing confident output distributions. arXiv preprint arXiv:1701.06548 (2017)
19. Shin, Y., Qadir, H.A., Aabakken, L., Bergsland, J., Balasingham, I.: Automatic colon polyp detection using region based deep CNN and post learning approaches. IEEE Access **6**, 40950–40962 (2018)
20. Tajbakhsh, N., Gurudu, S.R., Liang, J.: Automatic polyp detection in colonoscopy videos using an ensemble of convolutional neural networks. In: ISBI, pp. 79–83 (2015)
21. Tian, Z., Shen, C., Chen, H., He, T.: FCOS: fully convolutional one-stage object detection. In: ICCV, pp. 9627–9636 (2019)
22. Tomar, N.K., et al.: DDANet: dual decoder attention network for automatic polyp segmentation. In: Del Bimbo, A., et al. (eds.) ICPR 2021. LNCS, vol. 12668, pp. 307–314. Springer, Cham (2021). https://doi.org/10.1007/978-3-030-68793-9_23
23. Verma, V., et al.: Manifold mixup: better representations by interpolating hidden states. In: ICML, pp. 6438–6447. PMLR (2019)
24. Wang, D., et al.: AFP-Net: realtime anchor-free polyp detection in colonoscopy. In: ICTAI, pp. 636–643 (2019)
25. Wang, Y., Ma, X., Chen, Z., Luo, Y., Yi, J., Bailey, J.: Symmetric cross entropy for robust learning with noisy labels. In: ICCV, pp. 322–330 (2019)
26. Xia, X., et al.: Robust early-learning: hindering the memorization of noisy labels. In: ICLR (2020)
27. Xu, K., et al.: Show, attend and tell: neural image caption generation with visual attention. In: ICML, pp. 2048–2057. PMLR (2015)
28. Yang, Q., Zhang, J., Hao, W., Spell, G.P., Carin, L.: FLOP: federated learning on medical datasets using partial networks. In: KDD, pp. 3845–3853 (2021)
29. Yuan, Y., Meng, M.Q.H.: Automatic bleeding frame detection in the wireless capsule endoscopy images. In: ICRA, pp. 1310–1315 (2015)
30. Yue, Z., Zhang, H., Sun, Q., Hua, X.S.: Interventional few-shot learning. In: NeurIPS, vol. 33 (2020)
31. Zhang, C., Bengio, S., Hardt, M., Recht, B., Vinyals, O.: Understanding deep learning (still) requires rethinking generalization. Commun. ACM **64**(3), 107–115 (2021)
32. Zhang, D., Zhang, H., Tang, J., Hua, X.S., Sun, Q.: Causal intervention for weakly-supervised semantic segmentation. In: NeurIPS, vol. 33 (2020)
33. Zhang, H., Cisse, M., Dauphin, Y.N., Lopez-Paz, D.: Mixup: beyond empirical risk minimization. arXiv preprint arXiv:1710.09412 (2017)
34. Zhang, R., Zheng, Y., Poon, C.C., Shen, D., Lau, J.Y.: Polyp detection during colonoscopy using a regression-based convolutional neural network with a tracker. Pattern Recognit. **83**, 209–219 (2018)
35. Zhang, W., Wang, Y., Qiao, Y.: MetaCleaner: learning to hallucinate clean representations for noisy-labeled visual recognition. In: CVPR, pp. 7373–7382 (2019)
36. Zhang, Z., Sabuncu, M.R.: Generalized cross entropy loss for training deep neural networks with noisy labels. In: NeurIPS (2018)
37. Zhou, X., Liu, X., Wang, C., Zhai, D., Jiang, J., Ji, X.: Learning with noisy labels via sparse regularization. In: ICCV, pp. 72–81 (2021)
38. Zhou, Z., Shin, J., Zhang, L., Gurudu, S., Gotway, M., Liang, J.: Fine-tuning convolutional neural networks for biomedical image analysis: actively and incrementally. In: CVPR, pp. 7340–7351 (2017)

SD-LayerNet: Semi-supervised Retinal Layer Segmentation in OCT Using Disentangled Representation with Anatomical Priors

Botond Fazekas$^{(\boxtimes)}$, Guilherme Aresta, Dmitrii Lachinov, Sophie Riedl, Julia Mai, Ursula Schmidt-Erfurth, and Hrvoje Bogunović

Christian Doppler Laboratory for Artificial Intelligence in Retina, Department of Ophthalmology and Optometry, Medical University of Vienna, Vienna, Austria
{botond.fazekas,hrvoje.bogunovic}@meduniwien.ac.at

Abstract. Optical coherence tomography (OCT) is a non-invasive 3D modality widely used in ophthalmology for imaging the retina. Achieving automated, anatomically coherent retinal layer segmentation on OCT is important for the detection and monitoring of different retinal diseases, like Age-related Macular Disease (AMD) or Diabetic Retinopathy. However, the majority of state-of-the-art layer segmentation methods are based on purely supervised deep-learning, requiring a large amount of pixel-level annotated data that is expensive and hard to obtain. With this in mind, we introduce a semi-supervised paradigm into the retinal layer segmentation task that makes use of the information present in large-scale unlabeled datasets as well as anatomical priors. In particular, a novel fully differentiable approach is used for converting surface position regression into a pixel-wise structured segmentation, allowing to use both 1D surface and 2D layer representations in a coupled fashion to train the model. In particular, these 2D segmentations are used as anatomical factors that, together with learned style factors, compose disentangled representations used for reconstructing the input image. In parallel, we propose a set of anatomical priors to improve network training when a limited amount of labeled data is available. We demonstrate on the real-world dataset of scans with intermediate and wet-AMD that our method outperforms state-of-the-art when using our full training set, but more importantly largely exceeds state-of-the-art when it is trained with a fraction of the labeled data.

Keywords: Retinal layer segmentation · Semi-supervised learning · OCT

Supplementary Information The online version contains supplementary material available at https://doi.org/10.1007/978-3-031-16452-1_31.

L. Wang et al. (Eds.): MICCAI 2022, LNCS 13438, pp. 320–329, 2022.
https://doi.org/10.1007/978-3-031-16452-1_31

1 Introduction

Optical Coherence Tomography (OCT) is currently the main imaging modality for monitoring retinal disease and guiding treatment. With it, ophthalmologists can assess several imaging biomarkers including retinal layer thickness, an important maker for pathologies like Age-related Macular Degeneration (AMD), a leading cause of blindness worldwide [2]. However, the clinicians' workload and the large size of the acquired volumes make manual layer delineation almost prohibitive in clinical practice. Therefore, automated retinal layer segmentation methods have been pursued as soon as OCTs became widely available.

Initial automated layer segmentation approaches, such as the IOWA Reference Algorithms [9,17], relied on hand-crafted features, graph algorithms, and dynamic programming to estimate surface positions. These methods can fulfill hard constraints such as topological ordering, layer smoothness, or prior layer thickness. However, the reliance on hand-crafted image features hinders generalization to severe or rare pathologies, image acquisition noise, or artifacts. Over the past years, the emergence of deep learning-based (DL) segmentation models significantly reduced the need for handcrafted features. One of the first DL approaches [13] used a U-Net [12] to classify each pixel of the input image as one of 9 retinal layers, background or possibly fluid-filled pockets, which may lead to segmentation of layers on anatomically implausible locations. This can be circumvented with an edge detection network that predicts only a single location for a layer in an A-scan [16]. However, none of these two approaches accounted for hard anatomical constraints. Contrary to this, the method of He et al. [6,7] outputs per layer a pixel-wise labeling and a softmax mapping that encodes the most probable location of the layer boundary, with the two representations being decoupled. Layer ordering is imposed by predicting the positions of the shallower surface and iteratively rectifying all subsequent surfaces to ensure that they have higher depth, which significantly improved the state-of-the-art.

Despite the near expert-level performance of segmentation methods on healthy OCT scans or scans with common pathologies, current approaches struggle with severe or rare pathologies for which they often require a large number of annotated samples for training. However, acquiring annotated data is time-consuming and costly. Semi-supervised approaches address this problem by exploiting the abundantly available unlabeled data. A limited number of proposed methods for retinal layer segmentation make use of semi-supervised training by using a second network to generate an adversarial loss [10,14,15], but fail to incorporate retinal anatomical priors. A promising solution is to use disentangled learning, which has already been successfully applied to other medical imaging tasks. In particular, Chartsias et al. [3] proposed a disentangled representation learning model for cardiac image analysis, called Spatial Decomposition Network (SD-Net). The network creates a strictly disjoint representation of binary spatial anatomical information and non-spatial modality-dependent style. Subsequently, these two factors are used to reconstruct the original image. With a few labeled instances and an optional adversarial loss function, a subset of the anatomical factors can be encouraged to represent meaningful anatomical regions.

In this paper, we propose Spatial Decomposition Layer Segmentation Network (SD-LayerNet), a fully convolutional semi-supervised retinal layer segmentation approach that allows to significantly reduce the amount of annotated training data required to achieve state-of-the-art performance by using disentangled representations and anatomical priors. Specifically, our main contributions are 1. a **fully differentiable topological engine**, that allows converting surface positions to pixel-wise structured segmentations, while guaranteeing the correct topological ordering, enabling the coupled use of both 1D and 2D representations of the retinal layers to train the network; 2. a set of tailored retinal **anatomical priors** encoded as self-supervised loss terms, which improve the performance when training with very limited amounts of labeled data; and 3. evaluation of the method on a large clinical dataset with challenging **real-world intermediate and wet-AMD** cases.

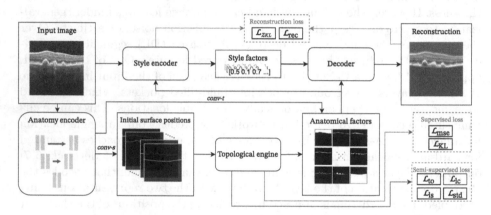

Fig. 1. Our network has two input branches. First, an anatomy encoder with two output branches is used for feature extraction. One output is directly used as a single spatial texture factor, while the other generates a probability map of the layer positions. A topological engine guarantees the correct ordering of the layers and generates the spatial maps of the layer. The second input branch of the network is connected to a style encoder that generates the style factors, which encodes the intensity values of the anatomical factors. The decoder generates the reconstructed image from the style and anatomical factors. Depending on whether layer annotations are available for the input image, a supervised loss (red arrow) or a self-supervised loss (blue arrow) is minimized. Regardless of the availability, the reconstruction loss (purple arrow) is always applied. (Color figure online)

2   Model Architecture

Our model (Fig. 1), uses both annotated and non-annotated images to learn to segment S retinal surfaces on OCT image by reconstructing input image from disentangled representation [3]. In particular, an anatomy encoder infers the initial surface positions and one textural factor. The topological engine converts the surface positions into 2D layer representations, to form with the textural factors the anatomical factors. These spatial factors, together with inferred style factors that encode gray-scale intensity, compose the disentangled representations from which the input image is reconstructed.

2.1 Anatomical Factor Generation

A Residual Attention U-Net [4] with four encoder and four decoder stages and PReLU activation is used as the feature extractor for the anatomical factor generation. The network has two output branches: 1. *conv-s* for surface position regression and 2. *conv-t*, for texture factor generation. The texture factor branch *conv-t* has a single sigmoid activated channel output, which is concatenated to the anatomical factors created from the surface position regressions, and is aimed at capturing the speckle noise present in the scans.

Layer Position Regression. Let W and H be the width and height of the input OCT slice (B-scan) with S surfaces to segment. For each B-scan, *conv-s* estimates a position distribution map $P_{W \times H \times S}$ via a column-wise (A-scan) softmax function [7]. In particular, for each A-scan i, $P(Y \mid i, s)$ is a probability mass function (PMF) that encodes the probability of Y taking A-scan position r for surface s. The surface position y_i^s at the A-scan i of surface s is then inferred as a mean value of Y, $y_i^s = \sum_r r \cdot P(r \mid i, s)$. Then, anatomical layer ordering is imposed by iteratively updating the inferred layer boundary positions, as in [6,7]: $y_i^s = y_i^{s-1} + \left| y_i^s - y_i^{s-1} \right|_+$.

Topologically Correct Anatomical Factors. We then use a novel *topological engine* to convert the surface probability maps P to S anatomical factors $M_{W \times H}$. The *topological engine* performs the column-wise top-down cumulative sum of each P^s, obtaining a representation C^s which has values close to 0 above y^s and close to 1 below it. Again, to guarantee the correct topological ordering, we iteratively update the generated surfaces: $M^s = \left| C^k + C^{k-1} - 1 \right|_+$. Then, to have mutually exclusive spatial maps for the retinal layers, we decompose the cumulative surface maps to layer maps iteratively by setting $M^s = M^s - M^{s+1}$.

The layer maps M and the texture factor are rounded to the nearest integers, forming the anatomical factors of the disentangled representation.

Supervised Training with Layer Annotations. During training, we alternate between a supervised and a self-supervised model update, depending on the availability of layer annotations. For supervised training, two loss terms are used: 1. $\mathcal{L}_{\mathrm{KL}}$, which describes the target distribution of $P(Y \mid i, s)$, and 2. $\mathcal{L}_{\mathrm{mse}}$, which penalizes wrongly regressed layer boundary locations with mean square error (MSE). For $\mathcal{L}_{\mathrm{KL}}$ in particular, we model $P(Y \mid i, s)$ as a normal distribution to accommodate possible pixel-wise imprecision of the annotations. For each A-scan i, the distribution's mean is the reference standard position μ_i^s of the surface and the standard deviation σ is a hyperparameter. The mean Kullback-Leibler (KL) divergence [8] is used as a loss term during the training to encourage the network to learn the target distribution [6], leading to the supervised loss:

$$\mathcal{L}_{\text{sup}} = \lambda_1 \mathcal{L}_{\text{KL}} + \lambda_2 \mathcal{L}_{\text{mse}} = \lambda_1 \sum_s \sum_r \sum_i P(r \mid i, s) \cdot P(i, s) \ln \frac{P(r \mid i, s)}{T(r \mid i, s)}$$
$$+ \lambda_2 \frac{1}{S \cdot W} \sum_s \sum_i (y_i^s - \mu_i^s)^2 \tag{1}$$

where $T(Y \mid i, s) \sim N(\mu_i^s \mid \sigma)$ is the target probability map containing a Gaussian normal distribution and λ are weighting factors.

Self-supervised Training with Anatomical Priors. We propose a set of tailored constraints to promote segmenting anatomically coherent surfaces. These are used whenever annotations are not available, and this extra supervision signal provided is especially important in scenarios with very limited training data.
1. *Topological ordering constraint.* Since retinal layers are strictly ordered, we encourage minimizing the number and magnitude of the mean topological ordering violations among A-scans: $\mathcal{L}_{\text{to}} = \frac{1}{W} \sum_s \sum_i |y_i^{s-1} - y_i^s|_+$.
2. *Surface continuity constraint.* To promote surface continuity, we penalize position differences between two adjacent A-scans larger than a layer specific constant c_s, derived from the training annotations: $\mathcal{L}_{\text{lc}} = \frac{1}{W} \sum_s \sum_i \left| |y_i^s - y_{i+1}^s| - c_s \right|_+$.
3. *Surface slope constraint.* We encourage the curvature of the surfaces to be within an expected range, as each of them have an inherent maximum slope, assuming B-scans with low inclination. For instance, normally, the maximum slope of the BM (Suppl. Fig. 1) is lower than of RPE in the presence of AMD. The annotated train data is used for computing a maximum expected slope o_s per layer for A-scans δ pixels apart (δ is a tunable hyperparameter). Each inferred surface slope greater than o_s is penalized: $\mathcal{L}_{\text{ls}} = \frac{1}{W} \sum_s \sum_i \left| \frac{|y_i^s - y_{i+\delta}^s|}{\delta} - o_s \right|_+$.
4. *Probability distribution standard deviation constraint.* We minimize the number of probable adjacent vertical positions for each surface on $P(Y|i, s)$ to encourage the network to settle at a specific layer boundary position and to predict a Gaussian with small variance, similarly to $\mathcal{L}_{\text{KL}}$. First, we compute the standard deviation for each A-scan i, $\hat{\sigma}_i^s$. We then penalize predicting locations with high uncertainty by introducing a maximum threshold for $\hat{\sigma}_i^s$: $\mathcal{L}_{\text{std}} = \sum_s \sum_i |\hat{\sigma}_i^s - t|_+$, where t is a tunable hyperparameter.

2.2 Image Reconstruction

Style Factor Generation. The style factor generation follows the modality factor generation in Chartsias *et al.* [3]. In particular, a Variational Autoencoder (VAE) generates the style factors, which are later used in the reconstruction part. During training, the loss term $\mathcal{L}_{z_{\text{KL}}}$ [3] minimizes the KL divergence of the estimated Gaussian distribution from the unit Gaussian.

Image Decoder. The image decoder block is similar to Chartsias *et al.* [3], where the style and the binarized anatomical factors are combined to create an image of the same size as the input. The fusion is achieved via a model conditioned with four FiLM [11] layers. This method only scales and offsets the intensities of the anatomical factors, ensuring that no spatial information is passed through the style factors. The reconstruction loss $\mathcal{L}_{rec}$ is the Mean Absolute Error of the pixel intensities of the original and reconstructed images between the predicted ILM and BM, the top-most and the bottom-most surfaces, to avoid the influence of the noisy region outside the retina.

The overall cost function **L** is a composition of the style encoder loss, the reconstruction loss and the mean of the supervised $\mathcal{L}_{sup} = \lambda_1 \mathcal{L}_{KL} + \lambda_2 \mathcal{L}_{mse}$ and self-supervised $\mathcal{L}_{self} = \lambda_3 \mathcal{L}_{to} + \lambda_4 \mathcal{L}_{lc} + \lambda_5 \mathcal{L}_{ls} + \lambda_6 \mathcal{L}_{std}$ loss:

$$\mathbf{L} = \lambda_7 \mathcal{L}_{zKL} + \lambda_8 \mathcal{L}_{rec} + \frac{1}{2} \left(\mathcal{L}_{sup} + \mathcal{L}_{self} \right)$$

3 Experimental Results

Dataset. The proposed method was trained and evaluated on an internal dataset of 459 volumetric OCT scans of 459 eyes spanning intermediate and late wet-AMD real-world clinical cases. The scans were acquired with Spectralis scanners (Heidelberg Engineering) consisting of $(512 \times 19 \times 496) - (1024 \times 49 \times 496)$ voxels covering a $6 \times 6 \times 2\,\mathrm{mm}^3$ volume. For 68 volumes, 7 B-scans uniformly spaced across the volume contained manual layer annotations by experts, totaling 476 annotated B-scans. The 68 volumes were randomly split into a training set, containing 54 volumes, and into validation and test sets, each containing 7 volumes. The remaining 391 scans without annotations were used for the self-supervised training set.

Training Details. The volumes were normalized volume-wise to zero mean and unit standard deviation. During training, B-scans were randomly flipped horizontally ($p = 0.3$) to augment the data.

The loss weight terms λ_7 and λ_8 are the same as in [3]. The remaining loss hyperparameters were optimized via grid-search on the validation set. In particular, these values were initially set to 1 and were either scaled up or down by 5 or 10. The network was trained for 50 epochs (approx. 1 h of training time) and the best-performing configuration was selected, leading to $\lambda_1 = \lambda_2 = 50, \lambda_3 = \lambda_4 = \lambda_5 = \lambda_8 = 1, \lambda_6 = \lambda_7 = 0.1$. The low value of λ_6 allows more flexibility in scenarios where a layer might be not present or invisible, and thus a larger $\hat{\sigma}_i^s$ is possible. The high values of λ_1 and λ_2 promote correct layer boundaries and allow to counter-balance the reconstruction loss, which could otherwise encourage layers with similar intensities to be in the same anatomical factor. For $\mathcal{L}_{std}$, $\mathcal{L}_{ls}$ and $\mathcal{L}_{KL}$ we used $t = 1$, $\delta = 10$ and $\sigma = 0.5$, respectively. These values were also determined with grid-search after fixing all λs. The values of c_s and o_s are presented in the supplementary material.

The training was done with a batch size of 14 with 7 labeled and 7 unlabeled samples, using a MADGRAD optimizer [5] with a learning rate of 10^{-4}. To mitigate training instabilities, a gradient norm clipping was applied with a maximum norm of 0.5. We trained all of the methods for 300 iterations and the models with the lowest average root mean squared error (RMSE) on the validation set were picked for testing.

The training was performed in a mixed-precision setting on an Nvidia GeForce RTX 2080 Ti GPU, with an Intel Xeon Silver 4114 CPU with 16 cores, under CentOS 7, using Python 3.8.8 and PyTorch 1.8.1. The training lasted for 6 h on this computer setup. The source code of our implementation is available at http://github.com/ABotond/SD-LayerNet.

Experiments. We compared our method to both supervised and a semi-supervised *baselines*. The supervised baseline was the state-of-the-art boundary regression method from He *et al.* [7], using an Attention Res-U-Net for feature extraction. To ease comparison, B-scan flattening and cropping were not performed, and instead, we use the same input as for our method. The semi-supervised baseline was SD-Net [3], which classifies the pixels into surfaces classes similarly to [13], but it is assisted with self-supervised training. We used the same optimizer and learning rate as for our method, while the other hyperparameter were kept from the original methods.

We conducted *ablation studies* on our method to assess the effect on the performance of the anatomical priors, texture factor, and image reconstruction. Further, we conducted an experiment by combining the method of He *et al.* with the additional priors.

To evaluate the methods' performance with a limited number of labeled samples, the networks were trained on a 50%, 25%, and 15% randomly reduced subset of the training set, while ensuring that all original training volumes were still represented. For instance, for the 15% training set a single B-scan was randomly selected from each of the annotated volumes. We conducted a statistical test with a linear mixed-effect model [1], which takes the interdependency of the B-scans from the same volume into account.

Results. Our baseline comparison study (Table 1) shows a significant improvement upon the two baseline methods in all subsets of the training set, with error reductions ranging from 18% when training on the full training set up to a 30% lower error rate when training on a reduced training set. In particular, our method, when trained on 15% of the training set, performed only 7% worse than the He *et al.* method trained on the full set, while yielding more consistent results, as indicated by the lower standard deviation. Also, the introduced prior knowledge allows for a more robust segmentation, specially on pathological regions (Fig. 2). These results support our hypothesis that incorporating a self-supervised paradigm, with disentangled learning, can considerably improve the data efficiency of layer regression methods.

The ablation study (Table 1) shows that the newly proposed anatomical priors $\mathcal{L}_{\mathrm{self}}$ and the texture factor contributed to lower the segmentation error. Indeed, $\mathcal{L}_{\mathrm{self}}$ improves the performance and consistency both of our method and

Table 1. Average B-scan-wise root mean square error (μm) and standard deviation of the proposed method and the baselines for different percentages of the training set. * indicates statistical difference to our method ($p < 0.05$)

Method	Subset size			
	15%	25%	50%	100%
SD-Net ≈ [3]	14.10 ± 11.26*	11.76 ± 8.06*	9.77 ± 5.43*	9.44 ± 5.20*
He *et al.* ≈ [7]	10.48 ± 5.95*	10.16 ± 6.96*	7.6 ± 4.18*	7.06 ± 3.44*
He *et al.* $+ \mathcal{L}_{self}$	10.35 ± 2.49*	8.63 ± 1.72*	7.38 ± 2.03*	6.86 ± 1.24*
Ours without *conv-t*	10.28 ± 4.34*	8.64 ± 2.33*	7.41 ± 2.03*	7.11 ± 1.87*
Ours without $\mathcal{L}_{self}$	8.12 ± 4.44	7.04 ± 3.57	6.55 ± 2.47	$\mathbf{5.79 \pm 1.33}$
Ours	$\mathbf{7.57 \pm 2.94}$	$\mathbf{6.95 \pm 1.69}$	$\mathbf{6.38 \pm 1.53}$	5.82 ± 1.32

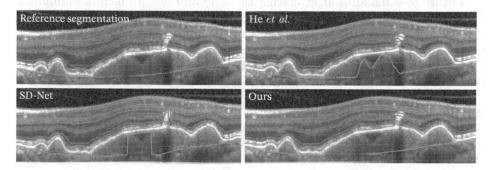

Fig. 2. Manual reference segmentations and models' predictions (from upper surface ILM to bottom surface BM).

of He *et al.* , indicating that this additional information is guiding the network to a better local optimum. Also, the texture factor (e.g. Fig. 3), alleviates the reconstruction burden and improves segmentation by enabling the anatomical factors to map solely the expected position and overall intensity of the layers.

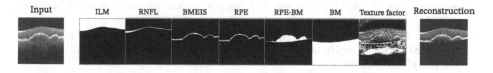

Fig. 3. A sample subset of the anatomical factors (six out of 12), and the texture factor for an intermediate AMD case.

4   Conclusion

Our data-efficient layer segmentation model outperforms the current state of the art by a large margin on our test set. In particular, the proposed fully-differentiable topological engine allows to use both 1D surface and 2D layer information in a coupled fashion to train the model. This module and the anatomical priors encoded on dedicated loss terms allow to efficiently make use of large amounts of unlabeled data by guiding the network to create mutually exclusive anatomically constrained spatial representations of the layers to reconstruct the input image. The applicability of the proposed method is not restricted to retinal layer segmentation but can be applied to any nested anatomy and where the thickness of a tissue is measured (e.g. inner and outer vessel lumen wall, cardiac wall, knee cartilage, etc.).

Future research aims at exploiting the style and texture factors to improve the generalization of the model. In particular, forcing the texture factor to have complete anatomical independence and a more dedicated use of the style factor may allow this method to be used for other tasks such as denoising, synthetic B-scan generation for data augmentation, and improved performance (or even image conversion) across different imaging devices.

Acknowledgements. The financial support by the Christian Doppler Research Association, Austrian Federal Ministry for Digital and Economic Affairs, the National Foundation for Research, Technology and Development, and Heidelberg Engineering is gratefully acknowledged.

References

1. Bates, D., Mächler, M., Bolker, B., Walker, S.: Fitting linear mixed-effects models using lme4. arXiv preprint arXiv:1406.5823 (2014)
2. Bressler, N.M.: Age-related macular degeneration is the leading cause of blindness. JAMA **291**(15), 1900–1901 (2004)
3. Chartsias, A., et al.: Disentangled representation learning in cardiac image analysis. Med. Image Anal. **58**, 101535 (2019)
4. Chen, X., Yao, L., Zhang, Y.: Residual attention u-net for automated multi-class segmentation of COVID-19 chest CT images. arXiv preprint arXiv:2004.05645 (2020)
5. Defazio, A., Jelassi, S.: Adaptivity without compromise: a momentumized, adaptive, dual averaged gradient method for stochastic optimization. arXiv:2101.11075 [cs, math], August 2021
6. He, Y., et al.: Fully convolutional boundary regression for retina OCT segmentation. In: Shen, D., et al. (eds.) MICCAI 2019. LNCS, vol. 11764, pp. 120–128. Springer, Cham (2019). https://doi.org/10.1007/978-3-030-32239-7_14
7. He, Y., et al.: Structured layer surface segmentation for retina OCT using fully convolutional regression networks. Med. Image Anal. **68**, 101856 (2021)
8. Kullback, S., Leibler, R.A.: On information and sufficiency. Ann. Math. Stat. **22**(1), 79–86 (1951). https://doi.org/10.1214/aoms/1177729694

9. Li, K., Wu, X., Chen, D., Sonka, M.: Optimal surface segmentation in volumetric images-a graph-theoretic approach. IEEE Trans. Pattern Anal. Mach. Intell. **28**(1), 119–134 (2006). https://doi.org/10.1109/TPAMI.2006.19

10. Liu, X., et al.: Semi-supervised automatic segmentation of layer and fluid region in retinal optical coherence tomography images using adversarial learning. IEEE Access **7**, 3046–3061 (2019). https://doi.org/10.1109/ACCESS.2018.2889321

11. Perez, E., Strub, F., de Vries, H., Dumoulin, V., Courville, A.: FiLM: visual reasoning with a general conditioning layer. In: Proceedings of the AAAI Conference on Artificial Intelligence, vol. 32, no. 1, April 2018. https://ojs.aaai.org/index.php/AAAI/article/view/11671

12. Ronneberger, O., Fischer, P., Brox, T.: U-Net: convolutional networks for biomedical image segmentation. In: Navab, N., Hornegger, J., Wells, W.M., Frangi, A.F. (eds.) MICCAI 2015. LNCS, vol. 9351, pp. 234–241. Springer, Cham (2015). https://doi.org/10.1007/978-3-319-24574-4_28

13. Roy, A.G., et al.: ReLayNet: retinal layer and fluid segmentation of macular optical coherence tomography using fully convolutional networks. Biomed. Opt. Express **8**(8), 3627–3642 (2017). https://doi.org/10.1364/BOE.8.003627

14. Sedai, S., Antony, B., Mahapatra, D., Garnavi, R.: Joint segmentation and uncertainty visualization of retinal layers in optical coherence tomography images using bayesian deep learning. In: Stoyanov, D., et al. (eds.) OMIA/COMPAY -2018. LNCS, vol. 11039, pp. 219–227. Springer, Cham (2018). https://doi.org/10.1007/978-3-030-00949-6_26

15. Sedai, S., et al.: Uncertainty guided semi-supervised segmentation of retinal layers in OCT images. In: Shen, D., et al. (eds.) MICCAI 2019. LNCS, vol. 11764, pp. 282–290. Springer, Cham (2019). https://doi.org/10.1007/978-3-030-32239-7_32

16. Sousa, J.A., et al.: Automatic segmentation of retinal layers in OCT images with intermediate age-related macular degeneration using U-Net and DexiNed. PLoS ONE **16**(5) (2021). https://doi.org/10.1371/journal.pone.0251591

17. Zhang, L., Sonka, M., Folk, J.C., Russell, S.R., Abrámoff, M.D.: Quantifying disrupted outer retinal-subretinal layer in SD-OCT images in choroidal neovascularization. Investig. Ophthalmol. Vis. Sci. **55**(4), 2329 2335 (2014). https://doi.org/10.1167/iovs.13-13048

Physiology-Based Simulation of the Retinal Vasculature Enables Annotation-Free Segmentation of OCT Angiographs

Martin J. Menten[1,2(✉)], Johannes C. Paetzold[1,2], Alina Dima[1],
Bjoern H. Menze[3], Benjamin Knier[4], and Daniel Rueckert[1,2]

[1] Lab for AI in Medicine, Klinikum rechts der Isar, Technical University of Munich, Munich, Germany
martin.menten@tum.de
[2] BioMedIA, Department of Computing, Imperial College London, London, UK
[3] Department of Quantitative Biomedicine, University of Zurich, Zurich, Switzerland
[4] Department of Neurology, Klinikum rechts der Isar, Technical University of Munich, Munich, Germany

Abstract. Optical coherence tomography angiography (OCTA) can non-invasively image the eye's circulatory system. In order to reliably characterize the retinal vasculature, there is a need to automatically extract quantitative metrics from these images. The calculation of such biomarkers requires a precise semantic segmentation of the blood vessels. However, deep-learning-based methods for segmentation mostly rely on supervised training with voxel-level annotations, which are costly to obtain.

In this work, we present a pipeline to synthesize large amounts of realistic OCTA images with intrinsically matching ground truth labels; thereby obviating the need for manual annotation of training data. Our proposed method is based on two novel components: 1) a physiology-based simulation that models the various retinal vascular plexuses and 2) a suite of physics-based image augmentations that emulate the OCTA image acquisition process including typical artifacts.

In extensive benchmarking experiments, we demonstrate the utility of our synthetic data by successfully training retinal vessel segmentation algorithms. Encouraged by our method's competitive quantitative and superior qualitative performance, we believe that it constitutes a versatile tool to advance the quantitative analysis of OCTA images.

1 Introduction

Optical coherence tomography angiography (OCTA) allows the non-invasive acquisition of high-fidelity volumetric images of the eye's circulatory system [29].

Supplementary Information The online version contains supplementary material available at https://doi.org/10.1007/978-3-031-16452-1_32.

It has become an important tool for ophthalmologists to diagnose and monitor ocular diseases that manifest themselves as pathological changes to the eye's vessels [9]. Furthermore, the retina has been described as "window to the body" as alterations to its vasculature have been linked to various neurological and cardiac diseases [13,16]. In order to improve the understanding and treatment of these conditions, it is crucial to automatically extract quantitative metrics that characterize the retinal vasculature. The calculation of many of these biomarkers requires a precise semantic segmentation of the blood vessels.

Recently, deep learning has seen wide-ranging success in the semantic segmentation of medical images, including the segmentation of blood vessels in angiographs. However, training of these algorithms is mostly based on large sets of annotated data, which are time-consuming to curate. Creating voxel-level annotations of the complex branching retinal vasculature in OCTA images is particularly cumbersome. Until now, only two publicly available OCTA datasets with voxel-wise annotations have been released [12,17]. With 226 and 500 images, respectively, these datasets are several orders of magnitude smaller than the largest medical image datasets and a dataset with three-dimensional annotations has not been published yet. There is a clear need for new strategies that are independent of manual labeling to further advance the quantitative analysis of OCTA images.

To address this need, we present a pipeline that can synthesize large amounts of realistic OCTA images with intrinsically matching ground truth labels (see Fig. 1). Our proposed method is based on two novel components: 1) a physiology-based simulation that models the various retinal vascular plexuses and 2) a suite of physics-based image augmentations that emulate the OCTA image acquisition process including typical artifacts.

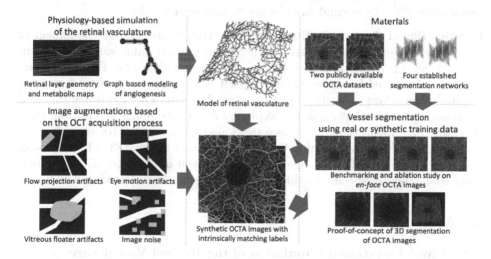

Fig. 1. Overview of the proposed method and conducted experiments.

We evaluate the utility of our synthetically generated data for the training of supervised vessel segmentation algorithms. In extensive benchmarking experiments involving four neural network architectures and two publicly available OCTA datasets, we compare the segmentation results when training on synthetic OCTA image-label pairs versus real OCTA images with expert-derived annotations. Additionally, we quantify the intrinsic scalability of our approach and investigate how it can facilitate segmentation of the retinal vasculature in three-dimensional OCTA images.

2   Related Works

Deep-Learning-Based Segmentation of OCTA Images. Similar to most segmentation tasks, convolutional neural networks constitute the top-performing methods for segmentation of tubular structures [4]. However, the adoption of supervised deep learning for retinal vessel segmentation in OCTA images has been limited due to a lack of annotated data [11,12,17]. Beyond supervised learning, Liu *et al.* have recently presented an unsupervised method for OCTA segmentation that does not rely on expert-derived labels [15]. However, their method requires multiple scans of the same subject acquired with scanners from different manufacturers, which are usually unobtainable in clinical practice.

Learning with Synthetic Data. One way to overcome data sparsity in machine learning is transfer learning from synthetically generated data. Here, models are pretrained on artificial data and then refined on a small set of real image-label pairs. In medical image segmentation, this approach has been successfully applied to the segmentation of brain tumors [14], endotracheal tubes [3] and catheters [7] as well as tubular structures, such as the whole mouse brain vasculature [32], the dermal vasculature [6] and neurons [20].

Physics-Based Augmentations. Another strategy to mitigate the impact of sparse data is image augmentation, where additional training samples are generated based on heuristic transformations of existing data [26]. However, many augmentations used for natural images do not translate to the medical domain as the underlying data acquisition processes are different. This motivates the need for transformations that emulate the physics of medical image acquisition. Such specialized augmentations have been developed for computed tomography [19], magnetic resonance tomography [24] and ultrasound imaging [31]. Even though the physics behind OCTA image acquisition is well understood [27], data augmentation schemes specific to this modality have not been introduced to date.

3   Methods

3.1   Physiology-Based Simulation of the Retinal Vasculature

In order to generate diverse and realistic models of the retinal vasculature, we adapt and extend a physiology-based simulation by Schneider *et al.* [23]. In the following, we briefly describe their method before presenting our key novel contributions that allow us to model the highly unique vasculature of the retina (see Fig. 2).

In Schneider *et al.*'s simulation, blood vessels are represented as a forest of rooted tree graphs. Each graph node encodes a vessel segment modeled as a cylindrical tube with a specific radius, length and position as well as connectivity information to its parent vessel and up to two children. These trees are grown iteratively in a multi-scale fashion. At each simulation step, the concentration maps of oxygen and vascular endothelial growth factor (VEGF) are calculated depending on the spatial configuration of the vessel trees. High VEGF concentration, which drives the growth of new blood vessels, will primarily occur in regions of low perfusion. To counteract the lack of oxygen, new vessels develop from nearby graph nodes via sprouting, elongation or bifurcation. Vessel formation adheres to rules derived from fluid dynamics that enforce morphologically plausible branching statistics.

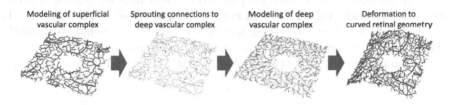

| Modeling of superficial vascular complex | Sprouting connections to deep vascular complex | Modeling of deep vascular complex | Deformation to curved retinal geometry |

Fig. 2. Main steps during the modeling of retinal vessel graphs. Additional examples can be found in the supplementary material.

Sequential Simulation of the Retinal Vascular Complexes. The inner retina is supplied with blood by four vascular plexuses, which can be grouped into two complexes: the supervicial vascular complex (SVC) and the deep vascular complex (DVC) [2,9]. We sequentially simulate these vascular complexes according to their order in blood stream direction.

The SVC features several large arterioles that branch out as they run towards the center of the retina. Its simulation is initialized with large vessel stumps that are radially distributed along the edges of the volume. The SVC leads to the DVC, which primarily consists of smaller, sprawling vessels. After the SVC's simulation has converged, we calculate the chance of each vessel node to form a vertical sprout following the global branching statistics [23]. These sprouts are used as initial seeding vessels for the simulation of the DVC. We have heuristically tuned the simulations' hyperparameters so that the generated vasculature models mimic the morphological statistics of the SVC and DVC, respectively. We provide the two sets of hyperparameters and rationale for these settings in the supplementary material.

Modeling of Regions with Low Angiogenesis. The outer retinal layers, which are responsible for the sensing of light, are not directly perfused. Furthermore, all retinal plexuses feature a region devoid of blood vessels at their center, the foveal avascular zone, so that light can pass through to the photoreceptor layers [30]. The lack of angiogenesis in these regions is induced by enforcing a reduced secretion of VEGF using binary masks. The shape of these masks is based on previously reported sizes for the retinal layers and the foveal avascular zone [22].

Deformation to the Retinal Layer Structure. We model both vascular complexes inside thin rectangular volumes before deforming the vessel graphs to the typical curved shape of the retina as it appears in OCT and OCTA images. To this end, we use the IOWA reference algorithms to extract retinal layer segmentations from anatomical OCT scans contained in the OCTA-500 dataset [1,5,10,12]. The SVC is sheared to adhere to the shape of the ganglion cell layer. The DVC is deformed to the relief of the inner nuclear layer. Afterwards, we remodel the entire vascular tree one final time in order to enforce physiologically correct branching angles and vessel thinning along blood flow direction.

Conversion to Gray-Scale Images. By running the simulation with varying starting conditions, retinal layer shapes and random number generator seeds, we are able to obtain a diverse set of realistic retinal vessel graphs. The graphs are converted to voxelized gray-scale images with matching ground truth labels. For the following experiments we generate both two-dimensional *en-face* images (i.e. maximum intensity projections onto the axial plane) and three-dimensional image volumes.

3.2   Image Augmentations Based on the OCTA Acquisition Process

Next, we apply a series of newly developed image transformations that simulate image features and artifacts introduced during OCTA acquisition (see Fig. 3). We briefly describe these physics-based augmentations below, while providing pseudo-code and hyperparameters in the supplementary material.

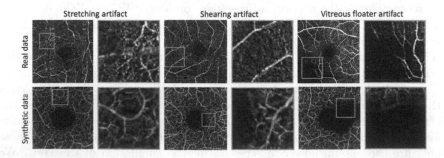

Fig. 3. *En-face* OCTA images and close-up views of common artifacts in real OCT images from the ROSE dataset [17] and representative samples of our synthetically generated dataset. Additional examples can be found in the supplementary material.

Flow Projection Artifacts. OCTA resolves the temporal variation of successive scans of the same volume. Blood cells flowing through the vessels will display as bright signal, while stationary tissue will appear dark. However, as the imaging beam traverses the retina, blood vessels will cast a shadow onto the deeper parts of the retina. This shadow is detected as temporally changing signal and wrongly appears as blood flow in the calculated angiograph [27]. We simulate such artifacts by identifying all vessels inside the volume that exceed a certain radius. Subsequently, we increase the image brightness along the projection of these vessels in the imaging beam's direction.

Eye Motion Artifacts. Volumetric OCTA scans are usually acquired in a rasterized fashion, in which multiple B-scans and small imaging patches are merged together in a postprocessing step. Movement of the subject's eye or head during imaging may result in discontinuities between adjacent B-scans or so-called quilting artifacts at the border of the patches [27]. We simulate four different motion artifacts along random horizontal and vertical cuts of the synthetic images: shearing, stretching, buckling and whiteout. The first three are modeled by shifting the intensity values on one side of the cut perpendicular to the imaging direction. The latter one is modeled as uniform noise along the cut and emulates a complete signal decorrelation in a single B-scan.

Vitreous Floater Artifacts. During acquisition of retinal OCTA images, the light beam and its reflection pass through several transparent components of the eye, including the cornea, pupil, lens and vitreous. Opaque objects inside these structures, in particular vitreous floaters, can cause a loss of spatial coherence of the imaging beam that manifests itself as darkened areas in the image [27]. We model the typical thread-like shape of vitreous floaters as a graph of multiple connected line segments with random thickness, length and orientation. We determine the projection of the resulting polygon in imaging direction and reduce the signal in this region.

Background Signal Caused by Capillary Vessels. At its smallest scale, the circulatory system branches into numerous capillary vessels. OCTA scanners are typically unable to resolve these small blood vessels, which appear as milky background signal in the image [28]. It is computationally infeasible to simulate the entire capillary vasculature, so that the background of our synthetic images appears unrealistically empty. To account for this limitation, we add binomial noise, which is blurred by a Gaussian filter.

4 Experiments and Results

We evaluate the utility of our synthetic data in several benchmarking experiments using the publicly available ROSE-1 dataset [17]. We train supervised vessel segmentation algorithms using either synthetic OCTA image-label pairs ("synthetic") or real OCTA images with expert-derived labels ("real"). For all experiments we assess the algorithms' performance on real OCTA images by calculating accuracy (ACC), area under the receiver operating characteristic curve (AUC), F1-score (DICE) and the topology-aware centerline DICE (clDICE) [25].

We adapt network implementations, data preprocessing and hyperparameter settings from Ma *et al.*[1]. Diverging from their approach that uses a fixed number of training epochs, we introduce an independent validation split for model selection. As a result the absolute performance and relative rankings of the vary algorithms may slightly differ compared to their reported results. All results are reported as mean and standard deviation across five cross-validation splits.

We find that the use of synthetic data facilitates vessel segmentation in OCTA images across all four considered neural network architectures. However, the quantitative scores are consistently lower than those of networks that were trained on the same domain (see Table 1). Qualitatively, we find our segmentations to be superior (see Fig. 4). We suspect that this discrepancy is caused by a systematic difference in the datasets' annotations. The expert labels in the

Table 1. Performance of four segmentation networks trained on either synthetic image-label pairs or real images with expert-derived annotations.

Model	Training data	ACC	AUC	DICE	clDICE
U-Net [21]	Real	0.89 ± 0.01	0.91 ± 0.01	0.69 ± 0.02	0.60 ± 0.02
	Synthetic	0.80 ± 0.02	0.81 ± 0.01	0.54 ± 0.02	0.47 ± 0.02
ResU-Net [34]	Real	0.88 ± 0.01	0.90 ± 0.01	0.68 ± 0.02	0.59 ± 0.02
	Synthetic	0.84 ± 0.01	0.82 ± 0.02	0.56 ± 0.03	0.48 ± 0.04
CS-Net [18]	Real	0.89 ± 0.01	0.90 ± 0.01	0.69 ± 0.01	0.59 ± 0.02
	Synthetic	0.77 ± 0.04	0.81 ± 0.02	0.55 ± 0.02	0.48 ± 0.02
CE-Net [8]	Real	0.88 ± 0.01	0.88 ± 0.01	0.67 ± 0.02	0.58 ± 0.02
	Synthetic	0.85 ± 0.02	0.84 ± 0.02	0.59 ± 0.02	0.51 ± 0.04

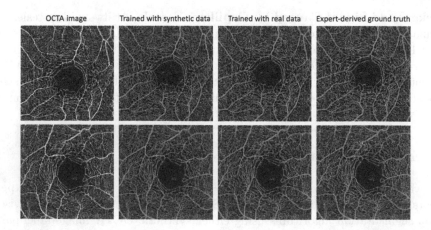

Fig. 4. Two representative test samples with segmentation maps overlaid in orange. Algorithms trained on synthetic data accurately segment capillary vessels.

---

[1] https://github.com/iMED-Lab/OCTA-Net-OCTA-Vessel-Segmentation-Network.

ROSE-1 dataset do not encompass the smallest capillaries, whereas these vessels are labeled in our synthetic dataset. Consequently, the networks trained on synthetic data label these important small vessels, whereas the baselines do not.

An advantage of our synthetic data pipeline is that it can easily generate large amounts of training data. In additional experiments, we show that network performance increases with training dataset size (see Table 2). We also observe that top-end network performance improves when pretraining networks on synthetic data before finetuning them on a small number of real samples. In further ablation experiments, we quantified the benefit of both newly introduced components. Using vessel trees without the typical structure of the SVC and DVC results in a decreased segmentation accuracy (see Table 3). Similarly, we find that leaving out the physics-based image transformations and training only with generic augmentations reduces performance.

Table 2. U-Net performance across different dataset types and training strategies.

Training data	Dataset size	ACC	AUC	DICE	clDICE
Synthetic	32	0.80 ± 0.02	0.81 ± 0.01	0.54 ± 0.02	0.47 ± 0.02
Synthetic	320	0.81 ± 0.02	0.83 ± 0.01	0.56 ± 0.01	0.48 ± 0.02
Synthetic	3200	0.81 ± 0.01	0.84 ± 0.01	0.57 ± 0.01	0.49 ± 0.02
Synthetic + finetuning	352	0.91 ± 0.01	0.91 ± 0.01	0.71 ± 0.01	0.62 ± 0.02
Real	32	0.89 ± 0.01	0.91 ± 0.01	0.69 ± 0.02	0.60 ± 0.02

Table 3. U-Net performance after ablating the physiology-based simulation of the retinal vasculature or the physics-based augmentations of our data synthesis method.

Configuration	ACC	AUC	DICE	clDICE
Proposed method	0.81 ± 0.02	0.83 ± 0.01	0.56 ± 0.01	0.48 ± 0.02
−vessel simulation	0.79 ± 0.01	0.80 ± 0.01	0.53 ± 0.01	0.45 ± 0.01
−augmentations	0.79 ± 0.01	0.70 ± 0.02	0.52 ± 0.01	0.47 ± 0.01

Finally, we train a 3D U-Net for vessel segmentation in volumes of the OCTA-500 dataset using only synthetic training data [11,12]. As of now, we are unable to benchmark on this task as there are OCTA datasets with volumetric labels are not available. Instead, we present initial qualitative results (see Fig. 5). These highlight the potential of our method to facilitate three-dimensional analysis of OCTA images; a task with enormous diagnostic potential which can only be rarely conducted due to a lack of suitable tools [33].

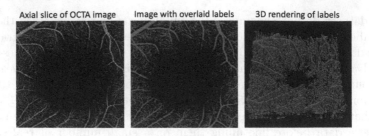

Fig. 5. Three-dimensional vessel segmentation of a volumetric OCTA image by a U-Net trained exclusively on our synthetic data.

5   Discussion and Conclusion

In this work we have presented a method to generate highly realistic, synthetic OCTA images. Our method models the retinal vasculature with excellent anatomical detail using a physiology-based angiogenesis model. Moreover, we simulate image features and artifacts resulting from the OCTA acquisition process using a set of physics-based image augmentations. While our synthetic OCTA images are still distinguishable from real images, they are accompanied by a fully characterized vascular graph. This intrinsically matched ground truth is highly advantageous when using the dataset for downstream tasks.

We demonstrate the promise of our approach by successfully training several segmentation algorithms without manual ground-truth annotations. In the future, our method can be tailored to emulate the characteristics of diverse clinical datasets. The vasculature simulation can be adapted to model the retinal morphology of specific populations, such as older subjects or patients with ocular, cardiac or neurological pathologies [9]. The image augmentations can be tuned to the hard- and software build into different OCTA scanners [28]. We believe that this versatility will enable application of our method beyond vessel segmentation and ultimately advance the quantitative analysis of OCTA in clinical practice.

Acknowledgments. Johannes C. Paetzold is supported by the DCoMEX project, financed by the Federal Ministry of Education and Research of Germany. Benjamin Knier is funded by the Else Kröner-Fresenius-Stiftung, the Gemeinnützige Hertie Foundation and received a research award from Novartis.

References

1. Abràmoff, M.D., Garvin, M.K., Sonka, M.: Retinal imaging and image analysis. IEEE Rev. Biomed. Eng. **3**, 169–208 (2010)
2. Campbell, J., et al.: Detailed vascular anatomy of the human retina by projection-resolved optical coherence tomography angiography. Sci. Rep. **7**(1), 1–11 (2017)

3. Frid-Adar, M., Amer, R., Greenspan, H.: Endotracheal tube detection and segmentation in chest radiographs using synthetic data. In: Shen, D., et al. (eds.) MICCAI 2019. LNCS, vol. 11769, pp. 784–792. Springer, Cham (2019). https://doi.org/10.1007/978-3-030-32226-7_87

4. Garcia-Garcia, A., Orts-Escolano, S., Oprea, S., Villena-Martinez, V., Martinez-Gonzalez, P., Garcia-Rodriguez, J.: A survey on deep learning techniques for image and video semantic segmentation. Appl. Soft Comput. **70**, 41–65 (2018)

5. Garvin, M.K., Abramoff, M.D., Wu, X., Russell, S.R., Burns, T.L., Sonka, M.: Automated 3-D intraretinal layer segmentation of macular spectral-domain optical coherence tomography images. IEEE Trans. Med. Imaging **28**(9), 1436–1447 (2009)

6. Gerl, S., et al.: A distance-based loss for smooth and continuous skin layer segmentation in optoacoustic images. In: Martel, A.L., et al. (eds.) MICCAI 2020. LNCS, vol. 12266, pp. 309–319. Springer, Cham (2020). https://doi.org/10.1007/978-3-030-59725-2_30

7. Gherardini, M., Mazomenos, E., Menciassi, A., Stoyanov, D.: Catheter segmentation in X-ray fluoroscopy using synthetic data and transfer learning with light U-nets. Comput. Meth. Program. Biomed. **192**, 105420 (2020)

8. Gu, Z., et al.: CE-Net: Context encoder network for 2D medical image segmentation. IEEE Trans. Med. Imaging **38**(10), 2281–2292 (2019)

9. Joussen, A.M., Gardner, T.W., Kirchhof, B., Ryan, S.J. (eds.): Retinal Vascular Disease. Springer, Heidelberg (2007). https://doi.org/10.1007/978-3-540-29542-6

10. Li, K., Wu, X., Chen, D.Z., Sonka, M.: Optimal surface segmentation in volumetric images-a graph-theoretic approach. IEEE Trans. Pattern Anal. Mach. Intell. **28**(1), 119–134 (2005)

11. Li, M., et al.: Image projection network: 3D to 2D image segmentation in OCTA images. IEEE Trans. Med. Imaging **39**(11), 3343–3354 (2020)

12. Li, M.: IPN-V2 and OCTA 500: methodology and dataset for retinal image segmentation. arXiv preprint arXiv:2012.07261 (2020)

13. Liew, G., Wang, J.J.: Retinal vascular signs: a window to the heart? Revista Española de Cardiología (Engl. Ed.) **64**(6), 515–521 (2011)

14. Lindner, L., Narnhofer, D., Weber, M., Gsaxner, C., Kolodziej, M., Egger, J.: Using synthetic training data for deep learning-based GBM segmentation. In: 2019 41st Annual International Conference of the IEEE Engineering in Medicine and Biology Society (EMBC), pp. 6724–6729. IEEE (2019)

15. Liu, Y., et al.: Variational intensity cross channel encoder for unsupervised vessel segmentation on OCT angiography. In: Medical Imaging 2020: Image Processing, vol. 11313, p. 113130Y. International Society for Optics and Photonics (2020)

16. London, A., Benhar, I., Schwartz, M.: The retina as a window to the brain-from eye research to CNS disorders. Nat. Rev. Neurol. **9**(1), 44–53 (2013)

17. Ma, Y., et al.: ROSE: a retinal OCT-angiography vessel segmentation dataset and new model. IEEE Trans. Med. Imaging **40**(3), 928–939 (2020)

18. Mou, L., et al.: CS-Net: channel and spatial attention network for curvilinear structure segmentation. In: Shen, D., et al. (eds.) MICCAI 2019. LNCS, vol. 11764, pp. 721–730. Springer, Cham (2019). https://doi.org/10.1007/978-3-030-32239-7_80

19. Omigbodun, A.O., Noo, F., McNitt-Gray, M., Hsu, W., Hsieh, S.S.: The effects of physics-based data augmentation on the generalizability of deep neural networks: demonstration on nodule false-positive reduction. Med. Phys. **46**(10), 4563–4574 (2019)

20. Paetzold, J.C., et al.: Transfer learning from synthetic data reduces need for labels to segment brain vasculature and neural pathways in 3d. In: International Conference on Medical Imaging with Deep Learning-Extended Abstract Track (2019)

21. Ronneberger, O., Fischer, P., Brox, T.: U-Net: convolutional networks for biomedical image segmentation. In: Navab, N., Hornegger, J., Wells, W.M., Frangi, A.F. (eds.) MICCAI 2015. LNCS, vol. 9351, pp. 234–241. Springer, Cham (2015). https://doi.org/10.1007/978-3-319-24574-4_28

22. Samara, W.A., et al.: Correlation of foveal avascular zone size with foveal morphology in normal eyes using optical coherence tomography angiography. Retina 35(11), 2188–2195 (2015)

23. Schneider, M., Reichold, J., Weber, B., Székely, G., Hirsch, S.: Tissue metabolism driven arterial tree generation. Med. Image Anal. 16(7), 1397–1414 (2012)

24. Shaw, R., Sudre, C.H., Varsavsky, T., Ourselin, S., Cardoso, M.J.: A k-space model of movement artefacts: application to segmentation augmentation and artefact removal. IEEE Trans. Med. Imaging 39(9), 2881–2892 (2020)

25. Shit, S., et al.: clDice - a novel topology-preserving loss function for tubular structure segmentation. In: Proceedings of the IEEE/CVF Conference on Computer Vision and Pattern Recognition, pp. 16560–16569 (2021)

26. Shorten, C., Khoshgoftaar, T.M.: A survey on image data augmentation for deep learning. J. Big Data 6(1), 1–48 (2019)

27. Spaide, R.F., Fujimoto, J.G., Waheed, N.K.: Image artifacts in optical coherence angiography. Retina (Philadelphia, Pa.) 35(11), 2163 (2015)

28. Spaide, R.F., Fujimoto, J.G., Waheed, N.K., Sadda, S.R., Staurenghi, G.: Optical coherence tomography angiography. Prog. Retin. Eye Res. 64, 1–55 (2018)

29. Spaide, R.F., Klancnik, J.M., Cooney, M.J.: Retinal vascular layers imaged by fluorescein angiography and optical coherence tomography angiography. JAMA Ophthalmol. 133(1), 45–50 (2015)

30. Tick, S., et al.: Foveal shape and structure in a normal population. Invest. Ophthalmol. Vis. Sci. 52(8), 5105–5110 (2011)

31. Tirindelli, M., Eilers, C., Simson, W., Paschali, M., Azampour, M.F., Navab, N.: Rethinking ultrasound augmentation: a physics-inspired approach. In: de Bruijne, M., et al. (eds.) MICCAI 2021. LNCS, vol. 12908, pp. 690–700. Springer, Cham (2021). https://doi.org/10.1007/978-3-030-87237-3_66

32. Todorov, M.I., et al.: Machine learning analysis of whole mouse brain vasculature. Nat. Meth. 17(4), 442–449 (2020)

33. Yu, S., et al.: Cross-domain depth estimation network for 3D vessel reconstruction in OCT angiography. In: de Bruijne, M., et al. (eds.) MICCAI 2021. LNCS, vol. 12908, pp. 13–23. Springer, Cham (2021). https://doi.org/10.1007/978-3-030-87237-3_2

34. Zhang, Z., Liu, Q., Wang, Y.: Road extraction by deep residual U-net. IEEE Geosci. Remote Sens. Lett. 15(5), 749–753 (2018)

Anomaly-Aware Multiple Instance Learning for Rare Anemia Disorder Classification

Salome Kazeminia[1,2], Ario Sadafi[1,3], Asya Makhro[4], Anna Bogdanova[4], Shadi Albarqouni[5,6,7], and Carsten Marr[1(✉)]

[1] Institute of AI for Health, Helmholtz Munich - German Research Center for Environmental Health, Neuherberg, Germany
carsten.marr@helmholtz-muenchen.de
[2] Technical University of Munich, Munich, Germany
[3] Computer Aided Medical Procedures, Technical University of Munich, Munich, Germany
[4] Red Blood Cell Research Group, Institute of Veterinary Physiology, Vetsuisse Faculty and the Zurich Center for Integrative Human Physiology, University of Zurich, Zurich, Switzerland
[5] Clinic for Diagnostic and Interventional Radiology, University Hospital Bonn, Bonn, Germany
[6] Helmholtz AI, Helmholtz Munich - German Research Center for Environmental Health, Neuherberg, Germany
[7] Faculty of Informatics, Technical University Munich, Munich, Germany

Abstract. Deep learning-based classification of rare anemia disorders is challenged by the lack of training data and instance-level annotations. Multiple Instance Learning (MIL) has shown to be an effective solution, yet it suffers from low accuracy and limited explainability. Although the inclusion of attention mechanisms has addressed these issues, their effectiveness highly depends on the amount and diversity of cells in the training samples. Consequently, the poor machine learning performance on rare anemia disorder classification from blood samples remains unresolved. In this paper, we propose an interpretable pooling method for MIL to address these limitations. By benefiting from instance-level information of negative bags (i.e., homogeneous benign cells from healthy individuals), our approach increases the contribution of anomalous instances. We show that our strategy outperforms standard MIL classification algorithms and provides a meaningful explanation behind its decisions. Moreover, it can denote anomalous instances of rare blood diseases that are not seen during the training phase.

Keywords: Multiple instance learning · Anomaly pooling · Rare anemia disorder · Red blood cells

1 Introduction

The appearance of human red blood cells changes directly with their volume. Typically red blood cells have a discoid concave shape, and as their volume

L. Wang et al. (Eds.): MICCAI 2022, LNCS 13438, pp. 341–350, 2022.
https://doi.org/10.1007/978-3-031-16452-1_33

increases or decrease in physiological conditions, they shrivel into star-shaped cells or swell into spherical shapes [9]. In hereditary hemolytic anemias (HHAs), a cell's membrane is not formed properly and cannot accommodate volume changes, resulting in the formation of anomalous morphologies. Membrane instability and reduced deformability are other factors in a number of HHAs, such as hereditary spherocytosis, sickle cell disease, and thalassemia, where improper membrane formation leads to irregularly formed cells.

Tools for close monitoring of blood samples in HHA patients is crucial for diagnosis [8], disease progression [4], and severity estimation [17]. However, since most cells in a patient's sample have no evident morphological feature relevant to the HHA, identifying hallmark cells is a needle-in-the-hay-stack search. Furthermore, presence of a few anomalous cells in a sample does not necessarily link to an underlying condition making the diagnosis even more challenging.

In addition, proper single cell annotation for supervised model training is a cumbersome, expensive task and introduces intra-expert variability. Thus, the automated analysis of blood samples is a perfect problem for multiple instance learning-based approaches. Multiple Instance Learning (MIL) is a weakly supervised learning method, where only bag-level labels are used [3]. Notably, a bag with a negative label does not contain any positive instance, while bags with a positive label may contain negative instances. In other words, the class of a bag depends on the existence of one or more class-related instance. Thus, the learning signal, back-propagated to the instance-level feature extractor may be very weak and ineffective. To address this problem, MIL-based deep classifiers require a large number of training data to perform promisingly [3]. Providing such data is particularly difficult in the case of rare disease. A possible solution is the deployment of intelligent pooling methods to magnify the learning signal back-propagated from informative instances [14]. In basic MIL classifiers, when the bag contains a small number of class-related instances, a typical max or average pooling cannot to provide such magnification [14].

Another requirement for health AI applications is explainability. MIL classifiers should thus be able to specify HHA-related structures of instances anomalies. Recently, attention-based pooling mechanisms showed a good performance in tackling both learning signal magnification and explainability challenges [10,14,16]. However, attention mechanisms are prone to fail in scenarios where only a few training samples are available, and consequently, the algorithm can not identify relevant instances in the bags correctly. In HHA classification, such a problem leads to noisy attention scores where lots of disorder-relevant (positive) cells receive low attention, and the distribution of attention on non-disorder (negative) cells would be non-uniform. Here, a strategy accounting for the diversity of disorder-relevant cells and data imbalance is required.

This paper introduces an anomaly-aware pooling method, which is able to address limitations of the attention mechanism with an efficient amount of training data. While instance-level information for positive bags is not available, we exploit negative bag labels that apply to all instances of the bag and estimate the distribution of negative instances using Bayesian Gaussian mixture models. By measuring

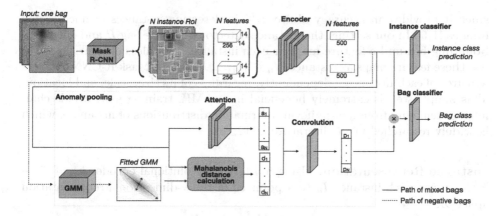

Fig. 1. Overview of our proposed anomaly-aware MIL classifier. A Mask R-CNN outputs detected instance bounding boxes and basic instance features. Then, an encoder maps those features to a latent representation. Dashed path: A GMM distribution is fitted to instances from negative bags B_{neg}, and its parameters are saved. Solid path: Attention scores $a_{n\in N}$ and anomaly scores $d_{n\in N}$ are estimated and combined through a convolution layer to generate pooling weights $p_{n\in N}$. Finally, a fully connected layer predicts the bag label.

the distance of instances to this distribution, we define an anomaly score that is used for pooling in addition to learned attention scores. Our method's performance is explainable by specifying the contribution of instances in the final bag classification. Also, our proposed anomaly score can specify anomalous instances that are rare and haven't been seen during the training. We make our code publicly available at https://github.com/marrlab/Anomaly-aware-MIL.

2 Method

Our MIL classifier f_θ consists of an instance detector, a deep instance feature extractor h_ψ, and an attention-anomaly pooling mechanism that assigns a contribution weight to each instance. The input of our classifier is a bag of instances $\{I_1, ..., I_N\} \in B$; the output is a class c_i from possible classes defined in C. In our target application, bags are red blood cells from brieghtfield microscopic images of blood samples, each containing between 12 to 45 cells (See Fig. 1).

2.1 Instance-Level Feature Extraction

Preprocessing. Since instance-level information plays a crucial role in bag classification and interpretation, we need to detect them and follow their footprint in the final classification result. For instance detection, we prefer two-stage object detection methods due to the higher accuracy of their performance in comparison with one-stage methods [5]. As a preprocessing step, any two-stage object detector can be used. We employ Mask R-CNN [6] with ResNet [7] backbone since it provides an accuracy above 91% in detecting instances in microscopic images [1,5]. In our setting, the instance detector takes the bag B and outputs a bounding box and a feature map for each instance, regardless of their class. We use these feature maps as instances $I_n \in \{I_1, ..., I_N\} = B$. Mask R-CNN extracts features of each instance independently, regardless of its size, scale, and location. This simple step is extremely beneficial in our MIL training as it avoids challenges stemming from non-uniform information distributions of instances, which is widely researched in the literature [2,12,18].

Instance Representation. Using a 4-layer convolutional encoder $h_\psi : \mathbb{R}^m \to \mathbb{R}^k$, we map each instance I_n to a point z_n in the k-dimensional representation space Z:

$$z_n = h_\psi(I_n), \quad n \in N \tag{1}$$

2.2 Anomaly-Aware Pooling

Negative Distribution Estimation. We estimate the distribution of negative instances in our latent space and detect anomalies by measuring their distance to this distribution. As a prior assumption, we consider a Gaussian Mixture Model (GMM) probability distribution on negative instance representations. Due to Bayes' rule, the posterior probability distribution would be a GMM as well. Therefore we fit a GMM model g_Γ on negative instance representations. To estimate Γ, we use an Expectation-Maximization (EM) algorithm that miximizes the likelihood $p(\Gamma|Z_{neg})$ given $Z_{neg} : \{z_j | I_j \in B_{neg}\}$

$$p(\Gamma|Z_{neg}) = \sum_i \tilde{\gamma}_i \mathcal{N}(\tilde{\mu}_i, \tilde{\Sigma}_i), \tag{2}$$

where $\tilde{\gamma}$, $\tilde{\mu}_i$, and $\tilde{\Sigma}_i$ are estimated weight, mean, and covariance matrix of a Gaussian distribution, characterizing the ith GMM component, respectively. When the algorithm converges, we save the model's parameters as a reference for anomaly scoring.

Anomaly Scoring. For anomaly scoring we measure the Mahalanobis distance between instances and the g_Γ

$$d_n = \sqrt{(z_n - \mu)^T \Sigma^{-1} (z_n - \mu)}, \tag{3}$$

where μ and Σ are mean and covariance of the g_γ distribution. We have chosen Mahalanobis distance over other distances since it considers the distribution's covariance in its distance measurement.

Attention. The attention mechanism is a method to extract meaningful instances contributing to the final decision of the model. Specially, in MIL it showed a good performance in both classification and interpretation of deep networks [10,13,14,16,19]. Our deep attention network v_ω estimates an attention score a_n for each instance I_n as

$$a_n = v_\omega(z_n). \tag{4}$$

Pooling. Our pooling mechanism combines attention a_n and anomaly d_n scores to estimate a contribution weight for each instance and conclude the latent representation of the bag:

$$z_B = \sum_{n=0}^{N} (W_{D_n} d_n + W_{A_n} a_{z_n}) z_n. \tag{5}$$

Here W_D and W_A are respectively learned parameters, to specify the intervention share of attention and anomaly scores. Finally, a fully connected layer f_θ maps the k-dimensional representation z_B to a class c_i (see Fig. 1). Both anomaly and attention scores of am instance are independently calculated and fed to a 1Œ1 convolution to estimate the final pooling weight of the corresponding instance. This makes our pooling method permutation invariant.

2.3 Optimization

The functionality of v_ω and fitting g_Γ on negative instances highly depends on the encoded instances by h_ψ. To boost the training procedure, we start with a single instance classifier (SIC) s_ζ using noisy labels for learning [16]. In other words, we assign the bag label to all of its instances and calculate a cross-entropy loss (CE_{SIC}) to optimize the model in the first epochs. Then, by increasing the epoch number e, we gradually decrease SIC's impact on the training and conversely increase the MIL cross-entropy loss (CE_{MIL}) contribution. Therefore, the final loss function, considering a dynamic coefficients $\beta(e)$, is defined as:

$$L(\theta, \zeta, \omega, \psi) = (1 - \beta(e))CE_{MIL} + \beta(e)CE_{SIC}, \tag{6}$$

3   Experiment

We applied our classifier on microscopic images of blood samples from HHA patients. In particular, we evaluated three aspects of our method's functionality: 1) classification, 2) explainability, and 3) rare anomaly recognition.

Dataset. Patients previously diagnosed with hereditary spherocytosis, xerocytosis, thalassemia, and sickle cell disease were enrolled in the CoMMiTMenT study. The study protocols were approved by the Medical Ethical Research Board

Table 1. Average classification performance of our proposed method compared to four baselines. The numbers show the mean value along with the standard deviation of metrics measured in 5 runs.

Method	Accuracy	F1-score	AU RoC
Att [10]	0.752 ± 0.009	0.741 ± 0.010	0.826 ± 0.009
Att + SIC [16]	0.770 ± 0.008	0.757 ± 0.009	0.808 ± 0.013
Anomaly	0.630 ± 0.029	0.604 ± 0.026	0.648 ± 0.025
Anomaly + Att	0.760 ± 0.019	0.743 ± 0.021	0.833 ± 0.006
Anomaly + Att + SIC	$\mathbf{0.787 \pm 0.015}$	$\mathbf{0.770 \pm 0.016}$	$\mathbf{0.854 \pm 0.008}$

of the University Medical Center Utrecht, the Netherlands, under reference code 15/426M and by the Ethical Committee of Clinical Investigations of Hospital Clinic, Spain (IDIBAPS) under reference code 2013/8436. Further blood samples of SCD patients were produced for MemSID (NCT02615847) clinical trial. The study protocol for it was approved by the Ethics committee of Canton Zurich (KEK-ZH 2015-0297) and the regulatory authority. Our dataset contains 3630 microscopic images taken from 71 patients/healthy individuals at different times and under variant treatments. The distribution of data in different classes is as follows: Sickle Cell Disease (SCD, 13 patients, 170 image sets), Thalassemia (Thal, 3 patients, 25 image sets), Hereditary Xerocytosis (Xero, 9 patients, 56 image sets), and Hereditary Spherocytosis (HS, 13 patients, 89 image sets). Also, we have a healthy control group (33 individuals, 181 image sets), used as negative bags.

Training. For training we considered 3–fold cross-validation and 100 epochs. We have two training sets: i) one set containing only control samples to estimate GMM, and ii) an other set containing a mixture of samples from all classes to train our network. We considered one GMM component with full covariance and iterated an EM algorithm up to 100 times. Mixed data are fed to the MIL classifier and every 5 epoch, control set is fed to the model to calibrate GMM parameters with updates. For optimization, we use the Adam optimizer [15] with the learning rate of 5×10^{-5} and weight decay of 10^5. We chose the dynamic SIC loss coefficient $\beta(e)$ as 0.95^e.

3.1 Classification

Our metrics for classification evaluation are average accuracy, F1 score, and area under the precision recall curve (AUC). Table 1 shows our results (Anomaly + Att + SIC) in comparison with other strategies proposed by Ilse et al. [10] (Att) and Sadafi et al. [16] (Att + SIC). In addition, as an ablation study, we show the performance of our proposed anomaly scoring without SIC loss (Anomaly + Att) and attention mechanism (Anomaly). The class-wise performance of our proposed method compared to other methods is shown in Fig. 2.

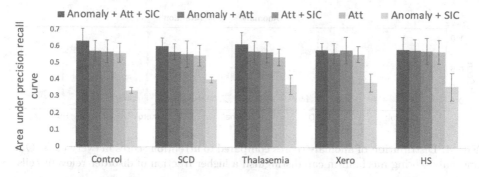

Fig. 2. Average and standard deviation of the class-wise area under precision recall curve in five runs. In all classes, our novel method outperforms others.

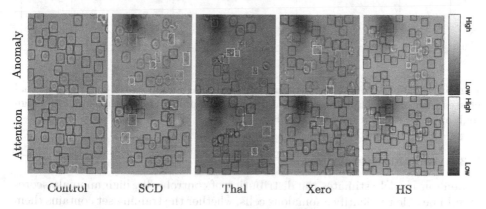

Fig. 3. Interpretation of bag classification at the instance level based on anomaly (top) and attention (bottom) scores. Compared with attention mechanism, disorder-relevant cells are more accurately scored by the anomaly mechanism.

3.2 Explainability

Our method's anomaly scoring mechanism is interpretable at the instance level. In Fig. 3, for each class, we visualized a sample image, in which anomaly and attention scores are depicted by the color of the cell's bounding box. The anomaly mechanism can distinguish class-related cells better than the attention mechanism, which is particularly striking for the SCD case, where irregular elliptoid cells are missed by the attention mechanism (Fig. 3). In Fig. 4 we show the distribution of scores assigned to cells in the test data. The frequency of both anomaly and attention scores are focused around zero, which is compatible with a majority of healthy cells (see also Fig. 4). On the other hand, for HHA, a small distribution of high scores notifies the anomalous cells. These cells show HHA properties.

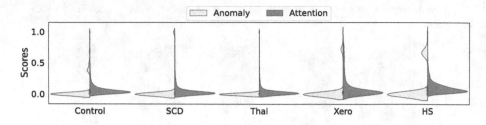

Fig. 4. Distribution of anomaly scores compared to attention scores in every class. Our anomaly scoring mechanism can distinguish a higher fraction of disorder-relevant cells.

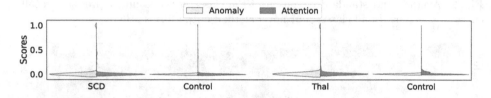

Fig. 5. Distribution of anomaly scores compared to attention scores for SCD and Thal classes when their samples were absent during the training. Our method still can assign high anomaly scores to abnormal cells.

3.3 Anomaly Recognition

When our model estimates the distribution of control cells, high anomaly scores should be able to identify anomalous cells, whether the training set contains them or not. This property of our method is useful for detecting anomalies in rare or unseen classes during training. To examine our method in this context, we trained the model with the two HHA classes SCD and Thalassemia, separately. Then, we tested the model with unseen class samples and measured their anomaly and attention scores. Figure 5 shows the results, where the small distribution of anomalous cells is clearly indicating anomaly awareness of the model. For both experiments, the distribution of scores in the control class is also shown.

3.4 CO2 Emission Related to Experiments

Experiments were conducted using our in-house infrastructure with a carbon efficiency of 0.432 $kgCO_2eq/kWh$. A cumulative 15 h of computation was performed on the Tesla V100-SXM2-32GB (TDP of 300W) hardware. Total emissions are estimated to be 1.94 kg CO_2eq. Estimations were conducted using the MachineLearning Impact calculator presented in [11].

4 Conclusion

We introduce anomaly-aware MIL, a simple method for enhancing classification of hereditary hemolytic anemias. Evaluations show that our method outperforms other MIL classifiers and provides an instance-level explanation for bag-level classification results. Moreover, our novel scoring mechanism identifies anomalies in rare disease, even if they have not been seen in training sets. An interesting future work would be to upgrade the anomaly scoring to deep-learning-based out-of-distribution detection method. Another interesting future work would be uncertainty estimation on anomalous instances, which might lead to a better understanding of models coverage in representation space.

Acknowledgements. The Helmholtz Association supports the present contribution under the joint research school "Munich School for Data Science - MUDS". C.M. has received funding from the European Research Council (ERC) under the European Union's Horizon 2020 research and innovation programme (Grant agreement No. 866411). CoMMiTMenT study was funded by the European Seventh Framework Program under grant agreement number 602121 (CoMMiTMenT) and from the European Union's Horizon 2020 Research and Innovation Programme. MemSID (NCT02615847) clinical trial was funded by the Foundation for Clinical Research Hematology for supporting the clinical trail at the Division of Hematology, University Hospital Zurich, and, partially, by the following foundations: Baugarten Zürich Genossenschaft und Stiftung, the Ernst Goehner Stiftung, the René und Susanna Braginsky Stiftung, the Stiftung Symphasis and the Botnar Foundation." Further funding for analysis of the obtained data was obtained European Union's Horizon 2020 Research and Innovation Programme under grant agreement number 675115-RELEVANCE-H2020-MSCA-ITN-2015/II2020-MSCA-ITN-2015.

References

1. Bessis, M.: Corpuscles: Atlas of Red Blood Cell Shape. Springer Science & Business Media (2012)
2. Bi, Q., et al.: Local-global dual perception based deep multiple instance learning for retinal disease classification. In: de Bruijne, M., et al. (eds.) MICCAI 2021. LNCS, vol. 12908, pp. 55–64. Springer, Cham (2021). https://doi.org/10.1007/978-3-030-87237-3_6
3. Campanella, G., et al.: Clinical-grade computational pathology using weakly supervised deep learning on whole slide images. Nat. Med. **25**(8), 1301–1309 (2019)
4. Fermo, E., Vercellati, C., Bianchi, P.: Screening tools for hereditary hemolytic anemia: new concepts and strategies. Expert Rev. Hematol. **14**(3), 281–292 (2021)
5. Fujita, S., Han, X.H.: Cell detection and segmentation in microscopy images with improved mask R-CNN. In: Proceedings of the Asian Conference on Computer Vision (2020)
6. He, K., Gkioxari, G., Dollár, P., Girshick, R.: Mask R-CNN. In: Proceedings of the IEEE International Conference on Computer Vision, pp. 2961–2969 (2017)
7. He, K., Zhang, X., Ren, S., Sun, J.: Deep residual learning for image recognition. In: Proceedings of the IEEE Conference on Computer Vision and Pattern Recognition, pp. 770–778 (2016)
8. Huisjes, R., van Solinge, W., Levin, M., van Wijk, R., Riedl, J.: Digital microscopy as a screening tool for the diagnosis of hereditary hemolytic anemia. Int. J. Lab. Hematol. **40**(2), 159–168 (2018)
9. Huisjes, R., et al.: Density, heterogeneity and deformability of red cells as markers of clinical severity in hereditary spherocytosis. Haematologica **105**(2), 338 (2020)

10. Ilse, M., Tomczak, J., Welling, M.: Attention-based deep multiple instance learning. In: International Conference on Machine Learning, pp. 2127–2136. PMLR (2018)
11. Lacoste, A., Luccioni, A., Schmidt, V., Dandres, T.: Quantifying the carbon emissions of machine learning. arXiv preprint arXiv:1910.09700 (2019)
12. Li, S., et al.: Multi-instance multi-scale CNN for medical image classification. In: Shen, D., et al. (eds.) MICCAI 2019. LNCS, vol. 11767, pp. 531–539. Springer, Cham (2019). https://doi.org/10.1007/978-3-030-32251-9_58
13. Lu, M.Y., et al.: AI-based pathology predicts origins for cancers of unknown primary. Nature **594**(7861), 106–110 (2021)
14. Lu, M.Y., Williamson, D.F., Chen, T.Y., Chen, R.J., Barbieri, M., Mahmood, F.: Data-efficient and weakly supervised computational pathology on whole-slide images. Nat. Biomed. Eng. **5**(6), 555–570 (2021)
15. Reddi, S.J., Kale, S., Kumar, S.: On the convergence of adam and beyond. arXiv preprint arXiv:1904.09237 (2019)
16. Sadafi, A., et al.: Attention based multiple instance learning for classification of blood cell disorders. In: Martel, A.L., et al. (eds.) MICCAI 2020. LNCS, vol. 12265, pp. 246–256. Springer, Cham (2020). https://doi.org/10.1007/978-3-030-59722-1_24
17. Sadafi, A., et al.: Sickle cell disease severity prediction from percoll gradient images using graph convolutional networks. In: Albarqouni, S., et al. (eds.) DART/FAIR -2021. LNCS, vol. 12968, pp. 216–225. Springer, Cham (2021). https://doi.org/10.1007/978-3-030-87722-4_20
18. Shi, X., Xing, F., Xie, Y., Zhang, Z., Cui, L., Yang, L.: Loss-based attention for deep multiple instance learning. In: Proceedings of the AAAI Conference on Artificial Intelligence, vol. 34, pp. 5742–5749 (2020)
19. Wu, Y., Schmidt, A., Hernández-Sánchez, E., Molina, R., Katsaggelos, A.K.: Combining attention-based multiple instance learning and gaussian processes for CT hemorrhage detection. In: de Bruijne, M., Cattin, P.C., Cotin, S., Padoy, N., Speidel, S., Zheng, Y., Essert, C. (eds.) MICCAI 2021. LNCS, vol. 12902, pp. 582–591. Springer, Cham (2021). https://doi.org/10.1007/978-3-030-87196-3_54

Unsupervised Domain Adaptation with Contrastive Learning for OCT Segmentation

Alvaro Gomariz[1](✉)(iD), Huanxiang Lu[1], Yun Yvonna Li[1], Thomas Albrecht[1],
Andreas Maunz[1], Fethallah Benmansour[1], Alessandra M. Valcarcel[2],
Jennifer Luu[2], Daniela Ferrara[2], and Orcun Goksel[3,4](iD)

[1] F Hoffmann-La Roche AG, Basel, Switzerland
alvaro.gomariz@roche.com
[2] Genentech Inc., South San Francisco, CA, USA
[3] Computer-assisted Applications in Medicine, ETH Zurich, Zurich, Switzerland
[4] Department of Information Technology, Uppsala University, Uppsala, Sweden

Abstract. Accurate segmentation of retinal fluids in 3D Optical Coherence Tomography images is key for diagnosis and personalized treatment of eye diseases. While deep learning has been successful at this task, trained supervised models often fail for images that do not resemble labeled examples, e.g. for images acquired using different devices. We hereby propose a novel semi-supervised learning framework for segmentation of volumetric images from new unlabeled domains. We jointly use supervised and contrastive learning, also introducing a contrastive pairing scheme that leverages similarity between nearby slices in 3D. In addition, we propose channel-wise aggregation as an alternative to conventional spatial-pooling aggregation for contrastive feature map projection. We evaluate our methods for domain adaptation from a (labeled) source domain to an (unlabeled) target domain, each containing images acquired with different acquisition devices. In the target domain, our method achieves a Dice coefficient 13.8% higher than SimCLR (a state-of-the-art contrastive framework), and leads to results comparable to an upper bound with supervised training in that domain. In the source domain, our model also improves the results by 5.4% Dice, by successfully leveraging information from many unlabeled images.

Keywords: Segmentation of 3D volumes · Semi-supervised learning

1 Introduction

Supervised learning methods, in particular UNet [20], for segmentation of retinal fluids imaged with Optical Coherence Tomography (OCT) devices have led to

---

Supplementary Information The online version contains supplementary material available at https://doi.org/10.1007/978-3-031-16452-1_34.

major advances in diagnosis, prognosis, and understanding of eye diseases [1, 10, 11, 21, 23]. However, training these supervised deep neural networks requires large amounts of labeled data, which are costly, not always feasible, and need to be repeated for each problem domain; since trained models often fail when inference data differs from labeled examples, so-called *domain-shift*, e.g. for images from a different OCT device [22]. Unsupervised domain adaptation aims to leverage information learned from a labeled data domain for applications in other domains where only unlabeled data is available. To this end, many deep learning methods have been proposed [25], mostly using generative adversarial networks, e.g. to translate visual appearance across OCT devices [19].

Contrastive learning (CL) aims to extract informative features in a self-supervised manner by comparing (unlabeled) data pairs in a feature subspace of a network [3, 5–7, 13–15, 18]. A widely-adopted CL framework, SimCLR [5], generates positive image pairs from the same image via image augmentations to minimize feature distances between these pairs, while maximizing their distance from augmentations of other images as negative samples. Other CL strategies aim to successfully learn without a need for negative pairs, SimSiam [7] being a representative example. CL is commonly used for pretraining models, typically using natural images such as ImageNet [9], which are then finetuned or distilled for downstream tasks, e.g. classification, detection, or segmentation [6].

Models pretrained with natural images are of limited use for medical applications, which involve images with substantially different appearances and often with 3D content, leading to a recent focus on application-specific approaches for CL pair generation in medical context [4, 8]. USCL [8] minimizes the feature distance between frames of the same ultrasound video, while maximizing the distance between frames of different videos, in order to produce pretrained models for ultrasound applications. USCL also proposes a joint semi-supervised approach, which simultaneously minimizes a contrastive and supervised *classification* loss. However, to be applicable for image segmentation, this method relies on subsequent finetuning, which is potentially sub-optimal for preserving the unlabeled information for the intended task of segmentation. In fact, there exist little work on CL methods on image segmentation without finetuning.

We hereby aim to improve segmentation quality of OCT datasets with limited manual annotations, but with abundant unlabeled data. We focus on unsupervised domain adaptation, where manual annotations exist for one device (source domain), but not for another (target domain). We achieve this with the following contributions: • We introduce a semi-supervised framework for joint training of CL together with segmentation labels (Sect. 2.1). • We propose an augmentation strategy that leverages expected similarity between nearby slices in 3D (Sect. 2.2). • We introduce a new CL projection head (Sect. 2.3) that aggregates features without losing spatial context, which produces results superior to the conventional spatial pooling strategy. Our contributions are tested on two large clinical datasets collected in trials using different OCT imaging devices.

2   Methods

2.1   Simultaneously Learning from Labeled and Unlabeled Data

As the segmentation backbone, we utilize the proven UNet architecture [20], which can be modeled as $F(\cdot)$ processing an image x to produce a segmentation map $p = F(x)$ to approximate an (expert-annotated) ground truth segmentation y. In the supervised setting, F is learned by minimizing a supervised loss $\mathcal{L}_{\text{sup}}$, which is for us the logarithmic Dice loss of labeled data in a domain D:

$$\mathcal{L}_{\text{sup}} = - \sum_{(p_i, y_i) \in D} \log \frac{2 \sum_{j \in \text{pixels}} y_i^j p_i^j}{\epsilon + \sum_{j \in \text{pixels}} (y_i^j + p_i^j)} \tag{1}$$

for all training images i in D, where ϵ is a small number to avoid division by 0.

Contrastive frameworks aim to learn features $h = E(x)$ with an encoder $E(\cdot)$ without the need of manually annotated labels y. We herein base our methods on the SimCLR framework [5]. In order to adapt the learned features h for our intended segmentation task, we replace the originally-proposed ResNet architecture for $E(\cdot)$ with the UNet encoder (illustrated in brown in Fig. 1a). A subsequent contrastive projection head $C(\cdot)$ maps the bottleneck-layer features to vector projections $z = C(h)$ on which the contrastive loss $\mathcal{L}_{\text{con}}$ is applied. This loss aims to minimize the distance between "positive" pairs of images (x_i', x_i'') created from each image x_i by a defined pair generator $P(\cdot)$ described further in Sect. 2.2 below, i.e. $P(x_i) = (x_i', x_i'')$. We employ a version of the normalized temperature-scaled cross entropy loss [18] adapted to our problem setting as:

$$L_{\text{con}}^{\text{CLR}} = \sum_{P(x_i),\ x_i \in D} \left(l(z_i', z_i'') + l(z_i'', z_i') \right) \tag{2}$$

$$l(z_i', z_i'') = - \log \frac{\exp\left(d(z_i', z_i'') / \tau \right)}{\sum_{x_i \in D} \mathbb{1}_{[k \neq i]} \exp\left(d(z_i', z_k'') / \tau \right)} \tag{3}$$

where $d(u, v) = (u \cdot v) / (\|u\|_2 \|v\|_2)$ and τ is the temperature scaling parameter.

In SimSiam, a learnable predictor $Q(\cdot)$ is applied on one projection to predict the other:

$$L_{\text{con}}^{\text{Siam}} = - \sum_{x_i \in D} \left(d(Q(z_i'), z_i'') + d(Q(z_i''), z_i') \right) \tag{4}$$

where the gradients from the second projection pairs are prevented from backpropagating for network weight updates (*stopgrad*).

We adapt the USCL joint training strategy, which was proposed for US video classification, to our segmentation task on 3D images by combining $\mathcal{L}_{\text{sup}}$ and $\mathcal{L}_{\text{con}}$ in a semi-supervised framework illustrated in Fig. 1a. Considering a source domain D^s and a target domain D^t, total loss $\mathcal{L}$ is calculated as follows:

$$\mathcal{L} = \frac{1}{2} \left(\underset{x \in D^s}{\mathcal{L}_{\text{con}}} + \underset{x \in D^t}{\mathcal{L}_{\text{con}}} \right) + \lambda \underset{(x,y) \in D^s}{\mathcal{L}_{\text{sup}}} \tag{5}$$

2.2   Pair Generation Strategy

Generation of pairs for the contrastive loss is key for successful self-supervised learning. We herein propose and compare different pair generation functions $P(\cdot)$ for volumetric OCT images, as illustrated in Fig. 1b.

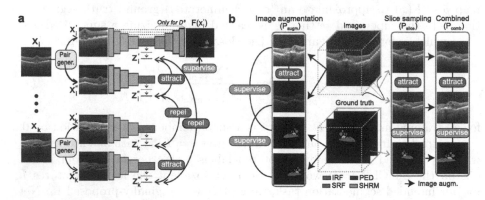

Fig. 1. Illustration of our CL methods. (a) Semi-supervised contrastive learning framework for unsupervised domain adaptation. Note that the *repel* modules do not apply to SimSiam. (b) Proposed pair generation methods for contrastive learning on 3D images.

We denote by P_{augm} an OCT adaptation of the pair formation typically employed for natural images (e.g., in SimCLR and SimSiam). Here, labeled slices in D^{s} and random slices in D^{t} are augmented with horizontal flipping ($p = 0.5$), horizontal and vertical translation (within 25% of the image size), zoom in (up to 50%), and color distortion (brightness up to 60% and jittering up to 20%). For color augmentation, images are transformed to RGB, and then back to grayscale.

We propose P_{slice} that leverages the coherence of nearby slices in a 3D volume for CL. Here, $x_i' = x_i$ for a slice index b_i' in 3D. Then, x_i'' is a slice from the same volume with the (rounded) slide index $b_i'' \sim \phi(b_i', \sigma)$, where ϕ is a Gaussian distribution centered on b_i', with standard deviation σ as a hyperparameter. Combining the two pairing strategies yields P_{comb} where P_{slice} is used first and the augmentations in P_{augm} are then applied on the selected slices.

2.3   Projection Heads to Extract Features for Image Segmentation

A projection head $C(\cdot)$ is formed by an aggregation function ρ^{agg} that aggregates features h to form a vector, which is then processed by a multilayer perceptron ρ^{MLP} to create projection z. Typical contrastive learning frameworks, e.g. SimCLR and SimSiam, use a projection (denoted herein by C_{pool}) where $\rho_{\mathrm{pool}}^{\mathrm{agg}} : \mathbb{R}^{w \times h \times c} \rightarrow \mathbb{R}^{1 \times 1 \times c}$ is a global pooling operation on the width w, height h, and channels c of the input features. Such projection C_{pool} may be suboptimal for learning representations to effectively leverage segmentation information, as backpropagation from $\mathcal{L}_{con}$ would lose the spatial context. Instead we propose C_{ch}, for which $\rho_{ch}^{agg} : \mathbb{R}^{w \times h \times c} \rightarrow \mathbb{R}^{w \times h \times 1}$ is a $1 \times 1 \times 1$ convolutional layer that learns how to aggregate layers, so the spatial context is preserved.

3 Experiments and Results

Dataset. We employ two large OCT datasets from clinical trials on patients with neovascular age-related macular degeneration. Images acquired using a *Spectralis* (Heidelberg Engineering) imaging device have $512 \times 496 \times 49$ or $768 \times 496 \times 19$ voxels, with a resolution of $10 \times 4 \times 111$ or $5 \times 4 \times 221$ µm/voxel, respectively. These were acquired as part of the phase-2 AVENUE trial (NCT02484690). Images acquired as part of another study, phase-3 HAR-BOR trial (NCT00891735), were acquired with a *Cirrus* HD-OCT III (Carl Zeiss Meditec) imaging device, which produces scans with $512 \times 128 \times 1024$ voxels and a resolution of $11.7 \times 47.2 \times 2.0$ µm/voxel. All slices (B-scans) from the two different devices are resampled to 512×512 pixels with roughly the same resolution of 10×4 µm/pixel. Select B-scans from Spectralis were manually annotated for fluid regions of potential diagnostic value: intraretinal fluid (IRF), subretinal fluid (SRF), pigment epithelial detachment (PED), and subretinal hyperreflective material (SHRM). More details on these datasets and the annotation protocol can be found in [17]. In our experiments, we use all training data from Spectralis as source domain D^s, and unlabeled images from Cirrus as target domain D^t. Labeled data from Cirrus is only used for the training of an *UpperBound* model for D^t. Data stratification used in our evaluations is detailed in the supplementary Table S1.

Implementation . Adam optimizer [16] was used in all models, with a learning rate of 10^{-3}. Dropout with $p = 0.5$ is applied before and after each convolutional block in the lowest UNet resolution level, as well as after the convolutions in the two subsequent resolution levels of the decoder. Group normalization [26] with 4 groups is used after each convolutional layer. After the aggregation function ϕ in $C(\cdot)$, two fully-connected layers are used with 128 units each, where the first one uses ReLU activation. We heuristically set $\lambda = 20$ and the standard deviation of ϕ for P_{slice} as $\sigma = 0.25$ µm, which is the range for which we observe roughly similar features across slices. Implementation is in Tensorflow 2.7, ran on an NVIDIA V100 GPU.

Metrics. We segment individual slices with 2D UNet, since (1) only some slices were annotated in OCT volumes; and (2) this enables our slice-contrasting scheme. Model performance was evaluated also slice-based, using the Dice coefficient and Unnormalized Volume Dissimilarity (UVD) on 2D slices. The latter measures the extent of total segmentation error (FP+FN) in each slice and is more robust to FP on B-scans with small annotated regions for individual classes. Averaging metrics across classes with a large variation may lead to bias. Thus, we first normalize each per-slice metric (m_i^c) for method i and class c by its class Baseline (m_{bas}^c), and then average these over all c and images on the test set.

All models with supervision were trained for 200 epochs, and the model at the epoch with the highest average Dice coefficient across classes on the validation set was selected for evaluation on a holdout test set.

Table 1. Evaluation on target domain D^t and source domain D^s across all classes, relative to Baseline (rel) and absolute values (abs), in red when metrics are inferior, and in bold for the best performance (excluding UpperBound). Supervised methods use labels from the domain in brackets. Dice is shown as %, and UVD as $\mu m^3 \times 10^2$.

Approach	Methods	Domain D^t				Domain D^s			
		Dice rel (abs)		UVD rel (abs)		Dice rel (abs)		UVD rel (abs)	
Supervised	UpperBound [D^t]	29.32	63.88	−8.93	8.67	-	-	-	-
	Baseline [D^s]	0.00	34.57	0.00	17.60	0.00	67.36	0.00	5.80
Adversarial	CycleGAN [24]	−6.53	28.04	2.51	20.10	−35.13	32.23	7.62	13.42
	DAN [2]	17.93	52.49	−5.25	12.34	−0.51	66.85	0.02	5.82
Finetuning (CL → supervision)	SimCLR [5]	14.01	48.58	−4.24	13.36	−3.48	63.88	0.48	6.28
	SimSiam [7]	11.41	45.97	−2.39	15.21	0.40	67.75	0.19	6.00
Joint (CL + supervision)	SegCLR(P_{augm}, C_{pool})	23.22	57.78	−5.91	11.68	−0.65	66.71	0.00	5.80
	SegSiam(P_{augm}, C_{pool})	−21.90	12.67	48.09	65.69	−46.58	20.78	48.31	54.11
	SegCLR(P_{slice}, C_{pool})	6.14	40.71	−2.81	14.79	−15.14	52.22	2.26	8.06
	SegCLR(P_{comb}, C_{pool})	27.21	61.77	−6.25	11.34	1.48	68.83	0.18	5.98
	SegCLR(P_{comb}, C_{ch})	**27.77**	**62.33**	**−6.71**	**10.88**	**1.93**	**69.28**	**−0.09**	**5.71**

3.1 Evaluation on the Unlabeled Target Domain

We first evaluate our proposed methods in the desired setting of unsupervised domain adaptation; i.e. models trained on $(x, y) \in D^s$ and $x \in D^t$ are evaluated on $y \in D^t$. Note that, although unlabeled for training, D^t has some ground truth annotations in the test set to enable its evaluation (see Table S1). In Table 1 and Table S2, *UpperBound* results for a supervised model trained on labeled data from the target domain are also reported for comparison. This labeled data, used here as a reference, is ablated for all other models. A supervised UNet model, *Baseline*, was trained only on the source domain D^s. Its poor performance on D^t confirms that the two domains indeed differ from supervised learning perspective.

Adversarial approaches are included as state-of-the-art baselines for unsupervised domain adaptation. CycleGAN [24] is adapted to our UNet using entire slices. Training converged with meaningful translated images from D^t to D^s, on which we run the pretrained UNet. Domain Adversarial Neural Network (DANN) includes a gradient reversal layer [12] with the design in [2] for segmentation. While DANN performs better than Baseline on D^t, CycleGAN is inferior. Our latter observation is contrary to that reported in [24], which is likely due to our Baseline being much superior to that of [24] (with a reported Dice of near zero).

Finetuning. Learning representations of D^t with SimCLR and SimSiam with subsequent finetuning on D^s shows a clear improvement over Baseline for all classes, confirming that these CL strategies are also valid when adapted to our

OCT dataset. SimCLR produces better results than SimSiam, suggesting that the use of negative pairs helps in learning better representations in our case.

Joint Training using the SimCLR framework and our above changes for a supervised loss for segmentation is herein called *SegCLR* (*SegSiam* for the Sim-Siam equivalent), which increases the number of parameters merely by 6.85% (7.33% for SegSiam). SegCLR(P_{augm}, C_{pool}) shows an overall improvement over finetuning. This is not the case for SegSiam(P_{augm}, C_{pool}), which suggests that the lack of negative pairs makes it difficult to simultaneously optimize $\mathcal{L}_{sup}$ and $\mathcal{L}_{con}$; e.g. minimizing $\mathcal{L}_{con}$ for only positive pairs may learn only simplistic features, which then would prevent $\mathcal{L}_{sup}$ from improving features for segmentation.

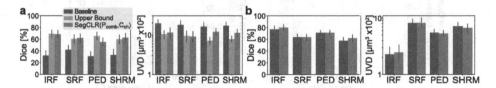

Fig. 2. Evaluation of models for the different classes on (a) target domain D^t and (b) source domain D^s. Black bars denote 95% confidence intervals.

Pair Generation. P_{slice} alone produces poorer results compared to P_{augm} alone, indicating that merely contrasting nearby slices does not facilitate extracting features useful for segmentation. Nevertheless, by applying both pair generation methods together, i.e. with P_{comb}, Dice and UVD results are overall superior to all the results above. This indicates that pairing nearby slices in our 3D images is a good complement to the typical image augmentation strategies.

Projections. We change the typical C_{pool} head with our proposed C_{ch} designed specifically for the segmentation task, which adds a mere 0.03% more parameters. While for IRF and PED (Table S2) this performs worse than SegCLR(P_{comb}, C_{pool}), the Dice and UVD metrics averaged across classes are overall the best for SegCLR(P_{comb}, C_{ch}), notably even surpassing the UpperBound in some cases (Fig. 2a). Hence, our proposed model could replace the UpperBound if and when no training data is available in the target domain, and in doing so only compromising the performance for PED (Fig. 2a).

3.2   Evaluation on the Labeled Source Domain

Herein we test the retention of segmentation information for the original source domain D^s, as shown in Table 1 (right-most column) and Fig. 2b. As expected, Baseline produces better results on D^s than on D^t, since it is evaluated in the same domain in which it was supervised. For finetuning, contrary to its relative performance on D^t, for D^s SimSiam produces better results than SimCLR. A reason could be SimSiam's use of only positive pairs leading to distinct features for each domain, which are later finetuned relatively more easily with segmentation supervision on D^s. Further observations on D^s corroborate their above-discussed counterparts for D^t; i.e. SegSiam fails; P_{slice} alone performs worse than P_{augm} alone; and combining them as P_{comb} performs the best. Our proposed SegCLR(P_{comb}, C_{ch}) model produces the best results across classes also for this source domain D^s, notably even surpassing the supervised Baseline. This shows that supervised information from the labeled domain is not forgotten (e.g. as a trade-off when learning from the unlabeled domain), but it is rather enhanced with the unlabaled data, despite the latter being from a different domain.

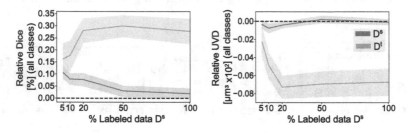

Fig. 3. Evaluation on D^s and D^t datasets with models trained on 5, 10, 20, 50, and 100% of labeled data from D^s. Herein volume percentages are reported. Results show the proposed SegCLR(P_{comb}, C_{ch}) relative to Baseline with same % of D^s labeled data.

3.3 Ablations on Amount of Labeled Data

We study below the effect that the amount of labeled data in D^s has on the performance of our semi-supervised learning framework. To this end, we randomly ablate parts of the training data in D^s. The validation set was fixed to avoid any bias on model selection. Results in Fig. 3 indicate that adding more labeled data from D^s in the training of our model has overall a positive effect on its effectiveness for segmentation of the target domain D^t. This is likely because $\mathcal{L}_{con}$ can adapt segmentation features to the D^t space only when these features are learned robustly with more labeled data, based on which $\mathcal{L}_{sup}$ can be minimized. The trend is somewhat the opposite for D^s: For the low data regime, $\mathcal{L}_{con}$ seems to help with feature extraction, even though the information comes from a different domain. However, as the amount of labeled data increases and $\mathcal{L}_{sup}$ is exposed to enough data from the source domain, any contrastive information contribution from a different unlabeled domain becomes relatively insignificant.

3.4 Segmentation Results Compared to Inter-grader Variability

Manual annotation of retinal fluids is challenging, leading to large variability in segmentation metrics even among human experts. We herein compare our proposed SegCLR(P_{comb}, C_{ch}) to inter-grader discrepancies. We employ a set of 44 OCT volumes, each fully annotated independently by 4 different graders.

These annotations are drawn from the same target domain D^t but come from a different clinical study than the dataset used in training, so a direct comparison is not possible. We evaluated segmentation metrics for graders by comparing them with one another. We deem our method within inter-grader variability when its metric for a class and image, with respect to any grader, is better than that of at least one human inter-grader metric (variation). Across images and classes, SegCLR(P_{comb}, C_{ch}) performs within such inter-grader variability in 65.34% and 48.30% of cases based on Dice and UVD, respectively.

4   Conclusions

Unsupervised domain adaptation for segmentation has been typically approached as finetuning on features learned via self-supervision from classification tasks. We propose herein a segmentation approach that is jointly supervised with existing data while being self-supervised with abundant unlabeled examples from a previously unseen domain. With our proposed slice-based pairing and channel-wise aggregation for contrastive projections, our model successfully adapts supervised labeled-domain info to an unlabeled domain, surpassing previous state-of-the-art adversarial methods and even approaching the performance of an upper bound. We also improve the results in the original labeled domain by leveraging the unsupervised (contrastive) info. These contributions will help reduce manual annotation efforts for segmentation of 3D volumes in new data domains.

References

1. Bogunovic, H., Venhuizen, F., Klimscha, S., Apostolopoulos, S., Bab-Hadiashar, A., et al.: RETOUCH: the retinal OCT fluid detection and segmentation benchmark and challenge. IEEE Trans. Med. Imaging **38**(8), 1858–1874 (2019)
2. Bolte, J.A., et al.: Unsupervised domain adaptation to improve image segmentation quality both in the source and target domain. In: IEEE Conference on Computer Vision and Pattern Recognition (CVPR) Workshops, pp. 1404–1413 (2019)
3. Caron, M., et al.: Emerging properties in self-supervised vision transformers. In: IEEE International Conference on Computer Vision (ICCV), pp. 9650–9660 (2021)
4. Chaitanya, K., Erdil, E., Karani, N., Konukoglu, E.: Contrastive learning of global and local features for medical image segmentation with limited annotations. In: Advances in Neural Information Processing Systems (NeurIPS), vol. 33, pp. 12546–12558 (2020)
5. Chen, T., Kornblith, S., Norouzi, M., Hinton, G.: A simple framework for contrastive learning of visual representations. In: International Conference on Machine Learning (ICML), pp. 1597–1607 (2020)
6. Chen, T., Kornblith, S., Swersky, K., Norouzi, M., Hinton, G.E.: Big self-supervised models are strong semi-supervised learners. In: Advances in Neural Information Processing Systems (NeurIPS), pp. 22243–22255 (2020)

7. Chen, X., He, K.: Exploring simple siamese representation learning. In: IEEE Conference on Computer Vision and Pattern Recognition (CVPR), pp. 15750–15758 (2021)
8. Chen, Y., et al.: USCL: pretraining deep ultrasound image diagnosis model through video contrastive representation learning. In: de Bruijne, M., et al. (eds.) MICCAI 2021. LNCS, vol. 12908, pp. 627–637. Springer, Cham (2021). https://doi.org/10.1007/978-3-030-87237-3_60
9. Deng, J., Dong, W., Socher, R., Li, L.J., Li, K., Fei-Fei, L.: ImageNet: a large-scale hierarchical image database. In: IEEE Conference on Computer Vision and Pattern Recognition (CVPR), pp. 248–255 (2009)
10. Fauw, J.D., Ledsam, J.R., Romera-Paredes, B., Nikolov, S., Tomasev, N., et al.: Clinically applicable deep learning for diagnosis and referral in retinal disease. Nat. Med. **24**(9), 1342–1350 (2018)
11. Fujimoto, J., Swanson, E.: The development, commercialization, and impact of optical coherence tomography. Invest. Ophthalmol. Vis. Sci. **57**(9) (2016)
12. Ganin, Y., Lempitsky, V.: Unsupervised domain adaptation by backpropagation. In: International Conference on Machine Learning (ICML), pp. 1180–1189 (2015)
13. Grill, J.B., et al.: Bootstrap your own latent-a new approach to self-supervised learning. In: Advances in Neural Information Processing Systems (NeurIPS), vol. 33, pp. 21271–21284 (2020)
14. He, K., Fan, H., Wu, Y., Xie, S., Girshick, R.: Momentum contrast for unsupervised visual representation learning. In: IEEE Conference on Computer Vision and Pattern Recognition (CVPR), pp. 9729–9738 (2020)
15. Khosla, P., et al.: Supervised contrastive learning. In: Advances in Neural Information Processing Systems (NeurIPS), vol. 33, pp. 18661–18673 (2020)
16. Kingma, D.P., Ba, J.: Adam: a method for stochastic optimization. In: International Conference on Learning Representations (ICLR) (2015)
17. Maunz, A., et al.: Accuracy of a machine-learning algorithm for detecting and classifying choroidal neovascularization on spectral-domain optical coherence tomography. J. Personal. Med. **11**(6), 524 (2021)
18. Oord, A.v.d., Li, Y., Vinyals, O.: Representation learning with contrastive predictive coding. arXiv preprint arXiv:1807.03748 (2018)
19. Ren, M., Dey, N., Fishbaugh, J., Gerig, G.: Segmentation-renormalized deep feature modulation for unpaired image harmonization. IEEE Trans. Med. Imaging **40**(6), 1519–1530 (2021)
20. Ronneberger, O., Fischer, P., Brox, T.: U-Net: convolutional networks for biomedical image segmentation. In: Navab, N., Hornegger, J., Wells, W.M., Frangi, A.F. (eds.) MICCAI 2015. LNCS, vol. 9351, pp. 234–241. Springer, Cham (2015). https://doi.org/10.1007/978-3-319-24574-4_28
21. Sahni, J.N., et al.: A machine learning approach to predict response to anti-VEGF treatment in patients with neovascular age-related macular degeneration using SD-OCT. Invest. Ophthalmol. Vis. Sci. **60**(11), PB094–PB094 (2019)
22. Schlegl, T., et al.: Fully automated detection and quantification of macular fluid in OCT using deep learning. Ophthalmology **125**(4), 549–558 (2018)
23. Schmidt-Erfurth, U., Waldstein, S.M.: A paradigm shift in imaging biomarkers in neovascular age-related macular degeneration. Prog. Retin. Eye Res. **50**, 1–24 (2016)
24. Seeböck, P., et al.: Using CycleGANs for effectively reducing image variability across OCT devices and improving retinal fluid segmentation. In: IEEE International Symposium on Biomedical Imaging (ISBI), pp. 605–609 (2019)

25. Wang, M., Deng, W.: Deep visual domain adaptation: a survey. Neurocomputing **312**, 135–153 (2018)
26. Wu, Y., He, K.: Group normalization. In: Ferrari, V., Hebert, M., Sminchisescu, C., Weiss, Y. (eds.) ECCV 2018. LNCS, vol. 11217, pp. 3–19. Springer, Cham (2018). https://doi.org/10.1007/978-3-030-01261-8_1

Machine Learning – Model Interpretation

Neuro-RDM: An Explainable Neural Network Landscape of Reaction-Diffusion Model for Cognitive Task Recognition

Tingting Dan[1,2], Hongmin Cai[2], Zhuobin Huang[2], Paul Laurienti[3], Won Hwa Kim[4], and Guorong Wu[1,5(✉)]

[1] Department of Psychiatry, The University of North Carolina at Chapel Hill, Chapel Hill, NC 27599, USA
grwu@med.unc.edu
[2] School of Computer Science and Engineering, South China University of Technology, Guangzhou 510006, China
[3] Department of Radiology, Wake Forest School of Medicine, Winston Salem, NC 27157, USA
[4] Computer Science and Engineering/Graduate School of AI, POSTECH, Pohang 37673, South Korea
[5] Department of Computer Science, The University of North Carolina at Chapel Hill, Chapel Hill, NC 27599, USA

Abstract. The functional neural imaging technology sheds new light on characterizing the neural activity at each brain region and the information exchange from region to region. However, it is challenging to reverse-engineer the working mechanism of brain function and behavior through the evolving functional neuroimages. In this work, we conceptualize that the ensemble of evolving neuronal synapses forms a dynamic system of functional connectivity, where the system behavior (aka. Brain state) of such a reaction-diffusion process can be formulated by a set of trainable PDEs (partial differential equations). To that end, we first introduce a PDE-based reaction-diffusion model (RDM) to jointly characterize the propagation of brain states throughout the functional brain network as well as the non-linear interaction between brain state and neural activity manifested in the BOLD (blood-oxygen-level-dependent) signals. Next, we translate the diffusion and reaction processes formulated in the PDE into a graph neural network, where the driving force is to establish the mapping from the evolution of brain states to the known cognitive tasks. By doing so, the layer-by-layer learning scenario allows us to not only fine-tune the RDM model for predicting cognitive tasks but also explain how brain functions support cognitive status with a great neuroscience insight. We have evaluated our proof-of-concept approach on both simulated data and functional neuroimages from HCP (Human Connectome Project) database. Since our neuro-RDM combines the power of deep learning and insight of dynamic systems, our method has significantly improved recognition performance in terms of accuracy and robustness to the non-neuronal noise, compared with the conventional deep learning models.

Keywords: Partial differential equation · Recurrent neural network · Functional MRI · Brain state recognition

© The Author(s), under exclusive license to Springer Nature Switzerland AG 2022
L. Wang et al. (Eds.): MICCAI 2022, LNCS 13438, pp. 365–374, 2022.
https://doi.org/10.1007/978-3-031-16452-1_35

1   Introduction

The human brain is a complex system that is supported by the vast wiring diagrams of white matter fibers [1]. Functional magnetic resonance imaging (fMRI) technology further allows us to characterize the coupling mechanism of brain functions on top of the structural connectomes by monitoring the fluctuations in blood-oxygen-level-dependent (BOLD) signal [2], which has been assumed to be proportional to the local average neuronal activity [3].

Understanding how cognition and behavior emerge from brain functions is a fundamental scientific problem in the field of neuroscience [4]. Since human cognition is influenced not only by external task demands but also latent brain states that change over time, uncovering hidden brain states and their time-varying functional fluctuation patterns in response to moment-by-moment changes in task demands becomes the gateway to understanding flexible and adaptive human cognition [5–7].

Striking efforts have been made to automatically detect the transition of brain state and recognize brain states using fMRI data. Current computational methods can be roughly grouped into model-based and data-driven approaches. Auto-regressive model [8] and the hidden Markov model [9] are two popular model-based statistical approaches to characterize the temporal dynamics of BOLD signals. At the cell level, ordinary differential equations (ODEs) have been used to model neural dynamics in the synaptic transmission mechanism for small species such as nematodes [10]. Although the ODE-based model introduces the explainability into understanding brain functions with the insight of system dynamics, the model parameters are often tuned empirically. On the other hand, data-driven approaches such as deep neural networks have been widely studied to detect the state change and recognize tasks from fMRI data [11]. For example, the evolving functional connectivity matrices are first decomposed using the predefined basis vectors in [12]. Then the coefficients after decomposition are used as the input to the recurrent neural network (RNN) brain state change detection. However, most of the deep learning models lack the explainability to interpret the underlying mechanism of functional dynamics.

There is a potential that an explainable neural network can be achieved by combining the power of mathematic models (with well-studied mechanisms) and deep neural networks (find the best model). In this context, we conceptualize that functional fluctuations manifested in the BOLD signals form a dynamic system. Specifically, we assume each brain region is associated with a latent region-specific state profile, which is the outcome of equilibrium between a diffusion process and a reaction process of evolving neuronal activities. Following the principle in systems biology, the evolution of brain functions can be formulated into a partial differential equation (PDE) of the reaction-diffusion model (RDM) [13]. Enlightened by the recent work of Neural-ODE [14], we first disassemble the non-linear processes in the RDM into the equivalent counterpart of neural network components. Then, we assemble them into a unified neural network architecture (coined as *neuro-RDM*), where the driving force of supervised learning is the prediction of brain state change or functional task recognition. Furthermore, cutting-edge deep learning components allow us to refine RDM from a machine learning perspective. To that end, we develop the machine intelligence of system-level explainability into a deep learning model, which is expected to yield new underpinnings of biological processes from a large amount of functional neuroimages.

The motivation of our *neuro-RDM* is demonstrated in Fig. 1. We train an RNN and our *neuro-RDM* to fit the temporal dynamics on the one-particle trajectory data generated from a Hamiltonian system. In the testing stage, we use the trained RNN and *neuro-RDM* to predict the entire trajectory based on the initial value, as shown in the middle and right panel of Fig. 1. It is clear that the system-level understanding can carve current deep models into a more trustable "black box", which is very beneficial in discovering novel mechanisms in neuroscience studies. We have evaluated our *neuro-RDM* on both simulated and real fMRI data, where we have enhanced the accuracy in predicting brain states with the reasonable interpretation of the functional dynamics even in the scenario with substantial external non-neuronal noise.

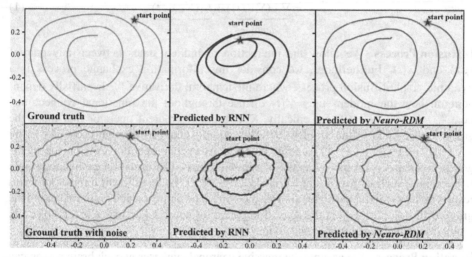

Fig. 1. The comparison between RNN (middle) and *neuro-RDM* (right) in predicting the one-particle trajectory generated from a Hamiltonian system with (top) and without noise (bottom).

2   Method

Suppose we partition the brain into N distinct regions. At each region, we observe the mean time course of BOLD signal $x_i(\tau)$ $(i = 1, \ldots, N)$ where τ is a continuous variable of time. Thus, the input to the deep model is a discretized time-varying signal matrix $X(t) = [x_i(t)]_{t=1}^{T} \in \mathbb{R}^{N \times T}$. The output is the label γ_c $(c = 1, \ldots, C)$ that is associated with one of C cognitive tasks. To establish the non-linear mapping between $X(t)$ and γ_c, we introduce a hidden state $v_i(t) \in \mathbb{R}^Q$ for each brain region, which can be regarded as the more intrinsic embedding vectors for predicting the label γ_c than using BOLD signal $X(t)$. In the perspective of neuroscience and dynamic systems, we conceptualize that the evolution of $V(t) = [v_i(t)]_i^N$ underlines the system behavior of functional fluctuations, where its principled mechanism can be modeled using systems biology approaches. In a nutshell, the whole-brain hidden states $V(t)$ act as a stepping stone that allows us to link the RDM to the deep learning model and achieve the trainable RDM (aka. *neuro-RDM*).

2.1 Reaction-Diffusion Model for Functional Dynamics

Convergence evidence shows that brain regions are closely connected to each other and form a functional connectome. It is a common practice to measure the connectivity strength w_{ij} for the link e_{ij} between i^{th} and j^{th} regions based on the statistical correlation between $x_i(t)$ and $x_j(t)$. Since each brain region is not isolated, it is reasonable to assume that the system behavior of time-varying hidden state $V(t)$ is the outcome of dynamic information exchange throughout the brain, which consists of a diffusion process and a reaction process:

$$\frac{dV}{dt} = \underbrace{\nabla \cdot (\nabla V(t))}_{diffusion} + \underbrace{f_\Theta(V, X, t)}_{reaction} \tag{1}$$

Diffusion Process. We allow the interaction of hidden states between any pair of $v_i(t)$ and $v_j(t)$. Furthermore, we consider this information exchange process is a dynamic graph diffusion process, where the temporal derivative $\frac{dV}{dt}$ is partially dependent on how the hidden states $V(t)$ diffuse throughout the functional connectome, i.e., $\frac{dV}{dt} = \nabla \cdot (\nabla V(t))$. Specifically, ∇ is a graph gradient operator that maps the graph embeddings to the amount of information exchanged through each link e_{ij} by $\nabla V(t)|_{e_{ij}} = w_{ij}(v_i(t) - v_j(t))$. After that, the divergence operator ($\nabla \cdot$) on top of the graph gradient $\nabla V(t)$ measures the whole-brain flux of information exchange at time t. Repeating such diffusion operation (i.e., $\nabla \cdot (\nabla V(t))$) a sufficient number of times results in identical hidden states all over the brain. The neuroscience intuition behind the graph diffusion term is that the activation pattern of neuronal activities is topologically aligned with the functional connectome.

Reaction Process. We assume the massive neuronal synapses at each brain region can be approximated by a non-linear function f that characterizes the reaction between BOLD signal $X(t)$ and hidden states $V(t)$ over time. In a neural network cliché, the non-linear interaction is often defined as $f_\Theta(t) = \sigma(\beta_1 V(t) + \beta_2 X(t) + \mu)$, where σ is a sigmoid function, and Θ are hyper-parameters including β_1, β_2, and μ.

Once the PDE model in Eq. (1) is fixed, the parameters Θ can be tuned based on domain knowledge. Since the cognitive task labels are not used to optimize the model parameters Θ, the conventional RDM model is limited in predicting cognitive status (such as state change [15] and recognition [16]) for fMRI studies. However, the recent work on graph neural networks (GNN) [17–19] sheds new light on connecting RDM to GNN that yields a trainable RDM as described next.

2.2 *Neuro-RDM*: A Trainable and Better RDM by Linking PDE with GNN

The diagram of RDM is shown in the left panel Fig. 2, where the diffusion and reaction processes are colored in gold and blue, respectively. It is worth noting that model parameters are not changed during the iterative updating of $V(t)$.

Trainable RDM: Translate from PDE to GNN. In the machine learning area, recent work [19, 20] shows that the diffusion process $\nabla \cdot (\nabla V(t))$ on the connectome (graph) domain is equivalent to the graph convolutions. Furthermore, the convolution kernel K (a $N \times N$ diagnal matrix) can be learned and make the diffusion $\nabla \cdot (K\nabla V(t))$ more adaptive to the observed data. The neural network backbone of RDM is shown in the right panel of Fig. 2, which consists of two major components. *First*, given the region-to-region functional connectivities $\left[w_{ij}\right]_{ij=1}^N$, graph convolution on the embedding vectors of hidden states $V(t)$ is eventually a fully-connected layer with learnable parameters $H \in \mathbb{R}^{Q_{in} \times Q_{out}}$ [18], where Q_{in} and Q_{out} denote the input and output dimensions of feature embeddings. *Second*, the output of the graph convolution layer is combined with the BOLD signals and feed to a fully-connected network, where the non-linearity of the interaction between $V(t)$ and $X(t)$ can be captured by a set of fully-connected layers.

It is clear that the deep neural network architecture casts the RDM into a supervised learning scenario by integrating the loss function for change detection and cognitive task recognition based on $V(T)$ (the final status of hidden states).

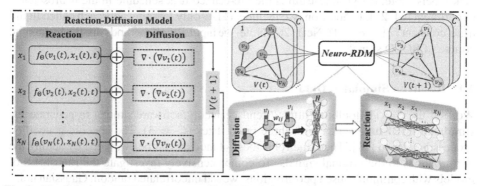

Fig. 2. The diagram of RDM implemented by PDEs (left) and the corresponding implementation using neural networks (right).

Neuro-RDM: **Revisit from GNN to PDE.** On the other hand, cutting-edge machine learning techniques allow us to refine RDM with the data-driven point of view. For example, the functional connectivity w_{ij} is fixed in the graph gradient and divergence operation. Here, we can go one step further to reformulate w_{ij} as the graph link attention p_{ij}. To achieve it, we first introduce a learnable node-wise attention vector $z_i \in \mathbb{R}^Q$. Following the graph attention mechanism in [21], the link-wise attention p_{ij} can be updated by $p_{ij} = \dfrac{\exp(LeakyReLU((z_i \odot v_i)^T z_j \odot v_j))}{\sum_{k \in \mathcal{N}_i} \exp(LeakyReLU((z_i \odot v_i)^T z_j \odot v_j))}$, where $\odot$ denotes Hadamard operator, $\mathcal{N}_i$ is the one-hop neighbor of ith node, and *LeakyReLU* denotes the leaky rectified linear unit. Recall that the matrix form L of Laplacian operator $\Delta = -\nabla \cdot \nabla$ in the graph domain is $L = D - W$, where $W = \left[w_{ij}\right]_{ij}^N$ is called adjacency matrix that is the pre-calculated connectivity degree and D is the diagonal matrix of row-wise summation of W. By plugging the self-attention hidden states $z_i \odot v_i(t)$ into the Laplacian operator, we devise the new PDE for graph diffusion process as $\frac{dV}{dt} = (P(V) - I)V(t)$, where I is a $N \times N$

identity matrix and $P = [p_{ij}]_{ij=1}^{N}$ is called graph attention matrix. Compared with W, P is dynamic and more robust to external noise as the hidden states $V(t)$ is a time-varying intrinsic feature representation. It is worth noting that the integration of the attention component in our *neuro-RDM* offers a new window to discover the novel mechanism of cognition and behavior in neuroscience studies.

3 Experiments

We have evaluated the performance of predicting cognitive tasks by our proposed *neuro-RDM* on both simulated data and task-based functional neuroimage data from HCP (Human Connectome Project) [22]. We compare the prediction accuracy between our *neuro-RDM* and two existing RNN-only methods: (1) classic long short-term memory (LSTM) network used for decoding brain state used in [16] and (2) a state classification network for detecting salient patterns over time and space (SPOTS) [23]. The loss function is formulated as the cross-entropy between the ground-truth and predicted cognitive task labels. Note, the ground-truth is the pre-defined task schedule in the neuroscience experiment [24, 25]. In addition, we include a PDE-only learning approach called liquid time-constant network (LTCNet) [26]. Note, the inputs of all methods are the mean time course of BOLD signal.

3.1 Result on Simulated Data

We first use SimTB toolbox (https://trendscenter.org/software/simtb/) to generate the simulated fMRI time series with three brain states ($C = 3$). The specific generation process is refer to [27]. Then, the robustness of models can be evaluated by adding the perturbations to the original signals. To comprehensively investigate the robustness of models with commonly-used perturbations, we add uncorrelated random Gaussian noise to the generated BOLD signals with an increasing level signal-noise ratios (SNR) from 60 to 0.5. A total 2000 instances are generated, splitting 900 training sets, 100 validation sets, and 1000 testing sets. Figure 3 demonstrates the state recognition accuracy results by our *Neuro-RDM* (red), LTCNet (green), SPOTS (blue), and LSTM (orange), where our *Neuro-RDM* consistently yields the highest accuracy in all settings of the noise levels. It is clear that PDE-based approaches (our *Neuro-RDM* and LTCNet) are generally

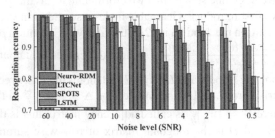

Fig. 3. The recognition accuracy of brain state with respect to noise levels by LSTM (orange), SPOTS (blue), LTCNet (green), and our *Neuro-RDM* (red). (Color figure online)

more robust to the noises, implying the importance of system-level neuroscience insight in deep learning. Since our *Neuro-RDM* optimizes the parameters in a layer-by-layer manner, the recognition accuracy is consistently higher than LTCNet.

3.2 Application on Task-Based fMRI Data

Data Description. We selected a total of 850 healthy subjects (splitting 425 training sets, 55 validation sets, and 370 testing sets) involved working memory task-based fMRI data from the HCP database. Each subject possesses two fMRI scans, including test and retest data. The working memory tasks in each fMRI scan include 2-back and 0-back task events of body, place, face, and tools, as well as fixation periods. Each fMRI scan contains 393 scanning time points and 268 brain regions parcellated by Yale functional atlas [28]. These brain regions are grouped into seven large-scale functional brain networks, including the central executive network (CEN), visual network (VN), sensorimotor network (SMN), default mode network (DMN), dorsal attention network (DAN), salience network (SN), and the basal ganglia network (BGN). To align with the learning task (i.e., recognizing functional tasks in Fig. 5), we truncate the long time course of BOLD signals (usually includes more than eight functional tasks) into a set of segments where each segment primarily covers one functional task.

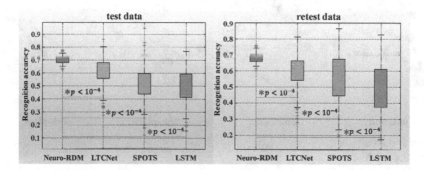

Fig. 4. The recognition performance of four methods on test and retest data.

Evaluating the Accuracy in Recognizing Cognitive Tasks. In this experiment, the training data is mixed with the test/retest fMRI data, which is to push the model to learn task-specific features. In the application stage, we apply the trained models for test/retest fMRI data separately. Figure 4 shows the recognition accuracies on test-scan (left) and restest-scan (right) by our *Neuro-RDM* (red), LTCNet (green), SPOTS (blue), and LSTM (orange), respectively. It is clear that our *neuro-RDM* consistently outperforms all the comparison methods with significant improvement (paired t-test: $p < 10^{-4}$) over the other three counterpart methods (indicated by '*').

Evaluating the Replicability in Brain Network Attention. Recall that we introduce attention p_{ij} for each link e_{ij} and attention z_i at i^{th} node in our *Neuro-RDM*. Thus, we first obtain the link-wise and node-wise attention for each subject, regardless of test-scan or retest-scan, which forms a brain circuit map associated with each functional task. Next, we average the task-specific attention maps for test-scans and for retest-scans separately, where we display the results (top: test-scans, bottom: retest-scans) for 0bk-body, 2bk-body, 0bk-place, and 2bk-place in Fig. 5. Specifically, the node size and edge thickness are proportional to the likelihood of being associated with the underlying functional task. The node color represents the association to the functional networks. It is apparent that the attention maps learned on test-scan and retest-scan are very similar in terms of a lot of common topological patterns, which indicates the replicability of our PDE-based deep model. Meanwhile, the default mode network (blue dots) and the central executive network (green dots) are highly repetitive (greater than 40% proportions) in all cognitive states, implying that they are highly related to the working memory tasks. It is worth noting that the associations between these identified brain circuits and cognitive status have also been frequently reported in neuroscience literature [29, 30].

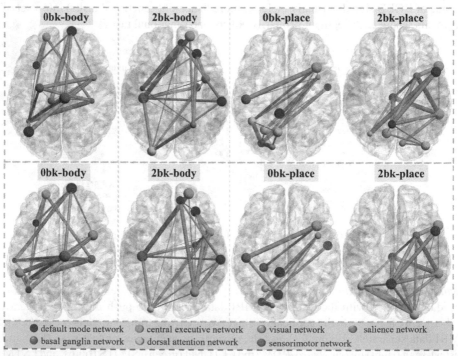

Fig. 5. The task-specific attention mappings of the brain circuits learned on test-scan (top) and retest-scan (bottom). Node size and edge thickness are proportional to the likelihood of being associated with the underlying functional tasks (from left to right: 0bk-body, 2bk-body, 0bk-place, and 2bk-place). (Color figure online)

4 Conclusion

In this work, we explore a new paradigm of developing the neuroscience insight of system dynamics into a deep learning framework. We put the spotlight on the reaction-diffusion model, which is used to capture the evolution of whole-brain neuronal activities. Our proposed *Neuro-RDM* is a two-way solution. We start from the classic PDE-based RDM model and present an equivalent network implementation. After that, the integration of widely-used machine learning components such as graph attention allows us to refine RDM that not only keeps mathematics insight but also becomes more adaptive to the observed neuroimaging data. Experimental results show that our *neuro-RDM* can achieve more accurate and robust task recognition results under a significant amount of non-neuronal noise than current methods that either use deep learning or PDE-based model only. In our future work, we will explore the clinic value of our *Neuro-RDM* in early diagnosing neurological disorders such as Autism and Alzheimer's disease from resting-state fMRI.

References

1. Sporns, O.: Networks of the Brain. MIT Press, Cambridge (2011)
2. van den Heuvel, M.P., Pol, H.E.H.: Exploring the brain network: a review on resting-state fMRI functional connectivity. Eur. Neuropsychopharmacology **20**(8), 519–534 (2010)
3. Heeger, D.J., Ress, D.: What does fMRI tell us about neuronal activity? Nat. Rev. Neurosci. **3**(2), 142–151 (2002)
4. Kitzbichler, M.G., et al.: Cognitive effort drives workspace configuration of human brain functional networks. J. Neurosci. **31**(22), 8259–8270 (2011)
5. Bressler, S.L., Menon, V.: Large-scale brain networks in cognition: emerging methods and principles. Trends Cogn. Sci. **14**(6), 277–290 (2010)
6. Shine, J.M., et al.: The dynamics of functional brain networks: integrated network states during cognitive task performance. Neuron **92**(2), 544–554 (2016)
7. Taghia, J., et al.: Uncovering hidden brain state dynamics that regulate performance and decision-making during cognition. Nat. Commun. **9**(1), 2505 (2018)
8. Zalesky, A., et al.: Time-resolved resting-state brain networks. Proc. Natl. Acad. Sci. **111**(28), 10341 (2014)
9. Vidaurre, D., Smith, S.M., Woolrich, M.W.: Brain network dynamics are hierarchically organized in time. Proc. Natl. Acad. Sci. **114**(48), 12827 (2017)
10. Wicks, S.R., Roehrig, C.J., Rankin, C.H.: A dynamic network simulation of the nematode tap withdrawal circuit: predictions concerning synaptic function using behavioral criteria. J. Neurosci. **16**(12), 4017 (1996)
11. Khosla, M., et al.: Machine learning in resting-state fMRI analysis. Magn. Reson. Imaging **64**, 101–121 (2019)
12. Li, H., Fan, Y.: Identification of temporal transition of functional states using recurrent neural networks from functional MRI. In: Frangi, A.F., Schnabel, J.A., Davatzikos, C., Alberola-López, C., Fichtinger, G. (eds.) MICCAI 2018. LNCS, vol. 11072, pp. 232–239. Springer, Cham (2018). https://doi.org/10.1007/978-3-030-00931-1_27
13. Kondo, S., Miura, T.: Reaction-diffusion model as a framework for understanding biological pattern formation. Science **329**(5999), 1616–1620 (2010)
14. Chen, R.T.Q., et al.: Neural ordinary differential equations. In: Advances in Neural Information Processing Systems (NIPS 2018), vol. 31 (2018)

15. Huang, Z., Cai, H., Dan, T., Lin, Y., Laurienti, P., Wu, G.: Detecting brain state changes by geometric deep learning of functional dynamics on riemannian manifold. In: de Bruijne, M., et al. (eds.) MICCAI 2021. LNCS, vol. 12907, pp. 543–552. Springer, Cham (2021). https://doi.org/10.1007/978-3-030-87234-2_51

16. Li, H., Fan, Y.: Interpretable, highly accurate brain decoding of subtly distinct brain states from functional MRI using intrinsic functional networks and long short-term memory recurrent neural networks. Neuroimage **202**, 116059 (2019)

17. Defferrard, M., Bresson, X., Vandergheynst, P.: Convolutional neural networks on graphs with fast localized spectral filtering. In: Proceedings of the 30th International Conference on Neural Information Processing Systems, pp. 3844–3852. Curran Associates Inc., Barcelona (2016)

18. Kipf, T.N., Welling, M.: Semi-supervised classificiation with graph convolutional networks. In: International Conference on Learning Representations ICLR (2016)

19. Chamberlain, B.P., et al.: GRAND: graph neural diffusion. In: 38th International Conference on Machine Learning, PMLR (2021)

20. Eliasof, M., Haber, E., Treister, E.: PDE-GCN: novel architectures for graph neural networks motivated by partial differential equations. In: 35th Conference on Neural Information Processing Systems (NIPS) (2021)

21. Veličković, P., et al.: Graph attention networks. In: International Conference on Learning Representations (2018)

22. Barch, D.M., et al.: Function in the human connectome: task-fMRI and individual differences in behavior. Neuroimage **80**, 169–189 (2013)

23. Chan, Y.H., Gupta, S., Kasun, L.L.C., Rajapakse, J.C.: Decoding task states by spotting salient patterns at time points and brain regions. In: Kia, S.M., et al. (eds.) MLCN/RNO-AI -2020. LNCS, vol. 12449, pp. 88–97. Springer, Cham (2020). https://doi.org/10.1007/978-3-030-66843-3_9

24. Dan, T., et al.: Learning brain dynamics of evolving manifold functional MRI data using geometric-attention neural network. IEEE Trans. Med. Imaging, 1–1 (2022). https://doi.org/10.1109/TMI.2022.3169640

25. Dan, T., et al.: Uncovering shape signatures of resting-state functional connectivity by geometric deep learning on Riemannian manifold. Human Brain Mapping **43**, 3970–3986 (2022)

26. Hasani, R., et al.: Liquid time-constant networks. arXiv preprint arXiv:2006.04439 (2020)

27. Lin, Y., et al.: Learning dynamic graph embeddings for accurate detection of cognitive state changes in functional brain networks. Neuroimage **230**, 117791 (2021)

28. Shen, X., et al.: Groupwise whole-brain parcellation from resting-state fMRI data for network node identification. Neuroimage **82**, 403–415 (2013)

29. Dai, C., et al.: Effects of sleep deprivation on working memory: change in functional connectivity between the Dorsal Attention, Default Mode, and Fronto-Parietal Networks. Front. Human Neurosci. **14**, 360 (2020). https://doi.org/10.3389/fnhum.2020.00360

30. Chai, W.J., Abd Hamid, A.I., Abdullah, J.M.: Working memory from the psychological and neurosciences perspectives: a review. Front. Psychol. **9**, 401 (2018). https://doi.org/10.3389/fpsyg.2018.00401

Interpretable Graph Neural Networks for Connectome-Based Brain Disorder Analysis

Hejie Cui[1], Wei Dai[1], Yanqiao Zhu[2], Xiaoxiao Li[3], Lifang He[4],
and Carl Yang[1(✉)]

[1] Emory University, Atlanta, USA
j.carlyang@emory.edu
[2] University of California, Los Angeles, USA
[3] The University of British Columbia, Vancouver, Canada
[4] Lehigh University, Bethlehem, USA

Abstract. Human brains lie at the core of complex neurobiological systems, where the neurons, circuits, and subsystems interact in enigmatic ways. Understanding the structural and functional mechanisms of the brain has long been an intriguing pursuit for neuroscience research and clinical disorder therapy. Mapping the connections of the human brain as a network is one of the most pervasive paradigms in neuroscience. Graph Neural Networks (GNNs) have recently emerged as a potential method for modeling complex network data. Deep models, on the other hand, have low interpretability, which prevents their usage in decision-critical contexts like healthcare. To bridge this gap, we propose an interpretable framework to analyze disorder-specific Regions of Interest (ROIs) and prominent connections. The proposed framework consists of two modules: a brain-network-oriented backbone model for disease prediction and a globally shared explanation generator that highlights disorder-specific biomarkers including salient ROIs and important connections. We conduct experiments on three real-world datasets of brain disorders. The results verify that our framework can obtain outstanding performance and also identify meaningful biomarkers. All code for this work is available at https://github.com/HennyJie/IBGNN.git.

Keywords: Interpretation · Graph neural network · Brain networks

1 Introduction

Brain networks (a.k.a the connectome) are complex graphs with anatomic regions represented as nodes and connectivities between the regions as links. Interpretable models on brain networks for disorder analysis are vital for understanding the biological functions of neural systems, which can facilitate early diagnosis

Supplementary Information The online version contains supplementary material available at https://doi.org/10.1007/978-3-031-16452-1_36.

of neurological disorders and neuroscience research [27]. Previous work on brain networks has studied models from shallow to deep, such as graph kernels [14], tensor factorizations [22], and convolutional neural networks [16,17,20].

Recently, Graph Neural Networks (GNNs) attract broad interest due to their established power for analyzing graph-structured data [19,34]. Compared with shallow models, GNNs are suitable for brain network analysis with universal expressiveness to capture the sophisticated connectome structures [4,26,38,43]. However, GNNs as a family of deep models are prone to overfitting and lack transparency in predictions, preventing their usage in decision-critical areas like disorder analysis. Although several methods have been proposed for GNN explanation [24,36,39], most of them focus on node-level prediction tasks and will produce a unique explanation for each subject when applied to graph-level tasks. However, for graph-level connectome-based disorder analysis, it is recognized that subjects having the same disorder share similar brain network patterns [15], which means disorder-specific explanations across instances are preferable. Moreover, brain networks have unique properties such that directly applying vanilla GNN models will obtain suboptimal performance.

In this work, we propose an interpretable GNN framework to investigate disease-specific patterns that are common across the group and robust to individual image quality. Meanwhile, the group-level interpretation can be combined with subject-specific brain networks for different levels of interpretation. As shown in Fig. 1, it is composed of two modules: a backbone model IBGNN which adapts a message passing GNN designed for connectome-based disease prediction and an explanation generator that learns a globally shared mask to highlight disorder-specific biomarkers including salient Regions of Interest (ROIs) and important connections. Furthermore, we combine the two modules by enhancing the original brain networks with the learned explanation mask and further tune the backbone model. The resulting model, which we term IBGNN+ for brevity, produces predictions and interpretations simultaneously.

Through experiments on three real-world brain disorder datasets (i.e. HIV, BP, and PPMI), we show our backbone model performs well across brain networks constructed from different neuroimaging modalities. Also, it is demonstrated that the explanation generator can reveal disorder-specific biomarkers coinciding with neuroscience findings. Last, we show that the combination of explanation generator and backbone model can further boost disorder prediction performance.

2   The Proposed Model

Problem Definition. The input to the proposed framework is a set of N weighted brain networks. For each network $G = (V, E, W)$, $V = \{v_i\}_{i=1}^{M}$ is the node set of size M defined by the Regions Of Interest (ROIs) on a specific brain parcellation [10,32], with each v_i initialized with the node feature x_i, $E = V \times V$ is the edge set of brain connectome, and $W \in \mathbb{R}^{M \times M}$ is the weighted adjacency matrix describing the connection strengths between ROIs. The model outputs

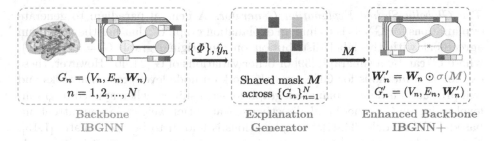

$G_n = (V_n, E_n, \boldsymbol{W}_n)$ Shared mask $\boldsymbol{M}$ $\boldsymbol{W}'_n = \boldsymbol{W}_n \odot \sigma(M)$
$n = 1, 2, ..., N$ across $\{G_n\}_{n=1}^{N}$ $G'_n = (V_n, E_n, \boldsymbol{W}'_n)$

Backbone   Explanation   Enhanced Backbone
IBGNN   Generator   IBGNN+

Fig. 1. An overview of our proposed framework. The backbone model is firstly trained on the original data. Then, the explanation generator learns a globally shared mask across subjects. Finally, we enhance the backbone by applying the learned explanation mask and fine-tune the whole model.

a brain disorder prediction $\hat{y}_n$ for each subject n and learns a disorder-specific interpretation matrix $\boldsymbol{M} \in \mathbb{R}^{M \times M}$ that is shared across all subjects to highlight the disorder-specific biomarkers.

The Backbone Model IBGNN. Edge weights in brain networks are often determined by the signal correlation between brain areas, which may have both positive and negative values, and thus cannot be handled correctly by conventional GNNs. To avoid this issue and better utilize edge weights in the GNN model, we design an edge-weight-aware message passing mechanism specifically for brain networks. Specifically, we first construct a message vector $\boldsymbol{m}_{ij} \in \mathbb{R}^D$ by concatenating embeddings of a node v_i and its neighbor v_j, and the edge weight w_{ij}:

$$\boldsymbol{m}_{ij}^{(l)} = \mathrm{MLP}_1\left(\left[\boldsymbol{h}_i^{(l)}; \boldsymbol{h}_j^{(l)}; w_{ij}\right]\right), \tag{1}$$

where l is the index of the GNN layer. Then, for each node v_i, we aggregate messages from all its neighbors $\mathcal{N}_i$ with the following propagation rule:

$$\boldsymbol{h}_i^{(l)} = \xi\left(\sum\nolimits_{v_j \in \mathcal{N}_i \cup \{v_i\}} \boldsymbol{m}_{ij}^{(l-1)}\right), \tag{2}$$

where ξ is a non-linear activation function such as ReLU, and $\boldsymbol{h}_i^{(0)}$ is initialized with node feature $\boldsymbol{x}_i$ reflecting the connectivity information in brain networks [5]. After stacking L layers, a readout function summarizing all node embeddings is employed to obtain a graph-level embedding $\boldsymbol{g}$. Formally, we instantiate this function with another Multi-Layer Perceptron (MLP) and residual connections:

$$\boldsymbol{z} = \sum\nolimits_{i \in V} \boldsymbol{h}_i^{(L)}, \qquad \boldsymbol{g} = \mathrm{MLP}_2(\boldsymbol{z}) + \boldsymbol{z}. \tag{3}$$

This backbone model IBGNN can be trained with the conventional supervised cross-entropy objective towards ground-truth disorder prediction, defined as

$$\mathcal{L}_{\mathrm{CLF}} = -\frac{1}{N}\sum\nolimits_{n=1}^{N}(y_n \log(\hat{y}_n) + (1 - y_n)\log(1 - \hat{y}_n)). \tag{4}$$

The Globally Shared Explanation Generator. A general paradigm to generate explanations for GNNs is to find an explanation graph G' that has the maximum agreement with the label distribution on the original graph $G = (V, E, \boldsymbol{W})$, where G' can be a subgraph [39] or other variations of G [24,40]. However, these explanation methods for GNNs mostly work on node-level prediction tasks and will produce a unique explanation graph for each subject when applied to graph-level tasks. On the other hand, directly using attention weights in some attention-based GNN models [34,41] as explanations is known to be problematic [1,13]. Note that brain networks have some unique properties. For example, the node number and order are fixed under a given atlas. Also, brain networks assume that subjects with the same brain disorder have similar brain connection patterns. Therefore, a globally shared explanation graph G' capture common patterns for specific disorders at the group level is preferable.

In this work, we propose to learn a globally shared edge mask $\boldsymbol{M} \in \mathbb{R}^{M \times M}$ that is applied to all brain network subjects in a dataset. Specifically, we maximize the agreement between the predictions $\hat{y}$ on the original graph G and $\hat{y}'$ on an explanation graph $G' = (V, E, \boldsymbol{W}')$ induced by a masking matrix $\boldsymbol{M}$, where $\boldsymbol{W}' = \boldsymbol{W} \odot \sigma(\boldsymbol{M})$, $\odot$ denotes element-wise multiplication, and σ denotes the sigmoid function. Formally this objective is implemented as a cross-entropy loss:

$$\mathcal{L}_{\text{MASK}} = -\frac{1}{N} \sum_{n=1}^{N} \sum_{c=1}^{C} \mathbb{1}[\hat{y}_n = c] \log P_{\Phi}(\hat{y}'_n = \hat{y}_n \mid G'_n), \tag{5}$$

where $\sum_{n=1}^{N} P_{\Phi}(\hat{y}'_n = \hat{y}_n \mid G'_n)$ represents the conditional probability that the backbone model Φ's prediction $\hat{y}'_n$ on the masked graph G'_n is consistent with the prediction $\hat{y}_n$ on the original graph G_n, C is the number of possible prediction labels. Besides, following the practice in GNNExplainer [39], we further apply two regularization terms $\mathcal{L}_{\text{SPS}}$ and $\mathcal{L}_{\text{ENT}}$ to encourage the compactness of the explanation and the discreteness of the mask values, respectively:

$$\mathcal{L}_{\text{SPS}} = \sum_{i,j} \boldsymbol{M}_{i,j}, \qquad \mathcal{L}_{\text{ENT}} = -(\boldsymbol{M} \log(\boldsymbol{M}) + (1 - \boldsymbol{M}) \log(1 - \boldsymbol{M})). \tag{6}$$

The final training objective is given as:

$$\mathcal{L} = \mathcal{L}_{\text{CLF}} + \alpha \mathcal{L}_{\text{MASK}} + \beta \mathcal{L}_{\text{SPS}} + \gamma \mathcal{L}_{\text{ENT}}, \tag{7}$$

where α, β and γ scale the numerical value of each loss item to the same order of magnitude to balance their influence. Our explanation generator will generate a globally shared edge mask that can be used for all testing graphs to investigate neurological biomarkers and highlight disorder-specific salient connections.

Enhancing the Backbone with the Learned Explanations. The learned explanation mask can further improve the disorder prediction considering that raw brain networked data inevitably contain random noise. Specifically, we enhance the original backbone by applying essential disorder-specific signals. We note that this strategy is compatible with any backbone model, not limited to our proposed IBGNN. We combined the aforementioned two modules so that predictions and interpretations are produced in a closed-loop for brain disorder analysis. We term the enhanced model by IBGNN+ hereafter.

The whole training pipeline is summarized in Fig. 1. The original brain networks are firstly input to train the backbone model. Then, a globally shared explanation mask is learned based on the backbone model Φ and prediction $\hat{y}_n$. Finally, we enhance the backbone model by highlighting salient ROIs and important connections on the raw data and tune the backbone model again.

3   Experiments

Dataset Acquisition and Preprocessing. We evaluate our framework using three real-world neuroimaging datasets of different modalities. Specifically, groups in each dataset have balanced age and gender portions and are collected with the same image acquisition procedure.

- *Human Immunodeficiency Virus Infection (HIV):* This dataset is collected from Early HIV Infection Study at Northwestern University. It includes fMRI imaging of 70 subjects, 35 of which are early HIV patients, and the others are seronegative controls. We perform image preprocessing using the DPARSF[1] toolbox. The images are realigned to the first volume, followed by slice timing correction, normalization, spatial smoothness using an 8-mm Gaussian kernel, band-pass filtering (0.01–0.08 Hz), and linear trend removing of the time series. We focus on the 116 anatomical regions of interest (ROI), and extract a sequence of responses from them. Finally, brain networks with 90 cerebral regions are constructed, where each node represents a brain region and links are created based on correlations between different brain regions.
- *Bipolar Disorder (BP):* This DTI imaging dataset is collected from 52 bipolar I subjects and 45 healthy controls. We use the FSL toolbox[2] for preprocessing which includes distortion correction, noise filtering, and repetitive sampling from the distributions of principal diffusion directions for each voxel. Each subject is parcellated into 82 regions based on FreeSurfer-generated cortical/subcortical gray matter regions.
- *Parkinson's Progression Markers Initiative (PPMI):* This large-scale, publicly available dataset[3] is from a collaborative study[4] to improve PD therapeutics. We consider brain imaging in the DTI modality of 754 subjects, 596 of whom are Parkinson's disorder patients, and the rest 158 are healthy controls. The raw data are aligned using the FSL eddy-correct tool to correct head motion and eddy current distortions. The brain extraction tool (BET) from FSL is used to remove non-brain tissue. The skull-stripped images are linearly aligned and registered using Advanced Normalization Tools (ANTs[5]).

---

[1] http://rfmri.org/DPARSF/.
[2] https://fsl.fmrib.ox.ac.uk/fsl/fslwiki/.
[3] https://www.ppmi-info.org/.
[4] https://www.michaeljfox.org/.
[5] http://stnava.github.io/ANTs/.

84 ROIs are parcellated from T1-weighted structural MRI using FreeSurfer[6] and the brain network connectivity is reconstructed using the deterministic 2nd-order Runge-Kutta (RK2) whole-brain tractography algorithm [42].

Experimental Settings. The proposed model is implemented using PyTorch 1.10.2 [29] and PyTorch Geometric 2.0.3 [9]. A Quadro RTX 8000 GPU with 48GB of memory is used for our model training. Hyper-parameters are selected automatically with the open source AutoML toolkit NNI[7]. We refer readers of interest to supplementary materials for implementation details. All reported results are averaged of ten-fold cross validation.

Table 1. Experimental results (%) on three datasets, where * denotes a significant improvement according to paired t-test with $p = 0.05$ compared with baselines. The best performances are in bold and the second runners are underlined.

Method	HIV			BP			PPMI		
	Accuracy	F1	AUC	Accuracy	F1	AUC	Accuracy	F1	AUC
M2E	$57.14_{19.17}$	$53.71_{19.80}$	$57.50_{18.71}$	$52.56_{13.86}$	$51.65_{13.38}$	$52.42_{13.83}$	$78.69_{1.78}$	$45.81_{44.17}$	$50.39_{2.59}$
MIC	$54.29_{18.95}$	$53.63_{19.44}$	$55.42_{19.10}$	$62.67_{20.92}$	$63.00_{21.61}$	$61.79_{21.74}$	$79.11_{2.16}$	$49.65_{45.10}$	$52.39_{2.94}$
MPCA	$67.14_{20.25}$	$64.28_{23.47}$	$69.17_{20.17}$	$52.56_{13.12}$	$50.43_{14.99}$	$52.42_{13.69}$	$79.15_{0.57}$	$44.18_{40.18}$	$50.00_{0.00}$
MK-SVM	$65.71_{47.00}$	$62.08_{47.49}$	$65.83_{47.41}$	$57.00_{48.89}$	$41.08_{13.44}$	$53.75_{48.00}$	$79.15_{0.57}$	$44.18_{40.18}$	$50.00_{0.00}$
GCN	$70.00_{12.51}$	$68.35_{13.28}$	$73.58_{9.49}$	$55.56_{13.86}$	$50.71_{11.75}$	$61.55_{28.77}$	$78.55_{1.58}$	$47.87_{44.40}$	$59.43_{8.64}$
GAT	$71.43_{11.66}$	$69.79_{10.83}$	$77.17_{49.42}$	$63.34_{49.15}$	$60.42_{47.56}$	$67.07_{45.98}$	$79.02_{1.25}$	$45.85_{43.10}$	$64.40_{46.87}$
PNA	$57.14_{12.78}$	$45.09_{19.62}$	$57.14_{12.78}$	$63.71_{411.34}$	$55.54_{414.06}$	$60.30_{411.89}$	$79.36_{41.84}$	$51.76_{410.32}$	$54.71_{46.77}$
BrainNetCNN	$69.24_{19.04}$	$67.08_{11.11}$	$72.09_{19.01}$	$65.83_{20.64}$	$64.74_{17.42}$	$64.32_{13.72}$	$55.20_{12.63}$	$\underline{55.45_{49.15}}$	$52.54_{10.21}$
BrainGNN	$74.29_{12.10}$	$73.49_{10.75}$	$75.00_{10.56}$	$68.00_{12.45}$	$62.33_{13.01}$	$74.20_{12.93}$	$69.17_{40.00}$	$44.19_{40.00}$	$45.26_{43.65}$
IBGNN	$\underline{82.14_{10.81}}^{*}$	$\underline{82.02_{10.86}}^{*}$	$\underline{86.86_{11.65}}^{*}$	$\underline{73.19_{12.20}}^{*}$	$\underline{72.87_{12.09}}^{*}$	$\underline{83.64_{9.61}}^{*}$	$\mathbf{79.82_{1.47}}$	$51.58_{44.66}$	$\underline{70.65_{46.55}}^{*}$
IBGNN+	$\mathbf{84.29_{12.94}}^{*}$	$\mathbf{83.86_{13.42}}^{*}$	$\mathbf{88.57_{10.89}}^{*}$	$\mathbf{76.33_{18.00}}^{*}$	$\mathbf{76.13_{18.01}}^{*}$	$\mathbf{84.61_{49.08}}^{*}$	$\underline{79.55_{41.67}}$	$\mathbf{56.58_{47.43}}^{*}$	$\mathbf{72.76_{46.73}}^{*}$

Baselines. We compare our proposed models, i.e., the backbone model IBGNN and the explanation enhanced IBGNN+, with competitors of both shallow and deep models. Shallow methods include M2E [22], MIC [31], MPCA [23], and MK-SVM [7], where the output graph-level embeddings are evaluated using logistic regression classifiers. We also include three representative deep graph models: GAT [35], GCN [19], PNA [3] and two state-of-the-art deep models specifically design for brain networks: BrainNetCNN [17] and BrainGNN [20].

Prediction Performance. The overall results are presented in Table 1. Both our proposed models yield impressive improvements over SOTA shallow and deep baselines. Compared with shallow models such as MK-SVM, our backbone model IBGNN outperforms them by large margins, with up to 11% absolute improvements on BP. Besides, the effectiveness of our brain network-oriented design is supported by its superiority compared with other SOTA deep models. Moreover, the performance of the explanation enhanced model IBGNN+ can further increase the backbone by about 9.7% relative improvements, which demonstrates that IBGNN+ effectively highlights the disorder-specific signals while also achieving the benefit of restraining random noises in individual graphs.

---

[6] https://surfer.nmr.mgh.harvard.edu/.

[7] https://github.com/microsoft/nni.

4   Interpretation Analysis

Neural System Mapping. The ROIs on brain networks can be partitioned into neural systems based on their structural and functional roles under a specific parcellation atlas, which facilitates the understanding of generated explanations from a neuroscience perspective. In this paper, we map the ROI nodes as defined on each dataset into eight commonly used neural systems, including Visual Network (VN), Auditory Network (AN), Bilateral Limbic Network (BLN), Default Mode Network (DMN), Somato-Motor Network (SMN), Subcortical Network (SN), Memory Network (MN), and Cognitive Control Network (CCN).

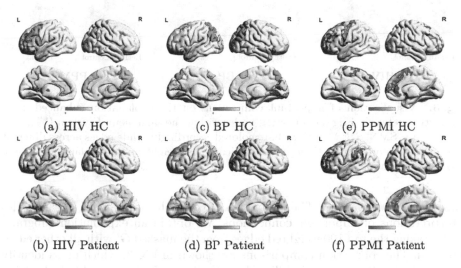

(a) HIV HC   (c) BP HC   (e) PPMI HC

(b) HIV Patient   (d) BP Patient   (f) PPMI Patient

Fig. 2. Visualization of salient ROIs on the explanation enhanced brain connection networks for Health Control (HC) and Patient. The color of regions represents ROI's average importance in the given group. The bright-yellow color indicates a high score, while dark-red indicates a low score. (Color figure online)

Salient ROIs. We provide both group-level and individual-level interpretations to understand which ROIs contribute most to the prediction of a specific disorder. On the group level, we rank the most salient ROIs on the learned explanation mask by calculating the sum of the edge weights connected to each node. Then on the individual level, we use the BrainNet Viewer [37] to plot the salient ROIs on the average brain connectivity graph enhanced by the learned explanation mask. For the HIV disease, anterior cingulate, paracingulate gyri, and inferior frontal gyrus are selected as salient ROIs. This complies with scientific findings that the regional homogeneity value of the anterior cingulate and paracingulate gyri are decreased [25] and lower gray matter volumes are found in inferior frontal gyrus in HIV patients [21]. The individual-level visualizations in Fig. 2(a)(b) show the difference between Health Control (HC) and HIV patients in those salient ROIs. For the BP disease, secondary visual cortex and medial to superior temporal gyrus are selected as salient ROIs. This observation is in line with existing studies that visual processing abnormalities have been character- ized in bipolar disorder patients [28,30], which is also confirmed in Fig. 2(c)(d). For the PPMI disease, rostral middle frontal gyrus and superior frontal gyrus are selected as salient ROIs and Fig. 2(e)(f) display the difference. This is in accor- dance with MRI analysis revealing a significant decrease in PD patients in the rostral medial frontal gyrus and superior, middle, and inferior frontal gyri [18]. All these observed salient ROIs can be potential biomarkers to identify brain disorders from each cohort.

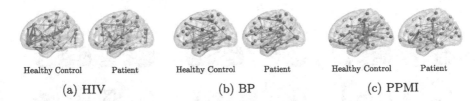

| Healthy Control   Patient | Healthy Control   Patient | Healthy Control   Patient |
| (a) HIV | (b) BP | (c) PPMI |

Fig. 3. Visualization of important connections on the explanation enhanced brain connection network. Edges connecting nodes within the same neural system (VN, AN, BLN, DMN, SMN, SN, MN, CCN) are colored accordingly, while edges across different systems are colored gray. Edge width indicates its weight in the explanation graph. (Color figure online)

Important Connections. The globally shared explanation mask M provides interpretations of important connections. We obtain an explanation subgraph G'_s by taking the top 100 weighted edges from the masked G' with all other edges removed. The connection comparisons are shown in Fig. 3, which helps identify connections related to specific disorders. For the HIV dataset, the explanation subgraph of patients excludes rich interactions within the DMN (colored blue) system. Also, interactions within the VN (colored red) system of patients are significantly less than those of HCs. These patterns are consistent with the find- ings in earlier studies [11,12] that connectivity alterations within- and between- network DMN and VN may relate to known visual processing difficulties for HIV patients. For the BP dataset, compared with tight interactions within the BLN (colored green) system of the healthy control, the connections within BLN system of the patient subject are much sparser, which may signal pathological changes in this neural system. This observation is in line with previous stud- ies [6], which finds that the parietal lobe, one of the major lobes in the brain roughly located at the upper back area in the skull and is in charge of processing sensory information received from the outside world, is mainly related to Bipo- lar disorder attack. Since parietal lobe ROIs are contained in BLN under our parcellation, the connections missing within the BLN system in our visualiza- tion are consistent with existing clinical understanding. For the PPMI dataset, the connectivity in the patient group decreases in the SMN (colored purple) system, which integrates primary sensorimotor, premotor, and supplementary motor areas to facilitate voluntary movements. This observation confirms existing neuroimaging studies that have repeatedly shown disorder-related alteration in sensorimotor areas of Parkinson's patients [2]. Furthermore, individuals with PD have lower connectivity within the DMN (colored blue) system compared with healthy controls, which is consistent with the cognition recession study on Parkinson's patients [8,33].

5   Conclusion

In this work, we propose a novel interpretable GNN framework for connectome-based brain disorder analysis, which consists of a brain network-oriented GNN predictor and a globally shared explanation generator. Experiments on real-world neuroimaging datasets show the superior prediction performance of both our backbone and the explanation enhanced models and validate the disorder-specific interpretations from the generated explanation mask. The limitation of the proposed framework might arise from the small size of neuroimaging datasets, which restraints the effectiveness and generalization ability of deep learning models. A direct future direction based on this work is to utilize pre-training and transfer learning techniques to learn across datasets. This allows for the sharing of information and explanations across different cohorts, which could lead to a better understanding of cross-disorder commonalities.

Acknowledgement. This research was partly supported by the internal funds and GPU servers provided by the Computer Science Department of Emory University and the University Research Committee of Emory University. Xiaoxiao Li was supported by NSERC Discovery Grant (DGECR-2022-00430). Lifang He was supported by ONR N00014-18-1-2009 and Lehigh's accelerator grant S00010293.

References

1. Bai, B., et al.: Why attentions may not be interpretable? In: SIGKDD (2021)
2. Caspers, J., et al.: Within-and across-network alterations of the sensorimotor network in Parkinson's disease. Neuroradiology **63**, 2073–2085 (2021)
3. Corso, G., et al.: Principal neighbourhood aggregation for graph nets. In: NeurIPS (2020)
4. Cui, H., et al.: BrainGB: a benchmark for brain network analysis with graph neural networks. arXiv preprint arXiv:2204.07054 (2022)
5. Cui, H., Lu, Z., Li, P., Yang, C.: On positional and structural node features for graph neural networks on non-attributed graphs. arXiv preprint arXiv:2107.01495 (2021)
6. Das, T.K., et al.: Parietal lobe and disorganisation syndrome in schizophrenia and psychotic bipolar disorder: a bimodal connectivity study. Psychiatry Res. Neuroimaging **303**, 111139 (2020)
7. Dyrba, M., et al.: Multimodal analysis of functional and structural disconnection in Alzheimer's disease using multiple kernel SVM. Hum. Brain Mapp. **36**, 2118–2131 (2015)

8. van Eimeren, T., et al.: Dysfunction of the default mode network in Parkinson disease: a functional magnetic resonance imaging study. Arch. Neurol. **66**, 877–883 (2009)

9. Fey, M., et al.: Fast graph representation learning with pytorch geometric. In: RLGM@ICLR (2019)

10. Figley, T.D., et al.: Probabilistic white matter atlases of human auditory, basal ganglia, language, precuneus, sensorimotor, visual and visuospatial networks. Front. Hum. Neurosci. **11**, 306 (2017)

11. Flannery, J.S., et al.: HIV infection is linked with reduced error-related default mode network suppression and poorer medication management abilities. medRxiv.org (2021)

12. Herting, M.M., et al.: Default mode connectivity in youth with perinatally acquired HIV. Medicine (2015)

13. Jain, S., et al.: Attention is not explanation. In: NAACL-HLT (2019)

14. Jie, B., et al.: Sub-network based kernels for brain network classification. In: ACM BCB (2016)

15. Kan, X., Cui, H., Lukemire, J., Guo, Y., Yang, C.: FBNetGen: task-aware GNN-based fMRI analysis via functional brain network generation. In: MIDL (2022)

16. Kan, X., Dai, W., Cui, H., Zhang, Z., Guo, Y., Yang, C.: Brain network transformer. arXiv preprint (2022)

17. Kawahara, J., et al.: BrainNetCNN: convolutional neural networks for brain networks; towards predicting neurodevelopment. NeuroImage **146**, 1038–1049 (2017)

18. Kendi, A.K., et al.: Altered diffusion in the frontal lobe in Parkinson disease. AJNR Am. J. Neuroradiol. **29**, 501–505 (2008)

19. Kipf, T.N., et al.: Semi-supervised classification with graph convolutional networks. In: ICLR (2017)

20. Li, X., et al.: BrainGNN: interpretable brain graph neural network for fMRI analysis. Med. Image Anal. **74**, 102233 (2021)

21. Li, Y., et al.: Structural gray matter change early in male patients with HIV. Int. J. Clin. Exp. Med **7**, 3362 (2014)

22. Liu, Y., et al.: Multi-view multi-graph embedding for brain network clustering analysis. In: AAAI (2018)

23. Lu, H., et al.: MPCA: multilinear principal component analysis of tensor objects. IEEE Trans. Neural Netw. **19**, 18–39 (2008)

24. Luo, D., et al.: Parameterized explainer for graph neural network. In: NeurIPS (2020)

25. Ma, Q., et al.: HIV-associated structural and functional brain alterations in homosexual males. Front. Neurol. (2021)

26. Maron, H., et al.: Invariant and equivariant graph networks. In: ICLR (2018)

27. Martensson, G., et al.: Stability of graph theoretical measures in structural brain networks in Alzheimer's disease. Sci. Rep. **8**, 1–15 (2018)

28. O'Bryan, R.A., et al.: Disturbances of visual motion perception in bipolar disorder. Bipolar Disord. **16**, 354–365 (2014)

29. Paszke, A., et al.: PyTorch: an imperative style, high-performance deep learning library. In: NeurIPS (2019)

30. Reavis, E.A., et al.: Structural and functional connectivity of visual cortex in Schizophrenia and bipolar disorder: a graph-theoretic analysis. Schizophr. Bull. Open **1**, sgaa056 (2020)

31. Shao, W., et al.: Clustering on multi-source incomplete data via tensor modeling and factorization. In: PAKDD (2015)

32. Shirer, W.R., et al.: Decoding subject-driven cognitive states with whole-brain connectivity patterns. Cereb. Cortex **22**, 158–165 (2012)
33. Tessitore, A., et al.: Default-mode network connectivity in cognitively unimpaired patients with Parkinson disease. Neurology **79**, 2226–2232 (2012)
34. Veličković, P., et al.: Graph attention networks. In: ICLR (2018)
35. Veličković, P., et al.: Deep graph infomax. In: ICLR (2019)
36. Vu, M.N., et al.: PGM-explainer: probabilistic graphical model explanations for graph neural networks. In: NeurIPS (2020)
37. Xia, M., et al.: BrainNet viewer: a network visualization tool for human brain connectomics. PLoS ONE **8**, e68910 (2013)
38. Yang, Y., et al.: Data-efficient brain connectome analysis via multi-task meta-learning. In: KDD (2022)
39. Ying, Z., et al.: GNNExplainer: generating explanations for graph neural networks. In: NeurIPS (2019)
40. Yuan, H., et al.: Explainability in graph neural networks: a taxonomic survey. arXiv.org (2020)
41. Yun, S., et al.: Graph transformer networks. In: NeurIPS (2019)
42. Zhan, L., et al.: Comparison of nine tractography algorithms for detecting abnormal structural brain networks in Alzheimer's disease. Front. Aging Neurosci. **7**, 48 (2015)
43. Zhu, Y., Cui, H., He, L., Sun, L., Yang, C.: Joint embedding of structural and functional brain networks with graph neural networks for mental illness diagnosis. In: EMBC (2022)

Consistency-Preserving Visual Question Answering in Medical Imaging

Sergio Tascon-Morales$^{(\boxtimes)}$, Pablo Márquez-Neila, and Raphael Sznitman

University of Bern, Bern, Switzerland
{sergio.tasconmorales,pablo.marquez,raphael.sznitman}@unibe.ch

Abstract. Visual Question Answering (VQA) models take an image and a natural-language question as input and infer the answer to the question. Recently, VQA systems in medical imaging have gained popularity thanks to potential advantages such as patient engagement and second opinions for clinicians. While most research efforts have been focused on improving architectures and overcoming data-related limitations, answer consistency has been overlooked even though it plays a critical role in establishing trustworthy models. In this work, we propose a novel loss function and corresponding training procedure that allows the inclusion of relations between questions into the training process. Specifically, we consider the case where implications between perception and reasoning questions are known a-priori. To show the benefits of our approach, we evaluate it on the clinically relevant task of Diabetic Macular Edema (DME) staging from fundus imaging. Our experiments show that our method outperforms state-of-the-art baselines, not only by improving model consistency, but also in terms of overall model accuracy. Our code and data are available at https://github.com/sergiotasconmorales/consistency_vqa.

Keywords: VQA · Consistency · Attention · Diabetic Macular Edema

1 Introduction

Visual Question Answering (VQA) models are neural networks that answer natural language questions about an image by interpreting the question and the image provided [1,7,11,22]. Specifying questions using natural language gives VQA models great appeal, as the set of possible questions one can ask is enormous and does not need to be identical to the set of questions used to train the models. Due to these advantages, VQA models for medical applications have also been proposed [6,8,12,13,24,28], whereby allowing clinicians to probe the model with subtle differentiating questions and contributing to build trust in predictions.

To date, much of the work in medical VQA has focused on building more effective model architectures [6,12,24] or overcoming limitations in medical VQA

Supplementary Information The online version contains supplementary material available at https://doi.org/10.1007/978-3-031-16452-1_37.

L. Wang et al. (Eds.): MICCAI 2022, LNCS 13438, pp. 386–395, 2022.
https://doi.org/10.1007/978-3-031-16452-1_37

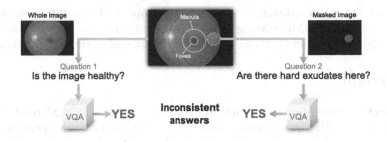

Fig. 1. VQA inconsistency in Diabetic Macular Edema staging from fundus photograph. While the VQA model correctly answers "Is the image healthy?" (left), it incorrectly answers yes to "Are there hard exudates here?" for a specified retinal region.

datasets [12,14,19,28]. Yet a critical component of VQA is the notion of *consistency* in the answers produced by a model. Here, consistency refers to a model's capacity to produce answers that are not self-contradictory. For instance, the task of staging diabetic macular edema (DME) from color fundus photograph illustrated in Fig. 1 involves identifying *perception* elements in the image (*e.g.*, "are there hard exudates visible near the macula?") to infer a disease stage, which can be expressed as a *reasoning* question (*e.g.*, "what is the stage of disease?"). Ultimately, for any VQA model to be trustworthy, it should be able to answer these without contradicting itself (*i.e.*, answer that the image is healthy, but also identify hard exudates in the periphery of the eye).

Consistency in VQA has been studied in the broader computer vision context [4,5,16,18,21], where the relation between perception and reasoning questions is unconstrained. That is, the answers to perception questions do not necessarily imply any information with respect to the reasoning question and vice-versa. In these broad cases, some methods have modeled question implications [16,18] or rephrased questions [21] by generating tailored question-answer pairs (*e.g.*, consistent data-augmentation). Alternatively, [5,23,27] used relations between questions to impose constraints in the VQA's embedding space. To avoid needing to know the relation between questions, [20] proposed to enforce consistency by making attention maps of reasoning and perception questions similar to one another. However, even though these approaches tackle unconstrained question relations, the ensuring of VQA models' consistency remains limited and often reduces the overall performance [20].

Instead, we propose a novel approach to enforce VQA consistency that is focused on cases where answers to the perception questions have explicit implications on reasoning question answers and vice-versa (*e.g.*, cancerous cells and severity of cancer found in H&E staining, or presence of hard exudates and DME staging). By focusing on this subset of question relations, our aim is to improve both the accuracy of our model and its consistency, without needing external data as in [4,14,18]. To do this, we allow questions to probe arbitrary image regions by masking irrelevant parts of the image and passing the masked image to the VQA model (see Fig. 1). To then enforce consistency, we propose a new loss function that penalizes incorrect perceptual predictions when reasoning ones are correct for a given image. To validate the impact of our approach, we test it in the context of DME staging and show that it outperforms state-of-the-art methods for consistency, without compromising overall performance accuracy.

2   Method

We present here our approach which consists of using a simple VQA model with a training protocol that encourages consistency among pairs of perception and reasoning questions. Figure 2 illustrates this VQA model and our training approach.

VQA Model. Following [2], our VQA model, $f : \mathcal{I} \times \mathcal{Q} \rightarrow \mathcal{P}(\mathcal{A})$, takes a tuple containing an image, $\mathbf{x}$, and a question, $\mathbf{q}$, to produce a distribution, $\mathbf{p} = f(\mathbf{x}, \mathbf{q})$, over a finite set of possible answers $\mathcal{A}$ (see Fig. 2(Top)). After encoding the inputs, the VQA model combines visual (v) and textual (q) features through an attention module (k) [26] that selects the visual features relevant to the question (v'). The final classifier receives a combination of the relevant features and the text features through a fusion module to predict the final distribution.

In some cases, questions may consider asking about content related to specific regions of the image (*e.g.*, "are there hard exudates in this region?"). To process these cases, the input image is masked so that the visible area corresponds to the region mentioned in the question while the rest of the image is set to zero. Training this model requires a dataset $\mathcal{T} = \{t^{(i)} = (\mathbf{x}^{(i)}, \mathbf{q}^{(i)}, a^{(i)})\}_{i=1}^{N} \subseteq \mathcal{I} \times \mathcal{Q} \times \mathcal{A}$ of images and questions annotated with their answers. The VQA loss is simply the cross-entropy between the predicted distribution and the real answer,

$$\ell_{\mathrm{VQA}}(\mathbf{p}, a) = H(\mathbf{p}, a) = -\log \mathbf{p}_a. \tag{1}$$

While this loss alone is sufficient to reach a reasonable performance, it ignores the potentially useful interactions that may exist among training questions.

Consistency Loss. We aim to improve the quality of our VQA model by exploiting the relationships between reasoning and perception questions at training time. To this end, we augment the training dataset with an additional binary relation $\prec$ over the set of questions $\mathcal{Q}$. Two questions are related, $\mathbf{q}^{(i)} \prec \mathbf{q}^{(j)}$, if $\mathbf{q}^{(i)}$ is a perception question associated to the reasoning question $\mathbf{q}^{(j)}$. From hence on, we refer to perception questions as *sub-questions* and reasoning questions as *main questions*.

Following the terminology in [20], an inconsistency occurs when the VQA model infers the main question correctly but the sub-question incorrectly. Using the entropy as a measurement of incorrectness, we propose to impose the consistency at training time by penalizing the cases with high $H^{(i)} = H(\mathbf{p}^{(i)}, a^{(i)})$ and low $H^{(j)} = H(\mathbf{p}^{(j)}, a^{(j)})$ when $\mathbf{q}^{(i)} \prec \mathbf{q}^{(j)}$. To do this, we use an adapted hinge loss that disables the penalty when $H^{(j)}$ is larger than a threshold $\gamma > 0$, but otherwise penalizes large values of $H^{(i)}$,

$$\ell_{\mathrm{cons}}(H^{(i)}, H^{(j)}) = H^{(i)} \max\{0, \gamma - H^{(j)}\}. \tag{2}$$

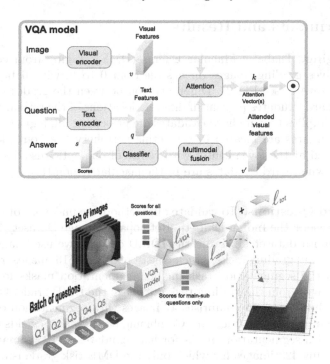

Fig. 2. *Top:* VQA model architecture. *Bottom:* Visualization of the training process with the proposed loss. The total loss, ℓ_{tot}, is based on two terms: the conventional VQA loss, ℓ_{VQA} and our proposed consistency loss term, ℓ_{cons}. The latter is computed only for pairs of main (reasoning) and sub (perception) questions. Training mini-batches consist of main and sub questions at the same time, whereby sub-questions can consider specific regions of the image. Unrelated questions (denoted with "ind") can also be included in training batches, but do not contribute to ℓ_{cons}.

The final cost function then minimizes the expected value of the VQA loss (1) for the elements of the training dataset and the consistency loss (2) for the pairs of training samples with $\prec$-related questions,

$$\mathbb{E}_{t \sim \mathcal{T}}[\ell_{\text{VQA}}(\mathbf{p}, a)] + \lambda \mathbb{E}_{(t^{(i)}, t^{(j)}) \sim \mathcal{T}^2}[\ell_{\text{cons}}(H^{(i)}, H^{(j)}) \mid \mathbf{x}^{(i)} = \mathbf{x}^{(j)}, \mathbf{q}^{(i)} \prec \mathbf{q}^{(j)}], \tag{3}$$

where $\lambda > 0$ controls the relative strength of both losses and $\mathcal{T}^2$ is the Cartesian product of $\mathcal{T}$ with itself, that is, all pairs of training samples.

To train, this cost is iteratively minimized approximating the expectations with mini-batches. The two expectations of Eq. (3) suggest that two mini-batches are necessary at each iteration: one mini-batch sampled from $\mathcal{T}$ and a second mini-batch of $\prec$-related pairs sampled from $\mathcal{T}^2$. However, in practice a single mini-batch is sufficient as long as we ensure that it contains pairs of $\prec$-related questions. While this biased sampling could in turn bias the estimation of the first expectation, we did not observe a noticeable impact in our experiments. Figure 2(Bottom) illustrates this training procedure.

3   Experiments and Results

DME Staging. Diabetic Macular Edema (DME) staging from color fundus images involves grading images on a scale from 0 to 2, with 0 being healthy and 2 being severe (see Fig. 3). Differentiation between the grades relies on the presence of hard exudates present in different locations of the retina. Specifically, a grade of 0 implies that no hard exudates are present at all, a grade of 1 implies that hard exudates are located in the retina periphery (*i.e.*, outside a circular region centered at the fovea center with radius of one optic disc diameter), and a grade of 2 when hard exudates are in the macular region [17].

Dataset and Questions. To validate our method, we make use of two publicly available datasets: the Indian Diabetic Retinopathy Image Dataset (IDRiD) [15] and the e-Ophta dataset [3]. From the IDRiD dataset, we use images from the segmentation and grading tasks, which consist of 81 and 516 images, respectively. Images from the segmentation task include segmentation masks for hard exudates and images from the grading task only have the DME grade. On the other hand, the e-Ophta dataset comprises 47 images with segmentation of hard exudates and 35 images without lesions. Combining both datasets yields a dataset of 128 images with segmentation masks for hard exudates and 128 images without any lesions, plus 423 images for which only the DME risk grade is available.

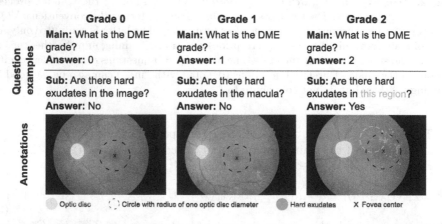

Fig. 3. DME risk grading Grade 0 is assigned if there are no hard exudates present in the whole image. Grade 1 is assigned if there are hard exudates, but only located outside a circle centered at the fovea with radius of one optic disc diameter. Grade 2 is assigned if there are hard exudates located within the circle. Examples of main and sub-questions are provided for each grade.

In this context, we consider main questions to be those asking "What is the DME risk grade?" when considering the entire image. Sub-questions were then defined as questions asking about the presence of the hard exudates. For instance, as shown in Fig. 3(Right), "Are there hard exudates in this region?" where the region designated contains the macula. In practice, we set three types of sub-questions: "are there hard exudates in this image?", "are there hard exudates in the macula?" and "are there hard exudates in this region?". We refer to these three questions as *whole*, *macula* and *region* questions, respectively. For the region sub-questions, we consider circular regions that can be centered anywhere, or centered on the fovea, depending on availability of fovea center location annotations. As mentioned in Sect. 1, to answer questions about regions, images are masked so that only the region is visible.

The total number of question-answer pairs in our dataset consist of 9779 for training (4.4% main, 21.4% sub, 74.2% ind), 2380 for validation (4.5% main, 19.2% sub, 76.3% ind) and 1311 for testing (10% main, 46.1% sub, 43.9% ind), with images in the train, validation and test sets being mutually exclusive.

Baselines, Implementation Details and Evaluation Metrics: We compare our approach to a baseline model that does not use the proposed ℓ_{cons} loss, equivalent to setting $\lambda = 0$. In addition, we compare our method against the attention-matching method, SQuINT [20], as it is a state-of-the-art alternative to our approach that can be used with the same VQA model architecture.

Our VQA model uses an ImageNet-pretrained ResNet101 [9] with input image of 448×448 pixels and an embedding of 2048 dimensions for the image encoding. For text encoding, a single-layer LSTM [10] network processes the input question with word encoding of length 300 and produces a single question embedding of 1024 dimensions. The multi-glimpse attention mechanism [26] uses 2 glimpses and dropout rate 0.25, and the multimodal fusion stage uses standard concatenation. The final classifier is a multi-layer perceptron with hidden layer of 1024 dimensions and dropout rate of 0.25. Hyperparameters λ and γ were empirically adjusted to 0.5 and 1.0, respectively.

All experiments were implemented using PyTorch 1.10.1 and run on a Linux machine with an NVIDIA RTX 3090 graphic card using 16 GB of memory and 4 CPU cores. All methods use the weighted cross-entropy as the base VQA loss function. Batch size was set to 64, and we used Adam for optimization with a learning rate of 10^{-4}. Maximum epoch number was 100 and we use early stopping policy to prevent overfitting, with a patience of 20 epochs.

We report accuracy and consistency [20] performances, using two different definitions of consistency for comparison. Consistency, C1, is the percentage of sub-questions that are answered correctly when the main question was answered correctly. Consistency, C2, is the percentage of main questions that are answered correctly when all corresponding sub-questions were answered correctly.

Results: Table 1 shows the results. We compare these results to the case in which the value of λ is 0, which corresponds to the baseline in which no additional

Table 1. Average test accuracy and consistency values for the different models. Results shown are averaged over 10 models trained with different seeds. Accuracy values are presented for all questions (overall), for main questions (grade) and for sub-questions (whole, macula and region). Both measures of consistency are shown as well.

Case	Accuracy					Consistency	
	Overall	Grade	Whole	Macula	Region	C1	C2
Baseline (no att.)	77.54	73.59	81.37	83.37	76.66	81.70	91.86
Baseline (att.)	81.46	80.23	83.13	**87.18**	80.58	89.21	96.92
Baseline (att.) + SQuINT [20]	80.58	77.48	82.82	85.34	80.02	88.17	94.62
Baseline (att.) + Ours ($\lambda = 0.5, \gamma = 1$)	**83.49**	**80.69**	**84.96**	**87.18**	**83.16**	**94.20**	**98.12**

Question	Type	Ans. GT	Ans. baseline	Ans. SQuINT	Ans. Ours
What is the DME grade?	main	0	0	0	0
Are there hard exudates in the image?	sub	NO	YES	NO	NO
Are there hard exudates in the macula?	sub	NO	NO	NO	NO
Are there hard exudates in this region?	sub	NO	NO	YES	NO
Are there hard exudates in this region?	sub	NO	YES	NO	NO

Question	Type	Ans. GT	Ans. baseline	Ans. SQuINT	Ans. Ours
What is the DME grade?	main	2	2	2	2
Are there hard exudates in the image?	sub	YES	YES	YES	YES
Are there hard exudates in the macula?	sub	YES	YES	YES	YES
Are there hard exudates in this region*?	sub	YES	NO	YES	YES
Are there hard exudates in this region*?	sub	YES	YES	YES	YES

*Regions located at fovea center, with radius smaller than 1 optic disc diameter (See Fig. 3)

Question	Type	Ans. GT	Ans. baseline	Ans. SQuINT	Ans. Ours
What is the DME grade?	main	0	2	0	0
Are there hard exudates in the image?	sub	NO	YES	YES	NO
Are there hard exudates in the macula?	sub	NO	NO	NO	NO

Question	Type	Ans. GT	Ans. baseline	Ans. SQuINT	Ans. Ours
What is the DME grade?	main	1	2	2	2
Are there hard exudates in the image?	sub	YES	NO	NO	NO
Are there hard exudates in the macula?	sub	NO	YES	YES	NO

Fig. 4. Qualitative examples from the test set. Inconsistent sub-answers are highlighted in red. Additional examples are shown in the supplementary material. (Color figure online)

loss term is used. For each case, we present the overall accuracy and the accuracy for each type of question, as well as the consistency values. Figure 4 illustrates the performance of each method with representative qualitative examples.

Table 2. Average test accuracy and consistency values for different values of the parameters λ and γ. The first row ($\lambda = 0$) corresponds to the baseline.

λ	γ	Accuracy					Consistency	
		Overall	Grade	Whole	Macula	Region	C1	C2
0	–	81.46	80.23	83.13	87.18	80.58	89.21	96.92
0.2	0.5	82.01	80.38	83.59	86.56	81.36	90.93	97.38
0.2	1	82.65	79.77	83.97	86.64	82.30	93.22	97.51
0.2	1.5	83.05	81.22	84.27	87.33	82.53	93.23	97.56
0.3	0.5	82.34	79.92	83.59	87.71	81.74	92.32	97.31
0.3	1	83.27	80.53	84.58	87.25	82.91	94.01	98.10
0.3	1.5	83.28	80.84	84.43	87.48	82.86	93.28	98.29
0.4	0.5	82.87	80.69	84.89	87.02	82.30	92.66	96.66
0.4	1	82.97	80.15	83.97	86.72	82.69	93.91	98.23
0.4	1.5	83.33	80.08	84.20	86.87	83.17	93.96	97.77
0.5	0.5	82.54	81.07	83.66	88.02	81.81	91.87	97.73
0.5	1	83.49	80.69	84.96	87.18	83.16	94.20	98.12
0.5	1.5	83.25	79.92	84.58	86.95	83.01	94.20	98.12

In general, we observe that our proposed approach yields increases in accuracy and consistency when compared to both the baseline and SQuINT. Importantly, this increase in consistency is not at the expense of overall accuracy. Specifically, this indicates that our loss term causes the model to be correct about sub-questions when it is correct about main questions. The observed increase in accuracy also indicates that our approach is not synthetically increasing consistency by reducing the number of correct answers on main questions [20]. We note that SQuINT results in a reduction in accuracy and consistency, which can be partially explained by the presence of region questions that are not associated to any main question. These questions, which exceed the number of main questions, may affect the constraint in the learned attention maps.

Table 2 shows the effect of λ and γ on the performance metrics. As expected, we notice that when λ increases, the consistency of our approach increases as well and will occasionally deteriorate overall accuracy. The impact of γ however is less evident, as no clear trend is visible. This would imply that the exact parameter value used is moderately critical to performances.

4 Conclusions

In this work, we presented a novel method for improving consistency in VQA models in cases where answers to sub-questions imply those of main questions and vice-versa. By using a tailored training procedure and loss function that measures the level of inconsistency, we show on the application of DME staging, that our approach provides important improvements in both VQA accuracy and consistency. In addition, we show that our method's hyperparameters are relatively insensitive to model performance. In the future, we plan to investigate how this approach can be extended to the broader case of unconstrained question relations.

Acknowledgments. This work was partially funded by the Swiss National Science Foundation through the grant # 191983.

References

1. Antol, S., et al.: VQA: visual question answering. In: Proceedings of the IEEE International Conference on Computer Vision, pp. 2425–2433 (2015)
2. Cadene, R., Dancette, C., Cord, M., Parikh, D., et al.: RUBi: reducing unimodal biases for visual question answering. Adv. Neural. Inf. Process. Syst. **32**, 841–852 (2019)
3. Decenciere, E., et al.: TeleoOhta: machine learning and image processing methods for teleophthalmology. IRBM **34**(2), 196–203 (2013)
4. Goel, V., Chandak, M., Anand, A., Guha, P.: IQ-VQA: intelligent visual question answering. In: Del Bimbo, A., et al. (eds.) ICPR 2021. LNCS, vol. 12662, pp. 357–370. Springer, Cham (2021). https://doi.org/10.1007/978-3-030-68790-8_28
5. Gokhale, T., Banerjee, P., Baral, C., Yang, Y.: VQA-LOL: visual question answering under the lens of logic. In: Vedaldi, A., Bischof, H., Brox, T., Frahm, J.-M. (eds.) ECCV 2020. LNCS, vol. 12366, pp. 379–396. Springer, Cham (2020). https://doi.org/10.1007/978-3-030-58589-1_23
6. Gong, H., Chen, G., Liu, S., Yu, Y., Li, G.: Cross-modal self-attention with multi-task pre-training for medical visual question answering. In: Proceedings of the 2021 International Conference on Multimedia Retrieval, pp. 456–460 (2021)
7. Goyal, Y., Khot, T., Summers-Stay, D., Batra, D., Parikh, D.: Making the V in VQA matter: Elevating the role of image understanding in visual question answering. In: Proceedings of the IEEE Conference on Computer Vision and Pattern Recognition, pp. 6904–6913 (2017)
8. Hasan, S.A., Ling, Y., Farri, O., Liu, J., Lungren, M., Müller, H.: Overview of the ImageCLEF 2018 medical domain visual question answering task. In: CLEF2018 Working Notes. CEUR Workshop Proceedings, CEUR-WS.org http://ceur-ws.org, Avignon, France, 10–14 September 2018
9. He, K., Zhang, X., Ren, S., Sun, J.: Deep residual learning for image recognition. In: Proceedings of the IEEE Conference on Computer Vision and Pattern Recognition, pp. 770–778 (2016)
10. Hochreiter, S., Schmidhuber, J.: Long short-term memory. Neural Comput. **9**(8), 1735–1780 (1997)
11. Hudson, D.A., Manning, C.D.: GQA: a new dataset for compositional question answering over real-world images. arXiv preprint arXiv:1902.09506, vol. 3(8) (2019)
12. Liao, Z., Wu, Q., Shen, C., Van Den Hengel, A., Verjans, J.: AIML at VQA-Med 2020: knowledge inference via a skeleton-based sentence mapping approach for medical domain visual question answering (2020)
13. Liu, F., Peng, Y., Rosen, M.P.: An effective deep transfer learning and information fusion framework for medical visual question answering. In: Crestani, F., et al. (eds.) CLEF 2019. LNCS, vol. 11696, pp. 238–247. Springer, Cham (2019). https://doi.org/10.1007/978-3-030-28577-7_20

14. Nguyen, B.D., Do, T.-T., Nguyen, B.X., Do, T., Tjiputra, E., Tran, Q.D.: Overcoming data limitation in medical visual question answering. In: Shen, D., et al. (eds.) MICCAI 2019. LNCS, vol. 11767, pp. 522–530. Springer, Cham (2019). https://doi.org/10.1007/978-3-030-32251-9_57

15. Porwal, P., et al.: Indian diabetic retinopathy image dataset (IDRiD) (2018). https://dx.doi.org/10.21227/H25W98

16. Ray, A., Sikka, K., Divakaran, A., Lee, S., Burachas, G.: Sunny and dark outside?! Improving answer consistency in VQA through entailed question generation. arXiv preprint arXiv:1909.04696 (2019)

17. Ren, F., Cao, P., Zhao, D., Wan, C.: Diabetic macular edema grading in retinal images using vector quantization and semi-supervised learning. Technol. Health Care **26**(S1), 389–397 (2018)

18. Ribeiro, M.T., Guestrin, C., Singh, S.: Are red roses red? Evaluating consistency of question-answering models. In: Proceedings of the 57th Annual Meeting of the Association for Computational Linguistics, pp. 6174–6184 (2019)

19. Sarrouti, M.: NLM at VQA-Med 2020: visual question answering and generation in the medical domain. In: CLEF (Working Notes) (2020)

20. Selvaraju, R.R., et al.: Squinting at VQA models: introspecting VQA models with sub-questions. In: Proceedings of the IEEE/CVF Conference on Computer Vision and Pattern Recognition, pp. 10003–10011 (2020)

21. Shah, M., Chen, X., Rohrbach, M., Parikh, D.: Cycle-consistency for robust visual question answering. In: Proceedings of the IEEE/CVF Conference on Computer Vision and Pattern Recognition, pp. 6649–6658 (2019)

22. Tan, H., Bansal, M.: LXMERT: learning cross-modality encoder representations from transformers. arXiv preprint arXiv:1908.07490 (2019)

23. Teney, D., Abbasnejad, E., Hengel, A.V.D.: On incorporating semantic prior knowledge in deep learning through embedding-space constraints. arXiv preprint arXiv:1909.13471 (2019)

24. Vu, M.H., Löfstedt, T., Nyholm, T., Sznitman, R.: A question-centric model for visual question answering in medical imaging. IEEE Trans. Med. Imaging **39**(9), 2856–2868 (2020)

25. Wang, P., Liao, R., Moyer, D., Berkowitz, S., Horng, S., Golland, P.: Image classification with consistent supporting evidence. In: Machine Learning for Health, pp. 168–180. PMLR (2021)

26. Xu, K., et al.: Show, attend and tell: neural image caption generation with visual attention. In: International Conference on Machine Learning, pp. 2048–2057. PMLR (2015)

27. Yuan, Y., Wang, S., Jiang, M., Chen, T.Y.: Perception matters: detecting perception failures of VQA models using metamorphic testing. In: Proceedings of the IEEE/CVF Conference on Computer Vision and Pattern Recognition, pp. 16908–16917 (2021)

28. Zhan, L.M., Liu, B., Fan, L., Chen, J., Wu, X.M.: Medical visual question answering via conditional reasoning. In: Proceedings of the 28th ACM International Conference on Multimedia, pp. 2345–2354 (2020)

Graph Emotion Decoding from Visually Evoked Neural Responses

Zhongyu Huang[1,2], Changde Du[1,2], Yingheng Wang[3,4],
and Huiguang He[1,2,5(✉)]

[1] Research Center for Brain-Inspired Intelligence, National Laboratory of Pattern Recognition, Institute of Automation, Chinese Academy of Sciences, Beijing, China
{huangzhongyu2020,huiguang.he}@ia.ac.cn
[2] School of Artificial Intelligence, University of Chinese Academy of Sciences, Beijing, China
[3] Department of Electronic Engineering, Tsinghua University, Beijing, China
[4] Department of Biomedical Engineering, Johns Hopkins University, Baltimore, USA
[5] Center for Excellence in Brain Science and Intelligence Technology, Chinese Academy of Sciences, Beijing, China

Abstract. Brain signal-based affective computing has recently drawn considerable attention due to its potential widespread applications. Most existing efforts exploit emotion similarities or brain region similarities to learn emotion representations. However, the relationships between emotions and brain regions are not explicitly incorporated into the representation learning process. Consequently, the learned representations may not be informative enough to benefit downstream tasks, e.g., emotion decoding. In this work, we propose a novel neural decoding framework, Graph Emotion Decoding (GED), which integrates the relationships between emotions and brain regions via a bipartite graph structure into the neural decoding process. Further analysis shows that exploiting such relationships helps learn better representations, verifying the rationality and effectiveness of GED. Comprehensive experiments on visually evoked emotion datasets demonstrate the superiority of our model. The code is publicly available at https://github.com/zhongyu1998/GED.

Keywords: Neural decoding · Graph neural networks · Brain · Emotion

1 Introduction

Human emotions are complex mental states closely linked to the brain's responses to our diverse subjective experiences. Generally, emotions can be perceived in various ways, such as visual signals [5], audio signals [4], physiological signals [10], or functional neuroimaging techniques [16]. Since functional magnetic resonance imaging (fMRI) has a high spatial resolution and allows a direct,

---

Supplementary Information The online version contains supplementary material available at https://doi.org/10.1007/978-3-031-16452-1_38.

L. Wang et al. (Eds.): MICCAI 2022, LNCS 13438, pp. 396–405, 2022.
https://doi.org/10.1007/978-3-031-16452-1_38

comprehensive assessment of the functions of individual brain regions, it is widely used to explore the relationships between emotions and brain regions.

Recently, Horikawa et al. [8] exploited linear regression to design a neural encoding and decoding model (Fig. 1), building a bridge between emotional experiences and the corresponding brain fMRI responses. The emotional experiences are evoked by videos, and each video was previously annotated by multiple raters using 34 emotion categories (e.g., joy, fear, and sadness; *multi-label*). As shown in Fig. 1, the decoding process aims to predict scores of individual emotions for presented videos from fMRI recordings, and the encoding process aims to predict responses of individual voxels for presented videos from emotion scores.

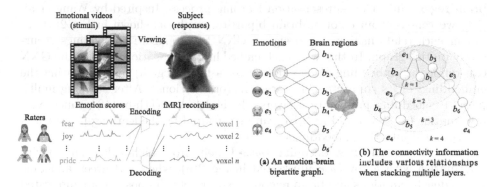

Fig. 1. Encoding and decoding visually evoked emotional responses in fMRI.

Fig. 2. A toy case of an emotion-brain bipartite graph and the connectivity information captured by embedding propagation layers.

Although Horikawa et al. [8] make great progress in emotion understanding, their linear regression model processes emotions independently and thus ignores their interconnections. A psychoevolutionary theory proposed by Plutchik [17] shows that different emotions are interrelated. For example, "amusement" is closer to "joy" and "satisfaction" than "horror" and "sadness". Thus, in multi-label emotion classification tasks, emotions with high correlations tend to be labeled together. A pioneering work [21] exploits Graph Neural Networks (GNNs) to model the dependencies between different emotions, and similarly, we can improve the emotion decoding tasks by incorporating such emotion correlations.

In addition, since we use the brain responses to decode emotions, it is intuitive to exploit the associations between different brain regions to promote our emotion decoding tasks. For example, previous studies [12, 16] demonstrate that the perception of aversive emotions (e.g., fear, anxiety) is processed in similar brain regions, such as the insula, amygdala, and medial thalamus. Accordingly, in fMRI-based emotion classification tasks, we can leverage the functional connectivity to analyze the associations between brain regions and construct brain networks [1]. In this way, different emotion categories correspond to different brain networks with more distinguishable graph topological properties and graph structural features. Several latest advances [3,13,15,22] apply similar ideas and achieve remarkable results in analyzing brain diseases and neurological disorders.

Despite their effectiveness, these approaches are insufficient to learn satisfactory emotion representations (or embeddings) for downstream emotion decoding tasks. The primary reason is that only the emotion similarities (i.e., correlations between different emotions) or brain region similarities (i.e., associations between different brain regions) are considered in the learning process. However, the embedding function lacks the explicit modeling of the relationships between emotions and brain regions. As a result, the learned embeddings may not be informative enough to benefit emotion decoding.

In this work, we propose to integrate the relationships between emotions and brain regions into the representation learning process. Inspired by Wang et al. [18], we construct an emotion-brain bipartite graph (as shown in Fig. 2(a)) to model such relationships and design a GNN to propagate embeddings recursively on this graph. In this way, each embedding propagation layer in the GNN can refine the embedding of an emotion (or a brain region) by aggregating the embeddings of its connected brain regions (or emotions). After stacking multiple (k) embedding propagation layers, the high-order (kth-order) connectivity information (as shown in Fig. 2(b)) can be captured by the learning process and incorporated into the embeddings.

Next, we explain how decoding tasks benefit from high-order connectivity information with a toy case illustrated in Fig. 2(a), where the green and blue nodes denote emotions and brain regions, respectively. Suppose we are interested in an emotion e_1 and aim to decode for e_1. Stacking one embedding propagation layer helps e_1 learn from its 1-hop neighbors b_1, b_2, and b_3 (immediately connected brain regions). And stacking two layers helps e_1 capture the information from its 2-hop neighbors e_2 and e_3 (potentially related emotions, since they have common neighbors b_2 and b_3, respectively). Now the emotion correlations between e_1 and e_2 (e_3) are captured, and the associations between different brain regions can be captured in a similar way. After stacking multiple layers, e_1 can capture most of the high-order connectivity information and perceive most nodes in the graph, thereby aggregating their embeddings and integrating the relationships between them into the neural decoding process. For example, after stacking four layers, all the emotions and brain regions have been perceived by e_1, and their information has been passed along the connected path, as shown in Fig. 2(b). Although we mainly take this idea for decoding tasks in this work, it can be similarly applied to encoding tasks, which is left for future work.

Our contributions can be summarized into three folds:

- We highlight the significance of exploiting the relationships between emotions and brain regions in neural decoding.
- We propose a novel neural decoding framework, Graph Emotion Decoding (GED), which builds a bridge between emotions and brain regions, and captures their relationships by performing embedding propagation.
- We verify the rationality and effectiveness of our approach on visually evoked emotion datasets. Experimental results demonstrate the superiority of GED.

2 Methodology

In this section, we present our proposed approach in detail. The pipeline of our approach is illustrated in Fig. 3. We first construct an emotion-brain bipartite graph with the fMRI recordings and emotion scores on the training set and initialize embeddings for all nodes. Then we stack multiple embedding propagation layers and refine the embeddings by integrating the relationships between nodes on the graph. At last, the refined emotion embeddings are fed into downstream emotion decoding tasks to predict the decoded emotion scores.

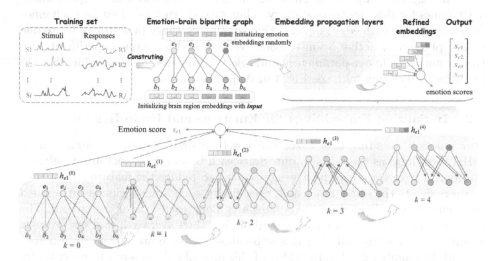

Fig. 3. The pipeline of Graph Emotion Decoding (GED). The component below illustrates how to propagate the information and predict an accurate emotion score s_{e_1} by stacking multiple embedding propagation layers. Each colored panel shows the results of k iterations of propagation starting from node e_1, where the colored nodes indicate that their information has been received by e_1, and the red arrows show the direction of information flow when aggregating neighborhoods from the previous layer. (Color figure online)

2.1 Constructing an Emotion-Brain Bipartite Graph

Let $G = (U, V, E)$ denote an emotion-brain bipartite graph. The vertex set of G consists of two disjoint subsets U and V, where U denotes the emotion set, and V denotes the brain region set. We use each vertex in U and V to represent an emotion category and a brain region, respectively. There are 34 emotion categories in our decoding task, and a total of 370 brain regions consisting of 360 cortical areas (180 cortical areas per hemisphere; defined by the Human Connectome Project (HCP) [6]) and 10 subcortical areas. The complete list of 34 emotion categories and 10 subcortical areas is presented in Table 2 of Appendix.

Lindquist et al. [14] find that when participants are experiencing or perceiving an emotion category, the activation in corresponding brain regions is greater than in a neutral control state. This evidence guides us to construct the edge set E in G as follows. First, on the training set, we classify each stimulus into the corresponding emotion category set according to its highest emotion score. If a stimulus gets the highest score in multiple emotion categories, it will be assigned to these sets simultaneously. Then, for each stimulus in each emotion category set, we sort brain regions in descending order by the average response of each brain region and select l brain regions corresponding to the top l average responses. Next, the potentially active brain regions for each emotion category are selected by voting. More specifically, the brain regions that got the top m votes among all stimuli in an emotion category set are taken as the potentially active ones for this emotion category. Thus we construct m edges for each emotion vertex, and each edge connects this emotion category (a vertex in U) to one of the potentially active brain regions (vertices in V). In our experiments, we treat l and m as hyper-parameters and select them based on the performance in one random training fold, see Fig. 4 in Appendix for details.

2.2   Initializing Embeddings for Emotions and Brain Regions

Our emotion decoding task takes the voxels in brain regions of interest from fMRI recordings as the initial input. Since each brain region contains a different number of voxels, we use the average pooling to reduce the feature size of each brain region to the same dimension. Specifically, each brain region is surrounded by a cuboid and divided into n equal parts along each axis of the cuboid. The responses of all voxels in each sub-cuboid are then averaged, and the average result is taken as the value of this sub-cuboid. If there are no voxels in a sub-cuboid, we simply take 0 as the value of this sub-cuboid. As a result, we initialize an embedding vector $\boldsymbol{h}_b^{(0)} \in \mathbb{R}^d$ for each brain region b, where $d = n \times n \times n$ denotes the embedding size. For each emotion e, we use Glorot initialization [7] to initialize its embedding vector $\boldsymbol{h}_e^{(0)} \in \mathbb{R}^d$, which can be refined by propagating embeddings on graph G and optimized in an end-to-end manner.

2.3   Embedding Propagation Layers

In general, GNNs follow a neighborhood aggregation strategy. They iteratively update the embedding of a node by aggregating embeddings of its neighbors, and each layer increases the size of the influence distribution by aggregating neighborhoods from the previous layer [20]. After k iterations of aggregation (stacking k layers), a node's embedding captures the structural information within its k-hop network neighborhood [19]. Hence, we can leverage GNNs to perform embedding propagation between the interrelated emotions and brain regions, thus refining their embeddings by integrating the relationships into the learning process.

For an emotion e and each of its connected brain regions $u \in \mathcal{N}_e$, where $\mathcal{N}_e$ denotes the set of 1-hop neighbors of emotion e in graph G, we take their embeddings $\boldsymbol{h}_e$ and $\boldsymbol{h}_u$ as the information to be propagated. Specifically, we consider e's own information $\boldsymbol{h}_e$ to retain its original features, and aggregate the information h_u along each edge (e, u) from e's neighborhood to refine e's embedding. We simply take the element-wise mean of the vectors in $\{h_e\} \cup \{h_u, u \in \mathcal{N}_e\}$ as our aggregation mechanism, commonly known as the "MEAN aggregator" [19]. Formally, the kth embedding propagation layer is:

$$a_e^{(k)} = \text{MEAN}\left(\left\{h_e^{(k-1)}\right\} \cup \left\{h_u^{(k-1)}, u \in \mathcal{N}_e\right\}\right), \quad h_e^{(k)} = \text{ReLU}\left(W^{(k)} \cdot a_e^{(k)}\right) \tag{1}$$

where $h_e^{(k)} \in \mathbb{R}^{d_k}$ is the hidden representation (embedding vector) of emotion e at the kth iteration/layer, and d_k is the embedding size of layer k with $d_0 = d$; $h_e^{(k-1)}, h_u^{(k-1)} \in \mathbb{R}^{d_{k-1}}$ are embedding vectors of emotion e and brain region u generated from the previous layer, respectively; $W^{(k)} \in \mathbb{R}^{d_k \times d_{k-1}}$ is a learnable weight matrix. And for a brain region b, we can similarly obtain the embedding by aggregating information from its connected emotions. In this way, each embedding propagation layer can explicitly exploit the first-order connectivity information between emotions and brain regions. After stacking multiple embedding propagation layers, the high-order connectivity information can be captured by the representation learning process and incorporated into the embeddings.

After propagating with K layers, we obtain a set of intermediate embeddings $\{h_e^{(0)}, h_e^{(1)}, \cdots, h_e^{(K)}\}$ from different layers for emotion e. Since the embeddings obtained in different layers reflect different connectivity information, they can flexibly leverage different neighborhood ranges to learn better structure-aware representations [20]. Thus, we combine these intermediate embeddings together to get the decoded emotion score s_e for emotion e, formulated as follows:

$$s_e = \sigma\left(\sum_{k=0}^{K} v_{(k)}^T h_e^{(k)}\right) \tag{2}$$

where $v_{(k)} \in \mathbb{R}^{d_k}$ denotes a learnable scoring vector for embeddings obtained in the kth iteration/layer, shared by all emotions; σ is the logistic sigmoid non-linearity, used to convert the result $\sum_k v_{(k)}^T h_e^{(k)}$ into an emotion score $s_e \in [0, 1]$ (also can be interpreted as the probability of the existence of emotion e).

3   Experiments

3.1   Dataset Description

We conduct experiments on visually evoked emotion datasets [8], which provide the measured fMRI responses to 2,196 visual stimuli (2,181 unique emotionally evocative short videos + 15 duplicates). For visual stimuli, the videos were originally collected by Cowen and Keltner [2]. Each video was previously annotated by a wide range of raters using self-report scales of 34 emotion categories (e.g., joy, fear, and sadness; *multi-label*). The human raters used binarized scores to report whether these emotions exist in each video, and the final emotion category scores were averaged among these raters, ranging between 0 and 1. The value of each emotion category score can be viewed as the intensity of this emotion. For fMRI responses, we use the fMRI data preprocessed by Horikawa et al. [8], where the value of each voxel represents the activity information of this voxel.

3.2   Experimental Setup

In general, there are two manners for emotion decoding, i.e., predict the emotion categories in a multi-label manner or predict the emotion scores in a regressive manner. Since human emotions are subjective mental states, different people usually have different feelings for the same stimulus. Even the same person may have different feelings for the same stimulus at different time periods. In view of these facts, we believe that it is more appropriate to predict the emotion score than the existence of a specific emotion. Accordingly, our experiments take the emotion scores obtained in Sect. 3.1 as the prediction targets and transform the multi-label classification task into a more rigorous regression task.

Evaluation Protocol. We perform decoding analyses between the fMRI responses to each visual stimulus and its emotion scores in a cross-validated manner. Specifically, we perform the 10-fold cross-validation on 2,196 pairs of {fMRI recordings, emotion scores} for each subject (a *within-subject* design). In each trial of 10-fold cross-validation, we use 1,976 random pairs (9 folds) as the training set to train a model and then take the remaining 220 pairs (1 fold) as the validation set (a.k.a. testing set) to evaluate the model. We repeat this process 10 times and use each fold as the testing set exactly once.

Evaluation Metric. We take the Mean Absolute Error (MAE) as our evaluation metric, which is widely used in regression tasks, defined as follows. Let $y_i \in \mathbb{R}^c$ and $\hat{y}_i \in \mathbb{R}^c$ denote the true and predicted (or decoded) emotion category scores for stimulus i, respectively, where c is the number of emotion categories. Let y_{ij} and $\hat{y}_{ij}$ denote the true and predicted score of a specific emotion e_j in stimulus i, respectively, where $\hat{y}_{ij} = s_{e_j}$ is calculated by Eq. (2). The MAE value (a.k.a. L1-norm) α is calculated as:

$$\alpha = \frac{1}{N} \sum_{i=1}^{N} \sum_{j=1}^{c} |y_{ij} - \hat{y}_{ij}| \tag{3}$$

where N denotes the number of stimuli.

Baselines. We compare our proposed model GED with several state-of-the-art baselines: Fully-connected Neural Network (FNN), Graph Convolutional Network (GCN) [11], BrainNetCNN [9], and BrainGNN [13]. FNN directly takes fMRI recordings as the input, mainly used to verify the effectiveness of other graph-based models. GCN takes a random graph as the input graph to verify the rationality of the graph construction in Sect. 2.1. The last two are state-of-the-art brain-network-based models, which are treated as our main baselines.

Table 1. Emotion decoding results (MAE, lower is better) in five distinct subjects.

Model	Subject 1	Subject 2	Subject 3	Subject 4	Subject 5
FNN	2.053 ± 0.059	2.071 ± 0.079	2.078 ± 0.086	2.039 ± 0.065	2.065 ± 0.078
GCN	1.817 ± 0.036	1.822 ± 0.028	1.819 ± 0.032	1.821 ± 0.028	1.818 ± 0.034
BrainNetCNN	1.723 ± 0.031	1.719 ± 0.034	1.736 ± 0.032	1.740 ± 0.031	1.741 ± 0.029
BrainGNN	1.678 ± 0.027	1.675 ± 0.026	1.684 ± 0.029	1.693 ± 0.026	**1.681 ± 0.024**
GED-1	2.010 ± 0.087	1.992 ± 0.076	2.014 ± 0.073	1.950 ± 0.092	2.010 ± 0.099
GED-2	1.755 ± 0.024	1.753 ± 0.028	1.769 ± 0.022	1.775 ± 0.022	1.778 ± 0.023
GED-3	1.675 ± 0.028	1.673 ± 0.029	1.684 ± 0.024	1.694 ± 0.027	1.698 ± 0.024
GED-4	**1.643 ± 0.028**	**1.647 ± 0.029**	**1.659 ± 0.026**	**1.668 ± 0.028**	1.674 ± 0.027

3.3   Performance Comparison

Table 1 presents a summary of the emotion decoding results. All models are evaluated using the standard 10-fold cross-validation procedure. We report the average and standard deviation of testing MAEs across the 10 folds (or 10 trials). The results show that our model achieves outstanding performance and outperforms baselines by a considerable margin in most subjects. Furthermore, we have the following observations and conclusions:

- FNN shows poor performance in all subjects, which indicates that traditional neural networks are insufficient to capture the complex relationships between emotions and brain regions. Other graph-based models consistently outperform FNN in all cases, demonstrating the importance of incorporating the relationships into the learning process.
- The brain-network-based models and GED all surpass GCN, which takes a random graph as the input graph. This fact highlights the importance of graph construction and verifies the rationality of our construction in Sect. 2.1.
- GED-4 significantly outperforms brain-network-based models in most cases (except Subject 5). This justifies the rationality of the analysis in Sect. 1 and the effectiveness of our model. However, GED performs on par with BrainGNN in Subject 5. The reason might be that Subject 5 was reluctant to use the custom-molded bite bar to fix his head, thus causing some potential head movements during fMRI scanning (see [8] for details). As a result, the head movements introduce noise to the collected fMRI responses and further affect the graph construction, leading to the sub-optimal performance.

3.4   Ablation Study

As the embedding propagation layer plays a pivotal role in GED, we perform ablation studies on GED to investigate how the layer size affects the performance. Specifically, we search the layer size in $\{1, 2, 3, 4\}$ and report the corresponding results in Table 1, where the suffix "$-k$" indicates the number of layers is k. As shown in Table 1, GED-1 exhibits better performance than FNN in all cases. Such improvement verifies that exploiting the relationships between emotions and brain regions can help learn better representations, thereby enhancing the decoding performance. After stacking two layers, GED can implicitly exploit both the emotion correlations and the associations between brain regions (as explained in Sect. 1), and thus GED-2 achieves substantial improvement over GED-1. Moreover, GED-2, GED-3, and GED-4 are consistently superior to GED-1 in all cases, and their performance gradually improves with the increase of layers. These facts justify the effectiveness of stacking multiple embedding propagation layers and empirically show that the high-order connectivity information can significantly facilitate the emotion decoding tasks.

4   Conclusion and Future Work

In this work, we propose a novel neural decoding framework, Graph Emotion Decoding (GED), which integrates the relationships between emotions and brain regions via a bipartite graph structure into the neural decoding process. Further analysis verifies the rationality and effectiveness of GED. In conclusion, we take an important step forward to better understand human emotions by using graph-based neural decoding models. It would be interesting to apply the proposed idea to the neural encoding process, and we leave the explorations of emotion encoding tasks for future work.

Acknowledgements. This work was supported in part by the National Natural Science Foundation of China (61976209, 62020106015), CAS International Collaboration Key Project (173211KYSB20190024), and Strategic Priority Research Program of CAS (XDB32040000).

References

1. Bullmore, E., Sporns, O.: Complex brain networks: graph theoretical analysis of structural and functional systems. Nat. Rev. Neurosci. **10**(3), 186–198 (2009)
2. Cowen, A.S., Keltner, D.: Self-report captures 27 distinct categories of emotion bridged by continuous gradients. Proc. Natl. Acad. Sci. **114**(38), E7900–E7909 (2017)
3. Cui, H., Dai, W., Zhu, Y., Li, X., He, L., Yang, C.: BrainNNExplainer: an interpretable graph neural network framework for brain network based disease analysis. In: ICML 2021 Workshop on Interpretable Machine Learning in Healthcare (2021)
4. Dellaert, F., Polzin, T., Waibel, A.: Recognizing emotion in speech. In: Proceeding of the 4th International Conference on Spoken Language Processing, vol. 3, pp. 1970–1973 (1996)
5. Ekman, P.: Facial expression and emotion. Am. Psychol. **48**(4), 384 (1993)
6. Glasser, M.F., et al.: A multi-modal parcellation of human cerebral cortex. Nature **536**(7615), 171–178 (2016)
7. Glorot, X., Bengio, Y.: Understanding the difficulty of training deep feedforward neural networks. In: Proceedings of the 13th International Conference on Artificial Intelligence and Statistics, pp. 249–256 (2010)
8. Horikawa, T., Cowen, A.S., Keltner, D., Kamitani, Y.: The neural representation of visually evoked emotion is high-dimensional, categorical, and distributed across transmodal brain regions. iScience **23**(5), 101060 (2020)

9. Kawahara, J., et al.: BrainNetCNN: convolutional neural networks for brain networks; towards predicting neurodevelopment. NeuroImage **146**, 1038–1049 (2017)
10. Kim, J., André, E.: Emotion recognition based on physiological changes in music listening. IEEE Trans. Pattern Anal. Mach. Intell. **30**(12), 2067–2083 (2008)
11. Kipf, T.N., Welling, M.: Semi-supervised classification with graph convolutional networks. In: Proceedings of the 5th International Conference on Learning Representations (2017)
12. von Leupoldt, A., et al.: Dyspnea and pain share emotion-related brain network. NeuroImage **48**(1), 200–206 (2009)
13. Li, X., et al.: BrainGNN: interpretable brain graph neural network for fMRI analysis. Med. Image Anal. **74**, 102233 (2021)
14. Lindquist, K.A., Wager, T.D., Kober, H., Bliss-Moreau, E., Barrett, L.F.: The brain basis of emotion: a meta-analytic review. Behav. Brain Sci. **35**, 121–202 (2012)
15. Ma, J., Zhu, X., Yang, D., Chen, J., Wu, G.: Attention-guided deep graph neural network for longitudinal Alzheimer's disease analysis. In: Martel, A.L., et al. (eds.) MICCAI 2020. LNCS, vol. 12267, pp. 387–396. Springer, Cham (2020). https://doi.org/10.1007/978-3-030-59728-3_38
16. Phan, K.L., Wager, T., Taylor, S.F., Liberzon, I.: Functional neuroanatomy of emotion: a meta-analysis of emotion activation studies in PET and fMRI. NeuroImage **16**(2), 331–348 (2002)
17. Plutchik, R.: A general psychoevolutionary theory of emotion. In: Theories of Emotion, pp. 3–33. Elsevier (1980)
18. Wang, X., He, X., Wang, M., Feng, F., Chua, T.S.: Neural graph collaborative filtering. In: Proceedings of the 42nd International ACM SIGIR Conference on Research and Development in Information Retrieval, pp. 165–174 (2019)
19. Xu, K., Hu, W., Leskovec, J., Jegelka, S.: How powerful are graph neural networks? In: Proceedings of the 7th International Conference on Learning Representations (2019)
20. Xu, K., Li, C., Tian, Y., Sonobe, T., Kawarabayashi, K.I., Jegelka, S.: Representation learning on graphs with jumping knowledge networks. In: Proceedings of the 35th International Conference on Machine Learning, pp. 5453–5462 (2018)
21. Xu, P., Liu, Z., Winata, G.I., Lin, Z., Fung, P.: EmoGraph: capturing emotion correlations using graph networks. arXiv preprint arXiv:2008.09378 (2020)
22. Zhang, Y., Tetrel, L., Thirion, B., Bellec, P.: Functional annotation of human cognitive states using deep graph convolution. NeuroImage **231**, 117847 (2021)

Dual-Graph Learning Convolutional Networks for Interpretable Alzheimer's Disease Diagnosis

Tingsong Xiao[1], Lu Zeng[1], Xiaoshuang Shi[1(✉)], Xiaofeng Zhu[1,2(✉)], and Guorong Wu[3,4]

[1] Department of Computer Science and Engineering, University of Electronic Science and Technology of China, Chengdu, China
{xsshi2013,seanzhuxf}@gmail.com
[2] Shenzhen Institute for Advanced Study, University of Electronic Science and Technology of China, Shenzhen, China
[3] Department of Psychiatry, University of North Carolina at Chapel Hill, Chapel Hill, NC, USA
[4] Department of Computer Science, University of North Carolina at Chapel Hill, Chapel Hill, NC, USA

Abstract. In this paper, we propose a dual-graph learning convolutional network (dGLCN) to achieve interpretable Alzheimer's disease (AD) diagnosis, by jointly investigating subject graph learning and feature graph learning in the graph convolution network (GCN) framework. Specifically, we first construct two initial graphs to consider both the subject diversity and the feature diversity. We further fuse these two initial graphs into the GCN framework so that they can be iteratively updated (*i.e.*, dual-graph learning) while conducting representation learning. As a result, the dGLCN achieves interpretability in both subjects and brain regions through the subject importance and the feature importance, and the generalizability by overcoming the issues, such as limited subjects and noisy subjects. Experimental results on the Alzheimer's disease neuroimaging initiative (ADNI) datasets show that our dGLCN outperforms all comparison methods for binary classification. The codes of dGLCN are available on https://github.com/xiaotingsong/dGLCN.

1 Introduction

Neuroimaging techniques (*e.g.*, magnetic resonance imaging (MRI)) is an effective way to monitor the progression of AD, so they are widely used for early AD diagnosis. Machine learning methods for early AD diagnosis usually include

---

T. Xiao and L. Zeng—Equal contribution.

Supplementary Information The online version contains supplementary material available at https://doi.org/10.1007/978-3-031-16452-1_39.

L. Wang et al. (Eds.): MICCAI 2022, LNCS 13438, pp. 406–415, 2022.
https://doi.org/10.1007/978-3-031-16452-1_39

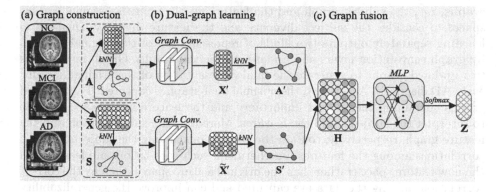

Fig. 1. The flowchart of the proposed dGLCN framework.

traditional methods and deep learning methods. Deep learning methods obtain higher diagnosis performance than traditional methods because of their powerful feature extraction capability with the help of large-scale subjects. For example, GCN generates discriminative representation for early AD diagnosis by aggregating the neighbor information of subjects [18,25,27]. However, previous methods for medical image analysis (including traditional methods and deep learning methods) still suffer from issues as follows, *i.e.*, limited and noisy subjects, and the interpretability.

Medical image analysis often suffers from the influence of limited and noisy subjects [1,20] because either subject labelling or feature extraction requires prior knowledge while experienced clinicians are always lacked. As a result, deep learning methods built on limited and noisy subjects easily result in the overfitting issue, and thus they influence the generalizability of the diagnosis model and the clinician's judgement [15]. However, few studies of medical image analysis have exploited them in the same framework.

Poor interpretability is a well-known drawback of deep learning methods. Existing methods mostly focus on post-hoc interpretation, where the interpretation model is built after the diagnosis model. In this way, the interpretation model will be re-built if the input changes. Hence, the post-hoc interpretation easily results in inflexible interpretation. Inspired by the interpretability of traditional methods, some deep learning methods employ either self-paced learning [26] or feature selection [16] to explore the subject diversity or the feature diversity. However, they usually require to have clean samples (*i.e.*, without noise) in the training process, so this might restrict their applications. In addition, these methods fail to jointly consider the subject diversity and the feature diversity in a unified framework, so that they cannot comprehensively capture the inherent correlations of the data and interpret the model.

To address the above issues, we propose to conduct dual-graph learning in the GCN framework (shown in Fig. 1), including graph construction, dual-graph learning and graph fusion. Specifically, graph construction constructs two initial graphs, *i.e.*, the subject graph and the feature graph, from the original feature space, to consider the subject diversity and the feature diversity. Dual-graph learning separately outputs two kinds of representation of the original features by graph convolution layers and updates two initial graphs. Graph fusion fuses two updated graphs to generate the final representation of the original data for early AD diagnosis. As a result, the optimal dual-graph is captured. The updated graphs containing the subject importance and the feature importance are able to interpret the subjects and the features. Moreover, the subject graph and the feature graph, respectively, contain the correlations among the subjects and the correlations among the features. Furthermore, such correlations are learnt from the new feature space (rather than the original feature space), thereby the correct correlations among the data are captured and can improve the generalizability of the model on the dataset with limited and noisy subjects. The contributions of this paper are summarized as follows:

– Our method is the first work to consider dual-graph learning by comprehensively capturing the correlations among the data to improve the generalizability and contain interpretability. In the literature, [7] focused on graph learning on a subject graph. [29] focused on learning a fixed feature graph and [4,5] focused on constructing a fixed dual-graph. In particular, these mentioned methods seldom consider the interpretability.
– Our method is able to identify the subjects and the brain regions related to the AD. Moreover, it can be easily applied to interpret other disease diagnosis on neuroimaging data.

2   Method

2.1   Graph Construction

We select the GCN framework as our backbone. The quality of its initial graph is very important as the graph stores the correlations among the data. In particular, if the correct correlations are captured, the quality of the graph is guaranteed. Recently, it is popular to construct the subject graph, which contains the correlations among subjects to indicate the subject diversity. That is, different subjects have distinct characteristics and contributions to the diagnosis model. Moreover, the higher the correlation between two subjects is, the larger the edge weight is. In this work, we extract node features based on region-of-interests (ROIs), which have structural or functional correlations to AD [19], so it is obvious that the features (*i.e.*, ROIs) are relevant. Moreover, distinct brain regions have different influence to AD. However, to the best of our knowledge, few methods focused on taking into account the correlations among ROIs (*i.e.*, the features) and the ROI diversity, but the feature graph can achieve both of them in this paper.

The graph is seldom provided in medical image analysis, so the graph should be constructed based on the information among the data. In this work, we construct the graphs where node features are the subject/features characteristics and the edge weight measures the correlation between two subjects/features. In particular, the higher the correlation between two subjects/features is, the larger the edge weight is. For simplicity, we employ the kNN method to construct both the subject graph $\mathbf{A} \in \mathbb{R}^{n \times n}$ and the feature graph $\mathbf{S} \in \mathbb{R}^{d \times d}$, where n and d denote the number of subjects and features.

2.2 Dual-Graph Learning

The initial graph obtained from the original feature space usually contains noise or redundancy, so its quality cannot be guaranteed. In this case, graph learning is an effective solution to improve its quality by iteratively updating it and the representation from the new feature space rather than the original feature space. As a result, graph learning is able to correctly capture the correlations among the data. For example, the graph learning convolutional network (GLCN) in [7] combines graph learning on the subject graph with the graph convolution in a unified network. In this paper, we conduct dual-graph learning to simultaneously update two initial graphs and the representation in this paper. To do this, we first separately update each graph by graph convolution layers and then fuse them for representation learning.

Subject Graph Update. Given the feature matrix $\mathbf{X} \in \mathbb{R}^{n \times d}$ and the initial subject graph $\mathbf{A}$, we employ graph convolutions to obtain

$$\mathbf{X}^{l+1} = \sigma(\mathbf{D}^{-1/2} \tilde{\mathbf{A}} \mathbf{D}^{-1/2} \mathbf{X}^l \mathbf{\Theta}^l) \tag{1}$$

where $\mathbf{X}^l \in \mathbb{R}^{n \times d_l}$ is a d_l-dimensional representation in the l-th layer and σ denotes the activation function. $\tilde{\mathbf{A}} = \mathbf{A} + \mathbf{I}_n$, where $\mathbf{I}_n \in \mathbb{R}^{n \times n}$ is the identity matrix, $\mathbf{D}$ and $\mathbf{\Theta}^l$, respectively, represents the degree matrix of $\tilde{\mathbf{A}}$ and the trainable parameters of the l-th layer. After obtaining the new representation $\mathbf{X}'$, we employ the kNN method to generate a subject graph $\mathbf{A}' \in \mathbb{R}^{n \times n}$, *i.e.*, the update of the initial subject graph $\mathbf{A}$.

Feature Graph Update. Given the feature matrix $\mathbf{X}$, we obtain its transpose as $\tilde{\mathbf{X}} = \mathbf{X}^T \in \mathbb{R}^{d \times n}$. In this paper, we design the feature graph $\mathbf{S} \in \mathbb{R}^{d \times d}$ to explore the correlations among features as AD is influenced by the complex correlations among ROIs (*i.e.*, features) [21]. Specifically, we regard the n-dimensional representation as the characteristics of the node (*i.e.*, the ROI information) and the edge weight as the correlation between two n-dimensional representation. After the two-layer graph convolution, the new representation of $\tilde{\mathbf{X}}$ is

$$\tilde{\mathbf{X}}^{l+1} = \sigma(\tilde{\mathbf{D}}^{-1/2} \tilde{\mathbf{S}} \tilde{\mathbf{D}}^{-1/2} \tilde{\mathbf{X}}^l \tilde{\mathbf{\Theta}}^l) \tag{2}$$

where $\tilde{\mathbf{X}}^l \in \mathbb{R}^{d \times n_l}$ is a n_l-dimensional representation in the l-th layer. $\tilde{\mathbf{S}} = \mathbf{S} + \mathbf{I}_d$, where $\mathbf{I}_d \in \mathbb{R}^{d \times d}$ is the identity matrix, $\tilde{\mathbf{D}}$ and $\tilde{\mathbf{\Theta}}^l$, respectively, represent the degree matrix of $\tilde{\mathbf{S}}$ and the trainable parameters of the l-th layer. After obtaining the new representation $\tilde{\mathbf{X}}'$, we utilize kNN method to generate a new feature graph $\mathbf{S}' \in \mathbb{R}^{d \times d}$, *i.e.*, the update of the initial feature graph $\mathbf{S}$.

2.3 Graph Fusion and Objective Function

Equation (1) and Eq. (2) learn the new representations of the original graph, which are further utilized to construct the subject graph and the feature graph separately. Meanwhile, the two graphs output the subject importance and the feature importance, respectively. In particular, the subject importance contains the weight of every subject while the feature importance involves the weight of every feature. Such importance can be used to interpret subjects and ROIs as well as can be fused into the original feature matrix for representation learning. To do this, we combine them (*i.e.*, $\mathbf{A}'$ and $\mathbf{S}'$) with $\mathbf{X}$ to have $\mathbf{H} \in \mathbb{R}^{n \times d}$ as

$$\mathbf{H} = \mathbf{A}'\mathbf{X}\mathbf{S}' \tag{3}$$

Compared with the original feature matrix $\mathbf{X}$, the new feature matrix $\mathbf{H}$ takes into account both the subject importance and the feature importance. Inspired by [12] and [11], we define $\mathbf{H}$ as follows by adding the original graphs (*i.e.*, $\mathbf{A}$ and $\mathbf{S}$) so that the updated graphs (*i.e.*, $\mathbf{A}'$ and $\mathbf{S}'$) have tiny variation in every iteration to achieve robust classification model.

$$\mathbf{H} = (\mathbf{A}' + \lambda_1 \mathbf{A})\mathbf{X}(\mathbf{S}' + \lambda_2 \mathbf{S}) \tag{4}$$

where λ_1 and λ_2 are parameters. After that, the new representation can be obtained by the MLP

$$\mathbf{H}^{l+1} = \sigma(\mathbf{H}^l \mathbf{W}^l) \tag{5}$$

where the $\mathbf{H}^l \in \mathbb{R}^{n \times d_l}$ denotes the representation of the l-th layer while $\mathbf{H}^0 = \mathbf{H}$. $\mathbf{W}^l \in \mathbb{R}^{d_l \times d_{l+1}}$ is the MLP parameters in the l-th layer.

After conducting the MLP, the output matrix $\mathbf{H}^L$ is derived. We further use the softmax function to obtain the label prediction $\mathbf{Z} = [\mathbf{z}_0, \mathbf{z}_1, ..., \mathbf{z}_{n-1}] \in \mathbb{R}^{n \times c}$, where $\mathbf{z}_i \in \mathbb{R}^c$ denotes the label prediction for the i-th subject, *i.e.*,

$$z_{ij} = \text{softmax}\left(h_{ij}^L\right) = \frac{\exp\left(h_{ij}^L\right)}{\sum_{m \in c} \exp\left(h_{im}^L\right)}. \tag{6}$$

where h_{ij} and z_{ij} represent the elements in the i-th row and the j-th column of $\mathbf{H}$ and $\mathbf{Z}$, respectively. The cross-entropy function is used to calculate the loss.

$$\mathcal{L}_{ce} = -\sum_{i \in N} \sum_{j=1}^{c} y_{ij} \ln z_{ij} \tag{7}$$

where y_{ij} is the element of the i-th row and the j-th column of the real label $\mathbf{Y}$.

We obtain optimal $\mathbf{A}'$ and $\mathbf{S}'$, where every element in $\mathbf{A}'$ represents the correlations between two subjects and every element in $\mathbf{S}'$ denotes the correlations between two ROIs. Moreover, they are symmetric matrices. Following [30], we first calculate the ℓ_2-norm value of every row in $\mathbf{S}'$ and then rank their ℓ_2-norm values. In this way, the features whose corresponded rows in $\mathbf{S}'$ with the top ℓ_2-norm values are regarded as important features. We can also obtain the important subjects by calculating the ℓ_2-norm value of every row in $\mathbf{A}'$. We did not follow [17] to set a sparse constraint on $\mathbf{S}'$ as the two ways output similar results in terms of feature importance while [17] is time-consuming.

3 Experiments

3.1 Experimental Settings

Our dataset from the ADNI (www.loni.usc.edu/ADNI) includes 186 ADs, 393 mild cognitive impairment patients (MCIs) and 226 normal controls (NCs). Moreover, 393 MCIs include 226 MCI non-converts (MCIn) and 167 MCI converts (MCIc). We use them to form four binary classification tasks, *i.e.*, AD-NC (186 vs. 226), AD-MCI (186 vs. 393), NC-MCI (226 vs. 393) and MCIn-MCIc (226 vs. 167) on the MRI data. The MRI data is first dealt with by the steps, *i.e.*, spatial distortion correction, skull-stripping, and cerebellum removal, and then segmented into gray matter, white matter, and cerebrospinal fluid. Finally, we use the AAL template [23] to obtain 90 ROIs for every subject.

The comparison methods include three traditional methods (*i.e.*, ℓ_1-norm support vector machines (ℓ_1-SVM) [28], self-paced learning (SPL) [10] and boosted random forest (BRF) [13]) and five deep methods (*i.e.*, graph convolutional networks (GCN) [9], graph attention networks (GAT) [24], dual graph convolutional networks (DGCN) [31], interpretable dynamic graph convolutional networks (IDGCN) [30] and sample reweight (SR) [22]).

We obtain the author-verified codes for all comparison methods and let them to achieve their best performance. Since the datasets used in this experiment do not provide a predefined subject graph, we construct it with the kNN method by setting $k = 30$. To avoid the over-fitting issue on the datasets with limited subjects, in all experiments, we repeat the 5-fold cross-validation scheme 100 times with different random seeds on all datasets for all methods. We finally report the average results and the corresponding standard deviation (std). We adopt four commonly used metrics to evaluate all methods, including classification accuracy, sensitivity, specificity and AUC.

3.2 Result Analysis

Table 1 shows the classification results of all methods on all datasets. First, our method achieves the best results, followed by SR, GCN, IDGCN, GAT, DGCN, BRF, SPL and ℓ_1-SVM, on all datasets for four evaluation metrics. Moreover, our improvement has statistically significant difference (with $p \leq 0.05$ by t-test) from every comparison method. For example, our method on average improves by 3.2% and 6.9%, respectively, compared to the best comparison method, *i.e.*, SR, and the worst comparison method, *i.e.*, ℓ_1-SVM. It indicates that it is feasible for our method to take into account both the subject diversity and the feature diversity as they benefit our method to comprehensively capture the complex correlations among the data, and thus improving the generalizability. Second, all deep learning methods (*i.e.*, SR, GCN, IDGCN, GAT, DGCN and our method) outperform traditional methods, *i.e.*, BRF, SPL and ℓ_1-SVM. For example, our method on average improves by 6%, compared to the best traditional method (*i.e.*, BRF), on all datasets in terms of four evaluation metrics. The reason is that (1) traditional methods are worse for representation learning than deep learning methods and (2) deep learning methods are still effective on the datasets with limited subjects and our method achieves the best generalizability.

Table 1. Classification results (average ± std) of all methods on four datasets.

Dataset	Metrics	ℓ_1-SVM	SPL	BRF	GCN	GAT	DGCN	IDGCN	SR	Proposed
AD-NC	ACC	$74.5_{\pm2.9}$	$75.1_{\pm1.3}$	$73.5_{\pm2.7}$	$82.5_{\pm1.8}$	$83.9_{\pm2.0}$	$79.6_{\pm3.0}$	$83.3_{\pm2.5}$	$82.8_{\pm2.7}$	$\mathbf{86.9_{\pm1.6}}$
	SEN	$76.8_{\pm1.1}$	$81.5_{\pm1.5}$	$79.7_{\pm2.3}$	$82.9_{\pm1.7}$	$84.1_{\pm1.1}$	$74.4_{\pm3.3}$	$82.6_{\pm2.4}$	$85.2_{\pm3.3}$	$\mathbf{85.9_{\pm1.6}}$
	SPE	$73.7_{\pm1.3}$	$70.7_{\pm2.0}$	$66.7_{\pm2.0}$	$83.7_{\pm2.7}$	$79.1_{\pm1.5}$	$85.8_{\pm2.4}$	$83.2_{\pm3.0}$	$78.4_{\pm1.3}$	$\mathbf{87.2_{\pm1.7}}$
	AUC	$74.7_{\pm1.5}$	$72.2_{\pm1.2}$	$73.2_{\pm2.6}$	$84.3_{\pm2.5}$	$81.6_{\pm1.9}$	$75.2_{\pm2.9}$	$83.5_{\pm2.8}$	$80.1_{\pm2.8}$	$\mathbf{90.6_{\pm2.5}}$
AD-MCI	ACC	$66.4_{\pm3.3}$	$67.1_{\pm2.3}$	$65.3_{\pm2.2}$	$67.3_{\pm2.0}$	$67.2_{\pm2.2}$	$68.0_{\pm2.7}$	$66.8_{\pm2.4}$	$67.6_{\pm2.8}$	$\mathbf{68.7_{\pm1.5}}$
	SEN	$66.7_{\pm4.2}$	$63.6_{\pm2.2}$	$67.6_{\pm2.4}$	$67.4_{\pm3.1}$	$65.2_{\pm1.9}$	$60.6_{\pm2.5}$	$64.2_{\pm2.5}$	$67.2_{\pm2.6}$	$\mathbf{68.5_{\pm1.6}}$
	SPE	$65.5_{\pm2.5}$	$72.1_{\pm2.5}$	$63.6_{\pm2.6}$	$65.8_{\pm2.2}$	$75.2_{\pm3.7}$	$\mathbf{77.3_{\pm3.1}}$	$74.4_{\pm1.7}$	$76.0_{\pm1.4}$	$74.8_{\pm2.4}$
	AUC	$59.7_{\pm3.0}$	$60.3_{\pm1.3}$	$62.1_{\pm2.3}$	$62.4_{\pm1.5}$	$60.6_{\pm2.4}$	$62.0_{\pm2.1}$	$61.6_{\pm2.6}$	$60.6_{\pm1.7}$	$\mathbf{65.5_{\pm2.8}}$
NC-MCI	ACC	$61.5_{\pm1.7}$	$63.9_{\pm1.4}$	$62.4_{\pm2.4}$	$62.4_{\pm1.7}$	$64.7_{\pm1.7}$	$63.5_{\pm3.1}$	$64.2_{\pm2.6}$	$64.4_{\pm2.5}$	$\mathbf{67.5_{\pm2.4}}$
	SEN	$57.5_{\pm2.2}$	$59.1_{\pm1.7}$	$61.4_{\pm1.7}$	$58.7_{\pm2.4}$	$55.4_{\pm1.6}$	$61.4_{\pm1.8}$	$58.0_{\pm2.5}$	$61.2_{\pm1.9}$	$\mathbf{61.7_{\pm1.5}}$
	SPE	$62.3_{\pm2.5}$	$64.5_{\pm2.0}$	$65.9_{\pm2.4}$	$64.3_{\pm1.5}$	$65.7_{\pm2.5}$	$58.2_{\pm1.4}$	$64.6_{\pm2.3}$	$65.6_{\pm2.2}$	$\mathbf{67.7_{\pm1.3}}$
	AUC	$59.5_{\pm2.3}$	$60.2_{\pm2.8}$	$65.6_{\pm2.4}$	$65.6_{\pm2.2}$	$62.4_{\pm2.8}$	$60.8_{\pm2.1}$	$58.5_{\pm1.9}$	$66.4_{\pm3.3}$	$\mathbf{69.2_{\pm2.8}}$
MCIn-MCIc	ACC	$62.1_{\pm2.4}$	$63.8_{\pm2.6}$	$63.7_{\pm3.1}$	$64.4_{\pm1.6}$	$63.9_{\pm2.4}$	$62.6_{\pm1.8}$	$63.9_{\pm2.6}$	$63.7_{\pm1.8}$	$\mathbf{67.7_{\pm2.4}}$
	SEN	$65.9_{\pm2.5}$	$61.1_{\pm2.1}$	$67.8_{\pm2.3}$	$\mathbf{67.9_{\pm1.9}}$	$66.6_{\pm1.4}$	$62.2_{\pm2.2}$	$62.9_{\pm1.6}$	$61.6_{\pm1.7}$	$64.0_{\pm2.5}$
	SPE	$63.0_{\pm2.7}$	$64.9_{\pm3.3}$	$62.2_{\pm3.5}$	$61.9_{\pm2.6}$	$55.9_{\pm2.2}$	$67.9_{\pm2.8}$	$66.5_{\pm1.6}$	$66.0_{\pm1.4}$	$\mathbf{69.9_{\pm3.1}}$
	AUC	$59.8_{\pm3.7}$	$62.2_{\pm3.2}$	$62.6_{\pm3.3}$	$62.8_{\pm2.0}$	$61.2_{\pm2.7}$	$61.7_{\pm1.6}$	$62.3_{\pm2.4}$	$62.5_{\pm2.5}$	$\mathbf{63.7_{\pm3.0}}$

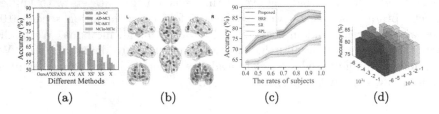

(a)   (b)   (c)   (d)

Fig. 2. Results of (a) Ablation study of 8 methods, (b) Top 20 ROIs selected by our method on AD-NC, (c) Subject interpretability of our method on AD-NC, and (d) our method with different parameter settings (*i.e.*, λ_1 and λ_2) on AD-NC.

3.3 Ablation Analysis

We use Eq. (4) (*i.e.*, $\mathbf{H} = (\mathbf{A}' + \lambda_1\mathbf{A})\mathbf{X}(\mathbf{S}' + \lambda_2\mathbf{S})$) to make Eq. (3) have a tiny variation in every iteration, so we generate 7 comparison methods to investigate the effectiveness of both the subject importance and the feature importance, *i.e.*, $\mathbf{H} = \mathbf{A}'\mathbf{X}\mathbf{S}'$, $\mathbf{H} = \mathbf{A}\mathbf{X}\mathbf{S}$, $\mathbf{H} = \mathbf{A}'\mathbf{X}$, $\mathbf{H} = \mathbf{A}\mathbf{X}$, $\mathbf{H} = \mathbf{X}\mathbf{S}'$, $\mathbf{H} = \mathbf{X}\mathbf{S}$, and $\mathbf{H} = \mathbf{X}$. We list the classification results of all eight methods in Fig. 2.(a) and Appendix A. First, dual-graph learning is very important in our method as the subject graph $\mathbf{A}'$ plays a greater role than the initial subject graph $\mathbf{A}$. Moreover, the feature graph has the same scenario. For example, the method of $\mathbf{A}'\mathbf{X}$ improves by 9% compared to that of $\mathbf{A}\mathbf{X}$, while the method of $\mathbf{X}\mathbf{S}'$ outperforms about 3%, compared to that of $\mathbf{X}\mathbf{S}$, in terms of classification accuracy, on dataset

AD-NC. Second, dual-graph learning is more effective than graph learning on one graph as more graphs could find more complex correlations among the data. Third, it is of great importance to add a portion of the initial graphs into the process of graph learning, mentioned in [3].

3.4 Interpretability

Feature Interpretability. We compare our method with three methods (*i.e.*, ℓ_1-SVM, BRF and IDGCN) to investigate their feature interpretability. To do this, since we repeat the 5-fold cross validation scheme 100 times to obtain 500 matrices of $\mathbf{S}'$, we select the top 20 features (*i.e.*, ROIs) from every experiment to obtain the frequency of every feature within 500 times. We list the ROIs selected by every method on all four datasets (*i.e.*, the third column) as well as the ROIs selected by all methods on all datasets (*i.e.*, the second column) in Appendix B and visualize top 20 ROIs selected by our method in Fig. 2.(b) and Appendix B. Obviously, ROIs selected by every method on all datasets are related to AD. For example, the hippocampal formation right is selected by all methods on all datasets and has been shown to be highly related to AD in [2]. In addition, compared to all comparison methods, our method selects much more ROIs, *e.g.*, the frontal lobe white matter and temporal lobe white matter, which are highly related to AD in [6,8,14]. Above observations suggest that our method is superior to all comparison methods, in terms of feature interpretability.

Subject Interpretability. We investigate the subject interpretability by evaluating the classification performance with different training rates. To do this, we first employ four methods with subject interpretability (*i.e.*, SPL, BRF, SR and Proposed) to output the subject importance within 500 experiments and then rank their importance in a descending order. With such an order, we increase the proportion of the training subjects from 40% to 100% and report the classification accuracy in Fig. 2.(c) and Appendix C. Obviously, all four methods achieve the highest accuracy when the training rates are between 70% and 90%. This indicates that there are noisy subjects in the datasets to affect the training process, and these methods can overcome this issue by learning the subject importance. In addition, our method always achieves the best results on all datasets with different rates as it is the most effective method to identify the noisy subjects, compared to all comparison methods.

3.5 Parameter Sensitivity Analysis

We investigate the parameter sensitivity by setting $k \in \{5, 10, ..., 35\}$, and $\lambda_1, \lambda_2 \in \{10^{-6}, 10^{-5}, ..., 10^{-1}\}$ and report the results in Fig. 2.(d) and Appendix D. First, our method is sensitive to the settings of k, but it achieves good performance while setting $k = 30$ on all datasets. Second, our method achieves the best performance with $\lambda_1 = 10^{-5}$ and $\lambda_2 = 10^{-3}$ on AD-NC, while is insensitive to them on other datasets. These cases are consistent with [3] of adding a portion of the initial graph into the process of graph learning.

4   Conclusion

In this paper, we propose a dual-graph learning method in the GCN framework to achieve the generalizability and the interpretability for medical image analysis. To do this, we consider the subject diversity and the feature diversity to conduct subject graph learning and feature graph learning in the same framework. Experimental results on the ADNI verify the effectiveness of our proposed method, compared to the state-of-the-art methods. In medical image analysis, imbalanced datasets are very common, *e.g.*, the number of normal controls (*i.e.*, majority class) is larger than the number of patients (*i.e.*, minority class), in the future, we will extend our method for interpretable medical image analysis on imbalanced datasets with limited subjects.

Acknowledgments. This work was partially supported by the National Natural Science Foundation of China (Grant No. 61876046), Medico-Engineering Cooperation Funds from University of Electronic Science and Technology of China (No. ZYGX2022YGRH009 and ZYGX2022YGRH014) and the Guangxi "Bagui" Teams for Innovation and Research, China.

References

1. Adeli, E., Li, X., Kwon, D., Zhang, Y., Pohl, K.M.: Logistic regression confined by cardinality-constrained sample and feature selection. IEEE Trans. Pattern Anal. Mach. Intell. **42**(7), 1713–1728 (2019)
2. Beal, M.F., Mazurek, M.F., Tran, V.T., Chattha, G., Bird, E.D., Martin, J.B.: Reduced numbers of somatostatin receptors in the cerebral cortex in Alzheimer's disease. Science **229**(4710), 289–291 (1985)
3. Chen, Y., Wu, L., Zaki, M.: Iterative deep graph learning for graph neural networks: better and robust node embeddings. In: NeurIPS, pp. 19314–19326 (2020)
4. Feng, J., et al.: Dual-graph convolutional network based on band attention and sparse constraint for hyperspectral band selection. Knowl.-Based Syst. **231**, 107428 (2021)
5. Fu, X., Qi, Q., Zha, Z.J., Zhu, Y., Ding, X.: Rain streak removal via dual graph convolutional network. In: AAAI, pp. 1–9 (2021)
6. Ihara, M., et al.: Quantification of myelin loss in frontal lobe white matter in vascular dementia, Alzheimer's disease, and dementia with Lewy bodies. Acta Neuropathol. **119**(5), 579–589 (2010)
7. Jiang, B., Zhang, Z., Lin, D., Tang, J., Luo, B.: Semi-supervised learning with graph learning-convolutional networks. In: CVPR, pp. 11313–11320 (2019)
8. Karas, G., et al.: Precuneus atrophy in early-onset Alzheimer's disease: a morphometric structural MRI study. Neuroradiology **49**(12), 967–976 (2007)
9. Kipf, T.N., Welling, M.: Semi-supervised classification with graph convolutional networks. In: ICLR (2017)
10. Kumar, M.P., Packer, B., Koller, D.: Self-paced learning for latent variable models. In: NeurIPS, pp. 1189–1197 (2010)
11. Liu, W., He, J., Chang, S.F.: Large graph construction for scalable semi-supervised learning. In: ICML (2010)

12. Liu, X., Lei, F., Xia, G.: MulStepNET: stronger multi-step graph convolutional networks via multi-power adjacency matrix combination. J. Ambient Intell. Human Comput., 1–10 (2021). https://doi.org/10.1007/s12652-021-03355-x
13. Mishina, Y., Murata, R., Yamauchi, Y., Yamashita, T., Fujiyoshi, H.: Boosted random forest. IEICE Trans. Inf. Syst. **98**(9), 1630–1636 (2015)
14. Mizuno, Y., Ikeda, K., Tsuchiya, K., Ishihara, R., Shibayama, H.: Two distinct subgroups of senile dementia of Alzheimer type: quantitative study of neurofibrillary tangles. Neuropathology **23**(4), 282–289 (2003)
15. Morgado, P.M., Silveira, M., Alzheimer's Disease Neuroimaging Initiative, et al.: Minimal neighborhood redundancy maximal relevance: application to the diagnosis of Alzheimer s disease. Neurocomputing **155**, 295–308 (2015)
16. Muñoz-Romero, S., Gorostiaga, A., Soguero-Ruiz, C., Mora-Jiménez, I., Rojo-Álvarez, J.L.: Informative variable identifier: expanding interpretability in feature selection. Pattern Recogn. **98**, 107077 (2020)
17. Nie, F., Huang, H., Cai, X., Ding, C.: Efficient and robust feature selection via joint 2, 1-norms minimization. In: NeurIPS, pp. 1813–1821 (2010)
18. Parisot, S., et al.: Disease prediction using graph convolutional networks: application to autism spectrum disorder and Alzheimer's disease. Med. Image Anal. **48**, 117–130 (2018)
19. Petersen, R.C., et al.: Memory and MRI-based hippocampal volumes in aging and AD. Neurology **54**(3), 581 (2000)
20. Qiu, S., et al.: Development and validation of an interpretable deep learning framework for Alzheimer's disease classification. Brain **143**(6), 1920–1933 (2020)
21. Reijmer, Y.D., et al.: Disruption of cerebral networks and cognitive impairment in Alzheimer disease. Neurology **80**(15), 1370–1377 (2013)
22. Ren, M., Zeng, W., Yang, B., Urtasun, R.: Learning to reweight examples for robust deep learning. In: ICML, pp. 4334–4343 (2018)
23. Tzourio-Mazoyer, N., et al.: Automated anatomical labeling of activations in SPM using a macroscopic anatomical parcellation of the MNI MRI single-subject brain. Neuroimage **15**(1), 273–289 (2002)
24. Veličković, P., Cucurull, G., Casanova, A., Romero, A., Liò, P., Bengio, Y.: Graph attention networks. In: ICLR (2018)
25. Wang, C., Samari, B., Siddiqi, K.: Local spectral graph convolution for point set feature learning. In: ECCV, pp. 52–66 (2018)
26. Yun, Y., Dai, H., Cao, R., Zhang, Y., Shang, X.: Self-paced graph memory network for student GPA prediction and abnormal student detection. In: Roll, I., McNamara, D., Sosnovsky, S., Luckin, R., Dimitrova, V. (eds.) AIED 2021. LNCS (LNAI), vol. 12749, pp. 417–421. Springer, Cham (2021). https://doi.org/10.1007/978-3-030-78270-2_74
27. Zeng, L., Li, H., Xiao, T., Shen, F., Zhong, Z.: Graph convolutional network with sample and feature weights for Alzheimer's disease diagnosis. Inf. Process. Manag. **59**(4), 102952 (2022)
28. Zhu, J., Rosset, S., Tibshirani, R., Hastie, T.J.: 1-norm support vector machines. In: NeurIPS, pp. 49–56 (2003)
29. Zhu, X., et al.: A novel relational regularization feature selection method for joint regression and classification in AD diagnosis. Med. Image Anal. **38**, 205–214 (2017)
30. Zhu, Y., Ma, J., Yuan, C., Zhu, X.: Interpretable learning based dynamic graph convolutional networks for Alzheimer's disease analysis. Inf. Fusion **77**, 53–61 (2022)
31. Zhuang, C., Ma, Q.: Dual graph convolutional networks for graph-based semi-supervised classification. In: WWW, pp. 499–508 (2018)

Asymmetry Disentanglement Network for Interpretable Acute Ischemic Stroke Infarct Segmentation in Non-contrast CT Scans

Haomiao Ni[1], Yuan Xue[2], Kelvin Wong[3], John Volpi[4], Stephen T.C. Wong[3], James Z. Wang[1], and Xiaolei Huang[1(✉)]

[1] The Pennsylvania State University, University Park, PA, USA
suh972@psu.edu
[2] Johns Hopkins University, Baltimore, MD, USA
[3] TT and WF Chao Center for BRAIN, Houston Methodist Cancer Center, Houston Methodist Hospital, Houston, TX, USA
[4] Eddy Scurlock Comprehensive Stroke Center, Department of Neurology, Houston Methodist Hospital, Houston, TX, USA

Abstract. Accurate infarct segmentation in non-contrast CT (NCCT) images is a crucial step toward computer-aided acute ischemic stroke (AIS) assessment. In clinical practice, bilateral symmetric comparison of brain hemispheres is usually used to locate pathological abnormalities. Recent research has explored asymmetries to assist with AIS segmentation. However, most previous symmetry-based work mixed different types of asymmetries when evaluating their contribution to AIS. In this paper, we propose a novel Asymmetry Disentanglement Network (ADN) to automatically separate pathological asymmetries and intrinsic anatomical asymmetries in NCCTs for more effective and interpretable AIS segmentation. ADN first performs asymmetry disentanglement based on input NCCTs, which produces different types of 3D asymmetry maps. Then a synthetic, intrinsic-asymmetry-compensated and pathology-asymmetry-salient NCCT volume is generated and later used as input to a segmentation network. The training of ADN incorporates domain knowledge and adopts a tissue-type aware regularization loss function to encourage clinically-meaningful pathological asymmetry extraction. Coupled with an unsupervised 3D transformation network, ADN achieves state-of-the-art AIS segmentation performance on a public NCCT dataset. In addition to the superior performance, we believe the learned clinically-interpretable asymmetry maps can also provide insights towards a better understanding of AIS assessment. Our code is available at https://github.com/nihaomiao/MICCAI22_ADN.

1 Introduction

Stroke is one of the leading causes of death and disability worldwide [10]. In the United States, about 795,000 people experience a new or recurrent stroke

---

H. Ni and Y. Xue—Contributed equally to this work.

L. Wang et al. (Eds.): MICCAI 2022, LNCS 13438, pp. 416–426, 2022.
https://doi.org/10.1007/978-3-031-16452-1_40

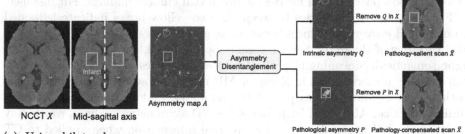

(a) Using bilateral symmetry of the human brain to detect abnormalities.

(b) Illustration of the proposed asymmetry disentanglement process. Different types of asymmetries can be removed from the input scan to obtain pathology-salient and pathology-compensated scans.

Fig. 1. Illustration of (a) different types of asymmetries in the human brain, and (b) our proposed asymmetry disentanglement framework. Asymmetry maps A, P, and Q in (b) are normalized for better visualization. (a) and (b) are from the same testing CT scan. (Color figure online)

every year, and 87% of all are acute ischemic strokes (AIS) [27]. Non-contrast CT (NCCT) images are routinely used to assess the extent of infarction in AIS patients [23]. For computer-aided AIS estimation in NCCT scans, accurate infarct segmentation is a crucial step. However, it is challenging to segment AIS infarct in NCCT scans. First, NCCT is more difficult to process than other medical image modalities such as MRI due to the low signal-to-noise and contrast-to-noise ratios of brain tissues [17]. Second, infarct regions can be confounded by normal physiologic changes, and the density and texture variations in involved brain areas may be subtle [19]. In clinical practice, to differentiate subtle abnormalities, clinicians often locate suspicious regions by comparing bilateral differences along the mid-sagittal axis (Fig. 1a).

Leveraging such prior knowledge that bilateral asymmetries can indicate potential lesions, recent symmetry-based AIS segmentation approaches [5,16, 19,22,23,28] have shown impressive progress. Clèrigues et al. [9] exploited brain hemisphere symmetry by inputting CT, CT perfusion images, and their horizontally flipped versions to a 2D-patch-based CNN to segment AIS. Kuang et al. [15] proposed a dense multi-path contextual GAN (MPC-GAN) to integrate bilateral intensity difference, infarct location probability, and distance to cerebrospinal fluid (CSF) for AIS segmentation.

Instead of exploring symmetry at the image level, Liang et al. [19] introduced a symmetry-enhanced attention network (SEAN) to segment AIS in NCCT images. The authors first ran a 2D alignment network to transform input images to be bilaterally quasi-symmetric in axial view. Then a symmetry-enhanced attention module was employed to capture both in-axial and cross-axial symmetry at the feature level. Though achieving promising results, most existing work simply fused all asymmetries, ignoring the fact that specific asymmetries caused by non-pathological factors cannot reveal clinical findings. For instance, in Fig. 1(b), the asymmetries between the two yellow boxes indicate left-sided infarction. However, differences between the green circles originate from the natural variation of the brain. Several recent approaches [4,6] explored how to highlight semantically-meaningful pathological asymmetries at the feature level to help identify abnormalities in X-ray or MR images. However, such feature-level pathological asymmetry has poor interpretability, making them less useful in clinical practice. Also, [4,6] both focused on 2D asymmetry analysis, which may fail to make full use of 3D spatial contextual information when applied to CT scans. Moreover, clinicians usually only look for asymmetry in voxels of the same tissue type, *e.g.*, within the grey matter or within the white matter. Such critical domain knowledge has not been investigated or utilized in the literature.

In this paper, we aim to address the aforementioned weaknesses in existing methods by proposing a novel asymmetry disentanglement network (ADN) to automatically separate pathological and intrinsic anatomical asymmetries in NCCT scans for AIS segmentation with tissue-type awareness. ADN performs asymmetry disentanglement at the image level and achieves high interpretability by directly outputting learned pathological and anatomical 3D asymmetry maps for clinical examination. Furthermore, when asymmetry maps are applied to remove different types of asymmetries from the original NCCT, pathology-salient or pathology-compensated images can be obtained (Fig. 1b). Validated by our experiments, performing segmentation on pathology-salient NCCTs shows a noticeable improvement over using original images. A key novelty of our framework is inspired by the observation that non-pathological asymmetries can be due to intensity differences between different types of tissues, uneven distribution of CSF, or inherent brain anatomical asymmetry. Thus we design a tissue-aware regularization loss function to incorporate tissue-type information into the training of ADN, which further encourages ADN to extract pathologically meaningful asymmetries. Coupled with ADN, an unsupervised 3D transformation network is also proposed to align NCCT scans to obtain the mid-sagittal plane for asymmetry estimation. We conduct extensive experiments on a public NCCT dataset AISD [19], and the results show that our proposed ADN can achieve state-of-the-art performance while successfully disentangling different types of asymmetries in a clinically interpretable way.

2   Methodology

Figure 2 shows the overview of our proposed framework ADN. In general, ADN includes three 3D volume-based modules: transformation network T for input alignment and the subsequent total asymmetry estimation, asymmetry extraction network D to detect pathological asymmetries and further separate different types of asymmetries, and segmentation network F for the final AIS segmentation. Network T is mainly based on a convolutional encoder while both D and F adopt an encoder-decoder architecture. For the input deskulled NCCT scan I, we first employ an unsupervised 3D transformation network T to align I and

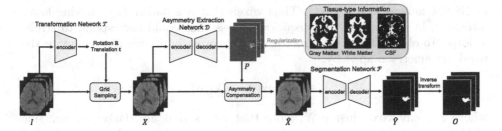

Fig. 2. Overview of the asymmetry disentanglement network (ADN). Tissue-type information is generated by SPM12 [2] and is only required during training.

generate a bilaterally quasi-symmetric scan X in which the mid-sagittal plane S is in the vertical center of the 3D volume space. We then feed X into the network $\mathcal{D}$ to extract pathological asymmetry map P. P is later used to calculate the intrinsic anatomical asymmetry map and then synthesize an intrinsic-asymmetry-compensated scan $\hat{X}$. We subsequently input $\hat{X}$ to network $\mathcal{F}$ to obtain the segmentation result $\hat{Y}$. We finally apply inverse transformation $\mathcal{T}^{-1}$ to $\hat{Y}$ for getting the final output O corresponding to the input I. During the training, we also leverage tissue segmentation results generated from an existing tool to provide extra regularization for network $\mathcal{D}$. The voxel intensities of NCCT images are normalized to be in the range of $[0, 1]$ for network processing and asymmetry computation.

Transformation Network $\mathcal{T}$. Since the input deskulled NCCT scan I is usually not perfectly centered in the volume space, to make better use of bilateral symmetry, we propose an unsupervised 3D transformation network $\mathcal{T}$ to align the mid-sagittal plane S to be in the vertical center of volume space for subsequent total asymmetry estimation. Different from the 2D alignment network in [19], which may be sensitive to texture variations in some slices, $\mathcal{T}$ utilizes 3D spatial contextual information and outputs parameters $\alpha \in \mathbb{R}^6$, which represents an affine transformation $(\mathbf{R}, \mathbf{t}) \in SE(3)$, where $\alpha_{1:3}$ are rotation angles and $\alpha_{4:6}$ are translations along x, y, and z axes. We then apply the output parameters α to generate bilaterally quasi-symmetric CT image $X = \mathcal{T}(I)$ using parameterized sampling grid [12]. Intuitively, when S is transformed to align with the vertical center plane, X should have the minimum difference from its horizontally flipped version X'. Thus we adopt the following loss function to train the 3D transformation network $\mathcal{T}$:

$$L_{\mathcal{T}} = \|X - X'\|_1, \tag{1}$$

where $\|\cdot\|_1$ is L1 loss. Note that $\mathcal{T}$ computes the 3D alignment in contrast to 2D, and no annotation is required for the training of $\mathcal{T}$.

Asymmetry Disentanglement. Based on X and its self-mirrored version X', we can compute a total asymmetry map A and further employ an asymmetry extraction network $\mathcal{D}$ to extract pathological asymmetry map P from A. Generally, the ischemic stroke areas appear darker than their contralateral regions in NCCT images (see Fig. 1a). Thus voxels that are darker (*i.e.*, having lower intensity) in X than X' are suspicious voxels that could correspond to stroke lesions. To obtain these asymmetric darker voxels in X, we first compute the total asymmetry map A by:

$$A_i = \max(X'_i - X_i, 0), \tag{2}$$

where i is any voxel inside X. Note that voxels that are darker on one side of the midsagittal plane have positive values in A, whereas the value of other voxels is set to zero. We obtain the pathological asymmetry map P through the trained network $\mathcal{D}$, *i.e.*, $P = \mathcal{D}(X)$. Then the map of asymmetry due to intrinsic anatomical asymmetry is $Q = A - P$. Again, in both P and Q asymmetric voxels have positive values and symmetric voxels have zero values. Next, we generate a new image $\hat{X}$ in which the intrinsic anatomical asymmetry is compensated or neutralized so that there is only pathological asymmetry in $\hat{X}$. $\hat{X}$ is defined as:

$$\hat{X} = X + Q = X + A - P. \tag{3}$$

Note that although $\hat{X}$ does not exist in reality since actual brain CTs always contain some normal anatomical asymmetry, using this synthetic $\hat{X}$ can make pathological asymmetries more salient and thus make accurate infarct segmentation easier as we will demonstrate in our experiments. Similarly, we can compensate for pathological asymmetry and generate a synthetic image $\tilde{X} = X + P$ that contains only normal anatomical asymmetry. Our proposed ADN encourages learned anatomical asymmetry and pathological asymmetry to be meaningful via implicit supervision from the final segmentation so that they should not affect pathology information presented in $\hat{X}$ or lead to false positives. Example asymmetry disentanglement results are shown in Figs. 1b and 4. We then input $\hat{X}$ to network $\mathcal{F}$ to obtain segmentation map $\hat{Y}$. The final segmentation O corresponding to the original I can be calculated by applying inverse transformation $\mathcal{T}^{-1}$ to $\hat{Y}$.

Training of Pathological Asymmetry Extraction Network $\mathcal{D}$ and Segmentation Network $\mathcal{F}$. Intuitively, one can utilize the infarct ground truth map G to train both $\mathcal{D}$ and $\mathcal{F}$ with binary cross-entropy loss:

$$L_{\mathcal{F}} = \mathcal{L}_{\text{bce}}(O, G) = \mathcal{L}_{\text{bce}}(\mathcal{T}^{-1}(\hat{Y}), G), \tag{4}$$

Since $\hat{Y} = \mathcal{F}(\hat{X}) = \mathcal{F}(X + A - \mathcal{D}(X))$, which is related to both $\mathcal{D}$ and $\mathcal{F}$, using the loss $L_{\mathcal{F}}$ can update both $\mathcal{D}$ and $\mathcal{F}$. However, this can lead to a trivial solution $P = \mathcal{D}(X) = A$, such that $\hat{X}$ is equivalent to X, downgrading the proposed model to a regular segmentation network. To ensure pathological asymmetry map P is clinically meaningful, we design a novel tissue-aware regularization loss function to provide extra constraints for the training of $\mathcal{D}$. This loss function is motivated by the fact that it is only meaningful to examine pathological asymmetry when the pair of mirroring voxels belong to the same tissue type. Thus P resulting from the network $\mathcal{D}$ should exclude asymmetry in voxels whose mirrored counterparts belong to a different tissue type. To utilize such same-tissue constraint, during training, we first employ an off-the-shelf tool, statistical parametric mapping SPM12 [2,3] and a CT brain atlas [24] to segment GM, WM, and CSF regions from X; these regions are represented as binary maps R_{GM}, R_{WM} and R_{CSF}. Then we improve these tissue segmentation results by removing the known stroke regions (based on ground truth G) from the GM, WM and CSF regions. The tissue-aware regularization loss for training $\mathcal{D}$ is designed by considering the following loss terms:

- Tissue-type constraint loss $L_{tissue} = \|P \cdot (R_{GW} + R_{CSF})\|_1$, which aims to make P exclude asymmetric voxels that belong to different tissue types and regions containing CSF. In particular, R_{GW} indicates GM voxels whose mirrored counterparts are WM voxels or WM voxels whose mirrored counterparts are GM voxels; R_{GW} can be obtained by computing the intersection of horizontally flipped R_{GM} and the original R_{WM}.
- Size constraint loss $L_{size} = \|\text{mean}(P) - \text{mean}(\mathcal{T}(G))\|_1$, which aims to keep P be of similar average size as ground truth.
- Asymmetry loss $L_{asymmetry} = \|P \cdot (1 - A)\|_1$, which is to constrain all symmetric regions (non-zero in $(1 - A)$) to have zero value in P so that P has non-zero only for asymmetric voxels.
- Intrinsic asymmetry loss $L_{intrinsic} = -\|\text{mean}(A - P)\|_1$, which is to encourage intrinsic anatomical asymmetries $Q = A - P$ to be as large as possible to contain all non-pathological asymmetries.

The final regularization loss function to train $\mathcal{D}$ is calculated by:

$$L_{\mathcal{D}} = L_{tissue} + L_{size} + L_{asymmetry} + L_{intrinsic}. \tag{5}$$

So the total loss function to jointly train $\mathcal{D}$ and $\mathcal{F}$ is:

$$L_{\mathcal{DF}} = L_{\mathcal{F}} + \lambda L_{\mathcal{D}}, \tag{6}$$

where λ is a scaling factor. For $L_{\mathcal{F}}$, we also add an extra generalized Dice loss function [25] to alleviate the class imbalance issue. Note that we only use tissue-type information during training. Using $L_{\mathcal{DF}}$, network $\mathcal{D}$ is trained to help maximize the segmentation accuracy of network $\mathcal{F}$ under the clinical constraints encoded in $L_{\mathcal{D}}$. Thus ADN can learn how to automatically separate different kinds of asymmetries in a clinically interpretable way.

3   Experiments

We validate our proposed method using AISD [19], a public non-contrast CT (NCCT) dataset of acute ischemic stroke (AIS), which includes 345 training scans and 52 testing scans. Ischemic lesions are manually contoured on NCCT by a doctor using MRI scans as the reference standard. The xyz spacing values are various in this dataset, where the x- and y-spacing values are $0.40 \sim 2.04$ mm,

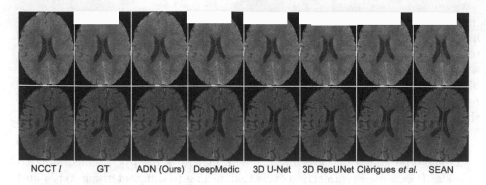

NCCT *I*   GT   ADN (Ours)   DeepMedic   3D U-Net   3D ResUNet Clèrigues *et al.*   SEAN

Fig. 3. Qualitative comparison of different methods on AISD. Segmented regions are marked by red contours. (Color figure online)

Table 1. Quantitative comparison of different methods on AISD. "Aligned" means whether the transformation is applied to the input CT to make it bilaterally quasi-symmetric.

Method	Aligned	Dice ↑	HD95 (mm) ↓
DeepMedic [13]	N	0.4412	58.20
3D U-Net [8]	N	0.4281	42.18
3D ResUNet [18]	N	0.4763	42.55
Clèrigues *et al.* [9]	Y	0.5051	43.17
SEAN [19]	Y	0.5047	40.07
3D ResUNet [18]	Y	0.4850	39.87
ADN w/o L_{tissue}	Y	0.5090	39.66
ADN (ours)	Y	**0.5245**	**39.18**

and z-spacing (slice thickness) varies from 3 to 10 mm. To ensure that each voxel represents a consistent volume throughout the whole dataset, after skull stripping, we resample all NCCTs to be $1.2 \times 1.2 \times 5\,\text{mm}^3$ and reshape them to be $256 \times 256 \times 40$ using the Python package `nilearn` [1]. To evaluate 3D segmentation performance, we employ two volume-based metrics Dice coefficient and Hausdorff distance with 95% quantile (HD95). The definitions of the metrics can be found in [26].

Implementation Details. Our implementation is based on `PyTorch` [21] framework. We implement transformation network $\mathcal{T}$ with four 3D residual blocks [11] followed by one fully-connected layer with `Tanh` activation to predict parameters α. The range of rotation degrees in xy plane is restricted to be no more than 60° and the translation distance is limited to be no more than half of the image size. For simplicity, we do not consider rotation and translation of input CT in z-axis. As a general framework, ADN can employ various networks as its backbone. Here we adopt the same architecture as 3D ResUNet [18] to implement asymmetry

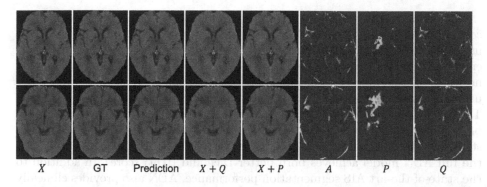

| X | GT | Prediction | X + Q | X + P | A | P | Q |

Fig. 4. Some asymmetry disentanglement results of our proposed ADN. X: aligned NCCT; GT: ground truth; Prediction: AIS segmentation by our method; $\hat{X} = X + Q$: pathology-salient NCCT; $\tilde{X} = X + P$: pathology-compensated NCCT; A: total asymmetry map; P: pathological asymmetry map; Q: intrinsic asymmetry map. Displayed asymmetry maps are normalized for better visualization.

extraction network $\mathcal{D}$ and segmentation network $\mathcal{F}$. Due to the GPU memory constraint, we first train unsupervised network $\mathcal{T}$ using Eq. (1) and then fix $\mathcal{T}$ and jointly train $\mathcal{D}$ and $\mathcal{F}$ using Eq. (6). The factor λ in Eq. (6) is set to be 10. All networks are trained with AdamW optimizer [20] with $(\beta_1, \beta_2) = (0.9, 0.999)$ and 5×10^{-4} weight decay. The initial learning rates are 1×10^{-5} for network $\mathcal{T}$ and 1×10^{-3} for network $\mathcal{D}$ and $\mathcal{F}$ and we adopt the poly learning rate policy [7] with a power of 0.9. We take the whole CT scan of size $256 \times 256 \times 40$ as input and the training batch is set to be 6. We only train models using the training set until convergence. More specifically, we terminate the training once the Dice of the training set remains mostly unchanged for 2 epochs. To help network $\mathcal{D}$ achieve good initialization and facilitate the joint training, at the first 2 epochs, we employ a warm-start strategy by using ground truth G to provide extra supervised cross-entropy loss for training $\mathcal{D}$.

Result Analysis. We compare our proposed ADN with current state-of-the-art methods, including 3D patch-based network DeepMedic [13], volume-based 3D U-Net [8] and 3D ResUNet [18], and symmetry-aware models Clèrigues et al. [9] and SEAN [19]. The comparison results are shown in Table 1 and Fig. 3. The original Clèrigues et al. is 2D-patch-based and it utilizes symmetry information by concatenating aligned CT patches with their mirrored versions. Here we adapt it to be 3D-volume-based by inputting both aligned CT and its horizontally flipped version to 3D ResUNet. We reimplement SEAN [19] according to their paper due to the lack of publicly available implementation. For the other models, we follow publicly available implementations. Note that both Clèrigues et al. and SEAN are based on aligned CT to better extract bilateral symmetry. All the aligned segmentation results will be inversely transformed to correspond to the original NCCT for final comparison. As shown in Table 1, ADN has achieved the best Dice and HD95, outperforming all other methods. We also show some qualitative results in Fig. 3.

To further verify the effectiveness of the proposed asymmetry extraction and compensation module, we conduct an ablation study by training a 3D ResUNet using aligned CT scans (see the third to the last line in Table 1). The only difference between this baseline and proposed ADN is the input to the segmentation network: 3D ResUNet uses the aligned CT scan (X in Fig. 2) as input while ADN uses the aligned CT scan with intrinsic asymmetry compensated ($\hat{X}$). Results in Table 1 demonstrate that using pathology-salient input can achieve a noticeably better Dice coefficient. We also demonstrate the effectiveness of tissue-type constraint loss by ablation study. Compared to the ADN model without using L_{tissue}, the full ADN model achieves both better Dice and HD95 scores. In addition to the state-of-the-art AIS segmentation performance, ADN also provides clinically interpretable asymmetry maps. We visualize some asymmetry disentanglement results of ADN in Fig. 4.

4   Discussion and Conclusion

We proposed a novel asymmetry disentanglement network, ADN, to separate different kinds of asymmetries in non-contrast CT (NCCT) images for effective acute ischemic stroke (AIS) infarct segmentation. Equipped with a clinically-inspired tissue-aware regularization loss function, ADN not only learns pathological and intrinsic anatomical asymmetry maps for clinical interpretation but also generates pathology-salient (and intrinsic asymmetry compensated) NCCT images for better AIS detection. We currently focus on NCCT because it is noisier and more challenging than other modalities when dealing with soft tissues. Besides CT, our ADN can be extended to other tasks/modalities that leverage bilateral asymmetries to identify abnormalities. Such tasks include but are not limited to stroke or multiple sclerosis (MS) in brain MRI [4], fractures in pelvic X-Rays [6], and infiltration in chest X-Rays [14]. One limitation of ADN that we observe is that it appears to ignore those bright bleeding spots inside stroke regions. With available annotations, bleeding spots could be detected by a network with inverse intensity change using the same architecture. We plan to explore bleeding spot detection and mitigate their effects in our future work.

References

1. Abraham, A., et al.: Machine learning for neuroimaging with scikit-learn. Front. Neuroinform. **8**, 14 (2014)
2. Ashburner, J., et al.: SPM12 manual. Wellcome Trust Centre for Neuroimaging, London, UK **2464**, 4 (2014)
3. Ashburner, J., Friston, K.: Multimodal image coregistration and partitioning-a unified framework. Neuroimage **6**(3), 209–217 (1997)
4. Bao, Q., Mi, S., Gang, B., Yang, W., Chen, J., Liao, Q.: MDAN: mirror difference aware network for brain stroke lesion segmentation. IEEE J. Biomed. Health Inform. **26**(4), 1628–1639 (2021)

5. Barman, A., Inam, M.E., Lee, S., Savitz, S., Sheth, S., Giancardo, L.: Determining ischemic stroke from CT-angiography imaging using symmetry-sensitive convolutional networks. In: Proceedings of the IEEE 16th International Symposium on Biomedical Imaging (ISBI 2019), pp. 1873–1877 (2019)
6. Chen, H., et al.: Anatomy-aware Siamese network: exploiting semantic asymmetry for accurate pelvic fracture detection in X-ray images. In: Vedaldi, A., Bischof, H., Brox, T., Frahm, J.-M. (eds.) ECCV 2020. LNCS, vol. 12368, pp. 239–255. Springer, Cham (2020). https://doi.org/10.1007/978-3-030-58592-1_15
7. Chen, L.C., Papandreou, G., Kokkinos, I., Murphy, K., Yuille, A.L.: DeepLab: semantic image segmentation with deep convolutional nets, atrous convolution, and fully connected CRFs. IEEE Trans. Pattern Anal. Mach. Intell. **40**(4), 834–848 (2017)
8. Çiçek, Ö., Abdulkadir, A., Lienkamp, S.S., Brox, T., Ronneberger, O.: 3D U-Net: learning dense volumetric segmentation from sparse annotation. In: Ourselin, S., Joskowicz, L., Sabuncu, M.R., Unal, G., Wells, W. (eds.) MICCAI 2016. LNCS, vol. 9901, pp. 424–432. Springer, Cham (2016). https://doi.org/10.1007/978-3-319-46723-8_49
9. Clerigues, A., Valverde, S., Bernal, J., Freixenet, J., Oliver, A., Lladó, X.: Acute ischemic stroke lesion core segmentation in CT perfusion images using fully convolutional neural networks. Comput. Biol. Med. **115**, 103487 (2019)
10. Feigin, V.L., et al.: Global, regional, and national burden of stroke and its risk factors, 1990–2019: a systematic analysis for the Global Burden of Disease Study 2019. Lancet Neurol. **20**(10), 795–820 (2021)
11. He, K., Zhang, X., Ren, S., Sun, J.: Deep residual learning for image recognition. In: Proceedings of the IEEE Conference on Computer Vision and Pattern Recognition, pp. 770–778 (2016)
12. Jaderberg, M., Simonyan, K., Zisserman, A., Kavukcuoglu, K.: Spatial transformer networks. In: Advances in Neural Information Processing Systems 28 (2015)
13. Kamnitsas, K., et al.: Efficient multi-scale 3D CNN with fully connected CRF for accurate brain lesion segmentation. Med. Image Anal. **36**, 61–78 (2017)
14. Kim, M., Park, J., Na, S., Park, C.M., Yoo, D.: Learning visual context by comparison. In: Vedaldi, A., Bischof, H., Brox, T., Frahm, J.-M. (eds.) ECCV 2020. LNCS, vol. 12350, pp. 576–592. Springer, Cham (2020). https://doi.org/10.1007/978-3-030-58558-7_34
15. Kuang, H., Menon, B.K., Qiu, W.: Automated infarct segmentation from follow-up non-contrast CT scans in patients with acute ischemic stroke using dense multipath contextual generative adversarial network. In: Shen, D., et al. (eds.) MICCAI 2019. LNCS, vol. 11766, pp. 856–863. Springer, Cham (2019). https://doi.org/10.1007/978-3-030-32248-9_95
16. Kuang, H., Menon, B.K., Sohn, S.I., Qiu, W.: EIS-Net: segmenting early infarct and scoring ASPECTS simultaneously on non-contrast CT of patients with acute ischemic stroke. Med. Image Anal. **70**, 101984 (2021)
17. Kuang, H., Najm, M., Menon, B.K., Qiu, W.: Joint segmentation of intracerebral hemorrhage and infarct from non-contrast CT images of post-treatment acute ischemic stroke patients. In: Frangi, A.F., Schnabel, J.A., Davatzikos, C., Alberola-López, C., Fichtinger, G. (eds.) MICCAI 2018. LNCS, vol. 11072, pp. 681–688. Springer, Cham (2018). https://doi.org/10.1007/978-3-030-00931-1_78
18. Lee, K., Zung, J., Li, P., Jain, V., Seung, H.S.: Superhuman accuracy on the SNEMI3D connectomics challenge. arXiv preprint arXiv:1706.00120 (2017)

19. Liang, K., et al.: Symmetry-enhanced attention network for acute ischemic infarct segmentation with non-contrast CT images. In: de Bruijne, M., et al. (eds.) MICCAI 2021. LNCS, vol. 12907, pp. 432–441. Springer, Cham (2021). https://doi.org/10.1007/978-3-030-87234-2_41

20. Loshchilov, I., Hutter, F.: Decoupled weight decay regularization. arXiv preprint arXiv:1711.05101 (2017)

21. Paszke, A., et al.: PyTorch: an imperative style, high-performance deep learning library. In: Advances in Neural Information Processing Systems 32 (2019)

22. Peter, R., et al.: A quantitative symmetry-based analysis of hyperacute ischemic stroke lesions in noncontrast computed tomography. Med. Phys. 44(1), 192–199 (2017)

23. Qiu, W., et al.: Machine learning for detecting early infarction in acute stroke with non-contrast-enhanced CT. Radiology 294(3), 638–644 (2020)

24. Rorden, C., Bonilha, L., Fridriksson, J., Bender, B., Karnath, H.O.: Age-specific CT and MRI templates for spatial normalization. Neuroimage 61(4), 957–965 (2012)

25. Sudre, C.H., Li, W., Vercauteren, T., Ourselin, S., Jorge Cardoso, M.: Generalised dice overlap as a deep learning loss function for highly unbalanced segmentations. In: DLMIA/ML-CDS 2017. LNCS, vol. 10553, pp. 240–248. Springer, Cham (2017). https://doi.org/10.1007/978-3-319-67558-9_28

26. Taha, A.A., Hanbury, A.: Metrics for evaluating 3D medical image segmentation: analysis, selection, and tool. BMC Med. Imaging 15(1), 1–28 (2015)

27. Virani, S.S., et al.: Heart disease and stroke statistics-2021 update: a report from the American Heart Association. Circulation 143(8), e254–e743 (2021)

28. Wang, Y., Katsaggelos, A.K., Wang, X., Parrish, T.B.: A deep symmetry convnet for stroke lesion segmentation. In: Proceedings of the IEEE International Conference on Image Processing (ICIP), pp. 111–115 (2016)

Regression Metric Loss: Learning a Semantic Representation Space for Medical Images

Hanqing Chao, Jiajin Zhang, and Pingkun Yan[✉]

Department of Biomedical Engineering, Center for Biotechnology
and Interdisciplinary Studies, Rensselaer Polytechnic Institute, Troy, NY 12180, USA
{chaoh,zhangj41,yanp2}@rpi.edu

Abstract. Regression plays an essential role in many medical imaging applications for estimating various clinical risk or measurement scores. While training strategies and loss functions have been studied for the deep neural networks in medical image classification tasks, options for regression tasks are very limited. One of the key challenges is that the high-dimensional feature representation learned by existing popular loss functions like Mean Squared Error or L1 loss is hard to interpret. In this paper, we propose a novel Regression Metric Loss (RM-Loss), which endows the representation space with the semantic meaning of the label space by finding a representation manifold that is isometric to the label space. Experiments on two regression tasks, *i.e.* coronary artery calcium score estimation and bone age assessment, show that RM-Loss is superior to the existing popular regression losses on both performance and interpretability. Code is available at https://github.com/DIAL-RPI/Regression-Metric-Loss.

Keywords: Medical image regression · Metric learning ·
Representation learning · Semantic representation · Interpretability

1 Introduction

Various clinical risk or measurement scores, such as coronary artery calcium (CAC) score [1], bone age [4], etc., have been widely used in clinical practice for quantifying the progression of diseases and pathological conditions [11]. Tasks for regressing such scores, *i.e.* estimating the continuous variables from medical images, are an important group of applications in medical image analysis [8]. Similar to other medical imaging applications like image segmentation and computer-aided diagnosis, where deep learning has reshaped the landscape of research by continuously pushing the performance to new record levels, deep neural networks (DNNs) have also been applied to regressing clinical scores [3,4,9].

Supplementary Information The online version contains supplementary material available at https://doi.org/10.1007/978-3-031-16452-1_41.

L. Wang et al. (Eds.): MICCAI 2022, LNCS 13438, pp. 427–436, 2022.
https://doi.org/10.1007/978-3-031-16452-1_41

However, compared with those relatively direct applications of DNNs for predicting discrete class labels, medical image regression is a more challenging task for DNNs due to the nature of predicting continuous quantity. Compared with the abundant options available for the classification tasks, choices for regression tasks are very limited. A majority of existing deep learning models for medical image regression are trained with Mean Squared Error (MSE) or L1 loss [3]. Although these models might have satisfactory performance, the high-dimensional feature representations learned by these deep models are hard to interpret. Recent studies on classification tasks have shown that imposing appropriate constraints can force deep learning models to learn more semantically meaningful representations [2,16,17]. A few works on medical image regression has tried to transplant popular distance metric learning losses such as N-pair loss [13] and triplet loss [7] by introducing an adaptable margin [3,18]. However, such adaptations lack theoretical foundations and cannot fully explore the inherent structure of the continuous label space. We argue that to learn a meaningful representation space for regression, a loss should be able to explore the structure of the continuous label space and reveal such structure in the representation space but not limited to changing the margin in loss functions.

In this paper, we propose a novel loss function suitable for regression problems, named Regression Metric Loss (RM-Loss). It guides the deep learning model to learn a low-dimensional manifold that has the same semantic meaning as the label, in the high-dimensional feature representation space. Specifically, the RM-Loss explicitly constrains the learned manifold and the label space to be isometric, *i.e.*, the geodesic distance between the representations of any two data points on the manifold is proportional to the Euclidean distance between their labels. Thus, each point on this manifold can be interpreted by the corresponding point in the label space. Assigning such a semantic meaning to the feature representation manifold is of the essence for label regression, which provides direct interpretability for the regression methods. With such a semantic representation, at the time of inference, the regression result of an input test sample can be computed based on its distance to the nearest neighbors on the training manifold, instead of using some uninterpretable fully connected layers for mapping its representations to an output value. In addition, since our proposed RM-Loss constrains the distance between data pairs, it automatically augments the number of training samples and helps the model explore relationships between samples. This in turn helps boost the model performance, especially on small datasets.

The key contributions of this paper are as follows. 1) We propose a novel loss for medical image regression tasks, the Regression Metric Loss (RM-Loss). It constrains a DNN model to learn a semantically meaningful manifold that is isometric to the label space. 2) At the inference time, the regression result is determined by the distance-weighted nearest neighbors. By providing the exact neighbor samples and their weights as an interpretation, such an approach would be more informative for clinical applications than only outputting a final score. 3) Experimental results on two clinical regression tasks over two large-scale public datasets, CAC score estimation from computed tomography images and bone age regression from X-ray images, show that the proposed RM-Loss achieved superior performance and interpretability.

2   Method

This section presents the details of our proposed RM-Loss. We aim to help a DNN learn a low-dimensional manifold in the high-dimensional feature representation space, which has the same semantic meaning as the label space.

2.1   Learning a Semantically Interpretable Representation Space

Let $\{(\boldsymbol{x}_i, \boldsymbol{y}_i)\}_{i=1}^N$ denotes a regression dataset of size N, where $\boldsymbol{x}_i$ is an input sample, for instance an image, and $\boldsymbol{y}_i \in \mathbb{R}^{d_y}$ is a d_y-dimensional label vector. We assume that the label space Y is a Euclidean space. Let $F : \boldsymbol{x}_i \mapsto \boldsymbol{f}_i$ represents a deep learning model that maps an input sample to a d_f-dimensional representation $\boldsymbol{f}_i$. The RM-Loss constrains the model such that all the representations $\{\boldsymbol{f}_i\}_{i=1}^N$ are on a Riemannian manifold M and the geodesic distance $G(\cdot, \cdot)$ between a pair of samples' representations $\boldsymbol{f}_i$ and $\boldsymbol{f}_j$ is proportional to the Euclidean distance between their corresponding labels $\boldsymbol{y}_i$ and $\boldsymbol{y}_j$. Thus, the key term for RM-Loss to minimize is

$$D_{ij}^o = |s \times G(\boldsymbol{f}_i, \boldsymbol{f}_j) - \|\boldsymbol{y}_i - \boldsymbol{y}_j\|_2|, \tag{1}$$

where s is a learnable parameter that will be optimized together with all other parameters in the deep learning model F. Equation 1 constraints the learned manifold M to be isometric to the label space Y. Furthermore, since M is a Riemannian manifold and Y is a Euclidean space, M is diffeomorphic to Y. It indicates that the learned manifold M will have the same topological structure as the label space Y. Therefore, we can interpret the high-dimensional feature representations on the manifold M by using the corresponding labels.

2.2   Local Isometry: From Geodesic to Euclidean Distance

The key challenge to minimize Eq. 1 is to calculate the geodesic distance $G(\cdot, \cdot)$ on the manifold M. Below we state a useful lemma of the isometry between a Riemannian manifold and a Euclidean space[1].

Lemma 1. *Let M be a connected complete Riemannian manifold, and E be a Euclidean space. If a differentiable mapping $h : M \to E$ is a local isometry, we have h as a global isometry.*

By Lemma 1, assuming the learned Riemannian manifold M is connected and complete, then as long as M is locally isometric to the label space Y, it will be diffeomorphic to Y. Furthermore, in the local neighborhood of $\boldsymbol{f}_i$ on M, $\mathcal{N}(\boldsymbol{f}_i)$, we approximate the geodesic distance $G(\boldsymbol{f}_i, \boldsymbol{f}_j), \boldsymbol{f}_j \in \mathcal{N}(\boldsymbol{f}_i)$ by the Euclidean

---

[1] The derivation of this lemma is provided in the Supplementary Material.

distance, $||\boldsymbol{f}_i - \boldsymbol{f}_j||_2$. In practice, instead of searching for neighbors of each point $\boldsymbol{f}_i$, we calculate D_{ij} for all sample pairs in a training batch and weight them by a Gaussian function according to their labels:

$$D_{ij} = |\ s \times ||\boldsymbol{f}_i - \boldsymbol{f}_j||_2 - ||\boldsymbol{y}_i - \boldsymbol{y}_j||_2\ |, \ \ w_{ij} = \exp\left(-\frac{||\boldsymbol{y}_i - \boldsymbol{y}_j||_2^2}{2\sigma^2}\right) + \alpha,$$

$$l' = \frac{\sum_{i=1}^N \sum_{j=1}^N w_{ij} D_{ij}}{\sum_{i=1}^N \sum_{j=1}^N w_{ij}}, \tag{2}$$

where l' shows the objective function of current RM-Loss, and σ and α are two hyper-parameters. The σ controls the size of the neighborhood. The α controls the curvature of the manifold to avoid self tangling, i.e., data points away from each other on the manifold will not be too close in the Euclidean space $\mathbb{R}^{d_f}$. We use the distance between labels instead of representations in w_{ij}, because at the beginning of training, the representations are randomly mapped to the $\mathbb{R}^{d_f}$ space. Using the label distance in w_{ij} guides the model to map the representations to a right manifold. When the right manifold is found, the w_{ij} can well depict the neighborhood of $\boldsymbol{f}_i$.

2.3   Hard Sample Pairs Mining

Similar to most of the distance metric loss, in the training process, the deep model F can quickly learn to correctly map the easy samples, rendering a large fraction of D_{ij} close to zero. These small terms will dramatically dilute the averaged loss value and slow down the training. Thus, we introduce a technique for mining the hard sample pairs to help the training focus on informative sample pairs. Specifically, only the sample pairs, whose weighted losses are greater than the batch average value, will be selected through a masking process as:

$$m_{ij} = \begin{cases} 1, & \text{if } w_{ij}D_{ij} > \bar{l}^{(k)} \\ 0, & \text{if } w_{ij}D_{ij} <= \bar{l}^{(k)} \end{cases}, \ \ \bar{l}^{(k)} = 0.9 \times \bar{l}^{(k-1)} + 0.1 \times \mathbb{E}^{(k)}(w_{ij}D_{ij}), \tag{3}$$

where k indicates the k-th iteration in the training, and $\bar{l}$ is the exponential moving average of the mean loss values of all the sample pairs in one training batch. Thereby, the full objective function of the RM-Loss is formulated as:

$$\mathcal{L} = \frac{\sum_{p=1}^N \sum_{q=1}^N m_{ij} w_{ij} D_{ij}}{\sum_{p=1}^N \sum_{q=1}^N m_{ij} w_{ij}}. \tag{4}$$

2.4   Making a Grounded Prediction

Because the learned manifold M is diffeomorphic to the label space Y, each point f_i on M and its neighborhood $\mathcal{N}^M(f_i) \subseteq M$ correspond to a unique point y_i on Y and a neighborhood $\mathcal{N}^Y(y_i) \subseteq Y$, respectively. This property assures that samples with similar representations (in $\mathcal{N}^M(f_i)$) have similar labels (in

$\mathcal{N}^Y(y_i)$). Therefore, we can use nearest neighbors (NN) to estimate the label for a test sample. We assume a neighborhood $\mathcal{N}^M(f_i)$ on M can be approximately regarded as a Euclidean space. Since the distance on M has specific semantic meaning defined by the label space, we apply distance-weighted NN within a fixed radius r^2. For a test sample t, its label $\hat{y}_t$ can be computed by:

$$\hat{y}_t = \frac{\sum_{f_i \in \mathcal{N}_r(f_t)} a_i y_i}{\sum_{f_i \in \mathcal{N}_r(f_t)} a_i}, \quad a_i = \exp\left(-\frac{\|f_i - f_t\|_2^2}{2(r/3)^2}\right) \tag{5}$$

where $\mathcal{N}_r(f_t)$ is the neighborhood of the test sample's representation f_t in the Euclidean representation space $\mathbb{R}^{d_f}$ with a radius r. f_i and y_i denote the representations and labels of the training samples in $\mathcal{N}_r(f_t)$.

3   Experiments

We evaluate the proposed RM-Loss from two aspects, *i.e.*, the regression performance and the quality of the learned space. The regression performance is measured by the **Mean Absolute Error** (MAE) and **R-squared** (R^2). The quality of the learned space is quantified by: 1) The **Averaged Rank-5 Difference** (D5) calculated by the label differences between each test sample and its 5 nearest neighbors from training samples. 2) The **Residual Variance** (RV) [15] defined as: $1 - \rho(G_M, D_Y)$, where $\rho(\cdot)$ is the Pearson correlation coefficient, G_M is the geodesic distance of all test sample pairs on the learned representation manifold M, and D_Y is the label Euclidean distance of the same set of test sample pairs. G_M is calculated following the original paper [15] by k-nearest neighborhoods. The k leads to the best (smallest) RV is selected. This measurement directly evaluates whether the manifold M and the label space Y are isometric.

3.1   Experimental Settings

Datasets. Two public datasets, RSNA Bone Age Assessment Dataset (BAA) [5] and NLST CAC score estimation dataset (CAC), are used for evaluation. **BAA Dataset:** Since the labels of original validation and test set of BAA dataset are not publicly available. We randomly split its original 12, 371 training images into training, validation, and test sets in a proportion of $7 : 1 : 2$. The input images are all resized into 520×400. In the training phase, the labels ($\in [4, 228]$) are z-score normalized. **CAC Dataset:** This dataset is originated from the National Lung Screening Trial (NLST) dataset [10]. It contains 43, 241 low dose chest CT images from 10, 395 subjects. These subjects are randomly split into training (7299, 70%, 30, 347 images), validation (1066, 10%, 4, 365 images), and test sets (2, 030, 20%, 8, 529 images). The heart region of each image is first segmented by a pre-trained U-Net [12]. The CAC in the heart region is further segmented by

---

[2] The algorithm proposed for efficient NN radius optimization for model selection is described in Supplementary Material.

another U-Net. Finally, a CAC score (Agatston score [1]) is calculated based on the size and intensity of the CAC. According to the clinical grading standard[3], the $\log_2$CAC scores ($\in [0, 13]$) are used as labels in the following experiments. In the training phase, the labels are scaled into $[-3.5, 3.5]$ ((label $- 6.5)/2$). The segmented heart region is cropped out and resampled into $128 \times 128 \times 128$ with a resolution of $1.6\,\text{mm} \times 1.6\,\text{mm} \times 1.07\,\text{mm}$.

Baselines. We compared our proposed RM-Loss with widely used MSE loss, L1 loss, ordinal regression loss (OrdReg) (225 heads for the BAA dataset; 26 heads for the CAC dataset), and the recently proposed adaptive triplet loss (ATrip) [18] (margin= 1). For the adaptive triplet loss, since it is applied on the representation space, in its original paper [18], it has to be applied together with L1 or MSE loss for final prediction. In our experiment, for fair comparison, we present the results of both ATrip+L1 and ATrip+NN, where NN is the same nearest neighbors algorithm used in our method. All the losses are compared on the exactly same baseline models. For the BAA dataset, the winning method of the RSNA Pediatric Bone Age Machine Learning Challenge [5] was used, which is a Inception Net V3 [14]. For the CAC dataset, a 3D-ResNet is applied [6]. Detailed structures of these two models are shown in the Supplementary Material.

Implementation Details. For all experiments, Adam with a learning rate of $1e - 4$ is applied as the optimizer. **BAA Dataset:** Unless otherwise stated, the σ and α in w_{ij} (Eq. 2) are set to be 0.5 and 0.1, respectively. The r in Eq. 5 is calculated as 0.162 by the algorithm described in Supplementary S-Fig 1. All the models are trained for $15,000$, $10,000$ iterations for the full and 10% size dataset[4], respectively, with a batch size of 64. **CAC Dataset:** Unless otherwise stated, the σ and α are set to be 1.5 and 0.1 respectively. The r in Eq. 5 is calculated as 0.291. All the models are trained for $30,000$, $10,000$ iterations for the full and 10% size dataset, respectively, with a batch size of 36. Our source code will be released on GitHub.

3.2   Main Results

Table 1 shows the regression performance and the quality of the learned representation space on the BAA and CAC datasets. The proposed RM-Loss achieved both best regression performance and highest space quality. These results support our claim that, the proposed RM-Loss can guide the model learn a representation manifold that have similar topological structure as the label space, and the predictions made based on this interpretable manifold are accurate. As a distance metric loss ATrip+NN achieved better performance than L1 on the CAC dataset, but not on the BAA dataset. A possible reason is that ATrip loss only controls the relative distance among anchor, positive, and negative triplets. For a classification task, this is enough to force the representations to cluster by groups. However, for a regression task, where the label space is continuous, this constrain cannot give the

---

[3] Agatston score: minimal: 1–10, mild: 11–100, moderate: 101–400, severe: >400.
[4] Details of using partial dataset are described in Sect. 3.4.

Table 1. Regression performance and quality of the learned space on the full-size BAA and CAC datasets. The best results are in bold.

Method	Regression performance				Space quality			
	BAA		CAC		BAA		CAC	
	MAE↓	R^2 ↑	MAE↓	R^2 ↑	D5↓	RV↓	D5↓	RV↓
MSE	7.021*	0.947	0.762*	0.930	8.872*	0.0690*	0.869*	0.1225*
L1	6.580*	0.952	0.668*	0.927	8.799*	0.0600	0.837*	0.1249*
OrdReg	7.061*	0.944	0.684*	0.937	9.368*	0.1450*	0.844*	0.1966*
ATrip+NN	6.799*	0.951	0.647*	0.939	9.022*	0.0617	0.834*	0.0874*
ATrip+L1	6.854*	0.949	0.660*	0.930	9.055*	0.0630*	0.855*	0.0813
RM-Loss (ours)	**6.438**	**0.954**	**0.617**	**0.944**	**8.614**	**0.0588**	**0.769**	**0.0806**

* $p < 0.05$ in the one-tailed paired t-test. The significant test was not applied on R^2.

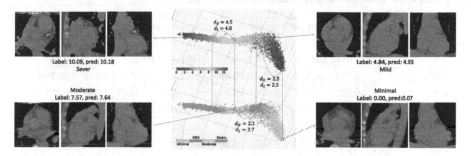

Fig. 1. Visualization of the learned representation space on the CAC dataset. Linear PCA was used for reducing the dimensionality to 3D for visualization. Two color maps are applied on the representations: a continuous color map indicating the original label (top), and a discrete color map shows the CAC score grading results (bottom). d_G and d_l represents the geodesic distance between representations and the Euclidean distance between labels, respectively. (Color figure online)

model a clear direction to optimize. Therefore, sometimes it can find a good representation but sometimes it cannot. The performances of ATrip+NN are better than ATrip+L1 on both datasets demonstrate the importance of using distance-weighted NN in the inference time. When applied together with L1, a distance metric loss cannot perform at its best.

To better understand the relationship between the learned representation space and the label space, we visualize the learned space and the corresponding sample cases in Fig. 1. The geodesic distance of the four sample cases is highly correlated with their label distance. The visualization of the space learned by other loss functions are included in the Supplementary Material.

3.3 Ablation Studies

In Table 2, we studied the influence of the two hyper-parameters (σ and α) and the hard sample pair mining on the BAA dataset. Similar results are observed on the CAC dataset, which are included in the Supplementary Material.

Table 2. Ablation study of σ, α, and m on BAA dataset. The best results are in bold.

σ	0.25	0.5	1.0	1.5	$+\infty$	0.5			
α	0.1					0.0	0.2	0.3	0.1
m	w/								w/o
MAE↓	6.555	**6.438**	6.642	6.759	6.823	6.496	6.591	6.741	6.520
R^2 ↑	0.953	**0.954**	0.952	0.951	0.950	**0.954**	0.953	0.951	0.953
D5↓	8.726	**8.614**	8.905	8.930	9.096	8.707	8.875	8.786	8.717
RV↓	0.0614	**0.0588**	0.0658	0.0659	0.0699	0.0650	0.0614	0.0677	0.0641

Table 3. The regression performance and the learned space quality on the 10%-size BAA and CAC dataset with the best results in bold.

Method	Regression performance				Space quality			
	10% BAA		10% CAC		10% BAA		10% CAC	
	MAE↓	R^2 ↑	MAE↓	R^2 ↑	D5↓	RV↓	D5↓	RV↓
MSE	8.721*	0.917	0.946*	0.895	11.204*	0.1054*	1.102*	0.1706*
L1	9.173*	0.906	0.875*	0.894	11.682*	0.1133*	1.028*	0.1529*
OrdReg	9.226*	0.908	0.849*	0.906	11.821*	0.2485*	1.010*	0.2189*
ATrip+NN	8.733*	0.911	0.861*	0.907	10.990	0.1018*	1.056*	0.1547*
ATrip+L1	9.017*	0.914	0.875*	0.908	11.208*	0.1016*	1.012*	0.1142
RM-Loss (ours)	**8.071**	**0.926**	**0.797**	**0.912**	**10.974**	**0.0878**	**0.971**	**0.1114**

$^{*}p < 0.05$ in the one-tailed paired t-test. The significant test was not applied on R^2.

σ: In Eq. 2, w_{ij} is calculated on the labels y_i and y_j. So the hyperparameter actually have the same semantic meaning as the label. Based on the role of w_{ij}, σ controls the size of region on the manifold. Since two Euclidean spaces can be mapped to each other with a linear mapping, σ indicates the degree that the representation space can be linearly related to the label space. A too large σ would decrease the non-linearity of the learned manifold such that its representation ability will be decreased, while a too small σ would cause overfitting. In Table 2, $\sigma = +\infty$ is equivalent to remove w_{ij} from Eq. 4, so that the model will tend to learn a linear space. It is worth noting that, our empirically found optimal σs on both two datasets are pretty close to the labels' diagnostic boundaries. In clinical practice, children with bone age more than 2 years (24 months) advanced or delayed are recommended to get a further diagnosis. By scaling with the standard deviation 41.2 we used on BAA dataset, a $\sigma = 0.5$ indicates a bone age difference of 20.6 months which is very close to 24 months. On the CAC dataset, since the label is log scaled, a $\sigma = 1.5$ indicates a 8 times difference, while according to the standard of Agatston score, a 10 times difference will increase or decrease one grade. α: The α also adjusts the linearity of the learned manifold, but in a global way. As shown in Table 2, an increase of α would cause a dramatic drop of the performance. However, a relatively small α can constrain the non-linearity of the manifold to avoid overfitting. Thus, we used a consistent $\alpha = 0.1$ on both two datasets. m: The last column in Table 2 shows that removing hard sample pair mining would cause a performance decrease.

3.4 Data Efficiency

In this section, we compare the performance of different losses when the training data is limited by using only 10% of the training and validation sets to train the models. The testing sets remain in full size. Table 3 shows that our proposed RM-Loss achieved much better regression performance than the other losses, due to its efficiency in exploring relationships between data pairs.

4 Conclusion

In this work, we proposed a novel distance metric loss originated for medical image regression tasks named as Regression Metric Loss (RM-Loss). By constraining data samples to have geodesic distances in the representation space corresponding to their Euclidean distance in the label space, the RM-Loss guides deep models to learn a semantically interpretable manifold. Experiments on two different regression tasks shows that the models trained with RM-Loss achieve both superior regression performance and high quality representation space.

Acknowledgements. This work was partly supported by National Heart, Lung, and Blood Institute (NHLBI) of the National Institutes of Health (NIH) under award R56HL145172.

References

1. Agatston, A.S., Janowitz, W.R., Hildner, F.J., Zusmer, N.R., Viamonte, M., Detrano, R.: Quantification of coronary artery calcium using ultrafast computed tomography. J. Am. Coll. Cardiol. **15**(4), 827–832 (1990)
2. Choi, H., Som, A., Turaga, P.: AMC-Loss: angular margin contrastive loss for improved explainability in image classification. In: Proceedings of the IEEE/CVF Conference on Computer Vision and Pattern Recognition Workshops, pp. 838–839 (2020)
3. Dai, W., Li, X., Chiu, W.H.K., Kuo, M.D., Cheng, K.T.: Adaptive contrast for image regression in computer-aided disease assessment. IEEE Trans. Med. Imaging **41**, 1255–1268 (2021)
4. Gilsanz, V., Ratib, O.: Hand Bone Age: A Digital Atlas of Skeletal Maturity. Springer, Heidelberg (2005). https://doi.org/10.1007/978-3-642-23762-1
5. Halabi, S.S., et al.: The RSNA pediatric bone age machine learning challenge. Radiology **290**(2), 498–503 (2019)
6. Hara, K., Kataoka, H., Satoh, Y.: Learning spatio-temporal features with 3D residual networks for action recognition. In: Proceedings of the IEEE International Conference on Computer Vision Workshops, pp. 3154–3160 (2017)
7. Hermans, A., Beyer, L., Leibe, B.: In defense of the triplet loss for person reidentification. arXiv preprint arXiv:1703.07737 (2017)

8. Litjens, G., et al.: A survey on deep learning in medical image analysis. Med. Image Anal. **42**, 60–88 (2017)

9. Liu, L., Dou, Q., Chen, H., Qin, J., Heng, P.A.: Multi-task deep model with margin ranking loss for lung nodule analysis. IEEE Trans. Med. Imaging **39**(3), 718–728 (2019)

10. National Lung Screening Trial Research Team, et al: Reduced lung-cancer mortality with low-dose computed tomographic screening. New Engl. J. Med. **365**(5), 395–409 (2011). https://doi.org/10.1056/NEJMoa1102873

11. Oprita, B., Aignatoaie, B., Gabor-Postole, D.: Scores and scales used in emergency medicine. practicability in toxicology. J. Med. Life **7**(Spec Iss 3), 4 (2014)

12. Ronneberger, O., Fischer, P., Brox, T.: U-Net: convolutional networks for biomedical image segmentation. In: Navab, N., Hornegger, J., Wells, W.M., Frangi, A.F. (eds.) MICCAI 2015. LNCS, vol. 9351, pp. 234–241. Springer, Cham (2015). https://doi.org/10.1007/978-3-319-24574-4_28

13. Sohn, K.: Improved deep metric learning with multi-class n-pair loss objective. In: Advances in Neural Information Processing Systems 29 (2016)

14. Szegedy, C., Vanhoucke, V., Ioffe, S., Shlens, J., Wojna, Z.: Rethinking the inception architecture for computer vision. In: Proceedings of the IEEE Conference on computer Vision and Pattern Recognition, pp. 2818–2826 (2016)

15. Tenenbaum, J.B., de Silva, V., Langford, J.C.: A global geometric framework for nonlinear dimensionality reduction. Science **290**(5500), 2319–2323 (2000)

16. Ye, M., Shen, J., Zhang, X., Yuen, P.C., Chang, S.F.: Augmentation invariant and instance spreading feature for softmax embedding. IEEE Trans. Pattern Anal. Mach. Intell. **44**(2), 924–939 (2020). https://doi.org/10.1109/TPAMI.2020.3013379

17. Zhang, Y., Choi, M., Han, K., Liu, Z.: Explainable semantic space by grounding language to vision with cross-modal contrastive learning. In: Advances in Neural Information Processing Systems 34 (2021)

18. Zheng, K., et al.: Semi-supervised learning for bone mineral density estimation in hip X-ray images. In: de Bruijne, M., et al. (eds.) MICCAI 2021. LNCS, vol. 12905, pp. 33–42. Springer, Cham (2021). https://doi.org/10.1007/978-3-030-87240-3_4

The (de)biasing Effect of GAN-Based Augmentation Methods on Skin Lesion Images

Agnieszka Mikołajczyk[1]([🖂]) [ID], Sylwia Majchrowska[2,3] [ID],
and Sandra Carrasco Limeros[2,3] [ID]

[1] Gdańsk University of Technology, Gabriela Narutowicza 11/12,
80-233 Gdańsk, Poland
agnieszka.mikolajczyk@pg.edu.pl
[2] Sahlgrenska University Hospital, Blå stråket 5, 413 45 Göteborg, Sweden
[3] AI Sweden, Lindholmspiren 3-5, 402 78 Göteborg, Sweden
{sylwia.majchrowska,sandra.carrasco}@ai.se

Abstract. New medical datasets are now more open to the public, allowing for better and more extensive research. Although prepared with the utmost care, new datasets might still be a source of spurious correlations that affect the learning process. Moreover, data collections are usually not large enough and are often unbalanced. One approach to alleviate the data imbalance is using data augmentation with Generative Adversarial Networks (GANs) to extend the dataset with high-quality images. GANs are usually trained on the same biased datasets as the target data, resulting in more biased instances. This work explored unconditional and conditional GANs to compare their bias inheritance and how the synthetic data influenced the models. We provided extensive manual data annotation of possibly biasing artifacts on the well-known ISIC dataset with skin lesions. In addition, we examined classification models trained on both real and synthetic data with counterfactual bias explanations. Our experiments showed that GANs inherited biases and sometimes even amplified them, leading to even stronger spurious correlations. Manual data annotation and synthetic images are publicly available for reproducible scientific research.

Keywords: Generative adversarial networks · Skin lesion classification · Explainable AI · Bias

1 Introduction

Deep learning-based approaches need a large amount of annotated data to perform well. High-quality images can be easily generated using publicly available

Supplementary Information The online version contains supplementary material available at https://doi.org/10.1007/978-3-031-16452-1_42.

L. Wang et al. (Eds.): MICCAI 2022, LNCS 13438, pp. 437–447, 2022.
https://doi.org/10.1007/978-3-031-16452-1_42

pretrained Generative Adversarial Networks (GANs). It seems especially useful in medical applications like skin lesion classification, detection of lung cancer nodules, or even brain tumor segmentation, where balanced data is a definite must-have.

However, if GAN's training set is biased, augmentation might backfire instead of helping. Bias is often defined as *a systematic error from erroneous assumptions in the learning algorithm* [17]. In this work, we focused primarily on bias in data and models. With the term 'bias in data,' we referred to four common data biases in machine learning (ML): *observer bias* which might appear when annotators use personal opinion to label data [15]; *sampling bias* when not all samples have the same sampling probability [17]; *data handling bias* when the way of handling the data distort the classifier's output; and *instrument bias* meaning imperfections in the instrument or method used to collect the data [11]. By 'bias in models', we referred to the broad term of the algorithmic bias [1]. Some sources define an algorithmic bias as amplifying existing inequities in, e.g., socioeconomic status, race, or ethnic background by an algorithm [19].

The problem of bias amplification is often mentioned e.g. in recommending engines [14], word embeddings [7], or any other discriminate model [16]. This leads to the question: if these models can amplify biases, does GANs do it too? If it does, how strongly GAN-augmented data affects the models?

Hence, to answer those questions, we studied the influence of data augmentation with unconditional and conditional GANs in terms of possible bias amplification. We analyzed with counterfactual bias insertion (CBI) GAN's ability to reproduce artifacts observed in a dataset, such as frames, pen markings, and hairs. In addition, we evaluated GANs in terms of fidelity, diversity, speed of training, and performance of classifiers trained on mixed real and synthetic data.

Our contributions are the following. Firstly, we performed the extensive research on the (de)biasing effect of using GAN-based data augmentation. Secondly, we introduced the dataset with manual annotations of biasing artifacts in six thousands synthetic and real skin lesion images, which can serve as a benchmark for further studies. Finally, we showed that the most represented biases in the real data are enhanced by the generative network whereas the least represented artifacts are reduced.

2   Related Works

Previous studies have showed that skin lesion datasets are not free from bias. Winkler et al. [26] proved that common artifacts like surgical pen markings are strongly correlated with the skin lesion type, influencing the model. Bissotto et al. [4] presented that certain artifacts in skin lesion datasets affect classification models so strongly that they achieve relatively good results even when the lesion is removed from the image. Using global explainability and CBI methods, Mikołajczyk et al. [18] examined how strongly artifacts can influence the training. The result showed that the model is strongly biased towards black frame artifacts, as inserting one into the image often leads to significant prediction shifts. Bevan et al. [3]

presented that skin tone is also a biasing factor that can influence the models. Considering the literature review, the most commonly mentioned artifacts are hair, rulers, frames, and others like gel bubbles or surgical pen markings. In the paper we examine and annotate those artifacts in Sect. 3.2.

Some works on measuring bias suggested simply comparing the performance metrics on biased and unbiased dataset [20]. But in a real-world scenario, it is usually not possible to access an unbiased dataset. Such an approach would require removing all biases before training. In the case of skin lesions, removing artifacts like black frames, surgical pen markings, and even hair is very difficult, especially when these artifacts are on top of the lesions. A CBI is a contrasting approach, where one needs to insert the bias instead [18]. CBI introduced a set of metrics that can be used to evaluate prediction shift after adding the bias to the input data: mean and median prediction shift and a number of *switched* predictions. Higher rates mean a higher risk of giving biased predictions. As those numbers do not indicate the accuracy or correctness of the predicted category, it is worth measuring the F_1 score, recall, or other performance metrics to observe if the accuracy is lower on the dataset with inserted bias.

The problem of instrument bias in melanoma classification for the ISIC2020 dataset was addressed before using different debiasing techniques for artifact bias removal [2]. However, the authors mitigated only two selected biases: the surgical marking and ruler. They investigated the generalization capabilities of the bias removal approaches across different CNN architectures and human diagnosis. On average, EfficientNet-B3, ResNet-101, ResNeXt-101, DenseNet, and Inception-v3 models reached better accuracy ($AUC \approx 0.88$) than experienced dermatologists, performing similarly amongst themselves. In these studies, artificial data was not utilized to augment real data.

The generation of synthetic data not only increases the amount of data and balances the dataset but also serves as an anonymization technique that facilitates its exchange between different institutions as a proxy dataset [5]. Despite many attempts to generate artificial samples of skin images, the evaluation methods for the generated data's quality, diversity, and authenticity are still unclear. In some works [8], researchers point out the inadequacies of commonly used open datasets, such as data imbalance, bias or unwanted noise and artifacts. As GANs are learning the distributions of all provided images, they might as well learn and generate those unwanted features.

3 Experiments

The main goal of the experiments was to examine if GAN-generated data makes classification models more prone to biases. We selected a skin lesion ISIC dataset for distinguishing between malignant and benign lesions. Our procedure consists of three main steps: data generation, manual artifacts annotation and counterfactual bias insertion. The steps are presented in Fig. 2. For the data generation, we explored unconditional and conditional settings and evaluated their performance in terms of fidelity, diversity and training speed. The generated data was examined in terms of bias inheritance, and further annotated with selected artifacts. We

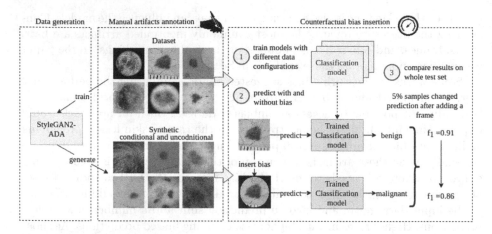

Fig. 1. The procedure behind (de)biasing effect of using GAN-based data augmentation

present the statistics and our remarks in the Sect. 3.2. Then, we train our classification models with different data configurations for both unconditional and conditional GANs: classic approach (training on the real data), augmentation approach (both real and synthetic data), and GANs-only (synthetic data). Each mode is tested how they respond to counterfactual bias insertion. The details behind CBI are presented in the Sect. 3.3 (Fig. 1).

3.1   Data and Training Details

All our experiments were performed using ISIC Archive challenges 2019 [9,10,24] and 2020 [22] data as our main datasets[1]. We splited that dataset randomly into a training set (30 118 samples) and a test set (7 530 samples) both for classification and generation tasks. In some experiments the training subset was augmented with artificial samples, while the test subset remained the same for all conducted studies[2] Detailed statistics are presented in Supplementary Table 1.

Image generation was performed using the StyleGAN2-ADA modified implementation from NVIDIA Research group[3]. The ADA mechanism stabilized training in limited data regimes that we faced in malignant samples. To select the best model, we considered both the Fréchet Inception Distance (FID) [12] and Kernel Inception Distance (KID) [6] metrics, along with training speed, similarly as proposed in [5]. Achieved results are presented in Supplementary Table 2.

As for the classification model, we used pre-trained EfficientNet-B2 [23] and trained it for 20 epochs with an early stopping with three epochs patience. We

---

[1] https://www.kaggle.com/nroman/melanoma-external-malignant-256.

[2] Data, annotations and additional results are publicly available on GitHub repository: https://github.com/AgaMiko/debiasing-effect-of-gans.

[3] https://github.com/aidotse/stylegan2-ada-pytorch.

used Adam optimizer with an adaptive learning rate initialized to 5e−4 and batch size 32.

3.2 Descriptive Statistics

To better understand a skin lesion dataset, or more precisely, the distribution of the artifacts, we have manually annotated 6000 real and synthetic images of skin lesions. We distinguish three main groups with two thousand annotations each: authentic images (real), synthetic images generated with unconditional GANs trained only on images from one class (GAN), and conditional GANs (cGAN). The exact numbers of annotated images are presented in Table 1.

Based on the literature, we selected four types of artifacts for annotations: hair, frames, rulers and *other* (see Fig. 2). *Hair* is defined as thick and thin hair of various colors, from light blond to black. Additionally, we annotated hair types: *normal, dense* (covering a significant part of an image) and *short* (shaved hair). *Frames* are black and white round markings around the skin lesion, black rectangle edges, and vignettes. *Rulers* can come in different shapes and colors, either fully or partially visible. *Other* are any other artifacts visible that are not as common as ruler marks, frames, and hair. It includes dermatoscopic gel or air bubbles, ink or surgical pen markings, patches and papers, dates and numbers, background parts, light reflection, and dust.

The annotation process was carried out by a trained professional working with the ISIC collection and identification of its biases for over 4 years. Additionally, we measured Inter-Annotator Agreement on a small subsample of data. The mean Cohen's kappa coefficient was over 70%, with the highest values on *ruler* annotations and lowest on the *other*.

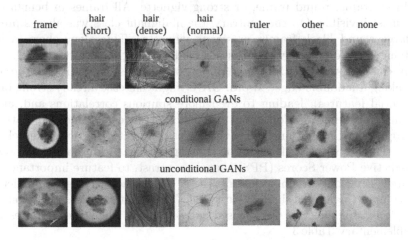

Fig. 2. Example artifacts in real and GAN generated data.

Interestingly, it seems that both, unconditional and conditional GANs, generate fewer artifacts than in the original images. Most rare or minor artifacts (like dust, paper, number, and dates) are never generated, leading to a significant decrease in the number of images with at least a single artifact. For instance, in unconditional GANs, almost half benign images were rendered without any artifacts. Moreover, in GANs, the artifacts are rarely correlated with each other, which means that there is usually one single artifact in the image at a time. The correlation calculated between each artifact and skin lesion type is presented in the Supplementary Table 4.

There is also a significant reduction in a number of hair and rulers generated in unconditional GANs and a slight one for conditional GANs. Short hair is pretty rare in the original dataset, but they almost entirely vanish in GAN-generated examples. Interestingly, manual annotations showed that conditional GANs seem to generate two rulers in one image of the benign class, which did not happen in the case of malignant skin lesions. This might be connected to the type of rulers annotated, as the GANs almost never generate small, partially visible rulers that are more common in real data.

Similarly, the surgical pen markings were generated only for the benign class in conditional and unconditional GANs, with no single example in the dataset with generated pen marking for the malignant class. The selectivity in artifacts generation can also be observed in the frame artifact. Frames are a common artifact strongly correlated with the skin lesion category: there are five times more examples of malignant skin lesions with frames than benign. This also affected the GANs training, as in the generated dataset, we observe much more images with frames for both GANs. Even more concerning is the fact that GANs generated only slightly visible vignettes or tiny, few pixel rectangular frames for benign moles. There was no single case of benign skin lesion generated with a large black frame, round frame, or strong vignette. All frames in benign class were almost invisible. On the contrary, the malignant class was always present with large round black frames or strong vignettes. This alone shows a huge amplifying effect on already pre-existing solid bias in the dataset.

This concludes that GANs might amplify strong biases but mitigate the small ones making it a double-edged sword. GANs might increase already strong biases (or essential features), leading to even more spurious correlations and, at the same time, loose information about insignificant tendencies and rare patterns. This property might be connected to the GANs architectures (such as kernel filter sizes) or the number of artifacts in the training dataset. Additionally, we provide the Predictive Power Scores (PPS) that, in contrast, to feature importance, are calculated using only a single feature (here: an artifact) trying to predict the target column (malignant/benign class) [25]. The result supports our conclusion about (de)biasing effect of GAN-based augmentation. The scores are presented in Supplementary Table 3.

Table 1. Statistics for manually labeled real and artificial images of malignant (mal) and benign (ben) class. cGAN refers to conditional GAN, while GAN – unconditional trained only on images from one class.

	Class	Hair (normal)	Hair (dense)	Hair (short)	Ruler	Frame	Other	None	Total
Real	ben	467	110	45	211	57	201	269	1000
	mal	444	50	51	287	251	402	141	1000
cGAN	ben	319	57	8	186	84	106	352	1000
	mal	223	29	8	110	365	128	328	1000
GAN	ben	190	43	4	94	78	257	412	1000
	mal	234	40	16	41	381	197	289	1000

3.3   Counterfactual Bias Insertion

The previous section identified three possible sources of bias in skin lesion classification: hair (regular, short, and dense), black frames, and ruler marks. We have tested several different ways and proportions of real to synthetic data to find the best performance metrics, as we wanted to mimic the realistic approach to data augmentation. We achieved the best scores when augmenting only the malignant class with 15k synthetic images. Achieved results are described in Table 2.

We use the CBI metrics [18] to measure bias influence. Frame bias insertion was done by adding a frame to an image. Hair and ruler insertion required more care to achieve a realistic look. We copied artifacts from the source image to the target image using provided segmentation masks [21]. We selected samples for each bias for a broader analysis, resulting in five frames, five types per hair type (regular, short, and dense), and five rulers. The segmentation masks used for the analysis are provided in Supplementary Fig. 1. The CBI was calculated for each image in the dataset, by inserting each of 25 biases. The mean CBI scores for each bias group are presented in Table 2. As the results strongly depended on the segmentation mask used, we also calculated standard deviation per bias.

Experiments allow understanding of how each artifact type affects the training, e.g., thin frames usually make predictions switch from malignant to benign, and large frames from benign to malignant. Rulers usually make predictions shift from malignant to benign, but in the GAN-augmented case, a thin ruler in the bottom causes prediction switch from benign to malignant.

The best performance and CBI scores were for real and augmented (aug. GAN) data. We also analyzed different augmentation policies and found that not every approach with augmentation gives better results than real data. Only the proposed approach did not provide worse CBI results than real. In all cases, the worst scores were observed for synthetic datasets. In general higher F_1 scores seemed to be a surprisingly accurate measure in case of vulnerability to biases. However, it also appears that quite a high score (90%) is needed to trust it: models with lower F_1 were not necessarily less biased.

Table 2. CBI metrics and F_1 scores measuring bias influence for each selected bias and type of training data: real data (real), augmented with synthetic images (aug.) and synthetic data (synth.), generated both with conditional (cGAN) and unconditional GANs (GAN) trained only on one class: benign (ben) or malignant (mal). Higher F_1 score means better performance, while higher number of switched images mean a higher bias influence.

Bias	Data	Switched					F_1 (%)			
		mean	std^a	median	mal to ben	ben to mal	F_1	aug	std^b	mean
Frame	real	129	119.39	77	24 (2.39%)	104 (1.60%)	91.99	88.97	4.01	90.48
	aug. cGAN	223	55.25	199	40 (3.88%)	183 (2.81%)	89.65	84.93	2.26	87.29
	aug. GAN	**59**	16.07	**51**	**22** (2.19%)	**37** (0.57%)	**91.52**	**90.49**	0.61	**91.01**
	synth. cGAN	290	43.97	271	125 (12.24%)	165 (2.54%)	80.39	79.28	1.26	79.84
	synth. GAN	413	33.17	404	297 (29.13%)	116 (1.78%)	76.04	74.99	0.82	75.51
Ruler	real	**81**	**86.76**	**29**	76 (7.48%)	**5** (0.07%)	**91.99**	88.59	4.30	**90.29**
	aug. cGAN	79	44.21	69	55 (5.43%)	24 (0.37%)	89.65	89.18	1.08	89.41
	aug. GAN	81	96.08	24	78 (7.60%)	3 (0.05%)	91.52	87.05	5.81	89.29
	synth. cGAN	200	137.26	151	194 (18.96%)	6 (0.09%)	80.39	78.31	5.11	79.35
	synth. GAN	154	109.89	107	65 (6.33%)	90 (1.38%)	76.04	74.69	1.82	75.36
Dense	real	**109**	**33.63**	118	90 (8.81%)	**19** (0.29%)	**91.99**	88.42	1.62	**90.20**
	aug. cGAN	439	269.40	459	96 (9.38%)	344 (5.28%)	89.65	78.85	9.04	84.25
	aug. GAN	122	28.48	113	74 (7.29%)	48 (0.73%)	91.52	87.03	1.42	89.28
	synth. cGAN	325	71.38	357	272 (26.66%)	52 (0.81%)	80.39	80.00	1.43	80.20
	synth. GAN	1089	651.43	1101	61 (5.97%)	1028 (15.79%)	76.04	59.94	10.27	67.99
Medium	real	**27**	**7.37**	**26**	17 (1.63%)	10 (0.15%)	**91.99**	91.60	**0.14**	**91.79**
	aug. cGAN	74	17.85	74	38 (3.74%)	36 (0.55%)	89.65	89.31	0.97	89.48
	aug. GAN	28	8.23	26	12 (1.19%)	16 (0.25%)	91.52	91.11	0.25	91.32
	synth. cGAN	163	47.93	177	113 (11.05%)	50 (0.77%)	80.39	80.49	1.84	80.44
	synth. GAN	284	141.58	298	46 (4.47%)	238 (3.66%)	76.04	73.51	3.20	74.78
Short	real	77	99.49	38	67 (6.52%)	10 (0.16%)	91.99	88.72	5.21	90.35
	aug. cGAN	180	114.84	224	12 (1.16%)	168 (2.59%)	89.65	84.73	3.56	87.19
	aug. GAN	**54**	**50.91**	**32**	**37** (3.64%)	**17** (0.26%)	**91.52**	**89.55**	**2.40**	**90.54**
	synth. cGAN	249	135.44	282	221 (21.67%)	28 (0.43%)	80.39	78.80	1.31	79.60
	synth. GAN	380	445.91	191	57 (5.62%)	323 (4.96%)	76.04	70.36	9.30	73.20

^{a}–standard deviation for *switched* metric for different bias types.
^{b}–standard deviation for F_1^{aug}. STD for F_1 is equal to 0.

Additionally, it is worth noticing that unconditional GANs performed better and were less prone to learn biases. Better performance might be connected with the lower Perceptual Path Length (PPL) [13] scores in unconditional GANs (see Supplementary Table 2). PPL measures the difference between consecutive images when interpolating between two random inputs. Lower PPL scores mean that the latent space is regularized better. Here, unconditional GANs have to learn the pattern distribution of only one class: either malignant or benign. We hypothesized this is also one of the reasons why unconditional GANs are better at capturing the consistency of the images. In contrast, cGANs seemed to link some biases to a one, specific class, resulting in a more biased dataset.

4   Conclusions

Descriptive statistics indicated that GANs amplified strong biases: large black frames, common dermoscopy artifacts, were never generated in benign skin lesions but were more prevalent in the generated dataset than in the original one. At the same time, the amount of clean images was much higher in the case of synthetic images. This observation and the manual exploration of generated artifacts implied that GANs also have debiasing properties, especially in the case of small, rare biases. In addition, for better reproducibility of our studies we provided manual annotations of biasing artifacts, which can serve as a benchmark for further studies. Future directions will be focused on generating unbiased data by learning directions for each of the biases in the latent space, to create a more complex, fair and diverse dataset.

The counterfactual bias insertion analysis supported the theory of GANs (de)biasing attributes. The study demonstrated an inverted correlation between the model's accuracy and bias robustness. This suggested that a well-trained model, even on biased data, is less likely to switch predictions after inserting biases. Ultimately, the best results in terms of accuracy and robustness were achieved for models trained on real data, or augmented with synthetic images produced by unconditional GANs. This shows that GANs can be successfully used to enrich data but should be monitored, as they can amplify preexisting inequities in data.

Acknowledgements. The research on bias reported in this publication was supported by Polish National Science Centre (Grant Preludium No: *UMO-2019/35/N/ST6/04052*). GANs trainings were conducted during first rotations of the *Eye for AI Program* thanks to the support of Sahlgrenska University Hospital and AI Sweden.

References

1. Baeza-Yates, R.: Bias on the web. Commun. ACM **61**(6), 54–61 (2018)
2. Bevan, P.D., Atapour-Abarghouei, A.: Skin deep unlearning: artefact and instrument debiasing in the context of melanoma classification. ArXiv abs/2109.09818 (2021)
3. Bevan, P.J., Atapour-Abarghouei, A.: Detecting melanoma fairly: skin tone detection and debiasing for skin lesion classification. arXiv preprint arXiv:2202.02832 (2022)
4. Bissoto, A., Fornaciali, M., Valle, E., Avila, S.: (De) constructing bias on skin lesion datasets. In: Proceedings of the IEEE/CVF Conference on Computer Vision and Pattern Recognition Workshops, p. 0 (2019)
5. Bissoto, A., Valle, E., Avila, S.: GAN-based data augmentation and anonymization for skin-lesion analysis: a critical review, April 2021
6. Bińkowski, M., Sutherland, D.J., Arbel, M., Gretton, A.: Demystifying MMD GANs (2021)

7. Bolukbasi, T., Chang, K.W., Zou, J.Y., Saligrama, V., Kalai, A.T.: Man is to computer programmer as woman is to homemaker? Debiasing word embeddings. Adv. Neural Inf. Process. Syst. **29**, 4349–4357 (2016)

8. Cassidy, B., Kendrick, C., Brodzicki, A., Jaworek-Korjakowska, J., Yap, M.H.: Analysis of the ISIC image datasets: usage, benchmarks and recommendations. Med. Image Anal. **75**, 102305 (2022). https://doi.org/10.1016/j.media.2021. 102305. https://www.sciencedirect.com/science/article/pii/S1361841521003509

9. Codella, N.C., et al.: Skin lesion analysis toward melanoma detection: a challenge at the 2017 international symposium on biomedical imaging (ISBI), hosted by the international skin imaging collaboration (ISIC). In: 2018 IEEE 15th international symposium on biomedical imaging (ISBI 2018), pp. 168–172. IEEE (2018)

10. Combalia, M., et al.: BCN20000: dermoscopic lesions in the wild. arXiv preprint arXiv:1908.02288 (2019)

11. He, J., van de Vijver, F.: Bias and equivalence in cross-cultural research. Online Read. Psychol. Cult. **2**(2), 2307–0919 (2012)

12. Heusel, M., Ramsauer, H., Unterthiner, T., Nessler, B., Hochreiter, S.: GANs trained by a two time-scale update rule converge to a local nash equilibrium. In: Guyon, I., et al. (eds.) Advances in Neural Information Processing Systems, vol. 30. Curran Associates, Inc. (2017). https://proceedings.neurips.cc/paper/2017/ file/8a1d694707eb0fefe65871369074926d-Paper.pdf

13. Karras, T., Laine, S., Aittala, M., Hellsten, J., Lehtinen, J., Aila, T.: Analyzing and improving the image quality of styleGAN. In: 2020 IEEE/CVF Conference on Computer Vision and Pattern Recognition (CVPR), pp. 8107–8116 (2020). https:// doi.org/10.1109/CVPR42600.2020.00813

14. Lloyd, K.: Bias amplification in artificial intelligence systems. arXiv preprint arXiv:1809.07842 (2018)

15. Mahtani, K., Spencer, E.A., Brassey, J., Heneghan, C.: Catalogue of bias: observer bias. BMJ Evid. Based Med. **23**(1), 23 (2018)

16. Mayson, S.G.: Bias in, bias out. YAle lJ **128**, 2218 (2018)

17. Mehrabi, N., Morstatter, F., Saxena, N., Lerman, K., Galstyan, A.: A survey on bias and fairness in machine learning. ACM Comput. Surv. (CSUR) **54**(6), 1–35 (2021)

18. Mikołajczyk, A., Grochowski, M., Kwasigroch, A.: Towards explainable classifiers using the counterfactual approach-global explanations for discovering bias in data. J. Artif. Intell. Soft Comput. Res. **11**(1), 51–67 (2021)

19. Panch, T., Mattie, H., Atun, R.: Artificial intelligence and algorithmic bias: implications for health systems. J. Glob. Health **9**(2) (2019)

20. Park, J.H., Shin, J., Fung, P.: Reducing gender bias in abusive language detection. arXiv preprint arXiv:1808.07231 (2018)

21. Ramella, G.: Hair removal combining saliency, shape and color. Appl. Sci. **11**(1), 447 (2021)

22. Rotemberg, V., et al.: A patient-centric dataset of images and metadata for identifying melanomas using clinical context. Sci. Data **8**(34) (2021). https://doi.org/ 10.1038/s41597-021-00815-z

23. Tan, M., Le, Q.V.: EfficientNet: rethinking model scaling for convolutional neural networks (2019). http://arxiv.org/abs/1905.11946, cite arxiv:1905.11946Comment. Published in ICML 2019

24. Tschandl, P., Rosendahl, C., Kittler, H.: The ham10000 dataset, a large collection of multi-source dermatoscopic images of common pigmented skin lesions. Sci. Data **5**(1), 1–9 (2018)

25. Wetschoreck, F., Krabel, T., Krishnamurthy, S.: 8080labs/ppscore: zenodo release, October 2020. https://doi.org/10.5281/zenodo.4091345
26. Winkler, J.K., et al.: Association between surgical skin markings in dermoscopic images and diagnostic performance of a deep learning convolutional neural network for melanoma recognition. JAMA Dermatol. **155**(10), 1135–1141 (2019)

Accurate and Explainable Image-Based Prediction Using a Lightweight Generative Model

Chiara Mauri[1](✉), Stefano Cerri[2], Oula Puonti[3], Mark Mühlau[4],
and Koen Van Leemput[1,2]

[1] Department of Health Technology, Technical University of Denmark,
Lyngby, Denmark
cmau@dtu.dk

[2] Athinoula A. Martinos Center for Biomedical Imaging, Massachusetts General
Hospital, Harvard Medical School, Charlestown, USA

[3] Danish Research Centre for Magnetic Resonance, Centre for Functional
and Diagnostic Imaging and Research, Copenhagen University Hospital Hvidovre,
Hvidovre, Denmark

[4] Department of Neurology and TUM-Neuroimaging Center, School of Medicine,
Technical University of Munich, Munich, Germany

Abstract. Recent years have seen a growing interest in methods for
predicting a variable of interest, such as a subject's age, from individual brain scans. Although the field has focused strongly on nonlinear
discriminative methods using deep learning, here we explore whether
linear generative techniques can be used as practical alternatives that
are easier to tune, train and interpret. The models we propose consist of
(1) a causal forward model expressing the effect of variables of interest
on brain morphology, and (2) a latent variable noise model, based on
factor analysis, that is quick to learn and invert. In experiments estimating individuals' age and gender from the UK Biobank dataset, we
demonstrate competitive prediction performance even when the number
of training subjects is in the thousands – the typical scenario in many
potential applications. The method is easy to use as it has only a single
hyperparameter, and directly estimates interpretable spatial maps of the
underlying structural changes that are driving the predictions.

1 Introduction

Image-based prediction methods aim to estimate a variable of interest, such as
a subject's diagnosis or prognosis, directly from a medical scan. Predicting a
subject's age based on a brain scan – the so called brain age – in particular has
seen significant interest in the last decade [12], with the gap between *brain* age
and *chronological* age being suggested as a potential biomarker of healthy aging
and/or neurological disease [12,25].

Methods with state-of-the-art prediction performance are currently based
on *discriminative learning*, in which a variable of interest x is directly predicted

L. Wang et al. (Eds.): MICCAI 2022, LNCS 13438, pp. 448–458, 2022.
https://doi.org/10.1007/978-3-031-16452-1_43

from an input image t. Although there are ongoing controversies in the literature regarding whether nonlinear or linear discriminative methods predict better [23, 28,32], recent years have seen a strong focus on nonlinear variants based on deep learning (DL), with impressive performances especially when the training size is very large [28]. Nevertheless, these powerful methods come with a number of potential limitations:

The Available Training Size is Often Limited: While methods for predicting age and gender can be trained on thousands of subjects using large imaging studies [4,14,16,21,24], in many potential applications the size of the training set is much more modest. In a recent survey on single-subject prediction of brain disorders in neuroimaging, the mean and median samples size was only 186 and 88 subjects, respectively [5]. Even in such ambitious imaging projects as the UK Biobank [4], the number of subjects with diseases such as multiple sclerosis is only projected to be in the hundreds in the coming years.

Discriminative Methods are Hard to Interpret: As opposed to *generative* methods that explicitly model the effect a variable of interest x has on a subject's image t, correctly interpreting the internal workings of discriminative methods is known to be difficult [3,6,20,22]. Whereas the spatial weight maps of linear discriminative methods, or more generally the saliency maps of nonlinear ones [8,17,33–38], are useful for highlighting which image areas are being used in the prediction process [20,29], they do not explain *why* specific voxels are given specific attention: Amplifying the signal of interest, or suppressing noninteresting noise characteristics in the data [22].

DL Can Be more Difficult to Use: Compared to less expressive techniques, DL methods are often harder to use, as they can be time consuming to train, and have many more "knobs" that can be turned to obtain good results (e.g., the choice of architecture, data augmentation, optimizer, training loss, etc. [28]).

In this paper, we propose a lightweight generative model that aims to be easier to use and more straightforward to interpret, without sacrificing prediction performance in typical sample size settings. Like in the mass-univariate techniques that have traditionally been used in human brain mapping [7,11,13,18], the method has a causal forward model that encodes how variables of interest affect brain shape, and is therefore intuitive to interpret. Unlike such techniques, however, the method also includes a linear-Gaussian latent variable noise model that captures the dominant correlations between voxels. As we will show, this allows us to efficiently "invert" the model to obtain accurate predictions of variables of interest, yielding an effective linear prediction method without externally enforced interpretability constraints [9,39].

The method we propose can be viewed as an extension of prior work demonstrating that naive Bayesian classifiers can empirically outperform more powerful methods when the training size is limited, even though the latter have asymptotically better performance [15,27]. Here we show that these findings translate to prediction tasks in neuroimaging when the strong conditional independence assumption of such "naive" methods is relaxed. Using experiments on age and gender prediction in the UK Biobank imaging dataset, we demonstrate empirically that, even when the number of training subjects is the thousands, our lightweight linear generative method yields prediction performance that is competitive with state-of-the-art nonlinear discriminative [28], linear discriminative [31], and nonlinear generative [40] methods.

2 Method

Let t denote a vectorized version of a subject's image, and $\phi = (x, \phi_{\backslash x}^T)^T$ a vector of variables specific to that subject, consisting of a variable of interest x (such as their age or gender), along with any other known[1] subject-specific covariates $\phi_{\backslash x}$. A simple generative model is then of the form

$$t = W\phi + \eta, \tag{1}$$

where η is a random noise vector, assumed to be Gaussian distributed with zero mean and covariance C, and $W = (w_x \; W_{\backslash x})$ is a matrix with spatial weight maps stacked in its columns. The first column, w_x, expresses how strongly the variable of interest x is expressed in the voxels of t; we will refer to it as the *generative* weight map. Taking everything together, the image t is effectively modeled as Gaussian distributed:

$$p(t|\phi, W, C) = \mathcal{N}(t|W\phi, C).$$

Making Predictions

When the parameters of the model are known, the unknown target variable x^* of a subject with image t^* and covariates $\phi_{\backslash x}^*$ can be inferred by inverting the model using Bayes' rule. For a binary target variable $x^* \in \{0, 1\}$ where the two outcomes have equal prior probability, the target posterior distribution takes the form of a logistic regression classifier:

$$p(x^* = 1|t^*, \phi_{\backslash x}^*, W, C) = \sigma(w_D^T t^* + w_o),$$

where

$$w_D = C^{-1} w_x$$

are a set *discriminative* spatial weights, $\sigma(\cdot)$ denotes the logistic function, and $w_o = -w_D^T(W_{\backslash x}\phi_{\backslash x}^* + w_x/2)$. The prediction of x^* is therefore 1 if $w_D^T t^* + w_o > 0$, and 0 otherwise.

For a continuous target variable with Gaussian prior distribution $p(x^*) = \mathcal{N}(x^*|0, \sigma^2)$, the posterior distribution is also Gaussian with mean

$$\sigma_x^2(w_D^T t^* + b_0), \tag{2}$$

where $b_0 = -w_D^T W_{\backslash x}\phi_{\backslash x}^*$ and $\sigma_x^2 = (\sigma^{-2} + w_x^T C^{-1} w_x)^{-1}$. The predicted value of x^* is therefore given by (2), which again involves taking the inner product of the discriminative weights w_D with t^*.

---

[1] For notational convenience, we include 1 as a dummy "covariate".

Model Training

In practice the model parameters W and C need to be estimated from training data. Given N training pairs $\{t_n, \phi_n\}_{n=1}^{N}$, their maximum likelihood (ML) estimate is obtained by maximizing the marginal likelihood

$$p\left(\{t_n\}_{n=1}^{N} | \{\phi_n\}_{n=1}^{N}, W, C\right) = \prod_{n=1}^{N} \mathcal{N}\left(t_n | W\phi_n, C\right) \tag{3}$$

with respect to these parameters. For the spatial maps W, the solution is given in closed form:

$$W = \left(\sum_{n=1}^{N} t_n \phi_n^T\right) \left(\sum_{n=1}^{N} \phi_n \phi_n^T\right)^{-1}. \tag{4}$$

Obtaining the noise covariance matrix C directly by ML estimation is problematic, however: For images with J voxels, C has $J(J+1)/2$ free parameters – orders of magnitude more than there are training samples. To circumvent this problem, we impose a specific structure on C by using a latent variable model known as factor analysis [10]. In particular, we model the noise as

$$\eta = Vz + \epsilon,$$

where z is a small set of K unknown latent variables distributed as $p(z) = \mathcal{N}(z|0, \mathbb{I}_K)$, V contains K corresponding, unknown spatial weight maps, and ϵ is a zero-mean Gaussian distributed error with unknown diagonal covariance Δ. Marginalizing over z yields a zero-mean Gaussian noise model with covariance matrix

$$C = VV^T + \Delta,$$

which is now controlled by a reduced set of parameters V and Δ. The number of columns in V (i.e., the number of latent variables K) is a hyperparameter in the model that needs to be tuned experimentally.

Plugging in the ML estimate of W given by (4), the parameters V and Δ maximizing the marginal likelihood (3) can be estimated using an Expectation-Maximization (EM) algorithm [30]. Applied to our setting, this yields an iterative algorithm that repeatedly evaluates the posterior distribution over the latent variables:

$$p(z_n | t_n, W, V, \Delta) = \mathcal{N}(z_n | \mu_n, \Sigma)$$

where $\mu_n = \Sigma V^T \Delta^{-1}(t_n - W\phi_n)$ and $\Sigma = (\mathbb{I}_K + V^T \Delta^{-1} V)^{-1}$, and subsequently updates the parameters:

$$V \leftarrow \left(\sum_{n=1}^{N} (t_n - W\phi_n)\mu_n^T\right) \left(\sum_{n=1}^{N} (\mu_n \mu_n^T + \Sigma)\right)^{-1}$$

$$\Delta \leftarrow \mathrm{diag}\left(\frac{1}{N}\sum_{n=1}^{N}(t_n - W\phi_n)(t_n - W\phi_n)^T - V\frac{1}{N}\sum_{n=1}^{N}\mu_n(t_n - W\phi_n)^T\right).$$

3   Experiments

In our implementation, we initialize the EM algorithm by using a matrix with standard Gaussian random entries for V, and a diagonal matrix with the sample variance in each voxel across the training set for Δ. For continuous target variables, we de-mean the target and use the sample variance as the prior variance σ^2. Convergence is detected when the relative change in the log marginal likelihood is smaller than 10^{-5}.

The method has a single hyperparameter, the number of latent variables K, that we set empirically using cross-validation on a validation set, by optimizing the mean absolute error (MAE) for regression and the accuracy for classification. Running times vary with the size of the training set N, which also influences the selected value of K – in our implementation, typical training runs in the full-brain experiments described below took between 2.8 and 16.3 min for $N = 200$ and $N = 1000$, respectively (CPU time for a single selected value of K; Matlab on a state-of-the-art desktop). Once the model is trained, testing is fast: Typically 0.01 s per subject when trained on $N = 1000$.

Comparing performance of an image-based prediction method with state-of-the-art benchmark methods is hampered by the dearth of publicly available software implementations, and the strong dependency of attainable performance on the datasets that are used [12]. Within these constraints, we conducted the following comparisons of the proposed linear generative method:

Nonlinear Discriminative Benchmark: As the main benchmark method, we selected the convolutional neural network SFCN proposed in [28], which is, to the best of our knowledge, currently the best performing image-based prediction method. The paper reports performance for age and gender prediction over a wide range of training sizes in preprocessed UK Biobank data (14,503 healthy subjects, aged 44–80 years), using a validation set of 518 subjects and a test set of 1036 subjects. For a training size of 12,949 subjects, the authors report a training time of 65 h on two NVIDIA P100 GPUs [28]. Although the method uses affinely registered T1-weighted scans as input ("affine T1s"), these are in fact skull-stripped and subsequently bias-field-corrected based on deformable registrations that are also available [4]. Because of this reason, and because the authors report only very minor improvements of their method when deformable T1s are used instead (~2.5% decrease in MAE for age prediction on 2590 training subjects), we compared our method using both affine and deformable T1s, based on a set-up that closely resembles theirs (validation set of 500 subjects, test set of 1000 subjects).

Linear Discriminative Benchmark: In order to compare against a state-of-the-art *linear* discriminative method, we selected the RVoxM method [31] because its training code is readily available [1] and its performance is comparable to the best linear discriminative method tested in [28]. RVoxM regularizes its linear discriminant surface by encouraging spatial smoothness and sparsity of its weight maps, using a regularization strength that is the one hyperparameter of the method. In our experiments, we selected the optimal value of this hyperparameter in the same way as we do it for the proposed method, i.e., by cross-validation on our 500-subject validation set. Typical training times were between 66 and 122 min for $N = 200$ and $N = 1000$, respectively (CPU time for a single selected value of the model's hyperparameter; Matlab on a state-of-the-art desktop).

Nonlinear Generative Benchmark: As a final benchmark, we compared against a variational auto-encoder (VAE) [40] that was recently proposed for age prediction, and that has training code publicly available [2]. It is based on a generative model that is similar to ours, except that its latent variables are expanded ("decoded") *nonlinearly* using a deep neural network, which makes the EM training algorithm more involved compared to our closed-form expressions [26]. In [40], the authors use T1 volumes that are cropped around the ventricular area (cf. Fig. 1 right), and they train their method on $\sim$200 subjects. We closely follow their example and train both the VAE and the proposed method on similarly sized training sets of warped T1 scans from the UK Biobank, cropped in the same way. There are two hyperparameters in the VAE model (dropout factor and L2 regularization), which we optimized on our validation set of 500 subjects using grid search. The training time for this method was on average 9.40 min for $N = 200$ with the optimal set of hyperparameters, using a NVIDIA GeForce RTX 2080 Ti GPU.

For each training size tested, we trained each method three times, using randomly sampled training sets, and report the average test MAE and accuracy results. For gender classification, we used age as a known covariate in $\phi_{\backslash x}$, while for age prediction no other variables were employed. All our experiments were performed on downsampled (to 2 mm isotropic) data, with the exception of RVoxM where 3 mm was used due to time constraints – we verified experimentally that results for RVoxM nor the proposed method would have changed significantly had the downsampling factor been changed (max difference of 0.32% in MAE between 2 mm and 3 mm across multiple training sizes between 100 and 1000). Since training code for SFCN is not publicly available, we report the results as they appear in [28], noting that the method was tuned on a 518-subject validation set as described in the paper.

4   Results

Figure 1 shows examples of the *generative* spatial map w_x estimated by the proposed method, along with the corresponding *discriminative* map w_D. The generative map shows the direct effect age has on image intensities, and reflects the typical age-related gray matter atrophy patterns reported in previous studies [19]. The discriminative map, which highlights voxels that are employed for prediction, is notably different from the generative map and heavily engages white matter areas instead. This illustrates the interpretation problem in discriminative models: the discriminative weight map does not directly relate to changes in neuroanatomy, but rather summarizes the net effect of decomposing the signal as a sum of age-related changes and a typical noise pattern seen in the training data (1), resulting in a non-intuitive spatial pattern [22].

Figure 2 shows the performances obtained by the proposed method, compared to the discriminative benchmarks RVoxM and SFCN, for age and gender prediction. Both our method and RVoxM achieve clearly worse results when they are applied to affine T1s compared to deformable T1s, whereas SFCN's performance is virtually unaffected by the type of input data (at least for age prediction with 2590 training subjects – the only available data point for SFCN with deformable T1s [28]). These results are perhaps not surprising, since both our method and RVoxM are *linear* predictors that do not have the same capacity as neural networks to "model away" nonlinear deformations that have not been removed from the input images (even though these are actually known and were used for generating the affine T1s).

Comparing the performances of the different methods, our generative model generally outperforms the linear discriminative RVoxM for both age and gender prediction, except when using very large training sets of affine T1s. For *nonlinear* discriminative SFCN, the situation is more nuanced: For age prediction, SFCN starts outperforming our method for training sets larger than 2600 subjects, while for more moderate training sizes our method achieves better performances when deformable T1s are used. For gender prediction, our method based on deformable T1s is competitive with SFCN even on the biggest training set sizes, although it should be noted that SFCN's results are based on affine T1s as its performance on deformable T1s for gender prediction was not tested[2] in [28].

Finally, Fig. 3 compares the age prediction results of our linear generative model with the nonlinear generative VAE, both trained on cropped deformable T1s. Our method clearly outperforms the VAE for all the considered training sizes, suggesting that, at least when only a few hundred training subjects are available, adding nonlinearities in the model is not beneficial.

5   Discussion

In this paper, we have introduced a lightweight method for image-based prediction that is based on a linear generative model. The method aims to be easier to use, faster to train and less opaque than state-of-the-art nonlinear and/or discriminative methods. Based on our experiments in predicting age and gender from brain MRI scans, the method seems to attain these goals without sacrificing prediction accuracy, especially in the limited training size scenarios that are characteristic of neuroimaging applications.

Although the method presented here is linear in both its causal forward model and in its noise model, it would be straightforward to introduce nonlinearities in the forward model while still maintaining numerical invertibility. This may be beneficial in e.g., age prediction in datasets with a much wider age range than the UK Biobank data used here. The method can also be generalized to longitudinal

---

[2] Nevertheless, SFCN's gender prediction, based on affine T1s, is reported by its authors to be the best in the literature.

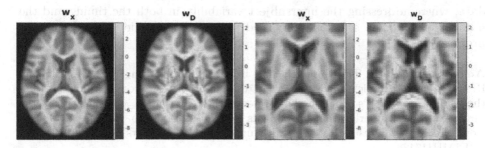

Fig. 1. Examples of *generative* maps w_x encoding age effects vs. the corresponding *discriminative* maps w_D predicting age, obtained on deformable T1s from 300 subjects and overlaid on the average T1 volume. Voxels with zero weight are transparent. Left: results on whole T1 images (used for comparing the proposed method with SFCN and RVoxM). Right: results on cropped T1s (used for comparing with VAE).

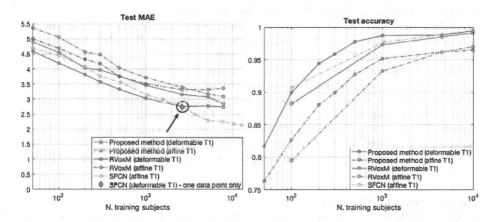

Fig. 2. Comparison of the proposed method, RVoxM and SFCN on an age prediction task (left) and on a gender classification task (right). For each method, results are shown for both affine and deformable T1 input data – except for SFCN for which the result for deformable T1s is only known for age prediction, in a single point (indicated by an arrow at 2590 subjects).

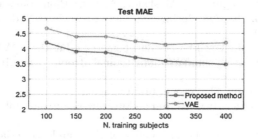

Fig. 3. Test MAE for age prediction obtained by the proposed method and VAE on cropped, deformable T1s.

data, where addressing the intersubject variability in both the timing and the number of follow-up scans is well suited for generative models such as the one proposed here.

Acknowledgments. This research has been conducted using the UK Biobank Resource under Application Number 65657. This project has received funding from the European Union's Horizon 2020 research and innovation program under the Marie Sklodowska-Curie grant agreements No. 765148 and No. 731827, as well as from the National Institutes Of Health under project numbers R01NS112161 and 1RF1MH117428.

References

1. https://sabuncu.engineering.cornell.edu/software-projects/relevance-voxel-machine-rvoxm-code-release/
2. https://github.com/QingyuZhao/VAE-for-Regression
3. Adebayo, J., et al.: Sanity checks for saliency maps. In: Bengio, S., Wallach, H., Larochelle, H., Grauman, K., Cesa-Bianchi, N., Garnett, R. (eds.) Advances in Neural Information Processing Systems, vol. 31. Curran Associates, Inc. (2018)
4. Alfaro-Almagro, F., et al.: Image processing and quality control for the first 10,000 brain imaging datasets from UK biobank. Neuroimage **166**, 400–424 (2018)
5. Arbabshirani, M.R., et al.: Single subject prediction of brain disorders in neuroimaging: promises and pitfalls. Neuroimage **145**, 137–165 (2017)
6. Arun, N., et al.: Assessing the trustworthiness of saliency maps for localizing abnormalities in medical imaging. Radiol. Artif. Intell. **3**(6), e200267 (2021)
7. Ashburner, J., et al.: Voxel-based morphometry-the methods. Neuroimage **11**(6), 805–821 (2000)
8. Baehrens, D., et al.: How to explain individual classification decisions. J. Mach. Learn. Res. **11**, 1803–1831 (2010)
9. Batmanghelich, N.K., et al.: Generative-discriminative basis learning for medical imaging. IEEE Trans. Med. Imaging **31**(1), 51–69 (2011)
10. Bishop, C.M., Nasrabadi, N.M.: Pattern Recognition and Machine Learning, vol. 4, Chap. 12. Springer, New York (2006)
11. Chung, M., et al.: A unified statistical approach to deformation-based morphometry. NeuroImage **14**(3), 595–606 (2001)
12. Cole, J.H., Franke, K., Cherbuin, N.: Quantification of the biological age of the brain using neuroimaging. In: Moskalev, A. (ed.) Biomarkers of Human Aging. HAL, vol. 10, pp. 293–328. Springer, Cham (2019). https://doi.org/10.1007/978-3-030-24970-0_19
13. Davatzikos, C., et al.: Voxel-based morphometry using the RAVENS maps: methods and validation using simulated longitudinal atrophy. NeuroImage **14**(6), 1361–1369 (2001)
14. Di Martino, A., et al.: The autism brain imaging data exchange: towards a large-scale evaluation of the intrinsic brain architecture in autism. Mol. Psychiatry **19**(6), 659–667 (2014)
15. Domingos, P., et al.: On the optimality of the simple Bayesian classifier under zero-one loss. Mach. Learn. **29**(2), 103–130 (1997)

16. Ellis, K.A., et al.: The Australian imaging, biomarkers and lifestyle (AIBL) study of aging: methodology and baseline characteristics of 1112 individuals recruited for a longitudinal study of Alzheimer's disease. Int. Psychogeriatrics **21**(4), 672–687 (2009)
17. Erhan, D., et al.: Visualizing higher-layer features of a deep network. Univ. Montr. **1341**(3), 1 (2009)
18. Fischl, B., et al.: Measuring the thickness of the human cerebral cortex from magnetic resonance images. PNAS **97**(20), 11050 (2000)
19. Fjell, A.M., et al.: High consistency of regional cortical thinning in aging across multiple samples. Cereb. Cortex **19**(9), 2001–2012 (2009). https://doi.org/10.1093/cercor/bhn232
20. Ghassemi, M., et al.: The false hope of current approaches to explainable artificial intelligence in health care. Lancet Digit. Health **3**(11), e745–e750 (2021)
21. Glasser, M.F., et al.: The human connectome project's neuroimaging approach. Nat. Neurosci. **19**(9), 1175–1187 (2016)
22. Haufe, S., et al.: On the interpretation of weight vectors of linear models in multivariate neuroimaging. Neuroimage **87**, 96–110 (2014)
23. He, T., et al.: Deep neural networks and kernel regression achieve comparable accuracies for functional connectivity prediction of behavior and demographics. NeuroImage **206**, 116276 (2020)
24. Jack Jr., C.R., et al.: The Alzheimer's disease neuroimaging initiative (ADNI): MRI methods. J. Magn. Reson. Imaging Off. J. Int. Soc. Magn. Reson. Med. **27**(4), 685–691 (2008)
25. Kaufmann, T., et al.: Common brain disorders are associated with heritable patterns of apparent aging of the brain. Nat. Neurosci. **22**(10), 1617–1623 (2019)
26. Kingma, D.P., et al.: Auto-encoding variational Bayes. arXiv preprint arXiv:1312.6114 (2013)
27. Ng, A.Y., et al.: On discriminative vs. generative classifiers: a comparison of logistic regression and Naive Bayes. In: Advances In Neural Information Processing Systems, pp. 841–848 (2002)
28. Peng, H., et al.: Accurate brain age prediction with lightweight deep neural networks. Med. Image Anal. **68**, 101871 (2021)
29. Ras, G., et al.: Explainable deep learning: a field guide for the uninitiated. J. Artif. Intell. Res. **73**, 329–397 (2022)
30. Rubin, D.B., et al.: EM algorithms for ML factor analysis. Psychometrika **47**(1), 69–76 (1982)
31. Sabuncu, M.R., et al.: The Relevance Voxel Machine (RVoxM): a self-tuning Bayesian model for informative image-based prediction. IEEE Trans. Med. Imaging **31**(12), 2290–2306 (2012)
32. Schulz, M.A., et al.: Deep learning for brains?: Different linear and nonlinear scaling in UK biobank brain images vs. machine-learning datasets. BioRxiv p. 757054 (2019)
33. Selvaraju, R.R., et al.: Grad-CAM: visual explanations from deep networks via gradient-based localization. In: Proceedings of the IEEE International Conference on Computer Vision, pp. 618–626 (2017)
34. Shrikumar, A., et al.: Learning important features through propagating activation differences. In: International Conference on Machine Learning, pp. 3145–3153. PMLR (2017)
35. Simonyan, K., et al.: Deep inside convolutional networks: visualising image classification models and saliency maps. In: Workshop at International Conference on Learning Representations (2014)

36. Smilkov, D., et al.: SmoothGrad: removing noise by adding noise. arXiv preprint arXiv:1706.03825 (2017)
37. Springenberg, J.T., et al.: Striving for simplicity: the all convolutional net. arXiv preprint arXiv:1412.6806 (2014)
38. Sundararajan, M., et al.: Axiomatic attribution for deep networks. In: International Conference on Machine Learning, pp. 3319–3328. PMLR (2017)
39. Varol, E., Sotiras, A., Zeng, K., Davatzikos, C.: Generative discriminative models for multivariate inference and statistical mapping in medical imaging. In: Frangi, A.F., Schnabel, J.A., Davatzikos, C., Alberola-López, C., Fichtinger, G. (eds.) MICCAI 2018. LNCS, vol. 11072, pp. 540–548. Springer, Cham (2018). https://doi.org/10.1007/978-3-030-00931-1_62
40. Zhao, Q., Adeli, E., Honnorat, N., Leng, T., Pohl, K.M.: Variational AutoEncoder for regression: application to brain aging analysis. In: Shen, D., et al. (eds.) MICCAI 2019. LNCS, vol. 11765, pp. 823–831. Springer, Cham (2019). https://doi.org/10.1007/978-3-030-32245-8_91

Interpretable Modeling and Reduction of Unknown Errors in Mechanistic Operators

Maryam Toloubidokhti[1]([⊠]), Nilesh Kumar[1], Zhiyuan Li[1],
Prashnna K. Gyawali[2], Brian Zenger[3], Wilson W. Good[3], Rob S. MacLeod[3],
and Linwei Wang[1]

[1] Rochester Institute of Technology, Rochester, NY, USA
{mt6129,nk4856}@rit.edu
[2] Stanford University, Stanford, USA
[3] The University of Utah, Salt Lake City, UT, USA

Abstract. Prior knowledge about the imaging physics provides a mechanistic *forward* operator that plays an important role in image reconstruction, although myriad sources of possible errors in the operator could negatively impact the reconstruction solutions. In this work, we propose to embed the traditional mechanistic forward operator inside a neural function, and focus on modeling and correcting its unknown errors in an interpretable manner. This is achieved by a conditional generative model that transforms a given mechanistic operator with unknown errors, arising from a latent space of self-organizing clusters of potential sources of error generation. Once learned, the generative model can be used in place of a fixed forward operator in any traditional optimization-based reconstruction process where, together with the inverse solution, the error in prior mechanistic forward operator can be minimized and the potential source of error uncovered. We apply the presented method to the reconstruction of heart electrical potential from body surface potential. In controlled simulation experiments and *in-vivo* real data experiments, we demonstrate that the presented method allowed reduction of errors in the physics-based forward operator and thereby delivered inverse reconstruction of heart-surface potential with increased accuracy.

Keywords: Inverse imaging · Forward modeling · Physics-based

1 Introduction

In traditional approaches to medical image reconstruction, prior knowledge about the underlying imaging physics plays an important role. We typically start

---

M. Toloubidokhti and N. Kumar—Contributed equally to this work.

Supplementary Information The online version contains supplementary material available at https://doi.org/10.1007/978-3-031-16452-1_44.

L. Wang et al. (Eds.): MICCAI 2022, LNCS 13438, pp. 459–468, 2022.
https://doi.org/10.1007/978-3-031-16452-1_44

with a *mechanistic forward operator* that defines the relationship between the unknown inverse solution and the external measurements, obtained by numerically solving mathematical equations governing the underlying imaging physics. The inverse problem of image reconstruction is then formulated as deterministic optimization or probabilistic inference leveraging these mechanistic forward operators [5,14]. Errors in these operators, arising from factors such as assumptions and imperfect knowledge associated with the underlying physics, heavily affect the optimization or inference processes [5]. Due to myriad sources of possible errors associated with the mechanistic operator, it is also non-trivial to attempt to directly minimize or correct these errors during the inverse process. The sources of error we considered represent the most prominent sources of errors in ECG imaging as concluded in literature [19]. These errors arise from different stages in the ECG imaging pipeline such as data acquisition, image segmentation, and forward modeling.

Alternatively, modern deep learning has shown great potential in medical image reconstruction across a variety of modalities [6,9,13,17]. These approaches do not rely on the correctness of any prior physics knowledge and directly learn the forward and/or inverse mapping from data. The neglect of available knowledge however must be compensated by a large number of labeled training pairs, which are often difficult to obtain in image reconstruction problems. Furthermore, the data-driven black-box reconstruction process leads to limited interpretability.

There has been substantial interest in combining the strength of deep learning with available prior knowledge of the imaging physics. For instance, in a traditional formulation of reconstruction problems utilizing mechanistic forward operators, existing works have explored the possibility to learn better regularizers for the optimization [4], or to learn the optimization gradient itself [12].

In this work, we are motivated to retain our prior knowledge of the known imaging physics, while focusing on modeling and correcting its unknown errors in an interpretable manner. To this end, we propose a hybrid mechanistic and neural modeling of the forward operator: given a mechanistic forward operator $\mathbf{H}_i$ obtained for instance by solving partial differential equations governing the imaging physics, we introduce a conditional generative model $\mathbf{H}_f = \mathbf{G}(\mathbf{H}_i, \mathbf{z}_r)$ that, in the form of a U-net [18], combining $\mathbf{H}_i$ and any unknown residual errors generated from the latent variable $\mathbf{z}_r$ as illustrated in Fig. 1.

Furthermore, we describe $\mathbf{z}_r$ with self-organizing maps (SOM) [11] to provide an interpretable model of the various potential sources that generate the errors. This hybrid and interpretable generative model is optimized via amortized variational inference. Once learned, the generative $\mathbf{G}(\mathbf{H}_i, \mathbf{z}_r)$ can be used in place of a fixed forward operator in any traditional optimization-based reconstruction process where, together with the inverse solution, the error in prior mechanistic forward operator can be minimized and the potential source of error uncovered (*e.g.*, to shed light on future data collection for a more accurate forward modeling).

We demonstrate this novel concept on the reconstruction of cardiac electrical potential from body surface potential [7,8]. A similar motivation was pursued in a previous work in this specific application (DAECGI) [20], where a conditional generative model was developed to learn the forward operator as a function of

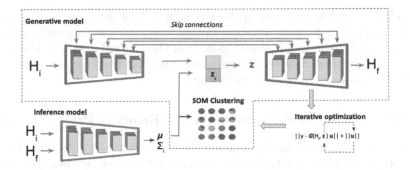

Fig. 1. Overview of IMRE network. Top: generative model; Bottom left: inference model; Bottom center: SOM clustering; Bottom right: Iterative optimization and reduction of errors in the generative model.

known geometry underlying the operator and an unknown latent variable. As a result, the generative model is not hybrid with the mechanistic forward operator, but mimics the mechanistic operator with a fully data-driven neural function of the input geometry. This modeling option also limits it to the particular application where the forward operator is a function of the underlying geometry. Furthermore, there was not an attempt to provide an interpretable modeling of the sources of error generation. In controlled simulation experiments and *in-vivo* real data experiments, we demonstrate that the presented method allowed reduction of errors in the mechanistic forward operator and recognition of the sources of errors. Furthermore, we demonstrated that the presented method improved the accuracy of the reconstructed heart-surface potential, in comparison to DAECGI as described in [20].

2   Method

As an application context of the proposed methodology, we focus on the reconstruction of cardiac electrical potential from body surface potential, also known as electrocardiographic imaging (ECGi). Considering the extracellular potential $\mathbf{u}$ on the heart surface as the electrical source, its relationship with body surface potential $\mathbf{y}$ is defined by the Laplace's equation [15]. Numerically solving this Laplace equation on the heart-torso geometry of any subject gives rise to the forward mechanistic operator $\mathbf{H}$ that relates heart surface potential to body-surface potential. The reconstruction of the $\mathbf{u}$ can then be formulated as:

$$\hat{\mathbf{u}} = \arg\min_{\mathbf{u}}\{\|\mathbf{y} - \mathbf{H}\mathbf{u}\| + \lambda \mathcal{R}(\mathbf{u})\} \tag{1}$$

where $\mathcal{R}(\mathbf{u})$ is the regularization term weighted by parameter λ.

We present Interpretable Modeling and Reduction of Unknown Errors in Mechanistic Operators (IMRE) for solving Eq. (1) which, as outlined in Fig. 1, consists of two components: 1) a generative model, shown in the dashed box, that models the unknown errors in the mechanistic forward operator in an interpretable manner, and 2) an iterative optimization scheme to jointly optimize the inverse solution and minimizes the error in the forward operator. Once optimized, we can further identify the potential source of errors owing to the use of SOM in the latent space of error modeling.

2.1   Interpretable Modeling of Unknown Errors in Prior Physics

The presented generative model respects the mechanistic forward operator and focuses on learning its potential errors, such as those caused by inaccuracy in the underlying heart-torso geometry or tissue conductivities. It is further enriched with a interpretable latent-space modeling to cluster possible sources of errors.

Generative Model: As outlined in the dashed box in Fig. 1, generation of the hybrid forward operator is 1) conditioned on the mechanistic forward operator $\mathbf{H}_i$ via a U-NET structure, and 2) augmented with a latent representation $\mathbf{z}_r$ that explains residual errors in the prior physics:

$$\mathbf{H}_f \sim p(\mathbf{H}_f|\mathbf{H}_i, \mathbf{z}_r), \quad p(\mathbf{z}_r) \sim \mathcal{N}(\mathbf{0}, \mathbf{I}) \tag{2}$$

The U-NET provides direct links from $\mathbf{H}_i$ to the decoder, allowing us to preserve the prior physics and focus on modeling its potential errors.

Self Organizing Maps (SOM): Considering that these errors can arise from several different sources, we further group sources of error $\mathbf{z}_r$ with a SOM [11]. SOM is an unsupervised machine learning algorithm that makes certain parts of the network respond similarly to the matching input patterns. We consider a SOM that consists of a set of $\mathbf{K}$ nodes $\mathcal{V} = \{\mathbf{v_1}, \mathbf{v_2}, ..., \mathbf{v_K}\}$ on a two-dimensional gird. To model $\mathbf{z}_r$, during training, a weight vector $\mathbf{w}_v$ is learned for each node $\mathbf{v}$ to store a specific type of the latent variable $\mathbf{z}_r$. Given the distribution of $\mathbf{z}_r$, its best matching unit (BMU) on SOM is found by:

$$v_{\text{BMU}} = \text{argmin}_{v \in \mathcal{V}} \|\mathbb{E}[\mathbf{z}_r] - \mathbf{w}_v\|^2, \tag{3}$$

Based on the BMU, weight vectors of each node $v \in \mathcal{V}$ (including the BMU) can be updated as:

$$\mathbf{w}_v \leftarrow \mathbf{w}_v + \gamma N(v, v_{\text{BMU}})(\mathbb{E}[\mathbf{z}_r] - \mathbf{w}_{v_{\text{BMU}}}), \tag{4}$$

where γ is the learning rate, and $\mathbf{N}(\mathbf{v}, \mathbf{v}_{\text{BMU}})$ is a neighborhood function (*e.g.*, Gaussian or triangular) that has higher value when $\mathbf{v}$ and $\mathbf{v}_{\text{BMU}}$ are closer on SOM, which can be loosely determined by SOM rules of thumb. At test time, the embedding of the test samples in the latent space are used to find the BMU in the SOM and assigning the error source label as discussed in Sect. 2.2.

Variatioanl Inference: We derive the modified evidence lower bound (ELBO) of the log conditional likelihood of $p(\mathbf{H}_f|\mathbf{H}_i)$ with β parameter as:

$$\log p(\mathbf{H}_f|\mathbf{H}_i) \geq \mathcal{L}_{ELBO} = E_{\mathbf{z}_r \sim q(\mathbf{z}_r|\mathbf{H}_i, \mathbf{H}_f)} p(\mathbf{H}_f|\mathbf{z}_r, \mathbf{H}_i) \\ -\beta D_{KL}(q(\mathbf{z}_r|\mathbf{H}_i, \mathbf{H}_f)\|p(\mathbf{z}_r)) \tag{5}$$

where we add a hyperparameter β to the second term. We use a variational distribution $q(\mathbf{z}_r|\mathbf{H}_i, \mathbf{H}_f)$, parameterized by an inference network as illustrated in the brown encoder in Fig. 1, to approximate the intractable posterior distribution. Mimicking the structure of a conditional variational auto-encoder (VAE), the conditioning of the encoder on $\mathbf{H}_i$ further encourages $\mathbf{z}_r$ to focus on learning the residual between $\mathbf{H}_i$ and $\mathbf{H}_f$. Overall, The first term in Eq. (5) encourages the reconstruction of the desired $\mathbf{H}_f$ given the mechanistic forward operator $\mathbf{H}_i$. The second term regularizes $q(\mathbf{z}_r|\mathbf{H}_i, \mathbf{H}_f)$ with a prior distribution $p(\mathbf{z})$, which we assume to be an isotropic Gaussian.

We also note that, without additional regularization, learning with the above loss can collapse to a trivial solution where the model may ignore the conditioning on $\mathbf{H}_i$ and learn to directly model $\mathbf{H}_f$ instead. To avoid this, we ask the model to generate $\mathbf{H}_i$ if the variational encoder is presented with a pair of identical operators (*i.e.*, no residual to be uncovered). This gives rise to a combined loss:

$$L = L_{ELBO} + \lambda_{reg} * L_{recon}(\mathbf{H}_i, \dot{\mathbf{H}}_i) \tag{6}$$

where $L_{recon}(\mathbf{H}_i, \hat{\mathbf{H}}_i)$ is the added regularization term with hyperparameter λ_{reg}.

2.2 Inverse Estimation with Simultaneous Error Reduction

When seeking the inverse solution for a given observation $\mathbf{y}$, we are interested in utilizing the (partially) known physics behind the mechanistic forward operator $\mathbf{H}_i$ without being bounded by its potential errors. To do so, while estimating the inverse solution $\mathbf{u}$, we simultaneously optimize the latent variable $\mathbf{z}_r$ in the conditional generative model $\mathbf{G}(\mathbf{H}_i, \mathbf{z}_r)$ to account for the errors in $\mathbf{H}_i$. After embedding the conditional generative model in Eq. (1), it is reformulated as:

$$\hat{\mathbf{u}} = argmin_{\mathbf{u}}\|\mathbf{y} - \mathbf{G}(\mathbf{H}_i, \mathbf{z}_r)\mathbf{u}\| + \lambda \mathcal{R}(\mathbf{u}); \tag{7}$$

where $\mathbf{G}(\mathbf{H}_i, \mathbf{z}_r)$ is the mean of $p(\mathbf{H}_i, \mathbf{z}_r)$. As a choice of $\mathcal{R}(\mathbf{u})$ in this initial study, we consider the second-order Laplacian operator over the heart surface to enforce the spatial smoothness of the inverse solution.

In each iteration, the algorithm updates $\mathbf{H}_f$ by optimizing $\mathbf{z}_r$ with the BOBYQA algorithm [3], a derivative-free iterative algorithm for finding the minimum of a function within given bounds. This is expected to continuously reduce the error in the initial mechanistic forward operator of $\mathbf{H}_i$. With each updated $\mathbf{H}_f$, the estimate of $\mathbf{u}$ is updated by the second-order Tikhonov regularization. The iterations continue until minimal changes are produced in $\mathbf{u}$ and $\mathbf{H}_f$ between consecutive updates, or until the maximum number of iterations is completed.

Error Source Detection with SOM: Once we get the optimized latent values for the possible error in $\mathbf{H}_i$, we predict the error type using the trained SOM. Specifically, given the optimized value of $\mathbf{z}_r$, we find its BMU on the SOM map.

We then identify the source of error associated with $\mathbf{z}_r$ using the source label from the majority members associated with its BMU. In case the node selected was not associated with any training samples, we look for the next BMU.

3 Experiments

IMRE is trained on mechanistic forward operators generated with controlled errors due to a variety of factors such as translation, rotations, inhomogenity, and scaling of the heart and torso geometries. It is then evaluated in simulated and *in-vivo* real data experiments.

3.1 Datasets

Synthetic Data: We used the open-source SCI-Run software [10] to generate 600 mechanistic forward operators using the boundary element method on given heart-torso geometries obtained by transforming a base human heart with rotations along the X-, Y- and Z-axes in the range of $[-50°,20°],[-50°,20°]$, and $[-80°,10°]$, respectively, and translation along X-, Y- and Z-axes in $[-60, 60]$ millimeters. We also performed torso scaling in range of $[0.9,1.4]$ and varying conductivity values in $[0,0.13]$ for introducing inhomogenuity. The forward operators are exhaustively paired and are split into 80–20 ratio for training and testing. To evaluate IMRE in ECGi estimation, we used Aliev-Panfilov (AP) model [1] to simulate the extracellular potential considering three different origins of activation and generated the body-surface potential data using $\mathbf{H}_f$ with 35 DB Gaussian noise. In total IMRE is evaluated for inverse estimation across 75 sets of simulated data.

Real Data: We evaluated the trained IMRE on human data samples of body-surface recordings of two CRT patients [2,16], given the ground-truth of the pacing location. We compared the performance of IMRE with DAECGI [20], and the initial forward operators $\mathbf{H}_i$ generated with SCIRun software.

3.2 Generative Model Training

We trained the two encoders and the decoder simultaneously for 100 epochs with a batch size of 64 and latent dimension of 16. The value of β is set to. 0.001 and λ to 0.02. Both encoders have the same architecture; five convolutional layers followed by four fully connected layers. The decoder consists of three fully connected layers followed by transpose convolutions for up-sampling. We should note that the VAE encoder and decoder are connected through skip-connections as visualized in Fig. 1.

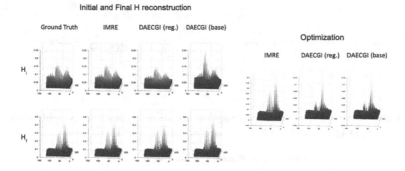

Fig. 2. Comparison of generative model accuracy. [20] is referred as DAECGI. Top left row shows reconstruction of $\mathbf{H}_i$ given no error, bottom right is $\mathbf{H}_f$ reconstruction and center right is optimized forward operator starting from $\mathbf{H}_i$.

Fig. 3. SOM pie chart: color of each node shows the dominant class in that particular node. Number of error classes are reduced for better visibility.

3.3   Evaluation of Generative Model

IMRE generative model is validated considering the following criteria: 1) successful reconstruction of $\mathbf{H}_f$, 2) generating diverse samples for any $\mathbf{H}_i$ and different residual errors $\mathbf{z}_\mathbf{r}$, and 3) reconstruction of $\mathbf{H}_i$ in the absence of error. Figure 2 compares our generative model with DAECGI which fails to reconstruct the $\mathbf{H}_i$ if not supplemented with proper regularization. This underscores our point that utilizing both the initial operator $\mathbf{H}_i$ and residual errors $\mathbf{z}_\mathbf{r}$ leads to a more accurate reconstruction of the final forward operator. The RMSE of $\mathbf{H}_i$ reconstruction given no error in each model is as follows; IMRE : 0.011, DAECGI with regularization (DAECGI(reg.)): 0.013, DAECGI without regularization (DAECGI(base)): 0.04 and for $\mathbf{H}_f$ reconstruction is; IMRE: 0.013, DAECGI(reg.): 0.013, DAECGI(base): 0.014 and the results after optimization is; IMRE: 0.011, DAECGI(reg.): 0.026, DAECGI(base): 0.026.

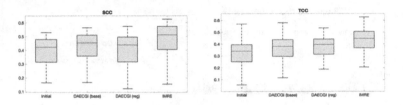

Fig. 4. Comparison of inverse reconstruction accuracy. From left to right: initial forward operator, DAECGI, DAECGI ith regularization, and IMRE (Ours).

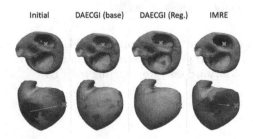

Fig. 5. Pacing location localization across two subjects presented in each row. From left to right, Initial ECGi solution, DAECGI with and without regularization, and IMRE final solution. The green and red cross are the ground-truth pacing locations. (Color figure online)

3.4   Evaluation of SOM

We use the Minisom [21] library for SOM implementation. After tuning the hyper-parameters, we used a SOM grid size of 40×40. We validated the SOM clustering ability by visualizing the clustered data samples in the SOM pie-chart. The clustering performance of this SOM map is crucial to identify the type of errors at test time. It is visible from Fig. 3 that the clusters are well-formed. Also, we note that the errors with an overlap in the error type are close to each other in nature. For example, the samples with both error type of x-translation and y-translation sometimes activate the nodes with x-translation or y-translation alone. The classification accuracy on the validation pairs in our simulation dataset is 71%.

3.5   Optimization: Inverse Estimation

After thorough validation of the generative model, we tested the complete optimization pipeline.

Synthetic Data Results: Since we have access to the ground forward operator in the synthetic data, we can easily compare the accuracy of the inverse solutions. Figure 4 compares the spatial and temporal correlation coefficients of inverse solutions obtained from initial forward operator, DAECGI with and without regularization, and IMRE, showing that IMRE outperforms the other methods.

Real Data Results: As we do not have the ground truth heart surface potential for the real data, we rely on plotting activation points shown in Fig. 5 to measure the effectiveness of different methods. The euclidean distance between each solution and the ground truth pacing location in Fig. 5 is; top - initial: 26.3, IMRE: 12.7; bottom - initial: 75.3, IMRE: 34.7. DAECGI failed in producing both results. It is evident from these results that our model shows significant improvement over initial H and DAECGI.

4 Conclusion

In this work, motivated by the importance of the physics underlying the forward and inverse imaging problems, we presented Interpretable Modeling and Reduction of Unknown Errors in Mechanistic Operators (IMRE). IMRE is a interpretable generative-model-based approach to image reconstruction that relies on the forward modeling physics but optimizes the underlying errors to deliver accurate inverse solutions. We showed that by separately modeling errors and forward operators, we can design a more interpretable neural network that leads to more accurate final solutions. This is an initial step towards interpretability in imaging and the current model is still not fully robust in detection of error types. Future work is required to investigate more sophisticated approaches for the interpretability of the latent space of residual errors.

Acknowledgement. This work is supported by the National Heart, Lung and Blood Institute (NHLBI) of the National Institutes of Health (NIH) under Award Number R01HL145590.

References

1. Aliev, R.R., Panfilov, A.V.: A simple two-variable model of cardiac excitation. Chaos Solitons Fractals **7**(3), 293–301 (1996). https://doi.org/10.1016/0960-0779(95)00089-5
2. Aras, K., et al.: Experimental data and geometric analysis repository-edgar. J. Electrocardiol. **48** (2015). https://doi.org/10.1016/j.jelectrocard.2015.08.008
3. Cartis, C., Fiala, J., Marteau, B., Roberts, L.: Improving the flexibility and robustness of model-based derivative-free optimization solvers (2018)
4. Chen, E.Z., Chen, T., Sun, S.: MRI image reconstruction via learning optimization using neural ODEs. In: Martel, A.L., et al. (eds.) MICCAI 2020. LNCS, vol. 12262, pp. 83–93. Springer, Cham (2020). https://doi.org/10.1007/978-3-030-59713-9_9
5. Formaggia, L., Quarteroni, A., Veneziani, A.: Complex Systems in Biomedicine. Springer, Milano (2006). https://doi.org/10.1007/88-470-0396-2
6. Ghimire, S., Dhamala, J., Gyawali, P., Sapp, J., Horacek, B., Wang, L.: Generative modeling and inverse imaging of cardiac transmembrane potential (2019)
7. Gulrajani, R.: The forward and inverse problems of electrocardiography. IEEE Eng. Med. Biol. Magaz. **17**(5), 84–101 (1998). https://doi.org/10.1109/51.715491
8. Horáek, B.M., Clements, J.C.: The inverse problem of electrocardiography: a solution in terms of single- and double-layer sources of the epicardial surface. Math. Biosci. **144**(2), 119–54 (1997)

9. Häggström, I., Schmidtlein, C., Campanella, G., Fuchs, T.: Deeppet: a deep encoder-decoder network for directly solving the pet image reconstruction inverse problem. Med. Image Anal. **54**, 253–262 (2019)

10. Institute, S.: sCIRun: A Scientific Computing Problem Solving Environment, Scientific Computing and Imaging Institute (SCI) (2016). http://www.scirun.org

11. Kohonen, T.: The self-organizing map. Proc. IEEE **78**(9), 1464–1480 (1990)

12. Lai, K.-W., Aggarwal, M., van Zijl, P., Li, X., Sulam, J.: Learned proximal networks for quantitative susceptibility mapping. In: Martel, A.L., et al. (eds.) MICCAI 2020. LNCS, vol. 12262, pp. 125–135. Springer, Cham (2020). https://doi.org/10.1007/978-3-030-59713-9_13

13. Lucas, A., Iliadis, M., Molina, R., Katsaggelos, A.K.: Using deep neural networks for inverse problems in imaging: beyond analytical methods. IEEE Signal Process. Magaz. **35**(1), 20–36 (2018). https://doi.org/10.1109/MSP.2017.2760358

14. Natterer, F., Wübbeling, F.: Mathematical Methods in Image Reconstruction. SIAM (2001)

15. Plonsey, R., Fleming, D.G.: Bioelectric Phenomena. McGraw-Hill (1989)

16. Potyagaylo, D., et al.: ECG adapted fastest route algorithm to localize the ectopic excitation origin in CRT patients. Front. Physiol. **10**, 183 (2019)

17. Ramanarayanan, S., Murugesan, B., Ram, K., Sivaprakasam, M.: DC-WCNN: a deep cascade of wavelet based convolutional neural networks for MR image reconstruction. In: 2020 IEEE 17th International Symposium on Biomedical Imaging (ISBI) (2020). https://doi.org/10.1109/isbi45749.2020.9098491

18. Ronneberger, O., Fischer, P., Brox, T.: U-Net: convolutional networks for biomedical image segmentation. In: Navab, N., Hornegger, J., Wells, W.M., Frangi, A.F. (eds.) MICCAI 2015. LNCS, vol. 9351, pp. 234–241. Springer, Cham (2015). https://doi.org/10.1007/978-3-319-24574-4_28

19. Throne, R., Olson, L.: The effects of errors in assumed conductivities and geometry on numerical solutions to the inverse problem of electrocardiography. IEEE Trans. Biomed. Eng. **42**(12), 1192–1200 (1995). https://doi.org/10.1109/10.476126

20. Toloubidokhti, M., et al.: Deep adaptive electrocardiographic imaging with generative forward model for error reduction. In: Ennis, D.B., Perotti, L.E., Wang, V.Y. (eds.) FIMH 2021. LNCS, vol. 12738, pp. 471–481. Springer, Cham (2021). https://doi.org/10.1007/978-3-030-78710-3_45

21. Vettigli, G.: Minisom: minimalistic and numpy-based implementation of the self organizing map (2018). https://github.com/JustGlowing/minisom/

Sparse Interpretation of Graph Convolutional Networks for Multi-modal Diagnosis of Alzheimer's Disease

Houliang Zhou[1], Yu Zhang[2], Brian Y. Chen[1], Li Shen[3], and Lifang He[1(✉)]

[1] Department of Computer Science and Engineering,
Lehigh University, Lehigh, PA, USA
{hoz421,lih319}@lehigh.edu
[2] Department of Bioengineering, Lehigh University, Lehigh, PA, USA
[3] Department of Biostatistics, Epidemiology and Informatics,
University of Pennsylvania, Pennsylvania, PA, USA

Abstract. The interconnected quality of brain regions in neurological disease has immense importance for the development of biomarkers and diagnostics. While Graph Convolutional Network (GCN) methods are fundamentally compatible with discovering the connected role of brain regions in disease, current methods apply limited consideration for node features and their connectivity in brain network analysis. In this paper, we propose a sparse interpretable GCN framework (SGCN) for the identification and classification of Alzheimer's disease (AD) using brain imaging data with multiple modalities. SGCN applies an attention mechanism with sparsity to identify the most discriminative subgraph structure and important node features for the detection of AD. The model learns the sparse importance probabilities for each node feature and edge with entropy, ℓ_1, and mutual information regularization. We then utilized this information to find signature regions of interest (ROIs), and emphasize the disease-specific brain network connections by detecting the significant difference of connectives between regions in healthy control (HC), and AD groups. We evaluated SGCN on the ADNI database with imaging data from three modalities, including VBM-MRI, FDG-PET, and AV45-PET, and observed that the important probabilities it learned are effective for disease status identification and the sparse interpretability of disease-specific ROI features and connections. The salient ROIs detected and the most discriminative network connections interpreted by our method show a high correspondence with previous neuroimaging evidence associated with AD.

Keywords: Sparse interpretation · Graph convolutional network · Neuroimaging · Multi-modality

1 Introduction

Neuroimaging pattern classification methods demonstrated recent advances in the prediction of Alzheimer's disease (AD) and mild cognitive impairment (MCI)

© The Author(s), under exclusive license to Springer Nature Switzerland AG 2022
L. Wang et al. (Eds.): MICCAI 2022, LNCS 13438, pp. 469–478, 2022.
https://doi.org/10.1007/978-3-031-16452-1_45

from the positron emission tomography (PET) and magnetic resonance imaging (MRI) scans [4, 8, 22]. Representing the brain as a connectivity graph have made a large improvements in understanding the brain mechanisms behind the diseases [3, 11, 16]. In this brain connectivity graph, nodes are regarded as the brain regions of interest (ROIs) and edges are regarded as the connectivity between those ROIs. This graph representation is highly compatible with the Graph Convolutional Network (GCN) based deep learning method, which has demonstrated the strong capabilities for analyzing the graph structured information [6, 10, 25].

In neuroimaging, GCN model has been widely used to analyze the brain connectivity graph, identify the salient ROIs and discover neurological biomarkers [3, 11]. In the graph classification problem, the explainability of GCN predictions plays an important role in identifying and localizing biomarkers that contribute most to the derivation of AD or MCI. Several graph based approaches have been proposed to interpret the GCN model (e.g., [13, 17, 21, 24, 27]). However, most of them did not target on the disease prediction. Generally, recent interpreting methods focused only on the single modality imaging data, and lacked a joint consideration between multi-modal node feature and their connectivity in brain disease analysis [3, 11]. Because the subjects within the same disease can share the similar abnormal patterns in the brain network, the group-level explanations are crucial for identifying the salient ROIs and discovering the most discriminative brain network connections related to AD and MCI. Recent studies also indicated that multi-modal brain imaging can provide essential complementary information to improve accuracy in disease diagnosis [2, 12, 26].

In this paper, we propose a sparse interpretable GCN framework (SGCN) for the identification and classification of AD using multi-modality brain imaging data. We utilize attention mechanism by importance probability with sparse technique to interpret the salient ROIs and identify the most discriminative subgraph structure for each subject in HC, AD, and MCI categories. In the results, our method exhibited high classification performance, and our ablation study demonstrated the effectiveness of mutual information loss and the sparsity of ℓ_1 and entropy regularization loss. Our interpretation method revealed that the hippocampus biomarker and the prominent network connections within Memory Network, Bilateral Limbic Network, and Default Mode Network were important for distinguishing HC, AD and MCI. The two-sample t-test on learned brain graph demonstrates that our proposed method with multi-modality imaging feature interprets the most discriminative connections between HC and AD group, suggesting that the multi-modality imaging information provide much more potential value for AD's diagnosis. These results point to applications for our method in the interpretation of ROIs and brain network connections from multi-modality imaging data.

The major contributions of this work can be summarized as follows: 1) the application of the sparse interpretation for the identification of salient ROIs and prominent disease-specific network connections; 2) the integration of multi-modality brain imaging data to construct the brain connectivity graph; 3) the extension of GCN model with importance probabilities for each node feature and edge to improve the performance of disease status prediction.

2 Methods

2.1 Data Acquisition and Preprocessing

In this work, the brain imaging data were obtained from the public Alzheimer's Disease Neuroimaging Initiative (ADNI) [15]. The neuroimaging data contained 755 non-Hispanic Caucasian participants in total, including 182 HC subjects, 476 MCI subjects, and 97 AD subjects respectively. The image data consisted of three modalities including structural Magnetic Resonance Imaging (VBM-MRI), 18 F-fluorodeoxyglucose Positron Emission Tomography (FDG-PET), and 18 F-florbetapir PET (AV45-PET).

In the preprocessing, the multi-modality imaging scans were aligned to each participant's same visit. Generally, all imaging scans were aligned to a T1-weighted template image, and segmented into gray matter (GM), white matter (WM) and cerebrospinal fluid (CSF) maps. They were normalized to the standard Montreal Neurological Institute (MNI) space as $2 \times 2 \times 2$ mm^3 voxels, being smoothed with an 8 mm FWHM kernel. We preprocessed the structural MRI scans with voxel-based morphometry (VBM) by using the SPM software [1], and registered the FDG-PET and AV45-PET scans to the MNI space by SPM. We subsampled the whole brain imaging and contained 90 ROIs (excluding the cerebellum and vermis) based on the AAL-90 atlas [19]. ROI-level measures were calculated by averaging all the voxel-level measures within each ROI.

2.2 Brain Graph Construction

In the construction of brain connectivity graph, all of three modalities are concatenated into the feature vector for each ROI. We define a graph adjacency matrix $A \in \mathbb{R}^{N \times N}$ and multi-modal node feature matrix $X \in \mathbb{R}^{N \times D}$, where N is the number of ROIs and D is the multi-modal dimension. The ROIs and their connectivity in the brain can be represented as an undirected weighted graph $G = (V, E)$. In the graph, the vertex set $V = \{v_1, \cdots, v_N\}$ consists of ROIs and the edges in E are weighted by the connection strength between ROIs. In our work, we define $\widetilde{G} = (V, \widetilde{E})$ based on the multi-modal information of the ROIs using K-Nearest Neighbor (KNN) graph method [26]. In the KNN graph, the edges are weighted by the Gaussian similarity function of Euclidean distances, i.e., $e(v_i, v_j) = \exp(-\frac{\|v_i - v_j\|^2}{2\sigma^2})$. We define N_i as the set of K nearest neighbors of vertex v_i. We use the weighted adjacency matrix A to represent the similarity between each ROI and its nearest similar neighboring ROIs. The element of weighted adjacency matrix A is represented as follows:

$$A_{i,j} = \begin{cases} e(v_i, v_j), & \text{if } v_i \in N_j \text{ or } v_j \in N_i \\ 0, & \text{otherwise.} \end{cases} \tag{1}$$

2.3 Sparse Interpretability of GCN

Importance Probabilities as the Interpretation. Given the weighted brain network G and node feature matrix X are normally very noisy, the original input

G and X into the GCN model Φ may not be entirely useful for the disease identification. Therefore, we postulate that an important subgraph $G_s \subseteq G$ and a subset of multi-modality feature $X_s = \{x_i | v_i \in G_s\}$ contribute most to the prediction of patients. To find the X_s and G_s, we propose to learn a globally shared multi-modality feature importance probability P_X, and the individual edge importance probability P_A based on the source and target node feature for each subject. We define $G_s = A \odot P_A$, and $X_s = X \odot P_X$. Then the prediction output $\hat{y}$ of the GCN model Φ can be expressed as: $\hat{y} = \Phi(A \odot P_A, X \odot P_X)$. In this equation, we translate the problem on exploring the subgraph and the subset of node feature into the inference of two importance probability P_X and P_A. We apply them on the individual brain network and node feature across all subjects in HC, AD, and MCI groups.

Because we assume that different modalities of each ROI have different contributions to the prediction of disease, we define the multi-modality feature importance probability $P_X \in \mathbb{R}^{N \times D}$, and $P_X = [p_1, p_2, ..., p_N]$, where $p_i \in \mathbb{R}^D, 1 \leq i \leq N$, denotes the feature probability for each ROI. Considering the joint connection between brain multi-modality node feature and their connectivity, we define the edge importance probability $P_A \in \mathbb{R}^{N \times N}$ for the node i and j as:

$$P_{A_{i,j}} = \sigma(v^T[x_i \odot p_i \| x_j \odot p_j]) \tag{2}$$

where $v \in \mathbb{R}^{2D}$ is the learnable parameter, p_i is multi-modality feature probability of node i, $\odot$ denotes the Hadamard element-wise product, and $\|$ denotes the concatenation. In this equation, the edge importance probability are adjusted by the combination of multi-modality node feature and their feature probability. It is beneficial to identify the important connections based on the information from multi-modality node feature.

Loss Function. In this part, we introduce the mutual information loss to determine the P_X and P_A, and the ℓ_1 and entropy regularization loss to induce the sparsity on them. The method to generate the interpretation of GCN is to find the subgraph G_s and the subset of node feature X_s, which has the maximum mutual information with the truth label distribution. Specifically, we train the importance probability P_X and P_A by maximizing the mutual information between the true label y on the original graph G and the prediction output $\hat{y}$ on the subgraph G_s and the subset of node feature X_s. We suppose there are C disease classes, and the mutual information loss $\mathcal{L}_m$ can be calculated as:

$$\mathcal{L}_m = -\sum_{c=1}^{C} \mathbb{1}[y = c] \log P_\Phi(\hat{y} = y | G_s = A \odot P_A, X_s = X \odot P_X) \tag{3}$$

The mutual information loss is optimized to infer importance probability P_X and P_A for the improvement of disease prediction. We further apply ℓ_1 and entropy regularization loss in order to induce the sparsity on P_X and P_A. The ℓ_1 regularization loss on P_X and P_A can be defined as:

$$\mathcal{L}_s = \|P_X\|_1 + \|P_A\|_1 \tag{4}$$

The element-wise entropy loss to encourage discreteness in probability values can be defined as:

$$\mathcal{L}_{P_A,e} = -(P_A \log(P_A) + (1 - P_A)\log(1 - P_A)) \tag{5}$$

where $\mathcal{L}_{P_A,e}$ denotes the entropy loss on P_A. The entropy loss $\mathcal{L}_{P_X,e}$ on P_X is defined as the same way. We summarize the entropy regularization loss as $\mathcal{L}_e = \mathcal{L}_{P_X,e} + \mathcal{L}_{P_A,e}$.

Both ℓ_1 and entropy regularization loss can induce the sparsity on P_X and P_A by driving the unimportant or noisy entries towards zero. In the meanwhile, the entropy regularization loss can induce the important feature and important edge to have higher probabilities towards one for the disease identification. Our final training objective can be defined as:

$$\mathcal{L} = \mathcal{L}_c + \lambda_1 \mathcal{L}_m + \lambda_2 \mathcal{L}_s + \lambda_3 \mathcal{L}_e \tag{6}$$

where $\mathcal{L}_c$ is the supervised cross-entropy disease prediction loss, and λ's are the tunable hyper-parameters as the penalty coefficients for the different regularization losses. The solution on loss function $\mathcal{L}$ is similar to the GCN method except for the parameters P_X and P_A. In our experiment, the importance probability P_X and P_A provide the interpretation for the salient ROIs and the prominent disease-specific brain network connections.

3 Results

Classification Performance. In our experiments, the whole data were separated into three groups, including HC vs. AD, HC vs. MCI, and MCI vs. AD, for the examination of SGCN's classification results. The one-against-one strategy was used to classify three different groups and compare the average classification results by using one, two or three modalities. This experimental design can measure the SGCN's performance on different numbers of modalities and on different groups. In the construction of the brain connectivity graphs, we set $K = 10$ to construct the KNN graph for each subject. We calculate the classification result by using a training framework, including three graph convolutional layers, three fully-connected layers with a dropout layer, and a softmax classifier. For the parameters of loss function, we set λ_1 to 1, λ_2 to 0.01, and λ_3 to 0.1 in each loss term. The 5-fold cross validation was performed. The experiment was repeated for 10 times to get the results. The average classification scores including accuracy, ROC-AUC, sensitivity, and specificity with their standard deviations are reported.

Tables 1, 2 and 3 show the classification results by using one, two and three modalities, respectively, where ± represents the standard deviation of evaluation scores in 5 folds. We compared our method with SVM using RBF kernel, Random Forest (RF), MLP and CNN models, which take vectorized adjacency matrices as inputs. We also compared our method with other GCN methods: GCN [10], GAT [20], and GraphSAGE [7]. The best classification performance was achieved by our method when using all three modalities. Based on these results, all modalities were used to evaluate the ablation study and the interpretability of our model.

Ablation Study. We conduct an ablation study to validate the effectiveness of each loss term of our model on the classification performance on three groups including HC vs. AD, HC vs. MCI, and MCI vs. AD. We reported the average score of the classification performance. In Table 4, we quantitatively measures the effectiveness of different losses on the identification of diseases. The mutual information loss $\mathcal{L}_m$ is crucial to find the important subgraph G_s and the important subset of node feature X_s to identify the specific disease. Without $\mathcal{L}_m$, the sensitivity score of our model will drop a lot from the results. We also ablate the sparse regularization loss $\mathcal{L}_s$ and $\mathcal{L}_e$, which leads to induce the important feature and important edge to have higher probabilities towards one, otherwise towards zero. Without them, the accuracy and sensitivity of classification performance will drop a little bit, and the interpretability of our model on the salient ROIs and the prominent brain network connections can become worse. The best classification performance was achieved when combining full loss terms together.

Interpretation of Salient ROIs. After training models for the ADNI datasets, to summarize the salient ROIs between HC and AD, we average the feature importance probability P_X across different modalities and obtain a set of scalar scores for each ROI. We then rank these scores in descending order and keep the top 20 salient ROIs. Figure 1(a-c) shows the salient ROIs in lateral, medial, and ventral view of brain surface by the single modality. Figure 1(d) illustrates the interpreted salient ROIs from all modalities. In Fig. 1(d), we found the hippocampus and the parietal lobe regions were important for the identification of

Table 1. One Modality. Classification comparison using VBM only.

Measures	SVM	RF	MLP	CNN	GCN	GAT	GraphSAGE	SGCN
Accuracy	.703 ±.045	.719 ±.028	.724 ±.062	.721 ±.035	.743 ±.068	.755 ±.072	.759 ±.065	**.772 ±.052**
ROC-AUC	.753 ±.061	.751 ±.029	.742 ±.049	.669 ±.115	.737 ±.052	.748 ±.049	.754 ±.054	**.761 ±.042**
Sensitivity	.522 ±.073	.568 ±.043	.615 ±.078	.611 ±.118	.702 ±.074	.708 ±.051	.714 ±.062	**.725 ±.053**
Specificity	.701 ±.078	.669 ±.039	.665 ±.036	.652 ±.084	.731 ±.045	.737 ±.053	.743 ±.068	**.751 ±.046**

Table 2. Two Modalities. Classification comparison using VBM and FDG.

Measures	SVM	RF	MLP	CNN	GCN	GAT	GraphSAGE	SGCN
Accuracy	.716 ±.043	.721 ±.041	.729 ±.049	.722 ±.037	.776 ±.052	.782 ±.049	.785 ±.053	**.797 ±.047**
ROC-AUC	.722 ±.054	.795 ±.036	.773 ±.057	.689 ±.085	.742 ±.042	.753 ±.039	.761 ±.041	**.801 ±.035**
Sensitivity	.443 ±.118	.591 ±.076	.621 ±.051	.597 ±.066	.705 ±.081	.712 ±.075	.725 ±.061	**.758 ±.067**
Specificity	.783 ±.048	.679 ±.074	.668 ±.046	.662 ±.067	.762 ±.045	.792 ±.053	.783 ±.068	**.817 ±.065**

Table 3. Three Modalities. Classification comparison using three modalities.

Measures	SVM	RF	MLP	CNN	GCN	GAT	GraphSAGE	SGCN
Accuracy	.723 ±.053	.726 ±.033	.728 ±.047	.756 ±.036	.787 ±.058	.795 ±.063	.803 ±.048	**.826 ±.038**
ROC-AUC	.788 ±.042	.811 ±.034	.765 ±.041	.679 ±.063	.779 ±.049	.792 ±.054	.797 ±.042	**.823 ±.034**
Sensitivity	.581 ±.087	.610 ±.054	.669 ±.043	.624 ±.102	.736 ±.085	.739 ±.073	.743 ±.065	**.782 ±.047**
Specificity	.767 ±.079	.682 ±.027	.648 ±.058	.685 ±.049	.801 ±.073	.807 ±.042	.819 ±.077	**.839 ±.054**

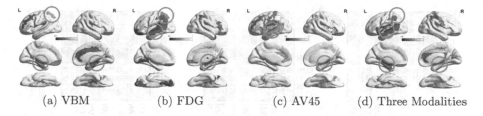

(a) VBM   (b) FDG   (c) AV45   (d) Three Modalities

Fig. 1. Interpreting top 20 salient ROIs based on the importance probability P_X between different modalities. The bright-yellow color indicates a high score. The common detected salient ROIs across different modalities are circled in blue. (Color figure online)

AD, which is consistent with previous evidence for the derivation of AD [9,14]. In Fig. 1, these ROIs are circled in blue. The right hippocampus has been detected by all single modality, and the score of this region in AV45 is larger. The left hippocampus has only been obtained in VBM. Meanwhile, the parietal lobes were identified in all single modalities except AV45. Combining all modalities detects all the above regions. These results suggest that combining all modalities can better support the interpretation of salient ROIs for biomarker detection.

Interpretation of Brain Network Connections. In the brain network analysis, the ROIs can be partitioned into the neural systems based on the structural and functional roles under a specific atlas, which are beneficial to verify our interpretation from the neuroscience perspective [23]. We mapped ROIs on the AAL-90 atlas into eight commonly used neural systems, including Visual Network (VN), Auditory Network (AN), Bilateral Limbic Network (BLN), Default Mode Network (DMN), Somato-Motor Network (SMN), Subcortical Network (SCN), Memory Network (MN) and Cognitive Control Network (CCN).

In Fig. 2, we measured the effectiveness of edge importance probabilities P_A on the identification of AD. The Fig. 2(a) shows the average KNN graph on AD group. The Fig. 2(b) shows the average sparse result by element-wise multiplying the KNN graph with P_A in our proposed method. The Fig. 2(c) illustrates the sparsity of average P_A, which induces the important network connections to have higher probabilities towards one and unimportant one towards zero. This result demonstrates the sparse effectiveness of P_A on the original KNN graph.

Table 4. Ablation study of loss terms on our sparse GCN model.

Model	Accuracy	ROC-AUC	Sensitivity	Specificity
SGCN(all)	.826 ±.038	.823 ±.034	.782 ±.047	.839 ±.054
SGCN(w/o $\mathcal{L}_s$)	.809 ±.045	.803 ±.049	.773 ±.051	.821 ±.075
SGCN(w/o $\mathcal{L}_e$)	.811 ±.043	.813 ±.042	.771 ±.046	.827 ±.052
SGCN(w/o $\mathcal{L}_s$ & $\mathcal{L}_e$)	.806 ±.059	.798 ±.038	.765 ±.053	.826 ±.045
SGCN(w/o $\mathcal{L}_m$)	.793 ±.047	.785 ±.067	.742 ±.064	.806 ±.071

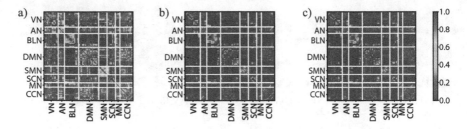

Fig. 2. Comparison between the KNN graph and the sparse interpretation of prominent brain network connections on AD group. (a) is the heatmap from the mean of KNN graph; (b) is the heatmap from the mean of sparse brain graph; (c) is the mean of probability P_A. The dark-red color indicates a high score. (Color figure online)

Two-sample t-tests were further applied on sparse brain graph in order to identify the most discriminative connections between HC and AD group. The Fig. 3(a) shows the t value of the discriminative connections by using all three modalities. In Fig. 3(b), we average the absolute t value of the discriminative connections within each module and normalize them to compare the interpretation using one, two, and three modalities respectively. The reported t value of one and two modalities are the average results from all single and double modalities. From the Fig. 3(b), we have the following observations. The t values are higher in VN, AN, DMN, CCN, MN, and SMN when using multiple modalities. In fact, the connections within MN disappear when only using a single modality, while they become the strongest one using all three modalities. Most discriminative connections within MN, SMN, DMN and CCN systems are found when using all three modalities instead of two or one modality. These discriminative connection patterns show a high correspondence with some previous neuroimaging evidence for the derivation of AD [5,14,18]. The connective patterns interpreted by our method within the neural systems between HC and AD are enhanced with additional modalities of imaging data.

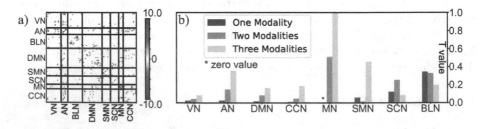

Fig. 3. (a) The significance difference of the most discriminative interpreted connections between HC and AD group were evaluated by two-sample t-tests with false discovery rate (FDR) corrected p-value < 0.05. The dark-red and dark-blue indicates the big positive and negative t values. (b) The normalized t value of the most discriminative ROI connections were reported by using multi-modalities in each neural system. (Color figure online)

4   Conclusions

In this paper, we proposed a sparse interpretable GCN framework for the identification and classification of Alzheimer's disease (AD) using multi-modal brain imaging data. We applied the attention mechanism by importance probability with sparse technique to interpret the salient ROIs and the prominent brain network connections. We found that the hippocampus region and the connections within MN, DMN, SMN, and CCN were consistent with established experimental findings [5,14]. We extended the current explanation method of GCN model to discover the neurological biomakers and identify the most discriminative network connections for multi-modal brain imaging analysis. Besides the promising classification performance, our interpretation of brain network connections demonstrated the most discriminative connective patterns between HC, MCI and AD groups. This suggests that our method can be applied to interpret the salient ROIs and prominent brain network connections with additional modalities of imaging data. Our approach is of wide general interest as it can be applied to other diseases when multi-modality data are available.

Acknowledgements. This work was supported in part by the National Institutes of Health [R01 LM013463, U01 AG068057, R01 AG066833].

References

1. Ashburner, J., Friston, K.J.: Voxel-based morphometry-the methods. Neuroimage **11**(6), 805–821 (2000)
2. Calhoun, V.D., Sui, J.: Multimodal fusion of brain imaging data: a key to finding the missing link(s) in complex mental illness. Biol. Psychiat. Cognit. Neurosci. Neuroimag. **1**(3), 230–244 (2016)
3. Cui, H., Dai, W., Zhu, Y., Li, X., He, L., Yang, C.: BrainNNExplainer: an interpretable graph neural network framework for brain network based disease analysis. In: ICML Workshop on Interpretable Machine Learning in Healthcare (2021)
4. Du, L., et al.: Multi-task sparse canonical correlation analysis with application to multi-modal brain imaging genetics. IEEE/ACM Trans. Comput. Biol. Bioinf. (2019)
5. Gaugler, J., James, B., Johnson, T.: Alzheimer's Disease Facts and Figures. Alzheimer's Association (2021)
6. Gilmer, J., Schoenholz, S.S., Riley, P.F., Vinyals, O., Dahl, G.E.: Neural message passing for quantum chemistry. In: ICML, pp. 1263–1272. PMLR (2017)
7. Hamilton, W., Ying, Z., Leskovec, J.: Inductive representation learning on large graphs. Adv. Neural Inf. Process. Syst. **30** (2017)
8. Izquierdo, W., et al.: Robust prediction of cognitive test scores in Alzheimer's patients. In: SPMB, pp. 1–7. IEEE (2017)
9. Jacobs, H.I., Van Boxtel, M.P., Jolles, J., Verhey, F.R., Uylings, H.B.: Parietal cortex matters in Alzheimer's disease: an overview of structural, functional and metabolic findings. Neurosci. Biobehav. Rev. **36**(1), 297–309 (2012)
10. Kipf, T.N., Welling, M.: Semi-supervised classification with graph convolutional networks. In: ICLR (2017)

11. Li, X., et al.: BrainGNN: interpretable brain graph neural network for FMRI analysis. Med. Image Anal. 102233 (2021)
12. Li, Y., Liu, J., Gao, X., Jie, B., Kim, M., Yap, P.T., Wee, C.Y., Shen, D.: Multimodal hyper-connectivity of functional networks using functionally-weighted lasso for MCI classification. Med. Image Anal. **52**, 80–96 (2019)
13. Luo, D., et al.: Parameterized explainer for graph neural network. In: NeurIPS (2020)
14. Mu, Y., Gage, F.H.: Adult hippocampal neurogenesis and its role in Alzheimer's disease. Molecul. Neurodegen. **6**(1), 1–9 (2011)
15. Mueller, S.G., et al.: The Alzheimer's disease neuroimaging initiative. Neuroimag. Clin. **15**(4), 869–877 (2005)
16. Rykhlevskaia, E., Gratton, G., Fabiani, M.: Combining structural and functional neuroimaging data for studying brain connectivity: a review. Psychophysiology **45**(2), 173–187 (2008)
17. Safai, A., et al.: Multimodal brain connectomics based prediction of Parkinson's disease using graph attention networks. Front. Neurosci. 1903 (2022)
18. Surendranathan, A., McKiernan, E.: Dementia and the brain. In: Alzheimer's Society (2019)
19. Tzourio-Mazoyer, N., et al.: Automated anatomical labeling of activations in SPM using a macroscopic anatomical parcellation of the MNI MRI single-subject brain. Neuroimage **15**(1), 273–289 (2002)
20. Veličković, P., Cucurull, G., Casanova, A., Romero, A., Lio, P., Bengio, Y.: Graph attention networks. arXiv preprint arXiv:1710.10903 (2017)
21. Vu, M.N., Thai, M.T.: PGM-explainer: probabilistic graphical model explanations for graph neural networks. In: NeurIPS (2020)
22. Wang, H., et al.: Sparse multi-task regression and feature selection to identify brain imaging predictors for memory performance. In: ICCV, pp. 557–562. IEEE (2011)
23. Xu, M., Wang, Z., Zhang, H., Pantazis, D., Wang, H., Li, Q.: A new graph gaussian embedding method for analyzing the effects of cognitive training. PLoS Comput. Biol. **16**(9), e1008186 (2020)
24. Ying, R., Bourgeois, D., You, J., Zitnik, M., Leskovec, J.: GNNExplainer: generating explanations for graph neural networks. In: NeurIPS, vol. 32, p. 9240. NIH Public Access (2019)
25. Zhang, M., Cui, Z., Neumann, M., Chen, Y.: An end-to-end deep learning architecture for graph classification. In: AAAI (2018)
26. Zhang, X., He, L., Chen, K., Luo, Y., Zhou, J., Wang, F.: Multi-view graph convolutional network and its applications on neuroimage analysis for Parkinson's disease. In: AMIA Annual Symposium Proceedings, vol. 2018, p. 1147. American Medical Informatics Association (2018)
27. Zhou, H., He, L., Zhang, Y., Shen, L., Chen, B.: Interpretable graph convolutional network of multi-modality brain imaging for Alzheimer's disease diagnosis. In: 2022 IEEE 19th International Symposium on Biomedical Imaging (ISBI), pp. 1–5. IEEE (2022)

Machine Learning – Uncertainty

FUSSNet: Fusing Two Sources of Uncertainty for Semi-supervised Medical Image Segmentation

Jinyi Xiang[1], Peng Qiu[2], and Yang Yang[1(✉)]

[1] Department of Computer Science and Engineering, Shanghai Jiao Tong University, Shanghai, China
yangyang@cs.sjtu.edu.cn
[2] Department of Vascular Surgery, Shanghai Ninth People's Hospital Affiliated to Shanghai Jiao Tong University, Shanghai, China

Abstract. In recent years, various semi-supervised learning (SSL) methods have been developed to deal with the scarcity of labeled data in medical image segmentation. Especially, many of them focus on the uncertainty caused by a lack of knowledge (about the best model), i.e. epistemic uncertainty (EU). Besides EU, another type of uncertainty, aleatoric uncertainty (AU), originated from irreducible errors or noise, also commonly exists in medical imaging data. While previous SSL approaches focus on only one of them (mostly EU), this study shows that SSL segmentation models can benefit more by considering both sources of uncertainty. The proposed FUSSNet framework is featured by a joint learning scheme, which combines the EU-guided unsupervised learning and AU-guided supervised learning. We assess the method on two benchmark datasets for the segmentation of left atrium (LA) and pancreas, respectively. The experimental results show that FUSSNet outperforms the state-of-the-art semi-supervised segmentation methods by over 2% on Dice score for pancreas data and almost reaches the accuracy obtained in fully supervised setting for LA data.

Keywords: Semi-supervised learning · Uncertainty-guided training · Medical image segmentation

1 Introduction

Automatic segmentation for medical images is a notoriously difficult job due to the lack of large-scale and high-quality labeled datasets, as collecting annotated data requires specific domain knowledge and can be prohibitively time-consuming, especially for volumetric data. To exploit the vast amounts of unlabeled data, semi-supervised learning (SSL) has received considerable attention [8,18].

Supplementary Information The online version contains supplementary material available at https://doi.org/10.1007/978-3-031-16452-1_46.

L. Wang et al. (Eds.): MICCAI 2022, LNCS 13438, pp. 481–491, 2022.
https://doi.org/10.1007/978-3-031-16452-1_46

One line of SSL methods focuses on consistency-based regularization [2, 11, 24], which employs consistency constraints over unlabeled data, like Π-model and temporal ensembling strategy [7], mean-teacher framework [18], and dual-task consistency network [10]. The other line relies on pseudo labeling [20], i.e. utilizing model's predictions for unlabeled data as their supervision. To alleviate overfitting and confirmation bias caused by pseudo labels, some studies aimed to generate good pseudo labels or data-label pairs [1, 17, 23, 25]; others proposed to utilize pseudo labels in an epistemic uncertainty (EU)-aware manner (EU refers to the ignorance of the model, which could be reduced by sufficient training samples or additional information [4]). For instance, Yu et al. [22] used Monte Carlo dropout to estimate an EU map, and imposed the consistency constraint between teacher and student network accordingly. Shi et al. [16] identified uncertain areas by using the outputs yielded by multiple decoders with cross-entropy (CE) losses, and treated certain and uncertain areas differently.

While epistemic uncertainty has caught great attention in SSL studies, the irreducible aleatoric uncertainty (AU) is often neglected in the existing segmentation systems. AU arises from inherent ambiguities and random effect in data itself, like blurry tissue boundaries in medical images. Kendall and Gal [5] studied uncertainties in computer vision and modeled AU through Bayesian deep learning models. Kohl et al. [6] proposed to combine U-Net with conditional variational autoencoder to model spatially correlated AU implicitly. Monteiro et al. [13] introduced an efficient probabilistic method for modelling AU by capturing joint distribution over entire label maps. In SSL scenarios, the lack of annotations makes models even more prone to this inherent uncertainty. Despite current progress in SSL models for medical image segmentation, the noisy and blurry cases have not been well addressed yet due to the ignorance of AU.

In this paper, we propose a novel semi-supervised segmentation framework integrating both EU and AU, corresponding to two training strategies, i.e. unsupervised EU-guided training and supervised AU-guided training. For the EU part, we design an EU assessment module to estimate an uncertainty mask. This module is an ensemble of decoders without Monte Carlo dropout. Instead of using differently weighted CE loss in [16], we use four decoders with different loss functions, resulting into more diverse predictions. Given the estimated mask, pseudo labels of certain areas can be directly used in training while consistency constraint is enforced over uncertain areas. For the AU part, we model AU by using multi-variate normal distribution and propose a new loss based on [13], leading to high efficiency and fast convergence. The two parts work together in the unified framework, FUSSNet, which exhibits distinct advantages over current SSL models. The contributions of this study are summarized below:

1) We propose FUSSNet for semi-supervised medical image segmentation, which enhances uncertainty-aware learning further by bringing AU into SSL. As far as we know, FUSSNet is the first attempt to fuse EU and AU for guiding the training in semi-supervised medical image segmentation.
2) We design a new EU assessment module based on an ensemble of decoders with different loss functions, which improves both the accuracy and efficiency of EU

assessment compared with the existing methods; and we also use a modified loss function in AU-guided learning to further reduces computation cost.

3) We apply FUSSNet to both CT and MRI datasets, which outperform the state-of-the-art SSL methods by a great margin.

2   Method

2.1   Problem Definition

Given a dataset $\mathcal{D}$, we have N labeled images and M unlabeled images, i.e. $\mathcal{D} = \{\mathcal{D}_l, \mathcal{D}_u\}$. We have image-label pairs $\mathcal{D}_l = \{(\boldsymbol{x}^i, \boldsymbol{y}^i)\}_{i=1}^{N}$ for labeled data and $\mathcal{D}_u = \{\boldsymbol{x}^i\}_{i=N+1}^{N+M}$ for unlabeled ones. Suppose each input image contains $H \times W \times D$ voxels, that is $\boldsymbol{x}^i \in \mathbb{R}^{H \times W \times D}$. And we have C classes to segment, which means $\boldsymbol{y}^i \in \{0, 1, \dots, C - 1\}^{H \times W \times D}$. We use $\hat{\boldsymbol{y}}$ to represent model's prediction.

2.2   The FUSSNet Framework

FUSSNet includes two training stages, namely pretraining and semi-supervised learning (SSL). The SSL part consists of three major components: i) the assessment for epistemic uncertainty (EU), ii) unsupervised learning for epistemic certain and uncertain areas, and iii) supervised learning by incorporating aleatoric uncertainty (AU) in the logit space. The overall architecture is shown in Fig. 1. The SSL stage proceeds in an iterative manner. In each iteration, we first estimate EU in images, i.e. delineating the EU mask. Based on the EU mask, we treat the certain and uncertain regions separately using pseudo label-based and consistency constraints-based training scheme, respectively. In the meantime, given the current parameters of networks, a supervised learning guided by AU is performed. Then, the total loss from the two parts are propagated backward to update the student model parameters.

2.3   Epistemic Uncertainty-Guided Training

Assessment of EU. Previous methods [16,19,22] have already demonstrated the necessity and benefits of using epistemic uncertainty as guidance when performing semi-supervised segmentation. They typically employ Monte Carlo (MC) dropout to derive an uncertainty weight map [19,22], which requires multiple forward passes leading to heavy computation burden. To reduce computation cost, we replace the MC dropout by an ensemble of four classifiers with different loss functions. In contrast to [16] that uses differently weighted cross-entropy loss, our four classifiers share the encoder but differ in loss functions, i.e. cross-entropy loss, focal loss [9], Dice loss, and IoU loss. Loss functions differ in directions of parameter optimization in high-dimensional space, thus providing diversified predictions in one forward pass. Then we regard the regions where the four predictions agree with each other as the epistemic certain regions. In this way, we not only slash computation cost but also capture the epistemic uncertainty in both pixel-level and geometry-level semantics.

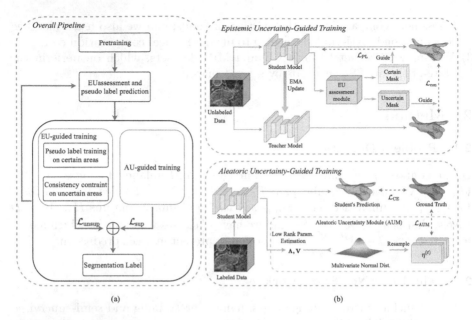

Fig. 1. Framework of the proposed method. (a) presents the overall pipeline of FUSS-Net and (b) shows the details of EU- and AU-guided training.

Training Schemes for Certain and Uncertain Regions. Here we treat the certain and uncertain regions identified by the EU assessment module separately. As illustrated in Fig. 1, we use the certain area of pseudo labels directly in training while enforcing a consistency between the student and teacher network in uncertain areas. For one thing, certain parts of pseudo labels have high confidence and using them could avoid the problems mentioned above (overfitting and confirmation bias). For another, uncertain areas are the regions where we need the models to reach consensus. For certain regions, we apply pseudo label (PL) training and get the loss tensor $\mathbf{L}_{PL}$ of size $H \times W \times D$. $\mathbf{L}_{con}$ corresponds to the consistency loss on uncertain regions, whose elements are computed by $\sum_{j}^{C}(\hat{y}_{ij}^{S} - \hat{y}_{ij}^{T})^2$, where $\hat{y}_{ij}^{S}$ and $\hat{y}_{ij}^{T}$ are the predictions at ith voxel for jth class by the student and teacher, respectively. The total loss for EU-guided learning $\mathcal{L}_{unsup}$ is defined in Eq. (1):

$$\mathcal{L}_{unsup} = \text{Mean}(\mathbf{M}^c \odot \mathbf{L}_{PL}) + \text{Mean}(\lambda(\mathbf{J} - \mathbf{M}^c) \odot \mathbf{L}_{con}), \qquad (1)$$

where $\mathbf{M}^c$ is the derived certain mask, i.e. a binary 3D tensor, whose 1-elements denote certain voxels. $\mathbf{J}$ is an all-ones tensor, λ adjusts the strength of consistency regularization, and $\odot$ is the element-wise product operation. Mean($\cdot$) averages over all non-zero elements and yields a scalar.

2.4   Aleatoric Uncertainty-Guided Training

As the aleatoric uncertainty is originated from inherent random effects, it is often modeled as a normal distribution [5]. Following the practice of [13], we assume a multivariate normal distribution as the prior distribution over the logit space, i.e., the input to the softmax function in the classifier. Let η denote the logits and x be the input, then we have $\eta \mid x \sim \mathcal{N}(\mu(x), \sigma(x))$ where $\mu(x) \in \mathbb{R}^{H \times W \times D \times C}$ and $\sigma(x) \in \mathbb{R}^{(H \times W \times D \times C)^2}$. Then the conditional log-likelihood can be approximated using Monte Carlo method as defined in Eq. (2) [13],

$$\log p(y \mid x) = \log \int p(y \mid \eta) p_\phi(\eta \mid x) d\eta \approx \log \frac{1}{T} \sum_{t=1}^{T} p(y \mid \eta^{(t)}), \quad (2)$$

where T is the number of sampling. In each iteration, we use the computed logits to estimate μ and σ, then perform sampling from the estimated distribution and get sampled outputs accordingly. The summation in Eq. (2) could be further transformed into a form using softmax function, which is used as the object function in [13]. However, it entails huge computation cost. Thus, we propose a new loss function Eq. (3) based on [13], which is proved to be the upper bound of the sum in Eq. (2) (see supplementary material). Consequently, optimizing our loss could also minimize the original negative log-likelihood.

Ground truth labels (y) are used as supervision for both original outputs yielded by the model and the sampled outputs, corresponding to $\mathcal{L}_{\text{CE}}$ (cross-entropy) and $\mathcal{L}_{\text{AUM}}$ (the loss for the AU module, as defined in Eq. (3) respectively. Then the loss is the sum of the two parts as shown in Eq. (4),

$$\mathcal{L}_{\text{AUM}} = -\sum_{t}^{T} \sum_{i}^{H \times W \times D} \sum_{j}^{C} y_{ij} \log(\text{softmax}(\eta_i^{(t)})_j), \quad (3)$$

$$\mathcal{L}_{\text{sup}} = \mathcal{L}_{\text{CE}} + \omega \mathcal{L}_{\text{AUM}}, \quad (4)$$

where ω controls the impact of aleatoric uncertainty. Finally, the loss function for the entire framework is a weighted sum of $\mathcal{L}_{\text{sup}}$ and $\mathcal{L}_{\text{unsup}}$.

3   Experiments and Results

Dataset. We evaluate our approach on two public benchmark sets, for the segmentation of pancreas [15] and left atrium [21], respectively. The pancreas dataset contains 82 contrast-enhanced abdominal CT scans with a 512×512 resolution. For preprocessing, we follow the steps of [8,16,24] and crop the scans based on ground truth with 25 unit enlarged margin and perform the same data splitting as [16], i.e. 62 scans for training and 20 scans for test. The left atrium dataset includes 100 3D gadolinium-enhanced MR images. Following [8, 10,20,22,24], we crop the images based on ground truth with enlarged margin, normalize them to zero mean and unit variance, and use 80 scans for training and 20 scans for test. For each dataset, we only use 20% of the training data with labels, namely 12 labeled scans for pancreas and 16 ones for left atrium.

Table 1. Performance comparison on the pancreas dataset.

Method	#Scans used		Metrics			
	Labeled	Unlabeled	Dice(%)	Jaccard(%)	ASD(voxel)	95HD(voxel)
V-Net	12	0	70.63	56.72	6.29	22.54
V-Net	62	0	82.53	70.63	1.88	6.01
MT [18] (NIPS'17)	12	50	75.85	61.98	3.40	12.59
UA-MT [22] (MICCAI'19)	12	50	77.26	63.28	3.06	11.90
SASSNet [8] (MICCAI'20)	12	50	77.66	64.08	3.05	10.93
RLSSS^a [1] [24] (MICCAI'21)	12	50	78.29	64.91	3.46	11.58
DTC [10] (AAAI'21)	12	50	78.27	64.75	2.25	8.36
CoraNet [16] (TMI'21)	12	50	79.67	66.69	1.89	7.59
FUSSNet (Ours)	12	50	**81.82**	**69.76**	**1.51**	**5.42**

^{a} As the data splitting and stride value of RLSSS are different from other methods in the table, we run the RLSSS model using its released code under the same settings as others.

Implementation Details. We implement our method with PyTorch using an NVIDIA GeForce RTX 2080TI GPU. V-Net [12] is adopted as the backbone network for easy implementation and fair comparison with other methods. We incorporate the Mean-Teacher [18] framework into FUSSNet, in which the student network is trained with Adam optimizer with a 0.001 learning rate and the teacher is updated with student's parameters using exponential moving average (EMA). For hyper-parameters, we set λ and β to 1 for both datasets, and only tune ω in our experiment. The value of ω is data-specific, 0.8 and 0.1 for pancreas and left atrium respectively. We randomly pick 2 labeled samples as val set to decide the specific value of ω, and then retrain the model using all labeled samples. To address the data scarcity issue, we randomly crop cubes of $96 \times 96 \times 96$ for the pancreas dataset and $112 \times 112 \times 80$ for the left atrium dataset for further training. During inference, we use the student model to predict, with the same sliding window strategy as [10,16,22] for fair comparison, i.e. $16 \times 16 \times 4$ for pancreas and $18 \times 18 \times 4$ for left atrium. No post-processing is performed for all models. Our code is available at https://github.com/grant-jpg/FUSSNet.

Results on Pancreas Dataset. Table 1 shows the comparison between FUSS-Net and 8 baseline models, all of which use V-Net as backbone. The first two rows list the results using two vanilla V-Net models in a fully supervised manner, which differ only in the number of labeled samples for training, i.e. 12 (the same as other methods) and 62 (all training samples), thus their performance can be regarded as the fully-supervised lower and upper bounds for semi-supervised approaches respectively. Here FUSSNet achieves the best results in terms of all metrics among all semi-supervised methods and outperforms the SOTA models by large margins. Compared to the latest method CoraNet [16], FUSSNet increases the Dice score by 2.15. We perform pairwise T-test between FUSSNet and CoraNet. All results show statistically significant better at 95% significance level (Suppl. Table 1). More importantly, the proposed framework performs even better than the theoretical upper bound (the second row) in terms of ASD and

Table 2. Performance comparison on the left atrium dataset.

Method	#Scans used		Metrics			
	Labeled	Unlabeled	Dice(%)	Jaccard(%)	ASD(voxel)	95HD(voxel)
V-Net	16	0	84.41	73.54	5.32	19.94
V-Net	80	0	91.42	84.27	1.50	5.15
MT [18] (NIPS'17)	16	64	88.23	79.29	2.73	10.64
UA-MT [22] (MICCAI'19)	16	64	88.88	80.21	2.26	7.32
SASSNet [8] (MICCAI'20)	16	64	89.54	81.24	2.20	8.24
LG-ER-MT [2] (MICCAI'20)	16	64	89.62	81.31	2.06	7.16
DTC [10] (AAAI'21)	16	64	89.42	80.98	2.10	7.32
3D G-S²Net [3] (MICCAI'21)	16	64	89.83	81.69	2.12	6.68
RLSSS [24] (MICCAI'21)	16	64	90.06	82.01	2.13	6.70
MC-Net [20] (MICCAI'21)	16	64	90.34	82.48	1.77	6.00
FUSSNet (Ours)	16	64	**91.13**	**83.79**	1.56	**5.10**

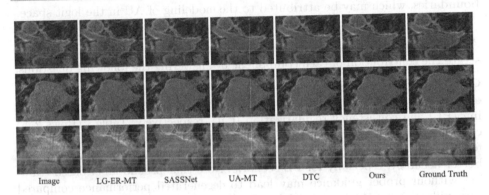

Image   LG-ER-MT   SASSNet   UA-MT   DTC   Ours   Ground Truth

Fig. 2. 2D visualization of the segmentation results of different semi-supervised models on the left atrium dataset. All models are trained with 20% labeled data.

95HD scores. The reason is perhaps that by modelling both kinds of uncertainty, AU in particular, our model is able to capture more information about segmentation surface even from limited annotations.

Results on Left Atrium Dataset. As the left atrium dataset is a widely used benchmark set, here we include more baseline models for comparison (Table 2). FUSSNet achieves the best performance again. As this task is relatively easier than pancreas segmentation and includes more data scans, the advantage of FUSSNet over other methods is not that much, while it is the only one that surpasses the theoretical upper bound in terms of 95 HD.

For a further illustration, Fig. 2 visualizes the segmentation results on three extreme noisy and blurry cases of the left atrium dataset. As can be seen, FUSS-Net has the closest segmentation to the ground truth, suggesting that the proposed EU assessment module and joint training strategies enable the model to exploit unlabeled data effectively and improve its robustness against the inher-

Table 3. Ablation study results on the pancreas dataset.

Method	Components indication		Metrics			
	SSL method	Mask	Dice(%)	Jaccard(%)	ASD(voxel)	95HD(voxel)
Epistemic uncertainly only	–	–	75.52	61.60	3.13	11.89
	PL	–	74.03	59.89	2.92	9.15
	PL	✓	79.64	66.94	2.32	7.22
	CR	–	78.70	65.61	1.89	7.40
	CR	✓	79.87	67.13	2.22	7.04
	PL + CR	✓	81.20	68.87	1.87	5.83
Aleatoric uncertainty only	–	–	79.22	66.25	1.93	5.94
EU + AU	PL + CR	✓	**81.82**	**69.76**	**1.51**	**5.42**

ent noise and ambiguity. Besides, FUSSNet generates more smooth segmentation boundaries, which may be attributed to the modeling of AU in the logit space.

Ablation Study. In this section, we conduct ablation experiments to demonstrate the contribution of each component by answering the following questions:

Q1: How does the EU assessment module behave? We investigate the effectiveness of the estimated EU mask under two scenarios using pseudo labeling (PL) and consistency regularization (CR), respectively. Table 3 (Rows 2–5) compares the results of using PL/CR for the whole images (without mask) and for only the certain or uncertain regions (with mask). The latter achieves much better accuracy, especially for PL scenario. Note that pseudo label-based training without proper guidance may lead to degenerated performance compared to vanilla V-Net (74.03 vs. 75.52 for Dice), which in part explains why CR are more preferred in recent SSL models [14]. Besides, FUSSNet with only EU part outperforms [16], which also uses an ensemble of classifiers (with CE losses) for EU assessment, indicating that our EU assessment strategy is more effective.

Q2: In EU-guided training, is it necessary to treat certain and uncertain regions differently? As Table 3 shows, 'PL+CR' (PL for certain and CR for uncertain regions) has enhanced performance compared to using PL/CR only. The results suggest that PL and CR have their own limitations and advantages, and a proper integration of them can bring more benefits to the model.

Q3: Does 'EU+AU' further improve model performance? As shown in Table 3, using both of them yields the best results. Actually, the performance gain brought by AU depends on the ambiguity in data. AU improves more on LA than Pancreas (Dice: 1.42, Jaccard: 2.39, ASD: 0.66, 95HD: 2.08), since the LA in MRI data are often more blurry, having no clear boundaries. Note that the two benchmark sets have relatively high quality, AU may contribute more to real world data.

4   Conclusion

In this paper, we present a general framework, FUSSNet, for fusing two sources of uncertainty in semi-supervised learning for medical image segmentation. It exhibits promising performance by integrating the unsupervised epistemic uncertainty-guided training and supervised aleatoric uncertainty-guided training. As unlabeled medical imaging data has accumulated rapidly, semi-supervised models have great potential to enhance the accuracy and efficiency of current segmentation systems. The components of FUSSNet can be further explored in the future work, including the estimation of uncertain regions, the teacher-student architecture, and the modeling for AU. The framework can also be extended to active learning and interactive segmentation clinical scenarios.

Acknowledgements. This work was supported by Clinical Research Program of 9th People's Hospital (JYLJ202010), Shanghai Science and Technology Innovation Action Plan (20Y11909600, 21S31904300), Clinical Research Plan of SHDC (SHDC2020CR6016-003), Shanghai Municipal Health Bureau Project (202040434). We thank the authors of [15] and [21] for sharing their datasets and [10,13,16] for their inspiring work and code repositories.

References

1. Berthelot, D., Carlini, N., Goodfellow, I., Papernot, N., Oliver, A., Raffel, C.A.: Mixmatch: a holistic approach to semi-supervised learning. Adv. Neural Inf. Process. Syst. **32** (2019)
2. Hang, W., et al.: Local and global structure-aware entropy regularized mean teacher model for 3D left atrium segmentation. In: Martel, A.L., et al. (eds.) MICCAI 2020. LNCS, vol. 12261, pp. 562–571. Springer, Cham (2020). https://doi.org/10.1007/978-3-030-59710-8_55
3. Huang, H., et al.: 3D graph-S^2Net: shape-aware self-ensembling network for semi-supervised segmentation with bilateral graph convolution. In: de Bruijne, M., et al. (eds.) MICCAI 2021. LNCS, vol. 12902, pp. 416–427. Springer, Cham (2021). https://doi.org/10.1007/978-3-030-87196-3_39
4. Hüllermeier, E., Waegeman, W.: Aleatoric and epistemic uncertainty in machine learning: an introduction to concepts and methods. Mach. Learn. **110**(3), 457–506 (2021)
5. Kendall, A., Gal, Y.: What uncertainties do we need in Bayesian deep learning for computer vision? Adv. Neural Inf. Process. Syst. **30**, 5574–5584 (2017)
6. Kohl, S., et al.: A probabilistic u-net for segmentation of ambiguous images. Adv. Neural Inf. Process. Syst. **31** (2018)
7. Laine, S., Aila, T.: Temporal ensembling for semi-supervised learning. arXiv preprint arXiv:1610.02242 (2016)
8. Li, S., Zhang, C., He, X.: Shape-aware semi-supervised 3D semantic segmentation for medical images. In: Martel, A.L., et al. (eds.) MICCAI 2020. LNCS, vol. 12261, pp. 552–561. Springer, Cham (2020). https://doi.org/10.1007/978-3-030-59710-8_54

9. Lin, T.Y., Goyal, P., Girshick, R., He, K., Dollár, P.: Focal loss for dense object detection. In: Proceedings of the IEEE International Conference on Computer Vision, pp. 2980–2988 (2017)

10. Luo, X., Chen, J., Song, T., Wang, G.: Semi-supervised medical image segmentation through dual-task consistency. In: Proceedings of the AAAI Conference on Artificial Intelligence, vol. 35, pp. 8801–8809 (2021)

11. Luo, X., et al.: Efficient semi-supervised gross target volume of nasopharyngeal carcinoma segmentation via uncertainty rectified pyramid consistency. In: de Bruijne, M., et al. (eds.) MICCAI 2021. LNCS, vol. 12902, pp. 318–329. Springer, Cham (2021). https://doi.org/10.1007/978-3-030-87196-3_30

12. Milletari, F., Navab, N., Ahmadi, S.A.: V-net: fully convolutional neural networks for volumetric medical image segmentation. In: 2016 Fourth International Conference on 3D Vision (3DV), pp. 565–571. IEEE (2016)

13. Monteiro, M., et al.: Stochastic segmentation networks: modelling spatially correlated aleatoric uncertainty. In: Larochelle, H., Ranzato, M., Hadsell, R., Balcan, M.F., Lin, H. (eds.) Advances in Neural Information Processing Systems, vol. 33, pp. 12756–12767. Curran Associates, Inc. (2020)

14. Rizve, M.N., Duarte, K., Rawat, Y.S., Shah, M.: In defense of pseudo-labeling: an uncertainty-aware pseudo-label selection framework for semi-supervised learning. In: International Conference on Learning Representations (2020)

15. Roth, H.R., et al.: DeepOrgan: multi-level deep convolutional networks for automated Pancreas segmentation. In: Navab, N., Hornegger, J., Wells, W.M., Frangi, A.F. (eds.) MICCAI 2015. LNCS, vol. 9349, pp. 556–564. Springer, Cham (2015). https://doi.org/10.1007/978-3-319-24553-9_68

16. Shi, Y., et al.: Inconsistency-aware uncertainty estimation for semi-supervised medical image segmentation. IEEE Trans. Med. Imaging (2021)

17. Sohn, K., et al.: Fixmatch: simplifying semi-supervised learning with consistency and confidence. Adv. Neural Inf. Process. Syst. **33** (2020)

18. Tarvainen, A., Valpola, H.: Mean teachers are better role models: weight-averaged consistency targets improve semi-supervised deep learning results. In: Proceedings of the 31st International Conference on Neural Information Processing Systems, pp. 1195–1204 (2017)

19. Wang, K., et al.: Tripled-uncertainty guided mean teacher model for semi-supervised medical image segmentation. In: de Bruijne, M., et al. (eds.) MICCAI 2021. LNCS, vol. 12902, pp. 450–460. Springer, Cham (2021). https://doi.org/10.1007/978-3-030-87196-3_42

20. Wu, Y., Xu, M., Ge, Z., Cai, J., Zhang, L.: Semi-supervised left atrium segmentation with mutual consistency training. In: International Conference on Medical Image Computing and Computer-Assisted Intervention, pp. 293–306. Springer (2021)

21. Xiong, Z., Xia, Q., et al.: A global benchmark of algorithms for segmenting the left atrium from late gadolinium-enhanced cardiac magnetic resonance imaging. Med. Image Anal. **67**, 101832 (2021)

22. Yu, L., Wang, S., Li, X., Fu, C.-W., Heng, P.-A.: Uncertainty-aware self-ensembling model for semi-supervised 3D left atrium segmentation. In: Shen, D., et al. (eds.) MICCAI 2019. LNCS, vol. 11765, pp. 605–613. Springer, Cham (2019). https://doi.org/10.1007/978-3-030-32245-8_67

23. Yun, S., Han, D., Oh, S.J., Chun, S., Choe, J., Yoo, Y.: Cutmix: Regularization strategy to train strong classifiers with localizable features. In: Proceedings of the IEEE/CVF International Conference on Computer Vision, pp. 6023–6032 (2019)

24. Zeng, X., et al.: Reciprocal learning for semi-supervised segmentation. In: de Bruijne, M., et al. (eds.) MICCAI 2021. LNCS, vol. 12902, pp. 352–361. Springer, Cham (2021). https://doi.org/10.1007/978-3-030-87196-3_33
25. Zou, Y., et al.: Pseudoseg: designing pseudo labels for semantic segmentation. In: International Conference on Learning Representations (2020)

CRISP - Reliable Uncertainty Estimation for Medical Image Segmentation

Thierry Judge[1](✉), Olivier Bernard[3], Mihaela Porumb[2], Agisilaos Chartsias[2], Arian Beqiri[2], and Pierre-Marc Jodoin[1]

[1] Department of Computer Science, University of Sherbrooke, Sherbrooke, Canada
thierry.judge@usherbrooke.ca
[2] Ultromics Ltd., Oxford OX4 2SU, UK
[3] University of Lyon, CREATIS, CNRS UMR5220, Inserm U1294, INSA-Lyon, University of Lyon 1, Villeurbanne, France

Abstract. Accurate uncertainty estimation is a critical need for the medical imaging community. A variety of methods have been proposed, all direct extensions of classification uncertainty estimations techniques. The independent pixel-wise uncertainty estimates, often based on the probabilistic interpretation of neural networks, do not take into account anatomical prior knowledge and consequently provide sub-optimal results to many segmentation tasks. For this reason, we propose *CRISP* a ContRastive Image Segmentation for uncertainty Prediction method. At its core, *CRISP* implements a contrastive method to learn a joint latent space which encodes a distribution of valid segmentations and their corresponding images. We use this joint latent space to compare predictions to thousands of latent vectors and provide anatomically consistent uncertainty maps. Comprehensive studies performed on four medical image databases involving different modalities and organs underlines the superiority of our method compared to state-of-the-art approaches. Code is available at: https://github.com/ThierryJudge/CRISP-uncertainty.

Keywords: Medical imaging · Segmentation · Uncertainty · Deep learning

1 Introduction

Deep neural networks are the *de facto* solution to most segmentation, classification and clinical metric estimation. However, they provide no anatomical guarantees nor any safeguards on their predictions. Error detection and uncertainty estimation methods are therefore paramount before automatic medical image segmentation systems can be effectively deployed in clinical settings.

In this work, we present a novel uncertainty estimation method based on joint representations between images and segmentations trained with contrastive

---

Supplementary Information The online version contains supplementary material available at https://doi.org/10.1007/978-3-031-16452-1_47.

L. Wang et al. (Eds.): MICCAI 2022, LNCS 13438, pp. 492–502, 2022.
https://doi.org/10.1007/978-3-031-16452-1_47

learning. Our method, *CRISP* (ContRastive Image Segmentation for uncertainty Prediction), uses this representation to overcome the limitations of state-of-the-art (SOTA) methods which heavily rely on probabilistic interpretations of neural networks as is described below.

Uncertainty is often estimated assuming a probabilistic output function by neural networks. However, directly exploiting the maximum class probability of the *Softmax* or *Sigmoid* usually leads to suboptimal solutions [7]. Some improvements can be made by considering the entire output distribution through the use of entropy [22] or by using other strategies such as temperature scaling [7].

Uncertainty may also come from Bayesian neural networks, which learn a distribution over each parameter using a variational inference formalism [10]. This enables weight sampling, which produces an output distribution that can model the prediction uncertainty. As Bayesian networks are difficult to train, they are often approximated by aggregating the entropy of many dropout forward runs [5,6]. Alternatively, a network ensemble trained with different hyper-parameters can also estimate uncertainties through differences in predictions [14].

In addition to modeling weight uncertainty, referred to as epistemic uncertainty, uncertainty in the data itself (aleatoric) can also be predicted [11]. However, it has been shown that these methods are less effective for segmentation [9].

Other methods explicitly learn an uncertainty output during training. DeVries and Taylor [4] proposed Learning Confidence Estimates (LCE) by adding a confidence output to the network. The segmentation prediction is interpolated with the ground truth according to this confidence. This confidence can also be learned after training by adding a confidence branch and finetuning a pre-trained network. This enables learning the True Class Probability which is a better confidence estimate than the maximum class probability [2].

Recent works have modeled the disagreement between labelers for ambiguous images [1,13]. Both these methods use a form of variational sampling to make their output stochastic. However, these methods require datasets with multiple labels per image to perform at their best. As these datasets are rarely available, we consider these methods out of scope for this paper.

With the exception of methods modeling disagreement, all other methods can be applied to classification and, by extension, to segmentation tasks with an uncertainty prediction at each pixel. In theory, uncertainty maps should identify areas in which the prediction is erroneous. However, as these methods produce per-pixel uncertainties, they do not take into account higher-level medical information such as anatomical priors. Such priors have been used in segmentation [17,25], but are yet to be exploited in uncertainty estimation. For instance, Painchaud et al. [18] remove anatomical errors by designing a latent space dedicated to the analysis and correction of erroneous cardiac shapes. However, this approach does not guarantee that the corrected shape matches the input image.

To this end, we propose *CRISP*, a method which does not take into account the probabilistic nature of neural networks, but rather uses a joint latent representation of anatomical shapes and their associated image. This paper will describe the *CRISP* method and propose a rigorous evaluation comparing *CRISP* to SOTA methods using four datasets.

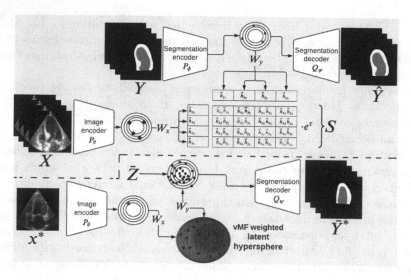

Fig. 1. Schematic representation of our method. Top depicts the training phase and bottom illustrate the uncertainty estimation on an input-prediction pair (x^*, y^*).

2   CRISP

The overarching objective of our method is to learn a joint latent space, in which the latent vector of an input image lies in the vicinity of its corresponding segmentation map's latent vector in a similar fashion as the "CLIP" method does for images and text [21]. As such, a test image x whose latent vector does not lie close to that of its segmentation map y is an indication of a potentially erroneous segmentation. Further details are given below.

Training. As shown in Fig. 1, at train time, *CRISP* is composed of two encoders: the image encoder P_θ and the segmentation encoder P_ϕ. They respectively encode an image x_i and its associated segmentation groundtruth y_i into latent vectors $\vec{z}_{x_i} \in \Re^{D_x}$ and $\vec{z}_{y_i} \in \Re^{D_y}$ $\forall i$. Two weight matrices $W_x \in \Re^{D_h \times D_x}$ and $W_y \in \Re^{D_h \times D_y}$ linearly project the latent vectors into a joint D_h-dimensional latent space where samples are normalized and thus projected onto a hypersphere. As such, the image latent vector $\vec{z}_{x_i}$ is projected onto a vector $\vec{h}_{x_i} = \frac{W_x \cdot \vec{z}_{x_i}}{\|W_x \cdot \vec{z}_{x_i}\|}$ and similarly for $\vec{z}_{y_i}$. A successful training should lead to a joint representation for which $\vec{h}_{x_i} \approx \vec{h}_{y_i}$.

During training, images and groundtruth maps are combined into batches of B elements, $\boldsymbol{X} = [x_1 x_2 ... x_B] \in \Re^{B \times C \times H \times W}$ and $\boldsymbol{Y} = [y_1 y_2 ... y_B] \in \{0,1\}^{B \times K \times H \times W}$ for images with C channels and K segmentation classes. As mentioned before, these batches are encoded by P_θ and P_ϕ into sets of latent vectors Z_X and Z_Y and then projected and normalized into sets of joint latent vectors H_X and H_Y.

At this point, a set of $2 \times B$ samples lie on the surface of a unit hypersphere of the joint latent space. Much like CLIP [21], the pair-wise distance between these joint latent vectors is computed with a cosine similarity that we scale by a learned temperature factor τ to control the scale of the logits. This computation is done by taking a weighted product between H_X and H_Y which leads to the following square matrix: $S = (H_X \cdot H_Y^T)e^\tau \in \Re^{B \times B}$. As shown in Fig. 1, the diagonal of S corresponds to the cosine similarity of the latent image vectors with their corresponding latent groundtruth vector while the off-diagonal elements are cosine similarity of unrelated vectors.

The goal during training is to push S towards an identity matrix, such that the latent vectors $\vec{h}_{x_i}$ and $\vec{h}_{y_j}$ lie on the same spot in the joint latent space when $i = j$ and are orthogonal when $i \neq j$. This would lead to similarities close to 1 on the diagonal and close to 0 outside of it. To enforce this, a cross-entropy loss on the rows and columns of S is used as a contrastive loss [21],

$$\mathcal{L}_{cont} = -\frac{1}{2}\left(\frac{1}{B}\sum_{i=1}^{B}\sum_{j=1}^{B} I_{ij}\log S_{ij} + \frac{1}{B}\sum_{i=1}^{B}\sum_{j=1}^{B} I_{ji}\log S_{ji}\right). \tag{1}$$

CRISP also has a segmentation decoder Q_ψ to reconstruct segmentation latent vectors, a critical feature for estimating uncertainty. This decoder is trained with a reconstruction loss $\mathcal{L}_{rec}$ which is a weighted sum of the Dice coefficient and cross-entropy loss. The model is trained end-to-end to minimize $\mathcal{L} = \mathcal{L}_{cont} + \mathcal{L}_{rec}$.

Uncertainty prediction. Once training is over, the groundtruth segmentation maps Y are projected one last time into the Z and H latent spaces. This leads to a set of N latent vectors $\bar{Z} \in \Re^{N \times D_v}$ and $\bar{H} \in \Re^{N \times D_h}$ which can be seen as latent anatomical prior distributions that will be used to estimate uncertainty.

Now let x^* be a non-training image and y^* its associated segmentation map computed with a predetermined segmentation method (be it a deep neural network or not). To estimate an uncertainty map, x^* is projected into the joint latent space to get its latent vector $\vec{h}_{x^*} \in \Re^{D_h}$. We then compute a weighted dot product between $\vec{h}_{x^*}$ and each row of $\bar{H}$ to get $\bar{S} \in \Re^N$, a vector of similarity measures between $\vec{h}_{x^*}$ and every groundtruth latent vector. Interestingly enough, the way CRISP was trained makes $\bar{S}$ a similarity vector highlighting how each groundtruth map fits the input image x^*.

Then, the M samples of $\bar{Z}$ with the highest values in $\bar{S}$ are selected. These samples are decoded to obtain $\bar{Y}^*$, i.e. various anatomically valid segmentation maps whose shapes are all roughly aligned on x^*. To obtain an uncertainty map, we compare these samples to the initial prediction y^*. We compute the average of the pixel-wise difference between y^* and $\bar{Y}^*$ to obtain an uncertainty map U.

$$U = \frac{1}{M}\sum_{i=1}^{M} w_i(\bar{y}_i^* - y^*) \tag{2}$$

As not all samples equally correspond to x^*, we add a coefficient w_i which corresponds to how close a groundtruth map y_i is from x^*. Since the joint latent space is a unit hyper-sphere, we use a von Mises-Fisher distribution (vMF)

[16] centered on $\vec{h}_{x*}$ as a kernel to weigh its distance to $\vec{h}_{y_i}$. We use Taylor's method [24] to define the kernel bandwidth b (more details are available in the supplementary materials). We define the kernel as:

$$w_i = e^{\frac{1}{b}\vec{h}_i^T\vec{h}_{x*}}/e^{\frac{1}{b}\vec{h}_{x*}^T\vec{h}_{x*}} = e^{\frac{1}{b}(\vec{h}_i^T\vec{h}_{x*}-1)}. \tag{3}$$

3 Experimental Setup

3.1 Uncertainty Metrics

Correlation. Correlation is a straightforward method for evaluating the quality of uncertainty estimates for a full dataset. The absolute value of the Pearson correlation score is computed between the sample uncertainty and the Dice score. In this paper, sample uncertainty is obtained by dividing the sum of the uncertainty for all pixels by the number of foreground pixels. Ideally, the higher the Dice is, the lower the sample uncertainty should be. Therefore, higher correlation values indicate more representative uncertainty maps.

Calibration. A classifier is calibrated if its confidence is equal to the probability of being correct. Calibration is expressed with Expected Calibration Error (ECE) computed by splitting all n samples into m bins and computing the mean difference between the accuracy and average confidence for each bin. Please refer to the following paper for more details [19].

Uncertainty-error mutual information. Previous studies have computed Uncertainty-error overlap by obtaining the Dice score between the thresholded uncertainty map and a pixel-wise error map between the prediction and the ground-truth segmentation map [9]. As the uncertainty error overlap requires the uncertainty map to be thresholded, much of the uncertainty information is lost. We therefore propose computing the mutual information between the raw uncertainty map and the pixel-wise error map. We report the average over the test set weighted by the sum of erroneous pixels in the image.

3.2 Data

CAMUS. The CAMUS dataset [15] consists of cardiac ultrasound clinical exams performed on 500 patients. Each exam contains the 2D apical four-chamber (A4C) and two-chamber view (A2C) sequences. Manual delineation of the endocardium and epicardium borders of the left ventricle (LV) and atrium were made by a cardiologist for the end-diastolic (ED) and end-systolic (ES) frames. The dataset is split into training, validation and testing sets of 400, 50 and 50 patients respectively.

HMC-QU. The HMC-QU dataset [3] is composed of 162 A4C and 130 A2C view recordings. 93 A4C and 68 A2C sequences correspond to patients with scarring from myocardial infarction. The myocardium (MYO) of 109 A4C (72

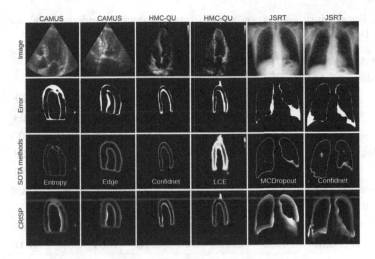

Fig. 2. From top to bottom: raw images, corresponding error maps, uncertainty estimation of SOTA methods and CRISP uncertainty. White indicates erroneous pixels in the error maps [row 2] and high uncertainty in the uncertainty maps [rows 3 and 4].

with myocardial infarction/37 without) recordings was manually labeled for the full cardiac cycle. These sequences were split into training, validation and testing sets of 72, 9 and 28 patients.

Shenzen. The Shenzen dataset [8] is a lung X-ray dataset acquired for pulmonary tuberculosis detection. The dataset contains 566 postero-anterior chest radiographs and corresponding manually segmented masks to identify the lungs. The dataset was split into training and validation sets of 394 and 172 patients.

JSRT. We use the Japanese Society of Radiological Technology (JSRT) [23] lung dataset which contains images and segmentation maps for 154 radiographs with lung nodules, and corresponding segmentation masks.

3.3   Implementation Details

CRISP was compared to several SOTA methods mentioned before. To make comparison fair, every method use the same segmentation network (an Enet [20] in our case). All methods were trained with a batch size of 32 and the Adam optimizer [12] with a learning rate of 0.001 and weight decay of 1e-4. We added early stopping and selected the weights with the lowest validation loss. The **Entropy** method was tested using the baseline network. We tested **MC Dropout** by increasing the baseline dropout value from 10% to 25% and 50% (we report best results with respect to the Dice score) and computing the average of 10 forward passes. For **LCE**, we duplicated the last bottleneck of the Enet to output confidence. The **Confidnet** method was trained on the baseline Enet pre-trained network. The full decoder was duplicated to predict the True Class Probability. For methods or metrics that require converting pixel-wise confidence (c) to

Table 1. Uncertainty estimation results (average over 3 random seeds) for different methods. Bold values indicate best results.

Training data	CAMUS			CAMUS			Shenzen		
Testing data	CAMUS			HMC-QU			JSRT		
Method	Corr. ↑	ECE ↓	MI ↑	Corr. ↑	ECE ↓	MI ↑	Corr. ↑	ECE ↓	MI ↑
Entropy	0.66	0.12	0.02	0.34	0.27	0.02	**0.89**	0.08	0.02
Edge	0.64	**0.06**	0.05	0.15	**0.08**	**0.06**	0.81	**0.05**	0.03
ConfidNet	0.34	0.08	0.04	0.36	0.17	0.04	0.69	0.09	0.01
CRISP	**0.71**	0.09	**0.20**	**0.41**	0.14	**0.06**	0.83	0.19	**0.11**
McDropout	0.67	0.13	0.03	0.26	0.26	0.02	**0.82**	**0.06**	0.03
CRISP-MC	**0.78**	**0.11**	**0.26**	**0.29**	**0.14**	**0.06**	**0.82**	0.21	**0.08**
LCE	0.58	0.44	0.08	**0.35**	0.37	**0.07**	0.87	0.37	0.06
CRISP-LCE	**0.59**	**0.08**	**0.15**	0.34	**0.13**	**0.07**	0.85	**0.18**	**0.11**

uncertainty (u), we define the relationship between the two as $u = 1 - c$ as all methods produce values in the range $[0, 1]$.

To highlight some limitations of SOTA methods, we also added a naïve method for computing uncertainty which we referred to as **Edge**. The uncertainty map for *Edge* amounts to a trivial edge detector applied to baseline predicted segmentation maps. The resulting borders have a width of 5 pixels.

As our **CRISP** method can be used to evaluate any image-segmentation pair, regardless of the segmentation method, we tested it on all the segmentation methods that produce different results (baseline, MC Dropout, LCE). This allows for a more robust evaluation as the evaluation of uncertainty metrics is directly influenced by the quality of the segmentation maps [9]. The value of M was determined empirically and kept proportional to the size of $\bar{Z}$. It can be noted, that the vMF weighting in the latent space attenuates the influence of M.

3.4   Experimental Setup

We report results on both binary and multi-class segmentation tasks. As our datasets are relatively large and homogeneous, Dice scores are consistently high. This can skew results as methods can simply predict uncertainty around the prediction edges. Thus, as mentioned below, we tested on different datasets or simulated domain shift through data augmentation.

Tests were conducted on the CAMUS dataset for LV and MYO segmentation. We simulated a domain shift by adding brightness and contrast augmentations (factor $= 0.2$) and Gaussian noise ($\sigma^2 = 0.0001$) with probability of 0.5 for all test images. We used the 1800 samples from the training and validation sets to make up the $\bar{Z}$ set and used $M = 50$ samples to compute the uncertainty map.

We also tested all methods trained on the CAMUS dataset on the HMC-QU dataset for myocardium segmentation. We added brightness and contrast augmentations (factor $= 0.2$) and RandomGamma (0.95 to 1.05) augmentations during training and normalized the HMC-QU samples using the mean and variance of the CAMUS dataset. We used the A4C samples from the CAMUS dataset (along with interpolated samples between ES and ED instants) to create the set of latent vectors $\bar{Z}$. This corresponds to 8976 samples, of which $M = 150$ were selected to compute the uncertainty map.

Finally, we tested our method on a different modality and organ by using the lung X-ray dataset. We trained all the methods on the Shenzen dataset and tested on the JSRT dataset. We normalized JSRT samples with the mean and variance of the Shenzen dataset. We used the 566 samples from the Shenzen dataset to form the $\bar{Z}$ set and used $M = 25$ samples to compute the uncertainty.

4 Results

Uncertainty maps are presented in Fig. 2 for samples on 3 datasets. As can be seen, *Entropy, ConfidNet*, and *MCDropout* have a tendency to work as an edge detector, much like the naive *Edge* method. As seen in Table 1, different methods perform to different degrees on each of the datasets. However, CRISP is consistently the best or competitive for all datasets for the correlation and MI metrics. ECE results for *CRISP* are also competitive but not the best. Interestingly, the trivial *Edge* method often reports the best ECE results. This is probably due to the fact that errors are more likely to occur near the prediction boundary and the probability of error decreases with distance. These results might encourage the community to reconsider the value of ECE for specific types of segmentation tasks.

Figure 3 shows the distribution of pixel confidence according to the well-classified and misclassified pixels. This figure allows for a better understanding of the different shortcomings of each method. It clearly shows that both MC Dropout and *Confidnet* methods produce over-confident results. On the other hand, LCE appears to produce slightly under-confident predictions which explains the higher mutual information value. Finally, *CRISP* is the only method that can clearly separate certain and uncertain pixels. These results are consistent with what is observed in Fig. 2 as both MC Dropout and *Confidnet* produce very thin uncertainty and LCE predicts large areas of uncertainty around the border. Only *CRISP* produces varying degrees of uncertainty according to the error.

It is apparent that there is a slight decrease in performance for *CRISP* on the JSRT dataset. This is most likely caused by the fact that the latent space is not densely populated during uncertainty estimation. Indeed, the 566 samples in $\bar{Z}$ might not be enough to produce optimal uncertainty maps. This is apparent in Fig. 2 where the uncertainty maps for the JSRT samples are less smooth than the other datasets that have more latent vectors. Different techniques such as data augmentation or latent space rejection sampling [18] are plausible solutions.

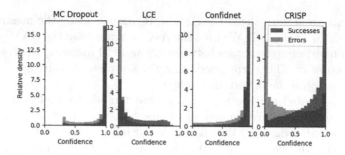

Fig. 3. Histograms of well classified pixels (Successes) and mis-classified pixels (Errors) for different methods on the HMC-QU dataset.

5   Discussion and Conclusion

While empirical results indicate that all methods perform to a certain degree, qualitative results in Fig. 2 show that most SOTA methods predict uncertainty around the prediction edges. While this may constitute a viable uncertainty prediction when the predicted segmentation map is close to the groundtruth, these uncertainty estimates are useless for samples with large errors. Whereas in other datasets and modalities, the uncertainty represents the probability of a structure being in an image and at a given position, lung X-Ray and cardiac ultrasound structures are always present and are of regular shape and position. This makes the task of learning uncertainty during training challenging as few images in the training set produce meaningful errors. Compared to other approaches, *CRISP* leverages the information contained in the dataset to a greater degree and accurately predicts uncertainty in even the worst predictions.

To conclude, we have presented a method to identify uncertainty in segmentation by exploiting a joint latent space trained using contrastive learning. We have shown that SOTA methods produce sub-optimal results due to the lack of variability in segmentation quality during training when segmenting regular shapes. We also highlighted this with the naïve *Edge* method. However, due to its reliance on anatomical priors, *CRISP* can identify uncertainty in a wide range of segmentation predictions.

References

1. Baumgartner, C.F., et al.: PHiSeg: capturing uncertainty in medical image segmentation. In: Shen, D., et al. (eds.) MICCAI 2019. LNCS, vol. 11765, pp. 119–127. Springer, Cham (2019). https://doi.org/10.1007/978-3-030-32245-8_14
2. Corbière, C., Thome, N., Bar-Hen, A., Cord, M., Pérez, P.: Addressing failure prediction by learning model confidence. In: Advances in Neural Information Processing Systems, vol. 32, pp. 2902–2913. Curran Associates, Inc. (2019)
3. Degerli, A., et al.: Early detection of myocardial infarction in low-quality echocardiography. IEEE Access **9**, 34442–34453 (2021)

4. DeVries, T., Taylor, G.W.: Learning confidence for out-of-distribution detection in neural networks. arXiv preprint arXiv:1802.04865 (2018)
5. Gal, Y., Ghahramani, Z.: Bayesian convolutional neural networks with Bernoulli approximate variational inference. arXiv preprint arXiv:1506.02158 (2015)
6. Gal, Y., Ghahramani, Z.: Dropout as a Bayesian approximation: representing model uncertainty in deep learning. In: Proceedings of the 33rd International Conference on International Conference on Machine Learning (ICML'16), vol. 48, pp. 1050–1059. JMLR.org (2016)
7. Guo, C., Pleiss, G., Sun, Y., Weinberger, K.Q.: On calibration of modern neural networks. In: Precup, D., Teh, Y.W. (eds.) Proceedings of the 34th International Conference on Machine Learning. Proceedings of Machine Learning Research, 06–11 August 2017, vol. 70, pp. 1321–1330. PMLR (2017)
8. Jaeger, S., Candemir, S., Antani, S., Wáng, Y.X.J., Lu, P.X., Thoma, G.: Two public chest x-ray datasets for computer-aided screening of pulmonary diseases. Quan. Imaging Med. Surg. **4**, 475 (2014)
9. Jungo, A., Reyes, M.: Assessing reliability and challenges of uncertainty estimations for medical image segmentation. In: Shen, D., et al. (eds.) MICCAI 2019. LNCS, vol. 11765, pp. 48–56. Springer, Cham (2019). https://doi.org/10.1007/978-3-030-32245-8_6
10. Kendall, A., Gal, Y.: What uncertainties do we need in bayesian deep learning for computer vision? In: Guyon, I., et al. (eds.) Advances in Neural Information Processing Systems, vol. 30, pp. 5574–5584. Curran Associates, Inc. (2017)
11. Kendall, A., Gal, Y.: What uncertainties do we need in bayesian deep learning for computer vision? In: Guyon, I., et al. (eds.) Advances in Neural Information Processing Systems, vol. 30. Curran Associates, Inc. (2017)
12. Kingma, D.P., Ba, J.: Adam: a method for stochastic optimization. In: Bengio, Y., LeCun, Y. (eds.) Proceedings of the 3rd International Conference on Learning Representations, ICLR 2015, San Diego, 7–9 May 2015, Conference Track (2015)
13. Kohl, S., et al.: A probabilistic u-net for segmentation of ambiguous images. In: Advances in Neural Information Processing Systems, vol. 31. Curran Associates, Inc. (2018)
14. Lakshminarayanan, B., Pritzel, A., Blundell, C.: Simple and scalable predictive uncertainty estimation using deep ensembles. In: Guyon, I., et al. (eds.) Advances in Neural Information Processing Systems, vol. 30. Curran Associates, Inc. (2017)
15. Leclerc, S., et al.: Deep learning for segmentation using an open large-scale dataset in 2d echocardiography. IEEE Trans. Med. Imaging **38**(9), 2198–2210 (2019)
16. Mardia, K.V., Jupp, P.E.: Directional Statistics. Wiley (1999)
17. Oktay, O., et al.: Anatomically constrained neural networks (ACNNS): application to cardiac image enhancement and segmentation. IEEE Trans. Med. Imaging **37**(2), 384–395 (2018)
18. Painchaud, N., Skandarani, Y., Judge, T., Bernard, O., Lalande, A., Jodoin, P.M.: Cardiac segmentation with strong anatomical guarantees. IEEE Trans. Med. Imaging **39**(11), 3703–3713 (2020)
19. Pakdaman Naeini, M., Cooper, G., Hauskrecht, M.: Obtaining well calibrated probabilities using bayesian binning. In: Proceedings of the AAAI Conference on Artificial Intelligence , vol. 29, no. 1 (2015)
20. Paszke, A., Chaurasia, A., Kim, S., Culurciello, E.: Enet: a deep neural network architecture for real-time semantic segmentation. arXiv preprint arXiv:1606.02147 (2016)
21. Radford, A., et al.: Learning transferable visual models from natural language supervision. arXiv preprint arXiv:2103.00020 (2021)

22. Settles, B.: Active learning literature survey. In: Computer Sciences Technical Report 1648. University of Wisconsin-Madison (2009)
23. Shiraishi, J., et al.: Development of a digital image database for chest radiographs with and without a lung nodule: receiver operating characteristic analysis of radiologists' detection of pulmonary nodules. Am. J. Roentgenol. **174**, 71–74 (2000)
24. Taylor, C.C.: Automatic bandwidth selection for circular density estimation. Comput. Statist. Data Anal. **52**(7), 3493–3500 (2008)
25. Zotti, C., Humbert, O., Lalande, A., Jodoin, P.M.: Gridnet with automatic shape prior registration for automatic MRI cardiac segmentation. In: MICCAI - ACDC Challenge (2017)

TBraTS: Trusted Brain Tumor Segmentation

Ke Zou[1,2], Xuedong Yuan[2(✉)], Xiaojing Shen[3], Meng Wang[4], and Huazhu Fu[4(✉)]

[1] National Key Laboratory of Fundamental Science on Synthetic Vision, Sichuan University, Chengdu, Sichuan, China
[2] College of Computer Science, Sichuan University, Chengdu, Sichuan, China
yxd@scu.edu.cn
[3] College of Mathematics, Sichuan University, Chengdu, Sichuan, China
[4] Institute of High Performance Computing, A*STAR, Singapore, Singapore
hzfu@ieee.org

Abstract. Despite recent improvements in the accuracy of brain tumor segmentation, the results still exhibit low levels of confidence and robustness. Uncertainty estimation is one effective way to change this situation, as it provides a measure of confidence in the segmentation results. In this paper, we propose a trusted brain tumor segmentation network which can generate robust segmentation results and reliable uncertainty estimations without excessive computational burden and modification of the backbone network. In our method, uncertainty is modeled explicitly using subjective logic theory, which treats the predictions of backbone neural network as subjective opinions by parameterizing the class probabilities of the segmentation as a Dirichlet distribution. Meanwhile, the trusted segmentation framework learns the function that gathers reliable evidence from the feature leading to the final segmentation results. Overall, our unified trusted segmentation framework endows the model with reliability and robustness to out-of-distribution samples. To evaluate the effectiveness of our model in robustness and reliability, qualitative and quantitative experiments are conducted on the BraTS 2019 dataset.

Keywords: Trusted segmentation · Uncertainty estimation · Brain tumor segmentation

1 Introduction

Brain tumor is one of the most common brain diseases and can be classified as primary, brain-derived, and brain metastatic tumors. Among the primary malignancies, Gliomas with different levels of aggressiveness, accounting for 81% of brain tumors [24]. Multiple Magnetic Resonance Imaging (MRI) modalities

Supplementary Information The online version contains supplementary material available at https://doi.org/10.1007/978-3-031-16452-1_48.

that provide complementary biological information are one of the clinical tools for sensing tumor-induced tissue changes. Accurate segmentation of lesion areas from different imaging modalities is essential to assess the actual effectiveness before and after treatment.

Recently, many researchers have made great efforts to accurately segment the brain tumor from multimodal MRI images. Most of the methods are based on Convolutional Neural Networks (CNN) [2,30,31]. U-Net [25] with skip-connections and its variants [23,32] are employed to improve performance of the brain tumor segmentation [5,31]. Recently, highly expressive Transformer has been applied to medical image segmentation [11], especially for brain tumor segmentation [30]. Although these models can improve the performance of segmentation, they are often prone to unreliable predictions. This is because these models use softmax to output predictions, which often leads to over-confidence, especially for error predictions [7,8,29]. Moreover, clinicians often not only need accurate segmentation result, but also want to know how reliable the result is, or whether the specific value of the reliability of the result is high or low. Above observations have inspired us to develop models that can accurately segment tumor regions while providing uncertainty estimations for the segmentation results.

Uncertainty quantification methods mainly include dropout-based [6,27], ensemble-based [16], evidential deep learning [26], and deterministic-based [29]. At the same time, many works are devoted to associating the uncertainty with brain tumor segmentation. A simple way to produce uncertainty for brain tumor segmentation is to learn an ensemble of deep networks [17,18]. On the downside, the ensemble-based methods require training the multiple models from scratch, which is computationally expensive for complex models. Some brain tumor segmentation methods introduce the dropout in the test phase to estimate lesion-level uncertainties [13,22]. Despite this strategy reduces the computational burden, it produces inconsistent outputs [15]. In addition, there is also a work that extends deep deterministic uncertainty [21] to semantic segmentation using feature space densities. Although the above methods quantify the uncertainty of voxel segmentation, they all focus on taking uncertainty as feature input to improve segmentation performance rather than obtaining the more robust and plausible uncertainty.

In this paper, we propose a Trusted Brain Tumor Segmentation (TBraTS) network, which aims to provide robust segmentation results and reliable voxel-wise uncertainty for brain tumor. Instead of directly outputting segmentation results, our model enables the output of the underlying network in an evidence-level manner. This not only estimates stable and reasonable voxel-wise uncertainty, but also improves the reliability and robustness of segmentation. We derive probabilities and uncertainties for different class segmentation problems via Subjective Logic (SL) [12], where the Dirichlet distribution parameterizes the distribution of probabilities for different classes of the segmentation results. In summary, our contributions are as follows:

(1) We propose a end-to-end trusted medical image segmentation model, TBraTS, for brain tumor aiming to quantify the voxel-wise uncertainty, which introduces the confidence level for the image segmentation in disease diagnosis.

(2) Our method could accurately estimate the uncertainty of each segmented pixel, to improve the reliability and robustness of segmentation.

(3) We conduct sufficient experiments on the BraTS2019 challenge to verify the segmentation accuracy of proposed model and the robustness of uncertainty quantification.[1]

2 Method

In this section, we introduce an evidence based medical image segmentation method which provides uncertainty for disease diagnosis. For the multi-modal voxel input, a backbone network is adopted to obtain segmentation results. Then, we elaborate on evidential deep learning to quantify the segmentation uncertainty to avoid high confidence values resulting from using softmax for prediction. At last, we construct the overall loss function.

2.1 Uncertainty and the Theory of Evidence for Medical Image Segmentation

One of the generalizations of Bayesian theory for subjective probability is the Dempster-Shafer Evidence Theory (DST) [4]. The Dirichlet distribution is formalized as the belief distribution of DST over the discriminative framework in the SL [12]. For the medical image segmentation, we define a credible segmentation framework through SL, which derives the probability and the uncertainty of the different class segmentation problems based on the evidence. Specifically, for brain tumor segmentation, SL provides a belief mass and an uncertainty mass for different classes of segmentation results. Accordingly, given voxel-based segmentation results $\mathbf{V}$, its $C+1$ mass values are all non-negative and their sum is one. This can be defined as follows:

$$\sum_{n=1}^{C} b_{i,j,k}^{n} + u_{i,j,k} = 1, \tag{1}$$

where $b_{i,j,k}^{n} \geq 0$ and $u_{i,j,k} \geq 0$ denote the probability of the voxel at coordinate (i, j, k) belonging to the n-th class and the overall uncertainty value, respectively. In detail, as shown in Fig. 1, $\mathbf{U} = \{u_{i,j,k}, (i, j, k) \in (H, W, F)\}$ means the uncertainty for the segmentation results $\mathbf{V}$. H, W, and F are the width, height, and number of slices of the input data, respectively. $\mathbf{b}^{n} = \{b_{i,j,k}^{n}, (i, j, k) \in (H, W, F)\}$ refers the probability of n-th class for the segmentation results $\mathbf{V}$. After that, the evidence $\mathbf{e}^{n} = \{e_{i,j,k}^{n}, (i, j, k) \in (H, W, F)\}$ for the segmentation results $\mathbf{V}$ is acquired by an activation function layer softplus, where $e_{i,j,k}^{n} \geq 0$. Then the SL associates the evidence $e_{i,j,k}^{n}$ with the Dirichlet distribution with the parameters $\alpha_{i,j,k}^{n} = e_{i,j,k}^{n} + 1$. Finally, the belief mass

---

[1] Our code has been released in https://github.com/Cocofeat/TBraTS.

and the uncertainty of the (i, j, k)-th pixel can be denoted as:

$$b_{i,j,k}^n = \frac{e_{i,j,k}^n}{S} = \frac{\alpha_{i,j,k}^n - 1}{S} \quad \text{and} \quad u_{i,j,k} = \frac{C}{S}, \tag{2}$$

where $S = \sum_{n=1}^{C} \alpha_{i,j,k}^n = \sum_{n=1}^{C} \left(e_{i,j,k}^n + 1\right)$ denotes the Dirichlet strength. This describes such a phenomenon that the more evidence of the n-th class obtained by the (i, j, k)-th pixel, the higher its probability. On the contrary, the greater uncertainty for the (i, j, k)-th pixel.

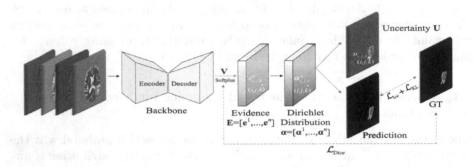

Fig. 1. The framework of trusted brain tumor segmentation.

2.2 Trusted Segmentation Network

The overall architecture of the proposed TBraTS network is shown as Fig. 1. As usual, We adopt the 3D backbone network (V-Net [20] or Attention-UNet [23]) to obtain the multi-class segmentation results. After that, we construct a trusted framework with SL [12] that induces probabilities and uncertainties for different classes of brain tumor segmentation results.

Backbone. Recently, U-Net and its variants were presented to tackle the segmentation problem of medical images. We compared the performances of 3D V-Net and Attention-UNet backbones under our trusted segmentation framework in the experiments. Furthermore, the backbones only performed down-sampling three times to reduce information loss and balance between GPU memory usage and segmentation accuracy. It is worth mentioning that our framework can be freely chosen by the designers with different backbones (such as 3D U-Net and TransUNet [3], etc.).

Uncertainty Estimation. For most brain tumor segmentation networks [2,28,30], the predictions are usually obtained by the softmax layer as the last layer. However, it tends to lead the high confidence even for the wrong predictions [7,29]. Our proposed TBraTS network avoids this problem well in the following way. Firstly, the traditional neural network output $\mathbf{V}$ is followed by an activation function layer to ensure that the network output is non-negative, which is regarded as the evidence voxel $\mathbf{E}$. Second, the SL provides a belief mass function that allows the model to calculate the uncertainty of the segmentation results for different classes. This provides sufficient evidences for clinicians to assist in diagnosing brain tumors. Specifically, as depicted in Fig. 1, the output result of the backbone network first passes through the layer of softplus, and then calculates the probability and uncertainty of its different categories by Eqs. 1 and 2.

Differences from Similar Methods. At last, we analyze the differences of our trusted segmentation network between the traditional brain tumor segmentation methods [28,30] and the evidential based methods [9,10,26]. Compared with the traditional brain tumor segmentation methods [28,30], we treat the predictions of the backbone neural network as subjective opinions instead of using a softmax layer to output overconfident predictions. As a result, our model provides voxel-wise uncertainty estimations and robust segmentation of brain tumor, which is essential for interpretability in disease diagnosis. Compared with the evidential deep learning method [26], we focus on trusted medical image segmentation and provide uncertainty estimations for 3D voxels. Meanwhile, we develop a general end-to-end joint learning framework for brain tumor segmentation with a flexible backbone network design. Compared with the similar evidential segmentation methods [9,10], we employ the subjective logic theory to explicitly model uncertainty rather than the belief function. Moreover, we verify the robustness of baselines (V-Net and Attention-UNet) with our proposed method under different Gaussian noise for brain tumor segmentation.

2.3   Loss Function

Due to the imbalance of brain tumor, our network is first trained with cross-entropy loss function, which is defined as:

$$\mathcal{L}_{ce} = \sum_{n=1}^{C} -y_m^n \log\left(p_m^n\right),$$ (3)

where y_m^n and p_m^n are the label and predicted probability of the m-th sample for class n. Then, SL associates the Dirichlet distribution with the belief distribution under the framework of evidence theory for obtaining the probability of different classes and uncertainty of different voxels based on the evidence collected from the backbone. As shown in [26], Eq. 3 can be further improved as follows:

$$\begin{aligned} \mathcal{L}_{ice} &= \int \left[\sum_{n=1}^{C} -y_m^n \log(p_m^n)\right] \frac{1}{B(\boldsymbol{\alpha}_m)} \prod_{n=1}^{C} p_m^{n\,\alpha_m^n-1} d\mathbf{p}_m \\ &= \sum_{n=1}^{C} y_m^n \left(\psi\left(\boldsymbol{S}_m\right) - \psi\left(\boldsymbol{\alpha}_m^n\right)\right) \end{aligned}$$ (4)

where $\psi\left(\cdot\right)$ denotes the *digamma* function. $\mathbf{p}_m$ is the class assignment probabilities on a simplex, while $B(\boldsymbol{\alpha}_m)$ is the multinomial beta function for the m-th sample concentration parameter $\boldsymbol{\alpha}_m$, and $\boldsymbol{S}_m$ is the m-dimensional unit simplex. More detailed derivations can be referenced in [26]. To guarantee that incorrect labels will yield less evidence, even shrinking to 0, the KL divergence loss function is introduced by:

$$\mathcal{L}_{KL} = \log\left(\frac{\Gamma\left(\sum_{n=1}^{C}\tilde{\alpha}_m^n\right)}{\Gamma(C)\sum_{n=1}^{C}\Gamma(\tilde{\alpha}_m^n)}\right) + \sum_{n=1}^{C}(\tilde{\alpha}_m^n - 1)\left[\psi(\tilde{\alpha}_m^n) - \psi\left(\sum_{n=1}^{C}\tilde{\alpha}_m^n\right)\right], \quad (5)$$

where $\Gamma(\cdot)$ is the *gamma* function. $\tilde{\alpha}_m^n = y_m^n + (1 - y_m^n) \odot \alpha_m^n$ denotes the adjusted parameters of the Dirichlet distribution, which is used to ensure that ground truth class evidence is not mistaken for 0. Furthermore, the Dice score is an important metric for judging the performance of brain tumor segmentation. Therefore, we use a soft Dice loss to optimize the network, which is defined as:

$$\mathcal{L}_{Dice} = 1 - \frac{2y_m^n p_m^n + \alpha}{y_m^n + p_m^n + \beta}, \quad (6)$$

So, the overall loss function of our proposed network can be define as follows:

$$\mathcal{L} = \mathcal{L}_{ice} + \lambda_p \mathcal{L}_{KL} + \lambda_s \mathcal{L}_{Dice}, \quad (7)$$

where λ_p and λ_s are the the balance factors, which are set to be 0.2 and 1.

3   Experiments

Data and Implementation Details. We validate our TBraTS network on the Brain Tumor Segmentation (BraTS) 2019 challenge [1,19]. 335 cases of patients with ground-truth are randomly divided into train dataset, validation dataset and test dataset with 265, 35 and 35 cases, respectively. The four modalities of brain MRI scans with a volume of $240 \times 240 \times 155$ are used as inputs for our network. The outputs of our network contain 4 classes, which are background (label 0), necrotic and non-enhancing tumor (label 1), peritumoral edema (label 2) and GD-enhancing tumor (label 4). We combined the three tumor sub-compartment labels to focus on the whole tumor's segmentation results. Our proposed network is implemented in PyTorch and trained on NVIDIA GeForce RTX 2080Ti. We adopt the Adam to optimize the overall parameters with an initial learning rate of 0.002. The poly learning strategy is used by decaying each iteration with a power of 0.9. The maximum of the epoch is set to 200. The data augmentation techniques are similar to [30]. For the BraTS 2019 dataset, all inputs are uniformly adjusted to $128 \times 128 \times 128$ voxels, and the batch size is set to 2. All the following experiments adopted a five-fold cross-validation strategy to prevent performance improvement caused by accidental factors.

Compared Methods and Metrics. Current medical image segmentation methods named U-Net (U) [25], Attention-UNet (AU) [23] and V-Net (V) [20] are used for the comparison of the brain tumor segmentation. The following different uncertainty quantification methods are compared with our method. (a) Dropout U-Net (DU) employs the test time dropout as an approximation of a

Bayesian neural network [6]. Similar to [22], DU applied Monte-Carlo dropout (p=0.5) on U-Net before pooling or after upsampling. (b) U-Net Ensemble (UE) quantifies the uncertainties by ensembling multiple models [16]. Although UE shares the same U-Net structure, it is trained with different random initialization on the different subsets (90%) of the training dataset to enhance variability. (c) Probabilistic U-Net (PU) learns a conditional density model over-segmentation based on a combination of a U-Net with a conditional variational autoencoder [15]. The following metrics are employed for quantitative evaluation. (a) The Dice score (Dice) is adopted as intuitive evaluation of segmentation accuracy. (b) Normalized entropy (NE) (c) Expected calibration error (ECE) [14] and (d) Uncertainty-error overlap (UEO) [14] are used as evaluation of uncertainty estimations.

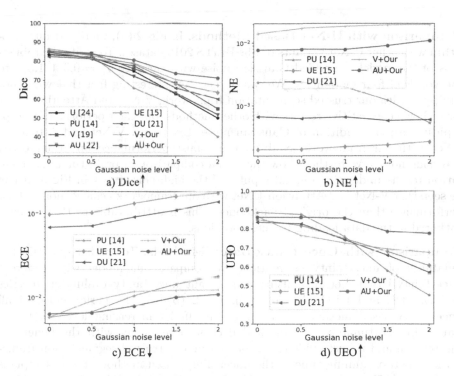

Fig. 2. The quantitative comparisons with U-Net based methods and uncertainty-based methods on the BraTS2019 dataset under vary noise degradation ($\sigma^2 = \{0, 0.5, 1, 1.5, 2\}$).

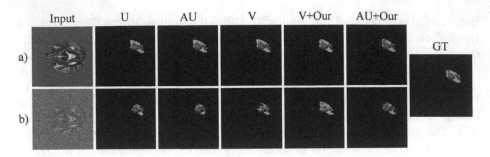

Fig. 3. The visual comparison of brain tumor segmentation results with different methods. a) Original input (T2 as an example); (b) Noised input under Gaussian noise ($\sigma^2 = 1.5$).

Comparison with U-Net Based Methods. In Fig. 2 (a), we report our algorithm with other U-Net variants on the BraTS 2019 dataset. To verify the robustness of the model, we added Gaussian noise with variance $\sigma^2 = 0.5, 1, 1.5, 2$ to the voxels of four modalities. We can observe an interesting fact that when not equipped with our trusted segmentation framework, V-Net and Attention-UNet have shown competitive results with other methods, but their performance drops rapidly with the addition of Gaussian noise. Excitingly, V-Net and Attention-UNet with our framework exhibit more robust performance under increased Gaussian noise. We further show the visual comparison of brain tumor segmentation results under the original input and the high noise input in Fig. 3. It can be seen that V-Net and Attention-UNet with our framework achieve more robust performance than the original backbones. This is attributable to the evidence gathered in the data leading to these opinions.

Comparison with Uncertainty-Based Methods. To further quantify the reliability of uncertainty estimation, we compare our model with different uncertainty-based methods, using the elegant uncertainty evaluation metrics of NE, ECE and UEO. As depict in Fig. 2 (b)-(d), the performance of all uncertainty-based methods decay gradually under increasing levels of Gaussian noise. Fortunately, our method decays more slowly with the benefit of the reliable and robust evidences captured by our trusted segmentation framework. The test running time of the uncertainty-based method on one sample is 0.015 mins (AU+Our), 0.084 mins (V+Our), 0.256 mins (PU), 1.765 mins (DU) and 3.258 mins (UE). It can be concluded that the running time of our framework is lower than other methods. This is due to the fact that PU and DU will sample at test time to obtain uncertainty estimations, while the UE obtains uncertainty estimations by ensembling multiple models. Moreover, to more intuitively demonstrate the reliability of uncertainty estimations, we show a visual comparison of brain tumor segmentation results from various methods. As shown in the fourth and fifth columns of Fig. 4, the V-Net and Attention-UNet equipped with our framework obtain more accurate and robust uncertainty estimations, even under strong Gaussian noise. The reason being the following two points, we did not use softmax for output which would lead to over-confidence; we employ a subjective logical framework to gather more favorable and robust evidences from the input.

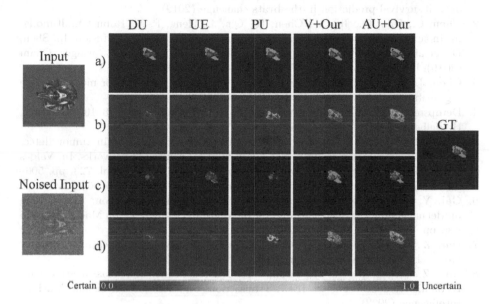

Fig. 4. The visual comparisons of MRI brain tumor segmentation results with uncertainty-based methods. a) Qualitative results of different methods with the original input (T2 as an example). b) Uncertainty maps for different methods with the original input (T2 as an example). c) Qualitative results of different methods under Gaussian noise with $\sigma^2 = 1.5$. d) Uncertainty maps for different methods under Gaussian noise with $\sigma^2 = 1.5$.

4   Conclusion

In this paper we presented an end-to-end trusted segmentation model, TBraTS, for reliably and robustly segmenting brain tumor with uncertainty estimation. We focus on producing voxel-wise uncertainty for brain tumor segmentation, which is essential to provide confidence measures for disease diagnosis. The theory of subjective logic is adopted to model the predictions of the backbone neural network without any computational costs and network changes. Furthermore, Our model learns predicted behavior from the perspective of evidence inference, through the connection between uncertainty quantification and belief mass of the subjective logic. Extensive experiments demonstrated that TBraTS is competitive with previous approaches on the BraTS 2019 dataset.

Acknowledgements. This work was supported by A*STAR Advanced Manufacturing and Engineering (AME) Programmatic Fund (A20H4b0141); Miaozi Project in Science and Technology Innovation Program of Sichuan Province (2021001).

References

1. Bakas, S., Reyes, M., Jakab, A., Bauer, S., et al.: Identifying the best machine learning algorithms for brain tumor segmentation, progression assessment, and overall survival prediction in the brats challenge (2019)
2. Chen, C., Dou, Q., Jin, Y., Chen, H., Qin, J., Heng, P.-A.: Robust multimodal brain tumor segmentation via feature disentanglement and gated fusion. In: Shen, D., et al. (eds.) MICCAI 2019. LNCS, vol. 11766, pp. 447–456. Springer, Cham (2019). https://doi.org/10.1007/978-3-030-32248-9_50
3. Chen, J., et al.: Transunet: transformers make strong encoders for medical image segmentation. arXiv preprint arXiv:2102.04306 (2021)
4. Dempster, A.P.: A Generalization of Bayesian Inference, pp. 73–104. Springer, Heidelberg (2008). https://doi.org/10.1007/978-3-540-44792-4_4
5. Dong, H., Yang, G., Liu, F., Mo, Y., Guo, Y.: Automatic brain tumor detection and segmentation using U-Net based fully convolutional networks. In: Valdés Hernández, M., González-Castro, V. (eds.) MIUA 2017. CCIS, vol. 723, pp. 506–517. Springer, Cham (2017). https://doi.org/10.1007/978-3-319-60964-5_44
6. Gal, Y., Ghahramani, Z.: Dropout as a Bayesian approximation: representing model uncertainty in deep learning. In: International Conference on Machine Learning, pp. 1050–1059. PMLR (2016)
7. Han, Z., Zhang, C., Fu, H., Zhou, J.T.: Trusted multi-view classification. In: International Conference on Learning Representations (2020)
8. Han, Z., Zhang, C., Fu, H., Zhou, J.T.: Trusted Multi-View Classification with Dynamic Evidential Fusion. IEEE Transactions on Pattern Analysis and Machine Intelligence (2022)
9. Huang, L., Ruan, S., Decazes, P., Denœux, T.: Evidential segmentation of 3D PET/CT images. In: Denœux, T., Lefèvre, E., Liu, Z., Pichon, F. (eds.) BELIEF 2021. LNCS (LNAI), vol. 12915, pp. 159–167. Springer, Cham (2021). https://doi.org/10.1007/978-3-030-88601-1_16
10. Huang, L., Ruan, S., Denoeux, T.: Belief function-based semi-supervised learning for brain tumor segmentation. In: International Symposium on Biomedical Imaging, pp. 160–164. IEEE (2021)
11. Ji, G.P., et al.: Video polyp segmentation: a deep learning perspective. arXiv (2022)
12. Jøsang, A.: Subjective logic: a formalism for reasoning under uncertainty, vol. 3 (2016)
13. Jungo, A., et al.: On the effect of inter-observer variability for a reliable estimation of uncertainty of medical image segmentation. In: Frangi, A.F., Schnabel, J.A., Davatzikos, C., Alberola-López, C., Fichtinger, G. (eds.) MICCAI 2018. LNCS, vol. 11070, pp. 682–690. Springer, Cham (2018). https://doi.org/10.1007/978-3-030-00928-1_77
14. Jungo, A., Reyes, M.: Assessing reliability and challenges of uncertainty estimations for medical image segmentation. In: Shen, D., et al. (eds.) MICCAI 2019. LNCS, vol. 11765, pp. 48–56. Springer, Cham (2019). https://doi.org/10.1007/978-3-030-32245-8_6
15. Kohl, S., et al.: A probabilistic u-net for segmentation of ambiguous images. Adv. Neural Inf. Process. Syst. **31** (2018)
16. Lakshminarayanan, B., Pritzel, A., Blundell, C.: Simple and scalable predictive uncertainty estimation using deep ensembles. Adv. Neural Inf. Process. Syst. **30** (2017)

17. McKinley, R., Rebsamen, M., Meier, R., Wiest, R.: Triplanar ensemble of 3D-to-2D CNNs with label-uncertainty for brain tumor segmentation. In: Crimi, A., Bakas, S. (eds.) BrainLes 2019. LNCS, vol. 11992, pp. 379–387. Springer, Cham (2020). https://doi.org/10.1007/978-3-030-46640-4_36

18. Mehrtash, A., Wells, W.M., Tempany, C.M., Abolmaesumi, P., Kapur, T.: Confidence calibration and predictive uncertainty estimation for deep medical image segmentation. IEEE Trans. Med. Imaging 39(12), 3868–3878 (2020)

19. Menze, B.H., Jakab, A., Bauer, S., Kalpathy-Cramer, J., et al.: The multimodal brain tumor image segmentation benchmark (brats). IEEE Trans. Med. Imaging 34(10), 1993–2024 (2015)

20. Milletari, F., Navab, N., Ahmadi, S.A.: V-net: Fully convolutional neural networks for volumetric medical image segmentation. In: International Conference on 3D Vision (3DV), pp. 565–571 (2016)

21. Mukhoti, J., van Amersfoort, J., Torr, P.H., Gal, Y.: Deep deterministic uncertainty for semantic segmentation. In: International Conference on Machine Learning Workshop on Uncertainty and Robustness in Deep Learning (2021)

22. Nair, T., Precup, D., Arnold, D.L., Arbel, T.: Exploring uncertainty measures in deep networks for multiple sclerosis lesion detection and segmentation. Med. Image Anal. 59, 101557 (2020)

23. Oktay, O., et al.: Attention u-net: learning where to look for the pancreas. arXiv preprint arXiv:1804.03999 (2018)

24. Ostrom, Q.T., Bauchet, L., Davis, F.G., Deltour, I., et al.: The epidemiology of glioma in adults: a "state of the science" review. Neuro-oncology 16(7), 896–913 (2014)

25. Ronneberger, O., Fischer, P., Brox, T.: U-Net: convolutional networks for biomedical image segmentation. In: International Conference on Medical Image Computing and Computer-Assisted Intervention, pp. 234–241 (2015)

26. Sensoy, M., Kaplan, L., Kandemir, M.: Evidential deep learning to quantify classification uncertainty. In: Proceedings of the 32nd International Conference on Neural Information Processing Systems, pp. 3183–3193 (2018)

27. Srivastava, N., Hinton, G., Krizhevsky, A., Sutskever, I., Salakhutdinov, R.: Dropout: a simple way to prevent neural networks from overfitting. J. Mach. Learn. Res. 15(1), 1929–1958 (2014)

28. Valanarasu, J.M.J., Sindagi, V.A., Hacihaliloglu, I., Patel, V.M.: Kiu-net: overcomplete convolutional architectures for biomedical image and volumetric segmentation. IEEE Trans. Med. Imaging (2021)

29. Van Amersfoort, J., Smith, L., Teh, Y.W., Gal, Y.: Uncertainty estimation using a single deep deterministic neural network. In: International Conference on Machine Learning, pp. 9690–9700. PMLR (2020)

30. Wang, W., Chen, C., Ding, M., Yu, H., Zha, S., Li, J.: TransBTS: multimodal brain tumor segmentation using transformer. In: de Bruijne, M., et al. (eds.) MICCAI 2021. LNCS, vol. 12901, pp. 109–119. Springer, Cham (2021). https://doi.org/10.1007/978-3-030-87193-2_11

31. Zhang, J., Jiang, Z., Dong, J., Hou, Y., Liu, B.: Attention gate resu-net for automatic MRI brain tumor segmentation. IEEE Access 8, 58533–58545 (2020)

32. Zhou, Z., Siddiquee, M.M.R., Tajbakhsh, N., Liang, J.: Unet++: redesigning skip connections to exploit multiscale features in image segmentation. IEEE Trans. Med. Imaging 39(6), 1856–1867 (2020)

Layer Ensembles: A Single-Pass Uncertainty Estimation in Deep Learning for Segmentation

Kaisar Kushibar$^{(\boxtimes)}$, Victor Campello, Lidia Garrucho, Akis Linardos, Petia Radeva, and Karim Lekadir

Department of Mathematics and Computer Science, University of Barcelona, 08007 Barcelona, Spain
`kaisar.kushibar@ub.edu`

Abstract. Uncertainty estimation in deep learning has become a leading research field in medical image analysis due to the need for safe utilisation of AI algorithms in clinical practice. Most approaches for uncertainty estimation require sampling the network weights multiple times during testing or training multiple networks. This leads to higher training and testing costs in terms of time and computational resources. In this paper, we propose Layer Ensembles, a novel uncertainty estimation method that uses a single network and requires only a single pass to estimate epistemic uncertainty of a network. Moreover, we introduce an image-level uncertainty metric, which is more beneficial for segmentation tasks compared to the commonly used pixel-wise metrics such as entropy and variance. We evaluate our approach on 2D and 3D, binary and multi-class medical image segmentation tasks. Our method shows competitive results with state-of-the-art Deep Ensembles, requiring only a single network and a single pass.

Keywords: Uncertainty estimation · Deep learning · Segmentation

1 Introduction

Despite the success of Deep Learning (DL) methods in medical image analysis, their black-box nature makes it more challenging to gain trust from both clinicians and patients [26]. Modern DL approaches are unreliable when encountered with new situations, where a DL model silently fails or produces an overconfident wrong prediction. Uncertainty estimation can overcome these common pitfalls, increasing the reliability of models by assessing the certainty of their prediction and alerting their user about potentially erroneous reports.

Several methods in the literature address uncertainty estimation in DL [1]. General approaches include: 1) Monte-Carlo Dropout (MCDropout) [7], which requires several forward passes with enabled dropout layers in the network

---

Supplementary Information The online version contains supplementary material available at https://doi.org/10.1007/978-3-031-16452-1_49.

during test time; 2) Bayesian Neural Networks (BNN) [6] that directly represent network weights as probability distributions; and 3) Deep Ensembles (DE) [13] which combines the outputs of several networks to produce uncertainty estimates. MCDropout and BNN have been argued to be unreliable in real world datasets [14]. Nonetheless, MCDropout is one of the most commonly used methods, often favourable when carefully tuned [8]. Despite their inefficiency in terms of memory and time, evidence showed DE is the most reliable uncertainty estimation method [1,4].

There have been successful attempts that minimised the cost of training of the original DE. For example, snapshot-ensembles [12] train a single network until convergence, and further train beyond that point, storing the model weights per additional epoch to obtain M different models. In doing so, the training time is reduced drastically. However, multiple networks need to be stored and the testing remains the same as in DE. Additionally, the deep sub-ensembles [23] method uses M segmentation heads on top of a single model (Multi-Head Ensembles). This method is particularly similar to our proposal – Layer Ensembles (LE). However, LE, in contrast to existing methods, exhibits the following benefits:

- Scalable, intuitive, simple to train and test. The number of additional parameters is small compared to BNN approaches that double the number of parameters;
- Single network compared to the state-of-the-art DE;
- Unlike multi-pass BNN and MCDropout approaches, uncertainties can be calculated using a single forward pass, which would greatly benefit real-time applications;
- Produces global (image-level) as well as pixel-wise uncertainty measures;
- Allows estimating difficulty of a target sample for segmentation (example difficulty) that could be used to detect outliers;
- Similar performance to DE regarding accuracy and confidence calibration.

2   Methodology

Our method is inspired by the state-of-the-art DE [13] for uncertainty estimation as well as a more recent work [3] that estimates example difficulty through prediction depth. In this section, we provide a detailed explanation of how our LE method differs from other works [3,13], taking the best from both concepts and introducing a novel method for uncertainty estimation in DL. Furthermore, we introduce how LE can be used to obtain a single image-level uncertainty metric that is more useful for segmentation tasks compared to the commonly used pixel-wise variance, entropy, and mutual information (MI) metrics.

Prediction Depth. Prediction Depth (PD) [3] measures example difficulty by training k-NN classifiers using feature maps after each layer. Given a network with N layers, the PD for an input image x is $L \sim [0, N]$ if the k-NN prediction for the Lth layer is different to layer at $L-1$ and the same for all posterior layer predictions. The authors demonstrated that easy samples (i.e. most common, in-distribution)

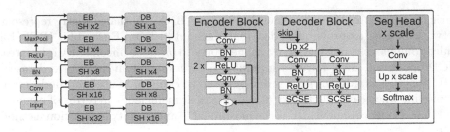

Fig. 1. LE built on top of U-Net like architecture. Encoder Block (EB) in orange and Decoder Block (DB) in green have internal structures as depicted in the boxes below with corresponding colours. Ten Segmentation Heads (SH) are attached after each layer output with an up-scaling factor depending on the depth of the layer. SCSE - Squeeze and Excitation attention module. BN - Batch Normalisation. (Color figure online)

have small PD, whereas difficult ones (i.e. less common or out-of-distribution) have high PD by linking the known phenomena in DL that early layers converge faster [15] and networks learn easy data first [22]. Using PD for estimating example difficulty is appealing, however, it requires training additional classifiers on top of a pre-trained network. Moreover, using the traditional Machine Learning classifiers (e.g. k-NN) for a segmentation task is not trivial.

We extend the idea of PD to a more efficient segmentation method. Instead of k-NN classifiers, we attach a segmentation head after each layer output in the network as shown in Fig. 1. We use a CNN following the U-Net [20] architecture with different modules in the decoder and encoder blocks. Specifically, we use residual connections [10] in the encoder and squeeze-and-excite attention [11] modules in the decoder blocks. Our approach is architecture agnostic and the choice of U-Net was due to its wide use and high performance on different medical image segmentation tasks.

Ensembles of Networks of Different Depths. DE has been used widely in the literature for epistemic uncertainty estimation. The original method assumes a collection of M networks with different initialisation trained with the same data. Then, the outputs of each of these M models can be used to extract uncertainty measurements (e.g. variance). As we have shown in Fig. 1, ten segmentation heads were added after each layer. Then, LE is a compound of M sub-networks of different depths. Since each of the segmentation heads is randomly initialised, it is sufficient to cause each of the sub-networks to make partially independent errors [9]. The outputs from each of the segmentation heads can then be combined to produce final segmentation and estimate the uncertainties, similarly to DE. Hence, LE is an approximation to DE, but using only one network model.

Layer Agreement as an Image-Level Uncertainty Metric. As we have stated above, LE is a combination of sub-networks of different depths. It can also be viewed as stacked networks where the parameters of a network f_t is shared by f_{t+1} for all $t \in [0, N)$, where N is the total number of outputs. This sequential connection of N sub-networks allows us to observe the progression of segmentation

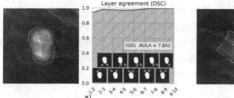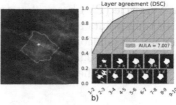

Fig. 2. Layer Agreement curve. a) A high contrast lesion: large AULA and low uncertainty. b) A low contrast lesion and calcification pathology is present: small AULA and higher uncertainty. Arrows represent the correspondence between layers 1 and 2, 2 and 3, etc. DSC – Dice Similarity Coefficient. Green contours are ground truths. (Color figure online)

through the outputs of each segmentation head. We can measure the agreement between the adjacent layer outputs – e.g. using the Dice coefficient – to obtain a layer agreement curve. Depending on the network uncertainty, the agreement between layers will be low, especially in the early layers (Fig. 2). We propose to use the Area Under Layer Agreement curve (AULA) as an image-level uncertainty metric. In the following sections, we demonstrate that AULA is a good uncertainty measure to detect poor segmentation quality, both in binary and multi-class problems.

3 Materials and Implementation

We evaluate our proposal on two active medical image segmentation tasks: 1) Breast mass for binary 2D; and 2) Cardiac MRI for multi-class 3D segmentation. We assess LE in terms of segmentation accuracy, segmentation quality control using AULA metric, and example difficulty estimation using PD. For all the experiments, except for the example difficulty, LE is compared against: 1) the state-of-the-art DE with M networks; 2) another single pass and single network Multi-Head Ensembles (MH) [23]; and 3) a plain network without uncertainty estimation (referred as Plain).

Datasets. We use two publicly available datasets for the selected segmentation problems. Breast Cancer Digital Repository (BCDR) [16] contains 886 Medio-Lateral Oblique (MLO) and CranioCaudal (CC) view mammogram images of 394 patients with manual segmentation masks for masses. Original images have a matrix size of 3328×4084 or 2560×3328 pixels (unknown resolution). We crop and re-sample all masses to patches of 256×256 pixels with masses centred in the middle, as done in common practice [19]. We randomly split the BCDR dataset into train (576), validation (134), and test (176) sets so that images from the same patient are always in the same set.

For cardiac segmentation, the M&Ms challenge (MnM) [5] dataset is utilised. We use the same split as in the original challenge – 175 training, 40 validation, and 160 testing. All the images come annotated at the End-Diastolic (ED) and End-Systolic (ES) phases for the Left Ventricle (LV), MYOcardium (MYO), and Right Ventricle (RV) heart structures in the short-axis view. In our experiments, both time-points are evaluated together. All MRI scans are kept in their original in-plane resolution varying from isotropic 0.85 mm to 1.45 mm and slice-thickness varying from 0.92 mm to 10 mm. We crop the images to $128 \times 128 \times 10$ dimensions so that the heart structures are centred.

Training. The same training routine is used for all the experiments, with only exception in batch-size: 10 for breast mass and 1 for cardiac structure segmentation. The network is trained for 200 epochs using the Adam optimiser to minimise the generalised Dice [21] and Cross-Entropy (CE) losses for breast mass and cardiac structure segmentation, respectively. For the multi-class segmentation, CE is weighted by 0.1 for background and 0.3 for each cardiac structure. An initial learning rate of 0.001 is set with a decay by a factor of 0.5 when the validation loss reaches a plateau. Common data augmentations are applied including random flip, rotation, and random swap of mini-patches of size 10×10. Images are normalised to have zero-mean and unit standard deviation. A single NVIDIA GeForce RTX 2080 GPU with 8 GB of memory is used. The source code with dependencies, training, and evaluation is publicly available.[1]

Evaluation. Testing is done using the weights that give the best validation loss during training. The final segmentation masks are obtained by averaging the outputs of individual networks in DE ($M = 5$). For DE we also tried $M = 10$, however, the performance was the same while the computational time increased. For both MH and LE the number of output heads is $M = 10$ and they are averaged to obtain the final outputs. For LE, we tried both averaging the sub-network outputs and using the well-known Simultaneous Truth And Performance Level Estimation (STAPLE) algorithm [24] that uses weighted voting. Both results were similar and for brevity we present only the version using averaging.

We evaluate LE, MH, and DE using the common uncertainty metrics in the literature – the pixel-wise variance, entropy, and MI, and they are summed for all pixels/voxels in cases where an image-level uncertainty is required. The AULA metric is used for LE. The network confidence calibration is evaluated using the Negative Log-Likelihood metric (NLL). It is a standard measure of a probabilistic model's quality that penalises wrong predictions that have small uncertainty [18]. Note that AULA can also be calculated by skipping some of the initial segmentation heads.

4   Results

Segmentation Performance and Confidence Calibration. Table 1 compares the segmentation performance of LE with MH, DE, and Plain models in terms of Dice Similarity Coefficient (DSC) and Modified Hausdorff Distance

---

[1] https://github.com/pianoza/LayerEnsembles.

Table 1. Segmentation and confidence calibration performance for Plain U-Net, MH, DE, and LE on BCDR and MnM datasets. The values for DSC, MHD, and NLL are given as 'mean(std)'. ↑ - higher is better, ↓ - lower is better. Best values are in bold. Statistically significant differences compared to LE are indicated by '*'.

Method	BCDR – breast mass segmentation			MnM – all structures combined		
	DSC ↑	MHD ↓	NLL ↓	DSC ↑	MHD ↓	NLL ↓
Plain	*0.865 (0.089)	*1.429 (1.716)	*2.312 (1.353)	0.900 (0.114)	**1.061 (2.693)**	0.182 (0.405)
MH	*0.865 (0.090)	*1.457 (1.826)	*2.191 (1.305)	*0.892 (0.128)	1.418 (3.865)	*0.228 (0.582)
DE	0.870 (0.090)	1.373 (1.762)	*0.615 (0.538)	*0.896 (0.129)	1.465 (4.856)	***0.157 (0.331)**
LE	**0.872 (0.084)**	**1.317 (1.692)**	**0.306 (0.250)**	**0.903 (0.103)**	1.302 (5.308)	0.173 (0.367)

Method	MnM – Structure-wise DSC ↑			MnM – Structure-wise MHD ↓		
	LV	MYO	RV	LV	MYO	RV
Plain	0.882 (0.131)	*0.804 (0.124)	*0.826 (0.151)	**1.313 (3.625)**	**1.303 (2.788)**	2.884 (10.888)
MH	*0.871 (0.149)	*0.798 (0.129)	0.827 (0.160)	1.693 (5.640)	1.651 (3.957)	2.148 (4.825)
DE	**0.885 (0.137)**	*0.804 (0.135)	0.829 (0.164)	1.536 (5.596)	1.500 (3.983)	**2.113 (5.671)**
LE	0.883 (0.128)	**0.809 (0.108)**	**0.832 (0.144)**	1.525 (5.861)	1.529 (5.497)	2.525 (8.925)

(MHD). Two-sided paired t-test is used to measure statistically significant differences with $\alpha = 0.05$. In breast mass segmentation, LE performs similarly to all other methods for both DSC and MHD metrics. The NLL of LE, however, is significantly better compared to others ($p < 0.001$). For cardiac structure segmentation, the combined DSCs for all methods are similar and MHD of Plain is slightly better. The NLL of LE (0.173 ± 0.367) is significantly better than MH (0.228 ± 0.582) with $p < 0.05$. The NLL of DE (0.157 ± 0.33) is significantly better than ours ($p < 0.05$), however, LE can achieve an NLL of 0.140 ± 0.23 by skipping less layers without compromising segmentation performance (see Fig. 3, right). In our experiments, skipping the first three and five outputs gave the best results in terms of correlation between uncertainty metrics and segmentation performance for breast mass and cardiac structure tasks, respectively (see Table 2). Skipping all but the last segmentation head in LE is equivalent to the Plain network. In terms of structure-wise DSC, all methods are similar for all the structures. Plain method has a slightly better MHD compared to other methods for the LV and MYO structures ($p > 0.05$), and DE is better for the RV structure compared to LE $p > 0.05$.

The ranking across all metrics in Table 1 are: LE (1.67), DE (2.17), Plain (2.58), MH (3.58), showing that on average LE is better than other approaches. Overall, segmentation performance of all four are similar and LE has a better confidence calibration. We note that both LE and MH are lightweight and single-pass, but they are structurally different. LE observes multiple levels of a network and combines information related to generalisation (from shallow layers) and memorisation (from deep layers) [3], whereas MH combines outputs from the same depth – equally expressive networks with the same number of parameters.

Segmentation Quality Control. We evaluate our uncertainty estimation proposal for segmentation quality control, similarly to [17], and compare it to the state-of-the-art DE. We do not compare the results with the MH method as its

Table 2. Spearman's correlation of segmentation metrics with uncertainty metrics for breast mass and cardiac segmentation tasks. Absolute highest values are shown in bold.

	BCDR				MnM			
	Entropy	MI	Variance	AULA	Entropy	MI	Variance	AULA
DE-DSC	−0.783	−0.785	**−0.785**	N/A	−0.323	−0.433	−0.377	N/A
LE-DSC	−0.615	−0.597	−0.620	**0.785**	−0.221	−0.207	−0.203	**0.649**
DE-MHD	0.762	**0.764**	0.763	N/A	0.401	0.499	0.447	N/A
LE-MHD	0.594	0.575	0.598	−0.730	0.309	0.313	0.300	**−0.571**

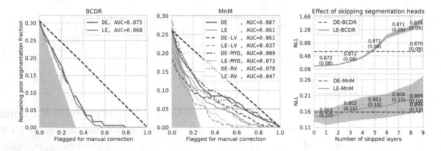

Fig. 3. Segmentation quality control for DE and LE. The following are averaged indicators for: random flagging (dashed black); remaining 5% of poor segmentations (dotted grey); and ideal line (grey shaded area). **The effect of skipping initial segmentation head outputs** on model calibration. Numbers on top of the lines represent DSC in 'mean (std)' format. Shaded areas are standard deviations for NLL.

performance is lower compared to DE (Table 1). We use the proposed AULA uncertainty metric to detect poor segmentation masks and the variance metric for DE. Figure 3 shows the fraction of remaining images with poor segmentation after a fraction of poor quality segmentation images are flagged for manual correction. We consider DSCs below 0.90 as poor quality for both segmentation tasks. We set the threshold for the cardiac structure following the inter-operator agreement identified in [2], and use the same value on the threshold for masses. As proposed in [17], the areas under these curves can be used to compare different methods. It can be seen that LE and DE are similar in terms of detecting poor quality segmentations, with LE achieving slightly better AUC for all the cases – mass, combined and structure-wise cardiac segmentations. Table 2 supports this statement by confirming high correlation between AULA and segmentation metrics. In BCDR, both are somewhat close to the averaged ideal line. For the cardiac structure segmentation, all the curves take a steep decline, initially being also close to the averaged ideal line indicating that severe cases are detected faster. In the case of the left ventricle, the remaining poor segmentation fraction is lower in DE in the range of [0.0; 0.1]. However, the curve takes a steeper decline reaching twice as less AUC. Moreover, as can be seen in Fig. 4,

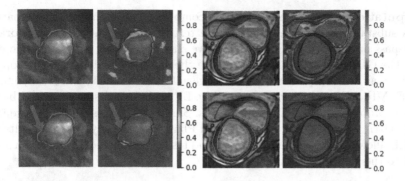

Fig. 4. Examples of visual uncertainty heatmaps based on variance for high uncertainty areas (red arrows) using LE (top) and DE (bottom) for breast mass and cardiac structure segmentation. Black and green contours correspond to ground truth. (Color figure online)

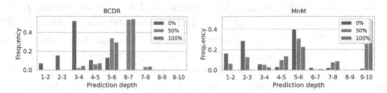

Fig. 5. PD distribution with 0%, 50%, and 100% of the images corrupted by Gaussian noise – MnM $\mathcal{N}(0.3, 0.7)$, BCDR Random Convolutions with kernel-size $(37, 37)$. Layer agreement threshold is 0.90 in terms of DSC for both datasets.

DE's uncertainty maps are overconfident, while LE manages to highlight the difficult areas. We believe that having such meaningful heatmaps is more helpful for the clinicians (e.g. for manual correction). More visual examples including entropy and MI are given in Appendix.

Example Difficulty Estimation. We evaluate example difficult estimation using PD by perturbing the proportion of images in the test set. We added random Gaussian noise to MnM dataset and used Random Convolutions [25] in BCDR as the model was robust to noise in mammogram images. Examples of perturbed images are provided in Appendix. Then, for a given sample, PD is the largest L corresponding to one of the N segmentation heads in a network, where the agreement between L and $L - 1$ is smaller than a threshold that is the same as in segmentation quality control. In this sense, PD represents the minimum number of layers after which the network reaches to a consensus segmentation. Figure 5 shows how the distribution of PD shifts towards higher values as the number of corrupted images increases in the test set for both BCDR and MnM datasets. Overall, cardiac structure segmentation is more difficult than breast mass segmentation while the latter is more robust to noise. This demonstrates how PD can be used to evaluate example difficulty for the segmentation task and detect outliers.

Computational Performance. The computational gain for LE compared to DE is substantial, both in training and testing due to the single network and single pass nature of LE. For training, we start measuring time after one epoch to let the GPU warm-up. Then, capture the training (including backprop) and test times as seconds per batch. The averaged times are 0.99, 0.23, 0.20, and 0.18 for DE, MH, LE, and Plain, respectively. LE is slightly faster than MH because the backprop is done at different depths. Similarly, the testing times are 0.240, 0.052, 0.047, 0.045 for DE, MH, LE, and Plain, respectively. These, results show that LE allows much efficient training and testing compared to DE and a similar speed to the Plain approach.

5 Conclusions

We proposed a novel uncertainty estimation approach that exhibits competitive results to the state-of-the-art DE using only a single network and outperforms another single-pass MH method. Compared to DE, our approach produces a more meaningful uncertainty heatmaps and allows estimating example difficulty in a single pass. Moreover, LE showed a considerable gain in terms of computational time for both training and testing. Experimental results showed the effectiveness of the proposed AULA metric to measure an image-level uncertainty measure. The capabilities of both AULA and PD were demonstrated in segmentation and image quality control experiments. We believe that the efficient and reliable uncertainty estimation that LE demonstrates will pave the way for more trustworthy DL applications in healthcare.

Acknowledgements. This study has received funding from the European Union's Horizon 2020 research and innovation programme under grant agreement No 952103.

References

1. Abdar, M., et al.: A review of uncertainty quantification in deep learning: techniques, applications and challenges. Inf. Fusion **76**, 243–297 (2021)
2. Bai, W., et al.: Automated cardiovascular magnetic resonance image analysis with fully convolutional networks. J. Cardiovasc. Magn. Reson. **20**(1), 1–12 (2018)
3. Baldock, R., Maennel, H., Neyshabur, B.: Deep learning through the lens of example difficulty. In: Advances in Neural Information Processing Systems, vol. 34 (2021)
4. Beluch, W.H., Genewein, T., Nürnberger, A., Köhler, J.M.: The power of ensembles for active learning in image classification. In: Proceedings of the IEEE Conference on Computer Vision and Pattern Recognition, pp. 9368–9377 (2018)
5. Campello, V.M., et al.: Multi-centre, multi-vendor and multi-disease cardiac segmentation: the M&Ms challenge. IEEE Trans. Med. Imaging **40**(12), 3543–3554 (2021)
6. Pinheiro Cinelli, L., Araújo Marins, M., Barros da Silva, E.A., Lima Netto, S.: Bayesian neural networks. In: Variational Methods for Machine Learning with Applications to Deep Networks, pp. 65–109. Springer, Cham (2021). https://doi.org/10.1007/978-3-030-70679-1_4

7. Gal, Y., Ghahramani, Z.: Dropout as a Bayesian approximation: representing model uncertainty in deep learning. In: International Conference on Machine Learning, pp. 1050–1059. PMLR (2016)
8. Gal, Y., et al.: Uncertainty in deep learning (2016)
9. Goodfellow, I., Bengio, Y., Courville, A.: Deep Learning. MIT Press (2016). http://www.deeplearningbook.org
10. He, K., Zhang, X., Ren, S., Sun, J.: Deep residual learning for image recognition. In: Proceedings of the IEEE Conference on Computer Vision and Pattern Recognition, pp. 770–778 (2016)
11. Hu, J., Shen, L., Sun, G.: Squeeze-and-excitation networks. In: Proceedings of the IEEE Conference on Computer Vision and Pattern Recognition, pp. 7132–7141 (2018)
12. Huang, G., Li, Y., Pleiss, G., Liu, Z., Hopcroft, J.E., Weinberger, K.Q.: Snapshot ensembles: Train 1, get M for free. In: International Conference on Learning Representations (2017). https://openreview.net/forum?id=BJYwwY9ll
13. Lakshminarayanan, B., Pritzel, A., Blundell, C.: Simple and scalable predictive uncertainty estimation using deep ensembles. In: Advances in Neural Information Processing Systems, vol. 30 (2017)
14. Liu, Y., Pagliardini, M., Chavdarova, T., Stich, S.U.: The peril of popular deep learning uncertainty estimation methods. In: Bayesian Deep Learning (BDL) Workshop at NeurIPS 2021 (2021)
15. Morcos, A., Raghu, M., Bengio, S.: Insights on representational similarity in neural networks with canonical correlation. In: Advances in Neural Information Processing Systems, vol. 31 (2018)
16. Moura, D.C., et al.: Benchmarking datasets for breast cancer computer-aided diagnosis (CADx). In: Ruiz-Shulcloper, J., Sanniti di Baja, G. (eds.) CIARP 2013. LNCS, vol. 8258, pp. 326–333. Springer, Heidelberg (2013). https://doi.org/10.1007/978-3-642-41822-8_41
17. Ng, M., Guo, F., Biswas, L., Wright, G.A.: Estimating uncertainty in neural networks for segmentation quality control. In: 32nd International Conference on Neural Information Processing Systems (NIPS 2018), Montréal, Canada, no. NIPS, pp. 3–6 (2018)
18. Quiñonero-Candela, J., Rasmussen, C.E., Sinz, F., Bousquet, O., Schölkopf, B.: Evaluating predictive uncertainty challenge. In: Quiñonero-Candela, J., Dagan, I., Magnini, B., d'Alché-Buc, F. (eds.) MLCW 2005. LNCS (LNAI), vol. 3944, pp. 1–27. Springer, Heidelberg (2006). https://doi.org/10.1007/11736790_1
19. Rezaei, Z.: A review on image-based approaches for breast cancer detection, segmentation, and classification. Expert Syst. Appl. **182**, 115204 (2021)
20. Ronneberger, O., Fischer, P., Brox, T.: U-Net: convolutional networks for biomedical image segmentation. In: Navab, N., Hornegger, J., Wells, W.M., Frangi, A.F. (eds.) MICCAI 2015. LNCS, vol. 9351, pp. 234–241. Springer, Cham (2015). https://doi.org/10.1007/978-3-319-24574-4_28
21. Sudre, C.H., Li, W., Vercauteren, T., Ourselin, S., Jorge Cardoso, M.: Generalised dice overlap as a deep learning loss function for highly unbalanced segmentations. In: Cardoso, M.J., et al. (eds.) DLMIA/ML-CDS -2017. LNCS, vol. 10553, pp. 240–248. Springer, Cham (2017). https://doi.org/10.1007/978-3-319-67558-9_28
22. Toneva, M., Sordoni, A., des Combes, R.T., Trischler, A., Bengio, Y., Gordon, G.J.: An empirical study of example forgetting during deep neural network learning. In: International Conference on Learning Representations (2019). https://openreview.net/forum?id=BJlxm30cKm

23. Valdenegro-Toro, M.: Deep sub-ensembles for fast uncertainty estimation in image classification. In: Bayesian Deep Learning (BDL) Workshop at NeurIPS (2019)
24. Warfield, S.K., Zou, K.H., Wells, W.M.: Simultaneous truth and performance level estimation (STAPLE): an algorithm for the validation of image segmentation. IEEE Trans. Med. Imaging **23**(7), 903–921 (2004)
25. Xu, Z., Liu, D., Yang, J., Raffel, C., Niethammer, M.: Robust and generalizable visual representation learning via random convolutions. In: International Conference on Learning Representations (2021). https://openreview.net/forum?id=BVSM0x3EDK6
26. Young, A.T., Amara, D., Bhattacharya, A., Wei, M.L.: Patient and general public attitudes towards clinical artificial intelligence: a mixed methods systematic review. Lancet Digital Health **3**(9), e599–e611 (2021)

DEUE: Delta Ensemble Uncertainty Estimation for a More Robust Estimation of Ejection Fraction

Mohammad Mahdi Kazemi Esfeh[1]([✉]), Zahra Gholami[1], Christina Luong[2], Teresa Tsang[2], and Purang Abolmaesumi[1]

[1] The University of British Columbia, Vancouver, BC, Canada
mahdik@ece.ubc.ca
[2] Vancouver General Hospital, Vancouver, BC, Canada

Abstract. Left Ventricular Ejection Fraction (LVEF) as a critical clinical index is widely used to measure the functionality of the cyclic contraction of the left ventricle of the heart. Limited amount of available specialist-annotated data, low and variable quality of captured ultrasound images, and substantial inter/intra-observer variability in gold-standard measurements impose challenges on the robust data-driven automated estimation of LVEF in echocardiography (echo). Deep learning algorithms have recently shown state-of-the-art performance in cardiovascular image analysis. However, these algorithms are usually overconfident in their outputs even if they provide any measure of their output uncertainty. In addition, most of the uncertainty estimation methods in deep learning literature are either exclusively designed for classification tasks or are too memory/time expensive to be deployed on mobile devices or in clinical workflows that demand real-time memory-efficient estimations. In this work, we propose Delta Ensemble Uncertainty Estimation, a novel sampling-free method for estimating the epistemic uncertainty of deep learning algorithms for regression tasks. Our approach provides high-quality, architecture-agnostic and memory/time-efficient estimation of epistemic uncertainty with a single feed-forward pass through the network. We validate our proposed method on the task of LVEF estimation on EchoNet-Dynamic, a publicly available echo dataset, by performing a thorough comparison with multiple baseline methods.

Keywords: Deep learning · Uncertainty · Delta method · Ensemble · Epistemic · Ejection fraction · Echocardiography · Ultrasound imaging

This work is funded in part by the Natural Sciences and Engineering Research Council of Canada (NSERC), and the Canadian Institutes of Health Research (CIHR).
M. M. Kazemi Esfeh and Z. Gholami—Joint first authorship.
T. Tsang and P. Abolmaesumi—Joint senior authorship.

L. Wang et al. (Eds.): MICCAI 2022, LNCS 13438, pp. 525–534, 2022.
https://doi.org/10.1007/978-3-031-16452-1_50

1   Introduction

1.1   Clinical Background

A human cardiac cycle consists of systole and diastole phases during which the ventricles of the heart contract and expand, respectively. LVEF (or simply EF) is defined as the ratio of the blood leaving the left ventricle during systole to the maximum amount of blood in the left ventricle in a cycle (end-diastolic volume). Typically, any EF in the range $EF = 65\% \pm 10\%$ is considered normal while lower values of EF indicate cardiac systole dysfunction. Studies show an inverse linear relationship between EF and heart failure (HF) and an association of ischemic stroke with very low EF ($EF \leq 15\%$) [28]. Cognitive aging, Alzheimer's and cerebrovascular disease are also linked to low-EF [11]. Timely and reliable evaluation of EF is essential as its lower values are linked to extremely dangerous outcomes and death.

1.2   Related Works

In the past decade, deep learning (DL) algorithms have achieved state-of-the-art performance in various applications, such as computer vision, medical imaging, autonomous driving, language analysis and so on. DL algorithms have specifically been used for cardiovascular image acquisition and analysis [18]. Although DL-based methods show promising performance, they usually suffer from overconfident predictions. These methods either do not give any uncertainty estimations, or their uncertainty estimates are poorly calibrated that cannot be directly employed in high-stakes clinical applications such as cardiovascular imaging [1,6,10,12–14,25,30]. The predictive uncertainty of DL methods is usually categorized into two separate classes, aleatoric uncertainty and epistemic uncertainty. Aleatoric uncertainty is the uncertainty of the model due to the inherent noise in data and cannot be reduced by collecting more data. On the other hand, epistemic uncertainty is the reducible uncertainty that originates from the model's lack of knowledge and can be explained away by collecting more data. Many works in the literature have attempted to address the problem of uncertainty estimation in DL by proposing methods to estimate calibrated uncertainties for DL. In [7], authors propose a method that uses dropout [26] layers at the inference time to estimate the epistemic uncertainty in DL which is equivalent to the uncertainty estimated by the Bayesian neural networks [6] under certain conditions. These methods usually give more calibrated uncertainties in comparison to the pure DL algorithms; however, they require many forward passes during the inference that makes them unsuitable for real-time applications. A few works also proposed deep ensembles (DE) approach to estimate the uncertainty in DL [16]. As discussed in [25], these methods usually give well-calibrated uncertainties, albeit they require evaluation of multiple models at the inference time along with a great amount of memory to store the parameters of these models, which prevents them to be deployed on smaller mobile devices. Several groups have aimed to alleviate these issues by proposing uncertainty estimation methods that are more time and/or memory-efficient.

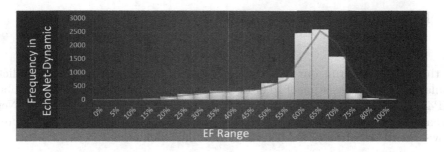

Fig. 1. The distribution of EF labels in EchoNet-Dynamic [21].

For instance, in [1,30] authors propose deterministic distance-based methods to capture the uncertainty of DL methods for classification tasks. The methods proposed in these works are not directly applicable to regression. Recently, [20] suggested an epistemic uncertainty estimation approach based on the Delta Method [15,31]. The authors of [20] propose to approximate the covariance matrix in the delta method by Hessian, outer-products of gradients and the Sandwich estimators [5,24]. Although their approach is mathematically rigorous, in real-world applications, the number of parameters of deep neural networks is usually very big, which can make their method either intractable or highly inaccurate.

1.3   Our Contribution

In this work, we propose a novel sampling-free approach to estimate the uncertainty of DL algorithms for regression tasks based on the Delta Method [31] and deep ensembles [16] for uncertainty estimation. We call our proposed method "Delta Ensemble Uncertainty Estimation (DEUE)". DEUE carries the pros of the above-mentioned methods while significantly mitigating their cons. DEUE is notably more time-efficient and much less memory-consuming at the inference time in comparison to DE. Also, grounded on the success of deep ensembles in epistemic uncertainty estimation [25], DEUE gives calibrated estimations of epistemic uncertainty while it eliminates the inaccuracies that approximating the covariance matrix by Hessian, outer-products of gradients and the Sandwich estimators impose on the estimated uncertainties. In addition, our model is scalable to arbitrary deep learning architectures without any limitations. Furthermore, DEUE is fundamentally different from the methods that are proposed in [2,7] as it does not assume any specific distribution or prior knowledge for the network output or the network parameters, it does not impose architectural constraints, and it does not need multiple forward-passes during the inference phase. Our main contributions can be summarized as proposing DEUE, a novel epistemic uncertainty estimation method for DL algorithms for regression tasks that 1) is neural architecture-agnostic; 2) is real-time and deterministic in a sense that it only requires one forward-pass at the inference time; 3) is memory-efficient; 4) is scalable and is not computationally intensive for large DL models as it does not rely on any numerical covariance estimation methods; and 5) estimates high-quality uncertainties, evaluated on EchoNet-Dynamic dataset.

2   Material and Methods

2.1   EF Dataset

In this study, We run our experiments on EchoNet-Dynamic [21], a publicly available dataset consisting of 10,031 echo exams captured in apical four-chamber (AP4) view. Multiple labels and annotations are provided with the EchoNet-Dynamic from which we only use the EF labels to run our experiments. Figure 1 shows the distribution of EchoNet-Dynamic data points.

2.2   Problem Definition and Method

A deep learning algorithm can be modeled as a learning algorithm $\mathcal{L}$ that maps a dataset D containing n data points each sampled from the joint distribution $\mathcal{P}_{(X,Y)}$ into a parametric function f_W which maps each x to its predicted label. Formally, one can write

$$f_W = \mathcal{L}(D_{X,Y}). \tag{1}$$

For simplicity of the notation, we only focus on single-output deep regression algorithms here. Hence, we assume each input $x \sim \mathcal{P}_X$ corresponds to a label $y \in \Re$ with $y \sim \mathcal{P}_{(Y|x)}$, where $\mathcal{P}_X$ is the distribution of input data and $\mathcal{P}_{(Y|x)}$ is the true conditional distribution of the label given input. In the following, we define the uncertainty of a deep learning algorithm.

Definition 1. *Assume the function f_W is the output of the deep learning algorithm $\mathcal{L}$ on dataset D with distribution $\mathcal{D}_{X,y}$. We define $U_{\mathcal{L}}(x)$, the uncertainty of $\mathcal{L}$ at any point x sampled from $\mathcal{P}_X$ as*

$$U_{\mathcal{L}}(x) := \mathbb{E}[(f_W(x) - y)^2] = \int (f_W(x) - y)^2 d\mathcal{P}_{(Y|x)}, \tag{2}$$

where $y \sim \mathcal{P}_{(Y|x)}$.

According to Definition 1, the uncertainty of a deep learning algorithm for each data point is defined as expected squared prediction error. This definition is natural as our ultimate goal with uncertainty estimation is to have a measure of how reliable the prediction of the model is for a specific input. In Definition 1, we assumed that the expectation is defined. We now deploy the Delta Method [31] to estimate the uncertainty of a DL model, assuming that W^* is the vector of optimal parameters of the DL model that approximates the true regressor f_{W^*}. Formally,

$$W^* \in \arg\min_W \mathbb{E}[L(f_W(x), y)] = \int L(f_W(x), y) d\mathcal{P}_{(Y|x)}, \tag{3}$$

for some loss function $L : \Re \times \Re \to \Re^+$, where $\Re^+$ is the set of non-negative real numbers. Approximating f_W by its first order Taylor's expansion in a small neighbourhood of W^*, we can write

$$\hat{y}_x := f_W(x) \simeq f_{W^*}(x) + g_{W^*,x}^T(W - W^*), \tag{4}$$

where $g_{W^*,x}$ denotes the gradient of $f_W(x)$ with respect to the parameters at W^* evaluated at x and $(.)^T$ is matrix transpose. The true label y_x for input x can be written as

$$y_x = f_{W^*}(x) + \epsilon_X, \tag{5}$$

where ϵ_x denotes the prediction error of the optimal model for input x. Combining Eqs. 4 and 5 we get

$$y_x - \hat{y}_x \simeq (f_{W^*}(X) + \epsilon_x) - (f_{W^*} + g_{W^*,x}^T(W - W^*)). \tag{6}$$

Canceling out f_{W^*} from the right hand side of Eq. 6, assuming independence of the two remaining terms, squaring and taking expectation from both sides, one gets

$$U_{\mathcal{L}}(x) = \mathbb{E}[(y_x - \hat{y}_x)^2] \simeq \mathbb{E}[(g_{W^*,x}^T(W - W^*))^2]. \tag{7}$$

Here, we assumed a deep enough DL model architecture and neglected the terms containing ϵ_x on the right hand side of Eq. 7. Note that, this is a reasonable assumption due to the expressive power of deep neural networks [8,19,22] and the fact that W^* represents optimal parameters. We can write

$$U_{\mathcal{L}}(x) \simeq \mathbb{E}[g_{W^*,x}^T(W - W^*)(W - W^*)^T g_{W^*,x}], \tag{8}$$

which yields

$$U_{\mathcal{L}}(x) \simeq g_{W^*,x}^T \Sigma g_{W^*,x}. \tag{9}$$

In Eq. 9, Σ represents the covariance matrix of the parameters of the model. Since the number of parameters of DL models is usually very large ($>10^4$), direct computation of the covariance matrix Σ is intractable. Several works have attempted to approximate Σ for DL models [3,17,20]. However, the methods proposed in these works are either highly inaccurate for large models and result in large error in uncertainty approximations, or are very time/memory expensive. Here, we assume the weights of the DL model are independent (mean-field approximation [32]). Also, according to the theoretical and empirical results [4], we expect the weights to have low variances. Hence, We sample multiple weights W_i, $i = 1, 2, \cdots, M$ as is suggested in [16], by training an ensemble of M DL models with the same architecture and different initializations. We assume all these M models are trained using a stochastic gradient method for enough number of epochs. Then, we approximate Σ by $\hat{\Sigma}_M$, a diagonal matrix with the same size as Σ, whose entries are empirical variances of weights of these M models, leading to

$$U_{\mathcal{L}} \simeq g_{W^*,x}^T \hat{\Sigma}_M g_{W^*,x}. \tag{10}$$

As it can be seen, the approximated uncertainty on the right-hand side of Eq. 10 still depends on the optimal parameters W^*. Since the optimization problem in 3 is non-convex, we usually do not have access to the optimal parameters W^*, and we need to approximate the right-hand side of Eq. 10. Consequently, we approximate $g_{W^*,x}$ by $g_{W,x}$. In our experiments, we use the parameters of the trained model with the best performance on the validation set as W and

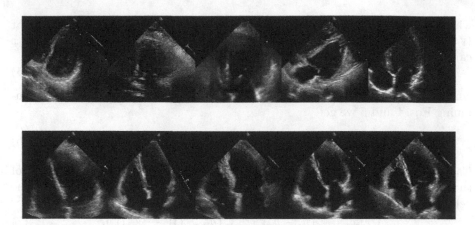

Fig. 2. A closer look at the frames of 5 videos with the highest epistemic uncertainty (top row) and the lowest epistemic uncertainty (bottom row) estimated by DEUE. The top row includes videos with wrong color-maps, wrong imaging angles and zoomed videos. On the other hand, the videos on the bottom are AP4-viewed high-quality videos.

compute the gradients (i.e. one of the M models in the ensemble). Then, the uncertainty of a DL model $\mathcal{L}$ can be approximated by DEUE as

$$U_{\mathcal{L}}(x) \simeq g_{W,x}^T \hat{\Sigma}_M g_{W,x}. \tag{11}$$

It is worth mentioning that in order to estimate the epistemic uncertainty using DEUE, one only needs to store the diagonal entries of $\hat{\Sigma}_M$ and the computations are of the order of vector-vector multiplication.

3   Experiments and Results

In order to compare the quality of the epistemic uncertainties estimated by our method to other available methods for the estimation of epistemic uncertainty in regression tasks, we choose ResNet18 [9] neural architecture with (2+1)D convolutional layers [27]. We specifically use this architecture as it has been used in [12,21] for the task of EF estimation and makes a better side-by-side comparison of the uncertainty estimations possible. This network takes 32 frames of size 112×112 sampled from echo videos and predicts a number as the output of the last fully-connected (FC) layer in the range $0\% \leq EF \leq 100\%$. We trained five copies of this network for 100 epochs using PyTorch [23], each with the hyper parameters suggested in [21] on 7,465 training samples of EchoNet-Dynamic with five different random parameter initialization as is suggested in [16] to get W_i, $i = 1, 2, \cdots 5$. We computed the empirical variance of each parameter using the weights of these networks. Using these variances we form the diagonal of matrix $\hat{\Sigma}_M$ in Eq. 11. We select the model that best performs in terms of mean squared error on the validation set of EcheNet-Dynamic, which contains 1,288 videos.

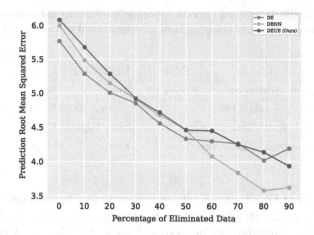

Fig. 3. Prediction root mean squared error of DE [16], DBNN [12] and DEUE against percentage of eliminated data from the test set of Echo-Net. Different percentage of the test data have been removed based on their associated epistemic uncertainties estimated by the respective models.

We use this model to compute the gradient of the output at the test input x using back-propagation, and substitute it in Eq. 11 to get the estimated epistemic uncertainty of the model on x. It is worth noting that DEUE does not change the training procedure, and it can be directly applied on any pre-trained model. On the top row of Fig. 2, 5 frames from the videos with the most epistemic uncertainty estimated by DEUE is shown. As it can be seen, these videos are captured from the wrong angle, have wrong color map, are zoomed-in and do not show the AP4-view. The images shown on the bottom row of Fig. 2 are frames of videos with the least amount of epistemic uncertainty estimated by DEUE. These videos in contrast to the videos on the top row are high quality, zoomed-out, AP4-viewed videos with the correct color maps. This suggests that the uncertainties estimated by DEUE agree with the quality of the associated input videos. In order to compare the calibration of the epistemic uncertainties estimated by DEUE to the ones estimated by the state-of-the-art deep ensembles (DE) [16] and Deep Bayesian Neural Networks (DBNN) [12], we train networks with the same architectures (ResNet(2+1)D) using these methods to get their uncertainty estimates on the test set of EchoNet-Dynamic.

The quality of the uncertainties estimated by DEUE on the test-set of Echonet-Dynamic, which contains 1,277 videos, is compared to the ones esti-mated by DE [16] and DBNN [12] in Fig. 3. As shown in this figure, the uncertain-ties estimated by all these methods benefit from similar amount of calibration. Even though a single deterministic deep regression model (DDR [21]) performs worse than the DE and DBNN in terms of prediction error, by rejecting only 30% of the test data using the respective estimated uncertainties, DEUE, DE and DBNN all show similar test error which shows that the uncertainties estimated by DEUE are highly-calibrated. This is while the computational cost and mem-

Table 1. A comparison between various epistemic uncertainty estimation methods for regression in terms of memory consumption, computational efficiency and architectural limitations.

	DDR [21]	DBNN [12]	DE [16]	**DEUE**
Need changes in architecture	N/A	Yes	No	No
Forward passes per prediction	1	Several (30)	Several (5)	1
Computational effort - inference	Low	Very High	High	**Low**
Memory consumption - inference	Low	Low	High	**Low**

ory consumption of DEUE at the inference time is significantly lower than those of the two other methods, which makes it superior for real-time applications and makes it a better candidate to be deployed on mobile devices. Computational cost and memory consumption of these models are compared in Table 1. In this work, the models were trained on four NVIDIA Tesla V100 GPUs with 32 GB of memory from UBC ARC Sockeye [29].

4   Conclusion

In this paper, we proposed DEUE, a novel architecture-agnostic method to estimate the epistemic uncertainty of deep learning algorithms. DEUE combines the benefits of the Delta method and deep ensembles approaches for epistemic uncertainty estimation in a memory/time-efficient manner. Also, being a general method that does not impose any architectural or computational constraints during the training and inference, DEUE is directly applicable to any deep regression model to capture the epistemic uncertainty associated with the model. We validated DEUE on EchoNet-Dynamic, a publicly available dataset, through a thorough side-by-side comparison to multiple state-of-the-art methods available in the literature. We also note that usage of DEUE is not limited to EF estimation task as it is a generic approach to estimate the epistemic uncertainty of DL algorithms and can be used to estimate the epistemic uncertainty associated with predicting any clinical index.

References

1. van Amersfoort, J., Smith, L., Teh, Y.W., Gal, Y.: Simple and scalable epistemic uncertainty estimation using a single deep deterministic neural network (2020)
2. Blundell, C., Cornebise, J., Kavukcuoglu, K., Wierstra, D.: Weight uncertainty in neural network. In: International Conference on Machine Learning, pp. 1613–1622. PMLR (2015)
3. Cardot, H., Degras, D.: Online principal component analysis in high dimension: which algorithm to choose? Int. Stat. Rev. **86**(1), 29–50 (2018)

4. Choromanska, A., Henaff, M., Mathieu, M., Ben Arous, G., LeCun, Y.: The loss surfaces of multilayer networks. In: Lebanon, G., Vishwanathan, S.V.N. (eds.) Proceedings of the Eighteenth International Conference on Artificial Intelligence and Statistics, Proceedings of Machine Learning Research, San Diego, California, USA, vol. 38, pp. 192–204. PMLR (2015). https://proceedings.mlr.press/v38/choromanska15.html
5. Freedman, D.A.: On the so-called "Huber Sandwich Estimator" and "robust standard errors.". Am. Stat. **60**(4), 299–302 (2006)
6. Gal, Y.: Uncertainty in deep learning. Ph.D. thesis, University of Cambridge (2016)
7. Gal, Y., Ghahramani, Z.: Dropout as a Bayesian approximation: representing model uncertainty in deep learning. In: International Conference on Machine Learning, pp. 1050–1059 (2016)
8. Hanin, B., Sellke, M.: Approximating continuous functions by ReLU nets of minimal width. arXiv preprint arXiv:1710.11278 (2017)
9. He, K., et al.: Deep residual learning for image recognition. In: Proceedings of the IEEE CVPR, pp. 770–778 (2016)
10. Jain, M., et al.: DEUP: direct epistemic uncertainty prediction. arXiv preprint arXiv:2102.08501 (2021)
11. Jefferson, A.L., et al.: Relation of left ventricular ejection fraction to cognitive aging (from the Framingham Heart Study). Am. J. Cardiol. **108**(9), 1346–1351 (2011)
12. Kazemi Esfeh, M.M., Luong, C., Behnami, D., Tsang, T., Abolmaesumi, P.: A deep Bayesian video analysis framework: towards a more robust estimation of ejection fraction. In: Martel, A.L., et al. (eds.) MICCAI 2020. LNCS, vol. 12262, pp. 582–590. Springer, Cham (2020). https://doi.org/10.1007/978-3-030-59713-9_56
13. Kendall, A., Gal, Y.: What uncertainties do we need in Bayesian deep learning for computer vision. In: NIPS, pp. 5574–5584 (2017)
14. Kendall, A., Gal, Y., Cipolla, R.: Multi-task learning using uncertainty to weigh losses for scene geometry and semantics. In: Proceedings of the IEEE Conference on Computer Vision and Pattern Recognition, pp. 7482–7491 (2018)
15. Khosravi, A., Nahavandi, S., Creighton, D., Atiya, A.F.: Comprehensive review of neural network-based prediction intervals and new advances. IEEE Trans. Neural Netw. **22**(9), 1341–1356 (2011)
16. Lakshminarayanan, B., Pritzel, A., Blundell, C.: Simple and scalable predictive uncertainty estimation using deep ensembles. In: Advances in Neural Information Processing Systems, vol. 30 (2017)
17. Levy, A., Lindenbaum, M.: Sequential Karhunen-Loeve basis extraction and its application to images. In: Proceedings 1998 International Conference on Image Processing. ICIP98 (Cat. No. 98CB36269), vol. 2, pp. 456–460 (1998). https://doi.org/10.1109/ICIP.1998.723422
18. Litjens, G., et al.: State-of-the-art deep learning in cardiovascular image analysis. JACC: Cardiovasc. Imaging **12**(8), 1549–1565 (2019)
19. Lu, Z., Pu, H., Wang, F., Hu, Z., Wang, L.: The expressive power of neural networks: a view from the width. In: Advances in Neural Information Processing Systems, vol. 30 (2017)
20. Nilsen, G.K., Munthe-Kaas, A.Z., Skaug, H.J., Brun, M.: Epistemic uncertainty quantification in deep learning classification by the delta method. Neural Netw. **145**, 164–176 (2022)
21. Ouyang, D., et al.: Interpretable AI for beat-to-beat cardiac function assessment. medRxiv (2019). https://doi.org/10.1101/19012419

22. Park, S., Yun, C., Lee, J., Shin, J.: Minimum width for universal approximation. arXiv preprint arXiv:2006.08859 (2020)

23. Paszke, A., et al.: PyTorch: an imperative style, high-performance deep learning library. In: Wallach, H., Larochelle, H., Beygelzimer, A., d' Alché-Buc, F., Fox, E., Garnett, R. (eds.) Advances in Neural Information Processing Systems, vol. 32, pp. 8024–8035. Curran Associates, Inc. (2019). http://papers.neurips.cc/paper/9015-pytorch-an-imperative-style-high-performance-deep-learning-library.pdf

24. Schulam, P., Saria, S.: Can you trust this prediction? Auditing pointwise reliability after learning. In: The 22nd International Conference on Artificial Intelligence and Statistics, pp. 1022–1031. PMLR (2019)

25. Snoek, J., et al.: Can you trust your model's uncertainty? Evaluating predictive uncertainty under dataset shift. In: Advances in Neural Information Processing Systems, pp. 13969–13980 (2019)

26. Srivastava, N., Hinton, G., Krizhevsky, A., Sutskever, I., Salakhutdinov, R.: Dropout: a simple way to prevent neural networks from overfitting. J. Mach. Learn. Res. 15(1), 1929–1958 (2014)

27. Tran, D., et al.: A closer look at spatiotemporal convolutions for action recognition. In: Proceedings of the IEEE CVPR, pp. 6450–6459 (2018)

28. Tullio, D., et al.: Left ventricular ejection fraction and risk of stroke and cardiac events in heart failure: data from the warfarin versus aspirin in reduced ejection fraction trial. Stroke 47(8), 2031–2037 (2016)

29. UBC Advanced Research Computing: UBC arc sockeye (2019). https://doi.org/10.14288/SOCKEYE. https://arc.ubc.ca/ubc-arc-sockeye

30. Van Amersfoort, J., Smith, L., Teh, Y.W., Gal, Y.: Uncertainty estimation using a single deep deterministic neural network. In: International Conference on Machine Learning, pp. 9690–9700. PMLR (2020)

31. Ver Hoef, J.M.: Who invented the delta method? Am. Stat. 66(2), 124–127 (2012)

32. Wainwright, M.J., et al.: Graphical models, exponential families, and variational inference. Found. Trends Mach. Learn. 1(1–2), 1–305 (2008)

Efficient Bayesian Uncertainty Estimation for nnU-Net

Yidong Zhao[1], Changchun Yang[1], Artur Schweidtmann[2], and Qian Tao[1(✉)]

[1] Department of Imaging Physics, Delft University of Technology,
Delft, The Netherlands
q.tao@tudelft.nl
[2] Department of Chemical Engineering, Delft University of Technology,
Delft, The Netherlands

Abstract. The self-configuring nnU-Net has achieved leading performance in a large range of medical image segmentation challenges. It is widely considered as the model of choice and a strong baseline for medical image segmentation. However, despite its extraordinary performance, nnU-Net does not supply a measure of uncertainty to indicate its possible failure. This can be problematic for large-scale image segmentation applications, where data are heterogeneous and nnU-Net may fail without notice. In this work, we introduce a novel method to estimate nnU-Net uncertainty for medical image segmentation. We propose a highly effective scheme for posterior sampling of weight space for Bayesian uncertainty estimation. Different from previous baseline methods such as Monte Carlo Dropout and mean-field Bayesian Neural Networks, our proposed method does not require a variational architecture and keeps the original nnU-Net architecture intact, thereby preserving its excellent performance and ease of use. Additionally, we boost the segmentation performance over the original nnU-Net via marginalizing multi-modal posterior models. We applied our method on the public ACDC and M&M datasets of cardiac MRI and demonstrated improved uncertainty estimation over a range of baseline methods. The proposed method further strengthens nnU-Net for medical image segmentation in terms of both segmentation accuracy and quality control.

Keywords: nnU-Net · Uncertainty estimation · Variational inference · Stochastic gradient descent

1 Introduction

Manually delineating the region of interest from medical images is immensely expensive in clinical applications. Among various automatic medical image segmentation methods, the U-Net architecture [24], in particular the self-configuring nnU-Net framework [14], has achieved state-of-the-art performance in a wide range of medical image segmentation tasks [2,5]. Nevertheless, the reliability of neural networks remains a major concern for medical applications, due to their

L. Wang et al. (Eds.): MICCAI 2022, LNCS 13438, pp. 535–544, 2022.
https://doi.org/10.1007/978-3-031-16452-1_51

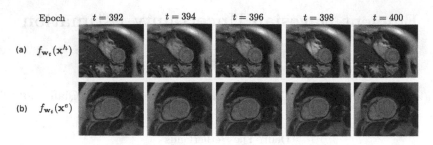

Fig. 1. We observe that the network checkpoints at various training epochs make diverse predictions when the network is uncertain on a *hard* input x^h (a). On the contrary, predictions of good quality on an *easy* input x^e enjoys consistency across checkpoints (b). We leverage this phenomenon to perform Bayesian inference and quantify uncertainty of network predictions.

over-parametrization and poor interpretability. Using the softmax output as a categorical probability distribution proxy is known to cause model miscalibration, which often leads to over-confidence in errors [21]. This can be problematic for large-scale medical image segmentation applications, where data are heterogeneous and nnU-Net may fail without notice. Accurate uncertainty estimation is highly important in clinical deployment of automatic segmentation models [16].

Previous efforts on uncertainty estimation of neural networks are categorized as either Bayesian or non-Bayesian [21]. Several non-Bayesian strategies have been proposed to quantify the predictive uncertainty in medical image segmentation. Guo *et al.* proposed to use temperature scaling [12] to mitigate the miscalibration in softmax. Probabilistic U-Net [17] aims at generating a set of feasible segmentation maps. Baumgartner *et al.* proposed a hierarchical model to learn the distribution in latent spaces and make probabilistic predictions [1]. However, these methods require modification of the original network, sometimes to a significant extent, therefore hard to be integrated with the well-configured nnU-Net.

Unlike non-Bayesian approaches, Bayesian neural networks (BNNs) learn the weight posterior distribution given the training data. At inference time, a probabilistic prediction is made, which delivers a natural epistemic uncertainty [4]. However, deriving weight posterior is an intractable problem, and Variational Inference (VI) [3] is often used for its approximation. The popular mean-field VI [4] doubles the network parameter assuming independence among weights, and can be unstable during training [23]. Gal *et al.* proposed Monte-Carlo Dropout (MC-Dropout) [9] as a VI proxy by enabling dropout layers at test time. The method is theoretically and practically sound, however, recent works [6,10,11] reported silent failure and poor calibration, with degraded segmentation performance. Deep Ensembles [18] estimate network uncertainty via averaging independently trained networks. It is robust [23] but highly costly in computation, especially for models which demand lengthy training themselves.

We propose a novel method for medical image segmentation uncertainty estimation, which substantially outperforms the popular MC-Dropout, while being

significantly more efficient than deep ensembles. We are inspired by the optimization theory that during stochastic gradient descent (SGD), the network
weights continuously explore the solution space, which is approximately equivalent to weight space posterior sampling [19,20,22]. While taken at appropriate
moments of SGD, the network can be sampled *a posteriori*, and uncertainty can
be reflected in the agreement among these posterior models, as illustrated in
Fig. 1. This generic methodology enables VI approximation on any network,
including the delicately-configured nnU-Net. The following contributions are
made:

- A novel VI approximation method that realizes efficient posterior estimation
  of a deep model.
- An extension to the nnU-Net for uncertainty estimation in medical image
  segmentation, with significantly improved performance over several baseline
  methods including MC-Dropout.
- Further improvement of the segmentation performance beyond the original
  nnU-Net, as showcased on cardiac magnetic resonance (CMR) data.

2   Methods

2.1   Bayesian Inference

Given a training dataset $\mathcal{D} = \{(\mathbf{x}_i, \mathbf{y}_i)\}_{i=1}^{N}$ with N image and segmentation label
pairs, the BNN fits the posterior $p(\mathbf{w}|\mathcal{D})$ over network weights $\mathbf{w}$. At inference
time, the probabilistic prediction on a test image $\mathbf{x}^*$ can be formulated as the
marginalization over parameter $\mathbf{w}$:

$$p(\mathbf{y}^*|\mathbf{x}^*, \mathcal{D}) = \int p(\mathbf{y}^*|\mathbf{x}^*, \mathbf{w})p(\mathbf{w}|\mathcal{D}) \, d\mathbf{w} \qquad (1)$$

We describe the proposed trajectory-based posterior sampling from $p(\mathbf{w}|\mathcal{D})$ in
Sect. 2.2 and our final multi-modal Bayesian inference based on cyclical training
in Sect. 2.3.

2.2   SGD Bayesian Inference

Single-modal Posterior Sampling. During the SGD training, the weights
first move towards a local optimum and then oscillate in the vicinity. The standard nnU-Net uses the polynomial learning rate decay scheme, in which the
learning rate approaches zero as the epoch increases. The vanishing learning rate
causes the network weights to converge. In order to make the weights explore a
wider neighborhood around the local optimum, we follow [15] to set the learning
rate to a constant value after γ fraction of the total epoch budget T. For each
training epoch $t \in [\gamma T, T]$, the weight checkpoint $\mathbf{w}_t$ is approximately a sample
drawn from a single-modal weight posterior: $\mathbf{w}_t \sim p(\mathbf{w}|\mathcal{D})$. In Fig. 1 (a) and (b),
we show the exemplar predictions made by various checkpoints on an *easy* and
a *hard* example, respectively.

Inference and Uncertainty Estimation. The $p(\mathbf{y}^*|\mathbf{x}^*, \mathbf{w})$ term in Eq. (1) corresponds to the model forward pass $f_\mathbf{w}(\mathbf{x})$ at weights $\mathbf{w}$. However, both the weight posterior and the integral are intractable for deep neural networks. In this work, we keep the intermediate weights (i.e. checkpoints) during SGD training as posterior samples after the learning stabilizes: $\mathbf{W} = \{\mathbf{w}_t | \gamma T < t \leq T\}$. Then, the Monte-Carlo approximation for the predictive posterior $p(\mathbf{y}^*|\mathbf{x}^*, \mathcal{D})$ can be computed by taking the discrete version of Eq. (1):

$$p(\mathbf{y}^*|\mathbf{x}^*, \mathcal{D}) \approx \frac{1}{n} \sum_{i=1}^{n} p(\mathbf{y}^*|\mathbf{x}^*, \mathbf{w}_{t_i}) \tag{2}$$

where $\mathbf{w}_{t_i} \in \mathbf{W}$ and n is the number of checkpoints out of the posterior sampling of the model. To generate the uncertainty map, we compute the entropy of the predictive $C-$class categorical distribution $H(\mathbf{y}_{i,j}^*)$ for each voxel (i, j), with 0 indicating the lowest uncertainty.

$$H(\mathbf{y}_{i,j}^*) = -\sum_{k=1}^{C} p(\mathbf{y}_{i,j}^* = k|\mathbf{x}^*, \mathcal{D}) \log_2 p(\mathbf{y}_{i,j}^* = k|\mathbf{x}^*, \mathcal{D}) \tag{3}$$

Stochastic Weight Averaging. An alternative to the prediction space averaging in Eq. (2) is the Stochastic Weight Averaging (SWA) [15], which takes average in the weight space instead: $p(\mathbf{y}^*|\mathbf{x}^*, \mathcal{D}) = p(\mathbf{y}^*|\mathbf{x}^*, \overline{\mathbf{w}})$, where $\overline{\mathbf{w}} = \frac{1}{n} \sum_{i=1}^{n} \mathbf{w}_{t_i}$, to construct a new aggregated model with improved performance [15]. After weight averaging, the network needs to perform one more epoch of forward passes to update the batch normalization layer parameters before inference.

2.3 Multi-modal Posterior Sampling

Cyclical Learning Rate. The traditional SGD converges to the neighborhood of a single local optimum, hence the checkpoints capture only a single mode of the weight posterior. The diversity in weight samples has proven beneficial for uncertainty estimation [7,8]. In order to capture a multi-modal geometry in weight space, we employ a cyclical learning rate [13] which periodically drives the weights out of the attraction region of a local optimum. However, the cosine annealing scheme proposed in [13] causes instability in the nnU-Net training. We divide the training epoch budget T to M cycles, each of which consumes $T_c = \frac{T}{M}$ epochs. A high restart learning rate α_r is set only for the first epoch in each training cycle. After γ fraction of T_c epochs, we keep the gradient update step constant. Our proposed learning rate scheme is formulated as Eq. (4):

$$\alpha(t) = \begin{cases} \alpha_r, & t_c = 0 \\ \alpha_0 \left[1 - \frac{\min(t_c, \gamma T_c)}{T}\right]^\epsilon, & t_c > 0 \end{cases} \tag{4}$$

where $t_c = t \bmod T_c$ is the in-cycle epoch number and the constant exponent ϵ controls the decaying rate of the learning rate.

Multi-modal Checkpoint Ensemble. In the cth training cycle, we collect checkpoints $\mathbf{W}_c = \{\mathbf{w}_t | \gamma T_c \leq t \bmod T_c \leq T_c - 1\}$. Then the aggregated checkpoints of all M training cycles $\mathbf{W} = \cup_{c=1}^{M} \mathbf{W}_c$ consist of multi-modal posterior samples in the weight space. We build an ensemble of n models via sampling $\frac{n}{M}$ intermediate weights from each mode $\mathbf{W}_c$ for $c \in \{1, 2, \ldots, M\}$. The multi-modal Bayesian inference is then performed as in Eq. (2). In comparison to [13], which collected one snapshot in each cycle, our method combines both local and global uncertainty of the weights.

3   Experiments

3.1   Experimental Setup

Datasets. We trained our network on the publicly available ACDC dataset[1] [2], which contains annotated end-diastolic (ED) and end-systolic (ES) volumes of 100 subjects. We randomly split 80% of The ACDC data for network training and kept the rest 20% to validate the in-domain (ID) performance. To evaluate the performance under a domain shift, i.e. out-of-domain (OOD), we also tested our method on the M&M dataset[2] [5] collected from different MRI vendors and medical centers. The annotated part includes 75 subjects collected from Vendor A (Siemens) in a single medical center and 75 scans by Vendor B (Phillips) from two medical centers.

Implementation Details. For CMR segmentation, we trained the 2D nnU-Net, with the proposed learning rate modulation in Sect. 2.2 and 2.3. During each training cycle, SGD with momentum was used for optimization with a batch size of 20. We set the initial learning rate as $\alpha_0 = 0.01$, the decay exponent $\epsilon = 0.9$ and the restart learning as $\alpha_r = 0.1$. We trained $M = 3$ cycles within a total training budget of $T = 1,200$ epochs, which is slightly higher than the standard nnU-Net which consumes $1,000$ epochs for a single model training. The learning rate kept at a constant level after $\gamma = 80\%$ of the epochs in each individual training cycle. We chose the latest $n = 30$ checkpoints (epoch Step 2) in the last training cycle to build a single-modal checkpoints ensemble (*Single-modal Ckpt. Ens.*). For a multi-modal weight sampling (*Multi-modal Ckpt. Ens.*), we aggregated the latest 10 checkpoints of all three training cycles. We took the single model prediction at the end of the training as the baseline (*Vanilla*). Temperature scaling (*Temp. Scaling*) with $\tau = 1.5$ was implemented as a calibration baseline as in [12]. We also compared our proposed method to MC-Dropout [9] and deep ensemble [18] (*Deep Ens.*). The dropout probability was set as $p = 0.1$ and $n = 30$ predictions were drawn for uncertainty estimation. A 5-model deep ensemble was trained on the ACDC training data with random initialization. We also evaluated the performance of *SWA* [15], which averages the posterior weights sampled during the last training cycle, and we used the softmax predictions for uncertainty estimation.

---

[1] https://www.creatis.insa-lyon.fr/Challenge/acdc.
[2] https://www.ub.edu/mnms.

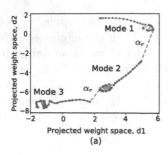 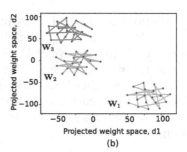

(a)   (b)

Fig. 2. (a) t-SNE plot of the weight space during SGD training. Dotted lines illustrate the transition between weight modes. (b) t-SNE plot of the posterior weights, which bounce in the neighborhood of different modes.

Evaluation Metrics. On each dataset, the segmentation performance was evaluated using the mean Dice coefficients of the three foreground classes, namely, left ventricle (LV), right ventricle (RV), and myocardium (MYO), over all volumes. We quantify the calibration performance through the expected calibration error (ECE) of voxels in the bounding box of all foreground classes in each volume [12,21]. We divided the voxels into 100 bins according to their confidence from 0% to 100%. The ECE is defined as the weighted average of the confidence-accuracy difference in each bin: $\text{ECE} = \sum_{s=1}^{100} \frac{|B_s|}{N_v} |\text{conf}(B_s) - \text{acc}(B_s)|$, where B_s defines the set of voxels whose confidence falls in the range $((s-1)\%, s\%]$, $\text{conf}(B_s)$ is the mean confidence of voxels in bin B_s, $\text{acc}(B_s)$ represents the classification accuracy of the voxels in B_s and N_v is the total number of voxels.

3.2   Results

Training Trajectory Visualization. We first present the training trajectory in the weight space to validate our concept of multi-modal posterior. Figure 2(a) shows the t-SNE plot of the weights of the last decoder layer in nnU-Net during the three training cycles. We observe that the cyclical training triggered a long-range movement in the weight space such that multiple local optima were visited. In Fig. 2(b) we demonstrate both local and global weight posterior distribution. In each training cycle, the weights did not converge to a single point but kept bouncing in a local neighborhood, conforming to [19,20]. The diversity in posterior modes is clearly shown by the three clusters in the t-SNE weight space. We note that similar behavior of multi-modality was also observed for posterior weights in other layers.

Segmentation and Calibration Performance. We list the average Dice coefficient of all methods in comparison in Table 1. The table demonstrates that except for MC-Dropout, which downgraded the performance slightly, the rest

Table 1. Dice coefficients on ID and OOD test sets.

Method	ACDC validation (ID)			M&M vendor A (OOD)			M&M vendor B (OOD)		
	RV	MYO	LV	RV	MYO	LV	RV	MYO	LV
Vanilla	0.911 ±0.052	0.904 ±0.026	0.944 ±0.035	0.830 ±0.119	0.810 ±0.043	0.897 ±0.063	0.878 ±0.077	0.844 ±0.054	0.894 ±0.076
SWA	0.913 ±0.054	0.910 ±0.023	0.948 ±0.033	0.856 ±0.093	0.808 ±0.041	0.896 ±0.061	0.879 ±0.067	0.845 ±0.050	0.897 ±0.069
MC-Dropout	0.906 ±0.061	0.901 ±0.028	0.940 ±0.043	0.810 ±0.146	0.810 ±0.049	0.896 ±0.066	0.880 ±0.079	0.844 ±0.058	0.891 ±0.081
Deep Ens.	0.915 ±0.051	0.912 ±0.023	**0.951** ±0.029	**0.857** ±0.089	0.816 ±0.041	0.902 ±0.062	**0.885** ±0.068	0.849 ±0.047	0.897 ±0.064
Ckpt. Ens. (Single)	**0.919** ±0.051	0.912 ±0.022	**0.951** ±0.032	0.851 ±0.100	0.816 ±0.041	0.902 ±0.061	0.883 ±0.070	0.850 ±0.048	**0.901** ±0.065
Ckpt. Ens. (Multi)	0.918 ±0.051	**0.913** ±0.024	**0.951** ±0.031	0.852 ±0.105	**0.818** ±0.043	**0.905** ±0.060	**0.885** ±0.069	**0.851** ±0.050	0.899 ±0.071

methods improved the segmentation performance in comparison to the Vanilla nnU-Net. The proposed checkpoint ensembles achieved overall the best performance except for the RV on Vendor A.

Table 2. ECE (%) on ID and OOD test sets.

Methods	ACDC validation (ID)	M&M vendor A (OOD)	M&M vendor B (OOD)
Vanilla	2.56	4.34	3.79
Temp. scaling	2.18	3.91	3.46
SWA	2.39	4.07	3.70
MC-dropout	1.70	3.41	2.95
Deep Ens	1.63	3.16	2.85
Ckpt. Ens. (Single)	**1.25**	2.83	2.69
Ckpt. Ens. (Multi)	**1.25**	**2.75**	**2.61**

The ECE scores are listed in Table 2. From the table, we can observe that the temperature scaling slightly improved the calibration performance. The results of Vanilla and SWA show that a single model was poorly calibrated compared to all 4 Bayesian methods. MC-Dropout improved calibration but was not as effective as Deep Ensemble. The proposed single-model checkpoint ensemble achieved the best performance on ID data, and the multi-modal checkpoint ensemble further improved the performance on OOD data.

Qualitative Results. Some representative examples of the segmentation and uncertainty maps are shown in Fig. 3. For the successful segmentation in Fig. 3(a), all methods highlighted the prediction borders as uncertain compared to regions, which conforms to our intuition in practice that different observers may have slightly different border delineations. Figure 3(b–d) show three cases in which the network failed, mainly in the RV region. In practice, this is the most common failure even with the state-of-the-art nnU-Net. We can observe that MC-Dropout frequently output low uncertainty in the area of wrong predictions (RV). Deep Ensemble correctly identified the uncertain areas in case (b) and (d). However, the limited number of models in Deep Ensemble may miss part of

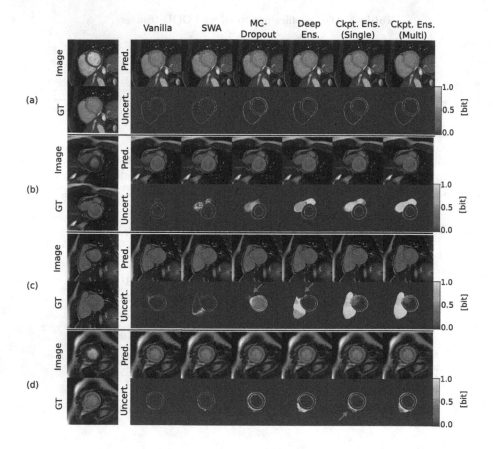

Fig. 3. Predictions (Pred.) and estimated uncertainty maps (Uncert.) on a successful case (a) and three partially failed cases (b–d). In case (a) all the methods highlighted the border as uncertain. MC-Dropout failed in all the three cases (b–d) to delineate RV, while reporting low uncertainty in the corresponding area. Deep Ensemble is robust but missed part of the uncertain areas in case (c). Multi-modal weight sampling detected the failed RV area more robustly than the single-modal version in case (d). (Color figure online)

the error, as shown in Fig. 3(c) (red arrow). We further demonstrate the benefit of multi-modality in weight space through Fig. 3(d) which shows an apical slice with a small RV. In this case, only deep ensemble and the multi-modal checkpoints ensemble successfully detected the uncertainty in RV region, while other methods just output high confidence, indicating "silent" failure, i.e. mistake that will escape notice in automatic segmentation pipelines.

In all three challenging cases, our proposed method robustly detected the nnU-Net failure on RV. Interestingly, we note that the estimated uncertainty map strongly correlated with true RV area, which is highly beneficial and informative for further manual contour correction in clinical practice.

4   Conclusion

In this work, we proposed an efficient Bayesian inference approximation method for nnU-Net, from the SGD training perspective. Our method does not require adapting the nnU-Net configuration and is highly efficient in computation. Our experimental results on both in-domain and out-of-domain cardiac MRI data proved its effectiveness, in comparison with established baseline methods such as MC-Dropout and Deep Ensemble. The proposed uncertainty estimation further strengthens nnU-Net for practical applications of medical image segmentation, in terms of both *uncertainty estimation* and *segmentation performance*.

Acknowledgement. The authors gratefully acknowledge TU Delft AI Initiative for financial support.

References

1. Baumgartner, C.F., Tezcan, K.C., Chaitanya, K., Hötker, A.M., Muehlematter, U.J., Schawkat, K., Becker, A.S., Donati, O., Konukoglu, E.: PHiSeg: capturing uncertainty in medical image segmentation. In: Shen, D., Liu, T., Peters, T.M., Staib, L.H., Essert, C., Zhou, S., Yap, P.-T., Khan, A. (eds.) MICCAI 2019. LNCS, vol. 11765, pp. 119–127. Springer, Cham (2019). https://doi.org/10.1007/978-3-030-32245-8_14

2. Bernard, O., et al.: Deep learning techniques for automatic MRI cardiac multi-structures segmentation and diagnosis: is the problem solved? IEEE Trans. Med. Imaging **37**(11), 2514–2525 (2018)

3. Blei, D.M., Kucukelbir, A., McAuliffe, J.D.: Variational inference: a review for statisticians. J. Am. Stat. Assoc. **112**(518), 859–877 (2017)

4. Blundell, C., Cornebise, J., Kavukcuoglu, K., Wierstra, D.: Weight uncertainty in neural network. In: International Conference on Machine Learning, pp. 1613–1622. PMLR (2015)

5. Campello, V.M., et al.: Multi-centre, multi-vendor and multi-disease cardiac segmentation: the M&MS challenge. IEEE Trans. Med. Imaging **40**(12), 3543–3554 (2021)

6. Folgoc, L.L., et al.: Is MC dropout bayesian? arXiv preprint arXiv:2110.04286 (2021)

7. Fort, S., Hu, H., Lakshminarayanan, B.: Deep ensembles: a loss landscape perspective. arXiv preprint arXiv:1912.02757 (2019)

8. Fuchs, M., Gonzalez, C., Mukhopadhyay, A.: Practical uncertainty quantification for brain tumor segmentation (2021)

9. Gal, Y., Ghahramani, Z.: Dropout as a Bayesian approximation: representing model uncertainty in deep learning. In: International Conference on Machine Learning, pp. 1050–1059. PMLR (2016)

10. Gonzalez, C., Gotkowski, K., Bucher, A., Fischbach, R., Kaltenborn, I., Mukhopadhyay, A.: Detecting when pre-trained nnU-Net models fail silently for Covid-19 lung lesion segmentation. In: de Bruijne, M., et al. (eds.) MICCAI 2021. LNCS, vol. 12907, pp. 304–314. Springer, Cham (2021). https://doi.org/10.1007/978-3-030-87234-2_29

11. Gonzalez, C., Mukhopadhyay, A.: Self-supervised out-of-distribution detection for cardiac CMR segmentation. In: Medical Imaging with Deep Learning (2021)

12. Guo, C., Pleiss, G., Sun, Y., Weinberger, K.Q.: On calibration of modern neural networks. In: International Conference on Machine Learning, pp. 1321–1330. PMLR (2017)
13. Huang, G., Li, Y., Pleiss, G., Liu, Z., Hopcroft, J.E., Weinberger, K.Q.: Snapshot ensembles: train 1, get M for free. arXiv preprint arXiv:1704.00109 (2017)
14. Isensee, F., Jaeger, P.F., Kohl, S.A., Petersen, J., Maier-Hein, K.H.: nnU-Net: a self-configuring method for deep learning-based biomedical image segmentation. Nat. Methods 18(2), 203–211 (2021)
15. Izmailov, P., Podoprikhin, D., Garipov, T., Vetrov, D., Wilson, A.G.: Averaging weights leads to wider optima and better generalization. arXiv preprint arXiv:1803.05407 (2018)
16. Jungo, A., Reyes, M.: Assessing reliability and challenges of uncertainty estimations for medical image segmentation. In: Shen, D., et al. (eds.) MICCAI 2019. LNCS, vol. 11765, pp. 48–56. Springer, Cham (2019). https://doi.org/10.1007/978-3-030-32245-8_6
17. Kohl, S.A., et al.: A probabilistic U-Net for segmentation of ambiguous images. arXiv preprint arXiv:1806.05034 (2018)
18. Lakshminarayanan, B., Pritzel, A., Blundell, C.: Simple and scalable predictive uncertainty estimation using deep ensembles. arXiv preprint arXiv:1612.01474 (2016)
19. Maddox, W.J., Izmailov, P., Garipov, T., Vetrov, D.P., Wilson, A.G.: A simple baseline for Bayesian uncertainty in deep learning. In: Advances in Neural Information Processing Systems 32 (2019)
20. Mandt, S., Hoffman, M.D., Blei, D.M.: Stochastic gradient descent as approximate Bayesian inference. arXiv preprint arXiv:1704.04289 (2017)
21. Mehrtash, A., Wells, W.M., Tempany, C.M., Abolmaesumi, P., Kapur, T.: Confidence calibration and predictive uncertainty estimation for deep medical image segmentation. IEEE Trans. Med. Imaging 39(12), 3868–3878 (2020)
22. Mingard, C., Valle-Pérez, G., Skalse, J., Louis, A.A.: Is SGD a Bayesian sampler? well, almost. J. Mach. Learn. Res. 22 (2021)
23. Ovadia, Y., et al.: Can you trust your model's uncertainty? Evaluating predictive uncertainty under dataset shift. arXiv preprint arXiv:1906.02530 (2019)
24. Ronneberger, O., Fischer, P., Brox, T.: U-Net: convolutional networks for biomedical image segmentation. In: Navab, N., Hornegger, J., Wells, W.M., Frangi, A.F. (eds.) MICCAI 2015. LNCS, vol. 9351, pp. 234–241. Springer, Cham (2015). https://doi.org/10.1007/978-3-319-24574-4_28

Improving Trustworthiness of AI Disease Severity Rating in Medical Imaging with Ordinal Conformal Prediction Sets

Charles Lu[1]([✉])[ID], Anastasios N. Angelopoulos[2][ID], and Stuart Pomerantz[1][ID]

[1] Massachusetts General Hospital, Boston, MA 02114, USA
{clu,spomerantz}@mgh.harvard.edu
[2] University of California, Berkeley, Berkeley, CA 94720, USA
angelopoulos@berkeley.edu

Abstract. The regulatory approval and broad clinical deployment of medical AI have been hampered by the perception that deep learning models fail in unpredictable and possibly catastrophic ways. A lack of statistically rigorous uncertainty quantification is a significant factor undermining trust in AI results. Recent developments in distribution-free uncertainty quantification present practical solutions for these issues by providing reliability guarantees for black-box models on arbitrary data distributions as formally valid finite-sample prediction intervals. Our work applies these new uncertainty quantification methods—specifically conformal prediction—to a deep-learning model for grading the severity of spinal stenosis in lumbar spine MRI. We demonstrate a technique for forming ordinal prediction sets that are guaranteed to contain the correct stenosis severity within a user-defined probability (confidence interval). On a dataset of 409 MRI exams processed by the deep-learning model, the conformal method provides tight coverage with small prediction set sizes. Furthermore, we explore the potential clinical applicability of flagging cases with high uncertainty predictions (large prediction sets) by quantifying an increase in the prevalence of significant imaging abnormalities (e.g. motion artifacts, metallic artifacts, and tumors) that could degrade confidence in predictive performance when compared to a random sample of cases.

Keywords: Conformal prediction · Uncertainty quantification · Deep learning

1 Introduction

Although many studies have demonstrated high overall accuracy in automating medical imaging diagnosis with deep-learning AI models, translation to actual

---

C. Lu and A. N. Angelopoulos—Equal contribution.

Supplementary Information The online version contains supplementary material available at https://doi.org/10.1007/978-3-031-16452-1_52.

ⓒ The Author(s), under exclusive license to Springer Nature Switzerland AG 2022
L. Wang et al. (Eds.): MICCAI 2022, LNCS 13438, pp. 545–554, 2022.
https://doi.org/10.1007/978-3-031-16452-1_52

clinical deployment has proved difficult. It is widely observed that deep learning algorithms can fail in bizarre ways and with misplaced confidence [12,16]. A core problem is a lack of *trust*—a survey of radiologists found that although they thought AI tools add value to their clinical practice, they would not trust AI for autonomous clinical use due to perceived and experienced unreliability [1].

Herein, we present methods for endowing arbitrary AI systems with formal mathematical guarantees that give clinicians explicit assurances about an algorithm's overall performance and most importantly for a given study. These guarantees are *distribution-free*—they work for any (pre-trained) model, any (possibly unknown) data distribution, and in finite samples. Although such guarantees do not solve the issue of trust entirely, the precise and formal understanding of their model's predictive uncertainty enables a clinician to potentially work more assuredly in concert with AI assistance.

We demonstrate the utility of our methods using an AI system developed to assist radiologists in the grading of spinal stenosis in lumbar MRI. Degenerative spinal stenosis is the abnormal narrowing of the spinal canal that compresses the spinal cord or nerve roots, often resulting in debility from pain, limb weakness, and other neurological disorders. It is a highly prevalent condition that affects working-age and elderly populations and constitutes a heavy societal burden not only in the form of costly medical care but from decreased workplace productivity, disability, and lowered quality of life. The formal interpretation of spinal stenosis imaging remains a challenging and time-consuming task even for experienced subspecialty radiologists due to the complexity of spinal anatomy, pathology, and the MR imaging modality. Using a highly accurate AI model to help assess the severity of spinal stenosis on MRI could lower interpretation time and improve the consistency of grading [10]. Yet, given the practical challenges of medical imaging that can degrade model performance in any given exam, the adoption of such tools will be low if clinicians encounter poor quality predictions without a sense of when the model is more or less reliable. To bolster such trust, we apply conformal prediction to algorithmic disease severity classification sets in order to identify higher uncertainty predictions that might merit special attention by the radiologist. Our main contributions are the following:

1. We develop new distribution-free uncertainty quantification methods for ordinal labels.
2. To our knowledge, we are the first to apply distribution-free uncertainty quantification to the results of an AI model for automated stenosis grading of lumbar spinal MRI.
3. We identify a correlation between high prediction uncertainty in individual cases and the presence of potentially contributory imaging features as evaluated by a neuroradiologist such as tumors, orthopedic hardware artifacts, and motion artifacts.

2   Methods

To formally describe the problem, let the input $X_{\text{test}} \in \mathcal{X}$, $\mathcal{X} = \mathbb{R}^{H \times W \times D}$ be an MR image and the ground truth label $Y_{\text{test}} \in \mathcal{Y}$, $\mathcal{Y} = \{0, ..., K - 1\}$ be an ordinal value representing the severity of the disease (higher values indicating greater severity). We are given a pre-trained model, $\hat{f}$, that takes in images and outputs a probability distribution over severities; for example, $\hat{f}$ may be a 3D convolutional neural network with a softmax function. Assume we also have a calibration dataset, $\{(X_i, Y_i)\}_{i=1}^{n}$, of data points that the model has not seen before. This calibration data should be composed of pairs of MR images and their associated disease severity labels drawn i.i.d. Given a new MR image X_{test}, the task is to predict the (unobserved) severity, Y_{test}. In the usual multi-class classification setting, the output is the label with the highest estimated probability, $\hat{Y}(x) = \underset{y \in \{1,\dots,K\}}{\arg\max} \hat{f}(x)_y$. However, $\hat{Y}(X_{\text{test}})$ may be wrong, either because the learned model $\hat{f}$ does not learn the relationship between MR images and severities properly or because there is intrinsic randomness in this relationship that cannot be accounted for by any algorithm (i.e. aleatoric uncertainty).

Our goal is to rigorously quantify this uncertainty by outputting a set of probable disease severities that is guaranteed to contain the ground truth severity on average. These *prediction sets* will provide *distribution-free* probabilistic guarantees, *i.e.* ones that do not depend on the model or distribution of the data.

Our approach, *Ordinal Adaptive Prediction Sets* (Ordinal APS), uses conformal prediction with a novel score function designed for ordinal labels. In particular, each prediction set will always be a contiguous set of severities, and for any user-specified error rate α, prediction sets will contain the true label with probability $1 - \alpha$ (similar to other conformal algorithms [18, 20]).

Imagine we had oracle access to the true probability distribution over severities $P(Y_{\text{test}} \mid X_{\text{test}})$ with associated density function $f(x)_y$. A reasonable goal might then be to pick the set with the smallest size while still achieving *conditional coverage*.

Definition 1 (conditional coverage). *A predicted set of severities $T(X_{\text{test}})$ has conditional coverage if it contains the true severity with $1 - \alpha$ probability no matter what MR image is input, i.e.,*

$$\mathbb{P}\left(Y_{\text{test}} \in T(x) \mid X_{\text{test}} = x\right) \geq 1 - \alpha, \text{ for all } x \in \mathcal{X}. \tag{1}$$

The clinical benefit of conditional coverage is that it essentially achieves a per-patient guarantee as opposed to one that is averaged across patients. Under conditional coverage, the uncertainty sets will work equally well for all possible subgroups such as subpopulations from different patient demographics.

Ignoring tie-breaking, we can succinctly describe the oracle prediction set as follows:

$$T^*(x) = \underset{\substack{(l,u) \in \mathcal{Y}^2 \\ l \leq u}}{\arg\min}\left\{ u - l : \sum_{j=l}^{u} f(x)_j \geq 1 - \alpha \right\}. \tag{2}$$

This set, T^*, is the smallest that satisfies (1). Ideally, we would compute T^* exactly, but we do not have access to f, only its estimator $\hat{f}$, which may be arbitrarily bad.

Naturally, the next step is to plug in our estimate of the probabilities, $\hat{f}$, to (2). However, because $\hat{f}$ may be wrong, we must calibrate the resulting set with conformal prediction, yielding a *marginal coverage* guarantee. Our procedure corresponds to greedily growing the set outwards from the maximally likely predicted severity.

Definition 2 (marginal coverage). *A predicted set of severities $\mathcal{T}$ has marginal coverage if it contains the true severity on average over new MRIs, i.e.,*

$$\mathbb{P}\left(Y_{\text{test}} \in \mathcal{T}(X_{\text{test}})\right) \geq 1 - \alpha. \tag{3}$$

Marginal coverage is weaker than conditional coverage since it holds only on average over the entire population, so coverage may be worse or better for some subgroups. While conditional coverage is, in general, impossible [6], we can hope to approximate conditional coverage by defining a set similar to $\mathcal{T}^*$ that uses $\hat{f}$. To that end, define a sequence of sets indexed by a threshold λ,

$$\mathcal{T}_\lambda(x) = \underset{\substack{(l,\,u) \in \mathcal{Y}^2 \\ l \leq u}}{\arg\min} \left\{ u - l : \sum_{j=l}^{u} \hat{f}(j|x) \geq \lambda \right\}. \tag{4}$$

Notice that as λ grows, the sets grow, meaning they are *nested* in λ:

$$\lambda_1 \leq \lambda_2 \implies \forall x, \ \mathcal{T}_{\lambda_1}(x) \subseteq \mathcal{T}_{\lambda_2}(x). \tag{5}$$

The key is to pick a value of λ such that the resulting set satisfies (2). The following algorithm takes as input $\mathcal{T}_\lambda$ and outputs our choice of λ:

$$\mathcal{A}(\mathcal{T}_\lambda;\ \alpha) = \inf \left\{ \lambda : \sum_{i=1}^{n} \mathbb{1}\left\{Y_i \in \mathcal{T}_\lambda(X_i)\right\} \geq \lceil (n+1)(1-\alpha) \rceil \right\}. \tag{6}$$

The quantity $\lceil (n+1)(1-\alpha) \rceil$, which is slightly larger than the naive choice $n(1-\alpha)$, corrects for the model's deficiencies (see [2] for more details). Using this algorithm, approximated in Algorithm 1, results in a marginal coverage guarantee.

Theorem 1 (Conformal coverage guarantee). *Let (X_1, Y_1), (X_2, Y_2), ..., (X_n, Y_n) and $(X_{\text{test}}, Y_{\text{test}})$ be an i.i.d. sequence of MRIs and paired severities and let $\hat{\lambda} = \mathcal{A}(\mathcal{T}_\lambda, \alpha)$. Then $\mathcal{T}_{\hat{\lambda}}$ satisfies (2), i.e., it contains the true label with probability $1 - \alpha$.*

This theorem holds for any data distribution or machine learning model, any number of calibration data points n, and any possible sequence of nested sets that includes $\mathcal{Y}$ (see the supplementary material for the proof).

In practice, Ordinal APS has two undesirable properties: computing $\mathcal{T}_\lambda(x)$ requires a combinatorial search of the set of possible severities, and $\mathcal{T}_\lambda(x)$ may not include the point prediction $\hat{Y}$. In practice, we therefore approximate Ordinal APS greedily as described in Algorithm 1. The algorithm always contains $\hat{Y}$

and requires only $\mathcal{O}(n)$ computations; furthermore, it usually results in exactly the same sets as the exact method in our experiments, which have a small value of K. Note that the approximate choice of $T_\lambda(x)$ described in Algorithm 1 is still nested, and thus we can still guarantee coverage (see corollary in the supplementary material).

Algorithm 1. Pseudocode for approximately computing $T_\lambda(x)$

Input: Parameter λ; underlying predictor $\hat{f}$; input $x \in \mathcal{X}$.
Output: $T_\lambda(x)$.

1:   $T_\lambda(x) \leftarrow \arg\max \hat{f}(x)$
2:   $q \leftarrow 0$
3: **while** $q \leq \lambda$ **do**
4:     $S \leftarrow \{\min T_\lambda(x) - 1, \max T_\lambda(x) + 1\}$
5:     $y \leftarrow \arg\max_{y' \in S} \hat{f}(x) \mathbb{1}\{y' \in \{1, ..., K\}\}$
6:     $q \leftarrow q + \hat{f}(x)_y$
7:     $T_\lambda(x) \leftarrow T_\lambda(x) \cup \{y\}$

---

3 Experiments

We compare Ordinal Adaptive Prediction Sets to two other conformal methods: *Least Ambiguous set-valued Classifier* (LAC) [19] and *Ordinal Cumulative Distribution Function* (CDF). LAC uses the softmax score of the true class as the conformal score function. LAC theoretically gives the smallest average set size but sacrifices conditional coverage to achieve this. Additionally, LAC does not respect ordinality and thus may output non-contiguous prediction sets, which are inappropriate in an ordinal setting such as disease severity rating. The Ordinal CDF method starts at the highest prediction score and then inflates the intervals by λ in quantile-space; in that sense, it is similar to a discrete version of conformalized quantile regression [13,17]. We only use the non-randomized versions of these methods.

We evaluate these three conformal methods on a deep learning system previously developed for automated lumbar spine stenosis grading in MRI, Deep-SPINE [15]. The deep learning system consists of two convolutional neural networks – one to segment out and label each vertebral body and disc-interspace and the other to perform multi-class ordinal stenosis classification for three different anatomical sites (the central canal and right and left neuroforamina) at each intervertebral disc level for a total of up to 18 gradings per patient. For each MRI exam, the associated radiology report was automatically parsed for keywords indicative of the presence and severity of stenosis for each of the 6 vertebral disc levels (T12-L1 through L5-S1) to extract ground truth labels for a total of 6,093 gradings. Each grading was assigned to a value on a four-point ordinal scale of stenosis severity: 0 (*no stenosis*), 1 (*mild stenosis*), 2 (*moderate stenosis*), and 3 (*severe stenosis*). An example of stenosis is included in the supplementary material.

For our experiments, we treat the stenosis grading model as a static model and only use it for inference to make predictions. We then process these predicted scores with the split-conformal techniques described in Sect. 2. This scenario would most closely reflect the clinical reality of incorporating regulated, third-party AI software medical devices, which would likely not permit users access to the AI model beyond the ability to make predictions.

3.1   Quantitative Experiments

We use the predicted softmax scores from a held-out set of MRI exams from 409 patients, comprising 6,093 disc level stenosis severity predictions to calibrate and evaluate each conformal method. We randomly include 5% of patients in the calibration set and reserve the remainder for evaluating coverage and set size. We evaluate performance at several different α thresholds, $\alpha \in \{0.2, 0.15, 0.1, 0.05, 0.01\}$, and average results over 100 random trials.

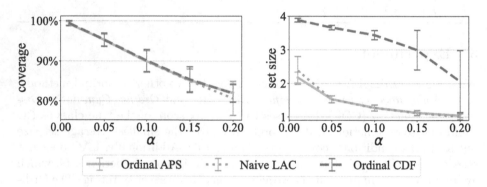

Fig. 1. Average coverage and set size of conformal prediction methods for $\alpha \in \{0.2, 0.15, 0.1, 0.05, 0.01\}$ (shown with $\pm$ 1 standard deviation).

As expected, all three conformal methods empirically achieve the desired marginal coverage as guaranteed by Theorem 1. However, Ordinal CDF requires a much larger set size to attain proper coverage than either Naive LAC or Ordinal APS for all values of α (shown in Fig. 1). In addition, while aggregate coverage is satisfied for each method, we find significant differences in class-conditional coverage (i.e. prediction sets stratified by the true stenosis severity label), which is shown in Fig. 2. We see that prediction sets for "mild stenosis" and "moderate stenosis" grades have lower average coverage and larger set sizes than prediction sets for "no stenosis" and "severe stenosis" grades. These differences may be partly attributed to the fact that the "no stenosis" class constitutes the majority of the label distribution (67%), so these cases may be easier for a model trained on this imbalanced distribution to classify. Additionally, "mild stenosis" and "moderate stenosis" grades may be more challenging to differentiate than "no stenosis" and "severe stenosis" grades, reflecting the greater inherent variability and uncertainty in the ground truth ratings.

We also compare coverage and distribution stratified by set size in Fig. 3. Stratifying by set size reveals that most predictions with Ordinal APS and Naive LAC contain only one or two grading predictions while Ordinal CDF mainly predicts a set of all four possible gradings (which always trivially satisfies coverage).

Lastly, we compare coverage and set size at the disc level with $\alpha = 0.1$ and find coverage inversely correlated to the prevalence of severe stenosis, which is most often found in the lower lumbar disc levels (see table in the supplementary material).

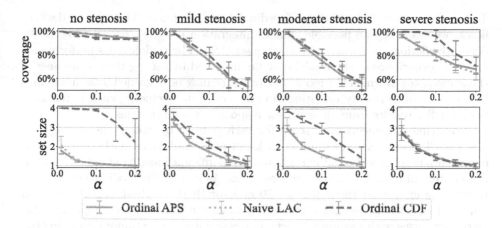

Fig. 2. Coverage and set size when stratified by ground-truth stenosis severity grading.

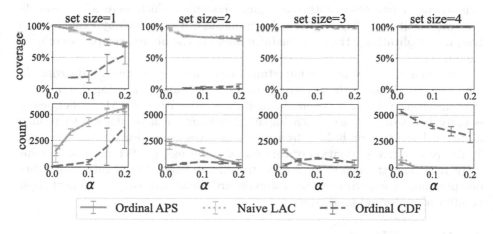

Fig. 3. Coverage and the number of prediction sets with a particular set size (coverage only shown for methods with at least one prediction set of a specific set size at the desired α).

Overall, we conclude that Ordinal APS performs similarly to LAC in both coverage and set size, and both Ordinal APS and Naive LAC outperform Ordinal CDF. The similarities between LAC and Ordinal APS are notable—they almost always result in the same sets, although the algorithms are quite different. This is unsurprising given that in our setting $|\mathcal{Y}| = 4$ and the model's accuracy is high, so bimodal softmax scores almost never happen. Therefore LAC and Ordinal APS do the same thing. This observation does not generalize; other ordinal prediction problems with more categories will have bimodal distributions and thus LAC and Ordinal APS will differ.

3.2   Clinical Review of High Uncertainty Predictions

To investigate the clinical utility of Ordinal APS to enhance AI-augmented workflows, we evaluate one possible clinical integration use case: flagging low confidence predictions (i.e. ones with a large set size). The radiologist's performance and user experience of the model may be improved by raising their awareness of those instances in which the model performance may be degraded by scan anomalies or when uncertainty quantification is very high, excluding such potentially poor quality results from their review responsibilities altogether.

We define an uncertainty score for each patient by taking the average set size for all disc levels and grading tasks. A neuroradiologist with >20 years of experience determined what constituted a "significant imaging anomaly" within the context of spinal stenosis interpretation. As a statistical validation of these results, we examined the report of 70 cases with the highest uncertainty and found 17 such anomalies: 11 cases with artifacts from metallic orthopedic hardware, four cases with motion artifacts, one case with a large tumor occupying the spinal canal, and one case with a severe congenital abnormality (achondroplastic dwarfism). In contrast, a random sample of 70 cases from the dataset only demonstrated five cases with significant anomalies which were all orthopedic hardware artifacts. This difference is significant with $p < 0.05$ by Fisher's exact test, and qualitatively the abnormalities found in the filtered samples were more extreme.

Our manual review of high uncertainty cases shows promise for improving the clinician experience with AI-assisted medical software tools using distribution-free uncertainty quantification. Rather than presenting all AI predictions as equally trustworthy, cases with higher uncertainty can be flagged to prompt additional scrutiny or hidden from the user altogether to maximize efficiency. While prospective evaluation of this use of conformal prediction in more clinically realistic settings will be needed to validate general feasibility and utility, our preliminary experiments are a step towards demonstrating the clinical applicability of conformal prediction.

4   Related Work

Conformal prediction was first developed by Vladimir Vovk and collaborators in the late 1990s [23,24] and we build most directly on the work of the Adaptive

Prediction Sets method [5,18] and the histogram binning method in [20]. The latter work is the most relevant, and it proposes an algorithm very similar to Algorithm 1 in a continuous setting with histogram regression. Our work also relies on the nested set outlook on conformal prediction [11]. The LAC baseline is taken from [19], and the ordinal CDF baseline is similar to the softmax method in [4], which is in turn motivated by [13,17]. Recently, uncertainty quantification has been promoted to facilitate trustworthiness and transparency in black-box algorithms, such as deep learning, for critical decision-making [8]. In particular, conformal prediction methods have been applied to a wide range of safety-critical applications such as reducing the number of false alarms in the detection of sepsis risk [21]. Distribution-free uncertainty quantification techniques such as conformal prediction sets have emerged as an essential tool for rigorous statistical guarantees in medical decision-making [2,3,7,9,14,22].

5 Conclusion

We show how conformal predictions can complement existing AI systems without further modification to the model to provide distribution-free reliability guarantees. We demonstrate its clinical utility in the application of flagging high uncertainty cases for automated stenosis severity grading. We hope this work promotes further studies on the trustworthiness and usability of uncertainty-aware machine learning systems for clinical applications.

References

1. Allen, B., Agarwal, S., Coombs, L., Wald, C., Dreyer, K.: 2020 ACR data science institute artificial intelligence survey. J. Am. Coll. Radiol. **18**(8), 1153–1159 (2021)
2. Angelopoulos, A.N., Bates, S.: A gentle introduction to conformal prediction and distribution-free uncertainty quantification. arXiv preprint arXiv:2107.07511 (2021)
3. Angelopoulos, A.N., Bates, S., Zrnic, T., Jordan, M.I.: Private prediction sets. arXiv preprint arXiv:2102.06202 (2021)
4. Angelopoulos, A.N., et al.: Image-to-image regression with distribution-free uncertainty quantification and applications in imaging. arXiv preprint arXiv:2202.05265 (2022)
5. Angelopoulos, A.N., Bates, S., Malik, J., Jordan, M.I.: Uncertainty sets for image classifiers using conformal prediction. In: International Conference on Learning Representations (ICLR) (2021)
6. Barber, R., Candès, E., Ramdas, A., Tibshirani, R.: The limits of distribution-free conditional predictive inference. Inf. Inference **10**(2), 455–482 (2021). https://doi. org/10.1093/imaiai/iaaa017
7. Begoli, E., Bhattacharya, T., Kusnezov, D.: The need for uncertainty quantification in machine-assisted medical decision making. Nature (2019). https://doi.org/10. 1038/s42256-018-0004-1
8. Bhatt, U., et al.: Uncertainty as a form of transparency: measuring, communicating, and using uncertainty, pp. 401–413. Association for Computing Machinery, New York (2021). https://doi.org/10.1145/3461702.3462571

9. Fannjiang, C., Bates, S., Angelopoulos, A., Listgarten, J., Jordan, M.I.: Conformal prediction for the design problem. arXiv preprint arXiv:2202.03613 (2022)

10. Fu, M., et al.: Inter-rater and intra-rater agreement of magnetic resonance imaging findings in the lumbar spine: significant variability across degenerative conditions. Spine J. **14** (2014). https://doi.org/10.1016/j.spinee.2014.03.010

11. Gupta, C., Kuchibhotla, A.K., Ramdas, A.: Nested conformal prediction and quantile out-of-bag ensemble methods. Pattern Recognit. **127**, 108496 (2021)

12. Hendrycks, D., Zhao, K., Basart, S., Steinhardt, J., Song, D.: Natural adversarial examples. In: CVPR (2021)

13. Koenker, R., Bassett Jr., G.: Regression quantiles. Econometrica J. Econom. Soc. **46**(1), 33–50 (1978)

14. Lu, C., Lemay, A., Chang, K., Hoebel, K., Kalpathy-Cramer, J.: Fair conformal predictors for applications in medical imaging (2022)

15. Lu, J., et al.: DeepSPINE: automated lumbar vertebral segmentation, disc-level designation, and spinal stenosis grading using deep learning. CoRR abs/1807.10215 (2018). http://arxiv.org/abs/1807.10215

16. Minderer, M., et al.: Revisiting the calibration of modern neural networks. arXiv preprint arXiv:2106.07998 (2021)

17. Romano, Y., Patterson, E., Candès, E.: Conformalized quantile regression. In: Advances in Neural Information Processing Systems 32: Annual Conference on Neural Information Processing Systems 2019, vol. 32, pp. 3543–3553. NIPS (2019). https://proceedings.neurips.cc/paper/2019/file/5103c3584b063c431bd1268e9b5e76fb-Paper.pdf

18. Romano, Y., Sesia, M., Candès, E.: Classification with valid and adaptive coverage. In: Larochelle, H., Ranzato, M., Hadsell, R., Balcan, M.F., Lin, H. (eds.) Advances in Neural Information Processing Systems, vol. 33, pp. 3581–3591. Curran Associates, Inc. (2020)

19. Sadinle, M., Lei, J., Wasserman, L.: Least ambiguous set-valued classifiers with bounded error levels. J. Am. Stat. Assoc. **114**, 223–234 (2019)

20. Sesia, M., Romano, Y.: Conformal prediction using conditional histograms. In: Advances in Neural Information Processing Systems 34 (2021)

21. Shashikumar, S., Wardi, G., Malhotra, A., Nemati, S.: Artificial intelligence sepsis prediction algorithm learns to say "i don't know". npj Digit. Med. **4** (2021). https://doi.org/10.1038/s41746-021-00504-6

22. Vazquez, J., Facelli, J.: Conformal prediction in clinical medical sciences. J. Healthc. Inform. Res. (2022). https://doi.org/10.1007/s41666-021-00113-8

23. Vovk, V., Gammerman, A., Shafer, G.: Algorithmic Learning in a Random World. Springer, New York (2005). https://doi.org/10.1007/b106715

24. Vovk, V., Gammerman, A., Saunders, C.: Machine-learning applications of algorithmic randomness. In: International Conference on Machine Learning, pp. 444–453 (1999)

Machine Learning Theory
and Methodologies

Poisson2Sparse: Self-supervised Poisson Denoising from a Single Image

Calvin-Khang Ta$^{(\boxtimes)}$, Abhishek Aich, Akash Gupta,
and Amit K. Roy-Chowdhury

University of California, Riverside, USA
{cta003,aaich001,agupt013}@ucr.edu, amitrc@ece.ucr.edu

Abstract. Image enhancement approaches often assume that the noise is signal independent, and approximate the degradation model as zero-mean additive Gaussian. However, this assumption does not hold for biomedical imaging systems where sensor-based sources of noise are proportional to signal strengths, and the noise is better represented as a Poisson process. In this work, we explore a sparsity and dictionary learning-based approach and present a novel self-supervised learning method for single-image denoising where the noise is approximated as a Poisson process, requiring no clean ground-truth data. Specifically, we approximate traditional iterative optimization algorithms for image denoising with a recurrent neural network that enforces sparsity with respect to the weights of the network. Since the sparse representations are based on the underlying image, it is able to suppress the spurious components (noise) in the image patches, thereby introducing implicit regularization for denoising tasks through the network structure. Experiments on two bio-imaging datasets demonstrate that our method outperforms the state-of-the-art approaches in terms of PSNR and SSIM. Our qualitative results demonstrate that, in addition to higher performance on standard quantitative metrics, we are able to recover much more subtle details than other compared approaches. Our code is made publicly available at https://github.com/tacalvin/Poisson2Sparse.

1 Introduction

Biomedical image denoising is a challenging inverse problem of recovering a clean noise-free image from its corresponding corrupted version. Current denoising strategies [4,28] assume that most prevalent noisy images can be modeled with additive Gaussian noise. Though this assumption shows reasonable performance for some applications, it is physically unrealistic for biomedical images as the

---

C.-K. Ta, A. Aich and A. Gupta—Joint first authors.
A. Gupta—Currently at Vimaan AI.

Supplementary Information The online version contains supplementary material available at https://doi.org/10.1007/978-3-031-16452-1_53.

L. Wang et al. (Eds.): MICCAI 2022, LNCS 13438, pp. 557–567, 2022.
https://doi.org/10.1007/978-3-031-16452-1_53

noise varies proportionally to the signal strength and is signal-dependent [12]. As the image acquisition process is discrete in nature, the data captured by the imaging sensors are often corrupted by shot noise which can be modeled as a Poisson Process [19,25]. Thus, Poisson denoising methods are of utmost importance in biomedical image processing and analysis.

Supervised deep learning approaches are proven to be effective for image denoising tasks [4,28] and are mostly developed on sophisticated neural networks. The performance of such approaches heavily relies on the availability of large datasets to train the networks. These large-scale datasets often involve data pairs of a clean image, X, and a noisy image, X_0. However in most practical settings, such as bio-imaging [2], it is difficult to obtain such data pairs. Hence in order to tackle such scenarios, self-supervised *internal learning* methods [17] have been introduced that attempt to employ randomly-initialized neural networks to capture low-level image statistics. Such networks are used as priors to solve standard inverse problems such as denoising for *single* images without requiring its clean counterpart.

Related Works. The general supervised approach for using deep learning based denoisers is to use Convolutional Neural Networks (CNNs) and given a dataset of clean and noisy images, to learn the mapping between them [1,4,9,28]. Recent works in self-supervised learning [15,16,27] have shown that even without the use of explicit ground truth, deep learning models can offer surprisingly strong performance in a range of tasks. Our work is largely inspired by works such as the Deep Image Prior [17] or Self2Self [20] in which a deep learning model is trained directly on a single test image with no additional datasets. The core assumption of such works is that the network is implicitly acting as the regularizer and empirical results show the network resists fitting to noise. Given such advantages of internal learning methods, *we propose a novel self-supervised approach to denoise biomedical images that follow the Poisson noise model.* Building on the implicit regularization of a network, we utilize sparse representations through the network design to handle Poisson Noise. Different from prior works [4,28], *we consider the scenario where only a single noisy image is collected with no corresponding ground-truth clean image and the noise is Poisson distributed.* We employ the sparse representations because, intuitively, an image will contain many recurrent patches and by finding a sparse representation of the image patches, we can represent it as a linear combination of elements in a dictionary. By utilizing this sparse coding framework, the dictionary elements will contain the basis vectors which minimize the reconstruction error and suppress the noise.

Contributions. We present a novel method for single image Poisson denoising which leverages a neural network's inductive bias. Specifically, we use the neural network to learn the dictionary elements that are resistant to the input noise by modeling similar and repetitive image patches. We then utilize sparse representations to reconstruct the image through learned dictionaries and further suppress input noise. By leveraging the internal learning strategy, our method gains two key advantages: *1)* we only need a single noisy input image which is desirable in many biomedical applications where data is scarce, and *2)* we can train our model in an entirely self-supervised manner with no ground-truth which makes our approach extremely practical. Experiments show our approach is able to outperform existing state-of-the-art methods significantly. We illustrate our method in Fig. 1 and summarize the same in Algorithm 1 in the supplemental material.

2   Proposed Methodology: Poisson2Sparse

Problem Statement. Given a single Poisson noisy input image, we aim to generate the corresponding clean image. We propose to utilize the patch recurrence property in an image to learn a dictionary that can be utilized to generate a sparse representation such that the clean image can be recovered. The dictionary elements will ideally represent a set of over-complete basis functions that can well represent the image. The sparse representation is then used to reconstruct the image using the learned dictionary to suppress the noise present in the input image [8, 22]. Let the Poisson noisy image be represented by $X_0 \in \mathcal{R}^{d \times d}$ and its corresponding vectorized form denoted by $x_0 \in \mathcal{R}^{d^2}$, where d is the image dimension size. Our objective is to learn a dictionary to obtain sparse representation of X_0 that can be utilized to recover an estimate of the clean image $\widehat{X}$. To this end, we incorporate an unrolled iterative optimization algorithm approximated using a neural network to learn the dictionary and decompose the noisy image representation into a sparse code. In this section, we first derive the dictionary-based sparse representation learning algorithm for the vectorized image, where we represent the learnable dictionary as $\mathcal{D} \in \mathcal{R}^{d^2 \times k}$ and the sparse vector as $\alpha \in \mathcal{R}^{k \times 1}$. Here, k is the number of elements in α. Next, we leverage the Convolution Sparse Coding model [3] to obtain an optimization solution where the dictionary is independent of the vectorized image dimension. This is done by changing the application of the dictionary $\mathcal{D}\alpha$ from a matrix-vector product into a convolution with M dictionaries $D \in \mathcal{R}^{k \times k}$ around M sparse feature maps $\Lambda \subset \mathcal{R}^{d \times d}$ [3].

Poisson-Based Optimization Regularizer. We assume that the pixel values of the noisy vectorized image x_0 are Poisson distributed random variables parameterized by pixel values of the ground truth vectorized image x at every i^{th} index of the image. This allows $x_0[i]$ to be modeled as $x_0[i] \sim \mathcal{P}(x[i])$ [8, 22] where $\mathcal{P}$ is the Poisson process defined as follows:

$$\mathcal{P}_{x[i]}(x_0[i]) = \frac{x[i]^{x_0[i]} \exp(-x[i])}{x_0[i]!} \tag{1}$$

In order to estimate a denoised clean vector $\widehat{x}$, we maximize the log-likelihood of (1). The maximum log-likelihood estimation for clean vector recovery is performed by minimizing the following optimization problem [21]

$$\min_{x} \left(\mathbb{1}^T x - x_0^T \log(x) \right) \text{ s.t. } x \succcurlyeq 0 \tag{2}$$

where $\mathbb{1} \in \mathcal{R}^{d^2}$ is a vector of ones, $\succcurlyeq$ denotes element-wise inequality, and $\log(\cdot)$ is applied element wise. However, the optimization problem defined in (2) is known to be an ill-posed problem [10, 26]. In order to address this, we follow a sparse representation approach [18] and aim to estimate $\hat{x}$ by computing an s-sparse vector α and a dictionary $\mathcal{D}$ such that $\hat{x} = \mathcal{D}\alpha$.

$$\min_{\mathcal{D},\alpha} \left(\mathbb{1}^T(\mathcal{D}\alpha) - x_0{}^T \log(\mathcal{D}\alpha) \right) \quad \text{s.t. } ||\alpha||_0 \leq s, \quad \mathcal{D}\alpha \succcurlyeq 0 \qquad (3)$$

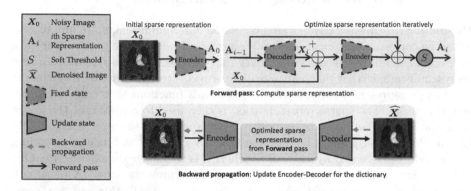

Fig. 1. Method Overview. Poisson2Sparse Optimization Steps: We optimize the sparse representation in the forward pass and then we update the encoder and decoder through back-propagation in an alternating manner.

This optimization problem in (3) is further relaxed by setting $\mathcal{D}\alpha = \exp(\mathcal{D}\alpha)$ to handle the non-negativity constraint [22]. Furthermore, the ℓ_0 constraint on α makes (3) an NP-hard problem [7]. Hence, we use the ℓ_1 relaxation as in [11], resulting in the following problem:

$$\min_{\mathcal{D},\alpha} \left(\mathbb{1}^T \exp(\mathcal{D}\alpha) - x_0{}^T(\mathcal{D}\alpha) \right) + \lambda||\alpha||_1 \qquad (4)$$

The above optimization problem in (4) now estimates $\hat{x}$ by solving for sparse prior α and dictionary $\mathcal{D}$. Inspired from the Iterative Shrinkage Thresholding Algorithm (ISTA) [6], we propose to solve for α and $\mathcal{D}$ in an alternating manner using a neural network based approach. In order to solve for α, traditional approaches [6] solve the following optimization problem

$$\min |\alpha|_0 \quad \text{s.t} \quad x = \mathcal{D}\alpha$$

However, trying to solve for that objective directly is difficult and a common approximation is the following objective using the ℓ_1 relaxation.

$$\arg\min_{\alpha} \left(\frac{1}{2}||x - \mathcal{D}\alpha||_2^2 + \lambda|\alpha|_1 \right) \qquad (5)$$

The ISTA algorithm aims to solve (5) via the update step $\alpha \leftarrow S(\alpha + \frac{1}{L}\mathcal{D}^T(x_0 - \mathcal{D}\alpha))$, where $L \leq \sigma_{\max}(\mathcal{D}^T\mathcal{D})$ and S is the soft threshold operator with a threshold of ϵ defined as $S_\epsilon(x) = \text{sign}(x)\max(|x| - \epsilon, 0)$. With this update step, the

ISTA algorithm iteratively refines the computed sparse code until a specified convergence criterion. However, in our problem formulation we work with images with dimension d making the dictionary $\mathcal{D} \in \mathcal{R}^{d^2 \times k}$ dependent on the size of the input image. To address this, we use the Convolutional Sparse Coding model as in [24] and replace the matrix-vector product with a convolution (denoted by $*$):

$$\mathcal{D}\alpha = \sum_j^M D_j * A_j = \boldsymbol{D} * \boldsymbol{A} \tag{6}$$

where $D_j \in \mathcal{R}^{k \times k}$ is filter convolved around a sparse feature map $A_j \in \mathcal{R}^{d \times d}$. This new form of the sparse code and application of the dictionary decouples the size of the dictionary from the input image size and removes the need to scale the model with respect to the image size and gives us the following update step:

$$\mathbf{A_i} \leftarrow S\big(\mathbf{A_{i-1}} + \boldsymbol{D}^T * (\boldsymbol{X_0} - \boldsymbol{D} * \mathbf{A_{i-1}})\big) \tag{7}$$

Using the ISTA approach, we can remove the need to optimize for α in (4) and rewrite the objective function, where $\odot$ is the Hadamard product, as

$$\min_D \big(\exp(\boldsymbol{D} * \mathbf{A}) - \boldsymbol{X_0} \odot (\boldsymbol{D} * \mathbf{A}) \big) \tag{8}$$

Poisson2Sparse Algorithm. To solve (8) using the ISTA algorithm, we represent $\boldsymbol{D} * \mathbf{A}$ using a neural network $\boldsymbol{f_\theta}$. The network $\boldsymbol{f_\theta}$ which contains a single encoder and decoder which computes the sparse representation $\mathbf{A}$ with respect to the network parameters which allows for learnable dictionaries $\boldsymbol{D}$ through backpropagation. Mathematically, this can be represented as $\boldsymbol{D} * \mathbf{A} = \boldsymbol{f_\theta}(\boldsymbol{X_0})$. The modified optimization problem (8), where we aim to enforce sparsity through the network structure implicitly, can be rewritten as

$$\min_\theta \big(\exp(\boldsymbol{f_\theta}(\boldsymbol{X_0})) - \boldsymbol{X_0} \odot \boldsymbol{f_\theta}(\boldsymbol{X_0}) \big) \tag{9}$$

which we will refer to as $\mathcal{L}_{Poisson}$ moving forward. Inspired by recent works in internal learning [17], we aim to use network $\boldsymbol{f_\theta}$ that will implicitly enforce sparsity through the network's structure. Hence, *we propose to adapt the internal learning approach via the ISTA algorithm.* Prior works [24] have demonstrated that by we can approximate computing the update step in the ISTA algorithm by replacing the D and term D^T with a decoder and encoder respectively in (7).

$$\mathbf{A} \leftarrow S\big(\mathbf{A} + Encoder(\boldsymbol{X_0} - Decoder(\mathbf{A}))\big) \tag{10}$$

Following [24], we approximate ISTA to a finite T number of iterations and by approximating the traditional update with (10) which naturally lends itself to a recurrent neural network-like structure where instead of passing in a T length sequence we are refining the sparse code $\mathbf{A}$ over T steps instead. This results in the network's forward pass that computes the sparse code as well as the application of the dictionary to the computed sparse code. The sparse code is then refined over a finite number of steps as opposed to being run until convergence in the traditional ISTA algorithm.

Poisson2Sparse Training. In order to train the network, we follow [13] and generate our input and target image pairs by using the random neighbor down-sampling. The random neighbor down-sampling is done by dividing the input image into $k \times k$ blocks and for each block, two adjacent pixels are selected and are used to create down-sampling functions denoted by g_1 and g_2. This down-sampling approach avoids learning the trivial identity solution where the network learns to simply map the input to output to solve (9). It creates image pairs that are similar in appearance but are slightly different in terms of the ground truth pixels. These image pairs can be seen as different realizations of the same noise distribution and by trying to minimize the loss function for these noisy pairs we can estimate the true ground truth signal. Optimizing (9) alone with the generated image pairs will result in blurry images due to the slight difference in the underlying ground truth and thus we incorporate the regularizer proposed in [13] which is defined as the following with strength μ_N.

Table 1. Quantitative Results show that we outperform both self-supervised works (DIP, Self2Self) and traditional work BM3D (best results in bold).

Dataset	λ	DIP	Self2Self	BM3D	Ours
		PSNR (dB)/SSIM			
*PINCAT	40	30.222/0.878	33.138/0.942	32.553/0.944	**34.309/0.957**
	20	26.495/0.765	30.067/0.893	31.448/0.911	**32.202/0.937**
	10	22.495/0.601	27.028/0.814	27.961/0.867	**30.005/0.898**
FMD	–	32.417/**0.916**	28.563/0.688	29.627/0.854	**32.980**/0.897
Average	–	27.907/0.790	29.699/0.834	30.397/0.894	**32.374/0.922**

$$\mathcal{L}_N = \| f_\theta(g_1(X_0)) - g_2(X_0) - g_1(f_\theta(X_0)) - g_2(f_\theta(X_0)) \|_2^2 \qquad (11)$$

We also add an L1 reconstruction loss which is referred as $\mathcal{L}_{L1}$ and it aids in the reduction of artifacts generated from (9). The overall loss function used to optimize the dictionary parameters f_θ which is applied per pixel is given as:

$$\mathcal{L} = \mathcal{L}_{Poisson} + \mathcal{L}_{L1} + \mu_N \mathcal{L}_N \qquad (12)$$

3 Experiments and Results

Datasets and Experimental Setup. We used the test set of the following datasets to evaluate our approach. *(a)* **Florescent Microscopy Denoising Dataset** (FMD) [29]: This dataset contains 12000 Fluorescence Microscopy images of size 512×512 containing noise where Poisson noise is dominant. The images contain real noise of varying strengths from across multiple microscopy modalities. In order to obtain clean images a common technique is to average multiple images for an effective ground truth. For this dataset this is especially appropriate as the samples are static which allows for accurate registration between the 50 images used to obtain the effective ground truth. *(b)* **PINCAT Dataset** [23]: This is a simulated cardiac perfusion MRI dataset with clean images of size 128×128. For this dataset, we added artificial noise (where the strength λ of noise indicates the maximum event count, with a lower λ indicating a higher noise). Specifically we can represent a noisy image as $X_0 = \frac{Z}{\lambda}$ where $Z \sim \mathcal{P}(\lambda X)$ and we tested with $\lambda = [40, 20, 10]$ following prior works [27].

Baselines and Evaluation Metrics. We use a traditional denoising approach, BM3D [5], and internal learning based approaches such as Deep Image Prior (DIP) [17] and Self2Self [20] as our baselines. While comparison to vanilla ISTA is also appropriate we found that the results were far worse than any of the methods previously mentioned despite its fast runtime and will leave those experiments in the supplementary material. In order to compare methods we use Peak Signal to Noise Ratio (PSNR) and the Structural Similarity Index (SSIM) as evaluation metrics.

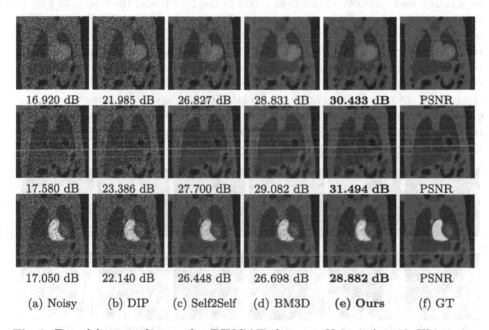

16.920 dB	21.985 dB	26.827 dB	28.831 dB	**30.433 dB**	PSNR
17.580 dB	23.386 dB	27.700 dB	29.082 dB	**31.494 dB**	PSNR
17.050 dB	22.140 dB	26.448 dB	26.698 dB	**28.882 dB**	PSNR
(a) Noisy	(b) DIP	(c) Self2Self	(d) BM3D	**(e) Ours**	(f) GT

Fig. 2. Denoising results on the PINCAT dataset. Noise is $\lambda = 10$. We can see that our method is able to recover finer details such as the ribs in the image.

Training Details. To optimize the network, we use the Adam optimizer [14] with a learning rate of 0.0001 and set $\mu_N = 2$ as done in [13]. We use a single convolutional layer for both the encoder and decoder with a kernel size of 3×3, stride of 1, and each layer has 512 filters. For the number of steps in the network, we empirically find that 10 gave us the best performance and we train the network over 5500 iterations. We used PyTorch for our implementation and the model was trained using a Nvidia RTX 2080 Ti for a total of 7 min for an image of size 128×128.

Table 2. Ablation studies. We tested the impact of each term in our loss function on the overall performance, indicated by a ✓.

Loss functions		Metrics			
$\mathcal{L}_{L1}$	$\mathcal{L}_{Poisson}$	PSNR (dB)	ΔPSNR	SSIM	ΔSSIM
✓	✓	32.202	–	0.9370	–
✓		31.565	−2.01 %	0.9335	−0.37 %
	✓	32.007	−0.61 %	0.9356	−0.14 %

Qualitative and Quantitative Results. From our experiments we are able to outperform existing state-of-the-art approaches for single image denoising by a significant margin in terms of the PSNR and SSIM. In Table 1, we can see that for all noise levels in the PINCAT dataset we are significantly outperforming other self-supervised and classical methods in terms of the PSNR and the SSIM. In Fig. 2, we show that our approach can recover the finer details around the rib-cage which other methods fail to recover to any meaningful degree. Additionally, we can see that in regions where the ground truth is of a single consistent value we are able to recover the region with a result that is much smoother than other methods where significant noise is still present in the final output. With the FMD dataset where the noise is not pure Poisson noise, we find that on average we are doing better than existing methods in terms of the PSNR. In terms of the SSIM, we are slightly underperforming when compared to the DIP but visual inspection shows that DIP in

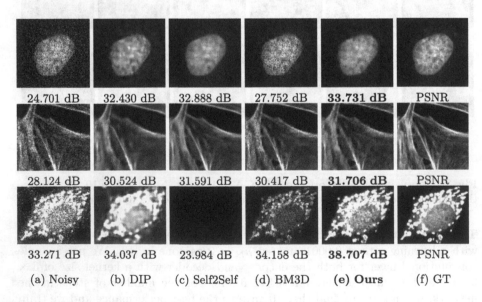

24.701 dB	32.430 dB	32.888 dB	27.752 dB	**33.731 dB**	PSNR
28.124 dB	30.524 dB	31.591 dB	30.417 dB	**31.706 dB**	PSNR
33.271 dB	34.037 dB	23.984 dB	34.158 dB	**38.707 dB**	PSNR
(a) Noisy	(b) DIP	(c) Self2Self	(d) BM3D	**(e) Ours**	(f) GT

Fig. 3. Denoising results on the FMD dataset. Note that for some cases, Self2Self failed to denoise the input image and returned only a blank image.

certain cases DIP will actually over-smooth the resulting image as shown in Fig. 3. We additionally found that Self2Self is unstable on many of the images resulting in blank images for a large portion of the dataset which explains the poor results shown in Table 1. Overall our method performs better than other self-supervised single image approaches for pure Poisson noise and is competitive in cases where the noise is not completely Poisson noise.

Ablation Studies. We performed ablation studies on our final loss function (12) in order to evaluate the performance of its components. We evaluate our approach using the same architecture for the full and ablated loss functions. Specifically, we test our full loss function, $\mathcal{L}_{Poisson}$, and $\mathcal{L}_{L1}$. For the experiments, we keep the regularizer $\mathcal{L}_N$ for all experiments and tested our results on the PINCAT dataset with Poisson noise with strength $\lambda = 20$. We use the same metrics used to evaluate the performance of our approach - PSNR, and SSIM. The results, as shown in Table 2, indicate that our Poisson-based loss is the key contributor to the performance of our overall approach; when it is removed we suffer the largest performance drop as opposed to removing the L1 reconstruction loss. This validates our motivation of using a specialized loss function for handling Poisson noise. In addition to this, we find that the inclusion of the L1 reconstruction loss does improve our performance to a level greater than any of the individual terms on their own. Qualitative results of the ablation studies are shown in the supplementary material.

4   Conclusion

In this paper, we introduce Poisson2Sparse, a self-supervised approach for single-image denoising for Poisson corrupted images. We explore the application of sparsity, in conjunction with internal learning-based methods for image enhancement, and show significantly superior performance to existing approaches. By only requiring a single noisy image, our method is practical in situations where the acquisition of clean data can be difficult. Our experiments validate our method as we are able to outperform existing state-of-the-art methods for self-supervised approaches under a variety of datasets and varying levels of Poisson noise, for example, by more $\sim$2 dB PSNR in average performance.

Acknowledgement. The work was partially supported by US National Science Foundation grants 1664172, 1762063, and 2029814.

References

1. Aich, A., Gupta, A., Panda, R., Hyder, R., Asif, M.S., Roy-Chowdhury, A.K.: Non-adversarial video synthesis with learned priors. In: Proceedings of the IEEE/CVF Conference on Computer Vision and Pattern Recognition (CVPR), June 2020
2. Aldaz, S., Escudero, L.M., Freeman, M.: Live imaging of drosophila imaginal disc development. Proc. Natl. Acad. Sci. **107**(32), 14217–14222 (2010)
3. Bristow, H., Eriksson, A., Lucey, S.: Fast convolutional sparse coding. In: 2013 IEEE Conference on Computer Vision and Pattern Recognition, pp. 391–398 (2013)

4. Chen, L., Lu, X., Zhang, J., Chu, X., Chen, C.: HINet: half instance normalization network for image restoration. In: Proceedings of the IEEE/CVF Conference on Computer Vision and Pattern Recognition (CVPR) Workshops, pp. 182–192, June 2021
5. Dabov, K., Foi, A., Katkovnik, V., Egiazarian, K.: Image denoising with block-matching and 3D filtering. In: Image Processing: Algorithms and Systems, Neural Networks, and Machine Learning. Society of Photo-Optical Instrumentation Engineers (SPIE) Conference Series, vol. 6064, pp. 354–365, February 2006
6. Daubechies, I., Defrise, M., De Mol, C.: An iterative thresholding algorithm for linear inverse problems with a sparsity constraint. Commun. Pure Appl. Math. J. Courant Inst. Math. Sci. **57**(11), 1413–1457 (2004)
7. Ge, D., Jiang, X., Ye, Y.: A note on the complexity of L_p minimization. Math. Program. **129**(2), 285–299 (2011)
8. Giryes, R., Elad, M.: Sparsity-based Poisson denoising with dictionary learning. IEEE Trans. Image Process. **23**(12), 5057–5069 (2014)
9. Gupta, A., Aich, A., Rodriguez, K., Reddy, G.V., Roy-Chowdhury, A.K.: Deep quantized representation for enhanced reconstruction. In: 2020 IEEE 17th International Symposium on Biomedical Imaging Workshops (ISBI Workshops), pp. 1–4. IEEE (2020)
10. Hansen, P.C.: Rank-Deficient and Discrete Ill-Posed Problems: Numerical Aspects of Linear Inversion. SIAM (1998)
11. Harmany, Z.T., Marcia, R.F., Willett, R.M.: This is spiral-tap: sparse Poisson intensity reconstruction algorithms-theory and practice. IEEE Trans. Image Process. **21**(3), 1084–1096 (2012)
12. Hasinoff, S.W.: Photon, Poisson noise (2014)
13. Huang, T., Li, S., Jia, X., Lu, H., Liu, J.: Neighbor2Neighbor: self-supervised denoising from single noisy images. In: Proceedings of the IEEE/CVF Conference on Computer Vision and Pattern Recognition (CVPR), pp. 14781–14790, June 2021
14. Kingma, D.P., Ba, J.: Adam: a method for stochastic optimization. CoRR arXiv:1412.6980 (2015)
15. Krull, A., Buchholz, T.O., Jug, F.: Noise2Void - learning denoising from single noisy images. In: 2019 IEEE/CVF Conference on Computer Vision and Pattern Recognition (CVPR), pp. 2124–2132 (2019)
16. Lehtinen, J., et al.: Noise2Noise: learning image restoration without clean data. In: Dy, J., Krause, A. (eds.) Proceedings of the 35th International Conference on Machine Learning. Proceedings of Machine Learning Research, 10–15 July 2018, vol. 80, pp. 2965–2974. PMLR (2018). https://proceedings.mlr.press/v80/lehtinen18a.html
17. Lempitsky, V., Vedaldi, A., Ulyanov, D.: Deep image prior. In: 2018 IEEE/CVF Conference on Computer Vision and Pattern Recognition, pp. 9446–9454 (2018)
18. Mairal, J., Bach, F., Ponce, J., Sapiro, G., Zisserman, A.: Non-local sparse models for image restoration. In: 2009 IEEE 12th International Conference on Computer Vision, pp. 2272–2279 (2009)
19. Pawley, J.B.: Fundamental Limits in Confocal Microscopy, pp. 20–42. Springer, Boston (2006). https://doi.org/10.1007/978-0-387-45524-2_2
20. Quan, Y., Chen, M., Pang, T., Ji, H.: Self2Self with dropout: learning self-supervised denoising from single image. In: Proceedings of the IEEE/CVF Conference on Computer Vision and Pattern Recognition, pp. 1890–1898 (2020)

21. Raginsky, M., Willett, R.M., Harmany, Z.T., Marcia, R.F.: Compressed sensing performance bounds under Poisson noise. IEEE Trans. Signal Process. **58**(8), 3990–4002 (2010)
22. Salmon, J., Harmany, Z., Deledalle, C.-A., Willett, R.: Poisson noise reduction with non-local PCA. J. Math. Imaging Vis. **48**(2), 279–294 (2013). https://doi.org/10.1007/s10851-013-0435-6
23. Sharif, B., Bresler, Y.: Adaptive real-time cardiac MRI using PARADISE: validation by the physiologically improved NCAT phantom. In: 2007 4th IEEE International Symposium on Biomedical Imaging: From Nano to Macro, pp. 1020–1023. IEEE (2007)
24. Simon, D., Elad, M.: Rethinking the CSC model for natural images. In: Advances in Neural Information Processing Systems, vol. 32 (2019)
25. Sjulson, L., Miesenböck, G.: Optical recording of action potentials and other discrete physiological events: a perspective from signal detection theory. Physiology **22**(1), 47–55 (2007)
26. Tikhonov, A.N., Goncharsky, A., Stepanov, V., Yagola, A.G.: Numerical Methods for the Solution of Ill-posed Problems, vol. 328. Springer, Cham (1995). https://doi.org/10.1007/978-94-015-8480-7
27. Xu, J., Adalsteinsson, E.: Deformed2Self: self-supervised denoising for dynamic medical imaging. In: de Bruijne, M., et al. (eds.) MICCAI 2021. LNCS, vol. 12902, pp. 25–35. Springer, Cham (2021). https://doi.org/10.1007/978-3-030-87196-3_3
28. Zamir, S.W., et al.: Multi-stage progressive image restoration. In: Proceedings of the IEEE/CVF Conference on Computer Vision and Pattern Recognition, pp. 14821–14831 (2021)
29. Zhang, Y., et al.: A Poisson-Gaussian denoising dataset with real fluorescence microscopy images. In: Proceedings of the IEEE/CVF Conference on Computer Vision and Pattern Recognition, pp. 11710–11718 (2019)

An Inclusive Task-Aware Framework for Radiology Report Generation

Lin Wang[1], Munan Ning[2], Donghuan Lu[2], Dong Wei[2], Yefeng Zheng[2], and Jie Chen[1,3]([✉])

[1] School of Electronic and Computer Engineering, Peking University, Shenzhen, China
[2] Tencent Jarvis Lab, Shenzhen, China
[3] Peng Cheng Laboratory, Shenzhen, China
chenj@pcl.ac.cn

Abstract. To avoid the tedious and laborious radiology report writing, the automatic generation of radiology reports has drawn great attention recently. Previous studies attempted to directly transfer the image captioning method to radiology report generation given the apparent similarity between these two tasks. Although these methods can generate fluent descriptions, their accuracy for abnormal structure identification is limited due to the neglecting of the highly structured property and extreme data imbalance of the radiology report generation task. Therefore, we propose a novel task-aware framework to address the above two issues, composed of a task distillation module turning the image-level report to structure-level description, a task-aware report generation module for the generation of structure-specific descriptions, along with a classification token to identify and emphasize the abnormality of each structure, and an auto-balance mask loss to alleviate the serious data imbalance between normal/abnormal descriptions as well as the imbalance among different structures. Comprehensive experiments conducted on two public datasets demonstrate that the proposed method outperforms the state-of-the-art methods by a large margin (3.5% BLEU-1 improvement on MIMIC-CXR dataset) and can effectively improve the accuracy regarding the abnormal structures. The code is available at https://github.com/Reremee/ITA.

Keywords: Report generation · Task-aware · Data imbalance

1 Introduction

A huge number of radiology reports are generated and used for healthcare [6] every day, leading to laborious, time-consuming, and tedious work for radiologists to write these reports [10]. Reducing the time spent on report writing could effectively improve the efficiency of radiologists and increase the chance of

Supplementary Information The online version contains supplementary material available at https://doi.org/10.1007/978-3-031-16452-1_54.

patients receiving prompt care. Therefore, automatic radiology report generation emerges as an attractive research direction [3,6] to provide radiologists with assistant information for timely and objective diagnosis.

With the rapid development of deep neural networks, a lot of efforts have been made to explore learning-based solutions for this challenging problem [12–14,16,22]. Some works started with transferring the image captioning methods to medical tasks [1,28]. Sharing similar frameworks, these approaches extract visual features from images with a convolutional neural network (CNN) and convert the latent visual representations to final reports through a recurrent neural network (RNN) model [13,22]. In addition, some advanced technologies are employed to boost the generation performance, such as the powerful attention mechanisms [13], memory-driven structure [5], and consistency-based constraint [23,25], to encourage the generation of inferentially consistent sentences.

Despite the progress made in generating fluent sentences, these studies omit an essential difference between medical report generation and other image captioning tasks, i.e., medical reports are more structured than natural image captions, which makes the radiology report generation a task-aware problem. Specifically, unlike the image captions where the images could have versatile descriptions, medical images of the same body part and modality should be described from the same aspects (usually based on anatomical structures), e.g., the chest X-ray images are usually described from seven aspects: heart, pleural, bone, lung, airspace, thoracic aorta, and foreign object. Neglecting such prior information, the descriptions generated by the image captioning methods could neglect the abnormality of some structures, affecting usability in clinical practice.

In this work, we propose an **Inclusive Task-Aware** framework (ITA) for radiology report generation. To begin with, for each specific dataset, a task distillation (TD) module is introduced to distill knowledge from this dataset and group the descriptions into several anatomical-structure-specific aspects. Subsequently, a task-aware report generation (TRG) module is proposed to generate the descriptions for each structure, instead of generating the overall report at once. Specifically, the module consists of a CNN-based embedding generator and a task-aware multi-head Transformer. In addition, a classification token (CLT) for identifying the abnormality of each structure is introduced to provide task-wise classification supervision for CNN and encoders, and guide the decoder to deliver structure-specific correct description. By making each head concentrate on generating the description of a specific structure, every structure is guaranteed to be inspected, and thus better described as demonstrated by the experiments.

Another major issue regarding the radiology report generation task is the severe data bias, i.e., not only the overall proportion of abnormal images to all images, but also the proportion of the descriptions of certain structures to those of others are small, resulting in various degrees of imbalance regarding different types of abnormalities. Previous studies [19–21] only attempted to resolve the former but omitted the latter, leading to inferior performance regarding the description of some abnormal structures. Through the multi-head Transformer of the proposed module, our method naturally achieves better sensitivities regarding the rare abnormalities. We additionally propose to introduce an auto-balance mask loss (ABL) to further boost the performance regarding the issue of different degrees of imbalance of various abnormalities.

In summary, this work makes the following contributions:

– We propose a novel inclusive task-aware framework (ITA) for the radiology report generation task. By enforcing each Transformer head to generate the description for a specific structure, every structure is guaranteed to be inspected for superior performance.
– An extra classification token (CLT) is additionally introduced to provide task-wise classification supervision and improve the correctness of the description.
– We introduce an auto-balance mask loss to further relieve the imbalance regarding various types of abnormalities.
– Extensive experiments are conducted on two widely used public datasets, which demonstrate the effectiveness of the proposed ITA framework.

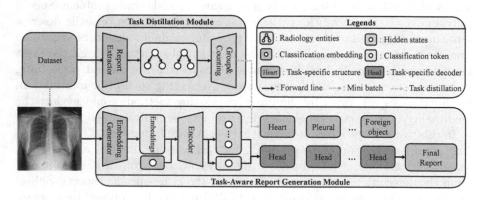

Fig. 1. Overview of the proposed framework.

2   Method

As shown in Fig. 1, the proposed framework consists of two parts, a task distillation (TD) module and a task-aware report generation (TRG) module. Specifically, TD extracts radiology entities from the dataset and disassembles the report into task-aware descriptions based on a knowledge graph. In addition, TRG extracts patch embeddings from the image, and transfers them to hidden states with a shared encoder and then generates task-wise sentences with a multi-head decoder. The detailed explanation of these parts, along with the classification token and the auto-balance mask loss are presented in the following sections.

2.1 Task Distillation Module

Following [29], we construct a TD module to transfer hand-written reports to structured reports where each sentence should describe a certain anatomical structure of the image and each structure of interest should be described. The TD module employs a knowledge graph [29] to group the descriptions in the reports to several entities for each structure, and specifies the final keywords with prior knowledge to ensure that all anatomical structures are covered. By grouping sentences according to the existing of these keywords, the ground truth report $\mathbf{R}$ of radiograph $\mathbf{X}$ can be disassembled into task-wise sections $\{r_1, r_2, ..., r_m\}$, where m represents the number of anatomical structures. Note that many clinical reports do not contain the descriptions for all the structures because radiologists tend to omit normal structures. Therefore, we supplement the missing descriptions with normal descriptions randomly selected from the entire training set.

2.2 Task-Aware Report Generation Module

With the disassembled descriptions, we propose to train a TRG module for the radiology report generation task. The TRG module is composed of an embedding generator and a task-aware multi-head Transformer, where each head corresponds to the description of a specific structure.

The embedding generator is composed of a CNN-based visual extractor f_V and a trainable linear projection f_P. Given a radiograph $\mathbf{X}$, if we set the dimension of embeddings to n, we get its corresponding patch embeddings as follows:

$$\{e_1, e_2, ..., e_n\} = f_P(f_V(\mathbf{X})), \tag{1}$$

where the output of the last convolution of visual extractor f_V is fed to the linear projection f_P and transferred to the patch embeddings $\{e_1, e_2, ..., e_n\}$.

The task-aware multi-head Transformer consists of a shared encoder and a multi-head decoder. The shared encoder is stacked by standard Transformer encoder blocks [27], transferring the patch embeddings to hidden states, which can be formulated as:

$$\{h_1, h_2, ..., h_n\} = f_E(\{e_1, e_2, ..., e_n\}), \tag{2}$$

where f_E denotes the shared encoder and $\{h_1, h_2, ..., h_n\}$ denotes the sequence of hidden states.

Unlike previous studies [4,5,19–21] which generates the overall report at once, each head of the multi-head decoder in our proposed TRG is only responsible for generating the description of a specific anatomical structure, such that the structures with fewer descriptions are not ignored. Specifically, each head is a modified version of the Transformer structure, where a relational memory and a memory-driven conditional layer [5] are used to effectively simulate doctors' clinical writing and generate professional descriptions. The generation of the task-specific descriptions $\mathbf{Y} = \{y_1, y_2, ..., y_m\}$ can be formulated as:

$$y_i = f_D^i(\{h_1, h_2, ..., h_n\}), i \in 1, ..., m \tag{3}$$

where f_D^i denotes the transformation function of header i.

The framework is optimized by minimizing the sum of cross-entropy loss for each structure as follows:

$$\mathcal{L}_{GEN}(\mathbf{R}, \mathbf{Y}) = -\sum_{i=1}^{m}\sum_{j=1}^{l_i} r_{ij} log(y_{ij}), \tag{4}$$

where l_i denotes the length of words in r_i, and r_{ij} and y_{ij} denote the j-th word in the ground truth and generated report, respectively. For each structure, the cross-entropy loss is calculated word by word until reaches the EOS (end-of-sentence) character in r_i.

2.3   Classification Token

When writing radiology reports, doctors usually decide whether there are abnormalities and then write diagnoses accordingly. Inspired by this, an extra classification embedding, similar to [9], is introduced into the encoders with the patch embeddings to generate the corresponding classification token which records the abnormal types:

$$\{h_1, h_2, ..., h_n\}, \{t_1, t_2, ..., t_m\} = f_E(\{e_1, e_2, ..., e_n\}, \{c_1, c_2, ..., c_m\}), \tag{5}$$

where the $\{c_1, c_2, ..., c_m\}$ denotes the classification embedding and $\{t_1, t_2, ..., t_m\}$ denotes the output classification token. The classification token is then fed into the decoder, concatenating with the hidden states, to provide high level feature for abnormal regions, and the report generation process can be revised as:

$$\{y_1, y_2, ..., y_m\} = f_D(\{h_1, h_2, ..., h_n\}, \{t_1, t_2, ..., t_m\}). \tag{6}$$

The classification token is optimized with the label obtained based on the TD module using the cross-entropy loss:

$$\mathcal{L}_{CLS}(g, p) = -\sum_{i=1}^{m} g_i log(p_i) \qquad \text{and} \qquad p_i = \text{MLP}(t_i), \tag{7}$$

where MLP denotes a multi-layer perceptron (MLP) head, g and p denote the classification label and prediction, respectively. By introducing the classification token, the framework distinguishes the structure-wise abnormality and generates correct reports.

2.4   Auto-Balance Mask Loss

Considering the high imbalance between normal and abnormal descriptions of several structures, we propose to introduce an auto-balance mask loss to resolve the data imbalance issue. If training directly with structured reports, with extreme data imbalance the networks tend to deliver trivial solutions by describing most structures to be normal. To address this issue, we propose an auto-balance mask loss by taking different degrees of sample imbalance of different structures into consideration. In order to balance the abnormal and normal samples of each structure separately, we propose to discard a normal sample of region i during training with a probability p_i, which is computed by:

$$p_i = max(1 - \alpha * \frac{N_a^i}{N_n^i}, 0), \tag{8}$$

where N_n^i and N_a^i denote the numbers of normal and abnormal samples of region i, respectively, and α is a hyperparameter, setting as $\alpha = 2$ empirically.

We train the framework by optimizing the weighted summation of generation and classification losses for each structure with a trade-off parameter λ:

$$\mathcal{L}_{ABL} = -\sum_{i=1}^{m} max(\delta(r_i), 1 - Rand(p_i)) * (\mathcal{L}_{GEN} + \lambda * \mathcal{L}_{CLS}), \tag{9}$$

where $\delta(r_i)$ returns 1 when the task-wise description r_i is abnormal otherwise returns 0, and $Rand(p_i)$ denotes a binary random number generator with a probability of p_i to generate 1. Intuitively, if the structure is abnormal, the loss will be added to the total loss directly; if the structure is normal, the loss is discarded with the probability p_i. In this way, the number of effective normal samples that are included in the total loss computation is re-balanced to approximately α times of the number of abnormal samples.

3   Experiments and Results

3.1   Datasets and Metrics

To validate the effectiveness of the proposed method, we conduct experiments on two public datasets. The **IU X-ray**[1] [7] consists of 7,470 chest X-ray images along with 3,955 radiology reports collected by Indiana University, which is randomly split into training, validation and testing sets with a proportion of 7:1:2 as [12,16,17]. **MIMIC-CXR**[2] [14] consists 473,057 chest X-ray images and 206,563 radiology reports of 63,478 patients from the Beth Israel Deaconess Medical Center, which is divided as the official splits [5]. The BLEU [26], METEOR [2], and ROUGE-L [18] are adopted to evaluate the performance of the proposed framework.

3.2   Implementation Details

The ResNet-101 [11] pretrained on ImageNet [8] is adopted as the visual extractor in our work, while other modules of the framework are randomly initialized. Both encoder and each decoder of the Transformer have three layers. The dimension of patch embeddings n and number of anatomical structures m are set to

---

[1] https://openi.nlm.nih.gov/.
[2] https://physionet.org/content/mimic-cxr/2.0.0/.

512 and 7, respectively. The ADAM optimizer [15] is adopted for parameter optimization. The learning rates of the visual extractor and other parameters are initially set to 5×10^{-5} and 1×10^{-4}, respectively, and decayed by 0.8 per epoch. The λ is set to 0.5. In order to balance the generation effectiveness and efficiency, the beam size is set to 3. Note that for IU X-Ray we concatenate two images of the same patient as two channels of the input to ensure consistency with the previous work. The proposed method is implemented on PyTorch 1.7 with an NVIDIA Tesla V100 GPU.

Table 1. Performance of our approach and other state-of-the-art methods.

Dataset	Methods	BLEU-1	BLEU-2	BLEU-3	BLEU-4	METEOR	ROUGE-L
IU-Xray [7]	HRGR [16]	0.438	0.298	0.208	0.151	–	0.322
	CMAS-RL [12]	0.464	0.301	0.210	0.154	–	0.362
	R2GEN [5]	0.470	0.304	0.219	0.165	0.187	0.371
	CMCL [19]	0.473	0.305	0.217	0.162	0.186	0.378
	CMN [4]	0.475	0.309	0.222	0.170	0.191	0.375
	CA [21]	0.492	0.314	0.222	0.169	0.193	0.380
	PPKED [20]	0.483	0.315	0.224	0.168	–	0.376
	ITA	**0.505**	**0.340**	**0.247**	**0.188**	**0.208**	**0.382**
MIMIC-CXR [14]	R2GEN [5]	0.353	0.218	0.145	0.103	0.142	0.277
	CMCL [19]	0.344	0.217	0.140	0.097	0.133	0.281
	CMN [4]	0.353	0.218	0.148	0.106	0.142	0.278
	CA [21]	0.350	0.219	0.152	0.109	**0.151**	0.283
	PPKED [20]	0.360	0.224	0.149	0.106	0.149	**0.284**
	ITA	**0.395**	**0.253**	**0.170**	**0.121**	0.147	**0.284**

3.3   Performance Evaluation

As presented in Table 1, the proposed framework is compared with several state-of-the-art radiology report generation methods. On both IU-Xray and MIMIC-CXR datasets, the proposed method outperforms other approaches by large margins on the BLEU metrics, and achieves the state-of-the-art performance on the ROUGE-L, demonstrating the effectiveness of the task-aware strategy. We notice that there is a slight decrease in METEOR compared with some other methods. It is because that the dictionary METEOR used to align synonym is obtained from natural language [24], which is lack of professional knowledge of medical field. Therefore, we argue that the current version of METEOR may not be appropriate to evaluate the quality of radiology generation task, and a specific medical dictionary for better evaluation will be established in our future work.

3.4   Ablation Study

To verify the effectiveness of each component, we perform an ablation study on MIMIC-CXR with the following variants as shown in Table 2: 1) 'R2GEN': the

Table 2. Ablation study of the proposed approach.

Dataset	Model	BLEU-1	BLEU-4	METEOR	ROUGE-L	ACC	F1-score
MIMIC-CXR [14]	R2GEN [5]	0.353	0.103	0.142	0.277	69.35	32.64
	TRG	0.373	0.117	0.143	0.279	69.51	38.48
	TRG+CLT	0.388	0.118	0.145	0.280	69.66	46.80
	TRG+CLT+ABL	**0.395**	**0.121**	**0.147**	**0.284**	**70.25**	**48.76**

R2GEN [5] as our baseline; 2) 'TRG': replacing the baseline decoder with the proposed task-aware multi-head decoder; 3)'TRG+CLT': adding the classification token into the sequence; 4) 'TRG+CLT+ABL': introducing the auto-balance mask loss for the optimization process. In addition to BLEU, METEOR and ROUGE-L, we also present the average accuracy ('ACC') and F1-socre of distinguishing between normal and abnormal structures. The steady improvement of performance on both report generation and abnormality classification metrics demonstrates the effectiveness of the task-aware framework as well as the additional classification supervision and the auto-balance mask loss.

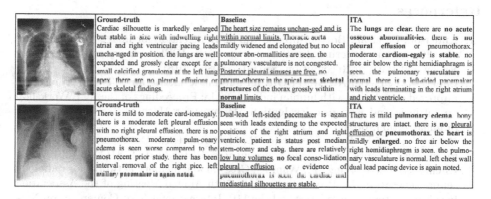

Fig. 2. Illustrations of reports from ground-truth, baseline and our ITA methods for two typical X-ray chest images. Different structures are marked with different colors. (Color figure online)

3.5 Qualitative Analysis

We further perform a qualitative analysis to perceptually understand the improvements. Two representative samples are displayed in Fig. 2, where we use different colors to differentiate descriptions of different structures, bold words for consistent sentences, and underlined words for inconsistencies. We can observe that the baseline generates trivial solutions for few structures and omits many other regions, whereas ITA correctly describes the omitted structures and finds the pacing device. We thus conclude that our approach can generate task-aware reports and alleviate the data bias of normal-abnormal sample imbalance.

4   Conclusion

In this study, we propose a novel framework for radiology report generation. Noticing the two essential differences between the radiology report generation and other image captioning tasks, we firstly apply a knowledge-graph-based task distillation module to disassemble the report into structure-wise descriptions. Subsequently, the task-aware report generation module is trained with the disassembled descriptions with each head corresponding to a separate structure, so that each structure could be better inspected and characterized. The performance is further boosted by introducing our proposed classification token and auto-balance mask loss. Extensive experiments on two public datasets demonstrate the superiority of the proposed framework compared with the state-of-the-art methods for radiology report generation, as well as the discriminative ability of abnormal structures.

Acknowledgements. This work is supported by the Nature Science Foundation of China (No.61972217, No.62081360152), Natural Science Foundation of Guangdong Province in China (No.2019B1515120049, 2020B1111340056).

References

1. Anderson, P., et al.: Bottom-up and top-down attention for image captioning and visual question answering. In: Proceedings of the IEEE Conference on Computer Vision and Pattern Recognition, pp. 6077–6086 (2018)
2. Banerjee, S., Lavie, A.: METEOR: an automatic metric for MT evaluation with improved correlation with human judgments. In: Proceedings of the ACL Workshop on Intrinsic and Extrinsic Evaluation Measures for Machine Translation and/or Summarization, pp. 65–72 (2005)
3. Brady, A., Laoide, R.Ó., McCarthy, P., McDermott, R.: Discrepancy and error in radiology: concepts, causes and consequences. Ulster Med. J. **81**(1), 3 (2012)
4. Chen, Z., Shen, Y., Song, Y., Wan, X.: Cross-modal memory networks for radiology report generation. In: Proceedings of the 59th Annual Meeting of the Association for Computational Linguistics and the 11th International Joint Conference on Natural Language Processing (Volume 1: Long Papers). pp. 5904–5914 (2021)
5. Chen, Z., Song, Y., Chang, T.H., Wan, X.: Generating radiology reports via memory-driven transformer. arXiv preprint arXiv:2010.16056 (2020)
6. Delrue, L., Gosselin, R., Ilsen, B., Van Landeghem, A., de Mey, J., Duyck, P.: Difficulties in the interpretation of chest radiography. In: Comparative Interpretation of CT and Standard Radiography of the Chest, pp. 27–49. Springer, Heidelberg (2011). https://doi.org/10.1007/978-3-540-79942-9_2
7. Demner-Fushman, D., et al.: Preparing a collection of radiology examinations for distribution and retrieval. J. Am. Med. Inf. Assoc. **23**(2), 304–310 (2016)
8. Deng, J., Dong, W., Socher, R., Li, L.J., Li, K., Fei-Fei, L.: ImageNet: a large-scale hierarchical image database. In: IEEE Conference on Computer Vision and Pattern Recognition, pp. 248–255. IEEE (2009)
9. Dosovitskiy, A., et al.: An image is worth 16x16 words: transformers for image recognition at scale. arXiv preprint arXiv:2010.11929 (2020)
10. Goergen, S.K., et al.: Evidence-based guideline for the written radiology report: methods, recommendations and implementation challenges. J. Med. Imaging Radiat. Oncol. **57**(1), 1–7 (2013)

11. He, K., Zhang, X., Ren, S., Sun, J.: Deep residual learning for image recognition. In: Proceedings of the IEEE Conference on Computer Vision and Pattern Recognition, pp. 770–778 (2016)
12. Jing, B., Wang, Z., Xing, E.: Show, describe and conclude: on exploiting the structure information of chest X-ray reports. arXiv preprint arXiv:2004.12274 (2020)
13. Jing, B., Xie, P., Xing, E.: On the automatic generation of medical imaging reports. arXiv preprint arXiv:1711.08195 (2017)
14. Johnson, A.E., et al.: MIMIC-CXR-JPG, a large publicly available database of labeled chest radiographs. arXiv preprint arXiv:1901.07042 (2019)
15. Kingma, D.P., Ba, J.: Adam: a method for stochastic optimization. arXiv preprint arXiv:1412.6980 (2014)
16. Li, C.Y., Liang, X., Hu, Z., Xing, E.P.: Hybrid retrieval-generation reinforced agent for medical image report generation. arXiv preprint arXiv:1805.08298 (2018)
17. Li, C.Y., Liang, X., Hu, Z., Xing, E.P.: Knowledge-driven encode, retrieve, paraphrase for medical image report generation. In: Proceedings of the AAAI Conference on Artificial Intelligence, vol. 33, pp. 6666–6673 (2019)
18. Lin, C.Y.: ROUGE: a package for automatic evaluation of summaries. In: Text Summarization Branches Out, pp. 74–81 (2004)
19. Liu, F., Ge, S., Wu, X.: Competence-based multimodal curriculum learning for medical report generation. In: Proceedings of the 59th Annual Meeting of the Association for Computational Linguistics and the 11th International Joint Conference on Natural Language Processing (Volume 1: Long Papers), pp. 3001–3012 (2021)
20. Liu, F., Wu, X., Ge, S., Fan, W., Zou, Y.: Exploring and distilling posterior and prior knowledge for radiology report generation. In: Proceedings of the IEEE/CVF Conference on Computer Vision and Pattern Recognition, pp. 13753–13762 (2021)
21. Liu, F., Yin, C., Wu, X., Ge, S., Zhang, P., Sun, X.: Contrastive attention for automatic chest X-ray report generation. arXiv preprint arXiv:2106.06965 (2021)
22. Liu, G., et al.: Clinically accurate chest X-ray report generation. In: Machine Learning for Healthcare Conference, pp. 249–269. PMLR (2019)
23. Lovelace, J., Mortazavi, B.: Learning to generate clinically coherent chest X-ray reports. In: Proceedings of the 2020 Conference on Empirical Methods in Natural Language Processing: Findings, pp. 1235–1243 (2020)
24. Miller, G.A.: WordNet: a lexical database for English. Commun. ACM **38**(11), 39–41 (1995)
25. Miura, Y., Zhang, Y., Tsai, E.B., Langlotz, C.P., Jurafsky, D.: Improving factual completeness and consistency of image-to-text radiology report generation. arXiv preprint arXiv:2010.10042 (2020)
26. Papineni, K., Roukos, S., Ward, T., Zhu, W.J.: BLEU: a method for automatic evaluation of machine translation. In: Proceedings of the 40th Annual Meeting of the Association for Computational Linguistics, pp. 311–318 (2002)
27. Vaswani, A., et al.: Attention is all you need. In: Advances in Neural Information Processing Systems, pp. 5998–6008 (2017)
28. Vinyals, O., Toshev, A., Bengio, S., Erhan, D.: Show and tell: a neural image caption generator. In: Proceedings of the IEEE Conference on Computer Vision and Pattern Recognition, pp. 3156–3164 (2015)
29. Zhang, Y., Wang, X., Xu, Z., Yu, Q., Yuille, A., Xu, D.: When radiology report generation meets knowledge graph. In: Proceedings of the AAAI Conference on Artificial Intelligence, vol. 34, pp. 12910–12917 (2020)

Removal of Confounders via Invariant Risk Minimization for Medical Diagnosis

Samira Zare$^{(\boxtimes)}$ (iD) and Hien Van Nguyen

University of Houston, Houston, TX, USA
szare836@uh.edu

Abstract. While deep networks have demonstrated state-of-the-art performance in medical image analysis, they suffer from biases caused by undesirable confounding variables (e.g., sex, age, race). Traditional statistical methods for removing confounders are often incompatible with modern deep networks. To address this challenge, we introduce a novel learning framework, named ReConfirm, based on the invariant risk minimization (IRM) theory to eliminate the biases caused by confounding variables and make deep networks more robust. Our approach allows end-to-end model training while capturing causal features responsible for pathological findings instead of spurious correlations. We evaluate our approach on NIH chest X-ray classification tasks where sex and age are confounders.

Keywords: Confounder removal · Invariant learning · Chest X-ray

1 Introduction

Deep neural networks for medical data analysis suffer from undesirable biases created by confounding variables. These models can use the confounders as shortcuts to establish spurious connections between clinically meaningless variables and diagnosis outcomes [8,15,17,25]. For example, when we train a model on a chest radiograph dataset where male patients are more likely to have a disease, the classifier can use breast regions to predict the absence of the disease. This behavior leads to a higher error rate for female patients [12]. Figure 1 provides empirical evidence to illustrate this problem. Specifically, while breast features are not clinically meaningful for performing chest radiograph diagnosis, deep networks rely heavily on these features as indicated by the visualization (see Sect. 3 for more experimental details). Other factors such as age [8,25], text markers on images [5,8], testing condition [6], institutions where data were collected, or even the pubertal development scale of subjects [25] may all function as confounders and impact the model performance. Relying on these confounders will significantly reduce the model's generalizability and reliability [12,20] because the model does not capture true pathologies underlying the diagnostic outcomes.

Supplementary Information The online version contains supplementary material available at https://doi.org/10.1007/978-3-031-16452-1_55.

Frequent deep learning methods simply assume that if confounders such as gender are not directly included to the training dataset, we can remove their effects. A key issue, however, is that strongly correlated features may act as proxies for confounders (e.g., inferring gender from chest x-ray images based on anatomical differences) [16]. Traditional statistical methods to mitigate the effects of confounders contain pre-processing, matching or stratification of input variables or post-processing of the outputs [1, 14]. However, because of the demand for end-to-end training schemes and large training datasets, these approaches have fallen out of favor with the machine learning community. How to eliminate confounding variables in deep networks remains an important research question. Recent methods use adversarial domain-invariant representation learning to remove the confounder [25]. However, when the class-conditional distributions of input features change between source and target domains, this approach cannot guarantee successful generalization [24].

Fig. 1. Activation heat-map visualization for a DenseNet121 trained on a Chest-Xray dataset confounded by sex. As marked in images, the model considers the breasts as abnormalities. This confounding effect culminated in higher false positive rate for females.

Invariant Risk Minimization (IRM) [4] is a robust framework for learning invariant features in multi-source domain adaptation. IRM relies on the idea that invariance is a proxy for causality; the causal components of the data remain constant (*invariant*) across environments. Although powerful, IRM requires a discrete set of *environments*, each corresponding to specific data distribution, during the training stage. As a result, one cannot directly apply this method to the confounder removal problem where pre-defined environments are unavailable.

To this end, we propose a novel strategy to optimally split the training dataset into different environments based on the available confounders (e.g., age, sex, test condition). We note that our method does not need the confounders during testing the model. Our experiments show that the generated environments facilitate IRM to learn features highly invariant to confounding variables. In addition, the original IRM formulation enforces the same conditional distribution among all classes, which potentially leads to learning unstable features as discussed in [3]. We propose the first conditional IRM method for medical images to relax this assumption and enable the model to learn more robust features specific to each diagnosis. The main contributions of this paper are as follows:

– We develop a novel confounder removal framework based on the invariant risk minimization theory. We extend this framework to accommodate class-

conditional variants, where the invariance learning penalty is conditioned on each class.
- We design a strategy for optimally splitting the dataset into different environments based on the maximum violation of the invariant learning principle.
- We compare the classification performance and visualization of our method to baseline CNN models trained under the traditional empirical risk minimization framework.

Related Works. Many recent studies in the medical domain raise the concern that deep learning models may have biases in their predictions. Larrazabal et al. [12] and Seyyed Kalantari et al. [20] provided experimental evidence that gender, race, age, and socioeconomic status of the patients confound the model predictions. They suggested the models should be trained on a multi-source balanced dataset to minimize the bias. While promising, creating large and diverse medical datasets is time-consuming and expensive. Examples of other techniques for removing the confounding factors are reweighting [21] and stratifying the batch sampling [17]. We note that these methods do not learn the invariant or causal medical pathologies underlying the disease. It can lead to a performance drop in the test environments where the spurious associations are different. Zhao et al. [25] used adversarial domain-invariant representation learning to remove the confounder via a min-max training approach. As mentioned, one major limitation of the adversarial learning method is that we cannot guarantee their successful generalization [24]. It is also possible for the predictor to move in a direction that helps the adversary decrease its loss [23]. Invariant Risk Minimization (IRM) [4] was proposed to overcome the limitations of adversarial domain-invariant representation learning. In this work, we are interested in evaluating the ability of IRM to remove the confounding effects in medical data analysis. Adragna et al. [2] previously utilized IRM to achieve fairness in comment toxicity classification. Our work is different in two ways: i) we introduce a strategy to define training environments when we have a collection of data, ii) we propose the class-conditional invariance learning penalty; our goal is to remove the association between the confounder and model prediction in a more proper way, as we will describe. We also note Rosenfeld et al. [18] argue that IRM does not improve over standard Empirical Risk Minimization in the non-linear setting. However, their theorem only indicates the existence of a non-invariant model that approximately satisfies the IRM criterion. This is similar to showing the existence of neural network parameters that fit the training set but do not generalize to the test set. This is not sufficient to question the efficiency of the method [11].

2   Removal of Confounders via Invariant Risk Minimization (ReConfirm)

In this section, we describe our approach for REmoval of CONFounders via IRM (ReConfirm). We first introduce the IRM approach from the perspective of confounder removal. Then, we will describe our strategy to split a dataset into training environments and our extensions to IRM. Suppose we have a set of training environments $e \in \mathcal{E}_{tr}$ and in each environment, datasets $D_e := \{(x_i^e, y_i^e)\}_{i=1}^{N_e}$

are generated from the same input and label spaces $\mathcal{X} \times \mathcal{Y}$ according to some distribution $P(X^e, Y^e)$. The environments differ in how the labels are spuriously correlated with the confounder variable c. For instance, in environment e_0, older people have a higher probability of being diseased, while in environment e_1, this association is reversed. We aim to find a predictor function $f : \mathcal{X} \to \mathcal{Y}$ that generalizes well for all confounded environments. Empirical Risk Minimization (ERM), which is the standard method for solving learning problems, minimizes the average loss over all training samples from all environments. On the other hand, IRM looks for features that remain invariant across training environments and ignores the confounding associations specific to each environment. It assumes that f is a compositional model $f := \omega \circ \Phi$, where $\Phi : \mathcal{X} \to \mathcal{Z}$ is the invariant data representation and $\omega : \mathcal{Z} \to \mathcal{Y}$ is the classifier on top of Φ. Using this notation, IRM minimizes the total risk of all training environments through a constrained optimization problem:

$$\min_{\Phi, \omega} \sum_{e \in \mathcal{E}_{tr}} R^e(\omega \circ \Phi)$$
$$\text{subject to} \quad \omega \in \operatorname*{argmin}_{\bar{\omega}} R^e(\bar{\omega} \circ \Phi), \text{ for all } e \in \mathcal{E}_{tr} \tag{1}$$

where $R^e := \mathbb{E}_{(X^e, Y^e) \sim D^e}[\mathcal{L}(f(X^e), Y^e)]$ is the risk for environment e and $\mathcal{L}$ is the loss function (e.g. cross entropy). To solve this bi-level optimization problem, the authors in [4] simplified Eq. 1 to:

$$\min_{\Phi} \sum_{e \in \mathcal{E}_{tr}} R^e(\omega \circ \Phi) + \lambda \|\nabla_{\omega|\omega=1.0} R^e(\omega \circ \Phi)\|^2 \tag{2}$$

where λ is a regularization hyperparameter and ω is a fixed dummy variable [4]. This formulation enables end-to-end network training. While IRM is a compelling approach for domain-generalization problems, we cannot immediately apply it to a medical dataset to remove the confounder variables. IRM requires a set of environments to find features that remain invariant across them. Thus, to take advantage of IRM in discovering the underlying medical pathologies in a confounded dataset, we have to create training environments. Environments should share the same underlying biomarkers that we expect our model to learn. However, they should differ in how the confounders generate spurious correlations. In what follows, we introduce our strategy to split the dataset to ensure learning invariant features while ignoring the confounding effects.

Creating Training Environments for ReConfirm. To use IRM to remove the spurious effects of confounders, we have to partition our dataset into different environments. Following [4,11], we use only two training environments: e_0 and e_1. The class label and the confounder have strong but spurious correlations in each environment. To construct the environment, we use the *invariant learning principle*. Specifically, ω is simultaneously optimal for all environments due to the constraint in Eq. 1. In addition, for regular loss functions like the cross-entropy and mean squared error, optimal classifiers can be expressed as conditional expectations of the output variable. Therefore, an invariant data representation function Φ must satisfy the below invariant learning principle:

$$\mathbb{E}[Y|\Phi(x) = h, e_0] = \mathbb{E}[Y|\Phi(x) = h, e_1] \tag{3}$$

where h is in the intersection of the supports of $\Phi(X^e)$. This condition means that IRM learns a set of features such that the conditional distribution of the outcomes given the predictors is invariant across all training environments. Given a collection of data, we seek partitions that maximally violate the invariance principle. This would be equivalent to the worst-case scenario on which we would like to train our model. We note that Creager et al. [7] show that maximizing the invariance principle violation corresponds to maximizing the regularization term in Eq. 2. Motivated by this observation, we maximize the following gap between our environments to find optimal environment splitting:

$$e_0, e_1 = \underset{e_0, e_1}{\operatorname{argmax}} \; g = \underset{e_0, e_1}{\operatorname{argmax}} \; \left| \mathbb{E}[Y|\Phi(x) = h, e_0] - \mathbb{E}[Y|\Phi(x) = h, e_1] \right| \tag{4}$$

Suppose our input X-ray (MRI, CT scan, etc.) images contain both authentic medical biomarkers and spurious confounding features. The worst-case classifier only relies on the confounder variable c to make predictions, i.e. $\Phi(x) = c$. Then the gap would be $g = \left| \mathbb{E}[Y|c, e_0] - \mathbb{E}[Y|c, e_1] \right|$. Therefore, we are looking for an environment partitioning strategy that maximizes g. One possible solution would be to define the environments based on the agreement between the confounder and the label [7]. This means, for example, in environment e_0, all diseased patients ($y = 1$) are old ($c = 1$) and healthy controls ($y = 0$) are young ($c = 0$), while in environment e_1, all diseased patients ($y = 1$) are young ($c = 0$), and healthy controls ($y = 0$) are old ($c = 1$). In this case, we have the maximum confounding association in each environment, and the gap is $g = 1$, which is its maximum value. The proof can be found in the supplementary materials.

Class-Conditional ReConfirm. While the IRM framework promotes invariant learning, it applies one penalty term to all classes (see Eq. 2). This formulation potentially leads to features that are less stable for each class [3]. To address this issue, we propose to use class-conditional penalties. Our formulation can correct confounding effects specific to each class while potentially promoting more diverse features. For instance, age (as a confounder) can impact healthy and diseased patients differently. Rather than learning a global effect as in IRM, our class-conditional method separately models each class's confounding influences. This way, we encourage our model to learn invariant medical pathologies only related to the diseased class (or healthy class as well), thus diversifying the learned features. The mathematical formulation of class-conditional ReConfirm is given as follows:

$$\min_{\Phi} \sum_{e \in \mathcal{E}_{tr}} R^e(\omega \circ \Phi) + \sum_{j=0}^{M-1} \sum_{e \in \mathcal{E}_{tr}} \lambda \|\nabla_{\omega|\omega=1.0} R^{e,j}(\omega \circ \Phi)\|^2 \tag{5}$$

where M is the number of classes and $R^{e,j}(\omega \circ \Phi)$ denotes the risk corresponding to samples from j-th class. A more systematic way to deal with the confounders is to remove their direct influence on the predictions. For example, we can remove the common effects of age or gender on chest X-ray images or brain MRIs while preserving their actual effects on the development of a disease [25]. We can condition our ReConfirm regularization only on the control class to achieve this behavior.

3   Results and Discussion

Dataset. We particularly evaluate the efficacy of our model on binary classification (normal versus abnormal) of frontal chest radiographs using the NIH Chest-Xray14 (NIH-CXR) dataset [22]. The abnormalities include 14 abnormal findings defined in [22]. This dataset contains age (0-95) and sex (Male and Female) as meta variables. It is shown that the deep learning models have poor performance on female patients and younger patients [12,20]. Given that some anatomical attributes (probably considering the breasts as abnormalities) and age-related alterations [9,13] are reflected in X-ray images, sex and age could be considered as confounders. In order to highlight the ability of our model to mitigate the effect of confounders on predictions, we created a subset of the NIH-CXR dataset where age and gender are confounders for the label. Figures 2 and 3 show the age and gender distributions within each class.

Implementation Details. We used a densely connected CNN (DenseNet) architecture [10], which has been shown to accomplish state-of-the-art results in X-ray image classification. We used the ImageNet setting to normalize all of the images, and standard online transformations to augment images while training. We also had the Adam optimizer with standard settings, a batch size of 96, a learning rate of 1×10^{-4}, and image size of 224×224. We use the same training settings across all models to ensure fair comparisons. The penalty coefficient λ and the number of training epochs to linearly ramp it up to its full value are among the hyperparameters for the ReConfirm method. Similar to [4,11], we found ramping in λ over several epochs and scaling down the ERM term by the penalty coefficient when it is more than 1 are useful for stable training. All codes will be available at https://github.com/samzare/ConfounderRemoval for research purposes.

Sex as Confounder. In our dataset, male patients are more probable to be in the diseased class, as shown in Fig. 2a. In order to remove the confounding association, we utilize ReConfirm and conditional variants. First, we construct our training environment based on the setting described in Fig. 2b. In environment e_0 all females are in the control group, while in e_1 this correlation is reversed. We have the ERM model as the baseline where the confounder effects are not removed. We expect that ERM predictions rely more on spurious correlations and consequently have lower performance compared to the variants of ReConfirm methods. We implement ReConfirm, class-conditioned ReConfirm conditioned on all classes (cReConfirm (all)), and only on the control class (cReConfirm $(y=0)$). Conditioning on all classes would encourage the model to specifically learn features that are invariant (among males and females) in each class. Also,

Table 1. Prediction performance of models trained on sex-confounded dataset.

	Whole Cohort			Male			Female		
	Accuracy	Precision	Recall	Accuracy	Precision	Recall	Accuracy	Precision	Recall
ERM	84.23	0.9010	0.7690	83.66	0.9051	0.7521	84.79	0.8971	0.7859
ReConfirm	86.69	**0.9278**	0.7958	85.92	**0.9352**	0.7718	87.46	0.9209	0.8197
cReConfirm (all)	86.41	0.9045	**0.8141**	85.63	0.9042	**0.7972**	87.18	0.9049	**0.8310**
cReConfirm (y = 0)	**87.18**	0.9244	0.8099	**85.92**	0.9153	0.7915	**88.45**	**0.9333**	0.8282

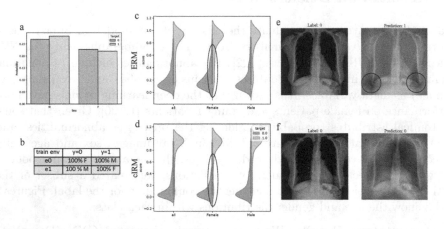

Fig. 2. Difference in sex distribution between normal and abnormal classes resulted in the baseline ERM learning the confounding effects, while cReConfirm removed this effect: **a.** sex distribution for each class, **b.** the ReConfirm environment setting, **c, d.** distribution of prediction scores. **e, f.** qualitative visualization of the learned features.

conditioning only on the control group helps the model learn the "normal" effects of sex that can be observed in the X-ray images (like the breasts). Table 1 lists the perfromance of all models for the balanced whole cohort, female and male patients separately. In the whole cohort setting, we have both male and female patients from both classes. We then restricted the test dataset to one sex to have a closer look at the model performance in each subgroup. We also have the results from worst-case scenarios where sex and class labels are strongly correlated in the supplementary materials. Overall, ReConfirm variants could achieve better performance compared to the ERM method. We could achieve an accuracy of 87.18% on the whole cohort with cIRM conditioned on the control group. To investigate more, we also have the score distributions (Fig. 2c, d) and GRAD-CAM [19] visualizations (Fig. 2e, f) for ERM and cReConfirm conditioned on the control group. Note that the score distributions show that the cReConfirm model is more confident in its predictions for all experiments (we used markers to illustrate the difference in Fig. 2). Activations also illustrate how the baseline ERM model is confounded by the sex-related anatomical features in the X-ray. As discussed by Larrazabal et al. [12], female patients are more likely

Table 2. Prediction performance of models trained on age-confounded dataset.

	Whole Cohort			Young			Old		
	Accuracy	Precision	Recall	Accuracy	Precision	Recall	Accuracy	Precision	Recall
ERM	82.77	0.884	0.7561	85.67	0.8481	0.7585	80.75	0.9012	0.7551
ReConfirm	86.05	0.8854	**0.8296**	**88.25**	0.8617	**0.8226**	84.52	0.8964	**0.8328**
cReConfirm (all)	85.46	0.9212	0.7771	86.53	**0.9091**	0.7170	84.72	0.9261	0.8041
cReConfirm (y=0)	**86.22**	**0.9237**	0.7911	87.97	0.8986	0.7698	**85.02**	**0.9349**	0.8007

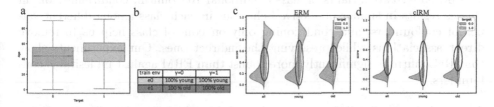

Fig. 3. Difference in age distribution between normal and abnormal classes confounded the baseline ERM while cReConfirm removed this effect: **a.** age distribution for normal and abnormal classes, **b.** the ReConfirm environment setting, **c, d.** distribution of prediction scores for ERM and cReConfirm conditioned on control class.

to have false positive predictions. Our visualizations can explain this confounding effect; the ERM model considered the breasts as abnormalities (see Fig. 3e), while using ReConfirm, we can learn more meaningful features (Fig. 3f). While ERM misclassified this case, cReConfirm could find more proper biomarkers and correctly classified the image. More results and visualizations can be found in the supplementary materials.

Age as Confounder. The average age of the diseased class is higher than the healthy controls (48.73 ± 16.77 vs. 42.61 ± 15.65), as shown in Fig. 3a. We construct our training environments based on the same strategy and the setting we used is described in Fig. 3b. In order to define the young and old groups, we set a threshold of 40 years old on the age; Seyyed Kalantari et al. [20] have shown that age groups under 40 experienced the highest performance disparities.

Table 2 lists the performance of all models for the balanced whole cohort, younger and older patients separately. The results from worst-case scenarios where age and class labels are strongly correlated are in the supplementary materials. We have ReConfirm, cReConfirm conditioned on all classes, and cReConfirm conditioned on the control group. Conditioning on all classes would preserve the diversity of learned features, while conditioning only on the control group would encourage the model to learn the normal aging effects on the lungs that can be captured in the X-ray images and confound the model. Overall, ReConfirm variants could achieve better performance compared to the ERM method. We have an accuracy of 86.22% on the whole cohort with cReConfirm conditioned on the control group. The score distributions (Fig. 3c, d) for ERM and cReConfirm conditioned on the control show that our cReConfirm model is more confident in its predictions for all experiments. More results and visualizations can be found in the supplementary materials.

4   Conclusion

In this work, we applied IRM to a binary chest X-ray classification task in order to evaluate its ability in removing the effect of confounder variables. We also proposed two variants of class-conditional ReConfirm; conditioning on all classes results in similar predictive behaviour in each class among different values of confounders, and conditioning only on control class help us to remove direct associations while preserving the indirect ones. Our experiments show that ReConfirm is significantly more robust than ERM against undesirable confounders.

Acknowledgements. This research was funded by the National Science Foundation (1910973).

References

1. Adeli, E., et al.: Chained regularization for identifying brain patterns specific to HIV infection. Neuroimage **183**, 425–437 (2018)
2. Adragna, R., Creager, E., Madras, D., Zemel, R.: Fairness and robustness in invariant learning: a case study in toxicity classification. arXiv preprint arXiv:2011.06485 (2020)
3. Ahmed, F., Bengio, Y., van Seijen, H., Courville, A.: Systematic generalisation with group invariant predictions. In: International Conference on Learning Representations (2020)
4. Arjovsky, M., Bottou, L., Gulrajani, I., Lopez-Paz, D.: Invariant risk minimization. arXiv preprint arXiv:1907.02893 (2019)
5. Badgeley, M.A., et al.: Deep learning predicts hip fracture using confounding patient and healthcare variables. NPJ Digit. Med. **2**(1), 1–10 (2019)
6. Bustos, A., et al.: xdeep-msi: explainable bias-rejecting microsatellite instability deep learning system in colorectal cancer. Biomolecules **11**(12), 1786 (2021)
7. Creager, E., Jacobsen, J.H., Zemel, R.: Environment inference for invariant learning. In: International Conference on Machine Learning, pp. 2189–2200. PMLR (2021)
8. DeGrave, A.J., Janizek, J.D., Lee, S.I.: Ai for radiographic covid-19 detection selects shortcuts over signal. Nat. Mach. Intell. **3**(7), 610–619 (2021)
9. Gossner, J., Nau, R.: Geriatric chest imaging: when and how to image the elderly lung, age-related changes, and common pathologies. Radiol. Res. Pract. 2013 (2013)
10. Huang, G., Liu, Z., Van Der Maaten, L., Weinberger, K.Q.: Densely connected convolutional networks. In: Proceedings of the IEEE Conference on Computer Vision and Pattern Recognition, pp. 4700–4708 (2017)
11. Krueger, D., et al.: Out-of-distribution generalization via risk extrapolation (rex). In: International Conference on Machine Learning, pp. 5815–5826. PMLR (2021)
12. Larrazabal, A.J., Nieto, N., Peterson, V., Milone, D.H., Ferrante, E.: Gender imbalance in medical imaging datasets produces biased classifiers for computer-aided diagnosis. Proc. Natl. Acad. Sci. **117**(23), 12592–12594 (2020)

13. Mihara, F., Fukuya, T., Nakata, H., Mizuno, S., Russell, W., Hosoda, Y.: Normal age-related alterations on chest radiography: a longitudinal investigation. Acta Radiol. **34**(1), 53–58 (1993)
14. Mohamad Amin, P., Ahmad Reza, B., Mohsen, V.: How to control confounding effects by statistical analysis (2012)
15. Pearl, J.: Causality. Cambridge University Press (2009)
16. Pedreshi, D., Ruggieri, S., Turini, F.: Discrimination-aware data mining. In: Proceedings of the 14th ACM SIGKDD International Conference on Knowledge Discovery and Data Mining, pp. 560–568 (2008)
17. Puyol-Antón, E., et al.: Fairness in cardiac MR image analysis: an investigation of bias due to data imbalance in deep learning based segmentation. In: International Conference on Medical Image Computing and Computer-Assisted Intervention, pp. 413–423. Springer (2021)
18. Rosenfeld, E., Ravikumar, P., Risteski, A.: The risks of invariant risk minimization. arXiv preprint arXiv:2010.05761 (2020)
19. Selvaraju, R.R., Cogswell, M., Das, A., Vedantam, R., Parikh, D., Batra, D.: Gradcam: Visual explanations from deep networks via gradient-based localization. In: Proceedings of the IEEE International Conference on Computer Vision, pp. 618–626 (2017)
20. Seyyed-Kalantari, L., Liu, G., McDermott, M., Chen, I.Y., Ghassemi, M.: Chexclusion: fairness gaps in deep chest x-ray classifiers. In: BIOCOMPUTING 2021: Proceedings of the Pacific Symposium, pp. 232–243. World Scientific (2020)
21. Wang, H., Wu, Z., Xing, E.P.: Removing confounding factors associated weights in deep neural networks improves the prediction accuracy for healthcare applications. In: BIOCOMPUTING 2019: Proceedings of the Pacific Symposium, pp. 54–65. World Scientific (2018)
22. Wang, X., Peng, Y., Lu, L., Lu, Z., Bagheri, M., Summers, R.M.: Chestx-ray8: hospital-scale chest x-ray database and benchmarks on weakly-supervised classification and localization of common thorax diseases. In: Proceedings of the IEEE Conference on Computer Vision and Pattern Recognition, pp. 2097–2106 (2017)
23. Zhang, B.H., Lemoine, B., Mitchell, M.: Mitigating unwanted biases with adversarial learning. In: Proceedings of the 2018 AAAI/ACM Conference on AI, Ethics, and Society, pp. 335–340 (2018)
24. Zhao, H., Des Combes, R.T., Zhang, K., Gordon, G.: On learning invariant representations for domain adaptation. In: International Conference on Machine Learning, pp. 7523–7532. PMLR (2019)
25. Zhao, Q., Adeli, E., Pohl, K.M.: Training confounder-free deep learning models for medical applications. Nat. Commun. **11**(1), 1–9 (2020)

A Self-guided Framework for Radiology Report Generation

Jun Li[1,2], Shibo Li[1(✉)], Ying Hu[1(✉)], and Huiren Tao[3]

[1] Chinese Academy of Sciences, Shenzhen Institute of Advanced Technology, Shenzhen, China
{jun.li,sb.li,ying.hu}@siat.ac.cn
[2] University of Chinese Academy of Sciences, Beijing, China
[3] Shenzhen University General Hospital, Shenzhen, China

Abstract. Automatic radiology report generation is essential to computer-aided diagnosis. Through the success of image captioning, medical report generation has been achievable. However, the lack of annotated disease labels is still the bottleneck of this area. In addition, the image-text data bias problem and complex sentences make it more difficult to generate accurate reports. To address these gaps, we present a self-guided framework (SGF), a suite of unsupervised and supervised deep learning methods to mimic the process of human learning and writing. In detail, our framework obtains the domain knowledge from medical reports without extra disease labels and guides itself to extract fined-grain visual features associated with the text. Moreover, SGF successfully improves the accuracy and length of medical report generation by incorporating a similarity comparison mechanism that imitates the process of human self-improvement through comparative practice. Extensive experiments demonstrate the utility of our SGF in the majority of cases, showing its superior performance over state-of-the-art methods. Our results highlight the capacity of the proposed framework to distinguish fined-grained visual details between words and verify its advantage in generating medical reports.

Keywords: Report generation · Data bias · Unsupervised learning · Clustering

1 Introduction

Medical images are essential to diagnose and find potential diseases. The radiologists' daily task includes analyzing extensive medical images, which supports the doctor in locating the lesions more precisely. Due to the increasing demand for medical images, radiologists are dealing with an unduly high workload. Nevertheless, writing reports is a time-consuming and knowledge-intensive mission. As a result, it's critical to develop an automatic and accurate report generation system to reduce their burden.

Recently, the success of image captioning has become a stepping stone in the development of medical report generation [1–4]. However, radiology images are similar, and the medical reports are diverse, leading to a data bias problem. Additionally, the long sentences with fewer keywords increase the difficulties of predicting reports. To address these problems, some methods [5, 6] used medical terminologies and report subject

© The Author(s), under exclusive license to Springer Nature Switzerland AG 2022
L. Wang et al. (Eds.): MICCAI 2022, LNCS 13438, pp. 588–598, 2022.
https://doi.org/10.1007/978-3-031-16452-1_56

headings as image labels to distinguish visual features. Yet, radiologists need to relabel the data, failing to lighten their workload.

To fill these gaps, we develop the first, to our knowledge, jointing unsupervised and supervised learning methods to mimic human learning and writing. Our framework includes Knowledge Distiller (KD), Knowledge Matched Visual Extractor (KMVE), and Report Generator (RG). KD simulates human behavior of acquiring knowledge from texts and uses an unsupervised method to obtain potential knowledge from reports. With the knowledge from KD, KMVE learns to extract text-related visual features. This module imitates the process of matching images and texts according to cognition. In the end, RG generates reports according to the image features. This process is similar to human self-improvement through comparative practice. Overall, the main contributions of our method are as follows.

- We present a self-guided framework, a platform of both unsupervised and supervised deep learning that is used to obtain the potential medical knowledge from text reports without extra disease labels, which can assist itself in learning fine-grained visual details associated with the text to alleviate the data bias problem.
- Inspired by human comparative practice, our SGF produces long and accurate reports through a similarity comparison mechanism. This strategy assists the framework in combining global semantics to generate long and complex sentences.
- Several experiments have been conducted to evaluate our framework. The comparison results outperform the state-of-the-art methods, showing the effectiveness of our framework. Furthermore, the results indicate that our approach can learn the visual features of each word and pay more attention to the keywords.

2   Related Works

Image Captioning. Most of the recent works are based on this classic structure [1], adding attention mechanisms to enhance local visual features [2], or creating a plurality of decoding passes to refine the generated sentences [4]. For example, an adaptive attention method [3] has been proposed to automatically switch the focus between visual signals and language. Lu et al. [4] used sentence templates to assist image captioning tasks. Recently, some works [7–9] have been proposed for more specific tasks. An anchor-caption mechanism [9] has been used to generate accurate text, such as numbers and time. Wang et al. [8] have developed a new approach to emulate the human ability in controlling caption generation. But all these methods [7–9] require image labels and bounding boxes of objects. It's difficult to transfer these methods in medical report generation because most medical reports do not have disease labels.

Medical Report Generation. Researchers have made a lot of attempts and efforts to fill these gaps. By using prior knowledge of chest discovery, Zhang et al. [10] established a graph model, and it could be injected into the network to enhance the text decoder. In [11], the graph model and disease keywords were changed to prior and posterior knowledge to assist report generation. Although these efforts have achieved good results, radiologists still need to label the data. When the dataset or disease changes, the data need to be labeled again. Undoubtedly, these methods [10, 11] have not fundamentally solved the data-labeling problem and failed to reduce the burden of radiologists. On the other hand, some strategies [12, 13] were used to enhance the encoder-decoder structure. Li et al. [12] applied reinforcement learning to strengthen network training. Wang et al. [13] designed a framework with two branches to enhance the fine-grained visual details, whose backbone is CNN-RNN [14]. However, the data-driven RNN structures designed in these works are easily misled by rare and diverse exceptions, and cannot effectively generate abnormal sentences. Recently, the transformer network [15] has laid a solid foundation in neural language processing and computer vision. In [16], a memory-driven unit was designed for the transformer to store the similarity of radiology images. This method only pays attention to the similarity of images while neglecting the diversity of text. In [17], a novel aligned transformer was proposed to alleviate the data bias problem. Yet, this method requires extra disease labels that are not suitable for other diseases.

3   Methods

Automatic report generation is a modality-changing process that aims to generate descriptive reports $R = \{y_1, y_2, \ldots, y_{N_r}\}$ from a set of images $I = \{i_1, i_2, \ldots, i_{N_i}\}$, where N_i and N_r are the total numbers of reports and images. As shown in Fig. 1, the self-guided framework consists of three parts: Knowledge Distiller (KD), Knowledge Matched Visual Extractor (KMVE), and Report Generator (RG).

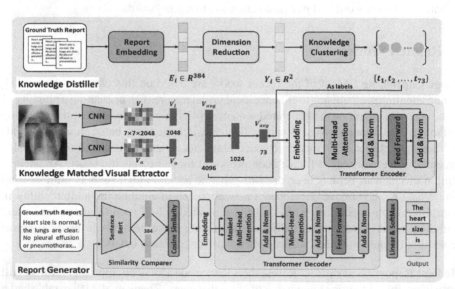

Fig. 1. Our proposed self-guided framework includes Knowledge Distiller (KD), Knowledge Matched Visual Extractor (KMVE), and Report Generator (RG).

3.1 Knowledge Distiller (KD)

KD is responsible for extracting the potential knowledge from the reports without any extra disease labels. The orange part of Fig. 1 provides an overview of the KD module that contains Report Embedding (RE), Dimension Reduction (DR), and Knowledge Clustering (KC). In RE, the Sentence-Bert (SB) [18] is considered as the embedding method to convert each report to numerical data $E_i \in R^{384}$. The reason for choosing SB as the embedding method in both KD and RG modules is that SB uses Siamese Networks. This structure can derive semantically meaningful sentence embedding vectors which are suitable for clustering and similarity comparison. In addition, SB is a multi-layer bidirectional transformer that has been well pre-trained on two large and widely covered corpora [19, 20], establishing new and most advanced performance in various natural language processing tasks. In DR, the Uniform Manifold Approximation and Projection (UMAP) algorithm [21] is applied for reducing the embedding vector E_i, which can be formulated as $Y_i = f_{UMAP}(E_i)$, $Y_i \in R^2$. The number of neighbors and the minimum distance between samples are set to 15 and 0 according to experience, which is robust enough in our training set. Dimension reduction is a common paradigm that can effectively handle the problem of high-dimensional embedding being difficult to cluster and requiring lots of computation in text clustering. Next, the Hierarchical Density-Based Spatial Clustering of Applications with Noise (HDBSCAN) algorithm [22] is used in KC to cluster the set of Y_i. HDBSCAN is very suitable for UMAP because UMAP retains many local structures in low-dimensional space, and HDBSCAN will not force clustering these data points. Furthermore, HDBSCAN has fewer and more intuitive hyperparameters and does not require the number of clusters to be specified. In the HDBSCAN algorithm, the minimum cluster size is set to 15, and the metric is set to Euclidean. Finally, the clustering results are marked as $T = \{t_1, t_2, ..., t_k\}, k = 73$. To identify whether the clustering result is reliable, we calculate the cosine similarity between each cluster. In Fig. 3 (c), the similarity matrix proves that each topic only shows a high degree of similarity to itself. For each t_i, it contains disease information and specific writing styles. The clustering results T can be regarded as the potential knowledge topics from the report.

3.2 Knowledge Matched Visual Extractor (KMVE)

KMVE is utilized to alleviate the mismatch feature diversity between the image and text. KMVE takes image pairs $I = \{i_m^1, i_m^2\}$, $i_m \in R^{N_i}$ as input, where the size of each image is $(3, 244, 244)$. The knowledge topics T from the KD module are adopted as the potential labels of the images. After this operation, the image-text matching process is converted to a classification task. With the knowledge topics as disease labels, the share weights Convolutional Neural Network (CNN) encoders can extract fine-grained visual features associated with text to alleviate the data bias problem. The pre-trained ResNet-101 [23] on ImageNet [24] is used as the backbone of CNN. In the beginning, the CNN extracts anteroposterior and lateral visual features $V_a, V_l \in R^{7 \times 7 \times 2048}$ from the share weights encoder, as shown in Fig. 1. Subsequently, a convolution layer with kernel size 7×7 and an average pooling layer are added to get the $V_a^{'} \in R^{2048}$ and $V_l^{'} \in R^{2048}$. These two vectors are concatenated together to get the global average features $V_{avg} \in R^{4096}$. To match the size of the knowledge topics T, the global average features V_{avg} are reduced to $V'_{avg} \in R^{73}$ by two average pooling layers. In sum, the KMVE loss can be formulated as:

$$\mathcal{L}_{KMVE} = -\sum_{i=1}^{k} \left(t_i \times \log\left(S_f(V'_{avg}) \right) \right) \tag{1}$$

where t_i is the potential label from T, $S_f(\cdot)$ is the SoftMax activation function. The global average features V_{avg} retain more information than V'_{avg}, and can obtain more fine-grained visual features from images. Therefore, the visual features V_{avg} are chosen as the input of the Report Generator.

3.3 Report Generator (RG)

RG is based on Transformer (TF) and Similarity Comparer (SC). TF is consisted with Transformer Encoder (TE) and Transformer Decoder (TD) [15]. In TE, the V_{avg} are converted into query, key, and value at first. Then the Multi-Head Attention (MHA) concatenates all head results together to acquire the visual details in different subspaces. After the MHA, the Residual Connections (RC) [23] and Layer Normalization (LN) [25] are used to fuse features. Besides, the Feed-Forward Network (FFN) is adopted at the end of each block. In TD, the outputs of the TE are converted to key and value. Meanwhile, the embedding matrix of the current input word token is utilized as the query. Like TE, the inputs are changed to vector h_m by the MHA. Next, the h_m is passed to FFN and LN, and it can be described as $h' = L_N(h_m + \Phi_{FFN}(h_m))$. Finally, the predicted word is formulated as: $y_t \sim p_t = S_f\left(h' W_p + b_p \right)$, where the W_p, b_p are the learnable parameters. In summary, the TF loss is as follows.

$$\mathcal{L}_{TF} = -\sum_{i=1}^{N_r} (y_i \cdot \log(p_i) + (1-y_i) \cdot \log(1 - p_i)) \tag{2}$$

Due to the long and complex sentences in the report, it is difficult to generate multiple semantic sentences only by the TF module. This is because it only pays attention to the local semantics of the previous words and ignores the overall semantics. Therefore, the SC module is developed to compare the differences between predicted report p and ground truth report y, which is helpful for the TF module to learn global semantic information. The SC module is mainly composed of the Sentence Bert, and its settings are the same as the KD module. After embedding, ground truth and predicted report are converted into vectors $y_e \in R^{384}$ and $p_e \in R^{384}$, respectively. Then, the cosine similarities between y_e and p_e are calculated. Besides, the RELU activation is added after the cosine similarity to ensure that the result is above zero. Thus, the similarity score S is simplified as $S = f_{relu}(f_{cs}(y_e, p_e))$, where f_{relu} and f_{cs} are the RELU activation and cosine similarity. In sum, the loss of the SC module is defined as follows.

$$\mathcal{L}_{SC} = -\sum_{i=1}^{N_r} \log(S_i) \tag{3}$$

4 Experiment

Dataset and Evaluation Metrics. Our experiments are conducted on the IU-Xray [26] public dataset. IU-Xray is a large-scale dataset of chest X-rays, constructed by 7,470 chest X-ray images and 3,955 radiology reports. The anteroposterior and lateral images associated with one report are used as data pairs. The dataset is split into train-validation-test sets by 7:1:2, and it is the same partition ratio in other methods.

To evaluate the quality of the generated report, the widely used BLEU scores [27], ROUGE-L [28], and METEOR [29] are implemented as the evaluation metrics. All metrics are computed by the standard image captioning evaluation tool [30].

Implementation Details. The experiments are conducted on PyTorch with NVIDIA RTX3090 gpu. for mha in the RG module, the dimension and the number of heads are respectively set to 512 and 8. Our maximum epoch is 50, and the training would stop when the validation loss does not decrease in 10 epochs. The training loss of the entire self-guided framework can be summarized as follows.

$$\mathcal{L}_{SG} = \mathcal{L}_{KMVE} + \mathcal{L}_{TF} + \mathcal{L}_{SC} \tag{4}$$

we apply the ADAM [31] for optimization and the training rate is set to $5e^{-4}$ and $1e^{-4}$ for the KMVE and RG, respectively. During the training process, the learning rate decays by a factor of 0.8 per epoch, and the batch size is set to 16.

5 Results

Performance Comparison. In Table 1, our results were compared to other state-of-the-art methods. All metrics reach the top except BLEU-1. The BLEU-1 to BLEU-4 analyze how many continuous sequences of words appear in the predicted reports. In our results, BLEU-2 to BLEU-4 significantly improved. Especially, the BLEU-4 is 4.7% higher than PPKED. One reasonable explanation is that our method ignores some meaningless words and pays more attention to the long phrases used to describe diseases. At the same time, the ROUGE-L is used to investigate the fluency and sufficiency of the predicted report. Our ROUGE-L is 3.9% higher than the previous outstanding method. It means that our approach can generate accurate reports rather than some meaningless word combinations. Furthermore, the METEOR is utilized to evaluate the synonym transformation between predicted reports and the ground truth. The METEOR also shows our framework is effective.

Ablation Study. Table 2 Shows the quantitative results of our proposed methods. It is observed that all evaluation metrics have increased after adding the KMVE module and the SC module separately. The highest metric increased by 5.8% and the lowest metric increased by 1%. Our framework combines the above two tasks to achieve the best performance. It is noteworthy that, the BLEU-1 metric has slightly decreased compared to "BASCE + SC". The reason for this result may be that the SC module is developed for joining the global semantics to overcome the long sentences problem. However, the KMVE module is designed to focus on fine-grained visual features between words. Therefore, the KMVE module might force SGF to pay attention to keywords in sentences, thus reducing the generation of meaningless words.

Table 1. Performance comparison. Best performances are highlighted in bold.

Methods	Year	BLEU-1	BLEU-2	BLEU-3	BLEU-4	ROUGE-L	METEOR
Transformer [15]	2017	0.414	0.262	0.183	0.137	0.335	0.172
H-Agent [12]	2018	0.438	0.298	0.208	0.151	0.322	-
CMAS-RL [14]	2019	0.464	0.301	0.210	0.154	0.362	-
SentSAT + KG [10]	2020	0.441	0.291	0.203	0.147	0.367	-
R2Gen [16]	2020	0.470	0.304	0.219	0.165	0.371	0.187
PPKED [11]	2021	**0.483**	0.315	0.224	0.168	0.376	0.190
SGF	-	0.467	**0.334**	**0.261**	**0.215**	**0.415**	**0.201**

Table 2. Ablation studies. "Base" refers to the vanilla Transformer. "KMVE" and "SC" stand for adding $\mathcal{L}_{KMVE}$ and $\mathcal{L}_{SC}$ loss, respectively. "SGF" refers to using $\mathcal{L}_{SG}$ as the loss. Best performances are highlighted in bold.

Methods	BLEU-1	BLEU-2	BLEU-3	BLEU-4	ROUGE-L	METEOR
Base	0.414	0.262	0.183	0.137	0.335	0.172
Base + KMVE	0.462	0.306	0.221	0.165	0.353	0.182
Base + SC	**0.472**	0.315	0.226	0.166	0.363	0.187
SGF	0.467	**0.334**	**0.261**	**0.215**	**0.415**	**0.201**

Visualization and Examples. Figure 2 shows examples of the generated reports in the test set. The red underlines are the aligned words between ground truth and generated reports. In the first example, neither transformer nor R2Gen can fully predict complete reports. however, our result is almost consistent with the ground truth. In the second example, the other two methods ignore "Non-calcified nodes", and only our prediction shows this lesion. In the third example, the result is still ahead of other methods and hits the most keywords. More importantly, the length of the predicted reports is significantly longer than the other two methods, which proves the proposed framework has distinct advantages in generating complex sentences. And it does not reduce the accuracy in key lesions prediction. Clearly, our method can generate readable and accurate reports from the images, and the results are consistent with Table 1.

Result Analysis. In Fig. 3, we analyzed the results from other aspects. Figure 3 (a) shows the heatmap of each predicted word in the test set. Our model distinguishes each word well and gives different attention to the image. The proposed method successfully attends the fine-grained visual features to describe the disease, such as "clear", "no" and "pneumothorax". For the meaningless words like "the", "are" and ".", our model assigns relatively low probabilities. It proves that KMVE can help the framework to distinguish image details and alleviate the data bias problem. Figure 3 (b) shows the comparison of cosine similarity and length radio. It can be observed that there is no linear relationship between the report length and similarity score. The increase in the report length will not affect the similarity score. Moreover, the predicted result length is consistent with the ground truth. Besides, the similarity on the test set is basically above 70%. It appears that our framework can overcome the obstacle of generating long and complex sentences in medical reports. Figure 3 (c) shows the similarity matrix of the KD module in the knowledge clustering step. It shows that each topic is highly correlated with itself and proves the reliability of clustering results.

Input Images	Ground Truth	Transformer	R2Gen	SGF
	The lungs are clear bilaterally. Specifically, no evidence of focal consolidation, pneumothorax, or pleural effusion. Cardio mediastinal silhouette is unremarkable. Visualized osseous structures of the thorax are without acute abnormality.	the lungs appear clear . the heart and mediastinum are normal . the mediastinum is unremarkable .	the lungs appear clear . there is no pleural effusion or pneumothorax . the heart and mediastinum are normal . the skeletal structures are normal	the lungs are clear bilaterally . no evidence of focal consolidation pneumothorax or pleural effusion . cardio mediastinal silhouette is unremarkable . visualized osseous structures of the thorax are without acute abnormality
	The heart size and pulmonary vascularity appear within normal limits. The lungs are free of focal airspace disease. No pleural effusion or pneumothorax is seen. No non-calcified nodules are identified.	heart size within normal limits . no focal airspace disease . no pneumothorax or effusions .	the heart size and pulmonary vascularity appear within normal limits . the lungs are free of focal airspace disease .	heart size and mediastinal contour within normal limits . no non-calcified nodules in the left lung base . no focal airspace consolidation pneumothorax or large pleural effusion . no acute osseous abnormality .
	Normal cardio mediastinal silhouette . there is no focal consolidation . there are no xxxx of a large pleural effusion . There is no pneumothorax . there is no acute bony abnormality seen .	the heart is normal in size . the mediastinum is unremarkable . the lungs are clear . there is no pleural effusion or pneumothorax .	cardiac and mediastinal contours are within normal limits . the lungs are clear . bony structures are intact .	the cardio mediastinal silhouette is within normal limits for size and contour . the lungs are normally inflated without evidence of focal airspace disease pleural effusion or pneumothorax . bony structures are within normal limits for patient age .

Fig. 2. Examples of the generated reports. Our results were compared with the ground truth and the other two methods: Transformer and R2Gen. Highlighted words are consistent parts.

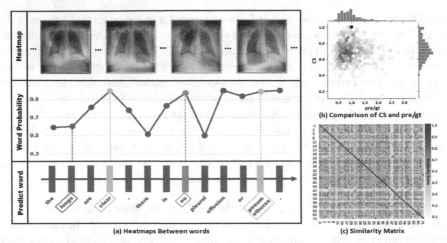

Fig. 3. (a) Heatmaps between words. Each word has different attention and probability in our model. (b) Comparison of cosine similarity and length radio. CS refers to the cosine similarity between predicted reports and ground truths. Pre/gt represents the ratio of predicted length to ground truth length. (c) Similarity Matrix. The similarity matrix of the KD module.

6   Conclusion

In this work, we propose a self-guided framework to generate medical reports, which imitates the process of human learning and writing. Our approach obtains the domain knowledge in an unsupervised way and guides itself to gain highly text-related visual features to solve the data bias problem effectively. Additionally, the RG can improve the performance through comparative practice, assisting itself in generating complex sentences. Experiment results exceed previous competing methods in most metrics, proving the superior efficiency of our framework. Besides, the result analysis further verifies that our framework can distinguish the fine-grained visual features among words, knowing the differences between keywords and meaningless vocabularies.

Acknowledgements. This work was supported in part by Key-Area Research and Development Program of Guangdong Province (No.2020B0909020002), National Natural Science Foundation of China (Grant No. 62003330), Shenzhen Fundamental Research Funds (Grant No. JCYJ20200109114233670, JCYJ20190807170407391), and Guangdong Provincial Key Laboratory of Computer Vision and Virtual Reality Technology, Shenzhen Institutes of Advanced Technology, Chinese Academy of Sciences, Shenzhen, China. This work was also supported by Guangdong-Hong Kong-Macao Joint Laboratory of Human-Machine Intelligence-Synergy Systems, Shenzhen Institute of Advanced Technology.

References

1. Vinyals, O., et al.: Show and tell: A neural image caption generator. In: Proceedings of the IEEE Conference on Computer Vision and Pattern Recognition, pp. 3156–3164 (2015)

2. Xu, K., et al.: Show, attend and tell: Neural image caption generation with visual attention. In: International conference on machine learning, pp. 2048–2057, PMLR (2015)
3. Lu, J., et al.: Knowing when to look: adaptive attention via a visual sentinel for image captioning. In: Proceedings of the IEEE Conference on Computer Vision and Pattern Recognition, pp. 375–383 (2017)
4. Lu, J., et al.: Neural baby talk. In: Proceedings of the IEEE Conference on Computer Vision and Pattern Recognition, pp. 7219–7228 (2018)
5. Liu, G., et al.: Medical-VLBERT: medical visual language BERT for covid-19 CT report generation with alternate learning. IEEE Trans. Neural Netw. Learn. Syst. 32(9), 3786–3797 (2021)
6. Yang, Y., et al.: Joint embedding of deep visual and semantic features for medical image report generation. IEEE Trans. Multimedia (2021)
7. Tran, A., et al.: Transform and tell: Entity-aware news image captioning. In: Proceedings of the IEEE/CVF Conference on Computer Vision and Pattern Recognition, pp. 13035–13045 (2020)
8. Chen, L., et al.: Human-like controllable image captioning with verb-specific semantic roles. In: Proceedings of the IEEE/CVF Conference on Computer Vision and Pattern Recognition, pp. 16846–16856 (2021)
9. Xu, G., et al.: Towards accurate text-based image captioning with content diversity exploration. In: Proceedings of the IEEE/CVF Conference on Computer Vision and Pattern Recognition, pp. 12637–12646 (2021)
10. Zhang, Y., et al.: When radiology report generation meets knowledge graph. In: Proceedings of the AAAI Conference on Artificial Intelligence, vol. 34, pp. 12910–12917 (2020)
11. Liu, F., et al.: Exploring and distilling posterior and prior knowledge for radiology report generation. In: Proceedings of the IEEE/CVF Conference on Computer Vision and Pattern Recognition, pp. 13753–13762 (2021)
12. Li, C. Y., et al.: Hybrid retrieval-generation reinforced agent for medical image report generation. Adv. Neural Info Process. Syst. 31 1537–1547 (2018)
13. Wang, Z., et al.: A self-boosting framework for automated radiographic report generation. In: Proceedings of the IEEE/CVF Conference on Computer Vision and Pattern Recognition, pp. 2433–2442 (2021)
14. Jing, B., et al.: Show, describe and conclude: on exploiting the structure information of chest X-ray reports. In: Proceedings of the 57th Annual Meeting of the Association for Computational Linguistics, pp. 6570–6580 (2019)
15. Vaswani, A., et al.: Attention is all you need. In: Advances in neural information processing systems, pp. 5998–6008 (2017)
16. Chen, Z., et al.: Generating radiology reports via memory-driven transformer. In: Proceedings of the 2020 Conference on Empirical Methods in Natural Language Processing (EMNLP), pp. 1439–1449 (2020)
17. You, D., et al.: Aligntransformer: hierarchical alignment of visual regions and disease tags for medical report generation. In: International Conference on Medical Image Computing and Computer-Assisted Intervention, pp. 72–82, Springer (2021)
18. Reimers, N., et al.: Sentence-BERT: sentence embeddings using siamese BERT-networks. In: Proceedings of the 2019 Conference on Empirical Methods in Natural Language Processing, pp. 671–688, Association for Computational Linguistics (2019)
19. Bowman, S.R., et al.: A large annotated corpus for learning natural language inference. arXiv preprint arXiv:1508.05326 (2015)
20. Williams, A., et al.: A broad-coverage challenge corpus for sentence understanding through inference. In: Proceedings of the 2018 Conference of the North American Chapter of the Association for Computational Linguistics: Human Language Technologies, vol 1 (Long Papers), pp. 1112–1122 (2018)

21. McInnes, L., et al.: UMAP: Uniform manifold approximation and projection for dimension reduction. arXiv preprint arXiv:1802.03426 (2018)
22. Campello, R.J., et al.: Density-based clustering based on hierarchical density estimates. In: Pacific-Asia Conference on Knowledge Discovery and Data Mining, pp. 160–172, Springer (2013)
23. He, K., et al.: Deep residual learning for image recognition. In: Proceedings of the IEEE Conference on Computer Vision and Pattern Recognition, pp. 770–778 (2016)
24. Deng, J., et al.: Imagenet: A large-scale hierarchical image database. In: 2009 IEEE Conference on Computer Vision and Pattern Recognition, pp. 248–255, IEEE (2009)
25. Ba, J.L., et al.: Layer normalization. arXiv preprint arXiv:1607.06450(2016)
26. Demner-Fushman, D., et al.: Preparing a collection of radiology examinations for distribution and retrieval. J. Am. Med. Inform. Assoc. **23**(2), 304–310 (2016)
27. Papineni, K., et al.: BLEU: a method for automatic evaluation of machine translation. In: Proceedings of the 40th Annual Meeting of the Association for Computational Linguistics, pp. 311–318 (2002)
28. Lin, C.-Y.: Rouge: A package for automatic evaluation of summaries. In: Text summarization branches out, pp. 74–81 (2004)
29. Banerjee, S., et al.: METEOR: an automatic metric for MT evaluation with improved correlation with human judgments. In: Proceedings of the ACL Workshop on Intrinsic and Extrinsic Evaluation Measures for Machine Translation and Summarization, pp. 65–72 (2005)
30. Chen, X., et al.: Microsoft COCO captions: Data collection and evaluation server. arXiv preprint arXiv:1504.00325 (2015)
31. Kingma, D.P., et al.: Adam: a method for stochastic optimization. arXiv preprint arXiv:1412.6980 (2014)

D'ARTAGNAN: Counterfactual Video Generation

Hadrien Reynaud[1,2]($\boxtimes$), Athanasios Vlontzos[2], Mischa Dombrowski[3], Ciarán Gilligan Lee[4], Arian Beqiri[5,6], Paul Leeson[5,7], and Bernhard Kainz[2,3]

[1] UKRI CDT in AI for Healthcare, Imperial College London, London, UK
`hadrien.reynaud19@imperial.ac.uk`
[2] Department of Computing, Imperial College London, London, UK
[3] Friedrich–Alexander University Erlangen–Nürnberg, Erlangen, Germany
[4] Spotify and University College London, London, UK
[5] Ultromics Ltd., Oxford, UK
[6] King's College London, School of BioEng and Imaging Sciences, London, UK
[7] John Radcliffe Hospital, Cardiovascular Clinical Research Facility, Oxford, UK

Abstract. Causally-enabled machine learning frameworks could help clinicians to identify the best course of treatments by answering counterfactual questions. We explore this path for the case of echocardiograms by looking into the variation of the Left Ventricle Ejection Fraction, the most essential clinical metric gained from these examinations. We combine deep neural networks, twin causal networks and generative adversarial methods for the first time to build D'ARTAGNAN (Deep ARtificial Twin-Architecture GeNerAtive Networks), a novel *causal* generative model. We demonstrate the soundness of our approach on a synthetic dataset before applying it to cardiac ultrasound videos to answer the question: "What would this echocardiogram look like if the patient had a different ejection fraction?". To do so, we generate new ultrasound videos, retaining the video style and anatomy of the original patient, while modifying the Ejection Fraction conditioned on a given input. We achieve an SSIM score of 0.79 and an R2 score of 0.51 on the counterfactual videos. Code and models are available at: https://github.com/HReynaud/dartagnan.

Keywords: Causal inference · Twin networks · Counterfactual video generation

1 Introduction

How would this patient's scans look if they had a different Left Ventricular Ejection Fraction (LVEF)? How would this Ultrasound (US) view appear if I turned the probe by $5\,°C$? These are important causality related questions that physicians and operators ask explicitly or implicitly during the course of an

Supplementary Information The online version contains supplementary material available at https://doi.org/10.1007/978-3-031-16452-1_57.

L. Wang et al. (Eds.): MICCAI 2022, LNCS 13438, pp. 599–609, 2022.
https://doi.org/10.1007/978-3-031-16452-1_57

examination in order to reason about the possible pathologies of the patient. In the second case, the interventional query of turning the probe is easy to resolve, by performing the action. However, in the first case, we ask a counterfactual question which cannot be answered directly. Indeed, it falls under the third and highest rung of Pearl's [23] hierarchy of causation.

Counterfactual queries probe into alternative scenarios that might have occurred had our actions been different. For the first question of this paper, we ask ourselves how the patient's scans would look if they had a different LVEF. Here, the treatment would be the different ejection fraction, and the outcome, the different set of scans. Note that this is a query that is *counter-to* our observed knowledge that the patients scans exhibited a specific LVEF. As such, standard Bayesian Inference, which conditions on the observed data without any further considerations, is not able to answer this type of question.

Related Works: Generating synthetic US images can be performed with physics-based simulators [6,8,12,18,27] and other techniques, such as registration-based methods [16]. However, these methods are usually very computationally expensive and do not generate fully realistic images. With the shift toward deep learning, Generative Adversarial Network (GAN)-based techniques have emerged. They can be based on simulated US priors or other imaging modalities (MRI, CT) [1,2,9,28–30] to condition the anatomy of the generated US images. Recently, many works explore machine learning as a tool to estimate interventional conditional distributions [3,15,17,35]. However, fewer works focus on the counterfactual query estimation. [19,22] explore the Abduction-Action-Prediction paradigm and use deep neural networks for the abduction step, which is computationally very expensive. [10] derive a parametric mathematical model for the estimation of one of the probabilities of causation, while [33] use [4] to develop deep twin networks. The computer vision field also has a lot of interest in conditional generation problems. [32,34] perform conditional video generation from a video and a discrete class. [11] uses an image and a continuous value as input to produce a new image. [15,25] introduce causality in their generation process, to produce images from classes.

Contributions: In this paper (1) We extend the causal inference methodology known as Deep Twin Networks [33] into a novel generative modelling method (Deep ARtificial Twin-Architecture GeNerAtive Networks (D'ARTAGNAN)[1]) able to handle counterfactual queries. (2) We apply our framework on the synthetic MorphoMNIST [7] and real-world EchoNet-Dynamic [21] datasets, demonstrating that our method can perform well in both fully controlled environments and on real medical cases. To the best of our knowledge, this is an entirely novel approach and task, and thus the first time such an approach is explored for medical image analysis and computer vision. Our work differentiates itself from all other generative methods by combining video generation with continuous conditional input in a new causal framework. This setup supports counterfactual queries to produce counterfactual videos using a semi-supervised approach which allows most standard labelled datasets to be used.

---

[1] D'Artagnan is the fourth Musketeer from the French tale "The three Musketeers".

2   Preliminaries

Structural Causal Models. We work in the Structural Causal Models (SCM) framework. Chapter 7 of [23] gives an in-depth discussion. For an up-to-date, review of counterfactual inference and Pearl's Causal Hierarchy, see [5].

As a brief reminder, we define a structural causal model (SCM) as a set of latent noise variables $U = \{u_1, \ldots, u_n\}$ distributed as $P(U)$, a set of observable variables $V = \{v_1, \ldots, v_m\}$ that is the superset of treatment variables X and confounders Z, i.e. $X, Z \subseteq V$. Moreover, we require a directed acyclic graph (DAG), called the *causal structure* of the model, whose nodes are the variables $U \cup V$, and its edges represent a collection of functions $F = \{f_1, \ldots, f_n\}$, such that $v_i = f_i(PA_i, u_i)$, for $i = 1, \ldots, n$, where PA denotes the parent observed nodes of an observed variable. These are used to induce a distribution over the observable variables and assign uncertainty over them.

Finally, the *do*-operator forces variables to take certain values, regardless of the original causal mechanism. Graphically, $do(X = x)$ means deleting edges incoming to X and setting $X = x$. Probabilities involving $do(x)$ are normal probabilities in submodel M_x: $P(Y = y \mid do(X = x)) = P_{M_x}(y)$.

Counterfactual Inference. The latent distribution $P(U)$ allows us to define probabilities of counterfactual queries, $P(Y_y = y) = \sum_{u \mid Y_x(u) = y} P(u)$. Moreover, one can define a counterfactual distribution given seemingly contradictory evidence and thereby state the counterfactual sentence "Y would be y (in situation $U = u$), had X been x". Despite the fact that this query may involve interventions that contradict the evidence, it is well defined, as the intervention specifies a new submodel. Indeed, $P(Y_x = y' \mid E = e)$ is given by [23] as $\sum_u P(Y_x(u) = y')P(u|e)$.

Twin Networks. As opposed to the standard *Abduction - Action - Prediction* paradigm, we will be operating under the Twin Model methodology. Originally proposed by Balke and Pearl in [4], this method allows efficient counterfactual inference to be performed as a feed forward Bayesian process. It has also been shown empirically to offer computational savings relative to abduction-action-prediction [14]. A twin network consists of two interlinked networks, one representing the real world and the other the counterfactual world being queried.

Given a structural causal model, a twin network can be constructed and used to compute a counterfactual query through the following steps: First, duplicate the given causal model, denoting nodes in the duplicated model via superscript $*$. Let V be observable nodes that include the treatment variables X and the confounders Z, and let $X^*, Z^* \subseteq V^*$ be the duplication of these. Also let U be the unobserved latent noise. Then, for every node v_i^* in the duplicated, or "counterfactual" model, its latent parent u_i^* is replaced with the original latent parent u_i in the original, or "factual", model, such that the original latent variables are now a parent of two nodes, v_i and v_i^*. The two graphs are linked only by common latent parents, but share the same node structure and generating mechanisms. To compute a general counterfactual query $P(Y = y \mid E = e, do(X = x))$, modify the structure of the counterfactual network by dropping arrows from parents of X^* and setting them to value $X^* = x$. Then, in the twin network with this modified structure, compute the probability $P(Y^* = y \mid E = e, X^* = x)$ via standard Bayesian inference techniques, where E are factual nodes.

3 Method

Deep Twin Networks. The methodology we propose is based on Deep Twin Networks. The training procedure and parametrization are borrowed from [33], which sets the foundation for our causal framework. Deep Twin Networks use two branches, the factual and the counterfactual branch. We denote our factual and counterfactual treatments (inputs unique to each branch) as X and X^*, while the confounder (input shared between both branches) is denoted by Z. We denote the factual and counterfactual outcomes as $\hat{Y}, \hat{Y}^*$ while the noise, injected midway through the network, and shared by both branches, is denoted by U_Y. This information flow sets Z as the data we want to query with X and X^*, to produce the outcomes $\hat{Y}$ and $\hat{Y}^*$. These variables will be detailed on a case-specific basis in Sect. 4. See Fig. 1 for a visual representation of the information flow.

Synthetic Data. Synthetic data allows for full control over the generation of both ground truth outcomes Y and Y^* along with their corresponding inputs X, X^* and Z. This makes training the Deep Twin Network trivial in a fully supervised fashion, as demonstrated in our first experiment.

Real-World Data. Theoretically, our approach requires labelled data pairs, but very few datasets are arranged as such. To overcome this limitation and support most standard labeled imaging datasets, we establish a list of features that our model must possess to generate counterfactual videos for the medical domain: (1) produce a factual and counterfactual output that share general visual features, such as style and anatomy, (2) produce accurate factual and counterfactual videos with respect to the treatment variable, and (3) the produced videos must be visually indistinguishable from real ones. In the following, we use the Echonet-Dynamic [21] dataset to illustrate the method, see Sect. 4 for details. We solve feature (1) by sharing the weights of the branches in the network, such that we virtually train a single branch on two tasks in parallel. To do so, we set the confounder Z as the input video and the treatment X as the labelled LVEF. We train the network to match the factual outcome $\hat{Y}$ with the input video. By doing so, the model learns to retain the style and anatomical structure of the echocardiogram from the confounder. This is presented as *Loss 1* in Fig. 1. For feature (2) we pre-train an expert network to regress the treatment values from the videos produces by the counterfactual branch, and compare them to the counterfactual treatment. The expert network's weights are frozen when training the Twin model, and alleviates the need for labels to train the counterfactual branch. This loss is denoted as *Loss 2* in Fig. 1. Finally, feature (3) calls for the well-known GAN framework, where we train a neural network to discriminate between real and fake images or videos, while training the Twin Network. This constitutes the adversarial *Loss 3* in Fig. 1 and ensures that the counterfactual branch produces realistic-looking videos.

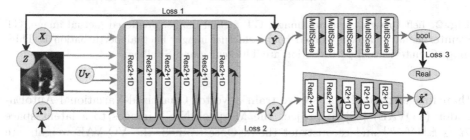

Fig. 1. The D'ARTAGNAN framework. The green variables are known, the orange are sampled from distributions and the blue are generated by deep neural networks. Factual path is in blue, counterfactual in red. (Color figure online)

With those 3 losses, we can train the generator (i.e. factual and counterfactual branches) to produce pairs of visually accurate and anatomically matching videos that respect their factual and counterfactual LVEFs treatment. To learn the **noise distribution** U_Y, we follow [13,33] and without loss of generality we can write $Y = f(X, Z, g(U'_Y))$ with $U'_Y \sim \mathcal{E}$ and $U_Y = g(U'_Y)$, where $\mathcal{E}$ is some easy-to-sample-from distribution, such as a Gaussian or Uniform. Effectively, we cast the problem of determining U_Y to learning the appropriate transformation from $\mathcal{E}$ to U_Y. For ease of understanding, we will be using U_Y henceforth to signify our approximation $g(U'_Y)$ of the true unobserved parameter U_Y. In addition to specifying the causal structure, the following standard assumptions are needed to correctly estimate $\mathbb{E}(Y|do(X), Z)$ [26]: (1) *Ignorability:* there are no unmeasured confounders; (2) *Overlap:* every unit has non-zero probability of receiving all treatments given their observed covariates.

4 Experimentation

Datasets. To evaluate D'ARTAGNAN, we use two publicly available datasets, the synthetic MorphoMNIST [7] and the clinical Echonet-Dynamic [21] dataset.

MorphoMNIST is a set of tools that enable fine-grained perturbations of the MNIST digits through four morphological functions, as well as five measurements of the digits. To train our model, we need five elements: an original image, a (counter-)factual treatment $X(X^*)$ and a corresponding (counter-)factual label $Y(Y^*)$. To generate this data, we take 60,000 MNIST images I_i and sample 40 perturbation vectors $p_{i,j}$ for the five possible perturbations, including identity, thus generating 2.4 million images $I_{p_{i,j}}$. The perturbation vectors also encode the relative positions of the perturbations, when applicable. We *measure* the original images to produce vectors m_i and one-hot encode the labels into vectors l_i. We decided to perform the causal reasoning over a latent space, rather

Fig. 2. Left to right: original image, GT factual image, predicted factual image, GT counterfactual image, predicted counterfactual image. Factual perturbation is Thinning, Counterfactual perturbation are Thickening and Swelling.

than image space. To do so, we train a Vector Quantized-Variational AutoEncoder (VQVAE) [20] to project the MorphoMNIST images to a latent space $\mathcal{H} \in \mathbb{R}^{(q \times h \times w)}$ and reconstruct them. Once trained, the VQ-VAE weights are frozen, and we encode all the ground-truth perturbed images $I_{p_{i,j}}$ into a latent embedding $\mathcal{H}_{i,j}$. Afterwards, the VQ-VAE is used to reconstruct the generated latent embeddings $\hat{Y}, \hat{Y}^*$ for qualitative evaluation purposes.

The clinical dataset Echonet-Dynamic [21] consists of 10,030 4-chamber echocardiography videos with 112×112 pixels resolution and various length, frame rates, image quality and cardiac conditions. Each video contains a single pair of consecutively labelled End-Systolic (ES) and End-Diastolic (ED) frames. Each video also comes with a manually measured LVEF. For our use case, all videos are greyscaled and resampled to 64 frames, with a frame rate of 32 images per second. All videos shorter than two seconds are discarded, and we make sure to keep the labelled frames. For the resulting 9724 videos dataset, the original split is kept, with 7227 training, 1264 validation and 1233 testing videos.

MorphoMNIST. For our synthetic experiment, we define a deep twin network as in [33] and follow the process we described in the Methods (Sect. 3). Regarding data organization, we use the elements defined in the section above. We set our confounder $Z_i = [l_i, m_i]$ to contain the one-hot encoded labels as well as the measurement of the original image. We sample two perturbation vectors $p_{i,m}$ and $p_{i,n}$ and their corresponding latent embeddings $\mathcal{H}_{i,m}$ and $\mathcal{H}_{i,n}$, where $n, m \in [\![0, 40[\![, n \neq m$. We set our input treatments as the perturbations vectors $(X = p_{i,m}, X^* = p_{i,n})$ and our ground-truth outcomes as the corresponding latent embeddings of the perturbed images $(Y = \mathcal{H}_{i,m}, Y^* = \mathcal{H}_{i,n})$. We sample $U_Y \sim [\mathcal{N}(0, 0.25) \bmod 1 + 1]$ and disturb the output of the branches of the neural networks that combine X and X^* with Z by multiplying the outputs of both with the same U_Y. With this setup, we generate factual and counterfactual perturbed MNIST embeddings from a latent description.

We assess the quality of the results by three means: (1) *Embeddings' MSE:* We sample a quintuplet (Z, X, X^*, Y, Y^*) and 1000 U_Y. The MSE between all $\hat{Y}_i$ and Y are computed and used to order the pairs $(\hat{Y}_i, \hat{Y}_i^*)$ in ascending order. We keep the sample with the lowest MSE as our factual estimate and compute the MSE between $\hat{Y}_0^*$ and Y^* to get our counterfactual MSE score. (2) *SSIM:* We use the Structural SIMilarity metric between the perturbed images $I_{gt} = I_{p_{i,j}}$, the images reconstructed by the VQVAE I_{rec} and the images reconstructed from the latent embedding produced by the twin network I_{pred} to get a quantitative score over the images. (3) *Images:* We sample some images to qualitatively assess best and worst cases scenarios for this framework. We show the quantitative results in Table 1(a), and qualitative results in Fig. 2 and in the appendix.

Table 1. Metrics for MorphoMNIST (a) and EchoNet-Dynamic (b) experiments.

Metric	Factual	Counterfactual
$MSE(Y, \hat{Y})$	2.3030	2.4232
$SSIM(I_{gt}, I_{rec})^{\dagger}$	0.9308	0.9308
$SSIM(I_{rec}, I_{pred})$	0.6759	0.6759
$SSIM(I_{gt}, I_{pred})$	0.6707	0.6705

(a) MSE and SSIM scores. †No ordering is performed as there is no noise involved.

Metric	Factual	Counterf.
R2	0.87	0.51
MAE	2.79	15.7
RMSE	4.45	18.4
SSIM	0.82	0.79

(b) D'ARTAGNAN LVEF and reconstruction metrics.

Echonet Dynamic. As stated in Sect. 3, our methodology requires an **Expert Model** to predict the LVEF of any US video. To do so, we re-implement the ResNet 2+1D network [31] as it was shown to be the best option for LVEF regression in [21]. We opt not to use transformers as they do not supersede convolutions for managing the temporal dimension, as shown in [24]. We purposefully keep this model as small as possible in order to minimize its memory footprint, as it will be operating together with the generator and the frame discriminator. The expert network is trained first, and frozen while we train the rest of D'ARTAGNAN. Metrics for this model are presented in the Appendix.

D'ARTAGNAN. We implement the generator as described in Sect. 3. We define a single deep network to represent both the factual and counterfactual paths. By doing so, we can meet the objectives listed in Sect. 3. The branch is implemented as a modified ResNet 2+1D [31] to generate videos. It takes two inputs: a continuous value and a video, where the video determines the size of the output. For additional details, please refer to Fig. 1 and the code.

Discriminator. We build a custom discriminator architecture using five "residual multiscale convolutional blocks", with kernel sizes 3, 5, 7 and appropriate padding at each step, followed by a max-pooling layer. Using multiscale blocks enables the discriminator to look at both local and global features. This is extremely important in US images because of the noise in the data, that needs to be both ignored, for anatomical identification, and accounted for to ensure that counterfactual US images look real. We test this discriminator both as a frame-based discriminator and a video-based discriminator, by changing the 2D layers to 3D layers where appropriate. We note that, given our architecture, the 3D version of the model requires slightly less memory but doubles the processing power compared to the 2D model.

Training the Framework. At each training step, we sample an US video (V) and its LVEF (ψ). We set our factual treatment, $X = \psi$ and our counterfactual treatment $X^* \sim \mathcal{U}(0, \psi - 0.1) \cup \mathcal{U}(\psi + 0.1, 1)$. The confounder Z and the factual ground truth Y are set to the sampled video such that $Z = Y = V$. We compute

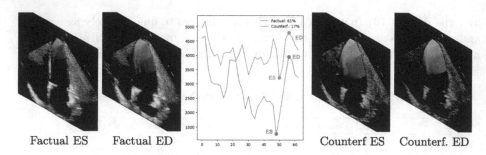

Fig. 3. Qualitative results for D'ARTAGNAN over the same confounder and noise. Left: factual ES and ED frames. Middle: left ventricle area over time, obtained with a segmentation network as in [21]. Dots represent where the corresponding frames were sampled. Right: counterfactual ES and ED frames. Anatomy is preserved across videos, while the LVEF fraction is different.

an L1 reconstruction loss (loss 1) between $\hat{Y}$ and $Y = V$. As we do not have ground truth for the counterfactual branch, we use the frame discriminator and the expert model to train it. Both models take as input the counterfactual prediction $\hat{Y}^*$. The expert model predicts an LVEF $\hat{\psi}$ that is trained to match the counterfactual input X^* with an L1 loss (loss 2). The discriminator is trained as a GAN discriminator, with $\hat{Y}^*$ as fake samples and V as real samples. It trains the generator with L1 loss (loss 3). The discriminator and expert model losses are offset respectively by three and five epochs, leaving time for the generator to learn to reconstruct V, thus maintaining the anatomy and style of the confounder. Our experiments show that doing so increases the speed at which the network is capable of outputting realistic-looking videos, thus speeding up the training of the discriminator that sees accurate fake videos sooner. Once the generator and discriminator are capable of generating and discriminating realistic-looking videos, the expert network loss is activated and forces the generator to take into account the counterfactual treatment, while the factual treatment is enforced by the reconstruction loss. The losses are also scaled, such that the discriminator loss has a relative weight of 3 compared to the reconstruction and expert loss.

Metrics. To match our three objectives, we evaluate this new task on 1) the accuracy of the anatomy and 2) the accuracy of the regressed LVEF. We obtain the best possible video by sampling 100 U_Y and keeping the $\hat{Y}^*$ with $\hat{\phi}^*$ closest to X^*. We then evaluate our metrics over those "best" videos. The anatomical accuracy is measured with SSIM and the LVEF precision is measured using R2, MAE and RMSE scores. Results are shown in Table 1b.

Qualitative. In Fig. 3 we show video frame examples to showcase the quality of the reconstructed frames, as well as how the anatomy and style are maintained.

Discussion. The predicted LVEF has an MAE of 15.7% which is not optimal. This can come from many factors such as the use of the same dataset to train the Expert model and D'ARTAGNAN, the limited number of real videos, or the limited size of the networks due to the necessity of working with three models at once. Those problems could be addressed with hyperparameter search, larger models, as well as additional medical data. For completeness, we compare the performance of D'ARTAGNAN with the literature [32,34], and run additional experiments (see Appendix) with an ablated version of our model for conditional video generation, where it achieves the best SSIM score of 0.72.

5   Conclusion

In this paper we introduce D'ARTAGNAN, a Deep Twin Generative Network able to produce counterfactual images and videos. We showcase its performance in both a synthetic and a real world medical dataset and achieve visually accurate results and high quantitative scores. In future work, we will explore other treatments, such as changing the heartbeat, as well as less constrained confounders, e.g. image segmentations.

Acknowledgements. This work was supported by Ultromics Ltd., the UKRI Centre for Doctoral Training in Artificial Intelligence for Healthcare (EP/S023283/1), and the UK Research and Innovation London Medical Imaging and Artificial Intelligence Centre for Value Based Healthcare. We thank the NVIDIA corporation for their GPU donations used in this work.

References

1. Abbasi-Sureshjani, S., Amirrajab, S., Lorenz, C., Weese, J., Pluim, J., Breeuwer, M.: 4d semantic cardiac magnetic resonance image synthesis on xcat anatomical model. arXiv preprint arXiv:2002.07089 (2020)
2. Amirrajab, S., et al.: Xcat-gan for synthesizing 3d consistent labeled cardiac MR images on anatomically variable xcat phantoms. arXiv preprint arXiv:2007.13408 (2020)
3. Assaad, S., et al.: Counterfactual representation learning with balancing weights. In: International Conference on Artificial Intelligence and Statistics, pp. 1972–1980. PMLR (2021)
4. Balke, A., Pearl, J.: Probabilistic evaluation of counterfactual queries. In: AAAI (1994)
5. Bareinboim, E., Correa, J.D., Ibeling, D., Icard, T.: On pearl's hierarchy and the foundations of causal inference. Columbia University, Stanford University, Tech. rep. (2020)
6. Burger, B., Bettinghausen, S., Radle, M., Hesser, J.: Real-time GPU-based ultrasound simulation using deformable mesh models. IEEE Trans. Med. Imaging **32**(3), 609–618 (2012)
7. Castro, D.C., Tan, J., Kainz, B., Konukoglu, E., Glocker, B.: Morpho-MNIST: quantitative assessment and diagnostics for representation learning. J. Mach. Learn. Res. **20**(178) (2019)
8. Cong, W., Yang, J., Liu, Y., Wang, Y.: Fast and automatic ultrasound simulation from CT images. Comput. Math. Methods Med. (2013)

9. Cronin, N.J., Finni, T., Seynnes, O.: Using deep learning to generate synthetic b-mode musculoskeletal ultrasound images. Comput. Methods Prog. Biomed. **196**, 105583 (2020)

10. Cuellar, M., Kennedy, E.H.: A non-parametric projection-based estimator for the probability of causation, with application to water sanitation in kenya. J. Roy. Statist. Soc. Ser. A (Statist. Soc.) **183**(4), 1793–1818 (2020)

11. Ding, X., Wang, Y., Xu, Z., Welch, W.J., Wang, Z.J.: CCGAN: continuous conditional generative adversarial networks for image generation. In: International Conference on Learning Representations (2020)

12. Gao, H., et al.: A fast convolution-based methodology to simulate 2-dd/3-d cardiac ultrasound images. IEEE Trans. Ultras. Ferroelect. Freq. Control **56**(2), 404–409 (2009)

13. Goudet, O., et al.: Learning functional causal models with generative neural networks. arXiv preprint arXiv:1709.05321 (2017)

14. Graham, L., Lee, C.M., Perov, Y.: Copy, paste, infer: a robust analysis of twin networks for counterfactual inference. In: NeurIPS Causal ML Workshop 2019 (2019)

15. Kocaoglu, M., Snyder, C., Dimakis, A.G., Vishwanath, S.: Causalgan: learning causal implicit generative models with adversarial training. In: International Conference on Learning Representations (2018)

16. Ledesma-Carbayo, M.J., et al.: Spatio-temporal nonrigid registration for ultrasound cardiac motion estimation. IEEE Trans. Med. Imaging **24**(9), 1113–1126 (2005)

17. Louizos, C., Shalit, U., Mooij, J., Sontag, D., Zemel, R., Welling, M.: Causal effect inference with deep latent-variable models. In: Proceedings of the 31st International Conference on Neural Information Processing Systems, pp. 6449–6459 (2017)

18. Mattausch, O., Makhinya, M., Goksel, O.: Realistic ultrasound simulation of complex surface models using interactive Monte-Carlo path tracing (2014)

19. Oberst, M., Sontag, D.: Counterfactual off-policy evaluation with Gumbel-max structural causal models. In: International Conference on Machine Learning, pp. 4881–4890. PMLR (2019)

20. Oord, A.v.d., Vinyals, O., Kavukcuoglu, K.: Neural discrete representation learning. arXiv preprint arXiv:1711.00937 (2017)

21. Ouyang, D., et al.: Video-based AI for beat-to-beat assessment of cardiac function. Nature **580**, 252–256 (2020)

22. Pawlowski, N., Castro, D.C., Glocker, B.: Deep structural causal models for tractable counterfactual inference. arXiv preprint arXiv:2006.06485 (2020)

23. Pearl, J.: Causality, 2nd edn. Cambridge University Press (2009)

24. Reynaud, H., Vlontzos, A., Hou, B., Beqiri, A., Leeson, P., Kainz, B.: Ultrasound video transformers for cardiac ejection fraction estimation. In: de Bruijne, M., et al. (eds.) MICCAI 2021. LNCS, vol. 12906, pp. 495–505. Springer, Cham (2021). https://doi.org/10.1007/978-3-030-87231-1_48

25. Sauer, A., Geiger, A.: Counterfactual generative networks. arXiv preprint arXiv:2101.06046 (2021)

26. Schwab, P., Linhardt, L., Karlen, W.: Perfect match: a simple method for learning representations for counterfactual inference with neural networks. arXiv preprint arXiv:1810.00656 (2018)

27. Shams, R., Hartley, R., Navab, N.: Real-time simulation of medical ultrasound from CT images. In: Metaxas, D., Axel, L., Fichtinger, G., Székely, G. (eds.) MICCAI 2008. LNCS, vol. 5242, pp. 734–741. Springer, Heidelberg (2008). https://doi.org/10.1007/978-3-540-85990-1_88

28. Teng, L., Fu, Z., Yao, Y.: Interactive translation in echocardiography training system with enhanced cycle-GAN. IEEE Access **8**, 106147–106156 (2020)
29. Tiago, C., Gilbert, A., Snare, S.R., Sprem, J., McLeod, K.: Generation of 3d cardiovascular ultrasound labeled data via deep learning (2021)
30. Tomar, D., Zhang, L., Portenier, T., Goksel, O.: Content-preserving unpaired translation from simulated to realistic ultrasound images. arXiv preprint arXiv:2103.05745 (2021)
31. Tran, D., Wang, H., Torresani, L., Ray, J., LeCun, Y., Paluri, M.: A closer look at spatiotemporal convolutions for action recognition. In: Proceedings of the IEEE Conference on Computer Vision and Pattern Recognition, pp. 6450–6459 (2018)
32. Tulyakov, S., Liu, M.Y., Yang, X., Kautz, J.: Mocogan: decomposing motion and content for video generation. In: Proceedings of the IEEE Conference on Computer Vision and Pattern Recognition, pp. 1526–1535 (2018)
33. Vlontzos, A., Kainz, B., Gilligan-Lee, C.M.: Estimating the probabilities of causation via deep monotonic twin networks. arXiv preprint arXiv:2109.01904 (2021)
34. Wang, Y., Bilinski, P., Bremond, F., Dantcheva, A.: Imaginator: conditional spatiotemporal GAN for video generation. In: Proceedings of the IEEE/CVF Winter Conference on Applications of Computer Vision, pp. 1160–1169 (2020)
35. Yoon, J., Jordon, J., Van Der Schaar, M.: Ganite: estimation of individualized treatment effects using generative adversarial nets. In: International Conference on Learning Representations (2018)

TranSQ: Transformer-Based Semantic Query for Medical Report Generation

Ming Kong[1(✉)], Zhengxing Huang[1], Kun Kuang[1,2], Qiang Zhu[1],
and Fei Wu[1,2,3,4]

[1] Institute of Artificial Intelligence, Zhejiang University, Hangzhou, China
`zjukongming@zju.edu.cn`
[2] Key Laboratory for Corneal Diseases Research of Zhejiang Province,
Hangzhou, China
[3] Shanghai Institute for Advanced Study of Zhejiang University, Shanghai, China
[4] Shanghai AI Laboratory, Shanghai, China

Abstract. Medical report generation, which aims at automatically generating coherent reports with multiple sentences for the given medical images, has received growing research interest due to its tremendous potential in facilitating clinical workflow and improving health services. Due to the highly patterned nature of medical reports, each sentence can be viewed as the description of an image observation with a specific purpose. To this end, this study proposes a novel ***Transformer-based Semantic Query*** (TranSQ) model that treats the medical report generation as a direct set prediction problem. Specifically, our model generates a set of semantic features to match plausible clinical concerns and compose the report with sentence retrieval and selection. Experimental results on two prevailing radiology report datasets, i.e., IU X-Ray and MIMIC-CXR, demonstrate that our model outperforms state-of-the-art models on the generation task in terms of both language generation effectiveness and clinical efficacy, which highlights the utility of our approach in generating medical reports with topics of clinical concern as well as sentence-level visual-semantic attention mappings. The source code is available at https://github.com/zjukongming/TranSQ.

Keywords: Medical report generation · Transformer · Auxiliary diagnosis · Deep learning

1 Introduction

Writing reports from medical images to describe normality and abnormality is a critical task in clinical practice. It is time-consuming and tedious for experienced doctors while error-prone for inexperienced ones [4]. Therefore, automatic report generation has become a prominent task in artificial intelligence-based clinical

Supplementary Information The online version contains supplementary material available at https://doi.org/10.1007/978-3-031-16452-1_58.

medicine to assist clinical decision-making, relieve the heavy workload, and alert doctors of the abnormality to avoid misdiagnosis and missed diagnoses.

Medical report generation aims to describe both normal and abnormal discoveries with a relatively structured pattern, which is highly related to the image caption task [2,6]. The difference is that it requires a much longer paragraph containing multiple sentences instead of one sentence, leading to a significant challenge for medical report generation. One way to alleviate this problem is to generate reports in a sentence-by-sentence manner for different abnormal performances. For instance, [13] introduced tag prediction to determine the semantic topic of sentence generation; [16,17] proposed to use manually extracted template to achieve sentence generation or retrieval. Although valuable, this category of models require hand-craft collation or definition of medical labels or knowledge, which is time-consuming and often incomplete. Another way is to utilize an encoder-decoder structure to generate the entire report in one go. For instance, [7] incorporated the relational memory to implicitly model and memorize the medical report patterns; [1,32] make report generation based on multi-label prediction for medical terms. [21] introduced a pre-constructed knowledge graph as the shared latent space to measure the relationship between images and reports. The downside of these solutions is that verbatim generation of long paragraphs remains a challenge, despite the improvements in Transformer-based models. Besides, most of them still rely on pre-defined medical terms. Interpretability is another critical concern. Note that providing visual explanations of definition-level or observation-level to the auto-generated report is essential for increasing the credibility and reliability of a medical report generation model. Unfortunately, existing methods have not effectively addressed this issue.

In this paper, we propose a **Trans**former-based **S**emantic **Q**uery (TranSQ) model that makes semantic queries to visual features to generate medical reports sentence-by-sentence. Specifically, medical images are first encoded into visual features; then a series of trainable semantic embeddings query the visual features through a transformer-based semantic encoder to generate the semantic features; finally outputs the selected sentences generated by retrieval. The sentence candidate selection is considered a direct set prediction problem, i.e., dynamically labeling the outputting selections according to the bipartite matching of semantic features and ground-truth sentences.

Experimental results on two benchmark datasets, i.e., IU X-Ray and MIMIC-CXR, confirm the validity and effectiveness of our approach. TranSQ achieves state-of-the-art performance on both natural language generation (NLG) and clinical efficacy (CE) metrics. Furthermore, it provides sentence-level visualized interpretations, enabling an intuitive and convincing correlation between attention maps and clinical concerns.

To summarize, the contributions of this study are as follows:

- We propose a novel TranSQ model for medical report generation, by learning visual embedding and semantic queries for the sentence candidate set. To the best of our knowledge, it is the first work that addresses the medical report generation in a candidate set prediction and selection manner.

- Extensive experiments show that TranSQ reaches state-of-the-art performance on both natural language generation and clinical efficacy.
- A sentence-level interpretation of medical report generation is fine-grained presented, which is more convincing and explainable than existing models.

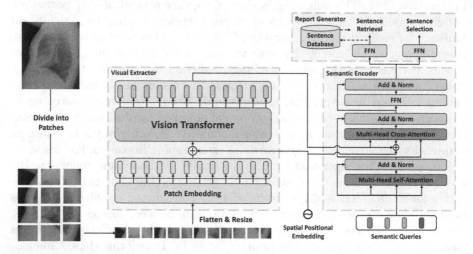

Fig. 1. The overall architecture of the TranSQ model that consists of the visual extractor, semantic encoder, and report generator modules.

2   Method

The problem of medical report generation can be decomposed into three steps: 1. Visual feature understanding; 2. Annotate observations with specific purposes to the visual features; 3. Describe each observation into a sentence and judge whether it deserves output. Accordingly, our proposed TranSQ model is partitioned into three major components: visual extractor, semantic encoder, and report generator, and its overall architecture is shown in Fig. 1.

2.1   Visual Extractor

Considering the practical need of generating reports from multiple images, we adopt the Vision Transformer (ViT) [10] as the visual encoder to achieve multi-modal adaptability. Specifically, given the input images $\mathcal{I}$, first we resize the images into a fixed resolution, then split each image into patches and flatten and reshape the patches into a sequence. A linear layer maps the sequence into a latent space and adds the learnable positional and modal embedding with the same dimensions. Thereafter, we obtain the final input to the ViT module denoted as $X = [x_1, \ldots, x_N]$, where N is the length of the input sequence.

The visual extractor follows the standard ViT structure, and each layer consists of a multi-head self-attention (MHSA) and a feed-forward network (FFN) sequentially. The visual extractor transforms the patch sequence into a visual feature sequence, denoted as $\mathbf{f}^v = [f_1^v, \ldots, f_N^v]$.

2.2   Semantic Encoder

Given the extracted visual features, we observe the valuable regions or features of the images with a set of K semantic queries $\mathbf{q} = [q_1, \ldots, q_K]$, where each query q_i corresponds with a latent topic definition. Note that since the semantic queries are permutation-invariant, the difference of the outputs comes from the value of semantic query embeddings, which are obtained by the training process. The semantic encoder transforms the semantic query set $\mathbf{q}$ into the semantic feature set, denoted as $\mathbf{f}^s = [f_1^s, \ldots, f_K^s]$.

The structure of the semantic encoder follows the structure of [5] to encode the semantic queries in parallel. Specifically, for each layer of the module, the inputs are first sent to a multi-head self-attention to consider the relevance and co-occurrence between latent topics. Then a multi-head cross-attention [29] implements the queries of the semantic features to the visual features. Finally, a feed-forward network (FFN) layer performs a transformation.

2.3   Report Generator

The report generator module achieves two tasks: to generate the sentence candidates and to predict the probability of sentence selection. In this work, sentence candidates are generated by the retrieval strategy. i.e., for each semantic feature f_i^s, convert it into sentence embedding $\hat{v}_i$ by a feed-forward network, and retrieval in the database to generate the candidate sentence $\hat{y}_i$. And sentence selection is achieved by a multi-label classifier to predict selection probabilities $\hat{p}_i$ from f_i^s.

The semantic encoder generates a fixed-size set of K semantic features, where K is significantly larger than the sentence number of a particular report to ensure sufficient diversity of the candidates. Denoting the ground truth report sentence set $\mathbf{y}$, the report generator needs to select appropriate subsets from $\hat{\mathbf{y}} = \{\hat{y}_i\}_{i=1}^K$ to compose the report paragraph. To solve the problem, We consider $\mathbf{y}$ also a set of size K padded with $\varnothing$ (empty string) to convert the problem into a bipartite matching between the two sets and search for the K elements permutation $\sigma \in \mathfrak{S}_K$ with the lowest cost:

$$\hat{\sigma} = \arg \min_{\sigma \in \mathfrak{S}_K} \sum_i^K \mathcal{L}_{match}(y_i, \hat{y}_{\sigma(i)}) \tag{1}$$

where $\mathcal{L}(y_i, \hat{y}_{\sigma(i)})$ is a pair-wise *matching cost* between the ground truth sentence y_i and a generated sentence candidate with index $\sigma(i)$.

The optimal assignment is computed efficiently with *Hungarian algorithm* [15], and the matching loss takes both sentence embedding similarity and the sentence selection probability into account, which is defined as:

$$\mathcal{L}_{match}(y_i, \hat{y}_{\sigma(i)}) = \mathbb{1}_{\{y_i \neq \varnothing\}} \mathcal{L}_{sim}(v_i, \hat{v}_{\sigma(i)}) - \mu \, \mathbb{1}_{\{y_i \neq \varnothing\}} \hat{p}_{\sigma(i)} \tag{2}$$

where $\mathcal{L}_{sim}$ is the evaluation of sentence embedding fitting and μ is the scale factor between sentence embedding fitting and sentence selection prediction.

We optimize the model following the best bipartite matching results. On the one hand, to optimize the sentence selection result to fit the optimal bipartite matching result; on the other hand, to reduce the discrimination between the ground truth and its optimal match sentence embeddings. We assign the selection labels for the K latent topics according to the bipartite matching result. i.e., for the candidate $\hat{y}_\sigma(i)$, its selection label $c_{\sigma(i)}$ is 1 if $y_i \neq \varnothing$, and is 0 otherwise. In summary, the loss function is a linear combination of a loss of sentence embedding similarities ($\mathcal{L}_{sim}$) and a loss of sentence selection ($\mathcal{L}_{cls}$), denoted as:

$$\mathcal{L}(\mathbf{y}, \hat{\mathbf{y}}) = \sum_{i=1}^{N} \left[\mathbb{1}_{\{y_i \neq \varnothing\}} \mathcal{L}_{sim}(v_i, \hat{v}_{\hat{\sigma}(i)}) - \lambda \mathcal{L}_{cls}(c_i, \hat{p}_{\hat{\sigma}(i)}) \right] \tag{3}$$

where λ is a scale factor between $\mathcal{L}_{sim}$ and $\mathcal{L}_{cls}$. Thanks to the effective representation of sentence embeddings learned by the large-scale pre-trained linguistic models, we apply the cosine embedding loss as $\mathcal{L}_{sim}$ to optimize the predictions to close to the corresponding ground-truth sentence embedding. And $\mathcal{L}_{cls}$ is a type of multi-label classification loss. Note that sentence selection labels are dynamic during training since sentence embedding and sentence selection probabilities change with the updating of model parameters, which increases the difficulty of training. At the same time, label co-occurrence and class distribution imbalance are also significant issues. In this work, we apply the *Distribution-Balanced Loss* (DB-Loss) [30] as the sentence selection loss $\mathcal{L}_{cls}$.

Accomplishing sentence retrieval and selection, we compose the medical report in a particular strategy that simply ranks the sentences by the average mentioned order of the corresponding semantic query type in the training set.

3   Experiment

3.1   Datasets, Metrics and Settings

Datasets. In this study, we validate our proposed model on two widely-used public benchmark datasets, i.e., IU X-ray[1] [9], and MIMIC-CXR[2] [14] for medical report generation. All protected health information (e.g., patient name and date of birth) was de-identified. For both experimental datasets, we exclude the samples without reports and then apply their conventional splits [17]. In particular, the IU X-ray dataset contains 7,470 chest X-ray images associated with 3,955 fully de-identified medical reports. Following the existing works [7,12,16,17], image-report pairs of the dataset to form the training-validation-testing sets are selected with 70%-10%-20%, respectively. The MIMIC-CXR dataset includes 377,110 chest x-ray images associated with 227,835 reports. The dataset is officially split into 368,960 images with 222,758 reports for the training set, 2,991 images with 1,808 reports for the validation set, and 5,159 images with 3,269 reports for the testing set.

---

[1] https://openi.nlm.nih.gov/.
[2] https://physionet.org/content/mimic-cxr/2.0.0/.

Table 1. Comparisons of TranSQ model with previous studies on IU X-RAY with NLG metrics. $\triangle$ denotes the improvements to the best baseline.

Method	BL-1	BL-2	BL-3	BL-4	MTR	RG-L
NIC [28]	0.216	0.124	0.087	0.066	–	0.306
AdaAtt [23]	0.220	0.127	0.089	0.068	–	0.308
Att2in [27]	0.224	0.129	0.089	0.068	–	0.308
$\mathcal{M}^2$ Trans. [8]	0.437	0.290	0.205	0.152	0.176	0.353
CoAtt [13]	0.455	0.288	0.205	0.154	–	0.369
HRGR [17]	0.438	0.298	0.208	0.151	–	0.322
CMAS-RL [12]	0.464	0.301	0.210	0.154	–	0.362
GDGPT [1]	0.387	0.245	0.166	0.111	0.164	0.289
Transformer [7]	0.396	0.254	0.179	0.135	0.164	0.342
CMCL [21]	0.473	0.305	0.217	0.162	0.186	0.378
R2Gen [7]	0.470	0.304	0.219	0.165	0.187	0.371
MedWriter [31]	0.471	0.336	0.238	0.166	–	0.382
PPKED [20]	0.483	0.315	0.224	0.168	0.190	0.376
AlignTransformer [32]	0.484	0.313	0.225	0.173	0.204	0.379
KGAE [21]	**0.519**	0.331	0.235	0.174	0.191	0.376
TranSQ-RS	0.484	0.332	0.236	0.171	0.206	0.359
TranSQ	0.484	**0.333**	**0.238**	**0.175**	**0.207**	**0.415**
$\triangle$	−0.035	+0.002	+0.003	+0.001	+0.003	+0.039

Baselines and Evaluation Metrics. We compare our approach with representative models for image captioning, such as NIC [28], AdaAtt [23], Att2in [27] and $\mathcal{M}^2$ Trans. [8], and state-of-the-art medical report generation models, such as CoAtt [13], HRGR [17], CMaAS-RL [12], GDGPT [1], CMCL [19], R2Gen [7], MedWriter [31], PPKED [20], AlignTransformer [32] and KGAE [21]. All the proposed metrics are referenced from the original paper. Besides, to prove that the performance of TranSQ comes from the precise predictions of the single sentences rather than the ordering strategy, we provide the 10-fold average performance of TranSQ prediction with random-ordered sentences, named TranSQ-RS.

To fairly compare with existing models, we follow the principle of existing works to evaluate the performance of our model in terms of both natural language generation (NLG) and clinical efficacy (CE). We measure the context matching by adopting the evaluation toolkit [6] to calculate the widely-used NLG metrics, i.e., BLEU [24], METEOR [3], and ROUGE-L [18]. The clinical efficacy is evaluated by Precision, Recall, and F1 score of the prediction on 14 categories [11], including thoracic diseases and support devices.

Implementation Details. We adopt the Vision Transformer model ViT-B/32 that pre-trained on *ImageNet-1K* to initialize the visual extractor. To match its setting, all the input images are resized into 384×384 and split into 32×32 patches. The visual extractor module extracts the flattened patch features into 768-dimension. Note that we used two images of one patient as input for the IU X-Ray dataset to ensure consistency with the experiment settings of previous work. The values of the other parameters of the model are randomly initialized. The sentence embeddings are generated by a pre-trained MPNet model [26], and all elements of the sentencing database are the sentences in the training sets.

Table 2. Comparisons of TranSQ model with previous studies on MIMIC-CXR with respect to NLG and CE metrics. $\triangle$ denotes the improvements to the best baseline.

Method	NLG Metrics						CE Metrics		
	BL-1	BL-2	BL-3	BL-4	MTR	RG-L	P	R	F-1
NIC [28]	0.299	0.184	0.121	0.084	0.124	0.263	0.249	0.203	0.204
AdaAtt [23]	0.299	0.185	0.124	0.088	0.118	0.266	0.268	0.186	0.181
Att2in [27]	0.325	0.203	0.136	0.096	0.134	0.276	0.322	0.239	0.249
$\mathcal{M}^2$ Trans. [8]	0.238	0.151	0.102	0.067	0.110	0.249	0.331	0.224	0.228
Transformer [7]	0.314	0.192	0.127	0.090	0.125	0.265	0.197	0.145	0.133
CMCL [21]	0.344	0.217	0.140	0.097	0.133	0.281			
R2Gen [7]	0.353	0.218	0.145	0.103	0.142	0.277	0.333	0.273	0.276
PPKED [20]	0.360	0.224	0.149	0.106	0.149	0.284	–	–	–
AlignTransformer [32]	0.378	0.235	0.156	0.112	0.158	0.283	–	–	–
KGAE [21]	0.369	0.231	0.156	**0.118**	0.153	**0.295**	0.389	0.362	0.355
TranSQ-RS	**0.423**	0.259	0.168	0.112	0.167	0.263	**0.482**	**0.563**	**0.519**
TranSQ	**0.423**	**0.261**	**0.171**	0.116	**0.168**	0.286			
$\triangle$	+0.045	+0.026	+0.015	−0.002	+0.010	−0.009	+0.093	+0.201	+0.164

We set the semantic query number K to 50 for the MIMIC-CXR dataset and 25 for the IU X-Ray dataset. For both datasets, we set the scale factor of bipartite matching loss $\mu = 0.5$ and the scale factor of loss function $\lambda = 1$. The hyper-parameters of DB-Loss followed the settings on the COCO-MLT dataset in [30]. In the training process of both datasets, the batch size is set to 64, and the optimizer is Adamw [22] with a learning rate of 1e-4 for parameter optimization with linear decay. All the experiments run on an Nvidia A100 GPU.

3.2   Results and Analyses

Comparison with Baselines. We evaluated the performance of our model (denoted as *TranSQ*) with the existing models on both IU X-Ray and MIMIC-CXR datasets. Table 1 reports the NLG metrics on IU X-Ray dataset, and Table 2 reports both NLG and CE results on MIMIC-CXR dataset, where *BL-n* denotes BLEU score using up to n-grams; *MTR* and *RG-L* denote METEOR and ROUGE-L, respectively; and *P*, *R* and *F-1* denote Precision, Recall and F1 Score, respectively. The results show that TranSQ achieves state-of-the-art neural language generation results. In terms of clinical efficiency on the MIMIC-CXR dataset, TranSQ achieves a 0.482 precision score, 0.563 recall score, and 0.519 F1-score, respectively, which significantly outperforms the state-of-the-art model KGAE [21]. The superior clinical efficacy scores demonstrate the capability of our model to generate higher quality descriptions for clinical abnormalities than existing models. Note that our method achieves the clinical efficacy improvement without introducing abnormality terms like other existing methods, which indicates that the trained latent topics can effectively and discriminately represent the actual abnormality definitions.

Besides, TranSQ achieves state-of-the-art performance on NGL metrics on both datasets even with random-ordered sentences, which indicates that the model performance improvements come from the precise predictions of single sentences rather than a well-designed sentence ordering strategy.

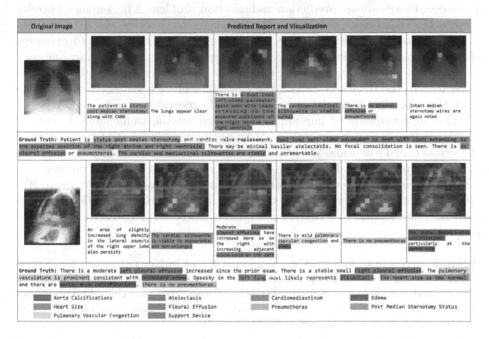

Fig. 2. Illustrations of the generated reports compared to the ground-truth reports and interpreted with the sentence-level visualizations. To better distinguish the content in the reports, different colors highlight the matched medical terms.

Visualized Interpretation. To further investigate the effectiveness of our model, we perform a qualitative analysis on some cases. Figure 2 shows two examples from the frontal and lateral viewed chest X-ray images from MIMIC-CXR as well as the comparison between ground-truth and generated reports, where the different colors on the texts indicate the matched medical terms. It is observed that the auto-generated descriptions are highly aligned with those written by radiologists about the critical medical concerns, including the relatively rare terms like "*Post Median Sternotomy Status*" and "*Aortic Calcification*".

As well, we present the visual-semantic attention maps for each sentence. It is evident that the textual description is highly consistent with the visual interests, indicating the strong correlation between visual and semantic representations. To the best of our knowledge, it is the first time to present the sentence-level visualized interpretations with respect to the medical report generation task. We argue that this interpretation form is more comprehensible and applicable than existing works with paragraph- or word-level interpretations.

4   Conclusion and Discussion

In this study, we propose a *Transformer-based Semantic Query* (TranSQ) approach to address the medical report generation problem. We consider the problem a sentence candidate set prediction and selection problem. The semantic encoder queries the visual features of the medical images to generate the semantic features for sentence retrieval and selection. The experiments verify the effectiveness of our approach, especially the significant improvements in the clinical efficacy metrics. In addition, our method can generate reliable sentence-level interpretations to help the doctors evaluate the credibility of each sentence, showing the clinical application potential as an auxiliary diagnostic approach.

The improvements of our approach depend on the tremendous success of large-scale pre-training research on the transformer. The initial parameters of the visual transformer and the sentence embedding generator are pre-trained on large-scale open-source data. Large-scale pre-training on the specific domain may benefit our model and related problems. Moreover, considering the expressive flexibility limitation of sentence retrieval, it deserves further attention to apply each semantic feature to a conditional linguistic decoder [25] to achieve sentence generation.

Acknowledgments. This work was supported in part by Key Laboratory for Corneal Diseases Research of Zhejiang Province, Key R & D Projects of the Ministry of Science and Technology (2020YFC0832500), Project by Shanghai AI Laboratory (P22KS00111), and the Starry Night Science Fund of Zhejiang University Shanghai Institute for Advanced Study (SN-ZJU-SIAS-0010).

References

1. Alfarghaly, O., Khaled, R., Elkorany, A., Helal, M., Fahmy, A.: Automated radiology report generation using conditioned transformers. Inf. Med. Unlocked **24**, 100557 (2021)
2. Anderson, P., et al.: Bottom-up and top-down attention for image captioning and visual question answering. In: Proceedings of the IEEE Conference on Computer Vision and Pattern Recognition, pp. 6077–6086 (2018)
3. Banerjee, S., Lavie, A.: Meteor: An automatic metric for MT evaluation with improved correlation with human judgments. In: Proceedings of the ACL Workshop on Intrinsic and Extrinsic Evaluation Measures for Machine Translation and/or Summarization, pp. 65–72 (2005)

4. Brady, A., Laoide, R.Ó., McCarthy, P., McDermott, R.: Discrepancy and error in radiology: concepts, causes and consequences. Ulster Med. J. **81**(1), 3 (2012)
5. Carion, N., et al.: End-to-end object detection with transformers. In: Vedaldi, A., Bischof, H., Brox, T., Frahm, J.-M. (eds.) ECCV 2020. LNCS, vol. 12346, pp. 213–229. Springer, Cham (2020). https://doi.org/10.1007/978-3-030-58452-8_13
6. Chen, X., et al.: Microsoft coco captions: data collection and evaluation server. arXiv preprint arXiv:1504.00325 (2015)
7. Chen, Z., Song, Y., Chang, T.H., Wan, X.: Generating radiology reports via memory-driven transformer. arXiv preprint arXiv:2010.16056 (2020)
8. Cornia, M., Stefanini, M., Baraldi, L., Cucchiara, R.: Meshed-memory transformer for image captioning. In: Proceedings of the IEEE/CVF Conference on Computer Vision and Pattern Recognition, pp. 10578–10587 (2020)
9. Demner-Fushman, D., et al.: Preparing a collection of radiology examinations for distribution and retrieval. J. Am. Med. Inf. Assoc. **23**(2), 304–310 (2016)
10. Dosovitskiy, A., et al.: An image is worth 16x16 words: transformers for image recognition at scale. arXiv preprint arXiv:2010.11929 (2020)
11. Irvin, J., et al.: Chexpert: a large chest radiograph dataset with uncertainty labels and expert comparison. In: Proceedings of the AAAI Conference on Artificial Intelligence, vol. 33, pp. 590–597 (2019)
12. Jing, B., Wang, Z., Xing, E.: Show, describe and conclude: on exploiting the structure information of chest x-ray reports. arXiv preprint arXiv:2004.12274 (2020)
13. Jing, B., Xie, P., Xing, E.: On the automatic generation of medical imaging reports. In: Proceedings of the 56th Annual Meeting of the Association for Computational Linguistics, vol. 1, pp. 2577–2586 (2018)
14. Johnson, A.E., et al.: Mimic-cxr-jpg, a large publicly available database of labeled chest radiographs. arXiv preprint arXiv:1901.07042 (2019)
15. Kuhn, H.W.: The Hungarian method for the assignment problem. Naval Res. Logist. Quart. **2**(1–2), 83–97 (1955)
16. Li, C.Y., Liang, X., Hu, Z., Xing, E.P.: Knowledge-driven encode, retrieve, paraphrase for medical image report generation. In: Proceedings of the AAAI Conference on Artificial Intelligence, vol. 33, pp. 6666–6673 (2019)
17. Li, Y., Liang, X., Hu, Z., Xing, E.P.: Hybrid retrieval-generation reinforced agent for medical image report generation. Adv. Neural Inf. Process. Syst. **31** (2018)
18. Lin, C.Y.: Rouge: a package for automatic evaluation of summaries. In: Text Summarization Branches Out, pp. 74–81 (2004)
19. Liu, F., Ge, S., Wu, X.: Competence-based multimodal curriculum learning for medical report generation. In: Proceedings of the 59th Annual Meeting of the Association for Computational Linguistics and the 11th International Joint Conference on Natural Language Processing (Volume 1: Long Papers), pp. 3001–3012 (2021)
20. Liu, F., Wu, X., Ge, S., Fan, W., Zou, Y.: Exploring and distilling posterior and prior knowledge for radiology report generation. In: IEEE Conference on Computer Vision and Pattern Recognition, pp. 13753–13762 (2021)
21. Liu, F., You, C., Wu, X., Ge, S., Sun, X., et al.: Auto-encoding knowledge graph for unsupervised medical report generation. Adv. Neural Inf. Process. Syst. **34** (2021)
22. Loshchilov, I., Hutter, F.: Fixing weight decay regularization in Adam. arXiv preprint arXiv:1711.05101 (2017)
23. Lu, J., Xiong, C., Parikh, D., Socher, R.: Knowing when to look: adaptive attention via a visual sentinel for image captioning. In: Proceedings of the IEEE Conference on Computer Vision and Pattern Recognition, pp. 375–383 (2017)

24. Papineni, K., Roukos, S., Ward, T., Zhu, W.J.: Bleu: a method for automatic evaluation of machine translation. In: Proceedings of the 40th Annual Meeting of the Association for Computational Linguistics, pp. 311–318 (2002)
25. Radford, A., et al.: Language models are unsupervised multitask learners. OpenAI blog **1**(8), 9 (2019)
26. Reimers, N., Gurevych, I.: Sentence-bert: sentence embeddings using siamese bert-networks. In: Proceedings of the 2019 Conference on Empirical Methods in Natural Language Processing (2019). https://arxiv.org/abs/1908.10084
27. Rennie, S.J., Marcheret, E., Mroueh, Y., Ross, J., Goel, V.: Self-critical sequence training for image captioning. In: Proceedings of the IEEE Conference on Computer Vision and Pattern Recognition, pp. 7008–7024 (2017)
28. Vinyals, O., Toshev, A., Bengio, S., Erhan, D.: Show and tell: a neural image caption generator. In: Proceedings of the IEEE Conference on Computer Vision and Pattern Recognition, pp. 3156–3164 (2015)
29. Wei, X., Zhang, T., Li, Y., Zhang, Y., Wu, F.: Multi-modality cross attention network for image and sentence matching. In: Proceedings of the IEEE/CVF Conference on Computer Vision and Pattern Recognition, pp. 10941–10950 (2020)
30. Wu, T., Huang, Q., Liu, Z., Wang, Y., Lin, D.: Distribution-balanced loss for multi-label classification in long-tailed datasets. In: Vedaldi, A., Bischof, H., Brox, T., Frahm, J.-M. (eds.) ECCV 2020. LNCS, vol. 12349, pp. 162–178. Springer, Cham (2020). https://doi.org/10.1007/978-3-030-58548-8_10
31. Yang, X., Ye, M., You, Q., Ma, F.: Writing by memorizing: Hierarchical retrieval-based medical report generation. arXiv preprint arXiv:2106.06471 (2021)
32. You, D., Liu, F., Ge, S., Xie, X., Zhang, J., Wu, X.: AlignTransformer: hierarchical alignment of visual regions and disease tags for medical report generation. In: de Bruijne, M., et al. (eds.) MICCAI 2021. LNCS, vol. 12903, pp. 72–82. Springer, Cham (2021). https://doi.org/10.1007/978-3-030-87199-4_7

Pseudo Bias-Balanced Learning for Debiased Chest X-Ray Classification

Luyang Luo[1]([✉]), Dunyuan Xu[1], Hao Chen[2], Tien-Tsin Wong[1], and Pheng-Ann Heng[1]

[1] Department of Computer Science and Engineering,
The Chinese University of Hong Kong, Hong Kong, China
`lyluo@cse.cuhk.edu.hk`
[2] Department of Computer Science and Engineering,
The Hong Kong University of Science and Technology, Hong Kong, China

Abstract. Deep learning models were frequently reported to learn from shortcuts like dataset biases. As deep learning is playing an increasingly important role in the modern healthcare system, it is of great need to combat shortcut learning in medical data as well as develop unbiased and trustworthy models. In this paper, we study the problem of developing debiased chest X-ray diagnosis models from the biased training data without knowing exactly the bias labels. We start with the observations that the imbalance of bias distribution is one of the key reasons causing shortcut learning, and the dataset biases are preferred by the model if they were easier to be learned than the intended features. Based on these observations, we proposed a novel algorithm, pseudo bias-balanced learning, which first captures and predicts per-sample bias labels via generalized cross entropy loss and then trains a debiased model using pseudo bias labels and bias-balanced softmax function. We constructed several chest X-ray datasets with various dataset bias situations and demonstrated with extensive experiments that our proposed method achieved consistent improvements over other state-of-the-art approaches (Code available at https://github.com/LLYXC/PBBL.).

Keywords: Debias · Shortcut learning · Chest X-ray

1 Introduction

To date, deep learning (DL) has achieved comparable or even superior performance to experts on many medical image analysis tasks [17]. Robust and trustworthy DL models are hence of greater need than ever to unleash their huge potential in solving real-world healthcare problems. However, a common trust failure of DL was frequently found where the models reach a high accuracy without learning from the intended features. For example, using backgrounds to

---

Supplementary Information The online version contains supplementary material available at https://doi.org/10.1007/978-3-031-16452-1_59.

distinguish foreground objects [19], using the gender to classify hair colors [20], or worse yet, using patients' position to determine COVID-19 pneumonia from chest X-rays [4]. Such a phenomenon is called *shortcut learning* [5], where the DL models choose unintended features, or *dataset bias*, for making decisions.

More or less, biases could be generated during the creation of the datasets [22]. As the dataset biases frequently co-occurred with the primary targets, the model might take shortcuts by learning from such spurious correlation to minimize the empirical risk over the training data. As a result, dramatic performance drops could be observed when applying the models onto other data which do not obtain the same covariate shift [13]. In the field of medical image analysis, shortcut learning has also been frequently reported, such as using hospital tokens to recognize pneumonia cases [25]; learning confounding patient and healthcare variables to identify fracture cases; relying on chest drains to classify pneumothorax case [16]; or leveraging shortcuts to determine COVID-19 patients [4]. These findings reveal that shortcut learning makes deep models less explainable and less trustworthy to doctors as well as patients, and addressing shortcut learning is a far-reaching topic for modern medical image analysis.

To combat shortcut learning and develop debiased models, a branch of previous works use data re-weighting to learn from less biased data. For instance, REPAIR [12] proposed to solve a minimax problem between the classifier parameters and dataset re-sampling weights. Group distributional robust optimization [20] prioritized worst group learning, which was also mainly implemented by data re-weighting. Yoon et al. [24] proposed to address dataset bias with a weighted loss and a dynamic data sampler. Another direction of works emphasizes learning invariance across different environments, such as invariant risk minimization [1], contrastive learning [21], and mutual information minimization [29]. However, these methods all required dataset biases to be explicitly annotated, which might be infeasible for realistic situations, especially for medical images. Recently, some approaches have made efforts to relax the dependency on explicit bias labels. Nam et al. [15] proposed to learn a debiased model by mining the high-loss samples with a highly-biased model. Lee et al. [11] further incorporated feature swapping between the biased and debiased models to augment the training samples. Yet, very few methods attempted to efficiently address shortcut learning in medical data without explicitly labeling the biases.

In this paper, we are pioneered in tackling the challenging problem of developing debiased medical image analysis models without explicit labels on the bias attributes. We first observed that the imbalance of bias distribution is one of the key causes to shortcut learning, and dataset biases would be preferred when they were easier to be learned than the intended features. We thereby proposed a novel algorithm, namely pseudo bias-balanced learning (PBBL). PBBL first develops a highly-biased model by emphasizing learning from the easier features. The biased model is then used to generate pseudo bias labels that are later utilized to train a debiased model with a bias-balanced softmax function. We constructed several chest X-ray datasets with various bias situations to evaluate the efficacy of the debiased model. We demonstrated that our method was effective and robust under all scenarios and achieved consistent improvements over other state-of-the-art approaches.

2 Methodology

2.1 Problem Statement and Study Materials

Let X be the set of input data, Y the set of target attributes that we want the model to learn, and B the set of bias attributes that are irrelevant to the targets. Our goal is to learn a function $f : X \to Y$ that would not be affected by the dataset bias. We here built the following chest X-ray datasets for our study.

Source-Biased Pneumonia (SbP): For the training set, we first randomly sampled 5,000 pneumonia cases from MIMIC-CXR [8] and 5,000 healthy cases (no findings) from NIH [23]. We then sampled $5,000 \times r\%$ pneumonia cases from NIH and the same amount of healthy cases from MIMIC-CXR. Here, the `data source` became the dataset bias, and `health condition` was the target to be learned. We varied r to be 1, 5, and 10, which led to biased sample ratios of 99%, 95%, and 90%, respectively. We created the validation and the testing sets by equally sampling 200 and 400 images from each group (w/ or w/o pneumonia; from NIH or MIMIC-CXR), respectively. Moreover, as overcoming dataset bias could lead to better external validation performance [5], we included 400 pneumonia cases and 400 healthy cases from Padchest [2] to evaluate the generalization capability of the proposed method. Note that we converted all images to JPEG format to prevent the data format from being another dataset bias.

Gender-Biased Pneumothorax (GbP): Previous study [10] pointed out that gender imbalance in medical datasets could lead to a biased and unfair classifier. Based on this finding, we constructed two training sets from the NIH dataset [23]: 1) **GbP-Tr1**: 800 male samples with pneumothorax, 100 male samples with no findings, 800 female samples with no findings, and 100 female samples with pneumothorax; 2) **GbP-Tr2**: 800 female samples with pneumothorax, 100 female samples with no findings, 800 male samples with no findings, and 100 male samples with pneumothorax. For validation and testing sets, we equally collected 150 and 250 samples from each group (w/ or w/o pneumothorax; male or female), respectively. Here, `gender` became a dataset bias and `health condition` was the target that the model was aimed to learn.

Following previous studies [11,15], we call a sample bias-aligned if its target and bias attributes are highly-correlated in the training set (e.g., (`pneumonia`, `MIMIC-CXR`) or (`healthy`, `NIH`) in the SbP dataset). On the contrary, a sample is said to be bias-conflicting if the target and bias attributes are dissimilar to the previous situation (e.g., (`pneumonia`, `NIH`) or (`healthy`, `MIMIC-CXR`)).

2.2 Bias-Balanced Softmax

Our first observation is that *bias-imbalanced training data leads to a biased classifier*. Based on the SbP dataset, we trained two different settings: i) SbP with $r = 10$; ii) Bias balancing by equally sampling 500 cases from each group. The

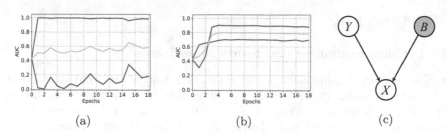

(a)   (b)   (c)

Fig. 1. We show (a) the testing results in AUC curves of a model trained on Source-biased Pneumonia dataset; (b) the testing results in AUC curves of a model trained with bias-balanced pneumonia dataset. We further show our causal assumption of data generation process in (c). Blue curves: results on bias-aligned samples; Red curves: results on bias-conflicting samples; Yellow curves: averaged results of bias-aligned AUC and bias-conflicting AUC. (Color figure online)

results are shown in Fig. 1a and Fig. 1b, respectively. Clearly, when the dataset is bias-imbalanced, learning bias-aligned samples were favored. On the contrary, balancing the biases mitigates shortcut learning even with less training data.

For a better interpretation, we adopt the causal assumption [14] that the data X is generated from both the target attributes Y and the bias attributes B, which are independent to each other, as shown in Fig. 1c. The conditional probability $p(y = j|x)$ hence can be formalized as follows:

$$p(y = j|x, b) = \frac{p(x|y = j, b)p(y = j|b)}{p(x|b)}, \tag{1}$$

where $p(y = j|b)$ raises a distributional discrepancy between the biased training data and the ideal bias-balanced data (e.g., the testing data). Moreover, according to our experimental analysis before, the imbalance also made the model favor learning from bias-aligned samples, which finally resulted in a biased classifier. To tackle the bias-imbalance situation, let k be the number of classes and $n_{j,b}$ the number of training data of target class j with bias class b, we could derive a bias-balanced softmax [6,18] as follows:

Theorem 1. *(Bias-balanced softmax [6]) Assume $\phi_j = p(y = j|x, b) = \frac{p(x|y=j,b)}{p(x|b)} \cdot \frac{1}{k}$ to be the desired conditional probability of the bias-balanced dataset, and $\hat{\phi}_j = \frac{p(x|y=j,b)}{\hat{p}(x|b)} \cdot \frac{n_{j,b}}{\sum_{i=1}^{k} n_{i,b}}$ to be the conditional probability of the biased dataset. If ϕ can be expressed by the standard Softmax function of the logits η generated by the model, i.e., $\phi_j = \frac{exp(\eta_j)}{\sum_{i=1}^{k} exp(\eta_i)}$, then $\hat{\phi}$ can be expressed as*

$$\hat{\phi}_j = \frac{p(y = j|b) \cdot \exp(\eta_j)}{\sum_{i=1}^{k} p(y = i|b) \cdot \exp(\eta_i)}. \tag{2}$$

Theorem 1 (proof provided in the supplementary) shows that bias-balanced softmax could well solve the distributional discrepancy between the bias-imbalanced training set and the bias-balanced testing set. Denoting M the number of training data, we obtain the bias-balanced loss for training a debiased model:

$$\mathcal{L}_{BS}(f(x), y, b) = -\frac{1}{M} \sum_{i=1}^{M} log \left(\frac{p(y = j|b) \cdot \exp(\eta_j)}{\sum_{i=1}^{k} p(y = i|b) \cdot \exp(\eta_i)} \right) \tag{3}$$

However, this loss requires estimation of the bias distribution on the training set, while comprehensively labeling all kinds of attributes would be unpractical, especially for medical data. In the next section, we elaborate on how to obtain the estimation of the bias distribution without knowing the bias labels.

2.3 Bias Capturing with Generalized Cross Entropy Loss

Inspired by [15], we conducted two experiments based on the Source-biased Pneumonia dataset with $r = 10$, where we set the models to classify data source (Fig. 2a) or health condition (Fig. 2b), respectively. Apparently, the model has almost no signs of fitting on the bias attribute (health condition) when it's required to distinguish data source. On the other hand, the model quickly learns the biases (data source) when set to classify pneumonia from healthy cases. From these findings, one could conclude that *dataset biases would be preferred when they were easier to be learned than the intended features.*

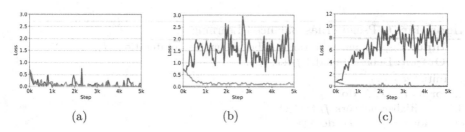

(a)   (b)   (c)

Fig. 2. Based on the SbP dataset, we show the learning curve of the vanilla model by setting the {target, bias} pair to be (a) {data source, health condition} and (b) {health condition, data source}. We also show in (c) the learning curve of a highly-biased model trained with GCE loss with the {target, bias} pair being {health condition, data source}. Blue curves: loss of bias-aligned samples; Red curves: loss of bias-conflicting samples. (Color figure online)

Based on this observation, we could develop a model to capture the dataset bias by making it quickly fit on the easier features from the training data. Therefore, we adopt the generalized cross entropy (GCE) loss [27], which was originally proposed to address noisy labels by fitting on the easier clean data and slowly memorizing the hard noisy samples. Inheriting this idea, the GCE loss could also quickly capture easy and biased samples than the categorical cross entropy (CE) loss. Giving $f(x; \theta)$ the softmax output of the model, denoting $f_{y=j}(x; \theta)$

the probability of x being classified to class $y = j$ and θ the parameters of model f, the GCE loss is formulated as follows:

$$\mathcal{L}_{\text{GCE}}(f(x;\theta), y = j) = \frac{1 - f_{y=j}(x;\theta)^q}{q}, \tag{4}$$

where q is a hyper-parameter. The gradient of GCE is $\frac{\partial \mathcal{L}_{\text{GCE}}(f(x;\theta),y=j)}{\partial \theta} = f_{y=j}(x;\theta)^q \frac{\partial \mathcal{L}_{\text{CE}}(f(x;\theta),y=j)}{\partial \theta}$ (proof provided in the supplementary), which explicitly assigns weights on the CE loss based on the agreement between model's predictions and the labels. As shown in Fig. 2c, GCE loss fits the bias-aligned samples quickly while yields much higher loss on the bias-conflicting samples.

2.4   Bias-Balanced Learning with Pseudo Bias

With the afore discussed observations and analysis, we propose a debiasing algorithm, namely Pseudo Bias Balanced Learning. We first train a biased model $f_B(x;\theta_B)$ with the GCE loss and calculate the corresponding receiver operating characteristics (ROC) over the training set. Based on the ROC curve, we compute the sensitivity $u(\tau)$ and specificity $v(\tau)$ under each threshold τ and then assign pseudo bias labels to each sample with the following:

$$\tilde{b}(f_B(x;\theta_B)) = \begin{cases} 1, & \text{if } f_B(x;\theta_B) \geq \text{argmax}_\tau(u(\tau) + v(\tau)); \\ 0, & \text{otherwise.} \end{cases} \tag{5}$$

Algorithm 1. Pseudo Bias Balanced Learning

    Input: θ_B, θ_D, image x, target label y, numbers of iterations T_B, T_D, N.
    Output: Debiased model $f_D(x;\theta_D)$.
1: Initialize $\tilde{b} = y$.
2: **for** n=1, $\cdots$, N **do**
3:    Initialize network $f_B(x;\theta_B)$.
4:    **for** t=1, $\cdots$, T_B **do**
5:        Update $f_B(x;\theta_B)$ with $\mathcal{L}_{\text{GCE}}(f_B(x;\theta_B), \tilde{b})$
6:    **end for**
7:    Calculate u, v, and τ over training set.
8:    Update pseudo bias labels $\tilde{b}$ with Eq. 5.
9: **end for**
10: Initialize network $f_D(x;\theta_D)$.
11: **for** t=1, $\cdots$, T_D **do**
12:    Update $f_D(x;\theta_D)$ with $\mathcal{L}_{\text{BS}}(f_D(x;\theta_D), y, \tilde{b})$
13: **end for**

Moreover, as the biased model could also memorize the correct prediction for the hard bias-conflicting cases [26], we propose to capture and enhance the bias via iterative model training. Finally, we train our debiased model $f_D(x;\theta_D)$ based on the pseudo bias labels and the bias-balance softmax function, with different weights from θ_B. The holistic approach is summarized in Algorithm 1.

3 Experiments

Evaluation metrics are the area under the ROC curve (AUC) with four criteria: i) AUC on bias-aligned samples; ii) AUC on bias-conflicting samples; iii) Average of bias-aligned AUC and bias-conflicting AUC, which we call balanced-AUC; iv) AUC on all samples. The difference between the first two metrics could reflect whether the model is biased, while the latter two metrics provide unbiased evaluations on the testing data.

Compared methods included four other approaches: i) Vanilla model, which did not use any debiasing strategy and could be broadly regarded as a lower bound. ii) Group Distribution Robust Optimization (G-DRO) [20], which used the bias ground truth and could be regarded as the upper bound. G-DRO divides training data into different groups according to their targets and bias labels. It then optimized the model with priority on the worst-performing group and finally achieved robustness on every single group. As in practical scenarios, the labels for the dataset biases may not be known, we also implemented iii) Learning from Failure (LfF) [15], which developed a debiased model by weighted losses from a biased model; and iv) Disentangled Feature Augmentation (DFA) [11], which was based on LfF and further adds feature swapping and augmentation between the debiased and biased models.

Model training protocol is as follows: We used the same backbone, DenseNet-121 [7] with pre-trained weights from [3], for every method. Particularly, we fixed the weights of DenseNet, replaced the final output layer with three linear layers, and used the rectified linear units as the intermediate activation function. We ran each model with three different random seeds, and reported the test results

Table 1. AUC results on SbP dataset. Best results without ground truth bias labels are emphasized in **bold**. † means the method uses ground truth bias labels.

Bias ratio	Method	Aligned	Conflicting	Balanced	Overall	External
90%	G-DRO† [20]	$70.02_{\pm 2.20}$	$89.80_{\pm 0.87}$	$79.94_{\pm 0.68}$	$80.23_{\pm 0.37}$	$90.06_{\pm 0.32}$
	Vanilla	$\mathbf{96.51}_{\pm 0.26}$	$31.21_{\pm 3.04}$	$63.86_{\pm 1.39}$	$69.84_{\pm 1.32}$	$71.57_{\pm 0.90}$
	LfF [15]	$68.57_{\pm 2.16}$	$\mathbf{87.46}_{\pm 2.17}$	$78.02_{\pm 0.18}$	$78.26_{\pm 0.18}$	$87.71_{\pm 2.66}$
	DFA [11]	$74.63_{\pm 4.61}$	$83.30_{\pm 3.96}$	$78.96_{\pm 0.33}$	$78.76_{\pm 0.15}$	$74.58_{\pm 7.56}$
	Ours	$76.82_{\pm 2.80}$	$85.75_{\pm 0.32}$	$\mathbf{80.49}_{\pm 0.20}$	$\mathbf{78.78}_{\pm 3.02}$	$\mathbf{89.96}_{\pm 0.69}$
95%	G-DRO† [20]	$68.65_{\pm 1.21}$	$89.86_{\pm 0.67}$	$79.26_{\pm 0.47}$	$79.8_{\pm 0.36}$	$90.16_{\pm 0.73}$
	Vanilla	$\mathbf{97.91}_{\pm 0.75}$	$20.45_{\pm 5.96}$	$59.18_{\pm 2.61}$	$67.11_{\pm 1.85}$	$68.61_{\pm 3.50}$
	LfF [15]	$69.56_{\pm 2.01}$	$\mathbf{86.43}_{\pm 1.67}$	$77.99_{\pm 0.18}$	$78.28_{\pm 0.22}$	$\mathbf{88.56}_{\pm 3.37}$
	DFA [11]	$69.04_{\pm 4.21}$	$84.94_{\pm 2.56}$	$76.99_{\pm 0.85}$	$77.26_{\pm 0.49}$	$76.37_{\pm 3.26}$
	Ours	$71.72_{\pm 6.65}$	$84.68_{\pm 3.49}$	$\mathbf{78.20}_{\pm 0.20}$	$78.04_{\pm 3.46}$	$82.65_{\pm 0.40}$
99%	G-DRO† [20]	$74.30_{\pm 2.28}$	$85.18_{\pm 1.26}$	$79.74_{\pm 0.55}$	$79.71_{\pm 0.40}$	$89.87_{\pm 0.64}$
	Vanilla	$\mathbf{99.03}_{\pm 0.95}$	$4.93_{\pm 3.68}$	$51.98_{\pm 1.60}$	$59.21_{\pm 3.76}$	$60.79_{\pm 0.98}$
	LfF [15]	$77.50_{\pm 11.08}$	$64.38_{\pm 8.75}$	$70.94_{\pm 1.30}$	$71.86_{\pm 1.72}$	$73.90_{\pm 4.42}$
	DFA [11]	$69.33_{\pm 1.74}$	$75.48_{\pm 2.61}$	$72.40_{\pm 0.48}$	$72.49_{\pm 0.45}$	$61.67_{\pm 6.86}$
	Ours	$72.40_{\pm 0.71}$	$\mathbf{77.61}_{\pm 0.45}$	$\mathbf{75.00}_{\pm 0.18}$	$\mathbf{74.70}_{\pm 0.14}$	$\mathbf{78.87}_{\pm 0.44}$

corresponding to the best validation AUC. Each model is optimized with Adam [9] for around 1,000 steps with batch size of 256 and learning rate of 1e-4. N in Algorithm 1 is empirically set to 1 for SbP dataset and 2 for GbP dataset, respectively. q in GCE loss is set to 0.7 as recommended in [27].

Table 2. AUC results on GbP dataset. Best results without ground truth bias labels are emphasized in **bold**. † means the method uses ground truth bias labels.

Training	Method	Aligned	Conflicting	Balanced	Overall
GbP-Tr1	G-DRO† [20]	$85.81_{\pm0.16}$	$83.96_{\pm0.17}$	$84.86_{\pm0.05}$	$84.93_{\pm0.01}$
	Vanilla	$89.42_{\pm0.25}$	$77.21_{\pm0.33}$	$83.31_{\pm0.05}$	$83.75_{\pm0.05}$
	LfF [15]	$88.73_{\pm1.34}$	$77.47_{\pm0.09}$	$83.10_{\pm0.64}$	$83.46_{\pm0.71}$
	DFA [11]	$86.12_{\pm0.46}$	$\mathbf{77.92_{\pm0.23}}$	$82.02_{\pm0.31}$	$82.23_{\pm0.30}$
	Ours	$\mathbf{90.17_{\pm0.42}}$	$77.07_{\pm1.73}$	$\mathbf{83.62_{\pm0.68}}$	$\mathbf{84.13_{\pm0.56}}$
GbP-Tr2	G-DRO† [20]	$83.76_{\pm1.59}$	$85.14_{\pm0.31}$	$84.45_{\pm0.65}$	$84.42_{\pm0.61}$
	Vanilla	$\mathbf{89.39_{\pm0.85}}$	$76.13_{\pm0.93}$	$82.76_{\pm0.78}$	$82.93_{\pm0.78}$
	LfF [15]	$87.25_{\pm0.62}$	$79.07_{\pm0.96}$	$83.16_{\pm0.45}$	$83.19_{\pm0.44}$
	DFA [11]	$80.44_{\pm0.58}$	$\mathbf{85.51_{\pm0.57}}$	$82.98_{\pm0.19}$	$83.09_{\pm0.21}$
	Ours	$86.34_{\pm0.64}$	$81.69_{\pm2.67}$	$\mathbf{84.02_{\pm1.01}}$	$\mathbf{84.03_{\pm0.97}}$

Quantitative results on Source-biased Pneumonia dataset are reported in Table 1. With the increasing of bias ratio, the vanilla model became more and more biased and severe decreases in balanced-AUC and overall-AUC was observed. All other methods also showed decreases on the two metrics, while G-DRO shows quite robust performance under all situations. Meanwhile, our method achieved consistent improvement over the compared approaches under most of the situations, demonstrating its effectiveness in debiasing. Interestingly, the change of external testing performance appeared to be in line with the change of the balanced-AUC and overall AUC, which further revealed that overcoming shortcut learning improves the model's generalization capability. These findings demonstrated our method's effectiveness in solving shortcut learning, with potential in robustness and trustworthiness for real-world clinic usage.

Quantitative results on Gender-biased Pneumothorax dataset are reported in Table 2. By the performance of the vanilla model, gender bias may not affect the performance as severely as data source bias, but it could lead to serious fairness issues. We observed that G-DRO showed robust performance on the two different training sets. Among approaches that do not use ground truth bias labels, our proposed method achieved consistent improvement over others with the two different training sets. The results also showed the potential of our method in developing fair and trustworthy diagnosis models.

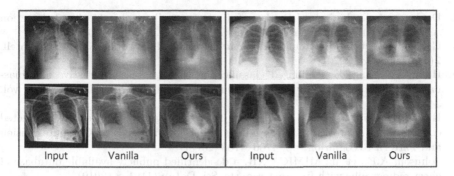

Fig. 3. Class activation map [28] generated from vanilla model and our method. Samples are from the SbP dataset (in blue box) and the GbP dataset (in red box), respectively. (Color figure online)

Qualitative results were visualized by class activation map [28], as shown in Fig. 3. It can be observed that vanilla model might look for evidence outside the lung regions, while our method could more correctly focus on the lung regions.

4 Conclusion

In this paper, we studied the causes and solutions for shortcut learning in medical image analysis, with chest X-ray as an example. We showed that shortcut learning occurs when the bias distribution is imbalanced, and the dataset bias is preferred when it is easier to be learned than the intended features. Based on these findings, we proposed a novel pseudo bias balanced learning algorithm to develop a debiased model without explicit labeling on the bias attribute. We also constructed several challenging debiasing datasets from public-available data. Extensive experiments demonstrated that our method overcame shortcut learning and achieved consistent improvements over other state-of-the-art methods under different scenarios, showing promising potential in developing robust, fair, and trustworthy diagnosis models.

Acknowledgement. This work was supported by Hong Kong Innovation and Technology Fund Project No. GHP/110/19SZ and ITS/170/20.

References

1. Arjovsky, M., Bottou, L., Gulrajani, I., Lopez-Paz, D.: Invariant risk minimization. arXiv preprint arXiv:1907.02893 (2019)
2. Bustos, A., Pertusa, A., Salinas, J.M., de la Iglesia-Vayá, M.: PadChest: a large chest x-ray image dataset with multi-label annotated reports. Med. Image Anal. **66**, 101797 (2020)
3. Cohen, J.P., et al.: TorchXRayVision: a library of chest x-ray datasets and models. arXiv preprint arXiv:2111.00595 (2021)

4. DeGrave, A.J., Janizek, J.D., Lee, S.I.: Ai for radiographic Covid-19 detection selects shortcuts over signal. Nat. Mach. Intell. **3**(7), 610–619 (2021)
5. Geirhos, R., et al.: Shortcut learning in deep neural networks. Nat. Mach. Intell. **2**(11), 665–673 (2020)
6. Hong, Y., Yang, E.: Unbiased classification through bias-contrastive and bias-balanced learning. In: Advances in Neural Information Processing Systems, vol. 34 (2021)
7. Huang, G., Liu, Z., Van Der Maaten, L., Weinberger, K.Q.: Densely connected convolutional networks. In: Proceedings of IEEE Conference on Computer Vision and Pattern Recognition, pp. 4700–4708 (2017)
8. Johnson, A.E., et al.: MIMIC-CXR, a de-identified publicly available database of chest radiographs with free-text reports. Sci. Data **6**(1), 1–8 (2019)
9. Kingma, D.P., Ba, J.: Adam: a method for stochastic optimization. In: Proceedings of International Conference on Learning Representations (2015)
10. Larrazabal, A.J., Nieto, N., Peterson, V., Milone, D.H., Ferrante, E.: Gender imbalance in medical imaging datasets produces biased classifiers for computer-aided diagnosis. Proc. Natl. Acad. Sci. **117**(23), 12592–12594 (2020)
11. Lee, J., Kim, E., Lee, J., Lee, J., Choo, J.: Learning debiased representation via disentangled feature augmentation. In: Advances in Neural Information Processing Systems, vol. 34 (2021)
12. Li, Y., Vasconcelos, N.: Repair: removing representation bias by dataset resampling. In: Proceedings of the IEEE/CVF Conference on Computer Vision and Pattern Recognition, pp. 9572–9581 (2019)
13. Luo, L., et al.: Rethinking annotation granularity for overcoming deep shortcut learning: a retrospective study on chest radiographs. arXiv preprint arXiv:2104.10553 (2021)
14. Mitrovic, J., McWilliams, B., Walker, J.C., Buesing, L.H., Blundell, C.: Representation learning via invariant causal mechanisms. In: International Conference on Learning Representations (2020)
15. Nam, J., Cha, H., Ahn, S.S., Lee, J., Shin, J.: Learning from failure: de-biasing classifier from biased classifier. In: Advances in Neural Information Processing Systems, vol. 33 (2020)
16. Oakden-Rayner, L., Dunnmon, J., Carneiro, G., Ré, C.: Hidden stratification causes clinically meaningful failures in machine learning for medical imaging. In: Proceedings of the ACM Conference on Health, Inference, and Learning, pp. 151–159 (2020)
17. Rajpurkar, P., Chen, E., Banerjee, O., Topol, E.J.: AI in health and medicine. Nat. Med. **28**(1), 31–38 (2022)
18. Ren, J., Yu, C., Ma, X., Zhao, H., Yi, S., et al.: Balanced meta-softmax for long-tailed visual recognition. Adv. Neural. Inf. Process. Syst. **33**, 4175–4186 (2020)
19. Ribeiro, M.T., Singh, S., Guestrin, C.: "Why should i trust you?" Explaining the predictions of any classifier. In: Proceedings of the 22nd ACM SIGKDD International Conference on Knowledge Discovery and Data Mining, pp. 1135–1144 (2016)
20. Sagawa, S., Koh, P.W., Hashimoto, T.B., Liang, P.: Distributionally robust neural networks for group shifts: on the importance of regularization for worst-case generalization. In: International Conference on Learning Representations (2020)
21. Tartaglione, E., Barbano, C.A., Grangetto, M.: End: entangling and disentangling deep representations for bias correction. In: Proceedings of the IEEE/CVF Conference on Computer Vision and Pattern Recognition, pp. 13508–13517 (2021)
22. Torralba, A., Efros, A.A.: Unbiased look at dataset bias. In: CVPR 2011, pp. 1521–1528. IEEE (2011)

23. Wang, X., Peng, Y., Lu, L., Lu, Z., Bagheri, M., Summers, R.M.: ChestX-ray8: hospital-scale chest x-ray database and benchmarks on weakly-supervised classification and localization of common thorax diseases. In: Proceedings of the IEEE Conference on Computer Vision and Pattern Recognition, pp. 2097–2106 (2017)
24. Yoon, C., Hamarneh, G., Garbi, R.: Generalizable feature learning in the presence of data bias and domain class imbalance with application to skin lesion classification. In: Shen, D., et al. (eds.) MICCAI 2019. LNCS, vol. 11767, pp. 365–373. Springer, Cham (2019). https://doi.org/10.1007/978-3-030-32251-9_40
25. Zech, J.R., Badgeley, M.A., Liu, M., Costa, A.B., Titano, J.J., Oermann, E.K.: Variable generalization performance of a deep learning model to detect pneumonia in chest radiographs: a cross-sectional study. PLoS Med. **15**(11), e1002683 (2018)
26. Zhang, C., Bengio, S., Hardt, M., Recht, B., Vinyals, O.: Understanding deep learning requires rethinking generalization. In: ICLR (2017)
27. Zhang, Z., Sabuncu, M.: Generalized cross entropy loss for training deep neural networks with noisy labels. In: Advances in Neural Information Processing Systems, vol. 31 (2018)
28. Zhou, B., Khosla, A., Lapedriza, A., Oliva, A., Torralba, A.: Learning deep features for discriminative localization. In: Proceedings of the IEEE Conference on Computer Vision and Pattern Recognition, pp. 2921–2929 (2016)
29. Zhu, W., Zheng, H., Liao, H., Li, W., Luo, J.: Learning bias-invariant representation by cross-sample mutual information minimization. In: Proceedings of the IEEE/CVF International Conference on Computer Vision, pp. 15002–15012 (2021)

Why Patient Data Cannot Be Easily Forgotten?

Ruolin Su[1(✉)], Xiao Liu[1], and Sotirios A. Tsaftaris[1,2]

[1] School of Engineering, University of Edinburgh, Edinburgh EH9 3FB, UK
{R.SU-1,Xiao.Liu,S.Tsaftaris}@ed.ac.uk
[2] The Alan Turing Institute, London, UK

Abstract. Rights provisioned within data protection regulations, permit patients to request that knowledge about their information be eliminated by data holders. With the advent of AI learned on data, one can imagine that such rights can extent to requests for forgetting knowledge of patient's data within AI models. However, forgetting patients' imaging data from AI models, is still an under-explored problem. In this paper, we study the influence of patient data on model performance and formulate two hypotheses for a patient's data: either they are common and similar to other patients or form edge cases, i.e. unique and rare cases. We show that it is not possible to easily *forget patient data*. We propose a targeted forgetting approach to perform patient-wise forgetting. Extensive experiments on the benchmark Automated Cardiac Diagnosis Challenge dataset showcase the improved performance of the proposed targeted forgetting approach as opposed to a state-of-the-art method.

Keywords: Privacy · Patient-wise forgetting · Scrubbing · Learning

1 Introduction

Apart from solely improving algorithm performance, developing trusted deep learning algorithms that respect data privacy has now become of crucial importance [1,15]. Deep models can memorise a user's sensitive information [2,10,11]. Several attack types [23] including simple reverse engineering [7] can reveal private information of users. Particularly for healthcare, model inversion attacks can even recover a patient's medical images [24]. It is then without surprise why a patient may require that private information is not only deleted from databases but that any such information is forgotten by deep models trained on such databases.

R. Su and X. Liu—Contributed equally.

Supplementary Information The online version contains supplementary material available at https://doi.org/10.1007/978-3-031-16452-1_60.

A naive solution to forget a patient's data is to re-train the model without them. However, re-training is extremely time-consuming and sometimes impossible [21]. For example, in a federated learning scheme [17], the data are not centrally aggregated but retained in servers (e.g. distributed in different hospitals) which may not be available anymore to participate in re-training.

As more advanced solutions, machine unlearning/forgetting approaches aim to remove private information of concerning data without re-training the model. This involves post-processing to the trained model to make it act like a re-trained one that has never seen the concerning data. Several studies have previously explored forgetting/unlearning data and made remarkable progress [5,8,9,18, 19]. When the concept of machine unlearning/forgetting was first developed in [5], they discussed forgetting in statistical query learning [12]. Ginart et al. [8] specifically deal with data deletion in k-means clustering with excellent deleting efficiency. Another approach is to rely on variational inference and Bayesian models [18]. Recently, Sekhari et al. [19] propose a data deleting algorithm by expanding the forgetting limit whilst reserving the model's generalization ability. Golatkar et al. [9] address machine unlearning on deep networks to forget a subset of training data with their proposed scrubbing procedure (shown in Fig. 1(a)), which adds noise to model weights that are uninformative to the remaining data (training data excluding the concerning data) to achieve a weaker form of differential privacy [6].

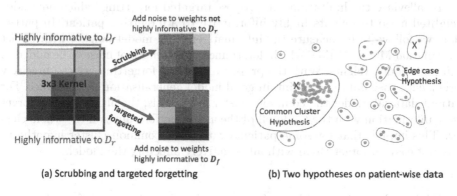

(a) Scrubbing and targeted forgetting   (b) Two hypotheses on patient-wise data

Fig. 1. (a) Visualisation of the scrubbing and targeted forgetting methods. $\mathcal{D}_r$ and $\mathcal{D}_f$ are the retaining data and the forgetting data. (b) Illustration of the two hypotheses. Blue contour delineates a big sub-population of similar samples within a *common cluster*; red contours denote several small sub-populations of distinct samples in *edge cases*. X and X are examples of samples to be forgotten. (Color figure online)

Different from previous work, we specifically consider the scenario of patient-wise forgetting, where instead of forgetting a selected random cohort of data, the data to be forgotten originate from a patient. We hypothesise (and show experimentally) that in a medical dataset, a patient's data can either be similar to other data (and form clusters) or form edge cases as we depict in Fig. 1(b).

These hypotheses are aligned with recent studies on long-tail learning [4,16], where different sub-populations within a class can exist with some being in the so-called long tail.[1] Subsequently, we will refer to these cases as *common cluster* and *edge case* hypotheses.

We first study the patient-wise forgetting performance with simple translation of an existing machine unlearning method developed in [9]. For patients under different hypotheses, forgetting and generalisation performance obtained after scrubbing [9] vary as detailed in Sect. 3. In particular, the scrubbing method removes information not highly related to the remaining data to maintain good generalisation after forgetting, which is a weaker form of differential privacy [6]. When forgetting a patient under common cluster hypothesis, adequate performance can be achieved with the scrubbing method by carefully tuning the level of noise added to the model weights. When forgetting an edge-case patient, the scrubbing method does not remove specifically the edge-case patient's information but noise will be introduced to model weights corresponding to most of the edge cases in the remaining dataset. Hence, the overall model performance will be negatively affected. In fact, we observed in our experiment that data of a large portion of patients are edge cases while for computer vision datasets, the selected random cohort of data to be forgotten usually falls in the common cluster hypothesis. This limits the application of the scrubbing method and possibly other machine unlearning approaches that designed specifically for vision datasets to patient-wise forgetting.

To alleviate the limitation, we propose targeted forgetting, which only adds weighted noise to weights highly informative to a forgetting patient. In particular, we follow [9] to measure the informativeness of model weights with Fisher Information Matrix (FIM), which determines the strength of noise to be added to different model weights. With the proposed targeted forgetting, we can precisely forget edge case data and maintain good model generalisation performance. For patient data fall under the common cluster hypothesis, the algorithm can forget their information with the trade-off of the model performance on the whole cluster. This implies that for some patients within the common cluster hypothesis, it is not easy to forget them without negatively affecting the model.

Contributions:

1. We introduce the problem of patient-wise forgetting and formulate two hypotheses for patient-wise data.
2. We show that machine unlearning methods specifically designed for vision datasets such as [9] have poor performance in patient-wise forgetting.
3. We propose a new targeted forgetting method and perform extensive experiments on a medical benchmark dataset to showcase improved patient-wise forgetting performance.

Our work we hope will inspire future research to consider how different data affect forgetting methods especially in a patient-wise forgetting setting.

---

[1] There is also a connection between edge cases and active learning [20], where one aims to actively label diverse data to bring more information to the model.

2   Method

Given a *training* dataset $\mathcal{D}$, a *forgetting* subset $\mathcal{D}_f \subset \mathcal{D}$ contains the images to be removed from a model $A(\mathcal{D})$, which is trained on $\mathcal{D}$ using any stochastic learning algorithm $A(\cdot)$. The *retaining* dataset is the complement $\mathcal{D}_r = \mathcal{D} \setminus \mathcal{D}_f$, thus $\mathcal{D}_r \cap \mathcal{D}_f = \emptyset$. Test data is denoted as $\mathcal{D}_{test}$. For patient-wise forgetting, $\mathcal{D}_f$ is all the images of one patient. Let $\mathbf{w}$ be the weights of a model. Let $S(\mathbf{w})$ denote the operations applied to model weights to forget $\mathcal{D}_f$ in the model, and $A(\mathcal{D}_r)$ be the *golden standard* model.

2.1   The Scrubbing Method

Assuming that $A(\mathcal{D})$ and $\mathcal{D}_r$ are accessible, Golatkar et al. [9] propose a robust scrubbing procedure modifying model $A(\mathcal{D})$, to brings it closer to a golden standard model $A(\mathcal{D}_r)$. They use FIM to approximate the hessian of the loss on $\mathcal{D}_r$, where higher values in FIM denote higher correlation between corresponding model weights and $\mathcal{D}_r$. With the FIM, they introduce different noise strength to model weights to remove information not highly informative to $\mathcal{D}_r$, and thus forget information corresponding to $\mathcal{D}_f$. The scrubbing function is defined as:

$$S(\mathbf{w}) = \mathbf{w} + \left(\lambda \sigma_h^2\right)^{\frac{1}{4}} F_{\mathcal{D}_r}(\mathbf{w})^{-1/4}, \tag{1}$$

where $F_{\mathcal{D}_r}(\mathbf{w})$ denotes the FIM computed for $\mathbf{w}$ on $\mathcal{D}_r$. Scrubbing is controlled by two hyperparameters: λ decides the scale of noise introduced to $\mathbf{w}$ therefore it controls the model accuracy on $\mathcal{D}_f$; σ_h is a normal distributed error term which simulates the error of the stochastic algorithm, ensuring a continuous gradient flow after the scrubbing procedure. Practically during experiments, the product of the two hyperparameters is tuned as a whole.

The Fisher Information Matrix F of a distribution $P_{x,y}(\mathbf{w})$ w.r.t. $\mathbf{w}$ defined in [9] is:

$$F = \mathbb{E}_{x \sim \mathcal{D}, y \sim p(y|x)} \left[\nabla_{\mathbf{w}} \log p_{\mathbf{w}}(y \mid x) \nabla_{\mathbf{w}} \log p_{\mathbf{w}}(y \mid x)^T \right] \tag{2}$$

To save computational memory, only the diagonal values for FIM are computed and stored. The trace of FIM is calculated by taking the expectation of the outer product of the gradient of a deep learning model. In a medical dataset, the FIM ($F_{\mathcal{D}_r}(\mathbf{w})$) is derived by summing up the normalised FIM of each patient's data in the retaining set $\mathcal{D}_r$ and take the expectation at patient-level. Therefore, weights highly related to the cluster's features show high values in FIM because several cluster patients within $\mathcal{D}_r$ are correlated to these weights. Whereas for edge cases, no other patients are correlated with the same weights as of these edge cases; thus, the aggregated values in FIM for weights corresponding to edge cases are relatively small.

A value within $F_{\mathcal{D}_r}(\mathbf{w})$ reflects to what extent the change to its corresponding weights $\mathbf{w}$ would influence the model's classification process on this set $\mathcal{D}_r$. Hence, if a model weight is correlated with multiple data and thus considered to be important in classifying these data, its corresponding value in FIM would be relatively high, and vice versa. This also explains that weights correlated to data under common cluster hypothesis hold larger value than edge case hypothesis. Therefore, when scrubbing an edge case from a model, weights correlated to other edge cases even within $\mathcal{D}_r$ are also less informative to the remaining data thus will be scrubbed as well, making the model performance be negatively affected.

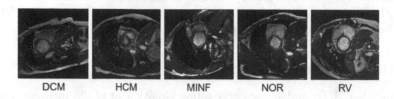

DCM   HCM   MINF   NOR   RV

Fig. 2. Example images of ACDC dataset. DCM: dilated cardiomyopathy. HCM: hypertrophic cardiomyopathy. MINF: myocardial infarction. NOR: normal subjects. RV: abnormal right ventricle.

2.2 The Targeted Forgetting Method

Based on the idea of scrubbing model weights, and the connection between the hessian of a loss on a set of data of a model and the extent to which the weights are informative about these data, we develop the targeted forgetting procedure. We assume access to the forgetting data $\mathcal{D}_f$ instead of $\mathcal{D}_r$. We believe that even in a real patient-wise forgetting scenario, temporary access to patient data is permissible until forgetting is achieved.

We compute FIM for $\mathbf{w}$ on $\mathcal{D}_f$ instead of $\mathcal{D}_r$ to approximate the noise added to model weights. Instead of keeping the most informative weights corresponding to $\mathcal{D}_r$ as in [9], our method precisely introduce noise to model weights highly informative about $\mathcal{D}_f$ (see Fig. 1(a)). Our proposed targeted forgetting is defined as:

$$S_T(\mathbf{w}) = \mathbf{w} + \left(\lambda_T \sigma_{h_T}^2\right)^{\frac{1}{4}} F_{\mathcal{D}_f}(\mathbf{w})^{1/4}, \tag{3}$$

where λ_T and σ_{h_T} are analogous parameters to λ and σ_h defined in Eq. 1.

Performance on the Two Hypotheses. *Common cluster hypothesis*: Targeted forgetting will add noise to the most informative model weights corresponding to $\mathcal{D}_f$ so it will also reduce model performance on the corresponding cluster in $\mathcal{D}_r$ and $\mathcal{D}_{test}$. *Edge case hypothesis*: Targeted forgetting will precisely remove information of an edge case and maintain good model performance. Results and discussion are detailed in Sect. 3.

3 Experiments

We first explore why scrubbing [9] works well on computer vision datasets but shows poorer performance on patient-wise forgetting. We conduct an experiment to demonstrate the intrinsic dataset biases of CIFAR-10 [14] and ACDC [3]. Then, we compare the forgetting and model performance after forgetting achieved using the scrubbing and our targeted forgetting methods.

Datasets: CIFAR-10 has 60,000 images (size 32 × 32) of 10-class objects. The Automated Cardiac Diagnosis Challenge (ACDC) dataset contains 4D cardiac data from 100 patients with four pathologies classes and a normal group. We split the 100 patients into training and testing subsets. Overall, by preprocess the patient data into 224 × 224 2D images, there are 14,724 images from 90 patients form D, and 1,464 images from 10 patients form $\mathcal{D}_{test}$. Patients in both sets are equally distributed across the five classes. Example images from the ACDC dataset are shown in Fig. 2. When conducting experiments under the patient-wise forgetting scenario, we only select one patient to be forgotten devising the forgetting set composed of all the images of the same patient.

Implementation Details: For CIFAR-10, we follow the implementation steps in [9]. When training the ACDC classifier, the model has a VGG-like architecture as in [22]. We use Cross Entropy as the loss function and use Adam optimizer [13] with $\beta_1 = 0.5$, $\beta_2 = 0.999$. During training we use data augmentation including random rotation, Gaussian blur, horizontal and vertical flip. We train all classifiers with a learning rate of 0.0001 for 13 epochs. The original model trained with all 90 patients has 0.00 error on $\mathcal{D}_r$ and $\mathcal{D}_f$, and 0.19 error on $\mathcal{D}_{test}$.

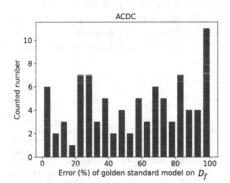 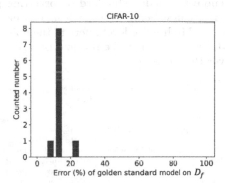

Fig. 3. Histograms of re-training experiments. The y-axis refers to the total number of patients/sets whose golden standard lies within an interval (e.g. [95,100]) of x-axis.

3.1 The Hardness of Patient-Wise Forgetting

Here we compare between CIFAR-10 and ACDC to show that some patient data are hard to learn and forget. For 90 patients in ACDC, we remove one patient's data and re-train a model on the remaining 89 to be the golden standard model, $A(\mathcal{D}_r)$. We then measure the error of the deleted patient on $A(\mathcal{D}_r)$. We repeat this for all 90 patients. For CIFAR-10, we select 10 non-overlapping sets from its training set, each with 100 images from the same class, to be the deleting candidates and repeat the re-train experiments. Data are hard to generalize by its golden model show high error on $A(\mathcal{D}_r)$ and thus should be hard to forget.

Results and Discussion: Figure 3 collects the findings of this experiment as histograms and shows the differences between the two datasets. Overall, for ACDC, the 90 individually measured results of classification error of a $\mathcal{D}_f$ on its corresponding golden model $A(\mathcal{D}_r)$ vary from 0% to 100%, whereas in CIFAR-10, the 10 experimental results only vary from 10% to 25%. High golden model error on a $\mathcal{D}_f$ means that the model is unable to generalise to this patient's data; thus, this patient is not similar to any other patients in the training set, and must belong to the edge case hypothesis. By considering a threshold of 50% on the error of the golden model, we find that > 60% **of patients in ACDC can be considered to belong to the edge case hypothesis.** This is remarkably different in CIFAR-10: golden model results concentrate at low error indicating that few edge cases exist. In addition, as discussed in Sect. 2.1, when dealing with edge cases, scrubbing can degrade model performance. This will explain the results of the scrubbing method: under-performance in ACDC because many patients fall under the edge case hypothesis.

Table 1. Forgetting results for four patients. We report Error $= 1-$Accuracy on the forgetting ($\mathcal{D}_f$) and test ($\mathcal{D}_{test}$) sets respectively. Scrubbing Method refers to the method of [9] whereas Targeted Forgetting refers to the method in Sect. 2.2. Red and blue denote the golden standard of forgetting performance for each row respectively, with performance being better when it is closer to the standard. With respect to error on $\mathcal{D}_f$ **High** noise level refers to the noise strength when a method reaches 1.00 error; **Medium:** 0.85 ± 0.05 error; and **Low:** 0.14 ± 0.05 error. The confidence bar is obtained over three experiments.

Patient ID	Error on	Golden standard	Noise level					
			Low		Medium		High	
			Scrubbing	Targeted forgetting	Scrubbing	Targeted forgetting	Scrubbing	Targeted forgetting
94	$\mathcal{D}_f$	1.000 ± 0.000	0.154 ± 0.005	0.174 ± 0.020	0.859 ± 0.010	0.851 ± 0.018	1.000 ± 0.000	1.000 ± 0.000
(Edge)	$\mathcal{D}_{test}$	0.237 ± 0.002	0.671 ± 0.012	0.223 ± 0.011	0.739 ± 0.007	0.291 ± 0.005	0.746 ± 0.008	0.316 ± 0.002
5	$\mathcal{D}_f$	0.809 ± 0.009	0.127 ± 0.022	0.121 ± 0.019	0.853 ± 0.020	0.857 ± 0.002	1.000 ± 0.000	1.000 ± 0.000
(Edge)	$\mathcal{D}_{test}$	0.253 ± 0.026	0.394 ± 0.017	0.269 ± 0.004	0.624 ± 0.015	0.407 ± 0.001	0.696 ± 0.002	0.506 ± 0.002
13	$\mathcal{D}_f$	0.202 ± 0.004	0.111 ± 0.006	0.092 ± 0.002	0.871 ± 0.018	0.850 ± 0.021	1.000 ± 0.000	1.000 ± 0.000
(Cluster)	$\mathcal{D}_{test}$	0.194 ± 0.001	0.361 ± 0.001	0.343 ± 0.007	0.590 ± 0.005	0.524 ± 0.013	0.694 ± 0.004	0.602 ± 0.016
9	$\mathcal{D}_f$	0.010 ± 0.002	0.176 ± 0.005	0.152 ± 0.009	0.892 ± 0.003	0.862 ± 0.005	0.998 ± 0.002	0.995 ± 0.005
(Cluster)	$\mathcal{D}_{test}$	0.233 ± 0.007	0.402 ± 0.012	0.442 ± 0.001	0.643 ± 0.006	0.613 ± 0.001	0.699 ± 0.005	0.656 ± 0.001

3.2   Patient-Wise Forgetting Performance

We focus on four representative patients using the analysis in Sect. 3.1: patients 94 and 5 that fall under the edge case hypothesis; and patients 13 and 9 fall under a common cluster hypothesis. Here we consider a stringent scenario: the re-trained golden standard model is not available for deciding how much to forget, so the level of noise to be added during scrubbing or forgetting is unknown. We adjust noise strength (low, medium and high) by modulating the hyperparameters in both methods to achieve different levels of forgetting.[2] We assess

---

[2] For our experiments we fix to introduce noise to 1% most informative weights (based on extensive experiments) when applying the targeted forgetting.

forgetting performance by comparing against golden standard models: A method has good forgetting performance by coming as close to the performance of the golden standard model on $\mathcal{D}_{test}$.

Is Targeted Forgetting Better for Forgetting Edge Cases? For edge cases, forgetting can be achieved (compared to the golden standard) at high level of noise with both methods. However, the scrubbing method significantly degrades the model generalisation performance. With targeted forgetting, good model generalisation performance on $\mathcal{D}_{test}$ at all noise levels is rather maintained. Additionally from Table 2 we observe that the scrubbing method adds more noise to model weights to forget an edge case. This further supports our discussion in Sect. 2.1 on how the scrubbing method negatively affects the overall model performance when forgetting edge case.

Table 2. The average noise value added to weights at High (when achieving 1.00 error on $\mathcal{D}_f$). Note that medium and low noise is with 66.7% and 30.0% of high noise level respectively.

Patient ID	High	
	Scrubbing	Targeted forgetting
94 (Edge)	2.33E−05	3.00E−06
5 (Edge)	1.65E−05	4.5E−06
13 (Cluster)	1.6E−05	8.66E−06
9 (Cluster)	1.43E−05	1.2E−05

Is Targeted Forgetting Better for Forgetting Common Cluster Cases? For common cluster cases, both methods can achieve standard forgetting with a near low level of noise with nice model's generalisation performance on $\mathcal{D}_{test}$, as shown in Table 1. For example for patient 13, the test error of two methods at low noise level is 0.361 and 0.343, which is close and relatively small. When the noise level grows to medium and high to forget more, although the test error with two methods still being close, it grows to a high value. Overall, when forgetting common cluster cases, the two methods show similar good performance at a standard level of forgetting and they both can forget more about a patient by sacrificing the model's generalisation.

Can Patient Data be Completely Forgotten? Overall, for edge cases, using targeted forgetting, the patient-wise data can be completely forgotten (achieving error higher than 0.80 (random decision for 5 classes in our case) on $\mathcal{D}_f$) without sacrificing the model generalisation performance. While for common cluster cases, it is less likely to forget the patient data as completely forgetting will result the significantly degraded generalisation performance with the scrubbing or our targeted forgetting. In fact, the level of noise added to the model weights affects the trade-off between model performance and respecting data protection. Higher noise leads to more information being removed, thus protecting the data better yet degrading the model accuracy. Therefore, the noise needs to be carefully designed such that a sweet spot between forgetting and generalisation performance can be achieved.

4 Conclusion

We consider patient-wise forgetting in deep learning models. Our experiments reveal that forgetting a patient's medical image data is harder than other vision domains. We found that this is due to data falling on two hypotheses: common cluster and edge case. We identified limitations of an existing state-of-the-art scrubbing method and proposed a new targeted forgetting approach. Experiments highlight the different roles of these two hypotheses and the importance of considering the dataset bias. We perform experiments on cardiac MRI data but our approach is data-agnostic, which we plan to apply on different medical datasets in the future. In addition, future research on patient-wise forgetting should focus on better ways of detecting which hypothesis the data of patients belong to and how to measure patient-wise forgetting performance with considering the two hypotheses.

Acknowledgements. This work was supported by the University of Edinburgh, the Royal Academy of Engineering and Canon Medical Research Europe by a PhD studentship to Xiao Liu. This work was partially supported by the Alan Turing Institute under EPSRC grant EP/N510129/1. S.A. Tsaftaris acknowledges the support of Canon Medical and the Royal Academy of Engineering and the Research Chairs and Senior Research Fellowships scheme (grant RC-SRF1819\8\25) and the [in part] support of the Industrial Centre for AI Research in digitalDiagnostics (iCAIRD, https://icaird.com) which is funded by Innovate UK on behalf of UK Research and Innovation (UKRI) [project number: 104690].

References

1. Abadi, M., et al.: Deep learning with differential privacy. In: Proceedings of the 2016 ACM SIGSAC Conference on Computer and Communications Security, pp. 308–318 (2016)
2. Arpit, D., et al.: A closer look at memorization in deep networks. In: International Conference on Machine Learning, pp. 233–242. PMLR (2017)
3. Bernard, O., et al.: Deep learning techniques for automatic MRI cardiac multi-structures segmentation and diagnosis: is the problem solved? IEEE Trans. Med. Imaging **37**(11), 2514–2525 (2018)
4. Buda, M., Maki, A., Mazurowski, M.A.: A systematic study of the class imbalance problem in convolutional neural networks. Neural Netw. **106**, 249–259 (2018)
5. Cao, Y., Yang, J.: Towards making systems forget with machine unlearning. In: 2015 IEEE Symposium on Security and Privacy, pp. 463–480 (2015). https://doi.org/10.1109/SP.2015.35

6. Dwork, C., Roth, A., et al.: The algorithmic foundations of differential privacy. Found. Trends Theor. Comput. Sci. **9**(3–4), 211–407 (2014)
7. Fredrikson, M., Jha, S., Ristenpart, T.: Model inversion attacks that exploit confidence information and basic countermeasures. In: Proceedings of the 22nd ACM SIGSAC Conference on Computer and Communications Security, pp. 1322–1333 (2015)
8. Ginart, A., Guan, M.Y., Valiant, G., Zou, J.: Making AI forget you: data deletion in machine learning. arXiv preprint arXiv:1907.05012 (2019)
9. Golatkar, A., Achille, A., Soatto, S.: Eternal sunshine of the spotless net: selective forgetting in deep networks. In: Proceedings of the IEEE/CVF Conference on Computer Vision and Pattern Recognition, pp. 9304–9312 (2020)
10. Hartley, J., Tsaftaris, S.A.: Unintended memorisation of unique features in neural networks. arXiv preprint arXiv:2205.10079 (2022)
11. Jegorova, M., et al.: Survey: leakage and privacy at inference time. arXiv preprint arXiv:2107.01614 (2021)
12. Kearns, M.: Efficient noise-tolerant learning from statistical queries. J. ACM (JACM) **45**(6), 983–1006 (1998)
13. Kingma, D.P., Ba, J.: Adam: a method for stochastic optimization. In: Proceedings of ICLR (2015)
14. Krizhevsky, A., et al.: Learning multiple layers of features from tiny images (2009)
15. Liu, X., Tsaftaris, S.A.: Have you forgotten? A method to assess if machine learning models have forgotten data. In: Martel, A.L., et al. (eds.) MICCAI 2020. LNCS, vol. 12261, pp. 95–105. Springer, Cham (2020). https://doi.org/10.1007/978-3-030-59710-8_10
16. Liu, Z., Miao, Z., Zhan, X., Wang, J., Gong, B., Yu, S.X.: Large-scale long-tailed recognition in an open world. In: Proceedings of the IEEE/CVF Conference on Computer Vision and Pattern Recognition, pp. 2537–2546 (2019)
17. McMahan, B., Moore, E., Ramage, D., Hampson, S., y Arcas, B.A.: Communication-efficient learning of deep networks from decentralized data. In: Artificial Intelligence and Statistics, pp. 1273–1282. PMLR (2017)
18. Nguyen, Q.P., Low, B.K.H., Jaillet, P.: Variational Bayesian unlearning. In: Advances in Neural Information Processing Systems, vol. 33 (2020)
19. Sekhari, A., Acharya, J., Kamath, G., Suresh, A.T.: Remember what you want to forget: algorithms for machine unlearning. arXiv preprint arXiv:2103.03279 (2021)
20. Settles, B.: Active learning literature survey (2009)
21. Shintre, S., Roundy, K.A., Dhaliwal, J.: Making machine learning forget. In: Naldi, M., Italiano, G.F., Rannenberg, K., Medina, M., Bourka, A. (eds.) APF 2019. LNCS, vol. 11498, pp. 72–83. Springer, Cham (2019). https://doi.org/10.1007/978-3-030-21752-5_6
22. Thermos, S., Liu, X., O'Neil, A., Tsaftaris, S.A.: Controllable cardiac synthesis via disentangled anatomy arithmetic. In: de Bruijne, M., et al. (eds.) MICCAI 2021. LNCS, vol. 12903, pp. 160–170. Springer, Cham (2021). https://doi.org/10.1007/978-3-030-87199-4_15
23. Truex, S., Liu, L., Gursoy, M.E., Yu, L., Wei, W.: Demystifying membership inference attacks in machine learning as a service. IEEE Trans. Serv. Comput. **14**(6), 2073–2089 (2019)
24. Wu, M., et al.: Evaluation of inference attack models for deep learning on medical data. arXiv preprint arXiv:2011.00177 (2020)

Calibration of Medical Imaging Classification Systems with Weight Scaling

Lior Frenkel and Jacob Goldberger[✉]

Faculty of Engineering, Bar-Ilan University, Ramat-Gan, Israel
{lior.frenkel,jacob.goldberger}@biu.ac.il

Abstract. Calibrating neural networks is crucial in medical analysis applications where the decision making depends on the predicted probabilities. Modern neural networks are not well calibrated and they tend to overestimate probabilities when compared to the expected accuracy. This results in a misleading reliability that corrupts our decision policy. We define a weight scaling calibration method that computes a convex combination of the network output class distribution and the uniform distribution. The weights control the confidence of the calibrated prediction. The most suitable weight is found as a function of the given confidence. We derive an optimization method that is based on a closed form solution for the optimal weight scaling in each bin of a discretized value of the prediction confidence. We report experiments on a variety of medical image datasets and network architectures. This approach achieves state-of-the-art calibration with a guarantee that the classification accuracy is not altered.

Keywords: Network calibration · Medical decision calibration · Network interpretability · Temperature scaling · Weight scaling

1 Introduction

A classifier is said to be calibrated if the probability values it associates with the class labels match the true probabilities of the correct class assignments. Modern neural networks have been shown to be more overconfident in their predictions than their predecessors even though their generalization accuracy is higher, partly due to the fact that they can overfit on the negative log-likelihood loss without overfitting on the classification error [6,9,16]. In a medical imaging application, we would like to defer images for which the model makes low-confidence predictions to a physician for review. Skipping human review due to confident, but incorrect, predictions, could have disastrous consequences [17]. The lack of connection between the model's predicted probabilities and the model's accuracy is a key obstacle to the application of neural network models to automatic medical diagnosis [2,12,24].

Various confidence calibration methods have recently been proposed in the field of deep learning to overcome the over-confidence issue. Post-hoc scaling approaches to calibration (e.g. Platt scaling [23], isotonic regression [29], and temperature scaling [6]) are widely used. They perform calibration as a post processing step by using holdout validation data to learn a calibration map that transforms the model's predictions to

---

This research was supported by the Ministry of Science & Technology, Israel.

L. Wang et al. (Eds.): MICCAI 2022, LNCS 13438, pp. 642–651, 2022.
https://doi.org/10.1007/978-3-031-16452-1_61

be better calibrated. Temperature scaling is the simplest and most effective calibration method and is the current standard practical calibration method. Guo et al. [6] investigated several scaling models, ranging from single-parameter based temperature scaling to more complex vector/matrix scaling. To avoid overfitting, Kull et al. [14] suggested regularizing matrix scaling with an L_2 loss on the calibration model weights. Gupta et al. [7] built a calibration function by approximating the empirical cumulative distribution using a differentiable function via splines. Most of these calibration methods extend single parameter temperature scaling by making the selected temperature either a linear or a non-linear function of the logits that are computed for the class-set (see e.g. [4,5]). Although network calibration is crucial for producing reliable automatic medical reports, there are only few works that directly address the issue of calibrating medical imaging systems (see e.g. [3,25,30]).

In this study we focus on calibration of neural networks that are applied for medical imaging tasks and propose an alternative to temperature scaling which we dub weight scaling. Weight scaling calibrates the network by computing a suitable convex combination of the original class distribution and the uniform distribution. We show that unlike temperature, vector and matrix scaling [14] and other recently proposed methods (e.g. [7]), we can obtain a closed form solution for the optimal calibration parameters. The proposed calibration does not change the hard classification decision which allows it to be applied on any trained network and guarantees to retain the original classification accuracy in all the tested cases. Unlike previous methods, if a network is more confident on one patient than the other, it remains more confident after the calibration. We evaluated our method against leading calibration approaches on various medical imaging datasets and network architectures using the *expected calibration error* (ECE) [19] calibration measure.

2   Calibration Problem Formulation

Consider a network that classifies an input image x into k pre-defined categories. The last layer of the network architecture is comprised of a vector of k real values $z = (z_1, ..., z_k)$ known as *logits*. Each of these numbers is the score for one of the k possible classes. The logits' vector z is then converted into a soft decision distribution using a *softmax* layer: $p(y = i|x) = \frac{\exp(z_i)}{\sum_j \exp(z_j)}$ where x in the input image and y is the image class. The output of the softmax layer has the mathematical form of a distribution. However, the network is not explicitly trained to compute the actual posterior distribution of the classes.

The hard decision predicted class is calculated from the output distribution by $\hat{y} = \arg\max_i p(y = i|x) = \arg\max_i z_i$. The network *confidence* for this sample is defined by $\hat{p} = p(y = \hat{y}|x) = \max_i p(y = i|x)$. The network *accuracy* is defined by the probability that the most probable class $\hat{y}$ is indeed correct. The network is said to be *calibrated* if for each sample the confidence coincides with the accuracy. For example, assume there are hundred images and for each we have a clinical prediction with identical confidence score of 0.9. If the network is well calibrated we expect that the network decision would be correct in ninety cases.

Expected Calibration Error (ECE) [19] is the standard metric used to measure model calibration. It is defined as the expected absolute difference between the model's accuracy and its confidence, i.e., $\mathbb{E}_{x,y} |\mathbb{P}(y = \hat{y}|x) - \hat{p}|$, where $\mathbb{P}$ is the true probability that the network decision is correct. In practice, we only have a finite amount of validation set samples $(x_1, y_1), ..., (x_n, y_n)$, with associated predictions and confidence values $(\hat{y}_1, \hat{p}_1), ..., (\hat{y}_n, \hat{p}_n)$. Hence, we cannot directly compute the ECE using this definition. Instead, we divide the unit interval $[0, 1]$ into m bins, where the ith bin is the interval $b_i = \left(\frac{i-1}{m}, \frac{i}{m}\right]$. Let $B_i = \{t|\hat{p}_t \in b_i\}$ be the set of samples whose confidence values belong to the bin b_i. The accuracy of this bin is computed as $A_i = \frac{1}{|B_i|} \sum_{t \in B_i} \mathbb{1} (\hat{y}_t = y_t)$, where $\mathbb{1}$ is the indicator function, and y_t and $\hat{y}_t$ are the ground-truth and predicted labels for x_t. A_i is the relative number of correct predictions of instances that were assigned to B_i based on their confidence value. Similarly, the confidence C_i is the average confidence values of all samples in the bin b_i, i.e., $C_i = \frac{1}{|B_i|} \sum_{t \in B_i} \hat{p}_t$. Note that if the network is under-confident at bin b_i then $A_i > C_i$ and vice versa. The ECE can be thus computed as follows:

$$\text{ECE} = \sum_{i=1}^{m} \frac{|B_i|}{n} |A_i - C_i| . \tag{1}$$

ECE is based on a uniform bin width. If the model is well trained then, hopefully, most of the samples lie within the highest confidence bins. Hence, low confidence bins are almost empty and therefore have no influence on the computed value of the ECE. For this reason, we can consider another metric, Adaptive ECE (adaECE) [20]:

$$\text{adaECE} = \frac{1}{m} \sum_{i=1}^{m} |A_i - C_i| \tag{2}$$

such that each bin contains $1/m$ of the data points with similar confidence values. Even though the drawbacks of ECE have been pointed out and some improvements have been proposed [7,15,21,31], the ECE is still used as the standard calibration evaluation measure.

3   Weight Scaling Based on the Predicted Confidence

Temperature Scaling (TS), is a simple yet highly effective technique for calibrating prediction probabilities [6]. It uses a single scalar parameter $T > 0$, where T is the temperature, to rescale logit scores before applying the softmax function to compute the class distribution. The optimal temperature T for a trained model, is found by minimizing the negative log likelihood for a held-out validation dataset. Alternatively, the adaECE measure can be used as the objective score when finding the optimal T. Let A_i and C_i be the accuracy and confidence of the validation-set points in the i-th set B_i. Denote the average confidence in bin i after temperature scaling of all the instances in B_i by a temperature T by $C_i(T)$:

$$C_i(T) = \frac{1}{|B_i|} \sum_{t \in B_i} \max_{j=1}^{k} \frac{\exp(z_{tj}/T)}{\sum_{l=1}^{k} \exp(z_{tl}/T)} \tag{3}$$

s.t. $z_{t1}, ..., z_{tk}$ are the logit values computed by the network that is fed by x_t. The optimal temperature T can be found by minimizing the following adaECE score:

$$L_{TS}(T) = \frac{1}{m}\sum_{i=1}^{m}|A_i - C_i(T)|. \tag{4}$$

The minimization is carried out by a grid search over the possible values of T. Direct minimization of the adaECE measure (2) on the validation set was shown to yield better calibration results than maximizing the likelihood on a validation set [18].

Ji et al. [11] extended TS to a bin-wise setting, denoted Bin-wise Temperature Scaling (BTS), by setting separate temperatures for each bin. BTS is trained by maximizing the log-likelihood function. We can also directly minimize the gap between the confidence and the accuracy in each bin by minimizing the following adaECE score:

$$L_{CTS}(T_1, ..., T_m) = \frac{1}{m}\sum_{i=1}^{m}|A_i - C_i(T_i)|, \tag{5}$$

We need to apply a grid search to find T_i that satisfies $A_i = C_i(T_i)$. We denote this calibration method Confidence based Temperature Scaling (CTS). Similar to the case of a single temperature, it can be shown that CTS consistently yields better calibration results than BTS. We use CTS as one of the baseline methods that are compared with the calibration method we propose next.

Varying the distribution temperature T from 1 to ∞ induces a continuous path from the original class distribution $p = (p_1, ..., p_k)$ to the uniform distribution $u = (1/k, ..., 1/k)$. The notion of temperature scaling of a distribution originated in statistical physics. There is no intrinsic reason to specifically use a temperature to make the network output distribution smoother. The relevant features of temperature scaling as a smoothing procedure are that the entropy increases monotonically and the confidence decreases monotonically as a function of T, the order of probabilities from smallest to largest is preserved in the smoothing operation and it is a continuous function of T. In this study we put forward a different way to make a distribution smoother. For each weight $\alpha \in [0, 1]$ we define a smooth version of the original distribution p as follow:

$$p_\alpha = \alpha p + (1 - \alpha)u. \tag{6}$$

Varying the weight α from 1 to 0 induces a different path from the class distribution p to the uniform distribution u. We denote the calibration approach based on shifting from p to p_α (6) as Weight Scaling (WS). The figure at the right shows the trajectories of temperature scaling and weight scaling from $p = [0.6, 0.3, 0.1]$ to $u = [1/3, 1/3, 1/3]$.

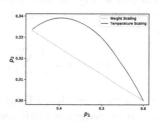

It can be easily verified that the entropy $H(p_\alpha)$ is a concave function of α and obtains its global maximum at $\alpha = 0$. Hence, as p_α moves from p to u, the entropy of p_α monotonically increases. The confidence after weight scaling by α is simply $\hat{p}_\alpha = \alpha\hat{p} + (1 - \alpha)1/k$ where $\hat{p}$ is the confidence before calibration.

Both temperature scaling and weight scaling preserve the order of the predicted classes and therefore do not change the original hard classification decision. Another

---

Algorithm 1. Confidence based Weight Scaling (CWS).

---

training input: A validation dataset $x_1, ..., x_n$ where each x_t is fed into a k-class classifier network to produce class distribution $p_{t1}, ..., p_{tk}$.
Compute the confidence values: $\hat{p}_t = \max_j p_{tj}, \qquad t = 1, ..., n$.
Order the points based on their confidence and divide them into equal size sets $B_1, ..., B_m$.
Compute the average accuracy A_i and confidence C_i based on the points in B_i, and compute the calibration weight:

$$\alpha_i = \max(0, \min(1, \frac{A_i - \frac{1}{k}}{C_i - \frac{1}{k}})), \qquad i = 1, ..., m$$

training output: weights $\alpha_1, ..., \alpha_m$ and a division of the unit interval into m bins.

Calibration procedure:
- Given a point x with class distribution $p_1, ..., p_k$, compute the confidence: $\hat{p} = \max_j p_j$.
- Find the index $i \in \{1, ..., m\}$ s.t. $\hat{p}$ is within the borders of i-th bin.
- The calibrated prediction is: $p(y = j|x) = \alpha_i p_j + (1 - \alpha_i)\frac{1}{k}, \qquad j = 1, ..., k$

---

desired property of a calibration method is preserving the order of clinical decisions in different patients based on the decision confidence. However, as it can easily be verified, a network that is more confident at patient x than at patient y can become less confident at x than y after a temperature scaling calibration using the same temperature in both cases. In contrast, since weight scaling is a monotone function of the confidence, it preserves the ranking of patients based on the clinical decision confidence after weight scaling by the same α.

We next use the adaECE score to learn a calibration procedure based on weight scaling instead of temperature scaling. In the case of weight scaling let

$$C_i(\alpha) = \frac{1}{|B_i|} \sum_{t \in B_i} \max_{j=1}^{k} (\alpha p_{tj} + (1 - \alpha)\frac{1}{k}) = \alpha C_i + (1 - \alpha)\frac{1}{k} \qquad (7)$$

be the confidence in bin i after scaling by a weight α where $p_{t1}, ..., p_{tk}$ are the softmax probability values computed by the network that is fed by x_t. In the case of single parameter weight scaling, we look for a weight α that minimizes the following adaECE score:

$$L_{WS}(\alpha) = \frac{1}{m} \sum_{i=1}^{m} |A_i - C_i(\alpha)| = \frac{1}{m} \sum_{i=1}^{m} |A_i - \alpha C_i - (1 - \alpha)\frac{1}{k}|. \qquad (8)$$

Here there is no closed form solution for the optimal α. In a way similar to CTS, we can allow assigning a different weight in each confidence bin. To find the weight set that minimizes the following adaECE score:

$$L_{CWS}(\alpha_1, ..., \alpha_m) = \frac{1}{m} \sum_{i=1}^{m} |A_i - C_i(\alpha_i)|, \qquad (9)$$

we can perform the minimization in each bin separately. To determine the number of bins we compute the adaECE score on the validation set and choose the number of bins that yields the minimal adaECE score. In the case of weight scaling (unlike temperature scaling) there is a closed form solution to the equation:

$$A_i = C_i(\alpha_i) = \alpha_i C_i - (1 - \alpha_i)\frac{1}{k} \tag{10}$$

which is

$$\alpha_i = \frac{A_i - \frac{1}{k}}{C_i - \frac{1}{k}}. \tag{11}$$

The definition of confidence as the probability of the most likely class implies that always $1/k \le C_i$. If $1/k \le A \le C_i$ then $\alpha_i \in [0, 1]$. In the (rare) case of accuracy less than random, i.e. $A_i < 1/k$, we set $\alpha_i = 0$ and in the (rare) case of under-confidence, i.e. $C_i < A_i$, we set $\alpha_i = 1$. The obtained calibration method is denoted Confidence based Weight Scaling (CWS) and is summarized in Algorithm box 1.

4 Experimental Results

We implemented the proposed calibration methods on various medical imaging classification tasks to evaluate their performance. The experimental setup included the following medical datasets:

- **ChestX-ray14** [28]: A huge dataset that contains 112,120 frontal-view X-ray images of 30,805 unique patient of size 1024×1024, individually labeled with up to 14 different thoracic diseases. The original dataset is multi-label. We treated the problem as a multi-class task by choosing the samples contain only one annotated positive label. We used a train/validation/test split of 89,696/11,212/11,212 images.
- **HAM10000** [27]: This dataset contains 10,015 dermatoscopic images of size 800×600. Cases include a representative collection of 7 diagnostic categories in the realm of pigmented lesions. We used a train/validation/test split of 8,013/1,001/1,001 images.
- **COVID-19** [22]: A small dataset of X-ray images obtained from two different sources. 127 COVID-19 X-ray images was taken from [1] and 500 no-findings and 500 pneumonia frontal chest X-ray images was randomly taken from the ChestX-ray8 database [28]. Here, we used a train/validation/test split of 901/112/112 images.

Each dataset was fine-tuned on pre-trained ResNet-50 [8], DenseNet-121 [10] and VGG-16-BN (with batch normalization) [26] networks. The models were taken from PyTorch site[1]. These network architectures were selected because of their widespread use in classification problems. The last FC layer output size of each of them was adjusted to fit the corresponding number of classes for each dataset. All models were fine-tuned using cross-entropy loss and Adam optimizer [13] with learning rate of 0.0001.

Compared Methods. WS and CWS were compared to TS, vector scaling (VS) and matrix scaling (MS) [14]. The optimal TS was found by minimizing the ECE score over a validation set [18]. We also implemented our CTS algorithm, which calculates the optimal temperature in each bin (5). Note that VS and MS may change the model's

---

[1] https://pytorch.org/vision/stable/models.html.

Table 1. ECE for top-1 predictions (in %) using 10 bins (with the lowest in bold and the second lowest underlined) on various medical imaging classification datasets and models with different calibration methods.

Dataset	Architecture	Acc (%)	Uncalibrated	TS	VS	MS	WS	CTS	CWS
ChestX-ray14	ResNet-50	52.7	2.14	2.14	2.00	3.67	2.13	<u>1.81</u>	**1.67**
	DenseNet-121	52.3	4.18	4.18	<u>2.99</u>	3.49	3.65	3.20	**2.75**
	VGG-16-BN	52.3	2.46	2.46	<u>1.81</u>	4.73	1.94	2.49	**1.79**
HAM10000	ResNet-50	88.8	5.17	<u>1.76</u>	5.28	3.08	3.53	1.93	**1.58**
	DenseNet-121	87.4	4.91	2.36	7.59	3.30	3.71	<u>2.00</u>	**1.71**
	VGG-16-BN	89.0	7.73	2.94	3.57	<u>1.78</u>	6.09	1.92	**1.59**
COVID-19	ResNet-50	91.1	6.08	**2.76**	21.39	15.35	4.65	3.99	<u>3.78</u>
	DenseNet-121	90.2	6.25	6.55	29.70	20.78	6.15	<u>5.69</u>	**4.65**
	VGG-16-BN	88.4	8.92	6.82	9.30	8.31	<u>4.27</u>	5.58	**4.09**

Table 2. adaECE for top-1 predictions (in %) using 10 bins (with the lowest in bold and the second lowest underlined).

Dataset	Architecture	Acc (%)	Uncalibrated	TS	VS	MS	WS	CTS	CWS
ChestX-ray14	ResNet-50	52.7	2.15	2.14	<u>1.95</u>	3.81	2.12	1.99	**1.69**

accuracy and reduce the initial performance, while the other methods preserve it. For each method we evaluated the ECE score (computed using 10 bins) after calibration of the test set. Although adaECE was used as the objective function in our algorithm, ECE is still the standard way to report calibration results, so we used it to compare our calibration results with previous studies.

Results. Table 1 shows the calibration results. CWS achieved the best results in almost all cases, except one where it reached the second best result. Moreover, the ECE score after WS calibration was lower than the ECE after TS in more than a half of the cases. ChestX-ray14 is a large dataset with many classes. We can see in this case the advantage of WS over TS that is not calibrating at all (the optimal temperature was $T = 1$). The results also show that vector and matrix scaling collapse when using a small amount of classes, such as the COVID-19 dataset. We next verified that the calibration performance of CWS is still better than the other compared methods when adaECE is used for evaluation. Table 2 shows calibration results in one case evaluated by the adaECE score.

An advantage of WS is that it preserves the order of confidence of two samples, unlike TS that may violate this order. Figure 1 presents two pairs of samples from HAM10000 with the same label (Benign keratosis). In each pair, the confidence of the first image before calibration was higher and after TS calibration the confidence became lower. Overall, TS changed the confidence order of 3% of the image pairs in the HAM10000 test dataset.

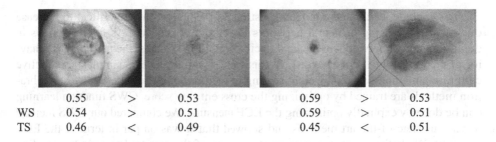

	0.55	>	0.53	0.59	>	0.53
WS	0.54	>	0.51	0.59	>	0.51
TS	0.46	<	0.49	0.45	<	0.51

Fig. 1. Two pairs of samples of benign keratosis taken from the HAM10000 dataset. For each image we show confidence before calibration (top row), after WS calibration (middle row) and after TS calibration (bottom row).

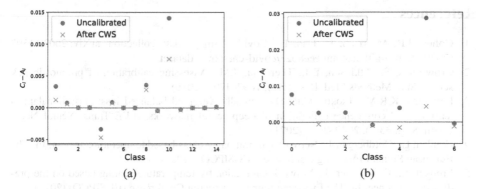

(a)   (b)

Fig. 2. Difference between average confidence C_i and average accuracy A_i for each class i of the (a) ChestX-ray14 and (b) HAM10000 datasets trained on ResNet-50.

We investigated the level of confidence of each class in the ChestX-ray14 and HAM10000 datasets. Figure 2 presents the difference between average confidence and average accuracy of each class before calibration and after applying the CWS algorithm for (a) ChestX-ray14 and (b) HAM10000 trained on ResNet-50. Positive difference symbolizes an over-confident class and negative difference represents an under-confident class. The labels of ChestX-ray14 are *Atelectasis, Cardiomegaly, Effusion, Infiltration, Mass, Nodule, Pneumonia, Pneumothorax, Consolidation, Edema, Emphysema, Fibrosis, PT, Hernia* and *No findings*. The labels of HAM10000 are *Actinic Keratoses, Basal cell carcinoma, Benign keratosis, Dermatofibroma, Melanoma, Melanocytic nevi* and *Vascular skin lesions*. The classes indexes of the model output displayed in Fig. 2 match this order. The results show that there are some classes in each dataset that are less calibrated than the others (like Emphysema in ChestX-ray14 and Melanocytic nevi in HAM10000) and some classes that are already relatively calibrated. They also show that CWS improves calibration for most of the classes and reduce the model's confidence in the few cases where the ECE gets higher.

To conclude, calibrated confidence estimates of predictions are critical to increase our trust in the using of neural networks for clinical decisions. As interest grows in deploying neural networks in medical decision making systems, the predictable behavior of the model will be a necessity. In this work, we introduced a simple and effective calibration method based on weight scaling of the prediction confidence. Most calibration methods are trained by optimizing the cross entropy score. CWS function learning can be done by explicitly optimizing the ECE measure. We compared our CWS method to various state-of-the-art methods and showed that it was on par in term of the ECE measure. We believe that it can be used in place of the standard temperature scaling method. In general, a calibrated prediction has a concrete probabilistic interpretation that hopefully enables practitioners build better trust on AI systems.

References

1. Cohen, J.P., Morrison, P., Dao, L.: Covid-19 image data collection. arXiv: 2003.11597 (2020). https://github.com/ieee8023/covid-chestxray-dataset
2. Crowson, C.S., Atkinson, E.J., Therneau, T.M.: Assessing calibration of prognostic risk scores. Stat. Methods Med. Res. **25**(4), 1692–1706 (2016)
3. Fernando, K.R.M., Tsokos, C.P.: Dynamically weighted balanced loss: class imbalanced learning and confidence calibration of deep neural networks. IEEE Trans. Neural Netw. Learn. Syst. **33**(7), 2940–2951 (2021)
4. Frenkel, L., Goldberger, J.: Network calibration by class-based temperature scaling. In: The European Signal Processing Conference (EUSIPCO) (2021)
5. Frenkel, L., Goldberger, J.: Network calibration by temperature scaling based on the predicted confidence. In: The European Signal Processing Conference (EUSIPCO) (2022)
6. Guo, C., Pleiss, G., Sun, Y., Weinberger, K.Q.: On calibration of modern neural networks. In: International Conference on Machine Learning (ICML) (2017)
7. Gupta, K., Rahimi, A., Ajanthan, T., Mensink, T., Sminchisescu, C., Hartley, R.: Calibration of neural networks using splines. In: International Conference on Learning Representations (ICLR) (2021)
8. He, K., Zhang, X., Ren, S., Sun, J.: Deep residual learning for image recognition. In: Proceedings of the IEEE Conference on Computer Vision and Pattern Recognition (CVPR) (2016)
9. Hein, M., Andriushchenko, M., Bitterwolf, J.: Why ReLU networks yield high-confidence predictions far away from the training data and how to mitigate the problem. In: Proceedings of the IEEE Conference on Computer Vision and Pattern Recognition (CVPR) (2019)
10. Huang, G., Liu, Z., Van Der Maaten, L., Weinberger, K.Q.: Densely connected convolutional networks. In: Proceedings of the IEEE Conference on Computer Vision and Pattern Recognition (CVPR) (2017)
11. Ji, B., Jung, H., Yoon, J., Kim, K., Shin, Y.: Bin-wise temperature scaling (BTS): improvement in confidence calibration performance through simple scaling techniques. In: IEEE/CVF International Conference on Computer Vision Workshop (ICCVW) (2019)
12. Jiang, X., Osl, M., Kim, J., Ohno-Machado, L.: Calibrating predictive model estimates to support personalized medicine. J. Am. Med. Inform. Assoc. **192**(2), 263–274 (2011)
13. Kingma, D.P., Ba, J.: Adam: a method for stochastic optimization. arXiv preprint arXiv:1412.6980 (2014)
14. Kull, M., Nieto, M.P., Kängsepp, M., Silva Filho, T., Song, H., Flach, P.: Beyond temperature scaling: obtaining well-calibrated multi-class probabilities with Dirichlet calibration. In: Advances in Neural Information Processing Systems (NeurIPs) (2019)

15. Kumar, A., Liang, P.S., Ma, T.: Verified uncertainty calibration. In: Advances in Neural Information Processing Systems (NeurIPs) (2019)
16. Lakshminarayanan, B., Pritzel, A., Blundell, C.: Simple and scalable predictive uncertainty estimation using deep ensembles. In: Advances in Neural Information Processing Systems (NeurIPs) (2017)
17. Minderer, M., et al.: Revisiting the calibration of modern neural networks. In: Advances in Neural Information Processing Systems (NeurIPs) (2021)
18. Mukhoti, J., Kulharia, V., Sanyal, A., Golodetz, S., Torr, P.H., Dokania, P.K.: Calibrating deep neural networks using focal loss. In: Advances in Neural Information Processing Systems (NeurIPs) (2020)
19. Naeini, M.P., Cooper, G., Hauskrecht, M.: Obtaining well calibrated probabilities using Bayesian binning. In: AAAI Conference on Artificial Intelligence (2015)
20. Nguyen, K., O'Connor, B.: Posterior calibration and exploratory analysis for natural language processing models. arXiv preprint arXiv:1508.05154 (2015)
21. Nixon, J., Dusenberry, M.W., Zhang, L., Jerfel, G., Tran, D.: Measuring calibration in deep learning. In: CVPR Workshops (2019)
22. Ozturk, T., Talo, M., Yildirim, E.A., Baloglu, U.B., Yildirim, O., Acharya, U.R.: Automated detection of COVID-19 cases using deep neural networks with X-ray images. Comput. Biol. Med. **121**, 103792 (2020)
23. Platt, J., et al.: Probabilistic outputs for support vector machines and comparisons to regularized likelihood methods. Adv. Large Margin Classifiers **10**(3), 61–74 (1999)
24. Raghu, M., et al.: Direct uncertainty prediction for medical second opinions. In: International Conference on Machine Learning (ICML) (2019)
25. Rousseau, A.J., Becker, T., Bertels, J., Blaschko, M.B., Valkenborg, D.: Post training uncertainty calibration of deep networks for medical image segmentation. In: International Symposium on Biomedical Imaging (ISBI) (2021)
26. Simonyan, K., Zisserman, A.: Very deep convolutional networks for large-scale image recognition. arXiv preprint arXiv:1409.1556 (2014)
27. Tschandl, P., Rosendahl, C., Kittler, H.: The HAM10000 dataset, a large collection of multi-source dermatoscopic images of common pigmented skin lesions. Sci. Data **5**(1), 1–9 (2018)
28. Wang, X., Peng, Y., Lu, L., Lu, Z., Bagheri, M., Summers, R.M.: Chestx-ray8: hospital-scale chest x-ray database and benchmarks on weakly-supervised classification and localization of common thorax diseases. In: Proceedings of the IEEE Conference on Computer Vision and Pattern Recognition (CVPR) (2017)
29. Zadrozny, B., Elkan, C.: Transforming classifier scores into accurate multiclass probability estimates. In: International Conference on Knowledge Discovery and Data Mining (KDD) (2002)
30. Zhang, F., Dvornek, N., Yang, J., Chapiro, J., Duncan, J.: Layer embedding analysis in convolutional neural networks for improved probability calibration and classification. IEEE Trans. Med. Imaging **39**(11), 3331–3342 (2020)
31. Zhang, J., Kailkhura, B., Han, T.Y.J.: Mix-n-Match: ensemble and compositional methods for uncertainty calibration in deep learning. In: International Conference on Machine Learning (ICML) (2020)

Online Reflective Learning for Robust Medical Image Segmentation

Yuhao Huang[1,2,3], Xin Yang[1,2,3], Xiaoqiong Huang[1,2,3], Jiamin Liang[1,2,3],
Xinrui Zhou[1,2,3], Cheng Chen[4], Haoran Dou[5], Xindi Hu[6], Yan Cao[1,2,3],
and Dong Ni[1,2,3(✉)]

[1] National-Regional Key Technology Engineering Laboratory for Medical
Ultrasound, School of Biomedical Engineering, Health Science Center,
Shenzhen University, Shenzhen, China
nidong@szu.edu.cn
[2] Medical Ultrasound Image Computing (MUSIC) Lab, Shenzhen University,
Shenzhen, China
[3] Marshall Laboratory of Biomedical Engineering, Shenzhen University,
Shenzhen, China
[4] Department of Computer Science and Engineering, The Chinese University of Hong
Kong, Hong Kong, China
[5] Centre for Computational Imaging and Simulation Technologies in Biomedicine
(CISTIB), University of Leeds, Leeds, UK
[6] Shenzhen RayShape Medical Technology Co., Ltd, Shenzhen, China

Abstract. Deep segmentation models often face the failure risks when
the testing image presents unseen distributions. Improving model robustness against these risks is crucial for the large-scale clinical application of deep models. In this study, inspired by human learning cycle,
we propose a novel online reflective learning framework (*RefSeg*) to
improve segmentation robustness. Based on the reflection-on-action conception, our RefSeg firstly drives the deep model to take action to obtain
semantic segmentation. Then, RefSeg triggers the model to reflect itself.
Because making deep models realize their segmentation failures during testing is challenging, RefSeg synthesizes a realistic proxy image
from the semantic mask to help deep models build intuitive and effective reflections. This proxy translates and emphasizes the segmentation
flaws. By maximizing the structural similarity between the raw input
and the proxy, the reflection-on-action loop is closed with segmentation
robustness improved. RefSeg runs in the testing phase and is general
for segmentation models. Extensive validation on three medical image
segmentation tasks with a public cardiac MR dataset and two in-house
large ultrasound datasets show that our RefSeg remarkably improves
model robustness and reports state-of-the-art performance over strong
competitors.

Keywords: Segmentation · Robustness · Online learning

Y. Huang and X. Yang—Contribute equally to this work.

© The Author(s), under exclusive license to Springer Nature Switzerland AG 2022
L. Wang et al. (Eds.): MICCAI 2022, LNCS 13438, pp. 652–662, 2022.
https://doi.org/10.1007/978-3-031-16452-1_62

1   Introduction

Deep learning has achieved great success in medical image segmentation [24]. However, deep models heavily depend on the training data and can easily suffer from serious performance degradation [5,16] when deploying to unseen test data with distribution shift, e.g., images acquired from different centers, devices, operators or acquisition protocols (Fig. 1). This risk greatly threats the reliable deployment of deep segmentation models in critical medical applications. To achieve robust segmentation, a plethora of methods have been proposed to address the risk and can be roughly categorized into three mainstreams.

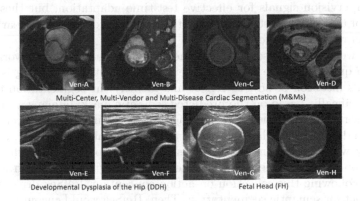

Fig. 1. Visualization of datasets from different vendors (Ven-A to Ven-H). Eight structures to be segmented include (1) M&Ms: left ventricle (LV, blue), left ventricular myocardium (MYO, green) and right ventricle (RV, red); (2) DDH: ilium (blue), lower limb (green), labrum (red) and co_junction (yellow); (3) FH: head (green). (Color figure online)

Domain Adaptation (DA) [7] typically aims to align distributions by using both source domain labeled data and target domain data. Most DA methods explore image or feature alignment and invariant feature extraction across domains. Regarding the label availability of target domain, DA can be summarized as supervised [12,20], semi-supervised [18] and unsupervised DA (UDA) [4,9,31]. Though UDA obtains promising performance on cross-domain medical images and does not require annotations of target domains, obtaining adequate amount of target images in advance can be tough for clinical practice.

Domain Generalization (DG) [1] only relies on source domains to train robust models that can directly generalize to different unseen domains. Though appealing, most existing methods need more than one source domain for training [23]. The alternatives are domain randomization [2,26] and adversarial learning [25] to systematically augment training samples to cover possible cases. Recently, Liu et al. [16] proposed a style-transfer based curriculum learning to enhance segmentation generalisation. Meta-learning based methods [14,15] were introduced to generalize segmentation models to unseen domains. Although effective, these methods often suffer from the problems of difficulties in controlling data generation, style image selection, and model over-fitting.

Test-time Adaptation (TTA) is an emerging topic that adapts a pre-trained model to each inference image at test time. Among the studies, test-time augmentation has preferred efficacy [16,19]. Although it is easy to implement, it cannot tightly mimic the unseen domains with limited augmentation combinations. Recently, self-supervised learning was introduced to remove the domain shift during testing [29]. Karani et al. [11] proposed an autoencoder to extract the anatomical prior for guidance. He et al. [8] introduced a set of adaptors to minimize the reconstruction errors. These methods made great efforts in exploring self-supervision signals for effective test-time adaptation, but these signals are still not accurate and strong enough to drive the deep model to clearly realize its segmentation failures for correction.

In this work, we propose a novel online Reflective Learning framework, named *RefSeg*, to quickly achieve robust segmentation at test time. RefSeg is inspired by human's intuition of how to reflect and identify the segmentation failure to refine. Specifically, based on the predicted semantic mask, humans would reflect and reconstruct an imaginary proxy image. If the segmentation is accurate, this proxy would present similar structures to the original input image, otherwise, this proxy would have remarkable flaws. This discrepancy drives the iterative reflection-on-action and helps humans to robustly segment images from unseen domains. Following this reflection-on-action conception, RefSeg drives the deep model to act for semantic segmentation. Then, RefSeg would encourage the deep model to reflect itself and identify segmentation flaws by synthesizing a realistic proxy image from the semantic mask. By maximizing the structural similarity between the raw input and the proxy, the deep model would be able to remedy its weakness and gradually converge towards a plausible segmentation.

Our RefSeg is an important extension of self-supervised learning. It significantly improves the efficacy of supervision signal by reflecting on the mask. Notably, the source domain information is only used for offline model training in RefSeg. During inference, RefSeg directly conducts online adaptation of the trained model to the unseen testing image by iteratively reflecting and refining the segmentation. We conduct extensive experiments on three segmentation tasks with public M&Ms Challenge [3] and two in-house large US datasets. We demonstrate that RefSeg is general in reducing the failure risk of deep segmentation models, remarkably improves the model robustness, achieves state-of-the-art results, and even approaches the supervised training upper bound on some tasks.

2   Methodology

Figure 2 shows the workflow of RefSeg. For each unknown-domain testing image, RefSeg drives the trained segmentor to produce segmentation heatmap. Then, a synthesizer leads the reflection process by generating a realistic proxy image based on the heatmap and the auxiliary sketch input. Our introduced structural similarity loss then measures the segmentation failure. Both the segmentor and synthesizer are then fine-tuned under this supervision for robust segmentation.

Segmentor for Differentiable Learning. As shown in Fig. 2, RefSeg is a general framework for k-class segmentation ($k \geq 2$, with background). Commonly, performing the non-differentiable *argmax* on the probability map can obtain the segmentation results. Here, to connect the gradient flow of the segmentation action path and synthesis reflection path for differentiable online learning cycle, we multiply probability map of each channel p_k by the corresponding ground truth label intensity value g_k and add them together (i.e., $\sum(p_k * g_k)$). Then, the k-class heatmap H_{att} with gradient can be produced.

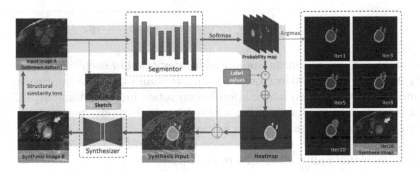

Fig. 2. The workflow of our proposed Reflective Learning framework (RefSeg).

Synthesizer for Informative Proxy. The source domain-trained segmentor suffers from failures in testing unseen-domain images. However, it is hard for the segmentor to reflect on its segmentation result and identify the failure. RefSeg provides an easy and intuitive reflection scheme through a synthesizer (see Fig. 2). It can generate a realistic proxy image, which translates and emphasizes the segmentation flaws. When the segmentation fails, it will be reflected in the synthesis image (yellow arrows in Fig. 2) in details. We believe that this reflection can provide informative and direct cues for failure risk evaluation. Specifically, inspired by [13], we adopt the Generative Adversarial Network (GAN) to synthesize proxy based on the heatmap and the sketches (like canny edge) obtained from the original input image. The heatmap indicates the target structures, while the sketch provides important support for realistic details. Same as the segmentor, the synthesizer is trained and validated on source domain.

Structural Similarity for Failure Evaluation. RefSeg reflects on the segmentation failure by quantifying the similarity between the input and synthesized proxy images. It is worth noting that, because the synthesizer is trained on the source domain, it can only translate the heatmap into the source domain by default. Therefore, as Fig. 2 shows, the input image comes from an unknown domain, while the synthesis image locates in the source domain. They naturally have unknown domain shifts. Regarding this challenge, inspired by multi-modal registration, we propose the structural similarity as measurement, rather than the pixel-level content similarities (like *L1* loss). Specifically, our similarity loss has the following main complementary components.

1) Normalized Cross-Correlation Loss (NCC). Invented to measure the similarity between an image and template, NCC has been extensively employed in image registration tasks [22]. The range of NCC is $[-1, 1]$, with -1 and 1 indicating perfect negative and positive correlation, respectively. Given the input image A and proxy image B, they both are divided into N sub-images with size n ($n = 9$ in our work). By calculating the CC of two corresponding sub-images ($A(x, y)$ and $B(x, y)$) and averaging N pairs, NCC loss can be formulated as:

$$L_{ncc}(A, B) = 1 - \frac{1}{N} \sum_{x,y} \frac{1}{\sigma_A \sigma_B} (A(x, y) - \mu_A)(B(x, y) - \mu_B), \tag{1}$$

where $\mu.$ and $\sigma.$ are the mean and standard deviation of each sub-image.

2) Mutual Information Loss (MI). MI comes from the information theory, measuring the shared information between two images (A and B) [27]. Different from the NCC that usually adopted in single-modal registration, MI is preferred in describing the common features shared among multiple modalities. The higher MI ($MI \geq 0$) means more information are shared between two images. Mathematically, MI can be defined as:

$$MI(A, B) = \sum_{a \in \mathcal{A}} \sum_{b \in \mathcal{B}} p(a, b) log \frac{p(a, b)}{p(a)p(b)}, \tag{2}$$

where a and b represent the intensity values of A and B, respectively. $p(\cdot)$ denotes the probability, relying on histogram-based calculation of pixel intensities, and thus is non-differentiable. For approximating MI in a differentiable way, we exploit the *Parzen window* formulation with *Gaussian* kernel to estimate $\tilde{M}I$ (refer to [28]). Then, the MI loss can be defined as $L_{mi}(A, B) = -\tilde{M}I(A, B)$.

3) Attention on Target Structures. In order to emphasize the target structures for segmentation in the structural similarity loss, we further propose to leverage the normalized heatmap $H'_{att} = H_{att}/255$ as the attention matrix to indicate the desired segmentation areas. Hence, the final image input to the similarity loss is $\hat{A} = (I + H'_{att}) \cdot A$, $\hat{B} = (I + H'_{att}) \cdot B$. I is the matrix with all the elements equal to 1. Therefore, our online RefSeg iteratively minimizes the final similarity loss on each testing image and remedies its segmentation failures for robustness as follows: $Loss = L_{ncc}(\hat{A}, \hat{B}) + L_{mi}(\hat{A}, \hat{B})$.

3   Experimental Results

Materials and Implementations. We validated RefSeg on three segmentation tasks (Fig. 1). For **Cardiac segmentation**, we employ cardiac MR images

Table 1. Datasets split for the training, validation and testing set of each experimental group (volumes/cases (slices/images)). The M&Ms dataset was split following the Challenge. The other two in-house datasets were split randomly at patient/case level.

		Training		Validation		Testing
M&Ms	A	75 (1738)	A	4 (98)	A	16 (360)
					B	40 (888)
	B	75 (1546)	B	10 (208)	C	40 (974)
					D	40 (1014)
DDH (E2F)	E	214 (402)	E	98 (180)	F	320 (649)
DDH (F2E)	F	220 (249)	F	100 (200)	E	312 (582)
FH (G2H)	G	75 (300)	G	31 (124)	H	199 (796)
FH (H2G)	H	150 (600)	H	49 (196)	G	106 (424)

from M&Ms Challenge [3], which aims to segment cardiac substructures including *LV*, *MYO*, and *RV*. The dataset consists of volumes acquired from four different vendors. We follow the experimental setting of the challenge to train on images from vendor A&B and test on images from all vendors A to D. For **DDH segmentation**, the aim is to segment *ilium, lower limb, labrum* and *co-junction*. We use one in-house dataset with images collected from two vendors E and F. For **FH segmentation**, the only structure to be segmented is *head*. We use another in-house dataset with images acquired from two vendors G and H. The two private datasets were manually annotated by experts using the Pair annotation software package [13]. We conduct bidirectional experiments for vendors on DDH and FH datasets for extensive evaluations, denoted as E2F, F2E, G2H and H2G. Dataset split information are listed in Table 1. For each split, the segmentor and synthesizer used the same training, validation and testing set.

We implemented RefSeg in Pytorch, using an NVIDIA TITAN 2080 GPU. All images were resized to 256×256. We chose Attention U-net [21] as a typical segmentor and trained it with Adam optimizer, learning rate $(lr) = 1e{-}3$ and batch size $= 8$. During offline training, segmentor was supervised by cross-entropy loss. The synthesizer was trained following [13], using Adam optimizer with batch size $= 4$. The lr for generator and discriminator are $1e{-}3$ and $1e{-}4$, respectively. Training epochs for segmentor and synthesizer are 100 and 400. We selected models with the best performance on validation sets to work with RefSeg. During the online testing, the lr for segmentor are $1e{-}4$, $1e{-}5$ and $1e{-}5$ for M&Ms, DDH and FH datasets, respectively. For synthesizers, the optimal lr are $1e{-}4$ for all datasets. RefSeg iterates for 10 steps in all experiments.

Quantitative and Qualitative Analysis. We evaluated the segmentation performance using Dice similarity coefficient (DICE) and Hausdorff distance (HD) for all the experiments. For M&Ms dataset, we added the Challenge criteria (*DICE score* and *HD score*) and *min-max (MM) score* ranking method for fair comparisons [3]. For each metric, the average results of substructures are reported. Table 2 compares RefSeg with other seven methods on M&Ms, including Attention U-net [21] (baseline), a recent robust segmentation method SCL [16], two state-of-the-art TTA methods DAE [11] and SDAN [8], and the top-3 methods on the Challenge leaderboard (i.e., P1–P3). Note that since we exactly follow the experimental setting of the M&Ms challenge, methods P1–P3 based on the heavy nnUNet [10] are strong comparisons. It can be observed that our proposed RefSeg improves over baseline by 4.81% and 1.95 mm in terms of the average DICE and HD score. Based on the *MM score*, RefSeg achieves the best performance among strong competitions. Moreover, RefSeg only requires 1.72 s (0.172 s/step). It is much faster than the P1 (26 s) and P2 (4.8 s).

Table 2. Comparisons on M&Ms Challenge (mean(std)) (DICE ↑: %, HD ↓: mm).

Methods	Vendor A		Vendor B		Vendor C		Vendor D		DICE	HD	MM
	DICE	HD	DICE	HD	DICE	HD	DICE	HD	score	score	score
SDAN [8]	86.59	12.04	85.23	11.63	77.23	14.06	82.68	11.64	81.94	12.51	24.74
	(4.51)	(3.88)	(7.91)	(5.59)	(17.78)	(8.34)	(6.48)	(6.26)			
Baseline [21]	87.19	11.55	87.05	9.78	79.52	13.53	83.82	9.80	83.49	11.33	47.03
	(5.10)	(3.48)	(5.36)	(3.15)	(14.46)	(11.92)	(5.10)	(4.11)			
DAE [11]	87.03	11.77	86.74	9.95	78.97	12.18	84.10	10.11	83.32	11.05	48.46
	(4.61)	(3.43)	(5.88)	(3.96)	(16.13)	(6.10)	(5.58)	(4.36)			
P3 [17]	87.85	12.59	88.68	9.87	86.47	10.46	86.41	13.97	87.05	11.89	67.26
	(4.25)	(12.28)	(5.29)	(3.61)	(5.54)	(6.50)	(5.07)	(16.85)			
P2 [30]	88.39	12.46	89.16	9.80	86.96	9.55	86.68	13.43	87.47	11.37	75.20
	(3.96)	(12.24)	(5.10)	(3.37)	(4.66)	(3.29)	(4.96)	(14.85)			
SCL [16]	88.42	9.80	87.64	10.24	86.48	10.59	86.79	11.20	87.10	10.60	79.84
	(3.23)	(3.53)	(4.69)	(2.98)	(6.00)	(5.19)	(3.67)	(4.89)			
P1 [6]	88.91	12.07	89.28	9.48	87.63	9.47	87.66	13.09	88.13	11.11	82.40
	(4.19)	(12.64)	(4.65)	(3.34)	(4.26)	(3.56)	(4.21)	(14.84)			
RefSeg-L1	84.73	14.10	85.01	12.44	78.05	19.17	81.09	11.53	81.33	14.66	0.00
	(6.92)	(6.72)	(5.78)	(5.01)	(9.82)	(18.64)	(5.27)	(4.51)			
RefSeg-N	88.27	10.37	87.92	9.84	81.97	12.95	85.37	9.71	85.15	10.92	62.82
	(5.02)	(4.85)	(4.63)	(3.47)	(9.85)	(12.62)	(3.76)	(4.02)			
RefSeg-M	88.65	11.21	88.02	9.98	83.08	13.70	86.74	8.05	86.05	10.78	70.60
	(3.55)	(3.49)	(3.09)	(2.84)	(8.68)	(15.96)	(3.42)	(3.61)			
RefSeg-NM	89.02	10.32	87.91	9.24	84.68	11.85	87.21	9.05	86.79	10.23	81.12
	(3.41)	(2.41)	(3.85)	(2.44)	(8.13)	(12.11)	(3.48)	(3.16)			
RefSeg	88.89	10.65	88.66	9.31	88.97	9.34	87.15	8.83	88.30	9.38	100.00
	(4.50)	(3.36)	(4.53)	(2.81)	(9.54)	(6.18)	(3.72)	(4.38)			

Table 3. Comparisons on DDH and FH datasets (mean (std)) (DICE: ↑ %, HD ↓: pixel).

Methods	DDH: E2F		DDH: F2E		FH: G2H		FH: H2G	
	DICE	HD	DICE	HD	DICE	HD	DICE	HD
Upper-bound	88.21	11.76	87.64	11.25	98.22	3.51	98.45	3.21
	(7.21)	(10.63)	(8.21)	(9.88)	(1.24)	(6.37)	(3.18)	(2.74)
Baseline [21]	83.47	13.51	72.54	15.99	90.17	6.97	97.53	5.43
	(5.91)	(10.74)	(16.07)	(16.98)	(16.53)	(10.79)	(1.76)	(4.23)
DAE [11]	83.35	7.04	71.48	20.47	73.04	14.88	97.61	3.43
	(5.57)	(6.17)	(14.20)	(18.84)	(36.69)	(25.51)	(1.22)	(1.92)
SDAN [8]	83.10	8.23	67.01	18.86	91.07	11.00	97.47	3.94
	(5.76)	(8.89)	(24.22)	(9.64)	(12.99)	(14.67)	(1.77)	(4.23)
SCL [16]	84.76	5.75	74.84	13.92	79.79	11.89	98.15	2.84
	(5.11)	(2.88)	(14.58)	(8.05)	(31.19)	(18.59)	(0.89)	(1.55)
nnUNet [10]	85.38	5.91	80.39	10.62	89.43	13.71	98.07	2.63
	(4.34)	(4.77)	(8.03)	(10.35)	(24.72)	(28.72)	(0.67)	(0.93)
RefSeg	87.86	6.91	81.56	14.34	97.31	3.74	98.26	3.07
	(3.01)	(9.24)	(8.52)	(14.57)	(4.58)	(5.94)	(0.81)	(4.35)

We conduct ablation experiments on M&Ms dataset (last 5 rows in Table 2) to analyze the contribution of each key design for the important component of structural similarity measurement in our method. We compare our RefSeg with four other variants, including similarity measurement with only L1 loss (RefSeg-L1), NCC loss (RefSeg-N), or MI loss (RefSeg-M), as well as that with both NCC

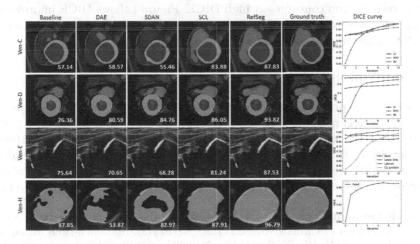

Fig. 3. Typical results of RefSeg. DICE values are shown at the right image corner.

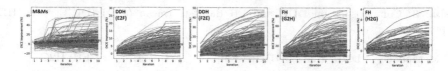

Fig. 4. DICE improvement curves of our RefSeg. One curve for one testing sample. The blue dot curve indicates the average DICE over all testing samples.

and MI losses but without the heatmap attention (RefSeg-NM). Compared with *baseline*, each of our proposed similarity losses and their combination can help improve the segmentation robustness, but RefSeg with L1 similarity loss is worse. It proves that maximizing the pixel-wise content similarity has adverse effects on RefSeg and our proposed structural similarity measurement captures important semantic information. We also note that the heatmap attention weight is effective in improving 1.51% on the DICE score (RefSeg-NM vs. RefSeg).

Table 3 reports the results of RefSeg and five competitors on DDH and FH datasets, including baseline [21], DAE [11], SDAN [8], SCL [16], and nnUNet [10]. *Upper-bound* represents the performance when training and testing on the target domain. Comparing *Upper-bound* with *baseline*, the performance degradation can be observed clearly in DICE index. RefSeg can significantly boost the performance over baseline and achieved the highest DICE in all tests, approaching the *Upper-bound* in E2F, G2H, and H2G. Although the performance degradation in H2G is not as serious as other tests (about 0.92% in DICE), our method can still achieve 0.73% and 2.36 pixel improvement in DICE and HD.

Figure 3 visualizes the segmentation results of baseline, DAE, SDAN, SCL and RefSeg on three datasets. Column *baseline* shows the severe segmentation failures. Though DAE, SDAN and SCL can improve model performance in some cases, they may fail in others and even perform worse than the baseline. From the DICE curves, we can see that RefSeg can significantly remedy the segmentation flaws iteratively and converges at high DICE. Figure 4 shows DICE improvement curves of RefSeg on all five experiment groups. The rising trend of the averaged blue dot curve validates the efficacy of RefSeg.

4   Conclusion

In this study, we propose a novel online reflective learning framework (RefSeg) to help deep models recognize segmentation failures and remedy. RefSeg is general in improving the model robustness against unseen imaging factors. Extensive experiments on three large datasets validate that RefSeg is effective and efficient, achieving state-of-the-art results over *nnUNet*. In the future, we will try to explore better similarity loss and extend the RefSeg to 3D segmentation tasks.

Acknowledgement. This work was supported by the grant from National Natural Science Foundation of China (Nos. 62171290, 62101343), Shenzhen-Hong Kong Joint Research Program (No. SGDX20201103095613036), and Shenzhen Science and Technology Innovations Committee (No. 20200812143441001).

References

1. Bergamo, A., Torresani, L.: Exploiting weakly-labeled web images to improve object classification: a domain adaptation approach. In: NeurIPS, pp. 181–189 (2010)
2. Billot, B., et al.: SynthSeg: domain randomisation for segmentation of brain MRI scans of any contrast and resolution. arXiv e-prints arXiv:2107.09559 (2021)
3. Campello, V.M.: Multi-centre, multi-vendor and multi-disease cardiac segmentation: the M&Ms challenge. IEEE TMI **40**(12), 3543–3554 (2021)
4. Chen, C., Liu, Q., Jin, Y., Dou, Q., Heng, P.-A.: Source-free domain adaptive fundus image segmentation with denoised pseudo-labeling. In: de Bruijne, M., et al. (eds.) MICCAI 2021. LNCS, vol. 12905, pp. 225–235. Springer, Cham (2021). https://doi.org/10.1007/978-3-030-87240-3_22
5. Dou, Q., Coelho de Castro, D., Kamnitsas, K., Glocker, B.: Domain generalization via model-agnostic learning of semantic features. In: NeurIPS, vol. 32 (2019)
6. Full, P.M., Isensee, F., Jäger, P.F., Maier-Hein, K.: Studying robustness of semantic segmentation under domain shift in cardiac MRI. In: Puyol Anton, E., et al. (eds.) STACOM 2020. LNCS, vol. 12592, pp. 238–249. Springer, Cham (2021). https://doi.org/10.1007/978-3-030-68107-4_24
7. Guan, H., Liu, M.: Domain adaptation for medical image analysis: a survey. IEEE T-BME **69**, 1173–1185 (2021)
8. He, Y., Carass, A., Zuo, L., et al.: Autoencoder based self-supervised test-time adaptation for medical image analysis. Media **72**, 102136 (2021)
9. Huo, Y., et al.: SynSeg-Net: synthetic segmentation without target modality ground truth. IEEE TMI **38**(4), 1016–1025 (2018)
10. Isensee, F., Jaeger, P.F., Kohl, S.A., Petersen, J., Maier-Hein, K.H.: nnU-Net: a self-configuring method for deep learning-based biomedical image segmentation. Nat. Methods **18**(2), 203–211 (2021)
11. Karani, N., Erdil, E., Chaitanya, K., Konukoglu, E.: Test-time adaptable neural networks for robust medical image segmentation. Media **68**, 101907 (2021)
12. Kushibar, K., et al.: Supervised domain adaptation for automatic sub-cortical brain structure segmentation with minimal user interaction. Sci. Rep. **9**(1), 1–15 (2019)
13. Liang, J., et al.: Sketch guided and progressive growing GAN for realistic and editable ultrasound image synthesis. MedIA **79**, 102461 (2022)
14. Liu, Q., Dou, Q., Heng, P.-A.: Shape-aware meta-learning for generalizing prostate MRI segmentation to unseen domains. In: Martel, A.L., et al. (eds.) MICCAI 2020. LNCS, vol. 12262, pp. 475–485. Springer, Cham (2020). https://doi.org/10.1007/978-3-030-59713-9_46
15. Liu, X., Thermos, S., O'Neil, A., Tsaftaris, S.A.: Semi-supervised meta-learning with disentanglement for domain-generalised medical image segmentation. In: de Bruijne, M., et al. (eds.) MICCAI 2021. LNCS, vol. 12902, pp. 307–317. Springer, Cham (2021). https://doi.org/10.1007/978-3-030-87196-3_29
16. Liu, Z., et al.: Style curriculum learning for robust medical image segmentation. In: de Bruijne, M., et al. (eds.) MICCAI 2021. LNCS, vol. 12901, pp. 451–460. Springer, Cham (2021). https://doi.org/10.1007/978-3-030-87193-2_43
17. Ma, J.: Histogram matching augmentation for domain adaptation with application to multi-centre, multi-vendor and multi-disease cardiac image segmentation. In: Puyol Anton, E., et al. (eds.) STACOM 2020. LNCS, vol. 12592, pp. 177–186. Springer, Cham (2021). https://doi.org/10.1007/978-3-030-68107-4_18

18. Madani, A., Moradi, M., Karargyris, A., Syeda-Mahmood, T.: Semi-supervised learning with generative adversarial networks for chest X-ray classification with ability of data domain adaptation. In: ISBI, pp. 1038–1042. IEEE (2018)

19. Moshkov, N., Mathe, B., Kertesz-Farkas, A., Hollandi, R., Horvath, P.: Test-time augmentation for deep learning-based cell segmentation on microscopy images. Sci. Rep. $10(1)$, 1–7 (2020)

20. Motiian, S., Piccirilli, M., Adjeroh, D.A., Doretto, G.: Unified deep supervised domain adaptation and generalization. In: ICCV, pp. 5715–5725 (2017)

21. Oktay, O., et al.: Attention U-Net: learning where to look for the pancreas. arXiv preprint arXiv:1804.03999 (2018)

22. Sarvaiya, J.N., Patnaik, S., Bombaywala, S.: Image registration by template matching using normalized cross-correlation. In: International Conference on Advances in Computing, Control, and Telecommunication Technologies, pp. 819–822. IEEE (2009)

23. Shankar, S., Piratla, V., Chakrabarti, S., Chaudhuri, S., Jyothi, P., Sarawagi, S.: Generalizing across domains via cross-gradient training. In: ICLR (2018)

24. Shen, D., Wu, G., Suk, H.I.: Deep learning in medical image analysis. Annu. Rev. Biomed. Eng. 19, 221–248 (2017)

25. Tobin, J., Fong, R., Ray, A., Schneider, J., Zaremba, W., Abbeel, P.: Domain randomization for transferring deep neural networks from simulation to the real world. In: IEEE IROS, pp. 23–30. IEEE (2017)

26. Volpi, R., Namkoong, H., Sener, O., Duchi, J., Murino, V., Savarese, S.: Generalizing to unseen domains via adversarial data augmentation. In: NeurIPS, pp. 5339–5349 (2018)

27. Wells, W.M., III., Viola, P., Atsumi, H., Nakajima, S., Kikinis, R.: Multi-modal volume registration by maximization of mutual information. Media 1, 35–51 (1996)

28. Xu, R., Chen, Y.W., Tang, S.Y., Morikawa, S., Kurumi, Y.: Parzen-window based normalized mutual information for medical image registration. IEICE Trans. Inf. Syst. $91(1)$, 132–144 (2008)

29. Yang, X., et al.: Generalizing deep models for ultrasound image segmentation. In: Frangi, A.F., Schnabel, J.A., Davatzikos, C., Alberola-López, C., Fichtinger, G. (eds.) MICCAI 2018. LNCS, vol. 11073, pp. 497–505. Springer, Cham (2018). https://doi.org/10.1007/978-3-030-00937-3_57

30. Zhang, Y., et al.: Semi-supervised cardiac image segmentation via label propagation and style transfer. In: Puyol Anton, E., et al. (eds.) STACOM 2020. LNCS, vol. 12592, pp. 219–227. Springer, Cham (2021). https://doi.org/10.1007/978-3-030-68107-4_22

31. Zhang, Y., et al.: Collaborative unsupervised domain adaptation for medical image diagnosis. IEEE TIP 29, 7834–7844 (2020)

Fine-Grained Correlation Loss
for Regression

Chaoyu Chen[1,2,3], Xin Yang[1,2,3], Ruobing Huang[1,2,3], Xindi Hu[4],
Yankai Huang[5], Xiduo Lu[1,2,3], Xinrui Zhou[1,2,3], Mingyuan Luo[1,2,3],
Yinyu Ye[1,2,3], Xue Shuang[1,2,3], Juzheng Miao[6], Yi Xiong[5], and Dong Ni[1,2,3(✉)]

[1] National-Regional Key Technology Engineering Laboratory for Medical Ultrasound,
School of Biomedical Engineering, Health Science Center, Shenzhen University,
Shenzhen, China
nidong@szu.edu.cn
[2] Medical Ultrasound Image Computing (MUSIC) Lab, Shenzhen University,
Shenzhen, China
[3] Marshall Laboratory of Biomedical Engineering, Shenzhen University,
Shenzhen, China
[4] Shenzhen RayShape Medical Technology Co., Ltd., Shenzhen, China
[5] Department of Ultrasound, Luohu People's Hosptial, Shenzhen, China
[6] School of Biological Science and Medical Engineering, Southeast University,
Nanjing, China

Abstract. Regression learning is classic and fundamental for medical
image analysis. It provides the continuous mapping for many critical
applications, like the attribute estimation, object detection, segmentation and non-rigid registration. However, previous studies mainly took
the case-wise criteria, like the mean square errors, as the optimization
objectives. They ignored the very important population-wise *correlation*
criterion, which is exactly the final evaluation metric in many tasks. In
this work, we propose to revisit the classic regression tasks with novel
investigations on directly optimizing the fine-grained correlation losses.
We mainly explore two complementary correlation indexes as learnable
losses: Pearson linear correlation (PLC) and Spearman rank correlation
(SRC). The contributions of this paper are two folds. First, for the PLC
on global level, we propose a strategy to make it robust against the outliers and regularize the key distribution factors. These efforts significantly
stabilize the learning and magnify the efficacy of PLC. Second, for the
SRC on local level, we propose a coarse-to-fine scheme to ease the learning of the exact ranking order among samples. Specifically, we convert the
learning for the ranking of samples into the learning of similarity relationships among samples. We extensively validate our method on two typical
ultrasound image regression tasks, including the image quality assessment and bio-metric measurement. Experiments prove that, with the
fine-grained guidance in directly optimizing the correlation, the regression performances are significantly improved. Our proposed correlation
losses are general and can be extended to more important applications.

C. Chen and X. Yang—Contributed equally to this work.

© The Author(s), under exclusive license to Springer Nature Switzerland AG 2022
L. Wang et al. (Eds.): MICCAI 2022, LNCS 13438, pp. 663–672, 2022.
https://doi.org/10.1007/978-3-031-16452-1_63

Keywords: Regression · Ultrasound image · Correlation Loss Functions

1 Introduction

Regression is a statistical method that attempts to determine the continuous mapping relationship between one dependent variable and another one. Regression has been explored as a fundamental solution for versatile medical image analysis, e.g. image quality assessment (IQA) [4], landmark localization [10,11], object detection [2], segmentation [6], bio-metric measurement (BMM) [15] and registration [1]. Figure 1 shows the tasks we accomplished with regression in this paper, including IQA and bio-metric estimation in fetal ultrasound (US) images.

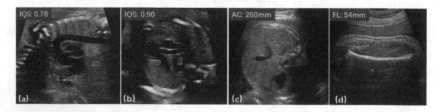

Fig. 1. The regression tasks considered in this paper. (a)–(b): IQA on fetal heart US images with IQS stands for image quality score. (c)–(d): AC and FL denote abdominal circumference and femur length of fetus in US images, respectively.

Lots of approaches have been devised for the regression. Dong et al. [5] proposed a regression forest to predict the landmark coordinates in brain MR. Wang et al. [13] formulated the spine segmentation as a boundary regression. In deep learning era, Cao et al. [1] designed deep networks to regress the deformation field. Korhonen et al. [14] built a deep transformer for IQA regression. In recent years, researchers explored to introduce extra information for case-wise supervision and improve the regression. Christian et al. [11] proposed to regress the Gaussian heatmap instead of coordinates for landmark detection. In [10], authors collected both landmark and classification cues to refine the location regression.

To the best of our knowledge, these medical regression studies mainly focus on learning the mapping among input and output for individual samples, but ignore the learning of the structured relationships over the dataset and among the samples. *Correlation* criterion at population level just fits the very capacities to describe the relationships, including linear relationship and ranking order. Recent work in computer vision community explored to directly optimize the correlation based objectives. V-MEON-SF [9] and Norm-In-Norm [7] approximated the Pearson linear correlation (PLC) based loss function on global level for regression. Although effective, their solution is sensitive to the outliers. Further, Engilberge et al. [3] use deep networks to directly regress the absolute ranking order with brute force. The solution is heavy and still overlooks the relative ranking among samples.

In this work, we propose to directly optimize the correlation in a fine-grained way to improve medical image regression. We mainly explore two complementary correlation indexes with novel formulations for maximization: PLC to regularize the strength of linear relationship and Spearman rank correlation (SRC) to further emphasize relative ranking order. Our contributions are two folds. First, for the PLC on global level, we propose a new design by customizing different optimization objectives for normal and outliers. Further, we propose to directly regularize the key distribution factors for regression. These composite efforts significantly stabilize the learning and strengthen the efficacy of PLC. Second, for the SRC on local level, we propose a lightweight, coarse-to-fine scheme to ease the learning of the relative ranking order among samples. Specifically, we transform the learning into the constraints on similarity relationships among samples. We extensively validate our method on two typical ultrasound image regression tasks, including the IQA and BMM. Experiments prove that, with the novel formulations in directly optimizing the correlation, our method can significantly improve the regression performances. Our proposed method is general and can be considered in more applications.

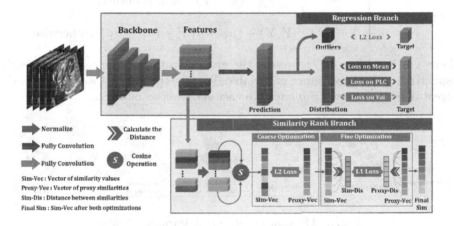

Fig. 2. Schematic view of our proposed method.

2   Methodology

Figure 2 provides an overview of our framework in the training phase. For a batch of image samples, the backbone firstly extracts feature tensors and then forwards them to the PLC based regression branch. The branch automatically identifies the outliers from normal samples and splits the batch into two parts. The normal part then receives the supervision from PLC loss. The feature tensors also flow into the similarity rank branch to constrain the ranking order. In testing, the regression branch would provide the final prediction.

2.1 Effective PLC Loss to Optimize Linear Relationship

PLC is used to measure the strength of linear relationship between two variables. We aim to take PLC as the objective to maximize and hence reduce the distribution discrepancy at global level. The basic definition of PLC between X and Y follows the Pearson index as follows:

$$PLC(X,Y) = \frac{\sum_{i=1}^{n}(X_i - \mu_X)(Y_i - \mu_Y)}{\sqrt{\sum_{i=1}^{n}(X_i - \mu_X)^2}\sqrt{\sum_{i=1}^{n}(Y_i - \mu_Y)^2}}, \tag{1}$$

where μ_X or μ_Y denotes the mean value of the variable. This definition is inherently very sensitive to the outliers in the prediction. The outliers mean the samples with predictions differ severely from the ground truth. Therefore, we propose to automatically identify and handle the outliers with customized loss for a stable training. For the rest clean samples, we move further to narrow the constraints on the distribution by minimizing the distance between means and variances, respectively. Finally, as Fig. 2 illustrates, the detailed definition of our reformed PLC loss is:

$$Loss_{PLC} = \begin{cases} \frac{1}{m}\sum_{i=1}^{m}(\hat{y}_i - y_i)^2, \text{ if } y_i \text{ is outlier,} \\ 1 - PLC^2(\hat{Y}, Y) + (\mu_{\hat{Y}} - \mu_Y)^2 + (\sigma_{\hat{Y}} - \sigma_Y)^2, \text{otherwise} \end{cases} \tag{2}$$

where $\hat{y} \in \hat{Y}$ and $y \in Y$ represent the ground truth and the regression result, respectively. σ is the variance of variable. We take the top 10% samples with the largest difference between $\hat{y}$ and y in each iteration as outliers.

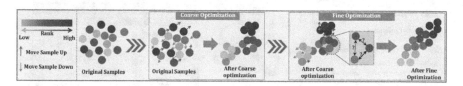

Fig. 3. The coarse-to-fine rank learning scheme.

2.2 Coarse-to-Fine SRC to Regularize Rank

A perfect regression should simultaneously satisfy the criteria from individual, global and peer levels. Previous methods mainly focus on optimizing the losses at individual level, like the mean square error, but ignore the correlation relationship. Our reformed PLC loss partially addresses the problem at global level, but still misses an important relationship at peer level, i.e., the ranking order. Our proposed SRC loss aims to solve this problem. The original SRC is defined to measure the strength of association between two ranked variables as $SRC(X,Y) = 1 - (6||\mathbf{rk}(X) - \mathbf{rk}(Y)||_2^2)/(n(n^2 - 1))$, where X and Y denote two variables, $\mathbf{rk}(\cdot)$ is the sorting operator, n is the sample number of the variable. Low SRC means X and Y matches each other on not only the value but also the strict rank. However, the discrete ranking involved loss is difficult to minimize, like the SRC which is non-differentiable in its original formulation. Moreover, how to describe the absolute and relative ranking for learning is challenging.

In this paper, we propose to transform the learning of the ranking order into the problem of regularizing the similarities among samples. This transformation provides not only a differentiable approximation for SRC, but also a new way for rank representation. Specifically, the sample similarity is represented by the cosine distance $\mathbf{S}(x_i, x_j)$ between feature vectors (Fig. 2). Notably, as shown in Fig. 3, to further ease the rank learning, we decompose the rank among samples into global and local rank and propose a coarse-to-fine learning scheme (Fig. 2).

Coarse Level for Global Rank. In the coarse level, as Fig. 3 shows, we aim to roughly regularize the global rank by adding constraints on sample similarity. Our hypothesis is that the samples with similar rank ground truth should have similar feature representations to some extent, while the images with dissimilar ranks should be pushed away from each other. We propose $\mathbf{P}(x_i, x_j) = \left[\frac{\mathbf{R}(x_i)}{\mathbf{R}(x_j)} \right]$ as a proxy similarity reference between sample i and j, where x_i is the feature vector, $\mathbf{R}(\cdot)$ denotes the vector's regression target. $[\cdot]$ is the reciprocal operation when the value is greater than 1.0. Based on our hypothesis and $\mathbf{P}(x_i, x_j)$, we can conduct the rough regularization on features to encourage the clustering and scattering of samples guided by the $\mathbf{R}(\cdot)$ (Fig. 3). The sample similarity $\mathbf{S}(x_i, x_j)$ should satisfy the following condition in this coarse level:

$$r(x_i, x_j) : \mathbf{P}(x_i, x_j) < |\mathbf{S}(x_i, x_j)| < \mathbf{P}(x_i, x_j) + \alpha \tag{3}$$

The parameter α is an interval and controls the margin. We set α to 0.25 in this study. Then, the first part of our SRC loss is defined as Eq. 4 for rough penalty:

$$L_C = (|\mathbf{S}(x_i, x_j)| - \mathbf{P}(x_i, x_j))^2, \text{ if } |\mathbf{S}(x_i, x_j)| \text{ not subject to } r(x_i, x_j). \tag{4}$$

Fine Level for Local Rank. L_C in coarse level set rough cluster and rank for samples. However, the exact rank in local range among samples is not reviewed. Therefore, when Eq. 3 is satisfied, we further propose to regularize the local rank for any tuple of sample features (x_i, x_j, x_k) in a fine level, as the triangle relationship shown in Fig. 3. Our intuitive motivation is that, if the target rank of the tuple (x_i, x_j, x_k) presents the relationship $\mathbf{R}(x_i) > \mathbf{R}(x_j) > \mathbf{R}(x_k)$, then the similarity metrics should accordingly satisfy the symmetric distance relationship of $\mathbf{S}(x_i, x_j) > \mathbf{S}(x_i, x_k)$ and $\mathbf{S}(x_j, x_k) > \mathbf{S}(x_i, x_k)$. Therefore, we can realize the sample ranking by constraining the similarities.

Inspired by the margin-based ranking loss [12], the difference between the similarities should be larger than a margin, in order to better distinguish the relationship between similar samples. Instead of using a fixed margin in [12], we propose to build an adaptive margin to better fit the diverse similarity relationships in regression task. Hence, we introduce the difference between the proxy similarity reference $\mathbf{P}(x_i, x_j)$ as the dynamic margin. We therefore build the following losses as the second part of our SRC to regularize the local rank:

$$L_{ascent} = max \{0, (\mathbf{P}(x_i, x_j) - \mathbf{P}(x_i, x_k)) - (|\mathbf{S}(x_i, x_j)| - |\mathbf{S}(x_i, x_k)|)\} \quad (5)$$

$$L_{descent} = max \{0, (\mathbf{P}(x_j, x_k) - \mathbf{P}(x_i, x_k)) - (|\mathbf{S}(x_j, x_k)| - |\mathbf{S}(x_i, x_k)|)\} \quad (6)$$

The tuple (x_i, x_j, x_k) in Eq. 5 and Eq. 6 is in its sorted version according to the ground truth rank. We considered both L_{ascent} and $L_{descent}$ as a bi-directional design for symmetric constraints on similarity relationships. Ablation studies in Table 2 validates the importance of this design. Finally, our SRC loss covering global and local rank, with coarse-to-fine learning scheme, is defined as:

$$Loss_{SRC} = \begin{cases} \frac{1}{m}\sum_{(i,j,k)}^{m}(L_{ascent} + L_{descent}), \text{otherwise} \\ \frac{1}{n}\sum_{(i,j)}^{n} L_C, \text{ if } |\mathbf{S}(x_i, x_j)| \text{ not subject to } r(x_i, x_j). \end{cases} \quad (7)$$

3   Experimental Results

3.1   Materials and Implementation Details

We evaluate the regression performance of the proposed framework on two typical ultrasound image-based regression tasks. The first one is IQA, consisting of 2000 images of right ventricular outflow tract (RVOT), 2000 images of pulmonary bifurcation (PB) and 4475 images of aortic arch (AA). The second task is BMM, including 5026 images of fetal head circumference (HC), 4551 images of fetal abdominal circumference (AC) and 6454 images of femur length measurement (FL). The pixel resolution of AC, HC and FL is $0.22 \times 0.22\,\text{mm}^2$, $0.18 \times 0.18\,\text{mm}^2$ and $0.17 \times 0.17\,\text{mm}^2$, respectively. Image quality score of IQA and measurement length of BMM were manually annotated by experts using the Pair annotation software package[8]. We randomly split the dataset into a training (60%), a validation (15%) and a test set (25%). All experimental results are based on three-fold cross-validation and presented in the form of mean(std).

We implement our method in Pytorch and train the system by Adam optimizer, using a standard server with an NVIDIA 2080Ti GPU. For optimization, we run 160 epochs with a stage-wise learning rate: initial value of 3e−4 and decaying to 25% of previous for every 70 epochs of training for all experiments. The batch size is set to 160 on all datasets. In addition, we employ a warm-up strategy to train the network with a basic loss function (i.e. Mean Square Error). Then, we introduce the correlation-based loss functions when the training meets both of the following conditions: 1) training for more than 30 epochs; 2) the PLC and SRC on the validation did not rise for 5 consecutive epochs. Data augmentation includes random rotation and random scaling. The input size of the image is 320×320 and the fixed size is generated by padding after scaling.

3.2   Quantitative and Qualitative Analysis

The performance is measured via three criteria for IQA task: PLC ↑, SRC ↑ and Kendall correlation (KLC ↑), and another two criteria are used for BMM task:

absolute error (AE ↓) and relative error (RE ↓). We use Resnet18 as the network for all methods. Ablation study was conducted by comparing the methods including Resnet18, Resnet18 with PLC loss (Res-PLC), Resnet18 with SRC loss (Res-SRC) and Resnet18 with PLC and SRC loss (Res-PLC-SRC). We also compared with NIN [7] and SoDeep [3] under the same warm-up strategy.

Table 1. Quantitative evaluation of mean(std) results for two regression tasks.

Methods		Resnet18	Res-PLC	NIN [7]	Res-SRC	SoDeep [3]	Res-PLC-SRC
ROVT	PLC	0.597(0.01)	0.616(0.02)	0.616(0.03)	0.602(0.01)	0.574(0.01)	0.659(0.01)
	SRC	0.551(0.02)	0.651(0.03)	0.628(0.01)	0.583(0.02)	0.670(0.02)	0.685(0.01)
	KLC	0.398(0.01)	0.477(0.02)	0.456(0.01)	0.422(0.01)	0.490(0.01)	0.506(0.00)
PB	PLC	0.622(0.04)	0.662(0.03)	0.570(0.03)	0.627(0.07)	0.565(0.08)	0.649(0.06)
	SRC	0.583(0.05)	0.615(0.04)	0.596(0.07)	0.627(0.07)	0.585(0.07)	0.648(0.05)
	KLC	0.420(0.04)	0.444(0.03)	0.425(0.06)	0.445(0.06)	0.418(0.06)	0.469(0.04)
AA	PLC	0.771(0.01)	0.808(0.01)	0.804(0.01)	0.801(0.01)	0.786(0.01)	0.820(0.01)
	SRC	0.796(0.03)	0.821(0.02)	0.814(0.02)	0.813(0.01)	0.810(0.03)	0.832(0.02)
	KLC	0.610(0.02)	0.632(0.02)	0.630(0.02)	0.628(0.01)	0.626(0.03)	0.642(0.01)
AC	PLC	0.977(0.03)	0.980(0.02)	0.962(0.03)	0.978(0.02)	0.966(0.03)	0.984(0.02)
	SRC	0.955(0.03)	0.963(0.02)	0.961(0.03)	0.962(0.02)	0.961(0.03)	0.968(0.02)
	KLC	0.855(0.07)	0.869(0.06)	0.860(0.07)	0.863(0.06)	0.867(0.04)	0.878(0.06)
	AE(mm)	5.74(6.38)	6.01(6.28)	68.36(6.67)	6.53(4.90)	39.18(5.08)	5.47(5.51)
	RE(%)	4.21(5.59)	4.43(5.54)	42.94(3.42)	5.23(5.89)	32.74(18.85)	3.86(4.73)
HC	PLC	0.995(0.00)	0.997(0.00)	0.994(0.00)	0.996(0.00)	0.988(0.01)	0.998(0.00)
	SRC	0.993(0.01)	0.995(0.00)	0.993(0.00)	0.995(0.00)	0.992(0.01)	0.996(0.00)
	KLC	0.943(0.03)	0.953(0.02)	0.933(0.01)	0.947(0.02)	0.945(0.03)	0.954(0.02)
	AE(mm)	2.07(1.04)	1.55(1.09)	32.44(2.24)	1.73(1.48)	25.96(3.06)	1.52(1.26)
	RE(%)	2.64(1.72)	1.96(1.51)	27.41(4.13)	2.40(2.69)	39.61(12.54)	1.85(1.42)
FL	PLC	0.975(0.02)	0.979(0.02)	0.978(0.01)	0.977(0.01)	0.972(0.01)	0.982(0.01)
	SRC	0.963(0.01)	0.973(0.01)	0.972(0.00)	0.970(0.01)	0.966(0.02)	0.978(0.01)
	KLC	0.850(0.03)	0.877(0.03)	0.873(0.04)	0.868(0.03)	0.883(0.02)	0.890(0.03)
	AE(mm)	1.73(1.04)	1.27(1.20)	14.55(1.49)	1.02(1.02)	5.00(1.04)	1.17(1.22)
	RE(%)	11.28(11.63)	8.09(11.82)	38.59(2.56)	9.40(15.98)	33.56(19.39)	7.02(11.32)

Table 1 compares the performance of the different methods on two regression tasks. Comparing Res-PLC and NIN [7] can prove that paying attention to outliers and explicitly constraining the mean and variance of the distribution can significantly improve model performance. Our proposed Res-SRC outperforms SoDeep [3] in overall comparison demonstrates that the Coarse-to-Fine strategy is more suitable for learning rank. Moreover, SoDeep and NIN perform poor in AE and RE is because they only focus on the rank correlation among predictions and labels, while ignore the value differences. This results in high correlation values, but poor AE and RE. According to Table 1, the superior performance of Res-PLC and Res-SRC compared to Resnet18 shows the efficacy of our proposed PLC loss and SRC loss separately. Furthermore, the Res-PLC-SRC achieved the best result on both regression tasks among all these methods further demonstrates the effectiveness and generality of our approach.

Table 2. Ablation results of SRC loss.

Methods		Resnet18	Res-SRC$_{ascent}$	Res-SRC$_{descent}$	Res-SRC
ROTV	PLC	0.597(0.01)	0.583(0.02)	0.562(0.01)	0.602(0.01)
	SRC	0.551(0.02)	0.569(0.01)	0.559(0.06)	0.583(0.02)
	KLC	0.398(0.01)	0.403(0.01)	0.403(0.05)	0.422(0.01)
PB	PLC	0.622(0.04)	0.531(0.09)	0.638(0.04)	0.627(0.07)
	SRC	0.583(0.05)	0.575(0.07)	0.625(0.05)	0.627(0.07)
	KLC	0.420(0.04)	0.408(0.05)	0.443(0.04)	0.445(0.06)
AA	PLC	0.771(0.01)	0.793(0.01)	0.785(0.02)	0.801(0.01)
	SRC	0.796(0.03)	0.793(0.00)	0.799(0.02)	0.813(0.01)
	KLC	0.610(0.03)	0.609(0.01)	0.614(0.02)	0.628(0.01)

Table 2 shows the ablation experiments on SRC loss. Res-SRC$_{ascent}$ indicates that only the ascent part in SRC loss was used, as shown in Eq. 5, and Res-SRC$_{descent}$ is the opposite. Experiments show that constraining both the ascent and descent parts simultaneously can achieve the best results. Figure 4 illustrates the consistency and correlation distribution map of three datasets in two regression tasks. Our proposed methods can reduce outliers very well and achieve excellent performance on correlation and consistency in various tasks.

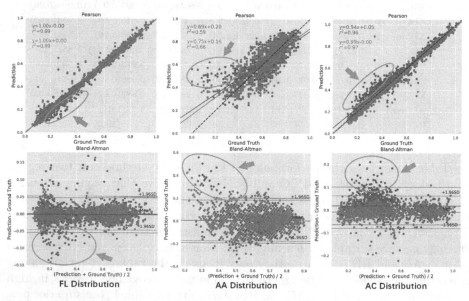

Fig. 4. Visualization of correlation and consistency. Blue dots are the Resnet18's result and red dots are our approach's result. Green circles indicate outliers. (Color figure online)

4 Conclusion

In this paper, we propose two correlation-based loss functions for medical image regression tasks. By constraining the outliers and explicitly regularizing the key distribution factors of normal samples, our proposed PLC loss exhibits powerful capabilities on regression tasks. Moreover, we propose a Coarse-to-Fine optimization strategy to ease the rank learning, which can further improve regression performance. Experimental results show that the simple network equipped with our proposed loss functions can achieve excellent performance on various medical image regression tasks.

Acknowledgement. This work was supported by the grant from National Natural Science Foundation of China (Nos. 62171290, 62101343), Shenzhen-Hong Kong Joint Research Program (No. SGDX20201103095613036), and Shenzhen Science and Technology Innovations Committee (No. 20200812143441001).

References

1. Cao, X., Yang, J., Zhang, J., Wang, Q., Yap, P.T., Shen, D.: Deformable image registration using a cue-aware deep regression network. IEEE Trans. Biomed. Eng. **65**(9), 1900–1911 (2018)
2. Ding, J., Li, A., Hu, Z., Wang, L.: Accurate pulmonary nodule detection in computed tomography images using deep convolutional neural networks. In: Descoteaux, M., Maier-Hein, L., Franz, A., Jannin, P., Collins, D.L., Duchesne, S. (eds.) MICCAI 2017. LNCS, vol. 10435, pp. 559–567. Springer, Cham (2017). https://doi.org/10.1007/978-3-319-66179-7_64
3. Engilberge, M., Chevallier, L., Pérez, P., Cord, M.: SoDeep: a sorting deep net to learn ranking loss surrogates. In: Proceedings of the IEEE/CVF Conference on Computer Vision and Pattern Recognition, pp. 10792–10801 (2019)
4. Gao, Q., et al.: Combined global and local information for blind CT image quality assessment via deep learning. In: Medical Imaging, vol. 11316, p. 1131615. International Society for Optics and Photonics (2020)
5. Han, D., Gao, Y., Wu, G., Yap, P.-T., Shen, D.: Robust anatomical landmark detection for MR brain image registration. In: Golland, P., Hata, N., Barillot, C., Hornegger, J., Howe, R. (eds.) MICCAI 2014. LNCS, vol. 8673, pp. 186–193. Springer, Cham (2014). https://doi.org/10.1007/978-3-319-10404-1_24
6. He, Y., et al.: Fully convolutional boundary regression for retina OCT segmentation. In: Shen, D., et al. (eds.) MICCAI 2019. LNCS, vol. 11764, pp. 120–128. Springer, Cham (2019). https://doi.org/10.1007/978-3-030-32239-7_14
7. Li, D., Jiang, T., Jiang, M.: Norm-in-norm loss with faster convergence and better performance for image quality assessment. In: Proceedings of the 28th ACM International Conference on Multimedia, pp. 789–797 (2020)
8. Liang, J., et al.: Sketch guided and progressive growing GAN for realistic and editable ultrasound image synthesis. Medical Image Analysis, p. 102461 (2022)
9. Liu, W., Duanmu, Z., Wang, Z.: End-to-end blind quality assessment of compressed videos using deep neural networks. In: ACM Multimedia, pp. 546–554 (2018)
10. Noothout, J.M., et al.: Deep learning-based regression and classification for automatic landmark localization in medical images. IEEE Trans. Med. Imaging **39**(12), 4011–4022 (2020)

11. Payer, C., Štern, D., Bischof, H., Urschler, M.: Regressing heatmaps for multiple landmark localization using CNNs. In: Ourselin, S., Joskowicz, L., Sabuncu, M.R., Unal, G., Wells, W. (eds.) MICCAI 2016. LNCS, vol. 9901, pp. 230–238. Springer, Cham (2016). https://doi.org/10.1007/978-3-319-46723-8_27

12. Schroff, F., Kalenichenko, D., Philbin, J.: FaceNet: a unified embedding for face recognition and clustering. In: Proceedings of the IEEE Conference on Computer Vision and Pattern Recognition, pp. 815–823 (2015)

13. Wang, Z., Zhen, X., Tay, K., Osman, S., Romano, W., Li, S.: Regression segmentation for m^3 spinal images. IEEE Trans. Med. Imaging **34**(8), 1640–1648 (2014)

14. You, J., Korhonen, J.: Transformer for image quality assessment. In: 2021 IEEE International Conference on Image Processing (ICIP), pp. 1389–1393. IEEE (2021)

15. Zhang, J., Petitjean, C., Lopez, P., Ainouz, S.: Direct estimation of fetal head circumference from ultrasound images based on regression CNN. In: Medical Imaging with Deep Learning, pp. 914–922. PMLR (2020)

Suppressing Poisoning Attacks on Federated Learning for Medical Imaging

Naif Alkhunaizi(iD), Dmitry Kamzolov(iD), Martin Takáč(iD),
and Karthik Nandakumar(✉)(iD)

Mohamed bin Zayed University of Artificial Intelligence, Abu Dhabi, UAE
{naif.alkhunaizi,kamzolov.dmitry,martin.takac,
karthik.nandakumar}@mbzuai.ac.ae

Abstract. Collaboration among multiple data-owning entities (e.g.,
hospitals) can accelerate the training process and yield better machine
learning models due to the availability and diversity of data. However,
privacy concerns make it challenging to exchange data while preserving confidentiality. Federated Learning (FL) is a promising solution that
enables collaborative training through exchange of model parameters
instead of raw data. However, most existing FL solutions work under
the assumption that participating clients are *honest* and thus can fail
against poisoning attacks from malicious parties, whose goal is to deteriorate the global model performance. In this work, we propose a robust
aggregation rule called Distance-based Outlier Suppression (DOS) that
is resilient to byzantine failures. The proposed method computes the distance between local parameter updates of different clients and obtains
an outlier score for each client using Copula-based Outlier Detection
(COPOD). The resulting outlier scores are converted into normalized
weights using a softmax function, and a weighted average of the local
parameters is used for updating the global model. DOS aggregation can
effectively suppress parameter updates from malicious clients without
the need for any hyperparameter selection, even when the data distributions are heterogeneous. Evaluation on two medical imaging datasets
(CheXpert and HAM10000) demonstrates the higher robustness of DOS
method against a variety of poisoning attacks in comparison to other
state-of-the-art methods. The code can be found at https://github.com/
Naiftt/SPAFD.

Keywords: Federated learning · Parameter aggregation · Malicious
clients · Outlier suppression

1 Introduction

Medical institutions often seek to leverage their data to build deep learning
models for predicting different diseases [10,23]. However, limited access to data
can impede the learning process [27] or introduce bias towards the local data
[18]. Hence, collaborative learning is vital to expand data availability and maximize model performance. Federated Learning (FL) [20] provides a paradigm

L. Wang et al. (Eds.): MICCAI 2022, LNCS 13438, pp. 673–683, 2022.
https://doi.org/10.1007/978-3-031-16452-1_64

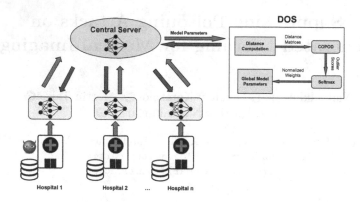

Fig. 1. Federated Learning (FL) in the presence of a malicious client. Distance-based Outlier Suppression (DOS) aggregation rule (right) can be applied to robustly aggregate local parameter updates.

where multiple institutions/devices can use their data to train local models and exchange their model parameters regularly with a central server. The server aggregates the local model parameters to update a global model, which is shared back to the clients. This allows all parties to preserve their data locally and offers better results while maintaining data privacy. Recent works have underscored the importance of FL in medical imaging [9,30].

Typically, FL algorithms (e.g., FedAvg [24]) operate under the assumption that clients participate in the protocol honestly and their data distributions are identical. However, the competitive nature of the participants makes them vulnerable to poisoning attacks. Real-world FL is susceptible to a variety of targeted/untargeted attacks [12,34] and byzantine faults [19]. Techniques proposed to tackle non-iid data [20] cannot handle malicious parties that attempt to deteriorate the global model performance. Though many robust aggregation rules have been proposed for byzantine-tolerant FL [5,14,33], such methods often require a careful choice of hyperparameters (e.g., prior knowledge of proportion of malicious clients) and are vulnerable to more sophisticated attacks [11].

The core contribution of this work is a novel robust aggregation rule called Distance-based Outlier Suppression (DOS) for byzantine-tolerant FL. The proposed framework (see Fig. 1) enables the central server to suppress local parameter updates from malicious clients during aggregation. The DOS framework is enabled by computing distances (Euclidean and cosine) between local parameter updates of different clients and detecting outliers in this distance space. A state-of-the-art, parameter-free outlier detection algorithm called COPOD [21] is applied to compute the outlier score for each client based on the above distances. Finally, the outlier scores are mapped to client-specific weights, and weighted average of local parameter updates is utilized for global model update. The proposed DOS aggregation rule demonstrates high robustness against diverse poisoning attacks under both iid (CheXpert) and non-iid (HAM10000) settings.

2   Related Work

Most FL algorithms aim to minimize the following loss function:

$$\min_{\theta \in \mathbb{R}^d} \left\{ \mathbf{F}(\theta) := \sum_{i=1}^{n} \alpha_i \mathbf{F}_i(\theta) \right\}, \tag{1}$$

where n is the number of clients, F_i is the loss function for the ith client, and α_i is a value between 0 and 1 that weights the contribution of the ith client. Popular aggregation rules such as FedAvg [24] either assign equal weights to all clients ($\alpha_i = 1/n, \forall\, i = 1, 2, \ldots, n$) or assign weights to the clients based on the relative size of their training sets. Such schemes have shown effective outcomes under the assumption of honest clients and iid data distributions. FedProx [20] was introduced to tackle heterogeneity and non-iid data across clients. Progressive Fourier Aggregation (PFA) was introduced in [6] to improve stability by preventing an abrupt drop in accuracy. While these methods promise convergence, they do not consider noisy parameters [32] or malicious parties that attempt to hinder learning or cause it to converge to poor local minima.

Since FL requires communication between the server and clients, it is susceptible to random network errors that can deliver abnormal parameters to the server or malicious parties that attempt to corrupt the learning process. Such failures are defined as Byzantine failures [19]. In such settings, there are two types of attacks: (i) targeted attacks that cause the global model to misclassify a selected class (e.g., backdoor attacks [2], model poisoning attacks [3,4], and data poisoning attacks [25]) and (ii) untargeted attacks that harm the model's performance across all classes [20]. Moreover, there are techniques designed to make the attack more stealthy [34]. Other potential attacks include label-flipping, where the model is trained on incorrect labels [12], and crafted model attacks [11] that formulate the attack as an optimization problem. In this paper, we mainly focus on untargeted attacks since they are more lethal to the learning process.

Several robust aggregation rules have been proposed to defend against Byzantine failures. Krum [5] selects the parameter update that is closest to the mean parameter update of all clients. Coordinate-Wise-Median [33] calculates the median because it is less sensitive to outliers as opposed to the mean. Trimmed Mean [33] sorts the parameter values and discards a fraction of each coordinate's smallest and largest values. Bulyan was proposed in [14] to further improve the robustness. However, most of these methods require hyperparameter selection (e.g., proportion of outliers to be discarded) and are susceptible to crafted model attacks [11]. More recently, Robust Federated Aggregation (RFA) [28], which relies on aggregation using the geometric median, and SparseFed [26], which uses global top-k update sparsification and device-level gradient clipping, have been proposed to mitigate poisoning attacks.

3   Proposed Method

We propose Distance-based Outlier Suppression (**DOS**), a robust FL aggregation rule (see Algorithm 1) that can defend against different untargeted poisoning

---

Algorithm 1. Distance-based Outlier Suppression (DOS)

Require: Initialize parameter vector $\theta^0 \in \mathbb{R}^d$ for global model
1: **for** $t = 0, 1, \ldots, T - 1$ **do**
2:    <u>Server:</u> Server broadcasts θ^t to all clients
3:    **for** all $i \in [n]$ in parallel **do**
4:       <u>Client i:</u> Learn local parameters θ_i^{t+1} using suitable local optimizer.
5:       Send $\hat{\theta}_i^{t+1}$ to server. Note that $\hat{\theta}_i^{t+1} \neq \theta_i^{t+1}$ for malicious clients.
6:    **end for**
7:    <u>Server:</u> **DOS** aggregation rule:
8:       Compute Euclidean and cosine distance matrices M_E and M_C, respectively
9:       Compute outlier scores $\mathbf{r}_E = COPOD(M_E)$, $\mathbf{r}_C = COPOD(M_C)$
10:      Compute average outlier score $\mathbf{r} = (\mathbf{r}_E + \mathbf{r}_C)/2$
11:      Compute normalized client weights as $w_i = \frac{\exp(-r_i)}{\sum_{j=1}^{n} exp(-r_j)}$
12:      Update global model based on weighted average of local parameters

$$\theta^{t+1} = \sum_{i=1}^{n} w_i \hat{\theta}_i^{t+1}$$

13: **end for**

---

attacks on FL as long as the proportion of clients experiencing byzantine-failures is less than 50%. Suppose that there are n clients in the FL setup, and their goal is to learn the global model parameters θ that minimizes the objective function in Eq. (1). Note that a proportion p of these clients ($p < 50\%$) can be malicious and may not share the same objective as the other honest clients. Similar to FedAvg, the global model parameters are initialized to θ^0. In each of the T communication rounds, the current global model parameters θ^t are broadcast to all clients. Each client $i \in [n]$ learns the local model parameters θ_i^{t+1} based on their local data using a suitable optimizer and sends $\hat{\theta}_i^{t+1}$ back to the server. While $\hat{\theta}_i^{t+1}$ is expected to be a faithful version of θ_i^{t+1} (except for known transformations like compression) for honest clients, this may not be the case for malicious clients. The server computes the updated global model parameters using the DOS aggregation rule. The proposed DOS aggregation rule consists of three key steps:

Distance Computation: The server starts with calculating the Euclidean and cosine distances between the local parameters sent by the clients as follows:

$$d_{ij}^E = ||\hat{\theta}_i - \hat{\theta}_j||_2, \qquad d_{ij}^C = 1 - \frac{\hat{\theta}_i^T \hat{\theta}_j}{||\hat{\theta}_i||_2 ||\hat{\theta}_j||_2},$$

where $i, j = 1, 2, \ldots, n$. Here, the time index t is skipped for convenience. The $(n \times n)$ distance matrices $M_E = [d_{ij}^E]$ and $M_C = [d_{ij}^C]$ are then computed and utilized for outlier detection. Unlike existing methods such as [5,14,33], where outlier detection is performed directly on the model parameter space, the proposed DOS method performs outlier detection in the distance space.

Outlier Score Computation: After exploring various anomaly detection methods such as Random Forest [29], Local Outlier Factor (LOF) [7], and K-means [22], we selected the Copula Based Outlier Detection (COPOD) method [21] due to several factors. Firstly, other methods require choosing the percentage of abnormal data points (in our case clients) in advance, whereas COPOD is parameter-free, thus making it more robust. Moreover, COPOD is known to be computationally efficient even in high dimensional settings because it utilizes the marginals of the joint distributions, thereby allowing for greater flexibility and individual modeling of each dimension. Finally, the COPOD method also has desirable interpretability properties since it is based on modeling the tail probabilities along each dimension. In general, the COPOD function takes a $(n \times d)$ matrix as input, where each row represents a sample and each column represents an attribute of the sample to produce a n-dimensional vector of outlier scores $\mathbf{r} = [r_1, r_2, \dots, r_n]$, where $r_i \in (0, +\infty)$ represents the relative likelihood that the sample i is an outlier (true outliers are expected to have larger values of r_i). In DOS, we compute $\mathbf{r}_E = COPOD(M_E)$ and $\mathbf{r}_C = COPOD(M_C)$ and average these two vectors to obtain the final outlier score $\mathbf{r} = (\mathbf{r}_E + \mathbf{r}_C)/2$.

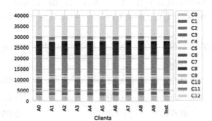 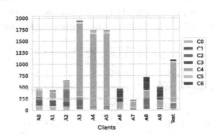

Fig. 2. Left: Distribution of the multiclass multilabel CheXpert dataset among clients where each stacked bar represents the number of positive cases for class 0 to 12. **Right:** Distribution of the multiclass HAM1000 dataset in non-iid case among clients where each stacked bar represents the number of samples for class 0 to 6.

Weighted Average Aggregation: Ideally, the local parameter updates of those clients with higher outlier scores must be suppressed and the local parameters of clients with lower outlier scores must be amplified. To achieve this goal, we apply a softmax function to the outlier score vector with a temperature parameter of -1 and use the resulting output as the normalized weights for each client, i.e.,

$$w_i = \frac{exp(-r_i)}{\sum_{j=1}^{n} exp(-r_i)}, \quad i = 1, 2, \cdots, n.$$

The local parameters of the clients are aggregated using the following rule:

$$\theta^{t+1} = \sum_{i=1}^{n} w_i \hat{\theta}_i^{t+1}.$$

4   Experiments

4.1   Datasets

CheXpert: CheXpert is a large chest X-ray dataset with uncertainty labels and expert comparison [17]. We use 'CheXpert-small', a multi-class multi-label dataset that contains 191,456 chest X-ray images for training. The dataset is imbalanced and has 13 pathology categories. In addition, it has a percentage of uncertain data, and [17] suggests either ignoring the uncertain labels during training or mapping all instances to zero or one. In our experiments, all uncertain labels were mapped to zero. The TorchXRayVision library [8] was used to preprocess the data, where every image has a 224 × 224 resolution. We divide the training images equally between the clients as shown in Fig. 2 (**Left**), where the last stacked bar represents the testing dataset that we use to measure the global model's performance after each round. We use the CheXpert dataset to evaluate our method in the iid setting.

Table 1. Area under the receiver operating characteristic curve (AUC) with different types of poisoning attack scenarios on the Chexpert dataset. T-M stands for Trimmed Mean [33]. The last column represents the average AUC over five presented scenarios.

	No attack	Label flip 10%	Mix attack 40%	Noise 40%	Noise & Scaled 40%	Avg
FedAvg	0.70	0.69	0.50	0.50	0.50	0.58
Median	0.70	0.69	0.69	0.69	0.54	0.66
T-M	0.70	0.69	0.69	0.50	0.50	0.62
Krum	0.66	0.66	0.64	0.63	0.67	0.65
DOS	**0.70**	**0.69**	0.68	**0.69**	**0.67**	**0.68**

HAM10000: HAM10000 is a multi-class dataset consisting of 10,015 dermoscopic images from different populations [31]. It consists of 7 categories of pigmented lesions where every image was resized to 128 × 128. The train-test split is 8,910 and 1,105 images, respectively. We use this dataset to test our method in the non-iid case as shown in Fig. 2 (**Right**).

4.2   FL Setup

In all our experiments, we assume $n = 10$ clients. The well-known ResNet-18 [16] model, as well as a custom Convolutional Neural Network (CNN) with two convolutional layers, a ReLU activation function, and two fully connected layers are used as the architectures for both global and local models. Each client only has access to its local dataset and the local models are trained using Stochastic Gradient Descent (SGD) [13] with a learning rate of 0.01. We implement all our experiments using the Pytorch framework [1]. Using a batch size of 16 for CheXpert, each client is trained for a total of 100 rounds with 1 local step in each round that goes through the entire dataset. As for the HAM10000 dataset, we iterate through the whole dataset with a batch size of 890 for each client. We train it for a total of 250 rounds with 5 local steps for each client. This experiment was performed to show that the batch size does not impact the DOS aggregation rule. The evaluation metric is the Area Under the Receiver operating characteristic curve (AUC), which is calculated after each round of communication on the testing dataset. For the CheXpert dataset [17], the AUC was calculated for each class and the macro average was taken over all classes. For the HAM1000 dataset [31], the average AUC was computed for all possible pairwise class combinations to minimize the effect of imbalance [15].

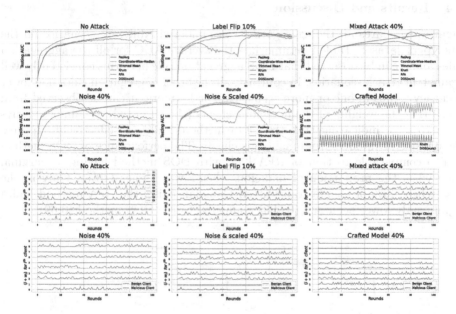

Fig. 3. Performance on CheXpert dataset using ResNet-18 model: The first two rows show AUC on a test set after each round for six scenarios in the following order (left to right): No Attack, Label Flip 10%, Mix Attack 40%, Noise 40%, Noise and Scaled 40%, and Crafted Attack 40%. The bottom two rows show the normalized weights of each client after each round.

4.3   Poisoning Attacks and Baseline Aggregation Rules

We assume that up to $p \leq 40\%$ of these clients could be malicious, i.e., at most 4 out of the 10 clients are malicious. We consider 5 different attacks on the CheXpert dataset: (i) **Label Flip** 10% - label-flipping by one of the clients, (ii) **Mix Attack** 40% - transmission of Gaussian noise by two clients and label-flipping by two clients, (iii) **Noise** 40% - transmission of Gaussian noise by four clients, (iv) **Noise and Scaled** 40% - transmission of a mix of Gaussian noise and scaled parameters by four clients, and (v) **Crafted** 40% - crafted model attack with four clients based on [11] (with the aggregation rule being unknown to the attacker). On the HAM1000 dataset, 2 attacks were considered: (i) **Noise** 30% - transmission of Gaussian noise by three clients, and (ii) **Mix Attack** 40% - transmission of Gaussian noise by two clients, scaled parameter by a factor of 100 by one client, and scaled parameter by a factor of -0.5 (directionally opposite to the true parameters) by one client. The robustness of the proposed DOS method was benchmarked against the following aggregation rules: FedAvg [24], Coordinate-Wise-Median [33], Trimmed Mean [33] and Krum [5]. For both datasets, a **No Attack** scenario was also considered to evaluate the performance of DOS when all the clients are benign (honest).

4.4   Results and Discussion

Figure 3 compares all the aggregation rules under six different scenarios on the CheXpert dataset. Table 1 summarizes the average AUC for all the aggregation rules and it can be observed that DOS aggregation rule performs consistently well against all attack scenarios. In contrast, all the other aggregation rules had lower accuracy values in one or more scenarios. Furthermore, it can be observed from Fig. 3 that the weights of the malicious clients (shown in red) are almost always close to zero, indicating that the DOS method is able to effectively suppress the parameter updates from malicious clients. The performance of DOS method is also comparable to that of RFA [28], with DOS method having a marginal edge when the proportion of malicious clients was higher (40%). Only in the case where 40% of clients transmitted Gaussian noise, the RFA method had a significantly lower accuracy (0.625) compared to the DOS method (0.69).

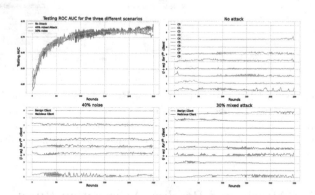

Fig. 4. Performance on HAM10000 dataset using a custom CNN model. The top-left plot shows AUC on the test set for DOS aggregation for the 3 scenarios. The normalized weights of each client after each round for the 3 scenarios are also depicted.

Figure 4 shows the performance of the DOS rule under three different scenarios on the HAM10000 dataset. In all cases, DOS performed with a high AUC score without dropping its overall performance. The main advantage of DOS lies in its ability to account for both Euclidean and cosine distance, thereby addressing both positive and negative scaling. It also successfully detects Gaussian noise attacks and label-flip attacks, leveraging the strengths of the COPOD method. Since DOS combines three different approaches, it is hard to design model poisoning attacks that can successfully circumvent it.

Proportion of Malicious Clients: Since our approach treats malicious weight updates as outliers, the protocol will fail when a majority of clients are malicious. We conducted experiments by fixing the number of clients and increasing the proportion of malicious clients from 10% to 60%, in steps of 10%. As expected, the DOS approach was robust until the proportion of malicious clients was less than or equal to 50% and failed when the proportion was 60% (e.g., for HAM10000 dataset, the AUC values were 0.695, 0.697, 0.696, 0.711, 0.710, and 0.554 for 10%, 20%, 30%, 40%, 50%, and 60% corruption, respectively. In comparison, the AUC without any attack was 0.70). This is the reason for choosing the proportion of malicious clients as 40% for most of our experiments. Thus, the DOS method is appropriate only for the honest majority scenario.

Different Number of Clients: We conducted experiments by fixing the proportion of malicious clients to 40% and increasing the number of clients from 5 to 40. The AUC values were 0.725, 0.700, 0.692, and 0.674 for 5, 10, 20 and 40 clients, respectively. We observe a minor degradation in accuracy when the number of clients increases and it requires more rounds to converge. Therefore, the DOS approach may be more suitable for cross-silo FL settings.

Non-IID Setting: We have conducted experiments under five different non-iid settings, where we randomly partition the HAM10000 dataset among 10 clients. For all the five experiments, the convergence trends and the final accuracy were similar (between 0.69 and 0.71) to the iid case, showing that the DOS method can work well in the non-iid setting.

4.5   Conclusions and Future Work

We presented Distance-based Outlier Suppression (DOS), a novel robust aggregation rule that performs outlier detection in the distance space to effectively defend against Byzantine failures in FL. We proved the effectiveness and robustness of our method using two real-world medical imaging datasets. In future, we aim to prove theoretical convergence and extend this framework to ensure fairness between FL clients, based on the contribution of their local datasets.

References

1. PyTorch: an imperative style, high-performance deep learning library
2. Bagdasaryan, E., Veit, A., Hua, Y., Estrin, D., Shmatikov, V.: How to backdoor federated learning. In: International Conference on Artificial Intelligence and Statistics, pp. 2938–2948. PMLR (2020)

3. Bhagoji, A.N., Chakraborty, S., Mittal, P., Calo, S.: Model poisoning attacks in federated learning. In: Proceedings of Workshop on Security Machine Learning (SecML) 32nd Conference Neural Information Processing Systems (NeurIPS), pp. 1–23 (2018)
4. Bhagoji, A.N., Chakraborty, S., Mittal, P., Calo, S.: Analyzing federated learning through an adversarial lens. In: International Conference on Machine Learning, pp. 634–643. PMLR (2019)
5. Blanchard, P., El Mhamdi, E.M., Guerraoui, R., Stainer, J.: Machine learning with adversaries: Byzantine tolerant gradient descent. In: Advances in Neural Information Processing Systems, vol. 30 (2017)
6. Chen, Z., Zhu, M., Yang, C., Yuan, Y.: Personalized retrogress-resilient framework for real-world medical federated learning. In: de Bruijne, M., et al. (eds.) MICCAI 2021. LNCS, vol. 12903, pp. 347–356. Springer, Cham (2021). https://doi.org/10.1007/978-3-030-87199-4_33
7. Cheng, Z., Zou, C., Dong, J.: Outlier detection using isolation forest and local outlier factor. In: Proceedings of the Conference on Research in Adaptive and Convergent Systems, pp. 161–168 (2019)
8. Cohen, J.P., et al.: TorchXRayVision: a library of chest X-ray datasets and models (2020). https://github.com/mlmed/torchxrayvision, https://github.com/mlmed/torchxrayvision
9. Dayan, I., et al.: Federated learning for predicting clinical outcomes in patients with COVID-19. Nat. Med. **27**(10), 1735–1743 (2021)
10. Esteva, A., et al.: Dermatologist-level classification of skin cancer with deep neural networks. Nature **542**(7639), 115–118 (2017)
11. Fang, M., Cao, X., Jia, J., Gong, N.: Local model poisoning attacks to {Byzantine-Robust} federated learning. In: 29th USENIX Security Symposium (USENIX Security 2020), pp. 1605–1622 (2020)
12. Fu, S., Xie, C., Li, B., Chen, Q.: Attack-resistant federated learning with residual-based reweighting. arXiv preprint arXiv:1912.11464 (2019)
13. Gardner, W.A.: Learning characteristics of stochastic-gradient-descent algorithms: a general study, analysis, and critique. Signal Process. **6**(2), 113–133 (1984)
14. Guerraoui, R., Rouault, S., et al.: The hidden vulnerability of distributed learning in byzantium. In: International Conference on Machine Learning, pp. 3521–3530. PMLR (2018)
15. Hand, D.J., Till, R.J.: A simple generalisation of the area under the roc curve for multiple class classification problems. Mach. Learn. **45**(2), 171–186 (2001)
16. He, K., Zhang, X., Ren, S., Sun, J.: Deep residual learning for image recognition. In: Proceedings of the IEEE Conference on Computer Vision and Pattern Recognition, pp. 770–778 (2016)
17. Irvin, J., et al.: CheXpert: a large chest radiograph dataset with uncertainty labels and expert comparison. In: Proceedings of the AAAI Conference on Artificial Intelligence, pp. 590–597 (2019)
18. Kaushal, A., Altman, R., Langlotz, C.: Health care AI systems are biased. Scientific American, vol. 17 (2020)
19. Lamport, L.: The weak Byzantine generals problem. J. ACM (JACM) **30**(3), 668–676 (1983)
20. Li, T., Sahu, A.K., Talwalkar, A., Smith, V.: Federated learning: challenges, methods, and future directions. IEEE Signal Process. Mag. **37**(3), 50–60 (2020)
21. Li, Z., Zhao, Y., Botta, N., Ionescu, C., Hu, X.: COPOD: copula-based outlier detection. In: 2020 IEEE International Conference on Data Mining (ICDM), pp. 1118–1123. IEEE (2020)

22. Likas, A., Vlassis, N., Verbeek, J.J.: The global k-means clustering algorithm. Pattern Recogn. **36**(2), 451–461 (2003)
23. Liu, Z., Xiong, R., Jiang, T.: Clinical-inspired network for skin lesion recognition. In: Martel, A.L., et al. (eds.) MICCAI 2020. LNCS, vol. 12266, pp. 340–350. Springer, Cham (2020). https://doi.org/10.1007/978-3-030-59725-2_33
24. McMahan, B., Moore, E., Ramage, D., Hampson, S., Arcas, B.A.: Communication-efficient learning of deep networks from decentralized data. In: Artificial Intelligence and Statistics, pp. 1273–1282. PMLR (2017)
25. Muñoz-González, L., et al.: Towards poisoning of deep learning algorithms with back-gradient optimization. In: Proceedings of the 10th ACM Workshop on Artificial Intelligence and Security, pp. 27–38 (2017)
26. Panda, A., Mahloujifar, S., Nitin Bhagoji, A., Chakraborty, S., Mittal, P.: SparseFed: mitigating model poisoning attacks in federated learning with sparsification. In: Proceedings of AISTATS, pp. 7587–7624 (2022)
27. van Panhuis, W.G., et al.: A systematic review of barriers to data sharing in public health. BMC Public Health **14**, 1144 (2014)
28. Pillutla, K., Kakade, S.M., Harchaoui, Z.: Robust aggregation for federated learning. IEEE Trans. Signal Process. **70**, 1142–1154 (2022)
29. Primartha, R., Tama, B.A.: Anomaly detection using random forest: a performance revisited. In: 2017 International Conference on Data and Software Engineering (ICoDSE), pp. 1–6. IEEE (2017)
30. Sheller, M.J., et al.: Federated learning in medicine: facilitating multi-institutional collaborations without sharing patient data. Nat. Sci. Rep. **10**(1), 12598 (2020)
31. Tschandl, P., Rosendahl, C., Kittler, H.: The HAM10000 dataset, a large collection of multi-source dermatoscopic images of common pigmented skin lesions. Sci. Data **5**(1), 1–9 (2018)
32. Wei, X., Shen, C.: Federated learning over noisy channels: convergence analysis and design examples. IEEE Trans. Cogn. Commun. Netw. **8**(2), 1253–1268 (2022)
33. Yin, D., Chen, Y., Kannan, R., Bartlett, P.: Byzantine-robust distributed learning: Towards optimal statistical rates. In: International Conference on Machine Learning, pp. 5650–5659. PMLR (2018)
34. Zhou, X., Xu, M., Wu, Y., Zheng, N.: Deep model poisoning attack on federated learning. Future Internet **13**(3), 73 (2021)

The Intrinsic Manifolds of Radiological Images and Their Role in Deep Learning

Nicholas Konz[1]($\boxtimes$) (iD), Hanxue Gu[1] (iD), Haoyu Dong[2] (iD),
and Maciej A. Mazurowski[1,2,3,4]($\boxtimes$) (iD)

[1] Department of Electrical and Computer Engineering, Duke University,
Durham, NC, USA
`{nicholas.konz,maciej.mazurowski}@duke.edu`
[2] Department of Radiology, Duke University, Durham, NC, USA
[3] Department of Computer Science, Duke University, Durham, NC, USA
[4] Department of Biostatistics and Bioinformatics, Duke University,
Durham, NC, USA

Abstract. The manifold hypothesis is a core mechanism behind the success of deep learning, so understanding the intrinsic manifold structure of image data is central to studying how neural networks learn from the data. Intrinsic dataset manifolds and their relationship to learning difficulty have recently begun to be studied for the common domain of natural images, but little such research has been attempted for radiological images. We address this here. First, we compare the intrinsic manifold dimensionality of radiological and natural images. We also investigate the relationship between intrinsic dimensionality and generalization ability over a wide range of datasets. Our analysis shows that natural image datasets generally have a higher number of intrinsic dimensions than radiological images. However, the relationship between generalization ability and intrinsic dimensionality is much stronger for medical images, which could be explained as radiological images having intrinsic features that are more difficult to learn. These results give a more principled underpinning for the intuition that radiological images can be more challenging to apply deep learning to than natural image datasets common to machine learning research. We believe rather than directly applying models developed for natural images to the radiological imaging domain, more care should be taken to developing architectures and algorithms that are more tailored to the specific characteristics of this domain. The research shown in our paper, demonstrating these characteristics and the differences from natural images, is an important first step in this direction.

Keywords: Radiology · Generalization · Dimension · Manifold

The original version of this chapter was revised: The name the author Maciej A. Mazurowski has been corrected; a middle initial has been added on request of the author. The correction to this chapter is available at
https://doi.org/10.1007/978-3-031-16452-1_70

Supplementary Information The online version contains supplementary material available at https://doi.org/10.1007/978-3-031-16452-1_65.

1   Introduction

Although using deep learning-based methods to solve medical imaging tasks has become common practice, there lacks a strong theoretical understanding and analysis of the effectiveness of such methods. This could be a potential problem for future algorithm development, as most successful methods for medical images are adapted from techniques solving tasks using natural image datasets [6]. Due to the apparent differences in relevant semantics between natural and medical domains [19], it is not clear what design choices are necessary when adapting these networks to medical images. This difference in domain is especially true when considering radiological images. Our goal is to provide a better, quantified footing for developing such radiology-specialized methods, by (1) analyzing the underlying structure of common radiological image datasets and determining how it relates to learning dynamics and generalization ability and (2) comparing these characteristics to common natural image datasets.

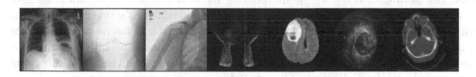

Fig. 1. Sample images from each dataset studied. From the left: CheXpert [15], OAI [22], MURA [24], DBC [25], BraTS 2018 [18], Prostate-MRI [28] and RSNA-IH-CT [10] (see Sect. 3).

The Manifold Hypothesis [5,9,29] states that high-dimensional data, such as images, can be well described by a much smaller number of features/degrees of freedom than the number of pixels in an image; this number is the *intrinsic dimension* (ID) of the dataset, which provides an estimate of the information content of the data [1]. This is central to deep computer vision because these abstract visual features can be learned from data, allowing inference and modeling in a tractable, lower-dimensional space. For example, dataset ID can be used as a lower bound for the dimensionality of the "noise" prior vector in generative adversarial networks (GANs) [23].

It is therefore important to study the relationship of the ID of datasets with the learning process of deep models. This was recently explored for standard natural image datasets [23], but a similarly comprehensive study has yet to be conducted for radiological image datasets, which is important because of the apparent differences between these two domains.

Contributions. Our contributions are summarized as follows.

1. We investigate the intrinsic manifold structure of common radiology datasets (Fig. 1), and find that their IDs are indeed much lower than the number of pixels, and also generally lower than for natural image datasets (Fig. 2).

2. We also find that classification is generally harder with radiology datasets than natural images for moderate-to-low training set sizes.
3. We show that classification performance is negatively linear to dataset ID within both data domains, invariant to training set size. However, the absolute value of the slope of this relationship is much higher for radiological data than for natural image data.
4. We test these linearity findings on a wide range of common classification models, and find that performance for radiological images is almost independent of the choice of model, relying instead on the ID of the dataset.

Our results show that while the ID of a dataset affects the difficulty of learning from this dataset, what also matters is the complexity of the intrinsic features themselves, which we find to be indicated by the sharpness of the relationship between generalization ability (GA) and ID, that is more severe for radiological images. Practically, this relationship could allow for an estimation of the number of annotations needed to create a training set for a model to achieve a desired GA, mitigating costly time spent labeling medical images. These findings give experimental evidence for the differences in intrinsic dataset structure and learning difficulty between the two domains, which we believe is the first step towards a more principled foundation for developing deep methods specially designed for radiology. We provide code for reproducing all results at https://github.com/mazurowski-lab/radiologyintrinsicmanifolds.

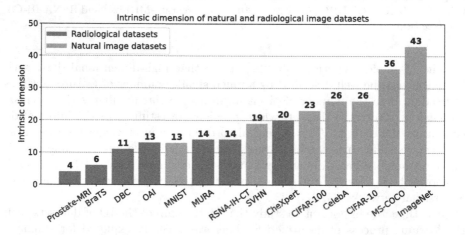

Fig. 2. Intrinsic dimension of radiological (blue) and natural image (orange) datasets, the latter from [23]. Figure recommended to be viewed in color. (Color figure online)

Related Work. Intrinsic dimension (ID) estimation methods ([3]), have only recently been applied to datasets used in modern computer vision, beginning with [23], which explored the ID of common natural image datasets and how it relates to learning ability and generalization. There have been a few studies of the

ID of medical datasets, *e.g.*, [7], but these are targeted at an individual modality or dataset. The most common ID estimator obtains a maximum-likelihood (MLE) solution for the ID by modeling the dataset as being sampled from a locally uniform Poisson process on the intrinsic data manifold [16]. Other estimators exist ([8,11]), but these are unreliable estimators for images [23], so we use the MLE estimator in this work. Note that we do not estimate dataset ID with some learned latent space dimension found by training an autoencoder-type model or similar; relatedly, we also do not study the ID of the learned feature structure, or parameters of a trained feature extraction model, *e.g.*, [1,4]. In contrast, we study the intrinsic, model-independent structure of the dataset itself.

2   Methods: Intrinsic Dimension Estimation

Consider some dataset $\mathcal{D} \subset \mathbb{R}^d$ of N images, where d is the *extrinsic dimension*, *i.e.*, the number of pixels in an image. The Manifold Hypothesis [9] assumes that the datapoints $x \in \mathcal{D}$ lie near some low-dimensional manifold $\mathcal{M} \subseteq \mathbb{R}^d$ that can be described by an intrinsic dimension $\dim(\mathcal{M}) = m \ll d$.

In order to obtain an estimate of m, [16] models the data as being sampled from a Poisson process within some m-dimensional sphere at each datapoint x; the density of points is assumed to be approximately constant within the radius of the sphere. Rather than specifying the radius as a hyperparameter, the authors set this radius to be the distance of the kth nearest neighboring datapoint to x (instead specifying k). By maximizing the likelihood of the data given the parameters of the Poisson model, we then obtain an ID for x of

$$\hat{m}_k(x) = \left[\frac{1}{k-1} \sum_{j=1}^{k-1} \log \frac{T_k(x)}{T_j(x)} \right]^{-1}, \tag{1}$$

where $T_j(x)$ is the ℓ_2 distance from x to its jth nearest neighbor. The authors of [17] then showed that MLE can be used again to obtain an estimate for the global dataset ID, as

$$\hat{m}_k = \left[\frac{1}{N} \sum_{i=1}^{n} \hat{m}_k(x_i)^{-1} \right]^{-1} = \left[\frac{1}{N(k-1)} \sum_{i=1}^{N} \sum_{j=1}^{k-1} \log \frac{T_k(x_i)}{T_j(x_i)} \right]^{-1}, \tag{2}$$

which is the estimator that we use for this work. Note here that k is a hyperparameter of the estimator; just as in [23] we set $k = 20$, a moderate value as recommended by [16]. This estimator has been validated on natural images using GANs [23], which we believe to also be valid for radiological images due to the commonality of intrinsic visual features measured by the ID that is unaffected by differences such as the number of channels or normalization. We do not use auto-encoders to estimate ID because they are trained to extract features suited for reconstruction, rather than features of class identity that would be used by a supervised classifier.

3 Datasets and Tasks

In this work, we use the common task of binary classification to analyze the effect of dataset intrinsic dimension on the learning of radiological images. We chose radiology datasets that are varied in modality and well-representative of the domain, while being large enough for a broad study of training set sizes for at least one realistic classification task. We explore using alternate tasks for the same datasets in Sect. 4.2.

The datasets are as follows. (1) CheXpert [15], where we detect pleural effusion in chest X-ray images. Next is (2) the Knee Osteoarthritis Initiative (OAI) [22], where we select the OAI-released screening packages 0.C.2 and 0.E.1 containing knee X-ray images. Following [2,30], we build a binary osteoarthritis (OA) detection dataset by combining Kellgren-Lawrence (KL) scores of $\{0,1\}$ as OA-negative and combining scores of $\{2,3,4\}$ as positive. (3) is MURA [24], where we detect abnormalities in musculoskeletal X-ray images. Next, (4) is the Duke Breast Cancer MRI (DBC) dataset [25], where we detect cancer in fat-saturated breast MRI volume slices; we take slices containing a tumor bounding box to be positive, and all other slices at least five slices away from the positives to be negative. We follow this same slice-labeling procedure for dataset (5), BraTS 2018 [18] where we detect gliomas in T2 FLAIR brain MRI slices. Dataset (6) is Prostate-MRI-Biopsy [28], where we take slices from the middle 50% of each MRI volume, and label each slice according to the volume's assigned prostate cancer risk score; scores of $\{0,1\}$ are negative, and scores of ≥ 2, which correlates with risk of cancer [21], are positive. Our final dataset (7) is the RSNA 2019 Intracranial Hemorrhage Brain CT Challenge (RSNA-IH-CT) [10], where we detect any type of hemorrhage in Brain CT scans. Sample images are shown in Fig. 1.

4 Experiments and Results

4.1 The Intrinsic Dimension of Radiology Datasets

We first estimate the intrinsic dimension (ID) of the considered radiology datasets; the results are shown in Fig. 2, alongside the natural image dataset results of [23]. For each dataset, we estimate the MLE ID (Equation (2)) on a sample of 7500 images such that there is an exact 50/50 split of negative and positive cases in the sample, to minimize estimator bias (although we found that when using fewer images, the estimates were little affected). Like natural images, we found the ID of radiological images to be many times smaller than the extrinsic dimension; however, radiological image datasets tend to have lower ID than natural images datasets. Intuitively, we found that modifying the dataset extrinsic dimension (resizing the images) had little effect on the ID.

4.2 Generalization Ability, Learning Difficulty and Intrinsic Dimension

We now wish to determine what role the intrinsic dimension (ID) of a radiology dataset has in the degree of difficulty for a deep model to learn from it, and how this compares to the natural image domain. As in [23], we use the test set accuracy obtained when the model has maximally fit to the training set as a proxy for the generalization ability (GA) of the model on the dataset. We train and test with each dataset separately on it's respective binary classification task (Sect. 3), for a range of models and training set sizes N_{train}, from 500 to 2000. We train for 100 epochs with the same hyperparameters for all experiments; further details are provided in the supplementary materials. For each experiment with a studied dataset, we sample 2750 images from the given dataset such that there is an exact 50/50 split of negative and positive images. From this, we sample 750 test images, and from the remaining 2000 images, we sample some N_{train} training examples.

Beginning with $N_{train} = 2000$ on ResNet-18, we plot the GA with respect to the dataset ID in Fig. 3, alongside the corresponding results for natural image datasets where binary classification was explored from [23]. Intriguingly, even across the range of tasks and datasets, we see that the relationship of GA with ID is approximately linear within each domain. Indeed, when fitting a simple ordinary least squares linear model

$$GA = a_{GA,ID} \times ID + b \tag{3}$$

to each of the two domains, we obtain a Pearson linear correlation coefficient of $R^2 = 0.824$ and slope of $a_{GA,ID} = -0.019$ for radiological images, and $R^2 = 0.981$ with $a_{GA,ID} = -0.0075$ for natural images.

When repeating the same experiments over the aforementioned range of N_{train} and ResNet models, we find that averaged over N_{train}, $R^2 = 0.76 \pm 0.05$, $a_{GA,ID} = -0.0199 \pm 0.0009$ and $R^2 = 0.91 \pm 0.12$, $a_{GA,ID} = -0.0077 \pm 0.0004$ (+ standard deviation) for the radiological and natural domains, respectively. These low deviations imply that even across a range of training sizes, both domains have a high, and mostly constant, correlation between GA and ID. Similarly, both domains have approximately constant slopes of GA vs. ID with respect to N_{train}, but between domains, the slopes differ noticeably.

On the left of Fig. 4, we show how GA varies with respect to N_{train} for datasets of both domains. We see that datasets with higher ID pose a more difficult classification task within both domains, i.e., more training samples are required to achieve some accuracy. However, between these two domains, radiological images are generally more difficult to generalize to than natural images, for these moderate-to-low training set sizes (that are typical for radiology tasks [27]). For example, OAI (ID = 13), MURA (ID = 14) and CheXpert (ID = 20), all prove to be more difficult than ImageNet, even though it has more than double the number of intrinsic dimensions (43).

This implies that the intrinsic dataset features described by these dimensions (and the correlations between them) can vary in learning difficulty between

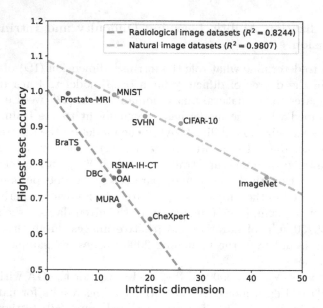

Fig. 3. Linearity of model generalization ability with respect to dataset intrinsic dimension, for radiological (blue) and natural (orange) image datasets, for $N_{\text{train}} = 2000$ on ResNet-18. Figure recommended to be viewed in color. (Color figure online)

domains, indicated by the aforementioned sharper slope $a_{\text{GA,ID}}$. Our results show that radiological images generally have more difficult intrinsic features to learn than natural images, even if the number of these intrinsic feature dimensions is higher for the latter.

We can also explore the dependence of generalization ability (GA) on both training set size N_{train} and ID, shown on the right of Fig. 4. [20] found that learning requires a training sample size that grows exponentially with the data manifold's ID; this implies that GA should scale with $\log N_{\text{train}}$. Indeed we see that GA is approximately linear with respect to ID and $\log N_{\text{train}}$: for each domain of radiological and natural, we find multiple linear correlation coefficients R^2 of 0.766 and 0.902 between these variables, respectively. Given some new radiology dataset, we could potentially use this to estimate the minimum annotations needed (N_{train}) to obtain a desired GA/test accuracy for the dataset, which would save costly labeling resources. However, extensive experiments would need to be conducted before this could be widely applicable, due to confounding factors such as if the chosen model has a high enough capacity to fully fit to the training set; as such, we leave such an investigation for future work.

Dependence on Model Choice. As mentioned, we repeated the same experiments with a number of additional models for the radiology domain, to see if these linear relationships change with different model choices. In addition to ResNet-18, we tested on ResNet-34 and –50 ([12]), VGG-13, –16 and –19 ([26]),

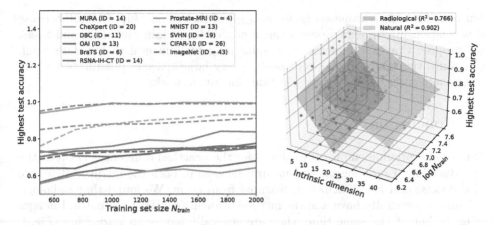

Fig. 4. Left: model generalization ability (GA) vs. training set size N_{train} for various radiological (solid line) and natural (dashed line) image datasets, using ResNet-18. **Right:** linearity of GA with respect to $\log N_{\text{train}}$ and dataset intrisic dimension. Accompanies Fig. 3; recommended to be viewed in color. (Color figure online)

Squeezenet 1.1 ([14]), and DenseNet–121 and –169 ([13]). Averaged over N_{train} and all models, we obtained $R^2 = 0.699 \pm 0.080$ and $a_{\text{GA,ID}} = -0.019 \pm 0.001$ (individual model results are provided in the supplementary materials). By the low deviations of both R^2 and the actual regressed slope $a_{\text{GA,ID}}$ of GA vs. ID, we see that the same linear relationship between GA and ID also exists for these models. We therefore infer that this relationship between classification GA and ID is largely independent of model size/choice, assuming that the model has a high enough capacity to fully fit to the training set.

Dependence on Task Choice. Logically, there should be other factors affecting a model's GA beyond the dataset's ID; *e.g.*, for some fixed dataset, harder tasks should be more difficult to generalize to. This section aims to determine how changing the chosen tasks for each dataset affects the preceding results. We will consider realistic binary classification tasks that have enough examples to follow the dataset generation procedure of Sect. 4.2. The datasets that support this are CheXpert—detect edema instead of pleural effusion, RSNA-IH-CT—detect subarachnoid hemorrhage, rather than any hemorrhage, and Prostate-MRI—detect severe cancer (score > 2), rather than any cancer. For robustness we will experiment on all three aforementioned ResNet models.

From switching all three datasets to their modified tasks, the linear fit parameters (averaged over N_{train}) changed as $R^2 = 0.76 \pm 0.05 \Rightarrow 0.78 \pm 0.15$ and $a_{\text{GA,ID}} = -0.0199 \pm 0.0009 \Rightarrow -0.012 \pm 0.002$ for ResNet-18; $R^2 = 0.77 \pm 0.07 \Rightarrow 0.76 \pm 0.21$ and $a_{\text{GA,ID}} = -0.019 \pm 0.001 \Rightarrow -0.011 \pm 0.003$ for ResNet-34; and $R^2 = 0.78 \pm 0.07 \Rightarrow 0.82 \pm 0.15$ and $a_{\text{GA,ID}} = -0.021 \pm 0.001 \Rightarrow -0.013 \pm 0.004$ for ResNet-50. We therefore conclude that the choice of task has some, but a small effect on the significance of the linear relationship of GA with ID (R^2), but can affect the parameters (slope $a_{GA,ID}$) of the relationship. Overall, because this relationship appeared over a range of models, training set sizes, and tasks, we propose that it originates from something fundamental to the data itself. Certainly, the choice of task represents a very large space of possibilities, so we leave more comprehensive investigations for future work.

5 Conclusion

Our results provide empirical evidence for the practical differences between the two domains of radiological and natural images, in both the intrinsic structure of datasets, and the difficulty of learning from them. We found that radiological images generally have a lower intrinsic dimension (ID) than natural images (Fig. 2), but at the same time, they are generally harder to learn from (Fig. 4, left). This indicates that the intrinsic features of radiological datasets are more complex than those in natural image data. Therefore, assumptions about natural images and models designed for natural images should not necessarily be extended to radiological datasets without consideration for these differences. Further study of the differences between these two domains and the conceptual reasons for why they arise could lead to helpful guidelines for deep learning with radiology. We believe that the results in this work are an important step in this direction, and they lay the foundation for further research on this topic.

References

1. Ansuini, A., Laio, A., Macke, J.H., Zoccolan, D.: Intrinsic dimension of data representations in deep neural networks. In: Advances in Neural Information Processing Systems, vol. 32 (2019)
2. Antony, J., McGuinness, K., Moran, K., O'Connor, N.E.: Automatic detection of knee joints and quantification of knee osteoarthritis severity using convolutional neural networks (2017)
3. Bac, J., Mirkes, E.M., Gorban, A.N., Tyukin, I., Zinovyev, A.: Scikit-dimension: a python package for intrinsic dimension estimation. Entropy **23**(10), 1368 (2021)
4. Birdal, T., Lou, A., Guibas, L.J., Simsekli, U.: Intrinsic dimension, persistent homology and generalization in neural networks. In: Advances in Neural Information Processing Systems, vol. 34 (2021)
5. Brand,M.: Charting a manifold. In: Advances in Neural Information Processing Systems, vol. 15 (2002)
6. Chrabaszcz, P., Loshchilov, I., Hutter, F.: A downsampled variant of imagenet as an alternative to the cifar datasets. arXiv preprint arXiv:1707.08819 (2017)
7. Cordes, D., Nandy, R.R.: Estimation of the intrinsic dimensionality of fmri data. Neuroimage **29**(1), 145–154 (2006)
8. Facco, E., d'Errico, M., Rodriguez, A., Laio, A.: Estimating the intrinsic dimension of datasets by a minimal neighborhood information. Sci. Rep. **7**(1), 1–8 (2017)
9. Fefferman, C., Mitter, S., Narayanan, H.: Testing the manifold hypothesis. J. Am. Math. Soc. **29**(4), 983–1049 (2016)

10. Flanders, A.E., et al. Construction of a machine learning dataset through collaboration: the rsna 2019 brain ct hemorrhage challenge. Radiol. Artif. Intell. **2**(3), e190211 (2020)
11. Gomtsyan, M., Mokrov, N., Panov, M., Yanovich, Y.: Geometry-aware maximum likelihood estimation of intrinsic dimension. In: Asian Conference on Machine Learning, pp. 1126–1141. PMLR (2019)
12. He, K., Zhang, X., Ren, S., Sun, J.: Deep residual learning for image recognition. In: Proceedings of the IEEE Conference on Computer Vision and Pattern Recognition, pp. 770–778 (2016)
13. Huang, G., Liu, Z., Van Der Maaten, L., Weinberger, K.Q.: Densely connected convolutional networks. In Proceedings of the IEEE Conference on Computer Vision and Pattern Recognition, pp. 4700–4708 (2017)
14. Iandola, F.N., Han, S., Moskewicz, M.W., Ashraf, K., Dally, W.J., Keutzer, K.: Squeezenet: alexnet-level accuracy with 50x fewer parameters and<0.5 mb model size. arXiv preprint arXiv:1602.07360 (2016)
15. Irvin, J., et al.: Chexpert: A large chest radiograph dataset with uncertainty labels and expert comparison. In: Proceedings of the AAAI Conference on Artificial Intelligence **33**, 590–597 (2019)
16. Levina, E., Bickel, P.: Maximum likelihood estimation of intrinsic dimension. AIn: dvances in Neural Information Processing Systems, vol. 17 (2004)
17. MacKay, D.J.C., Ghahramani, Z., Comments on'maximum likelihood estimation of intrinsic dimension'by e. levina and p. bickel,: The Inference Group Website, p. 2005. Cambridge University, Cavendish Laboratory (2004)
18. Menze, B.H., et al.: The multimodal brain tumor image segmentation benchmark (brats). IEEE transactions on medical imaging **34**(10), 1993–2024 (2014)
19. Morra, L., Piano, L., Lamberti, F., Tommasi, T.: Bridging the gap between natural and medical images through deep colorization. In: 2020 25th International Conference on Pattern Recognition (ICPR), pp. 835–842. IEEE (2021)
20. Narayanan, H., Mitter, S.: Sample complexity of testing the manifold hypothesis. In: Advances in Neural Information Processing Systems, vol. 23 (2010)
21. Natarajan, S., Priester, A., Margolis, D., Huang, J., Marks, L.: Prostate mri and ultrasound with pathology and coordinates of tracked biopsy (prostate-mri-us-biopsy) [data set] (2020). https://doi.org/10.7937/TCIA.2020.A61IOC1A. (Accessed: 21 Feb 2022)
22. Nevitt, M., Felson, D., Lester, G.: The osteoarthritis initiative. Protocol for the cohort study, vol. 1 (2006)
23. Pope, P., Zhu, C., Abdelkader, A., Goldblum, M., Goldstein, T.: The intrinsic dimension of images and its impact on learning. arXiv preprint arXiv:2104.08894 (2021)
24. Rajpurkar, P., et al.: Mura: large dataset for abnormality detection in musculoskeletal radiographs. arXiv preprint arXiv:1712.06957 (2017)
25. Saha, A.: A machine learning approach to radiogenomics of breast cancer: a study of 922 subjects and 529 dce-mri features. Br. J. Cancer **119**(4), 508–516 (2018)
26. Simonyan, K., Zisserman, A.: Very deep convolutional networks for large-scale image recognition. arXiv preprint arXiv:1409.1556 (2014)
27. Soffer, S., Ben-Cohen, A., Shimon, O., Amitai, M.M., Greenspan, H., Klang, E.: Convolutional neural networks for radiologic images: a radiologist's guide. Radiology **290**(3), 590–606 (2019)
28. Sonn, G.A.: Targeted biopsy in the detection of prostate cancer using an office based magnetic resonance ultrasound fusion device. J. urol. **189**(1), 86–92 (2013)

29. Tenenbaum, J.B., de Silva, V., Langford, J.C.: A global geometric framework for nonlinear dimensionality reduction. Science **290**(5500), 2319–2323 (2000)
30. Tiulpin, A., Thevenot, J., Rahtu, E., Lehenkari, P., Saarakkala, S.: Automatic Knee Osteoarthritis diagnosis from plain radiographs: a deep learning-based approach. Sci. Rep. **8**(1), 1727 (2018)

FedHarmony: Unlearning Scanner Bias with Distributed Data

Nicola K. Dinsdale[1]([✉]), Mark Jenkinson[2,3,4], and Ana I. L. Namburete[1]

[1] Oxford Machine Learning in NeuroImaging (OMNI) Lab,
University of Oxford, Oxford, UK
nicola.dinsdale@cs.ox.ac.uk
[2] Wellcome Centre for Integrative Neuroimaging FMRIB,
University of Oxford, Oxford, UK
[3] Australian Institute for Machine Learning (AIML), Department of Computer
Science, University of Adelaide, Adelaide, Australia
[4] South Australian Health and Medical Research Institute (SAHMRI),
North Terrace, Adelaide, Australia

Abstract. The ability to combine data across scanners and studies is vital for neuroimaging, to increase both statistical power and the representation of biological variability. However, combining datasets across sites leads to two challenges: first, an increase in undesirable non-biological variance due to scanner and acquisition differences - the *harmonisation problem* - and second, data privacy concerns due to the inherently personal nature of medical imaging data, meaning that sharing them across sites may risk violation of privacy laws. To overcome these restrictions, we propose **FedHarmony**: a harmonisation framework operating in the federated learning paradigm. We show that to remove the scanner-specific effects, for our scenario we only need to share the mean and standard deviation of the learned features, helping to protect individual subjects' privacy. We demonstrate our approach across a range of realistic data scenarios, using real multi-site data from the ABIDE dataset, thus showing the potential utility of our method for MRI harmonisation across studies. Our code is available at https://github.com/nkdinsdale/FedHarmony.

Keywords: Harmonisation · Federated learning · Domain adaptation

1 Introduction

Although some large scale projects, such as the UK Biobank, exist, the majority of neuroimaging datasets remain small. This necessitates the combination of data from multiple sites and scanners, both for statistical power and to represent the breadth of biological variability. However, combining data across scanners leads to an increase in non-biological variance, due to differences such as acquisition protocol and hardware [9,10,24]. Thus, we need *harmonisation methods* to enable joint unbiased analysis of data from different scanners and studies.

© The Author(s), under exclusive license to Springer Nature Switzerland AG 2022
L. Wang et al. (Eds.): MICCAI 2022, LNCS 13438, pp. 695–704, 2022.
https://doi.org/10.1007/978-3-031-16452-1_66

However, data cannot simply be pooled (combined) across imaging sites without ensuring compliance with data privacy laws, particularly if we wish to use representative clinical imaging data, as the sharing of medical images is covered by legislation such as GDPR [2] and HIPAA [13]. Federated learning (FL) has been proposed as a method to train models on distributed data [11], where data are kept on their local servers, the users train local models on their own private datasets and then share only the weights or gradients of the trained models. FL has the potential to become the standard paradigm for multisite imaging, with early studies demonstrating its feasibility in neuroimaging [18].

Direct translation of existing harmonisation methods into FL frameworks is non-trivial. Most deep learning methods for harmonisation are based on generative frameworks [3,12,26,27], and, although federated equivalents to GANs and VAEs are being developed [16,25], additional challenges exist for harmonisation approaches that require simultaneous access to source and target data [8]. Additionally, many methods require paired data – not possible with distributed data and unlikely to exist in large multisite studies. Further, most generative methods are data-hungry [3,27], which casts into doubt whether sufficient data would be available at local sites.

Alternative methods for harmonisation frame the task as a domain adaptation problem (DA) [5], as the goal mirrors the harmonisation problem: removal of information regarding domain (scanner or acquisition protocol) while retaining the true variance of interest (the biological signal). In [5], the DA approach has been demonstrated for a range of tasks and network architectures. The harmonisation approach in [5] is built upon the DA framework proposed in [20] and has since been translated into the federated setting [14]. In [14] the domain adaptation across local sites is achieved by sharing feature embeddings for local data points in a global shared knowledge bank, such that a global domain predictor can be trained. However, sharing the features still leads to privacy concerns [8], as images are potentially recoverable from the features. Many of the other FL DA methods proposed cannot be adapted for the harmonisation problem, as, for instance, they produce domain-specific models or ensembles [8,15,21,23], where the final predictions depend on the source of the data.

Therefore, we present FedHarmony: a method to adapt the harmonisation framework proposed in [5] for distributed data, while minimising shared information. We aim to train a model that performs equally well on the task of interest across all of the imaging sites while using features that are invariant to the imaging site, through a horizontal federated framework [22]. We show that by approximating the learned feature embeddings as Gaussian distributions, we can share only a mean and standard deviation per feature which, by definition, contain no identifying information for individual subjects. Alongside standard privacy-protecting approaches [7,19], sharing only these summary statistics would make the approach robust to honest-but-curious adversaries [22]. By demonstrating our approach, FedHarmony, for a range of data settings, we show its viability for data harmonisation for multisite distributed imaging studies.

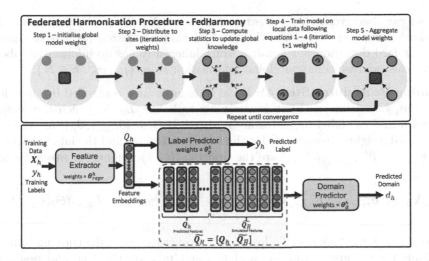

Fig. 1. FedHarmony Procedure and high level general network architecture.

2 Methods

Consider the scenario in which we have multisite MRI data, where the data for each site h are stored on their local server, for all sites H. For each site, we have pairs of training data $D_h = \{X_h, y_h\}$ where X_h is the input data and y_h is the label, and we consider each site to be a separate data domain. We wish to create a model that performs as well as possible on each imaging site, whilst having predictions that are invariant to the acquisition site. A global model is constructed, which following [5] is formed of a feature extractor (with weights θ_{repr}), a label predictor (θ_p) and a domain predictor (θ_d) (Fig. 1). This model is initialised randomly (step 1), and then the FedHarmony procedure begins, as shown in Fig. 1, with the global model weights for the three network components, $\theta_{repr,t}$, $\theta_{p,t}$ and $\theta_{d,t}$, being sent to the local sites; t indicates these are the current weights for iteration t and thus each site receives the same initialisation (step 2).

Update Global Knowledge Store (Step 3): To remove scanner information adversarially, the different sites' nodes need to have an understanding of the various scanner characteristics. Although there is precedent for achieving this through sharing the feature embeddings from local sites to the global site [14], we aim to minimise the quantity of shared information to help protect individual privacy. It has been shown that domain-specific characteristics can be encoded to enable contrastive learning [6], by sharing the mean and standard deviation of the feature embeddings following a BoxCox transformation [1] (an invertible transform which aims to make the distribution maximally Gaussian), suggesting that this might be sufficient information to also remove scanner information. However, in many multisite MRI studies, small amounts of local data are available that may be insufficient to fit a BoxCox transformation. Thus, we simplify the transformation by assuming that the features will already be normally distributed and that we can characterise $Q_h = featureExtractor(X_h, \theta_{repr,t})$ by their mean and standard deviations. Therefore the total information shared per site is a mean and standard deviation per feature, which inherently has no information about individuals, and we collate a global information store $\{\mu_h, \sigma_h : h \in H\}$.

Training Procedure (Step 4): Local training is then controlled by three loss functions, based on [5]. First is the main task loss L_p, in which the feature extractor and the label predictor are updated. If $\Theta_t = [\theta_{repr,t}, \theta_{p,t}]$ are the current global weights (iteration t) for the feature extractor and the label predictor, and $\Theta_{t+1}^h = [\theta_{repr,t+1}^h, \theta_{p,t+1}^h]$ are the updated $(t+1)$ weights for site h, then:

$$L_p(X_h, y_h; \theta_{repr,t+1}^h, \theta_{p,t+1}^h) = \frac{1}{N_h} \sum_{j=1}^{N_h} L_{task}(y_{h,j}, \hat{y}_{h,j}) + \mu L_{prox}(\Theta_t, \Theta_{t+1}^h) \quad (1)$$

where L_{task} is the task-specific loss function, averaged over the training samples available for the given site, N_h, and $y_{h,j}$ and $\hat{y}_{h,j}$ are the true and predicted labels for the jth example for the hth imaging site. L_{prox} is a proximal loss term based on FedProx [17] that penalises weight deviations from the global model that do not sufficiently improve the main task loss and has been shown to aid FL when the data is non-iid [17], as is inherently true for multisite MRI data, hence the harmonisation problem. Thus, if μ is a constant, weighting the contributions from the two losses, then:

$$L_{prox}(\Theta_t, \Theta_{t+1}^h) = ||\theta_{repr,t} - \theta_{repr,t+1}^h||^2 + ||\theta_{p,t} - \theta_{p,t+1}^h||^2 \quad (2)$$

The second loss function, L_d, then updates the domain predictor to be able to discriminate between the sites. Data is only available for the local site h and thus can only directly generate the features, Q_h, needed to train the domain predictor for this local site. For all the other sites $\check{H}$ we generate example features randomly using the shared knowledge store; thus, for site $\check{h}$ in $\check{H} : Q_{\check{h}} \sim \mathcal{N}(\mu_{\check{h}}, \sigma_{\check{h}})$. The generated features, $\widetilde{Q}_{\check{H}} = \{\widetilde{Q}_{\check{h}} \forall \check{h} \in \check{H}\}$ are then concatenated with the true features, Q_h, such that $\widetilde{Q}_H^h = [Q_h, \widetilde{Q}_{\check{H}}]$. The number of simulated subjects generated for each site $\check{h}$ is chosen randomly such that the final batchsize is twice that of the original; the features and corresponding domain (site) labels are then shuffled. We then update the parameters of the domain predictor, using categorial cross-entropy to assess the site information remaining in Q_h:

$$L_d(\widetilde{Q}_H^h, d; \theta_{d,t+1}^h) = - \sum_{h=1}^{H} \mathbb{1}[d = h] log(p_h) \quad (3)$$

where p_h are the softmax outputs of the domain classifier. The third loss is the confusion loss L_{conf}, which removes the site information, by penalising deviation in p_h from a uniform distribution:

$$L_{conf}(X_h, \theta_{d,t+1}^h; \theta_{repr,t+1}^h) = - \sum_{h=1}^{H} \frac{1}{H} log(p_h) \quad (4)$$

Therefore, the overall method can be considered to minimise the total loss function $L = L_p + \alpha L_d + \beta L_{conf}$ where α and β control the relative contributions of the different loss functions. The domain loss (Eq. 3) and the confusion loss (Eq. 4) act in opposition to each other, and so must be updated iteratively, with three iterations per epoch. The procedure is iterated through for E local epochs.

Weight Aggregation (Step 5): After each site has completed the E local epochs, the local weights are returned to the global node to be aggregated. In [5] it was shown that the harmonisation process was aided through evaluating each site separately in the loss function rather than averaging over all data points. Given that `FedAvg` [11] is equivalent to averaging over all training subjects for FL, we alter the aggregation to have equal contributions from each site: $\theta_{t+1} \leftarrow \frac{1}{H} \sum_{h=1}^{H} \theta_{t+1}^h$ where the aggregation is completed separately for θ_{repr}, θ_p and θ_d. We term this aggregation step `FedEqual`. Once the aggregation is complete, the training loops through stages 2–5 (Fig. 1) until convergence.

Semi-supervised Setting: We then explore the scenario where labels are only available for a subset of sites, which is realistic, as labels are expensive to generate in terms of time and expertise. Thus, we also consider the semi-supervised setting, adjusting the framework such that local training is only completed for sites with labels available, but we continue to update the global knowledge store for all sites. Therefore, the removal of the site information still considers all sites.

3   Implementation Details

For our experiments we use data from the ABIDE dataset[1] [4], for the task of age prediction, using T1 MR images as X and the ages as the labels y. The MR images from each site were processed using `FSL anat`[2]. Subjects were rejected where the pipeline failed or where data was missing. Four sites (Trinity, NYU, UCLA, Yale) were chosen for our experiments, so as to span both age distributions and subject numbers (Fig. 2). The data were split into training/validation/test sets as 70%/10%/20%, yielding a maximum of 127 subjects for training (NYU) and a minimum of 35 (Trinity). Our networks and baselines were all trained with 5-fold cross-validation until no improvement in the average mean absolute error (MAE) was reported on the validation data for all local sites. We present the results on the held-out testing data in all cases.

For the network, we used the VGG-based architecture used in [5][3]. The images were resized to (128, 240, 160) and normalised to have zero mean and unit standard deviation. As demonstrated by [5], the framework is flexible and should be applicable to many feedforward architectures and tasks, with age prediction being used to demonstrate the approach due to the availability of labels across many sites. The implementation was in Python 3.6.8 and PyTorch 1.10.2. The networks were trained on a 16 GB P100 GPU, taking up to 5 min per local

---

[1] Data from: https://fcon_1000.projects.nitrc.org/indi/abide/.

[2] https://fsl.fmrib.ox.ac.uk/fsl/fslwiki/fsl_anat.

[3] code from: https://github.com/nkdinsdale/Unlearning_for_MRI_harmonisation.

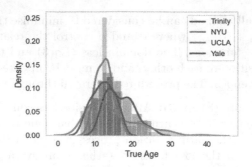

Fig. 2. Normalised age distributions for the 4 sites from the ABIDE dataset: Trinity: 49 subjects, 16.7 ± 3.6 years (range: 12–25), NYU: 182 subjects, 14.7 ± 6.6 (6–39), UCLA: 99 subjects, 12.5 ± 2.2 (8–17), Yale: 56 subjects, 12.2 ± 2.8 (7–17).

epoch (NYU), with a batchsize of 16, and requiring 50–75 rounds of communication to converge (`FedHarmomy` required 61 rounds and `FedAvg` required 56). The following hyperparameters were used for all experiments based on [5,17], with the same values applied for each local site: batchsize=16, learning rate=1×10^{-4} with Adam optimiser, local epochs (E)=10, μ=0.01, α=1, and β=100.

4   Results and Discussion

Fully Supervised: We first compared our method to several baselines: training on NYU data only (the largest site, representing where data cannot be shared and we have no federated learning framework), training on all sites normally (centralised data), `FedAvg` [11], `FedProx` [17] and our proposed `FedEqual` aggregation method. We also completed an ablation study, exploring the effect of the aggregation and proximal losses alongside the harmonisation. To compare methods, we evaluated both the mean absolute error (MAE), where we want the best performance possible across all sites, and the scanner classification accuracy (SCA): the performance of a domain classifier trained on Q at convergence, where the aim is to achieve random chance (25%). Note that the domain predictor was able to achieve 95% on the feature embeddings when the age prediction was trained with NYU only, and so is clearly able to identify scanner information.

Considering the results in Table 1, we were able train federated models (`FedAvg`) to perform as well as standard centralised training. `FedHarmony` led to improvement both in terms of average performance across all sites and in the reduction of SCA to close to random chance. This improvement indicates the success of the DA approach, as information from across sites is being used to aid predictions even though only summary statistics of the features are being shared. The ablation study shows the need for the three additions to the `FedAvg` baseline, with the L_{prox} (Eq. 2) being vital for both stability of training and the ability to remove scanner information. Figure 3 shows a PCA of Q comparing `FedAvg` and `FedHarmony`, where it is evident that the harmonisation increases the feature overlap of the different sites.

Table 1. Fully supervised results: Component represents additions relative to FedAvg [11]: Equal = Aggregation as FedEqual; Prox = Proximal Loss as Eq. 2; Harm = Harmonisation, otherwise local training only considers the main task loss. SCA = Scanner Classification Accuracy of domain classifier retrained on Q at the end of training, where random chance (25%) is the goal. NYU only and all sites = centralised training. FedHarmony is our proposed approach. * = significant improvement over next performing method (paired t-test, $p < 0.001$).

Method	Component			Site MAE				Average MAE	SCA (%)
	Equal	Prox	Harm	NYU n=40	Yale n=14	UCLA n=20	Trinity n=10		
NYU Only				5.26±4.37	2.38±1.42	3.22±2.26	9.66±7.89	5.13	95
All Sites				5.10±4.56	2.32±1.50	2.87±2.13	4.53±3.49	3.70	86
FedAvg [11]				5.26±4.74	**1.99±1.21***	2.57±1.88	4.94±3.80	3.69	64
FedProx [17]		✓		5.21±4.70	2.15±1.44	2.61±1.73	4.47±3.56	3.61	62
FedEqual	✓			6.07±3.99	2.06±1.31	2.61±2.30	5.43±3.00	4.06	42
Ablation A			✓	12.21±10.31	4.20±3.61	6.21±3.21	10.32±8.31	8.23	95
Ablation B	✓		✓	5.27±4.90	2.27±1.13	2.66±1.98	4.81±3.98	3.75	34
Ablation C		✓	✓	**4.93±4.31***	2.13±1.91	2.26±1.15	4.36±3.37	**3.42**	35
FedHarmony	✓	✓	✓	5.14±4.52	2.04±1.25	**2.13±1.45***	4.34±3.65	**3.42**	**29**

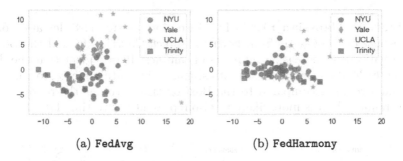

(a) FedAvg   (b) FedHarmony

Fig. 3. PCA of Q for FedAvg and FedHarmony, showing, as expected, increased overlap across sites with FedHarmony.

Semi-supervised: We then simulated two semi-supervised scenarios, where training labels were only available for a subset of the sites. First we considered when only one site had available training labels, NYU, as a multitarget DA task, which could for example represent when the organising site has labelled data. In Table 2 we compare to standard training (FedAvg and FedProx are equivalent to standard training for a single labelled site). Using FedHarmony, we were able to train the network to perform as well as fully supervised centralised training, while removing the scanner information, showing the power of the shared global knowledge. We also considered when three sites have labels and one does not (Trinity), for example, if a new site joins the study. FedHarmony led to improvement in performance again, even compared to having labels for all sites, while removing the scanner information. These results show the suitability of our approach across realistic data scenarios for multisite MRI studies.

Table 2. Semi-supervised results: *NYU only* = centralised training only NYU; *No Trinity* = centralised training no Trinity; *All sites* = centralised training. SCA = Scanner Classification Accuracy of domain classifier retrained on **Q** at the end of training, where random chance (25%). FedHarmony was trained locally for only labelled sites, and global shared information used for all sites. * = significant improvement over next performing method (paired t-test, $p < 0.001$).

Method	Site MAE				Average MAE	SCA (%)
	NYU n=40	Yale n=14	UCLA n=20	Trinity n=10		
a) Semi-supervised 1 site						
NYU Only	**5.26 ± 4.37**	3.22 ± 2.26	3.22 ± 2.26	9.66 ± 7.89	5.13	95
FedHarmony	**5.26 ± 4.15**	**2.20 ± 1.79***	**2.91 ± 1.56***	**4.09 ± 3.32***	**3.61***	30
b) Semi-supervised 3 site						
No Trinity	5.36 ± 4.65	**1.81 ± 1.66***	**1.83 ± 1.16***	7.29 ± 5.00	4.07	96
FedProx [17]	5.15 ± 4.76	2.15 ± 1.38	2.62 ± 1.82	5.96 ± 4.05	3.96	74
FedHarmony	**5.12 ± 4.60***	2.39 ± 1.67	2.16 ± 1.40	**4.69 ± 4.19***	**3.59***	26
All Sites	5.10 ± 4.56	2.32 ± 1.50	2.87 ± 2.13	4.53 ± 3.49	3.70	86

Suitability of Gaussian Fit: In Fig. 4 we plot the standard deviation of 100 mean estimates for Q_{NYU} from both the direct Gaussian fit and the BoxCox transformation for increasing numbers of samples. It is evident that the direct Gaussian fit leads to more consistent estimates, indicating increased suitability in low data regimes compared to the BoxCox transform, as the representation on the training data is more likely to also represent the testing data.

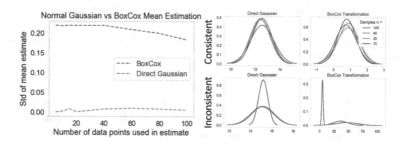

Fig. 4. We plot the standard deviation of 100 mean estimates of the fit for Q_{NYU}, for increasing numbers of random samples from the full Q_{NYU}, alongside consistent and inconsistent fits. Note: the estimated means will differ, as the BoxCox transforms the data to be maximally Gaussian rather than fitting the data.

5   Conclusion

We have presented **FedHarmony**, a method to allow harmonisation of MRI data in a federated learning scenario, through development of a domain adaptation approach with minimal information sharing, outperforming baseline and FL approaches across realistic data scenarios. Alongside standard privacy-protecting approaches, such as differential privacy, our approach would enable training models on multisite MRI data while maintaining individual subjects' privacy. Future work will explore application to different neuroimaging tasks.

Acknowledgement. ND is supported by a Academy of Medical Sciences Springboard Award. MJ is supported by the National Institute for Health Research, Oxford Biomedical Research Centre, and this research was funded by the Wellcome Trust [215573/Z/19/Z]. WIN is supported by core funding from the Wellcome Trust [203139/Z/16/Z]. AN is grateful for support from the UK Royal Academy of Engineering under the Engineering for Development Research Fellowships scheme and the Academy of Medical Sciences. The computational aspects of this research were supported by the Wellcome Trust Core Award [Grant Number 203141/Z/16/Z] and the NIHR Oxford BRC. The views expressed are those of the author(s) and not necessarily those of the NHS, the NIHR or the Department of Health.

References

1. Box, G.E.P., Cox, D.R.: An analysis of transformations. J. Roy. Stat. Soc. Ser. B (Methodol.) **26**(2), 211–252 (1964). https://doi.org/10.2307/2984418
2. Consulting I: General Data Protection Regulation (GDPR), Sep 2019. https://gdpr-info.eu/
3. Dewey, B., et al.: DeepHarmony: a deep learning approach to contrast harmonization across scanner changes. Magn. Reson. Imaging **64**, 160–170 (2019)
4. Di Martino, A., et al.: The Autism brain imaging data exchange: towards large-scale evaluation of the intrinsic brain architecture in Autism. Mol. Psychiatry **19**, 659–667 (2013). https://doi.org/10.1038/mp.2013.78
5. Dinsdale, N.K., Jenkinson, M., Namburete, A.I.: Deep learning-based unlearning of dataset bias for MRI harmonisation and confound removal. Neuroimage **228**, 117689 (2021). https://doi.org/10.1016/j.neuroimage.2020.117689
6. Dong, N., Voiculescu, I.: Federated contrastive learning for decentralized unlabeled medical images. In: de Bruijne, M., et al. (eds.) MICCAI 2021. LNCS, vol. 12903, pp. 378–387. Springer, Cham (2021). https://doi.org/10.1007/978-3-030-87199-4_36
7. Dwork, C.: Differential privacy. In: Bugliesi, M., Preneel, B., Sassone, V., Wegener, I. (eds.) Automata, Languages and Programming, pp. 1–12 (2006)
8. Feng, H., et al.: Kd3a: unsupervised multi-source decentralized domain adaptation via knowledge distillation. In: ICML (2021)
9. Han, X., et al.: Reliability of MRI-derived measurements of human cerebral cortical thickness: the effects of field strength, scanner upgrade and manufacturer. Neuroimage **32**, 180–94 (2006). https://doi.org/10.1016/j.neuroimage.2006.02.051
10. Jovicich, J., et al.: Reliability in multi-site structural MRI studies: effects of gradient non-linearity correction on phantom and human data. Neuroimage **30**, 436–43 (2006). https://doi.org/10.1016/j.neuroimage.2005.09.046

11. McMahan, H.B., Moore, E., Ramage, D., Hampson, S., y Arcas, B.A.: Communication-efficient learning of deep networks from decentralized data. In: AISTATS (2017)
12. Moyer, D., Ver Steeg, G., Tax, C., Thompson, P.: Scanner invariant representations for diffusion MRI harmonization. Magn. Reson. Med. **84**, 2174–2189 (2020). https://doi.org/10.1002/mrm.28243
13. Office for Civil Rights US: The hipaa privacy rule, Jul 2021. https://www.hhs.gov/hipaa/for-professionals/privacy/index.html
14. Peng, X., Huang, Z., Zhu, Y., Saenko, K.: Federated adversarial domain adaptation. ArXiv abs/1911.02054 (2020)
15. Peterson, D., Kanani, P.H., Marathe, V.J.: Private federated learning with domain adaptation. ArXiv abs/1912.06733 (2019)
16. Rasouli, M., Sun, T., Rajagopal, R.: Fedgan: Federated generative adversarialnetworks for distributed data. ArXiv, Jun 2020
17. Sahu, A., Li, T., Sanjabi, M., Zaheer, M., Talwalkar, A., Smith, V.: On the convergence of federated optimization in heterogeneous networks. ArXiv, Dec 2018
18. Sheller, M.J., Reina, G.A., Edwards, B., Martin, J., Bakas, S.: Multi-institutional deep learning modeling without sharing patient data: A feasibility study on brain tumor segmentation. In: Brainlesion: Glioma, Multiple Sclerosis, Stroke and Traumatic Brain Injuries, pp. 92–104 (2019). https://doi.org/10.1007/978-3-030-11723-8-9
19. Sweeney, L.: K-anonymity: a model for protecting privacy. Int. J. Uncertain. Fuzziness Knowl.-Based Syst. **10**(5), 557–570 (2002). https://doi.org/10.1142/S0218488502001648
20. Tzeng, E., Hoffman, J., Darrell, T., Saenko, K.: Simultaneous deep transfer across domains and tasks. In: ICCV (2015)
21. Yang, L., Beliard, C., Rossi, D.: Heterogeneous data-aware federated learning. ArXiv, Nov 2020
22. Yang, Q., Liu, Y., Chen, T., Tong, Y.: Federated machine learning: concept and applications. ACM Trans. Intell. Syst. Technol. **10**, 1–19 (2019). https://doi.org/10.1145/3298981
23. Yao, C.H., Gong, B., Cui, Y., Qi, H., Zhu, Y., Yang, M.H.: Federated multi-target domain adaptation. ArXiv (2021)
24. Yu, M., et al.: Statistical harmonization corrects site effects in functional connectivity measurements from multisite fMRI data. Hum. Brain Mapp. **39**, 4213–4227 (2018). https://doi.org/10.1002/hbm.24241
25. Zhang, K., Jiang, Y., Seversky, L., Xu, C., Liu, D., Song, H.: Federated variational learning for anomaly detection in multivariate time series. ArXiv, Aug 2021
26. Zhao, F., Wu, Z., Wang, L., Lin, W., Xia, S., Li, G.: Harmonization of infant cortical thickness using surface-to-surface cycle-consistent adversarial networks. In: Medical Image Computing and Computer Assisted Intervention - Conference Proceedings, pp. 475–483, Oct 2019
27. Zuo, L., et al.: Unsupervised mr harmonization by learning disentangled representations using information bottleneck theory. Neuroimage **243**, 118569 (2021). https://doi.org/10.1016/j.neuroimage.2021.118569

Fast Unsupervised Brain Anomaly Detection and Segmentation with Diffusion Models

Walter H. L. Pinaya[1]([✉]), Mark S. Graham[1], Robert Gray[2],
Pedro F. da Costa[3,4], Petru-Daniel Tudosiu[1], Paul Wright[1], Yee H. Mah[1,5],
Andrew D. MacKinnon[6,7], James T. Teo[3,5], Rolf Jager[2], David Werring[8],
Geraint Rees[9], Parashkev Nachev[2], Sebastien Ourselin[1],
and M. Jorge Cardoso[1]

[1] Department of Biomedical Engineering, School of Biomedical Engineering
and Imaging Sciences, King's College London, London, UK
walter.diaz_sanz@kcl.ac.uk
[2] Institute of Neurology, University College London, London, UK
[3] Institute of Psychiatry, Psychology and Neuroscience, King's College London,
London, UK
[4] Centre for Brain and Cognitive Development, Birkbeck College, London, UK
[5] King's College Hospital NHS Foundation Trust, London, UK
[6] St George's University Hospitals NHS Foundation Trust, London, UK
[7] Atkinson Morley Regional Neuroscience Centre, London, UK
[8] Stroke Research Centre, UCL Queen Square Institute of Neurology, London, UK
[9] Institute of Cognitive Neuroscience, University College London, London, UK

Abstract. Deep generative models have emerged as promising tools for
detecting arbitrary anomalies in data, dispensing with the necessity for
manual labelling. Recently, autoregressive transformers have achieved
state-of-the-art performance for anomaly detection in medical imaging.
Nonetheless, these models still have some intrinsic weaknesses, such as
requiring images to be modelled as 1D sequences, the accumulation of
errors during the sampling process, and the significant inference times
associated with transformers. Denoising diffusion probabilistic models
are a class of non-autoregressive generative models recently shown to produce excellent samples in computer vision (surpassing Generative Adversarial Networks), and to achieve log-likelihoods that are competitive with
transformers while having relatively fast inference times. Diffusion models can be applied to the latent representations learnt by autoencoders,
making them easily scalable and great candidates for application to high
dimensional data, such as medical images. Here, we propose a method
based on diffusion models to detect and segment anomalies in brain imaging. By training the models on healthy data and then exploring its diffusion and reverse steps across its Markov chain, we can identify anomalous areas in the latent space and hence identify anomalies in the pixel
space. Our diffusion models achieve competitive performance compared

---

Supplementary Information The online version contains supplementary material
available at https://doi.org/10.1007/978-3-031-16452-1_67.

with autoregressive approaches across a series of experiments with 2D CT and MRI data involving synthetic and real pathological lesions with much reduced inference times, making their usage clinically viable.

Keywords: Denoising diffusion probabilistic models · Unsupervised anomaly detection · Out-of-distribution detection · Lesion segmentation · Neuroimaging

1   Introduction

The segmentation of lesions in neuroimaging is an important problem whose solution is of potential value across many clinical tasks, including diagnosis, prognosis, and treatment selection. Ordinarily, segmentation is performed by hand, making this process time-consuming and dependent on human expertise. The development of accurate automatic segmentation methods is therefore crucial to allow the widespread use of precise measurements in clinical routine [17,31]. Over the last few years, deep generative models have emerged as promising tools for detecting arbitrary lesions and anomalies in data, dispensing with the necessity for either expensive labels or images with anomalies in the training set [2,15,16,30]. These generative models learn the probability density function of normal data and then highlight pathological features as deviations from normality.

Autoregressive models have recently achieved state-of-the-art results in generative modelling [5,18], and are being used to detect anomalies without supervision in real-world industrial image [28] and medical imaging [6,14,16]. By factorising the joint distribution of pixel/voxel intensities of an image as a product of conditional distributions $p(\mathbf{x}) = \prod_{i=1}^{n} p(x_i | x_{<i})$ (i.e., in an autoregressive way), the likelihood of images becomes tractable. We can thus directly maximise the expected log-likelihood of the training data, in contrast with Generative Adversarial Networks and Variational Autoencoders. In particular, transformers [27], with their attention mechanisms and proven expressivity, have set the state-of-the-art in autoregressive modelling for computer vision [9,20] and in unsupervised anomaly detection for medical imaging [16].

Despite their success, transformers still have some weaknesses intrinsic to their autoregressive nature. Due to the unidirectional bias of autoregressive models, the fixed order of sequence elements imposes a perceptually unnatural bias to attention in brain images, constrained to information from preceding elements in the sequence, [16] employed an ensemble of models with differently ordered versions of a unidimensional input derived from the multidimensional latent representation of vector quantized variational autoencoder (VQ-VAE). Summing across the ensemble improves performance, but at the cost of inference time (the authors used eight transformers to process each 2D image), hindering application in time-critical scenarios. This problem is accentuated with increased data dimensionality (e.g., when analysing 3D data), where even more transformers might be required to achieve good coverage of the image context. In many clinical contexts, such as live data quality control and clinical alerting systems, transformer-based inference times are too slow (>5 min) to make them clinically useful.

Another issue is the accumulation of prediction errors. The sequential sampling strategy introduces a gap between training and inference, as training relies on so-called teacher-forcing [4] or exposure bias [22], where the ground truth is provided for each step, whilst inference is performed on previously sampled elements. In anomaly segmentation, this training-inference gap can introduce significant accumulations of errors during the computation of the likelihoods, or in the sampling process involved when "healing" anomalous sequence elements, possibly affecting the quality and coherence of the generated anomaly-corrected images.

In this study, we use denoising diffusion probabilistic models (DDPM or diffusion models for brevity) [8,23] to create a fast approach that is clinically viable, to eliminate the unidirectional bias, and to avoid accumulated prediction errors during the "healing" process (i.e., the process that remove anomalies from the input image). In essence, DDPMs are trained to iteratively denoise the input by reversing a forward diffusion process that gradually corrupts it. These models are well-founded in principled probabilistic modelling and are able to generate diverse and high-quality images in computer vision [3,8,13]. Based on recent advances in generative modelling [4,7,19], we use a VQ-VAE [26] to compress the input image and model its latent space using at diffusion model. This approach uses DDPMs flexibly, rapidly, and efficiently in high dimensional data, such as 3D neuroimaging. In summary, we propose mechanisms to explore the capacities of DDPMs and perform extensive experiments on brain data with synthetic and real lesions.

2 Background

2.1 Compression Model

Based on previous works [16,19], we used a VQ-VAE to learn a compact latent representation that offers significantly reduced computational complexity for the

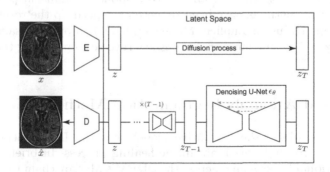

Fig. 1. The diffusion and reverse processes involved in our anomaly segmentation method, combining a compression model (autoencoder) and a DDPM.

diffusion model. It corresponds to only the autoencoder with discrete latent space from [26] (not including the PixelCNN part), where the encoder maps any given image, $\mathbf{x} \in \mathbb{R}^{H \times W}$, to a smaller dimensional latent representation $E(\mathbf{x}) = \mathbf{z} \in \mathbb{R}^{h \times w \times n_z}$. Next, we use the codebook (containing a finite number of embedding vectors $\mathbf{e}_k \in \mathbb{R}^{n_z}$, $k \in 1, ..., K$, where K is the size of the codebook) to perform an element-wise quantization of each latent variable onto its nearest vector $\mathbf{e}_k$, where k is selected using $k = argmin_j \|E(\mathbf{x}) - \mathbf{e}_j\|_2^2$, creating the quantized latent representation $\mathbf{z}$. Then, the decoder G reconstructs the observations $G(\mathbf{z}) = \hat{\mathbf{x}} \in \mathbb{R}^{H \times W}$. The encoder E, the decoder G, and the codebook can be trained end-to-end via $\mathcal{L}_{VQVAE} = \|\mathbf{x} - \hat{\mathbf{x}}\| + \mathcal{L}_{codebook} + \beta \|sg[\mathbf{e}_k] - \mathbf{z}_e\|$ where the operator sg denotes the stop-gradient operation. We used the exponential moving average updates for the codebook loss [26]. In our experiments, our encoder compresses the image data into a smaller latent representation by a factor of f.

2.2   Denoising Diffusion Probabilistic Models

In this study, we used the DDPM [8,23] to learn the distribution of the latent representation of healthy brain imaging. The DDPMs are a class of generative models that convert Gaussian noise into samples from a learned data distribution via a sequence of denoising steps ($p_\theta(\mathbf{x}_{0:T})$). For that, during training, we gradually destroy the structure of the training data via a fixed Markov chain over T diffusion steps ($q(\mathbf{x}_{1:T}|\mathbf{x}_0)$). Next, the reverse process is modelled as a Markov chain which learns to recover the original data $\mathbf{x}_0$ from the noisy input $\mathbf{x}_T$. This process can be efficiently learned by maximizing the variational lower bound on the log-likelihood. Following [8], we decomposed the as

$$\mathbb{E}[-\log p_\theta(\mathbf{x}_0)] \leq L := \mathbb{E}_q[\underbrace{D_{KL}(q(\mathbf{x}_T|\mathbf{x}_0)\|p(\mathbf{x}_T))}_{L_T}$$

$$+ \sum_{t>1} \underbrace{D_{KL}(q(\mathbf{x}_{t-1}|\mathbf{x}_t, \mathbf{x}_0)\|p_\theta(\mathbf{x}_{t-1}|\mathbf{x}_t))}_{L_{t-1}} - \underbrace{\log p_\theta(\mathbf{x}_1|\mathbf{x}_0)]}_{L_0} \quad (1)$$

where the term L_{t-1} penalises errors in one reverse step and requires a direct comparison between $p_\theta(\mathbf{x}_{t-1}|\mathbf{x}_t)$ and its corresponding diffusion process. Still, recently, different methods have been proposed to speed up the reverse process (e.g., Denoising Diffusion Implicit Models - DDIM), proposing samplers that reduce by $10\times \sim 50\times$ the number of necessary reverse steps during the sampling process [24].

3   Proposed Anomaly Segmentation Method

Our approach explores the generative model that the DDPM learns from a healthy dataset to guide the brain image healing process. In brief, we use the learned variational lower bound across the DDPM's Markov chain to identify the latent values that were unlikely to occur in the training set. We replace these unlikely values with more probable ones according to the DDPM, and then we use the latent spatial information to filter the residual maps (obtained from the difference between the original image and the healed image).

After training the VQ-VAE and DDPM on normal data, we use VQ-VAE to obtain the latent representation $\mathbf{z}$ of the test images. After that, we use the DDPM's forward process to obtain the noisy representations $\mathbf{z}_t$ across the Markov chain. For each step, we use the L_{t-1} values from Eq. 1 to verify how close each reverse step is to the expected Gaussian transition $q(\mathbf{x}_{t-1}|\mathbf{x}_t,\mathbf{x}_0)$. We observed that if the input image is from a healthy subject, the reverse process will only remove the added Gaussian noise, resulting in a low KL Divergence in L_{t-1}. However, if the image contains an anomaly, the reverse process removes part of the signal of the original anomalous regions. This signal removal does not follow the expected Gaussian transition, resulting in a high L_{t-1} in the anomalous regions. Using a threshold, we can create a binary mask indicating where the anomalies are and use it to guide the "healing" process.

To find an appropriate threshold, we first obtain the values of L_{t-1} for all our images in the healthy validation set. Instead of using the whole Markov chain, we focus on the steps t inside an intermediary range. As reported in [8], different t values are responsible for modelling different image features, where higher values are associated with large scale features, and the lower ones are responsible for fine details. In our study, we find that the range of $t = [400, 600]$ was less noisy than lower values ($t < 150$) and were more specific than high values ($t > 800$) to highlight anomalies across different experiments and lesion types. With the $L_{400,600} \in \mathbb{R}^{h \times w \times n_z \times 200}$, we compute the mean values inside the t range and across the n_z dimension. This results in a $\mathbf{v}^k \in \mathbb{R}^{h \times w}$ for each one of the validation samples k. Finally, we obtained our 2D threshold using the percentiles 97.5 of validation subjects $percentile_{97.5}(\mathbf{v}^{\text{validation set}}) = threshold \in \mathbb{R}^{h \times w}$. Similarly, the evaluated image has its $\mathbf{v}$ obtained, and its values were binarized using $m_{i,j} = 1$ if $v_{i,j} \geq threshold_{i,j}$, 0 otherwise.

The next step of our method is the healing process of the original $\mathbf{z}$. The goal is to inpaint the highlighted regions in $\mathbf{m}$ using the rest of the image as context. For that, we initialize our inpainting process with $t = 500$ (in our synthetic lesion tests, we observed that this starting point was enough to heal the lesions). Using the reverse process, we removed "noise" from the regions that have anomalies while keeping the rest as the original $\mathbf{z}_0$, i.e., $\mathbf{z}'_{t-1} \sim p_\theta(\mathbf{z}_{t-1}|\mathbf{m} \odot \mathbf{z}'_t + (1-\mathbf{m}) \odot \mathbf{z}_0)$. This way each step denoises the masked regions a little bit but keeps the rest of the image as original. The resulting $\mathbf{z}_0$ of this process is the latent variable with the anomalies corrected.

Then, we use the VQ-VAE to decode $\mathbf{z}(= \mathbf{z}_0)$ back to the pixel space $\hat{\mathbf{x}}'$ and obtain the pixel-wise residuals $|\mathbf{x} - \hat{\mathbf{x}}'|$. To clean areas that the DDPM did not specify as anomalous, we upsample our latent mask, smooth it using a Gaussian filter, and multiply it with the residuals. Finally, we can identify regions with anomalies of each brain image from the regions on the final residual maps with high values.

4 Experiments

4.1 Anomaly Segmentation and Detection on Synthetic Anomalies

In this experiment, we used the MedNIST dataset corrupted with sprites (details in Appendix C). We trained our models with "HeadCT" 9,000 images and we evaluated our method on 100 images contaminated with sprites.

Table 1 shows how each step of our method improves its performance. We measure the performance using the area under the precision-recall curve (AUPRC) as a sensible measure for segmentation performance under class imbalance. We also obtained the best achievable DICE score ($\lceil DICE \rceil$), which constitutes a theoretical upper-bound to a model's segmentation performance and is obtained via a greedy search for the residual threshold, which yields the highest DICE score on the test set. Step (a) corresponds to applying a series of reverse steps on z (no masks, neither masked inpainting). A significant improvement is observed when applying the upsampled mask to the residual maps (step b), and finally, we had the best results with our complete approach (step c). Our single model method has a significant higher performance compared to the transformer while showing a slightly better performance than the ensemble on the $\lceil DICE \rceil$ but a slightly smaller AUPRC. We also evaluate the anomaly detection performance of our models based on the mean KL Divergence of the images across the whole Markov chain. Using the corrupted images as near out-of-distribution class, our method obtained AUCROC = 0.827 and AUPRC = 0.702. These values are slightly worse than the transformer-based approach (AUCROC = 0.921 and AUPRC = 0.707).

4.2 Anomaly Segmentation on MRI Data

In this experiment, we trained our models on a normative dataset of 15,000 participants with the lowest lesion volume in the UK Biobank (UKB) [25]. We used

Table 1. Performance of DDPM-based method on synthetic dataset. The performance is measured with best achievable DICE-score ($\lceil DICE \rceil$) and area under the precision-recall curve (AUPRC) on the test set. The autoencoder downsampling factor is indicated by f.

Method	$\lceil DICE \rceil$	AUPRC
AE (Spatial) [2]	0.165	0.093
VAE (Dense) [2]	0.533	0.464
f-AnoGAN [21]	0.492	0.432
Transformer [16]	0.768	0.808
Ensemble [16]	0.895	**0.956**
DDPM ($f = 4$) (a) [ours]	0.777	0.810
DDPM ($f = 4$) (b) [ours]	0.908	0.950
DDPM ($f = 4$) (c) [ours]	**0.920**	0.955

Table 2. Performance on anomaly segmentation using real 2D MRI lesion data. We measured the performance using the theoretically best possible DICE-score ($\lceil DICE \rceil$). We highlight the best performance in bold and the second best with $\dagger$. The autoencoder downsampling factor is indicated by f.

	UKB	MSLUB	BRATS	WMH
VAE (Dense) [2]	0.016	0.039	0.173	0.068
f-AnoGAN [21]	0.060	0.034	0.243	0.048
Transformer [16]	0.104	0.234	0.328	0.269
Ensemble [16]	**0.232**	**0.378**	**0.537**	**0.429**
DDPM ($f = 4$) (b) [ours]	0.208†	0.204	0.469†	0.272
DDPM ($f = 4$) (c) [ours]	**0.232**	0.247†	0.398	0.298†

FLAIR images, and we evaluated our method on small vessel disease (White Matter Hyperintensities Segmentation Challenge (WMH) [10]), tumours (Multimodal Brain Tumor Image Segmentation Benchmark (BRATS) [1]), demyelinating lesions (Multiple Sclerosis dataset from the University Hospital of Ljubljana (MSLUB) [11]), and white matter hyperintensities (UKB) (details in Appendix C). Table 2 shows that our method performs as well as an ensemble of transformers on the same dataset used to train (i.e., UKB). It performs better than the single transformer on all datasets; however, the ensemble generalizes better.

4.3   Inference Time of Anomaly Segmentation on CT Data

In this experiment, we focused on analysing the inference time of our anomaly segmentation methods in a scenario where time consumption is critical for clinical viability: the analysis of intracerebral haemorrhages (ICH) (Fig. 2). We trained our models on CT axial slices that did not contain ICH from 200 participants from the CROMIS dataset [29]. To evaluate, we used 21 participants from CROMIS and the KCH and CHRONIC [12] datasets (details in Appendix C).

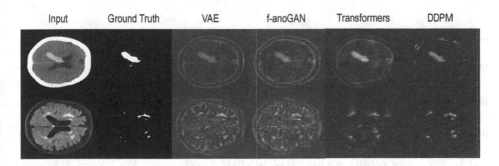

Fig. 2. Residual maps on the real lesions from CT and MRI images.

Table 3. Performance on anomaly segmentation using real 2D CT lesion data. We measured the performance using the theoretically best possible DICE-score ($\lceil DICE \rceil$). The autoencoder downsampling factor is indicated by f.

	CROMIS	KCH	ChroNIC	Time [s]	
VAE (Dense) [2]	0.185	0.353	0.171	<1	<1 min
f-AnoGAN [21]	0.146	0.292	0.099	<1	
DDIM ($f = 8$) (d) [ours]	**0.286**	**0.483**	**0.285**	12	
DDIM ($f = 4$) (d) [ours]	0.220	0.469	0.210	46	
DDPM ($f = 8$) (c) [ours]	0.284	0.473	0.297	81	1 min–10 min
DDPM ($f = 4$) (c) [ours]	0.215	0.471	0.221	324	
Transformer [16]	0.205	0.395	0.253	589	
Ensemble [16]	0.241	0.435	0.268	4907	>1 h
Transformer ($f = 4$) [ours]	0.356	0.482	0.116	8047	
Ensemble ($f = 4$) [ours]	0.471	0.631	0.122	>8000	

In Table 3, we divide our methods according to the inference time to process 100 slices from the KCH dataset (similar to the number occupied by the brain) on a single GPU (NVIDIA Titan RTX). All slices were fitted in a single minibatch for all models. We analysed different downsampling factors, and we added step (d) of our method where we use $L'_{400,600}$ (with only 50 values evenly spaced) and a DDIM to perform the reverse process (using 50 steps instead of 500). Our methods were able to perform in an acceptable time under 1 min. Using the DDIM sampler allowed us to significantly improve inference time while keeping a similar performance. All our methods were faster than the transformer-based approaches. As the length of the input sequence grows (changing from $f = 8$ to $f = 4$), the transformers potentially need to make more forward passes to replace the unlikely tokens. This limits their application of transformers in a higher resolution latent space (which would improve the ability to find smaller lesions). On the other hand, the number of forward passes that DDPM performs is constant for different resolutions, making it easier to scale.

5   Conclusions

We proposed a method to use DDPMs to perform anomaly detection and segmentation. The model performed competitively compared with transformers on both synthetic and real data, where it showed a better performance in most cases when compared to a single transformer. Our method holds promise in scenarios where the model prediction has time constraints, especially when using DDIMs. As pointed out in recent studies, anomaly detection methods are essential to obtaining robust performance in clinical settings[6]. We believe that our method's faster inference will help bring high-performance anomaly detection to the clinical front line. DDPMs have just recently caught the attention of the machine learning community, rivalling Generative Adversarial Networks in sample quality and autoregressive models in likelihood scores, built upon a solid theoretical foundation, and fitting within several different theoretical frameworks. We believe that DDPMs have the potential to be even further improved, bringing more advances to anomaly detection in a medical image.

Acknowledgement. WHLP, MG, RG, PW, SO, PN and MJC are supported by Wellcome [WT213038/Z/18/Z]. PTD is supported by the EPSRC Research Council, part of the EPSRC DTP, grant Ref: [EP/R513064/1]. YM is supported by an MRC Clinical Academic Research Partnership grant [MR/T005351/1]. PC is supported by SAPIENS Marie Curie Slowdowska Actions ITN N. 814302. PN is also supported by the UCLH NIHR Biomedical Research Centre. MJC and SO are also supported by the Wellcome/EPSRC Centre for Medical Engineering (WT203148/Z/16/Z), and by the GSTT NIHR BRC. This research has been conducted using the UK Biobank Resource (Project number: 58292). The models in this work were trained on NVIDIA Cambridge-1, the UK's largest supercomputer, aimed at accelerating digital biology.

References

1. Bakas, S., et al.: Identifying the best machine learning algorithms for brain tumor segmentation, progression assessment, and overall survival prediction in the brats challenge. arXiv preprint arXiv:1811.02629 (2018)
2. Baur, C., Denner, S., Wiestler, B., Navab, N., Albarqouni, S.: Autoencoders for unsupervised anomaly segmentation in brain mr images: a comparative study. Med. Image Anal. **69**, 101952 (2021)
3. Dhariwal, P., Nichol, A.: Diffusion models beat gans on image synthesis. In: Advances in Neural Information Processing Systems, vol. 34 (2021)
4. Esser, P., Rombach, R., Blattmann, A., Ommer, B.: Imagebart: bidirectional context with multinomial diffusion for autoregressive image synthesis. In: Advances in Neural Information Processing Systems, vol. 34 (2021)
5. Esser, P., Rombach, R., Ommer, B.: Taming transformers for high-resolution image synthesis. In: Proceedings of the IEEE/CVF Conference on Computer Vision and Pattern Recognition, pp. 12873–12883 (2021)
6. Graham, M.S., et al.: Transformer-based out-of-distribution detection for clinically safe segmentation (2021)
7. Gu, S., et al.: Vector quantized diffusion model for text-to-image synthesis. arXiv preprint arXiv:2111.14822 (2021)
8. Ho, J., Jain, A., Abbeel, P.: Denoising diffusion probabilistic models. Adv. Neural. Inf. Process. Syst. **33**, 6840–6851 (2020)
9. Jun, H., et al.: Distribution augmentation for generative modeling. In: International Conference on Machine Learning, pp. 5006–5019. PMLR (2020)
10. Kuijf, H.J., et al.: Standardized assessment of automatic segmentation of white matter hyperintensities and results of the wmh segmentation challenge. IEEE Trans. Med. Imaging **38**(11), 2556–2568 (2019)
11. Lesjak, Ž, et al.: A novel public mr image dataset of multiple sclerosis patients with lesion segmentations based on multi-rater consensus. Neuroinformatics **16**(1), 51–63 (2018)
12. Mah, Y.H., Nachev, P., MacKinnon, A.D.: Quantifying the impact of chronic ischemic injury on clinical outcomes in acute stroke with machine learning. Front. Neurol. **11**, 15 (2020)

13. Nichol, A.Q., Dhariwal, P.: Improved denoising diffusion probabilistic models. In: International Conference on Machine Learning, pp. 8162–8171. PMLR (2021)
14. Patel, A., et al.: Cross attention transformers for unsupervised whole-body pet anomaly detection with multi-modal conditioning (2021)
15. Pawlowski, N., et al.: Unsupervised lesion detection in brain ct using bayesian convolutional autoencoders (2018)
16. Pinaya, W.H.L., et al.: Unsupervised brain anomaly detection and segmentation with transformers. arXiv preprint arXiv:2102.11650 (2021)
17. Porz, N., et al.: Multi-modal glioblastoma segmentation: man versus machine. PLoS ONE **9**(5), e96873 (2014)
18. Ramesh, A., et al.: Zero-shot text-to-image generation. In: International Conference on Machine Learning, pp. 8821–8831. PMLR (2021)
19. Rombach, R., Blattmann, A., Lorenz, D., Esser, P., Ommer, B.: High-resolution image synthesis with latent diffusion models. arXiv preprint arXiv:2112.10752 (2021)
20. Roy, A., Saffar, M., Vaswani, A., Grangier, D.: Efficient content-based sparse attention with routing transformers. Trans. Assoc. Comput. Linguist. **9**, 53–68 (2021)
21. Schlegl, T., Seeböck, P., Waldstein, S.M., Langs, G., Schmidt-Erfurth, U.: f-anogan: Fast unsupervised anomaly detection with generative adversarial networks. Med. Image Anal. **54**, 30–44 (2019)
22. Schmidt, F.: Generalization in generation: A closer look at exposure bias. arXiv preprint arXiv:1910.00292 (2019)
23. Sohl-Dickstein, J., Weiss, E., Maheswaranathan, N., Ganguli, S.: Deep unsupervised learning using nonequilibrium thermodynamics. In: International Conference on Machine Learning, pp. 2256–2265. PMLR (2015)
24. Song, J., Meng, C., Ermon, S.: Denoising diffusion implicit models. arXiv preprint arXiv:2010.02502 (2020)
25. Sudlow, C., et al.: Uk biobank: an open access resource for identifying the causes of a wide range of complex diseases of middle and old age. PLoS Med. **12**(3), e1001779 (2015)
26. Van Den Oord, A., Vinyals, O., et al.: Neural discrete representation learning. In: Advances in Neural Information Processing Systems, vol. 30 (2017)
27. Vaswani, A., et al.: Attention is all you need. In: Advances in Neural Information Processing Systems, vol. 30 (2017)
28. Wang, L., Zhang, D., Guo, J., Han, Y.: Image anomaly detection using normal data only by latent space resampling. Appl. Sci. **10**(23), 8660 (2020)
29. Wilson, D., et al.: Cerebral microbleeds and intracranial haemorrhage risk in patients anticoagulated for atrial fibrillation after acute ischaemic stroke or transient ischaemic attack (cromis-2): a multicentre observational cohort study. T Lancet Neurol. **17**(6), 539–547 (2018)
30. You, S., Tezcan, K.C., Chen, X., Konukoglu, E.: Unsupervised lesion detection via image restoration with a normative prior. In: International Conference on Medical Imaging with Deep Learning, pp. 540–556. PMLR (2019)
31. Yuh, E.L., Cooper, S.R., Ferguson, A.R., Manley, G.T.: Quantitative ct improves outcome prediction in acute traumatic brain injury. J. Neurotrauma **29**(5), 735–746 (2012)

Reliability of Quantification Estimates in MR Spectroscopy: CNNs vs Traditional Model Fitting

Rudy Rizzo[1,2] (iD), Martyna Dziadosz[1,2], Sreenath P. Kyathanahally[3] (iD),
Mauricio Reyes[4,5] (iD), and Roland Kreis[1,2(✉)] (iD)

[1] MR Methodology, Diagnostic and Interventional Neuroradiology, University of Bern,
Bern, Switzerland
roland.kreis@insel.ch
[2] Translational Imaging Center, sitem-insel, Bern, Switzerland
[3] Data Science
for Environmental Research Group, Department of System Analysis, Integrated Assessment and
Modelling; EAWAG, Dübendorf, Switzerland
[4] Insel Data Science Center, Inselspital, Bern University Hospital, Bern, Switzerland
[5] ARTOG Center for Biomedical Engineering Research, University of Bern, Bern, Switzerland

Abstract. Magnetic Resonance Spectroscopy (MRS) and Spectroscopic Imaging (MRSI) are non-invasive techniques to map tissue contents of many metabolites in situ in humans. Quantification is traditionally done via model fitting (MF), and Cramer Rao Lower Bounds (CRLBs) are used as a measure of fitting uncertainties. Signal-to-noise is limited due to clinical time constraints and MF can be very time-consuming in MRSI with thousands of spectra. Deep Learning (DL) has introduced the possibility to speed up quantitation while reportedly preserving accuracy and precision. However, questions arise about how to access quantification uncertainties in the case of DL. In this work, an optimal-performance DL architecture that uses spectrograms as input and maps absolute concentrations of metabolites referenced to water content as output was taken to investigate this in detail. Distributions of predictions and Monte-Carlo dropout were used to investigate data and model-related uncertainties, exploiting ground truth knowledge in a synthetic setup mimicking realistic brain spectra with metabolic composition that uniformly varies from healthy to pathological cases. Bias and CRLBs from MF are then compared to DL-related uncertainties. It is confirmed that DL is a dataset-biased technique where accuracy and precision of predictions scale with metabolite SNR but hint towards bias and increased uncertainty at the edges of the explored parameter space (i.e., for very high and very low concentrations), even at infinite SNR (noiseless training and testing). Moreover, training with uniform datasets or if augmented with critical cases showed to be insufficient to prevent biases. This is dangerous in a clinical context that requires the algorithm to be unbiased also for concentrations far from the norm, which may well be the focus of the investigation since these correspond to pathology, the target of the diagnostic investigation.

Keywords: Magnetic Resonance Spectroscopy · Convolutional neural networks · Model fitting · Quantification · Reliability · Uncertainties

L. Wang et al. (Eds.): MICCAI 2022, LNCS 13438, pp. 715–724, 2022.
https://doi.org/10.1007/978-3-031-16452-1_68

1 Introduction

Magnetic Resonance Spectroscopy (MRS) and Spectroscopic Imaging (MRSI) are non-invasive methods for determining in-situ metabolic profile maps in humans or animals. A chemical-composition-specific response is evoked from localized tissue regions using an MRI scanner and allows the acquisition of a Voigt-damped time-domain signal, which results from a superposition of multiple metabolite signals. The resonance line patterns are metabolite-specific, reflecting the spin-systems, while their concentrations are proportional to the signal amplitude [1] (Fig. 1).

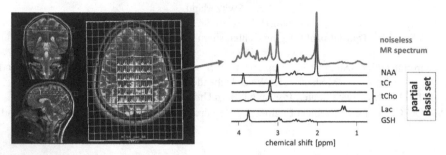

Fig. 1. MRSI acquisition with zoom-in to a sketch of a noiseless MR spectrum (real part) and relative spectral basis set outlined for five metabolites: N-Acetylaspartate (NAA), total-Creatine (tCr), total-Choline (tCho), Lactate (Lac), and Glutathione (GSH).

Quantification is traditionally based on parameter estimation with Model Fitting (MF), minimizing the difference between the data and a parameterized model function. Despite many fitting approaches [2–5], robust and accurate measurement of metabolite concentrations remains challenging [6, 7], mainly due to: (i) severely overlapping metabolite patterns, (ii) poor signal-to-noise ratio (SNR), and (iii) unknown background signals and peak lineshape (incomplete prior knowledge). As a result, the problem is ill-posed, and current techniques still hamper translation to clinical routine.

Supervised Deep Learning (DL) exploits neural networks to find key properties contained in large data sets and to generate complicated nonlinear mappings between inputs and outputs [8]. It thus requires no prior knowledge or formal assumptions. However, it is shown to be frequently biased towards the conditions prevalent in the datasets used in training [9]. DL in MRS quantification is increasingly explored [10–12] and has shown to speed up quantitation while reportedly preserving accurate estimates if compared to MF. Still, questions regarding the reliability of DL quantification have arisen.

Uncertainty measures provide information about how reliably or accurately a given algorithm performs a given task. This information in turn can be used to leverage the decision-making process for a user (e.g., how much to trust the estimated concentration of a metabolite) or to enable optimization of the acquisition technique or the algorithm employed to estimate results (e.g., focusing on areas of high uncertainty [13]). Given MRS restrictions to comply with clinical time frames, the repetition of multiple MRS measurements to determine repeatability is forbidding. Thus, estimates of uncertainty obtained from MRS model fitting of a single measurement are often taken as proxy:

the Cramer Rao Lower Bounds (CRLBs) [14] estimate uncertainties as function of the model (presumed to be true) and SNR; they represent the uncertainty limit for unbiased estimators. It is fundamental to access a CRLB-comparable uncertainty measure for MRS metabolite quantification by DL [15]. Neural network uncertainties originate from noise inherent in the data (aleatoric uncertainty) and uncertainty in the model parameters (epistemic uncertainty) [16, 17]. In the current work, an optimal-performance Convolutional Neural Network (CNN) architecture is designed to quantify metabolites, and metrics based on bias and spread of predicted distribution of concentrations are used to explain aleatoric uncertainties. Epistemic uncertainties are explored via Monte-Carlo dropout [18]. The reliability of MRS quantification is then compared between the two approaches. In-silico simulations guarantee knowledge of Ground Truth (GT).

2 Methods

2.1 Simulations

Spectral patterns were simulated for 16 metabolites recorded at 3T with a semi-LASER protocol [19, 20; TE = 35 ms, 4 kHz spectral width, 4096 points. To mimic pathological conditions, metabolite concentrations are varied independently and uniformly between 0 and twice a normal reference concentration for healthy human brain [1, 21–23]. A constant downscaled water reference (64.5 mM) is added at 0.5 ppm to ease quantitation. Macromolecular background (MMBG) signals and Gaussian broadening mimic in vivo conditions and were independently and uniformly varied (shim 2–5 Hz, MMBG amplitude ± 33%). Two datasets with 20'000 entries randomly split in training (80%), validation (10%), and testing sets (10%) are generated: one with independent, realistic white Gaussian noise realizations (time-domain water-referenced SNR 5–40), the other noiseless (Fig. 2).

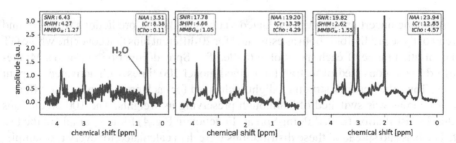

Fig. 2. Samples of realistic simulated spectra. SNR, shim, and MMBG intensity are indicated. Concentrations reported for 3 major metabolites in mM. Downscaled reference peak indicated.

High-frequency-resolved spectrograms [24] were used as input for the CNNs. A spectrogram is a complex, 2D time-frequency domain representation of a spectrum where each row reflects the frequency content of a specific time segment of the MRS signal. It is calculated using the Short-Temporal Fourier Transform (STFT), which allows for varying degrees of frequency and time resolution depending on the size of the Fourier analysis window. A large window size established through zero-filling is paired with a tiny overlap interval to maximize frequency resolution while compromising temporal resolution (Fig. 3).

2.2 Quantification via Deep Learning

Two Bayesian hyper-parameterized [25] shallow CNNs [26] were trained and tested with the two datasets. They had emerged as optimal DL quantification methods from 24 tested scenarios with different architectures, input forms, and active learning data augmentation. Relative concentrations are provided as output but referencing to the water signal yields absolute concentrations (Fig. 3). Training and validation sets were randomly assigned to train the CNN on a maximum number of 100 epochs and with batch normalization of 50. The learning rate was modulated via the adaptive moment (ADAM) estimation algorithm [27]. Mean-squared error (MSE) served as loss function. Visualization of training and validation loss over epochs combined with the implementation of early-stopping criterion monitoring minimization of validation loss with patience ten was used as a reference for tuning the network parameter space.

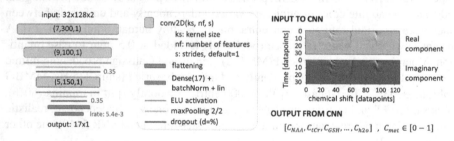

Fig. 3. Shallow CNN architecture, sample of input spectrogram, and output vector description.

Aleatoric uncertainties were evaluated via bias of the DL predictions from GT and spread of these predictions, both as estimated for 20 different bins that cover the whole GT concentration range of each metabolite (called Bin-Spread-Function in Fig. 4). Monte-Carlo dropout consisted of testing the trained model 100 times with activated dropout layers. Thus, the network structure slightly changed for each prediction (i.e., a different set of neurons was switched off) although preserving its weights. The 100 predictions yielded a distribution (called Point-Spread-Function in Fig. 4) for any sample in the test set. The bias and spread of these distributions were then calculated for every test sample, averaged for every GT value, and used as epistemic uncertainties. They highlight the susceptibility of predictions to model variation.

2.3 Quantification via Model Fitting

The test set spectra were fitted using fitAID [5]. The model consisted of a weighted sum of Voigt lines with fixed Lorentzian (GT value) and estimated Gaussian widths. Areas of the metabolites were restricted in $[-0.5 \cdot \mu, +2.5 \cdot \mu]$, where μ is the average concentration in the testing and training set distribution for each metabolite, aiming to bound the fitting condition to known prior knowledge, mimicking the implicit restrictions of DL algorithms. Bias from GT and CRLB are used as uncertainty measures.

a) aleatoric uncertainties

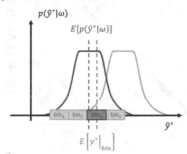

b) epistemic uncertainties

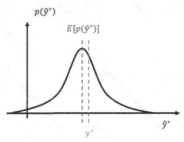

$p(\hat{y}^*|\omega)$: Bin-Spread-Function of prediction $\hat{y}^*$ for a certain ground truth binned concentration $y^*|_{bin}$ given fixed parameterized model ω.

$$\Delta(y^*|\omega)\Big|_{bin} = E[p(\hat{y}^*|\omega)] - y^*\Big|_{bin}$$

$$\Sigma(y^*|\omega)\Big|_{bin} = \sqrt{E[(\hat{y}^* - E[p(\hat{y}^*|\omega)])^2]}\Big|_{bin}$$

$p(\hat{y}^*)$: Point-Spread-Function of prediction $\hat{y}^*$ for a certain ground truth concentration y^* under small variations of the model ω.

$$\Delta(y^*) = E[p(\hat{y}^*)] - y^*$$

$$\Sigma(y^*) = \sqrt{(E[(\hat{y}^* - E[p(\hat{y}^*)])^2]}$$

Fig. 4. Distribution of uncertainties: bias (Δ) represents a deviation from ground truth, and spread (Σ) represents variability of predictions around their center: the expected value (E[·]).

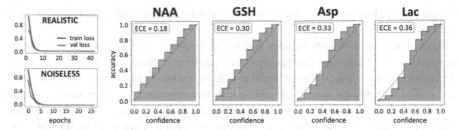

Fig. 5. Training and validation curves. Reliability diagrams and expected calibration error.

3 Results

Results are reported for four metabolites with progressively lower relative SNR: NAA, GSH, Asp, and Lac (c.f. Fig. 1). Figure 5 shows training and validation curves for both networks. Network calibration is investigated for regression, where the design is assumed to predict the Cumulative Distribution Function of relative metabolite concentrations [28, 29]. Reliability diagrams are reported for realistic simulations. Quantification of Lac and Asp is mildly overconfident for low concentrations and underconfident for high

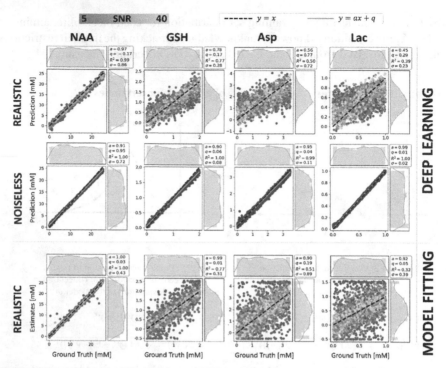

Fig. 6. Maps and marginal distribution of CNN predictions vs. GT for four metabolites and two datasets (realistic, noiseless) and model estimates vs. GT for the realistic case.

concentrations. However, the network can be considered well-calibrated for every target metabolite [13].

Figure 6 reports CNN predictions and MF estimates vs. GT values. A linear regression model is fit to estimate the quality of the prediction. Marginal distributions of GT and predicted values are displayed. Ideal predictions would display as a diagonal line ($y = ax + q$) with minimal spread (RMSE, σ). In line, distributions of predictions would mirror the uniform GT distributions. Considering the realistic case in DL and going from left to right, predicted distributions become less uniform and get more biased towards a mean expected value of the training range. This phenomenon is reflected in lower a and R^2 values and is emphasized for metabolites with low relative SNR (e.g., GSH, Asp, and Lac). Noiseless simulations show a significantly reduced bias. MF estimates show a better spread over the concentration range with a $\rightarrow$ 1 and q $\rightarrow$ 0 even for metabolites with low relative SNR. RMSE (σ) is lower in MF than DL for NAA but higher in the case of GSH, Asp, and Lac.

Figure 7 maps aleatoric and epistemic uncertainties as function of GT values for DL. Epistemic uncertainties indicate higher variability of predictions at the boundaries of the concentration ranges, which is paired with higher biases for aleatoric uncertainties. In the noiseless scenario, it is evident how the point-spread function is affected by a larger spread at the edges (i.e., U-shape). Training and testing with noise show the same trend if relative SNR is high enough. Model fitting appears unbiased (average bias as orange line) except for a small effect at the parameter boundaries and biased larger outliers (blue line) for metabolites with low SNR. CRLB are concentration-independent (linear fit parameter). Moreover, average CRLBs are confirmed to represent a lower bound to standard deviation (σ) of the fit error.

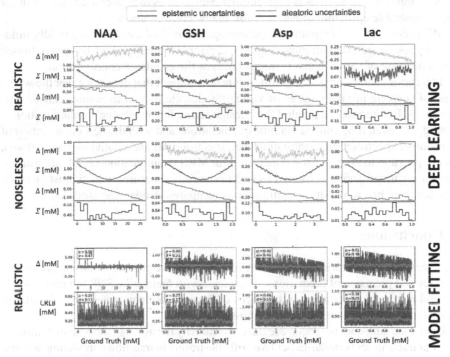

Fig. 7. CNNs' bias and spread of epistemic (green) and aleatoric (blue) uncertainties vs. GT values. MF bias and CRLBs vs. GT: single values (blue) and interpolated (orange). Estimated standard deviation (σ) of the bias can be compared to the estimated average (μ) CRLB. (Color figure online)

4 Discussion

Predicted concentrations should be unbiased, thus returning uniform distributions for uniform training and test data. However, our CNN predictions for real-world simulations tend towards the mean of the test data. Predictions at the boundaries of the testing range are folded back towards the mean value in case of strong uncertainty (i.e., low metabolite SNR), given the lack of knowledge outside the boundaries. Indeed, it is found that the prediction bias is influenced by the limited concentration ranges used in training: epistemic uncertainties indicate higher variability of predictions at the boundaries of the concentration ranges, which is paired with higher biases for aleatoric uncertainties. Though not exploring the exact same architecture, it is suspected that previous DL MRS approaches may show similar deficiencies [10–12]. An ideal noiseless scenario also shows similar findings: uncertainty is lower in absolute values compared to the realistic case, but a similar dependency on the concentration range is found (U-shape), confirming that the DL prediction constitutes a biased estimator with uncertainties that depend on the placement of the test case in the training range. Training and testing with noise show the same trend if relative SNR is high enough. Metabolites in high concentrations suffer from comparable epistemic spread as those in low concentrations.

MF is confirmed to be unbiased on average. Individual estimates are mildly influenced by restrained concentration ranges (i.e., prior knowledge). CRLBs are confirmed to be a measure of variance that is independent of the estimated concentration.

The current study considers a limited synthetic dataset that does not cover the whole range of possible in-vivo sources of variability despite its aim to mimic realistic performances. Furthermore, a single CNN design tuned for metabolite's quantification is investigated, even if optimized via multiple iterations and with the best combination of input/output spectroscopic information (i.e., spectrograms and relative concentrations), it is not possible to draw general conclusion for MRS quantification via DL algorithms. Uncertainty investigation is limited to two uncertainty measures, which must be taken with their benefits, reliability, and limitations compared to other measures [13].

5 Conclusions

Four measures for aleatoric and epistemic uncertainties are provided, partly representing accuracy and precision of predictions. They scale with metabolite SNR but hint towards bias and increased uncertainty at the edges of the explored parameter space for (these) DL methods in many cases, even at infinite SNR.

Deep Learning does not require feature selection by the user, but the potential intrinsic biases at training set boundaries act like soft constraints in traditional modeling, leading estimated values to an apparently precise (low mean deviation) estimate reflecting an expectation value over the normal concentration range used in training. This is dangerous in a clinical context that requires the algorithm to be unbiased to outliers, which may well be the focus of the investigation corresponding to pathological data.

Further investigation to access more stable predictions is needed: (i) training with even larger concentration ranges, such that the region of interest is well inside the training range where uncertainties are limited, (ii) consider ensemble of networks to strengthen network performances for outliers or (iii) implementation of Batch Nuclear-norm Maximization to improve discriminability and diversity of the predictions [30].

6 Data Availability Statement

The simulated datasets and network architecture that support the findings of this study are available at https://github.com/bellarude.

Acknowledgments. This work is supported by the Marie-Sklodowska-Curie Grant ITN-39 237 (Inspire-Med) and the Swiss National Science Foundation (#320030–175984).

References

1. de Graaf, R.A.: In Vivo NMR Spectroscopy: principles and techniques, 3rd ed., WILEY (2018)
2. Ratiney, H., et al.: Time-domain semi-parametric estimation based on a metabolite basis. NMR Biomed. **18**, 1–13 (2005)
3. Provencher, S.: Estimation of metabolite concentrations from localized in vivo. Magn. Reson. Med. **30**(6), 672–679 (1993)
4. Wilson, M., et al.: A constrained least-squares approach to the automated quantitation of in vivo 1h magnetic resonance spectroscopy data. Magn. Reson. Med. **65**(1), 1–12 (2011)
5. Chong, D.G.Q., et al.: Two-dimensional linear-combination model fitting of magnetic resonance spectra to define the macromolecule baseline using FiTAID, a Fitting Tool for Arrays of Interrelated Datasets. Magn. Reson. Mater. Physics, Biol. Med. **24**, 147–164 (2011)
6. Bhogal, A.A., et al.: 1H-MRS processing parameters affect metabolite quantification: the urgent need for uniform and transparent standardization. NMR in Biomed. **30**, e3804 (2017)
7. Marjanska, M., et al.: Results and interpretation of a fitting challenge for MR spectroscopy set up by the MRS study group of ISMRM. Magn. Reson. Med. **87**(1), 11–32 (2022)
8. Wick, C.: Deep Learn. Informatik-Spektrum **40**(1), 103–107 (2016). https://doi.org/10.1007/s00287-016-1013-2
9. Gyori, N.G., et al.: Training data distribution significantly impacts the estimation of tissue microstructure with machine learning. Magn. Reson. Med. **87**(2), 932–947 (2022)
10. Lee, H.H., et al.: Deep learning-based target metabolite isolation and big data-driven measurement uncertainty estimation in proton magnetic resonance spectroscopy of the brain. Magn. Reson. Med. **84**(4), 1689–1706 (2020)
11. Gurbani, S.S., et al.: Incorporation of a spectral model in a convolutional neural network for accelerated spectral fitting. Magn. Reson. Med. **81**, 3346–3357 (2018)
12. Hatami, N., Sdika, M., Ratiney, H.: Magnetic resonance spectroscopy quantification using deep learning. In: Frangi, A.F., Schnabel, J.A., Davatzikos, C., Alberola-López, C., Fichtinger, G. (eds.) Medical Image Computing and Computer Assisted Intervention – MICCAI 2018. Lecture Notes in Computer Science, vol. 11070, pp. 467–475. Springer, Cham (2018). https://doi.org/10.1007/978-3-030-00928-1_53
13. Jungo, A., et al.: Assessing Reliability and Challenges of Uncertainty Estimations for Medical Image Segmentation, arXiv:1907.03338v2. (2019)
14. Bolliger, C.S., et al.: On the use of Cramér-Rao minimum variance bounds for the design of magnetic resonance spectroscopy experiments. Neuroimage **83**, 1031–1040 (2013)
15. Landheer, K., et al.: Are Cramer-Rao lower bounds an accurate estimate for standard deviations in in vivo magnetic resonance spectroscopy? NMR Biomed. **34**(7), e4521 (2021)
16. Gal, Y.: Uncertainty in Deep Learning, University of Cambridge (2016)
17. Kendall, A.: What uncertainties do we need in Bayesian deep learning for computer vision? arXiv:1703.04977v2. (2017)
18. Gal, Y. et al.: Dropout as a Bayesian approximation: representing model uncertainty in deep learning, arXiv:1506.02142v6. (2016)
19. Soher, B.J., et al.: VeSPA: integrated applications for RF pulse design, spectral simulation and MRS data analysis. Proc. Int. Soc. Magn. Reson. Med. **19**(19), 1410 (2011)
20. Oz, G., et al.: Short-echo, single-shot, full-intensity proton magnetic resonance spectroscopy for neurochemical profiling at 4 T: validation in the cerebellum and brainstem. Magn. Reson. Med. **65**(4), 901–910 (2011)
21. Marjańska, M., et al.: Region-specific aging of the human brain as evidenced by neurochemical profiles measured noninvasively in the posterior cingulate cortex and the occipital lobe using 1H magnetic resonance spectroscopy at 7 T. Neuroscience **354**, 168–177 (2017)

22. Hoefemann, M., et al.: Parameterization of metabolite and macromolecule contributions in interrelated MR spectra of human brain using multidimensional modeling. NMR Biomed. **33**(9), e4328 (2020)
23. Oz, G., et al.: Clinical proton MR spectroscopy in central nervous system disorders. Radiology **270**(3), 658–679 (2014)
24. Kyathanahally, S.P., et al.: Deep Learning approaches for detection and removal of ghosting artifacts in MR Spectroscopy. Magn. Reson. Med. **80**, 851–863 (2018)
25. Snoek, J.: Practical Bayesian otimization of Machine Learning Algoirthms. In: 25th International Conference on Neural Information Processing System, vol. 2, pp. 2951–2959 (2012)
26. Espi, M., et al.: Exploiting spectro-temporal locality in deep learning based acoustic event detection. J. Audio Speech Music Proc. **26** (2015)
27. Kingma, D.P., et al.: Adam: A method for stochastic optimization. Arxiv:1412.6980. (2014)
28. Niculescu-Mizil, A., et al.: Predicting good probabilities with supervised learning. In: 22nd ICML, pp.7–11 (2005)
29. Kuleshov, V., et al.: Accurate uncertainties for deep learning using calibrated regression. In: 35th ICML (2018)
30. Cui, S., et al.: Towards discriminability and diversity: batch Nuclear-norm Maximization under label insufficient situations. Arxiv:2003.12237v1. (2020)

AdaTriplet: Adaptive Gradient Triplet Loss with Automatic Margin Learning for Forensic Medical Image Matching

Khanh Nguyen, Huy Hoang Nguyen$^{(\boxtimes)}$, and Aleksei Tiulpin

University of Oulu, Oulu, Finland
{khanh.nguyen,huy.nguyen,aleksei.tiulpin}@oulu.fi

Abstract. This paper tackles the challenge of forensic medical image matching (FMIM) using deep neural networks (DNNs). FMIM is a particular case of content-based image retrieval (CBIR). The main challenge in FMIM compared to the general case of CBIR, is that the subject to whom a query image belongs may be affected by aging and progressive degenerative disorders, making it difficult to match data on a subject level. CBIR with DNNs is generally solved by minimizing a ranking loss, such as Triplet loss (TL), computed on image representations extracted by a DNN from the original data. TL, in particular, operates on triplets: anchor, positive (similar to anchor) and negative (dissimilar to anchor). Although TL has been shown to perform well in many CBIR tasks, it still has limitations, which we identify and analyze in this work. In this paper, we introduce (i) the AdaTriplet loss – an extension of TL whose gradients adapt to different difficulty levels of negative samples, and (ii) the AutoMargin method – a technique to adjust hyperparameters of margin-based losses such as TL and our proposed loss dynamically. Our results are evaluated on two large-scale benchmarks for FMIM based on the Osteoarthritis Initiative and Chest X-ray-14 datasets. The codes allowing replication of this study have been made publicly available at https://github.com/Oulu-IMEDS/AdaTriplet.

Keywords: Deep learning · Content-based image retrieval · Forensic matching

1 Introduction

Content-based image retrieval (CBIR) describes the long-standing problem of retrieving semantically similar images from a database. CBIR is challenging due to the diversity of foreground and background color, context, and semantic

---

K. Nguyen and H.H Nguyen—Equal contributions.

Supplementary Information The online version contains supplementary material available at https://doi.org/10.1007/978-3-031-16452-1_69.

L. Wang et al. (Eds.): MICCAI 2022, LNCS 13438, pp. 725–735, 2022.
https://doi.org/10.1007/978-3-031-16452-1_69

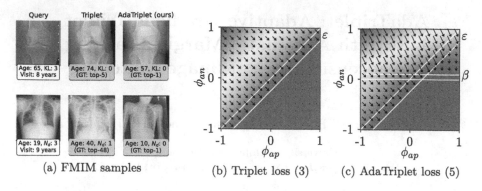

(a) FMIM samples   (b) Triplet loss (3)   (c) AdaTriplet loss (5)

Fig. 1. Comparisons between the Triplet loss and our AdaTriplet loss. (a) Top-1 retrieved results. Green: if a ground truth (GT) is the top-1 in the ranked retrieval list, orange: otherwise. KL indicates the grade of knee osteoarthritis severity. N_d is the number of thorax diseases. (b-c) 2D loss surfaces and negative gradient fields of the two losses. Each point is a triplet. Loss values are represented by colors (increasing from purple to red). The arrows are negative gradient vectors.

changes in images [19]. Besides general computer vision [18,22], in the domain of medicine, content-based medical image retrieval (CBMIR) is growing [3,27], due to the increasing demand for effectively querying medical images from hospital picture archive and communication systems (PACS) [10].

In CBMIR, given a medical image (query), one aims to search in a database for images that are similar disease-wise or belonging to the same subject. The former problem is related to diagnostic applications, and the latter problem is of interest for forensic investigations. Hereinafter, we name this problem forensic medical image matching (FMIM). Unlike general CBIR, matching longitudinal medical imaging data of a person is challenging due to aging, progression of various diseases or surgical interventions (Fig. 1a). Therefore, the FMIM domain poses new challenges for CBIR.

Deep learning (DL)-based methods have made breakthroughs in various fields, and in particular metric learning, which is the backbone of CBIR [3,12, 22,27]. The aim of DL-based metric learning is to train a functional parametric mapping f_θ from the image space $\mathbb{R}^{C \times H \times W}$ to a lower-dimensional feature space $\mathbb{R}^D$. In this feature space, representations of semantically similar images are close, and ones of irrelevant images are distant. In our notation, C, H and W represent the number of channels, height, and width of an image, respectively.

The loss function is the central component of metric learning [13], and there exist two major types: (i) those that enforce the relationships between samples in each batch of data during stochastic optimization – *embedding losses* [9,12,19, 25,27] and (ii) *classification losses* [6,22,28]. Two fundamental embedding losses that previous studies have built upon are Contrastive loss (CL) [4] and Triplet loss (TL) [9]. The idea of the CL, is to minimize the feature space distance between similar data points, and maximize it for the dissimilar ones. The TL, on the other hand, considers every triplet of samples – anchor, positive and negative, and aims to ensure that the distance between the anchor and positive samples is smaller than the distance between the anchor and negative ones.

In many practical applications, although the TL is more commonly used than the CL [1,24,26], it also has limitations. Firstly, the TL depends on a "margin" hyperparameter, which is usually fixed and needs to be chosen empirically. Secondly, as we show in this work, the TL ignores the magnitude of the pair-wise distances, thus may overlook the case where anchors and negative samples are too close. In this paper, we tackle these limitations, and summarize our contributions as follows:

1. We theoretically analyze the TL, and propose *an adaptive gradient triplet loss*, called AdaTriplet, which has appropriate gradients for triplets with different hardness. That characteristic makes our loss distinct from the TL, as illustrated in Fig. 1.
2. To address the issue of selecting margin hyperparameters, we propose a simple procedure – AutoMargin, which estimates margins adaptively during the training process, and eliminates the need for a separate grid-search.
3. Through a rigorous experimental evaluation on knee and chest X-ray image forensic matching problems, we show that AdaTriplet and AutoMargin allow for more accurate FMIM than a set of competitive baselines.

2 Methods

2.1 Problem Statement

Let $\mathbf{X} \times \mathbf{Y} = \{(\mathbf{x}_i, y_i)\}_{i=1}^{N}$ be a dataset of medical images $\mathbf{x}_i$'s $\in \mathbb{R}^{C \times H \times W}$ and corresponding subjects' identifiers y_i's with $|\mathbf{Y}| \leq N$. We aim to learn a parametric mapping $f_\theta : \mathbb{R}^{C \times H \times W} \rightarrow \mathbb{R}^D$ such that $\forall(\mathbf{x}_i, y_i), (\mathbf{x}_i', y_i), (\mathbf{x}_j, y_j) \in \mathbf{X}_{train} \times \mathbf{Y}_{train}, \mathbf{X}_{train} \subset \mathbf{X}, y_i \neq y_j$,

$$d(f_\theta(\mathbf{x}_i), f_\theta(\mathbf{x}_i')) < d(f_\theta(\mathbf{x}_i), f_\theta(\mathbf{x}_j)). \tag{1}$$

The learned mapping f_θ is expected to be generalizable to $\mathbf{X}_{test} = \mathbf{X} \setminus \mathbf{X}_{train}$ where $\mathbf{Y}_{test} \cap \mathbf{Y}_{train} = \varnothing$. Often, $\mathbf{x}_i$ is called an anchor point, $\mathbf{x}_i'$ – a positive point, and $\mathbf{x}_j$ – a negative point. Hereinafter, they are denoted as $\mathbf{x}_a, \mathbf{x}_p$, and $\mathbf{x}_n$, respectively. For simplicity, we also denote $\mathbf{f}_a = f_\theta(\mathbf{x}_a), \mathbf{f}_p = f_\theta(\mathbf{x}_p), \mathbf{f}_n = f_\theta(\mathbf{x}_n)$, $\phi_{ap} = \mathbf{f}_a^\mathsf{T} \mathbf{f}_p$, and $\phi_{an} = \mathbf{f}_a^\mathsf{T} \mathbf{f}_n$.

2.2 Triplet Loss

Let $\mathcal{T} = \{(\mathbf{x}_a, \mathbf{x}_p, \mathbf{x}_n) \mid y_a = y_p, y_a \neq y_n\}$ denote a set of all triplets of an anchor, a positive, and a negative data point. For each $(\mathbf{x}_a, \mathbf{x}_p, \mathbf{x}_n) \in \mathcal{T}$, the Triplet loss is formulated as [2,9]:

$$\mathcal{L}_{\text{Triplet}} = \left[\|\mathbf{f}_a - \mathbf{f}_p\|_2^2 - \|\mathbf{f}_a - \mathbf{f}_n\|_2^2 + \varepsilon\right]_+, \tag{2}$$

where $[\cdot]_+ = \max(\cdot, 0)$, and ε is a non-negative margin variable. Following common practice, we normalize all feature vectors, that is $\|\mathbf{f}_a\|_2 = \|\mathbf{f}_p\|_2 = \|\mathbf{f}_n\|_2 = 1$,

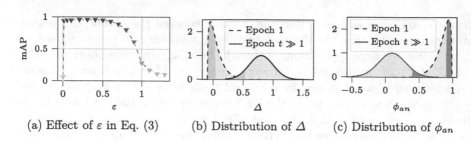

(a) Effect of ε in Eq. (3)   (b) Distribution of Δ (c) Distribution of ϕ_{an}

Fig. 2. (a) The sensitivity of the Triplet loss (3) with the change of ε. (b-c) The convergences of distributions of $\Delta = \phi_{ap} - \phi_{an}$ and ϕ_{an} under our loss. Yellow and blue areas, specified by Eqs. (7) and (8), indicate hard triplets and hard negative pairs, respectively. (Color figure online)

as well since we can then derive that $\varepsilon \in [0, 4)$. Thereby, we can convert Eq. (2) to a slightly different objective, which is identical to optimize, but allows us to identify limitations of the TL.

Proposition 1. *Given* $\|\mathbf{f}_a\|_2 = \|\mathbf{f}_p\|_2 = \|\mathbf{f}_n\|_2 = 1$, *minimization of the Triplet loss* (2) *corresponds to minimizing*

$$\mathcal{L}^*_{\text{Triplet}} = [\phi_{an} - \phi_{ap} + \varepsilon]_+, \ \varepsilon \in [0, 2). \tag{3}$$

Proof. See Suppl. Section 1.

Instead of depending on L2 distances between feature vectors as in (2), the TL in Eq. (3) becomes a function of the cosine similarities ϕ_{ap} and ϕ_{an} (i.e. $\cos(\mathbf{f}_a, \mathbf{f}_p)$ and $\cos(\mathbf{f}_a, \mathbf{f}_n)$, respectively). In Fig. 1b, we graphically demonstrate the 2D loss surface of the TL (3) with $\varepsilon = 0.25$, treating ϕ_{ap} and ϕ_{an} as its arguments.

2.3 Adaptive Gradient Triplet Loss

The TL in Eq. (3) only aims to ensure that the distance between the feature vectors $\mathbf{f}_a$ and $\mathbf{f}_p$ is strictly less than the distance between the anchor and a negative $\mathbf{f}_n$. Such a formulation, however, allows for the existence of an unexpected scenario where both the distances are arbitrarily small. We present a simple intuition of the scenario in Suppl. Figure 1. Although increasing the margin ε should enlarge the distance of negative pairs, our empirical evidence in Fig. 2a shows that using $\varepsilon > 0.5$ results in a significant drop in performance. Therefore, we propose to explicitly set a threshold on the *virtual angle* between $\mathbf{f}_a$ and $\mathbf{f}_n$, that is $\angle(\mathbf{f}_a, \mathbf{f}_n) \geq \alpha$, where $\alpha \in [0, \pi/2]$, which is equivalent to $\cos(\mathbf{f}_a, \mathbf{f}_n) - \cos(\alpha) \leq 0$. To enforce such a constraint, we minimize the following loss

$$\mathcal{L}_{\text{an}} = [\phi_{an} - \beta]_+, \tag{4}$$

where $\beta = \cos(\alpha) \in [0, 1]$. Using this additional term, we introduce *an adaptive gradient triplet loss*, named AdaTriplet, that is a combination of $\mathcal{L}^*_{\text{Triplet}}$ and $\mathcal{L}_{\text{an}}$:

$$\mathcal{L}_{\text{AdaTriplet}} = [\phi_{an} - \phi_{ap} + \varepsilon]_+ + \lambda [\phi_{an} - \beta]_+ , \tag{5}$$

where $\lambda \in \mathbb{R}_+$ is a coefficient, $\varepsilon \in [0, 2)$ is a strict margin, and $\beta \in [0, 1]$ is a relaxing margin.

Proposition 2. *Consider $\|\mathbf{f}_a\|_2 = \|\mathbf{f}_p\|_2 = \|\mathbf{f}_n\|_2 = 1$. Compared to the Triplet loss, the gradients of AdaTriplet w.r.t. ϕ_{ap} and ϕ_{an} adapt the magnitude and the direction depending on the triplet hardness:*

$$\left(\frac{\partial \mathcal{L}_{\text{AdaTriplet}}(\tau)}{\partial \phi_{ap}}, \frac{\partial \mathcal{L}_{\text{AdaTriplet}}(\tau)}{\partial \phi_{an}} \right) = \begin{cases} (-1, 1 + \lambda) & \text{if } \tau \in \mathcal{T}_+ \cap \mathcal{P}_+ \\ (0, \lambda) & \text{if } \tau \in (\mathcal{T} n \mathcal{T}_+) \cap \mathcal{P}_+ \\ (-1, 1) & \text{if } \tau \in \mathcal{T}_+ \cap (\mathcal{T} n \mathcal{P}_+) \\ (0, 0) & \text{otherwise} \end{cases}, \tag{6}$$

where $\mathcal{T}_+ = \{(\mathbf{x}_a, \mathbf{x}_p, \mathbf{x}_n) \mid \phi_{an} - \phi_{ap} + \varepsilon > 0\}$ and $\mathcal{P}_+ = \{(\mathbf{x}_a, \mathbf{x}_p, \mathbf{x}_n) \mid \phi_{an} > \beta\}$.

Proof. See Suppl. Section 2.

In Fig. 1c, we illustrate the negative gradient field of AdaTriplet with $\varepsilon = 0.25, \beta = 0.1$, and $\lambda = 1$. As such, the 2D coordinate is partitioned into 4 subdomains, corresponding to Eq. (6). The main distinction of the AdaTriplet loss compared to the TL is that our loss has different gradients depending on the difficulty of hard negative samples. In particular, it enables the optimization of easy triplets with $\phi_{an} > \beta$, which addresses the drawback of TL.

2.4 AutoMargin: Adaptive Hard Negative Mining

Hard negative samples are those, where feature space mapping $f_\theta(\cdot)$ fails to capture semantic similarity between samples. Recent studies have shown the benefit of mining hard or semi-hard negative samples for the optimization of TL-based metric learning methods [19,25]. These approaches rely on using *fixed* margin variables in training, which are selected experimentally. In this work, we hypothesize that learning the margin *on-line* is not only more computationally efficient, but also allows gaining better results [7,17,28].

In AdaTriplet, instead of defining hard negatives as the ones for which $\phi_{an} > \phi_{ap}$, we have enforced the numerical constraint on the value of ϕ_{an} itself. Empirically, one can observe that this constraint becomes easier to satisfy as we train the model for longer.

Let $\Delta = \phi_{ap} - \phi_{an}$, we rewrite (5) as $\mathcal{L}_{\text{AdaTriplet}} = [\varepsilon - \Delta]_+ + \lambda [\phi_{an} - \beta]_+$. During the convergence of a model under our loss, the distributions of Δ and ϕ_{an} are supposed to transform as illustrated in Figs. 2b and 2c, respectively. Here, we propose adjusting the margins ε and β according to the summary statistics of the Δ and ϕ_{an} distributions during the training:

$$\varepsilon(t) = \frac{\mu_\Delta(t)}{K_\Delta}, \qquad (7) \qquad \beta(t) = 1 + \frac{\mu_{an}(t) - 1}{K_{an}}, \qquad (8)$$

where $\mu_\Delta(t)$ and $\mu_{an}(t)$ are the means of $\{\Delta \mid (\mathbf{x}_a, \mathbf{x}_p, \mathbf{x}_n) \in \mathcal{T}\}$ and $\{\phi_{an} \mid (\mathbf{x}_a, \mathbf{x}_p, \mathbf{x}_n) \in \mathcal{T}\}$ respectively, and $K_\Delta, K_{an} \in \mathbb{Z}_+$ are hyperparameters.

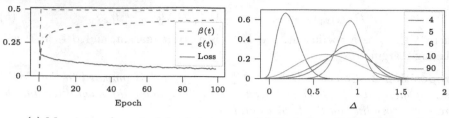

(a) Margins and our training loss   (b) Evolution of distribution of Δ

Fig. 3. Effects of AdaTriplet and AutoMargin. Colors in (b) represent epochs.

The difference in $\varepsilon(t)$ and $\beta(t)$ can be observed from their definition: we aim to enforce the triplet constraint with the highest possible margin, and this progressively raises it. Simultaneously, we want to increase the virtual thresholding angle between anchors and negative samples, which leads to the decrease of $\beta(t)$. We provide a graphical illustration of adaptive margins in Figs. 2b and 2c using yellow and blue colors, respectively.

3   Experiments

3.1   Datasets

Knee X-ray Dataset. The Osteoarthritis Initiative (OAI) cohort, publicly available at https://nda.nih.gov/oai/, comprises $4,796$ participants from 45 to 79 years old. The original interest of the cohort was to study knee osteoarthritis, which is characterized by the appearance of osteophytes, joint space narrowing, as well as textural changes of the femur and tibia. We used X-ray imaging data collected at baseline, 12, 24, 36, 48, 72, and 96-month follow-up visits. The detailed data description is presented in Suppl. Table 2. We utilized KNEEL [21] to localize and crop a pair of knees joints from each bilateral radiograph. Our further post-processing used augmentations that eventually produces input images with a shape of 256×256 (see Suppl. Table 1a for details).

Chest X-ray Dataset. ChestXrays-14 (CXR) [23] consists of $112,120$ frontal-view chest X-ray images collected from $30,805$ participants from 0 to 95 years old. The radiographic data were acquired at a baseline and across time up to 156 months. The training and test data are further described in Suppl. Table 2. To be in line with the OAI dataset, we grouped testing data by year, and used the same set of augmentations, yielding 256×256 images.

3.2   Experimental Setup

We conducted our experiments on V100 Nvidia GPUs. We implemented our method and all baselines in PyTorch [15] and the Metric Learning library [14]. Following [13], the same data settings, optimizer hyperparameters, augmentations, and feature extraction module were used for all the methods. We utilized

Table 1. Ablation studies (5-fold Cross-Validation; OAI dataset). CMC means CMC top-1. * indicates the results when the query and the database are 6 years apart. N_s is the number of scanned hyperparameter values.

(a) Impact of $\lambda\mathcal{L}_{an}$				
λ	mAP*	CMC*	mAP	CMC
0	95.6	93.4	96.6	93.6
0.5	96.1	94.4	96.9	94.6
1	**96.3**	**94.6**	**97.0**	**94.7**
2	94.5	92.1	95.6	92.3

(b) Triplet loss			
Method	N_s	mAP	CMC
Q1	1	27.3	14.9
Q2	1	87.7	76.9
WAT [28]	4	96.5	93.5
Grid search	4	**96.6**	93.6
AutoMargin	2	**96.6**	**93.7**

(c) AdaTriplet loss			
Method	N_s	mAP	CMC
Q1	1	94.3	89.4
Q2	1	88.9	79.5
Grid search	16	**97.0**	**94.8**
AutoMargin	4	**97.1**	94.7

(a) On OAI test set   (b) On CXR test set

Fig. 4. Performance comparisons on the test sets of OAI and CXR (mean and standard error over 5 random seeds). Detailed quantitative results are in Suppl. Tables 4 and 5.

the Adam optimizer [11] with a learning rate of 0.0001 and a weight decay of 0.0001. We used the ResNet-18 network [8] with pretrained weights to extract embeddings with D of 128 from input images. We trained each method in 100 epochs with a batch size of 128. For data sampling in each batch, we randomly selected 4 medical images from each subject. We thoroughly describe lists of hyperparameters for all the methods in Suppl. Table 1b.

To evaluate forensic matching performance, we used mean average precision (mAP) [20], mAP@R [13], and cumulative matching characteristics (CMC) accuracy [5]. All experiments were run 5 times with different random seeds. All test set metrics represent the average and standard error over runs.

3.3 Results

Impact of $\mathcal{L}_{an}$. We performed an experiment in which we varied the coefficient λ in the AdaTriplet loss (5). The results on the OAI test set in Table 1a show that $\lambda = 1$ yielded the best performances according to both the mAP and CMC metrics. Notably, we observed that the differences are more apparent when querying images at least 6 years apart from images in the database. We thus set $\lambda = 1$ for our method in all other experiments.

Impact of AutoMargin. AutoMargin is applicable for both TL and Ada-Triplet, and we investigated its impact in Tables 1b and 1c. For baselines, we used the Q1 and Q2 quartiles of distributions of Δ and ϕ_{an} to define the margins ε and β, respectively. In addition, we performed exhaustive grid searches for the two losses' margins. Besides the naïve baselines, we compared our method to the weakly adaptive triplet loss (WAT) [28], which also allows for dynamic margin adjustment in the TL. Based on Suppl. Table 3, we set the constants (K_Δ, K_{an}) of AutoMargin to $(2, 2)$ and $(2, 4)$ for OAI and CXR, respectively.

AutoMargin helped both the losses to outperform the quartile-based approaches. Compared to the grid search, our method was at least 2-fold more efficient, and performed in par with the baseline. In the TL, AutoMargin was 2 time more efficient and achieved better results compared to WAT. Furthermore, on the independent test sets, the combination of AdaTriplet and AutoMargin gained substantially higher performances than WAT (Fig. 4).

Effects of Our Methods in Training. We demonstrate the behaviour of Ada-Triplet and AutoMargin during training of one of the runs of the OAI experiments in Fig. 3. Specifically, under our adaptive hard negative mining, the margin β drastically increased from 0 to 0.5 in a few epochs. While β was stable after the drastic increase in value, the margin ε gradually grew from 0 and converged around 0.4. As a result, our loss improved rapidly at the beginning, and continuously converged afterwards (see Fig. 3a). During the process, the mean of Δ shifted away from 0 to 1 while its variance increased at first, and then gradually decreased (Fig. 3b).

Comparison to Baselines. Finally, We compared our AdaTriplet loss with AutoMargin to competitive metric learning baselines such as SoftTriplet [16], ArcFace [6], TL (Triplet) [9,19], CL (Contrastive) [4], WAT [28], and Selectively Contrastive Triplet (SCT) [25]. Whereas SoftTriplet and ArcFace are classification losses, the other baselines are embedding losses. In Fig. 4, our empirical results show that the classification losses generalized poorly on the two test sets, especially on chest X-ray data. On both test sets, our loss outperformed all baselines across years. Notably, on the OAI data, the differences between our method and the baselines were more significant at later years. We present more detailed results in Suppl. Tables 4 and 5. Moreover, we demonstrate the retrieval results of our method alongside the baselines in Fig. 1a and Suppl. Figure 2.

4   Discussion

In this work, we analyzed Triplet loss in optimizing hard negative samples. To address the issue, we proposed the AdaTriplet loss, whose gradients are adaptive depending on the difficulty of negative samples. In addition, we proposed the AutoMargin method to adjust margin hyperparameters during training. We applied our methodology to the FMIM problem, where the issue of hard negative samples is evident; many medical images may look alike, and it is challenging to capture relevant fine-grained information. Our experiments on two medical datasets showed that AdaTriplet and AutoMargin were robust to visual changes caused by aging and degenerative disorders. The main limitation of this work is that we did not test other neural network architectures, and used grayscale images. However, as recommended in [13], we aimed to make our protocol standard to analyze all the components of the method. Future work should investigate a wider set of models and datasets. We hope our method will be used for other CBMIR tasks, and have made our code publicly available at https://github.com/Oulu-IMEDS/AdaTriplet.

Acknowledgments. The OAI is a public-private partnership comprised of five contracts (N01- AR-2-2258; N01-AR-2-2259; N01-AR-2- 2260; N01-AR-2-2261; N01-AR-2-2262) funded by the National Institutes of Health, a branch of the Department of Health and Human Services, and conducted by the OAI Study Investigators. Private funding partners include Merck Research Laboratories; Novartis Pharmaceuticals Corporation, GlaxoSmithKline; and Pfizer, Inc. Private sector funding for the OAI is managed by the Foundation for the National Institutes of Health.

We would like to thank the strategic funding of the University of Oulu, the Academy of Finland Profi6 336449 funding program, the Northern Ostrobothnia hospital district, Finland (VTR project K33754) and Sigrid Juselius foundation for funding this work. Furthermore, the authors wish to acknowledge CSC - IT Center for Science, Finland, for generous computational resources.

Finally, we thank Matthew B. Blaschko for useful discussions in relation to this paper. Terence McSweeney is acknowledged for proofreading this work and providing comments that improved the clarity of the manuscript.

References

1. Bai, X., Yang, M., Huang, T., Dou, Z., Yu, R., Xu, Y.: Deep-person: learning discriminative deep features for person re-identification. Pattern Recogn, **98**, 107036 (2020)
2. Chechik, G., Sharma, V., Shalit, U., Bengio, S.: Large scale online learning of image similarity through ranking. J. Mach. Learn. Res. **11**(3), 1109–1135 (2010)
3. Choe, J., et al.: Content-based image retrieval by using deep learning for interstitial lung disease diagnosis with chest ct. Radiology **302**(1), 187–197 (2022)
4. Chopra, S., Hadsell, R., LeCun, Y.: Learning a similarity metric discriminatively, with application to face verification. In: 2005 IEEE Computer Society Conference on Computer Vision and Pattern Recognition (CVPR 2005), vol. 1, pp. 539–546. IEEE (2005)
5. DeCann, B., Ross, A.: Relating roc and cmc curves via the biometric menagerie. In: 2013 IEEE Sixth International Conference on Biometrics: Theory, Applications and Systems (BTAS), pp. 1–8. IEEE (2013)
6. Deng, J., Guo, J., Xue, N., Zafeiriou, S.: Arcface: Additive angular margin loss for deep face recognition. In: Proceedings of the IEEE/CVF Conference on Computer Vision and Pattern Recognition, pp. 4690–4699 (2019)
7. Harwood, B., Kumar BG, V., Carneiro, G., Reid, I., Drummond, T.: Smart mining for deep metric learning. In: Proceedings of the IEEE International Conference on Computer Vision, pp. 2821–2829 (2017)

8. He, K., Zhang, X., Ren, S., Sun, J.: Deep residual learning for image recognition. In: Proceedings of the IEEE Conference on Computer Vision and Pattern Recognition, pp. 770–778 (2016)
9. Hoffer, E., Ailon, N.: Deep metric learning using triplet network. In: Feragen, A., Pelillo, M., Loog, M. (eds.) SIMBAD 2015. LNCS, vol. 9370, pp. 84–92. Springer, Cham (2015). https://doi.org/10.1007/978-3-319-24261-3_7
10. Hostetter, J., Khanna, N., Mandell, J.C.: Integration of a zero-footprint cloud-based picture archiving and communication system with customizable forms for radiology research and education. Acad. Radiology **25**(6), 811–818 (2018)
11. Kingma, D.P., Ba, J.: Adam: A method for stochastic optimization. arXiv preprint arXiv:1412.6980 (2014)
12. Liang, Y., et al.: Exploring forensic dental identification with deep learning. In: Advances in Neural Information Processing Systems, vol. 34 (2021)
13. Musgrave, K., Belongie, S., Lim, S.-N.: A metric learning reality check. In: Vedaldi, A., Bischof, H., Brox, T., Frahm, J.-M. (eds.) ECCV 2020. LNCS, vol. 12370, pp. 681–699. Springer, Cham (2020). https://doi.org/10.1007/978-3-030-58595-2_41
14. Musgrave, K., Belongie, S., Lim, S.N.: Pytorch metric learning (2020)
15. Paszke, A., et al.: Pytorch: An imperative style, high-performance deep learning library. In: Advances in Neural Information Processing Systems, vol. 32 (2019)
16. Qian, Q., Shang, L., Sun, B., Hu, J., Li, H., Jin, R.: Softtriple loss: Deep metric learning without triplet sampling. In: Proceedings of the IEEE/CVF International Conference on Computer Vision, pp. 6450–6458 (2019)
17. Roth, K., Milbich, T., Ommer, B.: Pads: Policy-adapted sampling for visual similarity learning. In: Proceedings of the IEEE/CVF Conference on Computer Vision and Pattern Recognition, pp. 6568–6577 (2020)
18. Saritha, R.R., Paul, V., Kumar, P.G.: Content based image retrieval using deep learning process. Cluster Comput. **22**(2), 4187–4200 (2018). https://doi.org/10.1007/s10586-018-1731-0
19. Schroff, F., Kalenichenko, D., Philbin, J.: Facenet: A unified embedding for face recognition and clustering. In: Proceedings of the IEEE Conference on Computer Vision and Pattern Recognition, pp. 815–823 (2015)
20. Schütze, H., Manning, C.D., Raghavan, P.: Introduction to information retrieval, vol. 39. Cambridge University Press Cambridge (2008)
21. Tiulpin, A., Melekhov, I., Saarakkala, S.: Kneel: knee anatomical landmark localization using hourglass networks. In: Proceedings of the IEEE/CVF International Conference on Computer Vision Workshops, pp. 0–0 (2019)
22. Tzelepi, M., Tefas, A.: Deep convolutional learning for content based image retrieval. Neurocomputing **275**, 2467–2478 (2018)
23. Wang, X., Peng, Y., Lu, L., Lu, Z., Bagheri, M., Summers, R.M.: Chestx-ray8: hospital-scale chest x-ray database and benchmarks on weakly-supervised classification and localization of common thorax diseases. In: Proceedings of the IEEE Conference on Computer Vision and Pattern Recognition, pp. 2097–2106 (2017)
24. Wu, C.Y., Manmatha, R., Smola, A.J., Krahenbuhl, P.: Sampling matters in deep embedding learning. In: Proceedings of the IEEE International Conference on Computer Vision, pp. 2840–2848 (2017)
25. Xuan, H., Stylianou, A., Liu, X., Pless, R.: Hard negative examples are hard, but useful. In: Vedaldi, A., Bischof, H., Brox, T., Frahm, J.-M. (eds.) ECCV 2020. LNCS, vol. 12359, pp. 126–142. Springer, Cham (2020). https://doi.org/10.1007/978-3-030-58568-6_8

26. Yuan, Y., Chen, W., Yang, Y., Wang, Z.: In defense of the triplet loss again: Learning robust person re-identification with fast approximated triplet loss and label distillation. In: Proceedings of the IEEE/CVF Conference on Computer Vision and Pattern Recognition Workshops, pp. 354–355 (2020)
27. Zhang, K., et al.: Content-based image retrieval with a convolutional siamese neural network: Distinguishing lung cancer and tuberculosis in ct images. Comput. Biol. Med. **140**, 105096 (2022)
28. Zhao, X., Qi, H., Luo, R., Davis, L.: A weakly supervised adaptive triplet loss for deep metric learning. In: Proceedings of the IEEE/CVF International Conference on Computer Vision Workshops (2019)

Correction to: The Intrinsic Manifolds of Radiological Images and Their Role in Deep LearningCorrection

Nicholas Konz ⓘ, Hanxue Gu ⓘ, Haoyu Dong ⓘ,
and Maciej A. Mazurowski ⓘ

Correction to: Chapter "The Intrinsic Manifolds of Radiological Images and Their Role in Deep Learning" in: L. Wang et al. (Eds.): *Medical Image Computing and Computer Assisted Intervention – MICCAI 2022*, LNCS 13438, https://doi.org/10.1007/978-3-031-16452-1_65

In the originally published version of chapter 65, the middle initial was missing in the name of the author Maciej A. Mazurowski. This has been corrected.

The updated original version of this chapter can be found at
https://doi.org/10.1007/978-3-031-16452-1_65

Author Index

Printed in the United States
by Baker & Taylor Publisher Services